OST OMNES ALIAS AEDITIONES ACCVRATISSIM
VIA LATINA
PORTA LATINA
PORTA CAPENA
VIA OSTIENSIS
PORTA TRIGEMINA
AQVA CRABRA
NAVMACHIA
PISCINA PVBLICA

ATLAS OF THE ROMAN WORLD

CHRONOLOGICAL TABLE

This table is supplemented by the list of emperors that appears on pp. 98–99.

	800 BC	600 BC	500 BC	400 BC	300 BC	200 BC
ROME AND ITALY	Foundation of Rome trad. 753 Tarquin I 616–579 Growth of the city	Servius Tullius 579–534 Reorganization of the tribes, army and civic constitution Tarquin II 534–509 Beginning of the Republic 509 Rome dominant in Latium	Latins defeated at Lake Regillus 499 Incursions of Sabines, Aequi and Volsci Domination of the patricians Campania overrun by Samnites 420 Siege and capture of Veii 405–396	Rome sacked by Gauls Patricians and plebeians share the consulship Latin War 340 Latin League dissolved, Campania incorporated in Roman state 338 Roman colonization and conquest of Italy 334–264 Second Samnite War 327–304	Third Samnite War 298–290 Pyrrhus' invasion 280–275 Early Roman coinage (from c. 280) First Punic War 264–241 Gauls invade Italy 225 Second Punic War 218–202	Trials of the Scipios 187 Censorship of the Elder Cato 184 Direct taxation on Roman citizens abolished 167 Tribunates of Ti. and C. Gracchus 133, 123–122 Marius consul 7 times: 107, 104–100, 86 Defeat of Cimbri and Teutones 102–101
	Villanovan hut urn, c. 800 BC	Head of Apollo from Veii, c. 500 BC				Coin of Hannibal c. 210 BC The Capitoline wolf, early 5th century BC
ART AND ARCHITECTURE	Primitive huts on the Palatine Rich orientalizing tombs at Caere, Praeneste etc. Roman Forum laid out; first permanent stone buildings in Rome	Temples of Diana, Fortuna and Mater Matuta c. 560 Walls of Servius Tullius (?) Temple of Jupiter Capitolinus 509 Etruscan tomb paintings → (to 200 BC)	Temple of Saturn 497 Temple of Ceres 493 Temple of Castor 484 Temple of Apollo 431	Walls around Rome rebuilt 378 Temple C in Largo Argentina c. 350 Via Appia, Aqua Appia built 312 François Tomb at Vulci c. 320–310	Program of temple building in Rome 302–272 Roman fine pottery industry flourishes Tomb of the Scipios c. 280 Circus Flaminius 221	Greek art brought to Rome 200– Basilica Porcia built in the Roman Forum 184 Basilica Aemilia and Aemilian bridge 179 Temple of Fortuna at Praeneste c. 120
LATIN LITERATURE		Earliest Latin inscriptions c. 600	Laws of the Twelve Tables 451–450		Appius Claudius Caecus, orator Livius Andronicus, Naevius, Plautus, Ennius, Statius Caecilius and Pacuvius, playwrights and poets Cato, orator, historian, scholar	Terence and Accius, playwrights Lucilius, satirist L. Calpurnius Piso and Caelius Antipater, historians C. Gracchus, L. Crassus and Q. Hortensius, orators
AFRICA, SPAIN AND THE WESTERN MEDITERRANEAN	Foundation of Carthage trad. 814 Phoenician settlements in the western Mediterranean Greek colonization of Sicily and S Italy begins c. 750 Greek colony of Massilia (Marseilles) founded c. 600	Phocaean Greeks defeated at Alalia (Corsica) by the Etruscans and Carthaginians 535 First treaty between Rome and Carthage 509	Carthaginians defeated at Himera 480 Hieron defeats Etruscans at Cumae 474 Athenians defeated at Syracuse 413	Second treaty between Rome and Carthage 348 Timoleon drives Carthaginians from Sicily 344 Agathocles tyrant of Syracuse 317–289; invades Africa 310–307	Sicily becomes Roman province 241 Sardinia and Corsica overrun and formed into a province 238 Carthaginians build an empire in Spain 237–218 Romans occupy Carthaginian dominion in Spain and form two new provinces 206	Celtiberian and Lusitanian wars 197–133 Third Punic War 149–146; Carthage destroyed 146 First Sicilian Slave War 136–132 Jugurthine War 112–105 Second Sicilian Slave War 104–102
GAUL, BRITAIN AND CENTRAL EUROPE	Halstatt Culture		La Tène Culture Celtic invasion of northern Italy (and sack of Rome 390)		Gauls invade Macedonia, Greece and Asia Minor 279 Gallic invasion of Italy halted at Battle of Telamon 225	Roman conquest of Cisalpine Gaul 202–191 Gallia Narbonensis made a Roman province 121(?) Migration of Cimbri and Teutones c. 120–100 Roman campaigns in Dalmatia 118–117
GREECE AND THE EAST	First Olympiad 776 Homer, Hesiod c. 700 Age of Greek colonization (beginning c. 750) Age of Greek tyrants c. 655–510 →	Cyrus the Great establishes the Persian Empire c. 550–530 Sparta dominates the Peloponnese from c. 560 Pisistratus tyrant at Athens 546–528	Ionian Revolt 499–494 Persian invasions of Greece 490 and 481–479 Athenian Empire in the Aegean 478–404 Parthenon built 447–432 Peloponnesian War 431–404	Battle of Leuctra 371 Philip II makes Macedon the dominant power in Greece 359–336 Alexander the Great conquers the Persian Empire 333–323 Seleucid dynasty in Syria and Mesopotamia → Ptolemaic dynasty in Egypt →	Athens occupied by Macedonians 261 Romano-Illyrian wars 229–219 Attalid dynasty in western Asia Minor 281–133 Antigonid dynasty in Macedonia 277–167	Second Macedonian War 200–197 Syrian War 191–188 Third Macedonian War 172–168 Corinth destroyed 146

Special Features

List of Maps

Abbreviations of praenomina

A.	Aulus	P.	Publius
C.	Gaius	Q.	Quintus
Cn.	Gnaeus	Sex.	Sextus
D.	Decimus	Ser.	Servius
L.	Lucius	Sp.	Spurius
M.	Marcus	T.	Titus
M'.	Manius	Ti.	Tiberius

CONTENTS

Editor Graham Speake
Art editor Andrew Lawson
Map editors Liz Orrock, Zoe Goodwin
Text editor and index Jennifer Drake-Brockman
Design Adrian Hodgkins
Production Clive Sparling

Published by Phaidon Press Ltd, Littlegate House, St Ebbe's Street, Oxford, England, OX1 1SQ

Planned and produced by Equinox Ltd, Mayfield House, 256 Banbury Road, Oxford, England, OX2 7DH

British Library Cataloguing in Publication Data
Cornell, Tim
Atlas of the Roman world.
I, Title II. Mathews, John.
937'.06 DG210
ISBN 0–7148–2152–7

Origination by MBA Ltd, Chalfont St Peter, Bucks, England, and David Brin Ltd, London

Filmset by Keyspools Ltd, Golborne, Lancs, England

Maps drawn and originated by Lovell Johns Ltd, Oxford

Printed in Spain by Graficromo, S.A., Córdoba

Frontispiece Mosaic of a Nile landscape, from Pompeii.

ATLAS OF THE ROMAN WORLD

by Tim Cornell and John Matthews

Phaidon · Oxford

100 BC	AD	100 AD	200 AD	300 AD	400 AD	500 AD
Social War 91–89 Civil War: Sulla dictator 83–82 Revolt of Spartacus 73–71 First Triumvirate 60 Civil War: Caesar dictator 49–44 Murder of Caesar 44 Second Triumvirate 43 Reign of Octavian/ Augustus 31 BC–14AD	Julio-Claudian dynasty 27 BC–68 AD Fire of Rome 64 Flavio-Trajanic dynasty 69–117 Eruption of Vesuvius 79	Antonine emperors 117–93	Severan emperors 193–235 Roman citizenship extended to all free inhabitants of the provinces 212 Usurpations and fragmentation of the imperial office 235–84 Tetrarchy established by Diocletian 293	"Great Persecution" of Christians 303–05 Freedom of worship restored 313 Constantine sole ruler of the Empire 324–37 Failed pagan revival of Julian 361–63 "Disestablishment" of paganism 382 Division of the Empire 395	Imperial court shifted to Ravenna 402 Visigoths under Alaric sack Rome 410 Rome pillaged by Vandals 455 Deposition of last Roman emperor of the west 476 Barbarian kings at Ravenna 476–540	Byzantine reconquest of Italy 540
Augustus as Pontifex, late 1st century BC		The Colosseum, 79 AD		Diocletian and Maximian, c. 300 AD		Mosaic of Justinian at Ravenna, c. 560 AD
Tabularium 78 Theater of Pompey 55 Forum of Caesar 46 Arch of Augustus 21 Baths of Agrippa 19 Theater of Marcellus 17 Ara Pacis Augustae 9 Forum of Augustus 2	Augustan building program at Rome Colosseum dedicated 79	Trajan's Forum dedicated 112 Pantheon rebuilt 118–28 Hadrian's Villa at Tivoli 126–34	Severan building at Leptis Magna Baths of Caracalla built at Rome 216 Aurelian builds walls around Rome 271	Arch of Constantine Church-building programs at Rome, Jerusalem and Constantinople	Mosaics in churches at Ravenna	St Sophia rebuilt at Constantinople 537
Cicero, orator, philosopher Caesar, orator, historian Lucretius, poet and philosopher Sallust and Livy, historians Catullus, Virgil, Horace, Tibullus, Propertius, Ovid, poets	The "Silver Age" of Latin literature Seneca the Elder, orator Persius, Lucan, Martial, poets Pliny the Elder, natural historian Pliny the Younger, letter writer Tacitus, historian	Juvenal, poet Suetonius, historian Apuleius, novelist	Ulpian, Papinian, jurists Tertullian, Christian apologist	Ausonius and Claudian, poets Lactantius, Christian apologist Ambrose, Jerome and Augustine, Christian writers Symmachus, orator Ammianus Marcellinus, historian	Jerome's Vulgate completed c. 404 Orosius, historian Servius and Macrobius, scholars Theodosian code compiled 429/37 Sidonius Apollinaris, poet	Boethius, philosopher Cassiodorus, historian and administrator
Sertorius' "revolt" in Spain 80–72 Defeat of Pompeian forces in Spain (49) and Africa (46) Battle of Munda 45 Sextus Pompey controls W Mediterranean 40–36 Conquest of NW Spain by Agrippa 27–19	Annexation of Mauretania 42		Expansion of Roman settlement in North Africa	Origins of Donatist schism 311/12	Vandals enter Spain Vandal kingdom at Carthage 439	Byzantine conquest of Vandal kingdom in Africa 533 Byzantine conquest of southern Spain 554
Caesar's conquest of continental Gaul 58–51; expeditions to Britain 55–54 Noricum and Raetia become provinces 16–15 Tiberius conquers Pannonia 12–9	Rebellion of Vindex 68 Roman occupation of Britain 43 Frontier in Germany advanced Danube frontier of Illyricum consolidated Dacian wars 86–92	Province of Dacia formed 107 Marcomannic wars of M. Aurelius Barbarian invasion of Dacia 167	Breakaway Gallic "empire" 259–73 Britain in rebellion (Carausius and Allectus 287–96) Rise of Trier as Gallic capital Dacia ceded to the Goths 272	Goths allowed to settle within the Empire's boundaries 376 Battle of Hadrianople fought 378	Gothic regime in southern Gaul Britain abandoned by Romans and colonized by Saxons Burgundians occupy middle Rhône valley Hunnish "empire" under Attila	Franks drive Visigoths from Gaul 507 Slav, Bulgar and Avar incursions
Mithridatic Wars 88–84, 83–82, 74–63 Pompey's conquest of the east 66–63 Pompey defeated at Pharsalus 48 Brutus and Cassius defeated at Philippi 42 Antony defeated at Actium 31	First Jewish revolt 66–73 Temple in Jerusalem destroyed 70 Josephus, Jewish historian	Second Jewish (Bar-Kochba) revolt 132–35 Province of Meso-potamia formed 165 Plutarch, Pausanias, Greek writers "2nd Sophistic" work in Greek literature	Rise of Sasanian dynasty in Persia Palmyrene rebellion 266–72 Heruli invade Attica and Peloponnese 267 Cassius Dio, Herodian, Greek historians Eusebius, Christian apologist	Council of Nicaea 325 Constantinople consecrated as new imperial capital 330 Visigothic invasion of Greece 395 Eunapius, Greek historian	Hunnish invasions Council of Chalcedon convened 451 Olympiodorus, Priscus, Malchus, Greek historians	Persian attacks on Asia Minor Slav raids in the Balkans Nika riots 532 Zosimus, Procopius, Greek historians

INTRODUCTION

The purpose of this Atlas is to give a comprehensive general view of the Roman world in its physical and cultural setting. It covers the period from the foundation and early development of the city of Rome, through its expansion and conquest of Italy and the Mediterranean, the establishment of imperial rule by Augustus and the subsequent emergence of a new political and religious order, to the collapse of the west and the recovery of Italy from Germanic kings by a Christian Byzantine emperor. Our survey is built upon a historical narrative, for which a broadly chronological structure seemed appropriate, given the sheer length of the period (over 1300 years) described and the scale of the changes in question. We hope, however, that the manner in which we have written, and our choice and presentation of illustrations, maps and special features, have resulted in an integrated and balanced picture in which thematic interpretation is at least as prominent as historical narrative.

For the same reason – the length and variety of the period covered – joint authorship seemed a necessity, at least if the Atlas were to possess across more than a fraction of its range any of that sense of immediacy which comes from direct acquaintance with the latest research. While we have tried constantly to write for the general reader, we have indicated areas of specialist controversy and made our position clear.

Our own research interests, respectively in the earlier republican and later imperial periods, should mean that our book is not biased, as many are, in favor of the "central," but rather of the "outer," periods of Roman history. The section on the provinces of the Roman Empire is directed to the Empire of the 2nd century AD (though here too tracing change and development in the choice and description of individual sites); but in general we have found ourselves writing with greater relish of those periods which lie at the beginning and the end of the history of the Roman world. We have given perhaps greater attention to the problems of the nature of archaic Roman society and to the Christianization of the Empire after Constantine than to the civil wars of the late Republic and the dynastic politics of the Julio-Claudians, and we make no apology for this.

The historian Ammianus Marcellinus criticized those philosophers who wrote books on the vanity of human ambition and put their names to them. As historians ourselves, however, and sharing Ammianus' regard for the true recollection of facts, we think that it will be helpful to indicate which of us is responsible for which part of the book. Tim Cornell has composed the survey of the Roman Republic and of the Empire until the death of Augustus, and has chosen the material and written the captions for the maps, illustrations and special features that go with it, and in addition for the features on Pompeii, Ostia and Roman religion. John Matthews is responsible in the same terms for the description of and illustrative material for the Empire after Augustus and for Part Three, on the provinces of the Empire. We have worked independently, though with firmly agreed guidelines and with every effort to achieve compatibility.

We have learned much from each other, and also acknowledge with pleasure the collaboration of members of the editorial team, especially Andrew Lawson, with whom we have discussed the choice and presentation of illustrations with a mutual understanding of historical and artistic aims which has delighted us; Liz Orrock and Zoe Goodwin for their preparation of cartographic material from briefs which were probably the more obscure and confusing, the fuller we tried to make them; and Graham Speake, whose editorial suggestions have much influenced the design of the book. In addition, Ray Davis compiled the material for the map on the distribution of estates listed in the *Liber Pontificalis*, Michael Whitby for the map on the eastern frontier in the time of Justinian, and Margaret Roxan has advised us on matters connected with the distribution of the Roman army. Other scholars have helped us in a variety of ways, notably Benjamin Isaac, Kenan Erim and Brian Croke, and many others who may not always have been aware of the purpose of the inquiries addressed to them by authors who have, in the course of writing, become more sharply aware how little they themselves know.

PART ONE

EARLY ITALY AND THE ROMAN REPUBLIC

SWITZERLAND
AUSTRIA
FRANCE
YUGOSLAVIA
ITALY
ALGERIA
TUNISIA
MONACO
SAN MARINO
ALPS
DOLOMITES
LIGURIAN ALPS
APENNINES
Valle d'Aosta
Piemonte
Liguria
Lombardia
Trentino–Alto Adige
Venezia–Euganea
Friuli–Venezia–Giulia
Emilia–Romagna
Toscana
Marche
Umbria
Lazio
Abruzzo
Molise
Campania
Puglia
Basilicata
Calabria
Corsica (Fr)
Sardinia Sardegna
Sicily Sicilia
LIGURIAN SEA
TYRRHENIAN SEA
ADRIATIC SEA
MEDITERRANEAN SEA
Gulf of Venice
Strait of Bonifacio
Strait of Messina
Sicilian Channel
Tuscan Archipelago
Elba
Ischia
Capri
Ustica
Lipari Is
Egadi
Pantelleria
Krk
Cres
Brac
Hvar
Rome
Milan
Turin
Genoa
Venice
Florence
Naples
Palermo
Bologna
Mt Blanc 4807
Matterhorn 4477
Ortles 3899
Amiata 1738
Corno 2914
GRAN SASSO D'ITALIA
Amaro 2795
MONTAGNA DELLA MAIELLA
Vesuvius 1277
Etna 3323
PROM. DEL GARGANO
TAVOLIERE DELLA PUGLIA
2000m
1000m
200m
0
3899 mountain peak (meters)
international boundary
regional boundary
scale 1:4 250 000
0 150 km
0 100mi

A CITY DESTINED TO GROW GREAT

The geography of Italy

The most important feature of the historical geography of Italy is the close interaction of plain, hill and mountain. Only about one-fifth of the total land surface of Italy is officially classified as plain (that is, land below 300 meters), and of this lowland area more than 70 per cent is accounted for by the valley of the Po. Of the rest, about two-fifths is classified as mountain (land over 1000 meters), and the remaining two-fifths as hill (land between 300 and 1000 meters). The alternation of these types of relief and their distribution throughout the country create a great diversity of climatic conditions and sharp contrasts in the physical appearance of the landscape from one region to another.

Italy is separated from central Europe by the great barrier of the Alps. In spite of their altitude these mountains have not kept Italy isolated from the rest of the continent. Although the winter snows make them impenetrable for more than half the year, most of the passes have been known since the earliest times; movements of people across the Alps have taken place throughout history, sometimes on a very large scale, for example during the incursions of the Celts and the Cimbri in the republican period and the barbarian invasions in the 5th and 6th centuries of our era.

Although there can be no doubt about the basic geographical unity of the Italian mainland to the south of the Alps, it is convenient to draw a distinction between "continental Italy," which consists of the valley of the Po and its surrounding mountain fringes — the Alps in the north, the Apennines in the south — and "peninsular Italy," which comprises the rest of the country apart from the islands. The two areas are different in climate and physical topography, as well as in cultural and economic development.

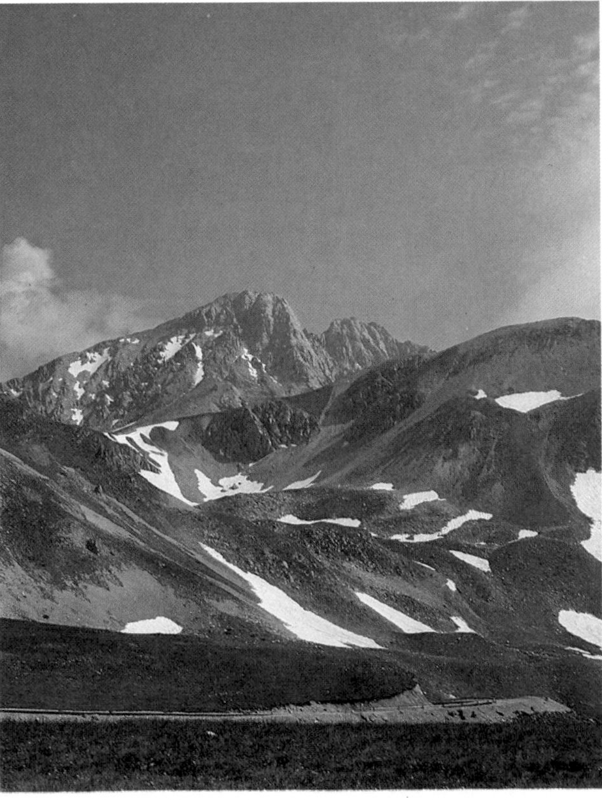

Right The Gran Sasso d'Italia. At nearly 3000 meters the Gran Sasso (the "Great Crag") dominates the central Apennine range and is the highest point in the Italian peninsula.

Peninsular Italy enjoys a typically "Mediterranean" climate, which is characterized by mild winters, hot summers and a moderate annual rainfall; this rainfall is however concentrated in heavy precipitations during the winter months, so that fierce drought occurs in June, July and August. Continental Italy on the other hand belongs climatically to central Europe. It has much greater extremes of temperature; the severe cold of the winter is matched by the intense heat of the summer, when temperatures are as high as those of the peninsula. Annual rainfall is no heavier than in some parts of peninsular Italy, but it is more evenly distributed through the seasons. The most telling sign of the climatic distinction between the two areas is that the olive tree, which is grown almost everywhere in peninsular Italy and along the Ligurian riviera, is not to be found north of the Apennines.

Today the Po plain is the most productive agricultural district in Italy. Its economic predominance certainly goes back to ancient times, and writers such as Strabo dwell on its fertility, the size of its population and the prosperity of its towns. Communications are made easy by the Po river itself, then as now navigable as far as Turin. In antiquity the region was well wooded, and its abundant acorns fed the herds of swine that supplied most of the meat consumed in the city of Rome. However in the lower part of its course the Po runs through a wide flood plain, and widespread inundations are prevented only by means of canals and dikes. It is clear that in pre-Roman times the lower part of the Po valley was marshy and subject to flooding, especially in Emilia and the Veneto; the marshes on the south side of the river formed a serious obstacle to Hannibal's invading army in 218 BC. But after the Roman conquest the land was reclaimed by a system of canals and dikes which the censor M. Aemilius Scaurus had constructed in the area between Parma and Modena in 109 BC. Further schemes were carried out by the emperor Augustus and his successors, and during the 1st century of our era northern Italy was one of the most prosperous areas of the Empire.

Continental Italy is bounded on its southern side by the Apennines, a system of massifs which runs the whole length of the peninsula from the Ligurian Alps to the straits of Messina, and continues beyond the straits along the north coast of Sicily. In doing so the mountains adopt a serpentine course. In the north they extend in a straight line which cuts obliquely across the peninsula from the Ligurian riviera in the west almost as far as Rimini in the east; at this point they curve gently round towards the south and run parallel with the Adriatic coast, reaching their highest peaks in the Abruzzi region at the Gran Sasso d'Italia (2914 meters) and the Montagna della Maiella (2795 meters). From there they once again cut diagonally across the peninsula to reach the Tyrrhenian coast in Lucania, and thence they extend into Calabria and on into Sicily.

In terms of physical features, then, the difference between continental Italy and peninsular Italy can be summed up in the observation that the former is essentially a large lowland plain surrounded by mountains, while the latter consists of a central mountain chain surrounded by small coastal plains.

As far as peninsular Italy is concerned, the coastal plains have a historical importance out of all proportion to their relative area. Broadly speaking the Apennines divide the peninsula into two separate lowland zones. The main central chain of the Apennines is much closer to the eastern than the western seaboard, and for a distance of about 350 kilometers from Rimini to the Biferno river there is only a very narrow lowland strip, about 30 kilometers wide, between the coast and the mountains of the interior. On the western side, however, the Apennines descend gently and irregularly into the lowland plains of Latium and Campania and the hilly but fertile land of Etruria.

In the south of the peninsula, from Molise and the northern edge of the Gargano promontory, the Apennines run almost due south into Lucania and Calabria (the "toe"). To the east of this line lies the second main lowland area of peninsular Italy, the region of Apulia, which stretches from the plain of the Tavoliere around Foggia to the tip of the Salentine peninsula (the "heel").

In general the Tyrrhenian side of Italy enjoys certain natural advantages over the Adriatic side; as a consequence the northwestern lowland area (Campania-Latium-Etruria) has been culturally favored by comparison with the southeastern district of Apulia. These differences relate largely to climate and to the nature of the soil. The main climatic difference lies in the general distribution of rainfall. Taking the country as a whole it can be said that the north is wetter than the south, and, except in the Alpine regions, the west is wetter than the east. This general pattern is complicated by the fact that more rain falls on the high ground than on the plains; but for the present purpose it is sufficient to note the general trend, which can be illustrated by comparing the average annual rainfall of La Spezia on the northwest coast (115 centimeters) with that of Ancona on the Adriatic (64 centimeters), or that of Naples (79 centimeters) with that of Bari (60 centimeters).

The Tyrrhenian coast is moreover fortunate in being served by relatively large rivers, at least two of which, the Tiber and the Arno, were navigable waterways in classical antiquity. The streams which flow into the Adriatic on the other hand are mostly dried up in the summer, and in winter become raging torrents which erode the thin soil from the upland slopes. The Adriatic coast is at a further disadvantage in having no good harbors.

The consequence of this natural imbalance has been that the western side of Italy has played a more prominent part in the history of civilization than the east, ever since the earliest Greek colonists rejected the desolate Adriatic coast and chose to make their homes on the Ionian and Tyrrhenian shores.

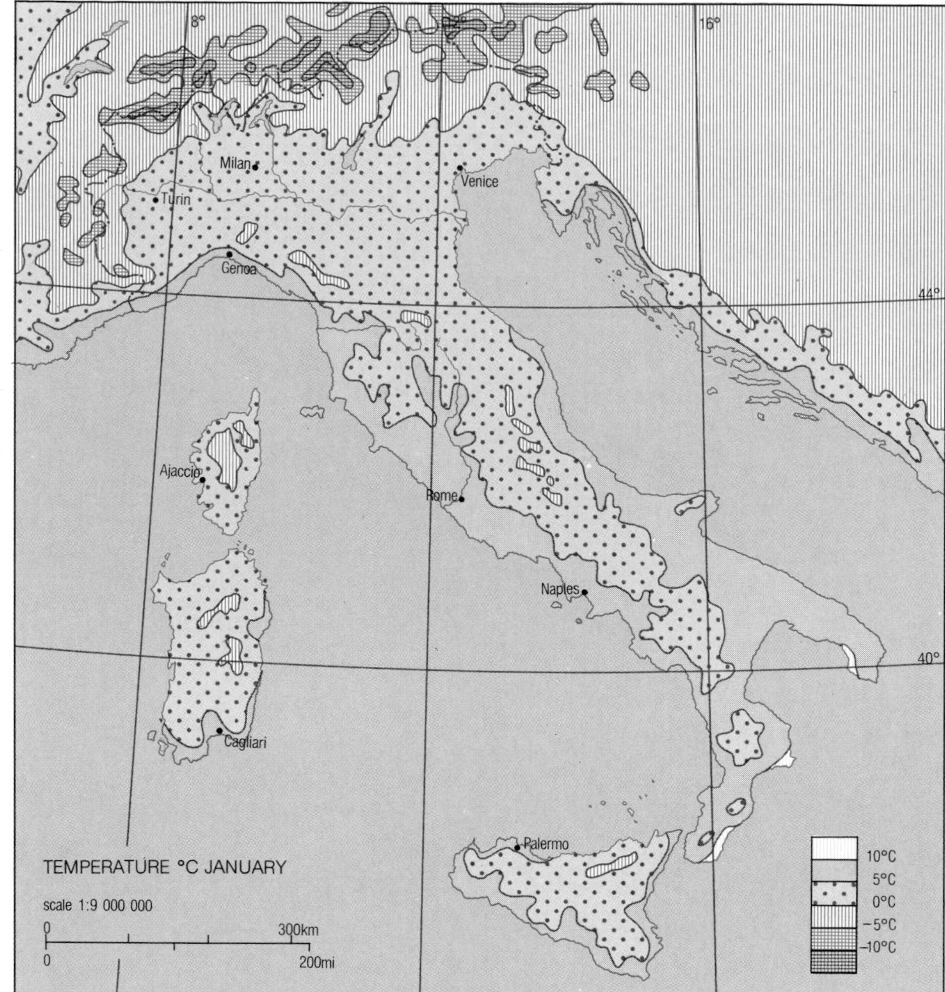

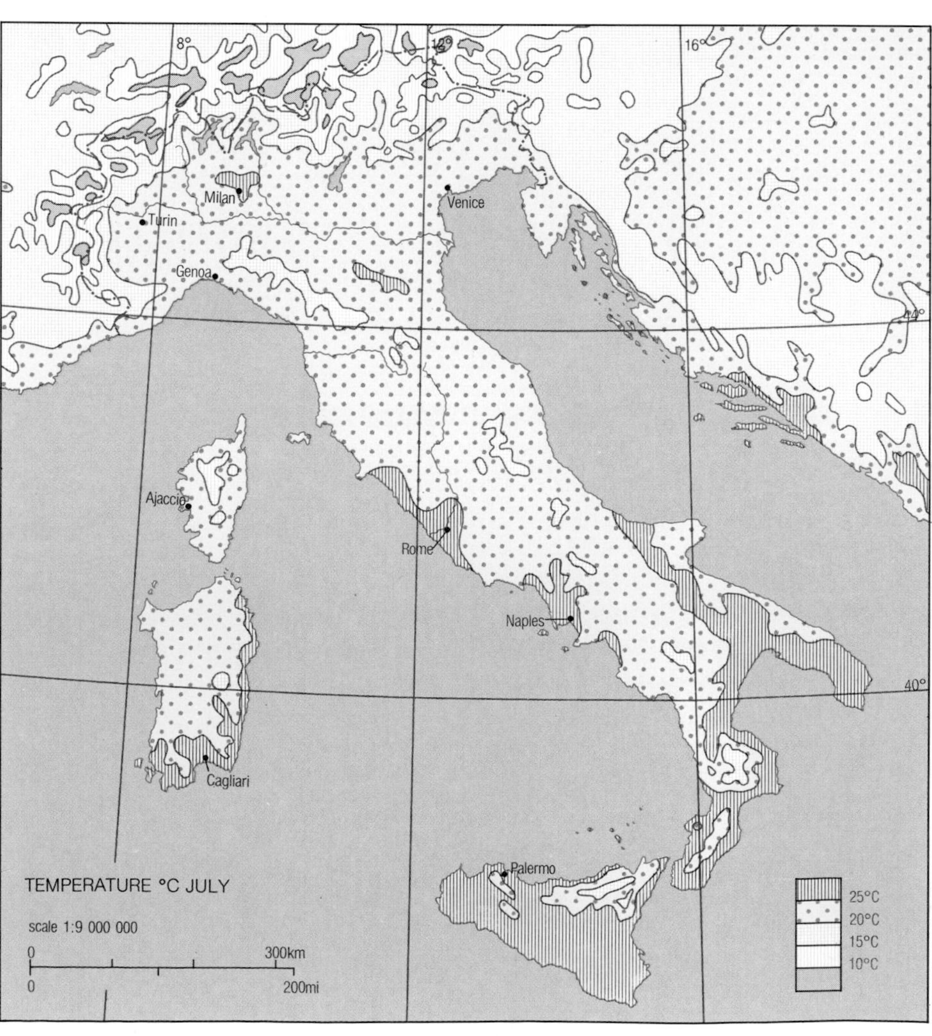

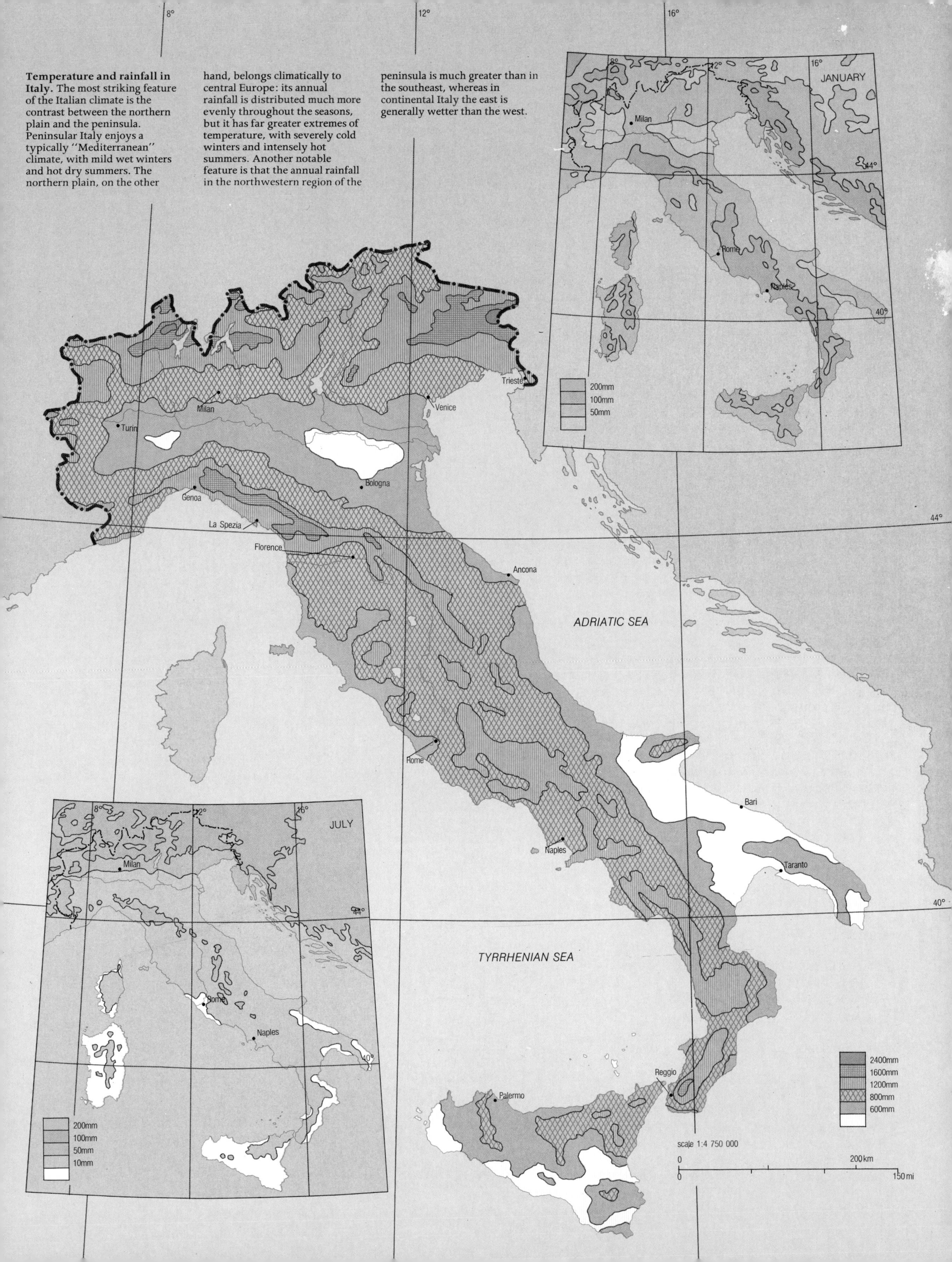

Temperature and rainfall in Italy. The most striking feature of the Italian climate is the contrast between the northern plain and the peninsula. Peninsular Italy enjoys a typically "Mediterranean" climate, with mild wet winters and hot dry summers. The northern plain, on the other hand, belongs climatically to central Europe: its annual rainfall is distributed much more evenly throughout the seasons, but it has far greater extremes of temperature, with severely cold winters and intensely hot summers. Another notable feature is that the annual rainfall in the northwestern region of the peninsula is much greater than in the southeast, whereas in continental Italy the east is generally wetter than the west.

The earliest traces of human activity on the site of Rome were found near the Tiber island, which marks an ancient crossing place. The first bridge, the Pons Sublicius, which was situated downstream, was traditionally ascribed to King Ancus Marcius. The ruins of a republican bridge, the Pons Aemilius (2nd century BC), can still be seen (in the foreground). The island itself has long been connected with the art of healing. A temple to Aesculapius, the Greek god of healing, was established there after a plague in 293 BC; and a famous hospital (16th century) still stands on the island.

Apulia has always been a backward region. It has the lowest rainfall of all the regions of peninsular Italy (an annual average ranging between 57 and 67 centimeters), and suffers badly from drought, especially in the barren and riverless uplands of the Murge, the limestone plateau between Bari and Taranto. In Cicero's day (the 1st century BC) Apulia was the "most sparsely populated part of Italy" (*Letters to Atticus* 13.4), and throughout antiquity it remained culturally isolated and politically unimportant.

The other main lowland area of peninsular Italy lies to the west of the central Apennines and occupies the regions of Campania, Latium and Tuscany. These regions exhibit a variety of physical features. A network of volcanic hills and mountains runs down the western side of Italy from Mount Amiata in southern Tuscany to the still active Vesuvius on the bay of Naples. The greater part of this system consists of extinct volcanoes surrounded by volcanic tuff plateaus and interspersed with a series of crater lakes, the main examples being lakes Bolsena, Vico and Bracciano in south Etruria, Albano and Nemi to the south of Rome in the Alban hills, and Lake Averno in the Campi Flegrei to the west of Naples. The volcanic soil of this central region contains essential natural fertilizers (phosphates and potash) and is extremely productive. Along the Tyrrhenian coast is a series of small alluvial plains, while the interior of the region is traversed by an interconnected chain of elevated basins which borders the eastern side; the most important of these alluvial valleys are the upper Arno between Florence and Arezzo, the Val di Chiana, the middle Tiber, and the Liri, Sacco and Volturno valleys which connect Latium and Campania.

These river valleys are also natural corridors of communication, and together they form the main longitudinal route along the western side of Italy which is followed today by the main railroad track and the Autostrada del Sole between Florence and Naples. The chief natural lines of communication from the coast to the interior also run along the river valleys, and above all along the Tiber. The lower Tiber valley is the nodal point of the network of natural communications of central Italy, and it was inevitable that the lowest available crossing of the Tiber, which occurs at Rome, should become an important center. A defensible position with a good supply of fresh water, it dominated the crossing point at the Tiber island, where the first bridge, the Pons Sublicius, was constructed in the reign of King Ancus Marcius. In historical times this part of the city comprised the commercial harbor (the Portus) and the cattle market (the Forum Boarium). It was also the site of the "Great Altar" of Hercules, which was supposedly founded by the natives of the region in gratitude to Hercules, who had slain Cacus, the giant of the Palatine. The legend implies that the Forum Boarium was an important meeting

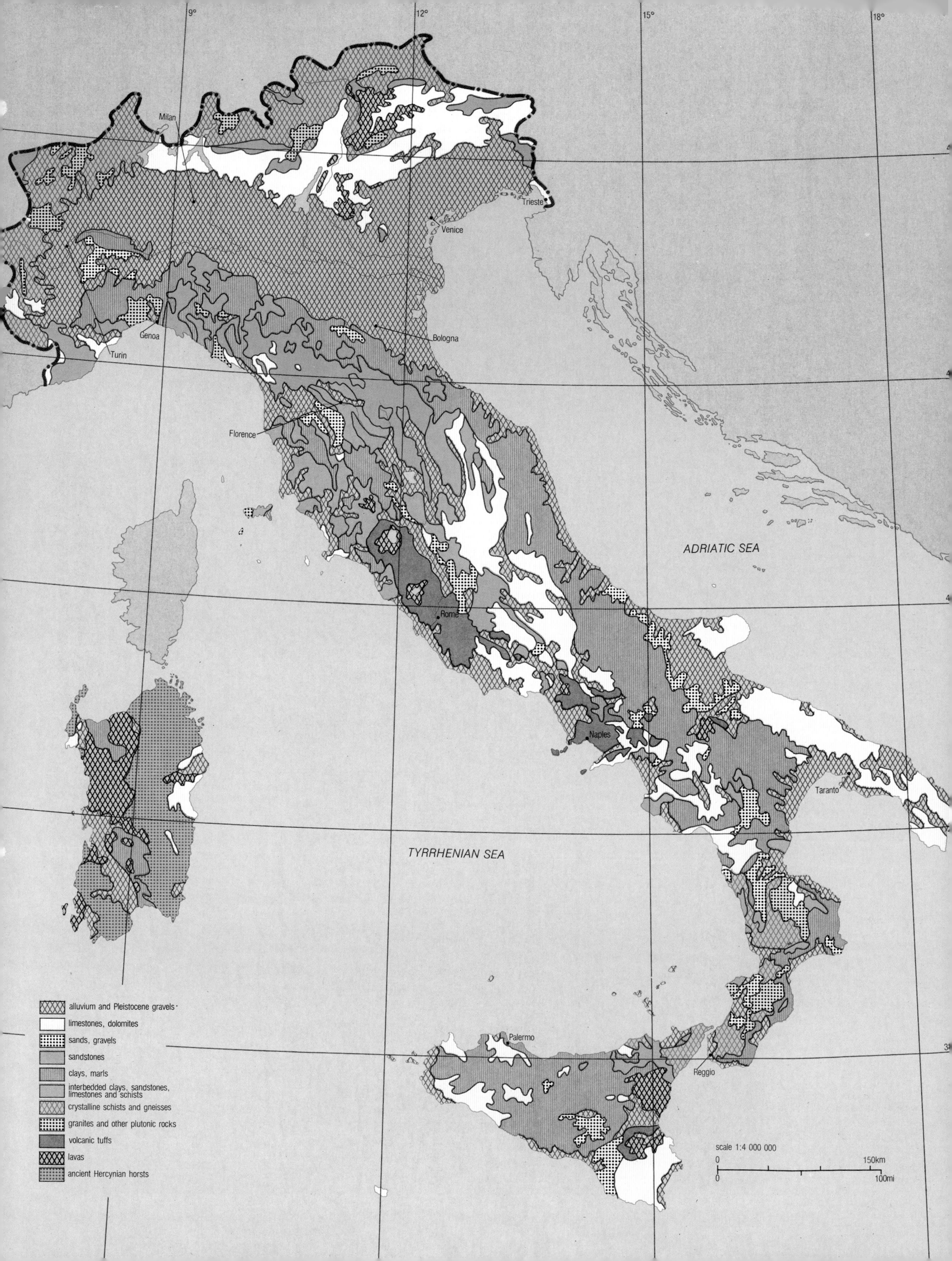
9°
12°
15°
18°
Milan
Trieste
Venice
Genoa
Turin
Bologna
Florence
ADRIATIC SEA
Rome
Naples
Taranto
TYRRHENIAN SEA
Palermo
Reggio
alluvium and Pleistocene gravels
limestones, dolomites
sands, gravels
sandstones
clays, marls
interbedded clays, sandstones, limestones and schists
crystalline schists and gneisses
granites and other plutonic rocks
volcanic tuffs
lavas
ancient Hercynian horsts
scale 1:4 000 000
0
150km
0
100mi

Above The story of the miraculous rescue of Romulus and Remus became a favorite theme in Roman art. This relief on a stone altar of the 2nd century AD shows the shepherd Faustulus discovering the twins and the she-wolf near the Palatine.

Left: The geology of Italy. The geology of Italy is mainly determined by that of the Apennines, the great chain of mountains that forms the backbone of the peninsula. The Apennines consist largely of limestone, sandstone and clay in the northern and central districts, and of granite in Calabria. The western foothills of the Apennines in Tuscany are rich in mineral deposits; while further south along the shores of the Tyrrhenian Sea there is a series of volcanic zones, extinct in the region of Lazio from Mt Amiata to the Alban hills south of Rome, but still active in the area of Mt Vesuvius, which has erupted on several occasions since the great explosion of 24 August 79 AD.

place which was frequented before the city of Rome was founded.

The natural advantages of the site were clearly recognized by the Romans themselves. Thus Livy, in a speech which he puts into the mouth of Camillus: "Not without reason did gods and men choose this spot for the site of our city — the salubrious hills, the river to bring us produce from the inland regions and sea-borne commerce from abroad, the sea itself, near enough for convenience yet not so near as to bring danger from foreign fleets, our situation in the very heart of Italy — all these advantages make it of all places in the world the best for a city destined to grow great" (Livy 5. 54. 4).

The foundation of Rome

The beginnings of Rome have been the object of inquiry, speculation and controversy since historical writing first began. As early as the 5th century BC Greek historians included Rome among the foundations of the Trojan hero Aeneas, who was thought to have fled to Italy after the sack of Troy. Aeneas was in fact only one of several mythical adventurers who were said to have wandered around the western Mediterranean and to have founded settlements along its shores. Whether any historical reality lies behind these legends is doubtful, but they were popular with the Greek reading public and eventually took root also in Rome.

The Romans themselves produced no historical literature until about 200 BC when a senator of illustrious family, Q. Fabius Pictor, wrote the first history of Rome. The work, written in Greek, does not survive, apart from a few quotations. Fabius Pictor probably consulted priestly archives, the records of the leading aristocratic families and the accounts of Greek historians; these sources, together with the evidence of popular oral tradition and of archaic inscriptions, monuments and relics, are likely to have formed the basis of his account of Rome's earliest history. Fabius Pictor attributed the foundation of the city to Romulus. According to the traditional story, Romulus was abandoned as a child on the banks of the Tiber, together with his twin brother Remus. The infants were saved when they were suckled by a she-wolf, and then rescued by shepherds among whom they spent their early years in the hills overlooking the left bank of the river. It was here that Romulus later founded the city that bore his name, after killing his brother in a petty quarrel.

This famous story was part of the oldest native tradition, and was well established as part of the city's heritage many years before the time of Fabius Pictor. But at a certain point (the dating is uncertain) the story of Aeneas was accepted locally and grafted onto the native tradition. The result was a version which eventually became canonical: Aeneas arrived in Latium where he founded the city of Lavinium; after his death his son Ascanius founded Alba Longa, where his descendants ruled as kings for over 400 years. Romulus and Remus belonged to this line, being the sons of the god Mars and the daughter of one of the kings of Alba.

This contrived assemblage of folk tale and conjecture was put together in the course of the 3rd century BC. A version of it certainly appeared in Fabius Pictor, and it was handed down and developed in later historical works until it received definitive treatment in the hands of Virgil, Ovid and Livy. Historical elements in the story are hard to discern. As has been said, the part played by Aeneas and the Trojans is almost certainly pure fiction, although some scholars see in it a dim memory of contacts between the Aegean world and Italy in the Mycenaean age. The prominence of Lavinium and Alba Longa does however reflect the importance which these places had as religious centers in early times; it is striking that some of the earliest archaeological traces of permanent settlement in Latium have been found precisely at Lavinium and in the area of the Alban hills. It should be noted, however, that the very earliest Latin sites also include Rome, which cannot at present be shown to be later than either Lavinium or the Alban hills sites. The developed tradition held that all the historic centers of Latium were colonies of Alba Longa and that Rome was the latest; but the supposed chronological interval between the foundations of Alba and Rome is a purely artificial construction based on the discrepancy between the conventional Greek date (1182 BC) for the Trojan War, in which Aeneas took part, and the firmly held belief of the Romans that their city was founded in the 8th century BC. The consequence was that a dynasty of kings of Alba had to be fabricated in order to fill the gap of more than 400 years between Aeneas and Romulus.

Most Roman writers believed that the city was founded in the 8th century BC, although there was disagreement about the exact year. Fabius Pictor placed it in 748 BC, but other alternatives (753, 751, 728) were canvassed by his successors. The date which finally became standard (753) was proposed by the scholar M. Terentius Varro at the end of the Republic. Traces of primitive huts have been found on the Palatine hill, traditionally the site of Romulus' settlement, dating from the 8th century BC; but other finds, mostly from tombs in the valley of the Forum, seem to indicate that the site had been occupied from at least the 10th century. The archaeological evidence does however seem to confirm that the Palatine was the first part of the city to be permanently settled. Thus it can be said that some of the elements of the foundation story may be based on fact, although Romulus himself cannot be considered historical. But the belief that the city came into being through a deliberate act of "foundation" made it necessary to postulate a founder; the same mechanical process required that Romulus must have created some of the basic institutions of the city. Thus the senate, the tribes, the *curiae* and so on are attributed to him by our sources, which are effectively saying that these institutions were as old as the city itself. In this they were probably correct.

Since the work of Theodor Mommsen in the last century it has been recognized that our tradition is basically sound on the history of the constitution, but is less reliable when dealing with political and military events. But even the most sensational and romantic parts of the traditional story may contain elements of historical fact, as an extreme example will illustrate. A few months after the founding of the city, so we are told, there occurred the rape of the Sabine women, a notorious escapade that led to a war between the Romans and the Sabines and then to a reconciliation between them and the joint rule of their respective leaders, Romulus and Titus Tatius. This story, fantastic though its details are, forms part of a considerable body of evidence which suggests that the population of early Rome contained a significant Sabine element; for example the Latin language exhibits many signs of Sabine influence, most strikingly in certain basic domestic words such as *bos* ("ox"), *scrofa* ("sow") and *popina* ("kitchen").

Secondly, the union of Romans and Sabines under the joint rule of Romulus and Titus Tatius must be considered in the light of the many indications that Rome came into existence as the result of a fusion of two communities, the one on the Palatine, the other on the Quirinal – or perhaps rather through the incorporation of the latter by the former. That Rome was originally a double community is the view of our sources (Livy (1.13.4) writes of the *geminata urbs*, "the two-fold city"), and is confirmed by the dualism of certain archaic institutions. Thus for example the Salii, the "dancing priests" of Mars, were divided into two groups – the Salii of the Palatine and the Salii of the Quirinal. This primitive dualism may also be reflected in the fact that the Roman citizens were also called "Quirites."

The early kings

After Romulus' death the kingship was held in turn by men of Sabine and Latin extraction. The Sabine Numa Pompilius, Rome's second king, is presented in the tradition as a pious man whose peaceful reign saw the creation of the major priesthoods and religious institutions of Rome, and in particular of the calendar. He was succeeded by the Latin Tullus Hostilius, a fierce warrior who fought an epic struggle against Alba Longa, Rome's mother-city, and finally destroyed it. The next king was Ancus Marcius, a Sabine, who was remembered by tradition for extending Roman territory as far as the coast and for the foundation of Ostia at the mouth of the Tiber.

With the exception of the shadowy Romulus these early kings are probably historical. Admittedly they no longer emerge from the legends as real flesh-and-blood personalities – it is obvious for instance that the pacific Numa and the bellicose Tullus are little more than contrasting stereotypes – but we need not doubt that the kings of Rome did include men named Numa Pompilius, Tullus Hostilius and Ancus Marcius. The traditions that linked their names with particular institutions and military achievements may well be correct in essentials. Above all the stories are set against a background of authentic constitutional practice, and it is possible to piece together a coherent and plausible reconstruction of the political and social organization of Rome under the early kings.

Political and social organization

We are told that Romulus chose a hundred "fathers" to advise him; these men formed the first senate, and their descendants were known as patricians. He also divided the people into three tribes, called Ramnes, Tities and Luceres, which were in their turn subdivided into 30 smaller units (ten in each tribe) called *curiae*. The *curiae* were local divisions, but membership was also determined by kinship. This means, probably, that in origin the *curiae* consisted of groups of neighboring families. They also functioned as constituent units of a primitive assembly, the *comitia curiata*. Romulus is also said to have organized an army of 3000 infantry (*milites*) and 300 cavalry (*celeres*), each tribe contributing 1000 and 100 men respectively. The tribal contingents were commanded by tribunes (*tribuni militum, tribuni celerum*).

At the head of the state was the king. Kingship in early Rome was not hereditary. On the death of a king the functions of government were carried on by the senators, each one in turn holding office for a period of five days, with the title *interrex* ("between-king"), until a suitable successor could be found. The essential test of his suitability was religious. According to Livy, the normal procedure was for the augurs (experts in divination) to ask the gods to give their assent by sending suitable signs (auspices). Thus the king was "inaugurated," a word that has passed into our language. Finally, the king's position was confirmed by a vote of the *comitia curiata*.

The king had political, military, judicial and religious functions, and the powers he exercised in these spheres can be summed up in the concept of *imperium*. This *imperium* was a kind of divine or magical authority which could only be conferred by inauguration and the taking of auspices. As for the senate, its role seems to have been confined during the monarchic period to that of advising the king. It was said however to possess *auctoritas*, a kind of religious prestige which the fathers exercised in approving and ratifying the decisions of the *comitia curiata*; and they played a fundamental role in nominating the king through the *interrex*, who was one of their number. When the king died (or if, during the Republic, both consuls happened to die before any replacement could be inaugurated) it was said that "the auspices returned to the fathers."

The fathers represented groups of great social importance called *gentes*. The *gens* was essentially a kinship group consisting of families which traced their descent back to a common ancestor and expressed their relationship in the use of a common name. The individual members of the *gentes* in fact had two names: a personal name or *praenomen* (e.g. Marcus, Gnaeus, Titus) and a gentile name or *nomen* in the form of a patronymic (hence Marcius, Naevius, Titius). We may compare the names of the Scottish clans – MacDonald, MacGregor, etc. The two-name system is found also among other Italic peoples, and must imply that they too had *gentes*.

In the historical period the *gentes* practiced their own religious rites and festivals, and had their own distinctive customs in matters such as burial of the dead. Their origin and their character in early times are however matters of dispute. Some scholars have argued that the *gens* was a primordial unit which existed before the emergence of the state; on this view it functioned as an autonomous political and economic organization, possessing its own territory and its own recognized leader. Some residual traces of this hypothetical "gentile organization" survived into the republican period, and can be seen for example in the exploit of the Fabian *gens*, which in 479 BC fought a private war against the town of Veii. The notion of the *gentes* existing "before the

This terracotta head of Hermes is from a 6th-century statue group which stood on the roof of a temple at Veii. The sculptures are popularly attributed to Vulca, a famous Veientine artist of the time who was summoned to Rome by King Tarquin to make the cult statue of Jupiter for the temple on the Capitol.

The *fasces* (bundles of rods and axes) symbolized the powers of the chief magistrates, and were carried by their attendants (lictors). According to tradition the *fasces* were among the royal insignia borrowed from the Etruscans, a tradition confirmed by the discovery of an iron model of *fasces* in the Etruscan town of Vetulonia.

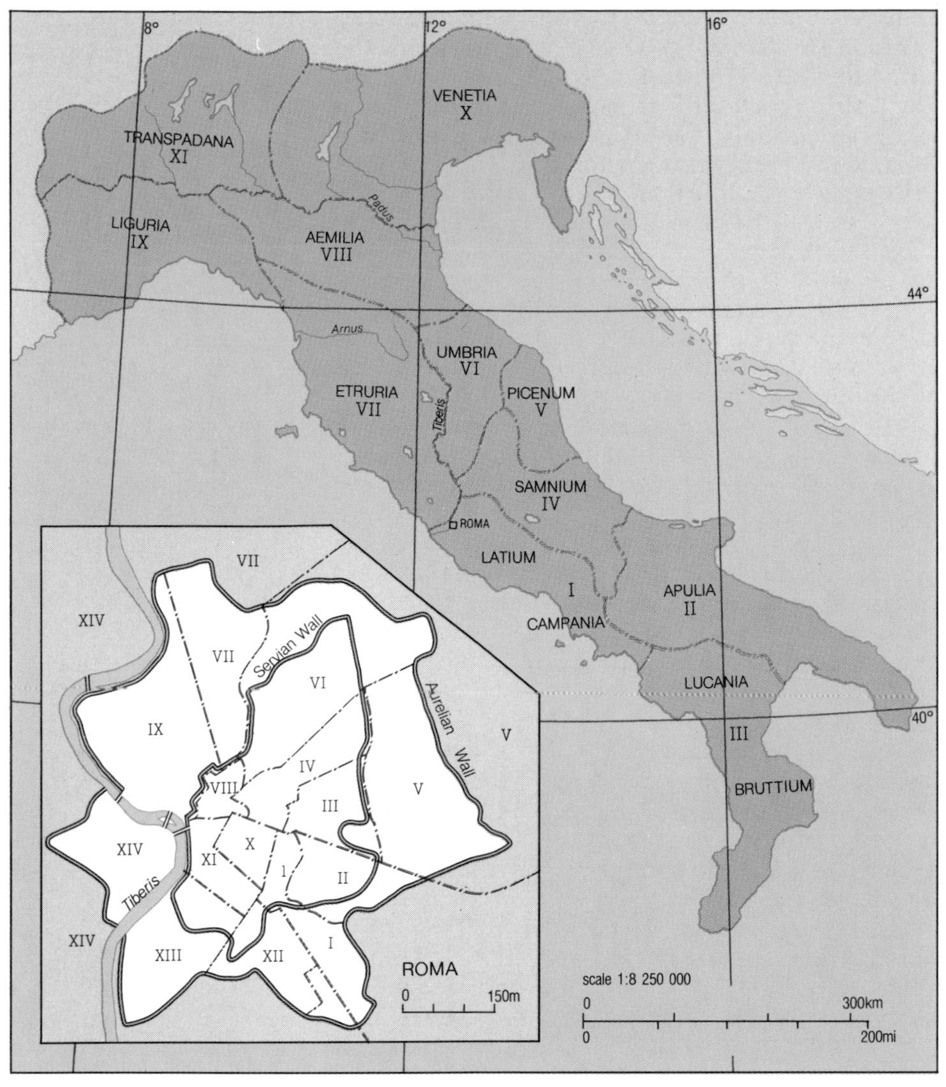

The Regions of Rome

I Porta Capena
II Caelimontium
III Isis et Serapis
IV Templum Pacis
V Esquiliae
VI Alta Semita
VII Via Lata
VIII Forum Romanum
IX Circus Flaminius
X Palatium
XI Circus Maximus
XII Piscina Publica
XIII Aventinus
XIV Trans Tiberim

Augustan regions of Italy and regions of Rome. In early times, Italy was a country of great linguistic, ethnic and cultural diversity. With the unification of the country under Roman rule this primitive disunity was largely, but not entirely, submerged; traces of it were, and still are, preserved in the names of the Italian regions. The first formal division of Italy into regions was made by the emperor Augustus, who divided the country into 11 administrative districts. The city of Rome was similarly divided into 14 regions for administrative purposes.

state" is however very speculative, and their position in relation to the tribes and *curiae* is uncertain.

In historical times the family, not the *gens*, was the basic unit of Roman society. The Roman *familia* comprised the whole household, including property as well as persons, and was under the control of the head of the household, the *paterfamilias*. The *paterfamilias* exercised a virtually unrestrained authority over all members of the household, who were said to be in his power (*in potestate*). His sons, even though they might be mature adults with children of their own, had no independent legal status or rights of property, and were not released from their father's authority until his death, whereupon they became *patres familiarum* in their own right. The father's power (*patria potestas*) included the right to kill members of his family or to sell them into slavery. He was subject only to moral constraints and the limits of custom; for example on important matters he was traditionally expected to consult the advice of senior relatives and friends, although he was under no obligation to follow it. He represented the family in its relations with other families and with the community as a whole; and he performed, on behalf of the family, the necessary rituals and sacrifices to his departed ancestors and to the gods. The family was thus a kind of miniature state, with the *paterfamilias* as priest, judge and source of law.

Private ownership of property, and its concentration in the hands of the *paterfamilias*, are taken for granted as original features of Roman society by our historical tradition, and are presupposed in the earliest surviving legal texts. Nevertheless it is still possible that this represents a secondary development from a time when property, especially land, was held in common by the *gens*. There may be a shadowy reflection of this in the provision of the Twelve Tables (450 BC) that if a *paterfamilias* died intestate and without heirs, his property should go back to the *gens*. In any case nothing prevents us from assuming that in the archaic period there was much greater solidarity among the constituent families of a *gens*, that they occupied neighboring properties and that the most influential of the *patres* exercised some sort of *de facto* leadership over the *gens* as a whole.

The power and influence of the leading aristocratic *gentes* derived partly from the support of large numbers of dependants called clients (*clientes*). *Clientela* was one of the oldest Roman institutions and was traditionally ascribed to Romulus. The relationship between patron and client was based on moral, rather than legal, constraints, the client having been accepted into the "good faith" (*fides*) of the patron. A client can be defined as a free man who entrusted himself to the protection of another man and in return paid him respect and performed certain services. In the late Republic these services consisted of political support and personal attendance, but in earlier times the obligations of clients were apparently much more extensive.

The status of both patron and client was hereditary and passed on from one generation to another. It is possible moreover that at first clients belonged within the structure of the *gens* alongside the *gentiles* properly so called, and that they too bore the gentile name. There is some evidence that in the archaic period clients were assigned portions of land which they cultivated on behalf of their patrons and were also obliged to perform military service; it was among their clients that the great *gentes* of the early republican period recruited their private armies.

The development of the city

In the earliest period Rome was a small village or collection of villages on the Palatine and neighboring hills. Similar settlements existed at other sites in Latium Vetus, and excavations have recently begun to give us some idea of their character. The villages consisted of small groups of thatched huts clustered together in defensible positions on the hills overlooking the Roman campagna.

The daily life of these hut villages, which probably consisted of no more than a few hundred persons at most, was very basic. Subsistence was provided by primitive agriculture (the chief crops being emmer wheat, barley, peas and beans) supplemented by raising stock (chiefly goats and pigs), fishing, hunting and gathering. Domestic production saw to the provision of pottery, textiles and other household necessities. Sharp differences of wealth or status are not apparent in the evidence.

From about 770 BC onwards the volume of evidence (still mainly from cemeteries) begins to increase, indicating a rise in the population. Secondly there are signs of more intensive contacts with the outside world, especially with the Greek

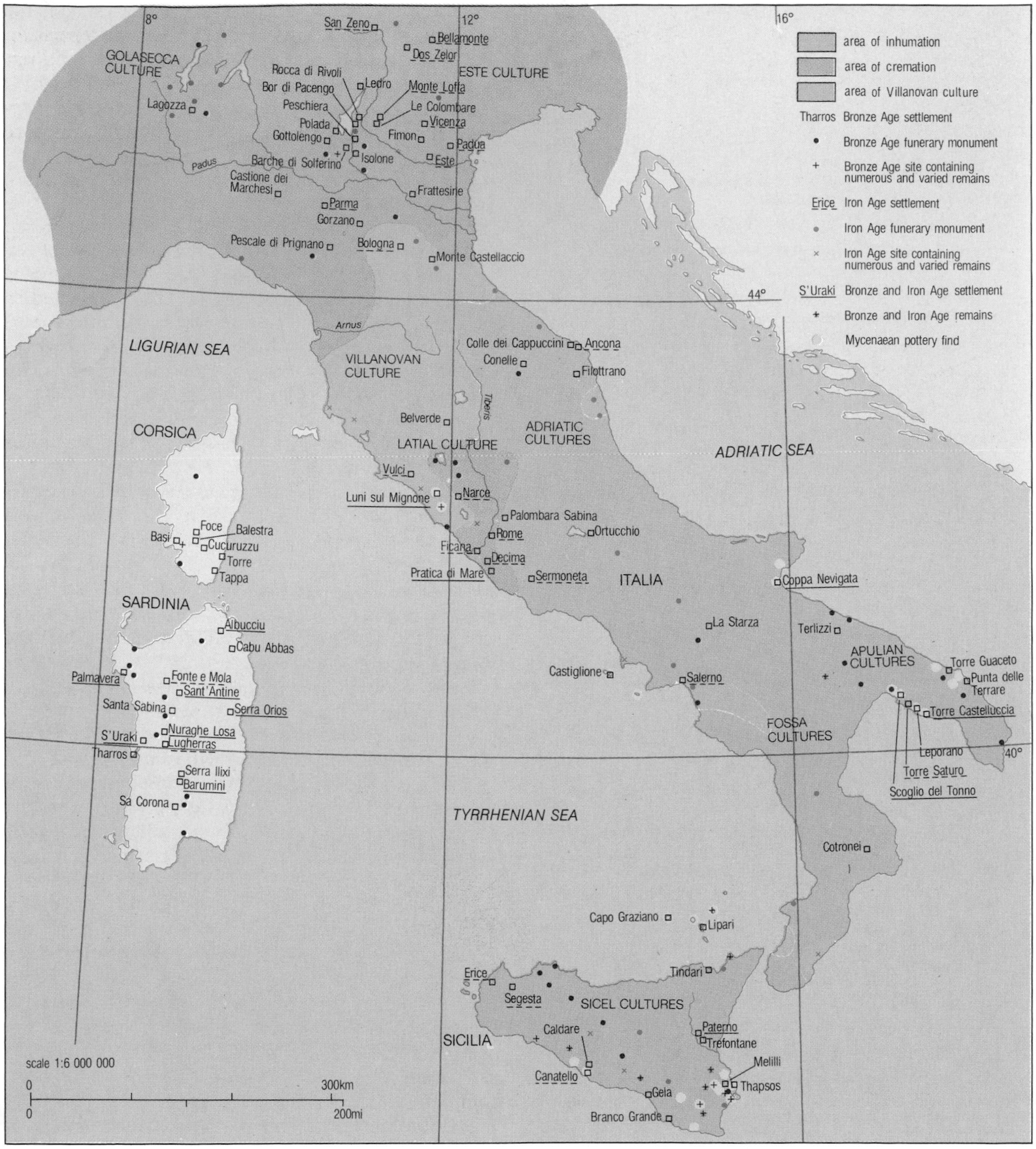

Bronze and Iron Age sites in Italy. Italy during the Bronze Age shows a remarkable uniformity in its material culture. The large number of mountain sites has led to the use of the term "Apennine culture" to describe the civilization of the Italian Bronze Age, which seems to have been based largely on a transhumant pastoral economy. With the beginning of the Iron Age in the first millennium BC the evidence becomes more abundant, indicating a general increase in the size and number of settlements, and the emergence of locally differentiated cultures. These can be broadly divided into two groups, according to the type of burial rites used. Inhumation (the "Fossa cultures") was generally practiced in southern Italy and in the Adriatic regions, while cremation (the "urnfield cultures") was the rule in northern Italy, Etruria and Umbria west of the Tiber.

colonies of Campania. Other features of the period include increasing specialization of craft production (for example the use of the potter's wheel), and the emergence of economically differentiated social classes. The latter phenomenon begins to appear in the second half of the 8th century and becomes increasingly evident in the 7th. The evidence comes from tombs of exceptional richness which have been unearthed in many sites in Latium, especially during the last few years. These tombs contain extraordinarily rich personal ornaments and show the progressive formation of a dominant aristocracy which had succeeded in concentrating the economic surplus of the community into its own hands and perpetuating its domination through inheritance.

During this period the villages on the hill tops became large nucleated settlements, and in a number of cases received the protection of artificially constructed fortifications in the form of terraces, earthworks and ditches. This development no doubt occurred also at Rome, which had expanded considerably from the original Palatine village, and by the middle of the 7th century included the valley of the Forum, the Quirinal, parts of the Esquiline and probably also the Caelian.

Towards the end of the 7th century BC there is evidence of a major change in the physical aspect of the settlement, which now began to take on the appearance of a fully urbanized community. In various parts of the city the huts were replaced by more substantial houses with stone foundations, timber frames and tiled roofs. In the area of the Forum the huts were demolished and in their place a formal public square was laid out. Traces of the foundations of temples, public buildings and sanctuaries have been unearthed, together with fragments of roof-tiles, terracotta antefixes and decorated architectural friezes.

The later kings

The first appearance of these changes coincides in date with the accession of Tarquinius Priscus, or

Coin of 54 BC issued by Marcus Brutus, the future murderer of Caesar. The reverse type shows his ancestor L. Junius Brutus, consul in 509 BC and one of the founding fathers of the Republic. The obverse celebrates the aristocratic ideal of *libertas*, here portrayed as a goddess.

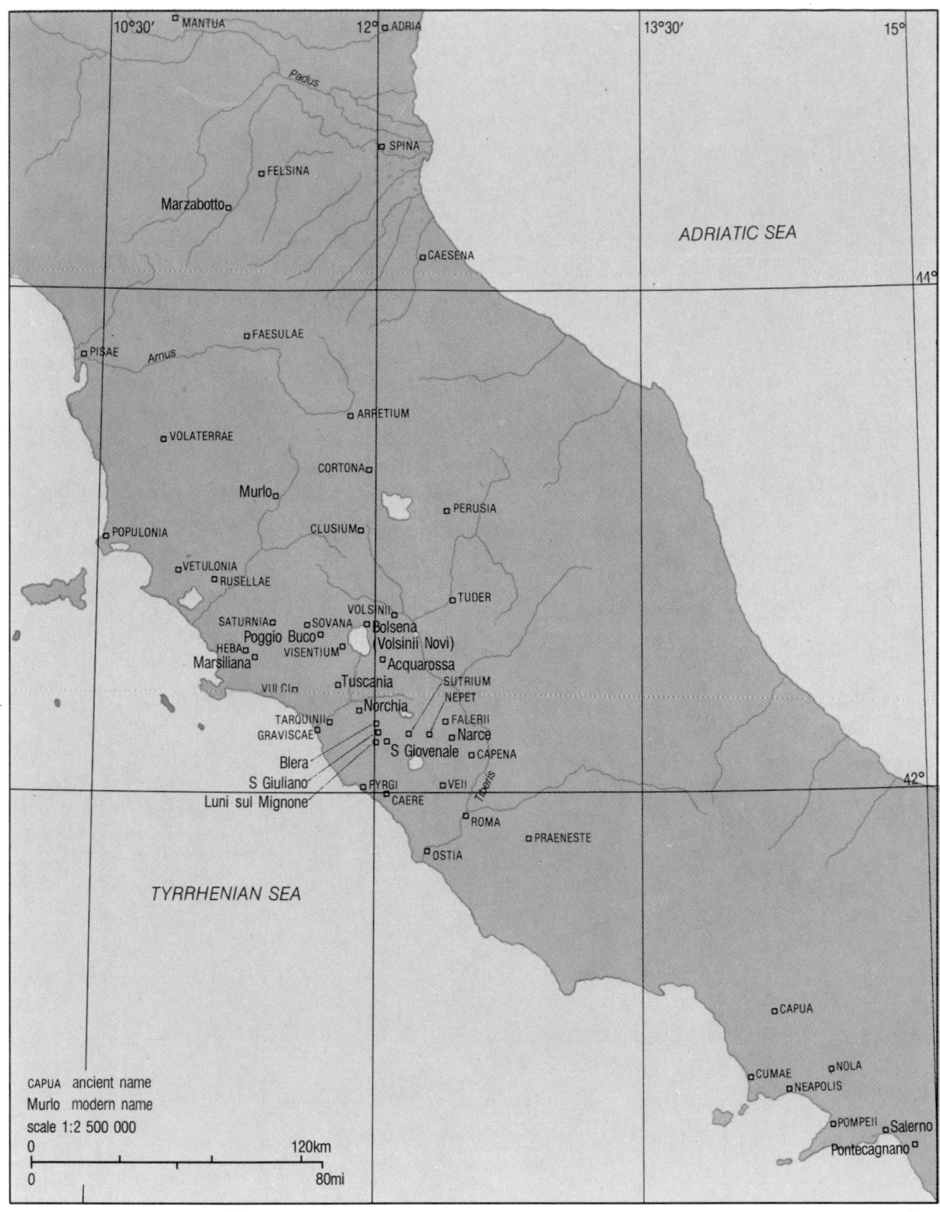

Etruria and Etruscan cities, 6th century BC. The Etruscan civilization grew up in the region bounded by the Tyrrhenian Sea in the west, the Arno in the north, and the Apennines and the Tiber in the east and south. Politically speaking, the region was divided into powerful independent city-states which reached the height of their power during the 6th century BC. Etruscan settlements were also established in the Po valley, including Felsina (Bologna), Mantua and Ravenna, and in Campania, where the main centers were Capua, Nola and Pompeii, and a number of sites near Salerno.

Tarquin I (traditional dates 616–579 BC), who according to our sources transformed the appearance of the civic center of Rome. The archaeological evidence thus provides a general confirmation of the historical tradition, which can in fact be shown to contain much genuine information about the last century of the monarchy. The last kings undoubtedly belong to history, although it should be noted that the personal history of the kings themselves contains many uncertain elements.

Tarquinius Priscus was an Etruscan who migrated to Rome where he was accepted in the most influential circles, and was at length chosen as king on the death of Ancus Marcius. He ruled for more than 35 years, and was eventually succeeded by Servius Tullius, a man of obscure origin who seized power in a palace revolution following the assassination of Tarquin. The long and successful reign of Servius was brought to a violent end when he too was murdered, in a coup engineered by his son-in-law and successor, Tarquin II, who was either the son or grandson of Tarquin I. Known to posterity as Tarquin the Proud, the second Tarquin was a brutal and despotic ruler who was finally overthrown in 509 BC by a group of aristocrats who established a republican government.

This is a fairly straightforward story; the reality may have been more complex. For example the emperor Claudius unearthed some information about a king of Rome called Mastarna, who did not appear in the traditional list of seven kings enshrined in the writings of the historians. His evidence suggests that there may have been more than three kings of Rome in the 6th century BC, and that the dynastic history of the period was more confused than the tradition alleges.

The same is true of the downfall of the monarchy. This event is said to have occurred as a result of the outrage caused by the rape of Lucretia by one of Tarquin's sons. Tarquin was expelled but tried to return to Rome with the aid of Lars Porsenna of Clusium. Although the conventional histories maintained that Porsenna's attack was repelled by the Romans, thanks largely to Horatius and his two companions who held the bridge, there was a variant tradition which asserted that Porsenna actually succeeded in capturing Rome. The unpalatable version is less likely to have been invented than the more patriotic (and romantic) one, and it may even be that the overthrow of the monarchy was occasioned not by the fate of Lucretia but by the invading army of Lars Porsenna. However that may be, the anecdotal details of the story are only of secondary importance. What matters is that the main structural elements are sound, and permit us to make generalizations about the character of Roman society in the late regal period.

The first point to note is that a perceptible change takes place in the character of the monarchy itself. The later kings based their position on popular support and challenged the power and privileges of the aristocrats. Thus Tarquin I obtained the throne by canvassing among the masses, and enrolled new men in the senate. Servius Tullius and Tarquin II went further by openly flouting traditional procedures and launching an all-out assault on the aristocracy. Both seized power by illegal means and ruled without bothering to obtain the assent of the gods or the vote of the *comitia curiata*. Tarquin II completely ignored the advice of the senate, put to death its most prominent members and generally behaved like a typical tyrant. The most obvious comparison is in fact with the tyrants who were ruling in many of the Greek cities during this same period.

Like the Greek tyrants, the last three kings of Rome pursued an ambitious foreign policy, patronized the arts and embarked on extensive and grandiose building projects. The Greek tyrants also attempted to legitimize their position by claiming the special personal favor of the gods; for example, Pisistratus of Athens presented himself as a protégé of Athena. In the same way, it seems, Servius Tullius claimed a special relationship with the goddess Fortuna, to whom he built a temple in the Forum Boarium (excavations have in fact revealed part of the foundations of an archaic temple in this part of the city, dating precisely from the mid-6th century BC).

But the most important element of tyranny was its populist character. The tyrants expropriated the wealth of their aristocratic opponents and distributed it among their friends and supporters; at the same time they attacked oligarchic privileges and extended the franchise to wider groups. It is against this general background that Servius Tullius' "constitutional reforms" should be viewed. Servius is said to have created the *comitia centuriata*, a new assembly in which citizens were distributed in voting units called centuries and classified according to the amount of property they owned and for military purposes according to the weapons and armor they were able to afford.

The sources attribute to Servius an elaborate system which comprised five classes of infantry graded according to ascending levels of wealth and bearing different types of arms; in this form it certainly reflects later conditions, and cannot date back to the 6th century. But there is no reason to doubt that Servius introduced the centuriate organization. It is probably to him that we should attribute a simpler system, of which some traces survive in antiquarian sources, in which there was only one class of infantry; this was composed of men who owned a minimum amount of property and were called *adsidui*, to distinguish them from the poor, who were *infra classem* ("beneath the class") and excluded from the army. The poor were called *proletarii*, since they produced only offspring (*proles*).

According to the most widely accepted interpretation of the meager evidence, the class of infantry originally comprised 60 centuries (in later times this was the standard complement of a Roman legion), and the cavalry formed an additional six centuries. It is logical to assume that at the time of its introduction the century was a body of 100 men; this means that at the time of Servius Tullius Rome had a potential fighting force of 6000 infantry and 600 cavalry.

The reform was probably connected with the introduction of improved military techniques and a disciplined method of fighting in close formation. The Romans are said to have learned these new tactics from the Etruscans, who had themselves adopted the methods of the Greek heavy infantry, the so-called hoplites. The hoplites, like Servius' *adsidui*, were men who had sufficient property to equip themselves with arms. The introduction of the new techniques gave these men the means to bring about political changes, and it is often, and rightly, suggested that the tyrants were able to seize power and challenge the aristocrats because they were supported by the hoplites.

Servius is also said to have changed the basis of citizenship by creating new local tribes to which the citizens were assigned on the basis of residence. This had the effect of enfranchising large numbers of immigrants and others who were not members of the *curiae* and had hitherto been excluded from the citizen body. From this time onwards the old "Romulean" tribes and the *curiae* became increasingly obsolete.

The popular and anti-aristocratic character of the regime of the last kings is confirmed by the Romans' later attitude to the institution of kingship. In the republican period the very idea of a king was viewed with an almost pathological dislike. It is hard to believe that this was due solely to the popular memory of the second Tarquin's misdeeds; it is much more likely to be an element of the powerful aristocratic ideology of the ruling class of the Republic. This class was dominated by a narrow oligarchy of "nobles" who claimed the exclusive right to compete for positions of power and influence, and dignified this state of affairs with the name of "liberty" (*libertas*). The Romans were always conscious of the basic incompatibility of monarchy and *libertas*, and by taking precautions against the incidence of the former they hoped to defend and preserve the latter. The tradition is very likely correct when it states that two of the first acts of the new leaders of the Republic were to make the people swear an oath never to allow any man to be king in Rome and to legislate against anyone aspiring to a monarchical position in the future. But what was truly repugnant to the nobles was the thought of one of their number attempting to elevate himself above his peers by attending to the needs of the lower classes and winning their support by taking up their cause.

This explains why all the serious charges of monarchism (*regnum*) in the Republic were leveled against mavericks from the ruling elite whose only offense, as far as we can see, was to direct their personal efforts and resources to the relief of the poor. This was the case with the unfortunate Sp. Cassius, put to death in 486 BC, with Sp. Maelius, executed in 440, and with M. Manlius, who suffered a similar fate in 382. Later the murders of the

The "Lapis Niger," Rome's oldest public document. The fragmentary stone inscription, which was found under an area of black marble paving in the Forum, dates probably from the early 6th century BC. The text is in very archaic Latin and cannot be fully understood; but it seems to be some sort of ritual prescription for the performance of a cult or the maintenance of a sanctuary.

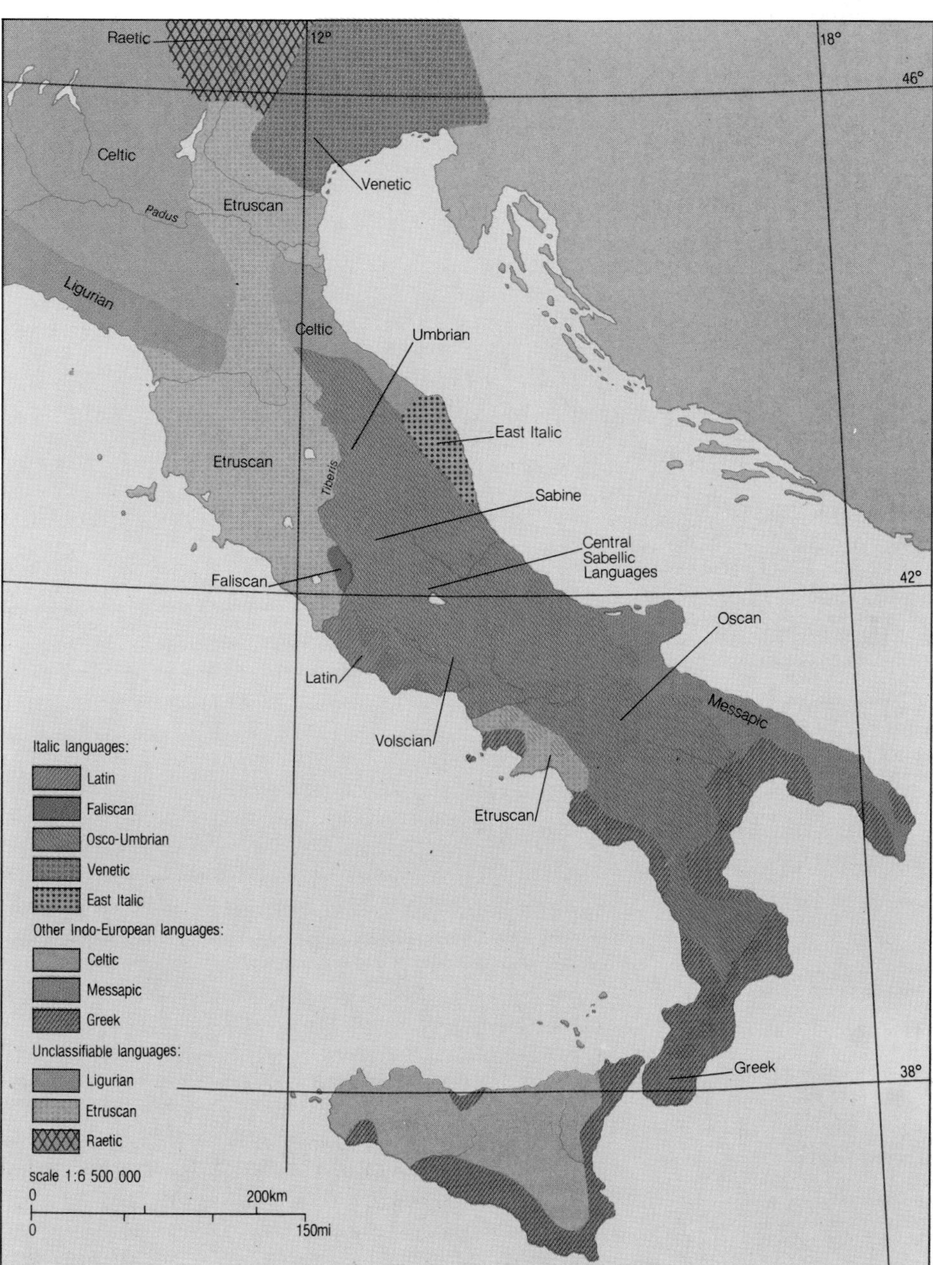

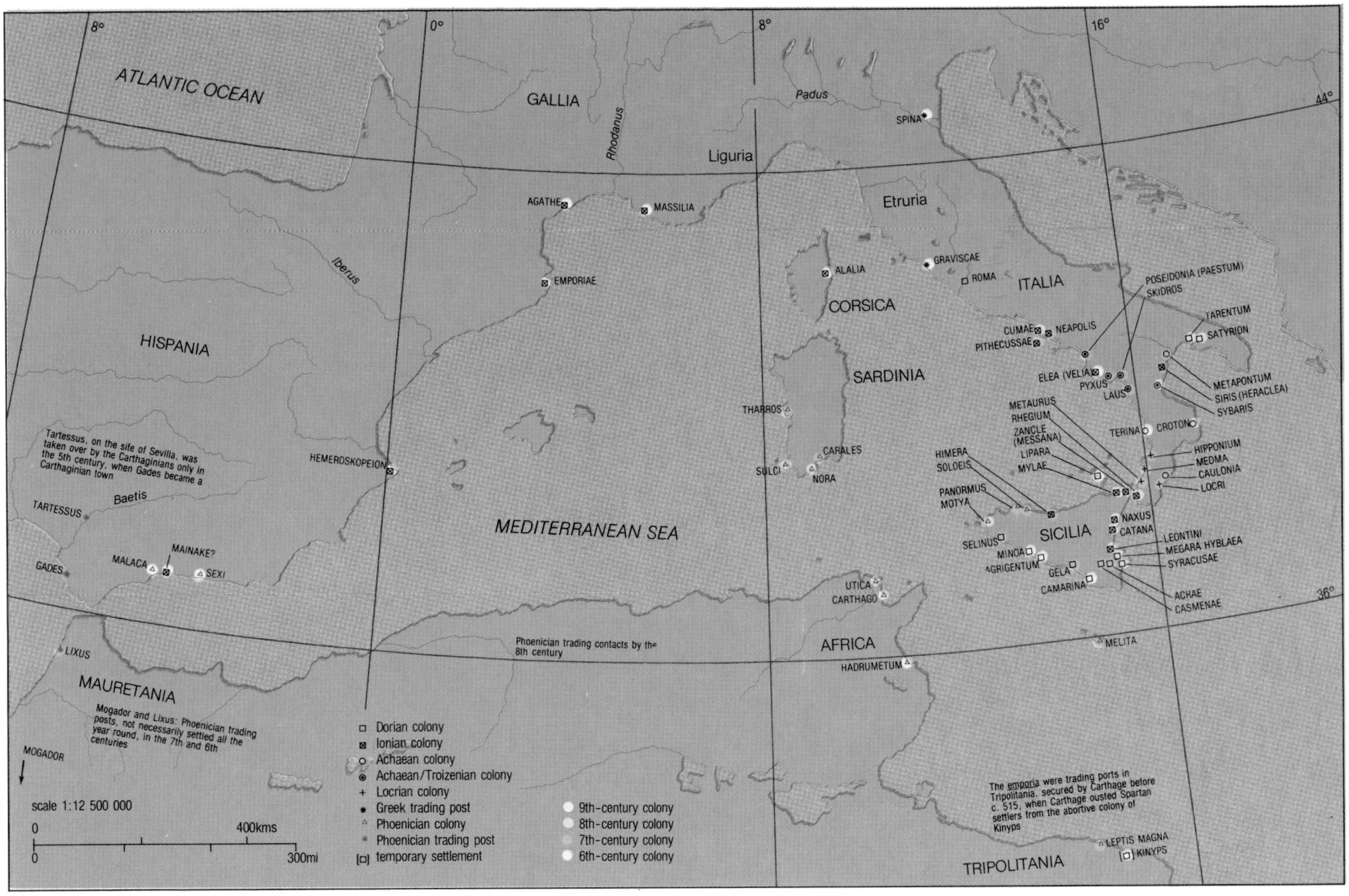

Greek and Phoenician colonies in the western Mediterranean.

Coin of P. Porcius Laeca, 110 or 109 BC. *Provocatio*, the right of appeal to the people, was considered a fundamental element of Roman citizenship. The coin shows *provocatio* in action, and bears the legend *"provoco"* ("I appeal").

Left: The languages of pre-Roman Italy, 450–400 BC. Before the Roman conquest, Italy was a country of great ethnic, cultural and linguistic diversity. Our knowledge of the languages of pre-Roman Italy is very limited, but by examining the meager evidence of inscriptions, place-names and other indications, scholars have been able to divide the early Italian languages into distinct groups. The main division is between Indo-European and non-Indo-European languages (the chief example of the latter being Etruscan).

Gracchi were justified also on the grounds that the brothers had aimed at kingship. However absurd this charge may have been in actuality, it was not made simply for rhetorical effect. At the time it was no doubt genuinely believed by those whose openly expressed hatred of kingship concealed a profound subconscious fear of the lower classes.

Early Rome and the Etruscans

The traditional view, which sees the end of the monarchy as an aristocratic reaction against a tyrannical regime, is undoubtedly more convincing than a modern theory which regards the expulsion of the Tarquins as a moment of national liberation, and the end of a period of Etruscan domination in Rome. It is true that the Tarquins were of Etruscan origin, but this does not mean that they were the puppets of some Etruscan power that had subordinated Rome to its rule. Tradition maintains that Rome was an independent city under the kings, and there is absolutely no evidence to suggest the contrary (apart from the brief episode of Lars Porsenna).

On the other hand it is clear that the cultural life of Rome was strongly influenced by the civilization of Etruria, a fact which is fully admitted by the tradition. For example the royal insignia, particularly the *fasces*, the bundles of rods and axes which symbolized the awesome powers of the holder of *imperium*, were borrowed from Etruria, as were the games, the ceremony of the triumph and certain religious cults and practices. Etruscan goods were imported into Rome; large quantities of *bucchero* pottery have been found in excavations, and there is evidence that local wares began to be produced in imitation. Etruscan influence is also evident in architecture and the decorative arts, and the presence of Etruscan craftsmen is indicated by the story that Tarquin II summoned a Veientine sculptor named Vulca to make the cult statue for the great temple of Jupiter.

A few Etruscan inscriptions have been found in Rome, but the majority of the inhabitants were Latin-speaking. The Latin language shows very few traces of Etruscan influence, which would be surprising if the city had been under Etruscan rule for any length of time. Moreover, Latin was the language of public documents, for example the inscription from beneath the so-called Lapis Niger, which dates from the early 6th century BC. That a number of Etruscan families took up residence in Rome is demonstrated by the presence of Etruscan names among the consuls of the early years of the Republic. This proves incidentally that the end of the monarchy did not entail the wholesale expulsion of Etruscans from the city.

The evidence shows that the Romans were apparently willing to accept immigrants into their society. This curious feature of archaic Rome, which is fully recognized by the historical tradition, seems also to have been characteristic of some of the Etruscan cities, where inscriptions have revealed the presence of families of Greek, Latin and Italic origin. The evidence seems to imply a kind of horizontal social mobility, by which individuals and groups could move freely from one community

An important archaic inscription was discovered in 1977 during excavations at the temple of Mater Matuta at Satricum in southern Latium. The preserved part of the text reads: "the comrades of Publius Valerius dedicated this to Mars." The P. Valerius in question may be the great P. Valerius Publicola, one of the first consuls of the Republic; but the real importance of the text is that it confirms the picture of a society dominated by bands of warriors owing their allegiance to aristocratic leaders and clans.

to another and expect to be accepted and integrated into the social structure even at the highest levels. Thus the simple story of how the elder Tarquin made a purely personal decision to leave Tarquinia and seek his fortune in Rome is another case in which the ancient tradition turns out to be more credible than the modern theories which aim to replace it.

The origins of the Roman Republic

In 509 BC a group of aristocrats expelled Tarquin and put an end to the monarchy. In its place they devised the curious institution of a collegiate magistracy, in which two men shared the supreme power. The consuls, as they later came to be called (originally they were known simply as "praetors," but the term consul will be used here to avoid confusion), were elected by the *comitia centuriata* and held office for a year. Reelection for consecutive terms was not permitted. The consuls held *imperium* (they were still obliged to submit to the formality of a vote of the *comitia curiata*) and they inherited from the kings all the outward marks of sovereignty, although in order to avoid the appearance of having merely substituted two kings for one, the Republic's founders arranged that the consuls should take it in turns to hold the *fasces*.

But the power of the consuls was limited in other, more substantial, ways. According to the tradition, in the very first year of the Republic a law was passed which gave citizens the right of appeal (*provocatio*) to the people against a decision of a magistrate. Some scholars doubt the authenticity of this law, treating it as a fictitious anticipation of similar laws passed in 449 and 300 BC; but there is no proof of this, and the tradition is certainly not unbelievable as it stands. The consul's freedom of action was restricted by the fact that his office was both collegiate and annual. The twin principles of "collegiality" and "annuality" became basic elements of Roman constitutional practice, and were applied to all subsequent magistracies, the only (partial) exception being the dictatorship. The collegiate principle meant that the intentions of any one consul could be frustrated by the intervention of his colleague, since it was agreed that in any dispute the negative view should prevail. The limitation of the consul's term to one year also reduced his chances of making mischief, and ensured that continuity of government and the direction of policy rested with the senate, from which the consuls were chosen and to which they afterwards returned. Strictly speaking the senate could do no more than advise the consuls, but since its most influential members were men who had themselves been consuls its advice effectively bound those who held the office for the time being. The senate was a living embodiment of the Roman tradition and a repository of political wisdom and experience. In practice it was the governing body of Rome, the magistrates being merely its executive officers.

The exception to these basic rules was the dictatorship, instituted in about 500 BC. In cases of extreme emergency a dictator could be appointed by the consuls to act on his own as supreme commander and head of state. He had an assistant, the Master of the Horse, who commanded the cavalry but was strictly subordinate to the dictator. There was no appeal against a dictator, and he was not hampered by colleagues; on the other hand his term of office lasted for only six months.

Among other magistrates were the quaestors, who assisted the consuls and were chosen by popular election from 447 BC onwards, and the censors, first elected in 443. The censors performed tasks which had formerly been carried out by the consuls; the most important of these duties was to conduct a census of the community, to assess the rights and obligations of the citizens and to assign them to their appropriate tribes and centuries. The censors were elected at intervals of four to five years, and held office for 18 months.

The new system was a very sophisticated set of political institutions which, as far as we know, had no obvious parallels in the Greek world or in Etruria. For this reason a number of scholars have doubted whether a unique institution like the consulship could have been simply invented out of nothing at the start of the Republic; they have argued instead that the consulship developed gradually out of a more primitive system in which the state was governed by an annual dictator or a single chief magistrate (*praetor maximus*). But there is no convincing evidence to support these theories.

In fact there are good grounds for thinking that the founding fathers of the Republic were far from being political illiterates. One of their most daring innovations was the appointment of an official who would take care of the former king's religious responsibilities. This official was called the *rex sacrorum* ("king of the sacrifices"). His functions were purely religious and he was not allowed to hold any other office. This ban was no doubt designed to prevent any possibility of the title "king" being associated with a position of political power. In the words of A. Momigliano, whose view of the matter is followed here, "the double consulate was not a usual form of government and implies a certain maturity. It is the maturity of the men who created the *rex sacrorum* in order to isolate and therefore sterilize the sacral power of the kings. We see an alert and ruthless aristocracy at work at the beginning of the Roman Republic."

Coin of L. Cassius Caecianus (102 BC). The bust of Ceres on the obverse recalls the dedication of the plebeian temple of Ceres on the Aventine by Sp. Cassius in 493 BC.

Yet for all its sophistication the new system was not able, and indeed was not primarily intended, to guarantee well-ordered and stable government. On the contrary, the political and military history of Rome in the first half-century of the Republic is a confused picture of turmoil and disorder. It seems that the strong centralized authority which had been established by the kings disintegrated with the fall of Tarquin, and gave way to a revival of disorderly competition between powerful individuals and groups, who were able to resume their activities independently of the control of the state and to operate with private armies of dependants and clients.

The best illustration of this situation is the story of the Sabine leader Attius Clausus, who migrated to Rome in 504 BC with 5000 clients and dependants; taking the name Appius Claudius he was admitted to the senate, and became the ancestor of the Claudian *gens*. Other examples of the same phenomenon include the attempted coup d'etat of Appius Herdonius, who in 460 BC occupied the Capitol with a band of 4000 clients, and the private war of the Fabii and their clients, who in 477 BC were massacred by the Etruscans at the battle of the Cremera river. The political importance of the Fabii at this period is confirmed by the fact that for seven consecutive years down to 479 BC (when the Cremera campaign began) one of the consuls was always a Fabius; after the disaster no Fabii held the chief magistracy until 467.

The general picture of a society dominated by closed groups or bands under aristocratic leadership can now be confirmed by a recently discovered inscription from Satricum which records a dedication to Mars by "the comrades of Publius Valerius." The inscription dates from around 500 BC, which raises the interesting possibility that the Publius Valerius referred to might be the celebrated P. Valerius Publicola, one of the founding fathers of the Republic. The important point however is that we have here a group of men who define themselves not as citizens of a state or as members of an ethnic group, but as comrades of an individual leader. The Latin word *sodales*, here translated "comrades," implies a group bound together by a strong sense of solidarity and devoted to the service of a leader or leaders. The same word is also used by Livy to describe the followers of the Fabii at the Cremera. Such groupings are found in many aristocratic societies: we may compare for instance the Celtic *ambacti* ("surrounders") who accompanied the Gallic chieftains, and were regarded as equivalent to clients by Caesar (*Gallic War* 6. 15).

It seems that this kind of society flourished for a brief period following the disintegration of the centralized and ordered regime of the kings. Many of the civic institutions established under the later kings must have fallen into abeyance when the aristocrats took over in 509 BC. One is bound to assume, for instance, that the centuriate system of Servius Tullius had become rather shadowy and ineffectual in the days when the Fabii marched out to the Cremera with their clients. But the aristocratic fling came to an end in the second quarter of the 5th century. This must have happened partly as a result of the catastrophe at the Cremera, which was in fact only one of a series of military reverses. But the main challenge to the aristocratic order came from a completely new factor which began to make itself felt in these years: this factor was the newly organized strength of the *plebs*.

The rise of the *plebs*

The domestic history of Rome during the first two centuries of the Republic is entirely dominated by the conflict between the patricians and the plebeians. Although the surviving sources have a good deal to tell us about this epic struggle, conventionally known as the "struggle between the orders," the unfortunate fact is that we are not really in a position to understand it. The explanation of this paradox is that the main issues of the conflict were resolved long before the first historians of Rome were even born, so that they themselves had only a very hazy idea of the nature of the events they were attempting to describe. The surviving narratives are full of misleading anachronisms and distortions; there are very few certain facts, and any modern reconstruction is bound to be largely hypothetical.

We should be able to understand the history of the conflict much better if we knew how to define patricians and plebeians. What the sources have to say about the origins of the distinction is certainly inadequate and at least partly wrong. They tell us that the patricians were the descendants of the original senators chosen by Romulus. There is a certain element of truth in this, in as much as the patricians were a group of senatorial families with certain hereditary privileges, one of which was probably the right to a place in the senate. The senate in fact was composed of two groups, the "fathers" and the "conscripts" (*patres et conscripti*), of whom only the former were patricians. If the patrician "fathers" were hereditary senators, the *conscripti* were probably the equivalent of life-peers.

The patrician senators had certain prerogatives in the historical period of the Republic. For example, they chose the *interrex*, whenever one was needed, and he was himself always a patrician. They monopolized the priesthoods and had the exclusive right to take the auspices, and it was they who possessed the *auctoritas* by which decisions of the *comitia* were approved. From this it seems that the original definition of patrician status was the hereditary possession of certain religious privileges; these must have been granted to a particular group of families during the monarchy, when the *interregnum* was a regular and important institution.

It does not however follow that the Roman ruling class was exclusively patrician from the earliest times. This possibility seems to be excluded by the fact that four of the kings, and some of the early consuls, including Brutus himself, were plebeians – or, at least, bore names which were later considered plebeian. The most probable reconstruction is that the priestly families of the patriciate took a leading part in establishing the Republic, and gradually extended their influence during its first years, no doubt making full use of their religious prerogatives, until they acquired a virtual monopoly of political power. In the period down to 486 BC 77 per cent of the consuls were patricians; the proportion increased to over 90 per cent in the years between 485 and 445. The disgrace and execution of Spurius Cassius, the plebeian consul of 486 BC, may have been a part of this process, which has been called the "closing of the patriciate." The final stage came in 450 with the ban on intermarriage between the orders.

The rise of the *plebs* was a parallel development, but its origins are even more obscure. The term *plebs* is sometimes used in our sources to designate all Roman citizens who were not patricians, but that was almost certainly not its original meaning. In classical Latin the word also has the more specific sense of "the masses" or the "common people," for example in such phrases as *plebs urbana* ("city mob"). It is probable that the *plebs* was in origin a particular group of underprivileged persons. It is perfectly possible, indeed likely, that the original *plebs* was not a well-defined group at all, but rather a heterogeneous body of poor, weak and vulnerable men of diverse origins and backgrounds. They probably included peasants, craftsmen, shopkeepers, traders and the like. To search for the remote "origins" of the *plebs* is almost certainly the wrong approach to the problem. The important point is that the plebeians enter history in the early years of the Republic, when they emerge as an organized movement; and it is by describing this organization and investigating its aims that we can best hope to understand the Roman *plebs*.

In 494 BC the plebeians, weighed down by debt and arbitrary oppression, withdrew in a body from the city and occupied the Sacred Mount (or, according to an alternative tradition, the Aventine). There they formed themselves into what amounted to a self-contained state, or "state within a state." They created an assembly, the *concilium plebis*, and chose their own officials, known as tribunes. There were probably only two tribunes at first, but their number was later increased to ten. The tribunate came into being through what the Romans called a *lex sacrata*. This was a collective resolution reinforced by a solemn oath of those who made it. The plebeians swore to protect their tribunes and invoked curses on anyone who should harm them. The tribunes thus became "sacrosanct."

The *lex sacrata* is otherwise known as a feature of primitive military organization among the Italic peoples. Among the Samnites, for example, we find bands of warriors who were sworn to obey their leaders and to follow them to the death. There are also clear affinities with the bands of comrades or *sodales* who, as we saw, attended the aristocratic leaders of the early Republic. It is probably not fanciful to suggest that the plebeians, who were excluded from these groups and enjoyed no special aristocratic protection, resolved to form a rival organization which would counterbalance the tightly knit groupings on which the patricians' power rested.

The patricians themselves constituted a small minority of the total population of the city (Roman antiquarians reckoned that there were 136 patrician families in existence in 509 BC), and they were only able to control the state because of the support they received from their clients. The latter seem in many cases to have been fairly well off and owed their position to the patrons on whom they were dependent; they thus had a vested interest in preserving the status quo. The clients of the patricians could afford arms and were enrolled in the Servian *classis*, which they were probably able to dominate. This explains how the patricians retained their privileged position and survived with their throats uncut for over 200 years.

The organization of the *plebs* was an immensely powerful and potentially revolutionary instrument of change. Its strength derived ultimately from its collective solidarity, not from any statutory authorization, although the patricians were eventually compelled to recognize the plebeian institutions by a series of enactments such as the *lex Publilia* of 471 BC and the Valerio-Horatian laws of 449. The final stage of this process occurred in 287, when the resolutions of the plebeian assembly (*plebiscita*) were given the full force of law. The ultimate weapon of the *plebs* was "secession," an extreme form of civil disobedience which was resorted to no less than five times between 494 and 287 BC. On these occasions the *plebs* withdrew en masse from the city to the Aventine, which became a center of plebeian activity.

In 493 BC, following the first secession, a temple to Ceres, Liber and Libera was dedicated at the foot of the Aventine by Spurius Cassius, who was consul in that year. The temple became an important plebeian cult center, and was also used as a treasury and archive. At the same time the *plebs* created two officials, called aediles, whose job it was to look after the upkeep and administration of the temple (*aedes*).

The tribunes of the *plebs* became extremely important. Although they were not magistrates in the strict sense, and had no *imperium*, they did possess an effective power (*potestas*) which allowed them to act as if they were magistrates. They were able to enforce their will by coercion (*coercitio*); they could impose fines, imprisonment and perhaps even the death penalty. Because of their personal inviolability they were able to protect individual plebeians against ill-treatment by the consuls by giving them "assistance" (*auxilium*). Moreover, they were able to "intercede" in the general legislative, deliberative and executive procedures of the official organs of the state, and thus in effect bring its business to a standstill. This was the famous tribunician "veto" (*intercessio*).

The chief aims of the plebeians' agitation in the early years were to obtain relief from debt and a more equitable distribution of economic resources, especially land. In the matter of debt the plebeians seem to have been particularly concerned with a form of debt-bondage called *nexum*. This practice is not clearly defined by our sources, who do not seem to have understood it very well themselves. The most likely interpretation is that *nexum* was a contract whereby a free man offered his services as security for a loan; if he failed to repay the loan (at an agreed rate of interest) he could be made to work off the debt. The *nexus* was not a slave, in that he remained a citizen and, at least in theory, retained his legal rights. But the condition of *nexum* became very widespread and was the source of intense bitterness, perhaps because the *nexi* were in practice subjected to all kinds of abuse and found it almost impossible to obtain release from the situation of bondage once it had been established. Plebeian agitation against *nexum* continued until it was finally abolished by a *lex Poetilia* in either 326 or 313 BC.

The second major grievance of the *plebs* was land-

Rome and its neighbors during the monarchy. The extent of Rome's territory in the early regal period (say around 700 BC) was commemorated in the festival of the *Ambarvalia*, a kind of "beating the bounds" ceremony held every year in May, in which Roman priests (the "Arval Brethren") traced a boundary which extended for a few kilometers around the city. According to our sources conquests under the kings took the confines of Roman territory as far as the Alban hills to the south, and westwards as far as the Tiber mouth, where a fort was established at Ostia by Ancus Marcius. The map shows the approximate extent of the territories of the various Latin communities at the end of the monarchy. The boundaries as shown are conjectural, and follow the lines suggested by K. J. Beloch, who estimated their respective areas as follows (in square kilometers): Rome 822, Tibur 351, Praeneste 262·5, Ardea 198·5, Lavinium 164, Lanuvium 84, Labici 72, Nomentum 72, Gabii 54, Fidenae 50·5, Tusculum 50, Aricia 44·5, Pedum 42·5, Crustumerium 39·5, Ficulea 37. These figures are accepted here as being of the correct order of magnitude. Rome thus occupied more than one third of the territory of Latium Vetus, and was the leading power in the region. This general picture is confirmed by archaeological evidence, which suggests that Rome was a rich and powerful state at the end of the 6th century, and by the text of the treaty with Carthage (509 BC), in which Rome's hegemony in Latium is explicitly recognized.

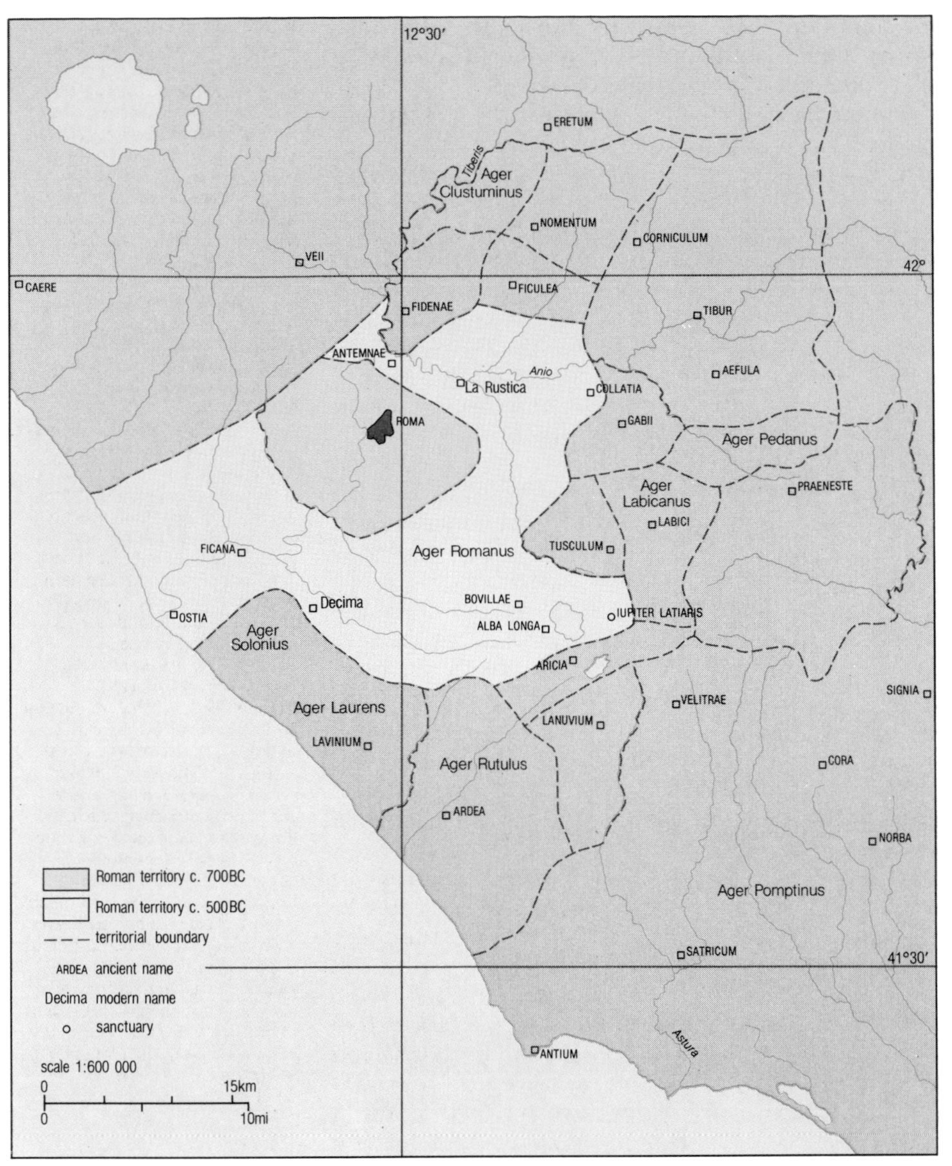

hunger. According to tradition the amounts of land held by peasants in early Rome were extremely small. Romulus is said to have given to each of his followers a plot of land measuring two *iugera* (1 *iugerum* = 0·25 hectares = 0·625 acres) as a *heredium* (hereditary estate). Other sources imply that the normal size of a peasant farm in early times was seven *iugera*. But since even this larger figure is less than half the minimum that would be required to provide subsistence for a family, we must assume that the peasants had access to some other land. The most likely explanation is that the peasants depended on access to public land, the *ager publicus*. This was land belonging to the state, originally acquired by conquest, which could be occupied for farming and grazing by individuals. But it seems that in the early period the public land was occupied by the wealthy patricians, who simply annexed it to their estates and reduced the poor to dependence by extracting from them a payment in kind for the use of the land. Agitation for the redistribution of *ager publicus* is recorded on many occasions during the 5th century BC. These reports should not be dismissed as anachronistic retrojections of conditions in the age of the Gracchi. Land-hunger, poverty and debt were enduring features of Roman society which were present from the earliest times.

The *plebs* also demanded the codification and publication of the law. Agitation for this measure led in 451 to the suspension of the constitution and the appointment of ten legislators (the "Decemvirs"). The Decemvirs were in power for two years, in which they published 12 "tables" of laws. In 450 however they began to abuse their position and were themselves overthrown. In 449 the consuls L. Valerius and M. Horatius passed a series of laws which reaffirmed the rights of the citizens and recognized the plebeian institutions.

The Twelve Tables were the foundation of Roman law. The full text does not survive, but can mostly be reconstructed from quotations. These take the form of terse injunctions and prohibitions in archaic language. For example: "If he summons him to court, let him go. If he does not go, summon a witness. Then he shall seize him" (1.1). "If he has maimed another's limb, unless he settles with him, let there be retaliation" (8.2). The Twelve Tables were not a systematic code in a modern sense. The main topics dealt with are: the family, marriage and divorce; inheritance, ownership and transfer of property; torts and delicts; debt, slavery and *nexum*. On the other hand the whole subject of public law was omitted.

The Twelve Tables are a mixture of codification and innovation. The chief innovation was the prohibition of intermarriage between patricians and plebeians. This enactment aroused a storm of protest, and was soon repealed by the tribune C. Canuleius (445 BC). Apart from this clearly exceptional clause, the Tables gave equality of rights to all free citizens, which is what the plebeians had demanded. But it was still left to the individual to get his opponent to court, and to execute judgment himself. Moreover the appropriate forms of action were not set out in the code, and remained mysterious to the majority of Romans. In these circumstances weak and vulnerable citizens would have found little protection in the law, and must have continued to depend on the patronage of the rich and powerful.

Rome and its neighbors

Under the early kings Rome was a small, primitive settlement whose external relations were confined to local wars and petty disputes with immediate neighbors. Tradition records campaigns against Etruscan Veii, whose territory lay across the Tiber from Rome, and against the settlements of the "Ancient Latins" to the northeast of Rome in the region between the Tiber and the Anio. These settlements (such as Antemnae, Corniculum, Ficulea, etc.) are repeatedly named in accounts of the wars of the early kings, but they disappear from the record as Rome's horizons become wider in the 6th century.

In very early times Rome's territory extended for about 7 kilometers in each direction and measured about 150 square kilometers altogether. But this area was considerably enlarged during the regal period. Tullus Hostilius overran Alba Longa and added its territory to that of Rome, while Ancus Marcius carried the boundaries of the Roman state as far as the coast, incorporating as he went the settlements of Tellenae, Politorium and Ficana. In the 6th century BC Rome extended its influence over a wide area, and began to have dealings not only with the historic centers of Latium, such as Tibur,

Lavinium and Ardea, but also with the cities of Etruria and Magna Graecia. It had commercial links with Carthage, and in the reign of one of the Tarquins established friendly relations with the Greek colony of Massilia (Marseille) which persisted down to imperial times.

Servius Tullius is said to have founded a sanctuary of Diana on the Aventine which was to be a common cult center for a federation of Latin states under Roman leadership. The foundation of this cult, together with the names of the Latin cities that took part, was recorded on an archaic inscription which could apparently still be seen on the Aventine in the time of Augustus.

The precinct of Diana was only one of several cult places which were shared in common by some or all of the Latin peoples. The most venerable of these sanctuaries was that on the Alban Mount (Monte Cavo), where every year representatives of the Latin states would assemble to celebrate a common festival in honor of Jupiter Latiaris. Other common cults of a similar kind were celebrated at Lavinium, at Ardea and at Mount Corne near Tusculum. These festivals gave expression to a sense of kinship among the Latins, who shared the same language and culture and a belief in a common racial origin. It is likely that Servius Tullius was attempting to exploit this ancient religious union for political purposes and to enhance the position of Rome by making it the new religious center of Latium. Our sources believe that under Servius Tullius Rome was the leading military power in Latium, and that his successor Tarquin II managed to achieve a formal hegemony over the other Latins. He is said to have established a political league or federation of Latin states with a central meeting place at the Grove of Ferentina (*Lucus Ferentinae*) near Aricia; he used this league to organize joint military enterprises under Roman leadership.

The view that Rome was already the chief city in Latium in the 6th century BC is almost certainly well founded. It is confirmed in the first place by what we know of the size of the city and its territory. Under Servius Tullius the *pomerium*, the sacred boundary of the city, was extended to include the Quirinal, the Viminal and the Esquiline. The resulting "city of the four regions" comprised a total area of about 285 hectares. Servius Tullius is also said to have surrounded Rome with a defensive wall. As yet there is no definite archaeological confirmation of this tradition. The so-called "Servian" wall, of which impressive remains are still visible, is of republican date, but may well follow the line of earlier fortifications. It is extremely unlikely that Rome was without any defenses in the monarchic period, since we know that other Latin settlements, such as Lavinium, had walls in the 6th century. The area enclosed by the circuit of the Servian walls is 427 hectares. Even allowing for the possibility that there were large open spaces within the walls which were not built up, there can be no doubt that Rome in the archaic period was a very large city indeed. A further indication of the size and prosperity of the city under Servius Tullius is the reformed military organization, which presupposed a force of 6000 infantry and 600 cavalry. Since these troops were recruited from the propertied classes and could afford to provide their own arms, we must assume that the total population, including women, children, old men, proletarians, slaves and resident aliens, was very considerable, perhaps over 30 000.

It has been estimated that by 500 BC Rome's territory embraced an area of some 822 square kilometers, which was included in the new tribal districts established by Servius Tullius. At the most probable level of productivity such an area ought to have been able to support a population of between 30 000 and 40 000 (at an average density of 40–50 per square kilometer), which is consistent with the figure already postulated in connection with the Servian army, and must be of the correct order of magnitude. The other Latin communities were very small by comparison. The largest of them, Tibur, possessed a territory which was less than half the size of Rome's. The Roman state in fact incorporated more than one-third of the total land surface of Latium Vetus in about 500 BC.

Further confirmation of Rome's power and standing at this time comes from a document preserved by the Greek historian Polybius (c. 200–118 BC). This is the text of a treaty between Rome and Carthage, which dates from the first year of the Republic. The treaty (which is almost certainly an authentic document) assumes that a number of Latin cities are subject to the Romans, who also claim to be able to speak on behalf of the Latins in general: "The Carthaginians shall not injure the people of Ardea, Antium, Lavinium, Circeii, Terracina or any other city of the Latins who are subjects of Rome. As for the Latins who are not subjects, they shall keep their hands off their cities, and if they take any such city they shall hand it over to the Romans unharmed. They shall build no fort in Latin territory. If they enter the territory in arms, they shall not spend a night there."

The treaty probably represents an attempt by the new republican regime to secure international recognition and to reaffirm Rome's hegemony in Latium. But it seems that the Republic's leaders were nevertheless unable to prevent the Latins taking advantage of Rome's temporary weakness and organizing a united resistance. This resistance was based on the existing league of states which met at the Grove of Ferentina, from which the Romans were now excluded. The anti-Roman alliance may well be connected with a document which records the dedication of a common shrine of Diana at Aricia by Egerius Baebius of Tusculum, who is styled "dictator of the Latins." This act could be seen as an attempt to establish a common cult of Diana which would replace the Aventine sanctuary at Rome and provide a religious focus for the coalition.

The ensuing struggle between Rome and the Latins culminated in an epic battle at Lake Regillus in 499 BC, where the Romans won a narrow victory. Five years later a treaty was drawn up by the Roman consul Spurius Cassius. The treaty was inscribed on a bronze pillar and set up in the Forum, where it remained until the time of Sulla. The two parties to the treaty were the Romans on the one side and all the Latin cities on the other. It stipulated peace between them, military cooperation against the attacks of third parties and an agreement to share the booty and other profits of successful wars. The treaty also gave legal backing to the community of private rights which had existed among the Latins since time immemorial. The traditional arrangement

Coins of c. 96 BC, recalling the victory of A. Postumius Albinus at Lake Regillus (499 BC). The types show a cavalry charge, and the divine twins Castor and Pollux, who were said to have fought on the Roman side, and later appeared watering their horses at a fountain in the Forum.

This inscribed gold tablet from the Etruscan port of Pyrgi records a dedication by the ruler of Caere, probably during the early 5th century BC. The text is in Etruscan, accompanied by a shorter version in Phoenician. This fact seems to indicate close relations between the Etruscans and the Phoenician-speaking Carthaginians; the Carthaginians had also made a treaty with Rome at the beginning of the Republic.

Northern Italy under Celtic occupation. A tradition much overlaid with legend informs us that the Celts were tempted to invade Italy by its rich agricultural products, and particularly wine. According to Livy the Gauls crossed the Alps before 500 BC, while Polybius dates the invasion to around 400. The truth lies somewhere in between, and it seems that in the course of the 5th century the main tribal groupings of what later became Cisalpine Gaul were established – the Insubres with their capital at Milan, the Boii around Bologna, the Cenomani with their centers at Brescia and Verona, and the Lingones and Senones along the Adriatic, in a region which came to be known as the *ager Gallicus*. The Celtic presence is confirmed archaeologically by finds that are widely distributed in small sites throughout northern Italy, but the principal concentrations are in Lombardy, Romagna and the valley of the upper Adige.

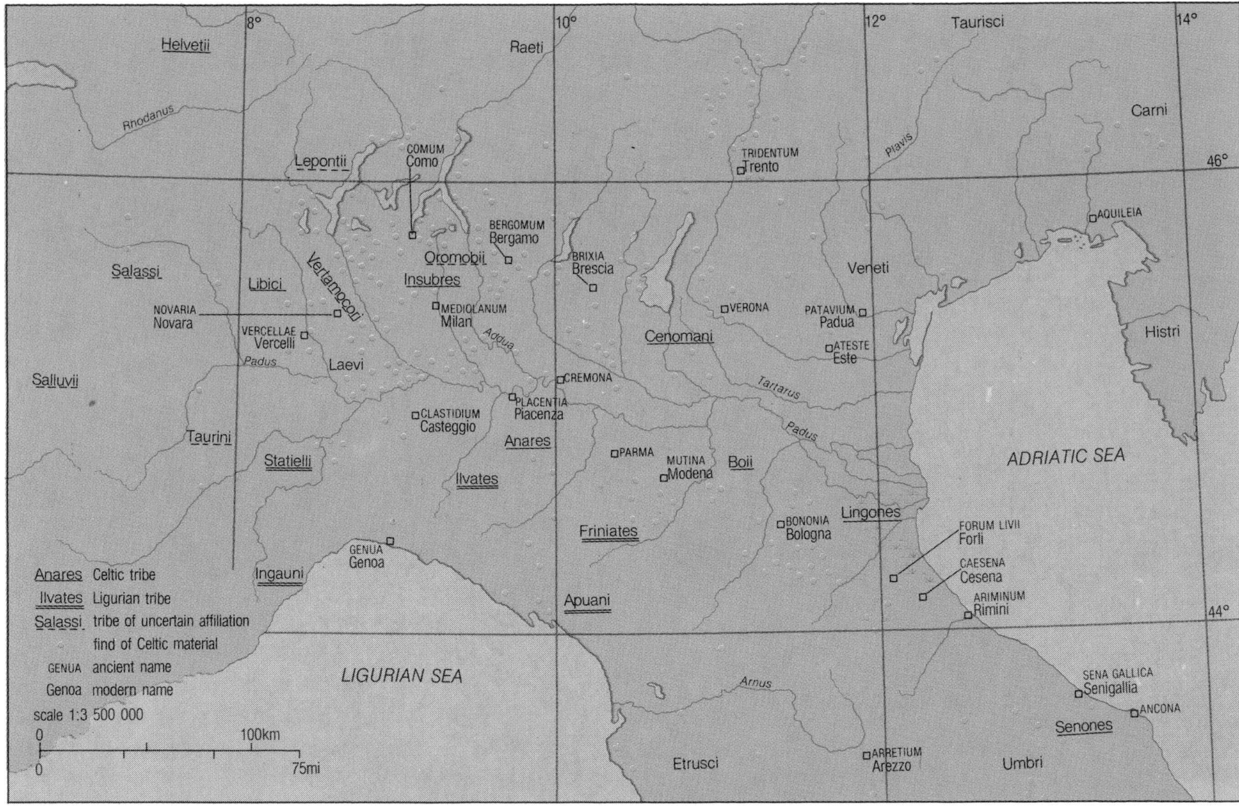

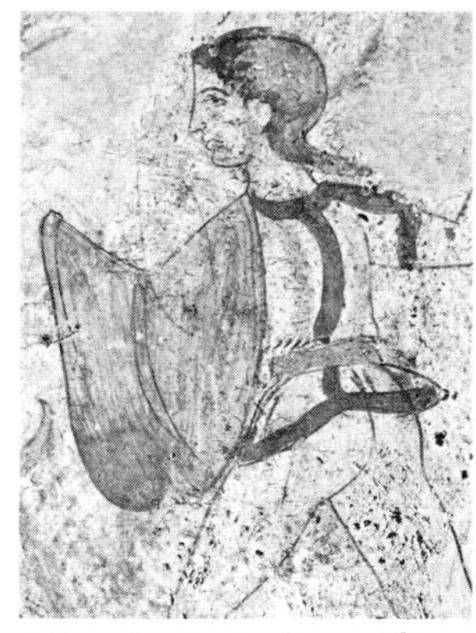

A Lucanian hunter from a 4th-century BC tomb painting near Paestum. The Lucanians were an Italic people related to the Samnites, who descended from the mountains of the interior into the coastal plains of southern Italy during the 5th century BC. By 400 most of the Greek cities on the Tyrrhenian coast (including Paestum) had been overwhelmed.

This coin of 43 BC shows the archaic cult statue of Diana in the grove at Aricia, which was a common shrine of the Latin peoples in early times. The goddess is represented in her three forms: Diana, Hecate and Selene.

was that an individual from one Latin community who happened to find himself in another could enjoy all the rights and privileges possessed by its inhabitants, and could become a full member of that community simply by taking up residence there. In later times these reciprocal rights were summed up in the juridical concepts of *conubium* (the right to contract a legal marriage with a partner from another state), *commercium* (the right to engage in commercial activity with full legal protection) and *migratio* (the right to become a citizen of another state by changing one's domicile). These rights were probably defined in the treaty of Sp. Cassius.

The treaty provided the basis for a new Latin league in which the Romans played the dominant part. It was administered jointly by representatives of Rome and the other Latins who continued to meet every year at the Grove of Ferentina to discuss matters of common interest and to organize joint military enterprises. The allied army probably consisted half of Romans and half of Latins, with the Romans supplying the commander. The evidence on this point is not however very clear, and it is in fact equally possible that the command alternated between Romans and Latins.

The military strength of the reorganized Latin League was soon put to the test. During the early years of the 5th century Latium was increasingly threatened by the incursions of enemies from beyond its borders, and in particular by the Sabines, the Aequi and the Volsci. The movement of these peoples into the plain of Latium was the consequence of a general expansion of the populations of the central and southern Apennines which had widespread repercussions. The Greek and Etruscan cities of Campania and the Greeks of the far south were also troubled at this time by increased pressure from the native peoples of the interior.

The infiltration of Sabines into Latium began in the monarchic period, and incursions are intermittently recorded down to the middle of the 5th century. A much more serious menace came from the Aequi and Volsci, whose appearance on the borders of Latium at the end of the 6th century caused a dramatic change in the fortunes of Rome and her Latin allies. The Volsci were an Italic people who spoke a dialect similar to Umbrian. Shortly before 500 BC they migrated from their Apennine homeland towards the coast and occupied the territory on the southern borders of Latium. The Volscian wars of this period form the setting for the romantic tale of Coriolanus, the proud Roman who left his homeland in disgust at the treatment he received from the plebeians, and went to join the Volsci, who recognized his worth and elected him as their leader. Coriolanus led the Volscian army on a victorious march through Latin territory to within eight kilometers of Rome, where only the entreaties of his mother persuaded him to spare his native city. The reality behind this famous episode is the memory of a Volscian invasion which threatened the existence of Rome. Subsequent Volscian incursions are recorded throughout the 5th century and beyond, but the high point of their activities was reached in the 490s and 480s BC.

The second major threat came from the Aequi, an Oscan-speaking people who lived in the upper Anio valley and the hills above Praeneste, from where they repeatedly descended into the plain. In 486 BC a tripartite alliance was formed on equal terms between Rome, the Latins and the Hernici, which was of decisive importance since the territory of the Hernici effectively separated the Aequi and the Volsci. During the later years of the 5th century the allies were gradually able to gain the upper hand against the Aequi and Volsci, allowing the Romans to concentrate their efforts in another direction.

Rome's great adversary on her northern border was the Etruscan city of Veii, situated on a rocky plateau some 15 kilometers to the north. Veii's territory stretched along the right bank of the Tiber as far as the coast, and the quarrel with Rome perhaps arose from the attempts of each to control the salt beds at the mouth of the river and the trade routes to the interior which ran along either side of the Tiber valley. During the 5th century a series of major wars is recorded, the first of which saw the massacre of the Fabii at the Cremera (477 BC) and ended in 475 with an inconclusive peace; the second ended in 426 when the Romans captured Fidenae, a Veientine outpost on the left bank of the Tiber about nine kilometers upstream from Rome. The decisive struggle soon followed, and culminated in the great siege of Veii, which in the Roman tradition is made to last for 10 years (405–396) and is associated with many legends and stories, some of which are borrowed from the Greek legend of the Trojan War. The final result was one of the crucial turning points in Roman history: Veii was captured and destroyed by the Roman general M. Furius Camillus, and her territory was annexed to that of Rome. The effect of the conquest was that the size of Rome's territory was doubled at a stroke. Rome was in a very strong position at the beginning of the 4th century BC. But only a few years after the capture of Veii, Rome itself was overtaken by a sudden and unexpected calamity.

The Gallic invasion

The movement of Celtic peoples across the Alps into northern Italy may have begun as early as the 6th century BC. This is Livy's view, although as yet there is no definite evidence of a Celtic presence in the Po plain before the 5th century. By 400 BC, however, the main tribal groupings (Insubres, Cenomani, Boii, Lingones, Senones) had established themselves in what later came to be known as Cisalpine Gaul, and were threatening the Etruscan settlements there. By about 350 BC most of the Etruscan cities in the Po valley, including Felsina (Bologna), had been overwhelmed by the Gauls, who had also begun to make occasional raids across the Apennines into peninsular Italy. One such raid took place in the summer of 390 BC, when a horde of Senones swept into Etruria, passed down the Tiber valley by way of Clusium and made for Rome.

On 18 July, which ever after was marked as an unlucky day in the Roman calendar, the Roman army which was sent to face the Gauls was routed at the Allia river. Three days later the Gauls arrived at the defenseless city and sacked it. Only the Capitol resisted capture and held out for some months; later generations of Romans told the story that a night attack by the Gauls was foiled when the cackling of the sacred geese aroused the garrison in the nick of time. Eventually the Gauls decided to leave, encouraged, so it is said, by the offer of a large payment of gold. A patriotic tale maintained that, just as the gold was being weighed out, a Roman army appeared on the scene and drove the Gauls away. This scratch force had been assembled by Camillus, who had been in exile at the time of the Allia, following accusations of dishonestly handling the spoils of Veii. The truth of the matter is probably that the Gauls were looking for plunder and had no intention of staying anyway. The story of Camillus' face-saving victory can be safely rejected; it may have been suggested by the fact that the Gauls were caught on their way back by an Etrucan army and soundly beaten. In any case, the Gauls went away, leaving the Romans to pick up the pieces.

Early Latium

Most of the communities of Latium Vetus seem to have originated in small hut villages on the low hills overlooking the plain. But very few of the habitation sites have so far been systematically investigated, and our knowledge is largely based on the finds from their cemeteries, which have been more intensively studied. These finds provide evidence for the development of the so-called "Latial culture" from the 10th to the 6th century BC. The typological classification of the grave-goods from these cemeteries has allowed scholars to divide the Latial culture into six archaeologically defined "phases": phase I, c. 1000–c.900 BC; phase IIA, c.900–c.830 BC; phase IIB, c.830–c.770 BC; phase III, c.770–730/720 BC; phase IVA, 730/720–640/630 BC; phase IVB, 640/630–580 BC. In the earliest phases (I–II) the settlements were no more than collections of thatched huts. But during phases III-IV they grew in size and sophistication, with the development of external contracts ("trade"), specialized craft production, and the emergence of a wealthy aristocracy. In the so-called "orientalizing" period (phases IVA and IVB) there is clear evidence of the development of fortified urban centers, which appear in our sources as the states of the Latin League.

Archaeological sites in Latium Vetus. In recent years our knowledge of early Latium has grown enormously as a result of intensive archaeological work. This has happened partly through the need to rescue as much as possible of the archaeological heritage of the Roman *campagna* before it is destroyed by urban growth and mechanized agriculture. During the last decade housing projects, road construction and other developments have revealed the existence of sites such as La Rustica, Acquacetosa Laurentina, Decima and Osteria dell'Osa, where rescue excavations have unearthed sensational finds. Systematic campaigns have also been carried out at Ficana and Pratica di Mare, and have greatly added to knowledge gained in earlier excavations.

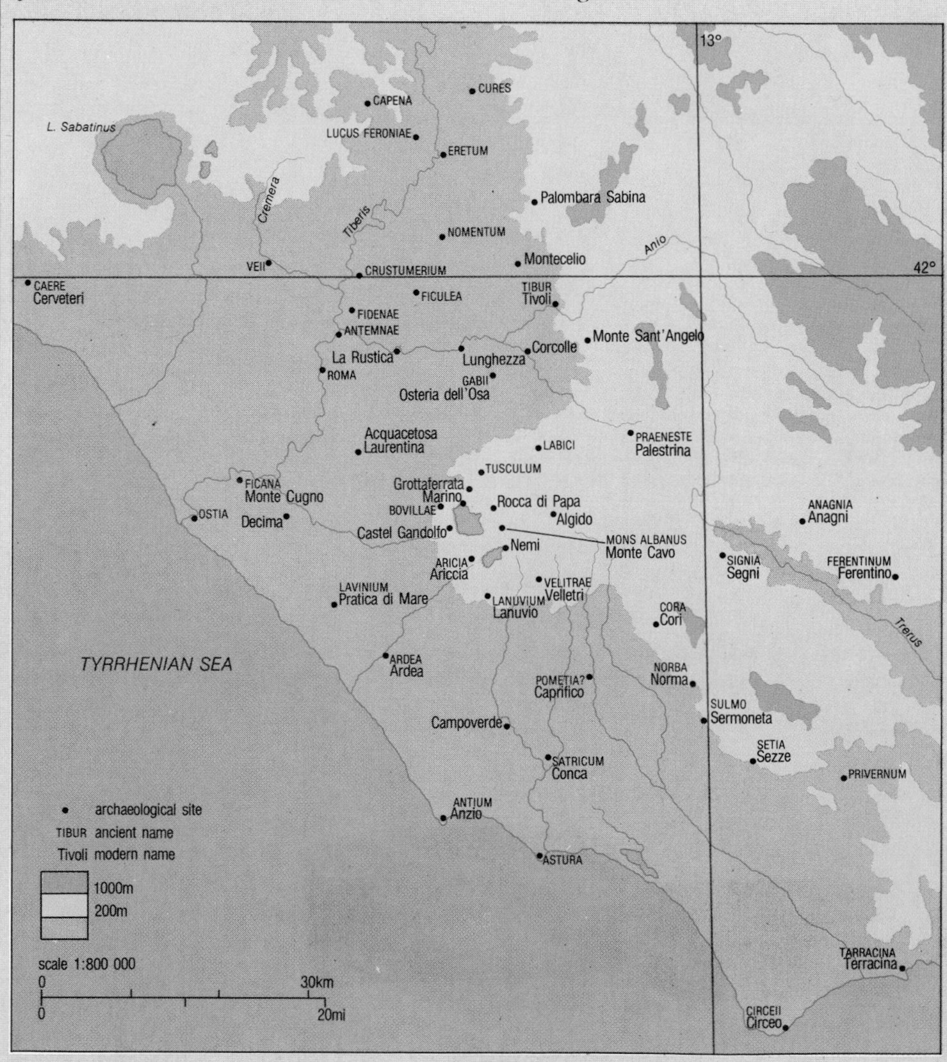

The "princely" tombs discovered in the 19th century at Palestrina contain an extraordinary amount of luxury prestige goods and testify to the wealth and power of the local aristocracy. This silver dish with Egyptian-style scenes from the Tomba Bernardini was perhaps manufactured in Cyprus. Early 7th century BC (phase IVA).

Below right The earliest tombs were cremations. The ashes of the dead were placed in hut urns together with miniaturized grave goods, including weapons, handmade pots and, in a few instances, terracotta figurines crudely modeled in the posture of making an offering. These examples are taken from tombs of phase IIA at Osteria dell'Osa.

Bottom left Carved ivory forearm from the Tomba Barberini at Palestrina, probably of Syrian manufacture and dating from the 7th century BC (phase IVA).

Bottom right In the later phases, cremation is replaced by inhumation, and the tomb furnishings become more elaborate. In phase III they begin to include metal vases and fine pottery, some of it imported from Greece and Etruria. Personal ornaments include brooches, pendants, silver spiral hair rings and glass and amber beads. The lady buried in the tomb shown here (La Rustica, end of phase III) was wearing a belt of sheet bronze.

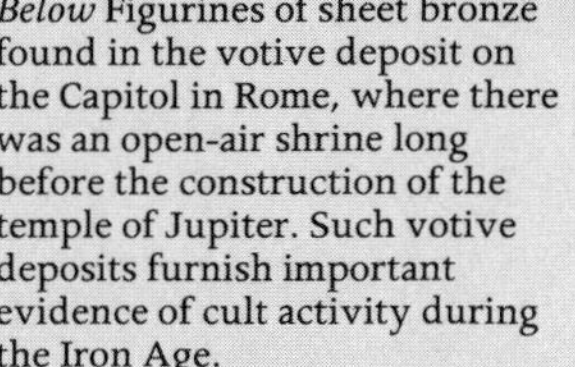

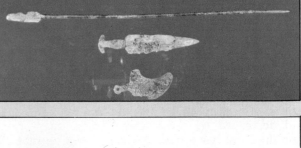

Below Figurines of sheet bronze found in the votive deposit on the Capitol in Rome, where there was an open-air shrine long before the construction of the temple of Jupiter. Such votive deposits furnish important evidence of cult activity during the Iron Age.

Right Cylindrical "cist" (container) from the Castellani Tomb at Palestrina (Phase IVA, mid-7th century BC). The cist, which is made of wood (restored) overlaid with strips of silver laminate, is a fine orientalizing piece, probably of Phoenician manufacture.

The Etruscans

Etruscan civilization is an enigma because of the paucity of our information. Etruscan literature, which once existed, has long since perished, and we have to rely on the statements of Greek and Roman writers (who were often ignorant or prejudiced) and the uncertain indications of archaeology. Most of the archaeological evidence comes from the elaborate cemeteries which lay outside the walls of the great Etruscan cities. The tombs of the noble families were richly furnished, and provide vivid testimony of the life-style of the upper classes. But the picture is one-sided: Etruscan society was based on the dependent labor of a class of rural serfs, of whom we know almost nothing; equally little is known about the character of the urban settlements, which have never been systematically investigated.

Below Aerial view of the Banditaccia cemetery outside Cerveteri (Caere). The cemetery was formally laid out like a city, with the tombs representing houses.

Bottom Tarquinia: Tomb of the Leopards. Painting of the early 5th century BC showing an aristocratic banquet.

Bottom right Tarquinia: Tomba dell'Orco I, early 4th century BC. Detail showing the head of a lady named Velia. The tomb probably belonged to the great noble clan of the Spurinnae.

Left The interior of the tombs at Caere contained features of standard domestic architecture, as can be seen in the Tomb of the Shields and Chairs (6th or 5th century BC).

Our knowledge of Etruscan art is enriched by the thousands of artifacts that have been found in the tombs. The Etruscans are especially noted for the high quality of their bronze sculptures. Examples are the warrior from Cagli (*below*) and the Chimaera from Arezzo (*bottom left*).

THE CONQUEST OF ITALY AND OF THE MEDITERRANEAN

The recovery of Rome

The effects of the Gallic sack are difficult to assess. The physical destruction of the city has, perhaps surprisingly, left little trace in the archaeological record, and may only have been superficial. The manpower losses at the Allia were probably not great, and would in any case have been made up within a few years. As early as 378 BC the Roman state was able to organize the building of a massive city wall, parts of which still survive. The wall, which was 10 kilometers long and enclosed the whole of the city, was made of squared stone blocks from the Grotta Oscura quarries in the territory of Veii. This region was still in Roman hands, and soon after the departure of the Gauls it was colonized by Roman settlers who were enrolled in four new tribes. At this date Roman territory measured some 1510 square kilometers. The city was well placed for a rapid recovery.

To the north of the former *ager Veientanus* lay the territory of the Etruscan city of Caere, which befriended the Romans at this time and aided their recovery. Rome's northern border was thus secured. In 383 BC it was able to found colonies to the north of Veii at Sutrium and Nepet, two strongholds which came to be known as the "gateways of Etruria."

On the other hand the Romans were confronted with serious difficulties in Latium. The Volsci and Aequi returned to the offensive, and the traditional accounts of the years following the Gallic sack make it clear that the alliance with the Latins and Hernici had ceased to function. But the Romans were able to hold their own, and won some important victories under the leadership of Camillus, whom later tradition regarded as the "second founder" of the city. A few events stand out. A Roman colony was established at Satricum in 385 and another at Setia in 382; in 381 Tusculum was given citizenship and its territory incorporated in that of Rome. But the circumstances of these events are unknown; the years following the Gallic sack constitute one of the most obscure periods in Roman history. It seems however that Rome had fully recovered its position by 358 BC, when the alliance with the Latins and the Hernici was renewed.

The recovery of Rome by the mid-4th century is indicated by the fact that it was able to conclude a second treaty with Carthage in 348. To the south Rome's horizon now extended beyond the borders of Latium. In 354 it made an alliance with the Samnites, an Oscan-speaking people who formed a powerful confederation of tribes in the region of the southern Apennines. The treaty probably defined the respective spheres of influence of the two sides and provided for cooperation against hostile third parties, such as the Gauls. Relations between the two powers became strained in 343, but it seems that after a brief period of hostilities (the so-called "First Samnite War," 343–341 BC) the Romans and Samnites renewed their alliance; they were then confronted in 340 by a hostile coalition of Latins, Campanians, Sidicini, Volsci and Aurunci. A bitter war ensued, which the Romans eventually won, with Samnite help, in 338 BC.

The settlement which was imposed on the losers was of crucial importance in that it established a pattern for the future development of Roman expansion in Italy. Some of the defeated Latin cities were incorporated in the Roman state, and their inhabitants made Roman citizens. Others retained their status as independent communities, although some were deprived of part of their territory. They remained allies of Rome, which effectively meant that they were obliged to provide military assistance in time of war, and they continued to possess the rights of *conubium* and *commercium* with Roman citizens; however they were no longer permitted to exercise such rights among themselves and were forbidden to have political relations with one another. Thus the old Latin League was finally dissolved, although the common religious festivals continued to take place under Roman supervision. The non-Latin peoples who had joined the struggle against Rome (the Volsci, Campanians and others) were incorporated in the Roman state, but were given only limited citizen rights. This half-citizenship, or "citizenship without suffrage" (*civitas sine suffragio*), meant that they had to fulfill all the military and financial obligations of citizens, but that they could not vote in the assemblies or hold office at Rome. By extending this form of limited citizenship to whole communities the Romans were able to enlarge their territory and to increase their manpower while maintaining the essential character of Rome as a city-state and conserving the integrity of her traditional political institutions. The incorporated communities also retained their own identity, and continued in

Above The republican city wall, of which large portions still remain, was constructed in 378 BC following the Gallic sack. The arches were probably added during the civil wars of the 80s BC.

Right: Wars of conquest and colonization in Italy 334–241 BC and (inset) central Italy in 338 BC. Rome's conquest of Italy involved incorporating defeated enemies as Roman citizens or compelling them to become allies. Large areas of territory were annexed from the allies and colonized by the Romans. Colonies had been founded since very early times at strategic points near the borders of Latium; after 338 BC Rome began to found colonies as military outposts in enemy territory. The colonists were drawn mainly from the Roman proletariat (although some allies also took part). They forfeited their citizenship in exchange for allotments of land in the new colony, which became an independent community. Colonies possessed the rights of *conubium* and *commercium*, and their status was equivalent to that of the old Latin communities; for this reason they were called "Latin colonies." The needs of coastal defense were met by the planting of small forts around the shores of Italy, each manned by a few hundred Roman citizens. In 311 BC they were backed up by a squadron of small ships under two commodores (*duoviri navales*). The coastal garrisons are misleadingly termed "colonies" in the sources; they are conventionally called "Roman" colonies, to distinguish them from the (much more important) "Latin" colonies.

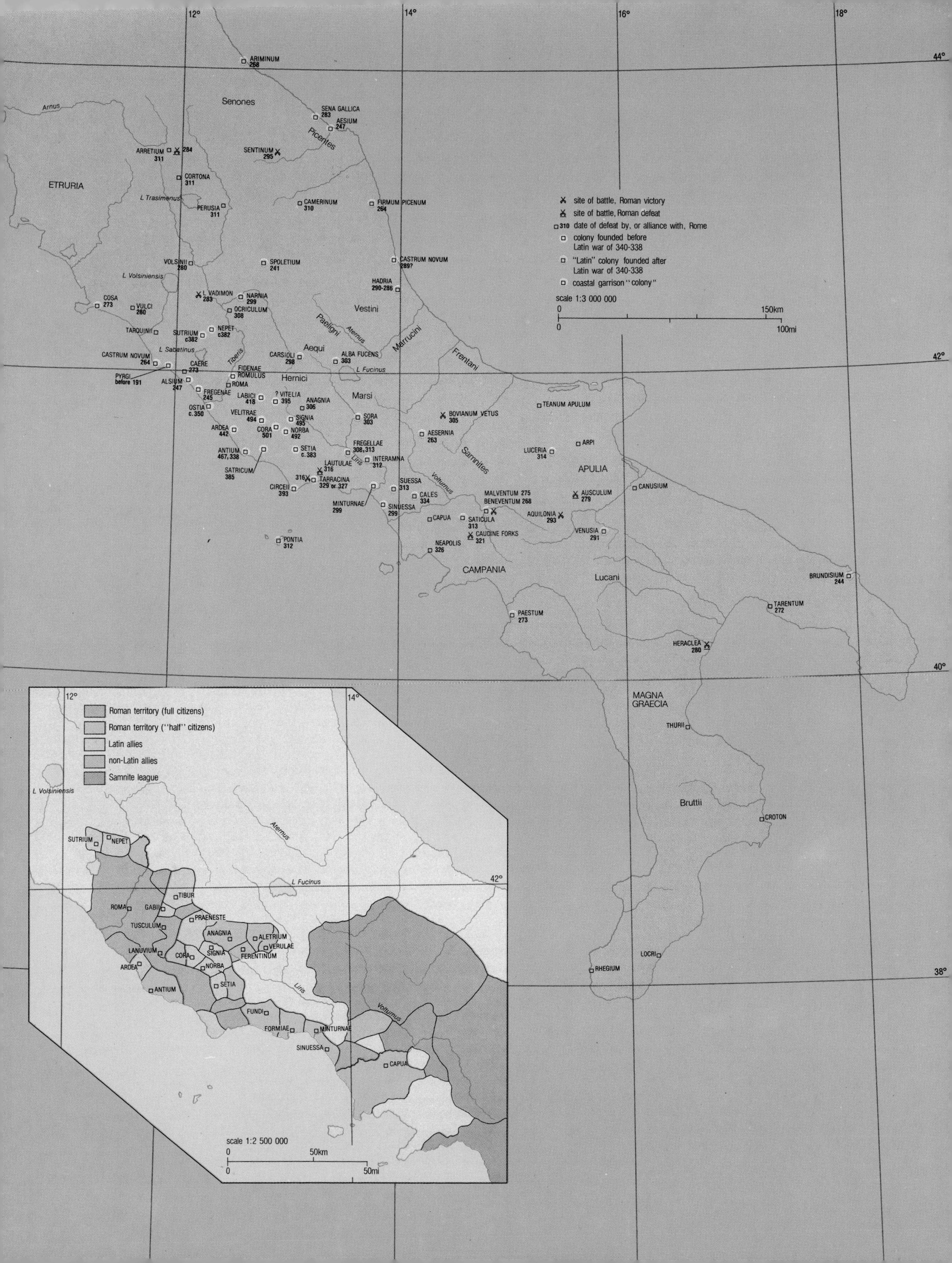

site of battle, Roman victory
site of battle, Roman defeat
310 date of defeat by, or alliance with, Rome
colony founded before Latin war of 340-338
"Latin" colony founded after Latin war of 340-338
coastal garrison "colony"
scale 1:3 000 000
0
150km
100mi
12°
14°
16°
18°
44°
42°
40°
38°
ARIMINUM 268
Arnus
Senones
SENA GALLICA 283
AESIUM 247
Picentes
ARRETIUM 311
284
SENTINUM 295
CORTONA 311
ETRURIA
L Trasimenus
PERUSIA 311
CAMERINUM 310
FIRMUM PICENUM 264
VOLSINII 280
SPOLETIUM 241
CASTRUM NOVUM 289?
L Volsiniensis
HADRIA 290-286
L VADIMON 283
NARNIA 299
COSA 273
VULCI 280
OCRICULUM 308
Vestini
TARQUINII
SUTRIUM c382
NEPET c382
Paeligni
Aternus
Marrucini
L Sabatinus
Aequi
Frentani
CASTRUM NOVUM 264
CAERE 273
Tiberis
CARSIOLI 298
ALBA FUCENS 303
PYRGI before 191
FIDENAE
ROMULUS
L Fucinus
ALSIUM 247
ROMA
Hernici
FREGENAE 245
LABICI 418
? VITELIA 395
ANAGNIA 306
Marsi
TEANUM APULUM
OSTIA c.350
BOVIANUM VETUS 305
VELITRAE 494
SIGNIA 495
SORA 303
ARDEA 442
CORA 501
NORBA 492
AESERNIA 263
FREGELLAE 308, 313
ARPI
ANTIUM 467, 338
SETIA c.383
INTERAMNA 312
LUCERIA 314
Samnites
SATRICUM 385
LAUTULAE 316
Liris
APULIA
316
TARRACINA 329 or 327
SUESSA 313
Volturnus
CIRCEII 393
CALES 334
MALVENTUM 275
BENEVENTUM 268
AUSCULUM 279
CANUSIUM
MINTURNAE 299
SINUESSA 299
CAPUA
SATICULA 313
AQUILONIA 293
VENUSIA 291
PONTIA 312
CAUDINE FORKS 321
NEAPOLIS 326
CAMPANIA
Lucani
BRUNDISIUM 244
TARENTUM 272
PAESTUM 273
HERACLEA 280
MAGNA GRAECIA
THURII
Bruttii
CROTON
LOCRI
RHEGIUM
Roman territory (full citizens)
Roman territory ("half" citizens)
Latin allies
non-Latin allies
Samnite league
L Volsiniensis
Aternus
SUTRIUM
NEPET
L Fucinus
TIBUR
ROMA
GABII
PRAENESTE
TUSCULUM
ANAGNIA
ALETRIUM
LANUVIUM
CORA
SIGNIA
VERULAE
FERENTINUM
ARDEA
NORBA
SETIA
ANTIUM
Liris
FUNDI
Volturnus
FORMIAE
MINTURNAE
SINUESSA
CAPUA
scale 1:2 500 000
0
50km
50mi

practice to govern themselves. These self-governing communities of Roman citizens were known as municipalities (*municipia*), and were the most important innovation of the settlement of 338 BC.

Domestic conflicts and political reforms

Although the Gallic sack proved in the long term to be only a minor setback, the immediate effects of wholesale destruction of property and economic disruption were severe, especially for the poor, and it is no surprise to read in Livy that in the aftermath of the catastrophe there was a renewed crisis of indebtedness among the *plebs*. Complaints against debt are frequently recorded during these years, and provide the setting for the story of M. Manlius, who was executed in 382 for attempting to make himself king. Although a patrician, Manlius had sided with the plebeians and had helped them by paying their debts from his personal fortune.

Plebeian agitation for the relief of debt led to riots in 378 BC, and in the later 370s to a period of political anarchy in which no magistrates were elected for at least a year. The Licinio-Sextian laws (367) provided for the short-term relief of debt; subsequent measures in 357, 352 and 347 attempted to regulate and to reduce interest rates. In 342 the *lex Genucia* made it illegal to lend at interest, but this law was doubtless impossible to enforce. Finally the system of debt-bondage (*nexum*) was abolished in 326.

In the event, however, what did most to alleviate the economic distress of the *plebs* was the acquisition by the state of new territory through military conquest, and its distribution in allotments to Roman citizens. On many occasions Livy records the agitation of the *plebs* for the distribution of such land, which was otherwise left as *ager publicus* and occupied by the rich. According to tradition the Licinio-Sextian laws of 367 BC imposed a limit on the amount of public land any one *paterfamilias* might occupy, and on the number of sheep or cattle he might graze on it.

Licinius and his colleague, L. Sextius, were celebrated in the Roman tradition for a whole series of laws, the most famous of which is supposed to have admitted plebeians to the consulship. The background to this reform is puzzling. In 445 BC it was apparently decided that in certain years the consulship should be suspended and that three or more "military tribunes with consular power" should be elected instead. We do not know why this new magistracy was introduced, or what determined the choice between the two types of magistracy in any given year. Livy suggests that the new office was to be open to plebeians, but in fact only patricians were elected as military tribunes in the first decades of the experiment. Moreover it is not certain that plebeians were ever legally ineligible for the consulship. The only certain facts are that military tribunes came to be elected more frequently than consuls towards the end of the 5th century (and invariably after 390), and that in the years after 400 they began to include increasing numbers of plebeians.

Licinius and Sextius seem in fact to have agitated for the restoration of the consulship as the regular chief magistracy, and to have demanded not only that it be open to plebeians, but that one of the two annual consulships should be reserved for plebeians. In other words they sought positive discrimination in favor of plebeian candidates. This amounted to an experiment in what we should call statutory power sharing.

The Licinio-Sextian proposals were finally enacted in 367 BC, and L. Sextius himself became the first plebeian consul under the new arrangement in 366. At this date the consuls were still known as praetors, or "consul-praetors." But in 367 a third praetor was created, junior to the two existing ones, who from now on were known simply as consuls. The praetorship thus became a separate magistracy, which in 337 BC was for the first time held by a plebeian. A plebeian dictator was elected in 356, and in 351 one of the censors was a plebeian. By the Licinio-Sextian laws two curule aediles were created, to work as civic officials alongside the plebeian aediles. The new aedileship was to be held in alternate years by patricians and plebeians. The principle of statutory power sharing was extended in 339 to the censorship and in 300 to the major colleges of priests, the augurs and the pontiffs. The equalization of the orders was finally accomplished in 287 BC, when plebiscites, the resolutions of the plebeian assembly, were given the force of law and made binding on the whole community.

One of the most important results of the legislation of 367 BC was the gradual formation of a new ruling elite which included the leading plebeian families. These families achieved distinction through the tenure of the senior "curule" magistracies (praetorship, consulship, dictatorship); the descendants of the holders of these offices were known as *nobiles* ("nobles"). The new patricio-plebeian nobility (as it is called) became a dominant group within the senate, and tended to regard the senior magistracies as its own preserve. But the exclusiveness of the nobility should not be exaggerated. One of the features that characterized it and distinguished it from the old patriciate was precisely the fact that new families were being continually admitted to its ranks.

The senate was also open to new blood; a significant percentage of senators will therefore always have been "new men" (i.e. first-generation senators). For a new man to reach the consulship was, naturally, a rare event; this fact should not however be taken as a sign that the consulship was a "hereditary" office. On the contrary, for the whole of the "classical" period of Roman history, say from c. 300 BC to 200 AD, only a minority of the consuls had consular fathers. In other words the nobility included a far greater number of families than would have been the case if office holding had been a hereditary privilege. The result was that the senior magistracies were extremely competitive, and the competition became more intense as time went on.

The patriciate survived as a prestigious and influential group of families within the nobility. Certain archaic priesthoods and offices (*rex sacrorum, interrex* and others) continued to be reserved exclusively for patricians, and it is to be noted that until 172 BC one of the consuls was always a patrician. As for the *plebs*, the organization that succeeded in obtaining equality of civil rights in the 4th century soon afterwards lost its revolutionary character. Its institutions were gradually integrated with those of the community as a whole, and its leaders, who before 367 BC had made common cause with the poor in their effort to gain access to the

Left Bronze statuette of a Samnite warrior, 6th or 5th century BC. He is clad in full armor – greaves, helmet, cuirass and belt – and a short leather tunic. He originally must have carried a shield and spear, but these are now lost, as is the crest of his helmet.

Below The best evidence for the appearance of Roman soldiers at this period is provided by these ivory plaques from Palestrina, dating probably from the first half of the 3rd century BC.

chief magistracies, now became part of the nobility. The office of tribune became equivalent to a junior magistracy, and was regarded as a stage in the career of an aspiring young plebeian noble. By about 300 most of the tribunes were probably members of the senate, and no doubt shared the outlook and interests of the senatorial class as a whole.

The conquest of Italy

The emergence of the nobility is one of the symptoms of a wholesale transformation of Roman society which occurred in the period between the settlement of the Latin War in 338 BC and the outbreak of the First Punic War in 264. This process of change coincided with, and was partly caused by, a remarkable, although poorly documented, series of military conquests which in the space of little more than half a century brought all of Italy under Rome's control.

In the years after 338 BC the Romans set about consolidating the gains they had acquired in the Latin War. Colonies were founded at Cales (334) and Fregellae (328) in the strategically vital region of the middle Liris valley. The settlers who took part in these colonies were drawn mainly from the Roman proletariat. They forfeited their Roman citizenship in exchange for an allotment of land in the new colony, which became an independent community. The colonies possessed the rights of *commercium* and *conubium*, and their status was equivalent to that of the old Latin cities; for this reason they were called "Latin colonies." Cales and Fregellae were the first of a long series of such Latin colonies, which contributed more than any other single factor to the consolidation and eventual unification of Italy under Rome.

The foundation of Fregellae in 328 immediately provoked a hostile reaction from the Samnites, and within a year a war had broken out which was to last intermittently for nearly 40 years. The conflict is conventionally divided into two parts: the Second and Third Samnite Wars (respectively 327–304 BC and 298–290 BC).

The Romans scored an early success in 326, when the government of the Greek city of Naples decided to expel a Samnite garrison and to call in the Romans. The result of this episode, the first formal contact Rome had had with a Greek community in Italy, was an extremely valuable alliance. It was followed by several years of inconclusive border warfare, until in 321 the consuls rashly embarked on a full-scale invasion of Samnite territory. The attempt ended in disaster when the Roman army was ambushed at the Caudine Forks and ignominiously forced to surrender. The patriotic Roman tradition attempted to compensate for this humiliation by fabricating a series of brilliant Roman victories in the following years. In fact it seems that peace was made on terms that clearly favored the Samnites, who gained possession of Fregellae, and that hostilities ceased until 316 BC.

The Romans used the lull to strengthen their position in Campania and to forge alliances with communities in northern Apulia (these included Arpi, Teanum Apulum and Canusium). The war was resumed in 316 with the Samnites taking the initiative. In 315 they invaded Latium and won a victory in a pitched battle at Lautulae near Terracina; but in the following year, after devastating Latin territory and advancing as far as Ardea, they were themselves defeated by the Romans. Fregellae was retaken in 313, and further Latin colonies were founded at Suessa Aurunca and Saticula (in 313), and at Interamna on the Liris and the island of Pontia (in 312). In 312 the censor Appius Claudius Caecus began the construction of the coast road from Rome to Capua which bears his name to this day (the Appian Way). From now on the Romans pressed ahead with a policy of encirclement, and were no longer in any serious danger of defeat, despite the intervention in 311 of some Etruscan and Umbrian cities. The Romans drove them back and retaliated with a vigorous advance up the Tiber valley into Etruria and Umbria. On the southern front a period of indecisive warfare against the Samnites was ended in 305 when the Romans captured the stronghold of Bovianum. Peace was made in the following year.

In the last years of the Second Samnite War the Romans began to strengthen their hold on the mountainous region of central Italy. In 306 a revolt of the Hernici was crushed, and their leading town, Anagnia, was incorporated with *civitas sine suffragio*; in the following years the peoples of the Abruzzi region were subdued, and one after another the Marsi, Paeligni, Marrucini, Frentani and Vestini were made allies of Rome. Particularly harsh treatment was reserved for the Aequi, whom the Romans overwhelmed in a lightning campaign in 304. Their territory was annexed and they ceased to exist as a separate people.

These conquests were reinforced by the construction of a military road from Rome to the Adriatic through the central Apennines (the Via Valeria, 306 BC), and by the foundation of Latin colonies at Sora (303), Alba Fucens (303) and Carseoli (298). An expedition into Umbria in 299 led to the foundation of another Latin colony at Narnia.

By 298 the Romans were once again fighting on two fronts. Annual compaigns in Etruria and Umbria are recorded from 302 onwards, and in 298 hostilities between Rome and the Samnites were resumed. One of the first actions of this war is recorded in the epitaph of L. Cornelius Scipio Barbatus, the consul of 298. The text, which was composed in the 2nd century BC, reads: "Lucius Cornelius Scipio Barbatus, begotten by his father Gnaeus, a brave and wise man, whose good looks matched his gallantry, who served you as consul, censor and aedile, captured Taurasia and Cisauna in Samnium, overran all Lucania and brought back hostages." The epitaph no doubt exaggerates the extent of Scipio's achievements, but it is to be preferred to the version of Livy (who makes him campaign in northern Etruria) and reflects the ever-widening scope of Roman operations.

The events of the Third Samnite War came to a head in 295 BC when the Samnites managed to get an army into northern Italy and to combine with the Etruscans and Umbrians who were still at war with Rome. At the same time they were able to take advantage of the presence of the Gauls, who had been making incursions across the Apennines since 299 BC. A grand anti-Roman coalition was formed, and its combined forces met a Roman army in a great battle at Sentinum in Umbria in the summer of 295. Victory went to the Romans, perhaps largely because of the absence of the Etruscans and

Umbrians, who had been drawn away by a diversionary maneuver; later tradition preferred to dwell on the heroic act of self-sacrifice by the consul P. Decius Mus, who "devoted" himself and the enemy forces to the infernal gods. After this the result of the war was no longer in doubt. The Samnites' territory was overrun and in 290 they came to terms. They were compelled to become allies of Rome and thus lost their independence; and they were deprived of all their territory that lay beyond the Volturnus river, which became the new frontier. This was in addition to the loss of a large area of land in southeast Samnium on which the Latin colony of Venusia had been founded in 291.

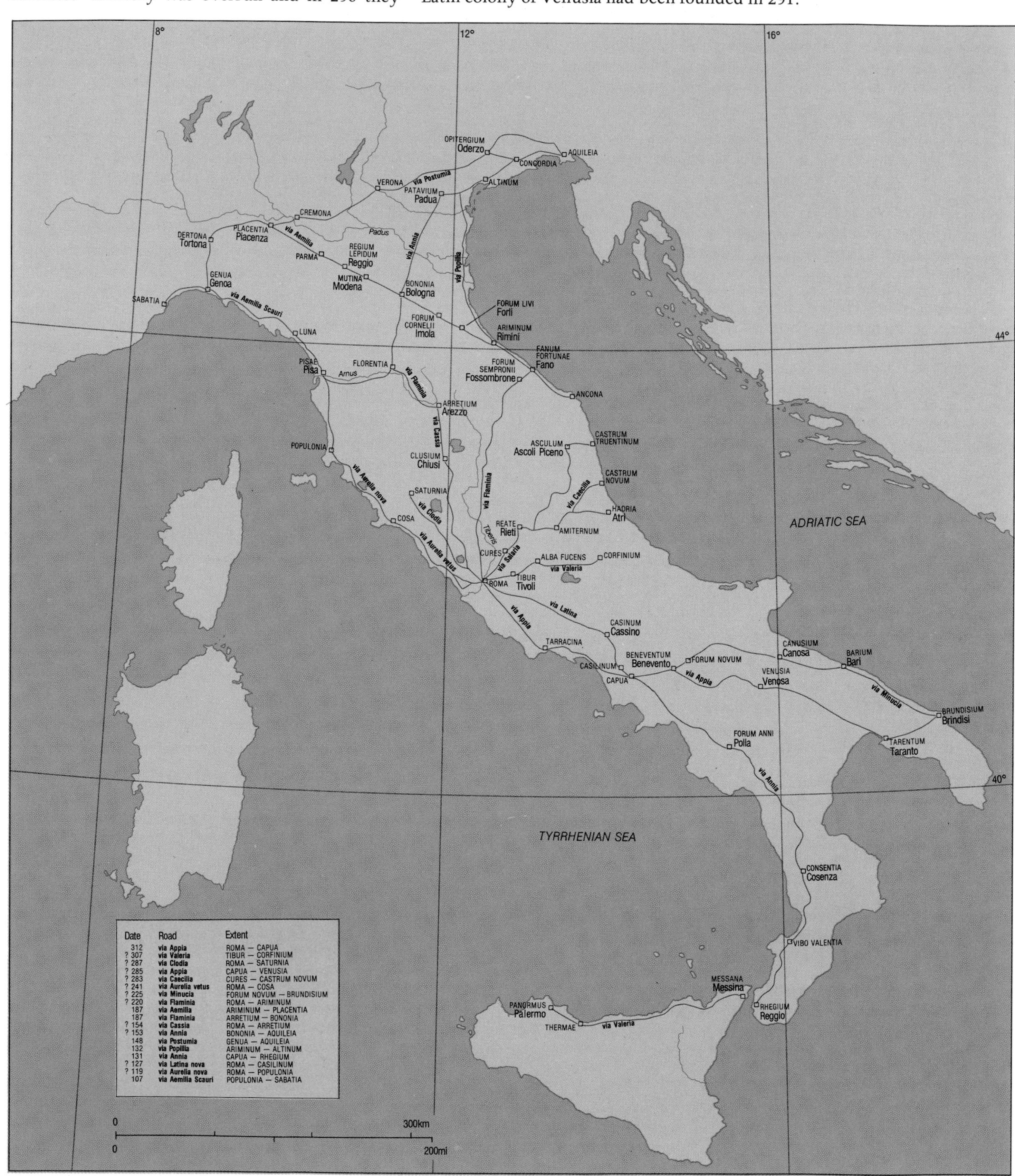

Date	Road	Extent
312	**via Appia**	ROMA — CAPUA
? 307	**via Valeria**	TIBUR — CORFINIUM
? 287	**via Clodia**	ROMA — SATURNIA
? 285	**via Appia**	CAPUA — VENUSIA
? 283	**via Caecilia**	CURES — CASTRUM NOVUM
? 241	**via Aurelia vetus**	ROMA — COSA
? 225	**via Minucia**	FORUM NOVUM — BRUNDISIUM
? 220	**via Flaminia**	ROMA — ARIMINUM
187	**via Aemilia**	ARIMINUM — PLACENTIA
187	**via Flaminia**	ARRETIUM — BONONIA
? 154	**via Cassia**	ROMA — ARRETIUM
? 153	**via Annia**	BONONIA — AQUILEIA
148	**via Postumia**	GENUA — AQUILEIA
132	**via Popillia**	ARIMINUM — ALTINUM
131	**via Annia**	CAPUA — RHEGIUM
? 127	**via Latina nova**	ROMA — CASILINUM
? 119	**via Aurelia nova**	ROMA — POPULONIA
107	**via Aemilia Scauri**	POPULONIA — SABATIA

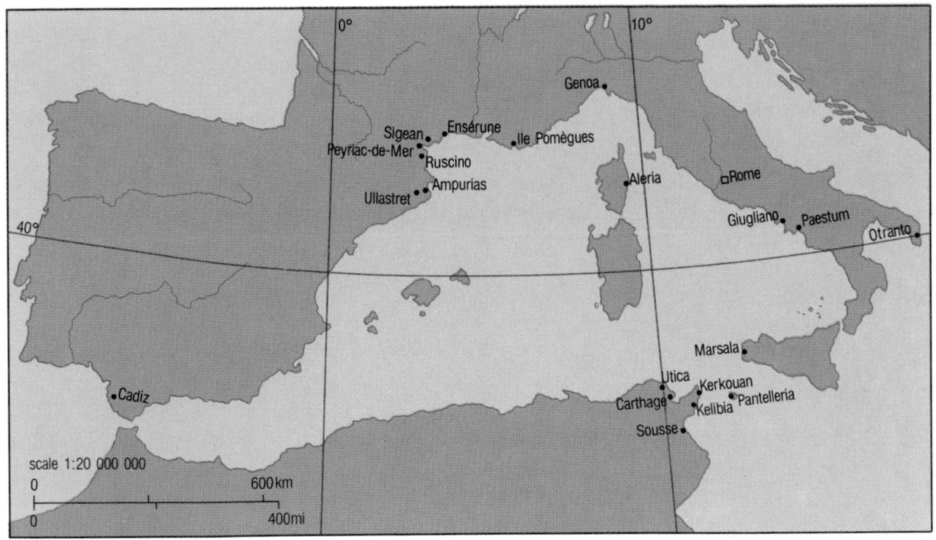

Above: Distribution of pottery made in Rome in the 3rd century BC. By the middle Republic Rome had become a major trading and manufacturing center. Among its products was fine pottery, which was exported throughout the western Mediterranean. One characteristic type of pottery, from a workshop known as the "Atelier des petites estampilles," has been found at numerous sites in central Italy, along the southern coast of France, in southern Spain, Corsica, Sicily and North Africa.

Left: Roman roads in the republican period. The earliest Roman roads were no doubt little more than tracks or strips of land along which a public right of way was recognized. Some, like the old Via Latina, which ran down the Sacco valley, followed natural lines of communication that had been used since time immemorial. The great Roman achievement was in the construction of straight, paved roads carried on bridges and viaducts, and through cuttings and tunnels. In this they were to some extent preceded by the Etruscans, whose settlements were linked by a network of well-built roads. The first great Roman highways were built in the age of the conquest, and had a strategic function, linking Rome to the Latin colonies. The roads and colonies together were the most important factor in the consolidation of the conquest. The second great age of road building in Italy came in the latter part of the 2nd century BC, and to some extent represents an investment of the profits of empire in public works, which provided employment for the proletariat as well as improved amenities for the community at large.

The Romans advanced relentlessly. In 290 the consul M'. Curius Dentatus conquered the Sabines and the Praetuttii, who were made Roman citizens *sine suffragio*; some of their land was seized and distributed to poor Romans. As a result of this episode Roman territory was extended right across the center of the peninsula to the Adriatic coast, where the Latin colony of Hadria was founded (between 290 and 286). In the poorly documented period that followed the Romans recorded victories against the Gauls and subdued the Etruscans and Umbrians, who were compelled to become allies.

Conflict with Magna Graecia

At the beginning of the 3rd century BC the Greek cities of southern Italy were in a state of advanced decline, resulting from the continuous pressure of hostile natives and centuries of internecine strife. The Romans became involved in the affairs of Magna Graecia in the 280s when the city of Thurii appealed to them for aid against the Lucanians; within a few years Locri, Rhegium and Croton had also placed themselves under Rome's protection. These developments were viewed with alarm in Tarentum, the most powerful of the Greek cities, which had for some time been suspicious of the growing power of Rome. In the face of this threat the Tarentines appealed for aid to King Pyrrhus of Epirus, an ambitious ruler who was himself on the lookout for an opportunity to increase his power.

Pyrrhus landed in 280 with a force of 25 000 men and 20 elephants. This was the first time that the Romans had had to face a fully trained Hellenistic army, and in the first engagement at Heraclea (280 BC) they were driven from the field, but not before they had inflicted heavy losses on their opponents. Pyrrhus then offered to make peace, but his terms were rejected by the Romans, who were persuaded by the aged Appius Claudius not to treat with him as long as he remained on Italian soil. Pyrrhus then attempted to march on Rome, and penetrated as far as Anagnia before turning back; Capua and Naples had closed their gates, and none of Rome's allies joined him. He must have begun to realize the size of the task he had set himself; Rome was a well-organized state with access to resources he could not hope to match. In 279 he won a second victory at Ausculum, but his losses were even greater than at Heraclea, and the battle had cost him more than the Romans.

In 278 he decided to abandon Italy for the time being and to try his hand in Sicily, where the Greek cities had requested his help against the Carthaginians. The result was a renewed alliance between Rome and Carthage. In Sicily Pyrrhus promised much but again achieved little, and when he returned to Italy in 275 he was met and defeated by a Roman army at Malventum (which was renamed Beneventum after the battle). Pyrrhus then sailed back to Greece where he continued to waste his talents in fruitless enterprises; his brilliant but ultimately worthless career came to an end a few years later when he was struck on the head and killed by a roof-tile during a street battle in Argos.

The unification of Italy

Following Pyrrhus' departure from Italy, the Romans pressed home their victory. Tarentum was besieged, and its fall (272 BC) marks the end of Italian independence. From this time on the whole peninsula, from the straits of Messina in the south to a line running from Pisa to Rimini in the north, was under Rome's control. Lucania and Samnium were secured by the foundation of colonies at Paestum (273), Beneventum (268) and Aesernia (263); two further colonies were founded at Brundisium (244) and Spoletium (241). The latter foundation occurred following a revolt by the city of Falerii, an isolated gesture of defiance which the Romans put down, with overwhelming force, in a campaign of only six days.

The general policy of the Romans during the Italian wars was a paradoxical blend of brutality and calculated generosity. Their victories entailed full-scale massacres (for example of the Aurunci in 314 BC or the Aequi in 304), extensive confiscations of territory and the mass enslavement of captives. For example on Livy's figures alone it is possible to calculate that over 60 000 individuals were enslaved during just five years of the Third Samnite War (297–293).

But the final settlement which Rome imposed on her vanquished enemies was enlightened and ultimately of considerable benefit to both sides. Those communities which were not incorporated in the Roman state with either full or half-citizenship were bound to Rome by treaties of alliance. As one might expect, many other states in Italy voluntarily entered into alliances with the Romans rather than suffer the consequences of a military defeat. In either case the allies were obliged to give military aid to Rome whenever it was required; in effect this meant that they lost their independence in the conduct of foreign policy and became vassal states, although they were left free to run their own internal affairs. On the other hand Rome imposed no taxes or tribute on them. The situation was in fact a kind of partnership in which the allies helped Rome to make further conquests and obtained a share of the profits. These profits included movable booty (including slaves) and land. Admittedly the land which was confiscated from defeated communities passed entirely into the possession of the Roman state, whereupon it was either sold, leased out as *ager publicus* or resettled by means of colonization or individual assignation, but it should be noted that the settlers who took part in these schemes included men from Latin and Italian allied states as well as Roman citizens. Thus it can be said that by being enrolled in the gang and invited to share the loot Rome's victims were in a way compensated for the losses they had originally suffered.

An important feature of the Roman organization in Italy was the senate's support for local aristocracies in the allied states. In their turn the propertied classes of the Italian communities turned naturally to Rome whenever their own interests were threatened. On several recorded occasions Roman military force actually intervened on behalf of the local ruling class to put down popular insurrections (for example at Arretium in 302 BC, in Lucania in 296 and at Volsinii in 264). In return the Romans expected, and usually received, the active cooperation of the ruling aristocracies in the allied communities. This convenient arrangement ensured the continuing loyalty of the allies to Rome. Even in the darkest days of the Second Punic War the majority of the allies remained faithful, in spite of Hannibal's repeated efforts to win them over to his side.

The most significant long-term result of the Roman conquest of the Italian peninsula was the gradual disappearance of its ethnic, linguistic and cultural differences. The progressive romanization of the indigenous peoples of Italy took place in the course of the following three centuries, and was more or less complete by the 1st century AD, apart from a few quaint survivals in remote areas. The first parts of Italy to be thus assimilated were the central districts whose inhabitants had been granted half-citizenship; they were gradually incorporated in the Roman body politic with full citizen rights, beginning with the Sabines in 268 BC.

The process of assimilation also affected the allies. It was not brought about by a deliberate or conscious policy of the Roman government; rather it was a natural result of the fact that men from the allied communities performed military service alongside Roman citizens, and under Roman commanders, sometimes for years on end. Moreover the dissemination of the Latin language and of Roman ways of life was promoted by the Latin colonies, which were distributed throughout allied territory. These colonies were founded as self-governing political units, but since the majority of the settlers were of Roman or Latin origin they in fact constituted romanized enclaves in which Latin was spoken and the Roman way of life was practiced.

The system of Latin colonies was linked to the network of military roads which were constructed in the wake of the conquest. These great roads, whose names (Appia, Aurelia, Flaminia, etc.) preserve the memory of the men who ordered them to be built, were primarily strategic in function, but had the secondary effect of improving communications generally and facilitating other forms of intercourse between the various regions of Italy. The inevitable result was the further spread of Roman ideas and practices.

Roman society in the age of the Italian wars

During the period of the wars of conquest Rome itself was transformed, and the characteristic political, social and economic structures of the middle Republic began to take shape. Political power was in the hands of an elite of patrician and plebeian nobles, who dominated the senate and the senior magistracies. These men included forceful political leaders who guided Rome's foreign policy and who worked to improve the lot of the lower classes. Examples are the plebeians Q. Publilius Philo and M'. Curius Dentatus, and the patrician Appius Claudius Caecus. Of the latter it has been said that he is "the earliest Roman to appear in our sources as a personality." His achievements, which are conveniently listed in an inscription dating from

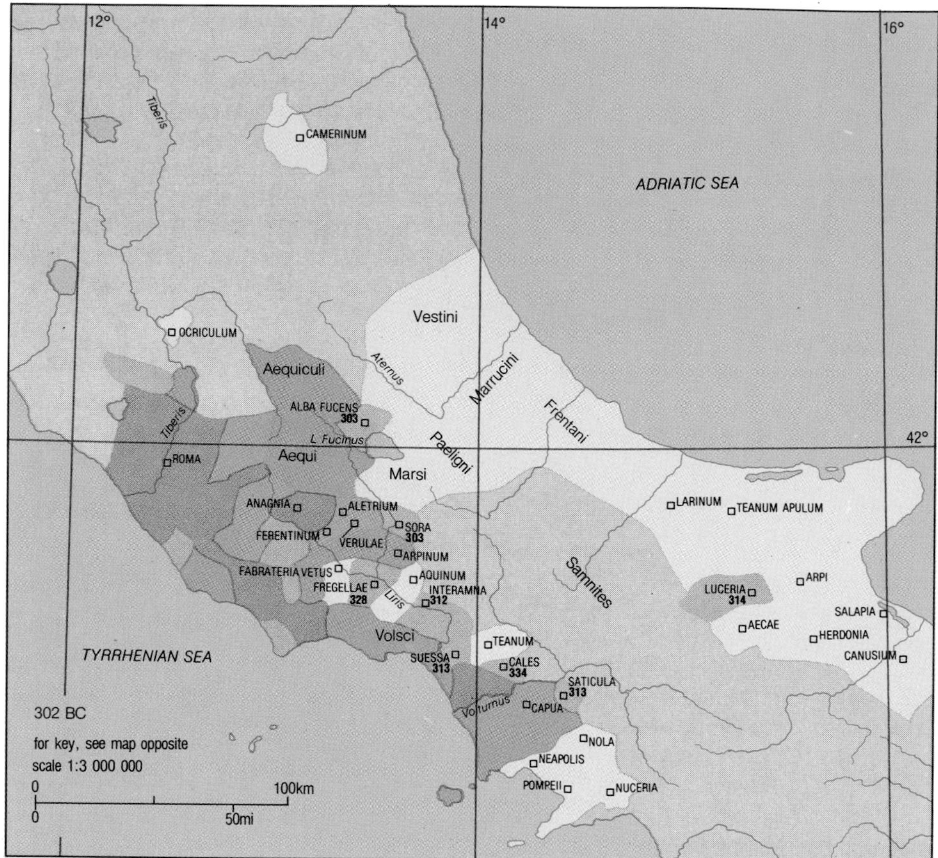

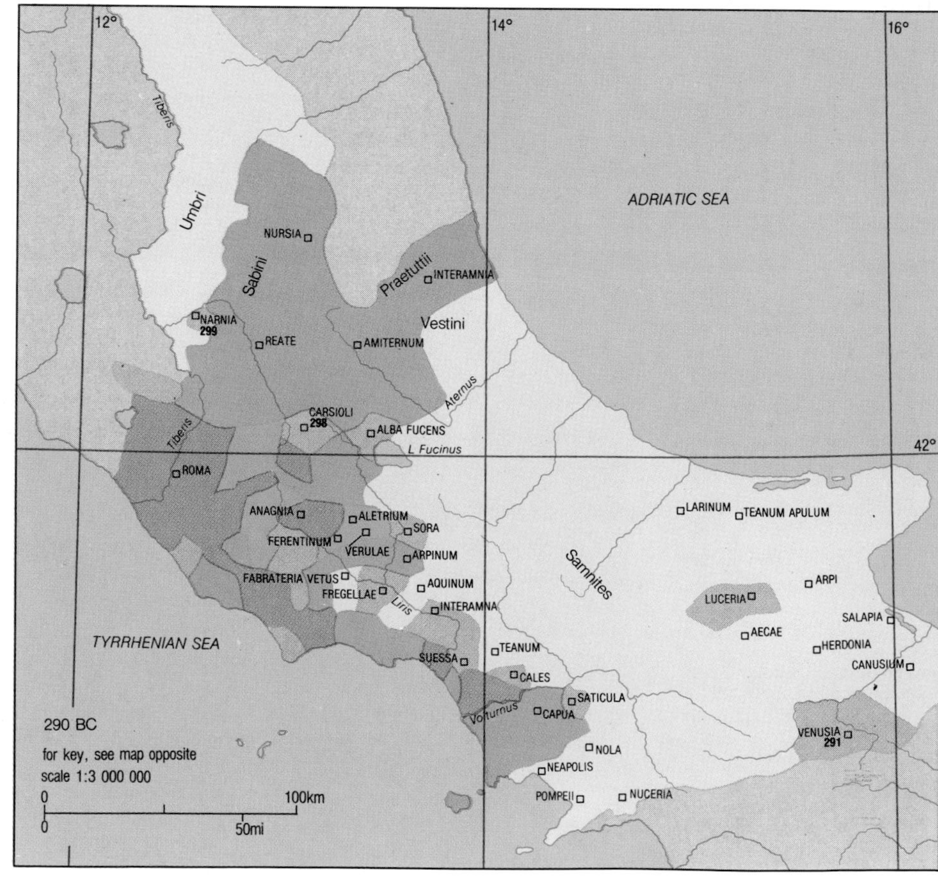

King Pyrrhus of Epirus (319–272 BC). Of all the Greek kings who ruled in the generations following Alexander the Great, Pyrrhus was the one who by general consent most closely resembled the legendary conqueror, not only in appearance and temperament, but also in ability. His defeat by the Romans in 275 created a sensation in the Greek world.

the reign of Augustus, are indeed impressive: "Appius Claudius Caecus, son of Gaius, censor, consul twice, dictator, interrex three times, praetor twice, curule aedile twice, quaestor, tribune of the soldiers three times. He captured several towns from the Samnites, and routed an army of Sabines and Etruscans. He prevented peace being made with King Pyrrhus. In his censorship he paved the Appian Way and built an aqueduct for Rome. He built the temple of Bellona."

The nobility was an elite within a wider ruling class, whose wealth and power were based on ownership of land. Its dominance was ensured by the peculiar structure of Roman political institutions. Rome was ruled by annual magistrates and a senate of ex-magistrates. The magistrates were chosen by popular election in voting assemblies in which all full citizens could participate. The voting assemblies (the various *comitia*) also had the power of decision on matters such as peace and war, on legislative proposals and in serious criminal cases. In theory the assembled Roman people was sovereign, but in practice the system was far from democratic. The *comitia* could only be summoned by magistrates, who alone had the right to address the people and to submit proposals. The assembled citizens had no right either to debate or to amend the proposals put to them. There was no freedom of speech.

But the most undemocratic aspect of the Roman assemblies was that the voting took place by groups. In the *comitia tributa* and the plebeian assembly, the *concilium plebis*, the constituent groups or voting units were the local tribes. The number of local tribes gradually increased as Rome acquired new territory, until in 241 BC the definitive figure of 35 was reached. This total was made up of four so-called "urban" tribes, and 31 "rural" tribes. The significance of this division is that only landowners were able to register in the rural tribes, while the landless inhabitants of the city were confined to the four urban tribes and thus had only minimal voting power, even though they probably formed a majority of those who attended the assemblies, which were held only in Rome. In this way the system artificially favored the wealthy landowners and discriminated equally against the urban proletariat and the far-flung peasant smallholders who for practical reasons were unable to attend the *comitia* in person. The voting units of the *comitia centuriata* were the 193 centuries, which were distributed among five economically defined

The growth of the Roman Confederacy. The "Roman Confederacy" is a label conventionally attached to the system of alliances and dependencies which the Romans built up during their conquest of the peninsula in the years 338–264 BC. Defeated enemies were either compelled to become allies, which meant that they had to contribute troops to Rome's armies, or incorporated in the Roman state as citizens. Newly incorporated citizens were given either full citizenship (*civitas optimo iure*) or "half citizenship" (*civitas sine suffragio*), which meant that they performed all the duties of citizens, such as tax paying and military service, but had only limited civil rights; for example they could not vote in the Roman assemblies. In the course of time the half citizens were given full citizen rights; this happened for example to the lowland Sabines in 268 BC, and to the people of Arpinum in 188 BC. It is probable that all communities of half citizens had been upgraded by the end of the 2nd century BC. With the extension of full citizenship the Romans created a series of new local tribes, in which they enrolled the new citizens as well as any existing citizens who were settled on areas of newly annexed territory. The local tribes functioned as constituent voting units in Roman political assemblies.

241 BC

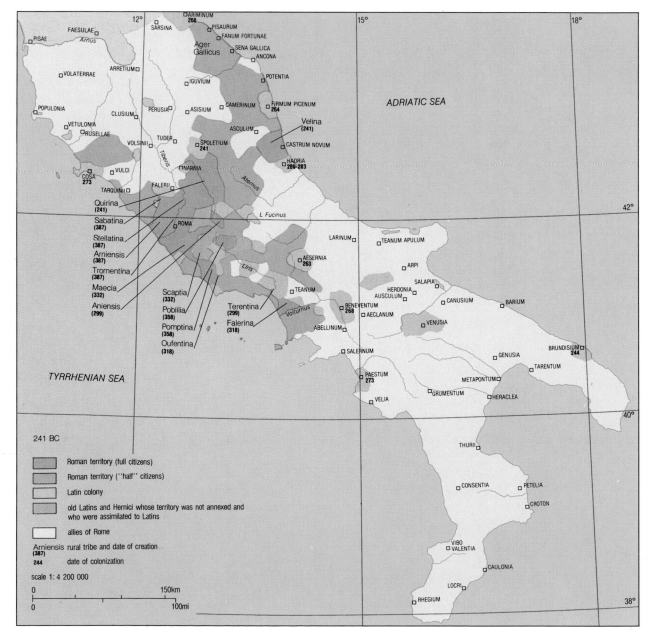

Roman territory (full citizens)
Roman territory ("half" citizens)
Latin colony
old Latins and Hernici whose territory was not annexed and who were assimilated to Latins
allies of Rome
Arniensis (387) rural tribe and date of creation
244 date of colonization
scale 1: 4 200 000
0 150km
0 100mi

classes; but the distribution was so arranged that the wealthiest class comprised the largest number of centuries, and thus dominated the assembly.

The division of property-owning citizens (*adsidui*) into five distinct classes is attributed by our sources to Servius Tullius (see above, p. 22), but in fact it was probably a later refinement connected with the institution of the *tributum*, a direct tax on the capital wealth of Roman citizens. The revenue which this tax yielded was used to provide pay for the army. The soldiers' pay, the *stipendium*, was traditionally introduced in 406 BC during the siege of Veii, in order to compensate the men for the loss of their normal income during the 10-year siege. This tradition reflects the fact that the Roman army was a part-time militia recruited from peasants who owned sufficient property to equip themselves, and who were registered for political and fiscal purposes in the five property classes.

It is important to understand that in many ancient city-states military service was regarded not as a burden but as a privilege and a mark of status. At the same time it was felt that a man's political rights should be commensurate with his contribution to the state. Thus the proletarian, who owned no wealth and was therefore necessarily free from the burden of taxation, was relieved of the obligation of military service and excluded from effective participation in political life. This kind of system, which was known in antiquity as timocracy, was based on the principle that "the higher one's census qualification, the greater one's military obligations and the wider one's political rights" (E. Gabba).

Wealth based on land was therefore the key to political power in republican Rome. This statement is not inconsistent with the fact that the political leaders of the late 4th and early 3rd centuries BC were looked upon in later times as models of parsimonious frugality and honest virtue. This they may have been, if the standard of comparison is the luxury and extravagance of the late Republic; but such men were in no sense poor. To that extent the stories about M'. Curius Dentatus, whose humble rustic dwelling was later to make a great impression on Cato, or C. Fabricius Luscinus, who contemptuously refused bribes offered by Samnite envoys who had found him cooking turnips for his supper, are misleading. In fact the later tradition was more concerned with the moral example which these men set than with their real economic status. An equally revealing story is the fate of P. Cornelius Rufinus, who was expelled from the senate in 276 BC because he owned 10 pounds of silver plate. Here the point is surely that the establishment disapproved not of Rufinus' wealth as such, but of the way he chose to display it.

In fact the decades on either side of 300 BC saw an unparalleled increase in the public and private wealth of the Romans. Their most obvious gain was in land. Roman territory, which after the conclusion of the Latin War in 338 BC had comprised 5525 square kilometers, had expanded by 264 BC to some 26 805 square kilometers, more than 20 per cent of the total land surface of peninsular Italy. Roman citizens also benefited directly from the foundation of Latin colonies, which by 241 BC occupied a further 10 000 square kilometers of confiscated land (according to the most probable modern estimates).

The population of Roman citizens grew accordingly. The recorded census figures, which first become plausible at the beginning of the 3rd century, suggest a total population of free Romans of between 750 000 and one million. At this date Rome itself was one of the largest cities of the Mediterranean, with a probable population of more than 150 000 persons. In order to provide for the needs of the inhabitants of the city it became necessary to construct aqueducts, the first of which was the Aqua Appia, built by Appius Claudius in 312, followed by the Anio Vetus, which M'. Curius Dentatus began in 272.

These public works were financed by the profits of war, which flowed into the city in the form of booty and indemnities, and gave rise to a program of public building on a scale which had not been seen since the great days of the Tarquins. The spoils of victory paid for the construction of at least 11 major temples between 302 and 272 BC, including those of Bellona (296), Jupiter Victor (295) and Victoria (294), which reveal the Romans' growing obsession with militaristic cults. Two of the temples which can now be seen in the Largo Argentina in Rome can be dated to around 300 BC and clearly belong to this series. The influx of wealth into the city must also have created a prosperous service sector, as well as generating a demand for luxury goods which was at least partly met by local production. This can be deduced from the survival of particular artifacts such as the Ficoroni *cista*, and of large quantities of Roman fine pottery, which has been found at many sites throughout the western Mediterranean.

This very fine bronze *cista* from Praeneste dates from the last decades of the 4th century BC. It bears two inscriptions: "Dindia Macolnia gave this to her daughter," and "Novios Plautios made me in Rome." The "made in Rome" label proves that Rome was at this date a major center for the production of high-quality goods.

The increasing economic prosperity and cultural sophistication of Rome in the early 3rd century BC can be illustrated by a number of important developments. The first is the growth of slavery. The mass enslavement of prisoners of war has already been mentioned, and demonstrates that the institution was well established and was being practiced on a large scale. By tradition freed slaves in Rome were admitted to the citizenship, though with limited civil rights; their offspring had full rights and were completely assimilated. An indication of the extent to which the citizen body was permeated by persons of servile origin is provided by the fact that in 312 Appius Claudius admitted sons of freedmen to the senate. At this date the majority of slaves were probably employed in domestic service in the houses of the rich and in trading and manufacturing enterprises in the city; but there is some evidence that slave labor was already being used on the land, to work the estates of the wealthy.

Secondly, during this period the Roman state began for the first time to issue coined money. The origin of Roman coinage is a difficult and controversial subject, but the most authoritative modern opinion seems to be that the earliest Roman coins appeared in about 280 BC. Before that date monetary transactions had taken place using uncoined metal which was measured by weight according to a fixed scale of units; the introduction of coinage simplified the system, so that it became possible to make payments, for example to soldiers or workmen, merely by counting out the required number of coins. An equally important aspect of coinage was that the circulation of money entailed the propagation of the legends and types which the minting authority chose to put on its coins. Coinage in other words provided a medium through which the state could advertise itself to the world at large. In 269 BC an issue of Roman silver coins bore as its reverse type a representation of the twins Romulus and Remus being suckled by the she-wolf. A slightly later series had the helmeted head of a female personification of Roma on the obverse, and a Victory on the reverse. Such types are signs of Rome's growing self-confidence and awareness of her enormous power.

Coinage was a Greek device, and Rome's adoption of it indicates the increasing influence of Greek culture on Roman life. This also manifests itself in monuments and artifacts which show that Roman craftsmen were imitating Greek styles and techniques, and in the direct importation of Greek religious cults, such as that of the healing god Aesculapius, to whom a temple was dedicated in 291 on the Tiber island. The cults of Victory were also based on Greek models. It is during this period that Hellenism began to become fashionable among the Roman elite. It is significant for example that some leading aristocratic families began to adopt Greek surnames such as Sophus, Philippus and Philo.

News of the sensational defeat of Pyrrhus by a hitherto little-known Italian republic made a tremendous impact on the Greek world. In 273 BC the king of Egypt, Ptolemy II Philadelphus, sent an embassy to Rome, no doubt as a fact-finding mission as well as a gesture of goodwill. The Romans replied with an embassy of their own to Alexandria; the three senators, unaccustomed to diplomatic protocol, were embarrassed when Ptolemy offered them gifts. At the court of Alexandria Rome and the Romans became a fashionable topic in intellectual and literary circles. Callimachus wrote a poem about a Roman called Gaius; Lycophron wrote an epic poem about a new Troy founded by the descendants of Aeneas; and the scientist Eratosthenes wrote about the "wonderful" system of government of the Romans. Meanwhile in Athens the historian Timaeus, a Sicilian exile, gave an important place to Rome in his monumental study of the peoples of the western Mediterranean, and also composed a separate monograph on the war between Rome and Pyrrhus (these works no longer survive). It was Timaeus more than anyone else who made Rome familiar to the Greeks. His realization of the importance of the new power in Italy derives from his knowledge of Sicilian affairs and from his perception of an impending conflict between Rome and Carthage, in which the fate of his native island would be decided.

Coin of T. Veturius (137 BC) recalling the agreement with the Samnites made by his ancestor T. Veturius Calvinus (consul 321 BC) after the surrender of his army at the Caudine Forks. The scene shows two warriors taking an oath by touching a pig (held by the kneeling figure in the center) with their swords.

Early Roman silver coins. The reverse of a silver didrachm of 269 BC (*below*) shows the she-wolf suckling the twins Romulus and Remus; a later issue, dating from the period of the First Punic War, shows the head of Roma, personified as an armed goddess (cf. Britannia), on the obverse (*left*), and a Victory with a palm branch and wreath on the reverse (*left below*). These types are signs of Rome's growing self-confidence and military power.

The struggle between Rome and Carthage

In 264 BC the Romans and their Italian allies became involved in a war with Carthage which arose from a petty incident in northeastern Sicily. This situation rapidly escalated into the first of a series of major wars which resulted in a dramatic change in the power politics of the Mediterranean world. Within less than 100 years the Romans had not only reduced Carthage to impotence; they had also humiliated all the major powers of the Greek east, and by 167 BC they were the effective rulers of the Mediterranean.

None of this was consciously planned. The crisis of 264 BC must have seemed at first sight a relatively minor affair. It arose when the Romans answered an appeal from the city of Messana (Messina). Originally a Greek city, Messana was at this date in the hands of some Oscan-speaking Italian mercenaries who had occupied it some 20 years earlier in a bloodthirsty coup. Not surprisingly the Mamertines, as these Italian adventurers called themselves, found few friends among the Greeks of Sicily, and when they were attacked by the Syracusans under King Hiero II, they were obliged to cast about for allies. Some of their leaders resolved to appeal to Carthage, the traditional enemy of the Sicilian Greeks; others argued in favor of calling in the Romans, whose sympathy they hoped to win by stressing the fact of their own Italian origin. The Carthaginians had every reason to be alarmed at the growing power of Rome, and when their small garrison in Messana was expelled by the Mamertines, they decided to form an alliance with Hiero, whose army was by now investing the city.

Hostilities began when a Roman army arrived at Messana and attacked the besieging forces. Initial Roman successes soon caused Hiero to change his mind; in 263 he abandoned his Carthaginian allies and went over to the Romans. Further Roman successes followed, and in 261 they captured the Carthaginian base at Agrigentum. By now both sides were fully committed to all-out war. Polybius tells us that after the fall of Agrigentum the Romans began for the first time to contemplate the possibility of driving out the Carthaginians and gaining complete control of Sicily. But they soon realized that they would be unable to carry out this plan as long as Carthage ruled the seas, and so with characteristic determination they resolved to build a fleet. By the beginning of 260 a fleet of 100 large warships (quinqueremes) was manned and ready for action, a remarkable achievement considering that hitherto the Romans had not possessed any naval forces to speak of.

In their first major naval engagement, at Mylae in 260 BC, the Romans under the consul C. Duilius won a memorable victory. This was followed by further victories, particularly at the battle of Ecnomus in 256, where the Carthaginian fleet was decisively beaten. But Rome's good fortune did not continue. An attempt to strike directly at Carthage by sending an invasion force to Africa under M. Atilius Regulus ended in failure, and turned into a complete disaster when the fleet sent to evacuate the army was wrecked in a storm on the return voyage (255). In Sicily itself the Romans managed to capture Panormus (Palermo) in 253, and two years later L. Caecilius Metellus won a decisive battle there, capturing over 100 elephants. But at sea they suffered further reverses, culminating in a disastrous battle at Drepana (249). Later in the same year the remainder of the fleet was almost entirely destroyed in a storm. The war dragged on inconclusively for the next few years, although the Carthaginians began to make some headway in Sicily under Hamilcar Barca, the father of Hannibal. But by the winter of 243–242 the Romans had recovered sufficiently to be able to resume the war at sea. A new fleet was built, and in 241 an overwhelming victory at the Aegates islands, off the western coast of Sicily, at last brought the war to an end. Under the peace terms offered by the victor C.

Lutatius Catulus, the Carthaginians agreed to evacuate Sicily, to return all Italian prisoners of war and to pay a large indemnity (the figure finally arrived at was 3200 talents, to be paid in 10 annual instalments).

Thus ended one of the most destructive wars in ancient history. The losses on both sides were enormous; at a conservative estimate the Romans and their allies lost over 100 000 men and more than 500 warships, and Carthaginian losses were probably nearly as great. The sufferings of the native Sicilians were undoubtedly appalling. Several major cities were sacked (Panormus, Agrigentum, Camarina, Selinus), and their populations enslaved. At Agrigentum in 261 the number of persons enslaved is said to have reached 25 000. In the opinion of Polybius the First Punic War was, "in terms of its duration, intensity and scale of operations, the greatest war in history."

The terms of Lutatius' treaty left the Carthaginians in an extremely weak position. They were shortly to suffer further as a result of a mutiny of their own mercenaries, which turned into a disastrous and bloody war (241–238). In 238 the Romans took advantage of this state of affairs and seized Sardinia, formerly a Carthaginian possession (an act for which there was not the slightest justification, according to Polybius). At the same time they began to reduce Corsica. After some fighting, these islands became Roman possessions, with the same status as Sicily.

Sicily had been the Romans' principal gain from their victory in 241. Apart from certain privileged cases, such as Messana and the kingdom of Syracuse, the various communities of Sicily became subjects and paid tribute to Rome in the form of a tithe. From 227 BC the administration of these overseas possessions was made the responsibility of magistrates with *imperium*, and two new praetorships were created for the purpose, one for Sicily and one for Corsica and Sardinia. The sphere in which a magistrate exercised his *imperium* was known as his "province" (*provincia*), a term which thus came to be used to describe Rome's overseas possessions. The praetor's job was to organize the defense of the province, to maintain law and order, and to supervise the collection of taxes.

While these matters were being settled the Romans turned their attention to northern Italy, where the Gauls had once again become restless. Their hostility was at least partly caused by an enactment of the tribune C. Flaminius (232 BC), which provided for the distribution of allotments of land in the *ager Gallicus* to Roman citizens and probably involved the eviction of Gauls who had occupied it as squatters since 283. In 225 an invading army of Gauls was heavily defeated at Telamon in Etruria and driven back across the Apennines. The Romans followed up their victory by advancing into the Po plain. Mediolanum (Milan) was captured in 222, and the process of integrating Cisalpine Gaul with the rest of Roman Italy was begun. In 218 two large Latin colonies were dispatched to Placentia (Piacenza) and Cremona. These had hardly been established, however, when Hannibal's army descended into Italy.

Following the two-fold disaster of the mercenaries' revolt and the loss of Sardinia, the Carthaginians had begun to create a new overseas

Top The old Phoenician city of Carthage, traditionally founded in 814 BC, was completely obliterated by Scipio Aemilianus in 146 BC. The standing remains date from the Roman period, when a new town was founded by Caesar. Recent excavations have however begun to reveal some traces of the old Punic city and its harbor installations.

Above Bronze bust of a Roman aristocrat (popularly known as "Brutus"), probably dating from the late 4th century BC.

Right: The First Punic War. The first great war between Rome and Carthage began when Rome intervened in a minor incident in Sicily in 264 BC. Since neither side was prepared to allow the island to fall into the possession of the other, the dispute rapidly escalated into a full-scale conflict. The Romans built a fleet and took to the seas in 260 BC; the war was then waged by land and sea for a further 20 years, with enormous losses on both sides. In the end Rome's resources proved greater than those of Carthage, and after the Roman victory at the Aegates islands in 241 BC the Carthaginians surrendered. The Romans occupied Sicily, which became their first province.

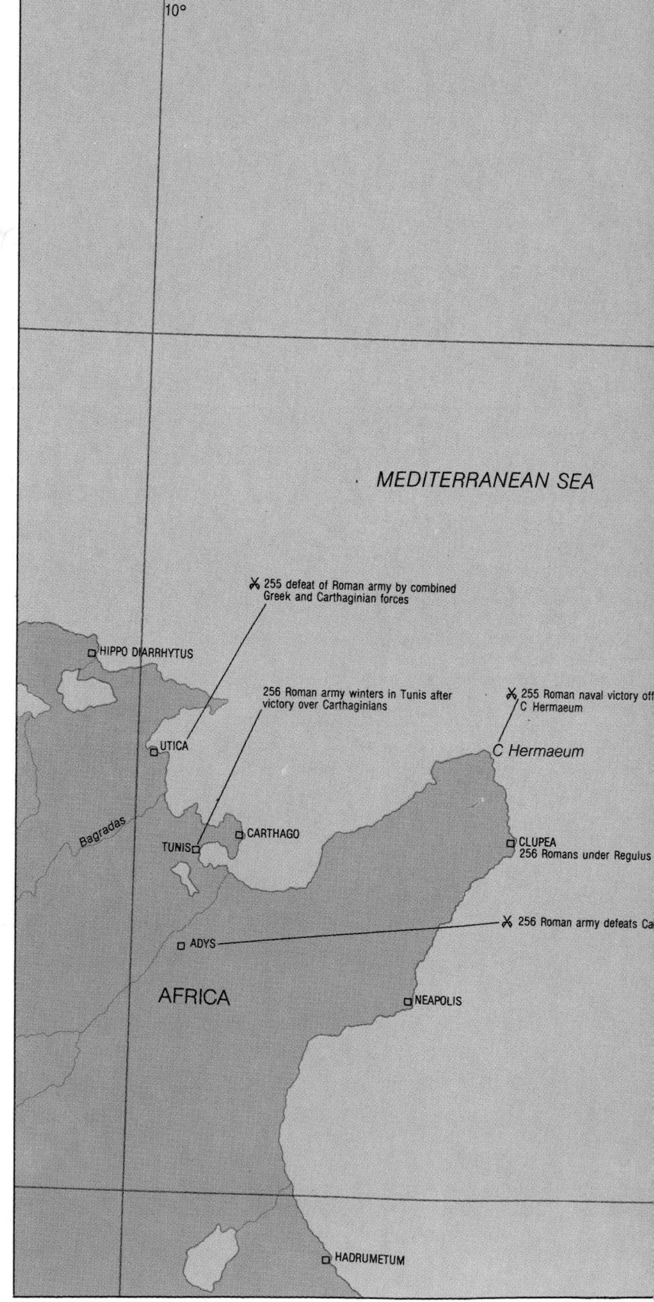

Coin of C. Metellus (125 BC) showing Jupiter in a chariot drawn by elephants. The type recalls the victory of L. Metellus at Panormus (Palermo) in 251 and the capture of over 100 Carthaginian war elephants.

empire in Spain. This enterprise was started in 237 by Hamilcar Barca, and was continued after his death by his son-in-law Hasdrubal. Rome kept a close watch on these developments, and in 226 it demanded, and received, assurances from Hasdrubal that the Carthaginians would confine their activities to the area south of the Ebro river. The real problems began when Hannibal, who succeeded Hasdrubal in 221, moved against the town of Saguntum (219). Saguntum was well to the south of the Ebro, but was nonetheless an ally of Rome. Hannibal ignored Rome's demands that he should not harm Saguntum, and when the city fell an embassy was sent to Carthage with an ultimatum demanding his surrender. Livy describes the dramatic scene in the Carthaginian senate. "Fabius [leader of the Roman delegation] laid his hand on the fold of his toga, where he had gathered it at the breast: 'Here,' he said, 'we bring you peace and war. Take which you will.' Scarcely had he spoken, when the answer no less proudly rang out: 'Whichever you please – we do not care.' Fabius let the gathered folds fall, and cried: 'We give you war.' The Carthaginian senators replied, as one man: 'We accept it; and in the same spirit we will fight it to the end.'"

The Romans probably hoped to fight Hannibal in Spain, and at the same time to put pressure on Carthage by sending an expeditionary force to Africa. But these plans were thwarted by Hannibal, who promptly marched his forces out of Spain and proceeded towards the frontiers of Italy. In the autumn of 218 BC he crossed the Alps with 20000 infantry and 6000 cavalry, and was immediately joined by the Gallic tribes of the northern plain, who had revolted from Rome on hearing news of his approach. With their help he won the first major engagements of the war, at the rivers Ticinus and Trebia, before the end of 218.

The attitude of the Gauls must have encouraged Hannibal, whose chief hope was that the Italian allies would rise up in rebellion against Rome. In 217 he advanced into Etruria and won a crushing victory at Lake Trasimene, but although he made a great show of the fact that his quarrel was solely with Rome, and freed all his non-Roman Italian

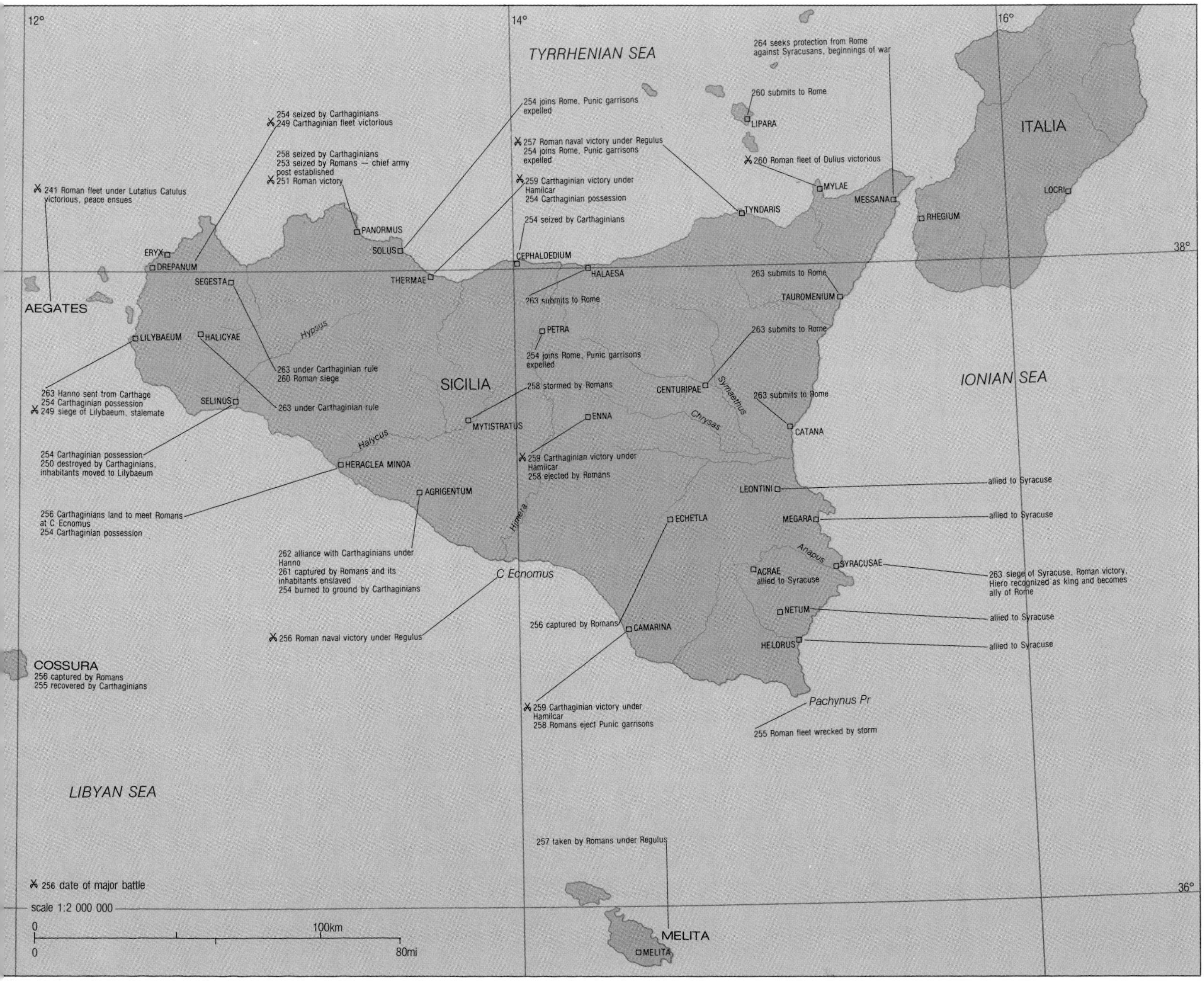

12°
14°
16°
38°
36°
TYRRHENIAN SEA
IONIAN SEA
LIBYAN SEA
SICILIA
ITALIA
AEGATES
COSSURA
256 captured by Romans
255 recovered by Carthaginians
MELITA
MELITA
257 taken by Romans under Regulus
264 seeks protection from Rome against Syracusans, beginnings of war
260 submits to Rome
LIPARA
260 Roman fleet of Duilius victorious
MYLAE
MESSANA
RHEGIUM
LOCRI
TYNDARIS
257 Roman naval victory under Regulus
254 joins Rome, Punic garrisons expelled
254 joins Rome, Punic garrisons expelled
259 Carthaginian victory under Hamilcar
254 Carthaginian possession
254 seized by Carthaginians
CEPHALOEDIUM
HALAESA
263 submits to Rome
254 seized by Carthaginians
249 Carthaginian fleet victorious
258 seized by Carthaginians
253 seized by Romans — chief army post established
251 Roman victory
PANORMUS
SOLUS
THERMAE
241 Roman fleet under Lutatius Catulus victorious, peace ensues
ERYX
DREPANUM
SEGESTA
LILYBAEUM
HALICYAE
Hypsus
263 under Carthaginian rule
260 Roman siege
263 under Carthaginian rule
263 Hanno sent from Carthage
254 Carthaginian possession
249 siege of Lilybaeum, stalemate
SELINUS
254 Carthaginian possession
250 destroyed by Carthaginians, inhabitants moved to Lilybaeum
Halycus
HERACLEA MINOA
256 Carthaginians land to meet Romans at C Ecnomus
254 Carthaginian possession
AGRIGENTUM
262 alliance with Carthaginians under Hanno
261 captured by Romans and its inhabitants enslaved
254 burned to ground by Carthaginians
C Ecnomus
256 Roman naval victory under Regulus
PETRA
254 joins Rome, Punic garrisons expelled
258 stormed by Romans
MYTISTRATUS
ENNA
259 Carthaginian victory under Hamilcar
258 ejected by Romans
Himera
ECHETLA
256 captured by Romans
CAMARINA
259 Carthaginian victory under Hamilcar
258 Romans eject Punic garrisons
263 submits to Rome
TAUROMENIUM
263 submits to Rome
CENTURIPAE
Symaethus
Chrysas
263 submits to Rome
CATANA
LEONTINI
allied to Syracuse
MEGARA
allied to Syracuse
Anapus
SYRACUSAE
263 siege of Syracuse, Roman victory, Hiero recognized as king and becomes ally of Rome
ACRAE
allied to Syracuse
NETUM
allied to Syracuse
HELORUS
allied to Syracuse
Pachynus Pr
255 Roman fleet wrecked by storm
256 date of major battle
scale 1:2 000 000
0
100km
0
80mi

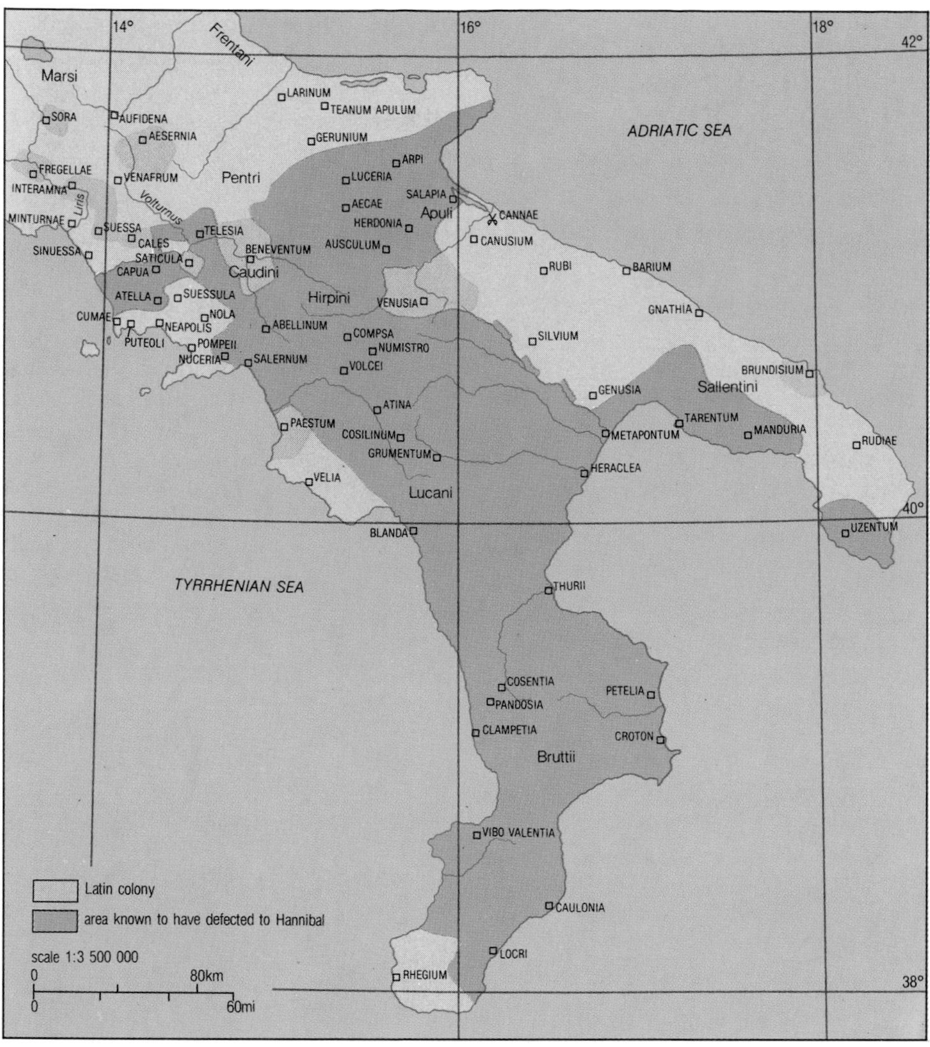

Italy during the war with Hannibal. During the early years of the war, Rome's Italian allies remained loyal, in spite of Hannibal's efforts to win them over. But the disaster of Cannae changed everything. Livy writes: "How much more serious was the defeat at Cannae than those which had preceded it can be seen by the behavior of Rome's allies: before that fatal day their loyalty had remained unshaken; now it began to waver, for the simple reason that they despaired of the survival of Roman power. The following peoples went over to the Carthaginian cause: the Atellani, Calatini, Hirpini, some of the Apulians, all the Samnites except the Pentri, the Bruttii, the Lucanians, the Uzentini, and nearly all the Greek settlements on the coast, namely Tarentum, Metapontum, Croton and Locri, and all the Gauls on the Italian side of the Alps." One should add that the greatest prize of all, the Campanian town of Capua, went over in 215. However the Romans began to recover lost ground almost immediately: by the time the Greek cities went over (212 BC), Rome had regained control of Samnium and northern Apulia; Capua fell in 211, Tarentum and Thurii in 209. By 206 Hannibal had been forced to retire to the extreme south, where he was confined to Bruttium.

prisoners, the allies still remained firmly loyal to the Romans. Hannibal had clearly miscalculated if he had been expecting a general revolt; in fact the upper classes of the allied communities felt that their interests lay with Rome, and at this stage they could see no advantage in joining an alien invader, especially one who had allied himself with the Gauls.

In 216 Hannibal won his greatest victory at Cannae in Apulia, one of Rome's worst military disasters, in which perhaps as many as 30 000 lost their lives (the ancient sources give much higher figures). After Cannae some defections did take place among the allies, and large areas of the south, including much of Samnium, Lucania and Bruttium, went over to Hannibal. Some towns in Apulia and, most important of all, Capua in Campania also seceded. At this point Hannibal might reasonably have expected that the Romans would sue for peace, and that he would be able to end the war with a settlement favorable to Carthage.

The Romans' blind refusal to admit defeat in any circumstances meant that Hannibal's enterprise was doomed, however much appearances might have suggested the contrary. He was able to win over more of Rome's allies (Tarentum and other Greek cities joined him in 212), and in 215 he received the support of Philip V of Macedon and of the kingdom of Syracuse, following the death of the aged Hiero II. But in spite of these successes, his general position became steadily weaker. This was because the Romans adopted a policy (devised by Q. Fabius Maximus, "the Delayer") of avoiding pitched battles and fighting a war of attrition. Time was on their side and all the circumstances favored them. They still had large reserves of manpower and supplies; Hannibal was cut off from his home base, and as yet none of the major ports had fallen into his hands. Rome's allies in Etruria, Umbria, Picenum and central Italy gave her solid support, and she was able to present a united front to the enemy, whereas the area controlled by Hannibal in the south was dotted with fortified loyalist enclaves, including most of the large towns and all of the Latin colonies. Hannibal could not afford to move too far from his base of operations in the south, whereas the Romans could ravage the territory of his allies almost at will, and reconquer them one by one. As Polybius noted, the Romans could divide their forces, but Hannibal could be in only one place at a time.

As the years went by the initiative gradually passed to Rome. In 211 Hannibal suffered a serious blow when Capua fell after a long siege. His attempt to relieve the city by a sudden march on Rome was a

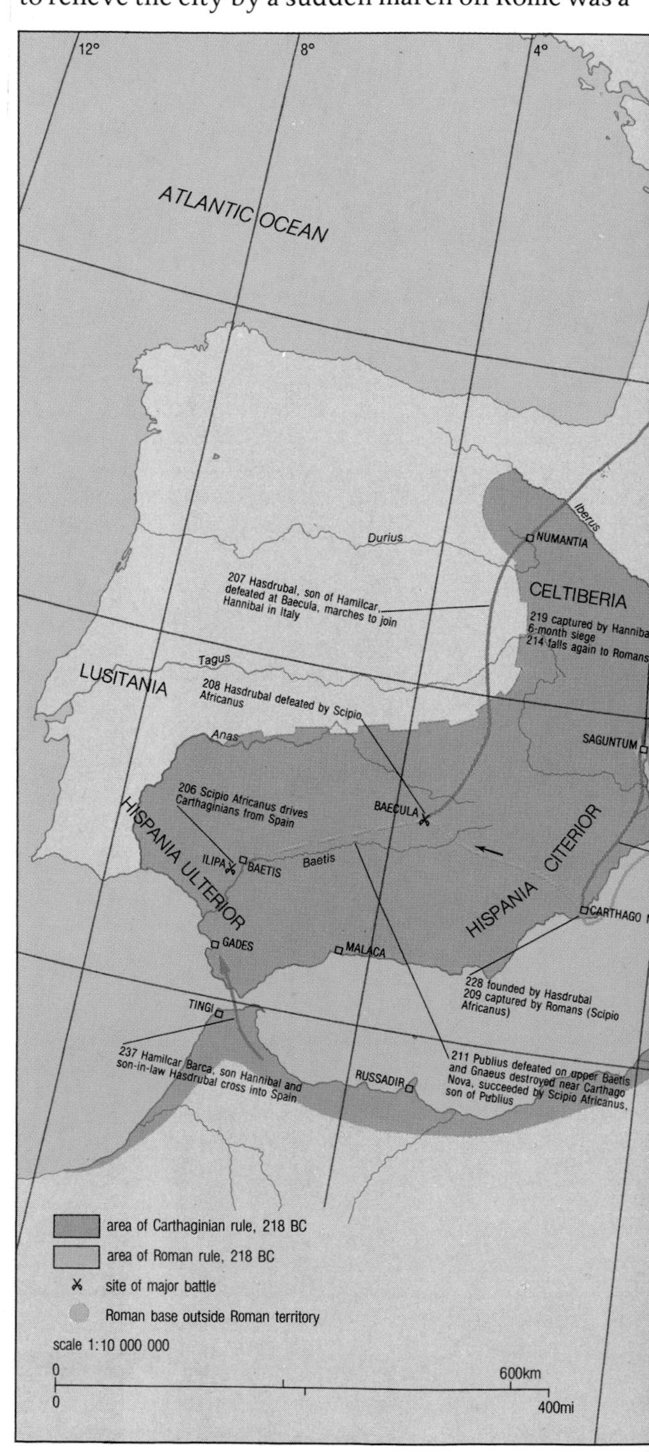

hopeless failure, although his appearance outside the walls caused consternation for a few days. Meanwhile the Romans were operating successfully against the Carthaginians in Sicily, where Syracuse was taken and sacked by M. Claudius Marcellus in 211, and a general revolt was crushed in 210. In Spain the Carthaginians had been held in check since 218 by a Roman expeditionary force under Publius and Gnaeus Scipio. In 215 they defeated Hasdrubal, Hannibal's brother, at Ibera, and in 214 they recaptured Saguntum. There was a serious setback in 211 when the Scipio brothers were defeated and killed, but the Romans immediately sent reinforcements to Spain and in 210 appointed as commander the young son and namesake of Publius Scipio, who at once embarked on a bold offensive strategy. In 209 he made a surprise attack on Carthago Nova (Cartagena) and captured it. In the following year he defeated Hasdrubal in a pitched battle at Baecula, but was unable to prevent him from taking his army out of Spain and setting off to join his brother in Italy. Hasdrubal crossed the Alps in the spring of 207 and advanced rapidly to the Adriatic, intending to rendezvous with Hannibal in Umbria. But before the two brothers and their forces could meet, Hasdrubal was caught by a Roman army under C. Claudius Nero at the Metaurus and was decisively defeated. By now there was no hope left for Hannibal, who retired to Bruttium. In 203 he yielded to the inevitable and, still undefeated, shipped his army back to Africa. His return was necessitated by the fact that the young Scipio, after driving the Carthaginians out of Spain in 206, had persuaded the senate to allow him to lead an invasion of Africa, which began in 204.

Hannibal returned to defend Carthage, which he had last seen in 237 BC at the age of nine. The final showdown occurred at Zama in 202, where in a closely contested battle Scipio's forces were finally victorious. Hannibal himself negotiated a peace

The Second Punic War. Hannibal's invasion of Italy in 218 BC took the Romans by surprise and foiled their plan of a direct attack on Carthage. But by waging a war of attrition against Hannibal in Italy, and adopting a bold offensive strategy in Spain and Sicily, culminating in the invasion of Africa in 204, the Romans gradually gained the upper hand. The Carthaginians failed to send reinforcements to Hannibal, and their allies (the Gauls of north Italy, Philip V of Macedon) proved ineffectual. Hannibal was eventually forced to abandon Italy in order to defend Carthage, and was finally defeated by Scipio Africanus near Zama in 202.

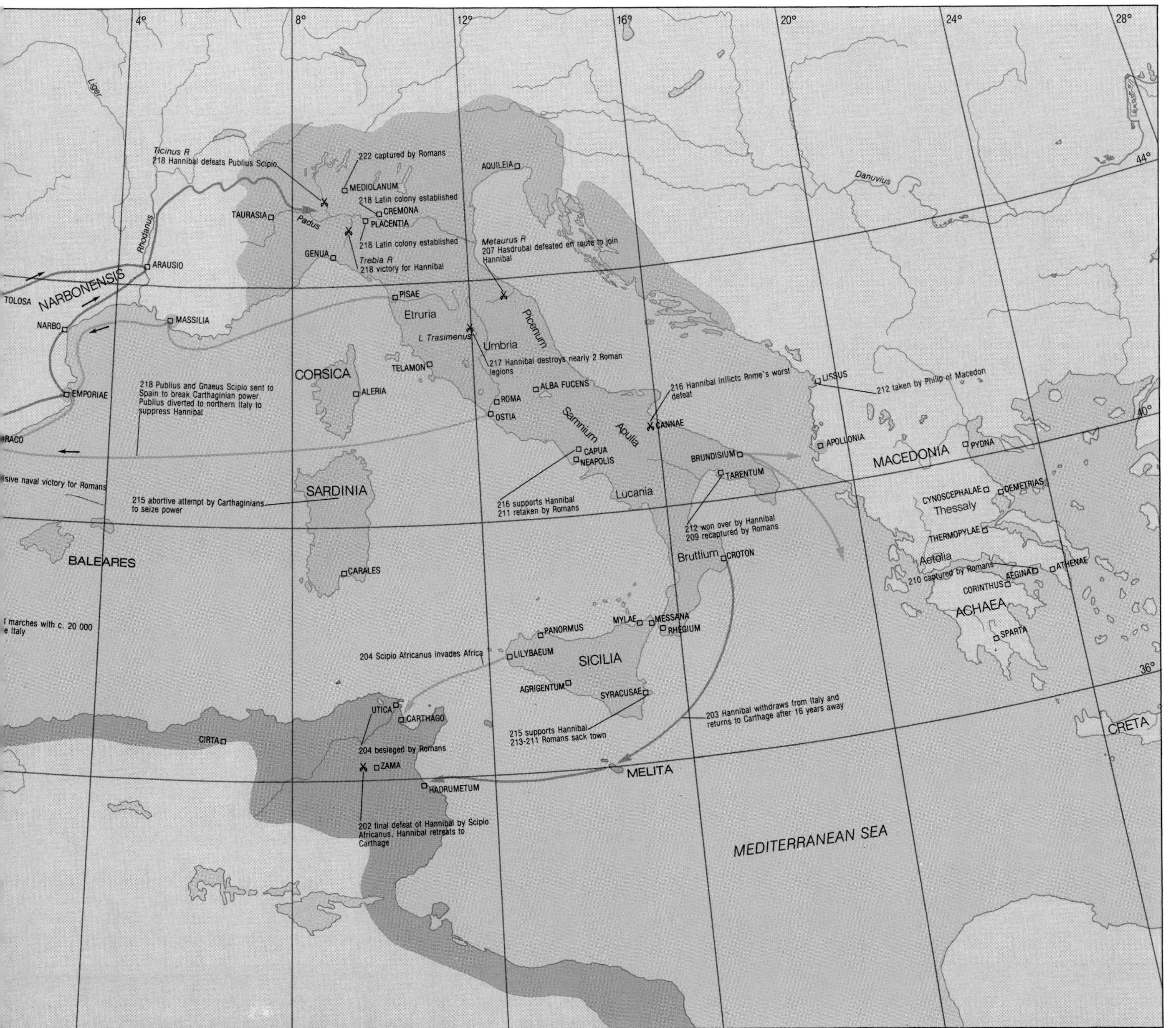

settlement, which confined Carthage to a restricted area of territory, deprived her of her fleet and imposed an indemnity of 10000 talents to be paid over a period of 50 years.

The growth of Roman imperialism

The peace settlement removed the threat of Carthage and brought relief to Italy, which had suffered extensive devastation and pillage during the 16 years of Hannibal's occupation. However, the victory over Carthage did not result in an immediate or drastic reduction in the scale of Rome's military commitments; in fact in the decades after 200 there were major wars in northern Italy, Spain, Sardinia and the eastern Mediterranean, in which large Roman armies were engaged, often for years on end. P.A. Brunt has pointed out that plausible estimates of the numbers of Italians in military service during this period "seem to show that the requirements for manpower were still enormous after the Hannibalic war had ended, and that in 191–190 they rose to much the same peak as in the gravest crisis of that struggle."

In 203 BC the Romans resumed the systematic conquest of Cisalpine Gaul, which had begun in 224 but was interrupted by Hannibal's invasion. Successive fierce campaigns in the Po valley ended in 191 with the defeat of the most powerful of the Cisalpine Gallic tribes, the Boii. Cremona and Placentia were reinforced and other colonies established, and in 187 the Via Aemilia (from which the present-day region of Emilia takes its name) was constructed from Placentia to Ariminum (Rimini). The Romans then turned to the task of conquering the warlike tribes of Liguria and the northern Apennines. This process was largely completed by 175, although resistance continued sporadically in some areas for a further 20 years. In 178–177 the Istrian peninsula was also overrun, following the establishment of a colony at the strategic site of Aquileia in 181.

In Spain Rome inherited from Carthage a substantial dominion in the southeast of the peninsula which required the presence of a permanent standing army, normally of two legions. This area was formed into two provinces, Hispania Ulterior and Hispania Citerior (Further and Hither Spain), after the Carthaginian withdrawal in 206. In 197 the number of annual praetors was raised from four to six, in order to provide regular magistrates to govern the new provinces. During these early years Spain was systematically looted by the Romans, who inevitably aroused the hatred of the native population. In 197 a revolt broke out in Further Spain which spread rapidly through both provinces and also involved the tribes of the interior. In spite of some energetic campaigning by Cato in 195, the war did not end until 179, when T. Sempronius Gracchus pacified the provinces and made an alliance with the Celtiberians. Twenty-five years of comparative peace ensued, until a new round of fighting began against the Lusitanians under their leader Viriathus (154–138), and a second war was fought against the Celtiberians (153–151). These wars proved immensely difficult and costly for the Romans, and disastrous for the Spaniards, who suffered countless atrocities. A final rebellion of the Celtiberians in 143 led to another lengthy and brutal war. One of the most unedifying chapters of Roman history was brought to a close in 133 BC when Scipio Aemilianus (the adoptive grandson of the victor of Zama) captured and destroyed Numantia, the chief stronghold of the Celtiberians. A permanent military presence continued to be necessary, however, and the northwestern corner of Spain remained unconquered until the time of Augustus.

It is clear that in the western Mediterranean the Romans had committed themselves to an aggressive policy aimed at enlarging their existing possessions at the expense of the native "barbarians." This led to an almost literally endless series of Gallic and Spanish wars. Mention should also be made of serious revolts among the natives of Sardinia (181–176 and 126 BC) and Corsica (181 and 166–163 BC). The conquest of Gallia Narbonensis (Provence) between 125 and 121 BC was a continuation of this policy, which led in the end to the occupation of all continental Gaul by Caesar (58–50 BC) and the invasion of Germany under Augustus. The Romans do not seem to have had any moral qualms about this activity, and the senate was evidently prepared to condone the harsh and often highly questionable methods of its commanders. In 151 BC Ser. Sulpicius Galba, who had massacred thousands of Lusitanians after they had surrendered to him, was acquitted at his trial although his guilt was palpable. Very few people in Rome cared much about what happened to the barbarians.

A rather more complex pattern of events developed in the eastern Mediterranean, where the Romans had further unfinished business at the end of the Hannibalic war. Here they were dealing with a culturally advanced world of established political communities which had emerged from the disintegration of the empire of Alexander the Great (356–323 BC). By the end of the 3rd century BC a relatively stable balance of power existed between the major kingdoms – the Antigonids of Macedon, the Attalids of Pergamum in Asia Minor, the Seleucids in Syria and Mesopotamia and the Ptolemies in Egypt. In the middle were the states of Greece and the Aegean, the most important of which were Athens, Sparta, Rhodes, the Achaean League (which comprised the cities of the northern Peloponnese) and the Aetolian League of northwest Greece.

Above Alba Fucens, founded as a colony in 303 BC in the territory of the Aequi, occupies a commanding position at the foot of Mt Velino (2487 meters). Belgian excavations since 1949 have revealed substantial remains of the city, which like most Roman colonies was built on a grid plan within a very impressive circuit of defensive walls. King Perseus of Macedonia was interned here after his surrender in 167 BC.

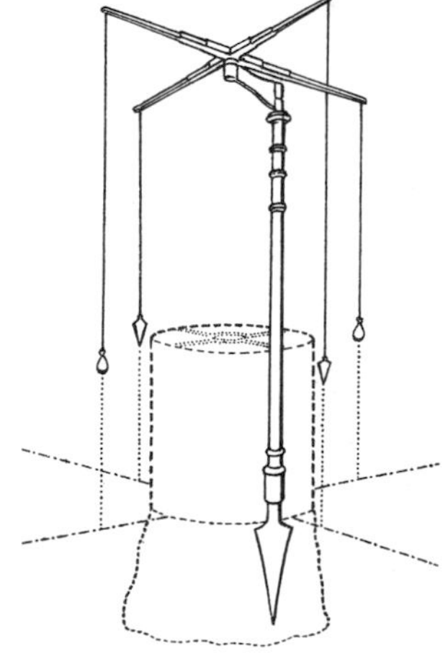

Below The *groma* was a Roman surveying instrument which allowed the surveyor to mark out lines at right angles to one another by taking sights from a central point.

Above The distribution of land to Roman colonists was based on a process of survey and division known as centuriation, whereby the land was marked out in large squares of 200 *iugera* (50 hectares) called *centuriae* (that is, areas embracing 100 2-*iugera* units). Traces of centuriation have been revealed by aerial photography in many parts of Italy and the provinces. This photograph shows centuriated land in Emilia.

Above right The grid plan of Roman colonies is reflected in the street plans of many Italian cities of colonial origin. One example is Florence, where the colony of Florentia was founded in the time of Augustus.

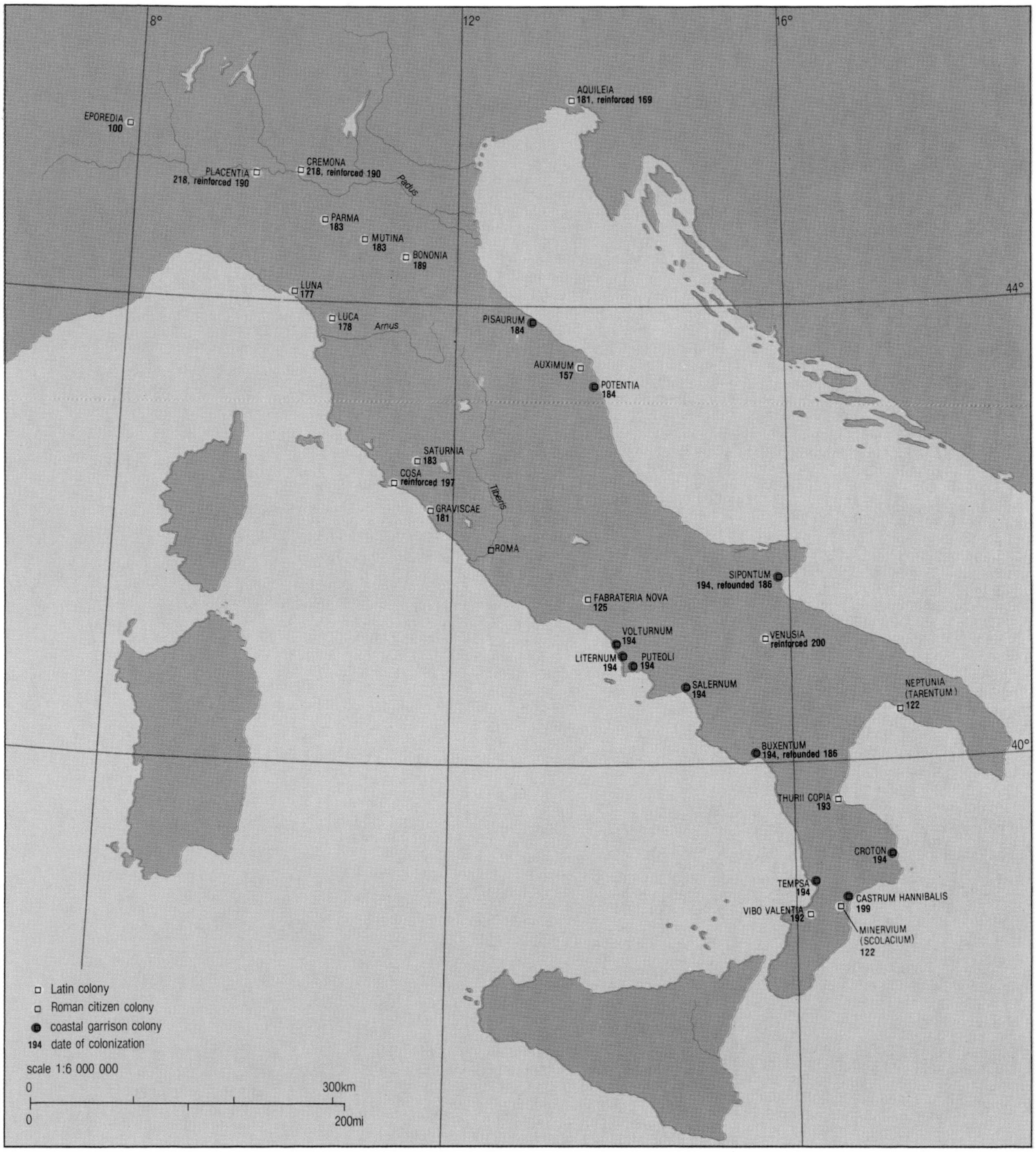

Right: Colonization in Italy, 2nd century BC. Rome's traditional policy of colonization continued after the Hannibalic war with the reinforcement of some existing Latin colonies and the founding of new ones at Vibo and Thurii in southern Italy. Notice the Roman habit of giving colonies optimistic names such as *Valentia* ("strength") and *Copia* ("plenty"). During the 190s a number of coastal garrison colonies were founded around the shores of south Italy to guard against the possibility of an invasion by the Seleucid King Antiochus III, who was thought to be capable of anything and was being advised by the hated Hannibal. The Roman occupation of Cisalpine Gaul and Liguria was consolidated in the usual way by the foundation of colonies; but because it was apparently becoming increasingly difficult to persuade Romans to give up their citizenship, the government stopped founding Latin colonies and began instead to found large colonies of Roman citizens. Parma and Mutina (183) were the first colonies of the new type, and Aquileia (181) was the last of the old. After the founding of Luna in 177 Roman colonization came to an abrupt end and was not resumed until the end of the century. The only exception was Auximum (157), whose date is doubted by some scholars.

8°
12°
16°
44°
40°
EPOREDIA 100
AQUILEIA 181, reinforced 169
PLACENTIA 218, reinforced 190
CREMONA 218, reinforced 190
Padus
PARMA 183
MUTINA 183
BONONIA 189
LUNA 177
LUCA 178
Arnus
PISAURUM 184
AUXIMUM 157
POTENTIA 184
SATURNIA 183
COSA reinforced 197
GRAVISCAE 181
Tiberis
ROMA
SIPONTUM 194, refounded 186
FABRATERIA NOVA 125
VOLTURNUM 194
VENUSIA reinforced 200
LITERNUM 194
PUTEOLI 194
SALERNUM 194
NEPTUNIA (TARENTUM) 122
BUXENTUM 194, refounded 186
THURII COPIA 193
CROTON 194
TEMPSA 194
CASTRUM HANNIBALIS 199
VIBO VALENTIA 192
MINERVIUM (SCOLACIUM) 122

Latin colony
Roman citizen colony
coastal garrison colony
194 date of colonization
scale 1:6 000 000
0 300km
0 200mi

Rome's first venture east of the Adriatic had occurred in 229 BC, when it declared war on Queen Teuta of Illyria, whose subjects had been engaging in piracy and molesting Italian traders. In two brief campaigns (the First and Second Illyrian Wars, 229–228 and 221–219 BC) Rome humbled the Illyrians and gained effective control of a number of Greek cities on the Illyrian coast. These developments aroused the suspicions of Philip V of Macedon, who in 215 took advantage of Rome's weakness after Cannae to form an alliance with Hannibal. The Romans responded in 211 by making an alliance with the Aetolians, old enemies of Philip, who undertook to prosecute the war on land with Roman naval support. Other Greek states soon joined the alliance, and the Romans found that they had successfully contained the threat of Philip without having to commit any large forces of their own. The Aetolians however felt that they were bearing the brunt of the war and were not receiving enough support from Rome; in 206 they decided to cut their losses and make their own peace with Philip. The Romans, still preoccupied with the problem of Hannibal, followed suit a year later.

Once Hannibal had been dealt with the Romans were free to turn their attention once again to the Balkans, where Philip had begun to build up his power in the Aegean and was making threatening moves in Illyria. In 200 the Second Macedonian War began. During two years of indecisive military action, the Romans were remarkably successful on the diplomatic front, winning the support of most of the states of central and southern Greece by making it known that their aim was to drive Philip out of Greece and to confine him to Macedonia. They were soon in a position to enforce this policy when they decisively defeated Philip at the battle of Cynoscephalae in 197 BC. At the Isthmian games of 196 the Roman commander T. Quinctius Flamininus dramatically proclaimed to an enthusiastic audience that the Romans intended to leave the Greek states free and independent. Two years were spent in implementing the settlement, and in 194 all Roman troops were withdrawn from the Balkans.

By this date considerable tension had built up between Rome and the Seleucid king Antiochus III, who had been operating in Asia Minor and in 196 had invaded Thrace. The two powers watched one another's movements with considerable anxiety; complex negotiations took place, accompanied by a propaganda campaign which modern observers have compared to the Cold War. In 192 the Aetolians, resentful because Flamininus had not permitted them to reoccupy some of their former territories evacuated by Philip, seized the fortress town of Demetrias and summoned Antiochus to free the Greeks from Rome. Antiochus saw his chance and responded by taking a small expeditionary force to Greece. Within a year he had been driven out of Greece by a Roman army which defeated him at Thermopylae. The Romans then invaded Asia under the command of L. Scipio (brother of Africanus, who accompanied the army), and defeated Antiochus in a pitched battle at Magnesia (190 BC). Antiochus was forced to withdraw beyond the Taurus mountains, to pay a huge indemnity and to surrender his elephants and fleet. In the following year the consul Cn. Manlius Vulso invaded the territory of the Galatians, killed large numbers of them and acquired enormous booty. In 188 a final settlement was reached with Antiochus, and a treaty signed, at Apamea. His former territories in Asia Minor were divided between Rhodes and Eumenes II of Pergamum, who had succeeded Attalus in 197. The Romans then withdrew entirely from Greece and Asia.

This remarkable sequence of events inevitably raises questions about the nature and purpose of Roman policy in the eastern Mediterranean, and more generally about the origins and growth of Roman imperialism. Broadly speaking, modern discussions of this subject fall into two categories. Some historians argue that the growth of the Roman empire was the accidental result of a predominantly defensive policy: the Romans made war in order to defend their interests, and those of their allies, against real or imagined threats. This view coincides to a certain extent with the Romans' own claim that they only fought "just wars." Other scholars however prefer to believe that imperialism was a bad habit which the Romans fell into because of their love of war and military glory, and their desire for land and booty. On this view their policy was consciously aggressive, and all the pious talk of "just wars" was either a cynical exercise in public relations or a naive fabrication of patriotic historians.

The ancient Greek city of Corinth was destroyed by Rome in 146 BC as an example to the rest of the empire. Roman Corinth, of which impressive remains survive, including the theater shown here, was founded as a colony by Julius Caesar. See below, p. 149.

The trouble with these two lines of interpretation is that they are solely concerned with the conscious aims and motives of the actors, who did not necessarily either understand or control the events in which they took part. Even on a conscious level such explanations are probably too schematic and elaborate. For example, it is unlikely that the Romans declared war on Macedon in 200 because they thought that Philip represented a threat to their interests, or because they were seeking a new outlet for aggressive action. A much simpler and more convincing motive is suggested by Livy: Philip's alliance with Hannibal in 215 was a "stab in the back" which could not be overlooked, and as soon as the Romans had dealt with Hannibal they crossed over to Greece and gave Philip the thrashing he deserved.

The most significant fact about the growth of the Roman empire is that it was the product of a continuous series of successful wars. We need to ask, therefore, not only why the Romans fought so many wars, but also why they were so successful. In the final analysis the answer to both questions is the same: the Romans had at their disposal a very efficient military machine and enormous reserves of manpower which could not be matched by their opponents. They had an almost infinite capacity for replacement, and could absorb huge losses, as the events of the Second Punic War demonstrated. Livy was absolutely right when he declared (with reference to Trasimene and Cannae): "No other nation in the world could have suffered so tremendous a series of disasters and not been overwhelmed."

Rome's military power depended ultimately on the system of alliances that resulted from its conquest of Italy. By making the allies active military partners rather than passive tribute-paying subjects the Romans committed themselves in advance to a career of militarism and conquest. They had built up a military organization which had

to be used if they were to derive any benefit from it; war and conquest thus became a logical necessity. In practice this meant that the Roman government could afford to use war as an instrument of policy in circumstances where other states might have been deterred by the risks or unable to sustain the losses that might be incurred. The constant practice of warfare on an ever-increasing scale led to even greater military effectiveness and expertise, and created a militaristic ethos that pervaded Roman society at every level.

The results of military success were an increase in territory, wealth (in the form of taxes, booty and indemnities), security and power. The Romans believed themselves entitled to these rewards, which compensated them for the expense and effort of the military operations that they had been compelled to undertake. The conquests were further justified by the benefits which Roman rule gave to the subjects of the empire: civilization to the barbarians, stability and order to the unruly Greeks. Everyone gained except those who were foolish or arrogant enough to resist.

tu regere imperio populos, Romane, memento
(hae tibi erunt artes), pacisque imponere morem,
parcere subiectis et debellare superbos.

("Remember, Roman, that it is for you to rule the nations. This shall be your task: to impose the ways of peace, to spare the vanquished and to tame the proud by war." Virgil, *Aeneid* 6. 851–53.)

Roman rule took different forms, according to circumstances. In the western Mediterranean, as we have seen, the Romans favored a policy of annexation, direct rule and a permanent military presence; in the Greek east, on the other hand, they tended to avoid annexation and preferred to rule indirectly through local governments which were left theoretically independent but were expected to act in the Roman interest. In fact the nominally free states of Greece were dependent on Rome in much the same way as clients were dependent on their patron (see above, p. 19); whether or not the Romans themselves used the terminology of *clientela* to describe their relations with other states, there is no doubt that the term "client states" accurately defines the position of the "free" allies controlled by Rome.

Nearly 20 years passed before the Romans felt any need for military intervention in the Greek world. Then in 171 a Roman army was sent across the Adriatic to deal with Perseus, who had in 179 succeeded his father Philip V in Macedon. The Romans are said to have been alarmed by the revival of Macedonian power, which had begun before Philip's death, and they became especially concerned when Perseus attempted to effect a reconciliation between himself and the Greek states. The allegation that his ultimate aim was to make war on Rome may be unfounded, although the Romans are unlikely to have been pleased by his appeal to the lower classes in the Greek cities; as in Italy, so too in Greece the Romans naturally tended to support the interests of the propertied classes (although there are some exceptions to this general pattern). Perseus had some initial successes, and was victorious in a pitched battle at Callinicus in 171, but in 168 he was decisively defeated at the battle of Pydna by L. Aemilius Paullus. The Macedonian army was almost totally destroyed, and Perseus himself surrendered shortly afterwards.

The settlement after the battle of Pydna was harsh and illustrates the extent to which Roman attitudes had changed since the 190s. Macedonia was divided up into four separate republics, and its population forced to pay tribute to Rome at half the rate that had been levied by Perseus. In this way the Romans obtained the benefits of direct rule without having to shoulder the burdens of administration and defense. A cruel fate was reserved for the Molossians of Epirus, who had joined Perseus after his victory at Callinicus. Their territory was systematically pillaged by Paullus' army, and the population was enslaved. A general purge of anti-Roman elements in the Greek states was then carried out. In particular, 1000 members of the upper class of the Achaean League were deported to Italy, where they were interned without trial. The most famous of these detainees was the historian Polybius. In Asia, Pergamum and Rhodes were punished with loss of territory. They had not taken part in the war, but they had been loitering with intent. Rome thus demonstrated that it would tolerate nothing less than complete obedience from its subjects.

By these methods the Romans were able to rule the Greeks indirectly for a further 18 years. Then in about 150 BC an uprising in Macedon under the leadership of a pretender named Andriscus prompted the Romans to intervene once more. Andriscus was defeated in 148, and Macedonia became a regular province. Two years later the Achaean League was crushed following a futile revolt, and its territory incorporated in the province. Corinth was sacked as an example to the rest of the world, and timocratic constitutions (see above, p. 42) were established instead of democracies in the Greek cities.

This was a crucial period in the growth of the Roman empire. In 150 BC the Third Punic War broke out when Rome intervened in a dispute between Carthage and Rome's friend and ally, King Masinissa of Numidia. At the insistence of the aged Cato, the Romans resolved to destroy the city. The Carthaginians put up a desperate resistance, but in the end the city fell to the Roman commander Scipio Aemilianus and was obliterated (146 BC). Its territory became the new province of Africa.

Archaic Rome

Reconstruction (after Gjerstad) of the frontal elevation of the great temple of Jupiter, Juno and Minerva, which was built by the Tarquins and dedicated by the first consuls in 509 BC. The building, which is some 64 meters long, 55 meters wide, and an estimated 40 meters high, was one of the largest archaic temples of the Mediterranean world. It survived intact until 83 BC, when it was destroyed by fire.

The earliest traces of habitation on the site of Rome consist of cremation graves in the Forum, which from the 10th century BC served as a burial ground for settlements on the surrounding hills. An early settlement on the Palatine is indicated by Iron Age hut foundations that have been found there, and by the tradition that Romulus founded his city on the Palatine. Later the Palatine settlement expanded to include the Forum, and from the 8th century the Esquiline became the chief cemetery. At the end of the 7th century the huts in the Forum were demolished, and a formal public square was laid out; the surrounding settlement also took on a more "urban" aspect, with the construction of permanent stone houses, temples and other public buildings. Tradition associated this development with the reign of Tarquin I (616–579 BC); according to Livy, Tarquin "made grants of land around the Forum to be used as private building sites, and built shops and porticoes." His successor Servius Tullius further enlarged the city, incorporating the Esquiline, Quirinal and Viminal hills, surrounded it with a wall and divided it into four regions. The archaeological record confirms the general picture of urban growth in the 6th century.

The "Capitoline Wolf." This archaic bronze masterpiece dates from around 500 BC and is possibly of Etruscan workmanship. The figures of the twins were added in the Renaissance, but there is good reason to think that the restoration is justified. If so, it follows that the legend of Romulus and Remus was already well established in Rome at the end of the regal period.

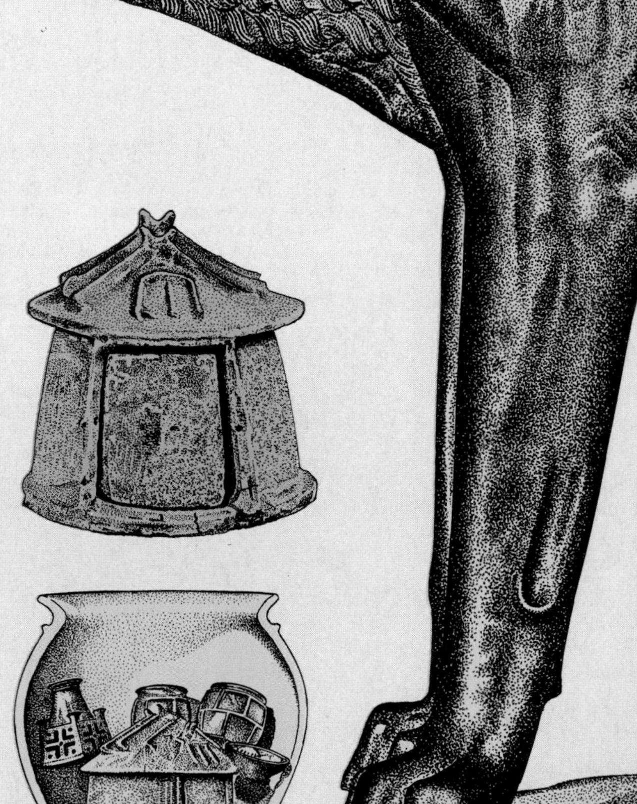

Left Traces of crude huts dating from the 8th century BC have been found on the Palatine, traditionally the site of Romulus' settlement. The Romans retained a memory of this primitive stage in the Casa Romuli (House of Romulus), a simple shepherd's hut lovingly preserved until the time of the Empire.

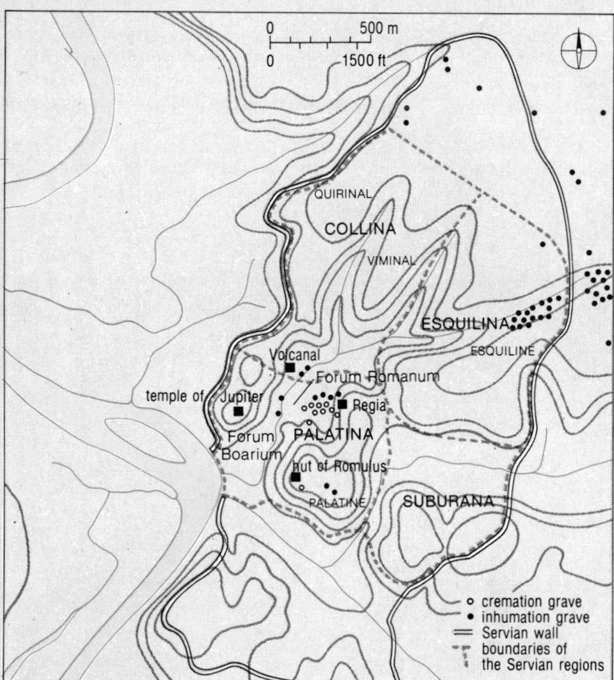

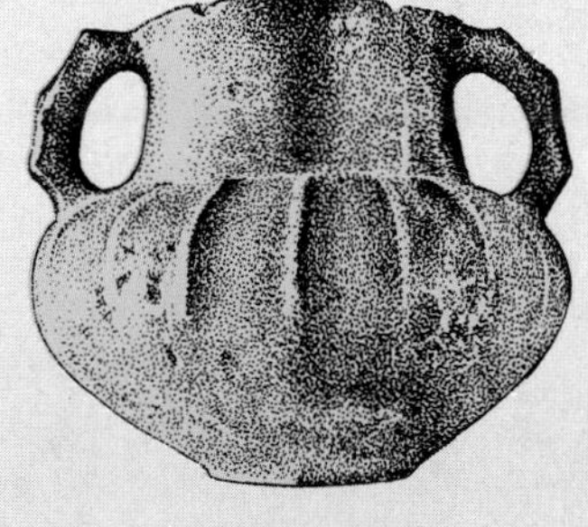

Above Two-handled impasto jar from an inhumation grave on the Esquiline – probably late 8th century BC.
Above right Hut urn from a cremation burial in the Roman Forum. Urns of this type are clearly meant to represent human dwellings: foundations of oval-shaped huts have been found on the Palatine.
Right Forum Tomb Y: a typical cremation grave. The hut urn and surrounding grave goods were placed in a large jar and buried in a pit; 10th-9th century BC.

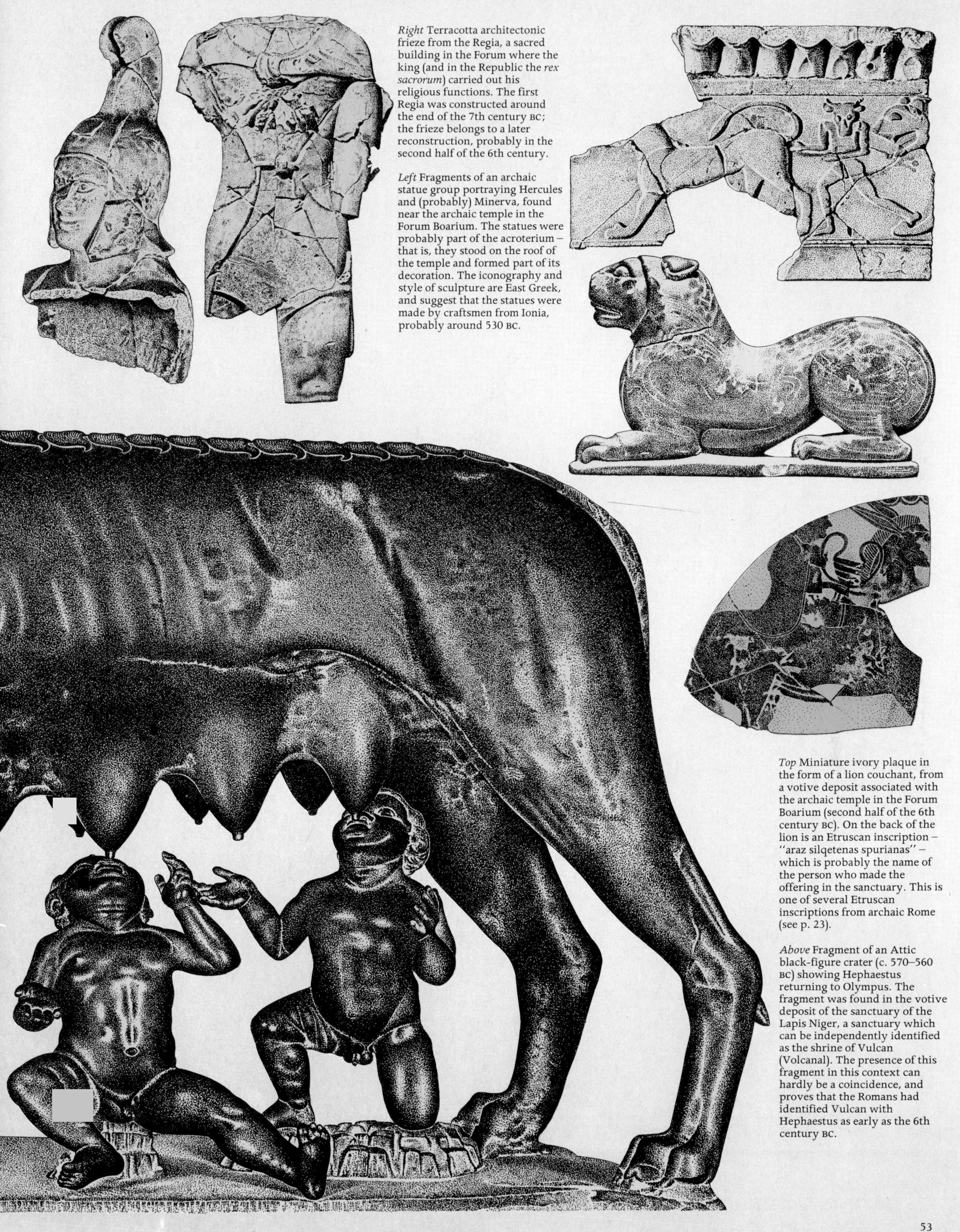

Right Terracotta architectonic frieze from the Regia, a sacred building in the Forum where the king (and in the Republic the *rex sacrorum*) carried out his religious functions. The first Regia was constructed around the end of the 7th century BC; the frieze belongs to a later reconstruction, probably in the second half of the 6th century.

Left Fragments of an archaic statue group portraying Hercules and (probably) Minerva, found near the archaic temple in the Forum Boarium. The statues were probably part of the acroterium – that is, they stood on the roof of the temple and formed part of its decoration. The iconography and style of sculpture are East Greek, and suggest that the statues were made by craftsmen from Ionia, probably around 530 BC.

Top Miniature ivory plaque in the form of a lion couchant, from a votive deposit associated with the archaic temple in the Forum Boarium (second half of the 6th century BC). On the back of the lion is an Etruscan inscription – "araz silqetenas spurianas" – which is probably the name of the person who made the offering in the sanctuary. This is one of several Etruscan inscriptions from archaic Rome (see p. 23).

Above Fragment of an Attic black-figure crater (c. 570–560 BC) showing Hephaestus returning to Olympus. The fragment was found in the votive deposit of the sanctuary of the Lapis Niger, a sanctuary which can be independently identified as the shrine of Vulcan (Volcanal). The presence of this fragment in this context can hardly be a coincidence, and proves that the Romans had identified Vulcan with Hephaestus as early as the 6th century BC.

CRISIS AND REFORM

The consequences of empire

Rome's conquest of the Mediterranean inevitably brought about profound changes in the political, social and economic life of Rome and Italy. At a political level, the senate's conduct of the war effort against Hannibal and its successful handling of subsequent foreign entanglements in the Greek east led to a general acceptance by the people of senatorial government; popular legislation and attacks on the established order were very infrequent in the century following the tribunate of C. Flaminius in 232 BC (see above, p. 44). The period was one of apparent political calm and stability, which Cicero was later to look back on as a kind of golden age of senatorial rule.

The senate itself was dominated by the nobles, who were divided up into competing factions. These groups took the form of *ad hoc* alliances of friends and kinsmen who united to promote particular policies and mobilized their clients and supporters to vote for favored candidates at the elections. The factions were certainly not permanent political parties, and although some "friendships" undoubtedly lasted longer than others, there is no good reason to suppose that Roman politics were dominated by permanent and hereditary alliances of noble families or *gentes*. Rivalry between individuals and groups was traditional and ensured a kind of equilibrium, but tensions within the senatorial oligarchy arose as the rewards for office increased and the competition for the senior magistracies intensified.

In the course of the Hannibalic war military necessity had given rise to the practice of prolonging the commands of successful generals beyond the statutory limit of one year. While this innovation may have been justified from a practical point of view, it clearly had dangerous political implications in that it allowed ambitious individuals like Scipio and Flamininus to break away from the constraints of the system of annual collegiate magistracies. These men also set themselves apart from their peers by affecting an ostentatious and luxurious life-style and parading their knowledge of Greek culture. Other nobles hastened to follow suit, and the results were intensified competition for office, self-enrichment, corruption and an indiscriminate cult of Hellenism. Opposition to these trends was led by Cato the Censor (234-149 BC), who deliberately adopted a simple and austere way of life in imitation of the great men of the past such as M'. Curius Dentatus (see above, p.42). Cato made fun of the frivolous exhibitionism of the Hellenists, advocated homespun virtues and showed a profound respect for native Italic traditions. His efforts to maintain the traditional cohesion of the oligarchy led him to mount a political attack on Scipio, who was eventually forced to retire from public life in 184 BC. Cato supported sumptuary laws and frequently spoke out against bribery, corruption and abuse of power.

Cato's opposition to Hellenism was not based on mere prejudice. He himself spoke Greek and understood Greek culture better than many of those whom he attacked; he actually favored the borrowing of Greek ideas, provided that they could be adapted to Roman needs. It was Cato who ordered the construction of Rome's first basilica, a building of Greek type, during his censorship in 184. This is one of many examples of public buildings in the Greek style which were erected during this period.

But the most striking example of the adaptation of Greek ideas to Roman needs is the growth of Latin literature, to which Cato himself made a decisive contribution. The earliest writer of literary Latin was Livius Andronicus, a Greek who was brought to Rome as a captive after the fall of Tarentum in 272 BC. Andronicus produced a Latin translation of the *Odyssey* and composed tragedies based on Greek originals. His example was followed by Cn. Naevius (c. 275–200 BC) and Q. Ennius (239–169), both of whom wrote epic poems as well as plays. It is noteworthy that these men were not native Latin speakers: Naevius was an Oscan-speaking Campanian and Ennius a Messapian from Rudiae. The same is true of the Umbrian T. Maccius Plautus, the Celtic Caecilius Statius, and the African P. Terentius Afer (Terence), all of whom produced Latin comedies in the Greek style during the early part of the 2nd century BC (those of Plautus and Terence are still extant). Other prominent figures of early Latin literature were the tragedians M. Pacuvius (220–c. 130 BC) and C. Accius (170–c. 90 BC) and the satirist C. Lucilius (c. 180–102 BC). Cato's achievement was the creation of Latin prose literature. His works included speeches, 142 of which were known to Cicero who greatly admired them, a work on agriculture which still survives and a historical work on Rome and Italy entitled *Origines*. Earlier Roman histories (for example, that by Fabius Pictor) had been written in Greek. A unique feature of the *Origines* was that it included the history of the Italian peoples as well as Rome.

Cato's efforts were thus directed towards a constructive exploitation of Greek cultural borrowings, and resistance to the corrupting influence of wealth, luxury and the pursuit of power, which he associated with Hellenism as the indirect products of military conquest. But Cato did not, as far as we can see, have any perception of a deeper and more serious consequence of Roman imperialism. During his lifetime the rural economy of Italy was being transformed by a process which eventually led to a major agrarian crisis. The most obvious symptoms of this development were the impoverishment and displacement of the Italian peasantry which resulted from more than half a century of continuous war.

Warfare affected the political economy of Italy in two distinct ways. First there were the direct effects of Hannibal's invasion, which resulted in extensive devastation of the countryside, especially in

Above This fine torso of Apollo from a temple at Falerii (late 4th or early 3rd century BC) is probably the work of a Greek sculptor from Magna Graecia. The piece illustrates the way in which central Italy was being influenced by Greek culture at this date, and is an excellent example of "Italo-Hellenic" art.

Above right The circular temple in the Forum Boarium (usually called, quite erroneously, the temple of Vesta) dates probably from the late 2nd century BC and is the earliest surviving example of a marble temple in Rome. The style is pure Greek.

southern Italy, and the annihilation of whole communities. For example, when Tarentum was captured by the Romans in 209 BC, the whole population was enslaved and a once flourishing city became a remote village. While devastation would not necessarily affect the productive capacity of agricultural land, the mere destruction of standing crops, buildings and livestock will have been sufficient in itself to ruin many peasant families and to depopulate large areas of territory. The indirect effects of continuous warfare were even more serious for the peasants, who had to bear the burden of prolonged military service. The traditional Roman army was a peasant militia which had proved adequate and efficient at a time when wars were local, seasonal conflicts against neighboring communities; but it was quite unsuited to Roman military needs during and after the Hannibalic war, when enormous numbers of soldiers were required to serve for years on end in distant areas of the Mediterranean.

It is estimated that the average size of the combined Roman and Italian army during the 35 years following the defeat of Hannibal was over 130000 men; this represents a very high proportion of the total adult male population of Italy. Of Roman citizens the average proportion of adult males in service at any one time during the last two centuries of the Republic is reckoned to have been around 13 per cent; this means that over half the adult males regularly served in the legions for at least seven years of their lives. Such a level of involvement in warfare was disastrous for the class of peasant smallholders. Many peasant families were thus deprived of essential manpower for long periods, or permanently, if their menfolk were killed in battle. Farms were neglected, debts were incurred and dispossession followed through sale or eviction. The process was hastened by the fact that the rich sought to invest the profits of successful war in Italian land. This led to the growth of large estates (*latifundia*) through the accumulation, by a few, of land which had formerly been worked by peasant smallholders.

Peasant families were driven out in large numbers by rich investors and were replaced on the land by slave labor. Slaves were in plentiful supply thanks to military victories and the resulting mass enslavement of defeated populations; they could be organized in gangs to provide the necessary labor for large-scale agricultural enterprises, they were relatively cheap and had the additional advantage of being exempt from conscription. Thus the development of the *latifundia* was facilitated by the influx of wealth and slaves, the products of victories which had been won by the efforts and sacrifice of Italian peasants who served in the army. As Keith Hopkins puts it, "Roman peasant soldiers were fighting for their own displacement."

The growth of the *latifundia* in the 2nd century BC was accompanied by new methods of farming, which were designed to provide absentee landlords with a cash income from the sale of surplus produce. The new regime is exemplified in Cato's work *On Agriculture,* a handbook aimed at proprietors of medium-sized estates (he specifies holdings of 25 and 60 hectares) worked by slaves and supervised by resident slave managers (*vilici*). Cato deals especially with the cultivation of vines and olives, which produce a good cash return but which require both a large initial capital outlay and relatively extensive holdings of land to allow economies of scale to be achieved. Equally profitable was the practice of cattle ranching and sheep grazing, which also required capital and large areas of land. Extensive pastures were available in southern Italy, where whole regions had been depopulated in the Second Punic War. Much of this land was technically *ager publicus*, having been confiscated by Rome from the allied states that had joined Hannibal, but the Roman government turned a blind eye to the expropriation of such land and did not enforce the legal restrictions on the size of holdings. It seems likely that the same thing happened to *ager publicus* in other parts of Italy.

Many of the displaced peasants migrated to the towns and cities of Italy, and especially to Rome, where opportunities for employment were being created by the lavish expenditure of the rich on luxuries, services, political bribes and entertainments. Public spending also contributed to the development of an urbanized market economy. The state's income, in the form of booty, indemnities and taxes, was immense; after the settlement of Macedon in 167 BC the *tributum* was abolished and direct taxes were not thereafter levied on the property of Roman citizens in Italy. A high proportion of public revenue was reinvested in further conquest, that is, spent on pay and supplies for the army. The rest was spent on the extensive public building projects which were undertaken in Rome and the towns of Italy throughout the 2nd century BC (there is no evidence for a decline in building activity in the 130s, as is sometimes supposed). The growth of the towns created a market for the produce of the estates of the rich, while the needs of the army accounted for much of the wool and leather produced on the ranch lands of southern Italy.

The towns and cities were also centers of craft production and small-scale industrial activity, which were probably based on slave labor. The principal market for manufactured goods was undoubtedly the army, which needed regular supplies of clothing, equipment and weapons. The organization of supplies was undertaken by private individuals and companies who competed for government contracts. These private contractors were known as "publicans" (*publicani*). They contracted for the construction and repair of public buildings, roads and other utilities, and it was they who bought the rights to exploit state-owned mines and to collect indirect taxes (such as tolls and harbor dues) and rents on public land. The contracts, which were let out every five years by the censors, were immensely lucrative and of great economic importance. Polybius tells us that there was hardly anyone in Rome who was not involved either in the sale of these contracts or in the kinds of business to which they gave rise. They brought wealth and power to the leading *publicani*, who formed an influential pressure group outside the senate (senators were not allowed to participate in public contracts).

The challenge of the Gracchi

The process of urbanization and the growth of a market economy produced a number of disturbing side effects which did not escape the notice of contemporaries. The continual displacement of peasant smallholders was worrying not only because of the human misery it caused but also because it led to a gradual decline in the numbers of potential recruits for the army, who were traditionally drawn from the class of *adsidui*; dispossessed peasants were reduced to the status of proletarians and were no longer qualified for army service. Difficulties in recruiting men for the legions are recorded on a number of occasions in the years after 150 BC. Secondly there was growing concern at the numbers of slaves who were being imported into Italy to work the land in place of the free peasants. In 136 BC a major uprising of slaves occurred in Sicily which involved tens of thousands of runaways and was only put down with extreme difficulty. Similar disturbances occurred in Italy at the same time, and Rome was faced with the threat of a general breakdown of law and order.

The problem of internal security, the increasing difficulties of recruitment and the wretched condition of the rural proletariat were the problems which Tiberius Gracchus set out to tackle during his tribunate in 133 BC. His carefully planned solution, a single agrarian law, was simple in conception, ostensibly moderate in form and potentially revolutionary in effect. Gracchus proposed to resettle the dispossessed peasants on allotments of public land. The necessary land was to be made available by enforcing the statutory limit (500 *iugera*) on the size of individual holdings of *ager*

Above Coin of P. Licinius Nerva (113/12 BC) showing citizens in an assembly passing along the gangway (*pons*) to cast their votes. The coin celebrates the system of secret ballot, which was introduced by a series of laws in the second half of the 2nd century BC.

Left The circular temple at Tivoli (Tibur) closely resembles that in the Forum Boarium in Rome (see p. 55), and dates from the same period. It shows that monumental buildings in the Greek style were being erected in the towns of Italy as well as in Rome.

Below The sanctuary of Fortuna Primigenia at Palestrina (Praeneste) was more impressive than any contemporary structure in Rome. The huge complex of buildings, dating probably from the last part of the 2nd century BC, is modeled on similar Hellenistic sanctuaries at Pergamum and Rhodes.

The land reforms of the Gracchi. The agrarian reforms of the Gracchi took place against a background of military crisis, rural impoverishment and mounting urban unrest. The free peasants of Italy were being driven from their land and replaced by slave labor on large estates; the results of this process were seen by Tiberius Gracchus on a journey through Etruria in 137 BC. A few years later a major slave revolt had broken out in Sicily, accompanied by minor uprisings in Rome and Italy.

Tiberius' solution was to reconstitute the free peasantry by distributing state-owned "public" land in small allotments to poor citizens. His agrarian law led to a political upheaval and his own death, but the land commission he set up was able to carry out its task, and has left evidence of its activities in the inscribed *termini* (boundary stones) which have been found in various parts of Italy. His brother Gaius continued his work, and also revived the tradition of founding colonies, at least two of which are known – at Scolacium (Minervium) and Tarentum (Neptunia).

12°
14°
16°
18°
42°
40°
38°
Arnus
Monte Giove
⊕474
Etruria
Tiberis
ROMA
137 BC: Tiberius Gracchus observes the desolation of the countryside and the slave gangs working in the fields during a journey through coastal south Etruria, and conceives the idea of reform
c.136 BC: uprising of 150 slaves in Rome: other revolts reported in Attica, Delos and elsewhere
MINTURNAE
SINUESSA
CAPUA
Arienzo
⊕468
Rocca San Felice
⊕⊕⊕473
c.136 BC: 450 slaves crucified after an uprising at Minturnae
133 BC: a rebellion of 4000 slaves is crushed at Sinuessa
Sant' Angelo
⊕467
Sicignano
⊕469
Polla
⊕⊕472
Barra
⊕470
Sala Consilina
⊕⊕⊕471, 472
Celenza Val Fortore
⊕ discovered 1973, listed in Année Epigraphique 1973 No. 222
centuriation has been revealed by aerial photography and fieldwork in various parts of northern Apulia and is probably to be associated with the work of the Gracchi as is now confirmed by the discovery of the boundary stone at Celenza Val Fortore
c.131 BC: inscription from Polla refers to the participation of runaway slaves from Italy in the Sicilian war, and to contemporary land-resettlement schemes
NEPTUNIA (TARENTUM)
colony founded by Gaius Gracchus
via Annia
MINERVIUM (SCOLACIUM)
colony founded by Gaius Gracchus
MESSANA
RHEGIUM
TAUROMENIUM
SICILIA
ENNA
CATANA
AGRIGENTUM
MORGANTINA
c.136 BC: 1st Sicilian Slave War broke out at Enna. Another revolt followed at Agrigentum. The insurgents, perhaps as many as 70 000, captured Morgantina, Tauromenium and probably Messana and defeated a Roman praetor who opposed them. Finally suppressed by the consul P. Rupilius in 132 BC
Roman territory 133 BC, including ager publicus
ager publicus annexed from disloyal allies after the 2nd Punic War
⊕ inscribed boundary stones recording the allocations of the Gracchan land commission
467 references are to the numbers of the inscriptions in A. Degrassi, Inscriptiones Latinae Liberae Rei Publicae Vol. 1. 1957
ROMA ancient name
Arienzo modern name
scale 1:4 500 000
0
150km
0
100mi

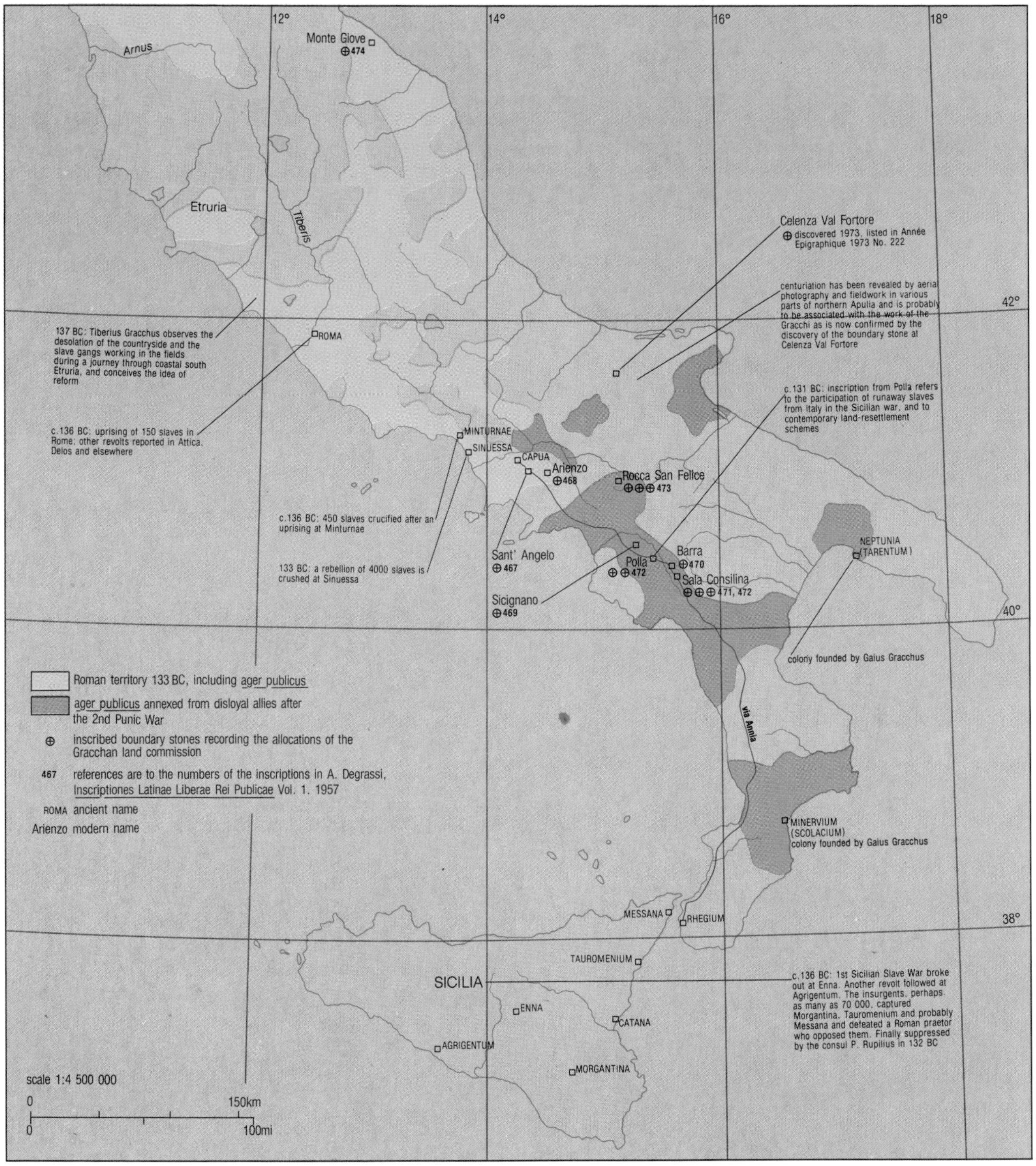

Overleaf The Roman Forum, seen through the arch of Septimius Severus, looking towards the temple of Vesta.

publicus and by reclaiming in the name of the state land held in excess of the limit. The task of reclamation was to be carried out by a commission of three men, who would then distribute small allotments to the poor. The beauty of the scheme was that it did not offend traditional rights of private property; on the contrary, it would only affect those who were already outside the law. In practice, however, Gracchus' bill was a major threat to the vested interests of many wealthy landowners, and intense opposition was aroused. On the other hand popular support was assured, especially among the rural poor, who flocked to Rome to vote for the bill. An attempt to veto the bill was foiled when Gracchus had the offending tribune voted out of office; the law was passed, and the land commission, consisting of Tiberius Gracchus himself, his brother Gaius and his father-in-law Appius Claudius, was duly set up.

But the opposition became alarmed at the political implications of what was happening. Gracchus had proposed his law without consulting the senate, as was customary; he had brushed aside the veto of a colleague by means that were possibly illegal; and he was now serving on his own land commission. Moreover he had not hesitated to make use of an unexpected windfall that occurred when Attalus III of Pergamum died, leaving his kingdom to the Romans. Gracchus immediately enacted that the bequest should be accepted, and the royal treasures distributed to the recipients of land allotments, to assist them in stocking their farms. The opposition was outraged by this unprecedented interference with the senate's traditional control of public finance. Finally, when Gracchus announced his intention to stand for a second tribunate for the following year, and to hint at further legislation, there was consternation and talk of *regnum* (see above, pp. 22–23). On the day of the election some leading senators and their attendants tried to break up the assembly, and in the ensuing riot Tiberius Gracchus and 300 of his supporters were killed. A general witch-hunt followed, in which many more Gracchan sympathizers were condemned by a special senatorial court of inquiry.

The sacrosanctity of the tribunate had been violated, and political conflict had ended in bloodshed for the first time in the history of the Roman Republic. Even so, it is unlikely that the full significance of the event was realized at the time. The land commission remained in being and continued its work (although not without difficulty), but in other respects the life of Rome appeared to return to normal. But the example of Tiberius Gracchus lived on, and soon began to be imitated by other tribunes. Within a few years an even more radical attack on the established order was mounted by Gaius Gracchus, Tiberius' younger brother. Gaius Gracchus held two successive tribunates (123 and 122 BC), in which he introduced a wide range of reforming legislation.

Gaius Gracchus' laws can be summarized under four main headings. First, a series of important measures aimed to promote the general welfare of the people. He passed an agrarian law which superseded that of his brother and provided in addition for the founding of colonies in Italy, at least two of which were actually established (at Minervium and Neptunia). A more radical step was the attempt to found a colony (Iunonia) on the site of Carthage. Other measures provided for a program of public works, the improvement of conditions of service in the army, the organization by the state of the corn supply of the city of Rome and the distribution of grain to the citizens at a fixed price, subsidized by the government. Secondly Gracchus attempted to increase the state's revenue, by imposing new customs tariffs and by enacting that the taxes of the immensely rich province of Asia (assessed as a tithe of its produce) should be collected by the *publicani*. Contracts were to be auctioned by the censors at Rome; in this way the state would receive a guaranteed income for five years, while the risks of fluctuations in the yield and the burden of administrative costs would be borne by the *publicani*. Gracchus' concern for public revenues arose from the need to finance his welfare schemes; his actions were guided by the principle that Rome's overseas possessions should be exploited to the full, and the proceeds used for the benefit of the people as a whole.

Thirdly Gaius attacked senatorial corruption and attempted to curb abuses of magisterial authority. He outlawed judicial conspiracy and enacted that special tribunals like that which had carried out the purge after his brother's death could not be constituted without popular authorization. Above all he reorganized the procedure for dealing with cases of peculation and maladministration by senatorial officials. In 149 BC a special standing committee of senators had been set up to deal with such offenses (prompted perhaps by the scandal of Ser. Galba: see above, p. 48). But experience had shown that senators were more concerned to cover up the nefarious activities of their peers than to see justice done, and the committee proved an inadequate safeguard against abuse. Gaius scrapped this convenient system of "internal inquiry," and replaced it with a regular criminal court manned by a jury from which senators were rigorously excluded. The jury was to be chosen from the equestrian order, that is from the propertied class. It was later asserted that Gracchus had split the ruling class, and given the state two heads. An unfortunate aspect of the new system was that the *publicani* became influential within the equestrian order, with the result that provincial governors who colluded with the *publicani* in robbing the provincials might hope to be acquitted if brought to trial in Rome. The reverse was also true; in 92 BC P. Rutilius Rufus was condemned for extortion by an equestrian jury after he had tried to check the abuses of the *publicani* in the province of Asia. The case was notorious and apparently the first of its kind; it is unlikely that such consequences could have been foreseen at the time of Gaius Gracchus.

Lastly, Gracchus attempted to widen the franchise by giving Roman citizenship to the Latins, and Latin rights to the other Italian allies. The proposal, which was not the first of its kind (an associate of Gracchus had proposed a similar bill in 125), was perhaps a response to expressions of discontent among the ruling class of the allied states, which had objected strongly to the activities of the Gracchan land commission. In any case the bill was rejected by the *plebs*, who did not wish to share their privileges. At this time (late in 122 BC) Gracchus was gradually losing support, and he failed to win a third tribunate for 121 BC. As soon as his tenure expired, an attempt was made to repeal some of his laws, beginning with the colony at Carthage. Gracchus and his supporters attempted to protest with a show of strength. The senate chose to view this as a threat to the state and ordered the consuls to see to it that the Republic suffered no harm. Gracchus and his friends fled to the Aventine, the old plebeian refuge (see above, p. 26), where they were rounded up and put to death; 3000 persons are said to have lost their lives in this grisly massacre.

The historical importance of Gaius Gracchus lies partly in the sheer volume and range of his legislation. Nothing like it had ever been seen before in Rome, and it was not to be repeated until the dictatorship of Julius Caesar. The whole Roman establishment had been shaken to its foundations, and there was no longer any doubt that the period of unchallenged oligarchic government that went back to the Hannibalic war was definitely at an end. The Gracchi had revived the traditional role of the tribunes as protectors of the *plebs*, and had asserted the people's right to legislate in its own interest on any matter whatsoever. Gaius Gracchus did not intend to remove the conduct of policy and administration from the senate and magistrates, but he hoped to make them more accountable to the people through the assemblies and by means of an independent judiciary which would be drawn from a class that was by definition outside politics.

The age of Marius and Sulla

Gaius Gracchus' miserable end was a victory for the most reactionary elements in the state. But their triumph was shortlived. Agitation by tribunes began again almost immediately, and the *populares* (political leaders who adopted the aims and methods of the Gracchi) were provided with an opportunity for a major assault in the years after 114 BC when

Rome was unexpectedly faced with a desperate military crisis. In that year the consul M. Porcius Cato (grandson of the famous censor) was disastrously defeated in Macedonia by the Scordisci, a Thracian tribe who had invaded the Roman province. At the same time news was received of a folk migration involving two Germanic tribes, the Cimbri and Teutones, who were reported to be approaching the borders of Italy. This created panic in the city, where attempts were made to appease the gods through archaic rituals, including that of human sacrifice. The same thing had happened at the time of the battle of Cannae, and the Romans clearly sensed that they were once again in extreme peril.

The senatorial oligarchy had acquired a position of unquestioned authority during the Hannibalic war, when it demonstrated competence in military leadership and organization, and skill in the conduct of foreign affairs. But these qualities were conspicuously lacking in the post-Gracchan senate. In 113 the consul Cn. Papirius Carbo risked a battle against the Cimbri at Noreia and suffered a calamitous defeat. Italy survived only because the Germans, for reasons of their own, decided to move westwards towards Gaul; but they returned a few years later, and defeated Roman armies in southern Gaul on three separate occasions (109, 107, 105). The last of these defeats, the battle of Arausio, was a massacre, and left Italy at the mercy of the Germans.

Meanwhile popular indignation had been aroused at Rome by the senate's handling of a crisis in North Africa, where a Numidian prince called Jugurtha had been making a nuisance of himself. The senate's role in this affair was a mixture of indecision, corruption and incompetence. When a Roman army was humiliatingly defeated by Jugurtha in 110, a tribune proposed that a special court of inquiry be set up, with equestrian jurors, to investigate the senate's conduct of foreign policy. As a result a number of leading nobles were exiled, including L. Opimius, the murderer of Gaius Gracchus. This event, which would have been unthinkable a generation earlier, was followed in 108 by the election of C. Marius to the consulship.

Marius was a "new man" (see above, p. 36) from the Volscian town of Arpinum. His election to the consulship was the result of a skillful campaign in which he attacked the nobility and made a positive virtue of his own lack of ancestry. Marius obtained a huge following and was not only elected to the consulship, but also appointed by plebiscite to take charge of the war against Jugurtha in place of the senate's nominee Q. Metellus, whom he had accused of incompetence (in this case probably unjustly). After some setbacks Marius defeated Jugurtha in 105, and was elected, in his absence, to a second consulship for 104. Since his departure from Rome

Rome and the Mediterranean world, c. 146–70 BC. Rome's triumphant march of imperial expansion came to an end with the destruction of Corinth and Carthage in 146 BC. The following generations saw the collapse of the political equilibrium that had prevailed since the end of the Hannibalic war, and at the same time witnessed an unprecedented series of military reverses. In the years 146–70 BC the Romans were faced with unrest and hostility in every part of the empire, and in attempting to respond, the ruling aristocracy showed itself corrupt and incompetent. The lowest point was reached in 105 BC when a Roman army was annihilated at Arausio by the German barbarians; at that moment Rome was faced with complete extinction. Almost equally serious was the revolt of the eastern provinces during Mithridates' advance in 88; this was a reaction to a generation of criminal exploitation and oppression by the Romans. These crises were resolved only by allowing able and ambitious individuals to reach positions of supreme power in the Roman state.

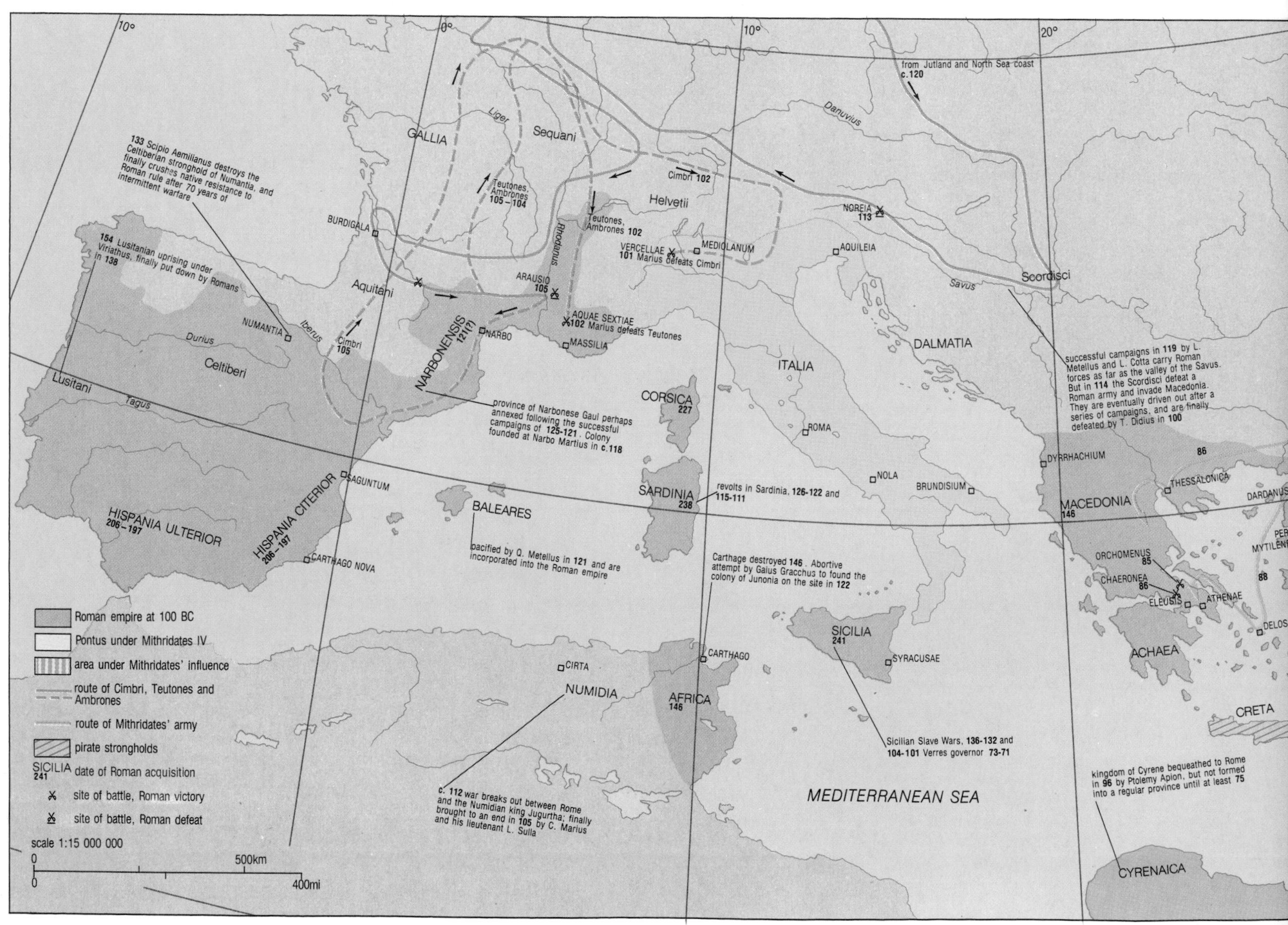

there had been a brief conservative reaction led by Q. Servilius Caepio, the consul of 106. But when Caepio was defeated in the following year at Arausio the oligarchy lost its nerve completely. Caepio became the first man since King Tarquin to have his *imperium* abrogated, and Marius, the people's hero, was appointed to save Italy from the Germans. The barbarian threat temporarily receded, however, and Marius was given the opportunity to carry out a systematic reform of the organization, training and equipment of the Roman army (104–102 BC). During this period he was reelected consul every year, contrary to all law and precedent, until finally he defeated the Teutones at Aquae Sextiae (102) and the Cimbri at Vercellae (101). Marius returned in triumph to Rome, and to a sixth consulship, in 100 BC.

Marius' victories were won by an army which he had turned into an efficient and disciplined fighting force. His military reforms had imposed professional standards on men who were already professionalized in a socio-economic sense. For his campaign against Jugurtha in 107 Marius had abandoned the traditional practice of raising troops from the class of *adsidui* and had simply enlisted volunteers from the proletariat. As we have seen, the numbers of *adsidui* had declined in the course of the 2nd century and had given rise to the agrarian reforms of the Gracchi. The Gracchi had attempted to revive the class of peasant smallholders, but they had not tackled the root cause of the problem. As P.A. Brunt points out, "There was an inherent contradiction in the Gracchan objective of increasing the number of Rome's peasant soldiers, when it was soldiering that did so much to destroy the peasantry." In any case the Gracchan scheme was repealed by a series of laws in the years following Gaius' death, and must be regarded, in the long term, as a failure. With a steadily declining peasantry the only way to solve the problem of recruitment was either to reduce the property qualification for military service, which indeed happened on a number of occasions before the 120s, or to ignore it altogether, as Marius did in 107. The evidence suggests that the army was already "proletarianized" by this date, and that Marius' action was merely the final stage in the formation of a professional army which was no longer based on the part-time service of the peasantry. The connection between ownership of property and military service was now completely broken, and soldiering became a form of employment for men who owned no land. The consequence however was that the proletarian armies began to demand some permanent reward for their services, and since the state was not prepared to institute a regular system of granting land allotments to discharged veterans, the men looked instead to their commanders to make provision for them. Thus the armies became instruments of political conflict in the hands of unscrupulous commanders, of whom there was no shortage in the late Republic.

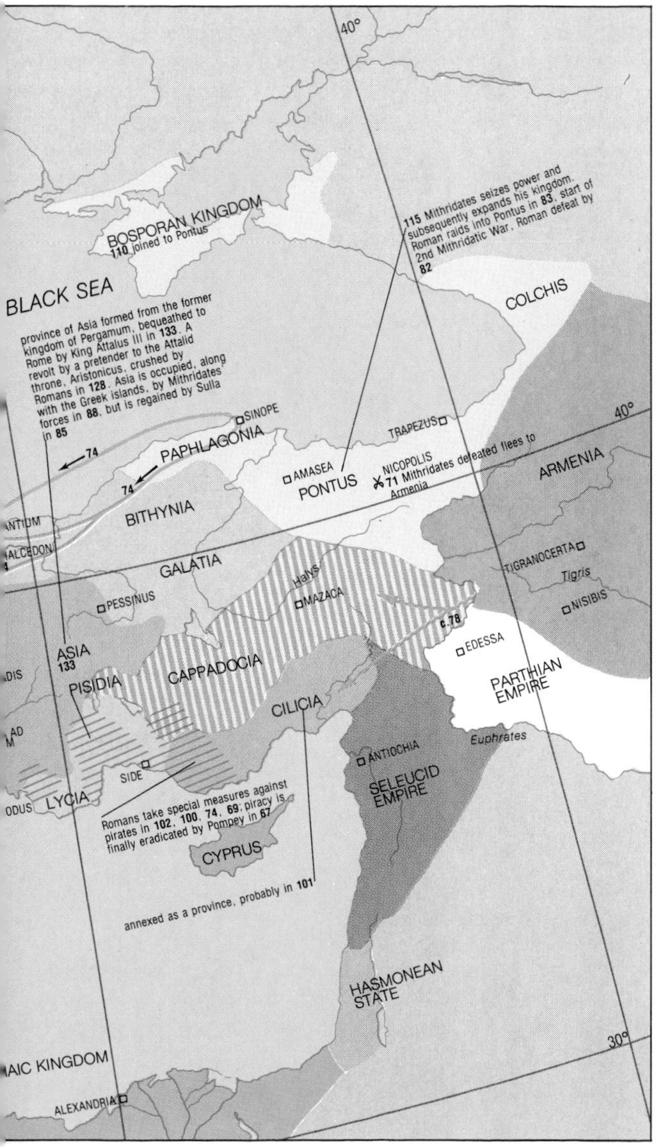

These consequences were certainly not foreseen by Marius, but some elements of the new situation became apparent immediately. In 103 a tribune, L. Appuleius Saturninus, had enacted that large allotments of land in Africa should be distributed to veterans of the Jugurthan war. During a second tribunate in 100 he proposed further distributions, and the foundation of colonies in the provinces, for veterans of the German wars and of a recent campaign in Sicily where a second slave revolt had taken place (104–101). These and other proposals received strong support from the veterans and were forced through the assembly with the help of mob violence. Later in the year matters got so bad that Marius was compelled to intervene to restore order. Saturninus and his associates surrendered, but Marius was unable to save them from a lynch mob. Saturninus' laws were then revoked by the senate. The end result was that Marius was discredited and his veterans never received their hoped-for rewards.

The profound shock of the German invasions exposed underlying tensions and divisions within Roman society and hastened the process of political breakdown. One such problem, which became critical in the decade following the battle of Vercellae, was a deterioration in relations between Rome and the Italian allies. In the Hannibalic war Rome had stood at the head of an alliance of free Italian communities and had led them to victory against the foreign invader. But during the far-flung wars of the 2nd century, in Spain, Greece, Asia and Africa, the notion of a defensive alliance began to fade. The allies gradually came to feel that they were no longer free partners, but subjects who carried the burden of wars in which they had no interest,

Coin of C. Fundanius (101 BC). The type shows C. Marius in a chariot celebrating his triumph over the Cimbri and Teutones.

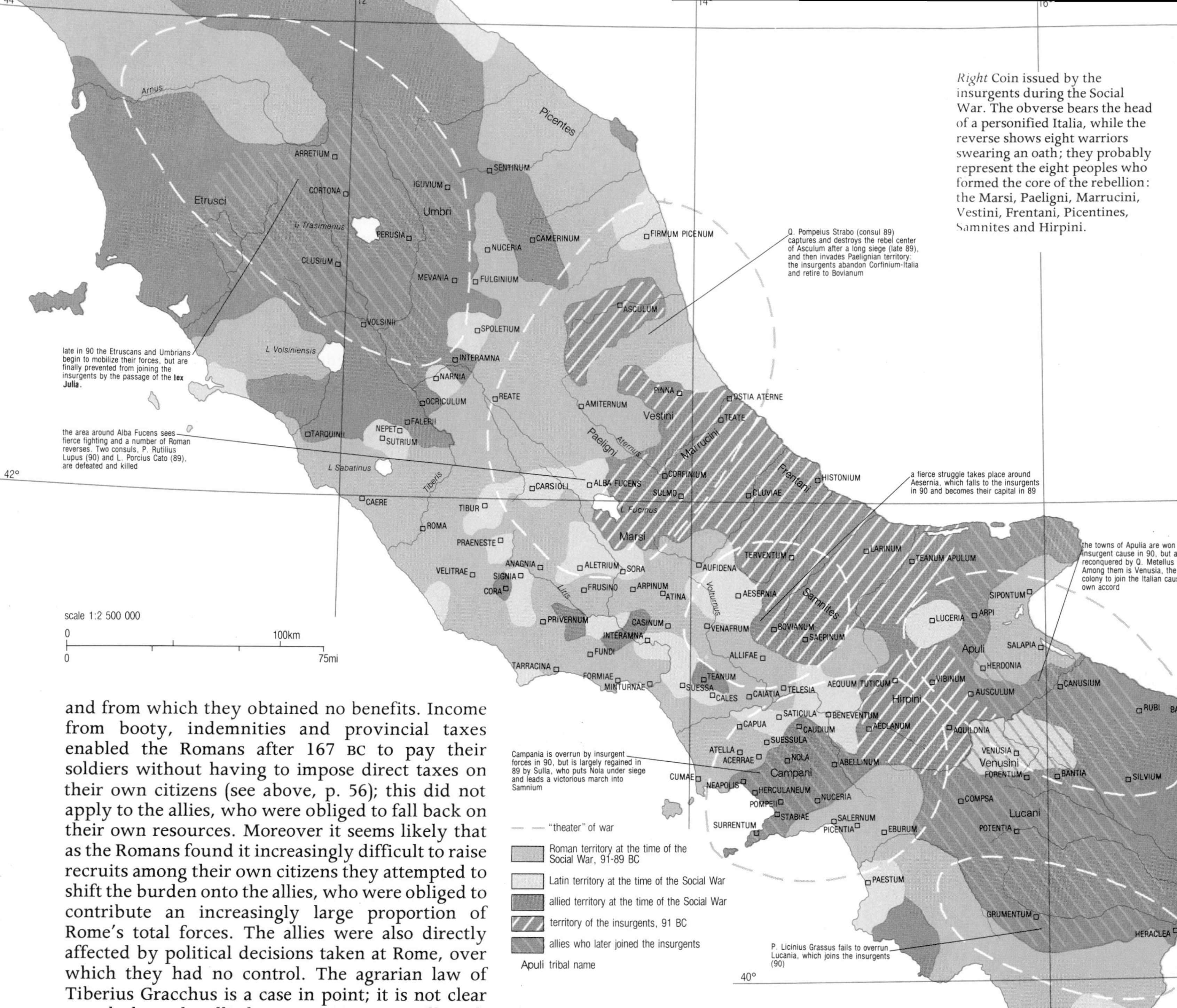

Right Coin issued by the insurgents during the Social War. The obverse bears the head of a personified Italia, while the reverse shows eight warriors swearing an oath; they probably represent the eight peoples who formed the core of the rebellion: the Marsi, Paeligni, Marrucini, Vestini, Frentani, Picentines, Samnites and Hirpini.

and from which they obtained no benefits. Income from booty, indemnities and provincial taxes enabled the Romans after 167 BC to pay their soldiers without having to impose direct taxes on their own citizens (see above, p. 56); this did not apply to the allies, who were obliged to fall back on their own resources. Moreover it seems likely that as the Romans found it increasingly difficult to raise recruits among their own citizens they attempted to shift the burden onto the allies, who were obliged to contribute an increasingly large proportion of Rome's total forces. The allies were also directly affected by political decisions taken at Rome, over which they had no control. The agrarian law of Tiberius Gracchus is a case in point; it is not clear exactly how the allied communities were affected, but our sources imply that many Italian landowners had been occupying *ager publicus* and were evicted by the land commission. Gaius Gracchus attempted, as we have seen, to compensate them by giving them Roman citizenship; his efforts were abortive, but it seems that the idea of obtaining Roman citizenship gradually caught on among the allies, for whom it became an increasingly attractive political goal. As citizens the Italians would gain the right of appeal against Roman magistrates, a say in the political process, direct access to the profits of empire (in particular the right to bid for public contracts) and the chance to enter the senate and the magistracies.

A general sense of resentment was no doubt accentuated by the German wars, which brought Romans and Italians together in a fight for survival and exposed the flagrant injustice of the allies' inferior status. It is probable that Marius appreciated this fact and was sympathetic to the allies' cause; it is also likely that Saturninus had intended to include them in his colonial settlements. If so, the annulment of Saturninus' laws will have been a bitter disappointment to the allies, who were alienated still further when the consuls of 95 BC cracked down on Italians who had unlawfully registered as Roman citizens. Finally in 91 the cause of Italian enfranchisement was taken up by the tribune M. Livius Drusus as part of a wider program, which included proposals for agrarian settlement in Italy and the provinces and a reform of the jury courts.

Unfortunately Drusus' attempts to win widespread support were inept, and succeeded only in arousing general hostility. The proposal to extend the citizenship had no chance and was probably never put to the vote. The death of his most influential supporter, the orator L. Crassus, left Drusus politically isolated; his laws were annulled by the senate on a legal technicality, and late in the year he was murdered in mysterious circumstances. For the allies, who had pinned all their hopes on Drusus, this was the last straw. Before the end of 91 an armed revolt had broken out.

The conflict which followed (it became known as

Right The Tabularium, one of the finest surviving republican buildings, stands at the western end of the Forum, backing on to the Capitol. The building, which was used as a record office and housed the state archives, was built in 78 BC by Q. Lutatius Catulus, and replaced an earlier structure that was destroyed by fire in 83 BC.

Italy and the Social War, 91–89 BC. The Social War (the War of the Allies) began in 91 BC following the persistent refusal of the Romans to grant the right of citizenship to their Italian allies. The insurgents formed themselves into an independent state called Italia, with its capital at Corfinium. The revolt was centered in the southern and central regions of the peninsula, and involved the Oscan-speaking peoples of the central Apennines (especially the Marsi), the Samnites and Lucanians, and the town of Asculum in Picenum. With the exception of Venusia, the Latin colonies remained loyal to Rome, as did the Greek cities; the Etruscans and Umbrians held back until the final stages of the war, and were the first to accept the Roman citizenship under the terms of the *lex Julia*.

the Social or Marsic War) was fiercely contested, and the Romans achieved a military victory only by conceding political defeat. In 90 BC the consul L. Julius Caesar passed a law granting Roman citizenship to all loyal communities and to any others which laid down their arms. By 89 the war was mostly over except for pockets of resistance in the south which were mopped up in the following years.

The Italian crisis had scarcely been resolved when news came of a disaster in the eastern provinces. For some years Rome had been keeping a watchful eye on the rise of the kingdom of Pontus under its powerful ruler Mithridates VI (121–63 BC). In 89 a Roman praetor had rashly provoked an attack on Mithridates, who retaliated by invading the province of Asia and ordering the massacre of all Romans resident there (88 BC). Our sources claim that 80000 persons were killed in a single day. This is a wild exaggeration: the actual number was probably in four figures, although even this is a conjecture.

By this date Romans and Italians were scattered throughout the Roman provinces as tax collectors, traders, moneylenders and landowners. They were very numerous in Sicily, which had been open to Roman exploitation since the 3rd century BC: at the time of the First Slave War (136 BC) many of the slave-owning landlords were Roman citizens of the equestrian class, and there were many Italian residents in the cities in the time of Verres, who governed Sicily in the late 70s. Their presence in North Africa is indicated by the story of the massacre of a group of Italian "businessmen" (*negotiatores*) at Cirta in 112 BC, which gave rise to the Jugurthan war. Soldiers often chose to settle in the provinces where they had served, especially in Spain, where there were a number of Italian communities. As for southern Gaul, Cicero tells us (in 74 BC) that "Gaul is packed with traders, crammed with Roman citizens. No Gaul does business independently of a citizen of Rome; not a penny changes hands without the transaction being recorded in the books of Roman citizens." Cicero classifies the Romans in Gaul as "publicans, farmers, ranchers and other businessmen." Italian businessmen were very numerous in the east, especially in Greece, the Aegean islands and western Asia Minor. For example in Greece an inscription of c. 103 BC shows that as much as 10 per cent of the land of the city of Messene was owned by Romans and Italians. An important center was the island of Delos, which the Romans had declared a free port in 167 BC as part of their policy of harming the trade of Rhodes (see above, p. 51). Delos became the center of the slave trade, and according to Strabo was able to handle more than ten thousand transactions in a single day. In the province of Asia itself many of the Italian residents would have been employed by the companies of *publicani*, who had been given the right to collect direct taxes there by the law of Gaius Gracchus. Their depredations were notorious (compare the case of the unfortunate Rutilius Rufus, above p. 58) and aroused the hatred of the native population, who willingly cooperated with Mithridates in the slaughter of 88. Mithridates was able to pose as a liberator of the Greeks against the hated Romans, "the common enemies of all mankind." By the end of 88 his forces had overrun the Aegean and invaded Greece.

The task of leading a Roman army against Mithridates was assigned to one of the consuls of 88, L. Cornelius Sulla. Sulla was an unprincipled and dissolute noble from an old patrician family (one of his ancestors was the notorious Rufinus – above p. 42). He had shown his ability as one of Marius' trusted lieutenants in the African and German campaigns, and had made a reputation for himself as a commander in the Social War. He was therefore well qualified for the task of dealing with Mithridates. However the decision came as a disappointment to Marius, who was still influential and had hoped that the command would be conferred on him. It was generally assumed that victory over Mithridates would be both easy and profitable, and Marius was especially annoyed that the prize should have gone to Sulla, with whom he had quarreled a few years previously.

In order to rectify this state of affairs Marius employed the services of a tribune, P. Sulpicius, who had entered office as a supporter of the *optimates* (the conservative elements in the senate) but for some reason had become embittered. Sulpicius proposed a series of laws, including one to give equal voting rights to the newly enfranchised Italians (they had been cheated of this by being confined to a restricted number of tribes) and another to appoint Marius in place of Sulla as commander in the forthcoming eastern campaign. Events then moved swiftly. Sulpicius' laws were passed amid violent scenes of street fighting. Sulla left to join his army at Nola in Campania, where he made a personal appeal to the troops. On receiving a favorable response he at once marched on Rome, which fell without a blow. Marius was taken completely by surprise, but managed to escape to Africa; Sulpicius was killed, and his laws were canceled. After enacting some constitutional measures which foreshadowed those of his dictatorship, Sulla left for the east.

As soon as his back was turned fresh dissensions broke out. One of the consuls of 87, L. Cornelius Cinna, attempted to revive Sulpicius' law on the new citizens, but was obstructed by his colleague Cn. Octavius, a supporter of Sulla. Rioting ensued and Cinna was forced to flee, but he found a willing ally in Marius, who had returned from Africa and was mobilizing his supporters. Cinna and Marius then marched on Rome in their turn, captured the city and massacred their opponents in a new reign of terror. Marius then entered his seventh consulship, but died after a few days (86 BC). His colleague Cinna attempted to restore some sort of normality: a fair deal was arranged for the new citizens, Sulla was declared an outlaw and an "official" army was sent to Asia under the command of L. Valerius Flaccus.

The events of the next few years are difficult to evaluate because the sources are heavily slanted in favor of Sulla. Part of the bias is due to Sulla's own memoirs, which do not survive but which clearly had a strong influence on the historical tradition. In Rome the government was controlled by Cinna, who was consul for four years in succession (87–84) and evidently had strong support. The upper classes seem at least to have acquiesced; at this stage few of the leading senators were prepared to go over to Sulla, and as far as we know none of them did so.

In the east Sulla succeeded in driving Mithridates' forces out of Greece after a victory at Chaeronea in 86 BC; in the same year Valerius Flaccus appeared with his army and began to campaign against Mithridates in Asia Minor. Flaccus was soon murdered by his own legate, C. Flavius Fimbria, but the war continued and Fimbria scored some notable successes. Sulla however made a peace treaty with Mithridates in 85 – on fairly generous terms – and then turned on Fimbria, whose troops deserted him. Sulla's settlement of Asia was extremely harsh; he allowed his troops to plunder almost at will and billeted them on the cities.

In 83 he returned to Italy, where he was joined by young opportunists such as M. Crassus and Q. Metellus Pius, and in particular by the young Pompey, who had raised three legions on his own initiative. The opposition was disorganized and poorly led (Cinna had been murdered in a mutiny in 84), and Sulla's support grew as it became increasingly clear that he was going to win. Even so there was bitter fighting in Italy, where the "Marians" were joined by the Samnites, and in the provinces, where they had a considerable following. But by the end of 82 Sulla was established in Rome after defeating the Samnites at the battle of the Colline Gate, and after the son of Marius had been defeated and killed at Praeneste. Resistance in Sicily and Africa was rapidly put down by Pompey, who was awarded a triumph (probably in 81) and greeted by Sulla with the title *Magnus* ("the Great").

In Rome Sulla carried out a purge of his opponents, who were hunted down and put to death without trial. The condemned persons were "proscribed," that is, their names were listed on public notices which declared them outlaws with a price on their heads. Thousands are said to have died, including over 40 senators and 1600 knights (*equites*); their property was confiscated and handed over to Sulla's supporters, many of whom made fortunes (an infamous example is Crassus). Sulla punished communities in Italy that had opposed him by confiscating their land and assigning it in allotments to his soldiers; 120 000 men are said to have been settled in colonies, mostly in Etruria and Campania.

In an attempt to regularize his position Sulla assumed the dictatorship, an office that had been in abeyance since the Second Punic War. Under its authority he introduced a series of laws (81 BC) which he hoped would create stability and prevent a recurrence of the disorders that had afflicted Rome since the time of Tiberius Gracchus. In particular he sought to defuse the tribunate, by severely limiting its powers of veto and legislation, and by not allowing tribunes to proceed to further offices. He drafted several hundred men from the equestrian order into the senate, and he gave the enlarged body (of about 600 members) the task of providing juries for the permanent courts, which were themselves thoroughly reorganized. A whole series of regular tribunals was set up to deal with particular public crimes: extortion, treason, bribery, embezzlement, fraud, assault, murder etc. Some of these were in existence before Sulla (for example the extortion court; see above, p. 58), but others were probably instituted by him.

Sulla established a regular order for the chief magistracies, and prescribed minimum ages for the quaestorship (30), praetorship (39) and consulship (42). Those who obtained the quaestorship were automatically admitted to the senate, and in order to maintain the number of senators at around 600 Sulla raised the number of annual quaestors to 20 (assuming therefore an average age at death of over 60). The number of praetors was raised from six to eight in order to provide governors for the increased number of provinces. Finally, he abolished the state-subsidized grain rations.

Sulla laid down the dictatorship at the end of 81, held the consulship in 80, retired into private life in 79 and died at the beginning of 78. His extraordinary career left a legacy of bitterness and hatred that overshadowed the last generation of the Roman Republic. It is remarkable that a man who in his own actions showed nothing but contempt for legality, human life and rights of property should have made such a determined effort to create order and stability. The result was undoubtedly a failure. In his efforts to cure the ills of the Republic Sulla attacked the symptoms but not the cause. Tribunician agitation during the previous half-century was the product of underlying discontent which could not be simply legislated out of existence. The enforced settlement of his veterans, so far from providing an armed guarantee of stability, merely created further unrest in the Italian countryside and furnished recruits for future revolutionary attempts. Sulla had established a governmental structure in which the senatorial oligarchy had more power than ever before, but it had originated in violence and bloodshed, and it was not borne up by any general consensus. Sulla's chief supporters were trimmers and opportunists who were among the first to exploit the weaknesses of his system as soon as he was gone; while the chief beneficiaries of his new order, the *optimates*, had neither the will nor the moral authority to make it work. In the words of E. Badian, "The Sullan oligarchy had a fatal flaw: it governed with a guilty conscience."

L. Cornelius Sulla (c. 138–78 BC) came from an old but not recently distinguished patrician family. He first rose to prominence as an associate of Marius, and served under him in the Jugurthine and Cimbric wars. His quarrel with Marius dates from the late 90s, and came to a head in 88 during his consulship, when Marius was appointed by a plebiscite to take over the command against Mithridates which had previously been conferred on him. Sulla responded by marching on Rome and forcing his enemies to give way. After four years' campaigning in the east he returned to a second civil war; his victory in 82 enabled him to establish a ruthless dictatorship.

Mithridates VI of Pontus (132–63 BC) succeeded his father while still a child in 120 BC. His career of expansion began when he overran most of the north coast of the Black Sea; he then occupied part of Armenia and turned his eyes towards Asia Minor. His chance came in 88, when he was able to advance into the province of Asia and to occupy the Aegean islands by posing as a liberator and exploiting the Greeks' hatred of the Romans. Defeated in successive campaigns by Sulla, Lucullus and Pompey, he was eventually driven to suicide in 63 BC.

PART TWO

FROM REPUBLIC TO EMPIRE

THE ROMAN REVOLUTION

The aftermath of Sulla and the rise of Pompey
Almost all effective opposition to Sulla had been wiped out by the end of 81 BC, with one significant exception. This was Q. Sertorius, a former confidant of Marius and Cinna, who had withdrawn from Italy in 83 at the approach of Sulla's armies and gone to his province in Spain. Temporarily driven out in 81, he returned in 80 and began a general revolt with the support both of the native Spaniards and of the Roman and Italian residents. Q. Metellus Pius, sent against him in 79, was unable to make any headway; in 77 the senate realized that reinforcements would have to be sent.

Meanwhile in Italy the government had had to deal with an uprising led by the consul of 78, M. Aemilius Lepidus, who had attempted to overthrow Sulla's arrangements and had found support among the dispossessed peasants in Etruria. Lepidus was fairly easily crushed by Pompey, who had been given a special command by the senate (77 BC), but Pompey then offered to take his army to Spain to help Metellus. Since he had a loyal army at his back the senate found his offer hard to refuse; late in 77 Pompey was appointed as "proconsul" to share the command against Sertorius.

Pompey's departure was followed by an uneasy period of oligarchic rule, interrupted by occasional agitation. In the east Rome annexed the provinces of Bithynia and Cyrene in 74, but was faced with another war against Mithridates, the conduct of which was assigned to L. Licinius Lucullus, formerly one of Sulla's henchmen. During this period the Roman world was also suffering from the depredations of pirates. But the most serious problem for the Roman government during the late 70s was the revolt of Spartacus, the last and greatest of the slave wars of classical antiquity. Spartacus was a Thracian gladiator who escaped in 73 and assembled a force of fugitive slaves on Mount Vesuvius. Within a short time he had an army of tens of thousands of slaves (our sources allege as many as 120 000), who roamed Italy for two years, pillaging as they went and inflicting defeat on the Roman forces that were sent against them (including two consular armies in 72). Finally the slaves were defeated in Bruttium by Crassus, who marched against them in 71 with an enormous army (eight or ten legions). Spartacus was killed, and over 6000 captured slaves were crucified along the Appian Way. The lines of crosses stretched from Rome to Capua. It should be noted that neither the revolt of Spartacus, nor the two uprisings in Sicily that preceded it (see above, pp. 56, 61), were genuine revolutionary movements, but rather pathetic attempts by the slaves to escape from their wretched condition and to take revenge on their masters. There is no sign of a conscious revolutionary ideology or of an articulate movement for the abolition of slavery as such.

In Spain Pompey and Metellus made slow progress until 72, when Sertorius was murdered by one of his own officers. Pompey rapidly concluded the war and took his army back to Italy, where he arrived in time to finish off some remnants of Spartacus' army. He and Crassus then joined forces and, although suspicious of one another, decided to stand together for the consulships of 70 BC. Pompey was not legally qualified for the office, as he was only 36 years old and had not held any other magistracy (indeed, he was not yet even a member of the senate). But the government, with the prudence of a man who hands over his wallet to a thief without waiting to be asked, waived the constitution in his favor.

Pompey was by now an immensely powerful figure. He was popular, gifted and handsome, and was already being compared to Alexander the Great. He had a loyal following not only among the

Above Pompey the Great (106–48 BC). "In his youth," writes his biographer Plutarch, "Pompey had a very engaging countenance, which spoke for him before he opened his lips. Yet that grace of aspect was not unattended with dignity, and amid his youthful bloom there was a venerable and princely air. His hair naturally curled a little before; which, together with the shining moisture and quick turn of his eye, produced a stronger likeness of Alexander the Great than that which appeared in the statues of that prince. So that some seriously gave him the name of Alexander, and he did not refuse it."

Below Monument of the early 1st century BC, known conventionally as the "Altar of Domitius Ahenobarbus." The frieze along one side shows scenes from a Roman census. On the left a citizen is being registered, while in the center the *lustrum* (purification) is being performed, with the sacrifice of a bull, sheep and pig. Possibly a monument of L. Gellius Publicola, censor in 70 BC.

Right: Colonization in Italy, 1st century BC. In the late Republic colonization became a device by which revolutionary leaders could reward the mass of their supporters. Sulla founded colonies for his veterans on land expropriated from his enemies; many of his colonies were established alongside existing cities, which became double communities (e.g. Pompeii). Sulla's example was followed by Caesar, Antony and Augustus.

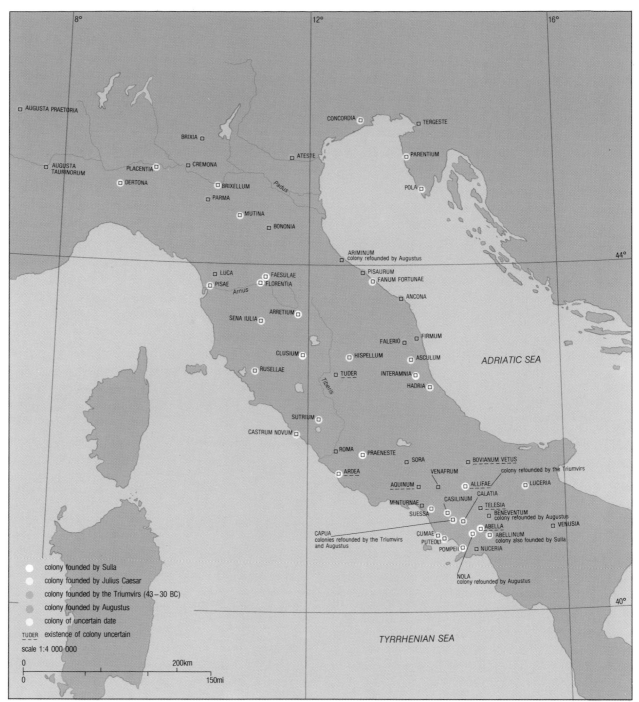

8°
12°
16°
44°
40°
AUGUSTA PRAETORIA
AUGUSTA TAURINORUM
PLACENTIA
DERTONA
BRIXIA
CREMONA
BRIXELLUM
PARMA
MUTINA
BONONIA
Padus
ATESTE
CONCORDIA
TERGESTE
PARENTIUM
POLA
ARIMINUM
colony refounded by Augustus
PISAURUM
FANUM FORTUNAE
ANCONA
LUCA
PISAE
FAESULAE
FLORENTIA
Arnus
ARRETIUM
SENA IULIA
FALERIO
FIRMUM
CLUSIUM
HISPELLUM
ASCULUM
ADRIATIC SEA
RUSELLAE
TUDER
INTERAMNIA
HADRIA
Tiberis
SUTRIUM
CASTRUM NOVUM
ROMA
PRAENESTE
SORA
BOVIANUM VETUS
colony refounded by the Triumvirs
ARDEA
VENAFRUM
AQUINUM
ALLIFAE
LUCERIA
CALATIA
MINTURNAE
CASILINUM
TELESIA
SUESSA
BENEVENTUM
colony refounded by Augustus
VENUSIA
ABELLA
CAPUA
colonies refounded by the Triumvirs and Augustus
CUMAE
PUTEOLI
ABELLINUM
colony also founded by Sulla
POMPEII
NUCERIA
NOLA
colony refounded by Augustus
TYRRHENIAN SEA
colony founded by Sulla
colony founded by Julius Caesar
colony founded by the Triumvirs (43–30 BC)
colony founded by Augustus
colony of uncertain date
TUDER existence of colony uncertain
scale 1:4 000 000
0 200km
0 150mi

Below M. Tullius Cicero (106–43 BC) came from a well-to-do family of Arpinum. Largely because of his extraordinary powers as an orator Cicero made his way to the consulship in 63 BC and became a prominent member of the senate. The leading intellectual figure of his generation, Cicero wrote not only speeches but also rhetorical and philosophical treatises; his voluminous correspondence survives as an invaluable record of the political life and high society of the period. A staunch upholder of the Republic, Cicero was brutally murdered in the proscriptions of 43 BC.

soldiers and the people, but also in the provinces, where he had shown moderation and respect for the native populations. He made it clear that he intended to reform Sulla's system, and that he wanted Crassus to be his colleague. After that, their election was a formality.

As consuls Pompey and Crassus restored the powers of the tribunate and supported a law which ended the senate's monopoly of the jury courts. Juries were to contain a mixture of senators (one-third) and equestrians (two-thirds). This move came in response to continuing evidence of the senate's unwillingness to check abuses by its own members. The conviction of C. Verres in 70 BC after three years of misgovernment in Sicily occurred in spite of obstruction by the *optimates*. In this infamous case the prosecution was led by Cicero, whose speech against Verres still stands as one of the most damaging indictments of official malpractice ever delivered.

After the defeat of Spartacus the problem of piracy became acute; by the early 60s the pirates had taken to making raids on the Italian coast, sacking villas and kidnapping travelers on the Appian Way. When the city's corn supply began to suffer, public opinion demanded action which led in 67 to the appointment of Pompey to a special command against the pirates. Pompey was granted wide-ranging powers and immense resources of men, money and supplies. Within three months he had completely cleared the seas of pirates, a truly astonishing feat of organization and tactics.

In the following year the tribune C. Manilius proposed that Pompey's command should be extended to allow him to finish the war against Mithridates. Mithridates was still at large, in spite of being driven out of the province of Asia by Lucullus in 70 BC. Lucullus had made himself unpopular with his troops by preventing them from looting the cities of the eastern provinces; he had also curbed the activities of the *publicani* who determined to ruin him. Manilius' proposal, which was supported by Cicero (now praetor), was overwhelmingly carried, and the unfortunate Lucullus was forced to make way for Pompey.

Pompey remained in the east for four more years. During this time he made short work of Mithridates, conquered all Anatolia and Syria and advanced as far south as Jerusalem, which he captured in 63. He annexed Syria, enlarged Cilicia, added Pontus to Bithynia and surrounded the new provinces with a ring of client kingdoms, which paid tribute to Rome. By this single campaign Pompey claimed to have raised the provincial revenues of the Roman state by 70 per cent. He brought back enormous quantities of booty, and was able to reward his soldiers by giving each of them a donative of 1500 denarii, equivalent to $12\frac{1}{2}$ years' pay. In all of this he acted largely on his own initiative, without consulting the senate, and generally behaved like an absolute monarch – which, in effect, is exactly what he was.

The political atmosphere in Rome during these years was dominated by thoughts of the absent Pompey, by fears of what he might do on his return and by the memory of Sulla. Tension was heightened by a monetary crisis (the reasons for which are unclear—we know merely that the amount of money in circulation had been declining since the 70s); there was a consequent squeeze on credit, widespread indebtedness and discontent among the poor. Social unrest and economic deprivation fostered complex political intrigue, in which Pompey's rivals attempted to build up their own positions during his absence. The most prominent of these men was Crassus, who was aided and abetted by the young Caesar.

In 63 Crassus and Caesar backed the proposal of a tribune to purchase land in Italy and the provinces for the settlement of the poor and of the veterans of Pompey's campaigns, which were now coming to an end. But the bill was successfully opposed by Cicero, on the rather perverse grounds that it was a threat to Pompey's interests, of which he was the self-appointed custodian. The activities of Crassus and Caesar aroused deep suspicion in conservative circles, and there was much sinister talk of conspiracies and threats to public order. The principal object of these fears, however, was a disreputable patrician named L. Sergius Catilina (Catiline), who stood for the consulship of 63 with a promise of agrarian reform and cancellation of debts. This threat united the propertied classes behind a rival candidate, Cicero, who was triumphantly elected in spite of being a "new man." When Catiline failed again at the elections for 62, he attempted to stage a coup d'etat, but the attempt was foiled by Cicero, who managed to arrest the ringleaders before they could strike. Catiline himself fled to Etruria where a general revolt had broken out; it was easily crushed and Catiline was killed. His associates in Rome were summarily executed on Cicero's orders. This act later aroused a storm of controversy, since as citizens the conspirators were entitled to a trial. Pompey was horrified when he heard the news and wrote a very frosty reply to Cicero's fulsome account of the affair.

The Catilinarian conspiracy reveals the extent of the problem of debt and poverty. Discontented groups included the victims of Sulla's expropriations, the families of the proscribed, Sulla's own veterans who had themselves fallen into debt, and the urban *plebs*, who were oppressed by high rents and appalling living conditions. The countryside of Italy had been extensively ravaged by war in the 20 years preceding the defeat of Spartacus. The high levels of conscription in the 70s and 60s hastened the continuing process of displacement, which agrarian legislation had done little to curb. Violence became endemic as desperate men turned to a life of crime. Gangsters and terrorists were active in the city of Rome, where there was no police force to maintain order. Indebtedness had also become a problem among the upper class, as increasing amounts of money were invested in the competition for high office, which promised huge rewards for the few who succeeded and ruin for the majority who failed. The careers of Catiline and his crew of frustrated nobles epitomize this unhealthy state of affairs.

At the end of 62 Pompey landed at Brundisium. There he disbanded his army, to everyone's relief, and returned to Rome for his triumph and what he probably hoped would be a life of ease and dignity as Rome's most respected statesman. If so, he was disappointed. He had hoped that the senate would ratify without question his settlement of the east, and would provide land allotments for his veterans.

Right Reconstruction of the great villa at Settefinestre in the territory of Cosa. Impressive standing ruins mark the site of this great establishment, which grew up in the 1st century BC as the center of a large estate. Since 1976 the villa has been the subject of a major program of excavation by a joint Anglo-Italian team. Preliminary results confirm that the villa was the center of an enterprise devoted to large-scale agricultural production (particularly wine production) using slave labor.

Gaius Julius Caesar (100–44 BC) belonged to a patrician family which traced its descent back to Aeneas. More recent political connections included Marius, his uncle by marriage, and Cinna, his father-in-law. As a young man Caesar incurred the enmity of Sulla, but managed to escape the proscriptions. In the post-Sullan period Caesar eagerly sought popularity: he associated himself with Pompey by supporting his cause, and he attached himself to Crassus, to whom he became heavily indebted. In 60 BC he formed an agreement with Pompey and Crassus which enabled him to obtain the consulship with their support, and to use the office to promote their interests. But the chief beneficiary of the "First Triumvirate" was Caesar, who engineered for himself a special command in Gaul, where his military successes ultimately provided him with a means to achieve absolute power. Caesar proved himself immensely gifted as an orator, writer, soldier, politician and administrator. He was completely unscrupulous in the pursuit of his own interests, and had nothing but contempt for the republican system of government, which he quite deliberately sought to destroy.

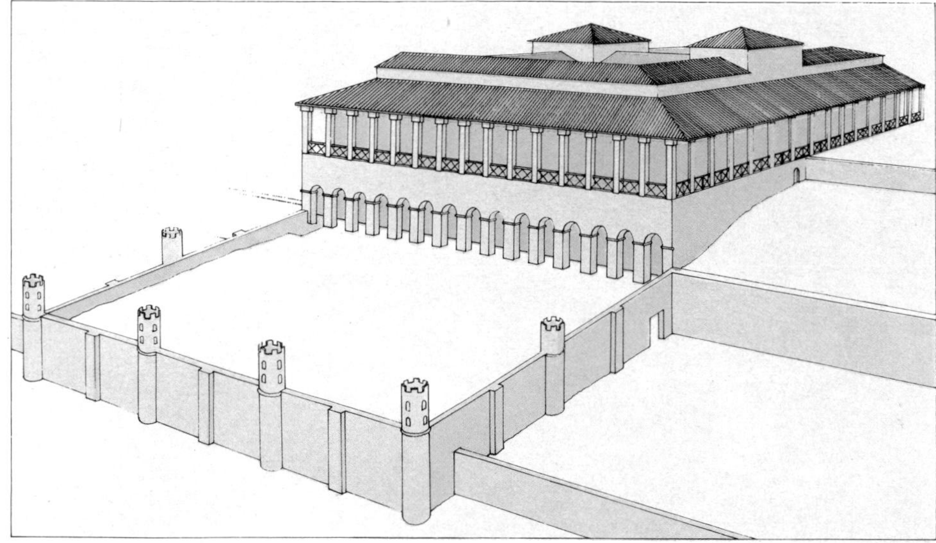

Fresco from Pompeii of a *villa marittima* (seaside villa), a type of luxury dwelling which became common in the last years of the Republic, when it became fashionable for wealthy Romans to spend time in relaxation away from the city. The great majority of these coastal villas were built around the Bay of Naples.

But his requests were met with obstruction and resistance from the *optimates,* led by Lucullus. Lucullus was aided by M. Porcius Cato, a posturing diehard whose principal distinction was his descent from Cato the Censor, whom he attempted to impersonate. These men and their friends managed to frustrate Pompey's wishes for a considerable time; in so doing they unwittingly contrived their own downfall and the destruction of the Republic.

The end of the Republic

The *optimates'* tactics eventually drove the frustrated Pompey into an informal alliance with Crassus and Caesar. This pact, now known as the First Triumvirate, was an informal arrangement of the traditional kind (see above, p. 24), but the particular combination of Pompey's immense popularity, Crassus' wealth and connections and Caesar's political acumen proved irresistible. Caesar gained the consulship of 59, and when in office introduced a legislative package which satisfied the wishes of all three partners. Pompey's eastern settlement was confirmed, and his veterans, together with large numbers of destitute families, were settled on the land by laws which resembled the abortive measure of 63. Another enactment provided for a reduction of the contract price for the taxes of Asia that had been agreed by the *publicani* in 61. The concession favored Crassus, who was probably financially involved. Finally, Caesar rewarded himself with a special command in Gaul and Illyricum for five years. During the year the triumvirate was strengthened by Pompey's marriage to Caesar's daughter, Julia; the triumvirs also secured the election of friendly consuls for the following year.

In 58 Caesar left for his province, where he embarked on the conquest of continental Gaul. In Rome the year 58 was dominated by the activities of the tribune P. Clodius (a member of the proud Claudian *gens,* who had had himself adopted into a plebeian family so that he could stand for the tribunate). Clodius built up a following among the urban *plebs,* in whose interest he passed several enactments, beginning with a radical corn law. The subsidized grain ration, introduced by C. Gracchus and subsequently abolished by Sulla, had been reinstated in a limited form in 73 and extended by Cato in 62. Now Clodius abolished the charge and transformed it into a regular dole. He legalized the formation of *collegia* (guilds or associations), which enabled him to mobilize the urban proletariat for political purposes. Other laws led to the exile of Cicero (for the murder of the Catilinarians) and the removal of Cato, who was sent on a mission to annex Cyprus. At first Clodius worked as an ally of the triumvirs, but he was in no sense their agent; towards the end of the year he launched a series of attacks on Pompey. In 57 Pompey enlisted the aid of another tribune, T. Annius Milo, who formed a rival band of ruffians and openly campaigned against Clodius' gangs on the streets. Clodius was thus held in check, and Pompey was able to arrange the recall of Cicero. In the same year (57) Pompey was given a special "command" for five years to organize the city's corn supply, a task which he undertook with characteristic efficiency, although shortages continued to occur from time to time.

In 56 Caesar summoned Crassus and Pompey to a meeting at Luca in Cisalpine Gaul, where their alliance was renewed. Pompey and Crassus became consuls in 55 and by a plebiscite received special commands for five years each. Crassus obtained Syria and the opportunity to lead a campaign against the Parthian empire. Pompey was awarded the Spanish provinces, which he decided to govern indirectly through legates (deputies appointed directly by himself), while he remained in Rome, continuing to administer the corn supply and able to watch over events in the city. Caesar's command in Gaul was prolonged for a second five-year term.

The renewed alliance soon began to show signs of strain. In 54 Pompey's wife, Julia, died, and the personal tie that linked him with Caesar was severed. A year later the triumvirate ceased to exist with Crassus' defeat and death at the battle of Carrhae (Harran), which ended his rash attempt to invade the Parthian empire. Increased tension between Pompey and Caesar was the inevitable result. Meanwhile violence and disorder prevailed at Rome, impeding the normal machinery of government; both 53 and 52 began without consuls.

Early in 52 Clodius and Milo met on the Appian Way and in the ensuing scrap Clodius was killed. The event provoked riots in which the senate-house was burned down. Finally the senate appointed Pompey sole consul, and order was eventually restored.

By this time Caesar's conquest of Gaul was almost complete, and his second five-year term was nearing its end. Fear of Caesar began to drive Pompey and the *optimates* closer together, as they tried to frustrate Caesar's aim of passing directly from his present command to a second consulship and thence (presumably) to a further long-term appointment. The senate sought instead to terminate his command, but its deliberations were vetoed by tribunes friendly to Caesar. Negotiations were prolonged but futile; it was clear that neither side was prepared to give way. Finally on 7 January 49 BC the senate passed the "Ultimate Decree," instructing the magistrates to see that the Republic suffered no harm. The Caesarian tribunes (one of whom was Mark Antony) fled from the city, and three days later Caesar crossed the Rubicon with his army and invaded Italy.

With the beginning of the Civil Wars the Republic, defined as the rule of magistrates, senate and people of Rome, was already dead. Since 60 BC control of affairs had passed from the oligarchy to the dynasts, who were supported by their private armies and vast *clientelae*, and were constitutionally provided for by special commands which freed them from the restrictions of the system of annual collegiate magistracies. The oligarchy that Sulla restored had shown itself to be irresponsible, corrupt, self-seeking and indifferent, and no longer commanded the respect or loyalty of any significant group in society. The propertied classes of Italy had no confidence in a regime which excluded their leading men from senior positions and was unable to guarantee order and stability; the poor happily surrendered their spurious freedoms and ineffectual political rights in favor of individual leaders who depended on them for support and who consequently took care to supply their material needs. The position of Pompey in the mid-50s, with his control of the corn supply, his sole consulship in 52 and his *imperium* in Spain (which in 52 was renewed for a further five years), already foreshadowed that of the emperors.

Portrait of a Gaul (once wrongly thought to be Vercingetorix) on a coin of 48 BC celebrating Caesar's victories.

The triumph of Caesar

Caesar's conquest of Gaul was a remarkable achievement. Its details are outlined in the seven books *On the Gallic War*, which Caesar published probably in 51 or 50 BC (an eighth book, on the events of 51–50, was published later by A. Hirtius). The work was no doubt intended to justify its author's actions and to increase his prestige in Rome, but it remains a masterly account of the progress of events. The campaign itself began in 58 when Caesar attacked the Helvetii, who, he thought, represented a danger to the Roman province. During the first three years he overran most of Gaul by proceeding in a roughly anticlockwise direction and subduing the tribes in Franche Comté and Alsace (58), in Belgium and

The rise of Julius Caesar: the events of the Gallic and civil wars (58–45 BC).

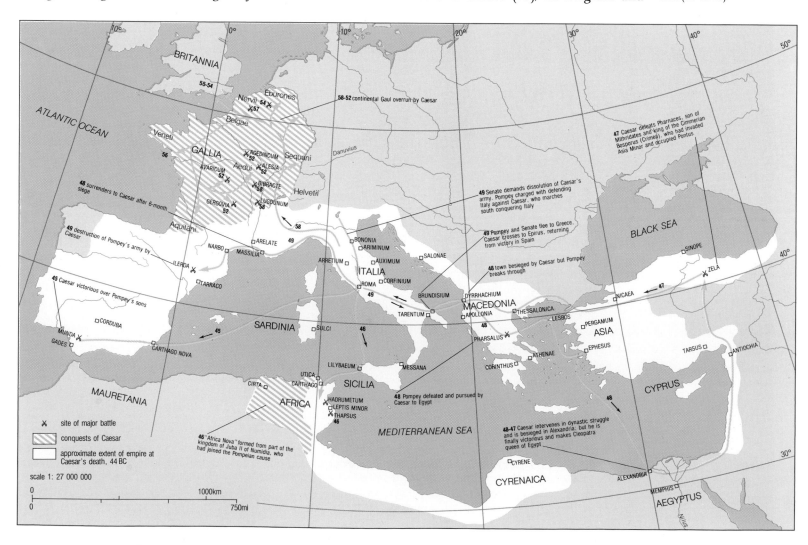

Coin issued in 43/2 BC by the liberators to celebrate the murder of Julius Caesar. It shows two daggers and a *pileus* (a kind of felt cap worn by freed slaves), and bears the legend *EID. MART.* ("the Ides of March").

Coin issued by Mark Antony in 39 BC. Antony's portrait on the obverse is matched on the reverse by that of Octavia, sister of Octavian, whom Antony married in 40 BC following the reconciliation of the two dynasts at Brundisium. The breakdown of the marriage in 36 led to a renewed breach between Antony and Octavian, and hastened the onset of civil war.

Normandy (57), and in Brittany and along the Atlantic seaboard (56). In 55 and 54 he ventured across the Rhine and also made two expeditions to southern England. On his return he was faced with a revolt among the Belgae which was put down after fierce fighting in 53. In 52 a serious revolt broke out in central Gaul under Vercingetorix, who was proclaimed supreme commander of the Gauls at Bibracte (near Autun); but later in the year Caesar managed to trap Vercingetorix in the fortress of Alesia in Burgundy, which the Romans captured after a month-long siege. In 51 the last remnants of Gallic resistance were dealt with, and Caesar was able to turn his attention to the political crisis. The Gauls were left for the time being as client states, subject to an annual tribute which amounted to ten million denarii.

When Caesar invaded Italy at the beginning of 49, Pompey chose not to face him, but instead staged a skillful withdrawal across the Adriatic and began to mobilize his forces in the Balkans. Thus Italy fell without a blow to Caesar, who entered Rome and seized the contents of the treasury. Then he made a rapid dash to Spain, where he defeated the Pompeian forces, before returning to Italy where he was appointed dictator. At the end of 49 he left for the east and the final showdown with Pompey. The decisive battle occurred in the summer of 48 at Pharsalus in northern Greece, where Caesar was victorious. Pompey fled to Egypt, where he was treacherously murdered. Caesar arrived shortly afterwards, to be greeted with the news of his rival's death. At Alexandria he intervened in a dynastic struggle, taking the side of Cleopatra who became his mistress. Despite fierce opposition he eventually succeeded in installing Cleopatra and her brother Ptolemy XIV on the throne of Egypt. Returning to Rome by way of Asia Minor, where he put down a revolt led by Pharnaces, a son of Mithridates, Caesar pardoned those (such as Cicero) who had joined Pompey, and settled affairs in the city. He then (late 47) left for Africa, where the Pompeians had established a base after defeating Caesar's lieutenants in 49. Caesar defeated the republicans at Thapsus and overran the province of Africa. The surviving Pompeians, including Pompey's two sons, escaped to Spain, but Cato, in a theatrical scene, committed suicide at Utica in order to deny Caesar the chance of pardoning him. On his return to Rome in 46 Caesar celebrated a magnificent triumph, but before the end of the year he was called away to Spain where Pompey's sons had raised an army. The republican cause finally came to grief on the field of Munda in 45; young Gnaeus Pompey was killed, but his brother Sextus lived to fight again. Caesar headed back to Rome, arriving early in October. Less than six months later he was assassinated.

During his brief sojourns in Rome Caesar launched a vast program of political, social and administrative reform, of which only a very brief summary can be given here. Urgent action was required to deal with poverty and debt. As early as 49 Caesar reduced debts by up to 25 per cent and decreed that for purposes of repayment property should be valued at prewar levels. A year's remission of rents was granted in 48, and probably again in 47. Large numbers of poor citizens and discharged veterans were to be settled on allotments and in colonies in Italy and especially in the provinces. Caesar's soldiers each received 5000 denarii at his triumph in 46, and the regular annual pay for legionary soldiers was raised from 120 to 225 denarii. Other measures regulated the corn dole, controlled the traffic in the city, banned the *collegia* (an exception was made for Jewish synagogues) and reformed the laws of extortion, treason and bribery. The system of contracting out the collection of direct taxes in Asia and other provinces was ended. The provinces were governed by legates appointed directly by Caesar himself. In 49 he granted Roman citizenship to all the inhabitants of Cisalpine Gaul (who had been excluded from the settlement after the Social War); he also enfranchised provincial communities, such as Gades in Spain, and he gave Latin rights to towns in southern Gaul and Sicily. He rewarded many of his supporters by admitting them to the senate, whose members rapidly increased to 900. He embarked on a series of grandiose building projects, the most impressive of which was a completely new Forum, centered around a temple of Venus Genetrix, the ancestress of the Julian house (the work on this project was begun in 54 and completed in 46). Western civilization owes to Julius Caesar the calendar of $365\frac{1}{4}$ days, which was introduced on 1 January 45 BC.

During his last years Caesar ruled as a king in all but name. In 46 he was made dictator for 10 years; in 44 he received the office in perpetuity. He was also consul in 48 and continuously from 46. Unprecedented and extravagant honors were heaped upon him by the senate. He was named "Superintendent of Manners" and "Father of the Fatherland"; the month in which he was born was renamed "Julius" (i.e. July). Although he eschewed the title *rex*, and rejected the "kingly crown" which Antony offered him at the Lupercalia in 44, he nonetheless adopted many of the trappings associated with kingship (such as a purple toga), had his statue placed among those of the old kings on the Capitol and issued coins bearing his portrait. He also began to institute cult honors for himself.

Caesar made no secret of his contempt for the Republic and its constitutional forms. He effectively nominated the magistrates, held the consular "elections" for several years in advance, summoned the senate merely in order to give notice of his decisions and silenced tribunes who attempted to oppose him. When a consul died on the last day of 45 BC, Caesar had another man elected for the remaining few hours. Such antics caused grave offense to men like Cicero who valued the traditions of the state. The murder of Caesar on the Ides of March 44 by a group of noble senators was a cruel and senseless act which unleashed a civil war even worse than the one that had just ended. But the deed was also very understandable. Caesar had it coming to him, and he probably knew it.

Antony and the new Caesar

Caesar's death was followed first by confusion and bewilderment, and then by a desperate struggle for power. The leading figures among Caesar's supporters were the surviving consul, Mark Antony, and the master of the horse, M. Aemilius Lepidus. Antony had the support of the army in Italy, which had been assembling for Caesar's projected Parthian expedition; he also won over the urban masses by

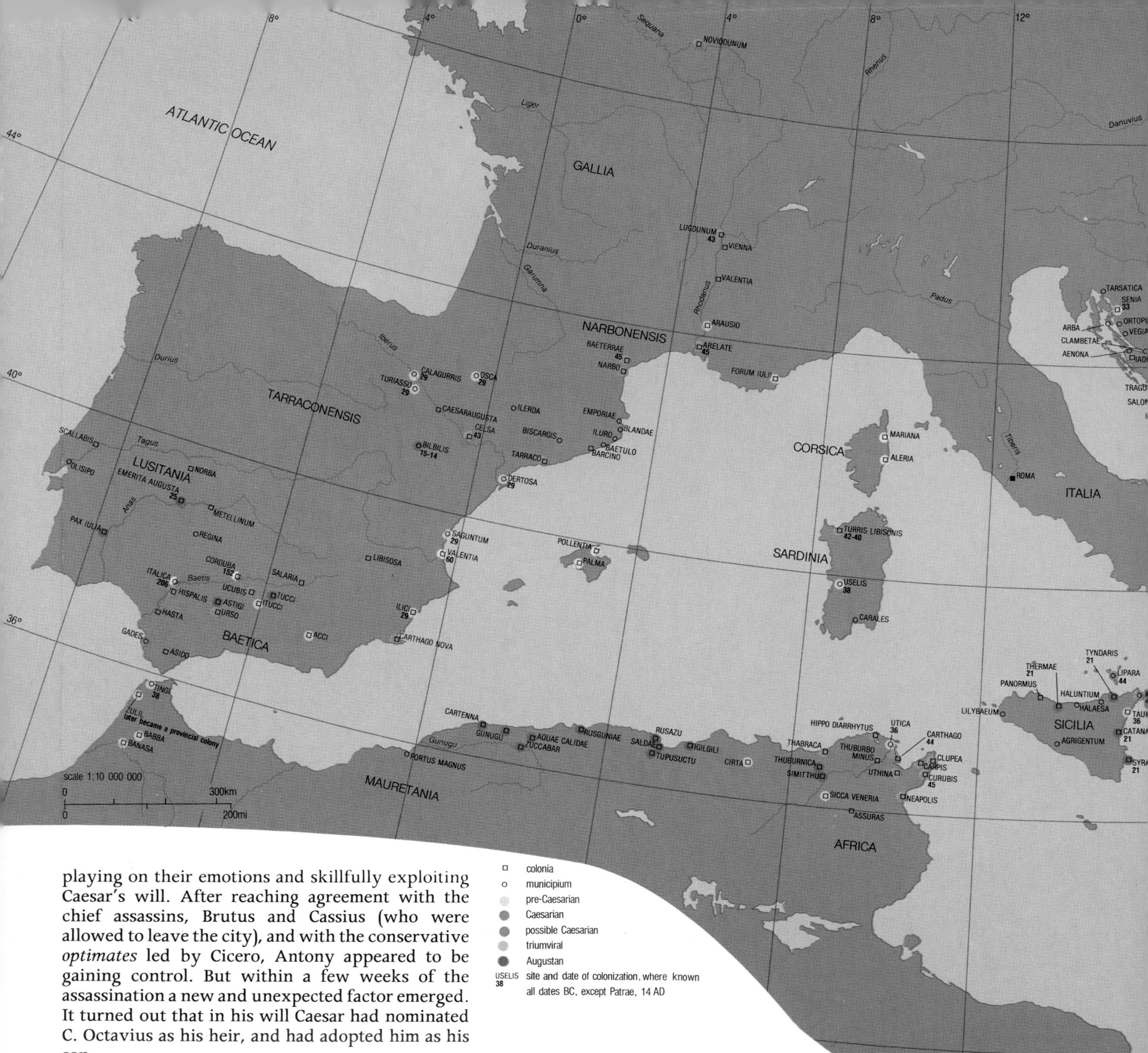

playing on their emotions and skillfully exploiting Caesar's will. After reaching agreement with the chief assassins, Brutus and Cassius (who were allowed to leave the city), and with the conservative *optimates* led by Cicero, Antony appeared to be gaining control. But within a few weeks of the assassination a new and unexpected factor emerged. It turned out that in his will Caesar had nominated C. Octavius as his heir, and had adopted him as his son.

Octavius was the grandson of Julius Caesar's sister; on his father's side he belonged to an obscure municipal family from Velitrae. In 44 Octavius was 19 years old, and was studying in Greece when he heard the news of the dictator's murder. He at once decided to return to Italy to claim his inheritance, ignoring his parents' advice to stay out of trouble. In Rome he was coolly received by Antony, who did not welcome his intrusion; this forced him into the arms of the *optimates*, who thought that they could use him in their struggle against Antony. Cicero wrote: "the boy is to be praised, honored, and kicked upstairs."

In 43 Antony went north to a provincial command in Gaul. In Rome Cicero launched a major attack on him (the so-called *Philippics*) and persuaded the senate to send an army against him under the consuls, together with Octavius. In two battles near Mutina Antony was defeated, but the consuls were killed; whereupon Octavius took over the army and demanded the consulship for himself. The senate declared Antony a public enemy but refused to accede to Octavius' demands; he therefore marched on Rome at the head of the army and obtained the consulship by force. At the same time he had his adoption ratified by the people, and formally became C. Julius Caesar Octavianus. Meanwhile other leading members of Caesar's party, such as Lepidus, aligned themselves with Antony. On his side Octavian had the support of the armies in Italy and of the *plebs*, who rallied to him as Caesar's heir.

Late in the year the Caesarian leaders decided to settle their differences and to present a united front against the senate and the liberators. Antony,

Emigration of Roman citizens to the provinces. The main social and economic problems that brought down the Republic were ultimately resolved by the enforced emigration of large numbers of free-born Italians to the provinces. Before Caesar's time overseas colonies (such as Narbo Martius, c. 118 BC) were few and controversial. Caesar however embarked on a policy of large-scale colonization in the provinces, and settled over 80 000 citizens and their families in over 30 colonies. These people included proletarians from the city as well as veterans. Caesar also granted Roman citizenship

to many native communities, especially in the western provinces, which thus acquired the status of *municipia*. Caesar's policy was carried out on an even greater scale by Augustus, who founded around 75 provincial colonies. In the *Res Gestae* he writes: "I founded colonies of soldiers in Africa, Sicily, Macedonia, both Spanish provinces, Achaea, Asia, Syria, Gallia Narbonensis and Pisidia."

Octavian and Lepidus were appointed as a triumvirate (a board of three for the organization of the state), whereupon they divided the empire among themselves, and purged their opponents by reviving Sulla's device of proscriptions. According to some sources as many as 300 senators (including Cicero) and 2000 knights met their deaths in the reign of terror that followed.

In 42 Octavian and Antony marched against Brutus and Cassius, who controlled the eastern provinces, and defeated them at Philippi. After the victory a new distribution of the empire occurred. Octavian received Italy and most of the western provinces, and the command against Sextus Pompey, who had occupied Sicily and had become a focus for resistance, while Antony took over the command against the Parthians in the east. Lepidus, "a slight unmeritable man," was fobbed off with Africa. In Italy Octavian attempted to settle the veterans of Philippi on land confiscated from certain specified towns. In this he was actively resisted by one of the consuls, Antony's brother Lucius, who eventually took up arms on behalf of the disgruntled Italians. After some months of fighting L. Antonius was besieged in Perusia (Perugia), which fell early in 40 BC; he himself was spared, but his followers were killed. Mark Antony himself arrived at Brundisium later in the year, but a full-scale conflict was averted when the soldiers refused to fight and forced the two leaders to settle their differences. The triumvirate was re-established, and the division between east and west confirmed.

The following year Antony led a campaign against the Parthians, which ended in failure in 36, although he did manage to overrun Armenia in 34. After that he stayed in Alexandria with Cleopatra, with whom he had become increasingly infatuated. Meanwhile Octavian managed to finish off Sextus Pompey (36), and conducted a successful campaign in Illyricum (35–33). From 33 onwards he consolidated his position in Italy, and initiated a propaganda war against Antony, making capital out of his affair with Cleopatra and exploiting Roman prejudice against Orientals. In 32 the towns of Italy took a personal oath of allegiance to Octavian and demanded his leadership in a national crusade against Antony and Cleopatra. The campaign itself, which shortly followed, ended in total victory at Actium in 31 BC; Antony and Cleopatra escaped to Alexandria, where they committed suicide.

The principate of Augustus

The victory of Actium left Octavian in complete control of the Empire. After a number of experiments in the next few years he succeeded in regularizing his position within the constitution. He avoided the overt absolutism of Caesar and was able to rule in the guise of a constitutional *princeps* ("first citizen"). He restored peace and prosperity and reigned unchallenged for 45 years until his death in 14 AD, by which time he had secured the succession of one of his own family and the continuation of a monarchical regime that was to last for centuries.

With the return of peace Octavian set about the enormous task of reconstructing a society shattered by 20 years of civil war. From the start he made it clear that he intended to restore the traditional form of the constitution. The difficulty was his own position of arbitrary authority, which was backed by overwhelming force but probably had no legal warrant. In January 27 BC Octavian announced that he was handing over the state to the senate and people. It was then agreed that he should be appointed to a special command for 10 years, with a "province" which included Spain, Gaul, Syria and Cilicia, areas which contained the bulk of the army and which he would govern through legates. Thus his position was legalized by a grant of *imperium* that had clear republican precedents (for example, Pompey in 55). He also continued to hold the consulship, and received various honors, including the title Augustus. In 23 a plot against his life was discovered; he decided to resign the consulship, no doubt because his perpetual tenure of the office was causing offense and was restricting the consulships available to other nobles. But he continued to govern his large province as proconsul, and in addition his *imperium* was made "greater" than that of other proconsuls. In the same year (23 BC) he received the power of the tribunes for life. In 19 BC he was granted the insignia (and perhaps also the full powers) of the consuls; evidently the fact that he was no longer seen to be holding the supreme office had caused disquiet among the people, who urged him to become perpetual consul or dictator.

In such matters he was very restrained, and made a show of refusing extravagant honors. For example in the *Res Gestae* (his account of his own achievements which was published after his death) he writes that on three occasions "the senate and people of Rome agreed that I should be appointed supervisor of laws and morals without a colleague and with supreme power, but I would not accept any office inconsistent with the custom of our ancestors." Augustus claimed that he had no more legal power than the other magistrates, but that he was preeminent in *auctoritas*; what he presumably meant was that his personal authority enabled him to assert his will without reference to his legal powers. Elections continued to take place, but were gradually reduced to a formality; by the end of his reign Augustus was in practice appointing most of the chief magistrates. Serious political opposition to the emperor was out of the question. By virtue of his tribunician power he had an absolute right of veto, but as far as we know he never needed to exercise it. *Auctoritas* was enough.

Silver denarius of c. 18 BC. The reverse type, two laurel branches and the legend "Caesar Augustus," commemorates the honors conferred on the emperor in 27 BC, when the senate decreed that the doorposts of his house should be decorated with laurel.

As the principate was established, the *Res Publica* was restored. The notion of a restored republic was not meant to conceal the domination of Augustus, but rather to signify the return of normal conditions after the chaos of the preceding 20 years, and the revived working of the machinery of government. Augustus reduced the size of the senate by removing "unworthy" members, and he restored the regular sequence of offices. Unlike Julius Caesar he treated the senate and its traditions with great respect. Provincial governors and other administrators were chosen from its ranks. The so-called "public" provinces were assigned by lot to proconsuls who governed for a year, while the "imperial" provinces (those within the emperor's *provincia*) were governed by legates appointed directly by Augustus, usually for periods of several years. The proconsuls and legates were normally either ex-praetors or (in the more important or prestigious provinces) ex-consuls. Senators were also used to command individual legions, and for a range of other administrative posts in Rome and Italy, for example the praetorian curators of the roads and prefects of the treasury, and the consular curators (of public works, aqueducts etc.). During the Empire the traditional magistracies became honorific titles with no serious duties attached to them; their function was to confer status on members of the senate and to qualify them for important military and administrative posts in the emperor's gift. The imperial senate was less important as a deliberative assembly than as a body of administrators.

For a number of other administrative tasks Augustus employed men of the equestrian order, first of all as his personal agents (procurators), and then increasingly as officials in his own provinces, for example as financial administrators and governors of small provincial districts, such as the Alps. Equestrians were also appointed to a range of very senior military and administrative posts which required men of proven ability whose loyalty was beyond question. Such posts were those of Prefect of the Praetorian Guard (the elite corps of soldiers who formed the emperor's official escort and garrisoned Italy), the Prefect of the Corn Supply (*annona*) and the Prefect of Egypt (the Empire's

The government of the Roman Empire. Of the division of the Empire the geographer Strabo (c. 63 BC–c. 21 AD) writes as follows: "Augustus divided the whole of his empire into two parts, and assigned one portion to himself and the other to the Roman people ... and he divided each of the two portions into several provinces, of which some are called 'imperial provinces' and the others 'public provinces.' To the imperial provinces Caesar sends legates and procurators, ... whereas to the public provinces the people sends praetors or consuls." The governors of the public provinces (actually called "proconsuls") were senior senators, and were chosen by lot to serve for one year; the legates who governed the imperial provinces were also high-ranking senators, but were directly appointed by the emperor and served until they were recalled. The legates included all the senior army commanders, since the imperial provinces contained nearly all the legions. The most significant exception to the pattern is Egypt, which was governed by an equestrian prefect, appointed by the emperor.

richest province and an exception in that it was not governed by a senator).

The class to whom the restored republic most appealed, and who benefited most by it, was the propertied class of Roman citizens who had formerly been excluded from public life under the republican oligarchy, the people, that is, who are normally defined as *equites*. The majority of these well-to-do Roman citizens now came not from Rome but from the towns and cities of Italy. Augustus himself belonged to a municipal family, and it was among the Italian gentry that he found his strongest support. His leading henchmen were typical examples: his schoolfriend M. Vipsanius Agrippa, an Italian of uncertain origin; C. Maecenas, an Etruscan from Arretium; T. Statilius Taurus from Lucania in south Italy. New families of Italian origin rose to prominence under Augustus in the senate and in the range of public appointments created for men of equestrian rank. M. Salvius Otho, the son of an equestrian, belonged to an old Etruscan family and entered the senate under Augustus; his son became emperor in 69. Similarly Vitellius, another of the emperors of 69, was descended from P. Vitellius of Nuceria in Campania, who was an equestrian procurator of Augustus.

The interests and aspirations of the Italian middle class were fulfilled by a national program of moral and spiritual regeneration. Augustus presented himself as a defender of the Roman tradition, and set out to restore the old state religion, the moral standards of family life and the legalistic forms of republican government. He revived ancient religious festivals and cult practices that had fallen into disuse, filled vacancies in the archaic priesthoods and repaired the temples and sacred buildings in the city of Rome. In 18 and 17 BC he introduced laws against sexual offenses; divorce was curbed and adultery made a public crime. He also imposed penalties on unmarried persons and rewarded couples who produced children. These provisions were modified by a consular law of 9 AD; wags did not fail to notice that the consuls who passed the law were both bachelors. A further source of embarrassment was the fact that the emperor's only daughter, Julia, was notorious for sexual conduct so scandalous that in 2 BC she was banished to an island. It is unlikely that the marriage laws were

designed to increase the birth rate; the legislation should rather be seen as an attempt to regulate the life-style of the upper classes, whose decadence and pleasure-seeking were notorious in the late Republic. The old idea that it was the duty of all Roman citizens to marry and have children thus became official policy. Augustus also introduced sumptuary laws and restricted excessive and indiscriminate manumissions of slaves.

Writers and artists promoted the ideals of the regime, and were actively encouraged by the emperor's friend Maecenas. The poets in his circle included Propertius, who wrote mostly love poems, but also praised Augustus, and Horace, whose poems are full of favorable references to the emperor and his policies. In 17 BC Horace composed the *Secular Hymn* for the great festival held in that year to celebrate the dawning of a new age (*saeculum*). The Hymn outlines the achievements of Augustus and welcomes the return of ancient virtues. The greatest of the Augustan poets was Virgil, whose works include pastoral poems (*Eclogues*), a didactic poem on farming (*Georgics*), and the *Aeneid*, an epic on the legend of Aeneas, the ancestor of the Julian *gens* and the legendary hero of the Roman tradition; the poem expounds the greatness of Rome and foreshadows the achievements of Augustus. These men were undoubtedly sincere in their praise of the new order. On the other hand the erotic poet Ovid earned the emperor's displeasure (especially with his poem on the *Art of Love*), and was banished from Rome in 8 AD. One of the most important literary figures of the age was the historian Livy, whose magnificent account of the story of Rome occupied 142 books. The narrative contained examples of great men and noble deeds, and brought out the sobering lessons of moral decline. The visual arts also flourished under Augustus, as painters, sculptors and architects were commissioned to beautify the city and give concrete expression to the ideals of the new age. Important examples of "official" art are the Altar of Peace and the statue of Augustus from Prima Porta, which are classical pieces of stylistic and technical perfection, but which have been criticized for their lack of warmth and vitality.

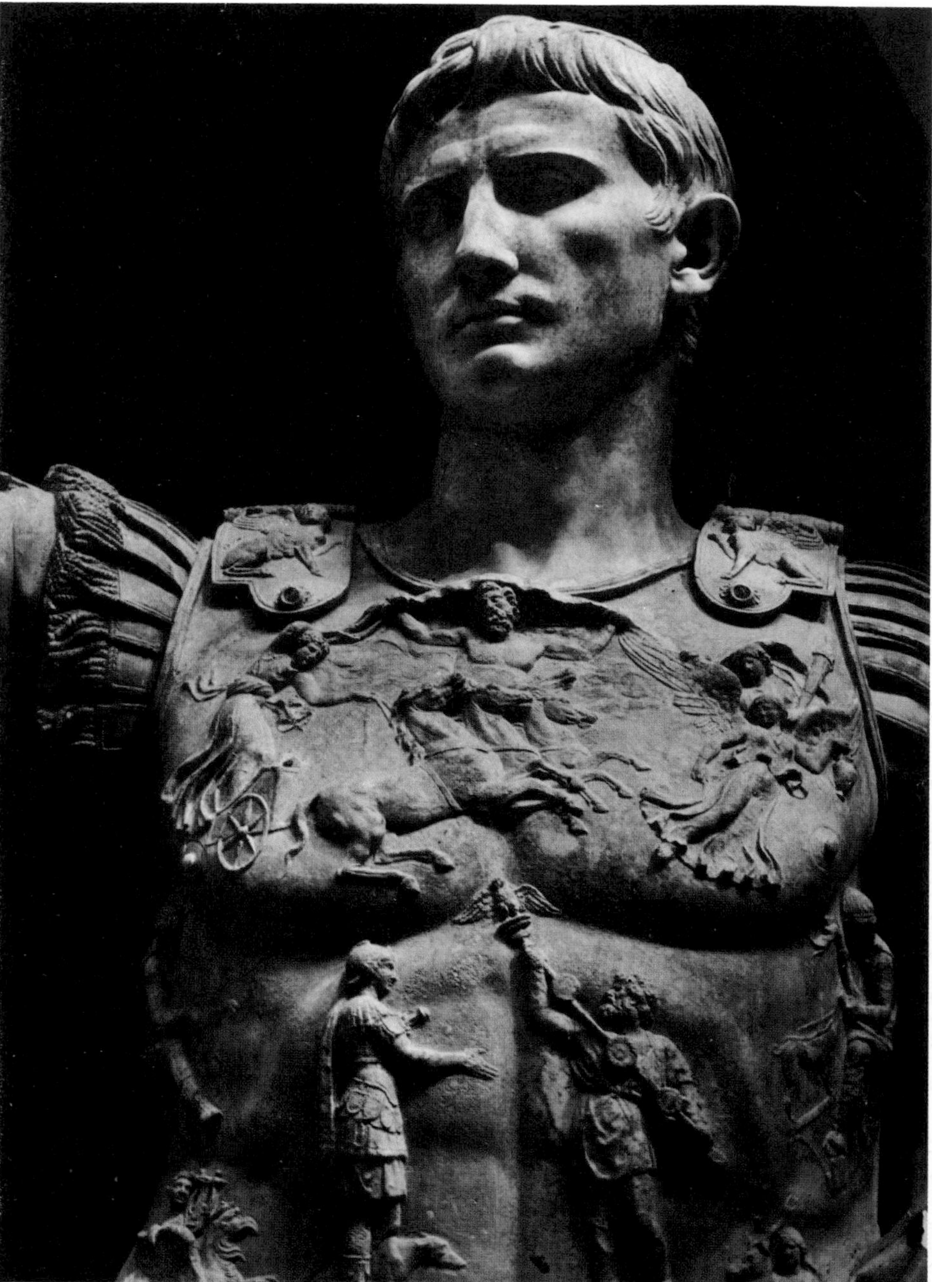

In Rome Augustus continued the work of Julius Caesar and carried out a vast program of public building. Temples, theaters, porticoes and triumphal arches were erected everywhere and justified the emperor's claim to have transformed Rome from a city of brick to one of marble. He constructed a new Forum (inaugurated in 2 BC), and developed the area of the Campus Martius; here the principal monuments were the Portico of Octavia, the Theater of Marcellus and his own Mausoleum. In the same district Agrippa constructed the Pantheon and the first of the great imperial baths. Agrippa also built two new aqueducts and supervised the city's water supply. At this time the population of the city was probably around one million persons, most of whom lived in appalling squalor. The great majority were housed in high-rise slum tenements which were poorly constructed and badly lit; they had no heating and were liable to collapse or catch fire at any moment. The living quarters of the poor were similar to lodging houses, with short-term tenancies, no security of tenure and exorbitant rents. The drainage system was rudimentary; the sewers (*cloacae*) ran beneath the streets, but only the houses of the rich were directly connected to them. Epidemics were frequent and destructive; excavations have unearthed mass graves containing thousands of corpses. There were no public hospitals or medical services. At night the streets were dark and dangerous; murder, housebreaking and mugging were frequent.

Augustus also followed Julius Caesar in taking responsibility for the city and its administration. He imposed a limit of 21 meters on the height of tenement blocks, and organized a fire brigade of 7000 *vigiles* ("watchmen") under an equestrian prefect. For administrative purposes the city was divided into 14 regions and 265 wards, which elected their own local officials. The task of policing the streets was given to a force of three "urban cohorts," under the command of the Prefect of the City, normally a senior ex-consul. Periodic flooding of the Tiber caused many deaths by drowning and undermined the foundations of the tenements; accordingly Augustus set up a conservancy board of senatorial "curators of the river banks." The corn supply was reorganized and eventually made the

Right The *Ara Pacis Augustae*. Of this great monument Augustus writes in the *Res Gestae*: "on my return from Spain and Gaul [13 BC] . . . the senate decreed that an altar of the Augustan Peace should be consecrated next to the Campus Martius in honor of my return, and ordered that the magistrates and priests and Vestal Virgins should perform an annual sacrifice there." The altar itself and the surrounding precinct are covered with reliefs illustrating aspects of the new age. The south frieze of the precinct wall shows a procession involving members of the imperial family, part of which is shown here. Identification of particular individuals is much disputed, but it is generally agreed that the dominant figure, who follows the attendants with his head covered, is Agrippa, accompanied by his young son Gaius Caesar. The other child in the picture is possibly Germanicus, standing between his parents Antonia Minor and Drusus.

Left Portrait of Augustus from Prima Porta (near Rome). There is much dispute about the meaning of the figures on the breastplate; but the central scene clearly represents the recovery of a Roman standard from a defeated barbarian. In the *Res Gestae* (see p. 74) Augustus writes: "By victories over enemies I recovered, in Spain and in Gaul, and from the Dalmatians, several standards lost by other commanders. I compelled the Parthians to restore to me the spoils and standards of three Roman armies, and to ask as suppliants the friendship of the Roman people."

Below The theater of Marcellus. The construction of the theater began under Julius Caesar, but it was completed by Augustus and dedicated to the memory of his nephew and designated successor Marcellus, who died in 23 BC.

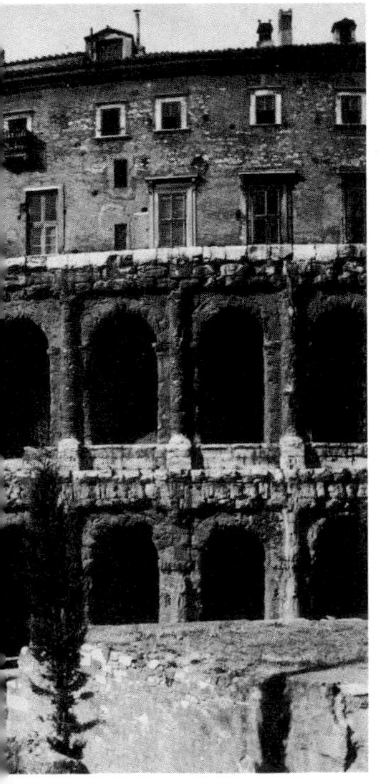

responsibility of a senior equestrian prefect. Free rations of corn were distributed to a group of registered male citizens, whose numbers were restricted to 200 000 in 2 BC. The *plebs* also received cash donations from time to time, and were kept entertained by games and shows. Their enthusiasm for the new regime was unbounded.

By the end of his reign Augustus had established strong and efficient government and had won the loyalty and respect of all classes at home and abroad. The provinces had been ruthlessly exploited under the Republic by governors and tax farmers who were not subject to any effective controls. The principate changed all that. The provincials were now offered peace, security, a focus for their loyalty and the prospect of strong government which could control its own officials and agents. Standards of provincial government were still far from ideal, but there is no reason to doubt that the new dispensation was universally welcomed in the provinces.

In 2 BC Augustus received the title *Pater Patriae* ("Father of the Fatherland"), a title which inevitably suggested the firm but kindly hand of a *paterfamilias* (above p. 19). The 19-year-old revolutionary leader who had seized power by force of arms was long forgotten. One of Augustus' greatest achievements was to neutralize the most potent forces of revolutionary change, and in particular the army. After Actium he drastically reduced the numbers of men under arms and settled discharged veterans in colonies in Italy and the provinces. The 28 legions (about 140 000 men) that were retained were stationed permanently on the frontiers together with a roughly equal number of auxiliaries (non-citizen troops, levied in the provinces). The army became a regular establishment, with a constant intake of new recruits, who served in the legions for a 20-year fixed term. On discharge they received grants of land or severance payments in cash. In 6 AD the system was institutionalized by the formation of a military treasury, which was funded in the first instance by a grant from the emperor himself, and subsequently replenished by the income from two new taxes levied on Roman citizens: a one per cent sales tax and a five per cent death duty. The new system took the army out of politics and made it loyal to the state and to the emperor, who remained its commander-in-chief and personally appointed its officers. The army maintained its allegiance to the heirs of Augustus, until the death of Nero in 68 when the civil wars were briefly renewed.

Augustus lived a simple, austere life; his character seems to have been somewhat cold and humorless. He was a good judge of character and was fortunate in his choice of friends and collaborators, most of whom remained faithful to him to the end. His family life was marked by tragedy and failure, although he retained the affection and trust of his third wife, Livia, throughout their 53 years of marriage. Although his health was generally poor, he lived to the age of 77; he died peacefully at Nola on 19 August 14 AD.

The Julio-Claudian dynasty, 14–68 AD

The accession of Tiberius was the first occasion on which the nature of the imperial office could be reviewed by a senate which, formally speaking, sanctioned its existence. The succession was from the beginning a matter of dynastic inheritance, cloaked in the legal forms provided by the senate. Augustus had first favored his nephew Marcellus, then his associate Marcus Agrippa, to whom he married his daughter Julia. When Agrippa also died (12 BC), Tiberius was induced reluctantly to take on Julia, divorcing his own wife to whom he was happily married, and it was the promotion of Julia's young sons by Agrippa, Gaius and Lucius, added to his dislike of Julia, which led to Tiberius' famed retirement in 6 BC to the island of Rhodes, where he devoted himself to leisure, and to the Greek culture which he loved. When Gaius and Lucius died, respectively in 2 and 4 AD, Tiberius, who had returned to Rome, was adopted by Augustus and in turn made to adopt Germanicus. On all these occasions, the senate was called upon to vote the legal powers, consisting of grants of *imperium* and the tribunician power, which secured the position of the chosen successors.

Tiberius, who lacked Augustus' ease of manner, was resentful at his treatment by Augustus and was known not to have been the first choice for the succession; he was also disliked for his proud aloofness and alleged capacity for dissimulation. The aspect of his principate for which he was most bitterly criticized was his conduct of the so-called law of *maiestas*. The republican *lex maiestatis* only very roughly corresponds to the modern concept of treason; it covered anything that might "diminish the majesty of the Roman people." Under the principate it was applied not only to rebellion and conspiracy but to disrespect for the emperor, and in some cases to libelous comments directed against senators. It could thus function as a very real curb on freedom of speech and the ability to criticize an emperor.

Accusations of *maiestas* were made in the senate, which by an assumed extension of its powers formed itself into a court of law and by a sort of quasi-judicial procedure conducted trials of those who were denounced. Tiberius himself attempted initially to restrain the use of *maiestas*. Only later, and especially after the fall of Tiberius' minister Sejanus in 31 AD, do we find the reign of terror for which his principate is notorious. Part of the difficulty was that Rome lacked a system of state prosecution, it being left to the initiative of the private citizen to bring an accusation. Further, the financial and, increasingly, the political inducements to prosecution were considerable. A successful accuser in a capital charge like *maiestas* received a share of the convicted man's estate and might hope to receive imperial favor for the elimination of opponents or critics of the regime. Yet it was the senate which conducted the "trials," often playing out its own enmities and feuds, and it was the senate, as much as the emperor, which deserves the discredit for the frequency of *maiestas* accusations under Tiberius.

Tiberius' death in 37 AD was greeted with jubilation both by the senate and by the people of Rome, for whom he had done little to make himself popular. Always remote in manner, for the last 10 years of his life he lived in seclusion on Capri in the company of intimate friends, mainly literary men and astrologers. The stories of his sexual habits on Capri may be set aside as the free invention of sources who knew that they could not be refuted, and that no one would wish to try.

The reign of Tiberius' successor Gaius (Caligula) began well but, apparently after an illness affecting the balance of his mind, degenerated into a capricious tyranny ended by his assassination in 41. Attempts have been made to view Gaius' principate in a rational light, to the extent of suggesting, for instance, that he proposed to transform the principate into a flamboyant Hellenistic monarchy of a type familiar from the east; such a project, if seriously entertained, would reflect flaws of political judgment scarcely more acceptable than insanity.

Claudius, unexpectedly made emperor after Gaius' murder, proved a serious and busy, even officious emperor who devoted himself to administrative improvements, public works – of which the most impressive was his development of the harbor at Ostia – and foreign conquest. His principate was criticized for the excessive power considered to be wielded by his personal freedmen, and for his encroachment on properly senatorial or "public" areas of activity, particularly judicial. The explanation for the prominence of freedmen may be that Claudius became emperor without possessing any sort of power base in senatorial or palace circles. At the moment of his proclamation by the Praetorian Guard, the senate was actually debating a restoration of the Republic, and viewed his intrusion with great resentment.

The businesslike and humane virtues of Claudius failed in popular estimation to outweigh his personal lack of dignity and the humiliating chaos of his private life. His second wife, Messalina, was executed after a conspiracy with a senator called Silius to replace Claudius; to the aftermath of this affair may be assigned many of the executions of senators and *equites* mentioned by contemporary sources. Claudius' third wife, his niece Agrippina, devoted herself to the advancement of her son by a previous marriage, Nero.

Nero's succession in 54 (Claudius having died, allegedly poisoned by a mushroom) was accompanied by promises to restore the Augustan principle of the division of powers between emperor and senate. For some time, especially during the ascendancy of his tutor, the Stoic philosopher Seneca, these promises were observed, but this was achieved largely by diverting Nero, unwisely as it turned out, to frivolous tastes. After Nero's vengeful murder of his mother in 59, the reign developed into an unhappy though colorful tyranny in which Nero indulged his passions for music and charioteering, and those senators and philosophers who opposed him were hounded to death. Through lavish expenditure, he retained his popularity with the people of Rome. The conclusion of peace with Parthia was commemorated by fantastic celebrations, during which the Armenian king Tiridates received his crown in person from the emperor. In 66 Nero undertook a successful tour of Greece, returning to Rome with more than 1600 crowns from theatrical and athletic victories. But his position was deteriorating. After the great fire of Rome in 64, he had ransacked Greece for works of art to embellish the restored city, and it was widely believed that Nero himself had some part in the burning of Rome in order to build himself a grandiose new capital in its ruins. Choosing the adherents of an unpopular new sect, the Christians, as plausible incendiaries (they believed in the imminent end of the world through fire), Nero found that the terrible punishments which he imposed, of death by burning in the arena, won them sympathy and more unpopularity for himself.

Throughout the Julio-Claudian period there was no real opposition to the institution of the principate as such, and no more than fleeting possibilities of a restoration of republican government. Stoic philosophy, of which the best-known proponent apart from Seneca was the senator Thrasea Paetus, encouraged participation in public life under the rule of a monarch. *Libertas*, the political ideal of this group, had evolved under the Empire from its republican sense of freedom from monarchical rule into the rights of free speech and criticism permitted under such rule. Involvement in

Claudius, found hiding in the palace after Caligula's murder in 41 AD, was taken to the praetorian barracks and proclaimed emperor. In the coin illustrated (*below*), one of several issues commemorating the episode, Claudius and a praetorian standard bearer clasp hands, with the legend "received by the praetorians."

The young Nero was in the early years of his reign guided by advisers including Seneca, the praetorian prefect Burrus, and by his mother Agrippina. The early coin issue (*below*) is remarkable for its explicit recognition of the position of Agrippina.

Right: The distribution of legions in the provinces. The table illustrates the location of Roman legions in the provinces at three different dates – 24, 74 and 150 AD. These dates have been chosen as representing periods of relative peace and stability. No account is taken of the temporary movement of legions at times of crisis, such as the civil wars of 68–69, or of short-term variations which distort the general pattern, for example the concentration of seven legions in Syria during the Jewish revolt of the 60s, and the build-up on the Danube frontier during the wars of 86–112. But the table nevertheless makes it clear that there was a long-term shift in the balance of forces between the western and eastern halves of the Empire, as the armies in Spain and Germany were reduced, and those in the Balkans and the east were increased. (The information for this table was kindly supplied by J. C. Mann and Margaret Roxan.)

Distribution of Legions in the Provinces

Provinces	24AD	74 AD	150 AD
AFRICA	III Augusta	III Augusta	III Augusta
SPAIN	IV Macedonica VI Victrix X Gemina	VII Gemina	VII Gemina
BRITAIN	—	II Augusta II Adiutrix IX Hispana XX Valeria Victrix	II Augusta VI Victrix XX Valeria Victrix
GERMANIA INFERIOR	I Germana V Alaudae XX Valeria Victrix XXI Rapax	VI Victrix X Gemina XXI Rapax XXII Primigenia	I Minervia XXX Ulpia
GERMANIA SUPERIOR	II Augusta XII Gemina XIV Gemina XVI	I Adiutrix VIII Augusta XI Claudia Pia Fidelis XIV Gemina	VIII Augusta XXII Primigenia
PANNONIA	VIII Augusta IX Hispana XV Apollinaris	XIII Gemina XV Apollinaris	Superior: I Adiutrix X Gemina Inferior: XIV Gemina II Adiutrix
DALMATIA	VII XI	IV Flavia	XIII Gemina
MOESIA	IV Scythica V Macedonica	I Italica V Alaudae V Macedonica VII Claudia Pia Fidelis	Superior: IV Flavia VII Claudia Pia Fidelis Inferior: I Italica V Macedonica XI Claudia Pia Fidelis
CAPPADOCIA	—	XII Fulminata XVI Flavia	XII Fulminata XV Apollinaris
SYRIA	III Gallica VI Ferrata X Fretensis XII Fulminata	III Gallica IV Scythica	III Gallica IV Scythica XVI Flavia
JUDAEA	—	X Fretensis	VI Ferrata X Fretensis
EGYPT	III Cyrenaica XXII Deiotariana	III Cyrenaica XXII Deiotariana	II Traiana
ARABIA	—	—	III Cyrenaica

Legions	24AD	74AD	150AD
I Adiutrix	(raised c. 68)	Germania Superior	Pannonia Superior
I Germana	Germania Inferior	(disappears c. 70)	
I Italica	(raised c. 66)	Moesia	Moesia Inferior
I Minervia		(raised c. 83)	Germania Inferior
II Adiutrix	(raised c. 70)	Britain	Pannonia Inferior
II Augusta	Germania Superior	Britain	Britain
II Traiana		(raised c. 104)	Egypt
III Augusta	Africa	Africa	Africa
III Cyrenaica	Egypt	Egypt	Arabia
III Gallica	Syria	Syria	Syria
IV Flavia	(raised c. 70)	Dalmatia	Moesia Superior
IV Macedonica	Spain	(disappears c. 70)	
IV Scythica	Moesia	Syria	Syria
V Alaudae	Germania Inferior	Moesia	(disappears c. 86)
V Macedonica	Moesia	Moesia	Moesia Inferior
VI Ferrata	Syria	Syria	Judaea
VI Victrix	Spain	Germania Inferior	Britain
VII	Dalmatia		
VII Claudia Pia Fidelis		Moesia	Moesia Superior
VII Gemina	(raised c. 68)	Spain	Spain
VIII Augusta	Pannonia	Germania Superior	Germania Superior
IX Hispana	Pannonia	Britain	(disappears c. 132?)
X Fretensis	Syria	Judaea	Judaea
X Gemina	Spain	Germania Inferior	Pannonia Superior
XI	Dalmatia		
XI Claudia Pia Fidelis		Germania Superior	Moesia Inferior
XII Fulminata	Syria	Cappadocia	Cappadocia
XIII Gemina	Germania Superior	Pannonia	Dalmatia
XIV Gemina	Germania Superior	Germania Superior	Pannonia Superior
XV Apollinaris	Pannonia	Pannonia	Cappadocia
XVI	Germania Superior	(disappears c. 70)	
XVI Flavia	(raised c. 70)	Cappadocia	Syria
XX Valeria Victrix	Germania Inferior	Britain	Britain
XXI Rapax	Germania Inferior	Germania Inferior	(disappears c. 92)
XXII Deiotariana	Egypt	Egypt	(disappears c. 125)
XXII Primigenia	(raised c. 40)	Germania Inferior	Germania Superior
XXX Ulpia		(raised c. 104)	Germania Inferior

political life became impermissible when a reign like Nero's declined into cruelty and tyranny, for it was impossible for a philosopher to serve such a tyrant without losing his fundamental integrity as a moral being. At this point it was his duty to withdraw from public life – a decision which, as in the case of Paetus, was tantamount to a declaration of dissent. His conspicuous absence from the senate was an important aspect of the denunciation which, in 66, led to his suicide. The death of Paetus closely followed the suicides of Seneca himself and his nephew, the poet Lucan. They had been suspected, with many others, of involvement in a plot to kill Nero and replace him with an obscure senator called Piso. This conspiracy, ruthlessly suppressed in 65, ushered in the decline of the last years of Nero and the end of the Julio-Claudian line.

In the spring of 68 a Gallic senator called Julius Vindex, who was then governing the province of Gallia Lugdunensis, circulated provincial commanders in an attempt to get them to revolt. His appeal was successful only with Galba, the elderly governor of Tarraconensian Spain, who allowed himself to be proclaimed emperor with the support of Vindex and the small garrison of Spain, to which he added a second legion, raised by himself. Vindex was suppressed near Vesontio (Besançon) by the governor of Upper Germany, Verginius Rufus, who was himself proclaimed emperor by his army but refused to accept. The most likely interpretation of Verginius Rufus' somewhat ambiguous conduct is that he was supporting Nero in a situation in which he did not know what was happening elsewhere. After Nero's suicide (9 June 68), Rufus gave his support to Galba, but was replaced as governor.

Vitellius, sent out by Galba as governor of Lower Germany, was proclaimed there at the beginning of 69. In the following month Otho, whom Galba had passed over for the succession, was put up at Rome by the Praetorian Guard, and Galba killed. His policies, however necessary, had been too strict and parsimonious to compensate for the unattractiveness of his character. After losing a preliminary skirmish to the advancing forces of Vitellius, Otho committed suicide (19 April), without waiting for the arrival in Italy of the Illyrian legions which might have saved him. Vitellius, however, soon found himself facing the carefully organized threat of Vespasian, who was proclaimed by the armies of the east at the beginning of July. Vespasian himself went to Alexandria, from where he controlled the corn supply to Rome, and won the west by a massive build-up of power in the Balkans, combined with a rapid strike into Italy itself. After his defeat at Bedriacum, Vitellius' resistance fell into ever-increasing disarray; he was killed when the forces of Vespasian entered Rome on 20 December 69. Domitian, Vespasian's son, was hailed as Caesar, and now Rome awaited its new Augustus, who arrived in October of the year 70. Last pockets of Vitellian resistance had been suppressed, and the rebellion in the Rhineland of a Batavian auxiliary commander, Julius Civilis, subdued. The armies had all had their say, and the civil wars were at an end.

Frontiers and the Roman army

The disbanding of the huge armies involved in the civil wars of the late Republic left Augustus with 26 legions, later increased to 28. With these relatively modest forces he embarked on a series of rationally planned campaigns to complete the pacification of provincial regions already partly won. Only after this was completed did Augustus divert his resources to expansion and conquest.

The first area to be pacified was northwestern Spain, with its mountain fastnesses and recalcitrant native tribes. On the completion of these difficult wars, in 19 BC, Augustus transferred part of his Spanish army to the German frontier and Illyricum, leaving Spain with a garrison of four legions. By the end of the Julio-Claudian period, this had dwindled to a single legion, stationed at León. Augustus next attended to Raetia and Noricum, regions posing a potential threat to the agriculture and settled communities of north Italy, as well as to communications with the crucial province of Illyricum. In the east, despite popular clamor for conquest, relations with Parthia were settled by diplomacy. The standards taken from Crassus at Carrhae were recovered (19 BC) and Roman interests were secured by client kings who were allowed effective independence in return for loyalty. The Herods of Judaea are the best-known example of Hellenistic kingdoms which enjoyed a late flowering under Roman patronage. After the death of Cleopatra, last of the Ptolemies, Egypt was ruled by prefects of equestrian rank, more or less as the personal domain of the emperors. Senators were not permitted even to enter it.

After his earlier campaigns, which Augustus sometimes attended in person, the armies were used to consolidate the Rhine frontier and push beyond it towards the Elbe river, and to pacify Illyricum. With this apparently achieved, a campaign was planned to annex the kingdom of Maroboduus, lying north of the Danube between Illyricum and the newly occupied parts of Germany. The entire northern frontier policy fell in ruins in 6 AD when Illyricum rose in revolt and the campaign against Maroboduus was abandoned. By 9 AD the revolt was suppressed, but in that year Quintilius Varus and his three legions were destroyed by the German chief Arminius at an unknown site in the Teutoburg forest. Varus has been charged with incompetence in allowing himself to be surprised. Little, however, is known of the circumstances, and it might be stated in mitigation that the revolt of Illyricum had left Varus isolated in a province which now protruded from the Rhine front as an exposed and vulnerable salient.

Julio-Claudian policy in the north was to consolidate the frontier through the establishment of legionary and auxiliary camps on the Roman bank and the tenure of bridgeheads across the river. The Danube frontier, after the recovery of Illyricum by Tiberius (6–9 AD), received the same treatment. The army in these and other newly conquered provinces became an effective agent for romanization, since the legionary camps generated informal settlements known as *canabae,* and in due course the foundation nearby of civilian towns (*municipia*); a particularly good example of this is Carnuntum on the Danube.

Augustus' recommendation not to extend the Empire was strictly observed by Tiberius, who nevertheless had to intervene in Thrace and to suppress a native rebellion in Numidian Africa led by a tribal leader, Tacfarinas. In the east, Tiberius

The arch of Titus at Rome was erected in commemoration of the triumph over the Jewish rebellion, achieved by Titus in 70 AD on behalf of his father Vespasian. Here are shown the spoils of the destroyed Temple being conveyed into Rome in the triumphal procession.

confirmed on the throne of Armenia a client king acceptable to Parthia. This was achieved by Germanicus, during an extensive tour of the east in which he also visited Palmyra and Petra, caravan cities with links in the Parthian empire.

The invasion of Britain undertaken by Claudius in 43 AD must have been planned very soon after he became emperor. Its motives have been much debated. It is unlikely, despite the high level of romanization achieved in Britain, that the province ever paid for its occupation, but this may not have been part of the Romans' calculations. It is possible that Claudius was eager for the glory of conquest to outweigh his other disadvantages as emperor. Certainly, he made much of the conquest, attending the campaign for a brief time (accompanied by elephants, which must have been an extraordinary sight to the Britons), naming his son Britannicus and in general receiving an unprecedented number of military salutations. Yet the most likely explanation is that Britain was linked more closely than seemed safe to the Belgic principalities of Gaul. There is evidence for much cross-Channel economic and political activity in the period before the conquest, and it may have seemed to Claudius and his advisers that Gaul would not be fully secure without the annexation also of Britain.

Claudius also reduced Mauretania to provincial status after disorders there following the death of a client king. This annexation, more significant than appears from the surviving sources, completed the pacification of the lands adjoining the western Mediterranean.

In the east, Nero inherited from Claudius involvement in renewed difficulties with Parthia and Armenia. After nearly a decade of military campaigns and complex shifts of diplomatic policy, the Parthian king Vologaeses agreed that his favored nominee Tiridates should visit Rome to receive his crown from Nero. By the agreement Armenia passed from the Roman into the Parthian sphere of influence, which is where it belonged by racial affinity.

Judaea, in the time of Augustus a client kingdom under Herod the Great, had after his death been made into a Roman province. It was given back by Claudius to his friend Herod Agrippa as a reward for his help during his accession as emperor, but after Agrippa's death in 44 Judaea once again became a Roman province. One of its governors was the Felix, brother of Claudius' freedman Pallas, before whom St Paul appeared (Acts 23:24ff). After some years of

The coin issue with the legend "IVD [aea] CAP [ta]," with its figures of disconsolate captives and a palm tree, celebrates the same event as the arch of Titus illustrated *opposite*. Similar types were issued by Hadrian after the suppression of the revolt of Bar-Kochba in 135 AD. For further description of Jerusalem, and of the fortress of Masada, captured in 73 AD, see pp. 162–63.

discontent Judaea rose in rebellion in 66, its suppression being committed to Vespasian and his son Titus. Interrupted by Vespasian's proclamation in 69, the defeat of the rebellion was completed by Titus with the destruction of the Temple in 70. The last stronghold, Masada, fell three years later after a long and bitter siege.

The subjugation of Britain was pursued with a severity which led to the rebellion of Boudicca in 60–61 AD, British anger being directed particularly against the veteran colony of Camulodunum (Colchester), which was seen as a symbol of Roman oppression, and the provincial capital, London. Subsequent, milder policy achieved the extension of Roman power to the line later taken by Hadrian's Wall. An attempt under the governorship of Agricola to achieve further annexations to the north was shortlived, since Domitian needed to recall a legion from Britain for service in Germany. The legionary fortress at Inchtuthill, built by Agricola, was occupied only very briefly, and in fact abandoned before its construction was finished.

These additions to the Empire were secured, as we have seen, by a trained professional army of less than 150 000 men with an approximately equal number of auxiliary troops recruited from various regions of the Empire and sometimes from client kingdoms, who often provided specialized fighting techniques. It was as small an army as could reasonably be employed, its size being controlled by economic and by political considerations. The economic factors relate to the problem of securing military pay from income from taxation and other sources. A soldier's pay did not increase between the times of Augustus and Domitian, who raised it by one-third, quite possibly at the cost of considerable financial strain (see below, p. 102). Throughout the first and more particularly the second and third centuries of the Empire, the army depended increasingly on additional payments received, for example, on the accessions of new emperors, and to a lesser extent from the spoils of active campaigning.

The dangers presented by an efficient but frequently inactive army were partly met by diverting its energies to works of construction, such as the building of roads and bridges, mining and digging canals, all of them useful in the economic development of the provinces, but not offering much in the way of excitement or financial reward. If Roman governors were sometimes impatient at the constraints imposed upon them, the soldiers were also very probably attracted when prospects of gain were offered by active campaigning, even in civil war.

The armies were established in legionary fortresses placed at intervals along the frontiers. No provincial legate had more than four legions at his disposal, which limited the chances of successful revolt against an established emperor who could be sure of the support of his other commanders. In settled times rebellions of provincial armies happened only occasionally and were easily suppressed. But when an emperor fell or was known to be insecure, as in 41, 68, 97, 193 and repeatedly in the 3rd century (see below, pp. 168–69), it was impossible to restrain the individual initiatives of provincial commanders and their armies. In 68–69 all the major army groupings except for that of Britain actively participated in civil war. As Tacitus remarked in a famous phrase, the secret had escaped, that emperors could be made elsewhere than at Rome.

In an obvious sense, the Roman emperors depended on the support of the army, and the unstated threat of military force was the reality behind the niceties of their constitutional position. Yet, the emperors of the 1st century – with the exceptions of Tiberius and Trajan, and to a lesser extent Vespasian – were not in general men of extensive military experience. In the same way, senatorial careers of the early Empire, which mingled civilian and military posts, and service in the provinces and at Rome, did not encourage the formation of a professionally self-conscious military elite. Some imperial legates, like Agricola and the writer on martial stratagems, Frontinus, were men of considerable military experience, systematically accumulated and put into practice. Yet such men remained attached to the life-style of Roman senators. They were men of private means, educated in the traditional culture of the civilian upper classes. A typical example is Pomponius Secundus, who governed Germany under Claudius. He was famous, wrote Tacitus, for his military triumphs, but still more so for the poetry which he composed. The contrast between this situation and that of the 3rd and 4th centuries could not be more marked.

The romanization of the west

The process known as "romanization" was the joint expression of imperial incentives and provincial wealth. The Romans did not use coercion to achieve it, but provided an example for imitation, with encouragement to the natives of the provinces to adopt Roman dress, to learn the Latin language and, to the differing degrees possible in different environments, to develop their settlements as urban centers. In the newly pacified west, the strongholds of native communities became the capitals of administrative districts known as *civitates*, based on the territories of the former tribes. Sometimes new cities took the place of inconvenient older sites. The Gallic hill-town of Bibracte (Mont Beuvray), for instance, yielded to the new foundation of Augustodunum (Autun), built by the Arroux river on a site far better suited to commercial activity. Similarly, in Noricum the native stronghold on the Magdalensberg was superseded by the new provincial capital, Virunum.

The Romans could provide civic institutions resembling those of the *municipia* of Italy. The new cities were given councils (*curiae*) composed of the wealthier members of local society, who on holding public office received the Roman citizenship and were formally enrolled in the ancient voting districts of Rome. The municipal office of *duumvir* appears in Gaul as the Celtic *vergobret* and in Punic Africa as *sufes*.

The political organization of the developing provinces was achieved through the existing upper classes. Many instances can be found of the political functions and civic munificence undertaken by the older nobility of the provinces. At Leptis Magna in Tripolitania the early theater and almost all the other public building of the 1st century were provided by members of wealthy Punic families. At Saintes (Mediolanum Santonum) in southwestern

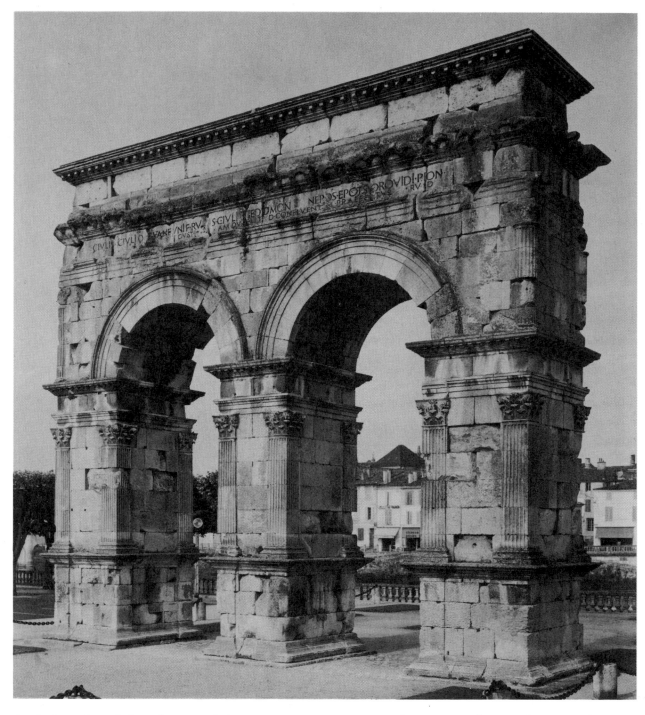

The triumphal arch of Saintes (*left*) bears on its frieze the commemorative inscription of C. Julius Rufus, whose family rises through C. Julius Otuaneunus, C. Julius Gedomo (the first citizen of the family, receiving this privilege from Julius Caesar) to Epotsorovidus, a chieftain of the Santones in the pre-Caesarian period. Rufus was also priest of Rome and Augustus at the altar of the Three Gauls at Lugdunum (see *opposite*) and is known to have contributed to the building of the amphitheater there.

Below A wooden votive offering preserved by the waterlogged conditions at the sanctuary of Sources-de-la-Seine near Dijon. The statue is an interesting example of the style of popular Celtic art in Roman Gaul, just as the vigor of the sanctuary itself is an expression of ancestral religious custom in the Roman Empire.

Gaul the triumphal arch erected in 18 AD was provided by the romanized grandson, C. Julius Rufus, of a Celtic notable who had acquired the citizenship from Julius Caesar.

The degree of urbanization achieved in the west differed greatly between those regions influenced by a Mediterranean and those influenced by a north European climate. In Africa urbanization proceeded rapidly, based in the province's eastern regions on the existing Punic communities and in Numidia on the development of native settlements, supplemented as always by Roman colonies. Spain too underwent rapid urban development, but in northern Gaul, the Belgic and German provinces and in Britain the process was slower. Many towns, such as Verulamium (near St Albans) in Britain, only produced extensive building in stone in the 2nd century. Nevertheless, Augustodunum, the capital of the Aedui, was already a center of Roman culture in the early 1st century; the sons of Gallic nobles were being educated there in the liberal arts when in 21 AD they were taken as hostages during a rebellion.

In the north, villa culture played a relatively more significant role than in the Mediterranean areas, and romanization should not be measured only by the degree of urban development. We must also estimate the advancement of material culture achieved in the villas, which was in its own way quite as impressive as that of the cities.

Two more factors are relevant to an assessment of the economic basis of romanization. The role of the army has arisen already, both in the provision of physical amenities like roads and bridges, and in the establishment of legionary camps which served as bases for urban development. Apart from the camps, with their adjacent *canabae* and, in due course, *municipia*, veterans retiring from the provincial armies tended to settle nearby and often became local gentry, the owners of villas and members of urban communities. The army's role as an agent of romanization can be seen clearly in

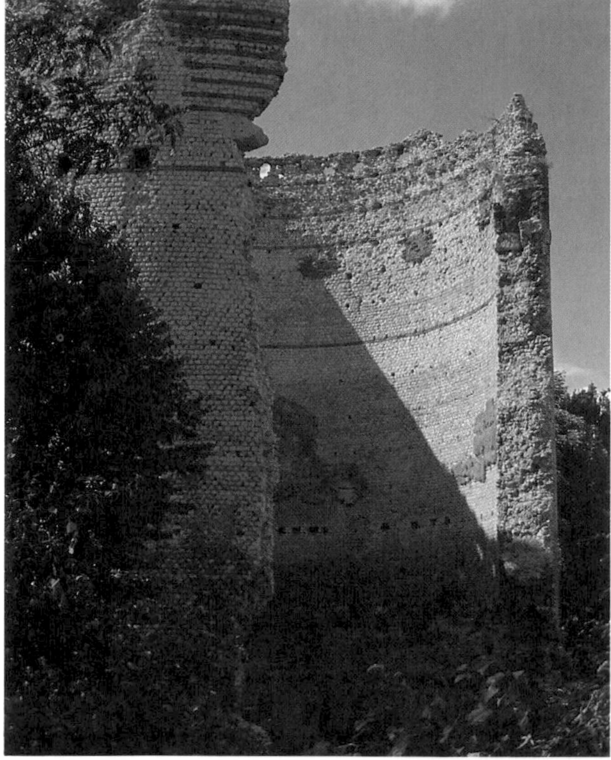

The temple of the goddess Vesunna at Périgueux (*right*), a stunning example of a Celtic shrine constructed during the early Roman period. Its huge circular cella or sanctuary was surrounded by an elaborate sacred precinct, of which the foundations survive. The ground plans of similar temples can be reconstructed from several sites in the former Celtic provinces of the Roman Empire.

The altar of Rome and Augustus at Lugdunum, founded in 10 BC, in association with a provincial council of the Three Gauls. Romanized tribal leaders held office as priests of Rome and Augustus, and with its annual festivities, held on 1 August, the altar had an important role in the unification of Gaul, and in the encouragement of its loyalty to Rome. The altar does not survive, but its general appearance is known from coin issues of Augustus (*above*). The nearby amphitheater of the Three Gauls has in recent years been cleared by excavation.

previously undeveloped regions like Pannonia and the Rhineland, and the plains of southern Numidia. In already urbanized areas like the east, soldiers were more involved in the social lives of the existing cities.

The second factor is that of Italian emigration under the later Republic, especially to Spain, Africa and Asia Minor. Civilians who had sought their fortune abroad, and veterans settled after campaigns in the provinces, often became very prosperous; their descendants were among the earliest to appear in the enlargement of the Roman ruling class by the admission of provincials to the senate in the first century of the Empire. The philosopher Seneca, the poet Lucan, the emperor Trajan, the first consuls from Africa – the Pactumeii brothers of Cirta – and many others, can be shown on the basis of their nomenclature to be descended from Italian families who had emigrated in the time of the Republic.

More frequently, provincial senators were members of indigenous local families taking their opportunity to express their wealth and social status at Rome. Claudius, who was particularly conscious of the process of the expansion from early times of the Roman ruling class, offered to the Aedui special privileges in seeking advancement through senatorial careers at Rome. The admission of Gauls, as of Spaniards and Africans, and later of Greeks and Orientals, to the Roman governing order, was part of a broader process, reflecting the steady advancement of the provinces under Roman rule and their absorption, to different degrees, of the classical ideal of political and civic life.

The limits of romanization must be defined as carefully as its extension. The regions of the Empire retained their own cultures and languages behind an often solid facade of romanization. The Celtic and Punic languages remained in use; a legal text of the early 3rd century states that wills made in either of these languages were valid. There is excellent evidence, throughout North Africa, for the survival also of a native language, described in modern discussions as Libyan or "Berber," though there is no way of judging how closely these native dialects resembled the modern Berber language. In the east, Celtic, according to the late evidence of St Jerome, was spoken in parts of Galatia, and in the time of Nero Paul and Barnabas were acclaimed by the inhabitants of the city of Lystra "in the Lycaonian language" (Acts 14:11). Beyond the Taurus mountains Syriac in its various forms was everywhere spoken throughout the time of the Roman Empire, from Antioch into Babylonia and southwards to Gaza, though it produced a written literature only with the rise of the Christian church in the later 3rd century.

The persistence of local art forms, especially in relief sculpture, is conspicuous, often contrasting strikingly with the more universalized forms of Roman imperial sculpture found in the provinces. The architecture of temples in the Celtic west retained a distinctive style quite unlike classical models, of a large central cella surrounded by an extensive precinct. The best surviving examples of this, at Autun and Périgueux, contrast dramatically with the classical temples at Nîmes and Vienne. The gods and goddesses of the west were often romanized native deities, as in the cases of the triple "mother-goddesses" and the "god with the hammer" of Roman Gaul, and the three hooded divinities of Britain. In Africa, Virgo Caelestis and Saturn were romanized versions of the Punic gods Tanit and Ba'al Hammon. The Gorgon-like face of the goddess Sulis-Minerva from the temple pediment at Aquae Sulis (Bath) is a particularly vivid expression of the persistence of Celtic decorative style in a romanized religious and civic context. Those aspects of native religious practice least compatible with Roman civilized ideals, such as druidism, were suppressed by government action, one of the few areas in which the Roman authorities forcibly intervened in the development of provincial life.

An influence in favor of unity was provided by the imperial cult, of which much is known from all parts of the Roman Empire. Based on regional capitals, such as Tarraco, Narbo, Ephesus (for Asia Minor) and Sardis (for Lydia), the imperial cult cleverly directed local patriotism into the channel of loyalty to Rome. The cult was administered by a provincial council, consisting of delegates from the cities, which met annually under the presidency of one of their number, the chief priest of the province for the year. The council was able not only to express its formal good wishes or condolences to the emperor as circumstances required, but also, as many inscriptions attest, to select and dispatch embassies to the emperor on matters of substantial interest to the communities of the province concerned.

The religious attitudes involved in the imperial cult differed between the western and eastern parts of the Empire. In the west, worship of the emperor was centered not directly on the emperor but on his *numen* or guardian spirit, and was coupled with reverence for the city (or the goddess) Roma. The emperor was regarded as divine (*divus*) only after his death, and then not invariably, since promotion of a dead emperor to the ranks of the gods depended on the attitude of his successor and the senate. In the

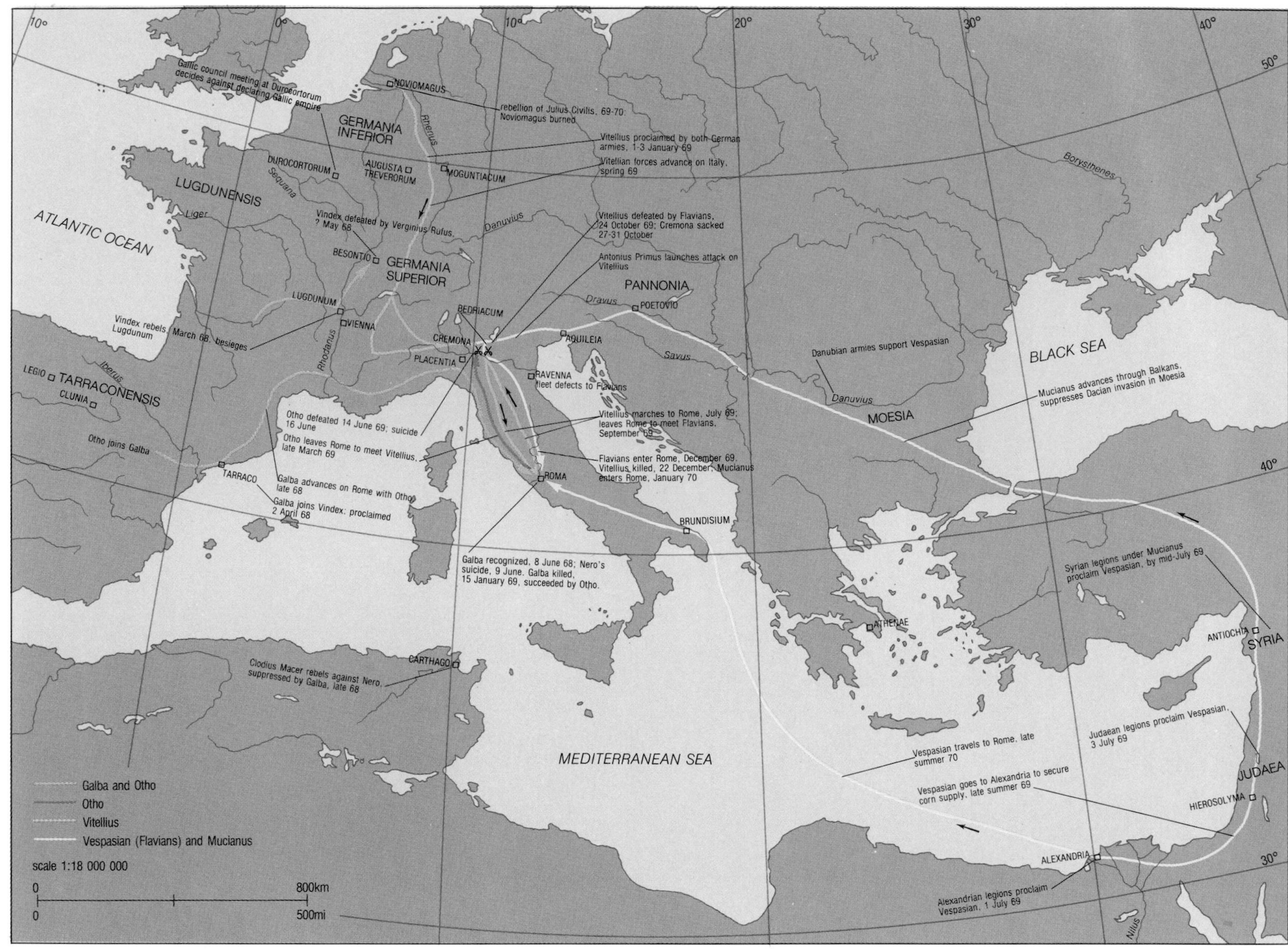
10°
0°
10°
20°
30°
40°
50°
40°
30°
Gallic council meeting at Durocortorum decides against declaring Gallic empire
NOVIOMAGUS
rebellion of Julius Civilis, 69-70: Noviomagus burned
GERMANIA INFERIOR
Rhenus
Vitellius proclaimed by both German armies, 1-3 January 69
Vitellian forces advance on Italy, spring 69
DUROCORTORUM
AUGUSTA TREVERORUM
MOGUNTIACUM
LUGDUNENSIS
Sequana
Liger
ATLANTIC OCEAN
Vindex defeated by Verginius Rufus, ? May 68
Danuvius
Vitellius defeated by Flavians, 24 October 69; Cremona sacked 27-31 October
BESONTIO
GERMANIA SUPERIOR
Antonius Primus launches attack on Vitellius
PANNONIA
Dravus
POETOVIO
LUGDUNUM
VIENNA
Vindex rebels, March 68, besieges Lugdunum
Rhodanus
BEDRIACUM
CREMONA
PLACENTIA
AQUILEIA
Savus
RAVENNA
fleet defects to Flavians
LEGIO
TARRACONENSIS
Iberus
CLUNIA
Otho defeated 14 June 69; suicide 16 June
Otho leaves Rome to meet Vitellius, late March 69
Otho joins Galba
Vitellius marches to Rome, July 69; leaves Rome to meet Flavians, September 69
Flavians enter Rome, December 69. Vitellius killed, 22 December; Mucianus enters Rome, January 70
TARRACO
Galba advances on Rome with Otho, late 68
Galba joins Vindex: proclaimed 2 April 68
ROMA
BRUNDISIUM
Galba recognized, 8 June 68; Nero's suicide, 9 June. Galba killed, 15 January 69, succeeded by Otho.
Borysthenes
Danubian armies support Vespasian
Danuvius
MOESIA
BLACK SEA
Mucianus advances through Balkans, suppresses Dacian invasion in Moesia
Syrian legions under Mucianus proclaim Vespasian, by mid-July 69
ATHENAE
ANTIOCHIA
SYRIA
CARTHAGO
Clodius Macer rebels against Nero, suppressed by Galba, late 68
MEDITERRANEAN SEA
Judaean legions proclaim Vespasian, 3 July 69
Vespasian travels to Rome, late summer 70
Vespasian goes to Alexandria to secure corn supply, late summer 69
JUDAEA
HIEROSOLYMA
ALEXANDRIA
Alexandrian legions proclaim Vespasian, 1 July 69
Nilus
Galba and Otho
Otho
Vitellius
Vespasian (Flavians) and Mucianus
scale 1:18 000 000
0
800km
0
500mi

The wars of 68–70 AD. The wars of 68–70 AD involved in turn all the main military groupings of the Empire, victory going to the most coherently mobilized. The chief exception was Britain, with potentially formidable but isolated forces. The single African legion was inadequate for serious contention, and Galba's modest forces, inherited by Otho, were unequal to the combined armies of the Germanies, frustrated in their attempts to proclaim Verginius Rufus and transferring their support to Vitellius. In being able to combine the eastern legions and those of the Danube, Vespasian had irresistible advantages, and he could also use his Italian connections to spread disaffection. The soldiers behaved in general with an obedience to their officers which suggests that they had no revolutionary aims of their own. The only serious provincial unrest after the revolt of Vindex was in the extreme northeast of Gaul, in the rebellion of the Batavian Julius Civilis, but even this failed to provoke a general revolt.

east, accustomed as it was to divinized Hellenistic monarchs, imperial worship was more direct. The inscription, published in 1963, recording the governorship of Judaea of Pontius Pilate, attests the existence at Caesarea of a "Tiberieum," or temple of Tiberius; this was an emperor more strongly opposed than most to the natural tendency toward direct worship of the emperor.

The concept of romanization can hardly be applied to the Greek east. Roman attitudes to the Greeks combined admiration for their cultural achievement (an admiration taken to unnecessary lengths by Nero), with a sort of patronizing affection. For their part the Greeks were impervious to the influence of Latin culture. Roman colonies founded in the east were Latin-speaking enclaves gradually absorbed by their Greek environment. Yet Greeks flocked to Rome to seek advancement under Roman patrons – men such as the geographer Strabo, the astrologer Thrasyllus and many poets, historians and others whose names are known. Greek and Oriental cultural and religious ideas flowed to Rome along the pacified Mediterranean. The 2nd century witnessed a tremendous flourishing of this Greco-Roman culture in the literary movement known as the Second Sophistic, with its associated artistic developments (see below, pp. 110–12). At the same time, men from the Greek east progressively took a greater share in government, emerging by the early 2nd century to become senators, consuls and provincial governors. The transference of the Roman ideal of government to the Greek east, which is the essence of Byzantium, had been anticipated in the days of the high Roman Empire.

It has been argued that the civil wars of 68–70 AD which brought to an end the Julio-Claudian dynasty, were an expression of provincial dissension in the Roman Empire. The notion that Vindex was a "nationalist" leader aspiring to establish a separatist "empire of the Gauls" is disproved by his coinage and by what can be seen of his policies and attitudes, which were traditionally Roman. Yet, in gathering his forces from the peasantry of the Gallic countryside, Vindex clearly betrays his position as a tribal dynast as well as Roman senator, and to this extent his rebellion was an expression, if not of nationalistic sentiment, certainly of the particular social structure of the part of Gaul from which he came. Yet the more significant aspect of the civil wars of 68–70 may be that, given these circumstances and the general disorder, there was not any nationalistic secession in the Roman provinces. The wars were fought between Roman armies under the command of their generals, and there was no serious likelihood that the Empire would fall apart.

Right A fanciful townscape from the cubiculum of the villa of Publius Fannius Sinister at Boscoreale.

Town Life at Pompeii

Pompeii was originally an Etruscan town, but was occupied in the 5th century BC by the Samnites. After this it remained a largely Oscan-speaking community until 80 BC when Sulla established a colony there. As a consequence it rapidly became romanized. Following its destruction in the eruption of 79 AD Pompeii lay buried (beneath a layer of ash and volcanic mud) until the 18th century.

The economy of Pompeii was principally based on the produce of its fertile hinterland, especially wine and olive oil. But it was also a flourishing industrial and trading center, the major industries being cloth manufacture and fulling. There is much evidence also of small-scale craft production, retailing and other service trades.

Like all Roman towns, Pompeii had a local government closely modeled on that of Rome. The ruling body was a town council (*ordo*) of 80–100 men (decurions), who were drawn from the propertied class and held office for life. The executive magistrates were two annually elected *duoviri* (equivalent to the Roman consuls), assisted by aediles who, like their Roman counterparts, administered public works. Slogans and graffiti survive to show that elections were lively affairs.

While the poor lived mostly in tiny apartments or in the *tabernae* (shops), which opened out on to the streets, the rich lived in luxurious town houses. The standard Pompeian house was centered on a large hall (*atrium*), opening out into a peristyle or colonnaded garden. The houses were richly decorated with murals, which provide the bulk of our knowledge of Roman painting. The paintings are divided into four chronological periods or "styles."

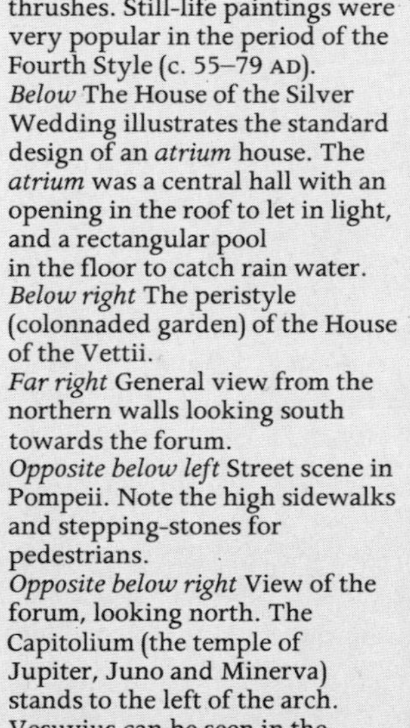

Right Still life with eggs and thrushes. Still-life paintings were very popular in the period of the Fourth Style (c. 55–79 AD).
Below The House of the Silver Wedding illustrates the standard design of an *atrium* house. The *atrium* was a central hall with an opening in the roof to let in light, and a rectangular pool in the floor to catch rain water.
Below right The peristyle (colonnaded garden) of the House of the Vettii.
Far right General view from the northern walls looking south towards the forum.
Opposite below left Street scene in Pompeii. Note the high sidewalks and stepping-stones for pedestrians.
Opposite below right View of the forum, looking north. The Capitolium (the temple of Jupiter, Juno and Minerva) stands to the left of the arch. Vesuvius can be seen in the background.

Republican Rome

The city of Rome underwent an extraordinary expansion during the Republic. Already a substantial settlement at the end of the 6th century, its population had risen to perhaps 100 000 by 300 BC, and was nearing the million mark in the time of Caesar. The squalid tenement blocks which dominated the imperial city were already making their appearance at the time of Hannibal. Public buildings – utilities, amenities, temples and decorative monuments – began to be constructed in large numbers in the time of Appius Claudius (who built the first aqueduct in 312), and continued on an ever-increasing scale, especially in the age of imperial expansion after the Second Punic War. Finally the dynasts of the 1st century BC, such as Sulla, Pompey and Caesar, embarked on building projects which changed the whole appearance of the city, in order to enhance their personal glory. But very few of the monuments of republican Rome survive to our time: they were mostly superseded in their turn by the even more grandiose building programs of the imperial age.

Top Marble relief from the Lacus Curtius ("Curtius' pond"). According to an ancient legend, a certain Curtius had once perished when he and his horse were swallowed by a chasm in the center of the Forum. One legend identified Curtius with a Sabine leader who fought in the war against Romulus; in another version of the story the event occurred in the 4th century BC and involved a Roman horseman. This relief illustrating the story, and dating from republican times, was found at the spot in the 16th century; it has since been moved to a museum and replaced by a replica.

Above The Forum Romanum was for centuries the center of Roman political and religious life. Its earliest monuments, such as the Lapis Niger (see p. 22), the temple of Vesta (*opposite*) and the Curia, date from the time of the kings. Here we see the Sacra Via, the oldest street in Rome, passing between the Lacus Curtius (left) and the Basilica Julia (right), built by Julius Caesar in 54 BC. Next to the basilica stand the three surviving columns of the republican temple of Castor, built on the site of an archaic temple which commemorated the victory at Lake Regillus in 499 BC. Dominating the skyline is the arch of Titus which belongs to the imperial period.

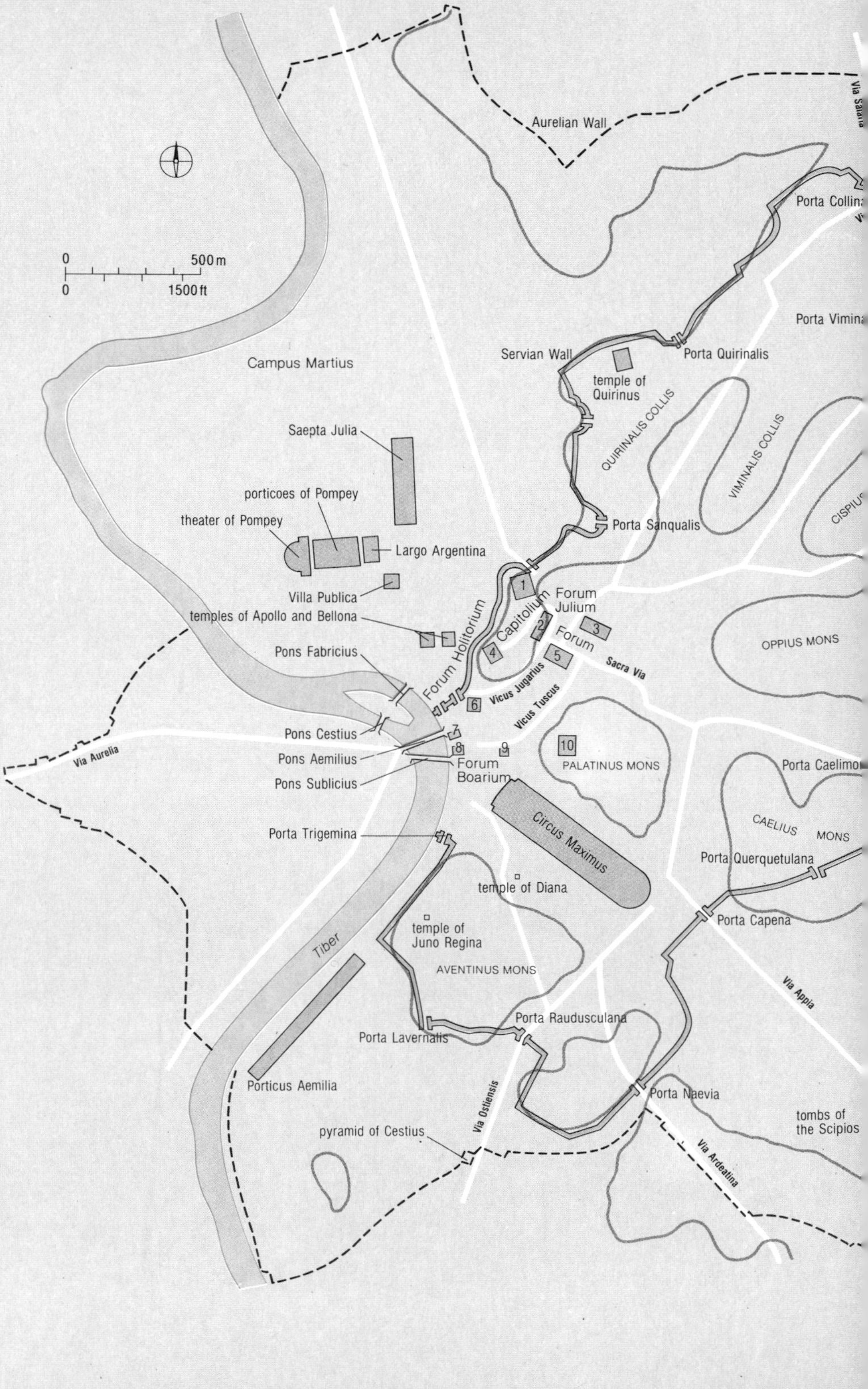

Right This well-preserved rectangular temple (early 1st century BC), commonly known as the temple of Fortuna Virilis, is more probably to be identified as the temple of Portunus, the deity associated with the nearby harbor.

Far right The forum of Caesar (dedicated in 46 BC) was dominated by a great temple of Venus, the mythical ancestor of the Julian house. An equestrian statue of the dictator stood in the center of the square.

Below right The monumental complex of the Largo Argentina came to light in the 1920s when excavations revealed four republican temples, ranging in date from the late 4th century to the end of the 2nd. The picture shows the remains of the 3rd-century temple A.

Far right The Pons Fabricius, connecting the left bank with the Tiber island, was built by L. Fabricius, supervisor of roads, in 62 BC.

Via Collatina

Porta Esquilina

Via Labicana

Via Praenestina

Via Tusculana

Via Latina

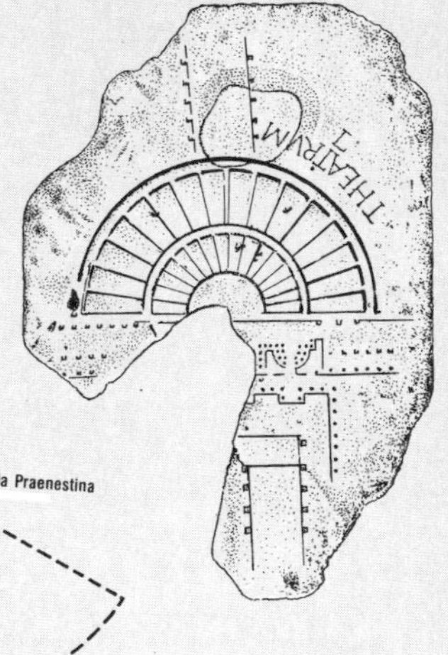

Above Rome's first stone theater was commissioned by Pompey and dedicated by him in 55 BC; little remains of the monument, but its layout can still be seen on a fragment of a 3rd-century marble plan of the city.

Above right The Milvian bridge (109 BC) stands to the north of Rome and carries the Via Flaminia towards Etruria and Umbria.

Right The Forum Romanum seen from the Palatine. Behind the columns of the temple of Castor stands the Curia or senate house begun by Sulla in 80 BC and rebuilt by Julius Caesar in 44.

Far right The temple of Vesta in the Forum. The site was associated with the cult of Vesta since the earliest times, although the surviving remains date from the imperial period.

1 temple of Juno Moneta
2 Tabularium
3 Basilica Aemilia
4 temple of Jupiter Capitolinus
5 Basilica Julia
6 temples of Fortuna and Mater Matuta
7 temple of Portunus
8 temple of Hercules Victor
9 Ara Maxima
10 temple of Cybele or Magna Mater

Early Imperial Rome

Imperial Rome was a huge conurbation with a probable population of over a million, most of whom lived in appalling conditions. The squalor of the slums contrasted with the magnificent public buildings erected by successive emperors, beginning with Augustus. According to Suetonius, "Augustus so embellished the city that his boast was justified: 'I left Rome a city of marble, though I found it a city of bricks.'" A further transformation occurred under Nero, following the disastrous fire of 64 AD. Tacitus tells us that "of the 14 regions into which Rome was divided [see map, p.19], only four remained intact [I, V, VI, XIV], three were destroyed to ground level [III, X, XI], and in the other seven a few houses survived, but half-burned and severely damaged." Nero began an energetic rebuilding program, which included a vast new palace, the Domus Aurea (the "Golden House"), which stretched from the Palatine to the Servian walls on the Esquiline. This area was later occupied by the temple of Venus and Roma (135 AD), the Colosseum (80 AD), and the baths of Trajan, built out of the ruins of part of the Golden House, after its destruction by fire in 104. The baths of Trajan were the first of three great thermal complexes (the others being the baths of Caracalla and the baths of Diocletian) which mark the grandiose culmination of Roman monumental architecture.

Right This fine representation of Marcus Aurelius is the only bronze equestrian statue surviving from classical times.

Far right Trajan's market is the name given to the multistoried complex of buildings overlooking the forum of Trajan and occupying a space which was carved out of the SW slopes of the Quirinal. The market consists of a great vaulted hall surrounded by shops and commercial premises; these stand behind a grandiose brick exedra which forms the eastern side of Trajan's forum. Like the forum and baths of Trajan, the whole complex was designed by the architect Apollodorus of Damascus.

The arch which dominates the western end of the Forum was built in 203 in honor of Septimius Severus and his sons Caracalla and Geta (whose name was erased from the inscription after his murder in 212). The reliefs show scenes from Severus' campaigns against the Parthians and Arabs.

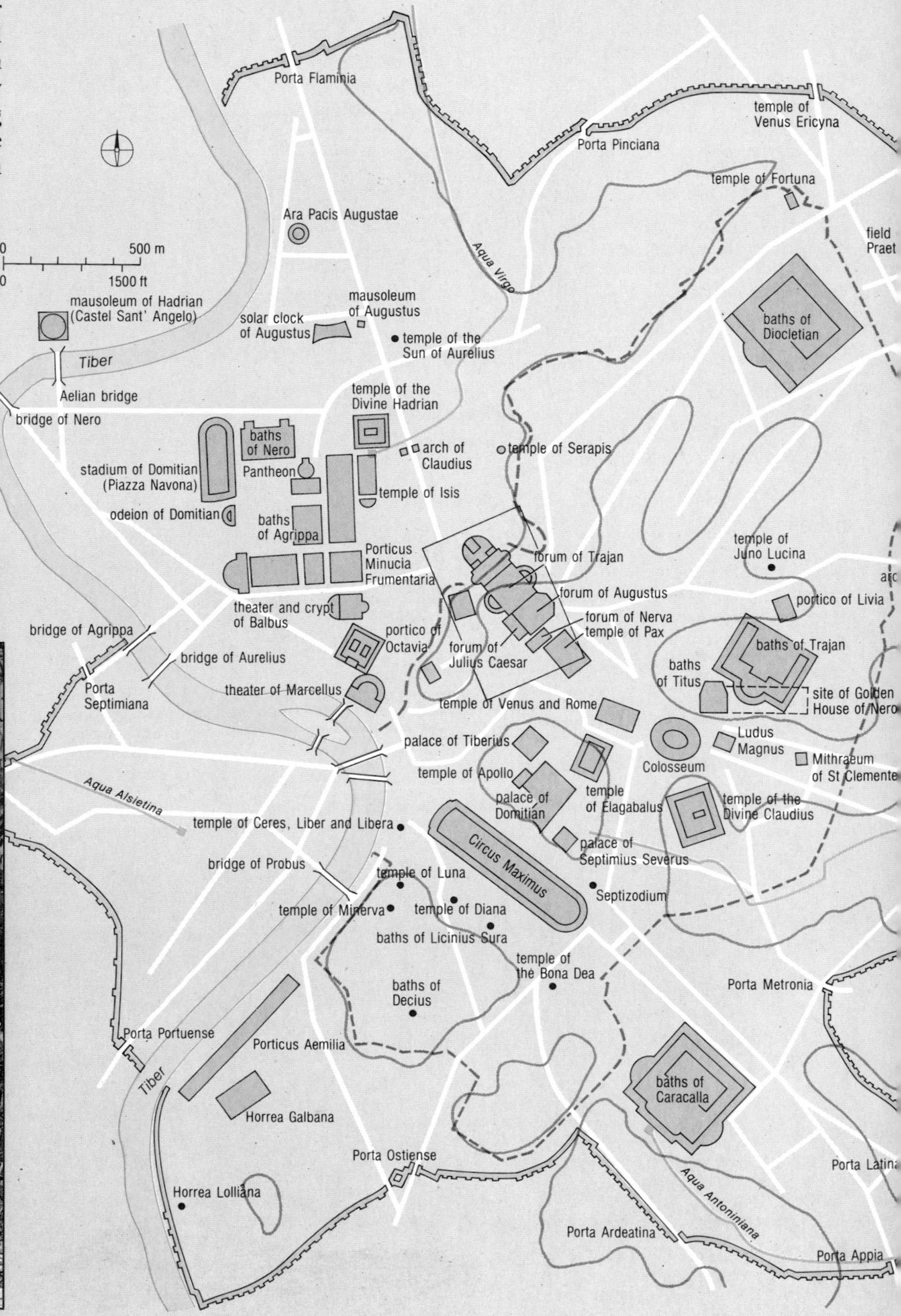

INSET
1 column of Trajan
2 libraries
3 Atrium Libertatis
4 equestrian statue of Trajan
5 temple of Venus Genetrix
6 temple of Antoninus and Faustina
7 Regia
8 temple of Julius Caesar
9 arch of Augustus
10 temple of Vesta
11 Atrium Vestae
12 temple of Castor
13 Argiletum
14 temple of Saturn
15 Rostra
16 arch of Septimius Severus
17 portico of the Di Consentes
18 temple of Vespasian
19 temple of Concord
20 Forum Romanum

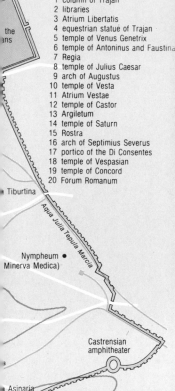

Tiburtina
Aqua Julia Tepula Marcia
Nympheum (Minerva Medica)
Castrensian amphitheater
Asinaria

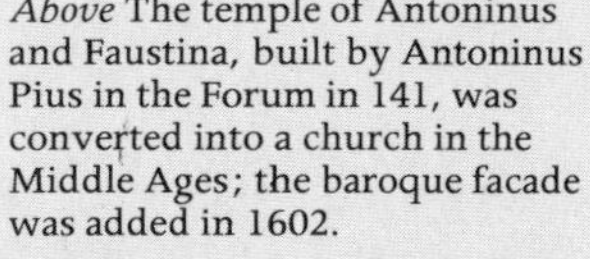

Above The temple of Antoninus and Faustina, built by Antoninus Pius in the Forum in 141, was converted into a church in the Middle Ages; the baroque facade was added in 1602.

Above right The Flavian amphitheater (the "Colosseum") was begun by Vespasian and completed by his sons Titus and Domitian. Over 50 meters high, it covered an elliptical area 188 by 156 meters. Officially opened in 80 AD, it could hold c. 70000 spectators.

Far right Trajan's column was erected in the emperor's new forum in 113 to commemorate his conquest of Dacia.

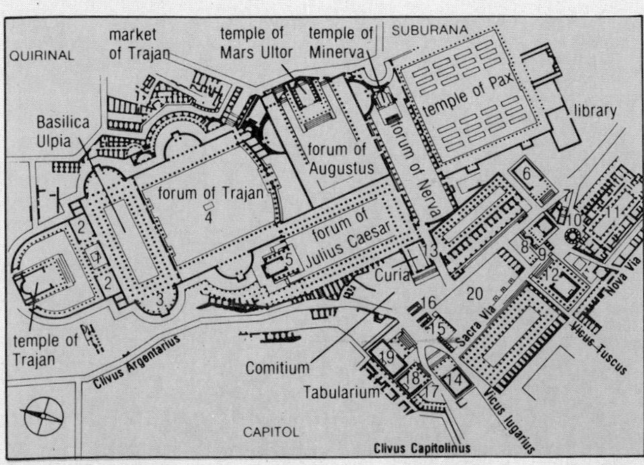

Above The Aqua Claudia, begun in 38 AD by Caligula and completed by Claudius in 52, brought water to the city from a source near Subiaco 68 kilometers away.

Right Detail of the model of ancient Rome in the Museo della Civiltà Romana, Rome. In the foreground is the Circus Maximus; beyond it are the imperial palaces on the Palatine. At the top of the picture, from left to right, are the Forum, the basilica of Maxentius, the temple of Venus and Roma, the Colosseum and the temple of the Divine Claudius.

Ostia: Port of Rome

Tradition ascribed the foundation of Ostia to King Ancus Marcius, but no trace of this early settlement has yet been found. The earliest remains belong to the coastal garrison "colony" (see p. 34) founded in the 4th century BC. Ostia was an important naval base in the Second Punic War, and expanded in the 2nd century as a commercial port serving the growing population of Rome. By the early Empire the river harbor could no longer cope with the volume of maritime traffic, so Claudius built a large artificial harbor some 3 kilometers to the north at Portus. This new harbor was itself enlarged under Trajan. Ostia flourished in the 2nd century, and its population almost doubled. High-rise tenement blocks appeared, and public buildings and amenities were constructed on a large scale. During the 3rd century, however, there was little new building, and some of the existing structures fell into disrepair. The population decreased, trade slumped, and the town gradually declined.

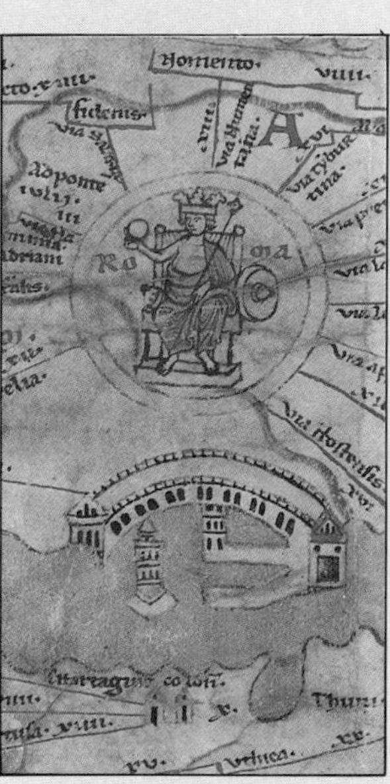

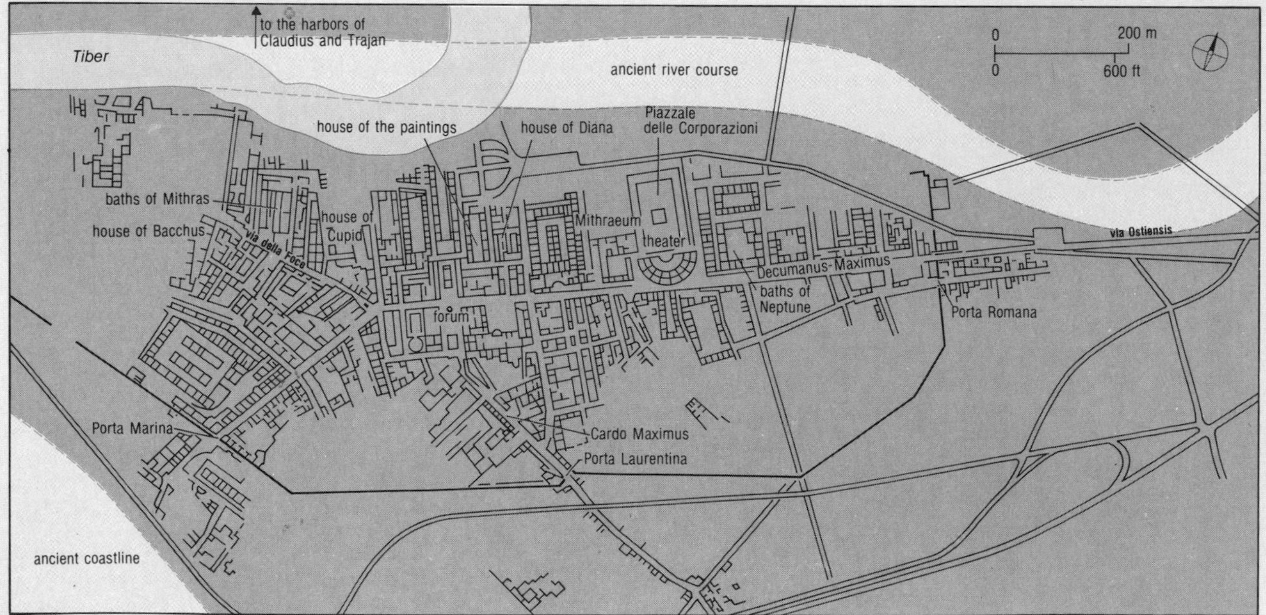

Top left The harbor at Portus in c. 350 AD, as shown on the medieval Peutinger map (see p. 116).

Above left Harbor scene on a marble relief of c. 200 AD, found near Trajan's harbor. The ship with furled sails on the right of the picture is being unloaded at the docks. On the left another ship sails into port while its crew sacrifice to celebrate their safe return. Note that the emblem of Rome, the wolf and twins, is twice depicted on the mainsail. A lighthouse (probably the one erected in the time of Claudius) can be seen in the background. The whole scene is dominated by the central figure of Neptune holding his trident.

Right Aerial view of Portus. The hexagonal plan of Trajan's inner basin can be clearly seen.

Below View of the Decumanus Maximus, the main street of Ostia.

Below Tomb painting from Ostia showing a river boat, the Isis Giminiana, being loaded with grain for the journey upstream to Rome. The captain, Farnaces, is shown holding the rudder in the stern. The representation of porters reminds us that many people in Rome and Ostia found employment in the docks.

Below center Mosaic (2nd century AD) in the Piazzale delle Corporazioni. This large colonnaded square in the town center was surrounded by shipping offices occupied by representatives of Roman and overseas trading companies. The offices are decorated with fine mosaics of nautical scenes.

An indication of the levels of maritime trade in the Mediterranean is given by the ancient wrecks discovered by underwater archaeology. The concentration in particular areas reflects the level of archaeological activity, and need not suggest that traffic was especially heavy in those waters or that they were particularly dangerous to ancient shipping! The chronological concentration of datable wrecks in the period 300 BC–300 AD illustrates the very high level of trade in classical times by comparison with earlier and later periods.

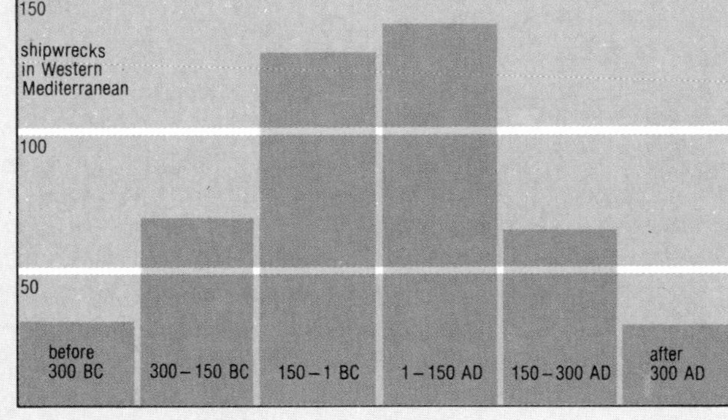

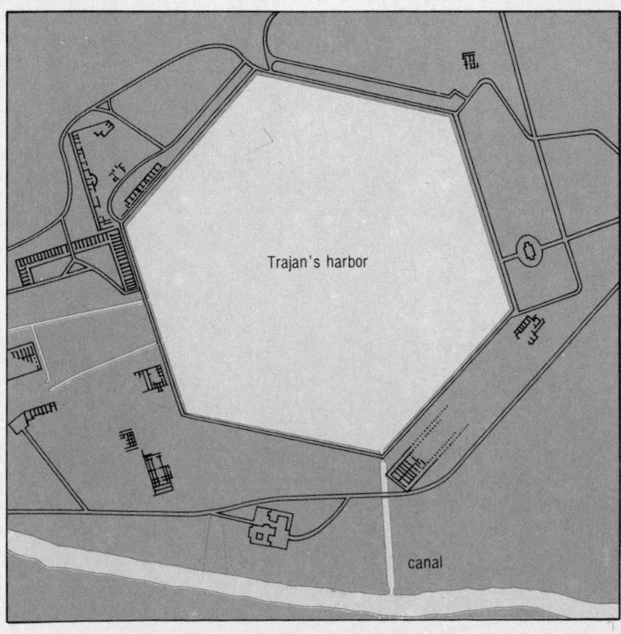

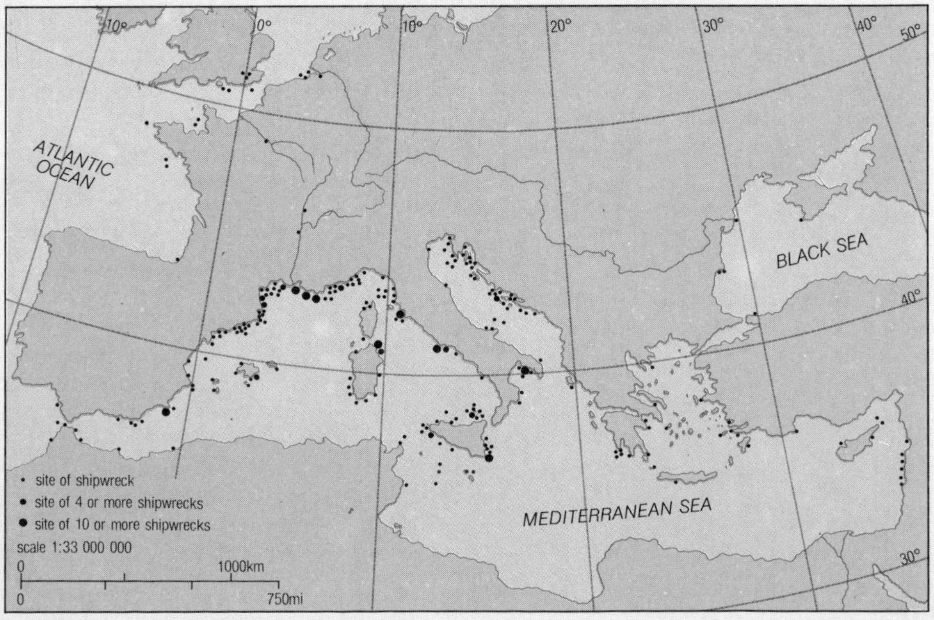

Festivals of the State Religion

From very early times the Romans adopted Greek cults and religious ideas. The first temple of Apollo was built in 431 BC during a plague. Apollo was especially favored by Augustus, who built a temple to him on the Palatine. Apollo is seen here (*below*), with his lyre, on a coin of c. 10 BC.

IMP
XII
ACT

The traditional pagan religion of Rome appears to us as a confused jumble of archaic ceremonies and rituals which were performed repetitively and mechanically as a means of ensuring the goodwill of the gods – what the Romans called the *pax deorum*. It was the duty of the *paterfamilias* to perform the appropriate rituals to propitiate the gods of the household, such as Vesta (the hearth), the Penates (the store cupboard) and the Lares (departed ancestors). A similar function was exercised on behalf of the community by the chief priests and magistrates. In the course of time an elaborate set of public cults became established, located at the hundreds of shrines and temples in and around the city. The priests were not a professional class, but members of the ruling aristocracy who also held magistracies and commanded armies. The more important of these priests included the pontiffs, who supervised the state festivals and the calendar, the augurs, who were concerned with divination, and the Decemviri Sacris Faciundis, who looked after sacred books and foreign cults. Other priests included the Flamines, the Arval Brethren, the Fetiales, the Salii, the Rex Sacrorum and the Vestal Virgins. All came under the authority of the Pontifex Maximus, who was the head of the state religion.

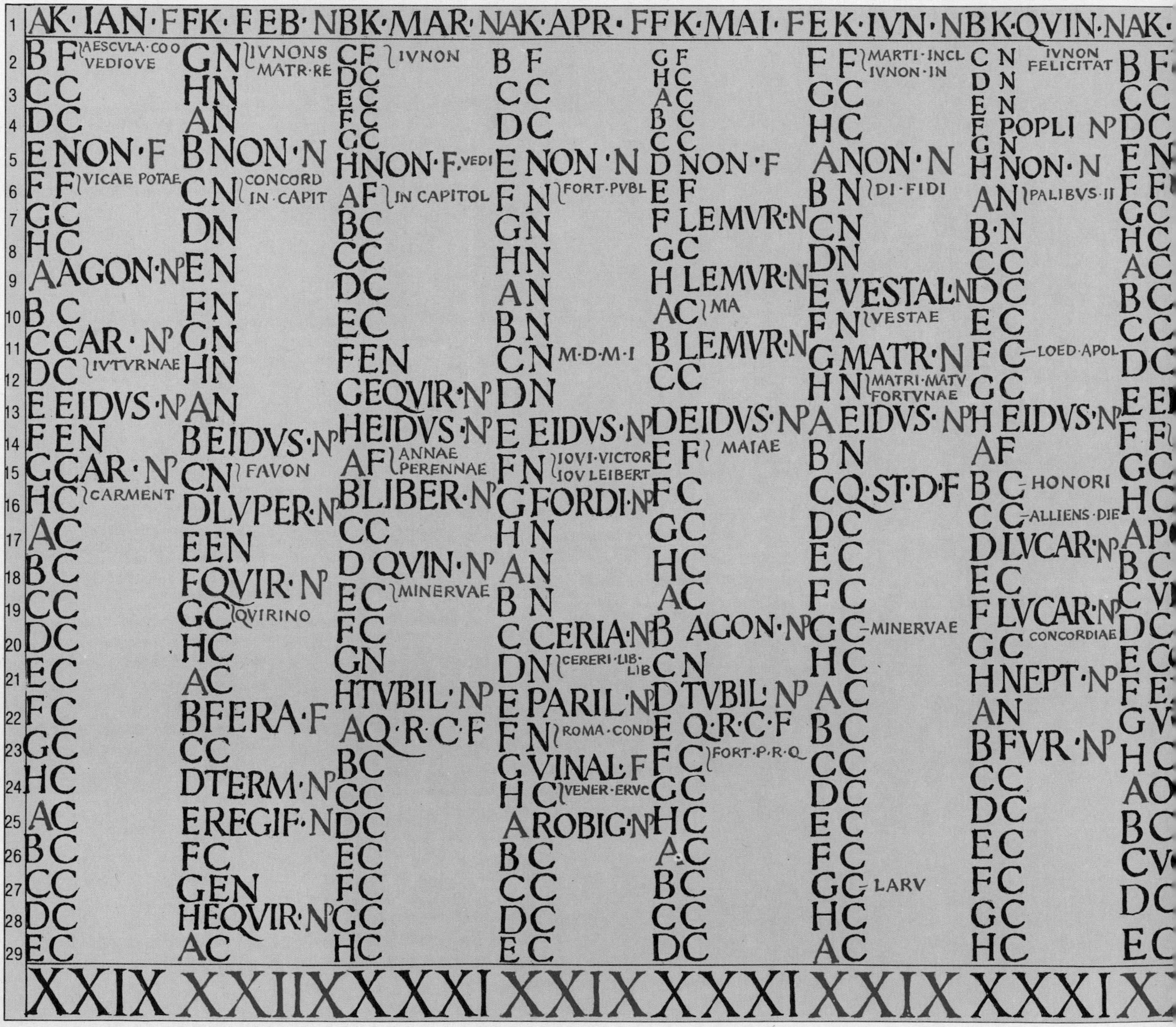
A K·IAN·F F K·FEB·N B K·MAR·N A K·APR·F F K·MAI·F E K·IVN·N B K·QVIN·N A K·
B F AESCVLA·CO VEDIOVE · C C · D C · E NON·F · F F VICAE POTAE · G C · H C · A AGON·N · B C · C CAR·N · D C IVTVRNAE · E EIDVS·N · F EN · G CAR·N · H C CARMENT · A C · B C · C C · D C · E C · F C · G C · H C · A C · B C · C C · D C · E C
G N IVNONS MATR·RE · H N · A N · B NON·N · C N CONCORD IN CAPIT · D N · E N · F N · G N · H N · A N · B EIDVS·N · C N FAVON · D LVPER·N · E EN · F QVIR·N · G C QVIRINO · H C · A C · B FERA·F · C C · D TERM·N · E REGIF·N · F C · G EN · H EQVIR·N · A C
C F IVNON · D C · E C · F C · G C · H NON·F·VEDI · A F IN CAPITOL · B C · C C · D C · E C · F EN · G EQVIR·N · H EIDVS·N · A F ANNAE PERENNAE · B LIBER·N · C C · D QVIN·N · E C MINERVAE · F C · G N · H TVBIL·N · A Q·R·C·F · B C · C C · D C · E C · F C · G C · H C
B F · C C · D C · E NON·N · F N FORT·PVBL · G N · H N · A N · B N · C N M·D·M·I · D N · E EIDVS·N · F N IOVI·VICTOR IOV LEIBERT · G FORDI·N · H N · A N · B N · C CERIA·N · D N CERERI·LIB·LIB · E PARIL·N · F N ROMA·COND · G VINAL·F · H C VENER·ERVC · A ROBIG·N · B C · C C · D C · E C
G F · H C · A C · B C · C C · D NON·F · E F · F LEMVR·N · G C · H LEMVR·N · A C MA · B LEMVR·N · C C · D EIDVS·N · E F MAIAE · F C · G C · H C · A C · B AGON·N · C N · D TVBIL·N · E Q·R·C·F · F C FORT·P·R·Q · G C · H C · A C · B C · C C · D C
F F MARTI·INCL IVNON·IN · G C · H C · A NON·N · B N DI·FIDI · C N · D N · E VESTAL·N · F N VESTAE · G MATR·N · H N MATRI·MATV FORTVNAE · A EIDVS·N · B N · C Q·ST·D·F · D C · E C · F C · G C MINERVAE · H C · A C · B C · C C · D C · E C · F C · G C LARV · H C · A C
C N IVNON FELICITAT · D N · E N · F POPLI·N · G N · H NON·N · A N PALIBVS·II · B·N · C C · D C · E C · F C LOED·APOL · G C · H EIDVS·N · A F · B C HONORI · C C ALLIENS·DIE · D LVCAR·N · E C · F LVCAR·N · G C CONCORDIAE · H NEPT·N · A N · B FVR·N · C C · D C · E C · F C · G C · H C
XXIX XXIIX XXXI XXIX XXXI XXIX XXXI

Divination based on the examination of entrails was an important part of both Roman and Etruscan religion. Etruscan diviners (*haruspices*) were considered especially expert and were regularly consulted by the Romans. This Etruscan mirror (*left*) shows the mythical seer Calchas in the guise of a *haruspex*.

Below Sacrifice of an ox, sheep and pig (*suovetaurilia*). From an early 4th-century monument of Diocletian, one of the last pagan emperors.

The six Vestal Virgins performed symbolic household tasks for the state. Above all they tended the sacred fire which burned continuously in a building in the Forum. Chosen between the ages of 6 and 10, the Vestals were bound to remain virgins for at least 30 years. Transgressors were buried alive.

K·SEPT·F	C K·OCT·N	B K·NOV·F	G K·DEC·N	G K·INT·F
GF	DF FIDE I	CF	HN	HF
HC	EC	DC	AN	AC
AC	FC	EC	BC	BC
B NON·F	GC	F NON·F	C NON·F	C NON·F
C F IOVI·STATORI	HC	GF	DF	DF
DC	A NON·F	HC	EC	EC
EC	BF IOVI·FVLGVR IVNON·QVIR	AC	FC TIBERINO GAIAE	FC
FC	CC	BC	GC	GC
GC	DC IVNON MON	CC	HC	HC
HC	E MEDI·NP	DC	A AGON·NP	AC
AN	FC	EC	BEN	BC
B EIDVS·NP	G FONT·NP	F EIDVS·NP	C EIDVS·NP	C EIDVS·NP
C F IOVI·O·M	HEN	GF FERON·FORT·PR	DF	DF
DN	A EIDVS·NP	HC	E CONS·NP	EC
EC	BF	AC	FC	FC
FC	CC	BC	G SATVR·NP	GC
GC	DC	CC	HC SATVRNO	HC
HC	E ARMI·NP	DC	A OPA·NP	AC
AC	FC	EC	BC OPI	BC
BC	GC	FC	C DIVAL·NP	CC
CC	HC	GC	DC LAR·PERM	DC
DC	AC	HC	E LARE·NP	E REGI·N
EC	BC	AC	FC DIAN·IVNON·R·INCAMP·TEMPE	FC
FC	CC	BC	GC	GEN
GC	DC	CC	HC	H EQVIR·NP
HC	EC	DC	AC	AC
AC	FC	EC	BC	
BC	GC	FC	CC	
	HC			
	AC			
XXIX	XXXI	XXIX	XXIX	XXVII

Before 46 BC, when Julius Caesar introduced the calendar we still use today, the Roman year consisted of 355 days, divided into 12 months: four of 31 days (March, May, Quintilis/July, October), one of 28 (February), and the rest of 29. In an attempt to keep the official calendar in line with the solar year the Romans used to insert an extra "intercalary" month of 22 or 23 days every other year. But this process was neither regularly nor competently carried out in practice, and the calendar was often seriously out of phase with the seasons. In order to make the necessary adjustment Caesar had to extend the year 46 BC by 90 days.

Our knowledge of the pre-Julian calendar is based partly on literary accounts and partly on an inscribed calendar from Antium, the *Fasti Antiates Maiores* (reconstructed *left*), the only pre-Julian calendar to survive.

Within each month there were three fixed points which originally corresponded with the phases of the moon. These were the Kalends, on the 1st day of the month, the Nones, on either the 5th or the 7th, and the Ides, on either the 13th or 15th. Days of the month were counted retrospectively (and inclusively) from these points. For example the battle of Cannae (2 August 216 BC) occurred on "the 4th day before the Nones of August" (for this reason the 4th day before the Nones was always considered unlucky). The months were also subdivided into "weeks" of eight days, with a market day (*nundinae*) every eighth day. On the calendars each day was marked with a letter from A to H, indicating its place in the nundinal cycle (see illustration). Besides the nundinal letter, each day was also marked with another letter or series of letters indicating whether it was a working day or a holiday. The letter F (*fastus*) marked an ordinary working day, the letter C (*comitialis*) one on which assemblies could be held. On days marked N (*nefastus*), however, certain types of public business were banned. Days marked EN (*endotercisus*) were split between the evening and morning, which were N, and the afternoon, which was F. The letters NP (probably *nefastus publicus*) usually designated the days of the great public festivals, the names of which were also included in abbreviated form – e.g. *TERMI* [*nalia*], *AGON*[*alia*], *FORDI*[*cidia*] etc. Apart from these fixed festivals (*feriae stativae*), there were a number of movable feasts (*feriae conceptivae*), such as the *Ambarvalia* (see above, p. 26), which did not appear in the calendar but were held on days which were determined each year by the pontiffs.

The festivals themselves were of very great antiquity, and most scholars would probably agree that the basic elements of the republican calendar date back at least as far as the 6th century BC. The festivals reflect the concerns of a simple agricultural community: to ensure the fertility of the soil and the health of the flocks, to promote childbirth, to placate the spirits of the dead, to avert disease and pestilence. A primitive warrior society is also implied in ceremonies such as the *Tubilustrium* (purification of the trumpets) on 23 March and 23 May, and the *Armilustrium* (purification of weapons) on 19 October. The rites performed at the various festivals were many and various; there was a good deal of mumbo jumbo, and by the late Republic the Romans themselves were unable to explain much of what they were doing or even to identify the gods who were being honored. Better-known festivals include the *Lupercalia* (15 February), a purification ceremony in which bands of naked youths ran around the Palatine, the site of the earliest settlement, striking any women they came across with strips of goatskin; and the *Saturnalia* (17 December), the forerunner of Christmas. At that time, according to Accius (see above, p. 54), "when people celebrate the day, they joyfully hold feasts throughout the countryside and towns, and each man waits upon his own slaves."

The Oriental Cults

The oriental religions which spread to Rome and the western provinces during the late Republic and early Empire belong to a world of ideas entirely different from the beliefs and practices of traditional Roman paganism. The traditional religions had fulfilled the needs of a simple agricultural society, and in their more advanced form gave sanction to the political activities and developing imperialism of the republican government of Rome; but they were increasingly found wanting in the cosmopolitan urban society of the Roman Empire. Oriental cults were first brought to the west by traders, merchants, and particularly slaves; it is significant that, for example, Eunus/Antiochus, the leader of the first Sicilian slave revolt (c. 136–132 BC), was a devotee of Atargatis, the "Syrian goddess," and derived much of his charisma from a claim to be her protégé. The large-scale manumission of slaves, and the spontaneous immigration occasioned by trade, led to the growth of sizable Greek and oriental communities in all the major cities of the western Empire, which became centers for the propagation of oriental cults, just as the Jewish communities of the Diaspora were centers for the spread of early Christianity. The movement of ideas was also facilitated by the ease of communication which Roman rule itself made possible.

The cult of the "Syrian goddess" was one of the most important of the increasingly popular mystery religions. Others include the Phrygian cults of Cybele and of Sabazios, the Egyptian Isis, and the Persian Mithras. One might add the Palestinian-Jewish cult of Christianity, which, although unique in certain respects, had much in common with the other oriental cults which were its rivals for a time.

The oriental cults differed from traditional paganism in that they made a direct appeal to the individual, offering him the chance of personal redemption through communion with the divine powers. The appeal to the personal convictions of the individual offered the possibility of conversion, which entailed ceremonies of initiation and the revelation of mysteries known only to a select and privileged group. There was a strong emphasis on ritual meals, on suffering as a means of atonement, and on ceremonies of purification. The most striking of the latter was the *taurobolium*, originally connected with the cult of Cybele, but later more generalized in usage; in a *taurobolium* the worshiper stood in a pit and was bathed in the blood of a bull sacrificed over him. He emerged from this rite in a state of purified innocence.

Part of the attraction of the mystery cults was that the initiate achieved an equality of status with his fellow believers which cut across existing social and ethnic barriers. Each of the mystery cults had elaborate rituals and liturgies, a complex theology and a doctrine of immortality; in short they were able to satisfy the aesthetic, intellectual and spiritual needs of all kinds of people in an often harsh and unjust world.

Mithraism originated in Persia and spread to the Roman Empire via Asia Minor in the 1st century AD. Mithras was a god of light, engaged in a permanent struggle with Ahriman, the evil prince of darkness. His role as creative god was symbolized in his slaying of the bull (*left*), whose flowing blood was the source of life and vegetation. The slaying took place in a cave, reflected in the underground location of Mithraic chapels, like the one beneath the church of St Clemente at Rome (*below*). Mithraism was an exclusively male cult, and was especially popular among soldiers, through whose agency it spread through the frontier provinces of the Empire. It possessed a rigid hierarchy of priesthoods and grades of initiation, and emphasized loyalty and discipline.

Right Relief showing an *archigallus*, or high priest of Cybele, with the robes and implements of his profession. The rites of the goddess were ecstatic and involved wild dancing, flagellation (notice the flail held by the *archigallus*) and self-mutilation. Those who went to the extreme of self-castration became her priests and were known as *galli*. From the first the Roman government suspected the strange new cult it had inadvertently admitted (see opposite). Originally Roman citizens were barred from the ceremonies and forbidden to join the ranks of fanatical eunuch priests, but this regulation was relaxed under the emperors.

The cult of Isis and her consort Osiris-Serapis, whose ceremonies are seen (*below*) in a wall painting from Herculaneum, was a hellenized version of an old Egyptian cult which spread through the Mediterranean world in the Hellenistic period. It was already established at Pompeii by 100 BC, and in Rome by the time of Sulla. The cult was repeatedly persecuted by the government until the time of Caligula, who officially recognized it and built a temple to Isis in the Campus Martius. The myth of Isis symbolized creation, in the death and resurrection of Osiris and Isis' conception of Horus over his body.

The Phrygian deity Sabazios was variously identified with Jupiter and Dionysus, and often confused with Attis. Characteristic of his cult were votive offerings of hands, covered with magical symbols, in this case (*below*) the signs of the Zodiac. They make the liturgical sign of benediction, with thumb and first two fingers extended.

Below The jackal-headed figure of the Egyptian god Anubis, on a tombstone from the 1st- and 2nd-century catacombs at Kom el-Shuqafa at Alexandria. In ancient Egyptian belief, Anubis was connected with the rituals of death and the afterlife and is here seen in the dress and with the pose of a Roman soldier. "Barking Anubis" was among the monstrous oriental deities ranged by Virgil among the supporters of Antony and Cleopatra against the ancestral Roman gods on the side of Octavian.

The earliest oriental cult to be established in Rome was that of Magna Mater or Cybele, which originated in Phrygia in Asia Minor and was introduced into the Roman state religion in 204 BC as a result of a prophecy that she would help the Romans against Hannibal. A goddess of the earth, Cybele is often portrayed (*right*) riding a chariot drawn by lions, symbolizing her role as mistress of wild beasts. Her consort, who rides beside her, was the vegetation god Attis, whose death and resurrection were reflected by the seasons and celebrated with frenzied and ecstatic rites.

The Emperors: Augustus to Justinian

The table expresses the changing nature of the imperial office: for its first two-and-a-half centuries, stable dynasties passing from one to another in a process accelerated by occasional civil war; in the 3rd century a rapid succession of short-lived emperors, their prospects of survival increasing towards the end of the century; and in the 4th and 5th centuries, after the flurry of the rise of Constantine, the restored stability of hereditary dynasties, based on the division of the Empire and collegiality of the imperial office.

The selected imperial portraits communicate the office as it was presented to successive contemporaries. The youthful paternalism of Augustus (here seen veiled as Pontifex Maximus) contrasts with the anxious thoughtfulness of Maximinus, an image picked up in more stylized form in the determined features of Diocletian and Maximian. The statue of Barletta in Italy has often been connected with Valentinian I, whom this tense, authoritarian character seems to fit; but the style is of the 5th rather than the 4th century, and the best candidate may be Marcian. Finally, the elderly Justinian, in an image of remote tranquillity.

Augustus

Maximinus

Diocletian and Maximian

27 BC–14 AD	Augustus	Julio-Claudian dynasty
14–37	Tiberius	
37–41	Gaius	
41–54	Claudius	
54–68	Nero	
68–69	Galba	
69	Otho, Vitellius	
69–79	Vespasian	Flavian, Nervo-Trajanic, and Antonine dynasties
79–81	Titus	
81–96	Domitian	
96–98	Nerva	
97–117	Trajan (97–98 with Nerva)	
117–38	Hadrian	
138–61	Antoninus Pius	
161–80	Marcus Aurelius (161–69 with Lucius Verus)	
180–92	Commodus	
193	Pertinax	Severan dynasty
193	Didius Julianus	
193–211	Septimius Severus	
211–17	Caracalla (211–12 with Geta)	
217–18	Macrinus	
218–22	Elagabalus	
222–35	Alexander Severus	

Period of political anarchy and disorder

235–38	Maximinus
238	Gordian I and II (in Africa)
238	Balbinus and Pupienus (in Italy)
238–44	Gordian III
244–49	Philip
249–51	Decius
251–53	Trebonianus Gallus
253	Aemilianus
253–60	Valerian
253–68	Gallienus (253–60 with Valerian)

WEST		EAST	
259–74	Gallic empire of Postumus, Victorinus, Tetricus	260–72	Palmyrene empire of Odaenathus, Zenobia, Vaballath

268–70	Claudius
270	Quintillus
270–75	Aurelian
275–76	Tacitus
276–82	Probus
282–83	Carus
283–84	Carinus and Numerian

284–305 Diocletian and Tetrarchy

WEST		EAST	
287–305	Maximian Augustus	284–305	Diocletian Augustus
293–305	Constantius Caesar	293–305	Galerius Caesar
305–06	Constantius Augustus	305–11	Galerius Augustus
305–06	Severus Caesar (306–07 Augustus)	305–09	Maximinus Caesar (309–13 Augustus)

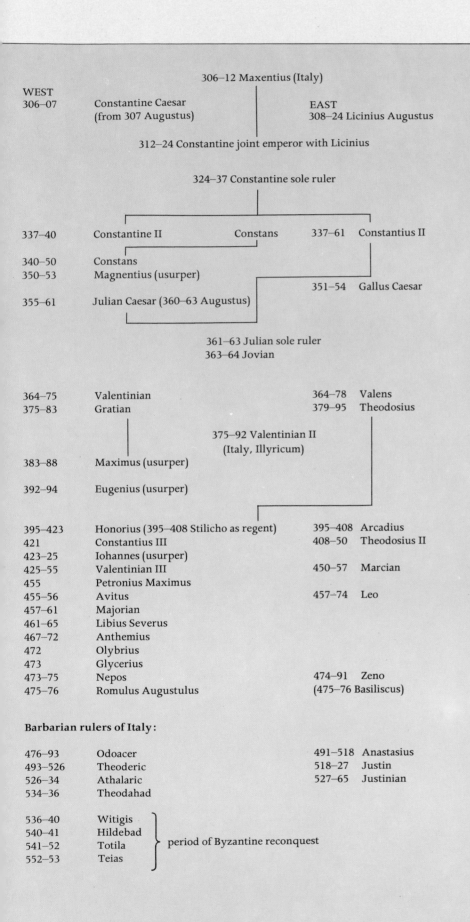

WEST			EAST	
		306–12 Maxentius (Italy)		
306–07	Constantine Caesar (from 307 Augustus)		308–24	Licinius Augustus
		312–24 Constantine joint emperor with Licinius		
		324–37 Constantine sole ruler		
337–40	Constantine II	Constans	337–61	Constantius II
340–50	Constans			
350–53	Magnentius (usurper)			
			351–54	Gallus Caesar
355–61	Julian Caesar (360–63 Augustus)			
		361–63 Julian sole ruler		
		363–64 Jovian		
364–75	Valentinian		364–78	Valens
375–83	Gratian		379–95	Theodosius
		375–92 Valentinian II (Italy, Illyricum)		
383–88	Maximus (usurper)			
392–94	Eugenius (usurper)			
395–423	Honorius (395–408 Stilicho as regent)		395–408	Arcadius
421	Constantius III		408–50	Theodosius II
423–25	Iohannes (usurper)			
425–55	Valentinian III		450–57	Marcian
455	Petronius Maximus			
455–56	Avitus		457–74	Leo
457–61	Majorian			
461–65	Libius Severus			
467–72	Anthemius			
472	Olybrius			
473	Glycerius			
473–75	Nepos		474–91	Zeno
475–76	Romulus Augustulus			(475–76 Basiliscus)

Barbarian rulers of Italy:

476–93	Odoacer		491–518	Anastasius
493–526	Theoderic		518–27	Justin
526–34	Athalaric		527–65	Justinian
534–36	Theodahad			
536–40	Witigis	period of Byzantine reconquest		
540–41	Hildebad			
541–52	Totila			
552–53	Teias			

Above Marcian (?)

Below Justinian

Trajan's Army

Apollodorus of Damascus, the designer of Trajan's column and of the monumental complex which provided its setting, was one of the great practical geniuses of antiquity. The column presents a narrative of the two Dacian wars of Trajan (101–02 and 105–06 AD) in the form of a continuous relief spiral over 200 meters in length. Though hard to see from ground level, the sculptures would originally have been viewed from galleries in the buildings of the Bibliotheca Ulpia surrounding it. Despite difficulties of detail, and in the almost complete absence of other evidence, the narrative of the Dacian campaign can be traced with considerable precision.

Apart from the interest of their narrative technique and artistic style, the reliefs are full of accurately perceived details of the Roman army at work. They illustrate not only the actual fighting but the marching, the building and engineering, the medical and transport facilities, and, not least, the religious observances, which framed the working life of the Roman army.

Throughout the series, the figure of Trajan recurs, usually accompanied by advisers: addressing and reviewing his troops, performing sacrifice, receiving embassies and prisoners, sometimes (as *right*) simply gazing forward with a studied calm foresight. He is presented as the "fellow soldier" of his men, and with this word, *commilitones*, he would address them in speeches.

The musicians (*below*) are from a procession associated with a sacrifice. Their instruments are valveless, but the leader of the band, who plays a pipe with a hollow mouthpiece, rather like a cornett, is using his right hand to produce a change of pitch or tone. The Legio III Augusta at Lambaesis in Africa had on its strength 39 trumpeters (*tubicines*) and 36 horn players (*cornicines*, as here).

Roman *ballistae*, resembling large crossbows, could attain considerable accuracy and range (up to 500 meters has been estimated). The two arms were operated by torsion springs of sinew cord, held in the drums at each side. Here two varieties are shown. *Below* a *ballista* is being brought up in a cart to be transferred to its prepared emplacement. The reconstruction (*right*), with its much sturdier carriage, is of a genuinely mobile version – a sort of Roman field gun, drawn by two mules.

In this scene (*below*), from the early stages of the first Dacian war, a camp is being built by legionaries, whose pikes, helmets and shields are propped up nearby. Some soldiers excavate a double ditch, carrying the earth away in baskets, while others construct the ramparts with squared pieces of turf, some of which are laid out in the foreground. The ramparts are stabilized with wooden cross-ties; the sculptor has shown the ends of these, apparently without understanding what they are. Trajan is shown looking out from his camp. To the left, more legionaries build a wooden bridge over a stream, beyond which (earlier in the narrative) is another, completed camp with its sentry. Below, a Dacian prisoner is brought to Trajan (off left) by two auxiliaries.

The detail (*below*), from the final assault on the Dacian capital of Sarmizegetusa, shows auxiliary troops leading the attack, both regular infantry, armed with short swords and rectangular shields, and archers clad in scale armor. The latter were recruited from the east, notably from the regions of Commagene, Emesa and Ituraea. Seen in their full context, they are covering the infantry from the rear, firing over their heads at the defending Dacians. Slingers and legionaries are also involved in the attack. As they appear on the column, legionaries wear rounded, while auxiliaries wear conical, helmets. Auxiliaries usually, though not in this instance, carry oval shields.

Left The standard bearer of a praetorian cohort. The shaft of his standard is decorated with the victory crowns won by his cohort, and with the image of the emperor, and is surmounted by the emblem of his unit.

Right Novaesium (Neuss), on the Rhine frontier in Lower Germany, was a typical permanent legionary fortress. Its neat barrack blocks accommodated upwards of 5000 legionaries divided into ten cohorts, and each of these into six centuries, nominally of 100 men but in practice rather smaller.

Above the most famous of all Roman military formations, the *testudo* or "tortoise," used for approaching the walls of an enemy in siege warfare. It is here being used in an attack on the citadel of a Dacian hill fort.

A POLITE AND POWERFUL EMPIRE

Imperial affairs

During the century and a half from 70 to 235 AD, the Roman Empire was by common consent at its height both of political and of cultural achievement. It was a period of slow development rather than of rapid change or spectacular events. Gibbon could write of the emperor Antoninus Pius (138–61) that he "diffused order and tranquillity over the greatest part of the earth," with the result that his reign provided few materials for history – "which is, indeed, little more than the register of the crimes, follies and misfortunes of mankind." Gibbon was thinking of regular narrative history with a military and political bias; yet, behind the obvious prosperity of the Antonine age, some of the changes which occurred in the military balance of the Empire in relation to its neighbors ultimately transformed the social basis of imperial power and led to the very different conditions of the 3rd century and late Empire. At the same time, in changes in the sensibilities of the 2nd century one detects the origins of some of the most distinctive cultural and religious features of late antiquity.

From a political point of view, this was a period of generally well-established imperial dynasties, the main moments of upheaval occurring in the civil wars of 69–70, which brought the Flavians to power, and of 193, from which emerged the dynasty of the Severi. The principle of succession under the Flavians was one of family inheritance, Vespasian being succeeded by his sons: the popular but short-lived Titus (79–81) and Domitian (81–96). The latter was a complex personality combining moral puritanism and religious archaism (he had an adulterous Vestal Virgin entombed alive) with a tyrannical intolerance which caused the last years of his reign to decline into a bloody persecution of those, especially philosophers, who expressed opposition to him. His denigration by the satirist Juvenal as a "bald Nero," lashing a half-dead world and enslaving Rome (*Satires* 4.38), was from this point of view at least not inappropriate.

The attractions of Nerva as imperial candidate upon the unexpected murder of Domitian in a palace plot (18 September 96) were in part his childlessness, which seemed to allow some room for political maneuver, as well as his personality and reputation as a mild, blameless senator. But Nerva's brief reign (96–98) was insecure and turbulent, and a major crisis and perhaps renewed civil war were only averted by his hasty adoption of Trajan, commander of the armies of Upper Germany. Trajan and his successor Hadrian, being without children, had recourse to adoption as a means of securing continuity of power; but both the accession of Hadrian in 117 and the preparations for his succession were marred by political unrest and the executions of potential rivals.

With the exceptions of Domitian and Commodus, the political conduct of the emperors of the Flavian and Antonine dynasties was relatively restrained, and opposition, though intermittently expressed, was not widespread. Hostility to the memory of Hadrian can be ascribed to the confusion and acrimony surrounding his attempts to secure the succession; his first choice, Aelius Caesar, adopted in 136 from an Italian senatorial family, died prematurely and was replaced by the later emperor Antoninus Pius. There was little unrest among the provincial armies, such as had brought Vespasian to power in 69 after the proclamations of other candidates in Spain, Germany, Africa and at Rome. Domitian had to suppress the rebellion of Antonius Saturninus in Germany in 89–90, and Marcus Aurelius was threatened by the uprising in the east in 175 of Avidius Cassius, governor of Syria. This rebellion, perhaps set afoot in the knowledge of Marcus' advancing age and the apparent unsuitability of Commodus for the succession, seems to have won some support in court circles close to Marcus himself. His wife Faustina was believed to be implicated, but Marcus refrained after Cassius' suppression from investigations that might have proved embarrassing.

The government of the Flavians and Antonines was characterized, again with relatively few exceptions, by restraint and sobriety. This was especially true of Vespasian, who alleged in support of his notorious financial parsimony the immense cost to the Empire of the civil wars of 69–70. But even Vespasian spent heavily on rebuilding at Rome, and the short reign of Titus was marked by lavish expenditure, especially on the occasion of the inauguration of the Flavian Amphitheater (the Colosseum), and on further rebuilding after a fire at Rome. Titus was also much praised for relief measures after the destruction of Pompeii and Herculaneum by the eruption of Vesuvius in 79. It has been argued that Domitian was confronted by serious financial crisis, perhaps consequent on his raising of military pay by one-third. This would indeed provide a motive for his prosecutions of senators, but the extent of the financial crisis, if it existed, remains uncertain. The Flavians also exacted responsible conduct from provincial governors, Domitian especially being insistent on this. The biographer Suetonius, no lover of Domitian, remarked that governors were at no time more restrained and honest than under this emperor.

The military policy of the Flavians shows care and consistent planning, especially in their redesigning of the frontier in the upper Rhine and Danube regions. Domitian's Dacian wars, at first catastrophic, with major defeats in 85 and 86, were later successful at the battle of Tapae (88), and prepared the way for Trajan's wars and annexation of Dacia. Among the terms agreed by Domitian with the Dacian king Decebalus was the provision to the Dacians of Roman engineers, an early instance of the "foreign aid programs" which have so often introduced outside influences to less advanced though previously independent peoples.

This silver sestertius was issued by the emperor Titus to commemorate the inauguration in 79 AD of the Flavian amphitheater. Begun by Vespasian as part of his embellishment and reconstruction of Rome after the civil wars of 68–70, the amphitheater could seat upwards of 70000 spectators, and remained in use until the 6th century.

A silver tetradrachm issued by Shimeon bar-Kosiba, or Bar-Kochba, the leader of the third Jewish revolt of 132–35 AD. The legends are (*above*) "Shimeon," with an image of the Temple facade, and (*below*) "of the freedom of Jerusalem."

The relief (*top*), from the *lararium*, or household shrine, of L. Caecilius Jucundus of Pompeii, vividly expresses the effect of the earthquake which in 62 AD damaged large parts of the city before its destruction by the great eruption of Vesuvius in 79.

The two Dacian wars of Trajan resulted in the annexation of Dacia as a Roman province (107 AD). Here, in a relief from Trajan's column (*above*), is shown part of the final battle against Decebalus, after which the Dacian king committed suicide. A recently published inscription records the exploit of the Roman soldier, Tiberius Claudius Maximus, who took Decebalus' head to Trajan.

The annexation of Dacia can be seen as a defensive maneuver in the overall strategic context of the northern frontiers of the Empire, but Trajan's wars of 101–02 and 106 were presented to the Roman public in a spirit of open imperialism; the sculptures of the Column of Trajan depict his campaigns with a wealth of detailed illustration covering all aspects of army life. The building of the Column, and of the Forum of Trajan in which it was placed, was largely financed by the royal treasures of the defeated Dacian king. Trajan's other military venture, an invasion of Parthia, apparently with annexation in mind, cannot be explained except as aggressive imperialism influenced by the desire to emulate Alexander the Great. Begun in 115, the project foundered in 117 with the emperor's illness and death in Cilicia, leaving unsecured annexations and unrest in Judaea, Egypt and Cyrenaica to be suppressed by Hadrian. Hadrian abandoned the attempt to conquer Parthia – if indeed Trajan had not already done so. After the second Jewish revolt of Bar-Kochba (132–35), he destroyed Jerusalem, establishing in its place the legionary camp of Aelia Capitolina.

In temperament Hadrian was very different from his predecessor. Trajan was a plain soldier, Hadrian a restless, inquiring intellectual with a deep love of Greek culture. During his 21-year reign, he traveled ceaselessly, visiting his armies all over the Empire (an inscription preserves a speech delivered by him to the soldiers stationed at Lambaesis in Numidia after he had reviewed them and watched their maneuvers) and cultural centers like Athens and Alexandria. The versatility of his tastes is well represented by his two most famous monuments: the imperial residence at Tibur (Tivoli), reflecting in its design the influence of his worldwide travels, and Hadrian's Wall, massively defining the military frontier of Britain and of the entire Roman Empire at its most northerly and remotest point.

By contrast with both Trajan and Hadrian, Antoninus Pius never left Italy while he was emperor; he lived quietly at Rome, devoted to the government of the Empire and surrounded by a sober household and honest family virtues. In this latter respect too he was unlike Hadrian, whose wife Sabina was neglected and unhappy, and whose relationship with the boy Antinous was notorious; Hadrian indeed named a town in Egypt after him, following Antinous' accidental death by drowning in the Nile. For the later years of his reign, Pius ruled jointly with his nephew and adoptive son, M. Annius Verus (Marcus Aurelius), and died peacefully in 161. Marcus ruled as joint emperor with his adoptive brother L. Verus until 169, when Verus died while returning with him from Germany, having previously conducted a successful Parthian campaign. From 177 until 180 Marcus ruled with his son Commodus. His reign brings out acutely the tensions which were increasingly to affect the Roman Empire and change the structure of its government. A Stoic philosopher and, both in ancient and modern times, one of the most admired of all Roman emperors, Marcus set out in Greek in his *Meditations* his most personal thoughts, as they occurred to him and without literary elaboration (their original title was simply "To himself"). He had not aspired to the office of emperor and did not much enjoy wielding the power which it gave, but through his philosophy possessed an immensely strong sense of the obligations of the station in life to which he had been called, and to which he owed the full exercise of his moral and intellectual powers. Marcus wrote the *Meditations* while involved in the wars against the northern enemies of Rome, the Quadi and Marcomanni, which for several years of his reign required his presence in the theater of war. The campaigns, like those of Trajan, were narrated on a column at Rome, in a coarser, but in some ways more vigorous and no less aggressive style than that of Trajan's Column; they were not for aggrandizement, but for the defense of the Empire against mounting pressure on the Danube frontier. This was to be the abiding pattern of Roman military history in the next century.

Marcus died at Vindobona (Vienna) in 180, while conducting these wars. His son and successor, Commodus, was criticized for the haste with which he made a settlement with the barbarians and returned to Rome. Commodus clearly preferred living at Rome to conducting campaigns on the frontiers. The history of his reign largely concerns his activities in the capital, especially conspiracies mounted against him and violently suppressed, his excessively lavish generosity in providing public games, to which he was personally devoted, the food riots which led him to sacrifice his favorite, the freedman Cleander, and the religious ambition which led to his adoption of Hercules as his personal deity and in due course to his identification of himself with the god; Commodus appears on coins and in statue busts dressed in a lionskin and wielding a club, as worn and carried by Hercules.

Commodus fell to a conspiracy on New Year's Eve

Above Marble bust of the emperor Hadrian, c. 120 AD.

Right Hadrian's villa at Tivoli (Tibur), well characterized as a group of freely related pavilions or as a "contrived architectural landscape" (B. Cunliffe), was influenced in its various stages by monuments admired by the emperor during his travels. The effect is sophisticated, cultured and rather nostalgic. Here is seen the "Canopus", reproducing an architectural feature seen at this Egyptian city. Hadrian's memories of Egypt were mixed, for his young lover Antinous, seen *below* in one of many idealized representations, was drowned there.

The boar-hunt roundel (*below center*), reused in the 4th-century arch of Constantine, shows Hadrian in a typical pose of imperial leisure. The Sasanian image shown below (p. 168) forms an interesting comparison.

Right The new Pantheon or "shrine of all the gods" at Rome, shown here in Panini's painting of c. 1750, is a Hadrianic masterpiece, although the original dedicatory inscription of Agrippa was allowed to remain. The diameter of the huge cupola – at over 45 meters the largest ever built by preindustrial methods – corresponds exactly to its height from the floor, so that it forms in effect the upper half of a perfect sphere. It is an image of the vault of the heavens, and the opening at its summit symbolizes the sun.

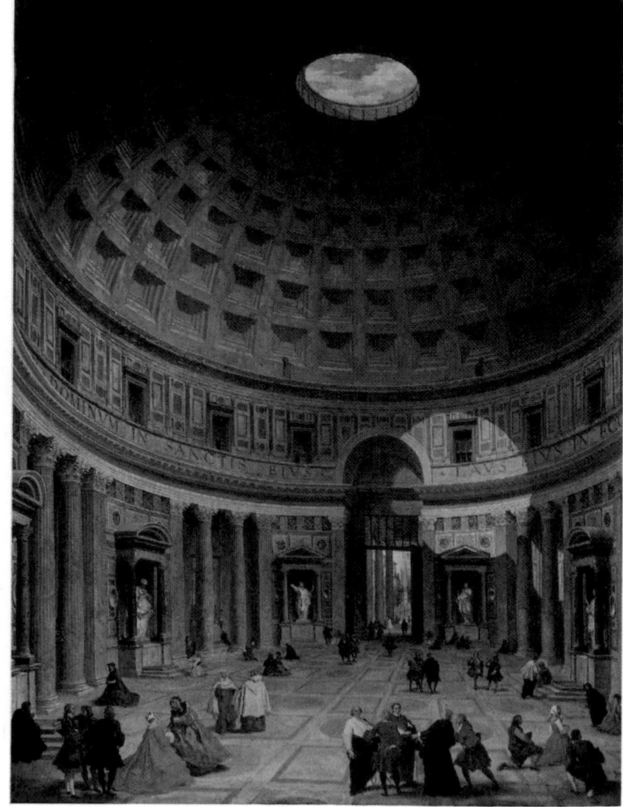

192. His successor, P. Helvius Pertinax, was a military officer whose service in the wars of Marcus Aurelius had raised him swiftly from equestrian rank to the consulship in 175. Pertinax failed to satisfy his supporters and, partly by the rigor of his policies, acquired too many new enemies; after less than three months in power he was murdered by the Praetorian Guard. He was succeeded by Didius Julianus, a hitherto respectable senator and the grandson of a great jurist of the time of Hadrian, who was able to raise the money to secure his acceptance by the Praetorians to the tune of 25 000 sestertii per man. At once, however, the armies of Pannonia proclaimed their commander, Septimius Severus, as emperor. In a rapid march to Italy Severus suppressed Julianus and then, in a pattern of civil war reminiscent of 69–70, defeated in battle his rivals Pescennius Niger, the commander of the armies of Syria, in 194, and Clodius Albinus, proclaimed in Britain but defeated near Lugdunum (Lyon), in 196. After overcoming Niger, Severus had already embarked on a campaign against Parthia, intending partly at least to divert public attention from civil war to a successful foreign conquest; he returned to the east after his victory over Albinus, in order to consolidate his conquests. The result of Severus' wars against the Parthians was the annexation of northern Mesopotamia and the setting of the Roman frontier at the Tigris, but he failed to capture the caravan city of Hatra further to the south.

Septimius Severus bestowed on his sons Caracalla and Geta official nomenclature implying continuity with the Antonine dynasty, and in early coin issues appears himself with the designation "son of the deified Marcus Pius." His reign was notable for his generous building programs and public expenditure, particularly at his native city of Leptis Magna in Tripolitania. He conducted military campaigns in Britain, where he died after a painful illness in 211. His successor Caracalla (M. Aurelius Antoninus) campaigned on the Rhine and Danube frontiers and visited Alexandria before embarking in 216 on a Parthian campaign. In the following year Caracalla was assassinated near Carrhae (Harran) in Syria, in favor of his Praetorian Prefect Macrinus.

As far as their domestic policies are concerned Septimius Severus and his son are not well regarded by the ancient sources; both he and Caracalla are reported, with some but not total exaggeration, to have put to death large numbers of senators and men of equestrian rank. Severus' deathbed advice to Caracalla was reputed to have been to preserve concord with his brother, enrich the armies and ignore the rest. Caracalla disregarded the first part of this advice, killing the young Geta in 212. As for the second part, the army was increased in size under the Severan emperors and better paid, and it received certain privileges, such as the right of soldiers to contract legal marriages while still in service. Despite the benefits received by the army it is not clear that the Severi particularly deserve the reputation which they have gained for "militarizing" the Roman Empire. More relevant to this process is the steady pressure on the northern frontiers which by its nature made the army more important and required its commanders to demonstrate military expertise to a degree not expected in the 1st and earlier 2nd centuries.

The commemorative medallion (*above*), issued in the last month of Commodus' reign, shows the emperor wearing the lion-skin headdress of Hercules. The reverse of the medallion, not illustrated, has Hercules with the features of Commodus and the legend "HERCULI ROMANO" – "to the Roman Hercules!"

The detail from the column of Marcus Aurelius (*above right*) shows a barbarian captive on the point of his dispatch by a Roman soldier. His face is distorted in agony and his outstretched right hand expresses despairing supplication; the movement of his hair suggests the shock of the impact of the spear in his back.

After the brief intermission of Macrinus (217–18), an eastern conspiracy produced an imperial candidate from among the Syrian relatives of Septimius Severus' wife, Julia Domna. This was Varius Avitus Bassianus, better known as Elagabalus, a boy priest from the temple of Elagabal, the indigenous god of Emesa (Homs). In a brief but eccentric reign, the most notable event was the importation to Rome of the black conical stone representing the god of Emesa, an event which is suggested on some coin issues of Elagabalus. The emperor is reported to have preceded on foot the carriage bearing the stone, walking backwards in obeisance. The more lurid of the stories told by some ancient sources on the reign of Elagabalus must be treated with caution, as must the fictionally idealistic picture which they present of Alexander Severus, Elagabalus' successor upon his murder in 222. Alexander, another easterner from the same family, was a weak emperor, dominated by his mother Julia Mammaea. After a fair start, his reign soon brought political disorder with the murder after little more than a year of his praetorian prefect, the jurist Ulpian, and continued without distinction. In 231 he set out on a campaign against Parthia but was compelled to return to face a more immediate threat on the Rhine frontier. At Moguntiacum (Mainz) in 235 he and his mother were murdered by the soldiers and a new emperor, C. Julius Maximinus, proclaimed. The conspiracy was inspired by the sheer insufficiency of Alexander to meet the military crisis facing the Empire, and the accession of the military officer Maximinus inaugurates a new phase of Roman history.

Military and economic expansion

Tacitus, writing in the early 2nd century, ascribed to the admirers of Augustus in 14 AD the view that the Roman Empire had already at the time of his death achieved a state of strategic completeness; the Empire was "enclosed by the Ocean or by distant rivers, with legions, provinces, fleets, all linked together and interconnected" (*Annals* 1.9). The validity of this judgment is debated, some critics thinking it more relevant to the situation in Tacitus' own day than to the time of Augustus. Apart from the conquest and annexation of Mauretania and Britain by Claudius – which might be taken to refine rather than to contradict the judgment reported by Tacitus – considerable improvements to the strategic defense of the Empire were made during the Flavian and Trajanic period. Under the Flavians, the agreement reached by Nero with Parthia in 66 AD, and the suppression of the Jewish revolt by Titus, were followed by an intensified occupation of Syria, the introduction of a garrison to Cappadocia for the defense of the upper Euphrates crossings and systematic road-building for purposes of military communication in the region between Palmyra, the cities of northern Syria and the Euphrates. In Germany an equally well-designed and carefully executed policy involved the annexation and fortification of the reentrant salient between the upper Rhine and Danube, the territory known as the *Agri Decumates*. This policy, begun by Vespasian, continued by Domitian and brought to completion in the first half of the 2nd century, permitted more economical and flexible deployments in the north, in that it became possible to release troops from the Rhine frontier to the Danube, where the military threat from barbarian peoples was more pressing and seemed likely to increase. Already under Nero a governor of Moesia had encountered kings "previously unknown and hostile" to the Romans, suppressed an "eastern movement" of Sarmatians and entered into diplomatic relations with Bastarnae, Roxolani and Dacians, and had settled 100000 Transdanubians on the Roman side of the river, with their wives, children and princes. The Dacian wars of Domitian prepared the way for those of Trajan, the outcome of which was the annexation of the kingdom of Decebalus as a new province, bounded in the east by the Aluta river (Olt), in the west by the Marisia (Mures) and Tisia (Theiss), and in the north and northeast by the barrier of the Carpathian mountains. This annexation, like the unfulfilled intention ascribed to Marcus Aurelius to create new provinces of Marcomannia and Sarmatia, can be interpreted as defensive. The province of Dacia secured the Roman bank of the Danube by forming a powerful salient, defined by natural geographical features, projecting into barbarian territory beyond the river.

In the east, Septimius Severus, as we have seen, established a new province of Mesopotamia covering the area south of Armenia as far east as the Tigris and as far south as Singara on the Djebel Sinjar. This acquisition was potentially provocative, in that it deprived the Parthians of what they regarded, and continued to regard, as their ancestral dominions, but it offered protection in depth to the Roman cities of Syria, which now stood far behind the front line. At the same time cities in Mesopotamia such as Nisibis (modern Nisaybin), Resaina and Singara were colonized. Particularly interesting is the Severan expansion into southern Numidia, which took the Romans westwards along the edge of the Sahara desert, for a short period as far as Castellum Dimmidi (the oasis of Messad). Aerial photography and field surveys on the southern and western fringes of the Aurès mountains, especially in the region of El Kantara and around the Chott el-Hodna, have revealed field-systems, irrigation works and settlement of the Roman period, on a scale and of a sophistication never achieved at any other time in history. Further north, in the plains between the Aurès mountains and the city of Sitifis (modern Sétif), can be traced large-scale settlement organized by imperial procurators through the medium of substantial townships, described on their inscriptions, of the later Severan period, as *castella*. The early 3rd century saw the greatest physical expansion of the Roman Empire and provides the most consistent evidence of the systematic exploitation of the agricultural resources of its border regions.

During the course of the first two centuries the provinces of the Roman Empire gained steadily in prosperity. A spectacular instance of this is the evidence for wine and oil imports, particularly from Spain, in the huge pile of broken pottery (50 meters in height) known as the Monte Testaccio or "Hill of Sherds" in the ancient warehouse quarter at Rome. In the 2nd and 3rd centuries, imports of olive oil from Numidian and proconsular Africa won a leading position in the popular market for this product. The great city of Thysdrus (El Djem) in proconsular Africa, with its immense amphitheater (the third largest in the Empire) of the early 3rd century and its rich mosaics, owed its prosperity to the expansion of the export trade in oil. In Numidia there developed on the same basis a thriving inland economy of substantial village communities and townships. For the Roman metropolitan market, supplies of African corn organized by imperial agents both in the province and in Rome, produced and shipped by specialized methods, vastly outweighed those brought from other sources or grown in Italy itself, though Africa did not gain proportionately from the transaction. Other parts of the Empire, like Britain and northern Gaul, Germany and the Danubian provinces, achieved a high standard of material culture, despite having begun as what would now be called underdeveloped countries.

As this survey implies, the wealth of the Roman Empire was based almost entirely on land. Commercial activity, though fundamental to the wealth of great trading cities like Alexandria, Palmyra and Dura-Europus, and an important part too of the prosperity of coastal cities like Leptis Magna in Tripolitania, did not rank with agriculture as a producer of wealth over the Empire as a whole. In any case the greater part of trade and commerce in the Empire was local in extent (the high costs of land transport would in themselves be enough to ensure this), and the commercial functions of the cities would often be performed by the landowners themselves and their agents. Industrial activity also, though more significant than sometimes assumed and obviously contributing to the material life-style of the Empire's cities, was not developed in such a way as to achieve large-scale production.

The visible urban prosperity of the Roman Empire was therefore based on the production of wealth by the labors of an agricultural population, of which relatively little is specifically known from the surviving evidence. The status of this agri-

The sun god of Emesa, shown on a coin of Elagabalus as a fire carried on a four-horsed chariot. Elagabalus had himself been boy-priest of the cult and, on becoming emperor, imported the god to Rome.

Provinces and frontiers of the Empire to 106 AD. On the completion of Trajan's Dacian wars, the Roman Empire had essentially reached its full extent. With the Flavian annexation of the "Agri Decumates," the northern land frontier was as short as it could be without the further advances into central Europe attempted, but abandoned, by Augustus. Dacia was less exposed than it looks, since its limits were based on geographical features and the Romans controlled the territory to the east and west of it; yet it was the only major province to be abandoned in the 3rd century (maps pp. 171 and 173). The only further acquisitions of any note after 106 AD were the annexation of Mesopotamia and some short-lived advances in Mauretania.

The formal distinction between "senatorial" and "imperial" provinces, though increasingly effaced in practice, remained valid, but the 2nd and 3rd centuries saw a considerable growth in their number, by division for ease of administration. Compare the provinces of the Severan and Tetrarchic periods (map p. 173).

cultural population varied widely, many being tenants of private landowners, whether local or absentee, or of the emperor, whose landed property throughout the Empire, acquired by gift, confiscation and intestacy, was very extensive. In the case of absentee landlords, the administration of estates would be performed by agents; in the case of imperial property by procurators. The oppressive behavior of imperial procurators in part of North Africa happens to be known from the inscriptions recording the successful attempts by the emperor's tenants, or *coloni*, to secure protection.

The degrees of wealth produced by agricultural exploitation varied very widely, providing at one extreme landowners of immense resources, like Herodes Atticus at Athens. At the same time many landowners, especially in smaller cities, barely reached the qualifying census for membership of the local council, or *curia*, the relatively modest figure of 100000 sestertii. At a level below that of curial status and economically continuous with it, it is clear that there existed in most parts of the Empire a free peasantry of sometimes quite substantial farmers and smallholders, owning their land and disposing of its produce in local markets.

An expression of the economic advance of the western provinces of the Empire during the first two centuries is to be found in the origins of the most significant Latin writers of the period. Following the two Senecas and Lucan from Corduba, the poet Martial and the writer on oratory Quintilian were also from Spain (respectively from the native towns of Bilbilis and Calagurris). Though an African origin has been suggested, the satirist Juvenal is more likely to have come from Aquinum in central Italy, and the younger Pliny was a Transpadane Italian from Comum. Tacitus, however, was a southern Gaul who married into a wealthy family from Forum Iulii (Fréjus). Africa provided a particularly rich contribution, with the biographer Suetonius coming from Hippo Regius in proconsular Africa, Fronto from Cirta, Apuleius from the Flavian colony of Madauros and the Christian polemicist Tertullian from Carthage. No known writer came from Pannonia until Victorinus, bishop of Poetovio (Ptuj, formerly Pettau) in the early 4th century, and Britain is absent from the register for almost another hundred years. Yet

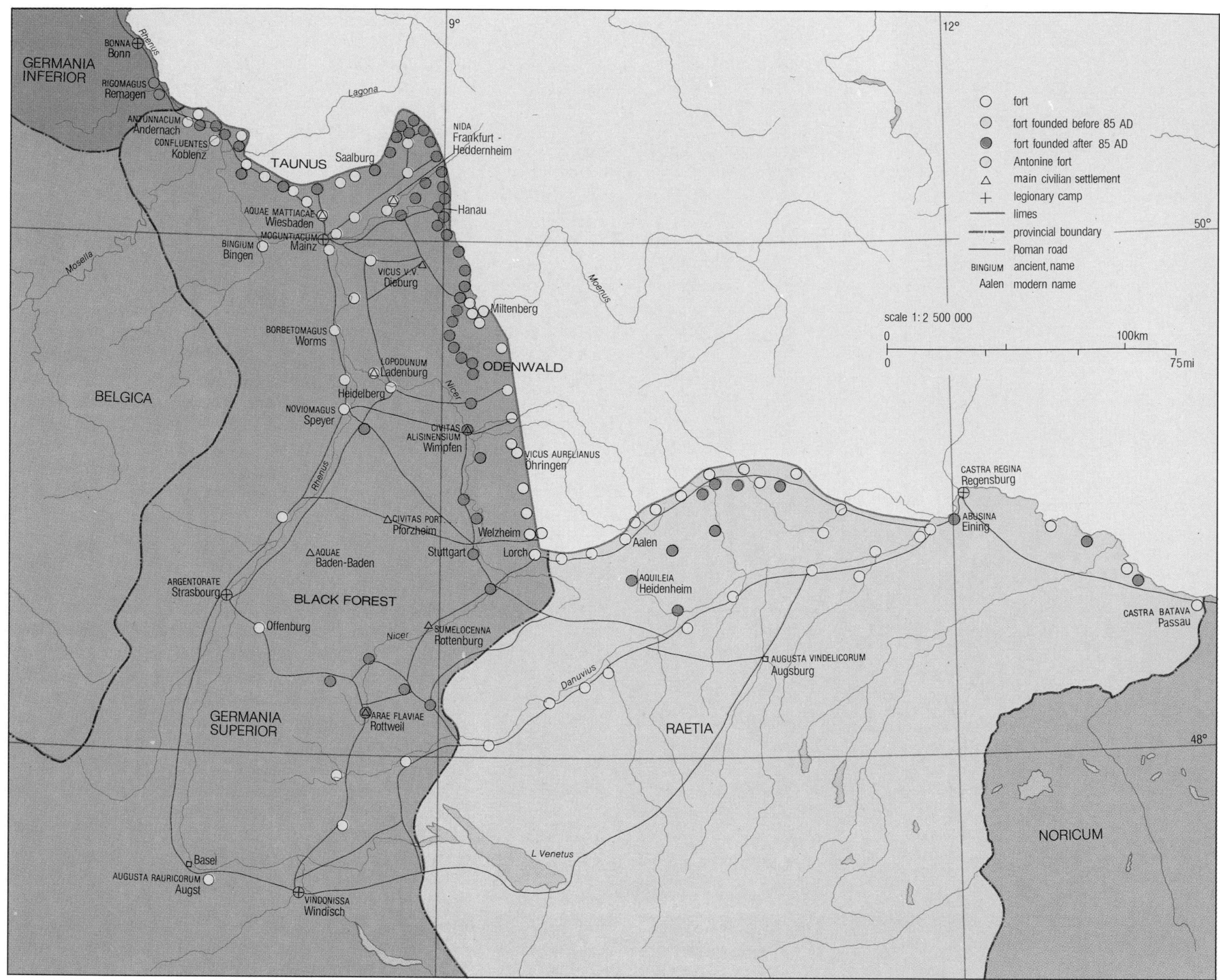

The German-Raetian *limes* from Vespasian to the Antonines. The map brings out the coherence of the advance of the *limes*, as the line of frontier forts is pushed forward from the Rhine and Danube to the advanced positions of the Antonine period. The greater east-west mobility provided by the new frontier, and the possibilities for greater freedom of military deployment, are also apparent. The advanced frontier was itself, however, based on no great physical barrier and was maintained largely by moral prestige. In the late Empire the annexed region was abandoned and frontier defense again based on the Rhine and Danube, heavily reinforced by fortification on and behind the rivers (see p. 192).

appearances can be deceptive. Central and western Gaul, after a long silence in the first three centuries, suddenly produced an efflorescence of distinguished writers in the 4th century, which is inexplicable unless the province had earlier possessed its share of literary culture. Britain produces the only known allusion on a Roman coin to Virgil as well as mosaic illustrations of episodes from the *Aeneid*, and its spoken Latin is argued to have been of a conspicuously high standard.

The steady extension of the Roman citizenship during the first two centuries of the Empire, by grants to individuals and to communities, meant that by the Severan period its possession had ceased to be a real asset or distinction. By a constitution of Caracalla, the *constitutio Antoniniana* of 212 AD, all free inhabitants of the Empire became Roman citizens. It is clear from the number of individuals who from this time appear in documents with the names M. Aurelius, after the official titulature of Caracalla, that many were enfranchised. The measure was nevertheless not of fundamental importance except, in the view of contemporaries (shared by modern critics), as a fiscal measure; Caracalla had thereby increased the numbers of the inhabitants of the Empire liable to taxation. The privileges previously inherent in the citizenship – such as the privilege claimed by St Paul of freedom from arbitrary beating by order of Roman officials (Acts 22:24ff.) – were maintained as part of a now more precise social distinction, that between men of "more honorable" and "more humble" status (*honestiores* and *humiliores*): the former can be broadly identified as the members of the curial class of the cities of the Empire. *Honestiores* were exempt from certain punishments, such as consignment to the state mines, corporal punishment and torture (except in certain defined cases such as treason), and execution by burning alive or exposure to wild beasts. The distinction between the two classes first appears in legal texts in the time of Hadrian, but it is evident that it was applied in practice before this, and reflects well-established Roman assumptions as to the differing values to be attached to men of different social rank.

The widening origins of the ruling classes

The origins of the emperors of the Flavian, Antonine and Severan dynasties reflect in social terms the steadily expanding political franchise and economic development of the Roman world. The Flavians came from municipal origins at Reate (Rieti), in old Sabine territory; Vespasian was said by Tacitus to have promoted an atmosphere of "domestic parsimony" typical of new men from Italy and the provinces after the excesses of the Julio-Claudian period. Trajan and Hadrian were from Spain, from the city of Italica in Baetica. Antoninus Pius was from Nemausus (Nîmes), an ancient tribal center and Roman colony in southern Gaul, and his dynasty, through the prematurely deceased Aelius Caesar and through Marcus Aurelius (whose grandfather was from Spain), presents an example of connections between wealthy provincial and Italian families such as often occurred in the first two centuries among the aristocracies of the west. Septimius Severus and his family widen the range still further. Severus himself was from Leptis Magna, an ancient Punic city which, through the generosity of its leading families, had very quickly asserted its prosperity and civic pride under the Roman Empire. It has been suggested that Septimius Severus was descended from a family of Italian émigrés to Africa in the time of the late Republic. This was indeed the background of several provincial senators at Rome, such as Seneca and the poet Lucan, perhaps also of the emperor Trajan; but it seems certain that Severus was in fact a member of a leading Punic family of Leptis, whose great-grandfather had come to Rome as a senator in the later 1st century. By his marriage to Julia Domna, whom he met while serving in Syria, Severus allied himself with a prominent Oriental family; we have already seen the political consequences of this marriage, in the rise to the imperial throne of the candidates of Syrian background, Elagabalus and Alexander Severus. The accession of the Danubian C. Julius Maximinus, popularly known as Maximin the Thracian, represents a new element in the widening of the social base of Roman political life which will be discussed later.

The imperial dynasties reflect the broadening provincial composition of the senatorial and equestrian governing classes of the Roman Empire. Statistical precision cannot be attempted on the basis of the surviving evidence, extensive though this is, but it is clear that those senators known in the Julio-Claudian period to come from central and northern Italy, southern Gaul and Spain, were followed under the Flavians by aspirants from Africa, where the city of Cirta (Constantine), with its huge and productive territory, plays a particularly prominent role. The Greek cities of Asia Minor, such as Ephesus and Pergamum, soon make their appearance; one family which has been studied in detail is that of the Plancii, from the less well-known city of Perge in Pamphylia. In the early 2nd century Trajan imposed a requirement, with what effect is not known, that all senators should possess a third of their landed property in Italy. He was evidently worried by the increasing numbers of provincial senators without connections in Italy, who were unlikely to commit themselves to the full obligations of a Roman senator.

Some parts of the Empire are conspicuously absent from the list of the provinces producing senators in this period. None came from northern or western Gaul, Germany or Britain, or from the Danubian provinces, though there is no reason to believe that these regions lacked the economic resources necessary to produce senators. Indeed, it had appeared to the critics of the policies of Claudius in the 1st century that many Gallic notables would, if admitted to the Roman senatorial order, eclipse their Italian counterparts in wealth (Tacitus, *Annals* 11.23). Sometimes, as in the case of Britain, sheer physical remoteness from the center of empire was obviously a factor, while elsewhere, as especially in Gaul, the existing social patterns were oriented towards local forms of expression, based on the countryside and on a developed villa economy rather than on the more urban life-style of the Mediterranean. In the case of Dalmatia, the coastal cities lacked the rich agricultural hinterland which might have generated the wealth necessary to the establishment of senatorial status. The economy of the inner Balkan area was and remained closely linked with the presence of the Roman army. The only known senator from Pannonia in the first two centuries was Valerius Maximianus, from Poetovio, who rose to senatorial rank, and to the consulship in 184 or 185, through his unbroken military service, especially in the wars of Marcus Aurelius. The case of Maximianus provides a good precedent for the transformation of the Roman governing class in the 3rd and 4th centuries. It is unlikely that he ever went to Rome to attend meetings of the senate or to assume his consulship, which he will have held in absence. Maximianus anticipates the growth of a provincial senatorial class in the late Empire, acquiring its rank from imperial service but not participating in the political and social life of the senate at Rome.

The widening social base of the governing class of the early Empire was thus an expression of two things: of the growth of provincial wealth as it developed under the *pax Romana* of the first two centuries, and of a tradition of service to the emperors and to the Empire which drew men into public careers and bestowed on them aristocratic status without involving them in the traditional duties of Roman senators. The importance of the senate in this development shifts from its political functions to its role as representing an order in Roman society.

Beside the regular senatorial career, broadly military or civil in its emphasis but with no clear or formal distinction between the two, developed similar opportunities for men of the equestrian order. These opportunities took them through posts known as procuratorships, of which something has already been seen; they were administrative positions connected with the emperors' possessions in the provinces but leading to a wide range of functions in which the procurator played an important role alongside the official governor of the province. It was the view of the jurist Ulpian that, in a fiscal matter involving the interests both of proconsul and of imperial procurator, the proconsul would "do better to abstain" (*Digest* 1.16.9). From such positions a procurator might advance to governorships of smaller provinces of equestrian status. The summit of the system of promotion was the high prefectures (see above, p. 74).

It is important not to exaggerate the degree of formalization implied by these careers. The crucial element in the promotion of an individual might, in this as in any other type of career, be his access to

Left Roman generals of the early imperial period, as in the Republic, were senators, from a society in which success in war was not reserved for professionals but was seen as part of an integrated style of life incorporating both civil and military distinction. Here, in the so-called "Clementia" sarcophagus from late 2nd-century Rome, the ideology is employed, as it were, in reverse: the deceased man is shown in the role of victorious general among his bodyguard and trophies, sparing his defeated enemies and being crowned by a figure of Victory.

Linguistic divisions of the Empire and physical conditions in relation to the distribution of cities. The distribution of urban settlement indicated is based on the physical development of cities rather than on their juridical status: the latter can disguise widely varying economic functions. In the most northerly provinces the importance of villa culture may yet again be emphasized (see p. 82). In the south and east, bordered by desert, the relationship between urbanization and the 250 mm isohyet, representing the limit of regular agricultural exploitation, is striking: cities lying outside this limit depend either on oases or on the delivery of water from distant mountains by major river systems. The correspondence of the olive-growing area with that of urbanization is also evident.

effective patronage, or the accident of the emperor's recognition of his merit at a fortunate moment, when others remained unnoticed. But a letter of appointment from Marcus Aurelius to a promoted procurator emphasizes his need to retain the emperor's favor by the vigor and integrity of his conduct. This clearly implies standards of conduct attaching to the office as such. The fact that the rank of procuratorships was defined by the salary attached to them – "centenariate" and "ducenariate" procurators, for instance, receiving respectively annual salaries of 100000 and 200000 sestertii – suggests that we have here at least the beginnings of a "bureaucratic" system. This is important in considering the origins of the late Roman state.

The financial qualifications required of candidates for political office ensured that members of this imperial "aristocracy of service" were still the products of the propertied upper classes. They were not specialized bureaucrats by background or training, but men educated in the traditional literary culture of the Roman Empire. It was assumed that a literary education provided the moral qualifications necessary for a good governor, and not until the late Empire were more specialized qualifications considered relevant.

Government and rhetoric

The actual processes of government of the Roman Empire remained much the same throughout the period from the Flavian to the Severan dynasties. The emperors did not customarily take major initiatives of their own, save in matters of military policy, nor were they equipped to do so. They neither possessed the means nor felt the need to consult public opinion; nor did they devise the instruments of active policy making which modern governments take for granted. Provincial governors administered their provinces at their own discretion, usually with only the most general guidelines from the emperors. The financial administration of the cities was one of the few areas where the emperors did intervene, and did so more intensively as time went on, partly by the appointment of officials instructed to supervise the financial management of the cities and partly by requiring the consent of the emperor or provincial governor to municipal decrees on financial matters. In general, the emperors governed by responding to approaches made to them. If a community wished to address itself to an emperor, it would do so by passing a decree in proper form by council and assembly and sending it to the emperor, either by letter through the governor of the province, or by sending an embassy mandated to present its case in support of the decree. Inscriptions show that the participating in and financing of embassies was one of the forms of civic munificence most frequently undertaken by the leading men of local communities.

The normal procedure for an embassy, as illustrated by many anecdotes and by the advice given in handbooks of rhetorical practice, was simply for it to appear before the emperor, present the decree and make its supporting case as persuasively as it could. This procedure naturally involved the use of rhetoric (which was precisely the art of persuasion), and it is against this background of practical utility that it is at least partly possible to understand the immense prestige enjoyed by rhetoric in the Empire of the Antonine age. The literary movement known as the "Second Sophistic" is characterized by an amalgamation of literary and philosophical cultures to produce what has well been called a form of "concert oratory," often indulged in purely for display purposes. The framework of reference of this oratory (which survives mainly in Greek, with some examples in Latin) was set in past literature, especially in Homer and the Greek writers and orators of the 5th and 4th centuries BC. When, as in one episode, an Arabian sophist, addressing the emperor Caracalla in Germany, compares himself to Demosthenes appearing nervously before Philip of Macedon, the

Roman coinage, as here in an issue of Trajan, sometimes exemplifies what a modern observer might call social policy. Here is illustrated the "alimentary scheme," by which financial benefits were provided, by entailment on local estates, for young boys and girls of Italian cities. The coin beautifully catches a spirit of charitable paternalism, as the children reach out their hands to receive their benefits from the emperor.

comparison can appear forced and remote; but it was understood by all present as apt for the occasion, and provided the background of sympathy and common understanding against which more practical issues could be determined. It has been supposed that, in making constant appeal to a distant past, Greeks of the Roman Empire were compensating for their lack of any significant political power in their own day. There is some truth in this; on the other hand, this cultural framework did provide a mode of communication between individuals, and between communities and their emperor.

Civic munificence: the nature of the Antonine age

The period from the Flavians to the Severans is that in which the material prosperity of the Roman Empire can be seen at its most impressive. The surviving ruins, largely dating from this period, of the cities of the provinces were in themselves the proof, for Gibbon, that these provinces were "once the seat of a polite and powerful empire." The building inscriptions associated with the monuments, as well as the commemorative inscriptions set up in honor of public benefactors, show that this civic grandeur was achieved through devotion to public duty and to the enhancement of their own prestige by the leading individuals of the cities. These worthies, who can be identified with the wealthier among the class of provincial councillors, took upon themselves in a spirit of willing generosity the provision not only of the material amenities of their cities, but of many of their social needs also, such as corn and wine distributions, the heating of public baths, the provision of games, the cleaning and lighting of the streets, the preservation of order in the countryside, as well as the supervision of many aspects of their financial and legal administration. It was men of this class who traveled abroad on embassies, offering this service too as an expression of civic pride and munificence.

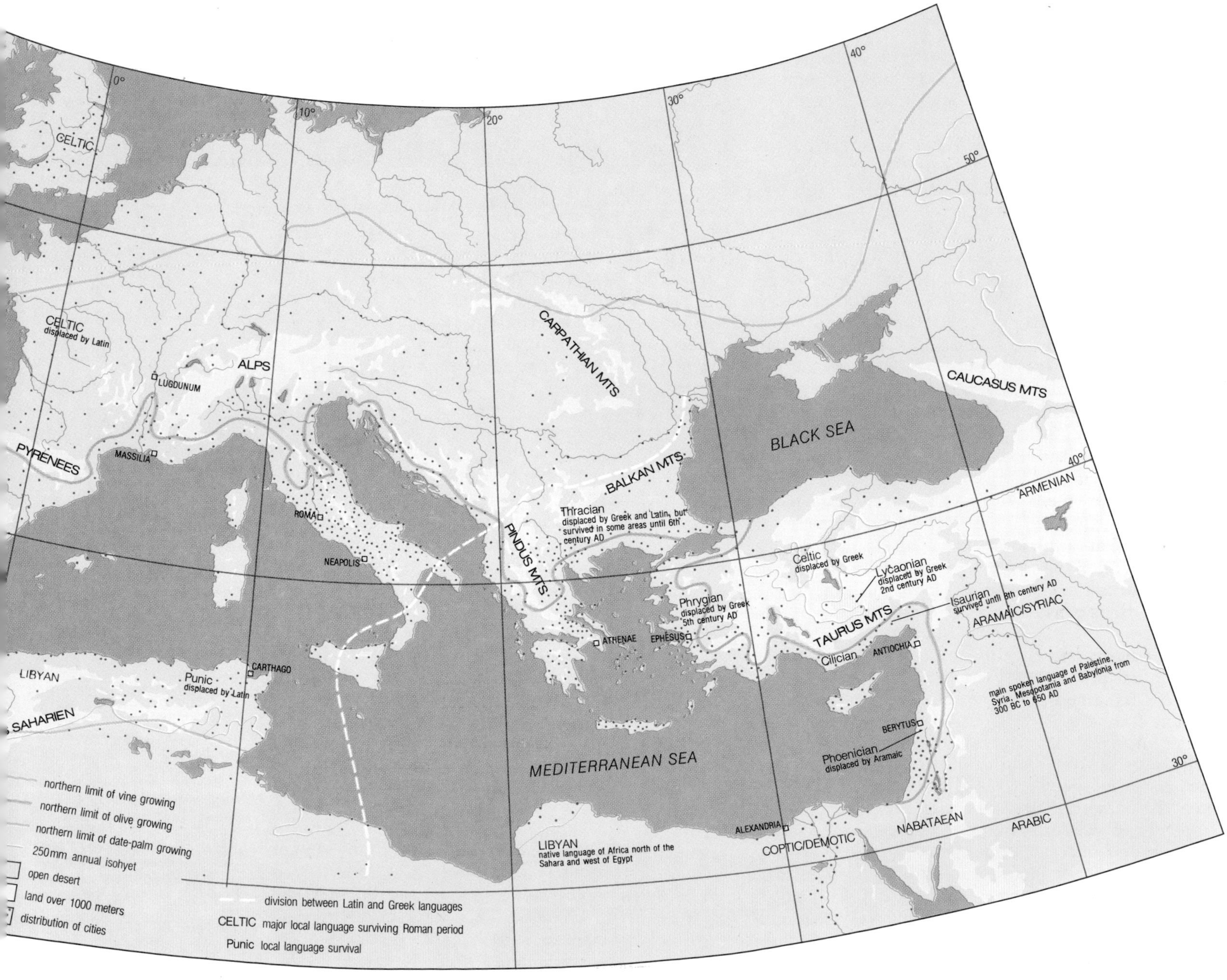

During the later 2nd and early 3rd centuries, evidence begins to appear that the spirit of munificence which sustained the public life of the cities of the early Empire was beginning to be replaced by a reluctance to assume civic offices and their associated duties. The full extent and causes of this tendency to avoid public office, which if it grew would threaten the essential nature of the civic prosperity of the Empire, are not fully understood. One factor appears to have been the growing influence within the class of decurions of a minority of particularly wealthy members of the order, known as *principales viri*, whose rivalries with each other and with their neighbors in other cities tended to raise the cost of munificence to a level which only they could reach; at the same time, through their political influence, they were more successful than their colleagues in gaining exemptions from the less attractive civic burdens.

Another possible factor was growing imperial influence on municipal affairs. From the later 1st century the emperors had begun to intervene more directly in the financial management of the cities, for example by sending out officials, or *curatores*, to supervise individual cities, and by imposing more specific terms of reference upon provincial governors. The correspondence of the younger Pliny, who was appointed governor of the province of Bithynia and Pontus under Trajan, illustrates the activities of a senatorial governor sent out with instructions to inquire closely into the finances of the cities of his province, "since many things," wrote Trajan, "appear in need of correction." This concern of the government with civic finances appears to have arisen from uncontrolled expenditure rather than financial stringency: the letters addressed to Trajan by Pliny show such problems as the mismanagement of civic funds, over-ambitious building projects begun and then abandoned and the embezzlement of public funds by individuals, rather than any shortage of money. If this was true of Bithynia-Pontus, it must have applied still more strongly to the adjacent, more spectacularly wealthy province of Asia Minor. Both Bithynia-Pontus and Asia Minor show another feature which inevitably attracted the emperors' attention; civic unrest generated within communities by the competition for influence among members of the upper classes, and by rivalry between cities, as, in Asia, between Ephesus and Smyrna, and in Bithynia, between Nicaea and Nicomedia. This led to faction fighting and to riots, which the emperors were obviously unable to ignore.

The civic prosperity of the Antonine age derived from a successful combination of two potentially contradictory features – public-spiritedness and individualism. The combination was based on the classical recognition of virtue as essentially public, or civic, in nature. At the same time, the 2nd century was marked by the development of a more personal conception of individualism (see below, pp. 176–77). It involved the increasing popularity, for instance, of religions of personal salvation, like the cult of Isis, commemorated in the tenth book of Apuleius' *Metamorphoses*, and, of course, Christianity. Another source, the *Dream Book* of Aelius Aristides, is a document of the relationship of an individual with a tutelary deity, the healing god Aesculapius, who in Aristides' account expresses himself personally, through dreams and visions, to his devotee. Aristides was a neurotic hypochondriac, but hypochondria is nothing if not a personal preoccupation; it has been well described as one of the more disquieting features of the Antonine age, embodied perhaps in the tremendous prestige of the doctor Galen. The individual fame, based on their personal talents, of the sophists and teachers of the Second Sophistic is well shown by the biographer of the sophists, Philostratus, who also wrote an account of the life and travels of a famous sage and wonder-worker, Apollonius of Tyana. Apollonius, to whom a cult was devoted and whose working of miracles later gained him comparison with Jesus Christ, can be set beside the philosophers and wise men of religious inspiration such as Peregrinus and Alexander of Abounoteichos, presented with satirical intent in the writings of Lucian.

The essential character of the Antonine age may then be summed up as residing in the balance which it achieved between private individualism and public munificence, the one seen as reinforcing the other. It is possible that the "slow and secret poison" that Gibbon detected in the age was not so much the disappearance of the spirit of liberty from a people over-indulged in peace, but the exuberant growth of a personal individualism, and the progressive weakening of the ideal of collective civic responsibility among many of those best placed to sustain it. In this period the lives of the cities and of their great individuals could flourish freely, and the Empire suffered no really damaging military threat, though the wars of Marcus Aurelius were a portent of what was to happen. It was in the 3rd century, after 235, and in the radically changed military, economic and political conditions which then came about, that the exuberance of the Antonine age was dissipated and a new social order evolved.

In an episode of the time of Nero, illustrated in the wall painting from Pompeii shown here, riots erupted between the Pompeians and visitors from neighboring Nuceria, in town for the gladiatorial games. The riots, in which the Pompeians' greater numbers gave them the advantage, so that "many Nucerians mourned the deaths of children or parents" and others were carried home injured (Tacitus), began with the exchange of insults at the games, but in the violence with which they developed they expressed a more deep-seated rivalry between the cities. This is suggested also by graffiti at Pompeii, such as "Nucerinis infelicia!" – "Bad luck to the men of Nuceria!" The episode resulted in the compulsory closure of the amphitheater for ten years. It illustrates the circumstances in which legitimate competition within and between cities could explode into destructive violence, and the restriction of local autonomy that could ensue.

PART THREE

PROVINCES OF THE EMPIRE

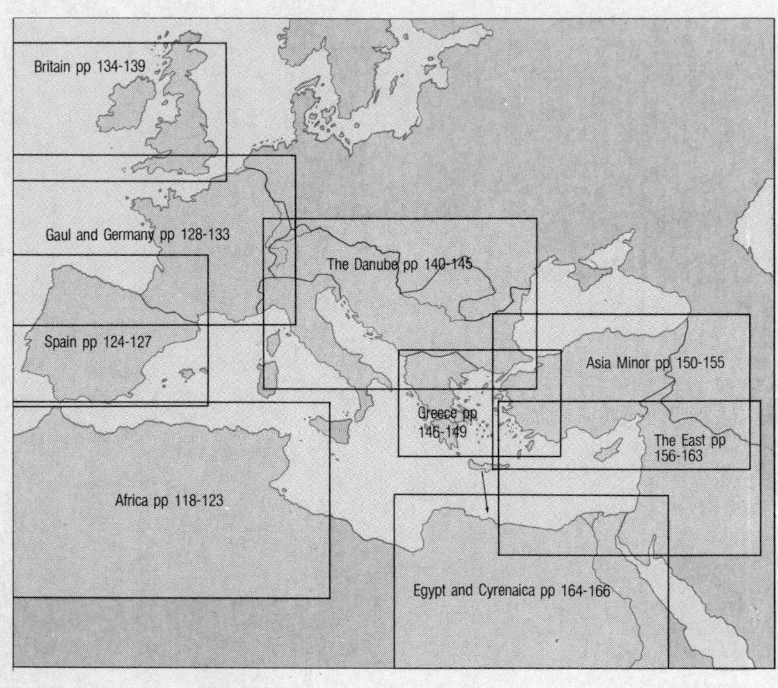

Communications in the Roman World

The direct, meticulously surveyed and engineered roads of the Roman Empire are among its most durable monuments: their distinctive traces exist everywhere from Scotland to the Syrian desert. They were often first constructed for military purposes. They also carried the *cursus publicus*, or imperial courier service for the use of authorized officials. For the general traveler they possessed staging posts, or *mansiones*, where towns were more than a day's traveling distance apart.

The roads quickly acquired economic uses and sustained a heavy volume of commercial traffic. Import taxes were levied at provincial frontiers, and in the late Empire officials were detailed to inspect vehicles to prevent overloading. The costs of maintaining the roads fell partly on the communities through which they passed, and which shared their benefits.

The economic importance of the roads was limited by the slowness and high costs of land transport, especially of bulk goods: it was cheaper to ship corn to Rome from Egypt and Africa than to bring it by land from southern Italy. Most of the commercial traffic on the roads of the Empire was of a local nature. The efficiency of the administration, too, was restricted by the physical speed with which messages could travel. Yet in the effectiveness of its communication the Roman Empire outclassed its predecessors, and long-distance contacts were better maintained then than at any subsequent time until the modern period.

Left The paved main street, or *decumanus*, of the Roman colony of Timgad (see p. 123). It led to the legionary camp of Lambaesis, and to the plains of southern Numidia, currently being developed by imperial initiative.

The milestone near the arch of Severus at Leptis Magna (*above*) marks the length of the road inland as 44 miles.

The horse-drawn carriage (*far left bottom*), on a Gallo-Roman relief, is reminiscent of a stage coach, with passengers seated on the roof as well as inside. Its simple solidity well evokes the laborious nature of travel by land even on the fine roads of the Roman Empire.

Trajan's bridge over the Danube at Drobeta (shown *far left top*, from the simplified representation on Trajan's column) was designed by the famous architect, Apollodorus of Damascus. The historian Cassius Dio thought it the greatest of Trajan's achievements: "it has 20 piers of squared stone, 150 feet high excluding the foundations, and 60 feet wide. These are placed 120 feet from each other and connected by arches." Its building was an engineering miracle, in water "so deep and full of eddies, and on a bed so muddy." When after Trajan's death the superstructure was demolished to reduce access from the Dacian side, the piers remained in place, "as if erected solely in order to demonstrate that there is nothing which human ingenuity cannot accomplish."

The roads of the Roman Empire, the "Devil's causeways" of the medieval period, frequently underlie the modern road systems of former provinces. Here (*center left*) the Fosse Way, the highway from Exeter to Lincoln, passes through Somerset, its direct course contrasting with the winding nature of the local roads seen in the photograph, and with the varied patchwork of the field system.

The Peutinger Map

The Peutinger map, a 13th-century copy of a late Roman original, owes its name to a town clerk of Augsburg, who inherited it in 1508 from the humanist scholar, Konrad Celtes. In the form of a continuous, elongated chart, 6·80 × 0·34 meters, the map shows the known world from Britain to

India, though the most westerly portions are missing. The distorted projection is well illustrated by the section (VI) shown here. The land masses appear as horizontal strips, separated by the Mediterranean and Adriatic seas. Mountains and rivers are indicated, and towns represented by little groups of buildings, as in the illustrations to the *Notitia Dignitatum* (see pp. 118, 124, and for the more elaborate images of Rome and Ostia, p. 92). The map should, however, not be seen as an attempt to attain geographical accuracy, though in detail it does sometimes achieve this. It is rather a schematic diagram for the traveler, indicating towns, the distances between them and their location in the road system. It relates to the geography of the Roman Empire in much the same way that a diagram of a metropolitan railway system may relate to the actual configuration of the districts which it serves.

AFRICA

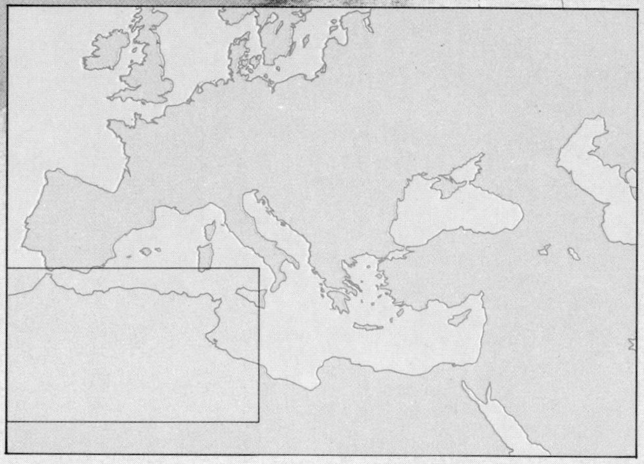

MEDITERRANEAN SEA
ICOSIUM
Algiers
CARTENNA
Ténès
IOL CAESAREA
Cherchell
TIPASA
AQUAE CALIDAE
ARSENARIA
TIGAVA
ZUCCABAR
Cheliff
QUIZA
CASTELLUM TINGITANUM
El Asnam
PORTUS MAGNUS
Oran
Mostaganem
MINA
TASACCURA
COLUMNATA
Tiaret
TINGI
Tangiers
RUSADDIR
Melilla
LIXUS
OPPIDUM NOVUM
SIGA
RIF
MAURETANIA TINGITANA
MAURETANIA CAESARIENSIS
NUMERUS SYRORUM
POMARIA
Tlemcen
ALTAVA
BANASA
Beht
COHORS BREUCORUM
THAMUSIDA
Subur
SALA
Rabat
VOLUBILIS
Fès
CASTELLUM DIMMI
Messad
Casablanca
Moulouya
HAUTS PLATEAUX
ATLAS SAHARIEN
MOYEN ATLAS
ATLAS MOUNTAINS
Marrakech
HAUT ATLAS
36°
34°
32°
30°
8°
4°
0°

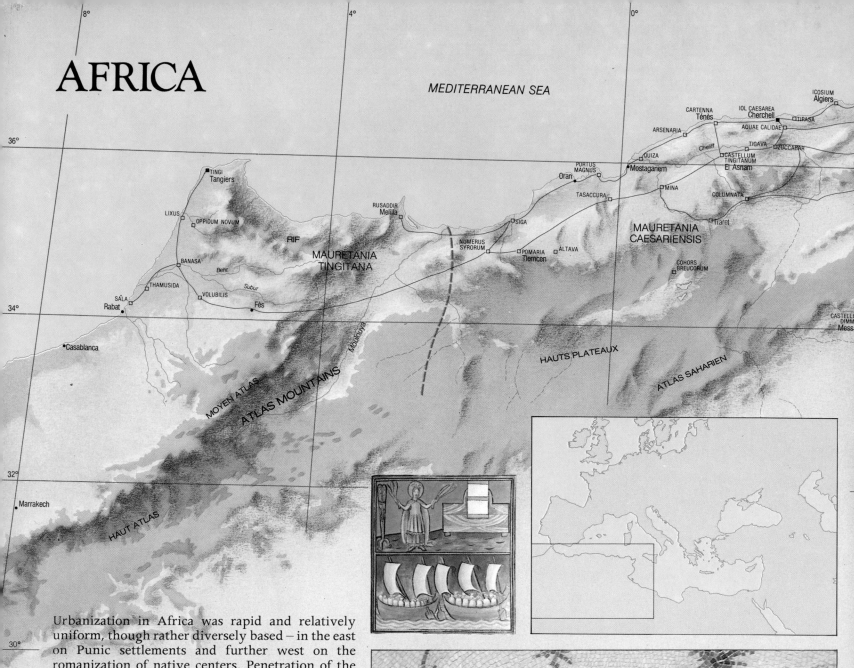

Urbanization in Africa was rapid and relatively uniform, though rather diversely based – in the east on Punic settlements and further west on the romanization of native centers. Penetration of the province followed the lie of the mountains, which run from west to east, allowing few easy communications from the interior to the sea. The Aurès mountains, encircled and penetrated during the 2nd century, were watched by the single legionary fortress of Lambaesis, with support from the colony at Timgad. The natives of the interior retained their identity: a confederation assembled during a 4th-century rebellion consisted, according to the historian Ammianus (29.5.28), of peoples "diverse in culture and in the variety of their languages," presumably dialects of "Libyan."

Romanized Africa was one of the most articulate of provinces. Renowned as the home of lawyers, it also produced many senators and *equites* and distinguished literary figures. Possessing links with the east, it received Christianity early, and in the 4th century, under the impulse of competition between Catholics and Donatists, developed an advanced episcopal structure.

The economy of Africa was closely linked with the outside world, not always to the advantage of the province. As well as its famed olive oil, profitably exported, Africa supplied Rome with corn under far less favorable terms. The evident wealth of the province would have been still greater, but for the profits that went overseas.

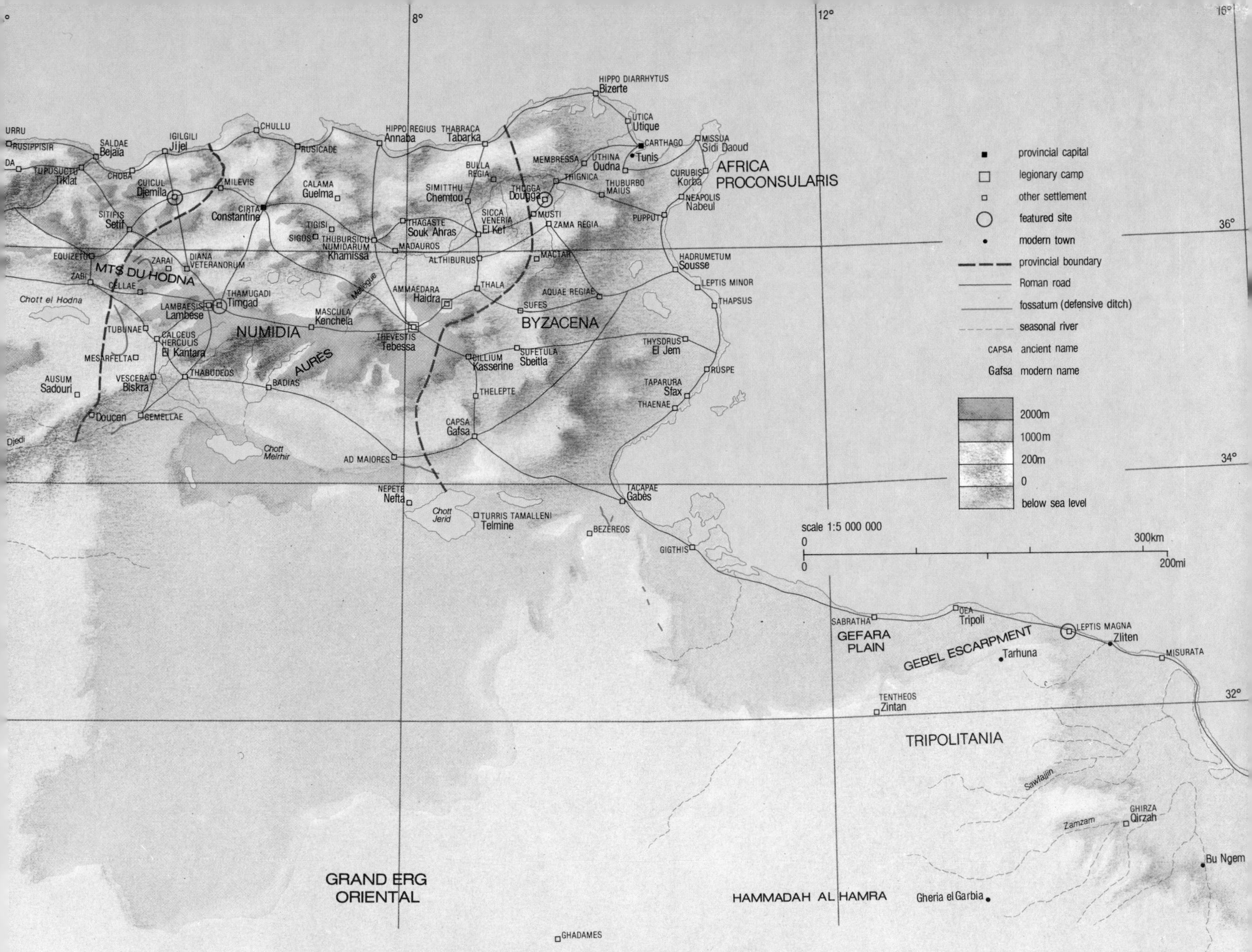

8°
12°
16°
HIPPO DIARRHYTUS
Bizerte
UTICA
Utique
CARTHAGO
Tunis
MISSUA
Sidi Daoud
HIPPO REGIUS
Annaba
THABRACA
Tabarka
RUSICADE
CHULLU
IGILGILI
Jijel
SALDAE
Bejaia
RUSIPPISIR
TUPUSUCTU
Tiklat
CHOBA
CUICUL
Djemila
MILEVIS
CALAMA
Guelma
BULLA REGIA
SIMITTHU
Chemtou
THUGGA
Dougga
MEMBRESSA
UTHINA
Oudna
THIGNICA
THUBURBO MAIUS
CURUBIS
Korba
NEAPOLIS
Nabeul
AFRICA PROCONSULARIS
SITIFIS
Setif
CIRTA
Constantine
TIGISI
SIGUS
THUBURSICU NUMIDARUM
Khamissa
THAGASTE
Souk Ahras
MADAUROS
SICCA VENERIA
El Kef
MUSTI
ZAMA REGIA
PUPPUT
EQUIZETUM
ZABI
ZARAI
DIANA VETERANORUM
MTS DU HODNA
CELLAE
ALTHIBURUS
MACTAR
HADRUMETUM
Sousse
Chott el Hodna
THAMUGADI
Timgad
LAMBAESIS
Lambese
MASCULA
Kenchela
AMMAEDARA
Haidra
THALA
AQUAE REGIAE
LEPTIS MINOR
THAPSUS
SUFES
NUMIDIA
TUBUNAE
CALCEUS HERCULIS
El Kantara
MESARFELTA
THEVESTIS
Tebessa
BYZACENA
AURÈS
CILLIUM
Kasserine
SUFETULA
Sbeitla
THYSDRUS
El Jem
AUSUM
Sadouri
VESCERA
Biskra
THABUDEOS
BADIAS
THELEPTE
RUSPE
TAPARURA
Sfax
THAENAE
Doucen
GEMELLAE
CAPSA
Gafsa
Djedi
Chott Melrhir
AD MAIORES
NEPETE
Nefta
Chott Jerid
TURRIS TAMALLENI
Telmine
TACAPAE
Gabès
BEZEREOS
GIGTHIS
SABRATHA
OEA
Tripoli
LEPTIS MAGNA
Zliten
MISURATA
GEFARA PLAIN
GEBEL ESCARPMENT
Tarhuna
TENTHEOS
Zintan
TRIPOLITANIA
Sawfajjin
Zamzam
GHIRZA
Qirzah
Bu Ngem
GRAND ERG ORIENTAL
HAMMADAH AL HAMRA
Gheria el Garbia
GHADAMES
36°
34°
32°

provincial capital
legionary camp
other settlement
featured site
modern town
provincial boundary
Roman road
fossatum (defensive ditch)
seasonal river
CAPSA ancient name
Gafsa modern name

2000m
1000m
200m
0
below sea level

scale 1:5 000 000
0 300km
0 200mi

The contours of the map show plainly the west–east alignment of the land. The "far west" of Mauretania, isolated by desert and sheer distance, was in the late Empire governed as part of the diocese of Spain.

The image from the *Notitia Dignitatum* (*above left*) neatly symbolizes the role of Africa in the 4th-century Empire. Surrounded by the insignia of the proconsul (for which see p. 202), the lady in the upper register brandishes ears of corn; below are the ships laden with bags of wheat, under sail for Rome.

The countryman pouring wine (*left*), seen on a mosaic in the Bardo Museum, Tunis, illustrates the changeless face of rural life. He sits before one of the thatched huts built in the traditional native style, called by their Punic name, *mapalia*.

Carthage drew water supplies from a source near Zaghouan, over 50 kilometers distant. The water was conveyed to the city by the magnificent aqueduct, seen here (*right*) as it crosses a shallow valley near Uthina, and stored there in huge covered cisterns.

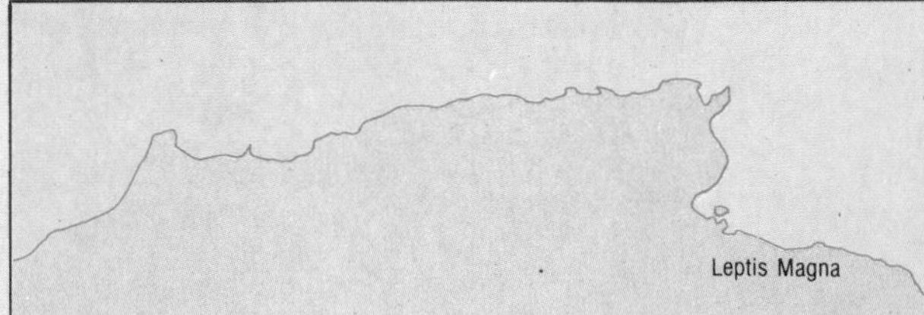

Leptis Magna

Leptis Magna, one of the group of three cities which gave its name to the district of Tripolitania (and to modern Tripoli), was a Punic foundation, perhaps of the 5th century BC. Little is known of its early history, but the wealth of Punic Leptis is shown by its payment of 1 talent a day to its overlord Carthage, and by the annual fine of 3 million pounds of oil later imposed by Julius Caesar on the city for its part in African resistance to him. The development of Leptis was continuous over the first two centuries of the Empire, with two particularly notable phases. In the first, under Augustus, monuments were provided by members of the Punic aristocracy which still dominated the city. The second was in the time of Leptis' most famous native, the emperor Septimius Severus, who visited the city, furnished a new forum and basilica, modernized the harbor and built the imposing colonnade leading from there to a monumental piazza by the Hadrianic baths.

In the late Empire Leptis remained prosperous, though with some retrenchment. It was the seat of the governor of Tripolitania and provides many inscriptions, but little new building, from this period. In the mid-4th century Leptis and its neighbors were troubled by tribal incursions from the desert. The fortunes of the city declined sharply under the Vandals, and by the time of the Byzantine reconquest the site was largely deserted.

The wealth of Leptis derived in part from trade and commerce. The main source of wealth, however, was agricultural development of the hinterland, based on the olive and on wheat.

The great Severan forum and basilica are seen (*above*) from the west, beyond (in the foreground) the market and Chalcidicum of the Augustan period. They, like the theater (*opposite*), were provided by members of the Punic aristocracy of the city. In the distance is a glimpse of the fertile coastal territory on which the wealth of Leptis depended. Shown *right* is a detail from one of a pair of pilasters of the Severan basilica, later reused to flank an apse of the church built in its ruins by Justinian. It shows scenes relating to Dionysus (Liber Pater), one of the patron gods of Leptis. A corresponding pair of pilasters shows scenes of the life of Hercules. The style of the sculpture has its closest affinities in the imperial art of Asia Minor.

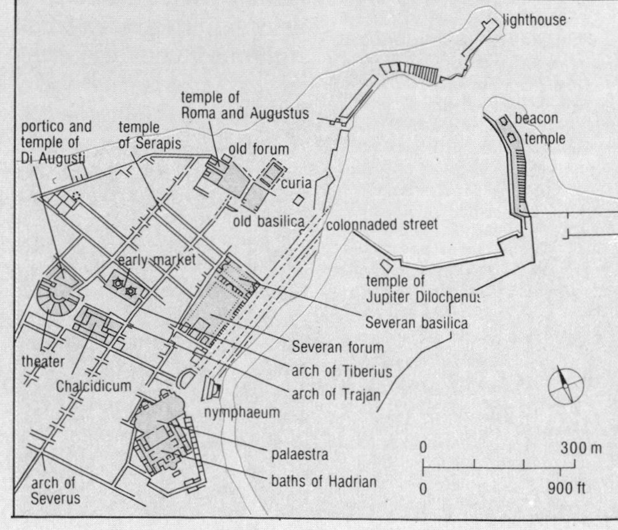

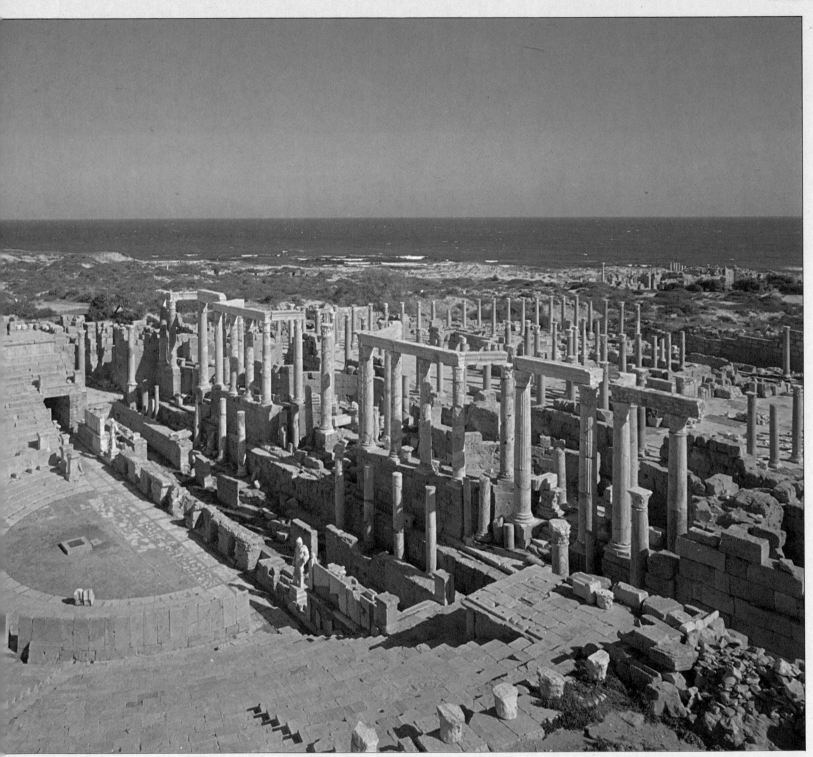

The Punic settlement was on the headland west of the harbor; the roads leading westward along the coast and to the country south of Leptis, and their influence on the later development of the city, are clearly visible on the plan of the site (*left*). The enlargement of the early settlement is suggested by the distance between the harbor and old forum and the theater, the latter built on the site of a Punic cemetery. The extent of the fully developed Roman city can only be appreciated with reference to the area still unexcavated. The circus stood at a distance of 1000 meters from the eastern habor mole, but the area between them remains unexplored.

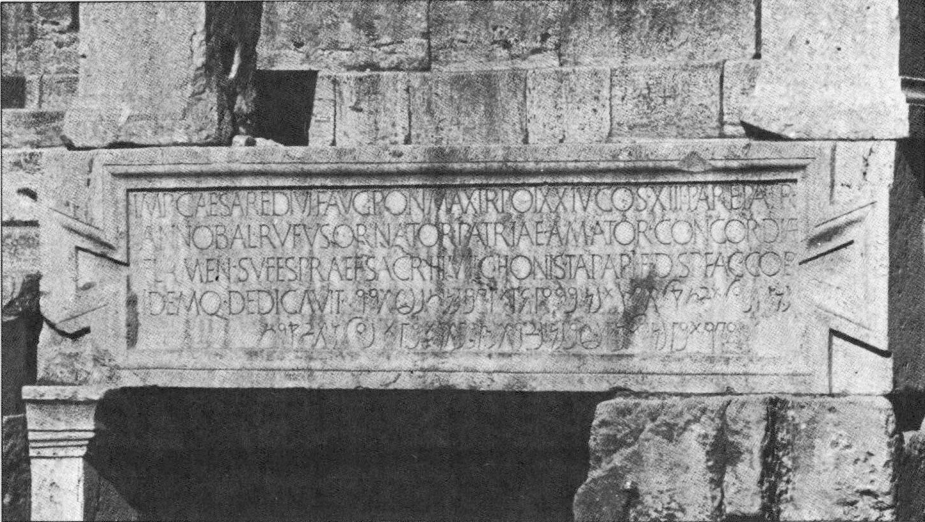

The theater (*above*) was built in 1/2 AD by the Punic noble Annobal Rufus, son of Himilcho Tapapius, whose dedicatory inscription, beautifully engraved in Latin and Punic, is pictured (*left*). Immediately behind the stage facade, added under the Antonines, is a courtyard and portico built in the time of Claudius to enclose a small temple of the Di Augusti, or deified emperors. The title "ornator patriae" in the inscription represents a traditional Punic expression commemorating civic munificence. The title "sufes," a civic magistracy equivalent to the Roman duumvirate, disappeared in 110 AD, when Leptis became a Roman colony. Its last bearer was the grandfather of Leptis' greatest benefactor, Septimius Severus.

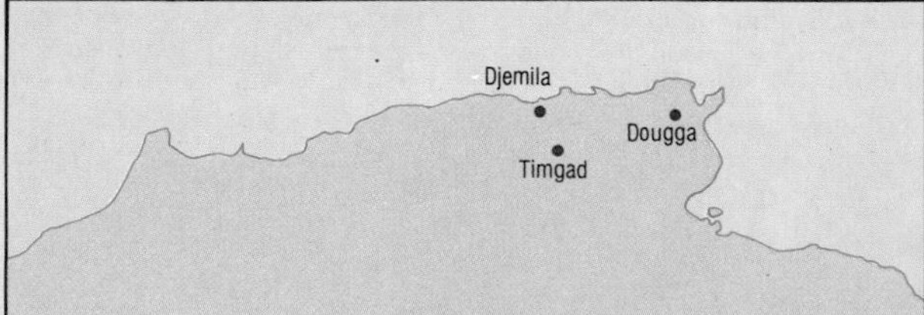

Dougga

Dougga (ancient Thugga) stands in a strong defensive position about 90 kilometers southwest of Carthage. A prosperous city long before the arrival of the Romans, its original population was a mixture of Punic and native Libyan: among its monuments is a mausoleum of the late 3rd or early 2nd century BC commemorating a Numidian prince, with an inscription in Punic and Libyan. After its annexation as part of the new province of Africa, the native inhabitants of Dougga continued to be governed by their own institutions, living side by side with a community of Roman citizens initially dependent on Carthage. Dougga became a formal municipality only in the early 3rd century. The irregular street plan (*below right*) and the buildings rising in terraces up the hillside reveal the native origins of the community. Nevertheless, Dougga acquired the standard amenities of a provincial Roman city – temple of the Capitoline gods, forum and senate house, and so on. The wealth of the city, derived from exploitation of the plains below, is expressed by the magnificence of some of its public buildings, notably the splendid theater, built in 168/9 AD, and the temple of Caelestis.

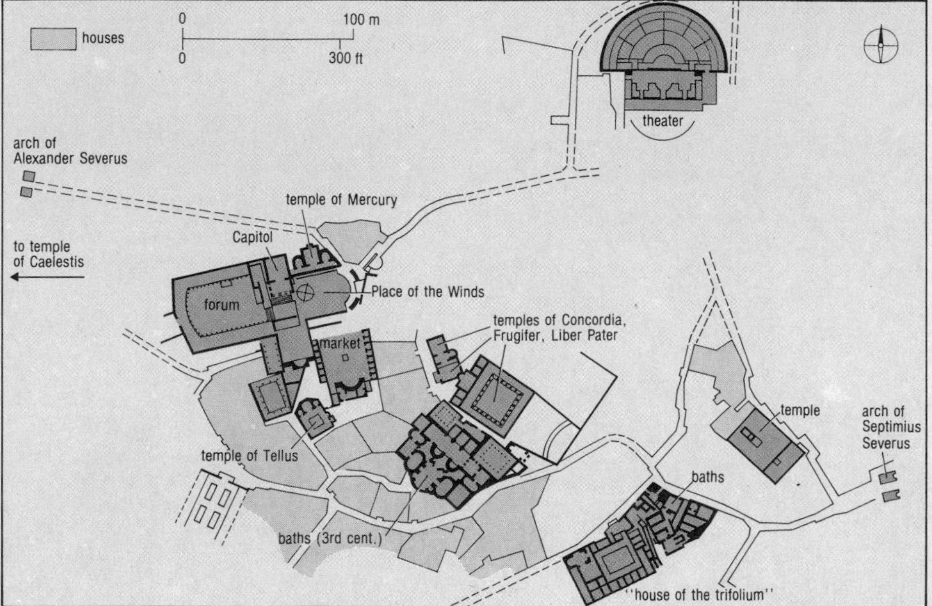

The street plan of Djemila clearly illustrates the city's course of development, the regular layout of the original foundation contrasting with the more casual pattern of the streets in the area of 2nd-century development. The architectural function of the Severan forum and basilica in unifying the now rather elongated city can also be clearly seen. The usual description of the southeast sector of the site as the "Christian quarter" is strictly misleading. The Christian monuments were built in the area of residential development of the 2nd century, but there is no reason to suppose that there was ever a time when this quarter of Djemila was Christian but the rest still pagan.

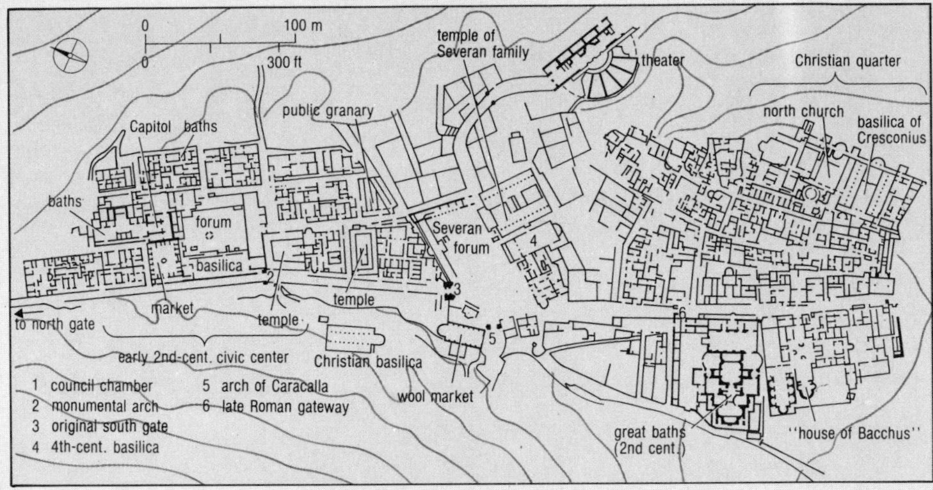

The Severan arch at Timgad (*below*) marked the entrance to the original colonial foundation on the road from Lambaesis. It occupies the site of the west gate which, with the west wall, had been overrun by the 2nd-century development of Timgad.

Djemila

Djemila (ancient Cuicul) was founded under Nerva or Trajan as one of a series of veteran colonies along the road leading from Sicca Veneria (El Kef) to Cirta (Constantine). Cuicul soon received additional settlers from other parts of Africa and rapidly outgrew its original site. It spread to the south and up the slope of the hill behind the colonial settlement; the 2nd-century theater and bath complex in this district drew the focus of the town away from its original center, balance being restored by the creation of a new forum, basilica and other monumental buildings in the Severan period. Cuicul retained its importance in the late Roman and Byzantine periods. Fourth-century churches and an episcopal residence were constructed in the south-east quarter of the city, and the houses both in this district and in the region of the old forum have produced late mosaics of high quality. The prosperity of Cuicul was presumably based on the exploitation of its agricultural resources.

The Capitoline temple of Dougga (*left, above*) was dedicated in 166/7 through the generosity of members of the same family which donated the theater. No doubt because of the hillside terrain of the city, the main forum and associated public buildings face its flank rather than front steps and pediment. The wall around the base of the temple dates from the time of the Byzantine reconquest of Africa. The mosaic (*left, below*), showing a man fishing from a rock with line and landing net, is from a room in the "House of Dionysus and Ulysses". It is a conventional design, intended to reinforce the maritime character of the scenes shown in other mosaics in the room, Ulysses passing the rock of the Sirens, and Dionysus' encounter with the Tyrrhenian pirates.

Timgad

The strictly regular layout of Timgad (ancient Thamugadi), shown as clearly in the aerial photograph (*left*) as in any site plan, demonstrates the circumstances of its foundation in 100 AD as a veteran colony by the Third Legion stationed at Lambaesis. By the mid-2nd century the settlement had already outgrown the limits of its original enclosure. As is especially clear on the western and southwestern sides, the new suburbs developed with a cheerful unconcern for the design of the military planners. The foundation was immensely successful and possessed every civilized amenity (including no fewer than 14 identified sets of bath buildings). It had a library, and in the 4th century among its many churches a great Donatist basilica.

SPAIN

Roman settlement of the Iberian peninsula was first directed to the eastern seaboard and to the valley of the river Baetis (Guadalquivir). The cities of these regions produced early senatorial families: an orator from Corduba founded one of the principal literary dynasties of early imperial Rome, while an imperial legate from Italica was father of the first provincial emperor.

The mountains to the north and northwest required subjugation, which was provided by Augustus' Cantabrian wars. Though also urbanized, these areas retained much of their indigenous character – Basque is a pre-Roman language – and a legion was maintained (at León) to ensure their contentment.

Partly in consequence of its small garrison, the contribution of Spain to the main political events of the Roman Empire did not match its social and economic importance. Rebellion there inaugurated the "year of the four emperors," and Spain played an important role in the political disintegration of the Empire in the early 5th century.

The peninsula yielded precious metals and copper, especially from mines in the Rio Tinto valley northeast of Huelva, and at Vipasca near Beja (Pax Iulia) in Portugal. Among other products, exports of wine to Rome reached massive proportions in the first two centuries.

Christianity came early. The records of the council of Elvira (Illiberris) in 306 provide evidence for the distribution (see p. 179), organization and moral concerns of the immediately pre-Constantinian church. In the Gallaecian emperor Theodosius Spain contributed Catholic intolerance, supported by legislation, to the christianization of the Empire, and in the ascetic teacher Priscillian the first "heretic" martyr.

The Spanish peninsula suffered considerably in the 5th-century invasion, but its centuries of Roman, followed by Gothic and Arab, occupation lend to its early cultural landscape an almost unique complexity.

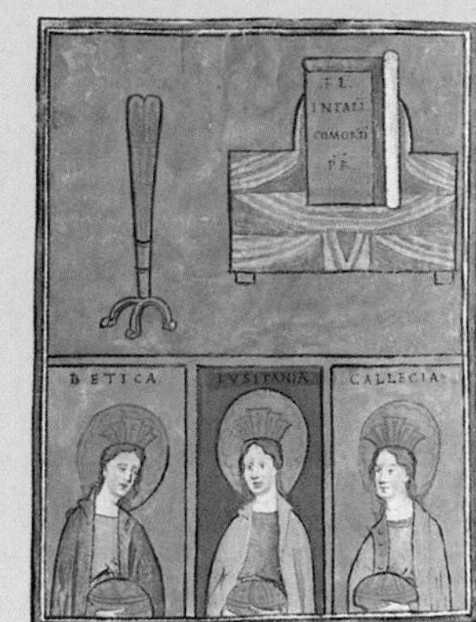

Above Spain in the *Notitia Dignitatum*. The provinces of the diocese are shown as ladies wearing mural crowns, carrying baskets – the fruits of the provinces in taxation. The *vicarius*, like the proconsul of Africa (p. 118), has the inkstand symbolizing judicial competence (see p. 203).

The splendid chariot team (*below*) is from a circus mosaic from a villa near Barcelona. Two of the horses' names are shown, Pa[n]tinicus ("Winner") and Calimorfus ("Beauty"): the substitution of *f* for *ph* is common in later Latin. Spain was in the 4th century a leading producer and exporter of racehorses.

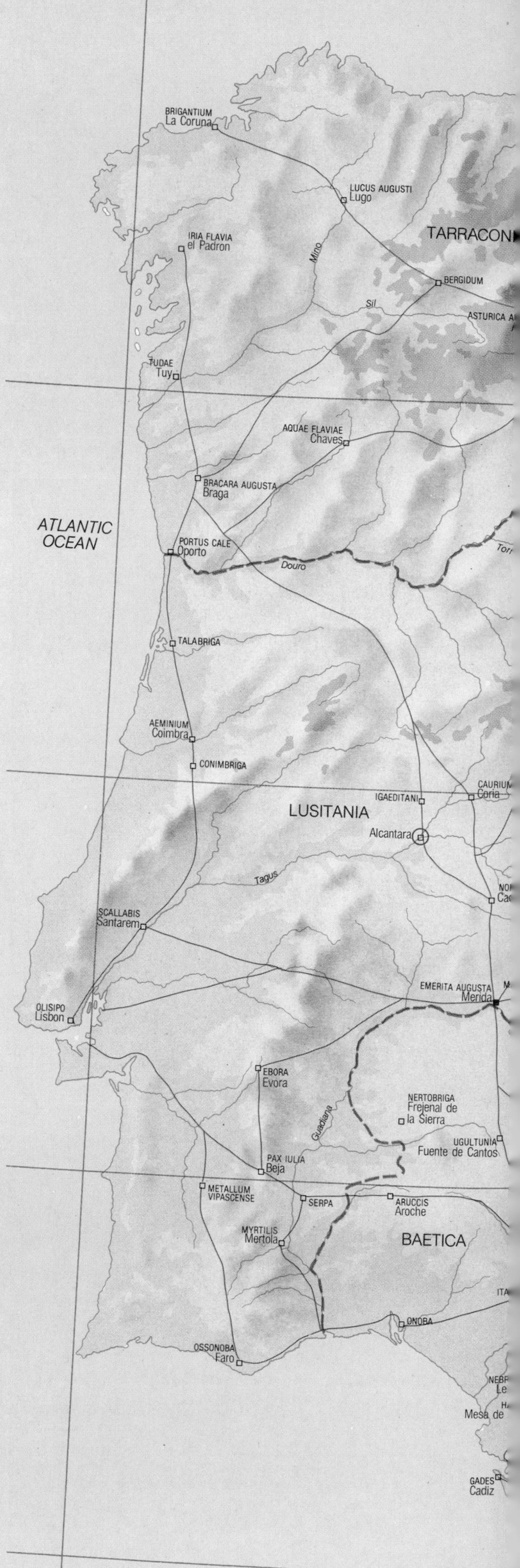

3°
0°
BAY OF BISCAY
GIGIA
Gijon
PORTUS VICTORIAE
FLAVIOBRIGA
NTABRIAN MOUNTAINS
IULIOBRIGA
Retortillo
UXAMA BARCA
Osma
ARACELI
Araquil
POMPAELO
Pamplona
PYRENEES
IACA
Jaca
IUNCARIA
Figueras
EMPORIAE
Ampurias
VIROVESCA
LIBIA
Leiva
VAREIA
LANCIA
SEGISAMO
Sasamon
CALAGURRIS
Calahorra
GRACCURIS
Alfaro
OSCA
Huesca
AESO
Avella
AUSA
Vich
GERUNDA
Gerona
42°
PALLANTIA
Palencia
SIERRA DE
LA DEMANDA
CASCANTUM
Cascante
TURIASSO
Tarazona
IESSO
Guisona
NUMANTIA
Soria
AUGUSTOBRIGA
CAESARAUGUSTA
Zaragoza
ILERDA
Lerida
BAETULO
Badalona
RAUDA
Roa
CLUNIA
Pisuerga
Duero
Ebro
Noguera
Valdeladuey
Remesga
SEPTIMANCA
Simancas
UXAMA ARGELA
Osma
CELSA
BARCINO
Barcelona
TERMES
BILBILIS
TARRACO
Tarragona
CAUCA
Coca
ARCOBRIGA
Arixa
SEGONTIA
Siguenza
DERTOSA
Tortosa
MEDITERRANEAN SEA
SEGOVIA
SIERRA DE GUADARRAMA
SERRANIA DE CUENCA
AVELA
Avila
COMPLUTUM
CARACA
ERCAVICA
40°
Minor
MAGO
POLLENTIA
Pollensa
BALEARES
PALMA
Maior
ERRA DE GREDOS
TITULCIA
Tagus
CAESAROBRIGA
Talavera de la Reina
SEGOBRIGA
Cabeza de Griego
TOLETUM
Toledo
SAGUNTUM
LEIRIA
(EDETA)
Liria
Turia
VALERIA
Valera Vieja
AUGUSTOBRIGA
Talavera la Vieja
VALENTIA
Valencia
MONTES DE TOLEDO
CONSABURA
Consuegra
Cabriel
Jucar
Guadiana
SAETABIS
Jatira
LAMINIUM
LIBISOSA
Lezuza
SALTIGIS
AD ARAS
DIANIUM
Denia
ORETUM
MIROBRIGA
Capilla
SISAPO
Almaden
TARRACONENSIS
LUCENTUM
Alicante
ILICI
Elche
Segura
BEGASTRUM
Cehegin
MELLARIA
Fuente Obejuna
CASTULO
Cazlona
SIERRA MORENA
EPORA
Montoro
CORDUBA
Cordoba
OBULCO
Porcuna
UCUBIS
TUCCI
Martos
ASTIGI
Ecija
CARTHAGO NOVA
Cartagena
BASTI
Baza
ACCI
Guadix
ILLIBERIS
Genil
URSO
Osuna
SIERRA NEVADA
ANTICARIA
Antequera
URCI
Huercal
ABDERA
Adra
MURGI
ARUNDA
Ronda
MALACA
Malaga
CALPE
Gibraltar
scale 1:3 400 000
0
200km
0
150mi
36°
38°
provincial capital
legionary camp
other settlement
featured site
provincial boundary
Roman road
BASTI ancient name
(EDETA) later name
Baza modern name
2000m
1000m
200m
0

Italica

Italica, the native city of Trajan and Hadrian, was the oldest community of Roman citizens in Spain, but came late to municipal status. Long overshadowed by the romanized native city of Hispalis (Seville), Italica underwent a transformation in the time of Hadrian. The city was redesigned in Hellenistic fashion. It acquired a huge amphitheater with a capacity of 25 000, hardly justified by the population of Italica itself, and fine town houses with elegant mosaics. The development of the city was always to some extent artificial; in the 3rd and later centuries Italica again yielded local primacy to Seville.

Below Fine mosaic floors of a house that has been excavated in the northern sector of Italica. They date from the time of Hadrian's embellishment of the city. Surviving sculptures are Greek in inspiration and it is possible that Greek craftsmen were employed.

Right The famous aqueduct at Segovia. Its 128 arches stride across the center of the city for 800 meters.

Below right The bridge at Alcantara over the Tagus river. Nearly 200 meters in length, it carried the Roman road between Norba and Conimbriga in Lusitania.

Segovia

Segovia, a relatively unimportant Roman town, formerly a Celtic stronghold, is famous mainly for its fine aqueduct, which brought water from a source about 16 kilometers distant to a distribution point, or *castellum*, from where it was fed to the township. Like the bridge of Alcantara it is a fine example of the transformation of civic amenities made possible by the combination of Roman engineering skills and local initiative. The pride of the people of Segovia in their aqueduct is evident: sculptured images of it are sometimes shown on their epitaphs.

Alcantara

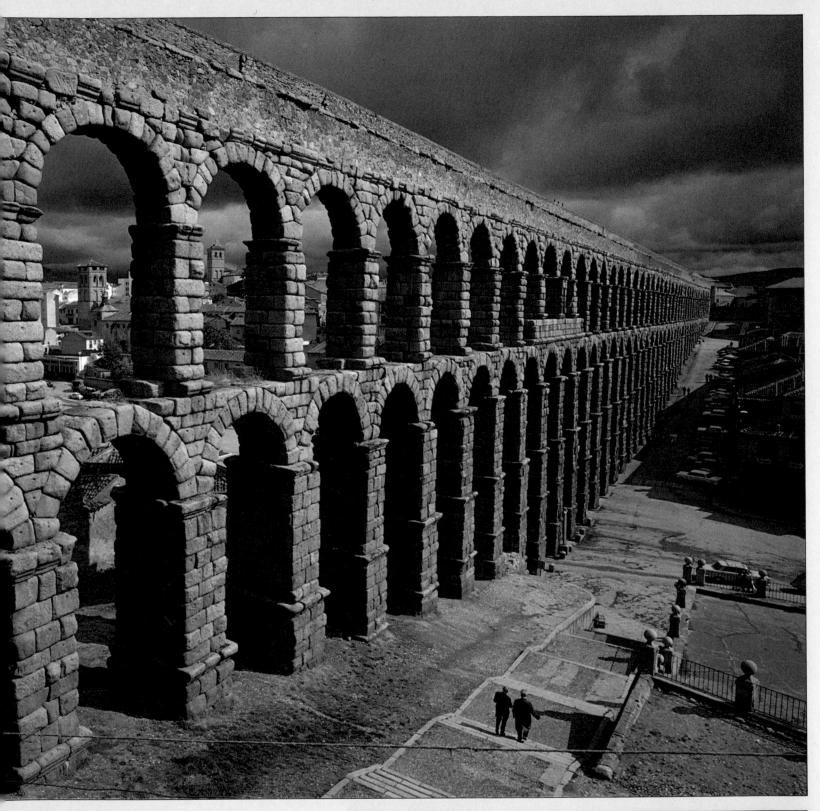

The bridge of Alcantara is a particularly notable instance of public initiative and cooperation under the Roman Empire, being built by 11 Lusitanian communities whose names were listed on inscriptions on the bridge. The height of the roadway above the water may seem excessive and wasteful, but in winter spate the river can rise almost to the level of the arches. The expertise and pride of the architect, C. Julius Lacer, are eminently justified: in an inscription at the site, he declared that his achievement would "last for ever through the ages."

GAUL AND GERMANY

The social history of the Gallic provinces was dominated by the geographical contrast between the urbanized south, already hellenized through cities like Massilia (Marseille) and Antipolis (Antibes), and the regions north and west of the Massif Central, known expressively as Gallia Comata – "long-haired Gaul." Here, with heavier open soils permitting large-scale agricultural exploitation, the countryside comes into its own. Cities are more widely separated and great villas like that of Estrées-sur-Noye (overleaf) and rural shrines like Sanxay are typical. A third area, the military zone adjoining the Rhine, fostered a population of soldiers and their dependants. These lived, married and often retired locally, requiring civilized comforts in their cities and country houses.

Despite the social conservatism of non-Mediterranean Gaul, a substantial commercial and trading class emerged, as suggested by many grave reliefs illustrating its activities. There was also technical innovation, in the use of waterpower and in agriculture (pp. 182–85).

In the late Empire the balance changed in favor of the north, as an imperial court based at Trier attracted increased financial and material resources, and was the center of a vastly increased bureaucratic establishment.

Below left The command of the Dux Tractus Armoricani in the *Notitia Dignitatum*. Armorica (roughly Brittany and Normandy) was not a province but a coastal command. Among the posts shown is the *litus Saxonicum* or "Saxon shore" (see p. 171).

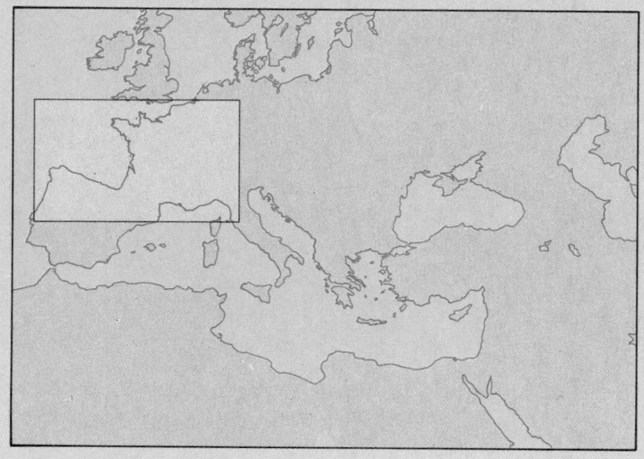

The bronze statuette from Trier (*below*), originally part of a larger group, shows a countryman, who is evidently working outdoors – possibly, as suggested by his forward movement and by his hands, which once held circular poles or handles, guiding a plow.

The city of Autun (Augustodunum) quickly emerged under the Empire as a center of liberal studies, with an early theater and amphitheater and a large wall circuit with well-proportioned monumental gates. One of these, the "Porte d'Arroux" leading north across the river, is shown *above*.

Rhineland glassware was often both very handsome and of extremely delicate workmanship. The jug shown (*above right*), with snake thread decoration, comes from Urdingen.

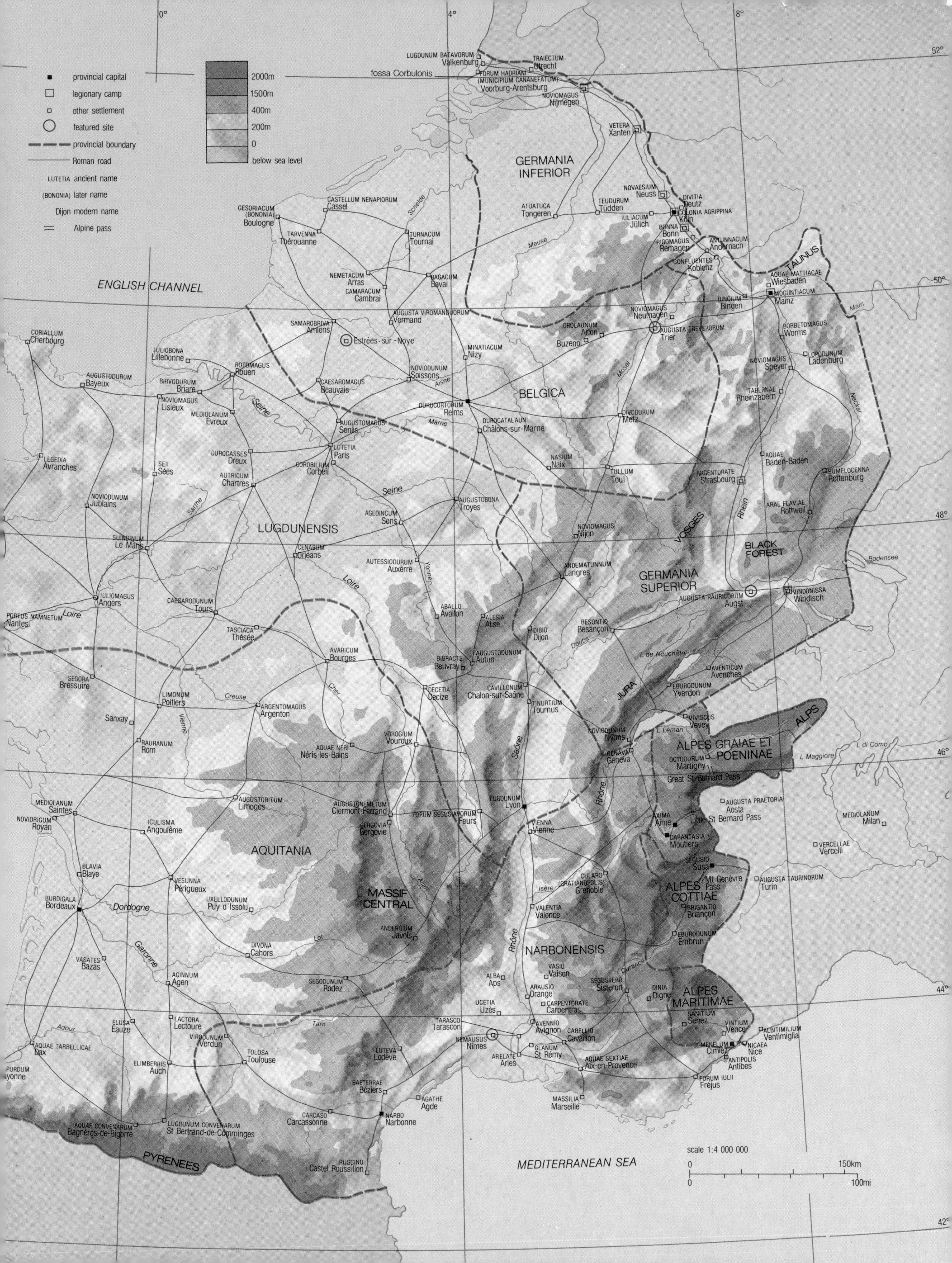
0°
4°
8°
52°
50°
48°
46°
44°
42°
provincial capital
legionary camp
other settlement
featured site
provincial boundary
Roman road
LUTETIA ancient name
(BONONIA) later name
Dijon modern name
Alpine pass
2000m
1500m
400m
200m
0
below sea level
ENGLISH CHANNEL
MEDITERRANEAN SEA
scale 1:4 000 000
0
150km
0
100mi
GERMANIA INFERIOR
BELGICA
LUGDUNENSIS
GERMANIA SUPERIOR
AQUITANIA
NARBONENSIS
ALPES GRAIAE ET POENINAE
ALPES COTTIAE
ALPES MARITIMAE
MASSIF CENTRAL
PYRENEES
ALPS
JURA
VOSGES
BLACK FOREST
TAUNUS
fossa Corbulonis
LUGDUNUM BATAVORUM
Valkenburg
TRAIECTUM
Utrecht
FORUM HADRIANI
(MUNICIPIUM CANANEFATIUM)
Voorburg-Arentsburg
NOVIOMAGUS
Nijmegen
VETERA
Xanten
NOVAESIUM
Neuss
DIVITIA
Deutz
COLONIA AGRIPPINA
Köln
ATUATUCA
Tongeren
TEUDURUM
Tüdden
IULIACUM
Jülich
BONNA
Bonn
RIGOMAGUS
Remagen
ANTUNNACUM
Andernach
CONFLUENTES
Koblenz
AQUAE MATTIACAE
Wiesbaden
MOGUNTIACUM
Mainz
BINGIUM
Bingen
NOVIOMAGUS
Neumagen
OROLAUNUM
Arlon
Buzenol
AUGUSTA TREVERORUM
Trier
BORBETOMAGUS
Worms
LOPODUNUM
Ladenburg
NOVIOMAGUS
Speyer
TABERNAE
Rheinzabern
DIVODURUM
Metz
AQUAE
Baden-Baden
SUMELOCENNA
Rottenburg
NASIUM
Naix
TULLUM
Toul
ARGENTORATE
Strasbourg
ARAE FLAVIAE
Rottweil
GESORIACUM
(BONONIA)
Boulogne
CASTELLUM NENAPIORUM
Cassel
TARVENNA
Thérouanne
TURNACUM
Tournai
NEMETACUM
Arras
CAMARACUM
Cambrai
BAGACUM
Bavai
AUGUSTA VIROMANDUORUM
Vermand
SAMAROBRIVA
Amiens
Estrées-sur-Noye
MINATIACUM
Nizy
CORIALLUM
Cherbourg
IULIOBONA
Lillebonne
ROTOMAGUS
Rouen
AUGUSTODURUM
Bayeux
BRIVODURUM
Briare
NOVIOMAGUS
Lisieux
CAESAROMAGUS
Beauvais
NOVIODUNUM
Soissons
DUROCORTORUM
Reims
MEDIOLANUM
Evreux
AUGUSTOMAGUS
Senlis
DUROCATALAUNI
Châlons-sur-Marne
LUTETIA
Paris
DUROCASSES
Dreux
COROBILIUM
Corbeil
LEGEDIA
Avranches
SEII
Sées
AUTRICUM
Chartres
AUGUSTOBONA
Troyes
NOVIODUNUM
Jublains
AGEDINCUM
Sens
NOVIOMAGUS
Nijon
SUINDINUM
Le Mans
CENABUM
Orléans
AUTESSIODURUM
Auxerre
ANDEMATUNNUM
Langres
IULIOMAGUS
Angers
CAESARODUNUM
Tours
PORTUS NAMNETUM
Nantes
ABALLO
Avallon
ALESIA
Alise
DIBIO
Dijon
BESONTIO
Besançon
AUGUSTA RAURICORUM
Augst
VINDONISSA
Windisch
TASCIACA
Thésée
AVARICUM
Bourges
BIBRACTE
Beuvray
AUGUSTODUNUM
Autun
SEGORA
Bressuire
DECETIA
Decize
CAVILLONUM
Chalon-sur-Saône
AVENTICUM
Avenches
EBURODUNUM
Yverdon
LIMONUM
Poitiers
ARGENTOMAGUS
Argenton
TINURTIUM
Tournus
VIVISCUS
Vevey
Sanxay
NOVIODUNUM
Nyons
GENAVA
Geneva
OCTODURUM
Martigny
Great St Bernard Pass
RAURANUM
Rom
VOROGIUM
Vouroux
AQUAE NERI
Néris-les-Bains
AUGUSTA PRAETORIA
Aosta
MEDIOLANUM
Saintes
NOVIORIGUM
Royan
AUGUSTORITUM
Limoges
AUGUSTONEMETUM
Clermont-Ferrand
FORUM SEGUSIAVORUM
Feurs
LUGDUNUM
Lyon
AXIMA
Aime
Little St Bernard Pass
MEDIOLANUM
Milan
ICULISMA
Angoulême
GERGOVIA
Gergovie
VIENNA
Vienne
DARANTASIA
Moutiers
VERCELLAE
Vercelli
BLAVIA
Blaye
SEGUSIO
Susa
Mt Genèvre Pass
AUGUSTA TAURINORUM
Turin
VESUNNA
Périgueux
CULARO
(GRATIANOPOLIS)
Grenoble
BURDIGALA
Bordeaux
UXELLODUNUM
Puy d'Issolu
VALENTIA
Valence
BRIGANTIO
Briançon
ANDERITUM
Javols
EBURODUNUM
Embrun
DIVONA
Cahors
VASATES
Bazas
ALBA
Aps
VASIO
Vaison
AGINNUM
Agen
SEGODUNUM
Rodez
ARAUSIO
Orange
SEGUSTERO
Sisteron
DINIA
Digne
CARPENTORATE
Carpentras
UCETIA
Uzès
SANITIUM
Senez
ELUSA
Eauze
LACTORA
Lectoure
TARASCO
Tarascon
AVENNIO
Avignon
CABELLIO
Cavaillon
VINTIUM
Vence
ALBINTIMILIUM
Ventimiglia
AQUAE TARBELLICAE
Dax
VIRODUNUM
Verdun
NEMAUSUS
Nîmes
GLANUM
St Rémy
CEMENELUM
Cimiez
NICAEA
Nice
ARELATE
Arles
AQUAE SEXTIAE
Aix-en-Provence
ANTIPOLIS
Antibes
LUTEVA
Lodève
TOLOSA
Toulouse
ELIMBERRIS
Auch
FORUM IULII
Fréjus
BAETERRAE
Béziers
AGATHE
Agde
MASSILIA
Marseille
CARCASO
Carcassonne
NARBO
Narbonne
AQUAE CONVENARUM
Bagnères-de-Bigorre
LUGDUNUM CONVENARUM
St Bertrand-de-Comminges
RUSCINO
Castel Roussillon
Schelde
Meuse
Mosel
Main
Neckar
Rhein
Aisne
Marne
Seine
Sarthe
Loire
Yonne
Doubs
L. de Neuchâtel
Bodensee
L. Léman
L. di Como
L. Maggiore
Creuse
Cher
Vienne
Allier
Saône
Rhône
Isère
Durance
Dordogne
Lot
Garonne
Tarn
Adour

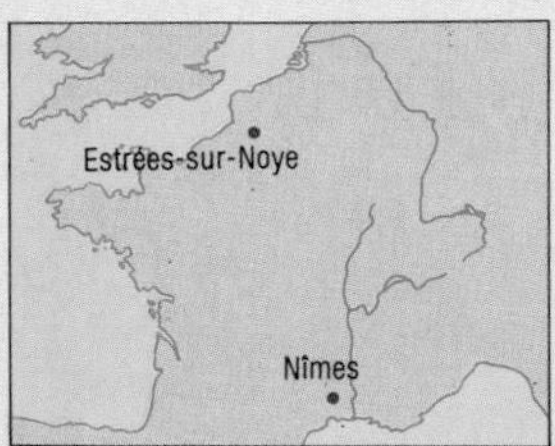

Estrées-sur-Noye

Despite its being a relatively unknown site of which nothing stands above ground, the great rural villa at Estrées-sur-Noye (Somme) is no less typical of the economic development of provincial life in the west than great cities like Nîmes and Trier. The villa is one of many in northern France surveyed in recent years by systematic aerial photography. *Below* appears an artist's reconstruction of the villa based on its actual site plan. It consists of a main residence, at the far end of the photograph, and before it a courtyard lined with cottages and storehouses. Near the front gateway is an isolated building, presumably a shrine. The whole complex is a self-sufficient farming establishment typical of the northern provinces of the Empire. The main difficulty in the interpretation of these sites, which can only be resolved by excavation, is to know how many were occupied simultaneously and how many were abandoned to be succeeded by others nearby. On any account, the density of rural occupation of northern Gaul was remarkably high.

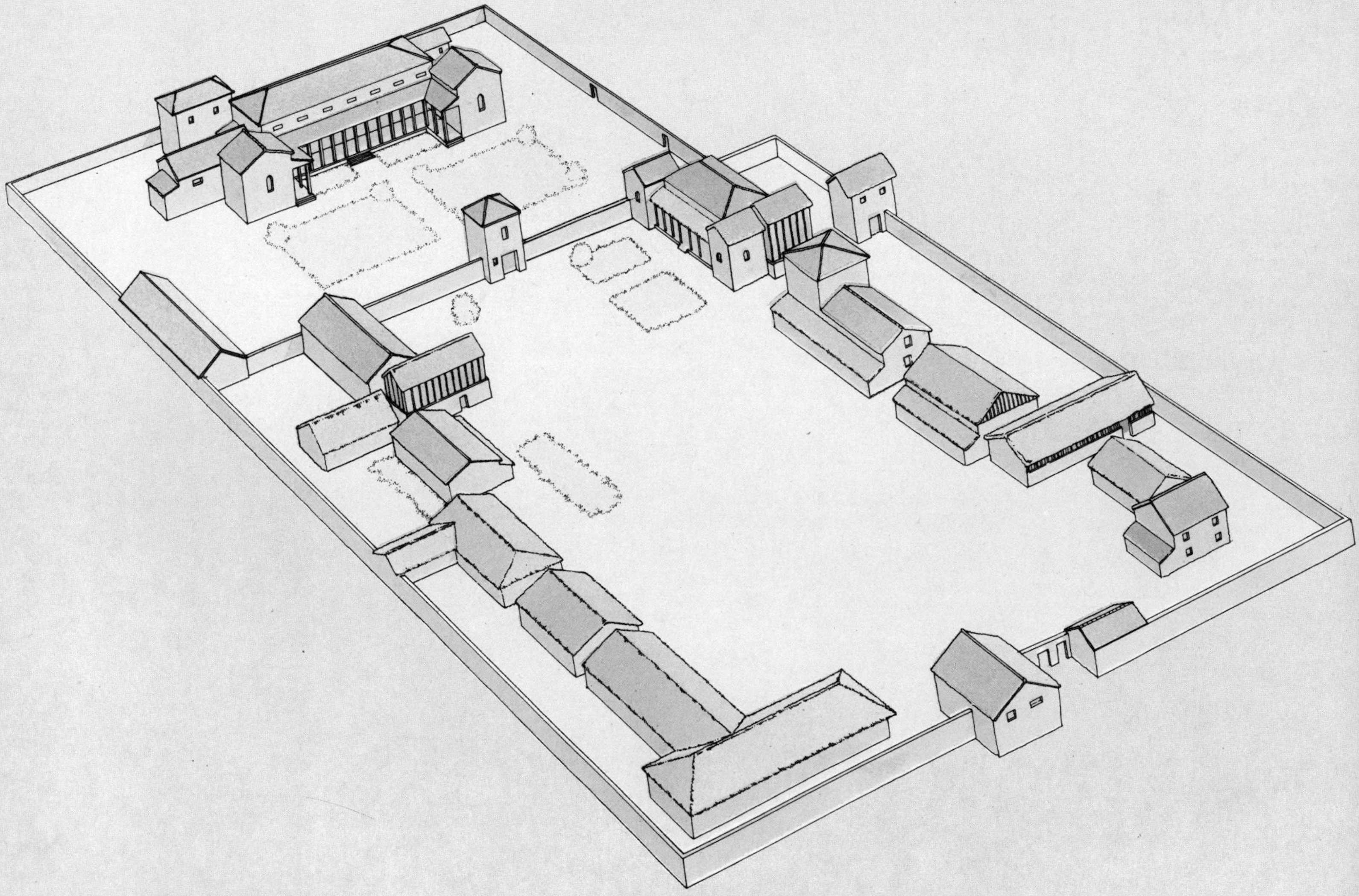

The famous aqueduct constructed in the time of Augustus over the river Gard (or Gardon) was part of a system which delivered water to Nîmes from a source near Uzès (see also p. 185). The accuracy of the surveying and engineering involved is most impressive; the water dropped only 17 meters over the distance of 50 kilometers for which it was conveyed. The local quarries from which the stone was brought for the construction of the aqueduct can still be seen.

After the capture of Alexandria by Octavian in 30 BC, Egyptian Greeks were settled at Nîmes; this is reflected by the coin issues showing the heads of Augustus and Agrippa with reverses (shown *left*) of a crocodile with the legend COL[onia] NEM[ausus]. The beautifully preserved temple in the forum of ancient Nîmes, known as the "Maison Carrée" (*left*), was dedicated to the princes Gaius and Lucius Caesar. It is a perfect example of classical style, conforming exactly to the proportions laid down by Vitruvius. The famous amphitheater of Nîmes (*top*), still used for bullfights, dates from the late 1st or early 2nd century.

Nîmes

Nîmes, ancient Nemausus, fell under Roman control in the late 1st century BC and became a colony of Roman citizens in the time of Augustus. Standing on the main road from Italy to Spain and with access to the Mediterranean, it was one of the most populous and important cities in southern Gaul. Its wealth nevertheless derived chiefly not from trade, in which it was surpassed by Narbonne, but from the exploitation of the agricultural potential of its territory; the early senators whom it produced can be shown, on the basis of their nomenclature, to have been romanized Gauls, the ancestral owners of the land, rather than Italian immigrants. The city was in the 2nd century the native city of the emperor Antoninus Pius. Apart from the other monuments illustrated on this page, Nîmes possessed an elaborate complex of baths and pools fed by the sacred spring of the god Nemausus. This, elaborately remodeled in the 18th century, can still be seen, but other public monuments, for example the circus which the city once possessed, are now lost.

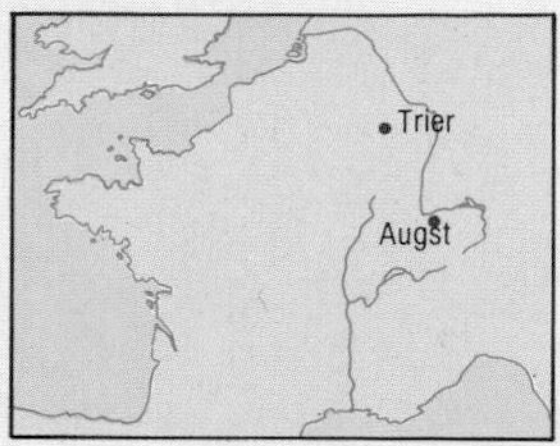

Augst

Augst (Augusta Rauricorum, in the later period simply Rauraci) was founded as a military colony in 44 BC by a lieutenant of Julius Caesar, partly as a safeguard for Caesar's recent conquests in Gaul. It was also important in the German wars conducted by Augustus and by the Flavians. The defensive advantages of the site are apparent from its contours: it is a plateau with steeply falling land on three sides, set back a little from the banks of the Rhine. Excavation is revealing a varied and well-equipped town with porticoed streets, theater and senate house, fountains, temples, two sets of baths and trading establishments including a sausage maker's. Like other sites in the northern provinces, Augst acquired substantial stone buildings only in the late 1st century AD. After the invasions of the mid-3rd century the apparently declining population concentrated in the smaller fortified settlement of Kaiseraugst; Ammianus Marcellinus described Rauraci in the 4th century as situated "on the very edge of the Rhine." Kaiseraugst should however not be regarded as an entirely separate settlement but rather as a contraction of the earlier one, involving a displacement from its monumental area.

The theater at Augst underwent various adaptations, visible in the aerial photograph and more fully on the site plan. It was first a small theater of orthodox design, with some of its seating in wood, then an amphitheater (or combined theater and amphitheater), and in its final transformation, c. 150 AD, a slightly larger classical theater with a capacity of 8000. To coincide with this phase a second amphitheater was built to the south. All this is a sign of a flourishing and expanding community. The city walls exist in two stretches but were never finished.

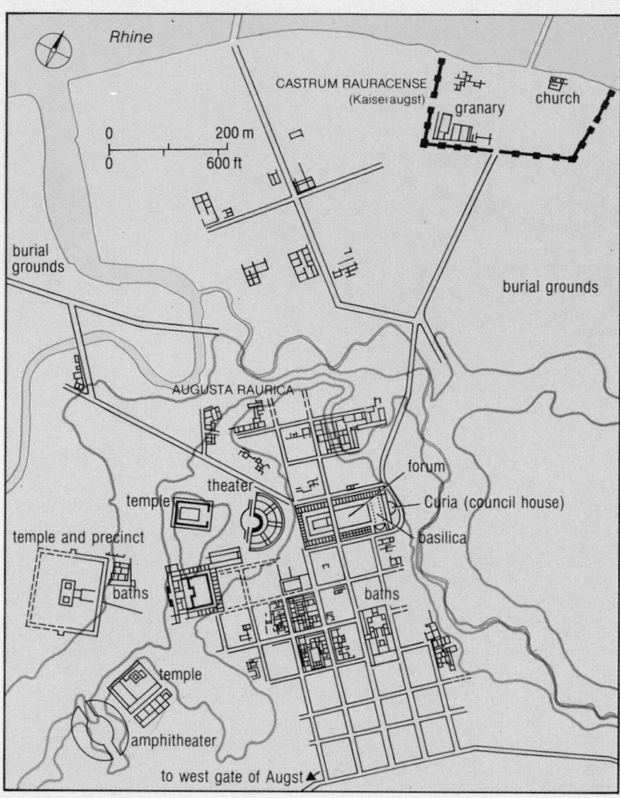

Trier

Trier was an ancient capital of the mixed Celtic, and possibly also Germanic, peoples of the Treveri; near the city stand important religious sanctuaries, including a native precinct, the Altbachtal, and a temple of Lenus Mars, a romanized native god. The name Augusta Treverorum derived from the presence of Augustus during his Gallic visit of 15–13 BC. In the early Empire the city flourished, owing its success to its position, on a waterway with easy access to the military establishments on the Rhine. To the early period belong the baths known as the Barbarathermen, the amphitheater and the remains of many elaborate private houses. Trier was in the first two centuries an important administrative center as the seat of the procurator of Belgica and the two Germanies, and several of its natives make appearances in written history. From the late 3rd century the city acquired a vastly enlarged role as the main imperial residence in the west. The emperors Constantius and especially Constantine the Great were particularly influential in this development, the most notable monuments from the time of Constantine being the great imperial basilica (Aula Palatina), the imperial baths, all of which formed part of a new "palace precinct," and several churches. An orator speaking at Trier in 310 evokes the atmosphere: "I see a great circus to rival the one at Rome, I see basilicas, forum, a seat of justice, rising to such heights as to be worthy neighbors of the stars. All of which are the fruits of your presence." As the imperial capital Trier attracted literary men, both as teachers and as civil servants. It drew embassies from the provinces, and churchmen like Martin of Tours and Ambrose of Milan went there on various errands. Until its transfer to Arles in the late 4th or early 5th century, the praetorian prefecture of Gaul, Britain and Spain, with its associated offices such as a mint and state workshops, had its seat at Trier. The position of the city, which had given it such great advantages in the earlier period, exposed it to the barbarian raids of the 5th century, and its decline as a Roman city was hastened by repeated barbarian sack.

Above In this painted fresco from Trier rural workers are seen outside a country house. One wears the hooded cloak seen in grave reliefs from the region and also from Britain. It was presumably as appropriate for the northern climate in those days as it would be now.

The great north gate of Trier (*far right*), known as the Porta Nigra or "Black Gate," and the city walls of which it formed part, are probably to be dated to the late 2nd or early 3rd century, but the gate is on any account an appropriate symbol of the later role of the city as imperial capital. In the Middle Ages it became a church, an apse being added to the east tower. The painted fresco (*right*), possibly representing the wife of Constantine, is from the Constantinian palace, on the site of the later cathedral.

BRITAIN

The conquest of Britain was in part provoked by its relations with Belgic Gaul, and its social history under the Roman Empire is an extension of that of its continental neighbor. The cities of Britain, though large in expanse, would undoubtedly have seemed more diffuse and less monumental than their Mediterranean counterparts. As in Gallia Comata, villas played a proportionately more important role, as the vehicles of commercial life and agents of romanization.

The continuing insecurity presented by the peoples of Wales and north of Hadrian's Wall meant that Britain always required a substantial military presence. The development of the province, indeed, falls into two halves. South of the Fosse Way, the road from Exeter to Lincoln, was civilian settlement; north and west of this line, occupation was generally under strong military influence.

As in the case of Gallia Comata but without the advantage of a late imperial presence, natives of Britain made little direct contribution to the political life of the Roman Empire except, in the 4th century, through repeated usurpation. Though Britain exported materials such as tin and lead, a little gold, and sometimes provided corn to the Rhine armies, it can hardly have covered the costs of its occupation. Yet we must not underestimate the intrinsic quality of romanization achieved there. The Roman cities and roads, built, it was supposed, by giants or the Devil, haunted the imagination of later writers. So an Anglo-Saxon poet (translated by R. Hamer) evokes the ruins of Roman Bath – "where long since/a host of heroes, glorious, gold-adorned .../shone in their armour, gazed on gems and treasure .../on this bright city with its wide domains ..."

In the symbols presented by the *Notitia Dignitatum* for the civil and military governors of Britain, the province is shown notionally as an island, with no attempt to achieve exact, or even relative, geographical accuracy in the location of the cities and forts. Shown here are the insignia of the Vicarius Britanniarum.

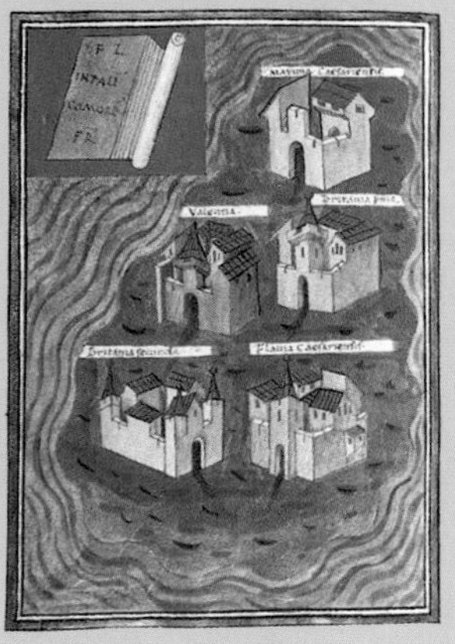

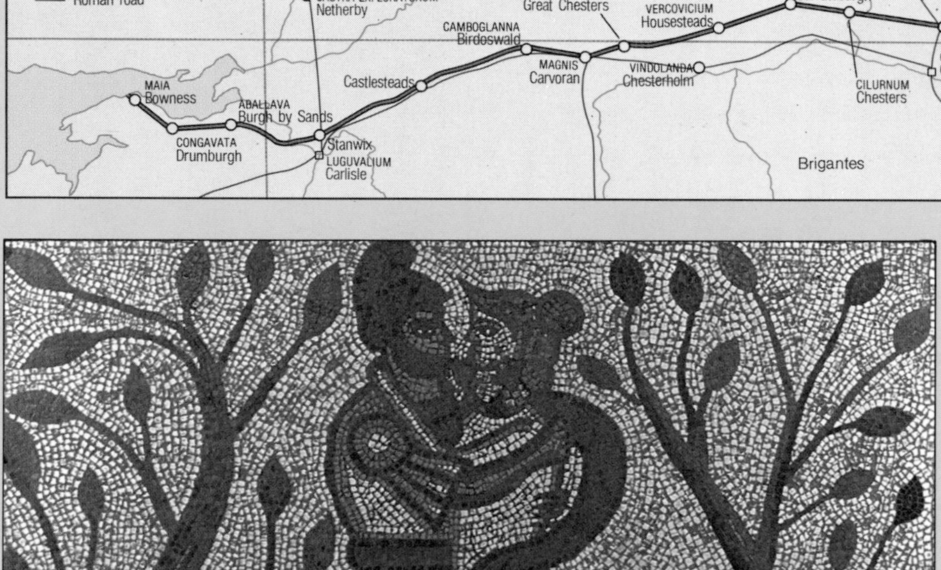

The Thetford treasure, discovered in 1979 beside the Icknield Way in Norfolk, is one of the largest hoards of Roman gold and silver to come to light in Britain. The quality of the working suggests that it was done on the Continent in the late 4th century. This gold buckle (*top*) has a hinged bow in the form of two confronted horses' heads and a rectangular plate with a relief of a dancing satyr.

The building inscription (*above*), from the fort of High Rochester north of Hadrian's Wall, records work done by a detachment of the Twentieth Legion from Chester. The crudely carved figures flanking the inscription are Mars and Hercules, appropriate military patrons. The date is probably early 3rd century, when there was much rebuilding after the British campaign of Septimius Severus.

The 4th-century mosaic (*above*) from the bath buildings of a villa in Somerset is part of a series illustrating the story of Dido and Aeneas. Apart from its mildly erotic appeal, the mosaic attests a knowledge of Virgil's *Aeneid* – or at least of its most romantic book. Augustine, too, as a student in 4th-century Africa, "wept on the death of Dido" (*Confessions* 1.13).

The strategic concept of Hadrian's Wall (inset map), of a patrolled linear frontier supported by an occupied military zone, has analogies with other 2nd-century frontiers, such as the Raetian palisade (p. 108). The wall, with its associated works, seems to be almost as concerned with what lay behind as beyond it. Possibly it was intended to separate and so control restless peoples on both southern and northern sides.

Hadrian's wall is seen (*overleaf*) looking east near Housesteads on a day of striking scenic contrasts. In conditions like these one can find some sympathy for the Palmyrenes and other Middle Easterners stationed there.

6°
4°
2°
0°
56°
54°
52°
55°
GRAMPIAN MOUNTAINS
Inchtuthil
Tay
Carpow
Antonine Wall
Inveresk
TRIMONTIUM
Newstead
SOUTHERN UPLANDS
BREMENIUM
High Rochester
CASTRA EXPLORATORUM
Hadrian's Wall
CILURNUM
Chesters
SEGEDUNUM
Wallsend
MAIA
Bowness
LUGUVALIUM
Carlisle
CORSTOPITUM
Corbridge
PONS AELIUS
Newcastle
CONCANGIUM
Chester le Street
CHEVIOT HILLS
ALAUNA
Maryport
VOREDA
Old Penrith
DERVENTIO
Papcastle
VERTERAE
Brough
LAVATRAE
Bowes
Tees
CUMBRIAN MTS
CATARACTONIUM
Catterick
YORKSHIRE MOORS
NORTH SEA
PENNINE CHAIN
ISURIUM
Aldborough
Ouse
EBURACUM
York
IRISH SEA
BREMETENNACUM
Ribchester
CALCARIA
Tadcaster
PETUARIA
Brough
LAGENTIUM
Castleford
MAMUCIUM
Manchester
NAVIO
Brough
AQUAE ARNEMETIAE
Buxton
LINDUM
Lincoln
VARAE?
St Asaph
DEVA
Chester
SEGONTIUM
Caernarvon
DERVENTIO
Littlechester
Trent
CAUSENNAE
Ancaster
BRANODUNUM
Brancaster
VERNEMETUM
Willoughby
THE FENS
VIROCONIUM
Wroxeter
LETOCETUM
Wall
RATAE
Leicester
DUROBRIVAE
Water Newton
VENTA
Caister
Caersws
Severn
VENONAE
High Cross
CAMBRIAN MTS
SALINAE
Droitwich
DUROVIGUTUM
Godmanchester
DUROLIPONS
Cambridge
Nene
Gt Ouse
Alcester
LACTODORUM
Towcester
Great Chesterford
MAGNIS
Kenchester
Wye
Llandovery
COTSWOLD HILLS
CAMULODUNUM
Colchester
Avon
MORIDUNUM
Carmarthen
GOBANNIUM
Abergavenny
BLESTIUM
Monmouth
GLEVUM
Gloucester
Alchester
CHILTERN HILLS
CAESAROMAGUS
Chelmsford
VENTA
Caerwent
VERULAMIUM
St Albans
NIDUM
Neath
ISCA
Caerleon
CORINIUM
Cirencester
Dorchester
LONDINIUM
London
Thames
AQUAE SULIS
Bath
CUNETIO
Mildenhall
CALLEVA
Silchester
DUROBRIVAE
Rochester
DUROVERNUM
Canterbury
RUTUPIAE
Richborough
DUBRIS
Dover
SALISBURY PLAIN
EXMOOR
SORVIODUNUM
Old Sarum
LEMANIS
Lympne
VENTA
Winchester
LINDINIS
Ilchester
CLAUSENTUM
Bitterne
PORTUS ADURNI
Portchester
SOUTH DOWNS
ANDERITA
Pevensey
NOVIOMAGUS
Chichester
Fishbourne
DARTMOOR
ISCA
Exeter
Maiden Castle
DURNOVARIA
Dorchester
ENGLISH CHANNEL
scale 1:2 700 000
0
150km
0
100mi
scale 1:800 000
30km
20mi
VINDOVALA
Rudchester
SEGEDUNUM
Wallsend
CONDERCUM
Benwell
PONS AELIUS
Newcastle
South Shields
ARBEIA
provincial capital
legionary camp
colonia
civitas capital
other important civil settlement
other settlement
featured site
Roman road
Roman road, course uncertain
Roman canal
Roman waterway
Roman wall
VENTA ancient name
Caerwent modern name
500m
200m
0
marsh

Silchester

Silchester (Calleva of the Atrebates) was the capital of one of the native states, or *civitates*, given as a client kingdom to the British chieftain Cogidubnus at the time of the Claudian conquest. The site, abandoned as an urban center after the Roman period, now consists of open fields, surrounded by the remains of the city walls, added to the existing earthen ramparts in the late 2nd or early 3rd century. Of modern buildings there is only a church and a farm near the east gate of the Roman town. The remains of the small amphitheater are visible nearby as a circular embankment. Its capacity has been calculated at about 2700, which might roughly represent the adult population. A recent estimate of the population of Silchester as 1000 seems far too low, and takes no account of the seasonal variations which must have been considerable in a rural center with such a large agricultural territory.

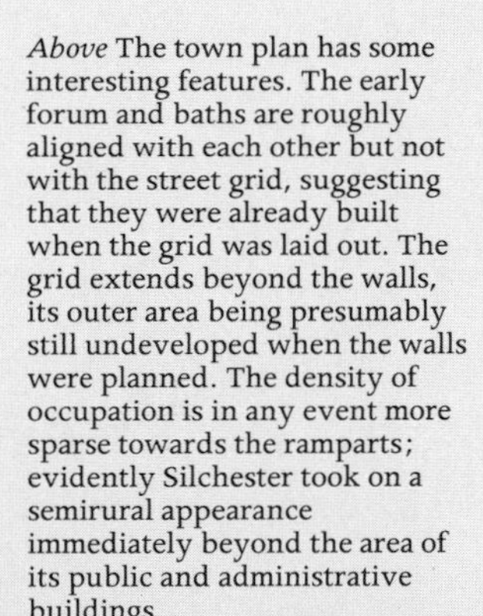

Right The bronze Silchester eagle, found in the Roman basilica, is evidently not, as was originally supposed, a legionary standard, but part of a larger statue once in the basilica complex.

Below The aerial photograph shows clearly the course of the Roman defenses of the 2nd/3rd century, the inner earthwork rendered superfluous by the early development of the town, and the regular street plan. The amphitheater is in the clump of trees at the far left corner of the site. The driveway crossing the site transversely is modern.

Above The town plan has some interesting features. The early forum and baths are roughly aligned with each other but not with the street grid, suggesting that they were already built when the grid was laid out. The grid extends beyond the walls, its outer area being presumably still undeveloped when the walls were planned. The density of occupation is in any event more sparse towards the ramparts; evidently Silchester took on a semirural appearance immediately beyond the area of its public and administrative buildings.

Below The Great Bath at Bath. Still fed by Roman conduits, it measures 24 by 12 m and is 1·8 m deep.

Below right The temple of the Celtic goddess Sulis, romanized as Minerva, was first discovered during the construction of the Pump Room at Bath in the late 18th century. The bearded male "Medusa" head here shown, with entwined serpents for hair, formed the striking central feature of the sculptured pediment of the temple. The decorative flair of Celtic art is applied with splendid effect to a somewhat adapted classical subject. The stylized vigor of the work is emphasized by the contrast with the calm poise of the classical head of Minerva also from Bath (*bottom*), a gilt-bronze piece, probably from a cult statue of the goddess, found in the Great Bath in the 18th century.

Bath

Roman Bath (Aquae Sulis), founded under the Flavians, was one of many settlements in the Roman Empire which owed their often long-lived prosperity to their medicinal springs. Parallels in the continental Empire, like Vichy and Néris-les-Bains in France, and in Germany Baden-Baden and Wiesbaden, can easily be found. Like them, Bath retained its popularity as a health and holiday resort into modern times, though the waters have recently been found contaminated by bacteria and unfit for use. Because of the continuous development of the city, little is known of Aquae Sulis apart from its well-preserved bath complex. The 2nd- or 3rd-century walls of the town survived, however, until the early 18th century.

Fishbourne

Its remains still suggest something of the sophistication of the palace at Fishbourne. The mosaic (*left*), showing sea monsters and a trident-bearing winged Cupid riding a dolphin, is in a room in the north wing reconstructed in the 2nd century. It is likely that more than one craftsman worked on the mosaic; this is suggested in particular by the different standards of workmanship visible in the sea horses in the north and south panels, the south panel being far better.

The Roman palace at Fishbourne in Sussex, by the main road leading west from Chichester (Noviomagus), has been spectacularly revealed by recent excavation. It stood at the head of a creek which at that time reached further inland than it does now, and was also the site of wooden granaries and a naval station associated on archaeological grounds with the Claudian conquest. The fully developed palace of the Flavian period was an enlargement of an earlier residence. It has been connected with the king Cogidubnus mentioned above – Roman citizen and friend of the emperor Claudius. The identification cannot be positively attested, but the magnificence of the palace – unsurpassed for its date in the west Roman provinces – makes Cogidubnus' candidacy for its ownership a strong one.

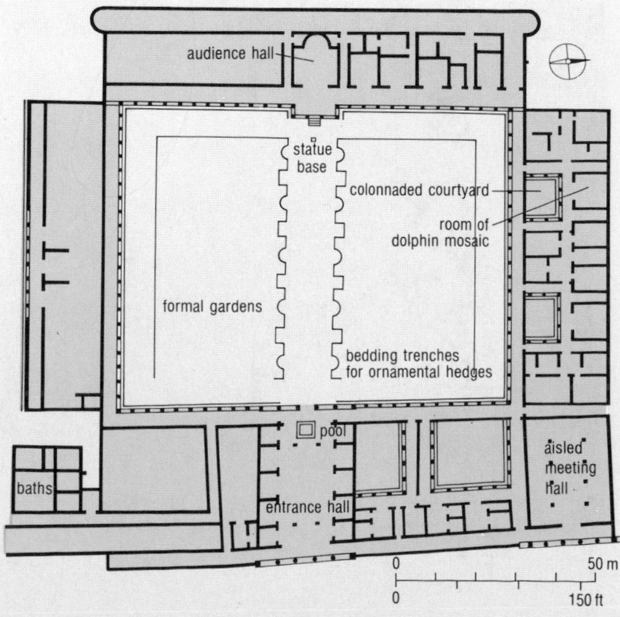

THE DANUBE

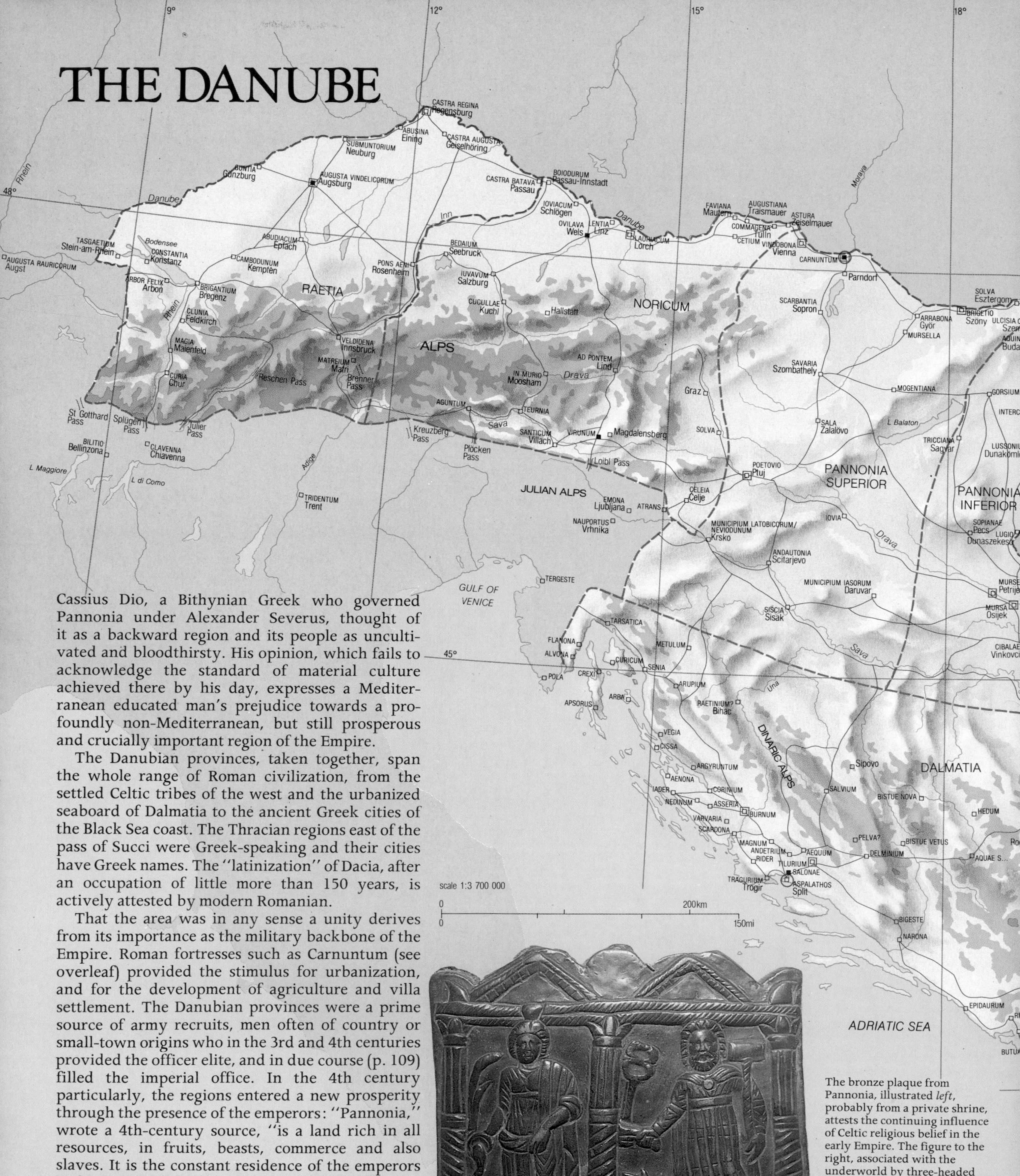

Cassius Dio, a Bithynian Greek who governed Pannonia under Alexander Severus, thought of it as a backward region and its people as uncultivated and bloodthirsty. His opinion, which fails to acknowledge the standard of material culture achieved there by his day, expresses a Mediterranean educated man's prejudice towards a profoundly non-Mediterranean, but still prosperous and crucially important region of the Empire.

The Danubian provinces, taken together, span the whole range of Roman civilization, from the settled Celtic tribes of the west and the urbanized seaboard of Dalmatia to the ancient Greek cities of the Black Sea coast. The Thracian regions east of the pass of Succi were Greek-speaking and their cities have Greek names. The "latinization" of Dacia, after an occupation of little more than 150 years, is actively attested by modern Romanian.

That the area was in any sense a unity derives from its importance as the military backbone of the Empire. Roman fortresses such as Carnuntum (see overleaf) provided the stimulus for urbanization, and for the development of agriculture and villa settlement. The Danubian provinces were a prime source of army recruits, men often of country or small-town origins who in the 3rd and 4th centuries provided the officer elite, and in due course (p. 109) filled the imperial office. In the 4th century particularly, the regions entered a new prosperity through the presence of the emperors: "Pannonia," wrote a 4th-century source, "is a land rich in all resources, in fruits, beasts, commerce and also slaves. It is the constant residence of the emperors and possesses great cities, like Sirmium ..."

Linking east and west, and also confronting barbarian invasion, the Danubian provinces are a constant test of the well-being of the Empire. It was on their stability that the survival of the Roman Empire, as Dio knew it, depended.

The bronze plaque from Pannonia, illustrated *left*, probably from a private shrine, attests the continuing influence of Celtic religious belief in the early Empire. The figure to the right, associated with the underworld by three-headed Cerberus, bears the mallet of a Celtic god roughly equivalent to the Roman Dis Pater, god of the underworld and night. The goddess with the snake is his consort, a Celtic version of Persephone, queen of the underworld.

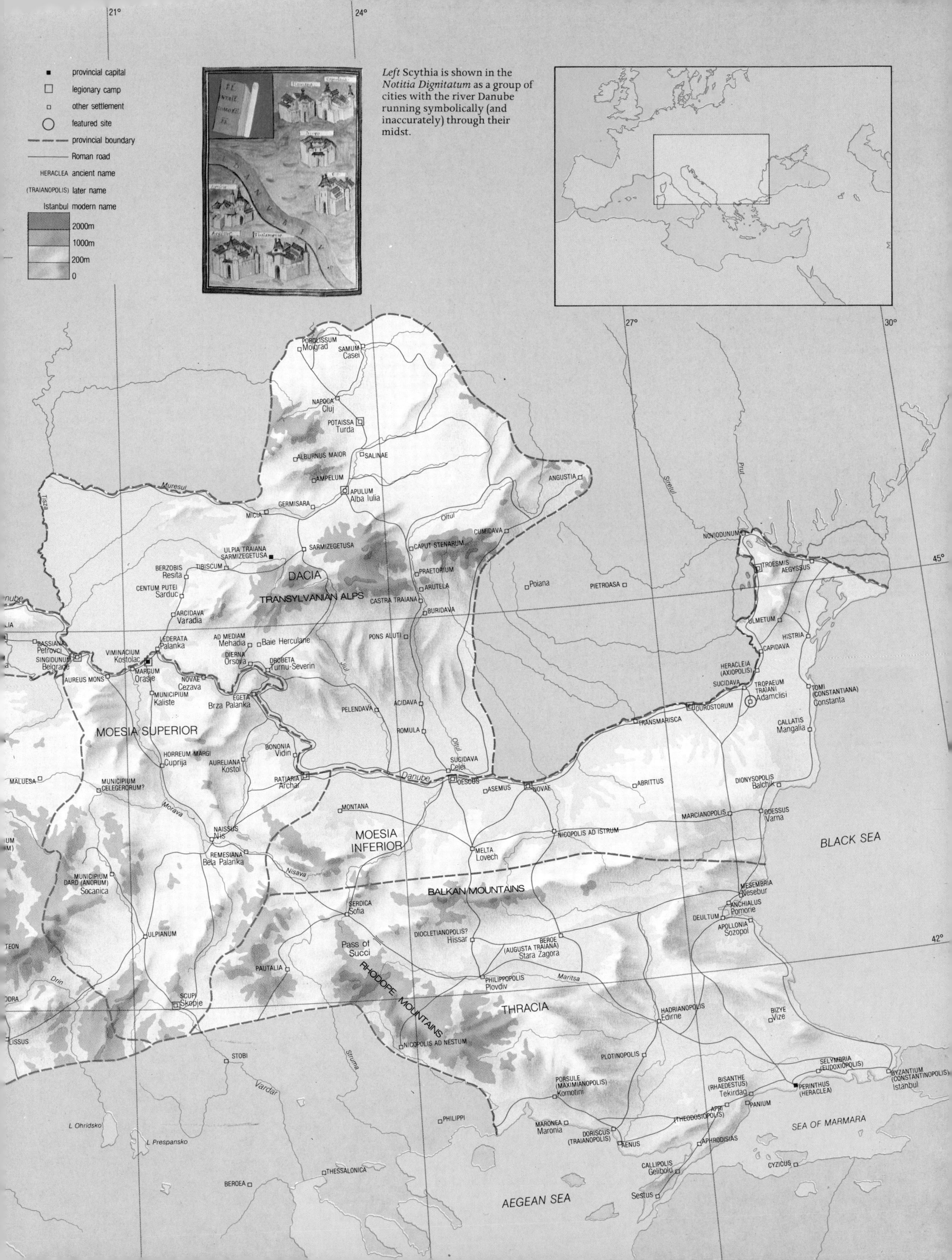

Left Scythia is shown in the *Notitia Dignitatum* as a group of cities with the river Danube running symbolically (and inaccurately) through their midst.

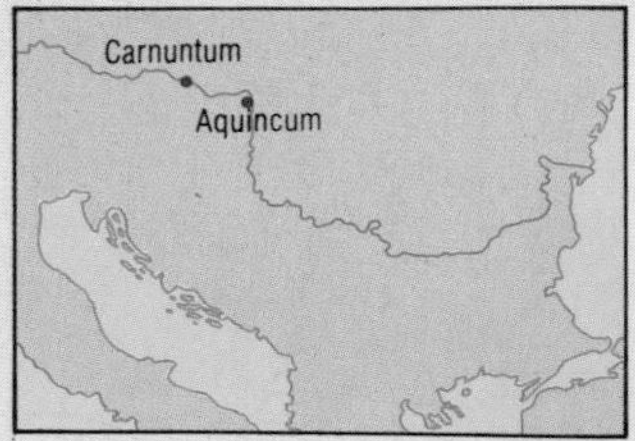

The aerial view of the *canabae* of the legionary fortress of Carnuntum (*below right*), with buildings and streets clearly seen as differences in the growth of standing crops, well indicates the spontaneous but substantial nature of the settlement. The main street forks as it enters the *canabae* from the southern gate of the fortress, which lies a little distance off the bottom of the picture, beyond a cleared area adjoining the rampart.

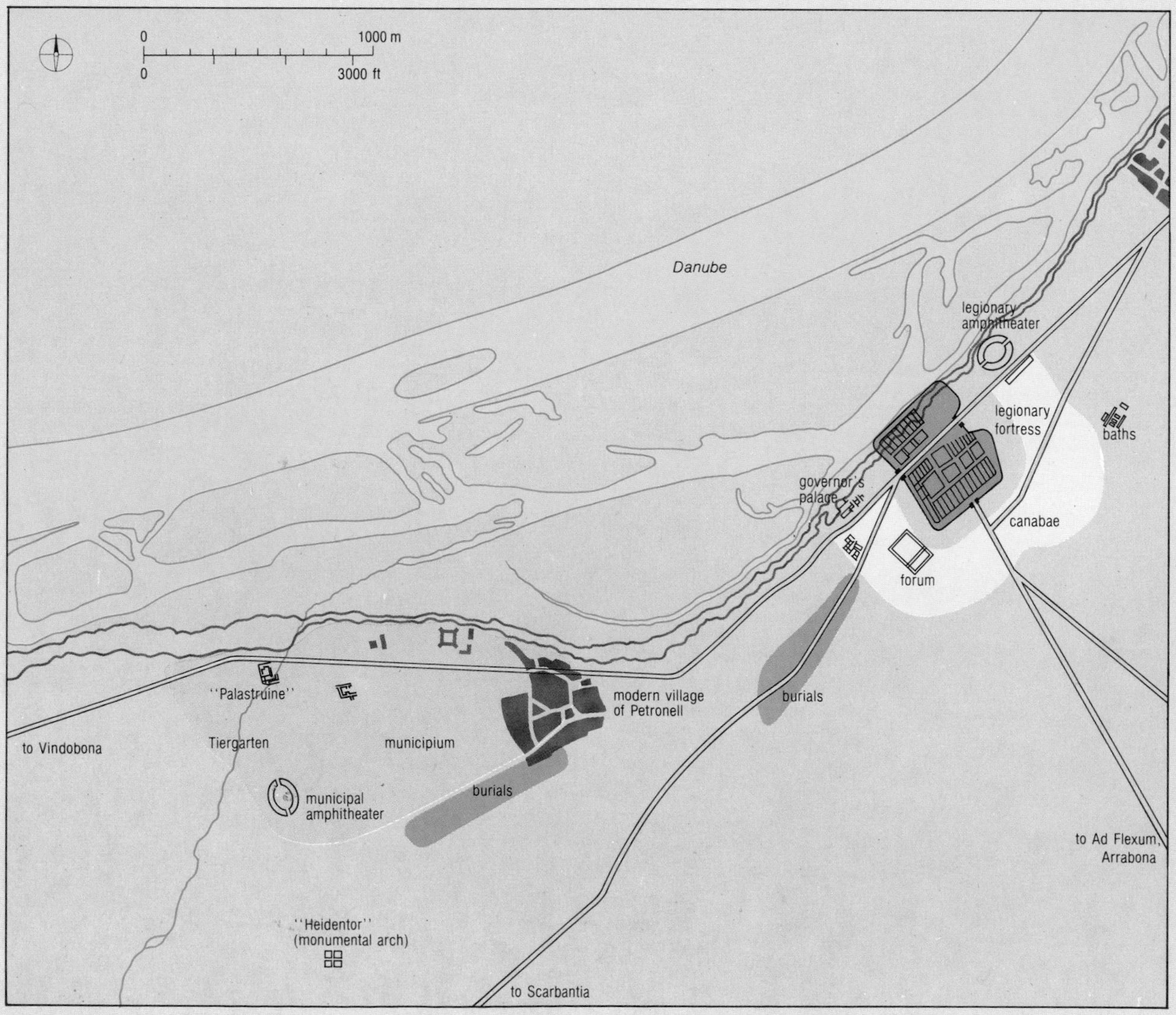

Carnuntum

Carnuntum and Aquincum illustrate a process of urban development characteristic of the northern military provinces of the Empire. Founded in the time of Tiberius as a legionary base on the Danube bank, the military camp of Carnuntum soon attracted settlers – traders, artisans, soldiers' concubines and others who saw their prospects of fortune in the vicinity of an establishment of 5000 men and more who received regular salaries from the Roman government. These immigrants congregated in informal settlements known as *canabae*, communities with no independent legal status but falling under the jurisdiction of the legionary legate. The civilian municipality, founded later, is to the west of the camp and *canabae*, its central area lying under the modern village of Petronell. It possessed its own amphitheater, provided in the 2nd century by an immigrant from Syrian Antioch named C. Domitius Zmaragdus, a decurion, or town councillor, of the municipality: 2nd-century Carnuntum was in its composite form a very substantial urban community.

It remained important until the time of the later Empire, although its military function was never lost. It was here that Marcus Aurelius undersigned the second book of his *Meditations* while engaged in war against the Quadi, and at Carnuntum Septimius Severus was proclaimed emperor in 193 AD. In the 4th century Ammianus Marcellinus described it as a "deserted and unkempt town" but militarily convenient. The emperor Valentinian spent three months there before moving on to Aquincum. Carnuntum was apparently abandoned with the Hunnish occupation of the plains to the north and Roman evacuation of the right bank of the Danube. Indeed, the presence of such well-appointed cities on the extreme fringes of the Roman Empire has often been seen as a standing temptation to the barbarian tribes who adjoined it.

The plan of Carnuntum (*below*) shows the relative positions of legionary camp and *canabae* and civilian *municipium* and suggests the overall size of the conurbation.

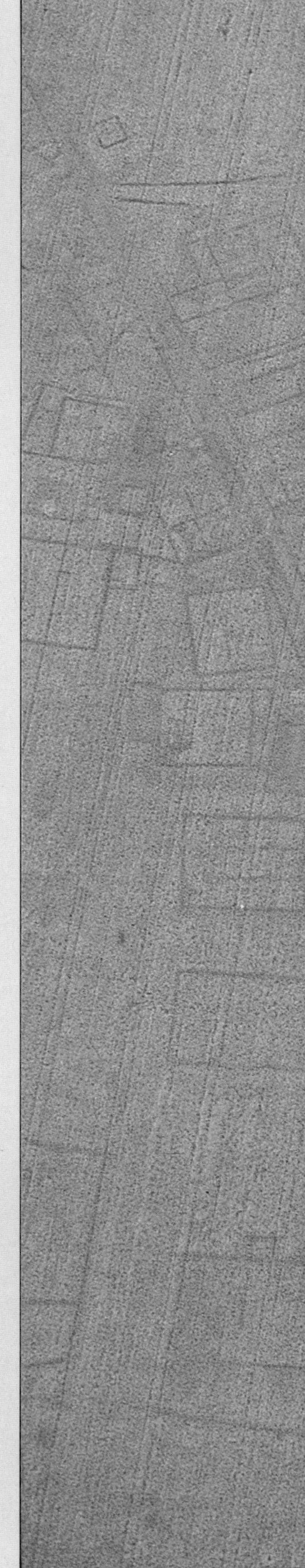

The civilian amphitheater of Carnuntum stood by the main road leading towards Vienna (Vindobona). In the aerial photograph (*bottom right*) the traces of extensive surrounding buildings are clearly visible.

Below This portable organ was found in the basement of the Collegium Centonariorum, or guild of firemen, and casts an intriguing light on the nature of its meetings. By coincidence, Aquincum also produced the touching epitaph set up by the legionary organist to his wife, a lady of musical accomplishments, in which "she alone excelled her husband."

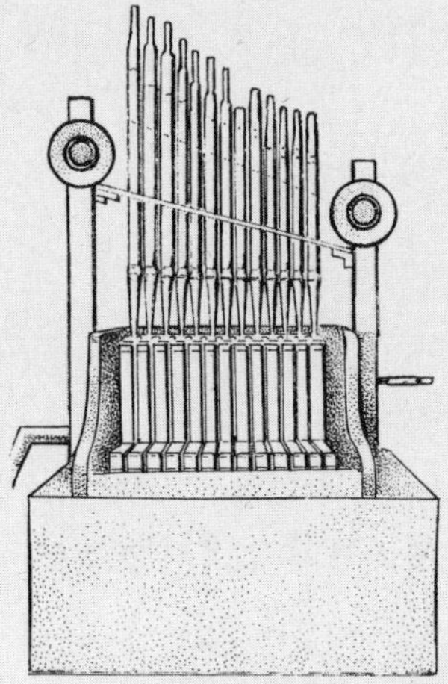

Aquincum

An identical process of development, from legionary camp and *canabae* to later *municipium*, took place at Aquincum as at Carnuntum. Here, too, as at Carnuntum, are two amphitheaters, military and civilian, the latter built after the foundation of the *municipium* in the 2nd century. Despite its annihilation by modern Budapest, Aquincum has furnished numerous artifacts, and richly decorated wall paintings which attest the standard of life achieved by the more opulent members of its society. Inscriptions also reveal the contribution to the civilian life of Aquincum which was made by veterans of the legion stationed there.

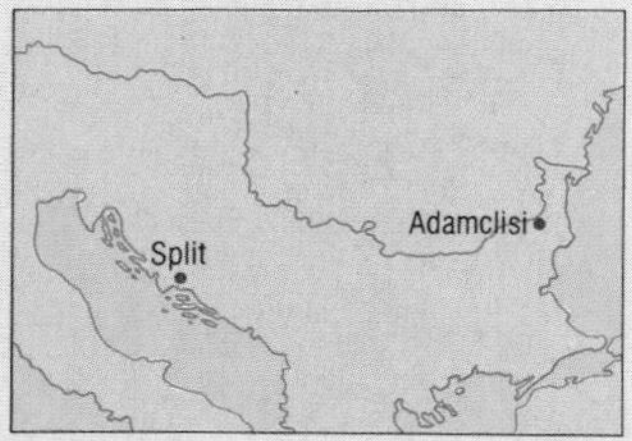

Split

Split, or Spalato, was originally a suburb of the city of Salona, an ancient tribal capital and in the Roman Empire a great city of Dalmatia. In the 4th to 6th centuries Salona was a notable center of late Roman Christianity, with monumental basilicas and many engraved sarcophagi, and in the 5th century was for a time the capital of an independent Dalmatian principality. Since medieval times the position of the two communities has been reversed, for with the development of Split as the nucleus of an urban settlement, Salona progressively became little more than a quarry for building materials. In modern times Split is a flourishing city while Salona is a deserted site.

The medieval town of Split (its ancient name, Aspalathos, the Greek name for the thorn plant which grew there, reflects the early Greek influence on this part of Dalmatia) grew in and around the seaside palace built by Diocletian for his retirement after his abdication from the imperial throne in 305. His octagonal mausoleum adjoining the peristyle (*below*) later became a Christian church – an ironic fate for the emperor whose last years had been spent in Christian persecution. The palace was laid out in strict Roman fashion like a military camp, with main streets crossing at right angles. It seems evident that, despite his reputation for simple tastes such as gardening, Diocletian was not deprived in retirement of the ceremonial grandeur that had attended him as emperor.

Above Diocletian, the builder of Split, as seen in a portrait bust from Nicomedia.

Right The architect Robert Adam was one of many European artists and designers to be attracted by the ruins of Diocletian's palace, and spent five eventful weeks in 1757 surveying and measuring the site. This is his reconstruction of the south facade of the palace, overlooking the sea. The artist has exercised some licence in clarifying the authentic parts of the ancient structure but his drawings give a good impression of the buildings at a time when they were better preserved than now. The architectural focus of the palace was formed by the colonnaded peristyle (*below*) which functioned as a ceremonial courtyard and, in due course, monumental approach to the mausoleum of Diocletian.

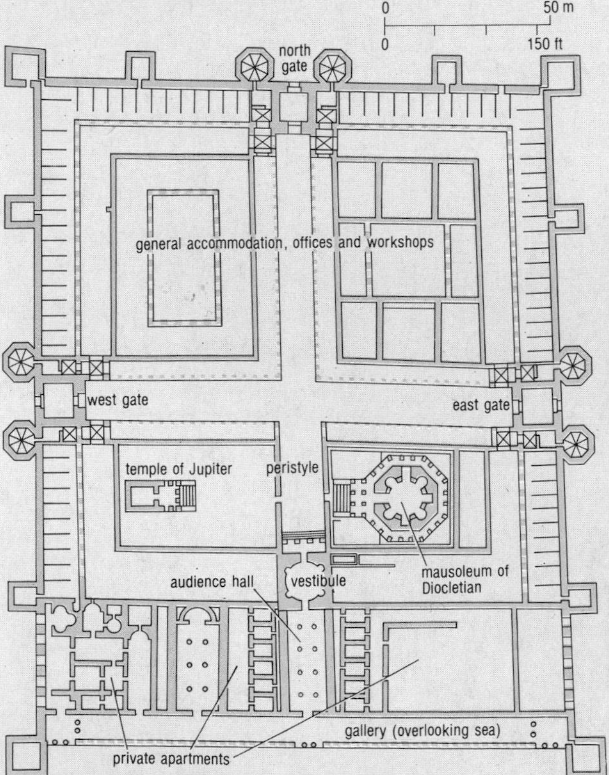

Below The "pastor bonus" (Good Shepherd) sarcophagus, found at Salona and now in the Archaeological Museum at Split. The quality of the carving (early 4th century) is superb, and it has been claimed that the same craftsman later worked on the arch of Constantine in Rome.

Adamclisi

The Roman city of Tropaeum Traiani, near Adamclisi in the Dobrudja, is known to have existed from the 2nd century until late antiquity. Destroyed by Gothic raids in the 3rd century, the city was rebuilt by Constantine and Licinius and in the later period possessed a number of fine churches. It took its name from the "Trophy of Trajan," of which a modern reconstruction is shown *below*. Erected by Trajan as a local reminder of his victories in the Dacian wars, it was also intended to mark retribution for the defeats suffered by Domitian. Nearby were built a mausoleum and commemorative altar, the latter containing the names of nearly 4000 soldiers killed in Domitian's Dacian wars.

Left The metopes of the Adamclisi trophy show scenes of warfare in a style which is a striking contrast with that of Trajan's column at Rome. Here are shown an auxiliary horseman dressed in chain mail, and sheep representing spoils of war. Some have argued that the metopes are Constantinian in date, connected with the late rebuilding of the city of Tropaeum Traiani; on any account they are a remarkable example of provincial style.

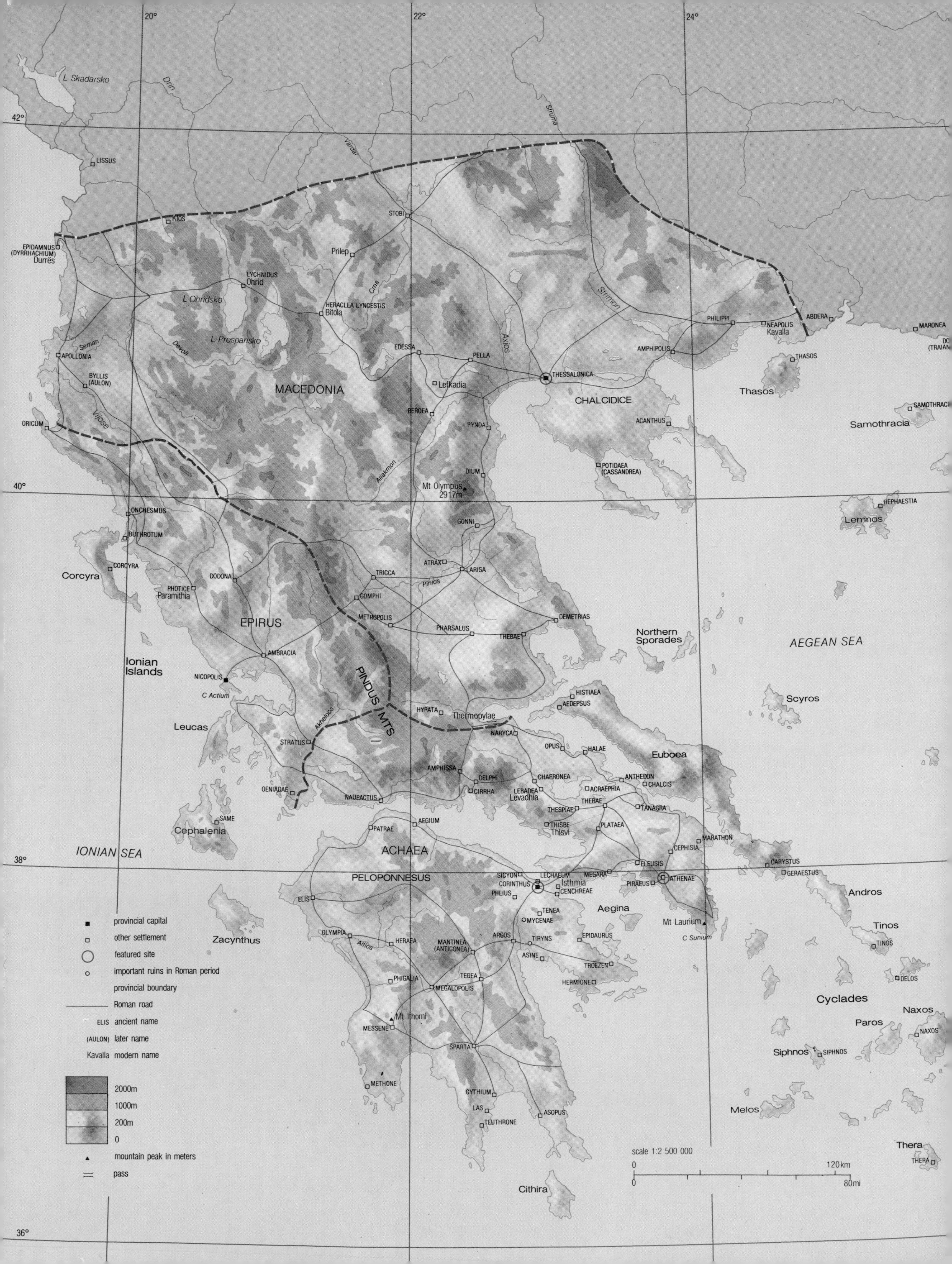

20°
22°
24°
42°
40°
38°
36°
L Skadarsko
Drin
Struma
Vardar
LISSUS
KIOS
STOBI
EPIDAMNUS (DYRRHACHIUM) Durrës
Prilep
LYCHNIDUS Ohrid
L Ohridsko
Crna
HERACLEA LYNCESTIS Bitola
Strimon
Seman
L Prespansko
Devoll
Axios
APOLLONIA
BYLLIS (AULON)
EDESSA
PELLA
PHILIPPI
NEAPOLIS Kavalla
ABDERA
MARONEA
AMPHIPOLIS
THASOS
Thasos
THESSALONICA
MACEDONIA
Lefkadia
CHALCIDICE
SAMOTHRACE
Samothracia
ORICUM
Vijose
BEROEA
PYNDA
ACANTHUS
Aliakmon
DIUM
POTIDAEA (CASSANDREA)
Mt Olympus 2917m
HEPHAESTIA
Lemnos
ONCHESMUS
GONNI
BUTHROTUM
Corcyra
CORCYRA
ATRAX
LARISA
DODONA
TRICCA
PHOTICE Paramithia
Pinios
GOMPHI
METROPOLIS
DEMETRIAS
EPIRUS
PHARSALUS
THEBAE
Northern Sporades
AEGEAN SEA
AMBRACIA
Ionian Islands
NICOPOLIS
C Actium
PINDUS MTS
HISTIAEA
AEDEPSUS
Scyros
HYPATA
Thermopylae
Akheloos
Leucas
NARYCA
STRATUS
OPUS
HALAE
Euboea
AMPHISSA
DELPHI
CHAERONEA
ANTHEDON
CHALCIS
OENIADAE
CIRRHA
LEBADEA Levadhia
ACRAEPHIA
NAUPACTUS
THESPIAE
THEBAE
TANAGRA
SAME
AEGIUM
THISBE Thisvi
PLATAEA
Cephalenia
PATRAE
MARATHON
ACHAEA
CEPHISIA
IONIAN SEA
CARYSTUS
ELEUSIS
GERAESTUS
PELOPONNESUS
SICYON
LECHAEUM
MEGARA
ATHENAE
CORINTHUS
Isthmia
PIRAEUS
Andros
PHLIUS
CENCHREAE
ELIS
Aegina
TENEA
MYCENAE
Mt Laurium
Tinos
C Sunium
OLYMPIA
HERAEA
ARGOS
TIRYNS
EPIDAURUS
Zacynthus
TINOS
Alfios
MANTINEA (ANTIGONEA)
ASINE
TROEZEN
TEGEA
DELOS
PHIGALIA
MEGALOPOLIS
HERMIONE
Cyclades
Naxos
Mt Ithomi
Paros
MESSENE
NAXOS
SPARTA
Siphnos
SIPHNOS
METHONE
GYTHIUM
LAS
ASOPUS
Melos
TEUTHRONE
Thera
THERA
Cithira
provincial capital
other settlement
featured site
important ruins in Roman period
provincial boundary
Roman road
ELIS ancient name
(AULON) later name
Kavalla modern name
2000m
1000m
200m
0
mountain peak in meters
pass
scale 1:2 500 000
0
120km
0
80mi

GREECE

The Roman conquest of Greece, starkly symbolized by Mummius' sack of Corinth in 146 BC and Sulla's capture of Athens 60 years later, was the culmination of a complex military, diplomatic and commercial involvement in the affairs of Greek cities and their leagues dating back to the 3rd century (see pp. 50–51). The resulting provinces, Achaea (initially including Epirus) and Macedonia, though both governed by proconsuls, differed in character. Achaea retained throughout the Roman period a special prestige based on the historic distinction of classical Greece. Macedonia, by contrast, was except for its western seaboard a remote and rural land, its society based on villages rather than cities; the latter, when they occurred in the interior, often developed in succession to native fortresses.

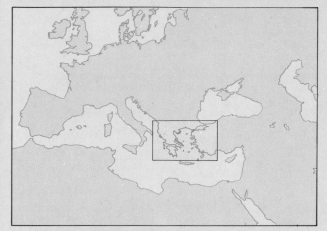

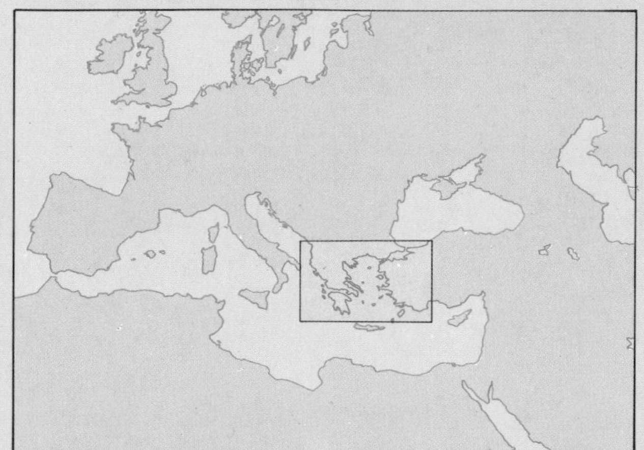

In some respects the Roman presence made possible the development of a greater material prosperity than before, or perhaps only of greater extremes of wealth. Certain families, like the Euryclid dynasty of Sparta and that of Herodes Atticus at Athens (see overleaf), acquired wealth on a scale far beyond anything achieved in classical times: in this respect Achaea follows the pattern yet more spectacularly achieved in the cities of Asia Minor. The writer Plutarch, from Chaeronea in Boeotia, is the counterpart of those literary figures from Asia Minor who flourished under the Empire: his works, especially the *Parallel Lives* in which a selected Greek is compared with a Roman, reflect the attitudes of a not unsympathetic Greek under Roman rule.

Some cities, like Corinth, Patrae and Thessalonica, acquired a progressively increasing prosperity, but others declined into insignificance, and in general the economic potential of Greece did not match that of Asia Minor, or of some newer provinces "opened up" by Roman exploitation.

In the 3rd century, and again in the late 4th, the peninsula suffered from barbarian invasion, that of Alaric in 395–97 being particularly destructive. By the mid-5th century Macedonia, passing firmly into the eastern sphere of influence and possessing in Thessalonica the new capital of Illyricum, had become a frontier against the barbarian north.

Above The symbols of the proconsul of Achaea, as shown by the *Notitia Dignitatum*. Achaea was one of only three provinces still governed in the late Empire by titular proconsuls (the others were Africa and Asia), a reflection of their prestige as senior senatorial provinces.

Above The old and the new in later Greco-Roman culture, seen in a fascinating 4th-century marble at Athens. Christ appears as Apollo with his lyre, in an unusually explicit piece of syncretism, but one in particular accord with the tradition of the cultural center of Greece.

Right The Roman road, the famous Via Egnatia, seen as it runs across Macedonia between Philippi and Neapolis. The road was strategically crucial in the civil wars of the late Republic (see p. 70), but under the Empire, with the consolidation of the frontier at the Danube, a more northerly route replaced it in military importance.

Athens

Tertullian's expression of the incompatibility of Christianity and classical culture, "What has Athens to do with Jerusalem?," epitomizes the moral and intellectual distinction of Athens which, surviving the destruction of the city's political power, remained the basis of its prestige in the Roman Empire. Many of the more important intellectual figures of all periods of the Empire studied, taught, or, as in the case of St Paul (Acts 17:16ff.), sought an audience there. The Eleusinian Mysteries retained their appeal; the emperors Hadrian and Julian the Apostate, and the late pagan senator Praetextatus (p. 193), were among the most famous of their many initiates.

Despite the benefactions of Hellenistic kings like Attalus of Pergamum, Roman Athens was very much a showpiece of imperial patronage, with its market of Caesar and Augustus, odeion of Agrippa and, provided by the philhellene Hadrian, gymnasium, Panhellenion or shrine of all the Greeks, magnificent library and, after a lapse of more than six centuries since it was started, temple of Olympian Zeus. A few years later Athens's own Herodes Atticus provided the odeion named for him, and a new stadium.

The philosophical tradition of Athens evolved in the late Empire into a mystic Neoplatonism influences by magical elements (see p. 177). Despite the damaging occupation of the city by Alaric, it remained in sufficiently good order to accommodate the 5th-century Neoplatonic school of Syrianus and Proclus, but this late efflorescence of its intellectual development, and the historic role of Athens as a shrine of classical learning, were ended in 529 by Justinian's closure of the schools.

Right Old and new in Roman Athens. Below the Acropolis, on which little new building was done among the masterpieces of Periclean Athens (a significant exception being a temple of Rome and Augustus), is seen the odeion of Herodes Atticus, given by the millionaire to his compatriots in about 160 AD.

Below left The "Tower of the Winds," or Horologion of Andronicus of Cyrrhus, built in the 1st century BC. It stood in an open space near the later market of Caesar and Augustus. It is decorated with reliefs of the eight winds, and was originally surmounted by a weathervane. Inside was a 24-hour clock driven by waterpower.

Below The cuirass of this torso of Hadrian, with the Acropolis in the background, stands for the Roman rather than the Greek in Hadrian's tastes. It shows figures of Victory, and the she-wolf with the twins, Romulus and Remus.

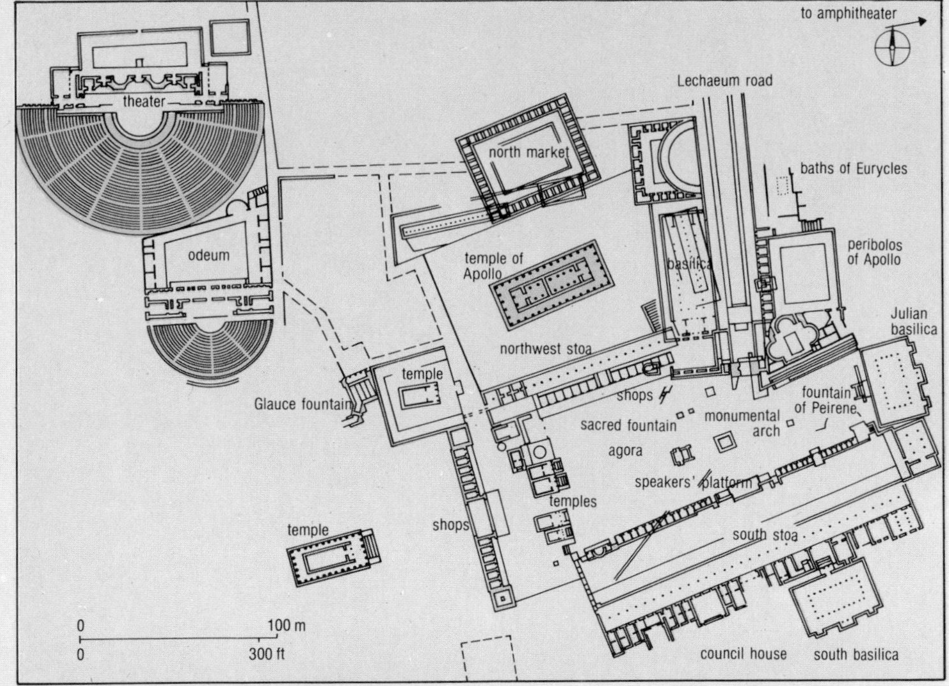

Corinth

Corinth (see plan, *left*) was refounded in 44 BC after its destruction by Mummius in 146, and became the capital of the province of Achaea, a distinction which reflects its earlier status as chief city of the Achaean League. It was here that St Paul appeared before the proconsul Gallio (Acts 18:12ff.). Its history under the Roman Empire is the rather generalized one of a great commercial city with wide connections. Nero visited it during his tour of Greece in 66 AD and initiated one of many unsuccessful attempts at different times to dig a canal through the Isthmus. Corinth was destroyed by an earthquake in 521 AD.

Thessalonica

Thessalonica, at the eastern end of the Via Egnatia, displaced Pella as both capital and main port of Macedonia. Though enjoying rapid civic development in the 2nd century and promoted as a Roman colony in the mid-3rd, its greatest magnificence came with the later shift of the resources of the Roman Empire towards the regions of the Bosphorus. As a Tetrarchic capital, Thessalonica acquired a palace complex including a hippodrome and the so-called octagon, possibly a throne room. This phase of its history illustrates the passion for building ascribed by Lactantius to Diocletian and more familiarly associated with Nicomedia in Asia Minor.

The city remained important as an occasional imperial residence. Riots, provoked by the imprisonment of a popular charioteer, resulted in the massacre in the hippodrome for which Theodosius was forced by Ambrose to do penance (p. 198). The third main phase of the physical enlargement of Thessalonica occurred in the mid-5th century, with its adoption in place of Sirmium as seat of the Illyrian prefecture. To this period belong the church of St Demetrius, a new palace for the use of the prefect, and the massive wall circuit.

Above The elegant arch of Hadrian, erected by the Athenians in his honor in about 130 AD, carries two inscriptions: on one side, facing the old city, "This is Athens, the ancient city of Theseus," and on the other, "This is the city of Hadrian and not of Theseus." It stands on a road by the precinct of the temple of Olympian Zeus. Hadrian clearly saw himself as the refounder of the city.

Right Monuments from the later phases of the growth of Roman Thessalonica. The triumphal arch of Galerius celebrates his victory over the Persians (see p. 171) with typical scenes of military and religious life. The Byzantine walls of Thessalonica (*far right*), long believed to be of 4th-century date, have now been associated with the promotion of the city as the seat of the prefecture of Illyricum after the abandonment of Sirmium.

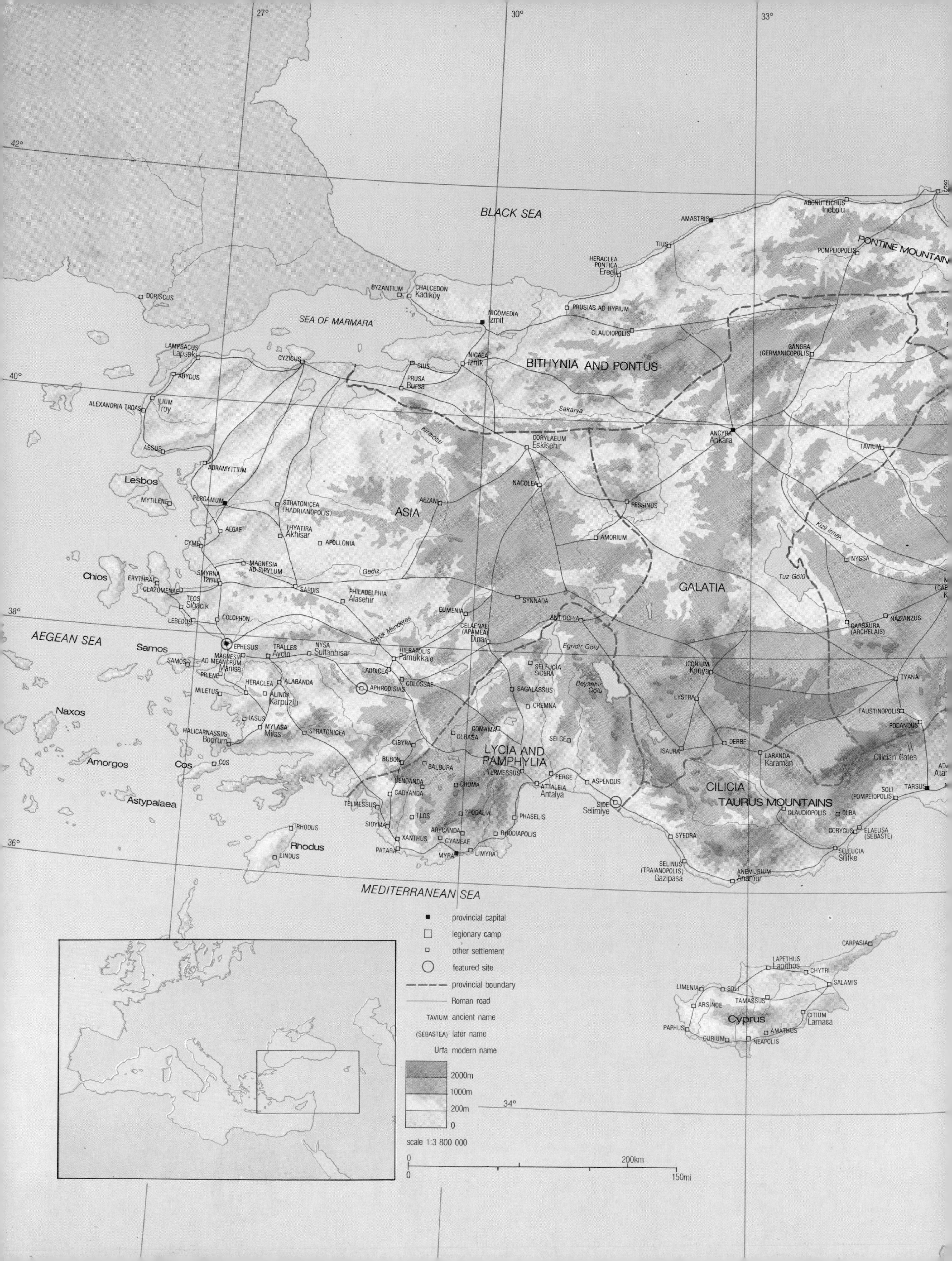
27°
30°
33°
42°
40°
38°
36°
34°
BLACK SEA
SEA OF MARMARA
AEGEAN SEA
MEDITERRANEAN SEA
BITHYNIA AND PONTUS
ASIA
GALATIA
LYCIA AND PAMPHYLIA
CILICIA
TAURUS MOUNTAINS
PONTINE MOUNTAIN
Cilician Gates
DORISCUS
BYZANTIUM
CHALCEDON
Kadiköy
NICOMEDIA
Izmit
PRUSIAS AD HYPIUM
CLAUDIOPOLIS
HERACLEA
PONTICA
Eregli
TIUS
AMASTRIS
ABONUTEICHUS
Inebolu
POMPEIOPOLIS
GANGRA
(GERMANICOPOLIS)
LAMPSACUS
Lapseki
ABYDUS
CYZICUS
CIUS
PRUSA
Bursa
NICAEA
Iznik
ALEXANDRIA TROAS
ILIUM
Troy
ASSUS
ADRAMYTTIUM
Lesbos
MYTILENE
PERGAMUM
STRATONICEA
(HADRIANOPOLIS)
AEGAE
THYATIRA
Akhisar
APOLLONIA
AEZANI
CYME
MAGNESIA
AD SIPYLUM
SMYRNA
Izmir
Chios
ERYTHRAE
CLAZOMENAE
TEOS
Sigacik
LEBEDUS
COLOPHON
SARDIS
PHILADELPHIA
Alasehir
Gediz
Sakarya
Kirmasti
DORYLAEUM
Eskisehir
NACOLEA
PESSINUS
AMORIUM
ANCYRA
Ankara
TAVIUM
Kizil Irmak
NYSSA
Tuz Gölü
NAZIANZUS
GARSAURA
(ARCHELAIS)
SYNNADA
EUMENIA
CELAENAE
(APAMEA)
Dinar
ANTIOCHIA
Egridir Gölü
Büyük Menderes
Samos
SAMOS
EPHESUS
MAGNESIA
AD MEANDRUM
Manisa
PRIENE
TRALLES
Aydin
NYSA
Sultanhisar
HIERAPOLIS
Pamukkale
LAODICEA
COLOSSAE
APHRODISIAS
MILETUS
HERACLEA
ALABANDA
ALINDA
Karpuzlu
Naxos
IASUS
MYLASA
Milas
STRATONICEA
HALICARNASSUS
Bodrum
Amorgos
Cos
COS
Astypalaea
SELEUCIA
SIDERA
Beysehir Gölü
SAGALASSUS
CREMNA
ICONIUM
Konya
LYSTRA
TYANA
FAUSTINOPOLIS
PODANDUS
COMAMA
OLBASA
CIBYRA
BUBON
BALBURA
SELGE
ISAURA
DERBE
LARANDA
Karaman
OENOANDA
CHOMA
TERMESSUS
PERGE
ASPENDUS
ATTALEIA
Antalya
CADYANDA
TELMESSUS
TLOS
?PODALIA
PHASELIS
SIDE
Selimiye
TARSUS
SOLI
(POMPEIOPOLIS)
CLAUDIOPOLIS
OLBA
CORYCUS
ELAEUSA
(SEBASTE)
SELEUCIA
Silifke
SIDYMA
ARYCANDA
CYANEAE
RHODIAPOLIS
XANTHUS
PATARA
MYRA
LIMYRA
RHODUS
Rhodus
LINDUS
SYEDRA
SELINUS
(TRAIANOPOLIS)
Gazipasa
ANEMURIUM
Anamur
CARPASIA
LAPETHUS
Lapithos
CHYTRI
LIMENIA
SOLI
SALAMIS
ARSINOE
TAMASSUS
Cyprus
CITIUM
Larnaca
PAPHUS
AMATHUS
CURIUM
NEAPOLIS
provincial capital
legionary camp
other settlement
featured site
provincial boundary
Roman road
TAVIUM ancient name
(SEBASTEA) later name
Urfa modern name
2000m
1000m
200m
0
scale 1:3 800 000
0
200km
0
150mi

ASIA MINOR

The expansion of Roman influence in Asia Minor, initiated by the acceptance of the legacy of Attalus of Pergamum (p. 57), proceeded steadily by annexation and the incorporation of client kingdoms, being defined in the east by the presence of Arsacid Parthia. With the wealth produced by agricultural exploitation, the cities of Roman Asia Minor expressed themselves with a vivid exuberance. Their leading citizens acquired immense and sometimes overbearing prestige. They served as effective spokesmen for their cities before the imperial authorities, and drew their communities into levels of expenditure which might, as in Bithynia, overstretch their means and invite Roman interference.

Further east, the picture changes. The Anatolian plateau was a land of villages and of a peasantry often sought as recruits for Roman armies. The mountains of Lycia and Pamphylia, Cilicia, and especially Isauria, harbored pastoralists who turned in hard times to brigandage, local raiding, and, in extreme cases, to revolt. Here were Roman colonies, outposts of Latin culture gradually absorbed by their Greek environment. To the east, Commagene and Lesser Armenia, attached to Cappadocia, were oriental principalities more closely aligned with the Syrian and Iranian east than with Greek Asia Minor.

Left The Isauria of the *Notitia Dignitatum* splendidly evokes the threat of the mountains to the security of the plains and coast of southern Asia Minor.

Below left The beautifully preserved theater of Aspendus in Pamphylia well illustrates the scale of expenditure and standards of construction achieved in 2nd-century Asia Minor.

Below Equally expressive of private opulence are the 4th-century mosaics in the "house of Eustolion" overlooking fields and the sea at Curium in Cyprus.

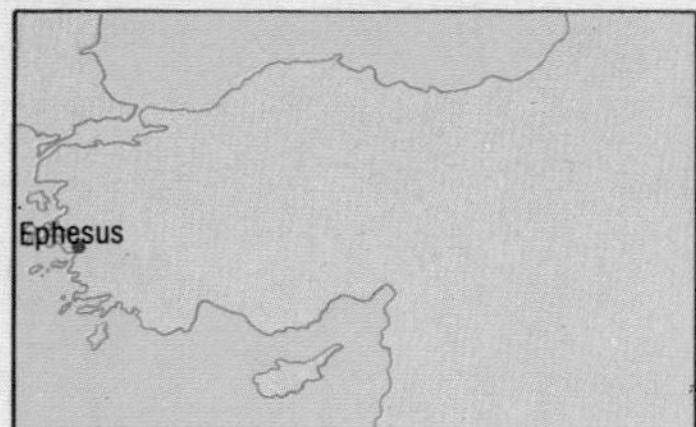

Ephesus

Ephesus, the first church of the Apocalypse, was also the home of the great temple of Artemis, one of the Seven Wonders of the World and a masterpiece of Hellenistic architecture in a predominantly Roman city, and of the legendary Seven Sleepers, who were supposed to have woken after centuries of slumber to find themselves living under a Christian government. The life of Roman Ephesus is revealed, not only by the extensive archaeological remains, but by inscriptions which show the munificence of the leading families and its rivalries with Smyrna for the title "first city" of Asia. The riot provoked by St Paul, in which the silversmiths roused the people in favor of their goddess, is an episode which reveals much of the life of this great eastern city (Acts 19:22ff.). The great theater (see *opposite*), in which the demonstration occurred, could seat 24 000 spectators. Among the many other facilities of the metropolis was the famous library of Celsus, dedicated in the early 2nd century in honor of Tiberius Julius Celsus Polemaeanus by his brother, also a Roman senator.

The city was attacked by Goths in the 3rd century, but recovered and passed undiminished into the Christian period. In the church of the Virgin Mary, built in the 4th century, met the council of Ephesus of 431 (see p. 000). The main street known as the Arkadiane, leading from the great theater to the harbor, dates from the early 5th century, and the church of St John, over the supposed tomb of the evangelist, was lavishly rebuilt by Justinian.

Ephesus suffered at various times from earthquakes, and in the end yielded to the double process of slow subsidence combined with accumulation of alluvial deposits. By these processes, the sea has retreated from the site, leaving the harbor silted up and many other remains, including the platform of the Artemision, in a waterlogged condition.

Below The road leading down to the Magnesian gate, on the line of the Hellenistic city wall (see plan). The procession of the festival of Artemis led by this gate from the Artemision to the great theater.

Bottom left The splendors of the more opulent residences of Ephesus are well illustrated by these mural paintings in a villa in the central area near the Agora.

Bottom right The entrance to the temple of Hadrian, built in the early 2nd century and restored, with additions, in the late 4th. The four bases before the temple carried statues of the Tetrarchs.

Left The view from the great theater along the Arkadiane to the harbor, which appears as a green swamp in the distance.

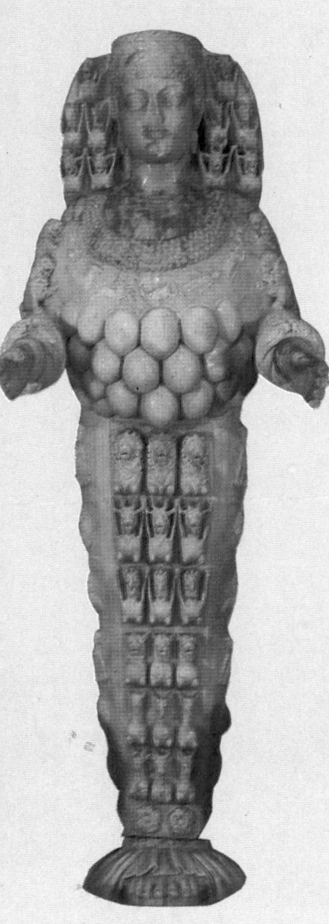

Above "Artemis of the Ephesians," seen in a Roman copy of the cult statue of the goddess, combines a classicizing archaism with a glimpse of a deeper past. The many breasts of this divine figure have little to do with the "Queen and Huntress, chaste and fair" of more orthodox classical conception.

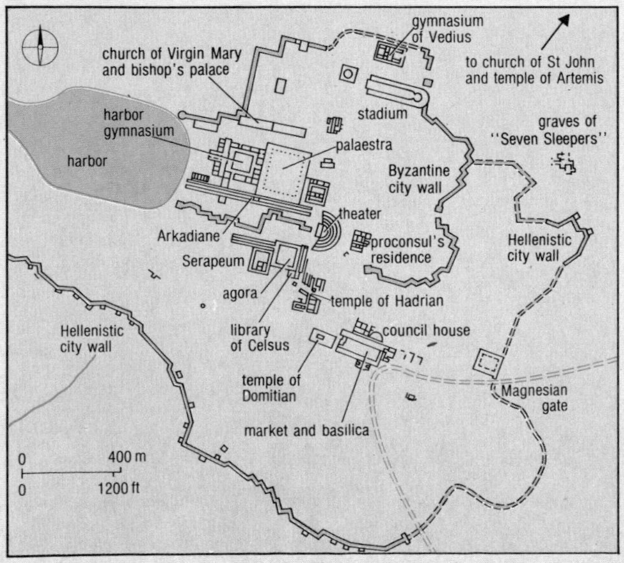

Left A detail of a more secular side of Ephesian life, the self-explanatory sign on the sidewalk advertising a brothel.

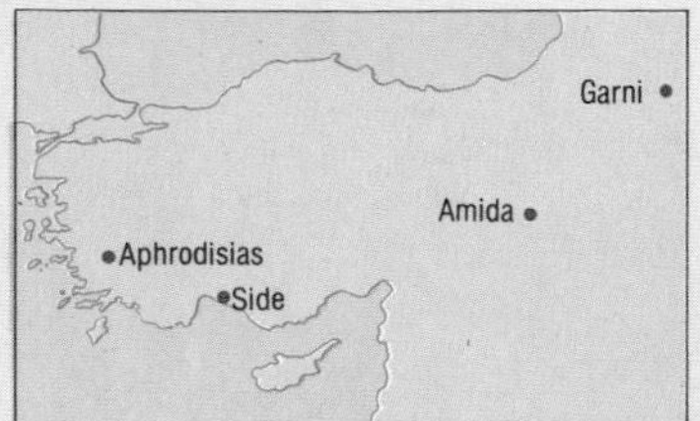

Aphrodisias

The Carian metropolis of Aphrodisias (the name of the modern hamlet at the site, Geyre, preserves the name of ancient Caria) was particularly favored not only by Roman emperors such as Augustus and Hadrian but by Sulla and Julius Caesar in the 1st century BC. Both these republican magnates, regarding themselves as protected by the goddess Venus, were drawn to favor a city whose name represents the "hellenization" of an ancient local deity. In this respect Aphrodisias may be compared with sites further east such as Heliopolis (p.161). The temple of Aphrodite, built in the 1st century BC, was embellished by a new precinct, provided by Hadrian; in the 6th century it was transformed into a church. The wall of the theater, also built in the 1st century BC, has produced later copies of many *senatus consulta* and imperial letters confirming the city's special privileges, and on a more mundane level parts of Diocletian's Edict on Maximum Prices (p.172).

The defensive wall enclosing the fine stadium but excluding other parts of the city was built in the 260s against Gothic invasion, but the city continued to flourish in the late Empire and only declined in the Byzantine period. The plan of Aphrodisias (*below*), consisting largely of open spaces, reflects the current state of excavation of this constantly productive site. In so far as a road system has been identified, the plan was apparently that of a normal late Hellenistic or early imperial city.

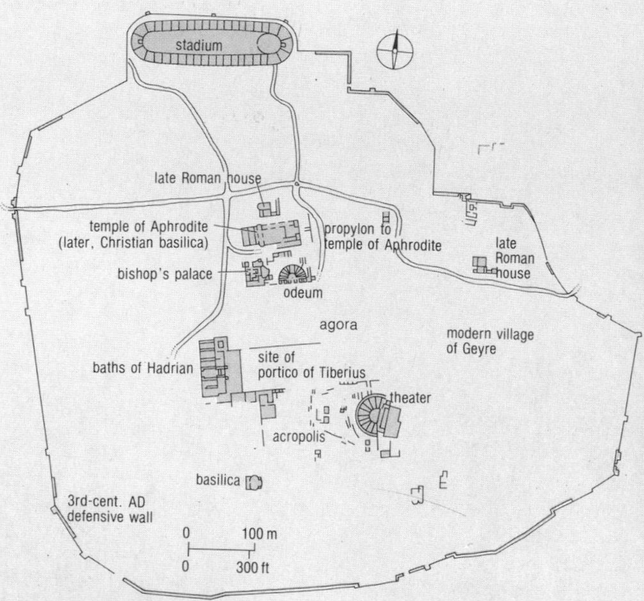

The theater of Aphrodisias (*below*) is built into the early acropolis, later a Byzantine fortress. It was adapted in the 2nd century AD to accommodate wild-beast and gladiatorial shows.

Aphrodisias was an important marble supplier and artistic center in the Roman Empire: its stylistic influence has been traced at Leptis Magna (p.120). Shown here is (*opposite top left*) the head of an imperial youth, possibly Britannicus, from the newly discovered temple of the Augusti.

Side

Side in Pamphylia stands on a narrow peninsula and possesses a mainly artificial harbor used, until their suppression by Pompey, by Cilician pirates. Unfortunately it was liable to silting and required constant dredging to keep it clear; an ancient saying, "a harbor of Side," signified a job continually in need of repeating. It also possessed a rather narrow entrance, and it is unlikely that the main part of the prosperity of the city came from maritime trade. Like its neighbors Aspendus (see p. 151) and Perge, Side was essentially a city of the Roman Empire; its theater, like that of Aphrodisias, was converted by the addition of a wall in the orchestra for wild-beast hunts and similar dangerous displays. In the late Empire a defensive wall was built across the narrowest part of the peninsula, passing just behind the agora, but the city continued to flourish beyond these limits and only declined with the Arab invasions.

Right A general view of the ruins of Side and the sea, suggesting mainly in its confusion the immense amount of work still to be done in Roman Asia Minor.

Amida

The previously unimportant city of Amida on the Tigris (*below*) was developed in the later years of Constantine as a nodal point in the defense of northern Mesopotamia and the Roman-controlled satrapies as far as Corduene (Kurdistan). It was besieged and captured in the Persian invasion of 359, but remained in Roman hands and after Jovian's surrender of Nisibis in 363 received some of its population. The wall circuit, much repaired in later times, is in essence that given it by Justinian. It is of dark basalt, hence a saying: "black the walls, and black the hearts of the men of Amida"!

Garni

Castellum Gorneae, Garni in Soviet Armenia, is the site of the classical building illustrated below (*left*), perhaps the 2nd-century tomb of a romanized client king. The place is mentioned by Tacitus as a fortification occupied by the Romans during the eastern campaign of Nero. It is the most easterly point reached by the Romans, unless we count the Flavian centurion from Melitene who, in unknown but intriguing circumstances, carved his name on a rock face near Baku.

THE EAST

Roman control of the east was built on the ruins of the Seleucid kingdom, incorporated by Pompey as the province of Syria, extended by the progressive absorption of "client kingdoms" friendly to Rome, such as Commagene and Judaea, and completed by the annexations of Arabia and Mesopotamia.

These provinces, taken together, comprised the western arc of the "Fertile Crescent," a region of ancient civilization running up the east Mediterranean seaboard, across Syria and northern Mesopotamia, and descending into Babylonia. Along this band of territory fell enough rain to permit systematic crop cultivation and the growth of cities. The open desert to the east and south of the Roman provinces, inhabited by transhumant and nomadic Bedouin, was otherwise penetrated only by caravans from trading cities, often, like Palmyra (see overleaf) and Hatra, based on oases.

Roman occupation made little real difference to the cultural life of the area. Greek remained the language of its upper classes, Syriac of the ordinary people in the towns and more particularly the countryside. Latin made little headway, though it was used at Berytus (Beirut), the home of Roman law in the east, and in the late Empire in the administrative capital of Antioch. Easterners, on the other hand, like Paul of Tarsus, Lucian of Samosata and the jurist Ulpian, found their way all over the Empire; while, writing of a less elevated level of society, the conservative Italian, Juvenal, complained that "the Orontes has flowed into the Tiber" (*Satires* 3.62)! Along the same route came some of the most innovative and important philosophical and religious ideas of the later Greco-Roman world.

The insignia given by the *Notitia Dignitatum* for the Dux Arabiae. Garrison towns are indicated in the usual manner; note the snakes and a pair of ostriches.

The frieze of a 5th-century mosaic from a villa at Daphne near Antioch (*bottom*) shows an itinerary from Antioch to this fashionable resort. Here are seen "the workshops of the martyr's shrine" (of St Babylos at Daphne), before which a reclining man, Markellos, is being served by an attendant named Chalkomas. Then comes "the Olympic stadium," "the private [baths] of Ardabourios," and "Kastalia" and "Pallas," the famous springs of Daphne. Below Kastalia is a semicircular basin with portico, possibly the nymphaeum built by Hadrian. The attractive "Still Life with Boiled Eggs" (*below*) is a detail from another mosaic from Daphne.

The upper-class family group (*right*), from a cave tomb at Edessa in Osrhoene, well expresses the cultural diversity of the Roman world. Its members, whose names are written in Syriac, wear the colorful robes, slippers, trousers and headgear evocative of an Iranian rather than Roman provincial background.

The view from the upper citadel (*opposite*) shows the commanding position of Edessa. Until the 3rd century it was ruled by an ancestral royal dynasty: a statue of Queen Shalmath, possibly wife of Abgar IX, "the Great" (179–216), surmounted one of the two free-standing columns on the citadel.

34°
36°
38°
40°
42°
38°
36°
34°
32°
30°
Tigris
Euphrates
SAMOSATA
Samsat
TUR ABDIN
BEZABDE
ANTINONOPOLIS
(CONSTANTINA)
EDESSA
Urfa
APAMEA
Birecik
ZEUGMA
BATNAE
CARRHAE
Harran
RESAINA
(THEODOSIOPOLIS)
NISIBIS
Nusaybin
CYRRHUS
EUROPUS
MESOPOTAMIA
SINGARA
ALEXANDRIA
AD ISSUM
ANTIOCHIA
Antakya
HIERAPOLIS
Membij
SELEUCIA PIERIA
BEROEA
Aleppo
BARBALISSUS
Mesken
NICEPHORIUM
(CALLINICUM)
Raqqa
Euphrates
CHALCIS
SOURA
Souriya
SYRIA
RESAPHA
(SERGIOPOLIS)
Risafe
ZENOBIA
Orontes
LAODICEA
APAMEA
Khabir
MEDITERRANEAN SEA
SERIANE
CIRCESIUM
Buseire
EPIPHANIA
Hama
ARETHUSA
ANTARADUS
RAPHANAEA
DURA-EUROPUS
EMESA
Homs
PALMYRA
TRIPOLIS
SYRIAN DESERT
DANABA
BYBLUS
BERYTUS
Beirut
HELIOPOLIS
Baalbek
SIDON
Saida
DAMASCUS
TYRUS
Tyr
CAESAREA PANEAS
PHAENAE
TRACHONITIS
PTOLEMAIS
Akko
L Tiberias
(Sea of Galilee)
DIOCAESAREA
TIBERIAS
HIPPOS
NAZARETH
CANATHA
El Qanawat
LEJJUN
GADARA
Um Qeis
ADRAA
Dera
CAESAREA MARITIMA
SCYTHOPOLIS
PELLA
BOSTRA
Busra
SAMARIA
Jordan
GERASA
Jarash
NEAPOLIS
APOLLONIA
JOPPA
Tel Aviv-Yafo
JUDAEA
DIOSPOLIS
JAMNIA
NICOPOLIS
JERICHO
PHILADELPHIA
Amman
AELIA
CAPITOLINA
Jerusalem
BETHLEHEM
HERODION
ESBUS
ASCALON
MADABA
Dead
Sea
GAZA
ELEUTHEROPOLIS
HEBRON
ENGEDI
RAPHIA
Rafah
CHERMELA
MASADA
RABBATHMOBA
Rabba
BEROSABA
Beersheba
CHARACMOBA
Karak
MAMPSIS
ELUSA
ARABIA
NESSANA
OBODA
PHAINON
NEGEV DESERT
PETRA
AILA
Elat
provincial capital
legionary camp
other settlement
featured site
provincial boundary
Roman road
EMESA ancient name
(CALLINICUM) later name
Homs modern name
2000m
1000m
200m
0
below sea level
seasonal river
scale 1:3 500 000
0
120km
0
100mi

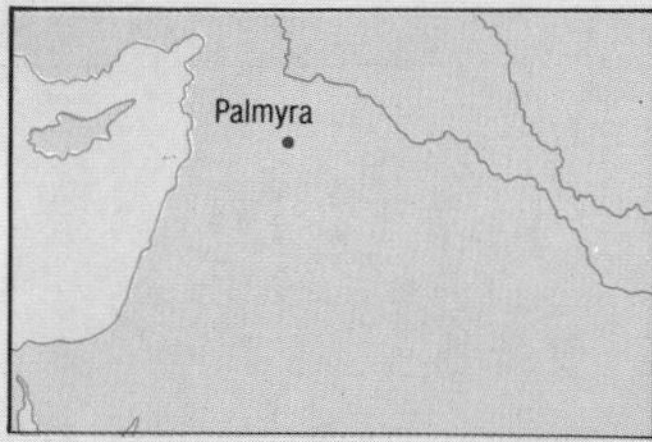

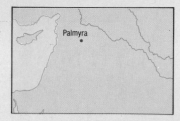

Palmyra

Palmyra or Tadmor, the "city of palms," produced under the Roman Empire a spectacular explosion of urban prosperity. Roman interest in Palmyra had begun as early as Mark Antony, who attacked it but failed to capture its legendary wealth, which was carried beyond the Euphrates by its mobile owners. In the earliest years of the Empire it could be regarded as an independent state between the empires of Rome and Parthia, but Germanicus visited it as Tiberius' envoy during his tour of the east in 18 AD and Palmyra was incorporated in the province of Syria. Its trading links with the east always gave it a degree of independence unusual for a Roman city. Its chief families organized the luxury caravan trade over the desert to the Euphrates and Mesene (Maisan) in the Persian Gulf, connecting there with the sea route to India. An inscription, written in both Palmyrene and Greek, tells how one merchant "on many occasions nobly and generously assisted the merchants, caravans and fellow citizens established at Vologesias," and had "defended from great danger the caravan recently arrived from Vologesias." The "danger" probably came from Bedouin tribesmen along the route.

In the 260s and 270s the Palmyrene dynasts Odaenathus, Vaballath and Zenobia established their city as the capital of an independent empire which performed important military services against the Sasanians. Palmyra was however destroyed by Aurelian and never regained prosperity.

The view from the northwest (*right*) well evokes the geographical setting and monumental splendor of the city. The great temple of Bel stands in the distance, built in 19AD on the tell, or ruin mound, which shows the antiquity of the settlement, with the colonnaded avenue leading from it through the city. On the near side of the temple is a group of buildings including the theater and, surrounded by columns, the agora (or caravanserai). Beyond the temple are the trees of the oasis, and the desert across which the caravans made their way to the Euphrates and the Persian Gulf.

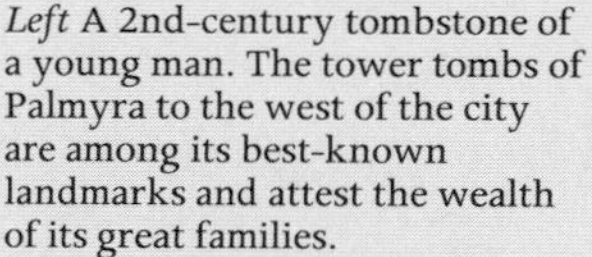

Left A 2nd-century tombstone of a young man. The tower tombs of Palmyra to the west of the city are among its best-known landmarks and attest the wealth of its great families.

Below Architectural fragment from Palmyra. The vine leaves and tendrils reflect oriental influence in their studied decorative symmetry.

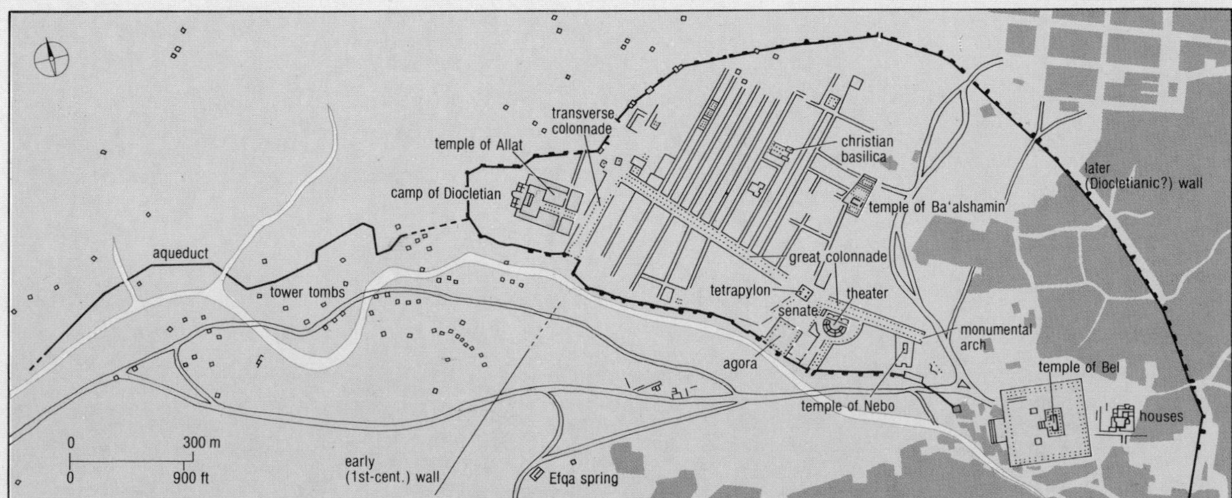

The most striking feature of the plan of Palmyra is its irregularity. The temple of Bel, the houses behind it, and the theater are out of alignment, and the arrangement of the theater and adjoining agora is asymmetrical. The great colonnade assumes three different directions and the transverse colonnade is not perpendicular to it. The explanation of the irregularity lies in the pattern of pre-Roman occupation of the site, itself dependent on the position of the oasis and location of the water sources. It has been suggested that the inhabitants had retained something of their Bedouin lifestyle, encamped in different areas of the site, which developed as different quarters of the Roman city.

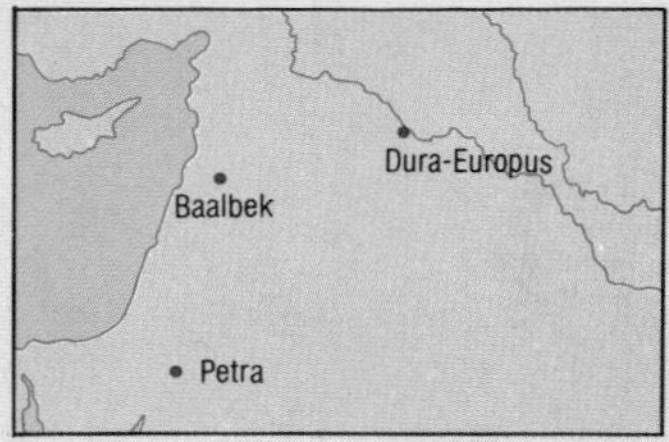

Dura-Europus

Dura on the Euphrates, named Europus by its Hellenistic settlers, was a city with, on one level, a clearly articulated history. Built as a fortress by the Seleucids in 300 BC, it fell in the 2nd century BC under Parthian, and from 165 AD, under Roman domination. In 256 it was destroyed by the Persians under Shapur I, and never resettled.

The sudden abandonment of Dura brings to an end the Roman phase of its existence, and the city has produced much evidence of Roman military organization. More significant, however, is the persistence of its indigenous Semitic character through all periods of foreign control. The rectangular agora was rapidly filled by the informal structures of a Levantine bazaar. The inscriptions are mostly in Greek, but Aramaic and Arabic dialects and Pahlavi are also represented. The same mixture occurs in the religious life of Dura. Apart from the Roman state cults, there was a synagogue, Mithraeum, and Christian house church.

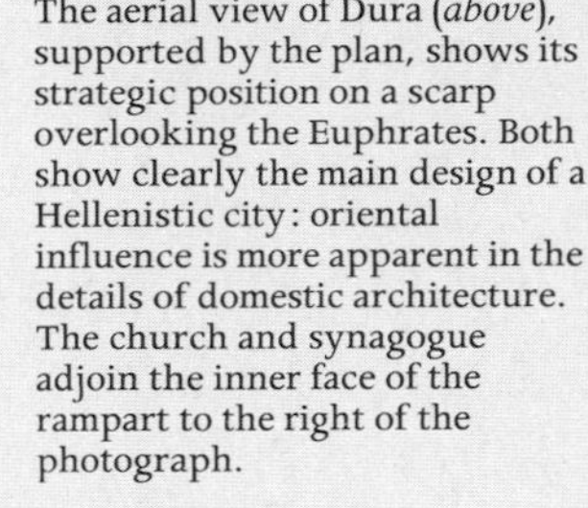

The aerial view of Dura (*above*), supported by the plan, shows its strategic position on a scarp overlooking the Euphrates. Both show clearly the main design of a Hellenistic city: oriental influence is more apparent in the details of domestic architecture. The church and synagogue adjoin the inner face of the rampart to the right of the photograph.

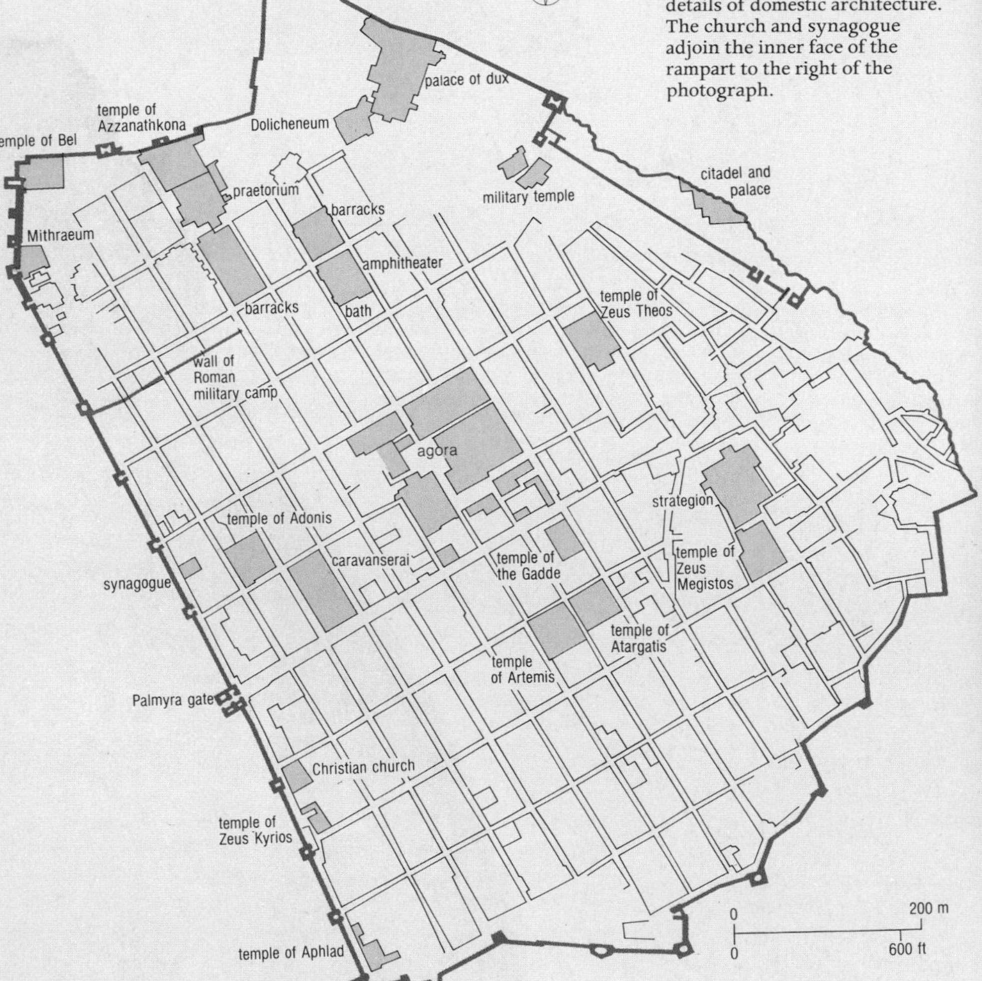

The wall paintings from the synagogue at Dura shown here portray (*top*) the discovery of the baby Moses in his reed boat on the river Nile and (*above*) the Ark of the Covenant under Philistine attack; the Philistine soldiers wear contemporary Sasanian military dress. The Jewish community had links with the Aramaic-speaking Jews of lower Mesopotamia, the presence of wall paintings in the synagogue suggesting in any case a less than strictly rigorous attitude to the teaching of the Law.

Right The view southeast from the platform of the temple of Jupiter-Baʿal. In the foreground is another temple, known as the temple of Bacchus, but most probably of Venus-Atargatis, one of the triad of Semitic deities worshiped at Heliopolis. The plan of the sacred precinct (*below*) illustrates the combination of open enclosures and *cellae* which, better than any individual architectural features, shows the "oriental" nature of the site. The Christian basilica was constructed in the late 4th century: Heliopolis was one of those cities where paganism maintained a long-lasting tenacity (see p. 194).

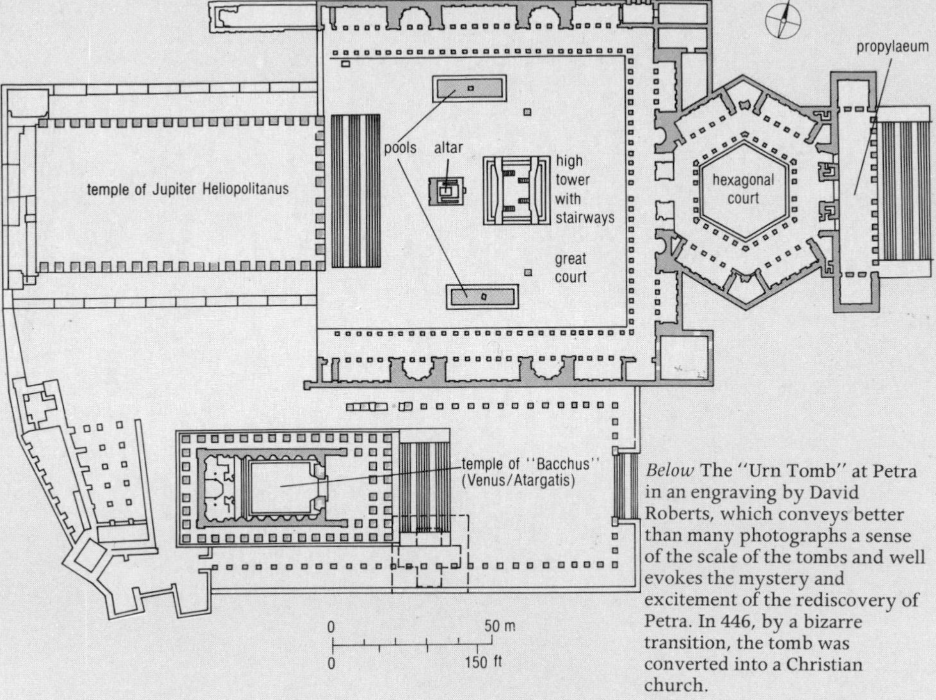

Below The "Urn Tomb" at Petra in an engraving by David Roberts, which conveys better than many photographs a sense of the scale of the tombs and well evokes the mystery and excitement of the rediscovery of Petra. In 446, by a bizarre transition, the tomb was converted into a Christian church.

Baalbek

Like Dura-Europus and Petra, Heliopolis (the ancient Baalbek) rose to prominence in the later Hellenistic and Roman periods, its main phase of civic development coming, as so often, in the 2nd and early 3rd centuries. Standing in the valley between the mountain massifs of Lebanon and anti-Lebanon, Heliopolis possessed the usual facilities of a large Greco-Roman council hall, theater and hippodrome, together with houses which have produced, especially from the late Roman period, fine mosaics, both classical and "orientalizing" in style.

The real claim of Heliopolis, however, is in its marvelous temple precinct, and especially in the temple of Jupiter-Baʿal, built like its counterpart at Palmyra (p. 158) during the 1st century AD on a tell, or ruin mound, which shows the antiquity of the site. Jupiter-Baʿal was one of a triad of divinities worshiped at the site: the others were Venus-Aphrodite, the classical equivalent of the Semitic Atargatis, and Mercury-Hermes, whose Semitic equivalent is not known.

Petra

Petra, the capital of the Nabataean kingdom visited by Germanicus Caesar in 18 AD, owed its development to the local kings of the later Hellenistic era whose achievement in urban settlement in Jordan and the Negev is currently becoming better appreciated. The great prosperity of Petra had derived from its role as a caravan city on the route from India to Rhinocorura (El Arish) and Gaza on the Mediterranean, but it seems that already by the 1st century AD such trade was taking the more northerly route by Palmyra or going by the Red Sea to Alexandria, and that the prosperity of Petra had reached its limit. The Roman remains are nevertheless impressive, with a theater and a colonnaded street leading by way of a triple-arched gateway to a sacred precinct. But Petra is most famous for its rock tombs, their facades evoking in massive relief the style of Hellenistic palaces.

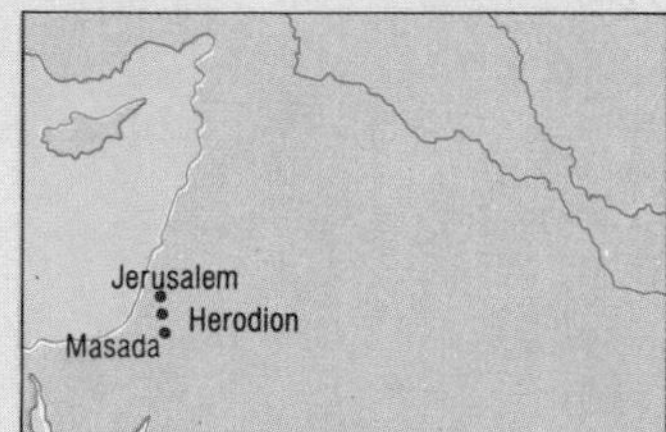

Jerusalem

Jerusalem, the ancient capital of King David, was described by the elder Pliny in the first century of the Roman Empire as "by far the most famous city, not only of Judaea, but of the east" (*Natural History* 5.70). This it owed largely to Herod the Great, who gave Jerusalem a quite spectacular magnificence, with extensions to its fortified area, a theater and amphitheater (presumably outside the walls), palaces and monumental buildings including the Temple, dominating the city from its massive platform. As these works suggest, Herod achieved a balance between Jewish and Greco-Roman culture hardly attempted by his Hasmonean predecessors. The independence of Judaea did not long survive Herod's death in 4 BC, before it was made into a Roman province with its capital at Caesarea, another of the cities rebuilt by Herod.

Jerusalem and its Temple were taken and destroyed by Titus during the Jewish revolt of 66–70 AD (see pp. 80–81), and the city occupied by the Tenth Legion. Under Hadrian it was refounded as a Roman colony with the name Aelia Capitolina. With the christianization of the Roman Empire it entered a new period of fame and prosperity through its association with the last teachings, death and resurrection of Christ. By the late 4th century Jerusalem was the object of frequent pilgrimage and site of monastic settlements, a phase of its history which continued into the Byzantine period. Notable benefactions were made by the exiled empress Eudocia (p. 217), and under Justinian. Jerusalem fell to the Arabs in 638 and was equally famous as a holy city of Islam.

Bottom Jerusalem, as it appears on a 6th-century mosaic map from Madaba in Jordan. Conspicuous among the monuments are the colonnaded main street of the Hadrianic city and the Church of the Holy Sepulcher midway along it, clearly recognizable by its rotunda (seen upside down as the picture is printed). The Wailing Wall (*below*) is actually the platform of the Temple, as extended by Herod the Great.

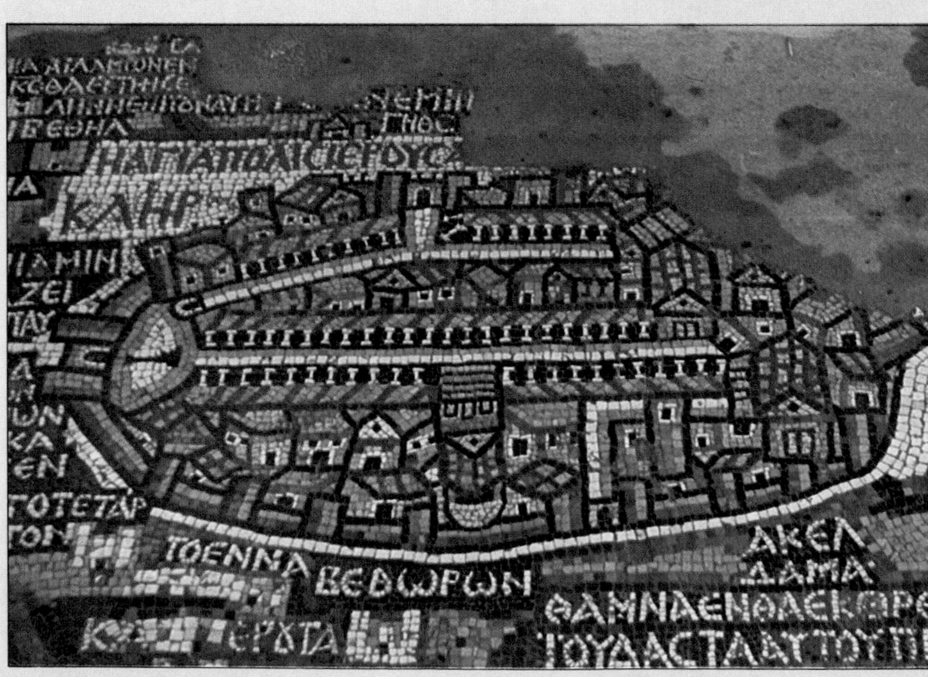

Herodion

The citadel of Herodion, built by Herod the Great 12 kilometers from Jerusalem and clearly visible from there, was the focal point of a large settlement "not inferior to a city," according to the historian Josephus. It was equipped with "diversions" or pleasure grounds, and water had to be taken there from some distance by aqueduct. The citadel itself contained an elaborate palace, with baths, synagogue and gardens, and was a clever feat of architectural deception. It was built upon and masked by an artificial mound added to the natural hilltop. The palace would reveal itself to a visitor only as he mounted the 200 steps of polished stone and entered through the deep-cut entrance by the main tower. It was among the residences in which Herod entertained M. Agrippa in 14 BC.

After his death, Herod was buried at Herodion – as some scholars believe, in the still unexcavated north tower. The site was one of the last strongholds in the Jewish revolt of 66–70 AD and was also occupied in the rebellion of Bar-Kochba.

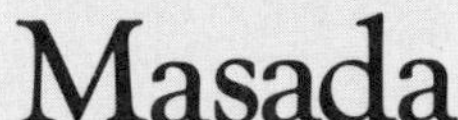

Masada

Masada, a spur of the barren mountains to the west of the Dead Sea, was used as a fortress by the Hasmoneans, but massively developed by Herod as a palace-cum-stronghold, to secure himself from challenges from both inside and outside his kingdom. The ruins contain extensive storehouses as well as heated baths, synagogue and two main palaces, the western with descending terraces perched dizzily on the edge of the precipice.

After Herod's death the palace was disused, but was taken by Zealots from the Roman garrison which occupied it at the beginning of the revolt of 66–70. The reduction of Masada was completed by Vespasian's legate Flavius Silva, only after a lengthy siege which ended (in 73) with the suicide of the defenders. A pottery fragment inscribed with the name of their leader, Ben Ya'ir, may possibly be one of the pieces by which the defenders drew lots to determine which ten of them would kill the others (390 in all, men, women and children), the last survivor of these ten taking his own life.

The aerial photograph of Herodion (*left*) clearly shows the four towers, and the artificial mound raised to their level. The north tower, in which Herod may lie buried, is to the right of the picture, with the approach and entrance to the palace visible beside it (the sloping ramp is modern).

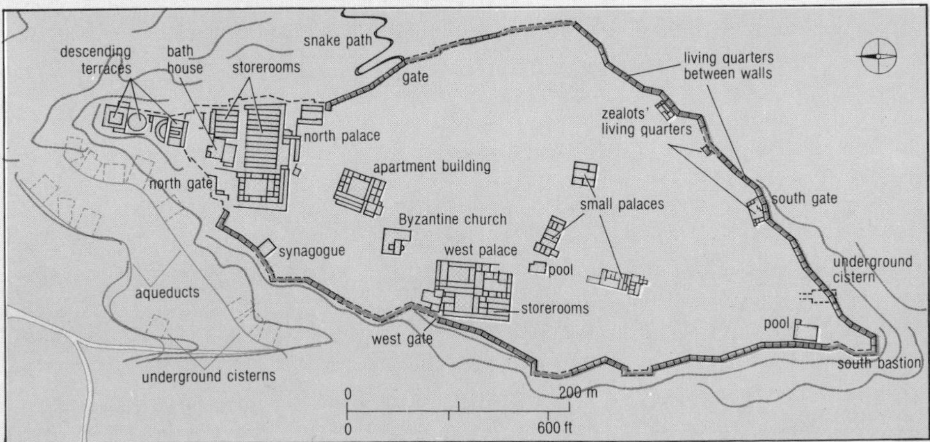

The aerial view of Masada (*far left*) shows some of the Roman siege fortresses, part of the wall of circumvallation and the huge ramp up which were moved the siege engines that finally ended the Zealot resistance. Josephus explains that the flat top of Masada was fertile and left clear for cultivation, so that the place should enjoy some self-sufficiency: the general truth of this is also clear from the plan (*left*). The summit is approached from the Dead Sea by the "Snake Path," the hair-raising nature of which is described by Josephus in vivid but possibly exaggerated terms (*Jewish War* 7.283). The western approach was easier, but blocked by Herod with a defensive tower.

EGYPT AND CYRENAICA

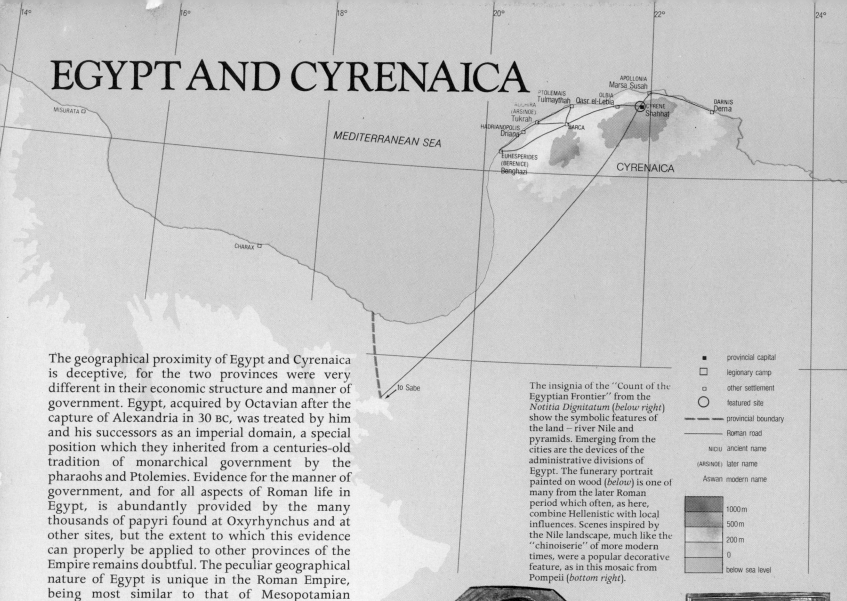

14° 16° 18° 20° 22° 24°

MISURATA
MEDITERRANEAN SEA
APOLLONIA
Marsa Susah
PTOLEMAIS
Tulmaythah
OLBIA
Qasr el-Lebia
AUCHIRA
(ARSINOE)
Tukrah
CYRENE
Shahhat
DARNIS
Derna
HADRIANOPOLIS
Driana
BARCA
EUHESPERIDES
(BERENICE)
Benghazi
CYRENAICA
CHARAX
to Sabe

The geographical proximity of Egypt and Cyrenaica is deceptive, for the two provinces were very different in their economic structure and manner of government. Egypt, acquired by Octavian after the capture of Alexandria in 30 BC, was treated by him and his successors as an imperial domain, a special position which they inherited from a centuries-old tradition of monarchical government by the pharaohs and Ptolemies. Evidence for the manner of government, and for all aspects of Roman life in Egypt, is abundantly provided by the many thousands of papyri found at Oxyrhynchus and at other sites, but the extent to which this evidence can properly be applied to other provinces of the Empire remains doubtful. The peculiar geographical nature of Egypt is unique in the Roman Empire, being most similar to that of Mesopotamian Babylonia. Linked by the Nile, its cities were more easily subjected to central control than those elsewhere; conversely, only under central control can the country achieve its full agricultural potential. The annual flooding of the Nile provided the essential rhythm of Egyptian life; it was officially measured at Elephantine by a gauge known as the Nilometer.

In Alexandria, Egypt had a great Hellenistic city. Elsewhere in the delta and in the Nile valley community life was founded on settlements, often described in the sources as "cities" but in reality resembling large villages. Greek culture penetrated Egypt through Alexandria to the cities of the Nile, but there is an essential distinction between the hellenized city populations of Egypt and the country folk, who retained their Egyptian language and in the late Empire produced the vernacular Coptic church.

Cyrenaica, the group of five cities known as the Pentapolis, was under the Empire governed together with Crete by a senatorial proconsul. The economic life of the Pentapolis was made possible by the well-watered coastal ridge known as the Gebel el Akdar. Though Cyrenaica seems in local terms rather remote, this was less true in the broader context of the eastern Mediterranean. Its cities flourished under the Roman Empire as they had under the Ptolemies, and the port of Apollonia in particular grew in importance as a link in the communications between the cities of proconsular Africa, Tripolitania and Alexandria.

The insignia of the "Count of the Egyptian Frontier" from the *Notitia Dignitatum* (*below right*) show the symbolic features of the land – river Nile and pyramids. Emerging from the cities are the devices of the administrative divisions of Egypt. The funerary portrait painted on wood (*below*) is one of many from the later Roman period which often, as here, combine Hellenistic with local influences. Scenes inspired by the Nile landscape, much like the "chinoiserie" of more modern times, were a popular decorative feature, as in this mosaic from Pompeii (*bottom right*).

provincial capital
legionary camp
other settlement
featured site
provincial boundary
Roman road
NICIU ancient name
(ARSINOE) later name
Aswan modern name
1000 m
500 m
200 m
0
below sea level

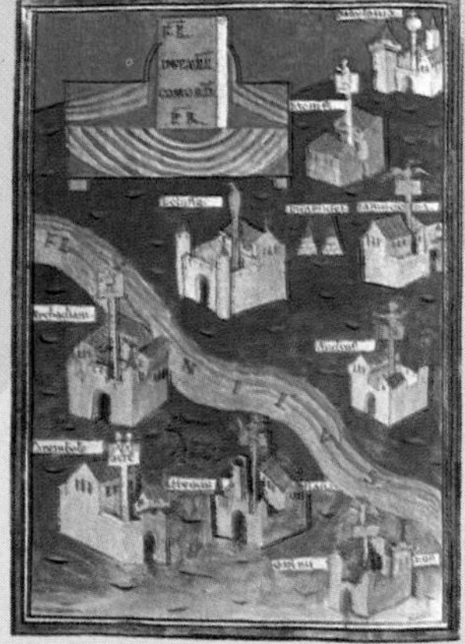

MEDITERRANEAN SEA
CISAMUM
Kastelli
CYDONIA
Khania
POLYRRHENIA
TARRHA
PHOENIX
SYBRITA
CNOSSUS
CHERSONESUS
CRETA
LYTTUS
GORTYN
ITANUS
MOCHLUS
HIERAPYTNA
Ierapetra
scale 1: 3 500 000
80km
40mi
RAPHIA
CASIUM
RHINOCOLURA
El-Arish
CANOPUS
NICOPOLIS
ALEXANDRIA
BUTO
SEBENNYTUS
SAIS
TANIS
BUSIRIS
THMUIS
PELUSIUM
PARAETONIUM
NAUCRATIS
TAPOSIRIS MAGNA
COMARUM
NICIU
ATHRIBIS
TERENUTHIS
HELIOPOLIS
BABYLON
CLYSMA
AILA
Elat
MEMPHIS
SINAI DESERT
QATTARA DEPRESSION
FAIYUM
CARANIS
DIONYSIAS
THEADELPHIA
ARSINOE
TEBTUNIS
HERACLEOPOLIS
AEGYPTUS
GULF OF SUEZ
Nile
ARABIAN DESERT
OXYRHYNCHUS
scale 1:4 000 000
200km
150mi
HERMOPOLIS
El Ashmunein
ANTINOOPOLIS
RED SEA
LYCOPOLIS
ANTAEOPOLIS
PANOPOLIS
PTOLEMAIS HERMIOU
El Manshah
TENTYRA
Dandara
COPTOS
HERMONTHIS
THEBAE
Luxor
LATOPOLIS
Isna
EILITHYOPOLIS
APOLLINOPOLIS MAGNA
THE GREAT OASIS
OMBOS
Kom Ombo
ELEPHANTINE
SYENE
PHILAE
Aswan
Nile

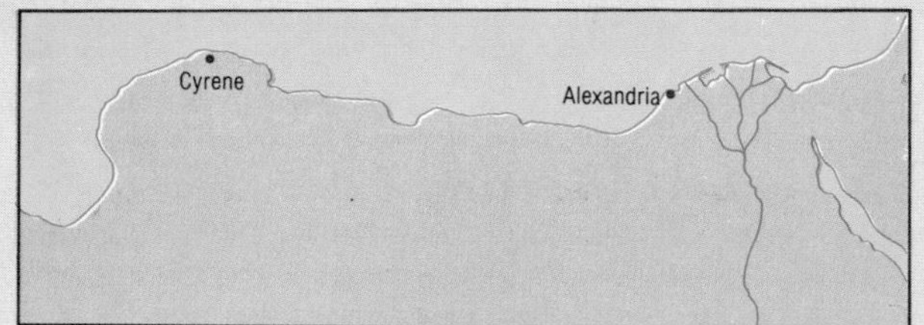

As with most Greek cities of the east Mediterranean, the visible remains of Cyrene are of the Roman period; yet the layout of the city is Hellenistic. In the photograph the "street of Battus" is seen as it passes the magnificent Caesareum, or temple of the imperial cult. Adjoining the Caesareum to the north is a basilica of Roman imperial date, to the west a small odeion, or recital hall, and across the "street of Battus" the Roman theater. It was obviously a most imposing civic center.

Alexandria

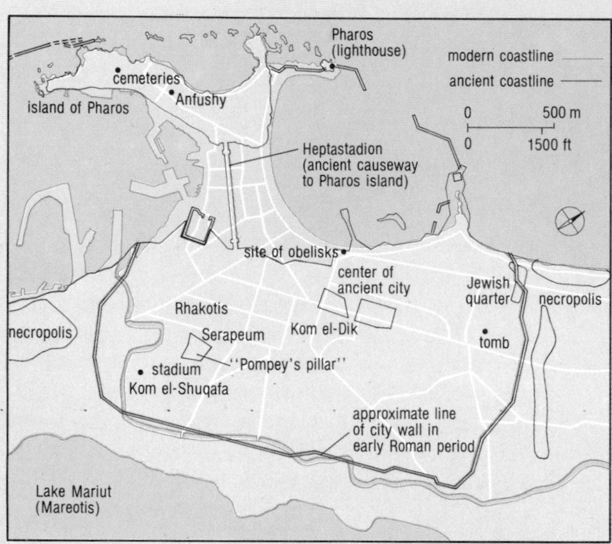

Alexandria, named for its founder Alexander the Great and vigorously developed by the Ptolemies, has been so successful a city that little archaeological trace of the ancient site remains. The ground plan, however, laid out by Dinocrates of Rhodes, was a famous example of Hellenistic urban design. Alexandria was in the Roman Empire an immense and exuberant metropolis, surpassed in size only by Rome, to which it was in intellectual distinction far superior. Its fortune came from trade; it was a clearing house for eastern imports, and in the Roman Empire dispatched the corn ships to Rome and, after 330 AD, to Constantinople. Prominent among its cosmopolitan population, the Jews possessed their own political organization and in 39 AD sent the philosopher Philo as ambassador to Caligula to protest about their treatment by the Greeks of Alexandria. Yet, as Philo shows, the Jews also were profoundly influenced by the persistent Hellenistic atmosphere of the city.

Cyrene

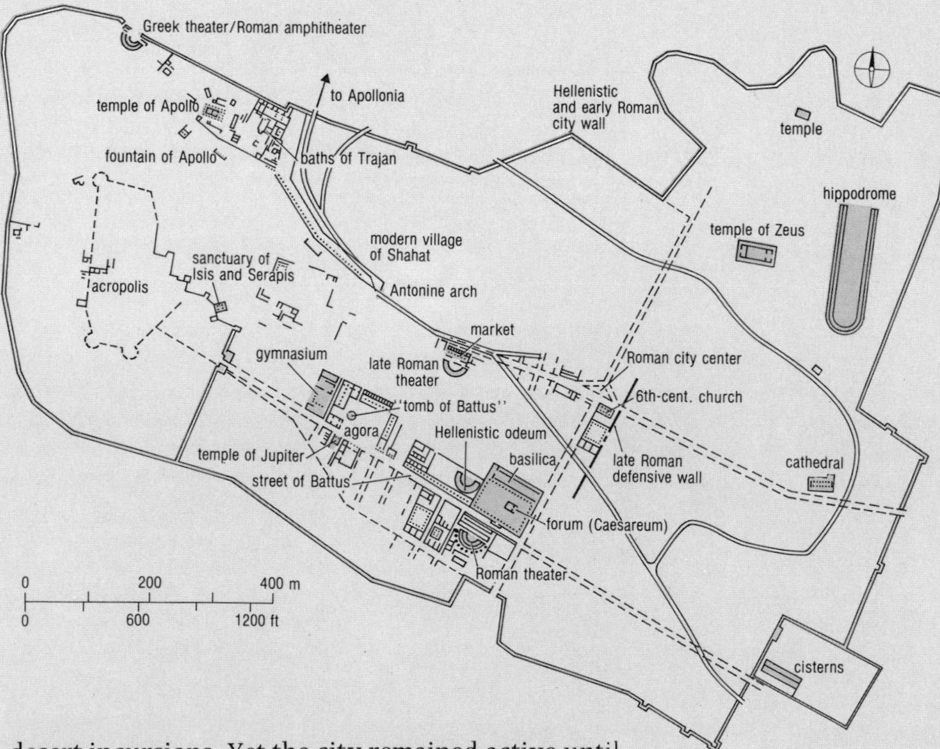

The prosperity of Cyrene was maintained for over a millennium after its foundation by Battus from Thera as one of the most famous and best-documented early Greek colonies. From the late 4th century it fell under a local dynasty of the Ptolemies, the last of whom bequeathed it to Rome in 96 BC. Its development under the Romans differed little from that of other Hellenistic cities. In the Jewish revolt of 115 AD it was occupied and badly damaged by a rebel leader; its recovery was assisted by the munificence of Hadrian. Damaged by earthquakes in the mid-3rd and mid-4th centuries, Cyrene, like its Tripolitanian neighbors, was afflicted in the late 4th and early 5th centuries by desert incursions. Yet the city remained active until the Byzantine period. It contained two Christian churches in the central area and a splendid cathedral with baptistery, which fell outside the Byzantine walls and served as a fortified outpost.

PART FOUR

THE EMPIRE IN DECLINE

DISORDER AND RECOVERY

Shapur I (240–72 AD), "king of kings" and inspirer of the resurgence against Rome of her ancestral enemy in the east, brings down a galloping stag on this beautiful silver and gilt presentation dish, perhaps the earliest of many showing Sasanian kings at their characteristic pleasure. The animals for hunting were kept in great walled parks, which often attract the attention of classical sources. The historian Ammianus Marcellinus, who visited Persia with the campaign of Julian in 363, commented on them and remarked also that the Persians "show nothing in their painting and sculpture than war and various forms of slaughter."

Maximinus to Carinus, 235–284

The half-century from the accession of Maximinus in 235 to the death of Carinus in 284 was a period of political disturbance made no easier for the modern historian by the fragmentary condition of its sources. Cassius Dio, particularly interesting on the personalities and events of his own time, comes to an end in the late 220s; the much less impressive history of the Syrian Herodian ends with the death of Maximinus in 238. The Greek historical works of an Athenian, Dexippus, were clearly of great interest, but survive only in the tantalizing fragments preserved by Byzantine epitomators. In the Latin tradition, the imperial biographies known as the *Augustan History*, often very informative on the 2nd century, are in the 3rd reduced to fiction and fantasy, the interest of which, great though it is, is not primarily of a historical order. Also writing in the later 4th century, a group of epitomators – Aurelius Victor, Eutropius and an anonymous successor of Victor – offer brief accounts of the 3rd century deriving from a lost Latin historian of the age of Constantine (died 337). The study of the interrelationship of these sources is however a technical and often controversial matter.

Any treatment of the 3rd century must necessarily be thematic, and cannot offer narrative and chronological precision. This is not necessarily a handicap. It is more serious that the historian is more or less forced to see the age in terms of that ill-used historical concept, an "Age of Transition," in that its meaning has to be inferred largely from what precedes and follows it. But contemporaries could not wait for the 4th century to tell them what their lives had been about; the historian must make some attempt to see the period in its own right and to read its character.

On a narrower view, that of the development of the imperial office, the 3rd century has been characterized as an age of anarchy. Between 235 and 284 there were 18 or more "legitimate" Roman emperors, holding office for an average of less than three years each; but this count is only a fraction of the story, for it leaves aside sons appointed to hold office with their fathers, and other colleagues, and it ignores usurpers and pretenders whose full number may never be known. Nearly all met violent deaths in civil or foreign war, or by conspiracy.

The circumstances and motives surrounding these monotonously repetitive events are often extremely obscure. Personal ambition alone can hardly account for the claims made by so many for an office which offered so few prospects of survival. Usurpations usually took place in areas of military occupation and barbarian invasion, especially among the armies of the Rhine and Danube. The phenomenon of usurpation should be regarded, not as an accumulation of acts of individual ambition, but as a facet of the structure of the Empire in this period.

The most obvious, and surely correct, interpretation is that usurpations were a response to the military pressures that increasingly beset the Empire. The incursions of the Goths into Asia Minor, of Alamanni and Franks into Gaul and Spain, of Heruli into Attica – whence they were repelled by local resistance led by the historian Dexippus – led to a need for effective power which a distant emperor could not supply, for locally provided finance and for imperial authority if negotiations with the invaders were to be successfully concluded. The independent Gallic empire of the 260s and 270s, established by the usurper Postumus, provided a better-organized response to the Germanic invasions than the legitimate emperor Gallienus, with his preoccupations in the east and with the Danube frontier, could hope to offer. It is a tribute to Gallienus' sense of reality as well as a comment on the limitations of his power, that he left his Gallic rival to get on with the job undisturbed.

In the east, there was a significant shift in the balance of power in the rise of a vigorous and ambitious new royal dynasty, that of the Sasanians under Shapur I, which succeeded in unifying and invigorating the Persian empire and in presenting an effective challenge after a long period in which the ascendancy had rested with the Romans. In 260 the emperor Valerian was taken prisoner by the Persians under Shapur I in a battle near Edessa; the figure of the humiliated Roman emperor, together with the supposed submission to Shapur of his predecessor Philip in 244, was portrayed on the monumental rock carvings at Bishapur and Naqsh-i-Rustam. From the mid-260s Gallienus, sole emperor after his father's capture, committed the defense of the eastern frontier to the Palmyrene dynast Odaenathus who, succeeded by Zenobia and Vaballath, governed a quasi-independent empire extending at its greatest from Egypt to southeastern Asia Minor.

The reign of Gallienus both illustrates the predicament of the Empire in the 3rd century and suggests the structural reforms by which it might be overcome. The reign was regarded by later sources as the time in which the frequency of rebellion had reached its climax, large tracts of Roman territory, in Spain, Gaul and Britain, and in the Orient, being governed as separate "empires." But this division of the Empire, with Gallienus holding Illyricum as the link between east and west, resembles the collegiate structure of the Tetrarchy and the 4th-century system of regional prefectures. The frequent usurpations were the painful early stages of the development of a collegiate imperial office, lacking only the adaptation of the ideal of imperial unity which made collegiality acceptable. One of the strangest aspects of the 3rd century was the determination and expenditure in manpower with which, despite their other preoccupations, legitimate emperors suppressed the claims to power of rivals who were in fact performing an effective local function.

The second development for which Gallienus was later criticized, was his alleged exclusion of the traditional Roman governing class, the senate, from the tenure of military power. One ancient source ascribes this to a "decree" of Gallienus forbidding senators from holding military commands, supposedly in order to keep the "best men" away from the armies. But this is much too simple a view: the elimination of senators from army commands in favor of men of equestrian rank and military background was part of a general process of change which can be traced back into the 2nd century, to the wars of Marcus Aurelius.

Economic aspects of the 3rd-century crisis

The condition of the Roman Empire in the later 3rd century can, on any account of its political history, only be described as critical. Within the tendency of provincial regions to split away into self-governing blocks, further levels of disaffection can also be perceived. In central Gaul, local rebels known as Bacaudae staged some sort of insurrection against imperial authority. In other parts of the Empire there is evidence for the flight of peasants from the land to take up more promising occupations such as banditry, and for an increase in the amount of deserted agricultural land. It is impossible to quantify the extent of these developments, as it is to assess the likelihood, based on the effects of plague and the incidence of war and disorder in the later 2nd and 3rd centuries, of a general decline in population, and therefore in the manpower available to the government and in the agricultural productivity of the Empire. Statistical evidence is lacking, and such tendencies are in any case unlikely to have affected the Empire uniformly in its different areas.

The most readily measurable expressions of the 3rd-century crisis are in economic developments. The later 3rd century saw a momentous weakening of the monetary system. The causes of this were complex, one of them being the Roman authorities' own lack of comprehension of any theory of monetary circulation, and so of the economic consequences of their own actions. The functioning of ancient coinage was based on the assumption that the value of a coin was that of its metal content: in this sense, one might regard the official legends stamped on the coins – as in the cases of the Lydian and early Greek coinages – as the state's guarantee of their purity and weight. But this assumption, if it was ever explicitly made, was not rigorously observed, for it was considered permissible, in times of a shortage of precious metals, to debase the coin by the admixture of base metal, without any idea of reducing its face value. This had been done, without disastrous consequences, by Nero, who issued silver denarii at a purity of 90 per cent, and increasingly by later emperors. Marcus Aurelius issued silver coin at a purity of 75 per cent, Septimius Severus at 50 per cent. But such things were noticed; Cassius Dio accused Caracalla of paying good gold coin in subsidies to barbarians and allowing debased silver to circulate in the Empire.

In the later 3rd century, an apparently severe shortfall in the supply of precious metals, combined with extremely heavy government expenditure, forced the emperors to issue an increasingly debased silver coinage in order to meet their financial needs. It is obvious that, with the recognition by the public that the coins were grossly overvalued in relation to their metal content, their value as currency would fall and prices rise. The result was an inflationary spiral in which an ever more heavily debased coinage pursued and then created still higher prices. In addition, coin of higher intrinsic value was hoarded and never returned as taxation, forcing still greater debasement as the government's access to sources of precious metal declined yet further.

Already by the time of Gallienus, the standard of purity of the silver denarius stood as low as 5 per cent. Before many years had passed, the government was reduced to issuing silver-plated copper coin. The inflation rate between the 2nd century and Diocletian's Prices Edict of 301 (see below, pp. 172–73) can be judged from a single, fairly reliable figure, deriving from the recorded price of wheat: a measure (*modius*) of wheat, normally valued in the 2nd century at about half a denarius, is listed in the Prices Edict – which gives a low estimate – at 100 denarii. The denarius was thus worth, at most, 0·5 per cent of its earlier value.

It is as difficult to comprehend how the government could persist with its self-destructive

A Persian view of Roman history. In this monumental rock carving from Naqsh-i-Rustam near the tomb of Darius the Great, Shapur publicizes his recent triumphs. He receives the obeisance of the emperor Philip (244), and holds by the right wrist Valerian, defeated and captured near Edessa in 260.

monetary "policy" as it is to see how, with the combination of inflation, high government spending and a shortage of precious metals, it could escape from it. The chief victim of the inflation was the government itself, as its tax receipts declined in real value and it was required to make large cash payments in salaries to its officials and soldiers. The government's solution was to secure its needs by exacting them directly in the form of requisitions of food and material supplies, transportation facilities and so on. Over the course of time these exactions became more regular and remained as a standard feature of the late Roman tax system.

An area of public life directly affected by the monetary collapse was the civic munificence which was the characteristic mark of the Empire in the Antonine age. Public building, the provision of shows and amenities and other such acts of public generosity, can be seen from an economic point of view as a means of disposing of large cash surpluses derived from agricultural production. Ancient society, as we have seen, lacked the variety of resources and instruments which in the modern industrial world absorb surpluses; there was little to do with surplus money except spend it, often ostentatiously. It is therefore not surprising that the collapse of the monetary system entailed a sudden and very noticeable decline in civic munificence during the later 3rd century. This does not merely imply a stabilization at an existing level of provision: the period is marked by a positive loss of public amenities and entertainments, as theaters and amphitheaters fall out of use, are filled with rubbish and their arcades inhabited by squatters. In some cases, as at Tours and Périgueux, the amphitheaters formed part of city defenses constructed in the later 3rd century, in response to invasions.

The transformation in the appearance of cities of the later Roman period, especially in the west, is sometimes taken to reflect a contraction of urban life also implied in the decline of civic munificence – especially when the process is accompanied by the continued prosperity and in some cases enlargement of great, self-sufficient rural villas. It is inferred that the civic dignitaries who had sustained the urban vigor of the Antonine age now neglected their cities in favor of a self-contained life with their dependants on their estates. Such inferences must be treated with extreme caution. It is true that, in Gaul at least, the cities underwent a transformation; instead of the expansive cities of the early Empire, with ostentatiously large wall circuits and imposing gateways intended more for show than for defense, there now appeared confined wall circuits enclosing the monumental area of the city, that is, only a small proportion of the actual urbanized area. The building materials include reused blocks and column drums from earlier public buildings now clearly out of commission, as well as funerary monuments, inscriptions and so on.

The provincial economies of northern Gaul, Germany and Britain were at all times dependent on a villa culture; archaeology and aerial surveys reveal the existence, especially in northern Gaul, of many self-contained country houses, equipped with storehouses and habitations for estate workers. This was the situation throughout Roman imperial history, and not merely the later period. Nor does the appearance of fortified citadels within the urban areas of late Roman towns imply that the economic functioning of the cities as such was permanently impaired. It is clear from many examples in Gaul that there was continued habitation of the urban areas outside the later wall circuits. Despite the apparent transformation of the cities of the western Roman Empire and elsewhere (for example at Athens, where the wall built after the Herulian invasion blocked the ancient Panathenaic Way), and despite the loss, for the economic reasons already described, of civic amenities, it should not be assumed that the 3rd-century crisis caused a permanent decline in urban life, leading to an enhancement of what are sometimes called the prefeudal or "seigneurial" aspects of the position of rural landowners.

It was argued in rather different terms by the great social and economic historian, Michael Rostovtzeff, that in the 3rd century an alliance was formed between the peasantry and a Roman army mainly recruited from the peasantry, directed against the cities and their propertied classes as the source of social and economic oppression. The interpretation owes much, as Rostovtzeff acknowledged, to the model provided by the activities of the Red Army in revolutionary Russia, which Rostovtzeff left in 1918. Applied to the Roman Empire of the 3rd century, it fails to convince, against the weight of evidence for the hostility felt by the peasantry towards an army which was invariably a more acute and more immediate oppressor than ever the cities had been. The army may have been recruited from the peasantry, but it behaved as an army, taking what it wanted from the land without too much reflection on its own social origins.

An extremely significant economic change, for which the military crisis of the Empire was responsible, was a shift of resources from the Mediterranean area to the frontier regions in which the wars were fought, and in which the emperors had of necessity to spend most of their time. Cities such as Trier on the Moselle, and Sirmium, Naissus and Serdica in the Danubian regions, emerge during the 3rd century in the role of regular imperial capital cities, a role which they retained in the 4th century. There was also a shift to the east. It was said that, before deciding on Byzantium, Constantine the Great had once favored Serdica as the site of a new capital city. Constantinople itself was the successor of Diocletian's Nicomedia; both sites held a strategic position between east and west, closely linked both with the Mediterranean and with the military land routes into Illyricum and eastwards to the Persian frontier.

In this shift of resources and of imperial interest, the ancient capital of Rome became increasingly isolated and, as an interesting consequence, under the dominance of its senatorial class it enjoyed an enhanced independence which made of it, in the absence of the emperors, still one of the most flourishing and lively of late Roman cities. But there can be no doubt that the 3rd century brought about a substantial shift of resources away from the Mediterranean towards the landbound northern frontier, which had for long been, but in the 3rd and 4th centuries was openly revealed as, the real military backbone of the Empire. The significant

The porphyry group of the "Tetrarchs," Venetian loot from Constantinople now set into the wall of the cathedral of San Marco, Venice. Though the identification of the group as Diocletian and his colleagues involves some difficulties, it beautifully captures the spirit of unity and "togetherness" required of late Roman emperors.

Right: Invasions and frontiers of the Empire in the 3rd century AD. The areas actually abandoned as a result of the mid-3rd-century crisis, of which the map gives a necessarily simplified impression, were surprisingly limited: the "Agri Decumates" in Germany, Dacia, and part of Mesopotamia (recovered by Galerius). The main effects were on the internal structure of the Empire. The immense length of the land frontier under simultaneous threat would necessitate devolution of power among "colleges" of emperors, and government would be carried on from military capitals in the frontier zones. In the 3rd century, usurpation secured a *de facto* devolution which "legitimate" emperors were reluctant to concede in principle. The Gallic and Palmyrene "empires" of the 260s and 270s formed, with the Balkan lands between, the self-financing and self-governing blocks represented in all essentials by the 4th-century prefectures (see map p. 173). Other rebellions, like those of the Quinquegentiani in Africa and the Bacaudae of central Gaul, arose from general uncertainty and required expenditure and effort in their suppression without affecting the structure of the Empire.

division in the Empire was as much that between the Mediterranean and the north as that between east and west, which ultimately provided the formal basis of its partition.

Diocletian and the Tetrarchy

The circumstances of the rise of Diocletian were, even for the 3rd century, melodramatic; he is said to have denounced and with his own hand struck down Numerian's praetorian prefect, Aper, before the eyes of the assembled army. This was in 284. Diocletian was proclaimed emperor at Nicomedia in the late summer of the year. The next spring he defeated the surviving emperor, Carinus, in Pannonia, and for the moment held unrivaled power. Nothing in this sequence of events gives any hint of the character of the reign of Diocletian as it was to emerge over the 20 years of vigorous government and reform on which the political structure of the late Roman state was based.

Diocletian's success was based on his recognition of the need to devolve power to colleagues. In 286 he promoted as Caesar another Illyrian officer, Maximian, and in the next year made him Augustus. Maximian devoted himself as co-emperor to the western part of the Empire, where he won victories over the Alamanni, while Diocletian confronted the Persians on the eastern frontier.

On 1 March 293 the arrangement which historians know as the "Tetrarchy" or "Rule of Four" came into being, when two more officers of Illyrian origin, Galerius and Constantius, were appointed Caesars. They held this rank below Diocletian and Maximian, by whom they were respectively adopted. Constantius put away his wife (or concubine) Helena, who took her young son Constantine to be educated in the east, and married a stepdaughter of the retired emperor Maximian, who was supporting his son Maxentius.

The devolution of power yielded most satisfactory results. Galerius fought the Goths on the lower Danube and in 297–98 won a spectacular victory over the Persians. His lucky capture of the harem of King Narses enabled him to negotiate a Roman frontier along the upper Tigris as far east as Kurdistan and Singara. Meanwhile Diocletian settled a revolt in Egypt, and in the west Constantius recovered Britain from the usurpation of Allectus and won victories on the Rhine frontier, and Maximian suppressed a native insurrection in Mauretania.

Diocletianic defense system: the "Saxon shore." The defense system of the "Saxon shore" (*litus Saxonicum*), anticipated in some respects by the British usurpers of the late 3rd century but developed and systematized by the Tetrarchs, was a means of coastal defense and surveillance designed to prevent the penetration of Saxon raids through the Straits of Dover to the coasts of southern Britain and northern Gaul. This map is derived from the commands of the "Counts" (*comites*) of the Saxon shore as given by the *Notitia Dignitatum*, but the number of actual forts listed here, especially in northern Gaul, is clearly incomplete. The former view that *litus Saxonicum* designates districts occupied and garrisoned by Saxons on behalf of the Romans is certainly mistaken.

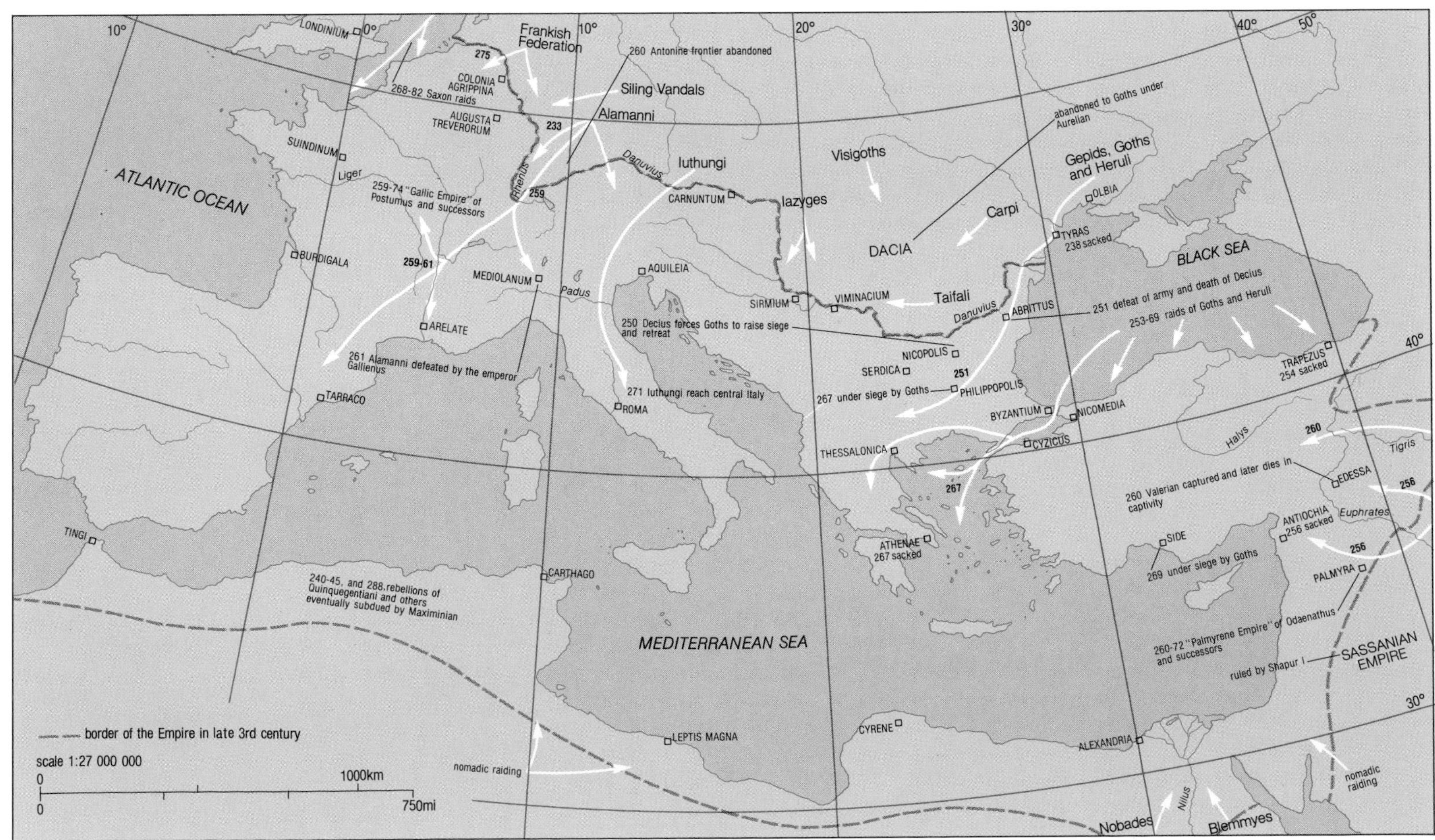

Top The rather crudely modeled but high-quality silver denarius of the British usurper Carausius is remarkable for the Virgilian echo, unique in Roman coinage, with which the province welcomes Carausius as its deliverer. "EXPECTATE VENI" is an allusion to the appearance of the ghost of Hector to Aeneas in a dream before the sack of Troy.

The medallion of Constantius, by contrast (*above*), shows the emperor in his turn being welcomed by LON [dinium], as the "Restorer of Eternal Light" – the "light" of legitimate government in place of the "tyranny" of Carausius and Allectus. The crossing of the Channel by Constantius is symbolized by a warship.

The formation of the Tetrarchy was a progressive achievement, in which the "centrifugal" tendencies in the structure of imperial power, so obvious in the 3rd century, were contained by being legitimized. In an act of self-denial perhaps more astonishing than any other of their achievements, Diocletian and Maximian resigned as Augusti in 305. Galerius and Constantius took their places and two new Caesars were appointed in an attempt to renew the Tetrarchy. The prompt collapse of these arrangements, described below, makes still more remarkable the mutual loyalty achieved by Diocletian and his colleagues. It seems evident that this was not the expression of any sudden change in the attitudes or structure of Roman society but that it was based on the personal and professional loyalty of Illyrian officers known to each other and prepared to accept the dominance of Diocletian.

The survival for 20 years of the government of Diocletian was the precondition for the extraordinary series of reforms which changed the entire tempo of Roman history and were the basis of late Roman government and social organization. Many of the reforms, taken in themselves, had precedents. In their reorganization of the army, for example, Diocletian and his colleagues pursued the development of a mobile field army to complement the role of static frontier garrisons. The promotion of a field army can be seen in the times of Gallienus and Aurelian, and was already implicit in the use made by the early emperors of legionary detachments (*vexillationes*) in active campaigning, while the main legion remained in its camp.

The distinction between a fully mobile field army and static frontier defense is fundamental to late Roman strategy. It has been thought that the frontier garrisons, sometimes referred to as *limitanei*, formed a sort of local militia, occupying land in return for their performance of military duties when required. It is now generally accepted that the word *limitanei* means simply "frontier troops," without these further and far-reaching implications. In certain regions, however, such as Tripolitania and Mauretania, where the defense system was manned by local federate tribesmen, the description of the frontier garrison as a "local militia" seems more apt.

Under the Tetrarchy the numerical strength of the army was greatly increased. A hostile contemporary witness, Lactantius, alleges that the army was quadrupled, and although this is an obvious exaggeration, modern writers are prepared to accept an increase of up to double. The implications of this increase for the problems of finance and supply are very evident, and lead naturally to the question of the monetary and tax reforms of the Tetrarchy.

The Tetrarchs did not at once succeed in stopping inflation, but by a combination of methods they checked it and left a partially stable monetary system to their successors. This was achieved by a series of monetary reforms, the most important of which was the creation of a new gold coin, struck at a high standard of purity at a rate of 60 coins to the pound of gold bullion. With a devaluation of one-fifth by Constantine, this system formed the basis of the stable gold currency of Byzantium. There was also a standard of silver coinage, which held its value relatively well in relation to gold, and of copper, which did not. The result was continuing inflation in prices as expressed in copper coin, the everyday currency of the Empire's populations. The complaints of the army provoked from Diocletian his Edict on Maximum Prices of 301. Inflation is naively ascribed in the Edict's preamble to "furious avarice . . . which with no thought for mankind hastens to its own gain and increase, not by years or months or days, but by hours and even minutes," and an attempt is made to impose maximum legal prices upon an immense range of products and services. Lactantius claimed that the Edict was an immediate and total failure as goods

The section of Diocletian's massive Prices Edict shown *below* lists maximum prices for a variety of plant and mineral products including sponge (used to make eye lotion), lime and fish glue, followed by the tariffs for sea transportation from Alexandria to Rome, Nicomedia and Byzantium.

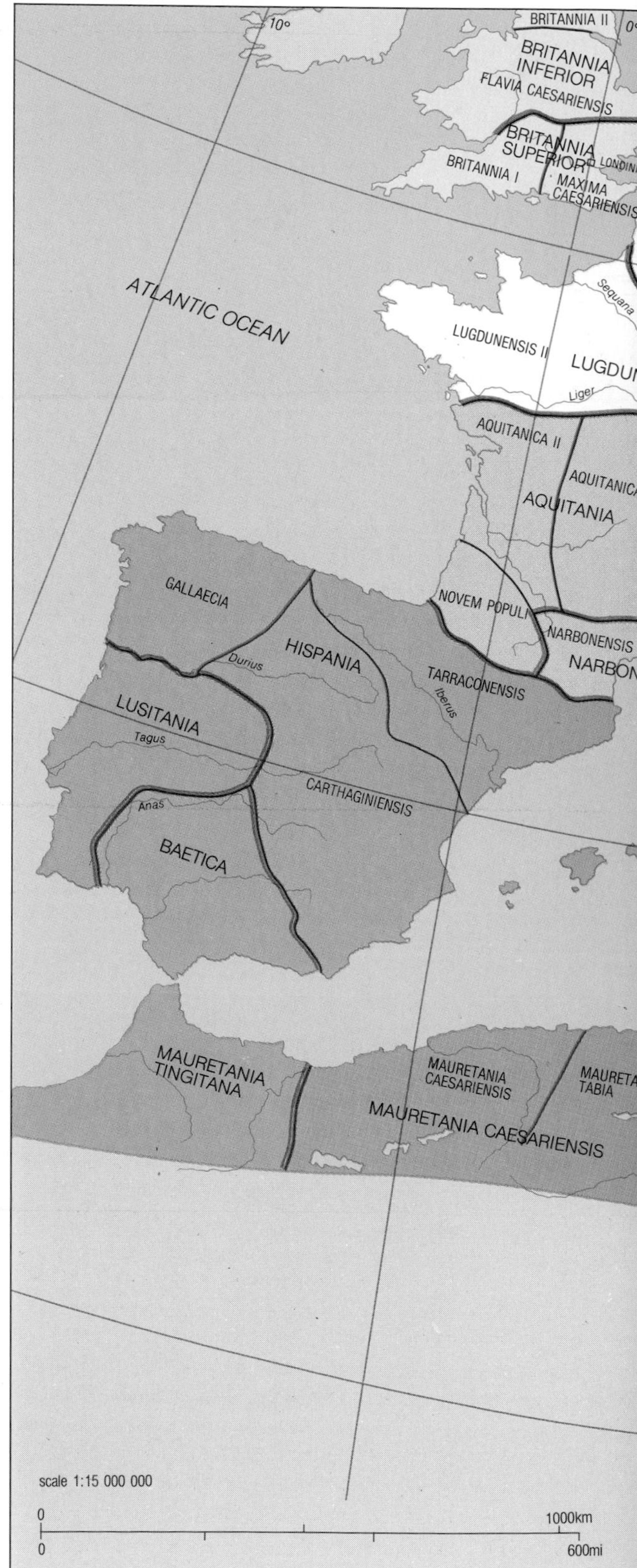

The later Empire in the time of Diocletian. The Diocletianic hierarchy of prefectures, dioceses and provinces is shown in relation to the provinces of the Severan period. The main changes are in the treatment of an enlarged Italy as a diocese with provinces, and in the abandonment to barbarian occupation of the "Agri Decumates" and Dacia, the name of the latter (and part of its population) being transferred to the Roman side of the Danube. The campaigns of Galerius, on the other hand, have added territory along the upper Tigris.

were driven off the market, and his opinion has generally been accepted. Yet the seriousness with which the government took its attempt to control inflation is demonstrated by the many sites which have produced fragments of this massive inscription. Its most effective contribution may have been psychological rather than economic, showing the willingness of a Roman government, after the trauma of the 3rd century, even to contemplate exerting its authority on such a scale and in such meticulous detail.

The implementation of such a complex piece of legislation clearly implies the possession by the government of considerable administrative manpower. This is equally clear in relation to the tax reforms of Diocletian and his colleagues. Again introduced progressively, and with allowance for regional variations and local custom, these reforms involved, in essence, the introduction of a standard unit of taxation, based on the labor (including women and slaves) and animal stock employed on agricultural land, and on the area of land exploited. The latter part of the assessment was variable, depending on the type of use to which the land was put – whether for cereal crops, vines, olives, grazing and so on. The figures were then combined to yield

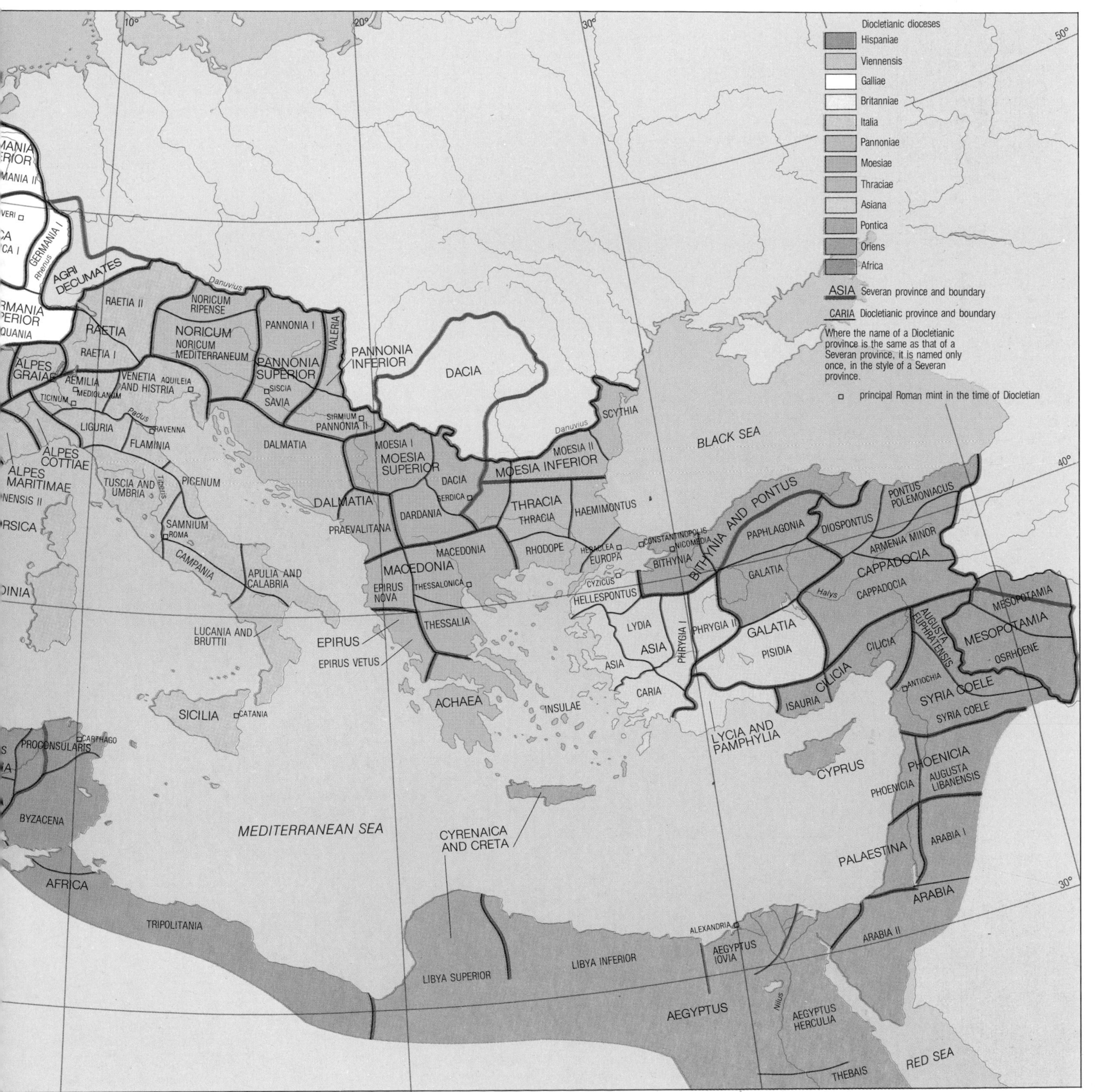

a unit of tax liability which made allowance for different modes of cultivation and degrees of fertility, and the actual rate of taxation was imposed uniformly at so much per unit. In the early 4th century, the city of Autun successfully petitioned Constantine for a reduction of its assessment from 32 000 to 25 000 units, its main argument being the amount of uncultivated land in its territory which had been included in the assessment.

In principle, this was an equitable method of taxation, based on the variable productivity of different types of land and of different modes of cultivation; it allowed, for the first time in Roman history, for rational budgeting. If the government could estimate in advance its financial obligations, then, by simply dividing this figure by the total number of tax units in the Empire (or any part of it), it could calculate each year the rate of taxation required to meet its predicted outlay. To what extent this ideal was achieved is another question. It is clear that there was often a shortfall in the taxes received, which the emperors remedied by making "supplementary assessments."

Various other forms of exaction existed alongside the new tax units. Additional taxes, not in themselves onerous, were levied on senatorial estates, and the emperors continued to receive cash and bullion on their various anniversaries; this was tantamount to additional taxation and clearly made a substantial contribution to imperial finance. As in the 3rd century, the government exacted by requisition services such as transportation facilities and the billeting of troops, and supplied most of the material needs of the armies and the bureaucracy by exacting produce directly from the land. Frontier garrisons were regularly supplied in kind from the estates of provincial landowners. Municipal services were devolved as an obligation onto local councils, which were also made responsible, against the personal fortunes of their members, for the collection and payment of taxation to the imperial authorities. The limitations of the system can be seen, not only from the need for the "special assessments" just mentioned, but from the frequency with which the emperors "wrote off" uncollected taxes by making remissions.

Lactantius alleged that as a result of Diocletian's tax reforms the Empire contained more tax-collectors than tax-payers. Despite Lactantius' obvious exaggeration, the enlargement of the imperial bureaucracy was one of the most characteristic features of the later Roman period (see below, pp. 199–200), and reflects the increased "incidence" of government on Roman society initiated under the Tetrarchy. The same development took place in the provincial administration. The division of the provinces already undertaken by the Severan emperors into smaller and more manageable units, was further pursued to produce a total of over 100 provinces, about twice their number in the 3rd century. Italy, for the first time in Roman history, was divided into provinces and subjected to regular taxation. The provinces were arranged in regional groups known as "dioceses," each under the authority of an official known as a *vicarius*, or "deputy" (of the praetorian prefect). The function of *vicarii* was apparently connected with taxation, since each diocese as a general rule housed an imperial mint, to which its product in monetary taxation was returned for restriking as new coin. One of the main functions of the praetorian prefecture of the 4th century was precisely the assessment and administration of regional taxation.

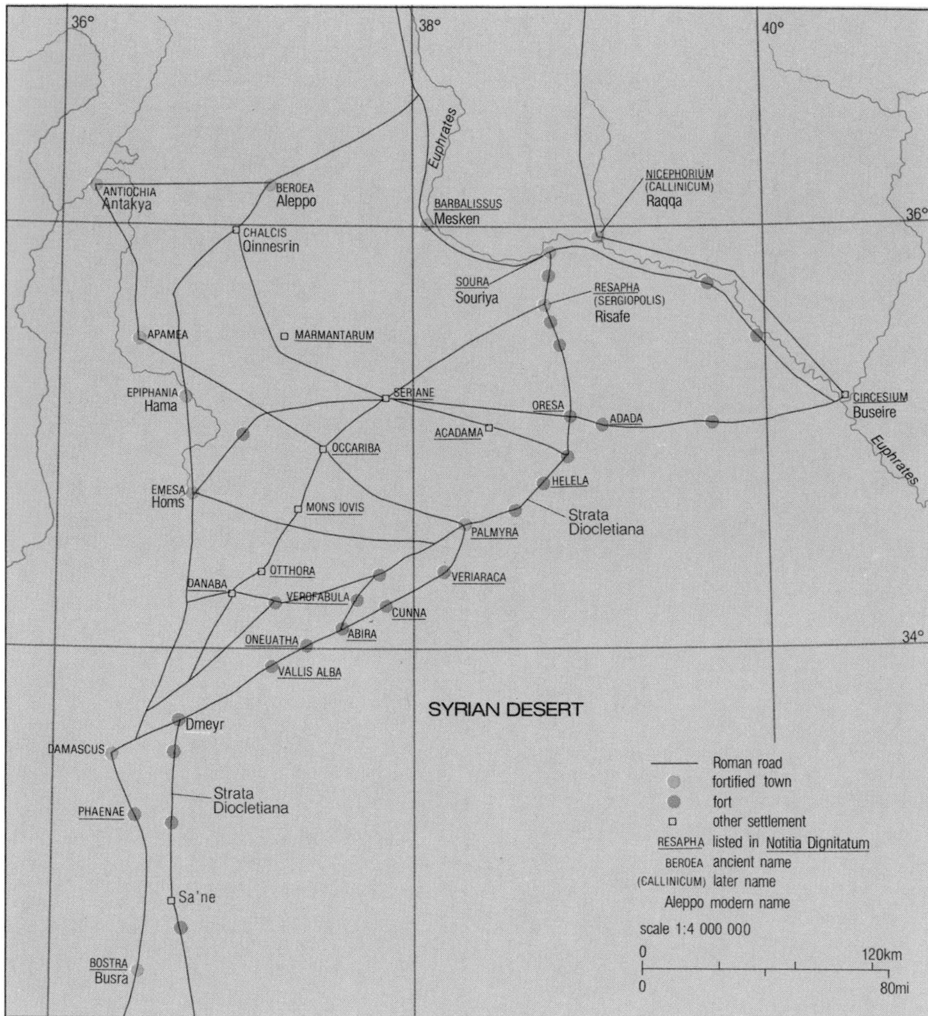

The eastern frontier of Diocletian (*strata Diocletiana*). The map shows the essentials of the Diocletianic eastern frontier, as reconstructed from the evidence of the *Notitia Dignitatum*, field archaeology and aerial surveys. There is nothing original in a garrisoned frontier based on a military road (the *strata Diocletiana*) lying in advance of and communicating with the cities which it defended. This line is in effect that of the Flavio-Trajanic period, and analogies with Diocletian's system can be found in late Roman Africa, where inscriptions show it evolving already in the 3rd century. Nevertheless, the eastern frontier required much new construction, as at Palmyra and Circesium, the latter in particular being seen as a crucial defensive point against Persian attack. It is uncertain to what extent the system was designed for security against local Bedouin, but this was evidently a factor in its operation, especially since the Bedouin ("Saracens" in our literary sources) might ally themselves with Persia.

The frontier was manned by regular frontier troops known as *limitanei*. Though these, like their African counterparts, certainly engaged in farming activities around their forts, there is no justification for describing them as a "peasant militia" engaging in military duties in return for assignments of land.

Many of the characteristics of the developed bureaucracy of the 4th century emerged progressively, under Constantine and his successors. But there is no doubt that its decisive enlargement is attributable to Diocletian, and reflects the intense governmental and legislative activity of his reign.

Late Roman ceremonial and art

Diocletian is credited by 4th-century sources with the introduction of a ceremony known as "adoration of the purple." In this an individual granted audience with the emperor was offered the edge of the imperial purple robe to kiss as an act of homage. The ceremony is taken by these sources to symbolize a change in the position of the Roman emperor from civil magistrate (a pretense maintained since the days of Augustus, but obviously with weakening force, especially during the military crisis of the 3rd century) to Oriental despot. *Adoratio purpurae* was only one aspect of a process whereby the late Roman emperors surrounded themselves by a much more elaborate ceremonial protocol than their predecessors. Although many of the individual elements in this development can be found in Roman practice of earlier periods, their combination marked a real change in the nature of the imperial office. The emperors' persons were attended by a religious aura; petitioners and panegyrists addressed their words to the "sacred ears" of the emperor, and replies, falling from his

This detail from the mosaics of the palace of Piazza Armerina in Sicily (see also p. 186) well conveys the color and brilliance of late Roman dress. A group of attendants awaits the embarkation of a captured animal; on their decorated tunics appear the embroidered emblems typical of the costume of their period. The mosaics are dated to the 4th century; it is widely argued that the villa was owned by the retired emperor Maximian, but this remains extremely uncertain.

"sacred mouth," were put into official rhetorical language by his "sacred secretariat." The official council of state was known as the *consistorium* because its members stood in the imperial presence. Diocletian, adopting the name "Jovius," presented himself as the vice-regent of Jupiter on earth; Maximian, his colleague, was "Herculius," representing the god who had by his untiring labors relieved mankind from terror and affliction. These titles were inherited by the respective junior members of the Tetrarchy. The language of administration becomes filled with abstractions, such as "Our Serenity," "Our Majesty," "Our Eternity," the emperors thereby being presented not as individual personalities but as the vehicles of the abstract virtues by which the Empire was protected. The emperors' victories in war become attached to them as a permanent attribute; they are "always victorious" (*semper victores*), even "extremely invincible," (*invictissimi*). The collegiality of the imperial office is strenuously asserted. Laws issued in one part of the Empire, though they may be of no interest at all to the other, bear the names of all the legitimate emperors of the time.

As part of the elaboration of the imperial office, the palaces became filled with officials and attendants of all kinds, who controlled and made difficult access to the emperor: This again contrasts with the earlier period, when a pretense at least was kept up that an emperor should be accessible to his subjects, and should find time to listen to their individual grievances. The enlarged administrative bureaucracy of the late Empire had as its counterpart a swelling palace staff, headed by "chamberlains" (*cubicularii*), who are often eunuchs (another sign of the "orientalization" of the imperial office); these individuals at times gained an immense and, in conservative opinion, scandalous influence.

The ceremonial elaboration of the late Roman imperial office did not come about in isolation. Late Roman public life in general was characterized by an increasing sense of "theatrical" effect; the emperors with their ceremonial audiences and great processions provide only the most spectacular examples. Many artistic expressions of this tendency, as in the mosaics from the palace at Piazza Armerina in Sicily or the marble intarsia from the audience hall at Rome of the consul Junius Bassus, illustrate how late Roman public life adopted a color and style, a theatrical panache more reminiscent of Renaissance Florence than of a classical city. Literary sources, like Ammianus Marcellinus' description of the fancy clothes worn by Roman aristocrats of the later 4th century, made of brightly colored, airy silk, with fringes and vividly embroidered figures, bear out this impression.

Ceremony is a mode of communication, and it is possible that in the late Roman period it functioned in a more positive and open way than is often assumed. It was not merely a reflection of the new despotism but it provided also a sense of identity to a new governing class, the imperial bureaucracy, which was still in the process of consolidation, and presented the imperial office to the late Roman public in a way which was found intelligible and reassuring. During the 3rd century the emperors must often have seemed very remote from the ordinary civilian populations of the Empire, and the prestige of their office can hardly have been unimpaired by the political disorders of the 3rd century. It may be that their emergence amid such splendor under the Tetrarchy and later was effective in persuading the late Roman public that imperial permanency was once again firmly established and confident.

Changes in the public presentation of the emperors appear to find expression in the art and iconography of the late Empire. During the 3rd and especially the 4th century, Roman public art is characterized by an increasing formalism both of feature and of design. The new style, of which the most obvious aspects are in the stiff, frontal presentation of human figures and the schematic arrangements of groups, together with a weakened sense of perspective, is already seen in the sculptures of the Arch of Septimius Severus at Leptis Magna (early 3rd century), and, more conspicuously, of the Arch of Constantine at Rome (c. 315). Here, the formality and simplicity of the sculptures are emphasized by their juxtaposition with works of the Antonine period, ransacked to embellish the new monument.

Affinities with the new style can be found in the provincial sculpture of the early Empire, but its prevalence in late Roman art is plausibly ascribed to the need to convey the enhanced ceremonial presentation of the emperors of that period, and in general the element of the theatrical. It is in this context that we can most readily understand the frontal poses, the calculated gestures, the neatly articulated rows of figures and carefully designed spaces of so much late Roman representational art. The increasingly stylized "expressionism" of individual portraiture seems also, at least in the case of imperial portraits, to reflect the development mentioned above, in which the emperors are seen less as individuals than as the embodiments of

This relief from the arch of Constantine at Rome illustrates the stiff "frontality" characteristic of much late Roman ceremonial art. The intention is deliberate: to define the roles of the various participants by separating the visual registers in which they respectively appear, and to represent the relationship between emperor and audience as a sort of theatrical set piece. The contrast with the more informal spontaneity of the 2nd-century sculptures incorporated in the arch is very marked (see p. 104).

certain virtues, the symbols of stereotyped abstractions.

Against this shift to a greater formalism, art historians have often seen the reign of Gallienus as marking a "renaissance" of classical style, not only in the fields of philosophy and literature, but also in the visual arts. The main stylistic feature in question is a renewed naturalism reminiscent of the art of the Antonine age, but with the addition of a greater emotional intensity, "an essentially romantic rendering of life in transience" (Gervase Mathew). Yet, apart from the difficulty of dating with sufficient accuracy the works under discussion, they may simply reflect an autonomous classical tradition, continuously developing in its own terms alongside the more "modernistic" developments in the visual arts. The evidence is far too insecure to support any such notion as that of a "renaissance," if by this is meant a movement with more or less consciously conceived aims and fostered by the deliberate support of the emperor and other patrons. It is better to see the various styles of 3rd-century art as expressions of diverse contemporaneous traditions pursued in their own right, not always as closely linked as the critic might suppose with the social and political situation which surrounded them, and ultimately far less easy to explain.

Religious developments

Writing in the early 2nd century, Plutarch had complained of the neglect of the ancient oracles of Greece, a situation which no doubt reflects the loss of the political independence of the Greek states. At Rome, the rise of Stoicism during the 1st century has been seen in terms of a shift of interest away from the state cults to a code of moral conduct deriving from concepts of individual duty, again as part of a response of a once great governing class, the senate, to its loss of political influence under the emperors.

These examples take us to the heart of religious changes of immense importance in the Roman Empire of the 2nd and 3rd centuries. New forms of devotion were drawn from the Greco-Oriental cultures of Egypt, Judaea and Syria, and from Mesopotamia – the cult of Isis and Osiris, Christianity and various forms of Gnosticism, later Mithraism and Manichaeism. Together with some of the more personal mystic cults from Asia Minor, like those of Dionysus and the Phrygian Great Mother, these seem to have become increasingly popular. They offered the individual a variety of attractions: hope of the salvation of his soul, in some cases exotic rituals of initiation to membership of a purified elite, allegorical myths explaining the cosmic order, a definition of the individual's place in the universe; sometimes, in their conception of the human soul as descended from a divine realm and trapped in a hostile world of matter or on a battleground between good and evil, they offered explanations of suffering and wickedness. The ancient public cults of the Greeks and Romans were interested in none of these matters.

The prevalence of the mystery cults has often been linked, more precisely, with the 3rd-century crisis. It has seemed natural to suppose that increasing disorder and insecurity in the outside world would have provoked a corresponding withdrawal by individuals into an inner life. Possibly, in addition, the failure of traditional belief to protect the Empire encouraged men to turn their attention to the mystery religions, to astrology, and, for their personal protection against misfortune, to magic arts, which are seen as increasing in popularity, both absolutely and relatively, in the later Roman period.

Such conclusions must be examined very critically. The evidence, being circumstantial and fragmentary, does not permit any proper analysis of the incidence of such beliefs in one period as opposed to another. The late Roman period, being in general more plentifully and more diversely documented than earlier periods, naturally reveals more cases, for example, of the use of magical practices. Further, such views as those just described are often linked to a more general conception of late Roman society as in an advanced stage of decline from the clear rationalism of the classical age, to an age of less "rational," more superstitious attitudes and beliefs. Such impressions may involve both the imposition of inappropriate concepts of rationalism, and a failure to appreciate the religious complexity of earlier Greco-Roman society.

The practice of magic and astrology was immemorial in ancient society. Government action against the magic arts, together with the expulsion of astrologers and "philosophers" from Rome, was already frequent in the 1st century, by which period a temple of Isis was standing in the central area of the city. Second-century sources are full of references to magical practices, action taken in response to dreams and many other "irrational" but, in the view of their practitioners, effective courses of action. The so-called "Chaldaean Oracles," a collection of utterances on the nature of the universe and of God, and on the techniques for raising the soul to God by the use of magical arts, were collected and circulated in the time of Marcus Aurelius. Indeed, if mysticism is linked too closely with the increasing misery of the 3rd century, it becomes difficult to account for Marcus himself, anxiously addressing his soul in the *Meditations*, in the prosperous days of the Antonine golden age.

The view that the popularity of the mystery religions was connected with the crisis of the 3rd century thus encounters the objection that, in many essential respects, they preceded it. It would be better to associate the development with the ever-increasing mobility of men and ideas in the Mediterranean world under the peaceful conditions provided by the Roman emperors as part of their unification of the Latin, Greek and Middle Eastern worlds. If there was a response on a religious level to the political and social crisis of the age, this is as likely to have taken the form of a reassertion of traditional values as a search for new ones. Such was the basis of the persecution of the Christians in the times of Decius and Diocletian (see below, p. 178), and of the Manichees by Diocletian. In his edict against the Manichees he denounced the wicked arrogance of these men who had set themselves against the common wisdom, opposing their new sect to the old-established religions and preferring their own beliefs to those long ago entrusted by the gods to mankind.

The emperors were not totally conservative. They had already reflected a widely held religious conviction of the age, in associating themselves with

The portrait bust from the theater of Dionysus at Athens has at different times been identified as a portrait of Christ, of an "unknown barbarian" (i.e. the representative of a "Semitic race"!), as a masterpiece of the Antonine age and of the "Gallienic renaissance" of the mid-3rd century. A more recent view is that it shows the emperor Gallienus himself in the guise of the god Serapis. The piece clearly looks back to the Hellenistic age through (or from) the age of the Antonines, with a "dreamy melancholy" of introspection which sets it firmly apart both from the severe modernism of the portrait bust shown *opposite* and from the uncomplicated clarity of the portrait of Aurelian (*below right*).

The coin of Aurelian (*right*) shows the emperor in military dress, wearing the radiate crown characteristic of the sun (see p. 188 for an example associated with Constantine). The reverse bears the legend "ORIENS AUG [ustus]," "rising emperor," with a rather spidery figure of the sun, again wearing radiate crown and carrying orb. The celestial imagery is confirmed by the appearance of a star in the field of the image.

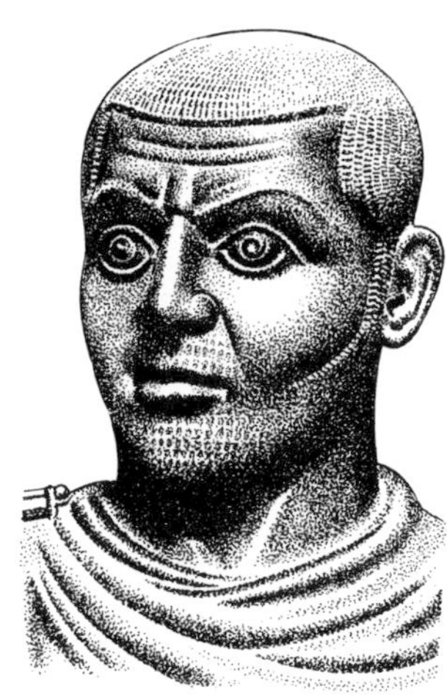

"Expressionism" in late Roman portraiture, as seen in a porphyry bust from Cairo of an unidentified emperor of the late 3rd or early 4th century. The modeling is notable for the abstract symmetry in which the personal character of the subject has been immersed. Though exaggerated and lively, the features are imposed statically on the surface of the material and their physiological structure has been simplified. There is no sense of the introspective complexity of mood so beautifully caught by the bust of "Gallienus" shown *opposite*.

certain particular gods under whose protection they lived. Commodus went so far as to identify himself with the god Hercules, but this was something of an eccentricity, as was the association of Elagabalus with the sacred stone of Emesa (see above, p. 105). From the mid-3rd century, particularly from the time of Gallienus, the emperors linked themselves with the "Unconquered Sun," whom they regarded as their familiar "companion" (*comes Augusti*). Aurelian established a public cult of the Sun at Rome, creating a new college of priests to administer it, which survived until the end of official state paganism. Diocletian and Maximian too associated themselves with the Unconquered Sun as well as with Jupiter and Hercules.

This tendency reflected both the popularity of Sun-worship, in the figure of Mithras, in the Roman army, and contemporary religious beliefs in which the sun was seen as identical with or the symbol of the ultimate deity, the source of physical life and intellectual illumination, of whose all-pervasive power the gods of the classical pantheon were the divine agents.

Contemporary philosophical developments, on a narrower definition, expressed the same tendencies as religious thought in general, in their pre-occupation with an array of doctrines set in an all-encompassing theology derived from Plato. Emphasis is given to the religious aspects of Platonic thought, especially to Plato's myths of the descent of the soul from the realm of divine Ideas to the world of matter and its longing to return to God. This "return of the soul" was to be achieved by rational contemplation or by the use of magical, or "theurgical," techniques designed to exploit the "symbols" of divine presence in the universe in physical objects, in numbers, magical spells and incantations. The former, purely intellectual, approach was that adopted by Plotinus, the founder of what is now known as Neoplatonism, a systematization of Platonic thought in terms of a hierarchy of different levels of being and of reality through which the soul must by contemplation make its way in its return to the "One," the supreme principle from which it was derived. Plotinus' most important follower in this approach was Porphyry, a Syrian from Tyre. The alternative and in every sense more popular method, that of the elevation of the soul by theurgy, was supported by the school of another Syrian, Iamblichus. The theurgical tradition of Iamblichus passed down to the 5th-century Athenian Neoplatonic school of Syrianus and Proclus.

For all these philosophers, Plato was not merely the dominant intellectual influence, but the "divine teacher," and they themselves were regarded as divinely inspired men. Their aims went beyond those of the traditional classical philosopher, in that they wanted to teach and to attain not merely virtue and goodness, but perfection. As divinely inspired men, they were believed to have special powers, enabling them to levitate, perform wonders, evoke the gods and receive divine oracles. Again, it must be emphasized, the origins of such a development must be sought at least as early as the Antonine age, in figures such as Apuleius and the miracle-working "philosophers" satirized by Lucian. It is best seen as an organic development in its own right, owing little or nothing to the insecurity of surrounding events; on the contrary, the origins of such rampant individualism as one sees in these movements are more satisfactorily ascribed to the leisure and security of an age of peace and prosperity like that of the Antonines.

The growth and persecution of Christianity

The 2nd and 3rd centuries were, for the Christian church also, a time of expansion. This was much more marked in the eastern provinces of the Empire, in Africa, and in those parts of the west most exposed to the Mediterranean, which as always bore the main current of intellectual and cultural influences from the east. The churches of the west were generally Greek-speaking until the end of the 2nd century. Bishop Hippolytus of Rome wrote in Greek; the early bishops of Lugdunum (Lyon) were Greek-speaking. Yet in Tertullian (?c. 170–220) the African church produced a major Latin writer, and it seems that, both there and in Italy, the Greek element in Christian congregations was by this time beginning to be overtaken by Latin-speaking local converts.

The growth of the church can be measured, from another point of view, by the 87 bishops who attended the council of Carthage organized by Bishop Cyprian in 256. At Rome the number of widows and orphans receiving charitable aid is put at 1500, which would suggest the existence of a substantial Christian community. At Antioch Bishop Paul, convicted of heresy and deposed in 268, is described by an opponent as lording it in his city as if he were an imperial procurator.

Some parts of the Empire, notably the European provinces of Pannonia, northern Gaul, Germany and Britain, were less immediately affected by Christianity, but it is clear that by 300 AD there were many districts in which its adherents formed at least a prominent minority.

The church historian Eusebius of Caesarea, writing soon after 300, remarked that the period since the reign of Decius had been one of peace and prosperity for the church, which the Devil had exploited by sowing dissension in its ranks. The persecution initiated by Decius was itself the first general attack against Christianity ever undertaken by the Roman government as a matter of deliberate policy. Earlier, persecution had been conducted on a local basis, often by governors under pressure from local populations and civic leaders. The existence of such action may be known to us only because the governor in question, like Pliny in the time of Trajan, consulted the emperor on points of procedure – what to do with Roman citizens who were admitted Christians, whether or not to countenance anonymously posted denunciations (on which point Trajan's reply was firmly in the negative). It is important not to underestimate the frequency of such local persecution. At the same time, it is essential to recognize that no emperor before Decius, in the mid-3rd century, mounted a centrally organized campaign against Christianity, and that until that time the issue was never particularly important in the mind of any Roman emperor.

The general causes of persecution are fairly clear, though it is not always easy to say why it occurred at a particular time. Tertullian complained that the Christians were blamed for any misfortune afflicting a community: "If the Tiber floods or the Nile fails to, the cry goes up: the Christians to the lion!" Outbreaks of plague, earthquakes or violent storms were other disasters which could be attributed in popular opinion to the withdrawal of the favor of the gods. For Romans believed that the universe was kept in balance only by the goodwill of the gods to men, which must be maintained by the collective piety of the community, that is, by the performance of duly established rituals and sacrifices. The Christians, a dissenting group who refused to participate in such rituals, were believed to be undermining the relations between the community and its gods, and by disturbing the "peace of the gods" (*pax deorum*) to be provoking the withdrawal of their protection.

In addition, the social and religious habits of Christians themselves caused suspicion. Their rituals were secret and involved the consuming of symbolic flesh and blood in the Eucharist: anti-Christian propagandists offer lurid allegations of cannibalism – "Thyestean banquets" (in Greek mythology Thyestes was served the bodies of his sons in a stew) – and of incest, since Christians were exhorted to love their brothers and sisters. Christians took mysterious oaths of loyalty to each other: it surprised Pliny to discover that the oath was "to commit neither theft, robbery, nor adultery, nor to betray a trust, nor to refuse to return a deposit on demand." They absented themselves from much of the social intercourse of a community, since this was linked up with the performance of religious rituals (Tacitus had already accused the Christians of a "hatred of the human race"); some Christian writers, like Tertullian, went so far as to maintain that a Christian should as a matter of fundamental principle have no part in the social life or culture of secular society. "What has Athens," he wrote, "to do with Jerusalem?" This was by no means the whole picture. Other Christian spokesmen argued that Christians too were loyal citizens, who paid their taxes and prayed to their own God for the emperor's safety. It is clear that not all Christians took Tertullian's rigorous view of classical culture and education; in this issue is anticipated one of the most important debates of the time of Christian empire (see below, pp. 194 ff.).

Decius' initiation of a persecution of the Christians, like the other evidence sketched above, suggests that Christianity was a relatively prominent religion, at least worth picking out as the cause of the Empire's ills. The reign of Decius coincided with the onset of serious military crisis, especially in the Gothic invasions, and it may be that it was felt necessary to reassert the loyalty of the Empire to its traditional gods. This feeling was possibly sharpened by a sense that the recent celebration of the millennium of Rome by the emperor Philip had not provided the confirmation of Rome's fortunes that might have been expected.

The actual process of persecution involved, first, the arrest and punishment of members of the clergy; later, all citizens were required to sacrifice to the gods of Rome and the emperor's genius, or guiding spirit. On the completion of sacrifice, a certificate (*libellus*) was issued to this effect; examples of these documents survive on papyrus. It was suspected, and must sometimes have happened, that *libelli* were obtained through bribery by Christians who did not wish to sacrifice but were terrified of the penal consequences. The clergy were also required to surrender the holy scriptures, but it does not appear that, in the Decian persecution, damage was done to church buildings. Many communities no doubt still met in the private houses of their wealthier members.

The persecution initiated by Decius was revived for a time by Valerian, but lapsed after Valerian's capture by the Persians (260). Among its victims was Cyprian of Carthage, who in the time of the Decian persecution had withdrawn from Carthage and escaped, but who under Valerian faced exile and, in 258, martyrdom by beheading. It nevertheless appears that it was relatively easy for a Christian to escape persecution by quietly disappearing for a time; the authorities were not equipped to track down everyone who might do this, especially if he were harbored by other members of his community. Presumably in this, as in the Great Persecution, some victims were Christians who actually wished to undergo martyrdom and thereby secure instant promotion to sainthood. This appears from the exasperated comments of Roman governors unwilling to impose execution and from the perplexity of Christian writers faced with the issue of voluntary martyrdom.

The Great Persecution of Diocletian is unlike that of Decius in that, although much more is known of the circumstances of its outbreak, the period of Diocletian's reign in which it began was not, from a political or military point of view, particularly critical or uncertain. There must be some truth in the allegation of contemporary Christian sources that the motivating force was Diocletian's junior colleague Galerius, stirred by a personal hatred of Christianity and imposing this attitude on the aging, weakening Diocletian. Diocletian's own wife and daughter were among those compelled to sacrifice as Christians or Christian sympathizers.

General persecution was occasioned by the failure of a sacrifice at Nicomedia, when an imperial official present was seen to cross himself to avert pollution by the rites. It is interesting to find the presence of Christianity in court circles so close to the emperor, and it may be that this was what disturbed and enraged Galerius. The first edict of persecution, dated 23 February 303, ordered the closure of churches and the surrender of the scriptures, and this was followed by an order to the clergy to perform sacrifice. So far only the ecclesiastical authorities were involved, but a third edict extended the obligation to sacrifice to all members of the Christian community. The edicts, posted at Nicomedia (where one was torn down by an angry Christian who was immediately executed by burning), were sent out to the praetorian prefects, passed on by them to provincial governors and by them to municipal officials for local enforcement. A papyrus from Oxyrhynchus records the experience of a Christian who came to Alexandria for litigation and found that all those appearing before the court were being made to sacrifice. He overcame this problem by empowering his brother, who was evidently not a Christian, to act on his behalf.

It is difficult to estimate the incidence of persecution and the numbers of those who suffered

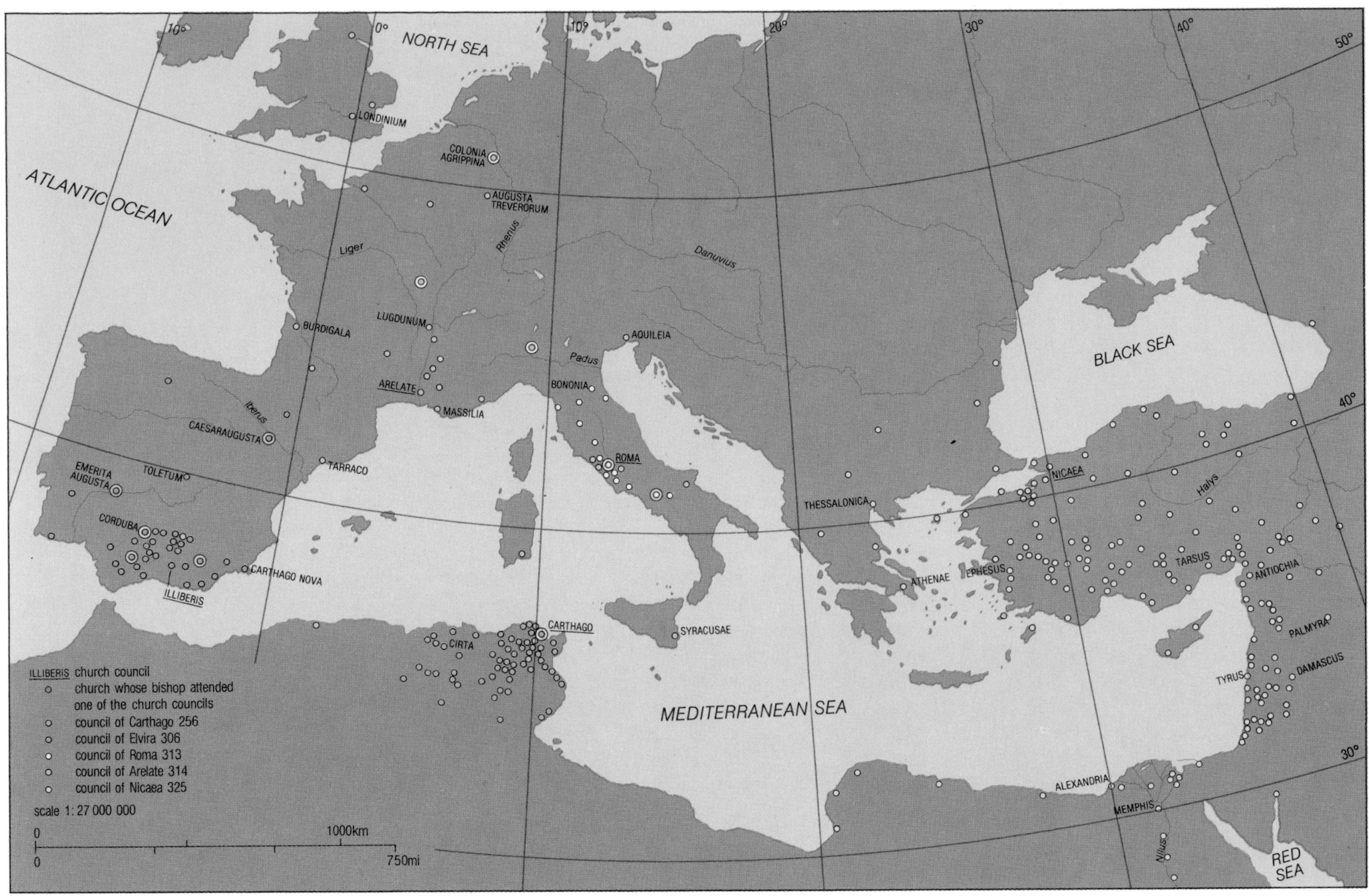

The distribution of Christian churches, 3rd and early 4th centuries AD. The purpose of the map is to indicate only those churches known to have attended the councils indicated. It omits churches recorded, sometimes reliably but often on late and untrustworthy evidence, as existing elsewhere, and gives no indication of the actual size of Christian communities. It suggests the "potential" rather than actual distribution of Christian churches, based on the evidence provided by the councils for certain regions. This evidence is obviously incomplete; one wonders, for example, what would have been revealed by a council held in southern Dalmatia. Nevertheless, the council of Nicaea gives a fair indication of the distribution of churches in the east at the outset of Constantine's reign there, and in other areas the distribution coincides sufficiently closely with the density of urbanization in the Empire (see p. 111) to suggest that the general impression is not a misleading one.

the penalties of exile, condemnation to the mines, mutilation or death. The picture given by Eusebius for the heavily Christianized provinces of Palestine and Egypt is that there were indeed many individual victims; in the case of Egypt, he mentions for instance two convoys, respectively of 97 and 130 Christians, men, women and children, being led off to hard labor in the state mines. Yet it seems unlikely that more than a small proportion of the Christian population in the Empire at large suffered penalties. What is clear is that the persecution was a central issue in public policy for several years and that its aftermath provided the Christian church with its main ideological preoccupation in the period after the granting of the peace of the church by Constantine and Licinius. The proper attitude to take to clergy who had compromised their faith by surrendering the scriptures, and to ordinary Christians who had sacrificed, and the rancorous disputes arising from allegations of such behavior, created the Donatist schism in North Africa and temporarily soured the life of many other churches.

The persecution was maintained by Galerius in the years after Diocletian's abdication, but was allowed to lapse in the regions controlled by Constantius (Gaul and Britain, where there were in any case few Christians) and the usurper Maxentius (Italy and Africa). In 311 Galerius fell ill of a terminal disease and, apparently in fear of death, suspended the persecution in terms which reveal clearly its original motivation. He had hoped by coercion to restore the Christians to a sound mind, but had discovered that, while they had been deprived of opportunities to worship their own God, they were not praying to the traditional gods either. He therefore restored freedom of worship, inviting Christians to pray to their God for his safety, their own and that of the Empire. Shortly afterwards Galerius died, the victim, according to gleeful Christians like Lactantius, of divine vengeance.

After Galerius' death the persecution was revived, with a somewhat different emphasis, by his successor Maximinus Daia. Maximinus received delegations from the cities petitioning for the persecution of Christians. The propaganda activities of pagans such as Theotecnus of Antioch, who circulated forged memoirs of Pontius Pilate full of blasphemies against Christ, give us a glimpse of the local feeling which may well have sustained the persecution for so many years. Maximinus also attempted, in anticipation of the policy of Julian the Apostate (see below, p. 191), to found a provincial priesthood charged with the administration of a restored paganism. Before any of the effects of these policies could be seen, Maximinus fell to the new emperor Licinius. In 313 Constantine and Licinius had issued a declaration of freedom of worship, and restored to the Christian church its confiscated property. This was the beginning of the peace of the church and the conversion of the Roman Empire to Christianity, welcomed with alacrity by Eusebius as the fulfillment of divine prophecy. But this is to anticipate the question of the conversion of Constantine which is to be discussed in the next chapter.

Roman Portraiture

The development of individual portraiture is generally considered one of the principal achievements of Roman art. This view is perhaps somewhat paradoxical, since the artists who produced the majority of the surviving portraits were in fact Greeks. But they were working under the patronage of wealthy Romans, and their work is a response to Roman needs and a reflection of Roman tastes. The distinguishing characteristic of this style of portraiture is an extreme realism, with a particular emphasis on the ugly and unattractive features of the subject. The origins of this "veristic" style are difficult to determine, but there is no doubt that it appealed strongly to the Romans, who liked to see themselves as a tough, honest, no-nonsense people.

During the late Republic and early Empire the realistic portrait style was adopted by all classes of society, including artisans, traders and freedmen, as can be seen from the numerous funerary portrait reliefs which are among the most characteristic expressions of plebeian art. In public portraiture there was a distinct change under Augustus and the Julio-Claudians, who favored a classicizing style of idealized portrait (see above, p. 76). But verism reappeared under the Flavians, and again in the 3rd century under Caracalla, who rejected the revived classicism that had prevailed since Hadrian and introduced a new harsh realism. Imperial portraits in the period of the 3rd-century crisis convey with remarkable frankness the energy, strength and vitality of the unsophisticated soldiers who ruled the Empire. But under Diocletian and his successors imperial portraits took on a fixed and abstract quality expressing the majesty of emperors separated from their subjects by an elaborate court ritual; in later imperial portraiture there is no longer any attempt to represent the real features of living men.

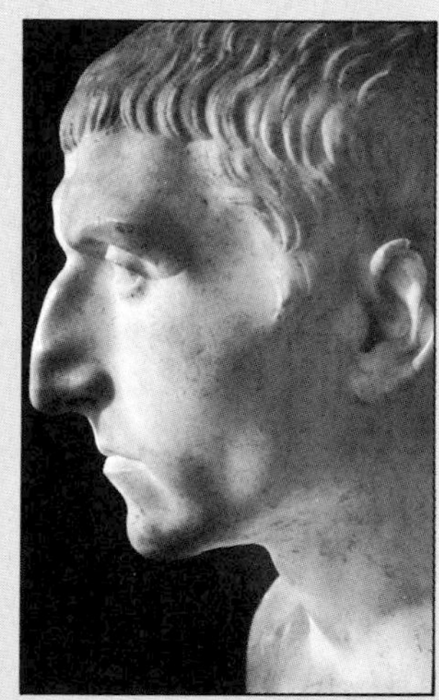

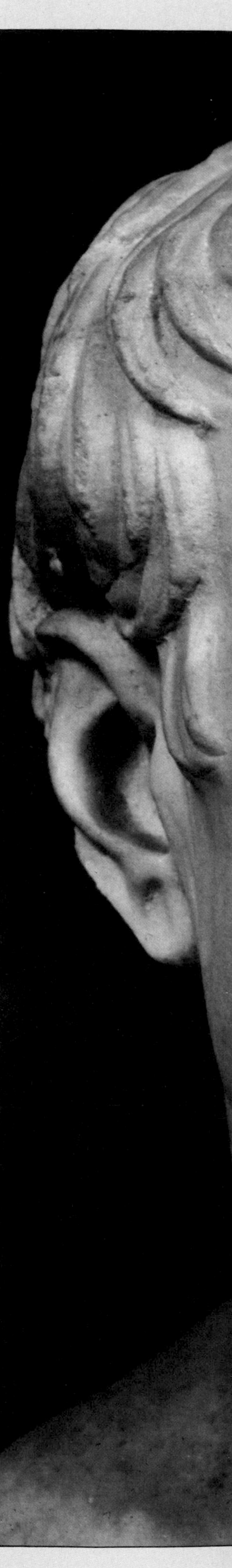

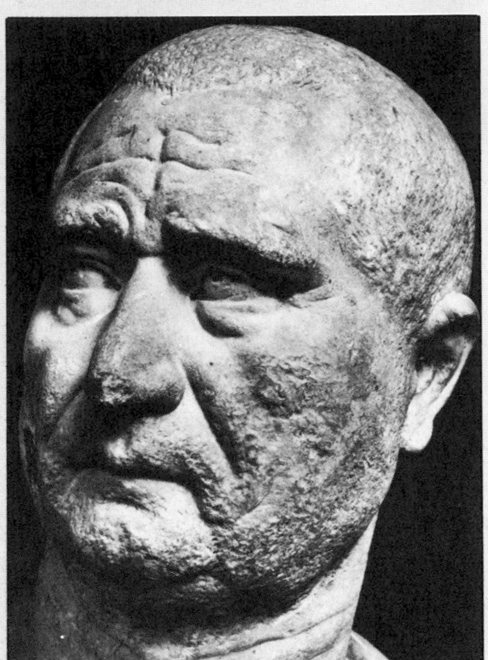

Everyday Life

Funerary monuments, especially from the western provinces of the Empire, frequently portray scenes of business life, carved in varied and often local styles but with much precisely observed detail. This selection well illustrates the generally small scale of production and exchange in the Roman world, often based on family units, with slave assistants and

The greengrocer.

The shopkeeper.

The blacksmith.

The ironmonger.

The apothecary.

There was no sharp distinction between the means of production and of distribution in the ancient world. Manufactured articles for sale, such as those displayed in the ironmonger's shop (*far left*), would be produced in workshops on the premises, like the smithy shown *above*. The relief *below* seems to show the payment or changing of money, perhaps in the form of rents paid to an agent; it distinguishes the figures who have come in from outside (shown in hooded cloaks) from those working indoors. In the butcher's shop (*below left*) the owner's wife (or is it a customer?) seems to be keeping records with a writing implement. Many examples of the yardarm, shown on the right of the relief, have been preserved.

The butcher.

The rent collector.

young apprentices; it was an economy of craftsmen rather than of industrial organization. The great state industries, such as the arms factories of the late Empire, were exceptional, and here too it is likely that the manufacturing process was not large-scale but a multiplication of small operations.

A carpenter's plane.

The bargeman.

In the smithy (*above*) an assistant is heating the forge with a pair of bellows, while shielded by a screen from the heat. The smith's tools are displayed separately, together with what appears to be one of his products, a spearhead. The carpenter's plane from Silchester (*top*) shows how little this implement has changed in design. Many reliefs survive of wine barrels being transported on boats; here (*left*) the barge is being pulled from a towpath by three men with ropes attached to a pivot, and steered by a helmsman. The large wine barrel (*right*), also from Silchester, is made of silver fir from the Pyrenees. It has survived through being reused as part of the lining of a well.

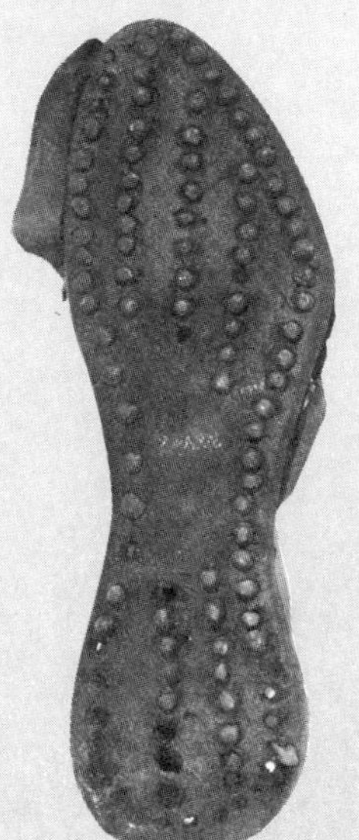

The sole of a boot.

The cobbler and the cord maker.

A wine barrel.

Mills and Technology

Roman society never developed an industrial economy, nor did it evolve any general theory of economic progress. It lacked the financial instruments necessary for industrial investment and was without such notions as productivity and consumer demand. It was not that the Romans were deficient in technical inventiveness or failed to apply it when a specific need was perceived and understood. In military technology, for example, ballistic and siege warfare reached a high level of sophistication and effectiveness. The Romans could produce stunning theatrical effects and their achievement in building and in water management speaks for itself. Yet manufacture continued to be pursued on a small scale, on the level of craft rather than industry.

This failure to develop an industrial technology is sometimes ascribed to the presence of slavery, which is argued to have removed the incentive to reduce labor costs by mechanization. Clearly, more is at issue than this. Many societies have lacked slavery but failed to industrialize, and in the Roman Empire there was often a surplus of free-born labor, especially in the large cities. When the need was felt, as in areas of lower population, the motive to economize on labor was present. It was partly for this reason that an agricultural writer recommended the reaping machine illustrated below.

There were practical limitations. Ancient society lacked an advanced metallurgical technology. Its mechanical devices were made of wood and not equipped to sustain the stresses undergone by power-driven machinery. The gears in the Barbegal water mills shown opposite were wooden, and held to their axles by lead plugs. They must have required constant repair and maintenance.

The *vallus* or reaping machine (*above*) was used in the flat, open plains of northeastern Gaul, from where all its known representations come. It operated by being pushed from behind, the tapered teeth cutting or tearing off the ears of corn and letting them fall in a container. The remainder of the plant was left to stand as tall stubble.

The ox-powered boat (*below*), with vertical capstans geared to paddle wheels, was one of a set of military inventions submitted to the emperors c. 370. The idea was ingeniously adapted in 537 by Belisarius who suspended paddle wheels from pairs of boats and used the waterpower to turn millstones on the boats.

The lifting device illustrated (*above*) is described by the architect Vitruvius. The beam or arm of the device is secured by guy ropes and the load borne by ropes on an arrangement of triple pulleys. In the case of heavier loads a geared windlass was used, operated in extreme cases by a man or men in a treadmill, as shown here in a reconstruction derived from a funerary relief from Syracuse.

The diagram (*left*) shows how the competing physical forces generated by a standing amphitheater in fact combine to reinforce its strength. The vertical forces exerted by the weight of the superstructure are transferred horizontally by the keystones of the arches; and these horizontal pressures, which would tend to force apart a single arch, are mutually self-supporting in the endless series of arches. The outward pressures which result from this are relatively insignificant, given the length of continuous circuit involved.

Rome was served by eight main aqueducts, bringing water from the hills east and south of the city. They were built over a period of hundreds of years, to keep pace with the increasing population of Rome. In the reconstruction (*right*) is shown the intersection of five aqueducts as they approach the city.

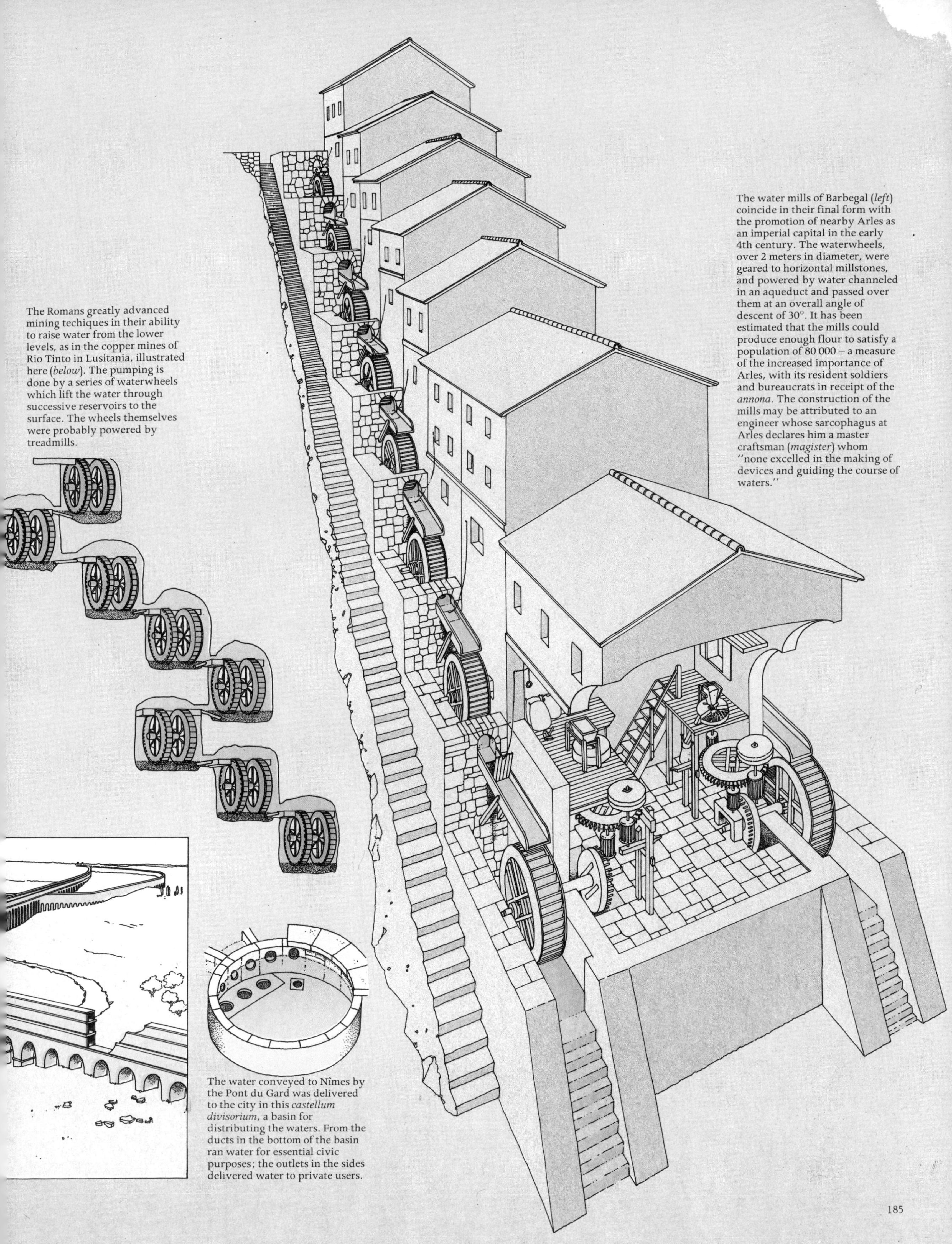

The Romans greatly advanced mining techiques in their ability to raise water from the lower levels, as in the copper mines of Rio Tinto in Lusitania, illustrated here (*below*). The pumping is done by a series of waterwheels which lift the water through successive reservoirs to the surface. The wheels themselves were probably powered by treadmills.

The water mills of Barbegal (*left*) coincide in their final form with the promotion of nearby Arles as an imperial capital in the early 4th century. The waterwheels, over 2 meters in diameter, were geared to horizontal millstones, and powered by water channeled in an aqueduct and passed over them at an overall angle of descent of 30°. It has been estimated that the mills could produce enough flour to satisfy a population of 80 000 – a measure of the increased importance of Arles, with its resident soldiers and bureaucrats in receipt of the *annona*. The construction of the mills may be attributed to an engineer whose sarcophagus at Arles declares him a master craftsman (*magister*) whom "none excelled in the making of devices and guiding the course of waters."

The water conveyed to Nîmes by the Pont du Gard was delivered to the city in this *castellum divisorium*, a basin for distributing the waters. From the ducts in the bottom of the basin ran water for essential civic purposes; the outlets in the sides delivered water to private users.

Public Shows

The satirist Juvenal's contempt for the taste of the Roman people for "bread and circuses" (*Satires* 10.81) is often cited by critics who cannot easily imagine the deprivation of urban poverty or the boredom of unemployment. In fact, public shows were not only a consolation for the underprivileged, but an extremely important aspect of the social life, and social relations, of a Roman city. They were provided by the local dignitaries, who thereby asserted their wealth and social prestige in rivalry with their peers, and established their patronage over the common people, whose gratitude was expressed by acclamations in theater, amphitheater or circus. In 1st-century Rome, the emperors could "undercut" the position of the senatorial aristocracy by their overwhelming generosity in providing shows – a position reversed in the late Empire, when the emperors rarely visited the city.

It is difficult to say whether the games relieved, or intensified, social tensions. They could explode into destructive violence, as in the riots between Pompeii and Nuceria under Nero (see p. 112), and civic disorders were often aggravated by the rivalries of local aristocrats. This provided one motive for the intervention of the emperors in the lives of provincial cities.

The games involved frantic danger and excitement, as in chariot races, and, in gladiatorial combats and wild-beast fights, systematic bloodletting. Exposure to beasts in the arena was a punishment reserved for slaves and the low-born, and for outsiders like the wretched desert tribesmen shown below. In other cases, combats between animals and men appear rather as feats of acrobatics, and one suspects that, as in modern professional wrestling, genuine combat was often presented with a certain histrionic contrivance. It is unlikely that those senators who presented themselves as gladiators under Nero took much risk with their lives, though in general it seems evident that a career as a gladiator was actually sought only by the desperate.

Scenes of gladiatorial combat, circus races and hunting shows are common in Roman decorative art. They give the artist the opportunity to show human and animal forms in vigorous action, and allow the patron to commemorate his munificence in providing the games. The mansion at Rome of the senator Junius Bassus produced the vivid marble intarsia shown *above*. Bassus as consul (in 331 AD) leads the parade. Behind him are the charioteers arrayed in the colors of their teams, or factions, whose fortunes were followed avidly by their partisans. The combat scene (*above left*) is from a mosaic at Bad Kreuznach in Germany, picturing various types of gladiatorial combat. Here in mid-action are a pair of gladiators armed in the "Samnite" fashion with sword, oblong shield and crested helmet. The extensive mosaics from the late Roman palace at Piazza Armerina in Sicily display hunting scenes: not only the ostriches shown here (*center left*), but tigers, antelopes and a rhinoceros are shown being loaded for export from Africa. The mosaic from Zliten in Tripolitania (*left*) is remarkable for its pitiless realism: captured desert tribesmen defenselessly exposed to beasts, and various forms of fighting with animals.

The wide-eyed circus audience shown *above* is captured from a mosaic of the Byzantine period from Gafsa (Capsa) in Tunisia. It does not attest the continuance of chariot racing in this 6th-century provincial town but derives from an earlier design, or conventional theme, associated with Roman Carthage.

Shown *above* on a papyrus from Oxyrhynchus is a 6th-century circus program. The attractions include six chariot races, interspersed by a parade, singing rope dancers (two appearances), gazelle and hounds, mime dancers and a troupe of athletes.

The amphitheater at El-Djem, ancient Thysdrus (*left*), was among the largest in the Empire. Built in the early 3rd century, it superseded an earlier structure already possessed by the city.

The ivory diptych of the Lampadii (*above*) is typical of the gifts which senatorial families would distribute to friends invited to their games, usually held to celebrate the public office of one of their members.

CONSTANTINE THE GREAT AND THE 4th CENTURY

The rise and conversion of Constantine

The retirement in 305 of the Augusti, Diocletian and Maximian, entailed the promotion in their place of the existing Caesars, Galerius in the east and Constantius in the west. At the same time, by a second tier of promotion, the relatively unknown Maximinus Daia and Severus became Caesars. This choice put at risk the loyalty and coherence of policy so laboriously achieved by Diocletian, for it involved the exclusion from the prospects of imperial power of Maxentius, son of the retiring Augustus Maximian, and Constantine, son of the promoted Constantius. The collapse of Diocletian's arrangements can be attributed in part to the personal ambitions of the disappointed candidates, but ambition must have its opportunity and it is perhaps as significant that the arrangements went against the general expectation, especially in the army, for the restoration of a directly hereditary succession.

In 305 Constantine, who was still residing in the east, was allowed by Galerius to join his father in Britain. In the following year Constantius died at York, and Constantine was proclaimed Augustus by the army, though he initially claimed from Galerius only the title of Caesar. Constantine at once embarked on the energetic civil wars which by 324 made him sole ruler of the Roman Empire. Crossing to Gaul, he won the support of the restless old Augustus, Maximian, and married his daughter, Fausta. Maximian had already supported his own son Maxentius in a proclamation at Rome before quarreling with him and joining Constantine, and it was not long before he turned against Constantine also and was forced to suicide (310). Constantine now marched against Maxentius and defeated him at the battle of the Milvian Bridge (28 October 312). Since Maxentius had himself earlier eliminated Severus, Constantine was now master of the entire west.

In the east, meanwhile, Galerius had died, and his successor Licinius shared the eastern empire with Maximinus Daia. Constantine and Licinius met for mutual recognition at Milan and agreed, among other things, to restore freedom of religious worship and allow the Christians to recover their property, confiscated in the Great Persecution. The two emperors lived in peace until 316 (Licinius in the meantime defeating Maximinus), when Constantine gained territory in the Balkans from Licinius, and from 317 until 324. In 324, however, Constantine moved against Licinius, defeating him at Hadrianople and in a sea battle at Chrysopolis, and from then until his death in 337 was sole ruler of the Empire, appointing as Caesars his sons Constantine, Constantius and Constans.

The rise of Constantine cannot be understood, even so far, without reference to his conversion to Christianity. The outward signs of this can be traced fairly closely. In the earliest stages of his quest for power, Constantine relied on a variety of claims of connections with the Tetrarchy. Then, after the suicide of Maximian in 310, a Gallic panegyrist announced that Constantine had experienced a vision of Apollo in a shrine somewhere in Gaul. Occurring in the same speech as a fabricated family connection with the emperor Claudius II (Gothicus), the vision would most naturally be taken as part of a double claim, for divine support, and for the legitimation of his quest for power at a time when, with the death of Maximian, Constantine most needed it. Our knowledge of the second phase depends ultimately on Constantine himself, in an account given late in his life to his Christian panegyrist, Eusebius of Caesarea. Constantine recalled how he had witnessed a vision of a cross standing over the sun, accompanied by the words, "Conquer with this," and the following night had been visited by a dream in which Christ explained to him the meaning of the vision. The third stage was another dream, experienced by Constantine on the evening before the battle of the Milvian Bridge. In this dream, he was told to paint on his troops' shields the Christian monogram (☧) and go to battle "armed with this sign." Doing so, he was victorious over Maxentius. To this point, Constantine's religious affiliations combined two tendencies. They were associated with the sun, the symbol of the all-powerful and all-embracing God of contemporary religious thought, and within this conception had come to focus on Christ as the particular representative of that power who had revealed himself and offered his support to Constantine.

The fourth, and most public, stage of the conversion involves a variety of pronouncements, by Constantine himself in his letters, by panegyrists and on monumental inscriptions, to the effect that his victories had been achieved by his piety to the One True God, to whom the emperor had now devoted himself. Two such statements among many are worth particular emphasis. The Arch of Constantine at Rome bears an inscription stating that the emperor had defeated the tyrant Maxentius "by the inspiration of the Divinity and the greatness of his [i.e. Constantine's] mind," and Constantine himself, writing in 314 to African bishops, measured by his own experience the extent of God's mercy. Referring directly to his conversion, the emperor wrote that there had originally been many things in himself which seemed to "lack justice," and which should have been rewarded with the fate that befalls all wickedness; but God had rescued Constantine from the darkness of ignorance and bestowed on him the salvation which he least deserved. Such statements in the emperor's own letters, in his legislation and in the comments of observers preclude any doubt that Constantine's "conversion," whatever its explanation in terms of his personal psychology, was an event publicized by the emperor, and recognized by contemporaries, as a genuinely religious experience with definite consequences.

Top Constantine and Trier, his early capital, in a gold medallion of 310/15. The emperor, with scepter, stands over the gate of the walled city, below which runs the river Moselle. On either side are defeated barbarians. The medallion of 313 (*above*) shows Constantine "the Unconquered" with his companion the sun, in an explicit recognition of the importance of the sun in Constantine's early religious development. On the shield is the four-horsed chariot of the sun.

Coin issues from later in Constantine's reign, as in this example of about 327 (*opposite top*), show him wearing a diadem, with an upward gaze symbolizing his intimacy with heaven. A medallion of 315, shown *opposite above* in the best of very few surviving examples, is generally taken to show the monogram (☧) on the crest of Constantine's helmet, but it is more likely that the apparent device is merely one of the rosette designs forming the crest. On Constantine's shield are Romulus and Remus with the she-wolf.

In his pronouncements, Constantine frequently emphasizes the personal nature of his relationship with the Christian God, as with the Apollo whom he had seen in his vision at the shrine in Gaul; the orator of 310, addressing Constantine, refers to this as a vision of "*your* Apollo" (*Apollinem tuum*). Further, dreams and visions were part of the regular "technology" of ancient religious experience – one of the standard means whereby the gods were accustomed to communicate with men. Many examples can be found of actions, of the widest possible variety, undertaken in response to dreams and visions. The conversion of St Paul on the road to Damascus is an obvious parallel to the experience of Constantine, but not all such divine messages were as sensational as these. However they are to be explained in terms of individual or collective psychology, it is clear that Constantine's experiences, in which he received revelations and instructions from his God, were part of the regular mode in which men of the ancient world believed these things to happen.

Constantine's religious attitudes were involved also in one of the most significant of all social and political events of antiquity, the foundation of Constantinople. The emperor had visited Rome in 315, for the celebrations of the 10-year anniversary of his rule. Repeating the visit in 326 after his victory over Licinius, Constantine offended the senate and people of Rome by refusing to attend a procession and sacrifice on the Capitol. His rupture with the old capital was followed by the deliberate promotion of Constantinople, the foundation of which, on the site of ancient Byzantium, he had already decided on before his visit to the west. The "New Rome" was built on seven hills, was divided into 14 city districts and possessed its own senate, which was further enhanced in dignity by Constantine's successor, Constantius. The city was dedicated in 330. Despite the report that secret pagan rites were involved in the consecration ceremonies (in 324), Constantinople was from the beginning a city without active pagan cults, except possibly for that of the "Tyche," or Fortune, of the city. Though it contained classical statuary collected from the cities of the east (including what was left of the tripod of Apollo from Delphi), this was "secularized" by being detached from its former religious associations, and the existing pagan temples of old Byzantium were put out of use. The new capital was a city of Christian worship and of great churches, among which those of Holy Peace (Hagia Eirene) and of the Apostles are the best-attested Constantinian foundations. The most famous of all, the church of Holy Wisdom (Hagia Sophia) was probably begun by Constantius.

Constantine's momentous visit to Rome was also connected in some way with a mysterious political crisis affecting his close family. In 326 his son Crispus was executed at Pola in Dalmatia. Then, a little later, Constantine's wife Fausta (Crispus' stepmother) also died, allegedly by being scalded to death in her bath. Not long afterwards, Constantine's mother Helena embarked on a visit, or pilgrimage, to the Holy Land. It has naturally been suspected that part of her intention was to expiate the guilt which had fallen on her family; indeed, the Greek pagan tradition, hostile to Constantine, could inaccurately but with evident plausibility assert that Constantine had been converted to Christianity in order to gain "instant forgiveness" for the murder of his relatives. Helena's visit was associated with a lavish program of church building at Jerusalem and at other places in the Holy Land, in which Constantine took an intense personal interest. He wrote to the bishop of Jerusalem on matters of design and furnishing, and promising financial and administrative help, transportation facilities and other assistance in the works. A pilgrim who went to Jerusalem from Bordeaux in 333 remarked on several occasions on the fine new churches, built by order of Constantine. The most celebrated was the church of the Holy Sepulcher, purporting to mark the very spot of Christ's burial; the church is shown by the 6th-century Madaba map as the dominating feature of Jerusalem. Within a few years of Constantine's death, fragments of the "True Cross" were also displayed at Jerusalem; on one occasion a pilgrim bent over as if to kiss the relic,

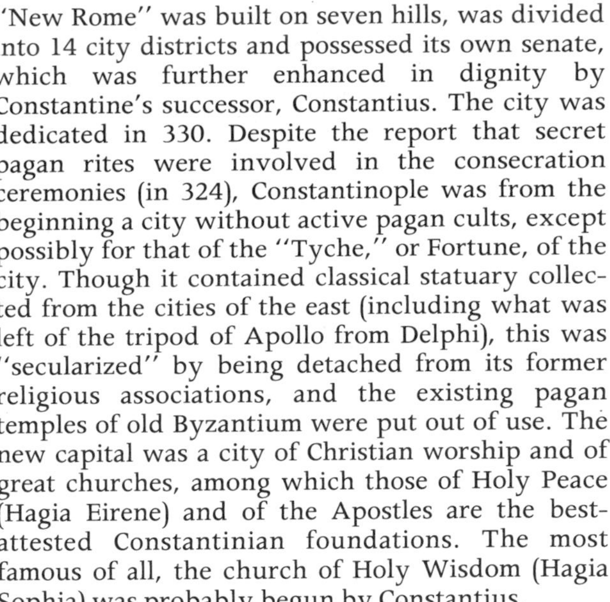

The arch of Constantine at Rome (*right*) was erected to mark the victory over the "usurper" Maxentius in 312. Some of the reliefs of the arch were reused 2nd-century pieces (cf. p. 104), but new sculptures were added which give a summary narrative of the campaign against Maxentius. Here are shown (*below right*) the siege of Verona and (*below*) a detail from a scene at Rome in which Constantine demonstrates his liberality by largesse. The officials take coin from a chest and hand it down for distribution, while one of them keeps a record of expenditure. The furrowed brows are presumably meant to suggest concentration rather than anxiety.

The city of Jerusalem, seen here (*above left*) in a mosaic from the triumphal arch of the 5th-century church of St Maria Maggiore at Rome, and its companion Bethlehem, stand for the churches of the circumcised and of the gentiles. Within the city appear its most distinctive Christian monuments, the Constantinian foundations also shown (*above*) in the relief from a Roman sarcophagus of St Peter being warned by Christ that he will thrice deny him before cockcrow. The three buildings to the left are identified as the church of the Holy Sepulcher and its baptistery, with domed rotunda (known as the Anastasis) over the supposed site of the burial of Christ. The prominence of the baptistery underlines the theme of repentance implied by Peter's denial of Christ.

then ran off with a piece between his teeth! The connection of Helena with the Invention of the Cross is, however, first found only in the last years of the 4th century; it is not part of the contemporary tradition.

Constantine was the founder of other famous churches: the Lateran basilica and St Peter's at Rome, and churches at Cirta (Constantine) in Numidia and at Trier, where he had spent some years in the early part of his reign. It was to Trier that Constantine had summoned the old teacher of rhetoric Lactantius, the author of works of Christian exegesis, and of a ferociously hostile pamphlet denouncing the persecutors of the Christians, to be the tutor of his son Crispus. Lactantius, an African, had taught rhetoric at Nicomedia, the capital city of Diocletian, before coming to Trier in 317 or earlier.

Both in the time of Constantine and throughout the 4th century, a decisive impulse in the process of the Christianization of the Empire was provided by the imperial court. Many of the supporters of Constantine at the highest levels, such as his praetorian prefect Ablabius and the Spaniard Acilius Severus, who was known to Lactantius and is the first known Christian prefect of Rome (326), were Christians whose example and influence undoubtedly had a great effect on the imperial court and through it on society at large. In addition, the bureaucracy drew its recruits from precisely those areas of society, the urban middle classes, in which Christianity had earlier made its deepest impact. In this sense, the conversion of Constantine, though in its own right a personal and unpredictable event, did not exercise its influence in a vacuum, but through the medium of what became one of the major social institutions of the late Empire (see below, p. 201).

The successors of Constantine

The policies of Constantine were not confined to matters of religion, though contemporary critics ascribed the many changes which he introduced in the administrative, financial and military organization of the Empire to the same restlessness of mind which led to his religious innovations. Constantine brought in new taxes, especially the *chrysargyron*, a monetary tax, which was bitterly criticized, on all forms of trade and commerce, and established the basic unit of gold currency, the *solidus*, at the new rate of 72 to the pound which it retained for centuries. In his military policy, Constantine further developed the role of a mobile field army, some believed at the cost of effective frontier defense. He conducted successful foreign wars against German tribes, and later against Goths and Sarmatians on the Danube frontier; his death in 337 took place in the midst of preparations for a major Persian campaign. Constantine was baptized on his deathbed, and his body was taken to Constantinople and buried there in his church of the Apostles. The memorials of the 12 were arranged, six on each side of the emperor, who thereby presented himself as a sort of thirteenth Apostle.

Through his father's second marriage to a stepdaughter of Maximian, Constantine possessed numerous half-brothers and nephews whom he sometimes used to further his political and diplomatic projects. Immediately after the emperor's death these relatives and most of their children were murdered, obviously by a concerted plan, leaving Constantine's own sons, Constantine II, Constantius and Constans as emperors respectively of Gaul with Spain and Britain, of the east, and of Illyricum with Italy. The most obvious direct beneficiary of the assassinations was Constantius, but he was under 20 years old at the time, and it seems more likely that those responsible were powerful politicians and generals who wished to preserve an orderly dynastic succession, free from disputes between different branches of the family.

Constantine II survived only three years before he was suppressed by Constans, who then ruled the west for a further 10 years. In 350 Constans himself fell to a military usurper, Magnentius. Constantius defeated Magnentius at Mursa (351) and Mons Seleucus (353), and became sole ruler of the entire Roman Empire, but it quickly became clear that, in the face of renewed German hostility, the western provinces required separate government by an emperor with local authority. In 355 Constantius overcame his personal dislike and appointed his nephew Julian, the son of one of those massacred in

Right: Mesopotamia and the campaigns of Julian, 363 AD. Julian's strategy in the Persian campaign of 363 was to divert the main army of Shapur by a feigned invasion of northern Assyria, then to attack Ctesiphon rapidly before the king could redeploy his forces. The plan foundered on the resistance of fortified cities like Pirisabora and the garrison near Besouchis, and on the Persians' willingness to obstruct Julian's passage by breaching river and canal banks and flooding the terrain. Julian reached Ctesiphon, but, threatened by the approach of the king's army, abandoned any attempt to take the city, burned the huge fleet which had carried his supplies down the Euphrates but was now an encumbrance, and turned north under constant Persian attack, to be killed in a skirmish. The map suggests the nature of the terrain, with ancient ruined cities left waterless by changing river courses, and complex canal systems. It also acknowledges a fact only fleetingly mentioned by classical sources on the campaign, the presence of a large Jewish population with its famous Rabbinical academies.

Julian the Apostate, seen here (*below*) as consul, appears on his coinage as the bearded philosopher-emperor, an image also taken up by the leader of another pagan "revival," the rhetorician Eugenius (*bottom*). Proclaimed in 392 by the Frankish general Arbogast and supported by members of the Roman aristocracy, Eugenius was defeated by Theodosius at the battle of the Frigidus river (394).

337, as Caesar in Gaul, summoning him from his studies at Athens.

Constantius intended that Julian should be in nominal control of the German wars, leaving their active management to the generals and other officials whom he appointed on his Caesar's behalf. Julian initially acquiesced, and under this arrangement achieved a great victory over the Alamanni near Strasbourg in 357, but as he became progressively more competent at and interested in warfare he asserted his personality more forcibly. Constantius, after visiting Rome in 357, returned to the east to meet a major invasion of Mesopotamia. Needing to strengthen the eastern armies, in 360 he requested reinforcements from Julian, whose response was his proclamation as Augustus, allegedly spontaneous and reluctantly accepted on his own part. In 361 Julian marched east against Constantius, and a potentially destructive civil war which Julian would probably have lost was averted by Constantius' death. He was still under 44 years of age.

Julian's short reign was one of frantic and in some ways ill-balanced activity. Disliking the elaborate ceremony of the imperial office, Julian severely reduced the size of the palace and bureaucratic staffs (the sources select barbers, cooks and eunuchs as the particular victims of these economies), and was strenuous in personally hearing judicial and other matters which were brought to his attention. His chief ambition as emperor was the restoration of the worship of the ancient gods, allied with a program of civic, moral and cultural renewal. His attempt to restore the Temple at Jerusalem was abortive, but restorations in other cities were successfully undertaken. Julian took the first steps towards the creation of a reformed pagan priesthood under which the temples would be administered; social and charitable institutions like those offered by the Christian churches were to be founded for the support of widows and the sick. Believing that a love of classical literature was incompatible with belief in Christianity, he issued an edict, which was widely criticized, forbidding Christians to act as teachers of literature and rhetoric. One of the greatest classical scholars of the day, Marius Victorinus, was forced to resign his chair of rhetoric at Rome, and became equally famous for his Christian doctrinal works; another, Prohaeresius of Athens, was also prevented from teaching but is said to have consulted the hierophant of Eleusis and to have learned that the emperor would not reign long.

Julian's personal religious sympathies were with the school of theurgical Neoplatonism propounded by Iamblichus (see above, p. 177). He was a devotee of Mithras and of Magna Mater, and wrote obscure allegorical tracts on their behalf as well as harsh polemical works against the Christians; the most famous of the latter, *Against the Galilaeans*, is only known from its refutation by a 5th-century writer, Cyril of Alexandria. He sacrificed with unrestrained enthusiasm to the pagan gods, and for this too he was criticized even by his supporters. It is far from certain what degree of sympathy he would have retained from pagans with different religious tastes from his own and more tolerant than he was of their opponents. His policies naturally incurred the bitter hostility of Christian writers, but before they could be fully implemented or their prospects of success demonstrated, the emperor was killed on his ambitious Persian campaign mounted from Antioch in 363.

Julian's successor, Jovian, was proclaimed by the army in Mesopotamia, in the crisis caused by Julian's death in battle. To secure the escape of the army from Persian territory, Jovian was obliged to cede territories in northern Mesopotamia, including five satrapies along the upper Tigris and all the land east of Nisibis and Singara; for these necessary concessions Jovian took the blame deserved by his predecessor. In contrast to Julian, Jovian was a Christian of apparently moderate temper, but before any real policies or attitudes could emerge he too was dead, overcome by the fumes in a recently plastered room in the house in Galatia where he was staying on his journey to Constantinople.

Jovian was succeeded by another military officer, Valentinian, who was nominated by a caucus of high military and civil officials and accepted without demur by the army. Valentinian appreciated the need to share the imperial power and selected as colleague his brother Valens, an apparently unpromising choice with the advantage that it seemed best suited to secure the loyalty between eastern and western parts of the Empire which recent experience had so clearly shown to be essential. In conferences held at Sirmium in the winter of 364/5, the emperors divided the provinces, army and administration between them. Valentinian then went to the Rhine frontier to confront the renewed barbarian threat which had followed the departure of Julian from Gaul in 361. Intent on the need to secure this frontier, Valentinian left his brother to meet and overcome from his own resources the usurpation of Procopius in 365.

The reign of Valentinian was devoted to the military defense of the Rhine frontier, and in its later years of the Danubian frontier of the Empire; his general Theodosius also suppressed a major barbarian incursion into Britain. Valentinian's policy is well attested by archaeology; it involved a

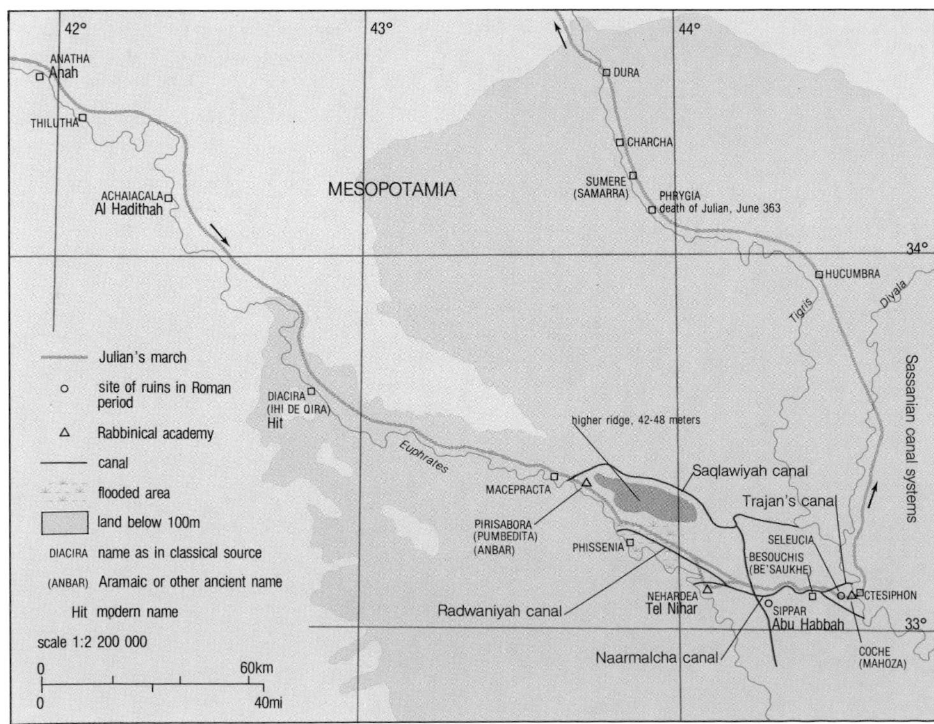

systematic program of fort construction, both along the rivers themselves and at sites lying behind them on routes of penetration into the Roman provinces, supported by punitive raids and reprisals in barbarian territory. His administration was generally characterized by rigor and thoroughness, not to mention the brutality now typical of late Roman government. Nonetheless, the attempts of Tripolitanian cities to confront tribal incursions from the desert were undermined by maladministration and corruption in both provincial and central government, Illyricum suffered from the oppressive administration of its praetorian prefect and Mauretanian Africa was threatened by a serious tribal rebellion, suppressed by Theodosius in 373–75. At Rome, Valentinian's organization of the corn supplies and his building projects won him a lasting reputation, but he provoked the hostility of the Roman nobility by instigating prosecutions there for magic and adultery from 369 onwards. Valentinian died in 375 of a stroke, brought on by his anger at the conduct of envoys of the Quadi whom he was receiving in his camp at Brigetio on the Danube.

The reign of Valens was concerned mainly with foreign wars, against the Goths, whom he attacked successfully in 367–69, and Persia, an indecisive conflict involving the status of Armenia. Valens, like his brother, conducted trials for magic, in which members of the eastern upper classes were involved. These trials involved genuine political dissent among members of the eastern intelligentsia rather than merely, as in the case of those conducted by Valentinian, the immoral behavior of the nobility. The crisis of the reign of Valens came in 376, when the emperor was persuaded to agree to the admission to the Empire of the Visigoths, pushed against the Roman frontier by the expansion of the Huns from their homelands east of the Dnieper river. The attractions of this policy to the emperor lay in the opportunity to acquire large numbers of recruits, which would allow the peasantry to remain on the land rather than be enrolled in the Roman army, and would thereby increase cash revenue from taxation. But the crossing of the Danube was inadequately supervised, the Goths flooded into Thrace in an uncontrolled mass and forced Roman armies to meet them in battle. In August 378 Valens himself encountered the Goths at Hadrianople (Edirne, in European Turkey). The battle was lost; Valens himself was killed and two-thirds of the Roman army destroyed.

In the crisis Theodosius, son of Valentinian's former general, was recalled from private life in Spain and made emperor (January 379). Theodosius

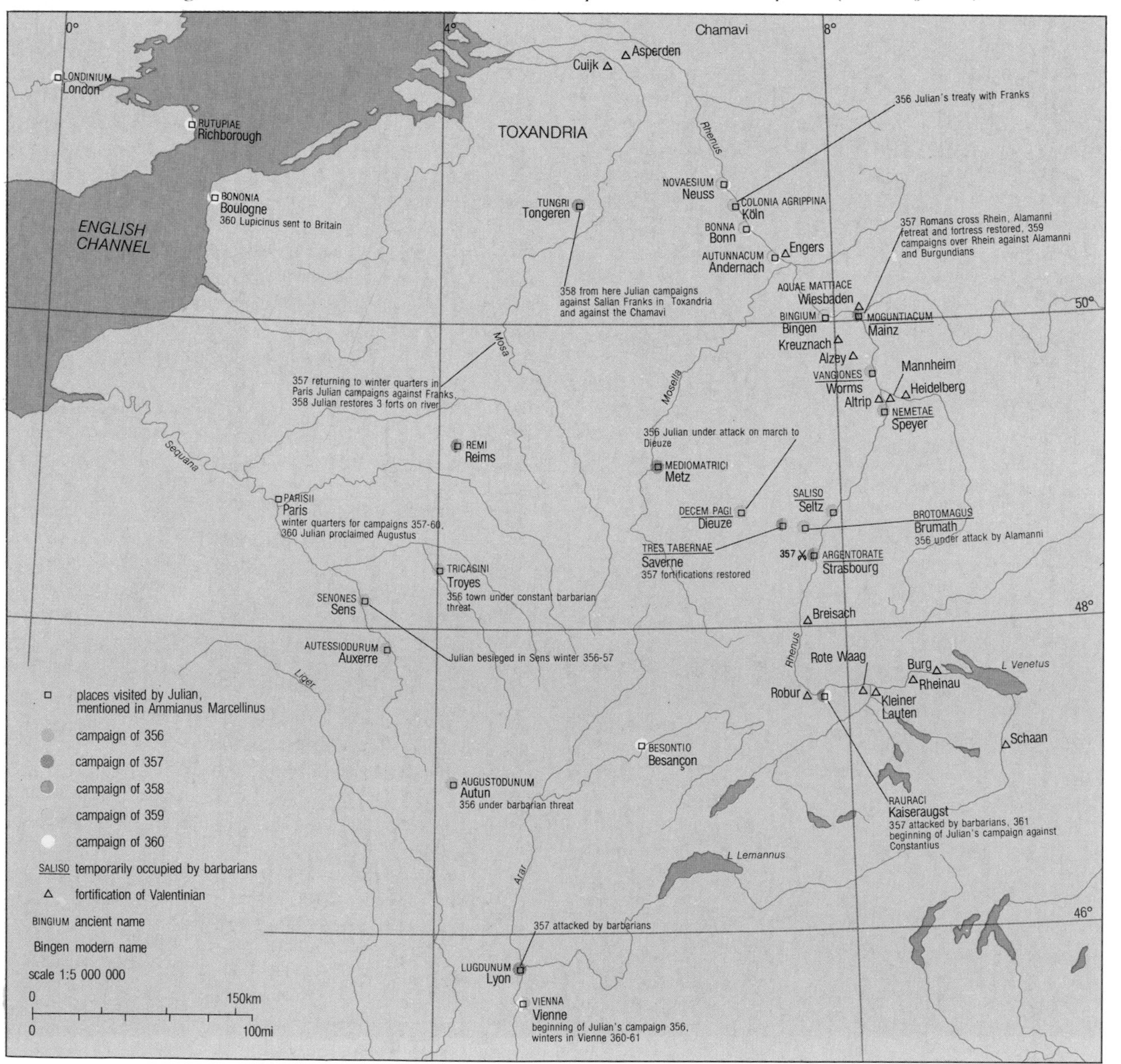

The German campaigns of Julian and Valentinian. On the appointment of Julian as Caesar in Gaul, after several years of political disturbance there, the area under barbarian occupation or threat reached as far west as Lyon, Autun, Sens and Troyes. Julian's campaigns reestablished the frontier as the Rhine, an achievement for which he claimed personal credit and deserved much of it, though there are several signs of his inexperience and the role of the advisers given him by Constantius was probably greater than Julian's admirers would admit. Julian's declaration of war against Constantius deprived Gaul of many troops, and the Persian campaign of 363, undertaken against the explicit advice of the praetorian prefect of Gaul, undermined much of his achievement. The situation was restored by the good sense and patience of Valentinian. It is likely however that the ancient sources, attracted by the personal glamor of Julian's achievements, underrepresent the less spectacular work which he put in hand, in engineering and the construction of frontier defenses.

The beautiful diptych leaf headed "SYMMACHORUM," with its companion "NICOMACHORUM" (in the Cluny Museum at Paris), commemorates some event, possibly a marriage, jointly involving these two leading late 4th-century families. The imagery is both pagan and classical. A priestess makes an offering at an altar, behind which is the oak tree symbolic of Jupiter, while the companion leaf presents images of Ceres and Cybele in a similar composition. Q. Aurelius Symmachus and Nicomachus Flavianus were champions of the traditional cults of Rome in this last generation of their existence. Flavianus fell in the pagan revival of Eugenius (392–94). Symmachus did not actively participate in the civil war and was able to retain his political influence during the last few years of his life and to use it in favour of some who had opposed Theodosius.

devoted the first years of his reign to the Gothic problem, and a treaty of alliance was concluded in 382, whereby the Goths were settled in Lower Moesia and allowed to serve in the Roman army as federates under their own tribal leaders. Theodosius also made a treaty with the Persians in 386. Both alliances are commemorated on the base of the obelisk of Theodosius at Constantinople, erected in 390.

In the west, Valentinian had been succeeded by his sons, Gratian and Valentinian II, then respectively aged 16 and four years old. Both were evidently controlled by their advisers, and Valentinian also by his mother, the forceful Justina, but neither regime made much impact on the government of the Empire, and in 383 that of Gratian fell to the usurper Maximus. Proclaimed in Britain, Maximus had Gratian murdered at Lyon, set up his court at Trier and hoped for recognition by Theodosius. In 387, however, he invaded Italy and unseated Valentinian, who fled to Theodosius. In response, Theodosius marched against Maximus in 388, defeated him and restored Valentinian, whom he sent to Gaul while he himself resided at Milan. Theodosius visited Rome in the summer of 389.

Returning to Constantinople in 391, Theodosius left Valentinian at Trier under the supervision of a Frankish general, Arbogast. In the next year the young emperor was found hanged, probably by suicide, and Arbogast elevated as Emperor Eugenius, a former teacher of rhetoric. Eugenius was used by a group of Roman senatorial supporters as the "front" for a pagan revival at Rome, but in September 394 their forces, under the command of Arbogast and the senator Nicomachus Flavianus, were defeated by Theodosius at the battle of the Frigidus (Wippach) river east of Aquileia. Theodosius came again to Milan and set up his court there, but in January 395 he died, apparently of heart disease, and left the Empire jointly in the hands of his young sons, Honorius in the west, and Arcadius, who ruled the east with equally nominal authority from Constantinople. From this time, if not already from 364, the Roman Empire can be considered effectively divided into eastern and western parts.

The Christianization of the Roman Empire

Writing in the late 4th century, Augustine remarked that the conversion of the Roman world to Christianity had happened "extremely fast." He was quite right in this, especially considering the extent to which the old pagan religion was embedded in the culture, moral values and social organization of classical antiquity. In the splendid chapter 15 of his *Decline and Fall*, Gibbon vividly described the difficulties faced by the early Christians, if they wished to keep their faith pure and yet take part in the regular life of society; in any social event in which they wished or were obliged to participate – weddings, funerals, litigation, "all the offices and amusements of society" – they would be drawn against their will into religious rituals and gestures, "infernal snares" from which they could not stand back without setting themselves apart from everyday life. From the same sources, the ancestral religion gained a tremendous tenacity when forced onto the defensive by an aggressive Christianity supported by the emperors. It proved almost impossible, for the purpose of government action, to isolate the religious elements from the social and cultural contexts with which they were so intimately linked. Constantine himself permitted the establishment of a temple of the second Flavian dynasty at Cirta in Numidia, and at Hispellum in central Italy, with the recorded proviso in the second case that the temple was to be kept free of any suspicion of the "contagion" of sacrifice. Imperial legislation throughout the 4th century, culminating in the laws of Theodosius in the 380s and early 390s, restricted and finally abolished pagan sacrifice; the ancient temples were closed and their estates confiscated, but it proved necessary to reiterate that the games and festivals traditionally associated with the temples were to continue, having been established "for the common enjoyment of all men." By a law of 382, the great temple at Edessa in Osrhoene was closed to religious observance, but maintained as a work of art and museum of antiquity. It was a situation with which the Christian emperors of the 4th century found themselves increasingly familiar.

The most conspicuous element of continuity with the pagan past in the emperors' own position was their retention of the title of *pontifex maximus*. The title was only abandoned by Gratian, probably as late as 382 under the influence of Bishop Ambrose, when an embassy came to Milan from Rome to offer him the pontifical robes. Gratian accompanied his refusal of the robes and rejection of the title *pontifex maximus* by more positive measures. He withdrew from the priestly colleges and Vestal Virgins the financial subsidies and other privileges which they had received for centuries, and removed from the senate-house the altar of Victory, where ever since the days of Augustus senatorial sessions had been inaugurated by a sacrifice. Gratian's action drew from the prefect of Rome, the pagan orator Symmachus, a petition of protest addressed on behalf of the senate to his successor, Valentinian II. Symmachus pressed the claims of the ancestral religion on grounds of custom and utility. The old gods, he argued, had defended Rome through the ages, and their support should not be casually set aside. Symmachus' arguments were unsuccessful against the assertion by Ambrose of the claims of an expanding religion under the patronage of an emperor whose Christian duty it was to support it. The pagan revival of Eugenius and Nicomachus Flavianus in 393–94 was no more than a last gesture of the pagan cause, which went down with its leaders at the battle of the Frigidus.

While the public battle was fought over the preservation of the ancient cults of the Roman state, the attitudes of the late pagans themselves were no less vitally involved with the so-called "Oriental" cults which they had adopted, sometimes in great profusion. The senator Praetextatus (died 384), as we know from his epitaph, combined priesthoods and initiations in no fewer than six Greek and Oriental mystery religions as well as four public priesthoods in the old state cults. These mystery cults, among which those of Magna Mater (Cybele), Mithras and Serapis were prominent, offered purification of the soul and a hope of eternal life to their initiates, and required of them a genuine religious devotion and, at their highest level, philosophical learning. For Praetextatus, as for Julian the Apostate, the gods of the pagan pantheon were united in a Neoplatonic interpretation as the diverse functions of the all-powerful Sun. Initiation into the cult of Magna Mater was by the rite known as the *taurobolium*, in which the initiate stood in a pit under a grille while a bull was slaughtered above him, spraying him with its blood. This rite especially drew the fire of Christian polemic, partly because of its intrinsically distasteful nature, but also because, like other such rites, it functioned as a sort of pagan "baptism" and showed that paganism, as expressed in these cults, had the capacity to appeal to the religious imagination of individuals as well as to the sense of public duty of Roman senators and priests.

Though judgments differ, it seems likely that at the time of Symmachus' appeal to Valentinian, the Roman senate was already, as Ambrose claimed, composed of a majority of Christians. There is at least no doubt as to the *direction* of the change, from paganism to Christianity, as a result of political and social pressure, genuine conversion (though recorded cases of this are rare) and, perhaps most pervasively effective, mixed marriages between Christians and pagans in which the Christian upbringing of the children secured the faith of the next generation.

Whatever point in the transition had been reached by the nobility of the city, the common people of Rome were surely Christianized by the second half of the 4th century, and took a lively interest in the life of its church (on one occasion riots over the election of a bishop of Rome left 137 corpses on the floor of one of the churches). This was also true of the populations of other great cities of the Empire. The case of Antioch is relatively well documented from the writings of the pagan rhetorician Libanius and the Christian priest John Chrysostom. Antioch contained a core of supporters of the old gods, among whom Libanius was prominent. Yet, as Julian the Apostate was shocked to find on arriving there in 362, the general population of the city, a large proportion of its aristocracy and no doubt the majority of the imperial officials there were already firmly Christianized by his day.

As to other Syrian cities, Carrhae was pagan and remained so until much later, while such cities as Heliopolis (Baalbek), Emesa, Arethusa and Berytus retained strong (if not always unanimous) traditions based on ancient cults, as, further south, did Gaza in Phoenicia. Edessa, on the other hand, with its traditions of St Thomas, its martyrs' memorials and its possession of the alleged letters written by Christ to King Abgar, was already strongly Christianized by the time of Julian; he refused even to visit it when invited to do so by an embassy in 363.

Elsewhere in the Empire, Athens retained pagan intellectual traditions into the 5th and 6th centuries; moreover, the rarity of Christian symbols on the many 4th-century clay lamps excavated in the Agora, and the absence of any definitely identified church building or of any well-known bishop in the same period, suggest that the general population also was resistant to Christianity. Alexandria, a center of study for Neoplatonic philosophy and the sciences, was at the same time a hotbed of Christian fanaticism, led by forceful bishops such as Athanasius, whose dominating influence in the city led on several occasions to his exile by the emperors. Apart from its intellectual traditions, Alexandria was notorious for its civic disorders, for which religious divisions no doubt provided yet further opportunities. In 391 a mob, led by monks and incited by the bishop, tore down the great statue and temple of Serapis in the city, one of the great marvels of the ancient world.

The evidence is less full for the western than for the eastern provinces. In the predominantly rural provinces of Gaul, bishops were by the later 4th century turning their attention to the evangelization of their communities, and such sources as the *Life of St Martin of Tours* by Sulpicius Severus show these efforts being directed against traditionally conservative rural areas, with the destruction of local shrines and the beginnings of the organization of parish churches based on townships and villages. The cities, as one would expect, were ahead of the countryside. To take one example, while waiting at Vienne in 360 to embark on his campaign against Constantius, Julian the Apostate, who had already secretly committed himself to paganism, maintained an open profession of Christianity and attended the services for Epiphany. He maintained this pretense in order not to alienate his support, an action which implies clearly that Vienne was a predominantly Christian city.

In Africa, where Christianity had gained an early hold (see above, p. 177), disputes between Catholics and Donatist schismatics seem to presuppose strongly Christianized communities, often with rival bishops, one belonging to each sect. But there were still in the late 4th century spokesmen for paganism, like Augustine's correspondent Maximus of Madauros, and as late as 408 anti-Christian riots occurred at Calama in Numidia when the bishop tried to break up a pagan procession. In general it seems clear that, although most parts of the Empire were predominantly Christian by the late 4th century, local pockets of pagan belief still persisted, often based on traditional associations with certain gods, and that at its more articulate levels paganism, though by now a minority interest, still presented a serious intellectual case requiring reasoned criticism.

Julian, like other Greek intellectuals, used the word *Hellen* ("Greek," that is, educated Greek), to mean a believer in the old gods. Julian's opinion was shared, from the opposite point of view, by Jerome, who argued that the acceptance of Christianity implied the rejection of classical culture and all its links with the pagan past. A third view, represented by the Christian bishop Gregory of Nazianzus, asserted that classical culture was the common possession of all men. Christians, he argued, were capable of appreciating classical literature and benefiting from it without succumbing to its dangers. They too were "Greeks" (Gregory challenged Julian's restrictive use of this word) and it was intolerable that they should be deprived of their heritage as educated human beings. Other writers, like Augustine, wrote tracts defining the use which could properly be made by Christians of classical culture, comparing it sometimes with the "gold of the Egyptians" seized by the children of Israel (Exodus 12:35), but it is clear that it was in effect the position of Gregory that was adopted by the majority. The importance of a classical education for recruitment into the Roman government, and of

Right Late Roman sarcophagi and mosaics, with their iconography of images often taken from the Old Testament and interpreted as a prefiguration of the *tempora Christiana*, provide vivid expressions of the Christian culture of late Roman society. Here are shown the three brothers of the Book of Daniel in the "burning fiery furnace" (*top left*), and Daniel in the lion's den on a 4th-century sarcophagus (*top right*) and on a 6th-century African mosaic (*center right*) – images of triumph over persecution frequently found on the monuments. On the sarcophagus of the Roman senator Petronius Probus, who died after baptism in about 390 and was buried in a family mausoleum at St Peter's (*center left*), Christ hands to the Apostles copies of the "New Law" of Christianity, an allusion interpreted by reference to the Tables of the Law broken and the new Tables received by Moses in Exodus. The detail of Pilate washing his hands, on a sarcophagus from the catacombs of Domitilla, is self-explanatory (*bottom left*), while Jonah and the whale, from an early 4th-century mosaic from the basilica at Aquileia (*bottom right*), symbolizes death and resurrection, or more specifically the salvation of the soul after baptism, an image of obvious appropriateness for a church.

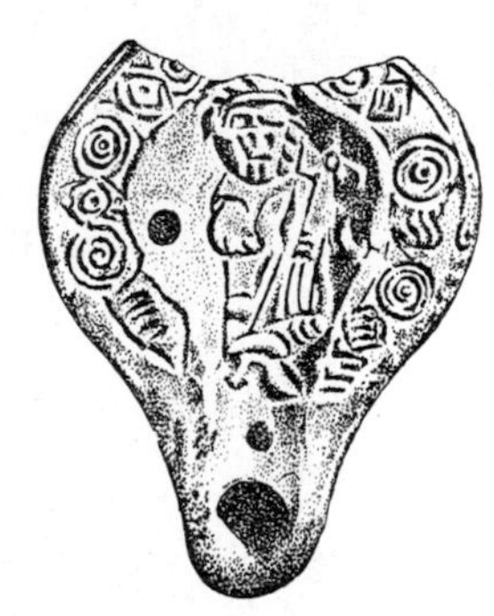

Above Christian and pagan motifs on lamps from the Athenian Agora: Athena, an early 4th-century type revived in the 5th (*top*) and St Peter (*bottom*; 5th century).

Left The Corbridge *lanx*, a rectangular presentation dish, is remarkable for the erudition of its mythological imagery. Its subject is the birth of Apollo and Artemis to Leto on the island of Delos; the "omphalos," or "navel" of the earth, is shown as a column behind the seated figure of Leto. It has been persuasively argued that the version of the legend shown, including the local Delian nymph Asteria (between Leto and Athena), involves a recondite knowledge implying active pagan belief rather than a merely formal classicism of taste. The gesture with which Athena addresses Artemis is very characteristic of the late Roman period.

rhetoric in its conduct, is no less conspicuous in the 4th and later centuries than it had been in the 2nd and 3rd. The examples of men such as Themistius the philosopher (a pagan) and the poet Ausonius (a Christian), who held office under the Christian emperors of the 4th century, could be multiplied many times over without difficulty.

At the same time, the 4th century saw the emergence of a specifically Christian culture, based on the Bible, expounded by bishops and developed in works of exegesis by Christian writers. Jerome's new Latin version of the Bible, the Vulgate, was a conscious attempt to provide a new Christian public with a scholarly and accurate translation; it was supported by a vast program of biblical commentaries, dedicated to Jerome's friends among the Christian aristocracy of Rome but clearly intended for a wider audience.

The Christianization of the Empire involved the acquisition of a new culture, based on the Bible, by a public which did not, in general, expect to lose its old one. This situation implies a certain difficulty in the interpretation of much of the surviving intellectual culture and artistic creation of the late Roman period. In cases where we do not know the religion of a poet, of the recipient of a literary dedication or of the owner of a villa containing mosaics with classical themes, it is tempting to infer this from the nature of the work of art of which he is the author or with which he is associated. On this basis, however, the poet Ausonius, whose work is full of classical themes, might be inferred to have been a pagan, though the evidence for his Christianity is explicit. The coexistence of a genuinely devout Christianity with a continuing love of classical culture was not only a possible but a frequent occurrence.

The church and the emperors

From the moment of the conversion of Constantine, the position of the Christian church in Roman society was transformed. By the so-called Edict of Milan (313) the church received back its property confiscated in the Great Persecution, and, beginning in Africa in the early years of Constantine's reign, acquired additional financial and other benefits from the emperor. The church gained for its clergy exemption from civic obligations (though a cleric was supposed on ordination to guarantee their performance by a substitute), bishops received rights of civil jurisdiction, with or without the consent of both parties. There is no doubting the practical benefits to litigants, who were released from what Constantine called the "interminable meshes of litigation" by this more speedy and honest method of jurisdiction. But there could be obvious abuses, as when Libanius complained of the activities of the bishop of Antioch, who by the exercise of episcopal jurisdiction settled land disputes in favor of the monks who had brought them to him. By their acquisition of such power, bishops quickly became prominent figures in their communities; their churches became important and, by their receipt of donations and legacies, often very wealthy institutions.

Jerome once made a tantalizing unfulfilled promise to write a history in which he would show how the church during the 4th century "grew richer in wealth and possessions but poorer in virtue." Jerome would have enjoyed the historian Ammianus Marcellinus' description of magnificently attired prelates parading around the city of Rome surrounded by crowds of admirers, and eating dinners fit for kings. In this, wrote Ammianus, they contrasted with the humbler and

Right Ambrose, bishop of Milan in the late 4th century, as he is presented, shortly after his lifetime, in a mosaic from the chapel of St Victor at Milan. Although it cannot be proved that it is a realistic portrait, the questioning but confident alertness of the features is a convincing expression of certain aspects at least of the character of this formidably gifted and determined man.

commendable manners of provincial clergy. Yet Jerome's own patron, Damasus (367–83), was not among those bishops of Rome least known for their sense of the high dignity of the office.

Jerome was also thinking of the religious divisions which beset the church in the 4th century. Constantine was dismayed at the outset of his reign by the division in the African church between Catholic and Donatist parties, the latter opposing the ordination as bishop of Carthage of a candidate who was believed to have surrendered the scriptures in the Great Persecution. This schism, which in the 4th century dominated the life of the African church, was only suppressed, amid much rancor, by the efforts of Augustine and his colleagues in the early 5th century, with the help of carefully managed councils supported by imperial legislation.

On his arrival in the east in 324, Constantine was at once confronted by the problem of Arianism. Arius, a priest of Alexandria, had developed theories concerning the nature of God, which owed much of their conceptual framework to Neoplatonic philosophy. He thought of the Trinity as a hierarchy of divine beings, with God the Father at its summit, and argued that the Son, or Logos, though existing before time, was created by the Father and subject to him. In this and related theological systems, the Son is seen as the Demiurge, or creating agency, and as the intermediary between the Father and the world of creation. Orthodox opinion refused to accept any such distinction between the members of the Trinity. At the Council of Nicaea, summoned in 325 to resolve the issue, Constantine himself offered the compromise formula that Father and Son were "consubstantial" (in Greek, *homoousios*) and succeeded in forcing its acceptance on all but two or three recalcitrant clergy, who were exiled. In the event, neither the Council of Nicaea, nor the Creed which it issued incorporating Constantine's formula, could reconcile the differences between the Arian and orthodox positions. The Arian movement remained the dominant opinion of the eastern Empire until Theodosius enforced a strictly "Nicene" definition of orthodoxy and eliminated Arianism as a serious issue in the east.

The emperors were obliged to participate closely in these theological controversies, and sometimes seem to have enjoyed doing so. They were constantly approached by ecclesiastical embassies, they summoned church councils, influenced their proceedings and used secular authority to impose their decisions, and deposed and exiled recalcitrant bishops like Liberius of Rome and Athanasius of Alexandria. Ammianus Marcellinus wrote, albeit with deliberate exaggeration, that in the time of Constantius the imperial transportation service, the *cursus publicus*, was near collapse because of the numbers of bishops traveling to and from synods with imperial permission.

Despite their involvement in the conduct of church councils and their use of the secular arm to enforce their outcome, and despite the great and threatening authority which they sometimes brought to bear on the church, the 4th-century emperors were never in the position of themselves defining official doctrine, nor were they in any way conceived of as heads of the church. Indeed, the position aspired to by Julian, who wrote letters to the priests of his reformed paganism showing them how they should dress and behave in public, what they should read and what doctrines they should accept, was far more theocratic and "Caesaropapist" than that of any of the Christian emperors.

In the west, Bishop Ambrose of Milan exerted great influence over the emperors who were at various times resident in the city. In 389, by publicly challenging Theodosius in his crowded cathedral at Milan, he forced the emperor to rescind an order to the bishop and congregation of Callinicum on the Euphrates to restore a synagogue which they had destroyed; the following year by similarly direct methods he made Theodosius perform penance for a massacre carried out by his soldiers at Thessalonica. Ambrose had a very clear conception of the duties of a Christian emperor, yet no contemporary source interprets any of these occasions as an issue of principle between "church" and "state." Despite the advantages won by the church and the immense influence exercised by certain bishops, the church acquired no recognized formal position in the constitutional structure of the late Roman state. Its relationship with the imperial government was and remained that of a privileged and well-organized pressure-group.

The ascetic movement

The end of persecution produced for the Christian community a dilemma as to the nature of spiritual virtue. A "martyr" in earlier times was precisely what the Greek word means, a "witness," one who publicly "confessed" his faith under the extreme threat of death. After persecution ended, a new form of expression was required by those Christians who still felt the need to confess their faith as vigorously as seemed to be implied by the New Testament. The Donatist movement in 4th-century Africa maintained the authentic attitudes of early Christianity, in a society in which the position of Christianity had been transformed, a position which evoked the more measured and realistic approach of their opponent Augustine. "Like frogs," he wrote, "they sit in their marsh, croaking 'We are the only Christians!'"

The need felt by some 4th-century Christians to belong to an elite of sanctity was partly answered by the growth of the ascetic movement. A sense of self-perfection by physical and intellectual discipline, as we have seen (p. 177), was a central aspect also of late classical philosophical practice; the emperor Julian, according to Ammianus Marcellinus, lived a life of quite conspicuous austerity, "as if he would soon return to the philosopher's cloak" (25.4.4). Yet the view maintained by late classical philosophy, of the physical body as an encumbrance to be mastered by discipline in order to free the mind for a higher contemplation of God, takes on in the Christian ascetic movement a more disquieting aspect. The body comes to be seen as actively hostile to the spirit, not merely to be trained by discipline but to be punished by extreme forms of ascetic behavior. The resulting body-spirit dualism led to suspicion of heresy. It was associated with the Gnostics and Manichees, according to whom the individual human being was the battleground of the opposing forces of good and evil, with the body, the vehicle of the evil forces, being the creation of the devil. The problem of the source of evil was central to Augustine's intellectual development; the difficulties inherent in the need to reach a proper balance in ascetic behavior are the subject of many treatises on virginity, and of letters of instruction written to prominent Christian laymen by spiritual advisers such as Jerome.

The main traditions in the development of the ascetic movement are represented by two men, both Egyptians: Pachomius and Antony. In the late 3rd century Pachomius had established a mode of living for societies of monks; they were organized in communities, owned essential possessions in common, satisfied their basic economic needs by their own labor, sold surpluses for charity and followed certain rules of religious and social conduct. This was the origin of the monastic movement, as further formulated in the *Rule* of Basil of Caesarea and in due course in the west by Cassian and Benedict, the founders of medieval monasticism. Antony, whose biography by Athanasius of Alexandria was immensely influential, represented the eremitic tradition in asceticism, living in increasing isolation from communal life and pursuing his spiritual perfection in solitary contemplation and self-imposed privation. The temptations of St Antony by the devil in the wilderness were a potent theme in the religious art of later ages.

The ascetic movement influenced the life of the 4th-century church in a variety of ways. Earlier in his religious career, Jerome had passed an unhappy period as a hermit in the Syrian desert. For Jerome, the monastic setting was the base for intellectual and academic work, for the writing of the translations and commentaries mentioned earlier and for the bitter theological controversies for which he was equally famous. For Jerome's contemporary Augustine, bishop of Hippo Regius in North Africa, a monastic community attached to the episcopal church was an environment for reading, meditation, discipline and communal living, from which new priests might emerge to become the bishops of the next generation. The community on the island of Lérins off the south coast of France performed a similar function in relation to the bishoprics of southern Gaul in the 5th century.

The establishment by Martin of Tours of the monastery of Marmoutiers (*maius monasterium*, the "greater monastery") in central Gaul introduces a further contribution of some importance made by the ascetic movement to late Roman society. From his association with the monastic life, Martin gained a reputation for spiritual authority going far beyond his office as bishop. He was believed to possess direct contact with divine power, by virtue of which he was able to perform miracles, and with which he charged his campaigns of aggressive evangelization. The activities of Martin bring out one of the most disturbing implications for traditional Roman society of the growth of the ascetic movement. Believing themselves to be directly inspired by the divine will, local monks banded together in some parts of the Empire to attack local shrines and pagan institutions. In doing so they were sometimes encouraged by the local bishop and apparently not restrained by the imperial authorities; on certain occasions, indeed, the local authorities gave their active support to these blatantly illegal activities. The Donatist controversy in North Africa produced the so-called "circum-

The distribution and influence of monasticism, 300–500 AD. The early diffusion of monasticism followed definite routes, often linked with geographical mobility arising out of ecclesiastical disputes. Contending bishops such as Athanasius of Alexandria from the beginning harnessed in their interests the prestige of the ascetic movement, while Hilary of Poitiers and Eusebius of Vercelli brought back the monastic example from their exiles in the east by the Arian Constantius II. The influence of other westerners such as Jerome, and of John Cassian in 5th-century Gaul, was linked with their respective roles in eastern theological controversies. The prestige of the ascetic was often seen as a challenge to episcopal authority, but bishops such as Martin of Tours and Augustine were able to harness the two and monasteries, like that of Lérins, became training grounds for episcopal office. The monastic traditions in 5th- and 6th-century Britain and Ireland reflect two phases: contacts between the Celtic peoples of Britain and those of western Gaul (represented also in the later diffusion of manuscripts from the Mediterranean to Ireland via the western sea routes), and the conversion of Saxon Britain begun by Augustine of Canterbury.

cellions," bands of crudely armed fanatics who went around shouting "Praise to God" and intimidating, injuring and sometimes killing Christians of the opposing party. For pagan observers, such "tyrants" were violating all standards of civilized behavior, moral and legal; it is in this that the reproach sometimes leveled against the monastic movement, that it promoted an attitude which undermined the morale of Roman society, can be appreciated most keenly.

This reproach forms part of a general criticism of the 4th-century church, that it attacked the moral purpose and the physical resources of the Roman Empire. It did this, so it is argued, by encouraging an ideology which was at its highest other-worldly and at its lowest antisocial in its violence against secular institutions and property, and by absorbing resources of finance and manpower which the imperial government could not afford to lose. As for the first part of this criticism, the notion that the church was other-worldly in the 4th century was, as we have seen, doubted by Jerome. The leaders of the church in this period seem to have lacked neither ambition nor a genuine sense of charity and public responsibility, while the bishops acquired certain rights, such as episcopal jurisdiction, which gave them a definite and useful role in secular society. The violence of Christians against their opponents, pagan or heretic, is as likely to have reinforced existing attitudes as to have undermined them; the more likely danger here is that of polarization rather than of indifference. As for the criticism that the church diverted resources and manpower from the state, this had best form part of a general discussion of the nature of the 4th-century Roman state and its relationship with Roman society.

The late Roman state and society

That the late Roman Empire was above all a bureaucratic state is universally admitted; by the term "bureaucratic" is meant that it was a government organized by departments (*officia*) with defined spheres of activity, served by salaried officials among whom promotion was by rules of seniority and precedence, that serving officials felt a sense of loyalty to their departments and that at the regular administrative levels there existed a high degree of continuity of service, whatever political upheavals might take place at higher levels. It was also, by a more everyday definition of bureaucracy, a government characterized by masses of paperwork. One particularly important source gives the impression that the organization of the government might even be appreciated as a work of art in itself; this tribute to bureaucratic self-awareness is the

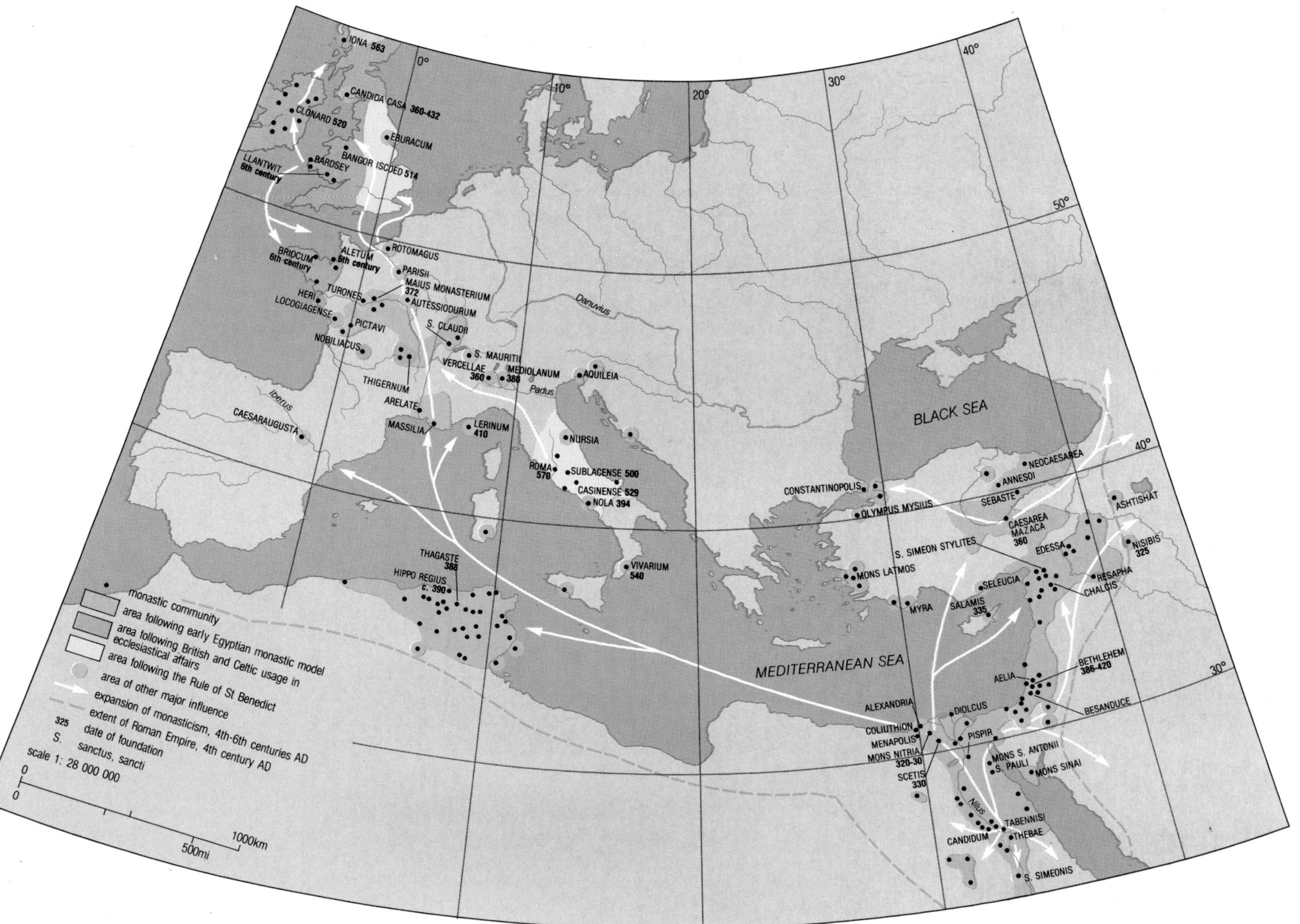

Notitia Dignitatum, a compilation, with illustrations of their insignia, of the administrative departments and military postings as they were at the end of the 4th and beginning of the 5th century.

The *Notitia Dignitatum* gives only a partial impression of the sheer scale of the operations of the late Roman government, whose agents must be numbered not only in those who held office at the imperial court, but throughout the provinces also: superintendents of provincial treasuries, accountants in charge of the supplying of regional armies, supervisors of mints and arms factories, officials sent out to draw up tax assessments, managers of imperial property and so on. Some, but not all, of these officials would be listed in another document, the *Laterculum minus* ("Register of Lesser Dignitaries"), which is mentioned once or twice by the *Notitia Dignitatum* but does not survive.

To the modern, as no doubt to the late Roman observer, the most obvious fact about the methods of this government, so elegantly illustrated in the *Notitia*, was the violence with which it tried to impose its will. The Theodosian Code, a compilation of 4th- and early 5th-century legislation made between the years 429 and 437 and covering all conceivable areas of legislative and administrative practice, provides a fearsome display of punishments. In two laws of Constantine, the hands of civil servants who accept bribes are to be cut off, and the mouths and throats of accessories to the abduction of unmarried girls are to be stopped with molten lead – outbursts of rhetorical aptness far from unparalleled in the Code and in other sources. Torture was regularly applied, not in its "proper" function of extracting truthful information in a court of law, but as a refinement before execution and as a punishment in itself. The use of such penalties and others is confirmed by many literary references, and especially by Ammianus Marcellinus, who takes us as close as any source to the atmosphere of terror with which the late Roman emperors defended their rights, especially when they feared that their position was being challenged by treason and its associated arts, magic and the reading of the future from horoscopes.

The moral tone of late Roman legislation was very little affected by the Christianization of the Empire. The influence of Christianity in individual cases can be seen very clearly. Constantine is said to have abolished the penalty of crucifixion and the breaking of legs, and one of his laws forbids branding on the face, "lest the image of divine beauty be disfigured." Laws were issued at various times in the 4th century on Sunday observance, and Easter amnesties were sometimes offered to criminals, certain categories always being excluded. It is possible, though far from certain, that increasingly harsh legislation on adultery, greater severity in divorce law and greater moral outrage on such matters as male prostitution and the immorality of actresses, were inspired by Christianity. In general, it is impossible to assert that late Roman legislation was more humane than earlier, and it is certain that in its treatment of religious dissent it became progressively more intolerant.

The political and social aims of late Roman legislation were in the emperors' own minds very clear: the maintenance of their own position and of public order, and the organization of society as best suited the needs of government. To this end, late Roman society was set out, as it were, as an array of economic instruments and agencies, each with its defined function in relation to the needs of the government.

The impression given by imperial legislation of the 4th century is that Roman society was more rigid and more firmly tied by hereditary obligation than ever before. It is possible however that the new image of late Roman society preserved in the laws is a reflection, less of actual changes in society itself, than in the needs of the government. There is no doubt that the *incidence* of late Roman government, as measured by its legislation and by the number of its officials, was far greater than at earlier times, and its impact more direct. Perhaps this should be seen as a consequence of the recognition by the imperial authorities of the late Roman period that they had more requirements to satisfy and more ends to meet, and they tried to achieve this by simply doing more governing.

Recent opinion is rightly inclined to emphasize two factors: the degree of social mobility still inherent in late Roman society, and, on the other hand, the conservatism of ancient society in general. As in many other times and places, sons tended to follow their fathers' occupations; bakers, soldiers, merchants and shipowners enjoyed certain advantages in life, a definite profession and a recognized role in society. It might not always be apparent that these attractions could be improved on. Still more evidently, peasant communities in any society are indifferent or resistant to change; they hang on to old ways of life and old modes of belief (it is no accident that the word *paganus*, used

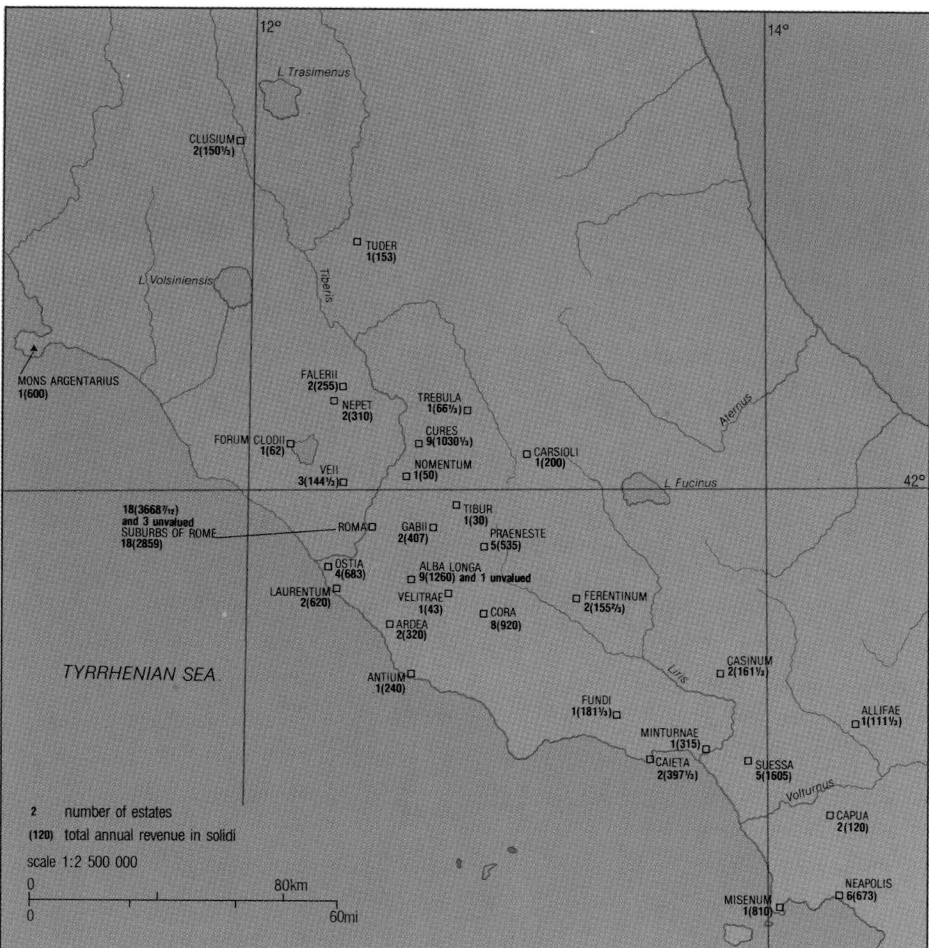

The early 6th-century compilers of the *Liber Pontificalis* were able to include in their biographies of the Roman bishops from 314 to 440 AD lists of the estates with which 16 churches at Rome and one each in Ostia, Albano, Capua and Naples were endowed by their founders. Apart from 36 properties elsewhere in the Empire, there are 122 in mainland Italy; in addition to the name and location of each estate the lists give in all but four cases the cash revenue that each was expected to produce.

The donor of 84 of these Italian properties is stated to have been Constantine. The other estates come from a senator Gallicanus, the will of a woman of high social standing named Vestina, and several of the popes themselves.

While there were doubtless many other unrecorded church endowments in this period, the surviving details show an ownership pattern of large numbers of small and scattered estates that is likely to be typical not merely of the imperial or private donors and the recipient churches but also of other wealthy families and corporations such as temples. Land was wealth, and could be accumulated by "casual" acquisitions over many generations. Constantine's estates include former properties of the emperors Augustus and Tiberius, Maecenas, senators of the early Empire, and a Christian whose land had been confiscated in time of persecution – and even the abandoned barracks of a legion since stationed elsewhere.

in Christian polemic to denote a believer in the old gods, actually means "villager" or "countryman").

However, it is possible to assemble many individual cases of social mobility of types debarred or discouraged by legislation, "success stories" of escapes from hereditary obligations: a baker becomes a provincial governor, the son of a town councillor a teacher of rhetoric (and later a bishop), a soldier becomes a monk and so on. The problem, as always, is one of quantification. The examples give a certain impression, which it is impossible to measure by anything approaching a scientific method. But the impression is worth something, especially since it is confirmed by examination of a topic that yields to more analytic discussion: the role of the imperial court itself, ironically in view of its aims for society, as a source of social mobility and of opportunities for evasion.

The *comitatus* appears in late Roman sources in a wide variety of guises: as the center of government, the scene of earnest discussions at moments of crisis, of litigation, the petitions of embassies, of political dispute and sudden death, but also as a sort of intellectuals' "club," attracting the gifted, ambitious and educated, fostering literary pursuits, providing the setting for elegant dinner parties as well as for the serious discussions of religious and philosophical matters such as those recorded for the court society of Milan in Augustine's *Confessions*. All of these are facets of its activity which can be readily attested from the ancient sources.

The court also functioned as an economic stimulus in those regions where it settled. The presence of an imperial court at Trier opened opportunities for a flock of aspirants from the cities of central and southwestern Gaul, which had in the early Empire taken little part in Roman political life. The same is true, in relation to the court of Constantinople, of the inland districts of Anatolia, where the Cappadocian bishops, Gregory of Nazianzus, Basil of Caesarea and Gregory of Nyssa, are expressions of the cultural and political "arrival" of a previously unassertive part of the eastern Roman Empire.

The role of the court is more fully illuminated by the letter-collections of some prominent figures in public life who had dealings with it: in the west, the orator Symmachus, and in the east, the rhetorician Libanius of Antioch and the Cappadocian bishops. From such sources it becomes clear that in addition to their role as imperial officials, many of the correspondents at court of these influential patrons were also the sources of benefits, privileges and exemptions for them and their friends. What can appear from the Theodosian Code as a caste-ridden society, rigidly defined by imperial legislation, often dissolves in the other evidence into a series of inconclusive running battles between the emperors and the intended objects of their legislation, the latter only too often using the emperors' own agents to defend themselves and maintain their privileges.

It would be misleading to describe this simply as "corruption," though the emperors were fully aware of the collusion of imperial officials with private vested interests, and tried to prevent it (by yet more legislation); it was simply the manner in which the government functioned in its social context. The late Roman Empire should be seen as a pluralist society with a multiplicity of vested interests, impinging on the government as effectively as their influence allowed. Two of the better-organized vested interests are worth mention.

The role of the Christian church, and the privileges won by it under the Christian emperors of the 4th century, have already been described. The church, with the bureaucracy itself, has been seen by some modern critics as one of the main sources of weakness in the late Empire, in that it attracted to its service men who would otherwise have been of use to the state. But bishops, like rhetoricians and charioteers, were among the great individualists of the late Empire. It is far from certain that they would have shone in the imperial service as brilliantly as they shone in the church, or that the imperial service would have gained perceptibly from their support as bureaucrats and officials. If Ambrose had become a praetorian prefect like his father, could he have expressed himself in that office with the panache allowed him by his bishop's *cathedra*?

The second main vested interest was the Roman senate, representing through an institution of no great political power but of immense historical prestige the interests of the landed nobility of Italy and the western provinces. (The senate of Constantinople, recruited from the landed families of the east, was always entwined with the eastern imperial court and never possessed the same corporate independence as did its counterpart at Rome.) Under the guidance of the prefect of Rome and of the *princeps senatus*, the leading senator in seniority and prestige, the senate governed Rome and a large part of central and southern Italy as its own domain. Senators possessed great landed wealth in Italy, Sicily and North Africa, and fortified their influence in these areas by governorships and by inherited ties of patronage. Through their economic influence, prestige, and their political organization based on the senate, the Roman aristocracy was able to exert great and continuing pressure on the emperors.

The immense wealth of the senatorial nobility of Rome cannot be over-emphasized; it was spent conspicuously on luxurious building, traveling in style, dressing ostentatiously and maintaining great household establishments with whole "armies" of slave attendants, and in largesse to colleagues and to the people of Rome, especially in financing public games. The cash incomes of some senatorial families from rentals on their estates ranged, according to one contemporary source, from 4000 pounds of gold to 1500 in the case of senators of "moderate" wealth, with another third which could be realized by the sale of surplus produce. Senatorial expenditure on public games was also lavish. The orator Symmachus, a senator of "moderate" wealth, laid out 2000 pounds of gold on his son's praetorian games in 401. At a time when the imperial government was increasingly handicapped by financial difficulty, the Roman senatorial class has justly received blame for its part in the political collapse of the western Empire. Yet it must be admitted that the role of the aristocracy of Italy during the period after the Visigothic invasion and sack of Rome in 410 was fundamental in achieving a degree of Roman continuity in that period. It was a role which came to an end only with the reconquest of Justinian.

The Bureaucracy

"A splendid theatre, filled with players of every character and degree": so Gibbon described the late Roman bureaucracy, referring especially to the illustrations of the *Notitia Dignitatum*, of which a selection is shown on these pages. The *Notitia*, or "Register of Civil and Military Dignities," was compiled in the mid-390s and its western sections used in the imperial administration until about 425. It then passed out of official use, but survived as part of a dossier of late Roman official and quasi-official documents copied in the 9th century. The examples shown here are from a manuscript in the Bodleian Library, Oxford, copied in 1436 from the 9th-century Carolingian manuscript. The successive illustrators of the manuscript clearly tried to show accurately the late Roman insignia, though they exercised some freedom in presenting certain decorative features such as clothing.

The administrative structure of the late Roman state, as presented in the *Notitia*, was headed by the emperor (here Constantius II, on a gold multiple struck at Nicomedia); usually there was a college of two or more emperors, ruling independently but maintaining a front of unity. The administration was from the time of Diocletian strictly divided between military and civil functions. The mobile field armies, east and west, were commanded by Magistri, or "Masters" of cavalry and infantry. Shown here are the insignia of the western Master of the Infantry and some of his troops' shield devices. Below the Magistri were the commanders, entitled Comites and Duces ("Counts" and "Dukes") of the regional armies, listed by the *Notitia* for all provinces. The Comes Domesticorum commanded the elite palace guard, again divided, as shown below, into horse and foot. The duties of the Castrensis were to maintain the palace establishment, a more complicated task than one might suppose, given the constant mobility of late Roman emperors.

Heading the civil administration were the praetorian prefects of Italy with Africa and Illyricum, Gaul with Spain and Britain, and of the east, from Thrace to Arabia. Their responsibilities extended both to court and to provincial administration, in the latter being much concerned with taxation. The Master of the Offices controlled the administrative staffs, regulated audiences with the emperor and coordinated the general running of the court administration. The Count of the Sacred Largesses controlled mints and mines, received monetary taxation and supervised the payment of donatives and cash salaries; another official, the Count of the Imperial Portfolio, administered state property. The Quaestor of the Sacred Palace was responsible for framing imperial communications in a suitable literary form and was himself often a well-known literary figure. The Primicerius Notariorum headed the corps of imperial secretaries, or "notaries."

The insignia of officials are shown as a set of codicils – letters of appointment set in gold and ivory frames and bearing the imperial portrait – or as a book with formulae of goodwill emblazoned on its cover, and scrolls. The codicils, and sometimes the books, are set on a table with patterned coverlet. In some cases an engraved ivory column appears standing on a tripod base. This was a ceremonial inkstand, symbolizing judicial competence.

The insignia of the Comes Domesticorum, shields resplendent in purple and gold, express his position in the palace establishment. The winged Victories bearing the imperial portrait are, from a Christian perspective, readily transformed into angels. The first two units shown under the western Magister Peditum, "Joviani" and "Herculiani," preserve the Tetrarchic titles Jovius and Herculius.

Provincial armies are represented by a symbolic city or group of cities. The duties of the Count of Italy, a late innovation, are represented by the Alps with their barricades (actual or symbolic), the Claustra Alpium. Belgica Secunda was the coastal region of northern France; the Litus Saxonicum or Saxon Shore was part of a system of coastal defense (see map p. 171).

For the Castrensis, pictures of palace furniture including an embossed silver casket containing perfume flasks.

Comes Domesticorum.

Comes Italiae.

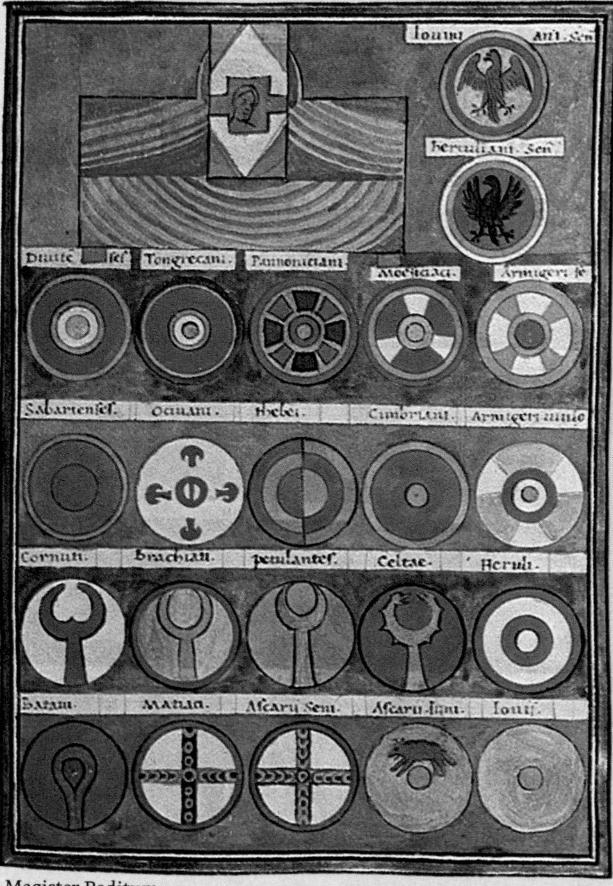

Magister Peditum.

Dux Belgicae Secundae.

Castrensis.

The three ladies, Italia, Africa and Illyricum, represent the dioceses under the praetorian prefect of Italy. Their baskets contain the tribute in taxation of the provinces. Their "modernized" dress is self-evident; equally so is the accuracy of detail preserved in other cases by the Carolingian and Renaissance copyists, who did not always understand what they reproduced. The consular province of Campania is shown, rather unusually, as a lady with shield and placard, sitting on a platform in a curtained alcove. The table with book is cunningly worked into the composition as part of the furniture of the alcove. Apulia and Calabria are the example given by the *Notitia* of a province governed at the rank of Corrector. The abbreviated legend on the book, slightly corrupted, reads "I [?] feliciter; Vale corrector iussu dominorum" ("Go [?] in prosperity; farewell, Corrector by order of our lords").

Italia, Illyricum, Africa.

Campania.

Apulia, Calabria.

Magister Officiorum.

Comes Sacrarum Largitionum.

Quaestor.

Primicerius Notariorum.

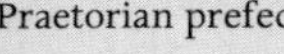
Praetorian prefect.

The insignia of the praetorian prefect, apart from the ceremonial inkstand and codicil mentioned above and a set of candlesticks, were a four-horsed carriage, as also boasted by the prefect of Rome. Such details as the decorative heads on the carriage have been faithfully, and in the case of the inkstand uncomprehendingly, represented. The arms factories (*fabricae*), shown as the preserve of the Master of the Officers, were in fact only acquired by him in 390; this is one argument for the dating of the *Notitia Dignitatum*. The various items of equipment – shields, arrowheads, breastplates – were manufactured in specialized workshops. The functions of the Quaestor are shown by scrolls and a column, perhaps optimistically inscribed "beneficial laws," and those of the Count of the Sacred Largesses by items of wealth in a form suitable for distribution – gold and silver coins, buckles, laurel leaves, presentation dishes. Also seen are bags of money with symbols of value and a money chest. The *Notitia* itself, or Laterculum Maius ("Greater Register"), is illustrated (*bottom right*) as a bound book with straps and tags to fasten it. Its maintenance was among the duties of the Primicerius Notariorum.

The City of Constantine

From the first days of its construction, Constantinople grew with amazing speed, commanding unlimited financial resources and attracting craftsmen and materials from the entire east. The Megarian colonists who had settled Chalcedon in the 7th century BC had been called "blind" for ignoring the richer site of Byzantium. In the context of the late Empire, however, the new city came into its own, standing between east and west, more particularly between Asia Minor and the northern land mass of the Balkans.

Its expansion saw a building "boom," evidently with much profiteering. Within a couple of generations, claimed critics, mansions built for its new nobility were already collapsing. Constantinople also acquired monumental squares and public buildings (see plan) with a notable absence of pagan temples but many Christian churches. A 5th-century source, the *Notitia* of Constantinople, lists 14 of these, together with 11 palaces of emperors and empresses, five markets, eight public and 153 private baths, 20 public and 120 private bakeries, 52 porticoes, 322 streets and 4388 houses.

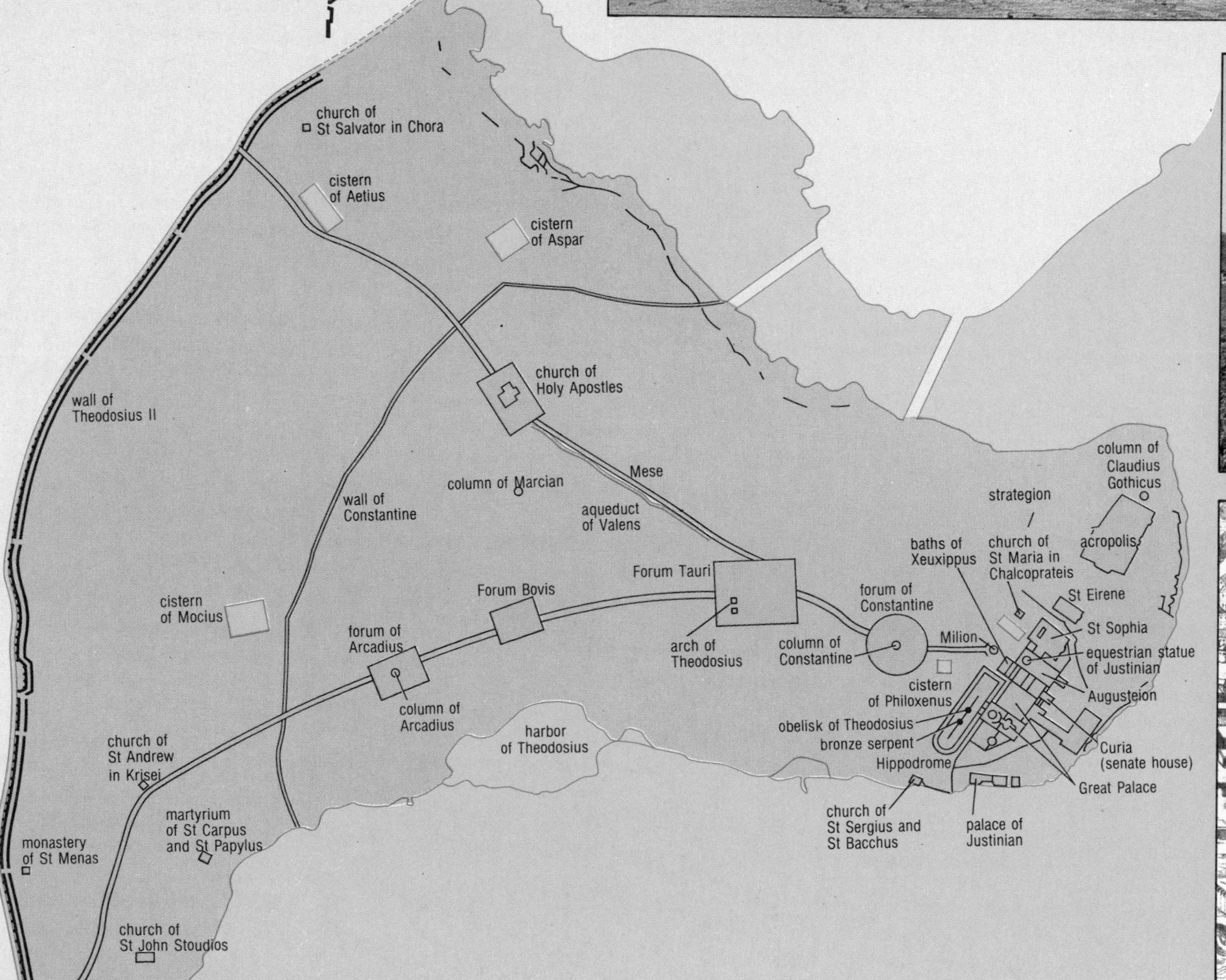

Below The frontispiece to the *Notitia* of Constantinople, as preserved in a manuscript of 1436. The vignette contains anachronisms, but well displays the configuration of the city, in which St Sophia and the Hippodrome are conspicuous. The equestrian statue is of Justinian.

The land walls of Constantinople (*below*) represent a doubling of the enclosed area of the city since its foundation by Constantine. Built in 413 by the Praetorian Prefect Anthemius, they were in 447 badly damaged by an earthquake and rebuilt within two months. The now vanished Hippodrome (*bottom*) is here seen in an engraving by Panvinio (c. 1580), showing the column of Justinian (here without its famous equestrian statue), the obelisk of Theodosius, which alone still survives *in situ*, and in the foreground the sea walls of Constantinople.

Justinian's new church of St Sophia (Holy Wisdom), the masterpiece of the architects Anthemius of Tralles and Isidore of Miletus, was consecrated in 537, five years after the destruction of its predecessor in the Nika riots (see p. 223). It is here seen (*below* and *opposite*) in two views published in 1852 by the architect Fossati, who had been commissioned by the sultan to supervise its restoration. Despite its massively imposing exterior (for contemporary historical accuracy the building must of course be imagined without the surrounding minarets), St Sophia is designed above all to be experienced from the inside; and here Fossati, choosing an ideal perspective, has beautifully conveyed its essential character – the rich splendor of the light, and the huge but harmonious space which it defines. These, and the dome, "floating as if suspended from heaven," were precisely the features which most appealed to a contemporary, the writer Procopius. The dome was, and remains, an architectural marvel; but it is worth recalling that the first attempt collapsed 20 years after its erection, to be replaced by the still more ambitious structure which stands today.

Late Imperial Rome

The "Calendar of the Year 354," whose dedicatory frontispiece is shown *below*, includes both traditional and Christian material. Its designer Furius Dionysius Filocalus, was a calligrapher also employed by Pope Damasus; his name appears on the fragmentary inscription also shown (*opposite*). Like his

VALEN TINE
FLOREAS IN DEO
VALENTINE
VALENTINE VIVAS FLOREAS
LEGE
VALENTINE VIVAS GAUDEAS
FELICITER

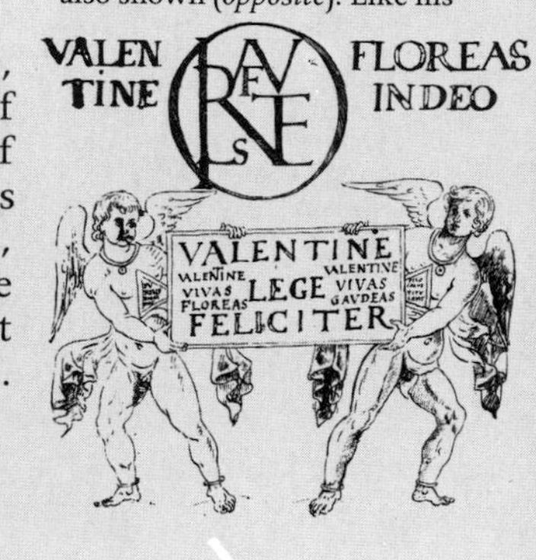

After the conversion of Constantine, Rome rapidly emerged as a great center of Christian culture. The vigor of the late imperial city was in part a consequence of the emperors' departure for their new capitals on the frontiers. In their absence from Rome – to its admirers still the "Eternal City" – its senatorial class and people asserted themselves with a lack of inhibition (not to mention periodic violence) lost since the late Republic. Simultaneously with its emergence as a Christian city, Rome also produced an efflorescence of classical culture, both literary and visual, and even a late revival of the ancestral pagan religion under a small group of pagan senators (see p. 193); but as the city was progressively christianized, old habits of patronage, intellectual and material, were transferred to the advantage of the Christian church, and great basilicas and martyr shrines were built everywhere.

Roman churches and their modern equivalents
t = titulus (parish church by c.500)

t Aequitii (Silvestri) = St Martino ai Monti
t Apostolorum = St Pietro in Vincoli
t Byzantis (Pammachii) = St Giovanni e St Paolo
t Fasciolae = St Nereo e St Achilleo
t Gaii = St Susanna
t Iulii iuxta forum Traiani = St Apostoli
t Iulii trans Tiberim = St Maria in Trastevere
Basilica Lateranensis = St Giovanni in Laterano
in Lucinis = St Lorenzo in Lucina
t Praxedis = St Prassede
S Stephani = St Stefano Rotondo sul Celio
t Vestinae = St Vitale

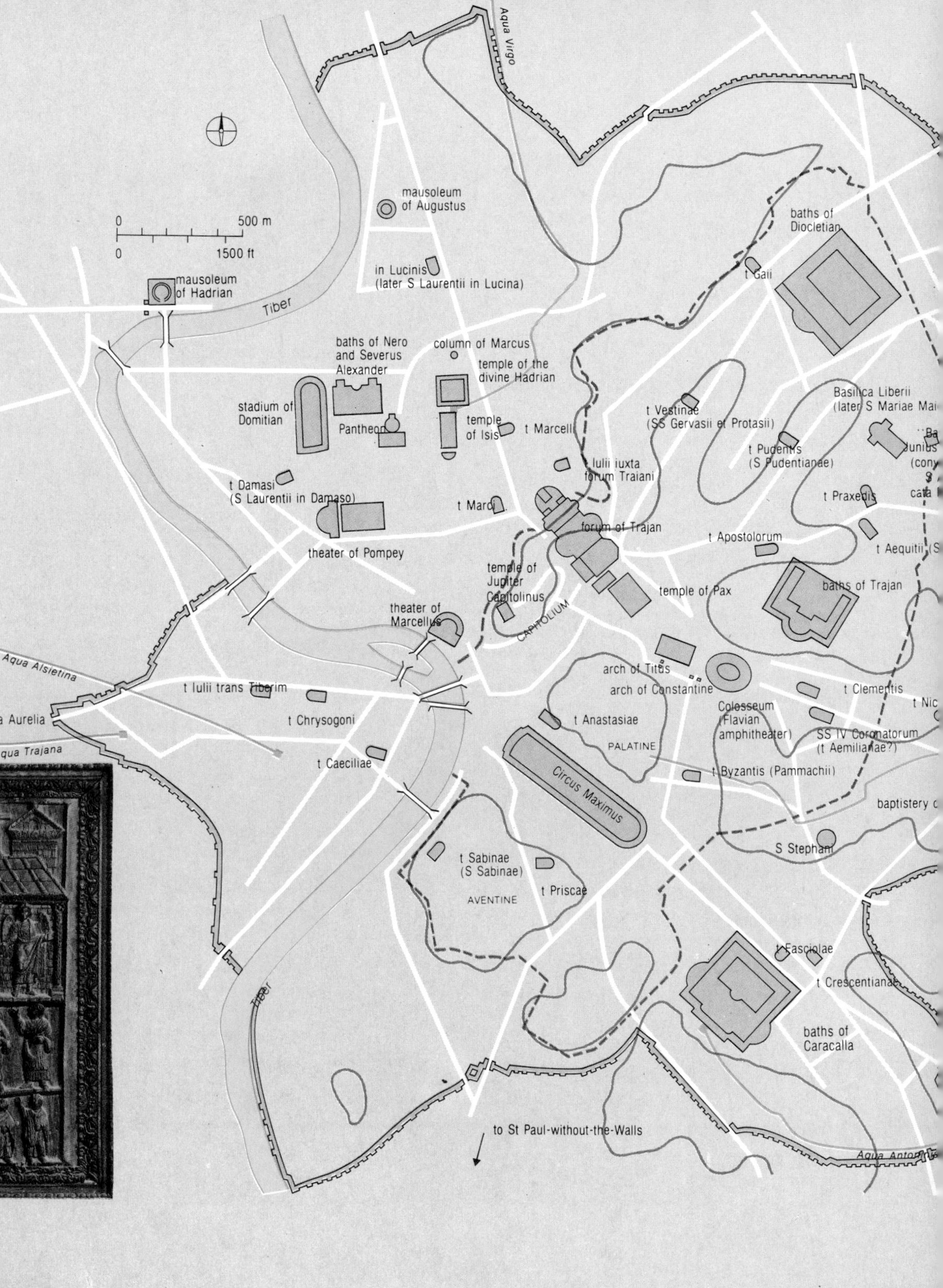

Aqua Virgo
mausoleum of Augustus
0 500 m
0 1500 ft
S Petri in Vaticano
mausoleum of Hadrian
Tiber
in Lucinis (later S Laurentii in Lucina)
baths of Diocletian
t Gaii
mausoleum of Anicii
baths of Nero and Severus Alexander
column of Marcus
temple of the divine Hadrian
stadium of Domitian
Pantheon
temple of Isis
t Marcelli
t Vestinae (SS Gervasii et Protasii)
Basilica Liberii (later S Mariae Mai
t Pudentis (S Pudentianae)
t Damasi (S Laurentii in Damaso)
Iulii iuxta forum Traiani
t Marci
t Praxedis
forum of Trajan
t Apostolorum
theater of Pompey
t Aequitii
temple of Jupiter Capitolinus
temple of Pax
baths of Trajan
theater of Marcellus
CAPITOLIUM
Aqua Alsietina
arch of Titus
arch of Constantine
t Iulii trans Tiberim
t Clementis
Porta Aurelia
t Chrysogoni
t Anastasiae
Colosseum (Flavian amphitheater)
SS IV Coronatorum (t Aemilianae?)
Aqua Trajana
PALATINE
t Caeciliae
Circus Maximus
t Byzantis (Pammachii)
baptistery
S Stephani
t Sabinae (S Sabinae)
t Priscae
AVENTINE
t Fasciolae
t Crescentianae
Tiber
baths of Caracalla
to St Paul-without-the-Walls
Aqua Antoniniana

The wooden door panels of the basilica of St Sabina, built in the 420s through the munificence of Peter, a wealthy priest from Illyricum, are among the most remarkable monuments of early Christian Rome. Seen below are (*left*) the ascent of Elijah in a "fiery chariot" (2 Kings 2:11), an Old Testament prefiguration of the ascension of Christ, and (*right*) an unexplained scene in which an angel presents an unidentified, but apparently lay, figure, who stands in the doorway of a sanctuary, to a waiting crowd, their hands raised in acclamation.

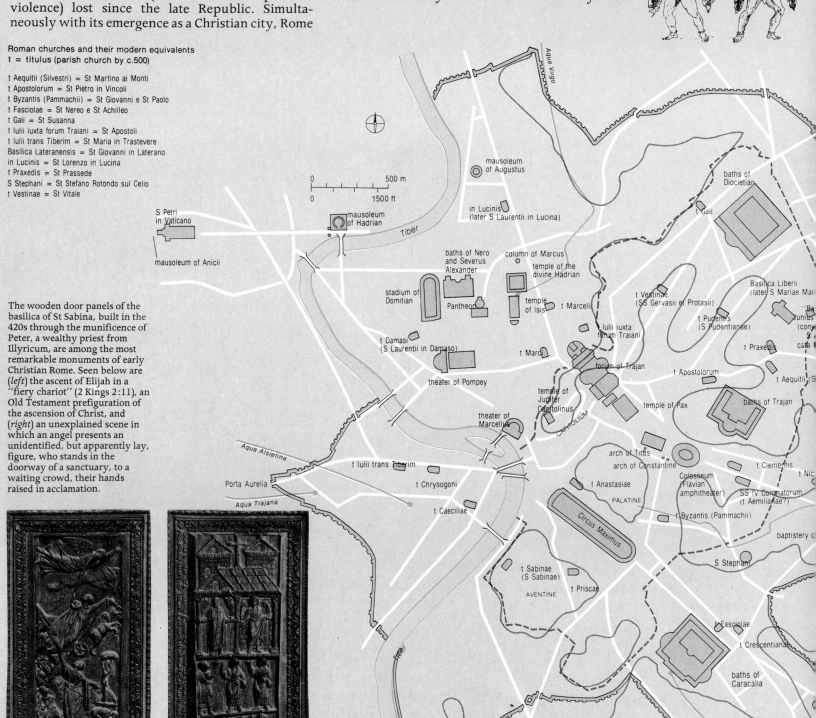

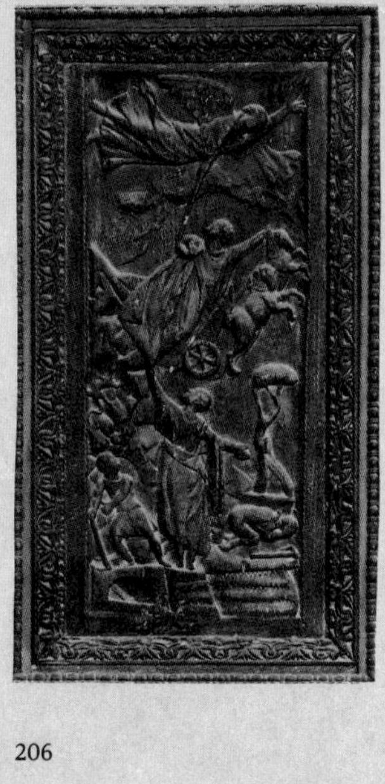

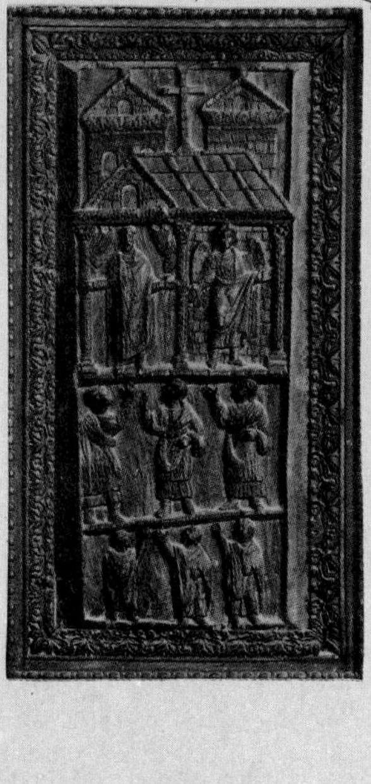

calendar, Filocalus illustrates the continuity of classical themes in the christianized culture of 4th-century Rome.

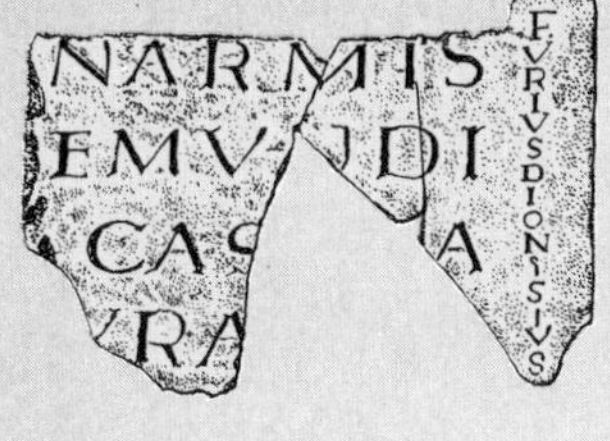

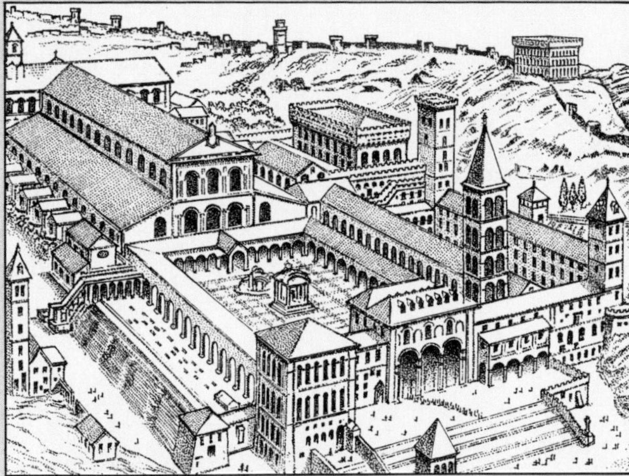

Artists' impressions sometimes offer the best available views of early churches subjected to subsequent rebuilding. Shown here are (*left*) old St Peter's, in a drawing of c. 1470, and (*below left*) the interior of St John Lateran, in a fresco by Dughet (c. 1660). Both churches were founded by Constantine.

Peter and Paul, the founders of Christian Rome, are sometimes described as the Christian counterparts of Romulus and Remus, and often appear together in iconography. Shown *below* is St Paul, in a mosaic from old St Peter's. He appears in his already conventional image as teacher rather than martyr.

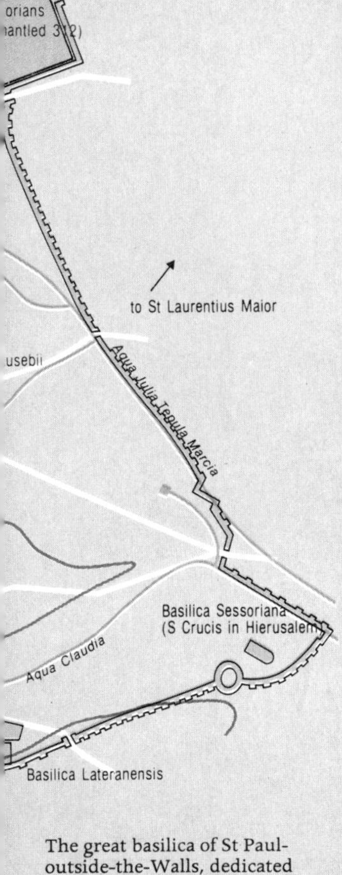

The great basilica of St Paul-outside-the-Walls, dedicated under Theodosius I but completed by his successor Honorius, is here seen in an engraving by Piranesi (c. 1750), particularly valuable since in 1823 the church was damaged by fire and its original form largely lost in the rebuilding. It was one of the finest new churches of late 4th-century Rome: Prudentius (c. 400 AD) well evokes the "royal splendor" of the place, its gilded beams, marble columns and brilliant mosaic frescoes, and the beauty of the light inside the church, "glowing like the rising sun."

THE FALL OF THE WESTERN ROMAN EMPIRE

Imperial disunity and barbarian threats

Theodosius I, who died at Milan in January 395, was the last emperor for over half a century who by military ability and force of character exerted any sustained personal control over the Roman Empire. It was in some ways ironic that his death should have left the Empire in the possession of two such nonentities as his sons: Arcadius, who nominally held power at Constantinople, and Honorius, emperor at Milan. The dynastic grip of Theodosius on the Empire had been further strengthened by his marriage, after the death of his first wife, to Galla, a daughter of Valentinian I. Their daughter, Galla Placidia, was born in 388.

At the time of his accession as senior Augustus, Arcadius was no more than 18, older by some years than Honorius. The later 4th century had accustomed the Empire to *Kinderkaiser* – emperors who assumed power in youth, even in infancy, and exercised it nominally, the actual government being conducted by great ministers of state and anyone who succeeded in establishing personal ascendancy. None of the successors of Theodosius possessed much individual personality, but yielded without resistance to the ceremonial constraints of their office and the influence of their advisers. Arcadius, who died in 408, was succeeded by his son Theodosius, who had been made co-Augustus in January 402, when he was less than one year old. Honorius, after a secluded reign of intense inactivity, died of disease in 423.It was maliciously said of him that he only recognized "Roma" as the name of his pet chicken. After the intermission of the usurpation of Johannes (423–25), the eastern court installed in the west the four-year-old Valentinian III, son of Galla Placidia by the gifted general Flavius Constantius.

The dynastic stability of the imperial office in this period, in itself impressive, was therefore secured at the cost of presenting to the Empire nominal emperors who lived in pampered seclusion and served merely to legitimize the powers of those ministers who succeeded in asserting their ascendancy. Several of these powerful ministers can be identified: in the east, among others, Theodosius I's former supporter Rufinus, the eunuch Eutropius, the praetorian prefect Anthemius, the urban and praetorian prefect Cyrus of Panopolis and Cyrus' enemy Chrysaphius, not to mention the influential women of the household of Theodosius II, his sister Pulcheria and wife Aelia Eudocia; in the west, a sequence of powerful military commanders, notably the half-Vandal Stilicho, Constantius, who became Augustus in 421, Flavius Aetius and the barbarian Ricimer.

The dynastic continuity achieved by the legacy of Theodosius did not prevent the usual political rivalries and violence among the supporters of the emperors, but its importance, in extremely difficult times, should not be underestimated. There were other conditions attached to the legacy, which between them provided the setting for the political and military history of the early 5th century: the division of the Empire between the courts of Constantinople and Milan (soon transferred to Ravenna), and the presence within the Empire of the Visigoths under their own national leaders, as a powerful military force owing service to the empire but also in a position to extract concessions from it.

In the years immediately after 395 Stilicho, in accordance with Theodosius' alleged dying wishes, claimed a "protectorate" over both western and eastern emperors. The hostility he thus incurred from the east was intensified by his attempts to secure for the west the recruiting grounds of eastern Illyricum, then administered from Constantinople. To pursue this project, Stilicho required the help of Alaric the Visigoth, who had invaded Greece in 395–97 and Italy in 401–02, escaped successive encounters with Roman armies and was still at large, seeking a secure homeland for his people. In 407 Stilicho was about to use Alaric to secure control of Illyricum, but the enterprise was prevented by major barbarian invasions in Gaul and by a usurpation in Britain. Alaric's demands for payment for his unused services, at first refused by the senate, led to his second invasion of Italy in 408. Stilicho was executed by the emperor's order in August 408 and his reputation assailed for his

Portrayed on contemporary ivory diptychs are (*above*) the half-Vandal general Stilicho with his wife and son, and (*overleaf*) his imperial master Honorius. Stilicho was dismissed and executed in 408 for alleged complicity with Alaric.

In winter 409/10 Alaric sponsored an imperial regime under a Roman senator, Priscus Attalus, against the intransigent government of Honorius at Ravenna. The medallion of Attalus (*below*), with its legend "INVICTA ROMA AETERNA," is an ironic commentary on the sack of Rome by Alaric only a few months later.

Barbarian incursions and settlements in the west. The character of the barbarian invasions was not uniform. Some, like that of the Vandals and Suebi, were aimed at the forcible seizure of land and property, while that of the Visigoths was an extended quest for settlement and recognition by the Romans.

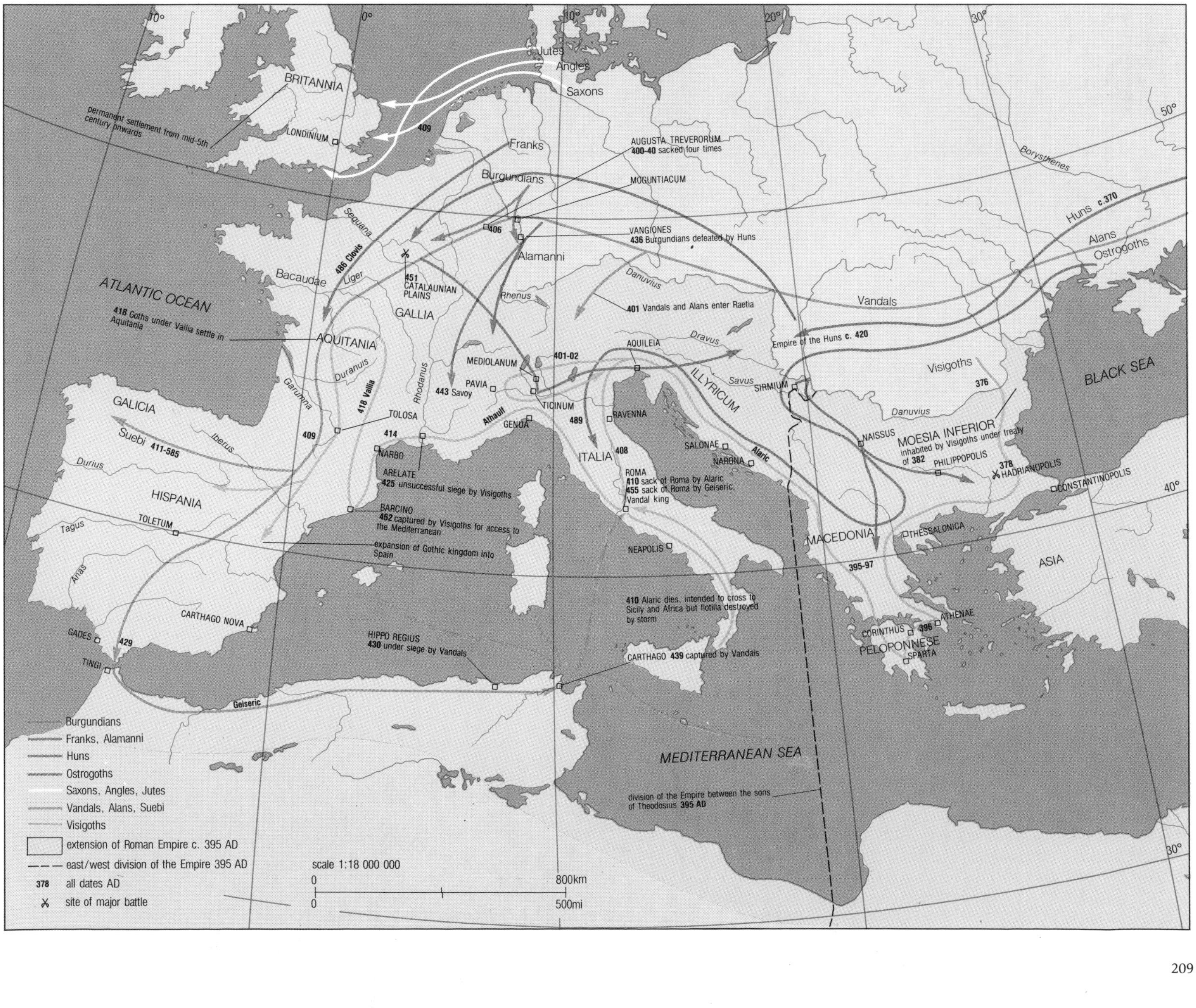

complaisant treatment of Alaric, but his successors in power proved incapable of meeting the barbarian threat. Stilicho's death was followed by three successive sieges of Rome, the last of these culminating in its capture and sack by Alaric in August 410.

It is worth trying to consider the situation from the viewpoint of the Goths themselves. Fourth-century sources show the Goths in the period before their entry into the Roman Empire as a quiet agricultural people, living in village communities, trading with and sometimes traveling as individuals to the Roman Empire. The migration of the Goths was caused by the pressure of the Huns from the east, and was not in any sense an aggressive move against the Roman Empire; this only emerged when the Goths were maltreated and oppressed by the Roman officials in charge of the crossing of the Danube.

The Goths may have seen the agreement of 382 as being with Theodosius himself rather than with the Roman government. The death of Theodosius placed Alaric in a precarious position, for he could not be sure that Theodosius' successors, whether in east or west, would honor the treaty. Throughout his relations with the regime of Honorius and Stilicho, Alaric pressed the same claims: land for his people to settle on, financial subsidies and the provision of food supplies. After the sack of Rome in 410, he pressed south, trying to secure a crossing to Africa, but died in southern Italy, and his successor Athaulf led the Goths from Italy into Gaul. Here, in 414, a Gothic regime was set up, with a puppet Roman emperor. It was based at Narbonne, where Athaulf married Theodosius' daughter Galla Placidia, a hostage from the sack of Rome, and proclaimed his policy of sustaining the Roman name by the force of Gothic arms. The following year the Goths were forced by naval blockade to abandon Narbonne for Spain. After Athaulf's assassination, his successor, Vallia, tried unsuccessfully to organize a crossing to Africa and finally, in 418, by agreement with the Roman government secured a settlement in southwestern Gaul, between the Garonne and the Loire. From the Gothic point of view it was not a very successful sequence of events, but they had in the end achieved what they wanted.

Though the sack of Rome had an immense emotional impact, it was from a strategic point of view very far from the worst disaster to afflict the Empire in these years. At the end of 406 a huge

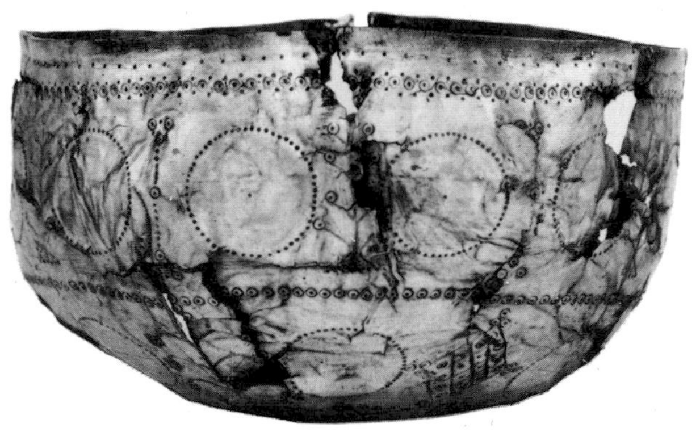

The silver bowl (*left*), reconstructed from the fragments into which it was broken, is from the "Coleraine hoard," a large deposit of silver coin, ingots and broken plate discovered in 1854. The coin series implies a 5th-century date (after 420), and the hoard may represent a cache taken as loot or paid in ransom after an Irish raid on western Britain or Gaul.

invasion of Germanic peoples, mainly Vandals, Suebi and Burgundians, crossed the Rhine, overwhelming Roman defensive positions, capturing cities in northern Gaul and the Rhineland and fanning out across Gaul to the southwest. By 409 the cities of Aquitania were threatened and the Suebi and Vandals forced their way over the Pyrenees into the rich, heavily urbanized provinces of Spain, the homeland of the dynasty of Theodosius. The whole of Gaul, as one contemporary put it, "burned in one vast funeral pyre," and letters of St Jerome to oppressed western provincials at this time reveal the disruption of material and family life caused by the invasions. Within a few years, the barbarian invaders of Spain were setting up kingdoms, competing for possession of the best lands, uprooting and scattering Roman landowners.

At the same time, local unrest in Britain and Saxon incursions around the coastline produced a series of imperial proclamations, as a result of which the usurper Constantine III crossed to Gaul in 407 and established his court at Arles, soon extending his power to Spain. Concerned at the time with the invasion of Alaric, the Italian government could do very little about the usurpation in Gaul.

After the proclamation of Constantine and his crossing to Gaul, Britain was never recovered as a Roman province. It was governed by men whom Roman sources describe as "tyrants," that is, local dynasts with a greater or lesser claim to continuity with Roman power, and from the mid-5th century it was progressively occupied from the east by the Saxons. The name of the shadowy Ambrosius Aurelianus survives to denote one of these post-Roman "tyrants" who resisted the Saxon encroachments in southwestern England. He may serve as a model for the "five princes" described by Gildas as wielding power in western Britain in the early 6th century, and for whatever truth lies behind the legendary figure of King Arthur.

In Gaul, Armorica (comprising Brittany and adjacent parts of the northwest) and a large part of the central region of the province were controlled after 410 by the insurgents known as the Bacaudae or by locally established barbarian enclaves. In 429 the Vandals crossed from Spain to Africa, and over the next few years worked their way eastwards towards Carthage. The bishop of Hippo, the now aged Augustine, died in 430 while his city was under Vandal siege.

The imperial government did what it could to counter these problems, but this was not very much. There is evidence for extensive recruitment by Stilicho among the barbarian peoples of the north, for the creation of emergency military commands in the frontier regions and for the calling-in and upgrading of provincial troops to meet the invasions of Italy. Roman generals conducted campaigns in Spain against the Vandals and Suebi. In this they were assisted by Visigothic federates, and it seems certain that the settlement of the Goths in southwestern Gaul was intended to provide a bulwark in the Roman interest against the unrest in Spain and against the Bacaudae in central and northwestern Gaul. In Africa, some resistance

IN NOMINE
XPI·VINCAS
SEMPER·
DN·HONORIO SEMP·AVG·
PROBVS·FAMVLVS·V·C·CONS·ORD·

After his deposition as western Roman emperor in 475, Julius Nepos, like his uncle before him, maintained himself for some years as head of an independent principality based on Salona in Dalmatia. Here (*top*) is shown a coin of Nepos issued at Milan on his behalf by Odoacer between 476 and 480, and also (*above*) a similar coin of the last officially recognized Roman emperor, Romulus Augustulus.

Left The western emperor Honorius (395–423), on an ivory diptych issued by Probus, consul in 406 AD. Honorius appears in military dress, a symbolic rather than actual reflection of his capacities. The legend on the *labarum* or standard, "In the name of Christ may you be ever victorious," is balanced by a winged victory who might also be interpreted as an angel.

to the advance of the Vandals was offered by an expedition sent from the east, but eastern Mauretania and Numidia were ceded to them in 435 and four years later, against the terms of the treaty, Geiseric seized Carthage and made himself master of proconsular Africa.

The establishment of the Huns from about 420 in the Hungarian plains north of the Danube, and the extension of their influence in succeeding years, threatened the land route between east and west which in the 4th century had been the military backbone of the Roman Empire, as well as access to traditional recruiting grounds. Treaties, involving the payment of subsidies, were conducted by the eastern government in about 430 with the Hunnish king Rua (or Rugila) and a few years later with his successors Bleda and Attila. Open war broke out in 441, in which Sirmium, Margus, Naissus and Philippopolis fell to the Huns, and again in 447. These wars were settled by the payment of increased subsidies, and by the Roman evacuation of territory on the Roman side of the Danube. The seat of the Illyrian prefecture was transferred from Sirmium to the coastal city of Thessalonica in Macedonia.

Because of their loose political organization and their lack of interest in settling within the Roman provinces, the Huns never achieved the devastating effect on the Roman Empire which they had once seemed to threaten. Their relations with the western court in the earlier 5th century were generally cooperative; they provided help to the troubled regime of Honorius in 409, supported the usurpation of Johannes and fought with the Romans against the Visigoths in the late 430s. Several figures prominent in western politics in this period had served some time as visitors or hostages among the Huns. In 451, after his agreement with the court of Constantinople, Attila advanced on the west but was defeated at the Catalaunian Plains (near Châlons-sur-Marne) by the combined forces of Romans, Visigoths and Burgundians. He retreated from Gaul, took and plundered Aquileia, Milan and Ticinum, but was persuaded by diplomacy and the threat of retaliation to withdraw from Italy. In 453 Attila died and the Hunnish empire fell apart.

The interest of the court of Constantinople in western affairs in this period was persistently, if not always effectively, expressed. In the time of Stilicho, Africa's adherence to the senior emperor of Constantinople had caused corn shortages at Rome until the "rebellion" was crushed by Stilicho. During the occupation of Italy by Alaric, Constantinople sent military aid to Honorius. The eastern government, under the influence of Galla Placidia, was responsible for suppressing the usurpation of Johannes and installing Valentinian III in 425. Valentinian was betrothed to the daughter of Theodosius, Licinia Eudoxia, and the marriage was performed at Constantinople in 437. On that occasion, western envoys went to Constantinople and returned in 438 with copies of the Theodosian Code, compiled by order of Theodosius II to bring coherence and chronological order to the confused mass of 4th- and early 5th-century imperial legislation. The compilers must necessarily have had to travel very widely to assemble the legislation from its scattered, often unofficial sources, and the Theodosian Code is one of the last constructive achievements of cooperation between east and west.

The eastern court attempted to prevent the capture of Africa by the Vandals, and was compelled to recall a second expedition in order to conduct its first war against Attila. The Vandals under Geiseric built up a powerful fleet, pillaged Rome in 455 and extended their piracy to Greece and the eastern Mediterranean. In 468 a major expedition was mounted against them from the east, with support from the west, but it ended disastrously, and a further entrenchment of Vandal power resulted from its failure.

The dynasty of Theodosius petered out in the east in 450, when Theodosius II died after a riding accident and was succeeded by emperors of a more traditionally military cast: Marcian (450–57), Leo (457–74) and the Isaurian Zeno (474–91). In the west the dynasty ended with the assassination of Valentinian III (455), who was succeeded by several short-lived emperors. After the reign of Libius Severus, creature of the barbarian magister Ricimer, the eastern government of Leo was responsible for the installation in the west of Anthemius (467–72); when Anthemius and Ricimer turned to civil war against each other, Leo tried to reconcile them through the mediation of Olybrius, a western senatorial exile living at Constantinople. Anthemius was however assassinated and Olybrius made emperor in his place. Upon the death of Olybrius a few months later, the eastern government dispatched Nepos to replace his successor Glycerius, but Nepos was deposed by the general Orestes. Orestes made his own son Romulus emperor, and Romulus' removal by Odoacer in 476 can be considered to symbolize the end of the Roman Empire in the west. From 476, Italy was controlled by barbarian kings holding court at Ravenna.

Reactions to the end of the western Empire

The reactions of contemporaries to the collapse of the western Empire varied widely. One writer, a Gallic landowner, Rutilius Namatianus, returned home by sea late in 417 to meet the challenge presented by the settlement of the Visigoths in his own part of southwestern Gaul. For Rutilius, there were grounds for optimism. Despite the destruction wrought by the invasions, which was still visible in Italy in broken bridges and abandoned lodging-houses, peace had been made with the Visigoths and life at Rome was beginning to return to normal. Rutilius' was perhaps the most optimistic of contemporary reactions. Optimism of a rather different kind was provided by a younger contemporary of Rutilius, the Spanish priest Orosius. In his polemical history of Rome, *Against the Pagans*, Orosius argued with painfully monotonous documentation that the misfortunes of the Roman Empire and of his own day, including the sack of Rome, were less serious than those of the old Roman Republic. He thus countered the imputation that the fall of Rome was the direct consequence of its abandonment of the traditional gods and adoption of Christianity. But it is clear from certain passages of the history, in which he allowed his personal reactions to appear, that Orosius did not regard the contemporary situation with any genuine optimism. He had escaped from Spain, amid great dangers, to go to North Africa, and was later unable to return to his native province because of the ferocity of the barbarian occupation. He deplored the possibility that the barbarian peoples might succeed in establishing their kingdoms in Spain. At one point he wrote with startling bitterness of the conquest of Gaul by Julius Caesar, putting into the mouth of a personified Gaul the complaint that "so did the Romans bow me down, that I cannot rise against the Goths." Orosius' history neither carried personal conviction nor coincided honestly with his own experience, but his work became the standard medieval handbook of Roman history of the classical as well as of the Christian period.

The autobiographical reflections of another Gaul, Paulinus of Pella, in his poem the *Eucharisticon,* or *Hymn of Thanks*, give a vivid impression of the experiences of one individual dispossessed by the invasions and reduced from the standing of a wealthy landowner to that of an impoverished monk at Marseille, selling the last of his once great properties to a Gothic purchaser. A compatriot from the northeast, the priest Salvian, writing in about 440, denounced the corruption of contemporary Roman society, which he contrasted with the honest purity of the barbarian occupiers of Gaul and Africa. The surviving Gallic landowners, the *curiales* (whom it is interesting to find still in existence), he described as "tyrants" as they extracted taxation from the peasantry. The peasants themselves, he alleged, sought refuge with the barbarians or with the Bacaudae. It is not easy to determine how accurately Salvian's polemical picture reflects the facts, but his recollection of lacerated corpses lying in the streets of Trier probably owes only too much to reality. Between 400 and 440 the city was sacked no less than four times by barbarian onslaught.

By far the most far-reaching and sophisticated response to the fall of Rome was given by Augustine. In his sermons on the sack of Rome, Augustine had evoked the sufferings of Job to show that the tribulations of Christian Romans were a testing of their faith by God. But it was clear that the sack, which appeared to some to reflect Rome's abandonment of the protection of the traditional gods, required a reasoned response from the Christian point of view; in his *City of God* Augustine gave this on an immense scale. In the first 10 books, Augustine put into perspective the achievement of pre-Christian Rome, especially the early republican period which was idealized by pagan contemporaries, and then presented a reasoned case against the philosophical claims of the pagan religions: in book 10, for instance, Augustine produced an intellectually stringent critique of the Neoplatonic philosophy of Porphyry. In the second part of the *City of God,* Augustine developed the conception of the "two cities," the "city of God" (*civitas dei*) and the "city of this world" (*civitas terrena*). For Augustine, the city of God was the "community of saints," living for the time being in the society of men; their actual identity, known only to God, would be revealed in the Last Days. The Latin word *civitas* is from some points of view better translated in the sense of "citizenship" rather than "city." The member of the heavenly community was like a foreigner (*peregrinus*) living on earth and, like a foreigner in a Roman city, subject to its laws, but owing his ultimate allegiance to the city of God to which he longed to return. For Augustine, secular society and government served certain basic material purposes in the preservation of lawful social life and the avoidance of disorder among imperfect men, but was ultimately neutral. As for the church itself, that was more like a sanatorium for the sick than a community of saints on earth; Augustine knew that his own church at Hippo contained many insincere Christians, and some whose presence within its walls was due mainly to fear of imperial legislation; these were the *ficti*, men whose conversion was "feigned" for safety and convenience, not as a matter of personal conscience. Even so, their presence in the church gave them a chance of salvation.

For modern historians as for contemporaries, the end of the Roman Empire has seemed to require explanation on the grand scale. How an empire of such resources, whose physical remains could be seen on all sides, had been brought down has preoccupied observers in most ages. In some ways, this preoccupation with the need for large-scale interpretation has hindered modern historical analysis, for its effect has been to suggest the possibility of some single interpretation which, of itself, could explain a historical transformation of immense complexity. Suggestions such as that of climatic change, and even of cumulative blood poisoning from lead piping, are only two of the more recent attempts to explain the fall of the Empire in terms of a single all-pervasive interpretation.

The solutions have often been moral, and have sometimes depended on a stated or assumed analogy between Roman society and a physical organism for which physical decline and death are a biological necessity. Voltaire, for instance, considered that the Empire had to end simply because all things must end. It is possible at once to discount the notion that the Roman Empire fell in consequence of the moral decline of its leaders. Had this been the case, the Empire would have been brought down by the Julio-Claudian emperors, or even in the late Republic, before the Empire, as we understand it, existed, for this was the heyday of Roman immorality. The emperors of the 3rd and 4th centuries were generally honest, hard-working men of great moral earnestness; one of the most striking facts about them is the almost complete absence of moral scandal attached to them by the ancient sources. The later Roman emperors and their supporters came from regions of conservative provincial virtues and were untouched by the decadence of metropolitan society.

For Gibbon, the decline of the Roman Empire was an eventual consequence of its political organization. The extent of physical coercion required to sustain the immense structure of the Empire had the effect of reducing the sense of liberty among its populations, so that when the crisis of invasion came they had lost all real interest in its preservation. At the same time, through a period (in the 2nd century) of sustained peace, the military classes lost the spirit of collective courage and the habit of obedience, while in the military crisis which followed, they were overindulged by the emperors.

The difficulty with this interpretation, as Gibbon himself conceded without pursuing its implications, is that it fails to explain how the Empire lasted so long. By a systematic increase in its exercise of power, it was able to survive the 3rd-century crisis and to enjoy a period of impressive vigor and of political, military and cultural renewal in the 4th century. The history of this immensely rich and complex period does not read as if it were faced irrevocably in the direction of decline.

The problem with Gibbon's and with other such long-term explanations is that, far from explaining the fall of the Empire, they only too easily turn into appreciations of its long survival. What is needed is something more precise and, no less important, something that will differentiate between the collapse of the western and the survival, for a further millennium, of the eastern Roman Empire.This requirement undermines the suggestion of Gibbon, developed in different terms by later historians, that the Christian church, by diverting men's ideals from civic to other-worldly aims, drew their interest away from the preservation of the Empire. Yet the influence of Christianity and of the Christian ideal was no less pervasive in the eastern Empire, which survived, than in the west, which did not. At the very least, such interpretations must be accompanied by an explanation of why the two parts responded differently to conditions that affected them both.

If we narrow the inquiry to the situation of the western government in the early 5th century, the problems of the Roman Empire are not difficult to comprehend. It is unlikely that it ever recovered from the loss of two-thirds of its eastern field army at Hadrianople (378); before this, there was the appalling waste of the unsuccessful Persian campaign of Julian and, earlier still, the civil wars of Constantius. In particular, the battle of Mursa (351), at which Constantius defeated Magnentius, was immensely destructive in manpower. When Valens agreed to the admission of the Goths to the Empire in 376, he was attracted by their potential as recruits for the Roman armies.

Shortage of military manpower was one of the basic conditions under which the Roman government was obliged to operate; it was this that compelled the Romans to accept the principle of Gothic service as federates. This solution, by creating a sort of Gothic "estate" within the Empire, made it increasingly difficult for the government to exercise a free response to external threats. During the early 5th century, the problem of relations with the Visigoths was at least as important an issue as how to deal with the external enemies of Rome, and inextricably entwined with it.

A major contribution to the weakness of the western government was the refusal of the senatorial landed class to carry its share of financial obligations. The senate of Rome was opposed to the raising of recruits from senatorial estates; it preferred instead to make a cash contribution and thus preserve intact its agricultural labor force, thereby maintaining its income. With the cash reluctantly provided by the senate, the government had to raise recruits from among barbarian peoples, and in particular to pay the subsidies demanded by Alaric. Yet at the same time the senate was opposed to the payment of these subsidies.

At a period when the imperial government was suffering from near bankruptcy, members of the Roman senatorial class continued to spend vast sums on public games, and failed to appreciate that they could not both refuse to provide recruits and object to the payment of subsidies to federate troops.

The effect of senatorial influence on the ability of the government to meet its difficulties was not only financial, but political, in that it became increasingly difficult for the government to present a unified front in its dealings with Alaric. The court behaved with an unpredictable inconsistency of which Alaric was quick to take advantage. In the eastern Empire, by contrast, although there was an assertive anti-Gothic faction and a serious Gothic rebellion (that of Gainas in 399–400), the government never depended on the Goths to the same extent as did the west in order to conduct its foreign wars. The east was comparatively free of invasion and since the eastern government retained control of the nearby recruit-producing regions of Thrace and Anatolia it never suffered from the shortages of military manpower which undermined the competence of its western counterpart. The civilization defended by east Roman policy, based on the eastern Mediterranean and its cities, coincided quite closely with the areas from which the defense was financed and mounted. In the west, on the other hand, the military resources of the Empire, in the inland provinces of the north, lay far from the regions in which most of its cultural life and financial resources lay. And finally, the eastern aristocracy, being less wealthy than that of the west and more consistently involved with the political and economic life of the imperial court, never came to form a separate estate such as was formed in the west by the senatorial class of Rome. It is in considerations like these, and not in general moral and religious reflections, that the reasons must be sought for the survival of the eastern Roman Empire while the west was weakened and dismembered.

Barbarian states in the post-Roman west

The barbarian states which established themselves in the Roman provinces of the west developed social and political characters very different from each other, some favorable to the survival of Roman manners and life-styles, other less so. In Gaul, the Visigothic regime in the southwest embarked on a process of consolidation and expansion.Theoderic died in the great war of 451 against Attila, but under his successor, Theoderic II, the Goths gained access to the Mediterranean by capturing Narbonne (462); a few years later they took Arles, the seat until then of the praetorian prefecture of the remaining Roman provinces of Gaul and a notable center of Roman culture in the west. Further up the Rhône valley lay the kingdom of the Burgundians, who settled in Savoy after a great defeat by the Huns, recorded by chronicle sources under the year 436. It is possible that this defeat is the remote historical basis for the German epic, the *Nibelungenlied*. Other barbarian enclaves, like those of the Alani near Orléans and in the region of Valence, occupied more tracts of land assigned to them from the territory of the old Roman cities. In northeastern Gaul, the forested lands beyond the Loire were controlled by the Bacaudae in what appear to have been independent principalities, governing themselves by their own laws.

The barbarian settlements in Gaul and elsewhere took place on the basis of *hospitalitas*, a sharing of

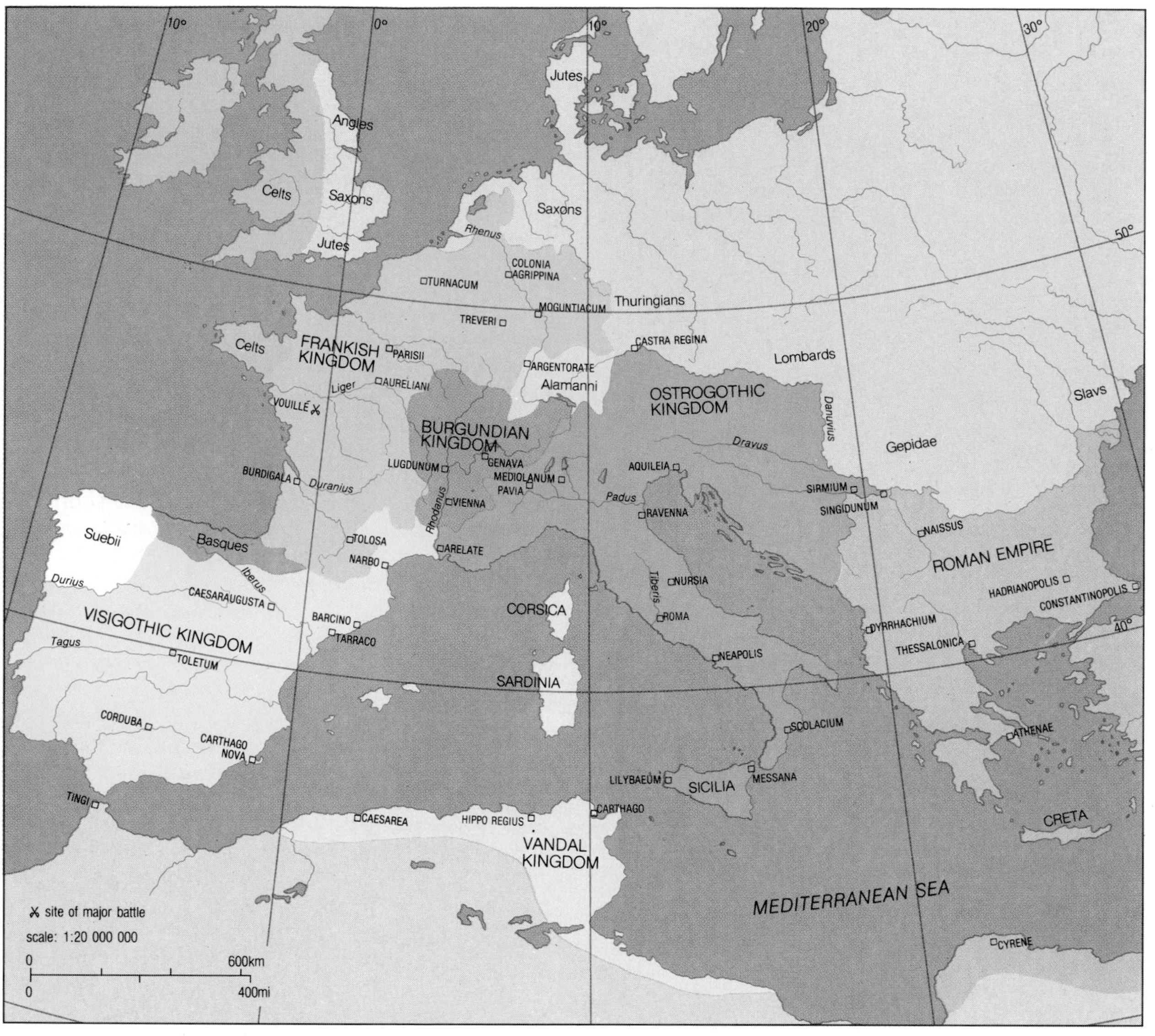

Political divisions of the Empire and barbarian occupation, 526 AD. At his death in 526, Theoderic the Ostrogoth exercised a protectorate over the Visigoths in Spain and was connected by marriage with Burgundians and with the Vandals in Africa. He had failed to prevent the expansion of the Franks under Clovis which had expelled the Visigoths from Gaul at the battle of Vouillé (507). The government of Constantinople was being drawn to reconquest by what it saw as the Arian Theoderic's persecution of his Catholic Roman subjects; but the conquest was first directed against another Arian regime. that of the Vandals, whose defeat provided a bridge with the west. In Britain it was an age of Celtic resistance to Saxons (the situation behind the original "King Arthur") and of migrations to western Gaul. The real threat to Italy came from the Lombards, and to the east from the Avars and Bulgars.

land between Roman landowner and his barbarian "guest." Unfortunately, little is known about the actual mechanics of the sharing of the land, or of the way in which the barbarian settlers were in practice distributed. Did they live in substantial barbarian enclaves – possibly on fringe land near forests – or did they scatter in smaller groups and as individual farmers on the estates and in the country-houses of Roman landowners? In the century of their occupation of Gaul before their expulsion by the Franks in the early 6th century, the Visigoths left little trace of their presence on the place-names of the region, and archaeological evidence of the Gothic settlement is scanty and indefinite. Yet the Visigothic court of Toulouse in the time of Theoderic II (453–66), which is described by a Gallic aristocratic visitor, Sidonius Apollinaris, was the scene of a colorful, opulent and in some ways quite cultured social life.

The actual manner of settlement was much less disruptive in Gaul than in Spain and Africa. The settlement of the Vandals and Suebi in Spain was attended by violence and disruption, from which little of Roman continuity appears. The fragmentary sources present none of the great landed dynastic families which are so common in 5th- and 6th-century Gaul. In Africa, the expansion of the Vandals to proconsular Africa was achieved at the cost of the widespread dispossession of Roman landowners. Many refugees found their way to the east as victims of this dispossession and of the religious persecutions conducted by the Vandals. The discontinuity was not complete. There is evidence of the continuance to the late 5th century of traditional forms of land tenure, by the Roman *lex Manciana*, on what had once been imperial estates in a rather remote region near the borders of southern proconsular Africa with Numidia. Other Roman landowners are occasionally recorded in the sources, and the early 6th-century Vandal court of Carthage became the focus of an intellectual and cultural life of some modest sophistication, its chief representative being the Latin poet Luxorius.

It is not very clear how the barbarian peoples of the Roman west were converted to Arian Christianity. The case of the Visigoths is easiest to understand, in that their earlier relations with and admission to the Roman Empire had been in the time of Valens, an Arian emperor; further, they had been evangelized by Ulfila, an Arian Gothic missionary (and translator of the Gothic Bible). But even this case is problematical. The government of Valens had few constructive relations with the Goths in the short period between their admission to the Empire and the battle of Hadrianople, and the treaty on which their later relations with the Romans were based was made with Theodosius, a pious Catholic emperor. It remains completely obscure why the Vandals, who crossed the Rhine by invasion late in 406, should have adopted Arianism. The Suebi and

This fine mosaic, from late 5th- or 6th-century Carthage, shows a landowner in Germanic costume setting out from his villa on a hunting expedition. The portrayal, if the landowner is indeed a Vandal, suggests a certain appreciation by the barbarian settlers of at least some aspects of the civilization which they found in Roman Africa.

Burgundians for some time remained pagan, while the Franks were converted directly from paganism to Catholic Christianity in the time of Clovis. There seems no reason to suppose that the barbarians were particularly attracted by the theological intricacies of Arian as opposed to orthodox Nicene doctrine. One is led to conclude that barbarian heresy had come to reflect their situation as settlers in Roman territory, their Christianity expressing shared interests with their Roman hosts, while their Arianism provided a point of distinction which limited the intimacy that could be achieved between them. Certainly, phases of more aggressively anti-Roman policy initiated by barbarian kings were expressed in persecutions of Catholics. This happened, especially, in Africa under King Huneric (477–84), and in Gaul under the aggressive Gothic regime of Euric II (466–84).

Roman continuity in Gaul was in the hands of the resident Gallo-Roman aristocracy, and their achievement was considerable. The letters of Sidonius Apollinaris, written in the second half of the 5th century, reveal an extensive network of political, cultural and theological contacts maintained among the members of this aristocracy. Some of these nobles, like Pontius Leontius of Bordeaux, preserved a Roman life-style in their villas and country-houses. The fortified country seat of Pontius, known to Sidonius as "Burgus" ("castle"; usually identified as Bourg-sur-Gironde), possessed walls and towers, porticoes with wall-paintings of Christian and classical themes, storehouses and a Christian chapel, and there are other such examples.

In Gaul the church also played a crucial role as the preserver of Roman continuity in the 5th and 6th centuries. When there was no longer an imperial court resident in Gaul, the incentive to obtain a classical education in order to secure professional advancement disappeared; with it went the motive for the cities to provide the educational facilities which they had maintained in the imperial period. The provision at least of a basic education was thus left in the hands of the church. Sometimes, as in the case of Sidonius Apollinaris at Clermont in 469, aristocrats became bishops of their cities and fulfilled urgent practical needs, securing food supplies, raising public morale in times of crisis and leading their cities against attack from the Goths. Sidonius himself was exiled and imprisoned by Euric II for his role in the resistance of Clermont in the 470s.

Sidonius' promotion as bishop after an active secular career (he had been prefect of Rome in 468) has often provoked scepticism as to the genuineness of his Christian piety, especially when combined with his obviously undiminished love of classical literature. But this would be a misconception. As we have already seen, the conversion of the Roman Empire to Christianity had taken place, despite some expressions of opposition from both sides, without the sacrifice of its classical culture. The real danger in assessing the promotion as bishop of a man like Sidonius is that of underestimating the level of genuine Christian piety which he had possessed as a layman. Like others, he made a conscientious, honest and useful bishop, whose contribution to the survival of his native city in a time of crisis was significant and admirable, and achieved not without danger to himself.

Others among Sidonius' friends made distinctive contributions to the relations of the Visigothic kingdom of Toulouse with the surviving Romano-Gallic population – men such as Leo of Narbonne, who was instrumental in devising the earliest known version of the "Roman Law of the Visigoths," an attempt to provide a simplified version of Roman law for the use of the Romans living under the Visigoths. Its successor, Alaric II's *Lex Romana Visigothorum* (506), was the chief source for knowledge of Roman law in the early medieval west. Similarly, the Burgundian law of King Gundobad, prepared in the late 5th century, was the most permanent legacy of a barbarian regime of whose internal history relatively little is known. Such achievements of Roman and barbarian collaboration in the 5th century were successful in preserving what could be preserved of Roman culture and religion without the support of Roman power, and prepared the way for the more permanent acceptance of Frankish rule by the old Roman provinces of Gaul.

Rome, Ravenna and Constantinople

In Italy, despite the loss of senatorial incomes from overseas estates, political and economic life continued very much as before, dominated by the court of Ravenna and by senatorial Rome. The sieges of Rome by Alaric had caused serious food shortages, especially when Africa too was blockaded or in rebellion, and failed to send the corn ships to Rome. On one occasion, the people assembled in the Circus Maximus had acclaimed the terrible words, "set a price on human flesh," meat being so scarce and its price so high.

Many senators with mainly provincial connections and sources of wealth must in these years have disappeared from Rome to secure what they could of their local possessions, leaving the capital and its public offices to be dominated by a small circle of clans of Italian origin, whose still great wealth derived from the possession of land retained in Italy and Sicily. Upon the initiative of these families, damaged parts of the city were rebuilt and public monuments, like the senate-house and the Colosseum, were restored. The Colosseum again became the scene of the elaborate hunting shows (*venationes*) put on by members of the nobility, by which they asserted their position as patrons and benefactors of the *populus Romanus*. There is evidence too that within a few years of the sack the population of Rome was again beginning to increase; refugees began to return and the public services of the city were restored.

Rome was the center of vigorous cultural and literary activity. To the third and fourth decades of the 5th century (and not, as was once thought, to the late 4th century) should be assigned the great commentary on Virgil by Servius, and the *Saturnalia* of Macrobius. To the same period belong also the *Fables* of Avienus, a Roman senator, and the preparation of the two illustrated Vatican manuscripts of Virgil's *Aeneid* known respectively as the *Virgilius Vaticanus* and the *Virgilius Romanus*. The classical revival of the time of Boethius and Cassiodorus in the early 6th century was thus the culmination of an interest in the preservation of classical learning maintained throughout the 5th century by members of the senatorial nobility and their literary clients.

The 5th century was also the time of the building of great new churches at Rome, monumental in design and decorated with elaborate mosaic sequences. Following the basilicas of the late 4th century, St Paul-outside-the-Walls and St Pudentiana, came the building of St Sabina and, shortly afterwards, of St Maria Maggiore. The dedication of the latter to the Virgin Mary reflected the support of Pope Sixtus for the Council of Ephesus (431), which confirmed her designation as Theotokos, "Mother of God."

The Christianization of the Roman aristocracy expressed itself in the 5th century in terms of an enhanced involvement in the organized life of the church of Rome. Roman senators are recorded with increasing frequency as the builders and benefactors of churches, and as participants in their regular liturgical activities. The suppression of the Pelagian heresy in 418 had put an end to a movement in which ascetic lay senators could take an independent role in dogmatic issues, and the period after this is characterized by the solidarity of the clergy of Rome with prominent lay members of the church, and of both with the Christian population of Rome.

Already in the early 5th century, the Spanish poet Prudentius had acclaimed Rome as the moral head of the Christian empire, possessing more relics of martyrs than any other city, great public processions in their honor and magnificently ornate churches. This ideal of Christian Rome was gradually deployed with increasing effectiveness by the bishops of the city in support of their claims of preeminence in the church. Pope Leo I (440–61) made notable contributions to this process in a series of sermons that presented the Roman saints, Peter and Paul, as the founders of Christian Rome, the counterparts of Romulus and Remus, and so provided an ideology appropriate for Rome's claims to be the Christian capital of the Empire. Pope Leo was also prominent politically, in particular as a member of the embassy which succeeded in averting the threatened invasion of Italy by Attila in 452.

From the very beginning of the 5th century, the imperial court lived in relative security at Ravenna; it moved there at the end of 402 in face of the threat posed by Alaric's first invasion of Italy, when Milan was actually beseiged by the Visigoths. Ravenna was one of a sequence of great maritime cities at the head of the Adriatic. Its predecessor was Aquileia, which by the 5th century was a neglected commercial site with a silted harbor but still, as Attila found, a considerable fortress. Ravenna's successors were medieval and Renaissance Venice and, in recent times, Trieste. For the emperors of the 5th century, the attraction of Ravenna lay in its defensive security; it was situated among marshes and lagoons, and only accessible from the landward side by a causeway. When the generals of Theodosius II took the place from the usurper Johannes in 425, their success was attributed to the help of an angel disguised as a shepherd, who showed them the way through the marshes.

Behind its natural and artificial defenses, 5th-century Ravenna became a great center of Christian culture. The churches of St John the Evangelist, attributed to the munificence of Galla Placidia, and the baptistery of Bishop Neon (otherwise known as the Baptistery of the Orthodox), with its mosaics symbolizing the rite of baptism, were constructed in the middle years of the 5th century. Other mosaics from the imperial palace, now lost, showed the marriage of Valentinian III with Licinia Eudoxia in 437. The so-called Mausoleum of Galla Placidia is probably not to be associated with her, but the building is of 5th-century date and its splendid mosaics have major iconographical significance. The most resplendent of the churches of Ravenna belong to the time of the Byzantine reconquest, but the town's origins as a center of Christian culture are to be sought in the 5th century.

The political relations between Constantinople and the west in the 5th century have already been described. The eastern Empire was free from major invasion, although Isaurian raids and incursions of desert peoples into Cyrenaica and southern Egypt caused great local difficulty and ultimately raised the question of Constantinople's ability to defend its more distant provinces. The philosopher and rhetorician Synesius of Cyrene was made bishop of Ptolemais in 411, having as local landowner been prominent in leading armed resistance to the incursions. The rebellion of the Goth Gainas was suppressed with some difficulty, and Theodosius' wars against Persia over the Armenian situation were resolved by diplomacy to enable him to meet the threat of the Huns, who in 422 ravaged Thrace. It was probably against the Hunnish threat that the new land walls of Constantinople had been completed in 413. The subsidies paid to the Huns under treaty were a relatively serious financial burden, but by no means as crippling as some have believed.

With such exceptions, the 5th century was a time of continued prosperity in the eastern Empire. Sardis in Asia Minor now entered a period of commercial and monumental expansion. Antioch also, on the evidence of the mosaics from its villas, continued prosperous, and imperial and private interest in the Holy Land led to a period of growing economic vigor based on the importation of capital from outside by pious pilgrims and tourists. After

Top The illustrated manuscript known as the *Virgilius Vaticanus* (Cod. Lat. 3225) is an outstanding monument of the interest in classical culture sustained in 5th-century Rome. Illustrated here is one of the most pathetic scenes in the *Aeneid*, Dido's preparation for suicide. With a knife in her hand, she reclines on the funeral pyre which, by a strange convention, seems to be indoors.

Above The church, monastery and pilgrimage center of St Simeon Stylites at Qalet Sem'an in Syria was built in the late 5th century around the pillar which until his death in 459 the stylite saint had occupied for 30 years, receiving visitors, offering advice to those who came for it, and undertaking prayer and meditation. The pillar on which the performance had taken place was enclosed in an octagonal open courtyard. The shrine was equipped with a guest house for visitors as well as the monastery and basilica illustrated here.

her political disgrace in 443, the empress Eudocia, wife of Theodosius II, lived in Jerusalem until her death in 460. She was responsible for many benefactions and ecclesiastical and monastic foundations in the Holy Land, and had also built a church at Constantinople. Athens, where Eudocia was born as Athenais, the daughter of a pagan sophist, was in the 5th century the center of the famous Neoplatonic school of Syrianus and Proclus, owing its allegiance to the theurgical tradition established by Iamblichus (see above, p. 177). After the sack of Athens by Alaric in 396, an attempt was made, especially by the praetorian prefect of Illyricum, Herculius (407–12), to repair and put in order some of its public buildings, including the Library of Hadrian.

Eudocia's supporter at Constantinople, the praetorian prefect Cyrus, was, like the empress, a classical poet of some reputation, and passionately devoted to Greek culture; John the Lydian, writing under Justinian, attributed to Cyrus the responsibility for abandoning Latin as the official language of the eastern administration – a significant step in the slow transition from the late Roman to a Greek Byzantine empire. Cyrus was also responsible for extending the new city walls of Constantinople to defend the sea frontage against the threat of Vandal piracy.

After Cyrus' loss of office in 441, probably because of his excessive popularity at Constantinople, he was consecrated bishop of a town in Phrygia, where he no doubt surprised his congregation by delivering what is probably the shortest, though perhaps not the least controversial, sermon on record: "Brethren, let the birth of our Savior Jesus Christ be honored in silence, because the Word of God was conceived in the Holy Virgin through hearing alone. Amen." Despite this splendidly contemptuous gesture, and despite the accusation of paganism leveled at him, as at Eudocia, at the time of his fall from power, Cyrus, on leaving his bishopric, returned to Constantinople and became famous there for his works of charity and for his support of the stylite saint, Daniel. The combination of classical literary and Christian religious tastes was a fundamental feature of Byzantine, as of late Roman, culture.

The most intractable, and in some ways most damaging problem to face the eastern Empire in this period was that of religious unity. The Arian heresy had been effectively suppressed by Theodosius I by the councils of Constantinople held in the early 380s, but its natural successors, the Nestorian and monophysite controversies, proved still more difficult to resolve. Nestorius, patriarch of Constantinople from 428, argued that of the two natures of Christ, divine and human, only the human was incarnate and suffered on the Cross. In consequence, the Virgin Mary, the mother of the human Christ, was not the mother of God, and Nestorius denied her the epithet Theotokos by which this concept was expressed. The doctrines of Nestorius were opposed with particular force by Cyril, patriarch of Alexandria. The imperial court was divided, but Nestorius was condemned and deposed at the Council of Ephesus in 431. After an unsuccessful attempt by Theodosius to reconcile the parties, Nestorius was exiled and his writings burned.

Over the next few years, the eastern church, under the influence of the Alexandrians, was drawn more strongly towards the so-called "monophysite" position, which, at the other extreme from Nestorianism, asserted the single indivisible nature of Christ, divine as well as human. The monophysite position was upheld by the Council of Ephesus in 449, called by Pope Leo the "robber council" (*latrocinium*) because his own views were ignored. Leo denounced the council to Valentinian III, and with his support complained to Theodosius. Only after Theodosius's death in 450 was any action taken.

The Council of Chalcedon in 451, held under the eye of the imperial court, was not allowed to develop with the same spontaneity as the two councils of Ephesus. Imperial commissioners presided over the sessions and imperial secretaries took down the proceedings. The "robber council" was denounced, the Alexandrians rejected and the so-called "Tome of Leo," presented to the council by papal legates, made the basis (or one of the bases) of the Creed of Chalcedon. At the same time the eastern bishops evaded the possible implications of their acceptance of the formula of Leo by explicitly defining the see of Constantinople as equal with that of Rome. Despite the objections of the papal legates and subsequently of Leo himself, the relevant canon (number 28) remained in force in the eastern church, thus denying the bishop of Rome's claim to supremacy.

The details of the disputes in the eastern church in this period are neither simple nor edifying. The intensity of the theological struggle cannot be explained without reference to personal rivalries and to the struggles of certain sees – Constantinople, Antioch and Alexandria – for preeminence. The patriarchs of Alexandria in particular conducted themselves with a domineering ruthlessness and lack of scruple fully worthy of the traditions of their see; Cyril of Alexandria carried his opinion against Nestorius at the first Council of Ephesus, partly by presents to various officials at the imperial court so lavish that he had to borrow 1500 pounds of gold to finance them. This was more than four times the annual subsidy first agreed between the government of Constantinople and the Huns in around 435.

The Council of Chalcedon was not successful in suppressing the theological divisions of opinion so powerfully held. The danger to the emperor lay in his failure to secure through it the religious unity to which he had so openly committed himself. Monophysitism, supported by an increasingly aggressive monastic movement, became entrenched in Coptic-speaking Egypt, in the Syriac-speaking churches of Palestine and Syria and in the Armenian church, while the Christian church in Persian Mesopotamia adopted Nestorianism. The combination of theological dissension and vernacular cultures in these regions makes one wonder whether there was a real possibility of an alliance between cultural and religious allegiances to produce a form of nationalistic sentiment against the government of Constantinople. The extent to which this created a weakness in the structure of the early Byzantine empire is debated, but the possibility of such a development clearly sets a question against the political integrity of an empire to which the enforcement of religious unity was so important.

Courtly Munificence at Ravenna

Ravenna had from the time of Augustus been the headquarters of one of the imperial fleets of Italy (the other was at Misenum), and had from then enjoyed a modestly flourishing life as a naval base. Though somewhat overshadowed as a commercial center by Aquileia, it was of obvious importance at such times as the civil wars of 68–70 AD.

The occupation of Ravenna as imperial capital can be dated precisely to 402 AD, after the siege of Milan which had exposed that city to the barbarian invasion of north Italy. Ravenna, tucked away among flats and marshes, surrounded by branches of the Po and linked to the mainland proper by a raised causeway, was nearly impregnable; it was taken only rarely, and then usually by treachery or collusion. For Sidonius Apollinaris it was a perverse city, in which the laws of nature had been reversed, where "walls fall flat and waters stand, towers float and ships are seated," while croaking frogs were citizens. More seriously, based on his security there, and on the direct sea link to Constantinople which always figured large in the advantages of Ravenna, Honorius was able to sit it out and defy Alaric when the latter's control of Italy seemed otherwise complete (see p. 209). The city was an equally secure refuge for the barbarian kings of Italy, and, after its capture in 540 by the armies of Justinian, for the Byzantine governors, or "exarchs" of the conquered province.

Throughout this time Ravenna witnessed a typically vigorous social and cultural life (not to mention periodic political violence) based on the presence of royal and imperial courts. Circus races there are described by Sidonius; the city received constant visitors; and its intellectual life is suggested by, among other evidence, the manuscripts known to have been revised there.

The churches of Ravenna span the times of the 5th-century emperors, the barbarian kings and the Byzantine reconquest, though the Byzantines did what they could to efface the memory, and the visual images, of their immediate predecessors.

Below A detail from a mosaic in St Vitale showing Justinian and his courtiers, in an image corresponding to that of Theodora and her attendants shown *opposite*. Members of the household guard are seen, one of them with resplendent monogrammed shield.

The church of St Apollinare Nuovo (*above center*), originally the palace church of Theoderic, was decorated with mosaic scenes of Ravenna which give some idea of its monumental grandeur. Here are (*left*) the harbor of Classis (Classe di Ravenna) and (*far right*) the palace of Theoderic, of which the facade may still be extant in the building known as the "palace of the exarchs" near the church. In the delicately carved balustrades from St Apollinare Nuovo (*above*) the peacocks and vine tendrils are symbols of eternal life. Also shown (*top*) is the elaborate marble throne of Bishop Maximianus (546–54).

The church of St Vitale, seen by the 9th-century chronicler Agnellus as beyond comparison in Italy, was begun at about the time of the death of Theoderic but dedicated in 547 or 548, after the reconquest of Italy by Justinian's generals. *Below* is shown Justinian's wife Theodora with her attendants, in an image symbolizing her generosity to the new church. The empress bears a golden chalice as her gift to the church, and on the rim of her robe appear the three wise men bearing gifts, in an allusion to Christian munificence. The scene is visualized as a procession from right to left across the narthex of the church, the end wall, with apse, and sides of the narthex being seen as if opened out. Theodora's head, with nimbus, appears almost, but not quite, in the center of the apse, as if it were itself a mosaic image there. The progress of the group is suggested by the gently increasing sway of the figures, by the curtain held aside by an attendant and, in a touch of brilliant imagination, by the sudden implied movement of the fountain.

The Ostrogothic King Theoderic rested after his death in 526 in the still standing mausoleum (*far left*) outside the walls of Ravenna. The immense size of the monolithic roof – 300 tons of Istrian stone – is remarked on by a contemporary source. The handles by which it was maneuvered into position can be seen around the rim. The palace of Theoderic is seen (*left*) in a mosaic from St Apollinare Nuovo. The figures of Theoderic and his court, removed after the Justinianic reconquest, can still be seen in outline.

THE OSTROGOTHIC KINGDOM AND THE BYZANTINE RECONQUEST

From 476, Italy was governed by Germanic kings, with their court at Ravenna. Odoacer, who had supplanted Romulus Augustulus, was himself defeated and killed by Theoderic the Ostrogoth after a long siege in which Ravenna was taken by treachery (493). Both kings ruled with consideration for the Italian peoples under their government, showing every sign of respect for the great Empire of whose impressive remains they found themselves masters. Senatorial life at Rome continued as before, the great urban offices being filled by members of the city aristocracy. The Colosseum was restored under Odoacer; entertainments and hunting displays were provided there, with chariot races in the Circus. These events are frequently illustrated on the ivory diptychs distributed by senators to commemorate the occasion. The involvement of the senate in the ecclesiastical politics of Rome grew ever more intense, as seen particularly in the disorders surrounding the election of Pope Symmachus against the claims of Laurentius (498) and in the diplomatic and theological negotiations attending the rapprochement with the eastern church which reached fruition after the emperor Justin's accession in 519.

Theoderic deserves his reputation as a humane and sympathetic ruler. He is compared by a contemporary source with the emperors Trajan and Valentinian – comparisons justified by his building restorations, in which, again, he encouraged and collaborated with members of the Roman nobility, and by his careful, restrained management of Rome and Italy. The key-word of the regime, *civilitas*, means the preservation of proper individual liberties under the protection of law. The senator Cassiodorus, a member of a line of imperial administrators, was employed by Theoderic to present his policies to the Roman public in official letters written in a highly wrought, metaphorical and, to modern eyes, extraordinarily affected style, which was nevertheless effective in maintaining an image of the regime as solicitous of the highest civilized values. From another point of view, the letters are the culmination of a long evolution of increasingly elaborate Roman "bureaucratese" which had been given its decisive impulse in the 4th century.

The reign of Theoderic also saw the preeminence of the philosopher Boethius, whose phenomenal achievement in the fields of theology, science and music, as well as in traditional philosophy, establishes him as one of the greatest minds ever produced by the ancient world, as well as a dominating influence in the Middle Ages. The fall of Boethius, described rather indirectly in his most famous work, *The Consolation of Philosophy*, was also a tragedy for Theoderic, whose reign ended in rancor and conflict between him and the senate. It is a misjudgment to regard the *Consolation* simply as a reversion by Boethius to traditional paganism; an examination of preoccupations about human fortune and the omniscience of God in the light of

"I, who once made poems in strength and hope, alas, now weeping must start sad songs." Boethius wrote his *Consolation* as a dialogue in prose and verse between himself and the lady Philosophy, who appears to him in prison. Here he is (*below*) as seen by a 12th-century illuminator of the opening page of the book, seated in his prison with a pair of writing tablets open before him.

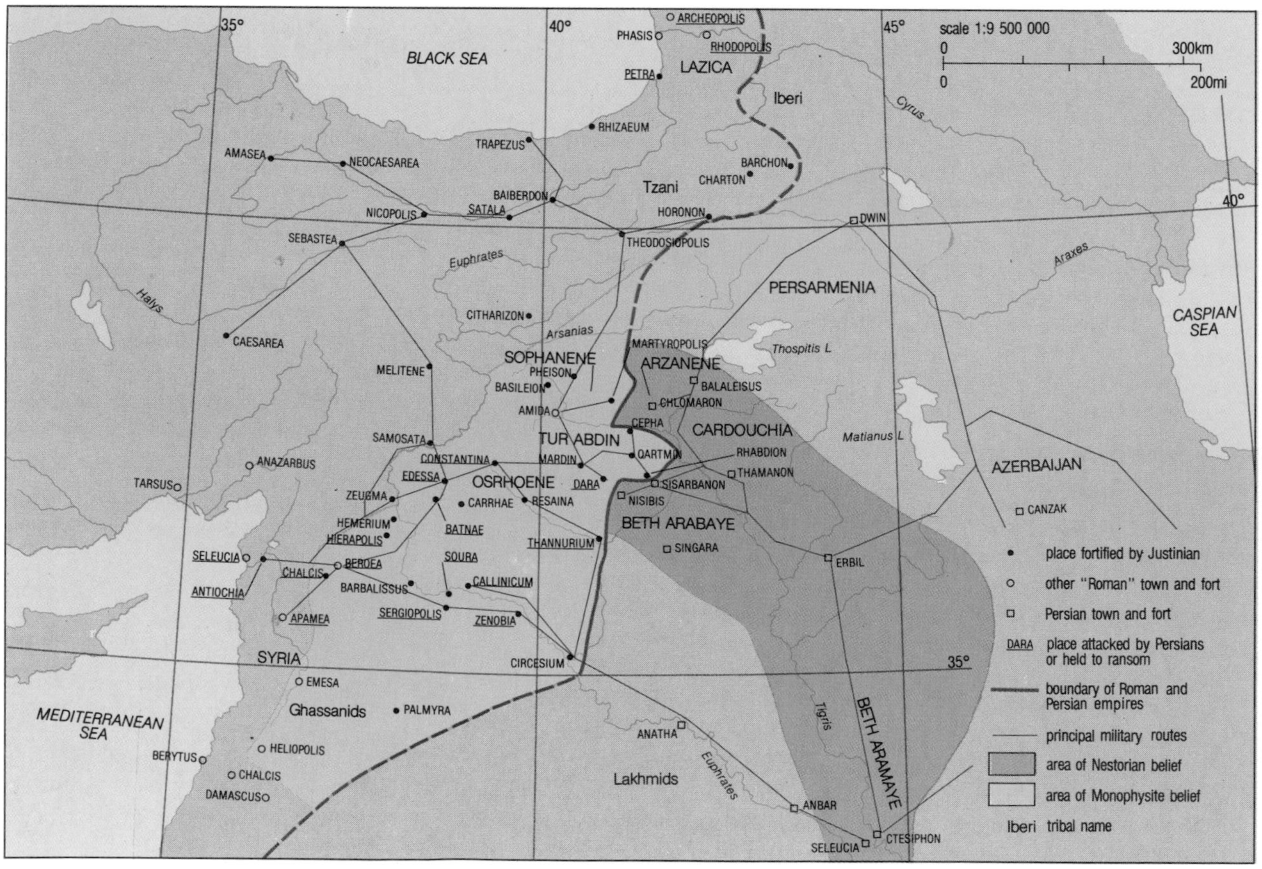

Left: Persia in the time of Justinian. For much of Justinian's reign the eastern Roman provinces had to withstand attacks by the Sasanians under their aggressive and successful Khusro I (531–79 AD). In the south limited Roman forces occupied a few strong points, while the Ghassanid Arab federation policed the desert approaches against raids by the Persian Lakhmid Arabs. In the center, the fortress of Dara, supported by the major military bases of Amida and Constantina and by the fortified salient of the Tur Abdin, opposed the Persian frontier city of Nisibis; yet the permanent garrisons were rarely sufficient to prevent Persian invasions, and the wealthy cities of Osrhoene and Syria were frequently threatened. Further north, the frontier bastions of Martyropolis, Citharizon and Theodosiopolis faced Arzanene and Persarmenia, and Justinian eventually established Roman control over the Tzani and Lazica, strategically important areas that could block nomad raids from across the Caucasus, and prevent Persian access to the Black Sea.

Above The diptych of Boethius' father Flavius Narius (?) Manlius Boethius, consul in 487. Upon his parents' early death, the young Boethius had been brought up in the family of Symmachus, consul in 485, whose daughter Rusticiana he married. After the execution of her husband, and shortly after that of Symmachus, Rusticiana devoted herself to charitable works.

the near certainty of its author's approaching execution, the work is a masterpiece of philosophical humanism.

The conflict between Theoderic and the senate was caused by a shift of ecclesiastical policy in the east, where the monophysite preferences of the old emperor Anastasius were replaced, on the accession of Justin I (519), by an aggressively "orthodox" policy which encouraged the previously estranged churches of the west to move closer to their eastern counterparts. This policy, encouraged with still greater energy by Justin's nephew and envisaged successor, Justinian, tended to ally senatorial Christian Rome with the Byzantine court, to the obvious unease of the Arian Theoderic. The diplomatic and other relations between east and west came, only too easily, to suggest political intrigue directed against the barbarian court of Ravenna by the Christian capitals of the Empire. It was Boethius' spirited defense of a senator accused of conspiracy with the east that led to his arrest and brutal execution by Theoderic in 523. In the previous year he had been given the post of *magister officiorum* at Ravenna and his sons made joint consuls, in an obvious and perhaps desperate attempt by Theoderic to maintain good relations between Ravenna and Rome in the face of overtures to Rome from Constantinople.

In the last year of his reign, Theoderic, in the hope of moderating the ecclesiastical policies of the eastern court, allowed Pope John I to visit Constantinople, but the visit, the first ever made by a pope of Rome to the eastern capital, was greeted there with terrific enthusiasm which further emphasized Theoderic's growing isolation from his Roman subjects. When John returned he was put under house arrest at Ravenna, and his death in confinement was closely followed by that of Theoderic himself (526).

In the west, Theoderic had confirmed his position by alliances and connections by marriage with the barbarian kings of Gaul, Spain and Africa. His attempts to unite the rulers of Gaul against the increasing threat of the Franks under Clovis failed. The Visigoths were heavily defeated by Clovis at the battle of Vouillé in southwestern Gaul (507). They were reduced to their territories in Spain, and the establishment of the Frankish kingdom in the old Roman provinces of Gaul was complete.

The successors of Theoderic maintained his sympathetic policies towards the city of Rome, but suffered from increasing conflict within the dynasty. The death of the young king Athalaric in 534, and the murder of his mother (and Theoderic's daughter) Amalasuntha by Theodahad, heralded the end of Visigothic rule. By 535 Justinian's general, Belisarius, was leading the campaigns of reconquest against the west.

Cassiodorus, having served both Athalaric and Theodahad as praetorian prefect, retired from political life in 537 and, after a possibly prolonged visit to Constantinople, returned to Italy to pursue the religious activities which have earned him a less ambiguous reputation than have his political commitments to barbarian kings. His earlier attempt to found a school of Christian learning at Rome having failed on account of the surrounding unrest of the wars of reconquest, Cassiodorus returned in advanced years to his family estates at Squillace in Calabria and founded there his famous monastic settlement of Vivarium. Here the essentials of classical learning were preserved alongside and as an integral part of the pursuit of a Christian holy life, a pattern of immense importance for the future of classical culture in medieval Europe.

The political history of the eastern Empire of the 6th century begins with the caution and stability of the reign of Anastasius, who administered the economy with such success and thrift as to leave a massive surplus on his death in 519. The reign of

Far right The diptych of Rufius Gennadius Probus Orestes, consul in 530 (the name Orestes also appears in the monogram). He sits enthroned in full consular dress, flanked by Rome and Constantinople. Below are symbols of largesse and, above the consul, the Ostrogothic King Athalaric and his mother Amalasuntha. The diptych illustrates both the favor of the later Ostrogothic regime to senatorial Rome, and the theme of east–west harmony – an association of ideas soon to be shattered by the Byzantine reconquest of Italy.

Left St Vitalis, the soldier martyr, receives the crown of martyrdom in a mosaic from the great 6th-century church dedicated to him at Ravenna (see also p. 218).

Top right The fortified monastery of St Catherine in Sinai, built by Justinian in 527. The foundation is eloquent of the piety of the emperor, but it is unlikely that the garrison did more than protect the monks against local disorder.

Below right The walls of Dara, the frontier fortress against the Persians often assigned to Justinian, but in fact certainly built in the time of Anastasius.

Justin I was notable for its abandonment of Anastasius' monophysite tendencies, with the consequences described above, and for the increasing influence of Justinian. Justinian's accession on his uncle's death in 527 initiated an explosion of energetic activity. Almost immediately after becoming emperor, he set in train the reorganization and codification of Roman law which remains as one of the Roman Empire's most imposing legacies as well as, in the *Digest*, a fundamental source of evidence for the social history of the classical Roman Empire itself. Justinian also turned his attention to the Persians, over whom Belisarius won a great victory in 530. In 532 the Romans and Persians signed an agreement known, with transparent optimism, as the "eternal peace." War broke out again later, and Justinian embarked on the building of a series of elaborate fortification works in northern Mesopotamia.

The reign of Justinian was almost cut short in 532 by riots of factions of circus supporters, directed initially against his unpopular ministers, especially the praetorian prefect and the quaestor Tribonian, a distinguished lawyer who had taken a leading role in the codification of the law. In the insurrection, known as the "Nika" ("Conquer!") riots from the chant of the crowds, another emperor was proclaimed, and Justinian was only saved by the determination of his wife Theodora, a former actress whom he had married years before he became emperor, and by his generals, Belisarius and Mundus, who led the troops under their command in an assault on the rioting crowds. Thousands of citizens were killed in the repression, and large parts of Constantinople burned. As in the burning of Rome under Nero, the damage provided the opportunity for magnificent rebuilding; Justinian's greatest work was the reconstruction of the church of St Sophia, described with such wonder by the historian Procopius. On seeing the interior of his new church Justinian exclaimed "Solomon, I have surpassed you!"

Justinian's reconquest of the west began with Africa, which, considering the fate of previous attempts, was taken from the Vandals with surprising ease in 533. The problem of Moorish rebellion, however, proved more intractable and took several more years to overcome. The murder of Amalasuntha by Theodahad provided a justification for extending the reconquest to Italy; in addition, the diplomatic traffic of recent years had established contacts between western senators and the eastern court, and there was also among the Latin-speaking community of Constantinople a group of senatorial exiles from the west, well placed to make contact with diplomatic visitors and to exert pressure on the eastern government.

The reconquest of Italy was much more difficult and laborious than that of Africa, and was attended by destruction and violence which cast the greatest doubt on the value, to the Italians themselves, of their incorporation into the Byzantine state. Justinian's general, Narses, eventually completed the reconquest in 553 by defeating King Teias, and the government of Italy was organized by the so-called "Pragmatic Sanction" of 554. The senatorial class of Rome, which had survived the 5th-century invasions and the establishment of the barbarian kingdom of Ravenna, makes no further appearance in history after the Byzantine reconquest. The resplendent greatness of Byzantine Ravenna, which became the seat of the new government, or "Exarchate," was achieved at the price of the impoverishment of Italy, and of Rome itself, which marks the end of the classical world. Little could be done to prevent the rapid occupation of Italy by the Lombards in the later 560s.

Justinian died in 565, the effective ruler of more traditionally Roman territory than any of his predecessors since the early 5th century. Yet the reality of his achievement is questionable. The costs of reconquest fell heavily on eastern resources, diverting armies from the Danubian and Persian fronts where their presence was more immediately necessary; moreover, the conquest itself was not in the best interests of the western provinces. The Byzantine Empire can be left to speak for itself in its survival for a further 900 years after the death of Justinian. As for Rome and Italy, where this book began, it is an irony that their latest period of prosperity, under the favorable eye of Germanic kings, was ended by a Byzantine court's repossession of them as impoverished provinces of a Roman Empire now governed from Constantinople.

A contemporary source alleges that Theoderic was illiterate and traced his name through a brass template. It seems certain that this is a misrepresentation, based on Theoderic's use of a template to draw the complicated monogram which appears on his coinage (*above*). Also shown (*below*) is the monogram of Odoacer.

The Roman Legacy

For Gibbon, the fall of the Roman Empire was "a revolution which will ever be remembered, and is still felt by the nations of the earth." At any moment until the rise of the modern industrial age, and in important respects beyond it, both parts of this statement were self-evidently true. Until quite recently "Tully's Offices" – the *De Officiis* of Cicero – could have been described as one of the most influential books in western culture, and it is still not unusual for a British civil servant, as was once normal for politicians, to know more about the history of the Roman world than about his own. That this can hardly be said to be a good thing is not the point: until the modern age its propriety would never have been questioned.

Even on a narrow understanding of what is meant by "Roman," the legacy of the Roman world to the languages, literary culture, architecture, government and religious life of medieval and modern Europe has been immense. On a broader view, comprising Roman influence as mediated through the Christian Greek world of Byzantium, its impact is even greater.

These two pages do not attempt to summarize the book which could be written on the Roman legacy in all its complexity: rather, they isolate particular examples, and suggest by implication where more may be found. The examples chosen are not unremittingly solemn. Awareness of a culture can, and should, reside in the trivial as well as the portentous, in the bizarre as well as ideal, not least in the affectionate as well as the forbidding.

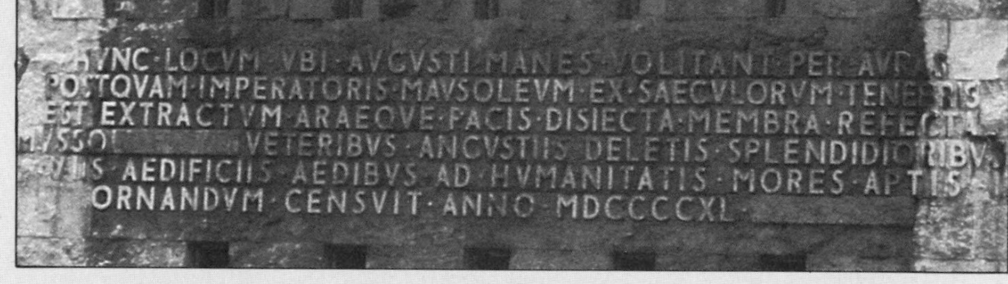

Ancient mythological and literary scenes in idealized landscapes were a frequent subject of classical painters, especially of the French school, as in this painting (*top*) of Aeneas at Delos by Claude (1600–82), in which the human figures do little more than provide the scale for a study of architectural forms in their landscape. The building in the middle distance bears some resemblance to Hadrian's Pantheon at Rome (p. 104). The engraving by Piranesi (*opposite top*), of two Roman roads flanked by funerary monuments piled up in an architectural extravaganza of obsessive profusion, reflects the renewed interest of the artist's time with the physical remains of Roman power. Its date, c. 1756, is close to that of Gibbon's musings on the Capitol which first moved his mind towards the writing of a history of Rome. The inscription in modern Rome (*above*) reproduces ancient Roman practice towards disgraced emperors: the name of Mussolini has been erased. An earlier and more sinister reminder of the reactionary tendencies of Rome in the 1920s is given by the group of proto-Fascists dressed up as legionary standard bearers (*left*). The publication in 1753 of Wood and Dawkins's *Ruins of Palmyra* made available to designers the immensely rich resources of this great eastern city. Here (*below*), in attenuated but unmistakable form, is Wood's engraving of a ceiling from the temple of Bel (cf. p. 158), as adapted for use in the dining room of Stratfield Saye House, Berkshire.

The triumphal arch, a universally acknowledged symbol of war and victory adopted from the Romans, here seen (*left*) in its French imperial version at Place Charles de Gaulle, Paris. On a less elevated level, manhole covers in Rome (*bottom left*) are still cast with the traditional legend SPQR: "Senatus Populusque Romanus." One particularly pervasive legacy of the Romans, the Julian calendar, is illustrated (*left*) in the so-called "Calendar of the Year 354" (see also p. 207), here seen at October with its list of public games and festivals and the image of Scorpio; the Zodiac itself is, through the Romans, a legacy of ancient Mesopotamia to the modern world. The last word goes to the Gauls, Astérix and Obélix, complaining during a journey to Lutetia Parisiorum of the damaging effects of Roman construction on the landscape. The village from which they came, near the garrison town of Laudanum in northern Gaul, is so far unexcavated though its life is well known from literary sources.

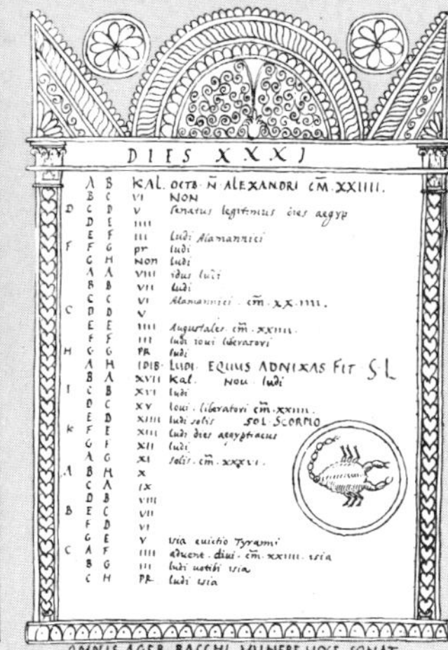

LIST OF ILLUSTRATIONS

Abbreviations: t = top, tl = top left, tr = top right, c = center, b = bottom etc.

All maps by Lovell Johns, Oxford.

All site plans by John Brennan, Oxford.

BIBLIOGRAPHY

The bibliography is from various points of view selective. It includes only books and not articles in learned journals, and with a very few exceptions mentions work written only in English. Even within these limitations, it expresses the authors' own choice of what seems to them especially important in a vastly more extensive field, concentrating first on the fundamental, and secondly on the most recent and (we hope) most accessible work. We hope nevertheless that it will provide a guide to more specialized work to those who need it, and to the general reader a way of following up topics which especially interest him.

Geography
As far as we know this is the first Atlas of the Roman world to be published, at least in English. But the Roman world is naturally covered in older historical and classical atlases, many of which are excellent and have been extensively used by us. These include H. Kiepert, *Atlas Antiquus* (Berlin 1882), A. A. M. van der Heyden and H. H. Scullard, *Atlas of the Classical World* (London 1959), G. Westermann, *Grosser Atlas zur Weltgeschichte* (Brunswick 1976), and C. McEvedy, *Penguin Atlas of Ancient History* (Harmondsworth 1967). There is no fully satisfactory treatment in English of the geography of ancient Italy and the Mediterranean. The best available is probably M. Cary, *The Geographic Background of Greek and Roman History* (Oxford 1949). The antiquated work of H. Nissen, *Italische Landeskunde*, 2 vols. (Berlin 1883–1902), is still useful in parts. The reconstruction of ancient landscape from field archaeology and air photography is the theme of J. Bradford's *Ancient Landscapes* (London 1957), which deals with Italy in particular. A very good selection of air photographs can be found in G. Schmidt, *Atlante aerofotografico delle sedi umani in Italia*, 2 vols. (Florence 1966–70). C. Delano Smith, *Western Mediterranean Europe* (London 1979), is a modern account of the historical geography of the area since the Neolithic age. The best general introduction to Mediterranean geography is probably M. and R. Beckinsale, *Southern Europe: the Mediterranean and Alpine Lands* (London 1975); the older work of E. C. Semple, *The Geography of the Mediterranean Region* (New York 1931), is still worth consulting. The most detailed account of Italian geography is the handbook published by the Admiralty, *Italy* (Naval Intelligence Division, Geographical Handbooks), 3 vols. (London 1944). The classic account of the historical role of the Mediterranean environment is F. Braudel, *The Mediterranean and the Mediterranean World in the Age of Philip II*, English trans. (London 1972).

Sources
The Loeb Classical Library includes the works of most classical and later authors, with text and parallel English translation. Several important texts, mainly of writers of the classical period, are also available in translation in the Penguin Classics series. Useful anthologies of translated texts and documents include N. Lewis and M. Reinhold, *Roman Civilisation*, 2 vols. (rev. ed., New York 1966), and A. H. M. Jones, *A History of Rome through the Fifth Century*, 2 vols. (London 1968). For a selection of documents on the early Christian church see J. Stevenson, *A New Eusebius: Documents Illustrative of the History of the Church to AD 337* (London 1957; often reprinted). Texts which bear on economic history are assembled and translated in T. Frank, *An Economic Survey of Ancient Rome*, vol. I (Baltimore, Md., 1927). Discussion of the value and reliability of the sources can be found in most textbooks on Roman history. On particular writers of the earlier period see P. G. Walsh, *Livy* (Cambridge 1961), F. W. Walbank, *Polybius* (Berkeley, Calif., 1972), and R. Syme, *Sallust* (Berkeley, Calif., 1968); for work on later writers see below. A. Momigliano, *Essays on Ancient and Modern Historiography* (Oxford 1977), contains some important studies of the sources for early Roman history; also useful is T. A. Dorey (ed.), *Latin Historians* (London 1966). On the interpretation of numismatic and papyrological evidence, especially, but by no means exclusively, important for the time of the Empire, see E. G. Turner, *Greek Papyri* (Oxford 1968), and J. P. C. Kent, B. Overbeck, A. U. Stylow, *Roman Coins* (London 1978).

General
The classic histories of Rome to the end of the Republic are T. Mommsen, *History of Rome*, trans. W. P. Dickson, 4 vols. (London 1861), G. De Sanctis, *Storia dei Romani*, 4 vols. (Turin/Florence 1907–53), and the collective *Cambridge Ancient History*, vols. VII–IX (Cambridge 1928–32). There are convenient one-volume histories of the entire period by A. Piganiol, *La Conquête romaine* (Paris 1927), A. E. R. Boak and W. G. Sinnigen, *History of Rome to AD 565*, 6th ed. (New York 1977), M. Cary and H. H. Scullard, *History of Rome*, rev. ed. (London 1975), and M. Grant, *History of Rome* (London 1979). The *Oxford Classical Dictionary*, 2nd ed. (Oxford 1970), is an invaluable work of reference.

Early Rome
The most up-to-date account in English is H. H. Scullard, *History of the Roman World 753–146 BC*, 4th ed. (London 1981). E. Gjerstad, *Early Rome*, 6 vols. (Lund 1953–75), presents all the archaeological evidence, but is unreliable in matters of interpretation. Specialized studies of early Italian archaeology (including Rome) are contained in D. and F. R. Ridgway (eds.), *Italy before the Romans* (London 1979); J. Reich, *Italy before Rome* (Oxford 1979), is a concise popular account. Also useful on early Rome: J. Heurgon, *The Rise of Rome to 264 BC* (London 1973), and R. M. Ogilvie, *Early Rome and the Etruscans* (London 1976). On the Etruscans there are good books by M. Pallottino, *The Etruscans*, 2nd ed. (London 1974), M. Cristofani, *The Etruscans* (London 1979), F. Coarelli (ed.), *Etruscan Cities* (London 1975), and M. Grant, *The Etruscans* (London 1980). E. Pulgram, *The Tongues of Italy* (Cambridge, Mass., 1958), has a good account of the languages of pre-Roman Italy.

The Republic
The best general account is M. Crawford, *The Roman Republic* (London 1978); see also A. H. McDonald, *Republican Rome* (London 1966). A. J. Toynbee, *Hannibal's Legacy*, 2 vols. (London 1966), is a wide ranging study of Roman society in the middle Republic. C. Nicolet, *Rome et la conquête du monde méditerranéen*, 2 vols. (Paris 1977–78), is the fullest modern account of the period 264–27 BC. On the fall of the Republic see R. Syme's classic, *The Roman Revolution* (Oxford 1939); also E. S. Gruen, *The Last Generation of the Roman Republic* (Berkeley, Calif., 1974), and, on the formation and attitudes of the nobility, M. Gelzer, *The Roman Nobility*, trans. R. Seager (Oxford 1975). For a clear and fully documented narrative of events see H. H. Scullard, *From the Gracchi to Nero*, 4th ed. (London 1976). Rome's conquest of Italy is seen from a regional point of view by E. T. Salmon, *Samnium and the Samnites* (Cambridge 1968), and W. V. Harris, *Rome in Etruria and Umbria* (Oxford 1971). E. T. Salmon, *Roman Colonisation under the Republic* (London 1969), is a good discussion of its subject. Juridical aspects of the conquest (and other matters) are treated in

A. N. Sherwin-White, *The Roman Citizenship*, 2nd ed. (Oxford 1973). The state of the Roman economy at the time of the Italian conquest is examined by C. G. Starr, *The Beginnings of Imperial Rome* (Ann Arbor, Mich., 1980).

On the Punic Wars see T. A. Dorey and D. R. Dudley, *Rome against Carthage* (London 1971), J. F. Lazenby, *Hannibal's War* (Warminster 1978), and B. Caven, *The Punic Wars* (London 1980). The growth of the Roman empire and the problem of Roman imperialism are dealt with by E. Badian, *Foreign Clientelae* (Oxford 1958), and *Roman Imperialism in the Late Republic* (Oxford 1968); W. V. Harris, *War and Imperialism in Republican Rome* (Oxford 1979). Notice also T. Frank, *Roman Imperialism* (New York 1914). For a clear account of the events see R. M. Errington, *The Dawn of Empire* (London 1971).

The social and economic consequences of empire are analyzed by P. A. Brunt, *Social Conflicts in the Roman Republic* (London 1971), and M. K. Hopkins, *Conquerors and Slaves* (Cambridge 1978). On the Gracchi see D. Stockton, *The Gracchi* (Oxford 1979), and A. H. Bernstein, *Tiberius Sempronius Gracchus* (Ithaca, N.Y., 1978). On the subject of slavery see M. I. Finley, *The Ancient Economy* (London 1973); J. Vogt, *Ancient Slavery and the Ideal of Man* (Oxford 1974: chapter 3 deals with the slave wars). T. Wiedemann, *Greek and Roman Slavery* (London 1981), is a collection of texts and documents in translation. The changing role of the army in the social structure of the Republic is discussed by E. Gabba, *Republican Rome: the Army and the Allies* (Oxford 1976). For a study of population figures, and of their importance for the social history of the Republic, see P. A. Brunt, *Italian Manpower 225 BC–AD 14* (Oxford 1971).

There are many good biographies of leading persons in the drama of republican history; only a selection can be given here: H. H. Scullard, *Scipio Africanus, Soldier and Politician* (London 1970); A. E. Astin, *Cato the Censor* (Oxford 1978), *Scipio Aemilianus* (Oxford 1967); P. A. L. Greenhalgh, *Pompey*, 2 vols. (London 1980–81); M. Gelzer, *Caesar* (Oxford 1969); M. Grant, *Julius Caesar* (London 1967), *Cleopatra* (London 1972); E. Rawson, *Cicero: a Portrait* (London 1975); D. R. Shackleton Bailey, *Cicero* (London 1971); W. K. Lacey, *Cicero and the End of the Roman Republic* (London 1978).

Aspects of Roman political thought and practice

C. Nicolet, *The World of the Citizen in Republican Rome* (London 1980); E. S. Staveley, *Greek and Roman Voting and Elections* (London 1972); L. R. Taylor, *Roman Voting Assemblies* (Ann Arbor, Mich., 1966); D. C. Earl, *The Moral and Political Tradition of Rome* (London 1967); C. Wirszubski, *Libertas as a Political Idea at Rome* (Cambridge 1950); E. Badian, *Publicans and Sinners* (Oxford 1972); L. R. Taylor, *Party Politics in the Age of Caesar* (Berkeley, Calif., 1966); A. W. Lintott, *Violence in Republican Rome* (Oxford 1968); J. A. Crook, *Law and Life of Rome* (London 1966); J. M. Kelly, *Roman Litigation* (Oxford 1966).

Roman society and culture

Intellectual life: R. M. Ogilvie, *Roman Literature and Society* (Harmondsworth 1980); T. Frank, *Life and Literature in the Roman Republic* (Berkeley, Calif., 1930); S. F. Bonner, *Education in Ancient Rome* (London 1977); H. I. Marrou, *A History of Education in Antiquity* (London 1956). Art and architecture: R. Bianchi Bandinelli, *Rome, the Centre of Power* (London 1970); G. M. A. Hanfmann, *Roman Art* (London 1964); D. Strong, *Roman Art* (London 1976); A. Boëthius, *Etruscan and Early Roman Architecture*, 2nd ed. (Harmondsworth 1978). Religion: R. M. Ogilvie, *The Romans and Their Gods* (London 1969); W. Warde Fowler, *The Religious Experience of the Roman People* (London 1911); H. H. Scullard, *Festivals and Ceremonies of the Roman Republic* (London 1981). The countryside: K. D. White, *Roman Farming* (London 1970); J. M. Frayn, *Subsistence Farming in Roman Italy* (Fontwell 1979); T. W. Potter, *The Changing Landscape of South Etruria* (London 1979); T. Ashby, *The Roman Campagna in Classical Times* (London 1927). The City: W. Warde Fowler, *Social Life at Rome in the Age of Cicero* (London 1922); U. E. Paoli, *Rome, Its People, Life and Customs* (New York 1963); J. Carcopino, *Daily Life in Ancient Rome* (London 1941); M. Grant, *The Roman Forum* (London 1970); S. B. Platner, T. Ashby, *A Topographical Dictionary of Ancient Rome* (Oxford 1929); E. Nash, *Pictorial Dictionary of Ancient Rome*, 2 vols., 2nd ed. (London 1968). Ostia: R. Meiggs, *Roman Ostia*, 2nd ed. (Oxford 1973); Pompeii: J. B. Ward Perkins and A. Claridge, *Pompeii AD 79* (New York 1978); M. Grant, *Cities of Vesuvius* (London 1971).

Augustus and the Julio-Claudians

The most convenient brief study of Augustus is by A. H. M. Jones, *Augustus* (London 1970); compare the more specialized discussions in his *Studies in Roman Government and Law* (Oxford 1960). Augustus' *Res Gestae* are translated and fully commented on by P. A. Brunt and J. M. Moore, *Res Gestae Divi Augusti: the Achievements of the Divine Augustus* (Oxford 1967). On Augustus' Julio-Claudian successors see B. M. Levick, *Tiberius the Politician* (London 1976), R. Seager, *Tiberius* (London 1972), A. Momigliano, *Claudius: the Emperor and His Achievement* (1934; reprinted with revised bibliography to 1959, Cambridge 1961), and B. H. Warmington, *Nero: Reality and Legend* (London 1969). Z. Yavetz, *Plebs and Princeps* (Oxford 1969), traces the political and social role of the people of Rome from late Republic to early principate. G. W. Bowersock, *Augustus and the Greek World* (Oxford 1965), studies the social, diplomatic and cultural relations of the new regime with the Greek east – compare also Fergus Millar, *The Emperor in the Roman World*, mentioned below – and Colin Wells, *The German Policy of Augustus: an Examination of the Archaeological Evidence* (Oxford 1972), its military policy on the Rhine frontier. On the literature and moral climate of Augustan Rome see Gordon Williams, *Tradition and Originality in Roman Poetry* (Oxford 1968). Miriam Griffin, *Seneca: a Philosopher in Politics* (Oxford 1976), is the best study of the problems of conscience raised by autocratic government; compare the work of Wirszubski, *Libertas* (mentioned above). Syme's *Roman Revolution* is as fundamental for the understanding of the early principate as it is for the fall of the Republic, and his marvelous *Tacitus*, 2 vols. (Oxford 1958), describes in rich detail the period covered by Tacitus – from the death of Augustus – as well as the historian's own milieu and time of writing in the Flavio-Trajanic age.

The Roman Empire, 70–306 AD

For the general history of the Empire from the Flavians to Constantine there is no real successor to H. H. Scullard's *From the Gracchi to Nero*, mentioned above. A. Garzetti, *From Tiberius to the Antonines* (Engl. ed. London 1974), covers in detail the period 14 to 192 AD, and H. M. D. Parker, *A History of the Roman World, AD 138 to 337* (2nd ed. London 1958), reaches the death of Constantine, but necessarily without reflecting recent advances in research. (It is worth noting that the familiar but now rather dated Methuen Roman histories will over the next few years be replaced by a series of new books.) The civil wars are described by K. Wellesley, *The Long Year, AD 69* (London 1975). A. R. Birley, *Septimius Severus, the African Emperor* (London 1971), is far more than a political study and also covers effectively much of the 2nd-century background. On the political and cultural history of the Flavio-Trajanic period Syme's *Tacitus* is in all ways fundamental, as, still, are his chapters on military history in the *Cambridge Ancient History*, vols. X and XI (1934 and 1936). On Trajan's wars L. Rossi, *Trajan's Column and the Dacian Wars* (London 1971), is full and most informative but with sometimes mediocre photographs. For the history and culture of Rome's eastern neighbor see R. Ghirshman, *Iran, from the Earliest Times to the Islamic Conquest* (Harmondsworth 1954) and *Iran: Parthians and Sassanians* (London 1962), and for Rome's eastern relations in their geographical and social context Freya Stark, *Rome on the Euphrates: the Story of a Frontier* (London 1966). The "anarchy" of the 3rd century is discussed in various works, notably the major books of Rostovtzeff and A. H. M. Jones mentioned below, and by R. MacMullen, *Roman Government's Response to Crisis, AD 235–337* (New Haven, Conn., and London 1976), and by Syme, *Emperors and Biography* (Oxford 1971).

On the role of the emperor in government and the development of governmental institutions and administrative hierarchies, see especially Fergus Millar, *The Emperor in the Roman World, 31 BC–AD 337* (London 1977). Millar may overstate the continuity of the conduct of the imperial office over this period and understate the impact of changing military needs on the emperors' role, on which see the absorbing study of E. N. Luttwak, *The Grand Strategy of the Roman Empire, from the First Century AD to the Third* (Baltimore, Md., and London 1976), and the very different perspective of R. MacMullen, *Soldier and Civilian in the Later Roman Empire* (Cambridge, Mass., 1963).

On the provincial prosperity of the Empire Gibbon's *Decline and Fall*, Chap. II, is still remarkable for its perceptiveness, and for its appreciation of the potential of archaeological and epigraphic evidence. The revolution in historical method made possible by the systematic study of material remains was essentially the work of Mommsen, substantial extracts from whose *Provinces of the Roman Empire* of 1885 are available in paperback with a useful introduction by T. R. S. Broughton (Chicago, Ill., and London 1968). Also fundamental, and incorporating a still wider range of material evidence, is M. Rostovtzeff, *The Social and Economic History of the Roman Empire* (2nd ed. by P. M. Fraser, Oxford 1957). The work of Mommsen is well appreciated by G. P. Gooch in *History and Historians in the Nineteenth Century* (2nd ed. London 1952), Chap. XXIV, and that of Rostovtzeff by A. Momigliano in his *Studies in Historiography* (London 1966), Chap. 5. For a comprehensive account of the regions of the Empire, with much citation of ancient sources, see Tenney Frank and others, *An Economic Survey of Ancient Rome*, 5 vols. (Baltimore, Md., 1933–40), and for a brief survey of its institutions and provincial diversities, Fergus Millar, *The Roman Empire and Its Neighbours* (2nd ed. London 1981). M. P. Charlesworth, *The Roman Empire* (Oxford 1951, reprinted with new bibliography, Oxford 1968), is also useful. The opportunities for economic and cultural life provided by the Roman pacification of the Mediterranean, and also the physical limitations imposed by natural conditions, are treated by L. Casson, *Ships and Seamanship in the Ancient World* (Princeton, N.J., 1971) and *Travel in the Ancient World* (London 1974); and the conditions of agricultural production by K. D. White in *Roman Farming* (London 1970), *Agricultural Implements of the Roman World* (Cambridge 1967) and *Farm Equipment of the Roman World* (Cambridge 1975). See also the *Oxford History of Technology*, Vol. II, edited by Charles Singer and others (Oxford 1956).

The changing nature of legal privilege in the context of the extension of the citizenship is studied by Peter Garnsey, *Social Status and Legal Privilege in the Roman Empire* (Oxford 1970), and by A. N. Sherwin-White, *The Roman Citizenship* (2nd ed. Oxford 1973); see also J. A. Crook, *Law and Life of Rome* (London 1967). R. Duncan-Jones, *The Economy of the Roman Empire: Quantitative Studies* (Cambridge 1974), provides excellent discussions of many aspects of civic munificence, especially on the cost of public works, and many useful papers by A. H. M. Jones are collected in his *The Roman Economy*, ed. P. A. Brunt (Oxford 1974). Syme's *Tacitus* (see above) is particularly good on the enlargement of the Roman governing class by provincial recruitment; see also his *Colonial Elites: Rome, Spain and the Americas* (London 1958).

On the prestige of rhetoric and its role in public communications, three recent books are especially notable: G. W. Bowersock, *Greek Sophists in the Roman Empire* (Oxford 1969); T. D. Barnes, *Tertullian: a Historical and Literary Study* (Oxford 1971); and E. Champlin, *Fronto and Antonine Rome* (Princeton, N.J., 1980). The attitudes of educated Greeks under Roman rule are discussed by C. P. Jones in *Plutarch and Rome* (Oxford 1971) and *The Roman World of Dio Chrysostom* (Cambridge, Mass., and London 1978), and by Fergus Millar, *A Study of Cassius Dio* (Oxford 1964).

On the huge topic of religious change and the rise of Christianity, a brief selection must suffice to convey the essentials. A. D. Nock, *Conversion: the Old and the New in Religion, from Alexander the Great to Augustine of Hippo* (Oxford 1933 and 1952), provides an introduction to new forms of religious experience, and F. Cumont, *Oriental Religions in Roman Paganism* (1911; reprinted New York 1956) and *The Mysteries of Mithras* (1903; reprinted New York 1956), still provides perhaps the most authoritative general treatment, despite recent criticism of some of his theories. See also E. R. Dodds, *Pagan and Christian in an Age of Anxiety* (Cambridge 1965), discussed, with the book of Frend mentioned below, by Peter Brown, *Religion and Society in the Age of St Augustine* (London 1972). Peter Brown's own *The Making of Late Antiquity* (Cambridge, Mass., and London 1978) tends, like much other recent work, to seek the origins of the new religious developments in the 2nd rather than in the 3rd century. J. H. W. G. Liebeschuetz, *Continuity and Change in Roman Religion* (Oxford 1979), is immensely rewarding for its care and thoughtfulness over a full four centuries of Roman religious experience. The best general description of the theory and practice of theurgy is by E. R. Dodds in his *The Greeks and the Irrational* (Berkeley, Calif., and London 1968), Appendix II.

On the rise of Christianity, W. H. C. Frend, *Martyrdom and Persecution in the Early Church* (Oxford 1965), is one of the most stimulating of all discussions of the subject, and H. Chadwick, *The Early Church* (Harmondsworth 1967), is clear, comprehensive and broad in scope. The two chapters of Gibbon, *Decline and Fall*, Chaps. XV and XVI, have survived the years marvelously well, and still make a fine introduction whose main lines are inherent in modern study. T. D. Barnes's *Tertullian*, mentioned above, is not only learned and precise but very vigorous and stimulating on the broader issues.

The Provinces of the Empire

On the provinces of the Empire, general surveys are provided by the works of Mommsen, Rostovtzeff, Millar and Tenney Frank mentioned above under "provincial prosperity of the Empire." For reference on individual sites, particularly useful are the *Princeton Encyclopaedia of Classical Sites*, ed. R. Stilwell and others (Princeton, N. J., 1976), and *Atlas of Classical Archaeology*, ed. M. I. Finley (London 1977). Both works contain bibliographical references and the latter has site plans and photographs.

As to books on individual provinces it is worth mentioning the series *Provinces of the Roman Empire* under the general editorship of S. S. Frere. This includes to date J. J. Wilkes, *Dalmatia* (London 1969), A. Mócsy, *Pannonia and Upper Moesia; a History of the Middle Danubian Provinces of the Roman Empire* (London 1974), G. Alföldy, *Noricum* (London 1974), and Sheppard Frere, *Britannia* (rev. ed. London 1978). See in addition C. H. V. Sutherland, *The Romans in Spain* (London 1939); Olwen Brogan, *Roman Gaul* (London 1963); Peter Salway, *Roman Britain* (Oxford 1981), and – among many other histories of Roman Britain – A. L. F. Rivet, *Town and Country in Roman Britain* (London 1958, reprinted 1966); P. Oliva, *Pannonia and the Onset of Crisis in the Roman Empire* (Prague 1962); R. F. Hoddinott, *Bulgaria in Antiquity: an Archaeological Introduction* (London 1975). On the eastern provinces: A. H. M. Jones, *The Greek City, from Alexander to Justinian* (rev. ed. Oxford 1966), and *The Cities of the Eastern Roman Provinces* (2nd ed. Oxford 1971); B. M. Levick, *Roman Colonies in Southern Asia Minor* (Oxford 1967); and various books by George Bean: *Aegean Turkey: an Archaeological Guide* (2nd ed. London 1979), *Turkey beyond the Maeander* (2nd ed. London 1980), *Lycian Turkey* (London 1978) and *Turkey's Southern Shore* (2nd ed. London 1979). J. H. W. G. Liebeschuetz, *Antioch: City and Imperial Administration in the Later Roman Empire* (Oxford 1972), has much also on the Syrian background. On Egypt, as well as the excellent chapter in Jones's *Cities of the Eastern Roman Provinces*, there is the brief account of H. Idris Bell, *Egypt, from Alexander the Great to the Arab Conquest: a Study in the Diffusion and Decay of Hellenism* (Oxford 1948).

The following are a selection of some of the more accessible works on the sites featured in the Atlas, arranged in the order of their appearance: D. E. L. Haynes, *The Antiquities of Tripolitania* (London 1955); R. Bianchi Bandinelli and others, *The Buried City: Excavations at Lepcis Magna* (Eng. trans. London 1970); E. M. Wightman, *Trier and the Treveri* (London 1970); G. C. Boon, *Silchester; the Roman Town of Calleva* (rev. ed. Newton Abbott 1974); B. Cunliffe, *Fishbourne: a Roman Palace and its Gardens* (London 1971); E. Vorbeck, L. Beckel, *Carnuntum: Rom an der Donau* (Salzburg 1973; in German, but with splendid aerial photographs, of which one is shown above, p. 143); J. and T. Marasović, *Diocletian Palace at Split* (Zagreb 1968); J. Travlos, *Pictorial Dictionary of Ancient Athens* (London and New York 1971); R. Day, *An Economic History of Athens under Roman Domination* (New York 1942). Research on the site of Ephesus is conducted by an Austrian school and the literature is almost all in German, but two books are worth recommending to English readers for their fine illustrations: W. Alzinger, *Die Ruine von Ephesos* (Berlin and Vienna 1972), and E. Lessing, W. Oberleitner, *Ephesos, Weltstadt der Antike* (Vienna and Heidelberg 1978). There is, however, a study of late Roman and Byzantine Ephesus in English: Clive Foss, *Ephesus after Antiquity: a Late Antique, Byzantine and Turkish City* (Cambridge 1979).

On the cities of the Orient: K. Michałowski, *Palmyra* (Eng. trans. London 1970); Iain Browning, *Palmyra* (London 1979); M. A. R. Colledge, *The Art of Palmyra* (London 1976). Robert Wood's *The Ruins of Palmyra, otherwise Tedmor, in the Desart*, of 1753, has been reproduced photographically (Farnborough 1971). See also J. Jeremias, *Jerusalem in the Time of Jesus* (Eng. trans. London 1969); Y. Yadin, *Masada: Herod's Fortress and the Zealots' Last Stand* (London 1966); M. Rostovtzeff, *Dura-Europos and Its Art* (Oxford 1938); A. Perkins, *The Art of Dura-Europos* (Oxford 1973); Clark Hopkins, *The Discovery of Dura-Europos* (New Haven, Conn., and London 1979); F. Ragette, *Baalbeck* (London 1980); N. Jidejian, *Baalbek: Heliopolis, "City of the Sun"* (Beirut 1975); Iain Browning, *Petra* (London 1973); and R. G. Goodchild, *Cyrene and Apollonia* (London 1963).

The Late Empire: Constantine to Justinian

There is no really good modern concise account of this period in English. Apart from the incomparable narrative presentation of Gibbon – abridged by D. M. Low (London 1960) – the best of the older accounts is perhaps that of J. B. Bury, *History of the Later Roman Empire, from the Death of Theodosius I to the Death of Justinian (AD 395 to 565)*, 2 vols. (London 1923, reprinted New York 1958). By far the best modern account of the 4th century is that of André Piganiol, *L'Empire chrétien* (2nd ed. by A. Chastagnol, Paris 1972), and of the 5th and 6th centuries the very good, though rather austere, work of E. Stein, *Histoire du bas-empire* (2nd ed. and trans. by J.-R. Palanque, Paris and Bruges 1959; reprinted Amsterdam 1968). The massive work of A. H. M. Jones, *The Later Roman Empire 284–602; a Social, Economic and Administrative Survey*, 3 vols. and maps (Oxford 1964; reprinted in 2 vols., Oxford 1973), is presented in abbreviated form in *The Decline of the Ancient World* (London 1966; reprinted 1975). Jones's work is notable above all for its appreciation of the bureaucratic nature of the late Roman state and also of the limitations of its power, and for his cool assessment of the reasons for its decline. In a totally different style, Peter Brown, *The World of Late Antiquity, from Marcus Aurelius to Muhammad* (London 1971), is a particularly challenging thematic study, skillfully illustrated.

Of individual emperors in this period, Constantine, Julian and Justinian have naturally attracted most attention: see on Constantine N. H. Baynes, *Constantine the Great and the Christian Church* (London 1931; reprinted with preface and bibliography by Henry Chadwick, Oxford 1972); A. H. M. Jones, *Constantine and the Conversion of Europe* (London 1948); R. MacMullen, *Constantine* (London 1970); A. Alföldi, *The Conversion of Constantine and Pagan Rome* (Oxford 1948, reprinted 1969). On Julian, recent biographies include those of R. Browning, *The Emperor Julian* (London 1975), and, with emphasis on Julian's character, G. W. Bowersock, *Julian the Apostate* (London 1978); though J. Bidez's *L'Empereur Julien* (Paris 1930; reprinted 1965) remains the most economically penetrating of studies, especially strong on the intellectual and religious background of Julian. On Justinian, R. Browning, *Justinian and Theodora* (London 1971).

Other works on the political and social history of the age include A. Alföldi, *A Conflict of Ideas in the Late Roman Empire: the Clash between the Senate and Valentinian I* (Oxford 1952) – extremely vivid, especially on the atmosphere of "terrorism" of late Roman government, though in some ways unreliable in its judgments – and John Matthews, *Western Aristocracies and Imperial Court, AD 364–425* (Oxford 1975). This is a study of the social context of the politics of the period but presents the narrative background and touches various other aspects of the age, especially the issue of Christianization (see below).

The literary and religious history of late antiquity is studied in several recent works, notably Peter Brown's wonderful *Augustine of Hippo* (London 1967), Alan Cameron's *Claudian: Poetry and Propaganda at the Court of Honorius* (Oxford 1970) and J. N. D. Kelly, *Jerome: His Life, Writings and Controversies* (London 1975). M. W. Binns (ed.), *Latin Literature of the Fourth Century* (London and Boston, Mass., 1974), contains chapters by different authors on Ausonius, Symmachus, Paulinus of Nola, Claudian and Prudentius, and on the religious and cultural background of their work. R. Syme, *Ammianus and the Historia Augusta* (Oxford 1968), ranges widely and to great effect among the varied literary products of the late 4th century. N. K. Chadwick, *Poetry and Letters in Early Christian Gaul* (London 1955), presents accounts of later 4th- and 5th-century writers, and the 5th-century poet and bishop, Sidonius Apollinaris, is the subject of C. E. Stevens's *Sidonius Apollinaris and His Age* (Oxford 1933). The Latin writers of the early 6th century have received recent attention from J. J. O'Donnell, *Cassiodorus* (Berkeley, Calif., and London 1979), Henry Chadwick, *Boethius: the Consolations of Music, Logic, Theology and Philosophy* (Oxford 1981), and in the symposium edited by Margaret Gibson, *Boethius: His Life, Thought and Influence* (Oxford 1981). Despite much specialized work, there are still in English no substantial general studies of writers as important as Ammianus Marcellinus and Procopius; on the first of these, however, E. A. Thompson, *The Historical Work of Ammianus Marcellinus* (Cambridge 1947), is one of the essential foundations for such study.

On late Roman art and ceremonial and responses to it, see the varying approaches and interpretations of H. P. L'Orange, *Art Forms and Civic Life in the Late Roman Empire* (Eng. trans. Princeton, N.J., 1965), R. Bianchi Bandinelli, *Rome: the Late Empire. Roman Art AD 200–400* (London 1971) – lavishly illustrated; S. MacCormack, *Art and Ceremony in Late Antiquity* (Berkeley, Calif., and London 1981); A. Grabar, *The Beginnings of Christian Art* (London 1967) and *Christian Iconography: a Study of Its Origins* (London 1969); and Gervase Mathew, *Byzantine Aesthetics* (London 1963).

The theme of the Christianization of the Empire is developed by F. van der Meer and Christine Mohrmann, *Atlas of the Early Christian World* (Eng. trans. London 1966), and by Diana Bowder, *The Age of Constantine and Julian* (London 1978), a useful introduction to the visual and archaeological evidence for the religious changes of the 4th century. A. Momigliano (ed.), *The Conflict between Paganism and Christianity in the Fourth Century* (Oxford 1963), contains some excellent papers on various aspects of this theme, as, still more so, does Peter Brown, *Religion and Society in the Age of St Augustine* (London 1972), a collection of the author's learned but vividly readable articles spanning the years 1961–70.

In the absence of any modern study of comparable scope, the classic of J. Geffcken, *The Last Days of Greco-Roman Paganism* (trans. S. MacCormack, Amsterdam, New York and Oxford 1978), remains fundamental; see also R. MacMullen, *Paganism in the Roman Empire* (New Haven, Conn., and London 1981). Though its central thesis has been challenged – though not abandoned by its author – W. H. C. Frend's *The Donatist Church: a Movement of Protest in Roman North Africa* (Oxford 1952; reprinted with additional bibliography 1971) remains a fine description of the effects of Christianization on the morale and integrity of an established church in its relations with a schismatic sect. On the duties and preoccupations of a bishop, F. van der Meer, *Augustine the Bishop* (Eng. trans. London 1961; reprinted 1978), is full and circumstantial, and on the ascetic movement Philip Rousseau, *Ascetics, Authority and the Church in the Age of Jerome and Cassian* (Oxford 1978), is a book which repays the closest attention and reflection. On the actual modes of the ascetic life, see for Egypt D. Chitty, *The Desert a City* (Oxford 1966), and for Syria A. Vööbus, *A History of Asceticism in the Syrian Orient*, Vol. II (Louvain 1960). Peter Brown's *The Cult of the Saints: Its Use and Function in Latin Christianity* (London 1981), is, as always, an arresting and profound, if at times rather intangible, treatment. One particularly interesting facet of Christianization, pilgrimage, is described and put into its cultural context by E. D. Hunt, *Holy Land Pilgrimage in the Later Roman Empire AD 312–460* (Oxford 1982).

For late imperial and early Christian Rome see R. Krautheimer, *Rome: Profile of a City 312–1308* (Princeton, N.J., 1980), and in general his *Early Christian and Byzantine Architecture* (3rd ed. Harmondsworth 1979); W. Oakeshott, *The Mosaics of Rome, from the Third to the Fourteenth Centuries* (London 1967). The fullest historical account of early Christian Rome is in French, by Ch. Piétri, *Roma Christiana: recherches sur l'Église de Rome, son organisation, sa politique, son idéologie, de Miltiade à Sixte II (311–440)*, 2 vols. (Paris and Rome 1978). On Ravenna, L. von Matt, *Ravenna* (Cologne 1971), with text, in German, by S. Bovini, but with splendid photographs. For Christianity and paganism in the life of 4th-century Antioch (and many other aspects of urban life) J. H. W. G. Liebeschuetz, *Antioch: City and Imperial Administration in the Later Roman Empire* (Oxford 1972), and for the life of a rapidly Christianized city J. B. Segal, *Edessa: the "Blessed City"* (Oxford 1970). Late Roman Jerusalem is described by Ch. Couäsnon, O.P., *The Church of the Holy Sepulchre in Jerusalem* (London 1974), and by J. Wilkinson, *Egeria's Travels: Newly Translated with Supporting Documents and Notes* (London 1971). The social life of Constantinople is explored by G. Downey, *Constantinople in the Age of Justinian* (London 1964), and by Alan Cameron, *Porphyrius the Charioteer* (Oxford 1971); cf. his *Circus Factions: Blues and Greens at Rome and Byzantium* (Oxford 1976).

On the barbarian invaders of the Roman Empire there are three especially illuminating books by E. A. Thompson: *A History of Attila and the Huns* (Oxford 1948), *The Visigoths in the Time of Ulfila* (Oxford 1966) and *The Goths in Spain* (Oxford 1969). Fifth-century relations between Rome and Constantinople are the theme of W. E. Kaegi, *Byzantium and the Decline of Rome* (Princeton, N.J., 1968); the background to the 6th-century reconquest is described in the books on Boethius and Cassiodorus mentioned above. For the barbarian settlements and the formation of the early medieval west see J. M. Wallace-Hadrill, *The Barbarian West 400–1000* (rev. ed. London 1967), and the various papers in his *The Long-Haired Kings* (London 1962); and W. Goffart, *Barbarians and Romans, AD 418–584: the Techniques of Accommodation* (Princeton, N.J., 1980).

GAZETTEER

19°06′E, 140
Doliche (Turkey), 37°04′N 37°22′E, 150
Domavia (Yugoslavia), 44°06′N 19°21′E, 140
Dorchester (U.K.), 51°39′N 1°10′W, 135
Dordogne R *see* Duranius R
Doriscus (Greece), (Traianopolis), 40°57′N 25°56′E, 140, 146, 150
Dorylaeum (Turkey), (Eskisehir), 39°46′N 30°30′E, 150
Dos Zelor 46°11′N 11°22′E, 20
Doubs R (France), 129
Doucen (Algeria), 34°36′N 5°05′E, 118
Douro/Duero R *see* Durius R
Drava R *see* Dravus R
Dravus R (Austria/Hungary/Yugoslavia), (Drava R), 10, 72, 84, 140, 208, 214
Drepanum (Sicily), (Trapani), 38°02′N 12°32′E, 45
Drin R (Yugoslavia/Albania), 140, 146
Drina R (Yugoslavia), 10, 140
Drobeta (Romania), (Turnu-Severin), 44°36′N 22°39′E, 140
Dubris (U.K.), (Dover), 51°08′N 1°19′E, 135, 171
Dubrovnik (Yugoslavia), 42°40′N 18°07′E, 10
Duna R *see* Danuvius R
Dura (Iraq), 34°29′N 43°48′E, 191
Dura-Europus (Syria), 34°46′N 40°46′E, 157
Durance R (France), 10, 129
Duranius R (France), (Dordogne R), 72, 75, 129, 208, 214
Durius R (Portugal/Spain), (Douro/Duero R), 47, 60, 72, 75, 124, 173, 208, 214
Durnovaria (U.K.), (Dorchester), 50°43′N 2°26′W, 135
Durobrivae (U.K.), (Rochester), 51°24′N 0°30′E, 135
Durobrivae (U.K.), (Water Newton), 52°32′N 0°21′W, 135
Durocasses (France), (Dreux), 48°44′N 1°23′E, 129
Durocatalauni (France), (Châlons-sur-Marne), 48°58′N 4°22′E, 129
Durocortorum (France), (Remi), (Reims), 49°15′N 4°02′E, 84, 107, 129, 192
Durolipons (U.K.), (Cambridge), 52°12′N 0°07′E, 135
Durostorum (Bulgaria), (Silistra), 44°06′N 27°17′E, 140
Durovernum (U.K.), (Canterbury), 51°17′N 1°05′E, 135
Durovigutum (U.K.), (Godmanchester), 52°19′N 0°11′W, 135
Dwin (U.S.S.R.), 40°04′N 44°44′E, 220
Dyme (Greece), 38°06′N 21°35′E, 72
Dyrrhachium *see* Epidamnus

Ebora (Portugal), (Evora), 38°34′N 7°54′W, 124
Ebro R *see* Iberus R
Eburacum (U.K.), (York), 53°58′N 1°05′W, 107, 135, 199
Eburodunum (France), (Embrun), 44°33′N 6°30′E, 129
Eburodunum (Switzerland), (Yverdon), 46°47′N 6°38′E, 129
Eburum (Eboli), 40°37′N 15°03′E, 62
Echetla (Sicily), 37°14′N 14°32′E, 45
Ecnomus, C (Sicily), 37°07′N 13°58′E, 45
Edessa (Greece), 40°48′N 22°03′E, 146
Edessa (Turkey), (Urfa), 37°08′N 38°45′E, 60, 150, 171, 199, 220
Egadi (Isl), 37°57′N 12°28′E, 10
Egeta (Yugoslavia), (Brza Palanka), 44°30′N 22°25′E, 140
Egridir Gölü (Turkey), 38°00′N 30°50′E, 150
Eilithyopolis (Egypt), 27°07′N 32°48′E, 164
Elaeusa (Turkey), (Sebaste), 36°32′N 34°12′E, 150
Elba (Isl), 42°45′N 10°15′E, 10
Elea (Velia), 40°08′N 15°11′E, 23, 41, 46
Elephantine (Egypt), 24°05′N 32°53′E, 164
Eleusis (Greece), 38°02′N 23°23′E, 60, 146
Eleutheropolis (Israel), 31°38′N 34°44′E, 157
Elimberris (France), (Auch), 43°40′N 0°36′E, 129
Elis (Greece), 37°54′N 21°22′E, 146
Elusa (France), (Eauze), 43°51′N 0°06′E, 129
Elusa (Israel), 31°06′N 34°39′E, 157
Elvira *see* Illiberis
Emerita Augusta (Spain), (Merida), 38°55′N 6°20′W, 72, 75, 107, 124, 179
Emesa (Syria), (Homs), 34°44′N 36°43′E, 157, 174, 220
Emona (Yugoslavia), (Ljubljana), 46°04′N 14°30′E, 10, 140
Emporiae (Spain), (Ampurias), 42°08′N 3°03′E, 23, 39, 47, 72, 124
Engedi (Israel), 31°28′N 35°23′E, 157
Enna (Sicily), 37°34′N 14°16′E, 45, 57
Engers (W. Germany), 50°27′N 7°29′E, 192
Ensérune (France), 43°38′N 3°49′E, 39
Ephesus (Turkey), 37°55′N 27°19′E, 60, 70, 75, 107, 111, 150, 179
Epidamnus (Albania), (Dyrrachium), (Durres), 41°18′N 19°28′E, 60, 70, 72, 146, 214
Epidaurus (Greece), 37°38′N 23°09′E, 146
Epidaurus (Yugoslavia), (Cavtat), 42°35′N 18°13′E, 72 140
Epiphania (Syria), (Hama), 35°09′N 36°44′E, 157, 174
Epora (Spain), (Montoro), 38°02′N 4°23′W, 124
Eporedia (Ivrea), 45°28′N 7°52′E, 49
Equizeto (Algeria), 35°59′N 5°04′E, 118
Erbil (Iraq), 36°12′N 44°01′E, 220
Ercavica (Spain), 40°25′N 2°27′W, 124
Eretum 42°08′N 12°37′E, 27, 30
Erice *see* Eryx
Eriza (Turkey), 39°44′N 39°30′E, 150
Erythrae (Turkey), 38°24′N 26°00′E, 150
Eryx (Sicily), (Erice), 38°03′N 12°35′E, 20, 45
Esbus (Jordan), 31°47′N 35°49′E, 157
Estrées-sur-Noye (France), 49°47′N 2°20′E, 129
Etna, Mt (Sicily), 37°45′N 15°00′E, 10
Euhesperides (Libya), (Berenice), (Benghazi), 32°07′N 20°05′E, 164
Eumenia (Turkey), 38°19′N 29°55′E, 150
Eupatoria (Turkey), (Magnopolis), (Erbaa), 40°42′N 36°37′E, 150
Euphrates R (Iraq/Syria/Turkey), 60, 72, 75, 150, 157, 171, 194, 220
Europus (Syria), 36°32′N 38°13′E, 157

Fabrateria Nova *see* Fregellae
Fabrateria Vetus 41°35′N 13°20′E, 40
Faesulae (Fiesole), 43°49′N 11°24′E, 41, 67
Falerii (Civita Castellana), 42°17′N 12°25′E, 21, 41, 62, 200
Falerio 43°07′N 13°33′E, 67
Fanum Fortunae (Fano), 43°51′N 13°01′E, 38, 41, 67
Faustinopolis (Turkey), 37°27′N 34°38′E, 150
Faviana (Austria), (Mautern), 47°24′N 14°50′E, 140
Felsina *see* Bononia
Ferentinum (Ferentino), 41°41′N 13°15′E, 30, 35, 40, 200
Ferrara 44°50′N 11°38′E, 10
Fès (Morocco), 34°05′N 5°00′W, 118
Ficana 41°44′N 12°21′E, 27, 30
Ficulea 41°57′N 12°38′E, 27, 30
Fidenae (Fidenae Romulus), (Castel Giueileo), 41°55′N 12°31′E, 27, 30, 35
Filottrano 43°16′N 13°31′E, 20
Fimon 45°29′N 11°29′E, 20
Firmum Picenum (Fermo), 43°09′N 13°44′E, 35, 41, 62, 67
Fishbourne (U.K.), 50°50′N 0°50′W, 135
Flanona (Yugoslavia), 45°11′N 14°26′E, 140
Flaviobriga (Spain), (Castro-Urdiales), 43°23′N 3°11′W, 124
Flaviopolis (Turkey), (Kadirli), 37°22′N 36°05′E, 150
Florence *see* Florentia
Florentia (Florence), 43°47′N 11°15′E, 10, 13, 16, 38, 67
Foce (Corsica), 41°50′N 9°04′E, 20
Foggia 41°28′N 15°33′E, 10
Fonte e Mola (Sardinia), 40°32′N 8°43′E, 20
Forentum 40°52′N 15°52′E, 62
Forli *see* Forum Livii
Formiae (Formia), 41°16′N 13°37′E, 35, 62
Forum Anni (Polla), 40°31′N 15°27′E, 38, 57
Forum Clodii (Materano), 42°09′N 12°09′E, 200
Forum Cornelii (Imola), 44°22′N 11°43′E, 38
Forum Hadriani (Netherlands), (Municipium Cananefatum), (Voorburg-Arentsburg), 52°04′N 4°22′E, 129
Forum Iulii (France), (Fréjus), 43°26′N 6°44′E, 72, 129
Forum Livii (Forli), 44°13′N 12°02′E, 10, 29, 38
Forum Novum 44°42′N 10°06′E, 38
Forum Segusiavorum (France), (Feurs), 45°44′N 4°13′E, 129
Forum Sempronii (Fossombrone), 43°42′N 12°48′E, 38
Frattesine 45°00′N 11°25′E, 20
Fregellae (Fabrateria Nova), (Ceprano), 41°33′N 13°32′E, 35, 40, 46, 49
Fregenae 41°52′N 12°12′E, 35
Frusino (Frosinone), 41°38′N 13°22′E, 62
Fucinus, L 42°00′N 13°45′E, 35, 40, 41, 200
Fulginium 42°57′N 12°43′E, 62
Fundi (Fondi), 41°22′N 13°27′E, 35, 62, 200

Gabii (Osteria dell Osa), 41°52′N 12°45′E, 27, 30, 200
Gadara (Jordan), (Um Qeis), 32°39′N 35°41′E, 157
Gades (Spain), (Cadiz), 36°32′N 6°18′W, 23, 39, 47, 70, 72, 75, 124, 208
Gangra (Turkey), (Germanicopolis), 40°35′N 33°37′E, 150
Garda, L di 45°30′N 10°45′E, 10
Gariannonum (U.K.), (Burgh Castle), 52°30′N 1°44′E, 171
Garonne R *see* Garumna R
Garsaura (Turkey), (Archelais), 38°20′N 34°02′E, 150
Garumna R (France), (Garonne R), 47, 72, 75, 129, 208
Gaza (Gaza Strip), 31°30′N 34°28′E, 157
Gediz R (Turkey), 150
Gela (Sicily), 37°04′N 14°15′E, 20, 23
Gemellae (Algeria), 34°35′N 5°39′E, 118
Genava (Switzerland), (Geneva), 46°13′N 6°09′E, 10, 129, 214
Geneva *see* Genava
Genil R (Spain), 124
Genoa *see* Genua
Genua (Genoa), 44°24′N 8°56′E, 10, 12, 13, 16, 29, 38, 39, 47, 75, 208
Genusia 40°35′N 16°45′E, 41, 46
Geraestus (Euboea Isl), (Greece), 37°59′N 24°31′E, 146
Gerasa (Jordan), (Jarash), 32°17′N 35°54′E, 157
Gergovia (France), (Gergovie), 45°47′N 3°05′E, 70, 129
Germanicia (Turkey), (Caesarea Germanicia), 37°34′N 36°54′E, 150
Germisara (Romania), 45°56′N 23°12′E, 140
Gerunda (Spain), (Gerona), 41°59′N 2°49′E, 124
Gerunium 41°38′N 15°08′E, 46
Gesoriacum (France), (Bononia), (Boulogne), 48°50′N 2°14′E, 129, 192
Ghadames (Libya), 30°10′N 9°30′E, 118
Gheria el-Garbia (Libya), 30°21′N 13°12′E, 118
Ghirza (Libya), (Qirzah), 31°00′N 14°39′E, 118
Gigia (Spain), (Gijón), 43°32′N 5°40′W, 124
Gigthis (Tunisia), 33°30′N 10°41′E, 118
S. Giovenale 42°13′N 12°03′E, 21
Giugliano 40°55′N 14°12′E, 39
Glanum (France), (St Rémy), 43°47′N 4°49′E, 129
Glevum (U.K.), (Gloucester), 51°53′N 2°14′W, 135
Gnathia 40°56′N 17°18′E, 46
Gobannium (U.K.), (Abergavenny), 51°50′N 3°00′W, 135
Golo R, 10
Gomphi (Greece), 39°23′N 21°36′E, 146
Gonni (Greece), 39°52′N 22°29′E, 146
Gorsium (Hungary), (Tac), 46°47′N 18°26′E, 140
Gortyn (Crete), 35°07′N 24°58′E, 107, 164
Gorzano 44°42′N 10°42′E, 20
Gottolengo 45°17′N 10°16′E, 20
Graccuris (Spain), (Alfara), 42°11′N 1°45′W, 124
Grannona (France), (Port en Bessin-Huppain), 49°21′N 0°45′W, 171
Graviscae 42°13′N 11°42′E, 21, 23, 49
Graz (Austria), 47°05′N 15°22′E, 10, 140
Great Chesterford (U.K.), 52°04′N 0°11′E, 135
Great Ouse R (U.K.), 135
Great St Bernard Pass (Switzerland/Italy), 42°52′N 7°11′E, 129
Grenoble *see* Cularo
Grottaferrata 41°47′N 12°40′E, 30
Grumentum (Grumento Nova), 40°17′N 15°53′E, 41, 46, 62
Guadalquivir R *see* Baetis R
Guadiana R *see* Anas R
Guntia (W. Germany), (Günzburg), 48°27′N 10°18′E, 140
Gunugu (Algeria), 36°32′N 1°32′E, 72
Gythium (Greece), (Yithion), 36°46′N 22°34′E, 146

Hadria (Atri), 42°35′N 13°59′E, 35, 38, 41, 67
Hadrianopolis (Libya), (Driana), 32°21′N 20°13′E, 164
Hadrianopolis (Turkey), (Edirne), 41°40′N 26°34′E, 140, 208, 214
Hadrumetum (Tunisia), (Sousse), 35°50′N 10°38′E, 23, 39, 45, 47, 70, 118
Halae (Greece), 38°41′N 23°10′E, 146
Halaesa (Sicily), 37°59′N 14°16′E, 45, 72
Halicarnassus (Turkey), (Bodrum), 37°03′N 27°28′E, 150
Halicyae (Sicily), 37°54′N 12°52′E, 45
Hallstatt (Austria), 47°34′N 13°39′E, 140
Haluntium (Sicily), 38°04′N 14°09′E, 72
Halycus R (Sicily), 45
Halys R (Turkey), (Kizil Irmak R), 60, 72, 75, 150, 171, 173, 179, 208, 220
Hanau (W. Germany), 50°08′N 8°56′E, 108
Hasta (Spain), (Mesa de Asta), 36°48′N 6°10′W, 72, 124
Heba (Magliano), 42°36′N 11°18′E, 21
Hebron (Jordan), 31°32′N 35°06′E, 157
Hedum (Yugoslavia), 44°03′N 18°18′E, 140
Heidelberg (W. Germany), 49°25′N 8°42′E, 108, 192
Helela (Syria), 34°46′N 38°41′E, 174
Heliopolis (Egypt), 38°08′N 31°18′E, 164
Heliopolis (Lebanon), (Baalbek), 34°00′N 36°12′E, 72, 157, 220
Helorus (Sicily), 36°51′N 15°07′E, 45
Hemerium (Syria), 36°42′N 38°04′E, 220
Hemeroskopeion (Spain), 38°51′N 0°07′E, 23
Hephaestia (Lemnos Isl), (Greece), 39°58′N 25°20′E, 146
Heraclea 40°14′N 16°41′E, 35, 41, 46, 62
Heraclea (Turkey), 41°02′N 27°59′E, 173
Heraclea (Turkey), 37°31′N 27°36′E, 150
Heraclea Lyncestis (Yugoslavia), (Bitola), 41°01′N 21°21′E, 146
Heraclea Minoa (Sicily), 37°24′N 13°17′E, 45
Heraclea Pontica (Turkey), (Eregli), 41°17′N 31°26′E, 72, 150
Heracleia (Romania), (Axiopolis), 44°20′N 28°03′E, 140
Heracleopolis (Egypt), 29°02′N 30°52′E, 164
Heraea (Greece), 37°36′N 21°51′E, 146
Herculaneum 40°46′N 14°22′E, 62
Herdonia 41°18′N 15°35′E, 40, 41, 46, 62
Heri (France), 47°03′N 1°56′W, 199
Hermaeum, C (Tunisia), 37°03′N 10°58′E, 45
Hermione (Greece), (Ermioni), 37°23′N 23°15′E, 146
Hermonthis (Egypt), 25°37′N 32°32′E, 164
Hermopolis (Egypt), (El Ashmunein), 27°47′N 30°47′E, 164
Herodion (Jordan), 31°41′N 35°14′E, 157
Hierapolis (Syria), (Membij), 36°32′N 37°55′E, 150, 157, 220
Hierapolis (Turkey), (Pamukkale), 37°57′N 28°50′E, 150
Hierapytna (Crete), (Ierapetra), 35°00′N 25°45′E, 164
Hieropolis Castabala (Turkey), 37°18′N 36°16′E, 150
Hierosolyma (Israel/Jordan), (Aelia Capitolina), (Jerusalem), 31°47′N 35°13′E, 75, 84, 157, 199
Himera (Sicily), (Thermae), 37°57′N 13°47′E, 23, 38, 45, 72
Himera R (Sicily), 10, 45
Hippo Diarrhytus (Tunisia), (Bizerte), 37°18′N 9°52′E, 72, 118
Hipponium (Vibo Valentia), 38°40′N 16°06′E, 23, 38, 40, 46, 49
Hippo Regius (Algeria), (Annaba), 36°55′N 7°47′E, 118, 199, 208, 214
Hippos (Lebanon), 32°44′N 35°43′E, 157
Hispalis *see* Tartessus
Hispellum (Spello), 42°59′N 12°41′E, 67
Histiaea (Euboea Isl), (Greece), 38°57′N 23°06′E, 146
Histonium 42°06′N 14°43′E, 62
Histria (Romania), 44°32′N 28°07′E, 140
Horonon (Turkey), 40°04′N 42°28′E, 220
Horreum Margi (Yugoslavia), (Cuprija), 43°56′N 21°21′E, 140
Hucumbra (Iraq), 33°51′N 44°31′E, 191
Hvar (Isl), (Yugoslavia), 43°18′N 16°36′E, 10
Hypata (Greece), 38°49′N 22°07′E, 146
Hypsus R (Sicily), 45

Iaca (Spain), (Jaca) 42°34′N 0°33′W, 124
Iader (Yugoslavia), (Zadar), 44°07′N 15°14′E, 72, 140
Iasus (Turkey), 37°17′N 27°35′E, 150
Iberus R (Spain), (Ebro R), 23, 47, 60, 72, 75, 84, 124, 173, 179, 214
Iconium (Turkey), (Konya), 37°51′N 32°30′E, 150
Icosium (Algeria), (Algiers), 36°50′N 3°00′E, 118
Iculisma (France), (Angoulême), 45°40′N 0°10′E, 129
Iesso (Spain), (Guisona), 41°47′N 1°18′E, 124
Igaeditani (Portugal), 39°56′N 6°54′W, 124
Igilgili (Algeria), (Jijel), 36°50′N 5°43′E, 72, 118
Iguvium (Gubbio), 43°21′N 12°35′E, 41, 62
Ilerda (Spain), (Lerida), 41°37′N 0°38′E, 70, 72, 124
Ilici (Spain), (Elche), 38°16′N 0°41′W, 72, 124
Ilipa (Spain), 37°28′N 5°56′W, 47
Ilium (Turkey), (Troy) 39°55′N 26°17′E, 150
Illiberis (Spain), (Elvira), 37°17′N 3°53′W, 124, 179
Iluro (Spain), 41°43′N 2°56′E, 72
Inchtuthil (U.K.), 56°32′N 3°23′W, 135
Ingila (Turkey), 38°11′N 40°12′E, 150
In Murio (W. Germany), (Moosham), 48°55′N 12°17′E, 140
Inn R (W. Germany/Austria), 140
Interamna 41°23′N 13°41′E, 35, 40, 45, 62
Interamna (Terni), 42°34′N 12°39′E, 10, 62
Interamnia (Teramo), 42°40′N 13°43′E, 40, 67
Intercisa (Hungary), 46°59′N 18°56′E, 140
Inveresk (U.K.), 55°58′N 2°56′W, 135
Iol Caesarea (Algeria), (Cherchell), 36°36′N 2°11′E, 75, 107, 118, 214
Iomnium (Algeria), 36°56′N 4°00′E, 118
Iona (U.K.), 56°19′N 6°25′W, 199
Iovia (Yugoslavia), 46°10′N 16°59′E, 140
Ioviacum (Austria), (Schlögen), 48°27′N 13°55′E, 140
Iovis Latiaris 41°46′N 12°42′E, 27
Iria Flavia (Spain), (el Padron), 42°44′N 8°40′W, 124
Isaura (Turkey), 37°12′N 32°15′E, 150
Isca (U.K.), (Caerleon), 51°37′N 2°57′W, 135
Isca (U.K.), (Exeter), 50°43′N 3°31′W, 135
Ischia *see* Pithecussae
Iseo, L d′ 45°35′N 10°08′E, 10
Isère R (France), 129
Isolone 45°15′N 10°42′E, 20
Issa (Yugoslavia), 43°02′N 16°12′E, 72
Issus (Turkey), 36°51′N 36°10′E, 150
Isthmia (Greece), 37°55′N 23°00′E, 146
Isurium (U.K.), (Aldborough), 54°30′N 1°41′W, 135
Italica (Spain), (Santiponce), 37°26′N 6°03′W, 72, 124
Itanus (Crete), 35°18′N 26°17′E, 164
Ithomi, Mt (Greece), 37°11′N 21°55′E, 146
Itucci (Spain), (Baena), 36°37′N 4°20′W, 172
Iuliacum (W. Germany), (Jülich), 50°55′N 6°21′E, 129
Iuliobona (France), (Lillebonne), 49°31′N 0°32′E, 129
Iuliobriga (Spain), (Refortillo), 43°03′N 4°09′W, 124
Iuliomagus (France), (Angers), 47°29′N 0°32′W, 129
Iuncaria (Spain), (Figueras), 42°16′N 2°57′E, 124
Iuvavum (Austria), (Salzburg), 47°48′N 13°03′E, 140

Jamnia (Israel), 31°45′N 34°48′E, 157
Jericho (Jordan), 31°51′N 35°27′E, 157
Jerid, Chott (Tunisia), 33°45′N 8°20′E, 118
Jiul R (Romania), 140
Joppa (Israel), (Tel Aviv-Yafo), 32°05′N 34°46′E, 157
Jordan R (Syria/Israel/Jordan), 157
Jucar R (Spain), 124
Julier Pass (Switzerland), 46°28′N 9°43′E, 140

Kelibia (Tunisia), 36°50′N 11°05′E, 39
Kelkit R (Turkey), 150
Kerkouane (Tunisia), 36°52′N 11°05′E, 39
Khabir R (Turkey/Syria), 157
Kinyps (Libya), 32°32′N 14°37′E, 23
Kirmosti R (Turkey), 150
Kizil Irmak R *see* Halys R
Klagenfurt (Austria), 46°38′N 14°20′E, 10
Kleiner Lauten (Switzerland), 47°36′N 8°15′E, 192
Klos (Albania), 41°28′N 20°10′E, 146
Kreuzberg Pass, 46°42′N 12°13′E, 140
Kreuznach (W. Germany), 49°49′N 8°01′E, 192
Krk (Isl), (Yugoslavia), 45°05′N 14°40′E, 10
Kupa R (Yugoslavia), 10
Kuria (Switzerland), (Chur), 46°52′N 9°32′E, 140

Labici 41°46′N 12°45′E, 27, 30
Lactodorum (U.K.), (Towcester), 52°08′N 1°00′W, 135
Lactora (France), (Lectoure), 43°56′N 0°38′E, 129
Lagentium (U.K.), (Castleford), 43°44′N 1°21′W, 135
Lagona R (W. Germany), 108
Lagozza 45°39′N 8°41′E, 20
Lambaesis (Algeria), (Lambese), 35°31′N 6°15′E, 118
Laminium (Spain), 39°01′N 2°54′W, 124
Lampsacus (Turkey), (Lapseki), 40°22′N 26°42′E, 72, 150
Lancia (Spain), 42°25′N 5°25′W, 124
Lanuvium (Lanuvio), 41°40′N 12°42′E, 27, 30, 35
Laodicea (Syria), (Latakia), 35°31′N 35°47′E, 157
Laodicea (Turkey), 37°46′N 29°02′E, 75, 150
Lapethus (Cyprus), (Lapithos), 35°20′N 33°11′E, 150
Lapurdum (France), (Bayonne), 43°30′N 1°28′W, 129
Laranda (Turkey), (Karaman), 37°11′N 33°13′E, 150
Larinum (Larino), 41°48′N 14°54′E, 40, 41, 46, 62
Larisa (Greece), 39°38′N 22°25′E, 146
La Rustica 41°53′N 12°35′E, 27, 30
Las (Greece), 36°41′N 22°31′E, 146
La Spezia 44°07′N 9°48′E, 10, 12
La Starza 41°10′N 15°02′E, 20
Latmos, Mons (Turkey), 37°33′N 27°35′E, 199
Latopolis (Egypt), (Isna), 25°16′N 32°30′E, 164
Laurentum 41°40′N 12°19′E, 200
Lauriacum (Austria), (Lorch), 48°14′N 14°29′E, 140
Laurium, Mt (Greece), 37°45′N 23°53′E, 146
Laus 39°54′N 15°47′E, 23
Lausanne (Switzerland), 46°32′N 6°39′E, 10
Lautulae 41°21′N 13°21′E, 35
Lavatrae (U.K.), (Bowes), 54°30′N 2°01′W, 135
Lavinium (Pratica di Mare), 41°40′N 12°30′E, 20, 27, 30
Lebadea (Greece), (Levadhia), 38°26′N 22°53′E, 146
Lebedus (Turkey), 38°04′N 26°55′E, 150
Lechaeum (Greece), 37°55′N 22°53′E, 146
Le Colombare 45°32′N 11°05′E, 20
Lederata (Romania), (Palanka), 44°52′N 21°24′E, 140
Ledro 45°33′N 10°34′E, 20
Lefkadia (Greece), 40°39′N 22°04′E, 146
Legedia (France), (Avranches), 48°42′N 1°21′W, 129
Leghorn 43°33′N 10°18′E, 10
Legio (Spain), (Leon), 42°34′N 5°34′W, 84, 124
Leiria (Spain), (Edeta), (Liria), 39°38′N 0°37′W, 124
Lejjun (Israel), 32°39′N 35°06′E, 157
Léman, L *see* Lemannus, L
Lemanis (U.K.), (Lympne), 51°05′N 1°02′E, 135, 171
Lemannus, L (France/Switzerland), (Léman, L), 46°45′N 7°00′E, 10, 129, 192
Lemnos (Isl), (Greece), 39°52′N 25°20′E, 146
Lentia (Austria), (Linz), 48°19′N 14°18′E, 140
Leontini (Sicily), (Lentini), 37°17′N 15°00′E, 23, 45
Leporano 40°23′N 17°20′E, 20
Leptis Magna (Libya), 32°38′N 14°16′E, 23, 118, 171
Leptis Minor (Tunisia), 35°39′N 10°54′E, 70, 118
Lerinum (France), (Iles de Lerins), 43°32′N 7°03′E, 199
Lesbos (Isl), (Greece), 39°15′N 26°15′E, 70, 150
Lesina, L di 41°53′N 15°30′E, 10
Letocetum (U.K.), (Wall), 52°40′N 1°50′W, 135
Leucas (Isl), (Greece), 38°40′N 20°17′E, 146
Libia (Spain), (Leiva), 42°21′N 3°04′W, 124
Libisosa (Spain), (Lezuza), 38°57′N 2°22′W, 72, 124
Liger R (France), (Loire R), 47, 60, 72, 75, 84, 129, 171, 173, 179, 192, 208, 214
Lilybaeum (Sicily), (Marsala), 37°48′N 12°27′E, 39, 45, 47, 70, 72, 214

Limenia (Cyprus), 35°09′N 32°33′E, 150
Limonum (France), (Pictavi), (Poitiers), 46°35′N 0°20′E, 129, 199
Limyra (Turkey), 36°20′N 30°11′E, 150
Lindinis (U.K.), (Ilchester), 51°01′N 2°41′W, 135
Lindum (U.K.), (Lincoln), 53°14′N 0°33′W, 135
Lindus (Rhodes Isl), (Greece), (Lindos), 36°05′N 28°05′E, 150
Lipara (Lipari Isl), (Lipari), 38°27′N 14°58′E, 20, 23, 45
Lipari (Isl), 38°30′N 14°57′E, 10
Liri R *see* Liris R
Liris R (Liri R), 10, 35, 40, 41, 46, 200
Lissus (Albania), (Lezhë), 41°47′N 19°39′E, 47, 72, 140, 146
Liternum 40°55′N 14°02′E, 49
Little St Bernard Pass (France/Italy), 45°40′N 6°53′E, 129
Lixus (Morocco), 35°12′N 6°10′W, 23, 118
Ljubljana *see* Emona
Llandovery (U.K.), 51°59′N 3°48′W, 135
Llantwit (U.K.), 51°25′N 3°30′W, 199
Locri 38°14′N 16°15′E, 23, 35, 41, 45, 46
Loibl Pass (Austria/Yugoslavia), 46°25′N 14°17′E, 140
Loire R *see* Liger R
Londinium (U.K.), (London), 51°30′N 0°10′W, 107, 135, 171, 173, 179, 192, 208
Lopodunum (W. Germany), (Ladenburg), 49°28′N 8°36′E, 108, 129
Lorch (W. Germany), 48°48′N 9°42′E, 108
Lot R (France), 129
Luca (Lucca), 43°50′N 10°30′E, 49, 67
Lucentum (Spain), (Alicante), 38°21′N 0°29′W, 124
Luceria (Lucera), 41°30′N 15°20′E, 35, 40, 46, 62, 67
Lucus Augusti (Spain), (Lugo), 43°00′N 7°33′W, 124
Lucus Feroniae 42°12′N 12°34′E, 30
Lugdunum (France), (Lyon), 45°46′N 4°50′E, 72, 75, 84, 107, 111, 129, 173, 179, 192, 214
Lugundum Batavorum (Netherlands), 52°14′N 4°25′E, 129
Lugdunum Convenarum (France), (St Bertrand-de-Comminges), 43°02′N 0°34′E, 70, 129
Lugherras (Sardinia), 40°06′N 8°48′E, 20
Lugio (Hungary), (Dunaszekesö), 46°06′N 18°49′E, 140
Luguvalium (U.K.), (Carlisle), 54°54′N 2°55′W, 135
Luna 44°02′N 10°02′E, 38, 49
Lunghezza *see* Collatia
Luni sul Mignone 42°19′N 11°47′W, 20, 21
Lussonium (Hungary), (Dunakömlöd), 46°38′N 18°51′E, 140
Lutetia (France), (Parisii), (Paris), 48°52′N 2°20′E, 129, 192, 199, 214
Luteva (France), (Lodève), 43°44′N 3°19′E, 129
Lychnidus (Yugoslavia), (Ohrid), 41°06′N 20°49′E, 146
Lycopolis (Egypt), 27°23′N 30°58′E, 164
Lystra (Turkey), 37°36′N 32°17′E, 72, 150
Lyttus (Crete), 30°08′N 25°23′E, 164

Macepracta (Iraq), 33°22′N 43°44′E, 191
Mactar (Tunisia), (Maktar), 35°51′N 9°12′E, 118
Madaba (Jordan), 31°44′N 35°48′E, 157
Madauros (Algeria), (M′Daourouch), 36°05′N 7°50′E, 118
Magdalensberg (Austria), 46°42′N 14°20′E, 140
Maggiore, L (Italy/Switzerland), 10, 129, 140
Magia (Switzerland), (Maienfeld), 47°01′N 9°32′E, 140
Magnesia ad Meandrum (Turkey), 37°46′N 27°29′E, 60, 150
Magnesia ad Sipylum (Turkey), (Manisa), 38°36′N 27°29′E, 150
Magnis (U.K.), (Carvoran), 54°58′N 2°20′W, 135
Magnis (U.K.), (Kenchester), 52°05′N 2°55′W, 135
Magnum (Yugoslavia), 44°03′N 15°59′E, 140
Mago (Menorca Isl), (Spain), (Mahon), 30°54′N 4°15′E, 124
Maia (U.K.), (Bowness), 54°22′N 2°55′W, 135
Maiden Castle (U.K.), 50°41′N 2°30′W, 135
Main R (W. Germany), 129
Mainake (Spain), (Velez Malaga), 36°47′N 4°06′W, 23
Maius Monasterium (France), 47°36′N 1°20′E, 199
Malaca (Spain), (Malaga), 36°43′N 4°25′W, 23, 47, 124
Maluesa (Yugoslavia), 43°51′N 20°03′E, 140
Malventum *see* Beneventum
Marne R (France), 129
Mampsis (Israel), 31°02′N 35°04′E, 157
Mamucium (U.K.), (Manchester), 53°30′N 2°15′W, 135
Manduria 40°24′N 17°38′E, 46
Mannheim (W. Germany), 49°30′N 8°28′E, 192
Mannu R (Sardinia), 10
Mantinea (Greece), (Antigonea), 37°27′N 22°23′E, 146
Mantua 45°10′N 10°47′E, 21
Marathon (Greece), 38°09′N 23°57′E, 146
Marcianopolis (Bulgaria), 43°20′N 27°36′E, 140
Marcis (France), (Marck), 50°57′N 1°57′E, 171
Mardin (Turkey), 37°34′N 40°29′E, 220
Margum (Yugoslavia), (Crasje), 44°44′N 21°08′E, 140
Mariana (Corsica), 41°23′N 9°10′E, 72
Marino 41°46′N 12°40′E, 30
Maritsa R (Bulgaria), 140
Marmantarum (Syria), 35°34′N 37°21′E, 174
Maronea (Greece), (Maronia), 40°56′N 25°32′E, 140, 146
Marrakech (Morocco), 31°49′N 8°00′W, 118
Marsala *see* Lilybaeum
Marsiliana 42°32′N 11°21′E, 21
Martyropolis (Turkey), 38°09′N 41°09′E, 220
Marzabotto 44°21′N 11°12′E, 21
Masada (Israel), (Mezada), 31°19′N 35°21′E, 157
Mascula (Algeria), (Khenchela), 35°22′N 7°09′E, 118
Massilia (France), (Marseille), 43°18′N 5°22′E, 23, 47, 60, 70, 75, 111, 129, 179, 199
Matianus, L (Iran), (Urmia, L), 37°40′N 45°30′E, 220
Matreium (Austria), (Matri), 47°06′N 11°28′E, 140
Matterhorn (Italy/Switzerland), 45°49′N 7°39′E, 10
S. Mauritii (France), 46°07′N 7°05′E, 199
Mazaca (Turkey), (Caesarea), (Kayseri), 38°42′N 35°28′E, 107, 150, 220
Mediolanum (Milan), 45°28′N 9°12′E, 10, 12, 13, 16, 29, 47, 60, 75, 129, 171, 173, 179, 199, 214
Mediolanum (France), (Évreux), 49°03′N 1°11′E, 129
Mediolanum (France), (Saintes), 45°44′N 0°38′W, 129
Mediomatrici *see* Divodurum
Medma 38°29′N 15°59′E, 23
Megalopolis (Greece), 37°24′N 22°08′E, 146
Megalopolis (Turkey), (Sebastea), (Sivas), 39°44′N 37°01′E, 150, 199, 220
Megara (Greece), 38°00′N 23°20′E, 146
Megara Hyblaea (Sicily), 37°12′N 15°10′E, 23, 45
Melilli (Sicily), 37°11′N 15°07′E, 20
Melita (Isl), (Malta), 23, 45, 46, 75, 214
Melitene (Turkey), (Malatya), 38°22′N 38°18′E, 150, 220
Mellaria (Spain), (Fuente Obejuna), 38°15′N 5°25′W, 124
Mellégue R (Tunisia), 118
Melos (Isl), (Greece), 36°42′N 24°26′E, 146
Melrhir, Chott (Algeria), 34°20′N 6°10′E, 118
Melta (Bulgaria), (Lovech), 43°08′N 24°45′E, 140
Membressa (Tunisia), 36°39′N 9°50′E, 118
Memphis (Egypt), 29°52′N 31°12′E, 70, 75, 164, 179
Menapolis (Egypt), 30°50′N 29°41′E, 199
Mesarfelta (Algeria), 35°09′N 5°31′E, 118
Mesembria (Bulgaria), (Nesebur), 42°39′N 27°43′E, 140
Messana (Zancle), (Messina), 38°13′N 15°33′E, 10, 23, 38, 45, 47, 57, 70, 72, 214
Messene (Greece), 37°11′N 21°58′E, 146
Messina *see* Messana
Metallum Vipascense (Portugal), 37°56′N 8°18′W, 124
Metapontum 40°23′N 16°50′E, 23, 41, 46
Metaurus (Gioia), 38°26′N 15°55′E, 23
Metaurus R, 47
Metellinum (Spain), (Medellin), 38°58′N 5°58′W, 72, 124
Methone (Greece), 36°49′N 21°42′E, 146
Metropolis (Greece), 39°20′N 21°50′E, 146
Metulum (Yugoslavia), 45°16′N 15°19′E, 140
Meuse R *see* Mosa R
Mevania (Bevagna), 42°56′N 12°37′E, 62
Micia (Romania), 45°57′N 22°40′E, 140
Milan *see* Mediolanum
Milazzo (Sicily), 38°16′N 15°14′E, 20
Miletus (Turkey), 37°30′N 27°18′E, 150
Milevis (Algeria), 36°32′N 6°15′E, 118
Miltenberg (W. Germany), 49°42′N 9°16′E, 108
Mina (Algeria), 35°44′N 0°35′E, 118
Minatiacum (France), (Nizy), 49°35′N 4°04′E, 129
Mineio R, 10
Minervium *see* Scolacium
Mino R (Spain), 124
Minoa (Sicily), 37°24′N 13°17′E, 23
Minturnae (Minturno), 41°16′N 13°45′E, 35, 46, 57, 62, 67, 200
Mirobriga (Spain), (Capilla), 38°50′N 5°05′W, 124
Misenum (Miseno), 40°46′N 14°06′E, 200
Missua (Tunisia), (Sidi Daoud), 36°52′N 10°57′E, 118
Misurata (Libya), (Misratah), 32°24′N 15°04′E, 118, 164
Mochlus (Crete), 35°11′N 24°54′E, 164
Modena *see* Mutina
Moenus R (W. Germany), 108
Mogador (Morocco), (Essaouita), 31°30′N 9°48′W, 23
Mogentiana (Hungary), 46°47′N 17°16′E, 140
Moguntiacum (W. Germany), (Mainz), 50°00′N 8°16′E, 84, 107, 108, 129, 192, 208, 214
Mons Albanus (Monte Cavo), 41°45′N 12°43′E, 80
Mons Argentarius (Monte Argentario), 42°23′N 11°11′E, 200
Mons Iovis (Syria), 34°45′N 37°25′E, 174
Mons Nitria (Egypt), 30°24′N 30°18′E, 199
Mons S. Antonii (Egypt), 28°56′N 32°19′E, 199
Mons Sinai (Egypt), (Jebel Musa), 28°32′N 33°59′E, 199
Montana (Bulgaria), 43°37′N 23°12′E, 140
Mont Blanc (France/Italy), 45°50′N 6°52′E, 10
Montecelio *see* Corniculum
Monte Castellaccio 44°12′N 11°42′E, 20
Monte Giove 43°53′N 11°26′E, 57
Monte Loffa 45°36′N 11°11′E, 20
Monte Sant′Angelo *see* Aefula
Mont Genèvre Pass (France/Italy), 44°56′N 6°45′E, 129
Mopsuestia (Turkey), 36°57′N 35°35′E, 150
Morava R (Yugoslavia), 140
Morgantina (Sicily), 37°10′N 14°45′E, 57
Moridunum (U.K.), (Carmarthen), 51°52′N 4°20′W, 135
Mosa R (France/Belgium/Netherlands), (Meuse R), 129, 192
Mosel R *see* Mosella R
Mosella R (France/Luxembourg/W. Germany), 108, 129, 192
Mostaganem (Algeria), 35°54′N 0°05′E, 118
Motya (Sicily), (S. Pantaleo), 37°53′N 12°29′E, 23
Moulouya R (Morocco), 118
Municipium (Yugoslavia), (Kaliste), 44°30′N 21°21′E, 140
Municipium Celegerorum (Yugoslavia), 43°44′N 20°41′E, 140
Municipium Dard(anorum) (Yugoslavia), (Socanica), 43°03′N 20°50′E, 140
Municipium Iasorum (Yugoslavia), (Daruvar), 45°36′N 17°14′E, 140
Municipium Latobicorum/Neviodunum (Yugoslavia), (Krsko), 45°58′N 15°30′E, 140
Municipium S(plonum) (Yugoslavia), 43°21′N 19°21′E, 140
Mur R (Austria), 10
Murat R (Turkey), 150
Muresul R (Romania), 140
Murgi (Spain), 36°46′N 2°35′W, 124
Murlo 43°09′N 11°23′E, 21
Mursa (Yugoslavia), (Osijek), 45°33′N 18°41′E, 140
Mursella (Hungary), 47°30′N, 17°27′E, 140
Mursella (Yugoslavia), (Petrijevci), 45°41′N 18°26′E, 140
Musti (Tunisia), (Henchir Mest), 36°25′N 9°15′E, 118
Mutina (Modena), 44°39′N 10°55′E, 10, 29, 38, 49, 67
Mycenae (Greece), 37°44′N 22°45′E, 146
Mylae (Sicily), 38°13′N 15°15′E, 23, 45, 47
Mylasa (Turkey), (Milas), 37°19′N 27°48′E, 150
Myra (Turkey), 36°17′N 29°58′E, 150, 199
Myrtilis (Portugal), (Mertola), 37°38′N 7°40′W, 124
Mytilene (Turkey), 39°06′N 26°34′E, 60, 150
Mytistratus (Sicily), 37°37′N 13°40′E, 45

Naarmalcha Canal (Iraq), 191
Nacolea (Turkey), 39°29′N 30°37′E, 150
Naissus (Yugoslavia), (Nis), 43°20′N 21°54′E, 140, 209, 214
Naples *see* Neapolis
Napoca (Romania), (Cluj), 46°47′N 23°37′E, 140
Narbo (France), (Narbonne), 43°11′N 3°00′E, 47, 60, 70, 72, 75, 107, 129, 209, 214
Narce 42°13′N 12°28′E, 20, 21
Narnia (Narni), 42°31′N 12°31′E, 35, 40, 41, 62
Narona (Yugoslavia), (Neretva), 43°02′N 17°39′E, 72, 75, 140, 209
Naryca (Greece), 38°48′N 22°43′E, 146
Nasium (France), (Naix), 48°43′N 5°16′E, 129
Naucratis (Egypt), 30°54′N 30°35′E, 164
Naupactus (Greece), 38°23′N 21°50′E, 146
Nauportus (Yugoslavia), (Vrhnika), 45°58′N 14°15′E, 140
Navio (U.K.), (Brough), 53°21′N 1°40′W, 135
Naxos (Naxos Isl), (Greece), 37°06′N 25°24′E, 146
Naxos (Isl), (Greece), 37°06′N 25°24′E, 146, 150
Naxus (Sicily), (Capo di Schiso), 37°49′N 15°17′E, 23
Nazianzus (Turkey), 38°16′N 34°23′E, 150
Neapolis (Naples), 40°50′N 14°15′E, 10, 12, 13, 16, 21, 23, 35, 40, 46, 47, 62, 111, 200, 209, 214
Neapolis (Cyprus), 34°40′N 33°03′E, 150
Neapolis (Greece), (Kavalla), 40°20′N 21°24′E, 146
Neapolis (Jordan), 32°13′N 35°16′E, 157
Neapolis (Tunisia), (Nabeul), 36°30′N 10°44′E, 45, 72, 118
Nebrissa (Spain), (Lebrija), 36°55′N 6°10′W, 124
Neckar R (W. Germany), 129
Nedinum (Yugoslavia), 44°06′N 15°31′E, 140
Nehardea (Iraq), (Tel Nihar), 33°04′N 44°11′E, 191
Nemausus (France), (Nîmes), 43°50′N 4°21′E, 129
Nemetacum (France), (Arras), 40°17′N 2°46′E, 129
Nemetae *see* Noviomagus
Nemi 41°43′N 12°43′E, 30
Nemrud Dagh (Turkey), 37°46′N 38°15′E, 150
Nene R (U.K.), 135
Neocaesarea *see* Cabira
Nepet (Nepi), 42°14′N 12°21′E, 21, 35, 62, 200
Nepete (Tunisia), (Nefta), 33°53′N 8°02′E, 118
Neptunia-Tarentum *see* Tarentum
Neretva R (Yugoslavia), 10
Nertobriga (Spain), (Frejenal de la Sierra), 38°10′N 6°39′W, 124
Nessana (Israel), 30°53′N 34°26′E, 157
Netum (Sicily), 36°53′N 15°05′E, 45
Neuchâtel, L de (Switzerland), 46°55′N 6°55′E, 129
Nicaea (Turkey), (Iznik), 40°27′N 29°43′E, 70, 150, 179
Nicaea (France), (Nice), 43°42′N 7°16′E, 10, 129
Nice *see* Nicaea
Nicephorium (Syria), (Callinicum), (Raqqa), 35°57′N 39°03′E, 157, 174, 220
Nicer R (W. Germany), 108
Niciu (Egypt), 30°39′N 30°45′E, 164
Nicomedia (Turkey), (Izmit), 40°47′N 29°55′E, 75, 107, 150, 171, 173
Nicopolis (Egypt), 31°19′N 30°04′E, 164
Nicopolis (Greece), 39°00′N 20°43′E, 146
Nicopolis (Jordan), 31°53′N 34°59′E, 157
Nicopolis (Turkey), (Susehri), 40°12′N 38°06′E, 60, 150, 220
Nicopolis ad Istrum (Bulgaria), (Nikjup), 43°14′N 25°40′E, 140, 171
Nicopolis ad Nestum (Bulgaria), 41°38′N 24°09′E, 140
Nida (W. Germany), (Frankfurt-Heddernheim), 50°06′N 8°41′E, 108
Nidum (U.K.), (Neath), 51°40′N 3°48′W, 135
Nile R *see* Nilus R
Nilus R (Egypt/Sudan/Uganda), (Nile R), 70, 75, 164, 171, 173, 179
Nisava R (Yugoslavia), 140
Nisibis (Turkey), (Nusaybin), 37°05′N 41°11′E, 60, 150, 157, 199, 220
Nobiliacus (France), (St Léonard), 45°50′N 1°29′E, 199
Noguera R (Spain), 124
Nola 40°55′N 14°32′E, 21, 40, 46, 60, 62, 67, 199
Nomentum 42°04′N 12°39′E, 27, 30, 200
Nora (Sardinia), 39°00′N 9°01′E, 23
Norba (Norma), 41°34′N 12°59′E, 27, 30, 35
Norba (Spain), (Caceres), 39°29′N 6°23′W, 72, 124
Norchia (Norcia), 42°47′N 13°05′E, 21
Noreia (Austria), (Neumark), 46°56′N 16°09′E, 60
Northern Sporades (Isl), (Greece), 146
Novae (Bulgaria), (Swisjtow), 43°36′N 25°22′E, 140
Novae (Yugoslavia), (Cezava), 44°36′N 21°54′E, 140
Novaesium (W. Germany), (Neuss), 51°12′N 6°42′E, 129, 192
Novaria (Novara), 45°27′N 8°37′E, 29
Noviodunum (France), (Jublains), 48°15′N 0°29′W, 129
Noviodunum (France), (Soissons), 49°23′N 3°20′E, 72, 129
Noviodunum (Romania), 45°10′N 28°50′E, 140
Noviodunum (Switzerland), (Nyons), 46°23′N 6°15′E, 129
Noviomagus (France), (Lisieux), 49°09′N 0°14′E, 129
Noviomagus (France), (Nijon), 48°03′N 5°31′E, 129
Noviomagus (Netherlands), (Nijmegen), 51°50′N 5°52′E, 84, 129
Noviomagus (U.K.), (Chichester), 50°50′N 0°48′W, 135
Noviomagus (W. Germany), (Nemetae), (Speyer), 49°18′N 8°26′E, 108, 129, 192
Noviomagus (W. Germany), (Neumagen), 49°51′N 6°55′E, 129
Noviorigum (France), (Royan), 45°38′N 1°02′W, 129
Nuceria (Nocera), 40°43′N 14°38′E, 40, 46, 62, 67
Numantia (Spain), (Soria), 41°46′N 2°28′W, 47, 60, 124
Numerus Syrorum (Algeria), 34°50′N 1°45′W, 118
Numistro 40°45′N 15°29′E, 46
Nuraghe Losa (Sardinia), 40°13′N 8°49′E, 20
Nursia (Norcia), 42°47′N 13°05′E, 40, 199, 214
Nysa (Turkey), (Sultanhisar), 37°52′N 28°10′E, 150
Nyssa (Turkey), 37°52′N 28°10′E, 150

Oboda (Israel), 30°50′N 34°44′E, 157
Obulco (Spain), (Porcuna), 37°52′N 4°11′W, 124
Occariba (Syria), 35°02′N 37°28′E, 210
Ocelum Duri (Spain), (Zamora), 41°30′N 5°45′W, 124
Ocriculum (Otricoli), 42°25′N 12°29′E, 35, 40, 62
Octodurum (Switzerland), (Martigny), 46°06′N 7°04′E, 129
Odessus (Bulgaria), (Varna), 43°12′N 27°57′E, 140
Oea (Libya), (Tripoli), 32°58′N 13°12′E, 118
Oeniadae (Greece), 38°23′N 21°12′E, 146
Oenoanda (Turkey), 36°49′N 29°38′E, 150
Oescus (Romania), 43°44′N 24°27′E, 140
Ofanto R, 10
Offenburg (W. Germany), 48°29′N 7°57′E, 108
Oglio R, 10
Ohridsko, L (Albania/Yugoslavia), 140, 146
Olba (Turkey), 36°42′N 33°55′E, 150
Olbasa (Turkey), 37°13′N 29°50′E, 72, 150
Olbia (Libya), (Qasr el-Lebia), 32°38′N 21°26′E, 164
Olbia (U.S.S.R.), 46°56′N 31°58′E, 171
Olisipo (Portugal), (Lisbon), 38°44′N 9°08′W, 72, 124
Oltul R (Romania), 140
Olympia (Greece), 37°38′N 21°39′E, 146
Olympus, Mt (Greece), 40°05′N 22°21′E, 146
Olympus Mysius (Turkey), 39°55′N 29°11′E, 199
Ombos (Egypt), (Kom Ombo), 24°26′N 32°57′E, 164
Ombrone R, 10
Onchesmus (Albania), 38°22′N 23°09′E, 146
Oneuatha (Syria), 34°01′N 37°30′E, 174
Onoba (Spain, (Huelva), 37°15′N 6°56′W, 124
Onnum (U.K.), (Halton), 55°01′N 2°01′W, 135
Opitergium (Oderzo), 45°57′N 12°29′E, 38
Oppidum Novum (Morocco), 35°04′N 5°57′W, 118
Opus (Greece), 38°39′N 23°00′E, 146
Oran (Algeria), 35°45′N 0°38′W, 118
Orchomenus (Greece), 37°43′N 22°18′E, 60
Oresa (Syria), 35°07′N 38°52′E, 174
Oretum (Spain), 38°46′N 3°46′W, 124
Oricum (Albania), 40°22′N 19°25′E, 146
Orolaunum (Belgium), (Arlon), 49°41′N 5°49′E, 129
Orontes R (Lebanon/Syria/Turkey), 157
Ortles, Mt 46°31′N 10°33′E, 10
Ortopla (Yugoslavia), 44°42′N 14°54′E, 72
Ortucchio 41°57′N 73°38′E, 20
Osca (Spain), (Huesca), 42°08′N 0°25′W, 72, 124
Ossonoba (Portugal), (Faro), 37°01′N 7°56′W, 124
Ostia 41°46′N 12°18′E, 21, 27, 30, 35, 47, 200
Ostia Aterne (Pescara), 42°27′N 14°13′E, 10, 62
Othona (U.K.), (Bradwell), 51°44′N 0°54′E, 171
Otranto 40°08′N 18°30′E, 39
Otthora (Syria), 34°22′N 37°08′E, 174
Ouse R (U.K.), 135
Ovetum (Spain), (Oviedo), 43°21′N 5°50′W, 124
Ovilava (Austria), (Wels), 48°10′N 14°02′E, 190
Oxyrhynchus (Egypt), 28°33′N 30°38′E, 164

Padua *see* Patavium
Padus R (Po R), 10, 14, 20, 21, 23, 29, 38, 47, 49, 67, 72, 75, 171, 173, 179, 214
Paestum (Poseidonia), 40°24′N 15°00′E, 23, 35, 39, 41, 46, 62
Palermo *see* Panormus
Pallantia (Spain), (Palencia), 41°01′N 4°32′W, 124
Palmavera (Sardinia), 40°36′N 8°18′E, 20
Palma (Mallorca Isl), (Spain), 39°35′N 2°39′E, 72, 124
Palmyra (Syria), 34°36′N 38°15′E, 75, 157, 171, 174, 179, 220
Palombara Sabina 42°10′N 12°46′E, 20, 30
Panaro R, 10
Pandosia 39°08′N 16°44′E, 46
Panium (Turkey), 40°55′N 27°28′E, 140
Panopolis (Egypt), 26°28′N 31°56′E, 164
Panormus (Sicily), (Palermo), 38°08′N 13°23′E, 10, 12, 13, 15, 23, 38, 45, 47, 72
Pantelleria *see* Cossura
Paphus (Cyprus), 34°45′N 32°25′E, 107, 150
Paraetonium (Egypt), 31°21′N 27°14′E, 164
Parentium (Yugoslavia), (Porec), 45°14′N 13°36′E, 67
Parisii *see* Lutetia
Parium (Turkey), (Kemer), 40°25′N 27°04′E, 72
Parlais (Turkey), 37°40′N 31°43′E, 72
Parma 44°48′N 10°19′E, 10, 20, 38, 49, 67
Parndorf (Austria), 47°59′N 16°52′E, 140
Paros (Isl), (Greece), 47°04′N 25°06′E, 146
Patara (Turkey), (Arsinoë), 36°06′N 28°05′E, 150
Patavium (Padua), 45°24′N 11°53′E, 10, 20, 29, 38
Paterno (Sicily), 37°34′N 14°55′E, 20
Patrae (Greece), 38°14′N 21°44′E, 72, 146
S. Pauli (Egypt), (Monastery of St Paul), 28°49′N 32°33′E, 199
Pautalia (Bulgaria), 42°22′N 22°40′E, 140
Pavia *see* Ticinum
Pax Iulia (Portugal), (Beja), 38°01′N 7°52′W, 72, 124
Pelendava (Romania), 44°18′N 23°47′E, 140
Pella (Greece), 32°27′N 22°30′E, 72, 146
Pella (Jordan), 32°27′N 35°37′E, 157
Pelusium (Egypt), 31°02′N 32°32′E, 164
Pelva (Yugoslavia), 43°50′N 17°04′E, 140
Pergamum (Turkey), (Bergama), 39°08′N 27°10′E, 60, 70, 75, 107, 150
Perge (Turkey), 36°59′N 30°46′E, 150
Perinthus (Turkey), (Heraclea), 40°59′N 27°57′E, 107, 150

INDEX

Page numbers in italics refer to illustrations or their captions.

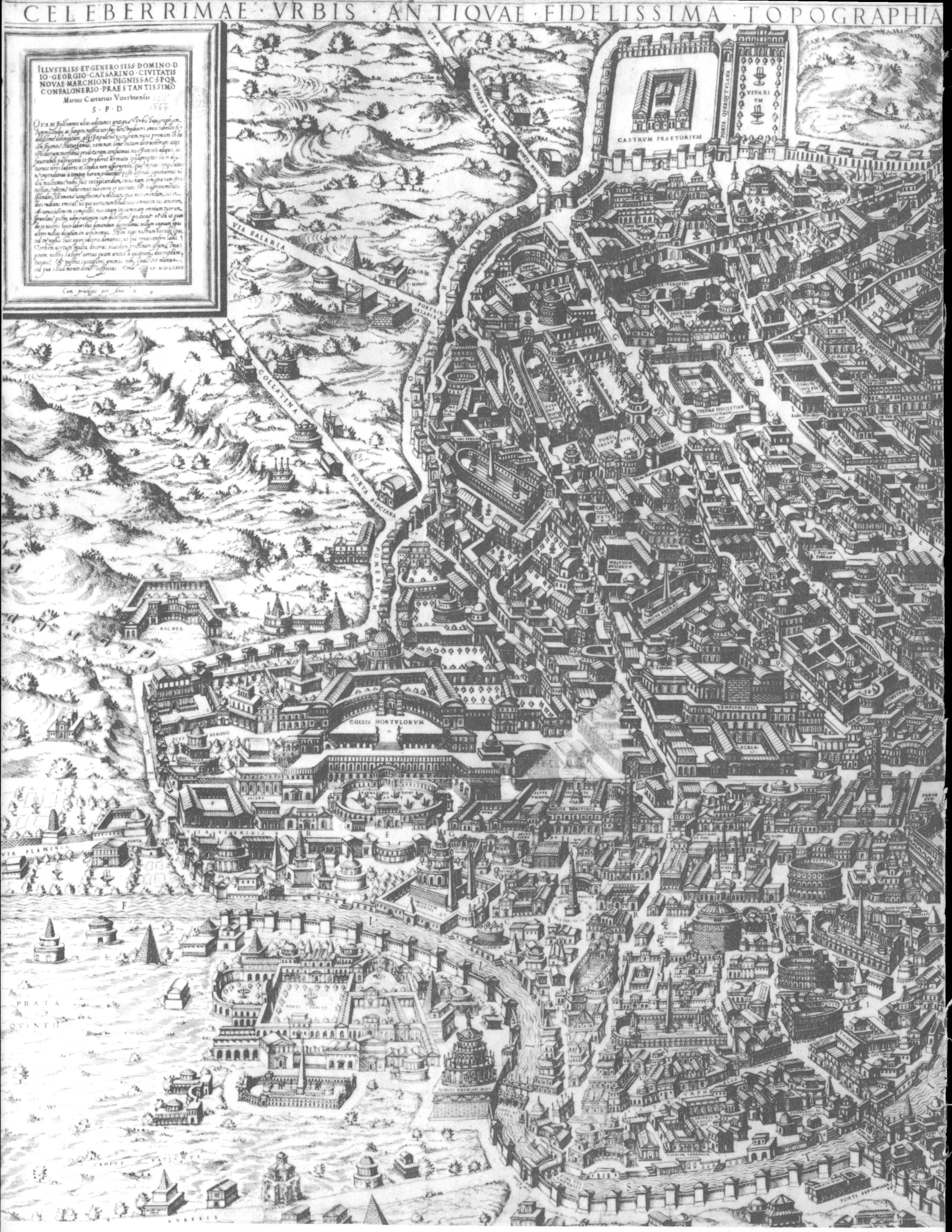
CELEBERRIMAE · VRBIS · ANTIQVAE · FIDELISSIMA · TOPOGRAPHIA
ILLVSTRISS·ET·GENEROSISS·DOMINO·D
IO·GEORGIO·CAESARINO·CIVITATIS
NOVAE·MARCHIONI·DIGNISS·AC·S·P·Q·R
CONFALONERIO·PRAESTANTISSIMO
Marius Cartarius Viterbiensis
S · P · D
CASTRVM PRAETORIVM
VIVARIVM
PORTA QVERQVETVLANA
VIA NVMENTANA
VIA SALARIA
PORTA SALARIA
VIA COLLATINA
PORTA PINCIANA
POMERIVM
BALNEA
AQVA VIRGO
COLLIS HORTVLORVM
THERMAE DIOCLETIAN
FORVM SALLVSTII
TEMPLVM SOLIS
VIA FLAMINIA
PRATA QVINTIA
CAMPVS VATICANVS
AVRELIA
MOLES HADRIANI
PORTA SEPTIMIANA

CLIFF RICHARD

The Biography

Cliff Richard

The Biography

STEVE TURNER

A LION BOOK

Published by
Lion Publishing plc
Sandy Lane West, Oxford, England
ISBN 0 7324 3982 1

First edition 1993
Second edition 1994
This updated edition 1998
10 9 8 7 6 5 4 3 2 1 0

A catalogue record for this book is available
from the British Library

Printed and bound in Great Britain by
Caledonian International Book Manufacturing, Glasgow

Steve Turner is a journalist, author and poet. He has written for many top music papers and journals, including *Rolling Stone*, *New Musical Express*, *Mojo* and *Q* magazine. He has also contributed music and travel articles to *The Times* and the *Independent*.

His books include: *Conversations with Eric Clapton*, *A Decade of The Who*, *Hungry for Heaven*, *U2: Rattle and Hum*, *Van Morrison: Too Late to Stop Now* and *A Hard Day's Write*.

Steve Turner's five poetry collections, including the best-selling *Up to Date* and the children's volume, *The Day I Fell Down the Toilet*, have established him as a notable modern poet. He lives with his wife and two children in west London.

*To my Dad and Mum, Gordon and Ivy Turner,
with thanks for all their love and encouragement,
and to the memory of George Hoffman*

Contents

Introduction

I was nine years old when I first became aware of Cliff Richard. I can remember hearing 'Living Doll' on the radio — the 'wireless' as we then called it — and have a clear memory of children singing 'Travellin' Light' on the way back home from junior school.

At that age I didn't know anything about Cliff having 'softened up' his sound. I had no knowledge of Little Richard, Jerry Lee Lewis, Chuck Berry and Gene Vincent because I hadn't heard Uncle Mac play their records on 'Children's Favourites', one of the few BBC wireless shows in those days to play pop records. All I knew was that Cliff wasn't like the Perry Como and Alma Cogan sound that seemed to dominate pop through my childhood, and I liked what I heard.

I also liked what I saw. I wanted a striped shirt like Cliff's ('too jazzy,' said Mum). I wanted pink socks ('girls' clothes,' said Mum). Most of all I wanted a hairstyle which swept back at the sides and tumbled forward at the front ('you're having a short back and sides and that's it,' said Mum).

I'd like to say that I have all Cliff's early singles in mint condition, but the fact is that in those days my parents had a gramophone that only played 78 rpm records. My first Cliff purchase (other than a comb in a grey plastic case bearing his image and signature) was the sheet music to 'Please Don't Tease'. It cost two shillings and I only bought it for the photograph on the cover.

It's easy to look back and see what a 'nice' boy Cliff really was, but at the time, to someone not yet in his teens, he seemed like forbidden fruit. The only people I knew who dressed in such outrageous colours and wore their hair without a clean parting were Teddy boys, Rockers and the boys who operated the bumper cars at fairgrounds.

These were the days, it must be remembered, when a solid-body electric guitar was regarded as a symbol of teenage discontent. Rock 'n' roll, whether original and from Memphis or derivative and from London, was nothing more than a 'noise' which the older generation associated with juvenile delinquency.

My parents certainly didn't see Cliff as a good thing. I'm sure they had never checked out his worthy opinions but he just looked like a rock 'n' roll person. I can remember wanting to buy a book about him (it must have been a paperback version of *It's Great To Be Young*, his 1960 autobiography) and my dad said, 'You don't want that. It'll be full of sex.' If only he had known.

I didn't meet Cliff until 1970, at a party in London. By this time I had started to write about rock music. We passed on the stairs and I stuck my hand out and said, 'Hi, I'm Steve Turner,' and Cliff stuck his hand out and just said, 'Hi'. It was then I realized that when you're as famous as Cliff you no longer have to bother giving your name. I saw him at various times after that during the early seventies, but didn't interview him until 1977 while he was recording his album *Small Corners*.

The genesis of this book, though, lies in a four-part documentary series for BBC TV called 'Cliff!' (1981) for which I was researcher and interviewer. I interviewed many of his friends and colleagues for these films, travelled with Cliff on the road, visited him at home and joined him on a tour of America.

At the end of it all I realized I would be well-positioned to write a much more comprehensive book about Cliff than had ever been written before. I had the access, I had the contacts and I had a pile of research material.

That Christmas I was given a copy of Albert Goldman's *Elvis*, a book which set new rigorous standards for rock biography. The previous 'definitive' biography of Elvis, written by Jerry Hopkins, had listed 112 interview sources and began the story at Elvis' birth.

Goldman listed 160 interviews and started the story with David Pressley (the original spelling of the family name) who had come to America some time during the 1740s.

Early in 1982 I made my first approach to Cliff's office suggesting there was room for a more expansive biography of Cliff than had been written before. They eventually agreed but there were long delays because they felt the market was saturated with Cliff products, and they didn't want fans to be overwhelmed.

Final approval wasn't given until March 1991. By this time I had amassed even more material, and had the additional perspective of having co-written a song for Cliff which became the title track of his album *Now You See Me . . . Now You Don't.*

I didn't come to the project with a prepared thesis. I wanted simply to provide as full a portrait of the man as I could, because I considered that anyone who had been that successful for that long was deserving of detailed investigation.

There were areas I was particularly interested in though, because I thought they offered clues both to his success and to his character.

There was the question of his enigmatic sexuality. If he were a bank manager or a captain of industry I wouldn't consider this relevant, but it is when you are dealing with a man who trades in romantic fantasy. Understandably people want to know why he has never married, or whether he's interested in women at all.

The fact that Cliff has survived so many changes in musical fashion is remarkable. He has been at the top of the music business for over thirty years, and yet his success in Europe and Australasia has not been repeated in America. I wanted to find out why.

Then there is Cliff's Christian faith — not very fashionable for a popular entertainer — and his image of being a 'nice guy'. Just how much of that is due to his upbringing, and how much is a result of his conversion to Christianity? I was intrigued to know if his faith had changed or matured over the years. And whether he's a nice guy when he's not on show.

Finally there is his youthfulness. His apparent failure to grow old has become an important part of his image. I wanted to discover how much his youthful looks have to be worked on now, and how bothered he is by changes in his appearance.

Since starting work on the book the two questions I've been asked most often are, 'Hasn't there already been a book about Cliff?' and 'Is it an authorized biography?' The answer in both cases is, . . . er, well, sort of.

There have been at least thirty books about Cliff published in Britain over the years. But surprisingly enough, only three of these are adult biographies, and none have been in-depth studies. In addition Cliff has written two autobiographies: *It's Great To Be Young* (1960) and *Which One's Cliff?* (1977). Both attempted a very different job from the book you now hold in your hand.

I felt that there was room for a more detailed account of Cliff's life because the expectations of a rock biography have been significantly raised by books such as Goldman's *Elvis* and *The Lives of John Lennon*, Philip Norman's *Shout* (the Beatles) and David Ritz's *Divided Soul* (Marvin Gaye). No longer is it sufficient to speak to half a dozen colleagues and stitch their comments together with material from newspaper cuttings.

For this book I carried out over two hundred interviews and discovered, very early on, that despite the volume of words written about Cliff over the years, I was not tramping a well-worn path. Almost all my interviewees had never been questioned about Cliff before. No one had spoken to his aunts, uncles, schoolfriends, childhood neighbours, former girlfriends and early business associates. No one had ever bothered tracing his family tree or tracking down the members of his early groups.

The book is authorized in as much I have had the full support and co-operation of Cliff and his management team during the writing, but they have not had authorial control and have no financial stake in the project.

I consider this to be the perfect arrangement. Without Cliff's blessing I would have had limited access to his friends, colleagues and office diaries. People are very suspicious about co-operating with unapproved biographers.

Yet if my involvement with Cliff had extended to include editorial approval the book would have lost any hope of objectivity. It's impossible to write an honest biography with the subject looking over your shoulder.

As it was, Cliff has given me as much of his time as I asked for. I was given an introductory letter to smooth the way in setting up interviews, and there has been no evidence of anyone having been warned against talking to me. In fact some interviews, like the one with Cliff's mother, Mrs Dorothy Bodkin, were organized on my behalf by the office.

It was very brave of Cliff to allow me to nose around in his past, digging up long-forgotten associations and asking impertinent questions. I hope that he discovers his trust has been rewarded with a book which accurately and fairly sums up his life so far.

Steve Turner

Acknowledgments

This book couldn't have been written without the support of Bill Latham who, in giving me the green light to go ahead with it, had to give the red light to a number of other well-qualified potential biographers.

It was Bill who ultimately had to reassure worried interviewees that I was alright when they called up to check with the office. Throughout the project he encouraged me to fight for objectivity knowing that this would be a difficult task in view of the closeness I had enjoyed with Cliff in the past.

Another vital support has been Gill Snow, secretary (and much, much more) to Cliff Richard. She has supplied me with phone numbers, answered all my little queries and opened the office diaries.

At Lion Publishing I'm grateful to Becky Winter not only for seeing the potential of a full-length biography of this kind but also for helping me focus my vision. Melanie Watson has overhauled the book for errors both historical and grammatical, and collected many of the photos.

All my interviewees deserve thanks for giving up time and information, but I must mention some who have given special help.

Cliff's mother, Mrs Dorothy Bodkin, had not been interviewed for twenty-five years but graciously consented to speak to me for this book.

Peter Gormley, famed for his reticence, not only gave me an interview but was ready at the end of a phone any time I had a query.

From Cliff's family I must thank Vincent Bridgwater for his time and the use of his photographs. Joyce Dobra not only lent me photographs from the Webb side of the family but gave me access to some documents and copies of birth certificates which greatly speeded up my completion of the family tree. Olive Dazely spent long hours on the phone telling me about life in India.

Delia Wicks, Janice Berry and Betty Clarke had never spoken of their romances with Cliff to anyone in the media before and I am grateful to them for their time and openness.

Ian 'Sammy' Samwell not only spoke to me frequently on the phone but met up with me in London and gave me a small suitcase full of photographs, cuttings, sheet music, and scrapbooks. A real gold mine!

Dick Teague, who thought I was a practical joker when I first called him to ask about the days when Cliff sang in his group, sent me invaluable information about the brief career of the Dick Teague Skiffle Group. This included pages from a diary kept by his father who managed their affairs, engagement sheets, letters and cuttings.

Royston Ellis was another great discovery. Back in Britain for a short break, he went through his cupboards and discovered all sorts of helpful photographs and cuttings. He lent me copies of his books *The Shadows By Themselves* and *The Big Beat Scene*, as well as an autographed proof copy of Cliff s *It's Great To Be Young*.

Ray Mackender, who has a great memory for the 'Oh Boy!' days, sent me lots of details about incidents he remembered and was always readily available to check facts.

There were some deleted albums and videos which I needed and Christine Whitehead, co-ordinator of Britain's Cliff Richard Fan Club, tracked them down and sent them to me.

Rachel Melville-Thomas cast a psychologist's eye over some of my research and Mick Brown, Richard Branson's biographer, was one of the first to encourage me to take on this book.

Of Cliff's current circle of close friends, Graham Disbrey was very generous with his time and Peter Graves was a reliable source of information when it came to dates of holidays and meetings. John

Davey very kindly photocopied material which helped me with the chronology of events around Cliff's Christian conversion.

Finally, much of the burden of this book has fallen on my family — daughter Lianne, son Nathan and wife Mo — and I thank them for their love and patience.

1

'Only a boy from Cheshunt'

Cliff Richard can't sleep. He's been lying in his bed for three hours but his mind won't switch off. He snaps on his bedside light and reaches out for a book. After two chapters the book is abandoned, the light is turned off and he again tries to drift into semi-consciousness. But something won't let him.

An hour later he's up and walking about the master bedroom. He puts on the television and watches Britain's only all-night channel with its mix of sport, chat shows and old movies. Still it doesn't tire him.

He has every reason to want this to be a good night's sleep for in just over twelve hours' time, on 16 June 1989, he will face his largest audience ever. That's what keeps him awake. It's not just the 72,000 fans who've been promised an event rather than a show, but the complexity of what he's planning to do on stage: working with ninety artists, singing forty-five songs, making five costume changes and moving in style from fifties high school hop to late eighties high-tech pop while everything is recorded and filmed.

It's already taken six weeks of rehearsals at Shepperton Studios but one technical hitch, spate of bad weather or dicky throat and The Event could go down in pop history as Almost The Event. The next forty-eight hours, he knows, could raise his career to even greater heights or have him written off as the man who flew too close to the sun.

By the time he leaves his bedroom at eight o'clock in the morning and goes down for breakfast he has had no sleep. The best he has been able to do has been to lie still on the bed for two hours conserving energy.

Already in the kitchen is Bill Latham, Cliff's longest-standing and most trusted friend. Although Latham is only two years older than Cliff, with his balding head and greying hair he looks like any middle-aged man could decently expect to.

Cliff appears to have defied the years. He doesn't have an extra ounce of fat on his frame, still walks with a youthful spring and hasn't yet been dealt the curse of a receding hairline, wrinkled flesh and double chin. He has grey flecks in his hair but most are hidden by lowlights.

After a light breakfast (two slices of toast and a coffee) Cliff showers, shaves and dresses in casual clothes (a T-shirt and shorts because the weather is bright). At 9.30 a stretch limo passes through the gates and draws up on the gravel outside the front door. In the driving seat is a chauffeur dressed in a grey peak cap. In the back is David Bryce, Cliff's professional manager.

Cliff leaves the house and climbs into the back of the limo next to Bryce. He doesn't have to worry about his costumes and personal effects as they've been taken ahead to Wembley Stadium by his personal assistant Roger Bruce.

At 10.30 Bruce calls through on the car phone to check on Cliff's progress. His first shock of the day has been to discover that a member of the pyrotechnic team has been badly burned while working on the firework display. A rope he was climbing snapped and he fell to the ground clutching an armful of explosives which went off on impact. The burns are so bad it's decided to cancel the display which was to close the show.

The limo arrives at Wembley and Bruce is at the back entrance to ensure that Cliff gets free access to the fenced-off backstage area. Promoter Mel Bush has had it designed to look like a small Mediterranean village with palm trees, fountains, open-air cafes, flowers, bushes, shrubs and a marquee.

Now on site, Cliff has a coffee in his dressing cabin which has been stocked by Bruce with everything he needs. There is shampoo and conditioner, perfumed soap, a dressing gown, monogrammed towels produced especially for the day, a hairdryer and his favourite brush and comb. In the fridge there are bottles of mineral water, cans of Dexters hypotonic drink and his preferred post-concert tipple of pineapple juice and champagne.

At midday he meets masseuse Linda Kay who has been hired to ease neck and shoulder tension. She uses manual lymphatic drainage, a massage that rids the body of toxins through the lymph system, and an electro-muscle stimulator to lift the contours of the face. A 'facelift without surgery' Cliff calls it. It tones his features up so well that some people think he's already been through make-up.

Wherever he goes on site he's surrounded by people making last-minute adjustments. He can't get it out of his head that he's the reason that they are all here today: ninety performing artists and 3,000 people checking tickets, selling goods, controlling the crowds, filming, recording and generally mounting the show.

After a light snack Cliff starts his soundcheck. The sun blazes down out of a clear blue sky. Everything seems perfect but he's so on edge he even forgets lines from his best-known songs. Few people who have worked with him have ever seen him so nervous.

The stadium has been made to look less cavernous by draping one end to create a huge arch beneath which Cliff will put on his most lavish and comprehensive performance yet. He knows he's one of only a few acts able to take on this venue with its daunting capacity of over 70,000.

But tickets for tonight's show sold out over a single weekend. Mel

Bush then took a further gamble — a second concert on the next night which also sold out. Cliff's nervousness is understandable: 144,000 people will see The Event.

Cliff is reluctant to give what he calls 'history lessons' in concert, which is why this isn't just another Cliff and the Shadows reunion. But for these two nights he will celebrate the start of his career with a short set based around the idea of the 'Oh Boy!' TV show which gave him his first national exposure in 1958.

The show's two resident vocal groups, the Dallas Boys and the Vernons Girls, have re-formed. Its MC Jimmy Henney will make the opening announcement, and there will be a special guest spot.

When Henney, dressed in a pale blue and white pullover, walks out on stage it is five o'clock. 'This is how it all began thirty years ago,' he announces and the band plays the opening chords of Buddy Holly's 'Oh Boy' as five Dallas Boys, in red satin bomber jackets and white trousers, strut out.

When they move back, two central doors burst open and Cliff dances out in a pink jacket, black shirt, pink belt, black trousers and pink socks: a tribute to the fashion he wore when he first sang 'Move It' on stage. A wave of applause rises from the crowd and Cliff beams with pleasure. As he steps back, a dozen Vernons Girls in party dresses, petticoats or shorts, sashay across the stage, all of them looking trim and elegant.

For the last verse the wispy-bearded Kalin Twins from America add their voices, walking on stage in black dinner jackets as if they've arrived late at the wrong party. They couldn't fail to remember that for the last show they did with Cliff, in October 1958, they were the chart toppers and he was the new boy.

A rumble of honky tonk piano chords announce 'Whole Lotta Shakin' Goin' On', the Jerry Lee Lewis hit which Cliff has performed ever since it was first released. In Jerry Lee's hands it was a crude song designated by rock critic Dave Marsh 'one of the strongest arguments for the idea that prudes really did have something to fear from rock 'n' roll'. In the hands of Cliff and the 'Oh Boy!' chorus it sounds about as threatening as Val Doonican singing the Sex Pistols' 'Anarchy In The UK'.

With the Kalins he sings the Everly Brothers' 'Bird Dog' and then takes off into a version of Elvis Presley's 1957 hit 'Let's Have A Party', with all the requisite bowing of legs and knocking of knees. During this song his fears evaporate. As he rolls and jerks across the stage he is the boy who never grew up, the boy who, in middle age, is still playing rock stars in the mirror.

After eight songs with the Shadows there is a short break and Cliff returns at 8.45 as dusk begins to fall. Lights play across the crowd, and a slow drum beat starts up as Cliff, dressed from neck to foot in white, strides purposefully across the stage, wreathed in dry ice. The jacket of his made-to-measure suit is studded with 2,000 diamantes, which now sparkle beneath the pyramid of lights.

Contrasted against his well-tanned face the shimmering white costume suggests he is a figure of purity, an unbesmirched survivor from another age. He looks magisterial and immaculate.

Two or three songs into the set he starts to loosen up, picking up on the energy of the crowd. He starts to work them a little, spinning around like a half-speed dervish and urging them to clap along.

Because the Shadows had declined to appear in the 'Oh Boy!' section (they argued it would spoil the effect of their later spot), Cliff invited two original Shadows, who hadn't played together with him since October 1961, to join in his set. Tony Meehan and Jet Harris are welcomed onto the stage.

Jet, gaunt and balding, saunters on in a Mississippi gambler's jacket and leather boots, his red guitar hanging over his right shoulder. Meehan settles behind his drum kit. 'This is the song that started it all off,' says Cliff, strapping on a white guitar and playing the rhythm line of 'Move It'. He's now played it so many times that it rarely sounds like the raw, earthy original.

The night sky is now pitch black, the show is reaching its climax. 'For thirty years you have given me a really glorious career,' Cliff says after singing 'I Just Don't Have The Heart' with the production team of Stock, Aitken and Waterman on backing vocals.

'What can I say? All I've been able to do in return is the best I can do. But the best I can do is not going to change your lifestyle in any way, it's not going to mean anything in any great eternal terms.

'I always feel that if I have one thing to offer that's of any value it's the message that God exists, that Jesus is alive and that he's yours if you want him. I've been criticized for saying that many times in situations like this but I thumb my nose at the criticism. Here are two songs I hope you like.'

He then sings the gospel songs 'God Put A Fighter In Me' by Graham Kendrick, Britain's best-known contemporary hymn writer, and 'Thief In The Night' by Paul Field.

That he bothers, at this climactic point in his biggest concert ever, to turn the attention away from himself, is evidence of the depth of his religious feelings. He would feel he had short-changed his fans if they left Wembley Stadium only thinking about how wonderful Cliff Richard is.

The finale comes with 'From A Distance'. Cliff stands on a plinth swathed in light while the rest of the night's performers congregate around him. During the instrumental passage, as the lights sweep the stage and flags flutter in the breeze, he grasps the radio mike close to his lips with both hands and then when he lets it drop it's clear that he's close to tears. He wants to smile but his mouth is going in the wrong direction.

He regains his composure long enough to get through the last verse and then when it's all over he says, 'Thank you. Good night and God bless,' and walks away wiping his eyes.

As soon as he is off stage Roger Bruce puts a coat over his shoulders and guides him towards his dressing cabin. Those who've been working on the site — cleaners, ticket collectors, police, first aiders — spontaneously line up and leave a path for him, applauding him as he moves between them.

When he gets to the cabin he flops onto a leather sofa and bursts into tears. Bruce puts his arms around Cliff's shoulders to comfort him and then he too begins to sob.

It's as if all the love and affection that Cliff has worked to generate over the past thirty years has just rolled over him in one single wave. It's at times like this that he says to himself: 'I can't believe all this is happening. I'm only a boy from Cheshunt.'

2

Roots in the Raj

The fact that the boy who became Cliff Richard was born in India and baptized Harry Rodger Webb has been presented a million times. But nothing has ever been said about how his parents, Rodger and Dorothy Marie, came to be on the subcontinent and there have been only the sketchiest descriptions of his grandparents.

Perhaps because of this it has often been rumoured that Cliff's dark good looks are due to mixed race. When he was a teenager in Cheshunt the question for his friends was not whether he had Indian blood, but from which parent it came. Most of them plumped for Mrs Webb because she was most like Cliff in appearance and had the same darker skin tone.

Cliff has never been a good source of information on family history because he has never been interested. The most he has ever said is that his grandparents were 'as English as roast beef,' and that it had been they who had made the move to India. He once told a journalist that he thought one of his grandfathers was born in Threadneedle Street, in the City of London, but that 'every time I pass through there all I can see are banks and insurance offices'.

The truth is that only one of his grandparents was born in England, but not in Threadneedle Street, and it's possible that some of his great-great-grandparents never knew any country other than India.

The mystery of the skin pigmentation is partly solved by the records of baptism, marriage and burial held by the India Office Library in London. They show that a great-grandmother on his mother's side was half Welsh and half Spanish, born to George David Smith and Emiline Josephine Rebeiro who had married in Calcutta in 1869. Photographs of her in middle age show that she had distinctively Mediterranean looks which passed to her children.

The Portuguese had planted themselves in India in 1510 when they captured Goa on the west coast and turned it into a colony. A steady flow of Portuguese and Spanish workers came to that first settlement and soon moved northwards to Bombay.

The British didn't come into India for another hundred years, when the East India Company began building trading posts and forts. Although the company hadn't intended to govern, merely to make money out of such commodities as spices, cotton, sugar, jute and silk, effectively it became an imperial power dividing the country into the presidencies of Bombay, Bengal and Madras and organizing its own massive private army.

By the time Victoria came to the throne in 1837, Westminster was firmly in control of India and the Crown had appointed a governor-general. Whereas the original merchants of the East India Company had set up in the ports and worked alongside the indigenous population, the Victorian imperialists had no such respect for the natives and their ways. They saw the Indians as people to be tamed.

Cliff's ancestors came to India as part of this exercise. His father's family came as part of the task force needed to build the railway system that would transform India from a collection of outposts to a modern nation. On his mother's side they came as soldiers, equipped to defend the British Empire against restless natives.

The earliest ancestor on record is Thomas Webb, Cliff's great-great-grandfather, who was born in London's East End in 1805. He became a book-keeper, married a woman called Mary Taynton, who was two years his junior, and lived at 2 Wilson's Place, a small cul-de-sac near Commercial Road in Limehouse. Here, in 1841, Mary gave birth to Cliff's great-grandfather, Thomas Benjamin Webb, the man who was to lead the Webb family to India.

Wilson's Place today is an area of lock-up garages with the outline of Canary Wharf visible in the distance. The houses that Thomas Benjamin Webb would have known were torn down long ago.

Nothing is recorded of his life until 1865 when he married Amelia Sophia Smart, a West Ham girl, and moved over the river to Woolwich where they settled at 135 Plumstead Road.

The 1871 census shows that Amelia was then a dressmaker and Thomas Benjamin was working as an engineer at the Woolwich Arsenal. This meant that they were affluent enough to employ a live-in nursemaid, Jane Brown, to look after their first child, probably their eldest son Thomas.

It was in this house in 1872 that Cliff's grandfather, Frederick William Webb, was born. Again we don't know much about his early life, but the stark facts show that he was frequently hit by tragedy. Two more children were born to his mother in quick succession. Then shortly after his second birthday she died, age thirty-three, of typhoid fever, leaving her husband with four children to care for.

In view of this new responsibility it's hard to account for what happened next. In 1877, the year Queen Victoria became empress of India, Thomas Benjamin packed his bags, left his children and went to work as a mechanical engineer on the South India Railway.

There may have been sound economic reasons for the move. The railway system in India was in its infancy and British labourers were being recruited to lay new track. Maybe the wages of an engineer at the Woolwich Arsenal weren't sufficient to cover the care and education of his children, whereas those of a covenanted engineer in India were. No one knows who looked after his children or whether he ever intended to return.

All that is known is that the young Frederick William received a grammar school education in Holborn and then, at the age of twelve, left England to join his father. On 10 April 1885 we find him in Perambur in South India where, according to the ecclesiastical returns, he was baptized by a chaplain of the Madras Railway. His brother later joined him, but the fate of his two siblings remains a mystery. Neither of them went to India or saw their father again.

Two years after Frederick William arrived in Perambur, further tragedy struck. On 27 August 1887 Thomas Benjamin was tending a damaged valve on an engine when it burst open. The escaping steam could have caused an explosion so he laid himself across it to prevent a disaster, and died of terrible injuries.

Thomas was buried the same day, which happened to be Frederick William's birthday. Conducting the funeral service was the same railway chaplain who had baptized the boy two years before. At fifteen Frederick was an orphan, alone in a still strange land, and with no means of returning to the familiar streets of South London.

No one alive today can remember him mentioning this calamitous time. 'We didn't ask our parents about their backgrounds in those days,' says his daughter Joyce Clarkson. 'It just wasn't done.'

The next entry in the ecclesiastical returns is Frederick's marriage in 1896 to Donella Eugenie Woodfall, Cliff's paternal grandmother. Donella Eugenie, known because of her initials as Dewy (a nickname that passed briefly to Cliff's oldest sister who was baptized Donella Eugenie Webb), had slightly oriental looks. Rumour had it they were due to a Burmese princess who had married into Donella Woodfall's mother's family. Her direct ancestry was Dutch and English but, if the Burmese connection is true, it would further explain Cliff's dark colouring.

Donella and Frederick started their married life in Negapatam but by 1899, when their first daughter Dorothy May was born, they had moved to Burma where Frederick William was involved in bridge construction in the capital city of Rangoon.

He was a handsome man with a commanding manner, but had a foul temper which sometimes lost him work. 'But there was another side to his character,' his granddaughter Joyce Dobra points out. 'He would spend a lot of time in the juvenile courts where he would bail out young men, take them home, get them good apprenticeships and see them on the right path.'

Donella Eugenie gave birth to a total of eleven children. Rodger Oscar Webb, Cliff's father, was born on 23 December 1904 at Tramway Quarters, Rangoon. Although it was company accommodation, the Webbs were well-off by the standards of their contemporaries back in England. They enjoyed the services of a cook, a bearer, a sweeper, a washer, and an *ayah*, the servant who looked after the small children.

They stayed in Burma until 1914 when the family began to move around Indian railway towns such as Howrah, Allahabad and Lucknow. By the time Rodger started at Allahabad High School his oldest brother, Harry, was seventeen and his youngest sister, Joyce, was a baby.

Frederick William was a tough disciplinarian who caned the boys and took the attitude that if girls misbehaved while boys were present it was the boys' fault for letting it happen. He kept his servants in order and told them that a spare glass eye which he kept in a drawer was able to see everything that they did in the house. (He had lost his left eye in an accident.)

He was also deeply religious, reading the Bible regularly and making notes of his studies in the margins. 'We were always taught from the Bible,' says his youngest daughter Joyce Clarkson. 'I remember having to go to Sunday school when I was young. The local priest, Reverend Vetichan, was a wonderful man and it was through him that we became regular churchgoers.'

The Webbs were a happy family and the children enjoyed the sheer fun of being let loose in a country of exotic smells, wild animals and brilliant sunshine. Rodger was often dragged around with his older brothers and sisters and unwittingly got involved in their mischief.

'Once they went to a Hindu cremation,' Joyce Dobra remembers being told. 'They hid in the bushes to watch and as the heat affected the muscles of the body being burned it began to sit up and the children fled in terror. Rodger was only a toddler and he had terrible nightmares for a long time afterwards.'

During the First World War life changed dramatically for the Webbs. Harry was sent to fight in Tanganyika, German East Africa. He was killed there in Dar es Salaam at the age of twenty. Around the same time Rodger's older brother Frederick died of typhoid at fifteen. The one bit of bright news was that Donella Eugenie was expecting yet another child, but even this turned into tragedy. She died of 'malarial cachexia and childbirth' in Lucknow. Eight months later the child, a little boy baptized Valentine, died of a heart defect.

Frederick William was badly affected by these tragedies. He locked himself away in a room alone for several weeks and drank heavily to numb the pain. 'When he finally came out his hair was absolutely white,' says Joyce Dobra.

Rodger must have left school around this time. No one is sure what he did immediately afterwards. His sister, Joyce Clarkson, thinks that he returned to Burma to work in a factory that made chocolate. What is certain is that he eventually took an office job with G.F. Kellner and Co., a Calcutta-based company described at the time as being 'wines, spirits and provision importers, wholesale and retail distributors'.

Established in India during the middle of the nineteenth century, Kellner's was well known to the European community for its railway catering. Rodger became a steward on trains travelling between Calcutta and Dehra Dun and then a regional manager, which is what he was doing when he met his future wife.

Cliff's maternal lineage is a military one. His grandmother, Dorothy Edith, was the daughter of William Brock Bridgwater and his wife Marie Beatrice. William Brock had been born in the Vale of Health, a beautiful hamlet tucked into a fold of Hampstead Heath.

He joined the army as a boy, trained in Ireland and went to India with the Essex Regiment. It was here he met Marie Beatrice Smith, a dark-eyed half-Spanish beauty who was living in the hill station of Naini Tal looking after the children of a high-ranking military officer. They fell in love and married in 1898 in Allahabad.

Their daughter, Dorothy Edith, was born with a club foot and grew up to be a short, plump girl. The children at school made fun of her and called her '*lungi*' ('lame one'). She visited England for operations to correct the foot but it only made matters worse. William Brock instead taught her to defend herself by giving her boxing lessons.

When the First World War broke out William was far too old to serve and had already done seven years' service in the army but he insisted on re-enlisting.

'They were taking people up to the age of forty,' remembers his son Vincent Bridgwater. 'He was forty-five and put his age down as forty and five months, and he was accepted.

'He returned to England where he was reunited with his family and then he was sent to France. He fought in the second battle of Ypres in April 1915 where the Germans used poison gas for the first time. He was gassed and the trench he was in was blown up. Fortunately he was discovered. They took him to hospital and found that he had broken his spinal cord. He came back to us in India in 1916 as a cripple.'

He spent the rest of his life in a wheelchair and Dorothy Edith had to look after him. Perhaps to escape the pressures of home life, at sixteen she married William Edward Dazely, a young soldier stationed in Bangalore with the Supply and Transport Corps. Nine months and three days later, in Lahore, she gave birth to a baby she had baptized Dorothy Marie.

Although she never discussed the marriage with her children, it can't have been happy. Two years after Dorothy Marie's birth there was a second daughter, Olive Queenie, born in Jubbulpore. Then in the spring of 1924 William Edward 'disappeared'.

Vincent Bridgwater, who was ten years old at the time, remembers being told that his brother-in-law had been sent up to the north-west frontier where British troops were defending themselves against Afghan tribesmen, and had never returned. There was no death certificate, he was told, because the body had never been found, but that in itself was not unusual in a conflict where soldiers were often captured and slashed to pieces with swords.

'He was attached to the army in some respect and he vanished,' he says. 'We never heard from him again. My sister and mother tried to find out where he was but they couldn't come up with anything. The army gave no details at all.'

Dorothy Marie and Olive Queenie grew up believing that their father was dead. They knew nothing about him because everything connected with him, including photographs, had been destroyed after he failed to return.

'She seemed to blame him for dying,' says Olive Queenie. 'She wouldn't talk about him and yet sometimes, when I had done something wrong, she would say, "You're just like your father". But how I was like my father I didn't know because I didn't know anything about him. I didn't even know what he looked like.'

It was only during research for this book that, after seventy years, the true story finally emerged. There are no records of a William Edward Dazely having died in India between 1924 and 1948 but there is a record of a William Edward Dazely arriving in Karachi in 1929 and marrying a 23-year-old woman named Maizie Sherard. Thirteen weeks later Maizie gave birth to a child. Mr Dazely's given age, thirty-three, was exactly that of Dorothy Edith's husband who had been born in Kirkee in February 1896. Significantly he described himself in the church register as a 'widower'.

Clearly he wasn't telling the truth, but whether he abandoned Dorothy Edith and his daughters or whether there had been an agreement to split up and start their lives anew will never be known. The fact that she harboured such long-lasting resentment towards him suggests that his disappearance was half expected.

Olive Queenie remembers overhearing her mother discussing the matter with an aunt. 'They were saying that he couldn't be dead and that he had only been reported missing,' she says. 'They were suggesting that he might still be alive and other bits of gossip.

'I used to ignore it and then one day a friend of the family showed my sister a photograph of him and she was more or less saying the same thing. I never believed it though. As far as I was concerned no one in the British Army could possibly get away from his family and live because he couldn't get out of the country.'

Yet he did manage to get away from his family. In Karachi he worked first as a policeman and later as a motor mechanic. He fathered five sons in fourteen years, though he was known always to have wanted a daughter.

In 1944 he moved his family to Poona and then four years later left for England where he settled in Balsall Heath, Birmingham, and worked as a storekeeper at the Rover factory in Solihull.

William Edward Dazely died of coronary thrombosis in 1969 never knowing that Cliff Richard was his grandson, and never having told his family about the wife and two daughters that he had left behind in Ambala in 1924. When, during the writing of this book, his family found out, the news was a great shock to them.

Within two years of William Edward's 'disappearance', Dorothy Edith had found a new love in Richard Dickson, an Anglo-Indian who claimed Indian royal blood. In 1927 their first daughter, Edna, was born.

As a chief inspector on the railway, Richard commanded respect, perks and a good salary. When the family travelled by rail they had their own special carriage and at home there were up to fifteen servants doing everything from cooking and washing to nursing the children and gardening.

Dorothy Marie and Olive Queenie loved him as if they had never had any other father.

'I had no feelings for my real father,' says Olive Queenie . 'The only father I knew was my step-father and I thought the world of him because he was a very clever person and he was very good to me.'

Dorothy Edith ruled her family with a rod of iron and had a fierce temper. 'When she went wild she would nearly kill you,' says Olive Queenie. 'People would have to grab hold of her to stop her. I remember once we were at a Railway Institute dance and a soldier turned and said something to my sister which involved referring to her as a "fair wench".

'My mother came up to this fellow and caught him right across his head with her hand. It sent him flying. He was enormous, she was only five-foot tall, but it sent him reeling backwards.

'She became known as "the battle-axe" but everyone respected her. She was good and kind but you couldn't act the fool and you couldn't use bad language when she was around. If she heard soldiers using bad language she would order them out of the room. She wasn't afraid of anyone.

'There was nothing religious about her morals though. She was just plain Victorian. My grandmother, on the other hand, was slightly of the religious kind. Behind her way of talking and teaching was always the Bible. Her point of view was that God wouldn't like that.

'She wasn't a Bible thumper but a lot of her goodness came from the fact that she always read the Bible and we all had to say our prayers at night before we went to sleep. If she wanted something done her way she would bring the Bible out to prove it.'

Dorothy Marie and Olive Queenie had spent most of their early life as boarders at the Lawrence Royal Military School in Sanawar, which offered a limited number of free places each year to children who had lost fathers in military service.

When William Edward Dazely went missing in 1924, Dorothy

Edith was living in an army cantonment in Ambala, close to Simla, and of the five Lawrence schools in India the one at Sanawar was the closest. Shortly after the two little girls entered the kindergarten their mother moved down to Asansol to be with Richard Dickson and so the girls spent their early years hardly ever seeing her.

'For the first few years we never went home at all,' remembers Olive Queenie. 'We were just kept at school because it was a good ten-day train journey to Asansol. We used to go for treks into Simla and further on up into the Himalayas. Then we went home when it was Christmas time but not for the summer holidays.'

Sanawar was a beautiful location high in the foothills of the Himalayas, close to the glamorous hill station of Simla where the Viceroy and his government spent their summers. The Lawrence school was mixed, and designed to produce soldiers, nurses and the wives of soldiers.

The two girls were very different. Dorothy Marie was outgoing, sporty and good at knitting and sewing, Olive Queenie was desperately shy and bookish. Dorothy Marie shone at tennis, badminton and hockey and was renowned as an aggressive team player, a quality that her son was to inherit along with her love of sport.

It was while at Sanawar that she started wearing glasses. 'Some children started calling her "four eyes" and "goggle eyes" but she was such a good fighter that very few of them would call her names except behind her back,' says Olive Queenie. 'She would fight anybody tooth and nail. I wouldn't fight anybody and I used to rely on her to defend me.'

Her second family now well established, Dorothy Edith decided in 1934 that it was time that the girls came to live at home, and they were enrolled in a local Roman Catholic school in Asansol, the Loretta Convent. It was at Asansol that Dorothy Marie was to meet her future husband.

3

'He was a terror for music'

Although she was an attractive girl with many admirers, especially from the nearby Catholic boys' school, Dorothy Marie had never loved a man before Rodger Webb. Up until then there had only been coy looks and flirtatious chatter. Actions more serious couldn't be contemplated in the climate of the times, especially with Dorothy Edith keeping a keen eye open for anything that might suggest misbehaviour.

It often fell to Vincent Bridgwater, her mother's younger brother, to discourage potential suitors. 'I had to warn some of them off because they weren't the type that I thought should be mixing with my niece,' he says.

Olive Queenie remembers the time: 'You could say she had boyfriends before Rodger but they were kept secret and they weren't boyfriends like young girls have nowadays. You didn't go out with them. You met them after school and cycled home with them or you'd go into the park and chat to them. To our way of thinking at the time they were boyfriends though.'

The British India of the thirties was still in a Victorian time warp. Children whose parents had grown up in Britain were considered terribly modern, and slightly dangerous. A girl was treated as a child until she was at least sixteen and then, on leaving school, she would be expected to clean, wash and darn at her parents' home until a man with an appropriate income came to ask for her hand in marriage. Except for those bold few who learned to type and thought in terms of a career, the late teens were spent learning how to be a housewife.

'We were terribly old-fashioned,' says Olive Queenie, looking back. 'The atmosphere we were raised in was the same one I was reading about in books written in nineteenth-century England.

'You weren't supposed to speak to a boy unless you were actually introduced to him and you certainly wouldn't be able to go out with a boy unless a *duenna* [governess and chaperone for young women] or your parents were with you. You weren't allowed to go out alone with a boy not even when you were engaged. I used to smile when Dorothy was engaged. She used to have to kiss Rodger in the sitting room. She couldn't go outside and kiss him.'

Dorothy met Rodger Webb in Asansol in 1936 when he came to visit his sister, Dorothy Cooke, who lived in the apartment above. The Cookes and the Dicksons had become close friends and were always in each other's homes. Now sixteen years old with dark bobbed hair and large flashing eyes, Dorothy Marie fell for this smartly-dressed man with his impeccable manners. She thought he looked like a matinée idol. 'He was a thorough gentleman,' she says. 'And handsome too.'

Remembers Olive Queenie, 'In those days he had smoothed-down hair and he was very good looking. He used to remind me of the actor Leslie Howard. He had the same bone structure.'

There were drawbacks though, the biggest being the difference in their ages. Rodger was thirty-one, almost twice Dorothy Marie's age and only two years younger than her mother. Then there was the question of distance. Rodger was based in Howrah, a district of Calcutta, and wouldn't be visiting Asansol more than twice a year. Dorothy Edith made it clear that much as she admired Rodger, she didn't think him a suitable boyfriend for her daughter.

Nevertheless Rodger and Dorothy Marie courted for three years, mostly by letter. When they were able to see each other in Asansol there wasn't much opportunity for intimacy because the visits were turned into huge family affairs with the Cookes, the Dicksons and the Webbs gathering to eat, sing and play parlour games. Rodger had a sister, Marjorie, and a brother Tom, who also lived in Howrah and they would travel up for these parties. They were quite unlike the debonair Rodger and were both, in their own way, eccentrics.

Tom appears to have been the black sheep of the family whose life consisted of a cycle of making money and giving up his job for a life of pleasure, before he eventually retuned home broke. Marjorie, who worked as a ticket collector on Howrah station, frightened the younger children with her loud voice and her strong language. She dressed in men's clothes and smoked a cigar. 'You didn't think a woman could be like me, did you?' she once asked a rather timid Olive Queenie. Neither Tom nor Marjorie ever married.

The two brothers were very close and teamed up to make music, Rodger with his guitar and mandolin, Tom singing while playing ukulele or banjo. Later, Tom would provide Cliff with one of his earliest musical memories by sitting at the foot of his bed and singing him to sleep.

To the impressionable Dorothy Marie, Tom was as smooth and accomplished as Bing Crosby and she would sit out on the steps of the quarters as he sang songs like 'Ramona', 'The Bells Of Sorrento' and 'Red Sails In The Sunset', while Rodger accompanied him and Marjorie huffed away on tissue paper and comb.

On 26 April 1939 Rodger and Dorothy Marie were married at St Paul's Church, Asansol, and moved north west to a large company bungalow in Dehra Dun. Life was wonderful for Dorothy Marie. Rodger was doing well in his job, managing the local Kellner's restaurant, and she was happy in her home where most of the housework was carried out by servants.

Although she had lived in India all her life she would never have known a native Indian as a close friend. The Indians had their homes on the outskirts of the big towns and lived entirely separate lives. Although she would have respected them there was no question of them being regarded as equals.

'The Indians didn't like the idea of a mixture of races,' says Olive Queenie. 'They thought that any white person who mixed with an Indian was trash, any white girl who went with an Indian man was trash to them. They wouldn't respect her. Similarly any of their girls who went with a white man was automatically considered trash.'

The largest employers in British India were the post and telegraph, the railways, the civil service and the army, and each occupation bred its own community.

'There was a very great class distinction,' Joyce Dobra remembers. 'I had the education of a civil servant and could get into almost any club. But because my father had been born in India he was looked down on by those who had been born in Europe. We in turn looked down on the railway people who, like the post and telegraph, lived in rented accommodation.

'There were very strict social codes laid down by the wives of army officers and diplomats. The rich Indians were allowed to socialize with the whites but even they weren't admitted to any of the clubs.'

Rodger and Dorothy Marie's club was the local Railway Institute where they regularly went to play cards or tennis and badminton. 'There were dances almost every day,' remembers Dorothy Marie. 'It was a lovely life.'

In 1940 she discovered she was pregnant. There were no large British hospitals in Dehra Dun, which then had a population of fewer than 250,000, so she planned to travel three hundred miles south east to Lucknow where Rodger's father was now living in retirement, to have the baby at the King's English Hospital in Victoria Street.

Britain was by now feeling the effects of the war with Germany. There had been skirmishes with fighter planes over south-east

England and bombs had been dropped on London. There was little danger of India being attacked but there was a feeling that the days of the British Empire might now be numbered.

When Dorothy arrived in Lucknow the local papers were running stories on the ambitions of the Axis (the alliance of Germany, Italy and Japan) to capture the oil fields of Iraq, and Mahatma Gandhi's plan to fast for the cause of Indian independence. The big films in town were Laurel and Hardy's *Saps At Sea* and *Broadway Melody Of 1940*, starring Fred Astaire.

On Monday 14 October 1940 Dorothy gave birth to the dark-haired boy who would one day be known as Cliff Richard. He weighed nine pounds. That day the Lucknow Pioneer printed the text of the first BBC radio broadcast by Britain's Princess Elizabeth which read, in part: 'When peace comes remember it will be for us, the children of today, to make the world a better and happier place.'

Rodger didn't see the new baby until his wife returned to Dehra Dun, where they agreed to name him Rodger Harry Webb — 'Harry' in memory of Rodger's eldest brother. This was the name they had prepared as they set off on Saturday 2 November to take the child to his baptism at St Thomas' Church.

'When I got to the church I saw his godmother and mentioned that I was naming him Rodger Harry,' remembers Dorothy Marie. 'She immediately said, "Oh no. I think it should be Harry Rodger." I just stood there unable to do anything and of course the vicar was holding the baby at the font as they do and I heard him saying, "I baptize thee Harry Rodger Webb." '

Harry was placid but tough. Many white children were susceptible to tropical disease but he remained strong and healthy, playing around the house under the eye of his ayah while his mother embroidered, sewed and knitted. She made all his clothes until he was six years old.

A year after Harry's birth she became pregnant again, this time returning to her mother in Asansol where, on 10 June 1942, she gave birth to a boy whom they named Frederick William, after Rodger's father.

The baby Frederick William hardly features in Cliff's biographies and autobiographies, the only mention coming in *It's Great to Be Young* where he says, 'Back in India Mum's second child had been a boy but the poor chap died very shortly after birth. Things like that don't mean much to children, and much as I wanted a brother then, I can't think what life would be like without my perky younger sister, Joan.'

There's disagreement over how long the child lived. Olive Queenie thinks he was over twelve months old. Dorothy Marie thinks it was less than three weeks. The ecclesiastical returns don't record his burial. He must have been alive at the age of eighteen days when he was baptized at St Paul's Church in Asansol.

He was born a 'blue baby' and never enjoyed full health. Often he cried all day. Dorothy Marie and Rodger went out dancing one night and returned to find him so ill that a doctor had to be called. The next morning young Frederick William was dead.

'Dorothy always felt she was to blame,' says Olive Queenie. 'But it would have made no difference if they had stayed at home that night. He would have died anyway.'

Dorothy Marie now thinks the death had a far deeper effect on Harry than she had at first thought.

'He was too young to explain what he was feeling but Rodger and I felt that he had lost something in that moment,' she remembers. 'I think he is always conscious that the brother he had was lost. When he was young he didn't show anything but when he grew older he would sometimes say, "I had a brother." Funnily enough when I was in Bermuda a few years ago I heard him say, "If my brother had lived he would now be forty." It's obviously never left him.'

After three years living in Dehra Dun Rodger was promoted, and the family moved to Calcutta where Kellner's had its headquarters in the prominent thoroughfare of Chowringhee Road. They were given a small first-floor apartment over a chocolate factory close by Howrah Station, Calcutta's teeming gateway to the rest of India, where a rickety wooden staircase on the outside of the building took them to their front door. Soon after moving in their first daughter, Donella Eugenie, was born.

Harry was remarkably even-tempered as a child. Interviewed in 1964 by Bob Ferrier for his book *The Wonderful World of Cliff Richard* his mother said, 'I never found any fault in that child. He never lied to us, he never hurt anybody, he still doesn't.' Today her opinion is much the same. 'He was very good,' she says. 'He has all his life been that way. He has always been very kind and I can honestly say that he has never driven me to despair like some children can.'

Yet he wasn't spineless. 'Cliff was undoubtably a toughie,' says Olive Queenie. 'He was always very fit and was able to weather all the sicknesses. His sister Donna had a habit of deliberately getting him into trouble with his mother and he would get soundly walloped but because he was such a tough little guy he never used to let on that he was innocent.'

In the summer months they would leave Calcutta and holiday in Lucknow with grandfather Webb and then go on to Buxar where grandmother Dickson was now living. These times away from home provided Harry with some of his few lingering memories of India — chasing bees, watching monkeys jumping in the branches of trees, fishing, flying kites and hearing tales of his father's exploits as a tiger hunter.

Rodger was a typical chauvinist of the period who expected everything to be done his way. He would come home from work and sit in his favourite chair while Dorothy Marie and the servants arranged things according to his wishes.

'If things weren't going exactly the way he wanted them to go he would become very Puritanical,' Olive Queenie recalls. 'He could be very strict with Dorothy. She would be quite tired by the time he came back home from work and yet he would want to go out to one of the company dances.'

It was in Howrah that Harry discovered that he could operate the family gramophone and sing along to records.

'He was pretty smart with that machine and would always choose the exact records that he wanted to hear,' says Dorothy Marie. 'He would wind it up himself. We asked him how he knew which records he liked and it was because he recognized different marks on the labels. After discovering the gramophone, music was his number one thing.'

His three favourite records were 'Ragtime Cowboy Joe' by Geraldo and his Orchestra featuring Dorothy Carless, 'Chewing A Piece Of Straw' by Jack Payne and his Orchestra and 'Jersey Bounce' by the Glenn Miller Orchestra.

'He was a terror for music,' remembers Olive Queenie . She was in the army, and used to take the children out for walks in Calcutta's Botanical Gardens when home on leave. 'He used to stand by the gramophone with his finger in the air beating time to the music as if he was a great conductor.'

On September 1945 Harry started at St Thomas' Church School in Church Road, Howrah, a building set among banana trees. He remembers one of the family servants, Habib, bringing his lunch up to him each day wrapped in a napkin.

He was already learning to speak Hindi, which his father spoke fluently, and at school he learned Bengali. His best friend Lal spoke no English and so all their conversations were in Hindi.

The war had only just ended, Japan had been crushed by two atomic bombs and the British, who had promised Home Rule to the Indians in return for their wartime co-operation, were now nervously working out the details of a transference of power.

For those like Rodger and Dorothy Marie who, although British by family origin had never known any other home but India, it was a worrying time. Their days living in the sun with servants at their beck and call were numbered because there would be no place for the old ruling class in an India run by Indians.

Harry began to notice that gradually schoolfriends were leaving, saying that they were going to a place called 'home' which was small, cold and thousands of miles away and which most of them had only read about in books.

The prospect of independence re-awakened old religious feuds. Under British rule the Moslem and Hindu factions had no power and so they set aside their differences. Now the Moslems were wanting to ensure that they would get their own state within the boundaries of the old British India.

In June 1946 the Moslem League voted to accept a British plan that granted them the territory of Pakistan but within seven weeks they withdrew their acceptance and accused Britain and the Congress Party of going back on their pledges. The All-India Moslem League in Bombay called for 'direct action' and set up a committee to launch a struggle 'as and when necessary'.

At this point violence spilled into the streets. Dorothy Marie was jostled while out shopping and Indians shouted at her, 'Go back to your own country white woman.' The young Harry was frightened. 'Leave her alone,' he screamed. 'She's my mummy.' The old India his parents knew, where the natives 'knew their place', was fast vanishing.

On 16 August 1946 riots came to the streets of Calcutta. The Moslem League mounted a Direct Action Day as a protest against the British Independence plan, and were attacked by Hindus. British troops and police had to fire on crowds as shops were burned and looted. In three days there was damage estimated at one million pounds, a death toll of 3,000 and 10,000 casualties. The Calcutta Fire Brigade dealt with 900 fires and the streets were littered with bodies.

The Webbs, who lived in a predominantly Sikh area, were terrified. A family of Moslems nearby had been attacked and killed by Hindus leaving only one boy who they could see was hiding in his garden. They kept him alive by dropping food parcels on a rope from their window at night and eventually got in touch with Dorothy Marie's uncle who was serving in the Calcutta Police and he came over in an armoured car to take the boy to safety.

'When he drove up we looked out of the window and we could see that there was human flesh hanging off the tracks of his vehicle,' remembers Dorothy Marie. 'It was a terrible sight. We could see a bit of the Hooglie River from our apartment but that day you couldn't see the water for dead bodies. It was dreadful.

'That was when we knew we had to leave eventually. We knew that if this was what it was going to be like then it wasn't going to be worth living in India.

'My uncle Harry made sure that we got safely out of our apartment and we went and stayed with Rodger's sister, Marjorie. But we hadn't been there for two days when threats were made to burn the place down. Some Moslems guided us out and they didn't hurt us but the whole street was strewn with dead bodies and glass and bricks. They took us to a cinema for safety.'

Thus began the speedy wind-down of British rule. In February 1947 Lord Louis Mountbatten was despatched from London to replace Field Marshal Lord Wavell as viceroy of India and to begin negotiations with Hindu and Moslem leaders over the future of their land.

Although the Hindus were fiercely resistant to the idea of partition it was obvious, with such hatred abroad, that this was the only workable solution. By June both the Congress Party, led by Pandit Nehru, and the Moslem League accepted a plan which would set up a state of West Pakistan in the north west and the much smaller state of East Pakistan in the north east.

On the stroke of midnight, on 14 August 1947, 163 years of British rule in India ended and the transference of power was complete.

But freedom for India didn't bring immediate peace. Months of turmoil followed as millions of refugees fled over the Indo-Pakistan borders in both directions and an estimated 400,000 Moslems and Hindus were slaughtered.

Into this India, on 21 November 1947, came Jacqueline Ann, the Webbs' second daughter. Two months later, in New Delhi, a Hindu fanatic assassinated Mahatma Gandhi, one of the inspirations behind the independence movement, as he made his way to a prayer meeting, thus precipitating a further series of riots. By now the British were streaming out of India towards destinations that they hoped would provide them with as good a life as they had left behind.

It was Rodger's inclination to go to Australia where Charlie Holder, one of the men who worked for him, had emigrated, but Dorothy Marie wanted to follow her mother to England where she had gone with her new family of seven, the youngest of whom was the same age as Harry.

A scheme had been set up where those who could prove British ancestry had half of their fare paid by the British government and so the Webbs put all their savings towards getting Bombay to London tickets and packed their few belongings into suitcases. They had always lived in company accommodation so there was no house to sell, no furniture to put into storage and most of the clothes they owned they knew would be hopelessly impractical in the English climate. Their pet dog was left with Dorothy Marie's uncle Vincent, who was staying on in India along with Tom and Marjorie Webb and Frederick William.

They left their home in Howrah for the last time on Saturday 21 August 1948 and took a train from Calcutta to Bombay where, three days later, they boarded their boat for England.

The *Ranchi* was a 23-year-old P&O passenger liner which had spent the war as an armed merchant cruiser and then as a troopship in the Middle East. This was its first round trip since being refitted as a passenger ship. (All other books have mistakenly identified this as the *Ranghi*.)

Built as a liner for 587 passengers, including a first-class section, it had been re-designed for 950 'tourist class' passengers, which meant that it was functional rather than luxurious. Rodger was told that this was to be the ship's last voyage before being scrapped — which wasn't true — and so they were pleasantly suprised to have a comfortable cabin to themselves. (The *Ranchi* stayed in service until the end of 1952 and was then sold to the British Iron and Steel Corporation.)

'The dining rooms were alright,' remembers Dorothy Marie. 'They had a cinema on board and I remember Cliff crawling under the tent without paying to see the films.

'He and I were quite ill when we started on the journey and couldn't even leave the cabin. We felt a little better during the middle of the journey and then when we reached the Bay of Biscay we both fell ill again.'

Having left Bombay on the evening of 24 August the *Ranchi* sailed through the Arabian Sea, arriving in Aden on the morning of the 29th where it docked for four hours, before setting off through the Red Sea towards the Suez Canal.

While sailing up the canal Harry learned how to whistle by imitating other passengers who cat-called the Egyptians watching from the banks. His father's response was to give him a memorable belt around the head. After a six-hour stop-over in Port Said on 2 September the liner made its way across the Mediterranean, arriving at Tilbury Docks at 6 a.m. on Monday 13 September.

The story that Cliff has always told is that after disembarking, his father hired a taxi to Carshalton with his last five pounds (or seven pounds as it was being reported in 1960) but Dorothy Marie remembers it differently.

She believes they were picked up by a private car from Tilbury and that their first few days in England were spent with an aunt of her mother's who lived somewhere in south-east London. It was only then that they made it down to Carshalton where the Dicksons,

Dorothy Marie's mother and her family, had set up home.

Harry's first impression of his new country was the typical one of those who had never seen the motherland — the striking appearance of vegetation after a lifetime surrounded by brown dust.

'I can remember nothing of the white cliffs of Dover or even of Tilbury,' he once said, 'but I shall never forget the green fields, the trees and the flowers; particularly the flowers on Carshalton station.'

More striking to Rodger and Dorothy Marie must have been the effects of the wartime rationing of clothes, food, petrol and confectionery, which was still in force, and the bomb sites which blighted London. This was not the colourful, confident Britain of the picture books but a nation suffering austerity.

The latest news in the *Wallington and Carshalton Times* was of a serious bread shortage and a worrying lack of telephones. Apparently there were only 8,000 phones in the whole area and even the chief engineer at the local exchange could not get one installed.

For Rodger, whose whole life had been spent promoting fine wines and good food, the prospects of work in the home country didn't look at all promising.

4

'Like a dream come true'

Richard and Dorothy Dickson had bought their three-bedroomed house at 47 Windborough Road, Carshalton, for £2,500 but it was barely big enough for them and their children — Edna, Jean, Nora, Vincent, Peggy, Geraldine and Christopher.

Then had come the news that Rodger and Dorothy Marie — their daughter and her family — were on their way with Harry, Donella and Jacqueline. It didn't seem possible that they could all fit into a suburban semi-detached so the neighbours at number 45, Norman and Elizabeth Luscombe, agreed to let the Webb family sleep in their small front bedroom until they found a home.

'The room was the size of a box,' remembers Dorothy Marie, 'and everything had to be done in that small space. Because the children were young I had to have a little cooker there to boil their milk and make them porridge.'

The arrangement didn't last long and the Webbs soon returned to number 47, where they were put in an equally small room. This meant that the Dicksons' house now had fourteen people sleeping in it, including two married couples and two children who were over twenty.

'We were sleeping all over the place,' remembers Vincent Dickson, the eldest son. 'We hadn't been in the house very long ourselves so it was a big upheaval.'

Soon after their arrival Harry started at Stanley Park Road Junior School which was only a five-minute walk away. Here he learned for the first time that he didn't have the milky-white skin that most English-born children had during the winter.

His deep tan hadn't stood out in India. In fact, there he had been the 'white boy'. But here in south-west London, where very few children had ever seen a person who wasn't white, he was thought exotic. The difference was accentuated by his Anglo-Indian accent.

Discovering that he was newly arrived from India his classmates concluded that he must be an Indian and, in 1948, the only Indians that British school children knew much about were the ones who threw tomahawks and attacked cowboys.

Harry was teased and asked where his head-dress was. It didn't make it any easier that most of his household were part-Indian and stood out in the street with their dark hair and brown skin.

To this day there are those in Carshalton who are convinced that Cliff is part Indian. 'I think there was Indian blood in him because the Dicksons were Indian weren't they?' says Dorothy Willis, who as Miss Olstead taught him in Sunday school.

The most effective way of gaining respect, Harry soon learned, was to hit back rather than to trade insults. Rodger wanted to lodge a formal complaint, especially after a teacher had said to his son, 'Come on Webb, you can't run off to your wigwam any more.' But Harry wanted to stand up for himself.

It was while in Carshalton that he had his first experience of evangelical Christianity. He had sung in the choir of St Thomas' in Howrah, a traditional Anglican church, but at Stanley Park Evangelical Mission, a crude corrugated hut in Stanley Road where he started to go to Sunday school, they talked about 'asking Jesus into your heart' and sang lively choruses.

'His interest in religion in those days was no more than any of the other kids in the class,' remembers Dorothy Willis, who taught him for half an hour each week. 'And he certainly had no thoughts of singing.'

In photographs taken at the time his Sunday school friends beam cheekily and confidently at the camera where he appears subdued and worried. His front teeth were beginning to protrude and he had a noticeably fang-like upper left tooth. His father had told him to straighten his teeth by sucking them in.

His insecurity was a natural part of finding a new place in the world. Back in India he had been treated like a prince by adult servants. Here he was being made to feel racially inferior by white children. Also his father was penniless and out of work and they had no home to call their own.

'The British in India were top dogs,' says his cousin Joyce Dobra. 'We were white and were always brought up with the idea that one day we would be going "back home to England". We were used to telling other people what to do. Our servants were all adults and yet we treated them as if they were children.'

Rodger finally found work as a wage clerk in a local hospital. It gave him money but it was a blow to the pride of a man who had been used to running the show. Dorothy Marie was so unhappy that she wondered whether it might not be best to find another country to live in.

'I was making all sorts of plans to leave England,' she admits. 'I had a brother-in-law who had gone somewhere in the East and he had written and said he could get Rodger a job. I wanted him to go.

'I told him that he could have a job and we'd have free accommodation but he felt that Britain was losing colony after colony and that soon that place would go. And it did.

'A year later my brother-in-law was in England himself and living not far from us but I still hated it here. Rodger hadn't wanted to come in the first place but he never once reproached me.'

Rodger's sister Dorothy Cooke and her husband had by now left

Asansol and were living at the opposite end of London in Waltham Cross, Hertfordshire, in a semi-detached house. They suggested easing the situation in Carshalton by having the Webbs stay with them.

Their local council was building a lot of rented accommodation as part of the post-war resettlement and they believed the Webbs could then be put on the waiting list. So, on Harry's ninth birthday, after one year and a month in Carshalton, they went to live with Dorothy and Ernest Cooke and their two boys, Rodger and Ernie.

It may have been slightly less cramped than the Dicksons' house but the Webbs still found themselves squatting in a small room with mattresses on the floor. The only difference was the glimmer of hope that within months they might get their own council house.

Harry was taken to the nearby King's Road school where his teacher was the second-year junior mistress Mrs Tonks.

'I'll always remember the day he came into my class,' she says. 'The headmaster, Harold Cooper, brought in this lad who was very dark with big brown eyes. He was holding his hand because he was quite young and he said to me, "Well, there you are Mrs Tonks. Here's another one for you," because the term had already started and I already had between thirty and forty children in the class. Harry stood there and he bowed. I'll never forget that. He bowed!'

One of Harry's new classmates was a tall blond-haired boy named Norman Mitham whose family lived near the Cookes. The two boys took to each other straight away. They shared a love of football and other sports and would stay close friends right through school, then becoming musical partners in Harry's first major venture.

Mitham remembers the racial taunting starting up again at Waltham Cross, this time with Harry being nicknamed 'Sabu' after the subject of Alexander Korda's 1937 documentary film *The Elephant Boy*.

'In those days anyone who didn't come from Waltham Cross was an alien,' he says. 'He was very unafraid of it all though. He didn't try to hide from the fact or kowtow to them. He stood up for himself. He could certainly lose his temper and he knew how to handle himself.'

On 6 January 1950, Rodger, who was now working as a clerk in the City for Eastwood's Ltd. at 158–160 City Road, filled out his first application form for a council house. He explained to Broxbourne Borough Council that his family of five had lived for a year with nine other people in a three-bedroomed house and now, with his wife expecting a fourth child, they were still having to live and sleep in one small bedroom.

They were added to the waiting list but by the summer he still hadn't heard anything so on 7 August he filed a second application. Christmas 1951 came and went without any news.

After fourteen months with the Cookes, tensions were rising, especially between the two women who found themselves trapped together in the house for long hours each day.

'We had to sleep on two mattresses which just fitted into the room and we had to stand on them when we got dressed,' says Dorothy Marie. 'She wouldn't let us use any other part of the house except to eat.'

Dorothy Marie began to get friendly with the woman next door, Marcelle Henrit, who was outraged that a young family was expected to live in such appalling conditions. Her son Bob Henrit (now drummer for the Kinks) remembers the time well.

'We had a family friend who was on the Waltham Abbey Council,' he says, 'and she started to pull some strings. She wasn't able to get anything going in Waltham Abbey itself but she had a friend in Cheshunt who she got in touch with and asked for things to be speeded up.'

In March 1951 things finally started to move. 'It all happened so quickly,' says Dorothy Marie. 'Within a week this fellow came and I told him that I couldn't take him over the house because that was out of bounds but he could come to the room where we all lived, slept, ate and drank.

'He got such a shock when he saw it. By that time Joan had been born and there was a line running across the room with nappies hanging out to dry, a burner to boil her milk and absolutely no room to move about.

'In two weeks' time we had the key to a brand-new council house. We went there to three bedrooms, a kitchen, bathroom and a huge living room downstairs. It was like a dream come true!'

Cheshunt, at that time a small town, is in the Lea Valley just north of London. It is only five miles from Enfield and a short train journey from Liverpool Street Station. After the war it had attracted some industry from the City and was a centre for garden nurseries.

The Bury Green estate, where the Webbs had been housed, represented the post-war ideal of reasonable rented accommodation surrounded by wide streets and playing areas for children. Hargreaves Close had eighteen houses, with number 12 part of a terrace at the far end looking down the close. The Webbs moved there on 11 April 1951 – two years after arriving in England.

Rodger and Dorothy Marie soon found work at Thorn Electrical Industries on the Great Cambridge Road in Enfield which incorporated the Ferguson Radio Corporation and Atlas Lighting. Rodger became a blue-collar worker in the credit control office while Dorothy Marie sorted components on the assembly line.

Their total wages barely added up to twenty pounds a week and it became a struggle to feed and clothe four children while furnishing a new home. Shoes had to be shared around, a lot of rice was eaten and Rodger improvised by making dining-room chairs and tables out of old packing cases he picked up at work for a pound. There was no television set, telephone nor gramophone.

'There was no furniture as such,' remembers Norman Mitham. 'When they first moved in you'd have to sit on boxes and quite often on the floor. None of us was rich but they probably had less than any of us.'

The values that the Webbs brought with them from India seemed strangely out of place in a world that was frantically trying to rid itself of Victorianism. Rodger didn't like the new air of informality. He was determined that in his family, at least, the old values of honesty, courtesy and diligence would be upheld.

Although not a church member, Rodger Webb had a firm belief, possibly inherited from his father, that the Bible was the supreme guide for living, and he would regularly read chapters of it to the children by the fireside in the evenings. When he admonished them it was always with an appeal to what the Bible said.

'He would always tell us that this was what God said,' recalls his daughter Jacqui. 'I remember him saying that we shouldn't do this or that because God wouldn't approve of it.

'I think he felt there was a lot wrong with the church system and that you didn't need to go to church in order to be a Christian. I suppose he sent us all to Sunday school because he felt that at least it was better for us to be doing something.'

This moral code was rigid and enforced quite severely at times. He demanded unquestioning obedience and was a stickler for the letter of the law. The children would be punished for being five minutes late. Harry would get a slap.

To his daughters, whom he never hit, he was a warm and friendly figure. 'I saw my dad as the most wonderful person in the world,' says Jacqui. 'What I most remember is sitting on his lap. He would always sit on the armchair and leave a little corner for me to sit on.'

But to Harry he was a prickly character who never openly displayed affection and in whose presence he was very wary. In some children this would have created wilful disobedience but in Harry it created respectful conformism. 'I knew I couldn't get away with anything,' he explains, 'and I never tried.'

He went to his mother for consolation. Whereas his father seemed old and crusty she was young, vivacious and attractive, and a big hit with the schoolfriends he would bring home for tea.

'She became a great guiding light for Cliff,' says Olive Queenie. 'In all the old-style families the father was respected. He was the master. He dished out the punishment. There wasn't the same close-knit attachment that there was with the mother.

'After coming to England things did drift between Cliff and his father because he saw a lot less of him than when he was in India. Rodger didn't have the time to take him out anywhere because he was either working or too tired.

'She adored Cliff and a bit of spoiling would go on. Sometimes Rodger would arrive home and find that Dorothy had allowed her son to do something which he had said he couldn't do.

'Cliff never argued back though. He would get chastised but wouldn't then turn round and say that his mother said he could do it. He knew that would have got her into trouble and Rodger could be very strict with her too.'

'His father could be unyielding,' remembers Mitham. 'If he wanted Cliff in by 9.30 and yet the film we wanted to see didn't end until 9.45 he'd say, "I don't care. It's 9.30 and that's that." Cliff would never argue with him. He set the law and that was it.'

'His family wasn't as flexible as most of ours were,' says Pete Bush, one of Harry's closest schoolfriends. 'We were the first generation to be a lot more free and easy with our parents but it didn't seem to apply to him. He respected his father but I think that it was respect out of fear rather than respect out of love.'

The Webbs stood out among their neighbours for their strictness. Harry didn't seem to enjoy the rough and tumble of life out on the streets and was only allowed out of the house at certain times to play. 'He was a mummy's boy,' says Ivy Clare, the Webbs' next-door neighbour. 'Mrs Webb had a real hold over him. I never saw him out at all.'

Another neighbour, Richard Holmes, had twin daughters who sometimes played with Joan and Jacqui.

'He may have had his own friends at school but I didn't see much of him playing outside,' he says. 'The only time I can remember seeing him is when he was flying his kite out in the close with his dad.' His daughter Linda confirms this. 'He just didn't mix with the other boys,' she says. 'He didn't play with other people outside.'

The only person who saw another side of Harry and his father was Norman Mitham. He remembers Rodger hiding coins around the house and getting the boys to find them. He also remembers being entranced by Rodger's stories of hunting tigers in India. 'To a boy in Cheshunt, hearing someone describe life in the jungle was quite amazing,' he says.

Norman and Harry would sometimes go 'scrumping' — stealing apples — or knocking on doors and running away. 'During the conker season we would fill our pockets with conkers and we would run down the road throwing conkers at people's front doors,' says Norman. 'I can remember he was absolutely over the moon one night because he had thrown a conker and it had hit a doorbell and made it ring.'

The biggest blow of Harry's early life came in the summer of 1952 when he failed the eleven-plus. The blow was all that much harder to take because it had been assumed that he would pass without any problem.

'I was top boy at my junior school,' he says. 'I have a book somewhere which I was given as a prize and then, within weeks, I had failed the eleven-plus and people below me had passed. I was shattered.'

In September 1952 he went to the newly-built Cheshunt County Secondary School which was taking in 800 pupils, and he soon fell in with a crowd of high achievers.

It was for his accomplishments on the sports field rather than in the classroom that Harry would be remembered. He played soccer for Hertfordshire, rugby football for the school, broke the over-13s javelin record with a throw of 106 feet 3 inches, was a top sprinter and had a reputation for fierce tackling that equalled his mother's tough tactics on the hockey pitches of Sanawar.

'He was good at football and played rugby like a lunatic,' says Brian Cooke. 'Also he was undoubtably the best scrapper in the school. You didn't play around with Harry Webb. I think he had to look after himself when he arrived in this country and that toughened him up.'

By the time he arrived in the second year, in September 1953, he was well established and popular. 'He was different from the other boys,' says his classmate Frances Slade. 'He seemed quieter and more gentle. He wasn't sloppy. I think a lot of it was due to his background in India. He was definitely the most polite and charming boy I knew.'

One woman Harry was able to charm was Jay Norris, a young English and drama teacher who, like Harry, had come to the Cheshunt school when it opened in 1952. They established a relationship which has never been broken and she was to become the first person to persuade him to get up on a stage and sing.

'I remember him coming to me one day because he hadn't done his homework,' she remembers. 'He had this really charming smile and he said something about having had to go out the night before and I said, "I'll tell you something, Webb. When you leave school you'll go into a job where the measure of success is smiling at women because you do it very well." '

Jay Norris had a unique ability in getting teenagers excited about poetry and drama. She read them Shakespeare and brought in a reel-to-reel tape recorder so that they could hear themselves recite. After school she ran a drama society which entered productions into local competitions.

'We were just an ordinary bunch of secondary modern kids,' says his schoolfriend John Vince, 'and she had us acting and singing and recording. We got to learn what a stage was and how to put theatrical make-up on. I'm sure a lot of kids today from backgrounds like ours wouldn't even know who Shakespeare was.'

Harry was only average at his schoolwork but he responded to Jay Norris. He joined the drama society and discovered that despite his shyness he had a real feel for acting.

His acting debut was in *The Price of Perfection* by Sheila Buckley in February 1954. This was followed up in October by A.A. Milne's *The Ugly Duckling* in which he played the chancellor and then, in February 1955, he had a part in *Willow Pattern* which won first prize in the Youth Drama Festival.

'He had the right kind of voice,' says Jay. 'He had a feeling for words and a feeling for putting something over. It's very rare to find a boy with a really good, interesting voice.'

'I think Jay was very instrumental in getting him motivated,' says Frances Slade. 'He was very shy when he first came to the school but she spotted something in him. He could read aloud so well.

'To get a class of idiots like us to sit down and listen to someone reading was quite something and she managed to get us all doing it with Shakespeare and the sorts of things you normally have to bludgeon kids with.'

Life at 12 Hargreaves Close had been complicated by the arrival of Harry's grandfather, Frederick William Webb, who was now in declining health. 'When everyone else left India in 1948 he didn't want to come to "Freezeland", as he called it. It was too cold,' says granddaughter Joyce Dobra. 'Then suddenly when he was about eighty he decided he wanted to come.'

He looked out of place in England. He insisted on wearing the lightweight linen suits he had always worn in India and with his long white beard and walking stick the local children believed he was Father Christmas. The fact that he frequently handed out sweets and apples to them reinforced the suspicion.

He took over the small front bedroom and Harry had to move in with his three sisters. It wasn't to be for long though. In 1954 Frederick went to stay with the Cookes where he died one morning of a sudden heart attack.

Dorothy Marie was now cycling every day to a wiring factory in Broxbourne where she would work until five o'clock. This meant that Harry had to look after Donna, Jacqui and Joan from the time they left school until she arrived home.

In September 1955 Jay Norris became Harry's form teacher and the school's Christmas production was to be A.A. Milne's *Toad of Toad Hall* based on Kenneth Grahame's *The Wind In The Willows*. Harry was her choice to play Ratty. 'That should tell you what sort of boy he was,' she says. 'Ratty was the sympathetic one, the nice one, the sensible one.'

The only problem was that if he took the part he would have to sing and although he had enjoyed singing since childhood he was not a confident performer. 'As far back as I can remember he had enjoyed music and he was always singing,' says Jacqui. 'But if anyone was around he would hide behind the settee. He wouldn't stand up and sing in front of our aunts and uncles if they could see his face.'

He told Jay that he wanted the part of Ratty but, unfortunately, he couldn't sing. 'I told him that was rubbish,' says Jay. 'I said, "It's actually quite simple. If you can't sing you can't play Ratty." Of course he did sing it and he sang it beautifully. I can see him now in his Ratty suit, twirling his tail.'

At the same time that Harry was fronting his first audience as a singer, a new form of American music had come over to Britain. It was called rock 'n' roll and 'Rock Around The Clock', a record by Bill Haley and the Comets, had come into the *Record Mirror* charts at number twelve on 15 October 1955 and had risen to the number one spot on 12 November, staying there through to the second week of January 1956.

Haley was a most unlikely looking hero for teenagers. Thirty years old, with an egg-shaped face, he appeared on stage in a tartan dinner jacket with a silk collar and had a precious kiss curl sprung on his forehead. With their receding hairlines, moustaches and spectacles, the Comets didn't look any more youthful.

Born in Michigan in 1925, Haley's musical background was in country and western but in 1951 he became the first white singer to cover a rhythm and blues song when he recorded Jackie Brenston's up-tempo song 'Rocket 88' with his group the Saddlemen.

At the time music like this made by blacks was categorized as 'race' music. It was produced mainly for what was then termed the 'negro' market, which didn't have the purchasing power to make an impact on the national charts.

'Rock Around The Clock' was recorded in New York on 12 April 1954, produced by Milt Gabler of Decca Records, and was an immediate hit in America. Its international success though happened only when the producers of *The Blackboard Jungle*, a film about rebellious New York schoolchildren, seized the opportunity of using what was then considered a novelty song over the credits.

The effect of Haley's record on British teenagers was profound. The pop music of the day was dominated by Rosemary Clooney, Dickie Valentine, Alma Cogan, Ruby Murray, Teresa Brewer and Frankie Laine who soothed rather than excited. It was music that appealed to those who had come through the war and were now looking forward to a future of peace, prosperity and family life.

But their children wanted something more vigorous and stirring. Rock 'n' roll, with its brash American sheen, pointed to the sort of future they wanted.

'I think we were all desperate for something new,' says Frances Slade . 'We all had been born either just before or during the war, many of us had experienced separation from our fathers, we had gone through rationing and everywhere looked grey. There was no colour anywhere. It was just dull, grey and boring.

'The word "teenager" had hardly been conceived. Entertainment for people in this age group was non-existent. We couldn't buy the clothes we wanted. The thing is, we didn't really know what we wanted. All we knew was that we wanted something different.

'Then along came Bill Haley and rock 'n' roll and suddenly there was something we could relate to and, what's more, it was something we could do.

'I think we were all being cloned into becoming very good safe little factory workers and office girls or, if possible, into doing some further education in order to become a teacher. But we weren't supposed to rock the boat because we were putting the country back together again. I think we just thought that there was more to it than that.'

Bill Haley inspired Harry. He never wanted to look like him or to emulate his stage act but at least he knew there was more to pop music than Jimmy Young singing 'The Man From Laramie'. For the real epiphany, the one that was to change his life, he had to wait. But only for another five months.

5

'I heard Elvis and the next step was to do it'

One Saturday, in May 1956, Harry was walking with friends in the Four Swannes area of Waltham Cross when he passed a Citroën, parked outside Asplan's the newsagents, with its engine ticking over and its radio playing. What he heard from that car radio transfixed him.

It was a pop song but it was unlike anything he had ever heard. It seemed like a surge of energy, an attitude transformed into noise. He had no idea what it was and had to tune in regularly to AFN (American Forces Network) to find out that it was 'Heartbreak Hotel', by an American singer named Elvis Presley. There were no BBC radio or television programmes at the time which were likely to play such music.

The effect of that moment has never left him. It marked a change in his aspirations. 'The day I first heard Elvis' voice I thought of it as a sound or an instrument,' he says. 'I had never heard anyone sing like that before. I had liked songs by Perry Como and Frank Sinatra but I had never wanted to be like them. When I heard Elvis the next step for me was to try to do it.'

Bill Haley had introduced the rhythm to the young white audience but Elvis brought the style. He was twenty-one when he cut

'Heartbreak Hotel' and had been recording for only eighteen months after having been discovered by Sam Philips whose Sun Record label in Memphis had released Jackie Brenston's 'Rocket 88' in 1951.

Philips' great idea — which must have been encouraged by Bill Haley's cover version of 'Rocket 88' — was to find a white boy with a black-sounding voice who could make rhythm and blues widely acceptable to the racially-prejudiced white community.

Hip white American teenagers were already tuning into black radio stations but as yet there were no artists they could identify with. There were no James Deans or Marlon Brandos singing rock 'n' roll.

Elvis was white with a voice that sounded black, and he looked great. He had the lips and nose of a young Greek god, held his long dark hair back with grease and wore flash pimp's jackets that would have branded a white man a homosexual in many parts of America.

'He had a strange kind of appeal to both sexes,' commented Jerry Leiber, who co-wrote many of his hits. 'He didn't intimidate or look too much like a grown man. He was innocent but still provocative. There was a feminine undertone to his features. He wasn't handsome, he was beautiful.'

Not that fifteen-year-old Harry even knew what Elvis Presley looked like in May 1956. All he knew was that he needed to buy a copy of 'Heartbreak Hotel' and he needed to try to sing like Elvis. The first that his friends knew about his Four Swannes experience was when he arrived at school one morning with the record begging them to listen to it.

'We had managed to commandeer the school record player,' says Frances Slade. 'We had it hidden in our stock room for months and we were allowed in school before everyone else because we were prefects. In Room 9 we used to have our own private club.'

Harry put 'Heartbreak Hotel' on the turntable and raved about his discovery. 'He came in at around half past eight and he played this record over and over again,' remembers Pete Bush. 'He then tried to mime to it. That to me was the first sign of his fascination for Elvis. He used to take the microphone from the tape recorder and sing through it as the record was playing.'

He soon saw photographs of Elvis in weekly magazines and developed a passion for wanting to look like him. He pushed Brylcreem through his dark hair, combed it back into a powerful wave and then practised curling his upper lip and staring moodily beneath lowered eyelids in the mirror over the fireplace.

'He used to keep asking us if he looked like Elvis,' remembers Jacqui. 'He used to do his little movements and then he'd say, "Do I look like Elvis? Do I look like Elvis?"'

There was a weekly dance on Saturday nights at Holy Trinity Youth Club in Waltham Cross. Harry would go with a group of friends and dance to chart records played on a small Dansette. Two of the girls, Betty Clarke and Freda Johnson, liked singing to the records and when Harry, John Vince and a girl called Beryl Molineux began to join in it took on the shape of an informal group.

They harmonized on songs like 'Water' by Frankie Laine and 'Only You' by the Hilltoppers but had a special affection for the doo-wop sounds of the Crew Cuts ('Sh-Boom') and the Teen Queens ('Eddie My Love').

Doo-wop was a convenient label to describe the new vocal harmony music coming out of New York from groups like the Clovers, the Moonglows, Frankie Lymon and the Teenagers and the Cleftones. It wasn't strictly rock 'n' roll but it was inspired by rhythm and blues and a lot of the groups were black.

There had been no serious intentions behind the sessions around the record player but when, in July 1956, Trinity Youth Club put on an Anglo-French dance as a fundraiser for Holy Trinity School the five were asked to perform a cabaret spot. They called themselves the Quintones, a suitably doo-wopish name, and began rehearsing in a friend's house.

'Harry would sing the song,' remembers John Vince, 'the girls would harmonize and I would do the boom-de-boom bass line.' One song, however, wouldn't require any help from the others. Harry was going to do 'Heartbreak Hotel' on his own.

When it came to the event on Bastille Day, 14 July 1956, at the Holy Trinity School in Waltham Cross, Betty Clarke suffered stage fright at the sight of an audience of 250 people and was substituted at the last minute by her friend Irene Fowler.

The brief performance, which included Harry's 'Heartbreak Hotel' solo spot, has gone down in history as his first concert. It also earned him his first publicity. The *Cheshunt Weekly Telegraph* carried a large photo of the Quintones with Harry clearly distinguishable in his light jacket and greased-back hair.

'The dance, which was in connection with the school's birthday and fete, also Bastille Day, raised £20 for the school funds,' ran the report above the picture.

'Posters, supplied by the French Embassy, advertising the day and the beauiful French countryside, decorated the hall, and the stage accommodating Jack de Benham and his band, represented a French cafe. Appropriate lighting completed a most effective scene.

'Cabaret turns were provided by members of the club; Mr Eric Frith, the leader, impersonated Liberace.

'Proceeds from the competition were given to the Duke of Edinburgh's playing fields fund.

'Refreshments were provided under the direction of Mrs Rix and Mrs Matthews.'

The Quintones rehearsed more than they played. The only other event that anyone is certain they performed at was the twenty-first birthday party at John Vince's sister Pamela, in September of that year. A photograph taken of the cake-cutting shows Harry still looking shy and out of place. While John Vince and his brothers are sniggering and wearing casual white shirts Harry is standing behind them in a dark jacket and tie with his lips gripped together.

Besides giving him his first performing experience the Quintones brought Harry closer to Betty Clarke, a petite girl with dark hair who he'd known since junior school in Waltham Cross. They had always liked each other but now they were both fifteen things became more serious.

'I think Betty Clarke was my first girlfriend,' he says. 'In those days you took bets on who you could catch and kiss. We used to say, "Well, if you're so crazy about her then grab her in the corridor during the break and kiss her."

'So from chasing girls, catching them and kissing them suddenly you found that you were with someone and you were seen as a couple. Betty and I were boyfriend and girlfriend and went to the pictures and to parties together.'

One of their first times together had been at the 1955 school lunch. 'It was usual that a boy and a girl would choose a member of staff to take to the lunch,' remembers Betty. 'This year both Harry and I had chosen to take Jay Norris and she said, "I think really it's Harry taking Betty!" At school we were just friends but then, at the youth club, we walked out together for a little while.

'He didn't send me flowers because none of us had that sort of money in those days, but he would send me cards and once he put a box of chocolates inside my desk at Christmas. It was just those little things that meant you were a closer friend than just an ordinary schoolfriend and other people regarded you as boyfriend and girlfriend.'

Teenage relationships in the fifties were still very innocent, unaffected by commercial pressure to couple up and become 'sexually active'. Over eighty per cent cent of English children still went to Sunday school, so in many cases there was a moral foundation for chastity, but the biggest fear was putting a girl 'in the family way', which inevitably meant an early marriage. Teenagers who went 'all the way' were generally considered a bit fast and not 'nice'.

Harry and his friends were definitely a 'nice' bunch who believed in socializing as a group rather than pairing off for intimate moments. With little money and no commercial teenage culture they spent their time swimming, walking, bike riding and going for picnics. They spent more time in one another's homes than they did in cafes or cinemas.

'We didn't have the opportunity to go to many different places so we used to take our bikes and go to Epping Forest,' says Betty. 'Sometimes we went out as a group. There weren't discos in those days only the record player down at the youth club.'

What struck Betty about Harry was his respect towards girls. He never used his good looks to flirt outrageously.

'He never pushed himself around,' she says. 'I think it was to do with the way he was brought up. He was taught that it wasn't nice to go out with one girl after another and that you should never take advantage of anyone.

'I'll always remember someone asking him whether he had a girlfriend and he said, "Yes. I've got her picture in my pocket," and he dived into his pocket and brought out a photograph of his mother.'

Most of the children in Harry's year, including Betty Clarke, left school that summer but he was included as part of an experimental group of fifteen pupils who stayed on to sit O levels. Their relationship didn't survive the summer holidays as Betty started courting another boy from the youth club.

'We parted good friends,' she says. 'We just went our separate ways. When I saw him on TV just a few years later I couldn't believe that I'd actually been out with him and he'd been in my home.'

'I'd always remember him whether or not he had become famous. Harry Webb was an important part of my schooldays.'

There were two other girlfriends from those days that he can still remember — Sheila Bevan and Heather Harman. 'Sheila was the girl that all the guys wanted to go out with,' he says. 'I also remember being besotted with Heather when we were doing *HMS Pinafore*. I went out with her for a short period.'

In the group that had stayed on in Jay Norris' fifth form there were thirteen boys — including John Vince, Pete Bush and Brian Cooke — and two girls — Janice Berry and Frances Slade.

They were an unusually close-knit form. Brian Cooke can remember the time when Pete Bush received a cuff around the head from a member of staff and the whole class walked out and protested to the headmaster. Groups of them would often go for tea at Jay's home.

'They were the first class that I knew I'd miss because they were so nice,' says Jay. 'We had been together such a long time and had developed a mutual trust and goodwill.'

Harry studied for O levels in Religious Education, English Language, English Literature and Maths, but he was never a star student. No one would have picked him out as a boy who was going to do great things.

'His problem wasn't in being lazy but in wanting to do too many other things so that he didn't want to sit down and do essays,' says Jay Norris. 'He was also extremely interested in rock 'n' roll. That didn't leave an awful lot of time for school work.'

At the age of sixteen Harry was a mixture of respectful conformism and determined individualism. In his reluctance to blaspheme, smoke, drink or argue back with his parents he seemed, even to his contemporaries, to be a little old-fashioned.

But no one mistook his politeness for compliancy, because beneath the well-mannered surface was grit. He showed this in his competitive nature on the sports field and in his reputation as a fighter.

'He was not a guy that you would upset,' says Cooke. 'He'd knock your block off. There was a really big lad in our class, and I remember that one day he said something Cliff didn't like, and Cliff punched him in the mouth.'

For his final Christmas play at Cheshunt School Harry took the part of Bob Cratchit in *A Christmas Carol*. It was then, according to Cooke, that the future rock 'n' roll star began to emerge.

'For his part in *A Christmas Carol* he had to dress up in tight black trousers and you suddenly noticed that the girls were looking at him as a bit of all right. Up until that time there had been nothing. During rehearsals he used to sing "Heartbreak Hotel" and "Hound Dog" just as a joke.'

A Christmas Carol earned him his first review. 'Harry Webb acted well as Bob Cratchit,' said the *Cheshunt Weekly Telegraph*, 'but he was rather let down by the make-up team and, hard as he worked, he could not dispel the impression that he was a teenager and not a harassed father.'

That Christmas he visited his grandmother in Carshalton and his aunt Ruth (married to Vincent Dickson) can remember him singing Tommy Steele's two hits 'Rock With The Caveman' and 'Singing The Blues', which were the first attempts at British rock 'n' roll, and telling her, 'I'm going to be famous one day.'

Although rock 'n' roll was being heard more frequently it was still considered a passing phase and wasn't receiving any specialized television coverage until '6.5 Special' started in February 1957 on BBC TV, the same month that Bill Haley arrived in Britain for his first tour.

Pete Bush remembers that by this time Harry was becoming very conscious of his looks. 'In our last year at school he became very meticulous about his appearance. He was always combing his hair. It wasn't a fashion show because none of us had a lot of money. It was just that he liked to keep looking good.'

There was enormous anticipation for Haley's concerts. The *Daily Mirror* had been orchestrating a publicity campaign which would culminate in the organization of a four-hundred-seater Rock 'n' Roll Special train. It was to travel from Waterloo Station in London to Southampton to greet Haley and the Comets when they docked on 6 February.

The film *Rock Around The Clock*, which starred Bill Haley, had gained notoriety because Teddy boys had decided that they shared an affinity with rock 'n' roll and were turning up at the cinemas to jive in the aisles and slash seats. The film was banned in some cities and Bill Haley was given space in the *Daily Mirror* to declare how sorry he was that his music had got people over-excited and to explain how virtuous it really all was.

In hyping Haley to such an extent the *Mirror* was walking a fine line between promoting a series of events and inciting teenage frenzy. When Haley finally arrived he was faced with a crowd of 5,000 at the dockside and more at Southampton station. The fans were so out of control at Southampton that he was virtually carried by the force of the bodies towards his train. All along the route to London those who'd read the *Mirror*'s timetable for the progress of the Rock 'n' Roll Special stood beside the tracks and waved.

The behaviour so alarmed Haley that he threatened to cancel the concerts if any rioting occurred. Strict security was enforced, dancing in the aisles was banned and the *Mirror* soberly advised its teenager readers to 'take it easy'. The warnings proved worthwhile. When he took to the stage at London's Dominion Theatre, Tottenham Court Road, there was a full house of 3,000 but no riots.

On 23 February Haley was able to write in *Melody Maker*: 'There haven't been any disturbances at the concerts. The boys and girls clap and they sing with us. That is the general pattern that we follow in our presentation. If we entertain the crowd, then the crowd will watch and listen quietly.'

The tour, as originally planned, was to be no more than a brief incursion but shortly before Haley arrived in Britain a further twelve dates were added, one of them at the Regal in Edmonton, just a few miles down the road from Cheshunt. Harry and his friends were in line for tickets the morning they went on sale, which was a school day.

The plan had been to go on to school but by the time they were served it was after midday so they killed the afternoon at Terry Smart's house. What they didn't know was that a member of staff had seen them in Edmonton and so the next day they received a dressing down from the headmaster, with the prefects among them temporarily losing their badges.

The concert was on Sunday 3 March 1957, and was an eye-opener for these sixteen year olds from Hertfordshire who had never been able to see a live rock 'n' roll performance.

'We were absolutely bowled over by the whole thing,' remembers Frances Slade. 'It was so exciting. At last there was something we could relate to instead of all this Guy Mitchell and Perry Como stuff that was being churned out at us.'

Haley was preceded by a fifty-minute set from the Vic Lewis Orchestra and then came on playing 'Razzle-dazzle' dressed in his tartan jacket. The volume, although low by today's standards, took the audience by surprise. *Melody Maker*'s Laurie Henshaw had described it as 'hitting the crowd like a battering ram' even though it only came through three small speakers.

Bass player Al Rex threw his stand-up bass around, eventually straddling it like a horse, while tenor sax player Rudy Pompilli climbed on his back in what appeared to be wild abandon to youngsters more accustomed to a band seated behind its music stands.

'What struck me was that everyone was standing up,' remembers Norman Mitham. 'It was electrifying. We'd never seen anything like it before. The sound seemed so full. We came home afterwards on the bus and talked about the concert for days.'

Says Cliff: 'I can still feel the excitement I felt that night. We were in the circle and we had to stand up to see and you could feel the balcony shake when he came out singing, "On your marks, get set, now ready, ready everybody, Razzle-dazzle . . ."

'It's hard for me now to think of anything that has been as good as that. There must have been, but that was my first encounter. I had never been to a concert before and suddenly everything we had heard on the radio was happening right before our eyes.'

In 1960 he wrote: 'This, I think, was the moment when I knew what I wanted to do above everything else in the world.'

The month of the Haley concert saw another musical phenomenon, skiffle, gripping Britain. Like rock 'n' roll it was an American music but its origins were further back in negro spirituals, folk songs and acoustic blues rather than the electrified Chicago blues.

Unamplified and largely unrecorded, skiffle tended to appeal to the better-educated and more middle-class teenagers who wore thick pullovers and corduroys rather than coloured shirts and drainpipes. They admired the music for its 'authenticity' and 'purity' and rather scorned rock 'n' roll because of its deliberate commercial appeal and its associations with Teddy boy hooliganism.

Nevertheless, that didn't stop the music papers from gleefully declaring the death of rock 'n' roll and predicting that skiffle would be the next big thing. The point was considered proven when the Vipers scored a hit with 'Cumberland Gap', Chas McDevitt with 'Freight Train' and Lonnie Donegan with 'Don't You Rock Me Daddy-O'.

Harry never really liked it. To him it was as far removed from rock 'n' roll as was opera. He bought Donegan's records but the releases that he really loved were those by Elvis, the Everly Brothers and the Platters. He could never have imagined himself singing skiffle.

6

'I unashamedly used skiffle'

During July and August 1957 Harry took a summer job picking tomatoes in a local garden nursery while waiting to hear how he had fared in his O level exams. He had a horrible feeling as he trudged home each night with his hands stained dark green that he could be doing a job like this for the rest of his life.

When the results came through they were a severe disappointment. His father opened the letter and broke the news that he had passed only in English Language. In real terms this left him no more qualified than his classmates who had gone out into the world after the fourth year. Career opportunities for people with one O level were limited. If he didn't take up an apprenticeship he was left with the options of being a manual labourer or an office junior.

Fearing the worst, his father had already been making enquiries at Thorn Electric and knew of a vacancy in the credit control department at Atlas Lighting. It was an unskilled position checking orders against the different trade discounts and passing the information on to regional despatch centres. It wasn't a demanding job but there were 'prospects' for the right hard-working lad and it brought in extra money for the still-struggling family. Most of his four pounds a week wage packet would be handed straight over to his mother.

Thorn Electric was a major employer in the area but didn't offer the ideal work environment for a sixteen-year-old boy. The average age of its workers at that time was forty and many of these were housewives working on the assembly lines. June Pearce, who, as June Turner, was a personnel officer when Harry joined the company, remembers him mainly because he was one of the few young people on the pay roll.

'He just seemed like most other young people of the day,' she says. 'He was very quiet, very polite and sort of orderly. He wasn't a tearaway by any means. He belonged to the Sports and Social Club and used to play a lot of badminton with his father.'

While sorting out the orders and looking up maps to find out where the closest despatch centre to Macclesfield was, he secretly dreamed of being Elvis. He had been doing his best to look like his idol, studying the photos that Donna was collecting and pinning up in the girls' bedroom, but he now wanted to be able to do what Elvis did — to sing, make records and appear in films.

He had been encouraged by singing with the Quintones but since then he had entered some local competitions as a solo act. In one talent show, held at the Capitol Theatre in Winchmore Hill, he had sung a version of Frankie Laine's 'A Woman In Love' and taken second place.

'I wasn't frustrated at the office,' he says, 'because I never thought about it that much. I was only thinking about becoming a singer. I was convinced I could do it but I was frustrated that I didn't know how to start. If only there had been a door marked "Show Business" with a list of vacancies posted outside. I had no way of knowing where to go. If there is such a thing as luck, that's where luck came in.'

Luck, in his case, came when his bicycle broke and he had to take the bus into work. On the top deck he met his schoolfriend, Frances Slade, who was now a student commuting daily to Hornsey College of Art. Somewhere between Cheshunt and Enfield, where Harry had to get off, Frances mentioned that the singer in the skiffle group her boyfriend Terry Smart was drumming for had just been called up to do his National Service and they were looking for a replacement. Harry's name had been brought up, apparently because Smart remembered from the school plays that he could sing. Harry indicated his interest and, the next evening, Smart came knocking at the front door of 12 Hargreaves Close.

Terry Smart was a year younger than Harry and had left school at fifteen to become a butcher's mate but he knew him from playing in the school's rugby football team and from playing the role of The Ghost Of Christmas Yet To Come in *A Christmas Carol*.

He had started drumming after seeing a trio playing at a wedding reception in the Flamstead End Community Hall. 'I sat watching the drummer and I thought, "That's what I want to do," ' he says. I used to have a paper round and I bought myself a bass drum, snare drum and high hat with my earnings. Later I bought a twenty-inch crash cymbal. A friend of my dad's had played drums in an army band and he used to come round and give me lessons.'

News that there was a drummer living on the estate came to the attention of Dick Teague, a fairly serious-minded accounts clerk whose big musical love was traditional jazz. When his younger brother Mick left the navy and bought a guitar he was inspired to start playing skiffle in the front room of his family's home at 19 Kingsley Avenue, with their mother Kathleen joining in on a washboard.

It wasn't long before the windows and doors were thrown open and friends would sit on the garden wall clapping along to these informal concerts. Eventually a neighbour complained to Broxbourne Borough Council who threatened the Teagues with eviction unless the music was halted at 10 p.m. each night.

By the time Smart was recruited in June 1957 it had become a fully-fledged skiffle group with the Teague brothers playing guitars, Terry Harness singing and playing guitar, Allan Crouch on washboard and Ken Simmons on tea-chest bass. An insurance salesman who was a friend of the Teague family heard the boys rehearsing and booked their first public appearance at a pub in Stoke Newington, North London, after which Dick's father, Walter Teague, began to manage the group, getting them regular work at local youth clubs, fêtes, pubs, jazz clubs and carnivals.

Terry Smart took Harry to meet the rest of the group at Frances Slade's home in Churchgate. 'It was an audition in a very loose sense of the word,' remembers Dick, who never had a high opinion of his group's musicianship.

'It would have been very presumptuous of us to consider we were auditioning someone. Basically it was a question of finding someone who could sing better than we could and none of us could sing a bloody note. Everybody was doing skiffle in those days. You didn't even have to be good at it.'

Harry turned up wearing a brown duffle coat and seemed shy and lacking in confidence as he ran through a couple of numbers in the front room of the bungalow, but his singing was distinct and impressive.

'There was a very musical, pleasant quality to his voice even then,' says Dick. 'As a matter of fact it wasn't the best sort of voice for the material we were doing, which often sounded better with a jazz voice that was slightly raspy and unpleasant. But Harry made everything he sang sound good.'

On 19 September 1957 Walter Teague wrote in the group's engagement diary: 'Harry introduced to group and enlisted right away. Good luck to the group's additional member.'

The next day Harry signed his first contract, a handwritten note made out on a sheet of paper torn from an exercise book. It read: 'We, the undersigned (members of Dick Teague's Skiffle group) hereby agree not to leave the group to take an individual engagement with any other musical concern without previously discussing the matter with the full group and its controlling manager.' It was signed by Harry Webb, Dick Teague, Mick Teague, Terry Harness, Allan

Crouch, Terry Smart and Ken Simmons.

British skiffle, which reached its commercial peak in 1957, had developed from a fascination with American folk blues and was pioneered by traditional jazz musicians like Ken Colyer (trumpet), who had spent time in New Orleans in 1952, Chris Barber (trombone) and Lonnie Donegan (banjo), which is why a jazzer like Dick Teague found himself getting involved. It was Donegan's 1955 recording of 'Rock Island Line' which triggered off the national craze when it became a hit.

'Rock Island Line' was the perfect skiffle number. It was frantic, it was easy to play and it was splattered with Americanisms. The story of how it was discovered by the American folklorist Alan Lomax, who picked it up from a convicted murderer called Huddie 'Leadbelly' Ledbetter in 1934, gave it absolute credibility in the eyes of the purists who liked to think that the best songs were written from the soul without any thought of posterity or financial reward.

Donegan, who played in Chris Barber's band, had initially been given a spot to play 'Rock Island Line' as a novelty interlude in Barber's programme of New Orleans jazz but by 1957 he was a major star in his own right with a string of top twenty hits including 'Lost John', 'Cumberland Gap' and 'Putting On The Style'.

Although the songs were inevitably American and skiffle was supposed to have started at rent parties (parties put on by impoverished musicians to raise money for their rent) in Chicago during the twenties, skiffle in the hands of Lonnie Donegan and his friends was a peculiarly British phenomenon which appealed not only because it was vibrant and unstuffy at a time when young people were looking for an excitement that would lift them out of the sea of post-war blandness, but because you didn't need to be an accomplished musician to play it and the equipment was inexpensive and largely improvised.

You could get by with three chords, a song book and a lot of enthusiasm. An upright bass could be made out of a used tea chest, a broom handle and a length of string, while percussion was produced by dragging a thimble across the ribbed metal of a domestic washboard.

It wasn't rock 'n' roll but it drew from the same well of black American culture and appealed to young people. It created a ready-made made audience for blues singers like Big Bill Broonzy, Sonny Terry, Brownie McGhee and Lonnie Johnson when they later came to England and led directly to the folk music revival of the early sixties.

It was also an ideal place for potential rock 'n' roll musicians to get started in Britain. Trade embargos introduced after the war meant that electric guitars weren't available in British music stores and few teenagers in this country had enjoyed the long exposure to black gospel music, country and western and blues that people like Elvis Presley and Chuck Berry had. Six months before Harry Webb joined Dick Teague, John Lennon had started singing skiffle with the Quarry Men, and was later joined by Paul McCartney.

Alan Lomax himself saw the movement in glowingly positive terms. In August 1957 he commented: 'Before skiffle, even three or four years ago, relatively few people in London made their own music. Singing and playing was for show-offs or professionals. Pub singers mulled over the dry bones of the Cockney music hall songs which had little meaning for the younger generation. Nowadays the young people of this country have songs they like to sing.'

Harry hated skiffle. It was too worthy and folkish for him and lacked the raw electric energy of Memphis rock 'n' roll. But he saw the sense in keeping his mouth shut about his personal musical preferences and regarding the job in Teague's group as his first step into show business. He even dared to think that maybe he could introduce a little rock 'n' roll into the act.

'For me it offered a way of singing,' he admits. 'Skiffle was just a vehicle to take me where I wanted to go. I couldn't have possibly sung like a skiffle singer. I didn't find it very exciting but I liked being able to sing in front of an audience. There wasn't another skiffle singer who looked like Elvis. I unashamedly used it to further my own ends.'

Once he had signed the contract he rehearsed every night, learning the words to such songs as Woody Guthrie's 'Bring A Little Water Sylvie' and the Donegan hits 'Rock Island Line' and 'Don't You Rock Me Daddy-O'. The group's sources were mainly the singles by Donegan and Ken Colyer's song book, *Skiffle Album*, which had the words and chords to such skiffle favourites as 'This Train', 'John Henry', 'Down By The Riverside' and 'The Grey Goose'.

'Before Harry joined the group Dick Teague's opinion was that they were "basically rubbish". His revised opinion was that they were "basically rubbish" but with an added "bit of quality". The speed at which the new singer could pick up songs amazed them all. 'We would pick a record we liked and work out the chords in rehearsal,' says Dick. 'Harry could come back the next day and he would know the piece inside out.'

One of the group's regular gigs over the coming months would be an 8.30 spot at the Flamstead End Youth Club during a Friday night jazz evening known as the Saints Rhythm Club.

'What used to happen was that while the jazz bands were on, the kids flopped round the hall looking bored,' says Dick. 'Then when the skiffle came on they would go mad dancing.' It was here, on 4 October, that Harry made his debut as the lead singer of a group.

With the departure of Terry Harness — after a couple of performances sharing the stage with Harry — the group had lost a guitarist. Harry couldn't yet play guitar but he did like to strap one over his shoulder and have it hanging behind him as he sang, Elvis Presley style.

'He used to embarrass me with it,' Dick admits.

Two weeks later Harry roped in Brian Parker, a friend from Cheshunt Secondary School who had played violin in the National Youth Orchestra, to play guitar. Parker was to go on to become an important figure in the rock 'n' roll scene around Cheshunt and Waltham Cross, playing with Dave Sampson and the Hunters and the Parker Royal Five before forming Unit Four Plus Two with an old school friend and scoring a number one hit in 1965 with 'Concrete and Clay'.

'I knew him mostly through sport at school,' says Parker. 'Then because I had owned a guitar for a couple of weeks he thought I must be very proficient and so he asked me to join.'

Over the next three months the Dick Teague Group played an average of twice a week and rehearsed furiously in between. A look at the date sheet meticulously kept by Walter Teague shows that they played Flamstead End Youth Club once a week and then usually played another local event such as a Boy Scouts' party, a dance at Goff's Oak or a function at Waltham Town Hall. The group's fee was one pound, raised to three pounds and five shillings for bigger events such as the one at the town hall.

At the same time they were entering local talent contests but finding themselves unplaced. On 22 October Walter Teague wrote rather proudly in his diary, 'Received confirmation of group's entry in Haileybury Boy's Club competition in Hoddesdon, which was a skiffle group contest with a first prize of a silver challenge cup autographed by Tommy Steele.'

On 2 November there was the forlorn addition 'Played in competition at Haileybury Club. Not in first 4 out of 12. Alleykats 3rd.' The Alleykats were their main local rivals.

Skiffle inspired dancing and quiet appreciation rather than screaming, but Harry was consciously introducing a rock 'n' roll element to his act by dressing sharp in patterned pullovers and emulating Elvis's pelvic thrusts. Sometimes, after his set, he would go out on the floor and dance with the girls but the partner most of the group remember him dancing with was his pretty fourteen-year-old sister Donella, who now called herself Donna and was catching the eye of all the local boys.

Surprisingly, in view of his Victorian contempt for the modern world, Rodger Webb supported Harry's skiffling, seeing in it perhaps some of the same unsophisticated fun that he had enjoyed in India with his brother Tom when they had played old Irish and Scottish folk tunes.

June Pearce remembers that he would regularly stop her at work to tell her how well his son was doing with his music.

'We used to have mid-morning breaks in the canteen and Mr Webb would come over and say that Harry was playing at such-and-such a place last night and they got on very well. He was obviously very proud of him.'

Yet, at the same time, he seemed surprised to find that Harry could succeed at something. Maybe his expectations had been progressively lowered through examination failures or maybe, with his own status in the world diminished, it was important for him to see Harry as a dependent child.

Walter Teague was taken aback when Rodger told his wife Kathleen that he was worried that Harry would hold the group back.

'He came along to one of the boys' local appearances,' remembers Walter, 'and he started talking to my wife. He said, "If only my son had the confidence that the rest of the group had, they would go far. But I'm afraid Harry will never do any good because he is so nervous." '

He was indeed nervous. In his early shows he found it hard to look directly at the audience and preferred to slink away afterwards. Although he was friends with Terry Smart and Brian Parker, whom he'd known from school, he never got close to anyone else in the group and didn't socialize with them.

Kathleen Teague remembers him as 'reserved and shy. He wouldn't push himself forward at all.' Her daughter Sheila picked up the same impression from seeing him rehearse at their home. 'I remember him with dark hair, jeans and a leather jacket just standing there looking very edgy. He used to have a nervous cough. They would hang a microphone from the light fixture in the middle of the room and start playing. I was extremely impressed with this boy's voice though. It seemed to boom out and fill the room.'

At twenty-two, Dick Teague was five years older than Harry. Whereas Harry couldn't wait to leave his office job and saw music as the key to his escape, Dick was rather happy in the accounts office of a local chemical company and was set against anyone taking the group too seriously. It had started out as fun, he thought, and when it stopped being fun the group should end.

Yet although he wasn't serious about a musical career he was serious about the type of music he thought they should play. He insisted that they be a 'purist' group not swayed by pop or gimmick songs. Dick Teague was a man for whom even Lonnie Donegan was suspected as a heretic. He had about as much interest in rock 'n' roll as Harry had in skiffle and thought that Elvis Presley was 'a great greasy wop'.

By December 1957 Harry was pushing Dick to let him sing 'Heartbreak Hotel' and 'All Shook Up' in a special spot. The suggestion appalled Dick, who saw it as a compromise with commercial pop. He wouldn't allow it. Already he was worried about Harry's swivelling hips and vocal 'uh-huh's which he found totally inappropriate for songs expressing the anxieties of rural blacks and dustbowl migrants.

'He had slightly long sideboards and he used to do himself up as a dead ringer for Elvis,' Dick remembers. 'When Harry started shaking himself about I got uptight about it because we were supposed to be a traditional jazz outfit. I was very old-fashioned for a young guy.'

In October, unknown to his sons, Walter Teague had written to the BBC requesting an audition for the 'Saturday Skiffle Club', an experimental half-hour show on the Light Programme, which was produced by Jimmy Grant and later turned into the highly influential pop and jazz show 'Saturday Club'. To Walter's surprise, a letter came back offering an audition at BBC's Studio 4, Maida Vale, on 13 January.

The first that Dick knew of the audition was when he arrived home from work and his father told him not to bother changing out of his office clothes as they were going straight out.

'All the others knew about it, but they knew I was a perfectionist. I thought the group was rubbish and that they were rushing to places I didn't want to go yet,' he says.

The group went to Maida Vale that evening and played 'Stackerlee Blues', 'Sporting Life', 'This Train' and 'This Little Light Of Mine' in front of a clerk from the variety booking section.

'It was ridiculous really. They asked us who the lead guitarist was but we didn't really have one,' says Dick. 'We were just a bunch of guys thrashing away on guitars. They asked who the lead singer was and so we stuck the mike on Harry and he took the lead while the rest of us stayed in the background churning out our rubbish. The woman who had auditioned us came down from her cubicle after we had finished and said to Harry, "You've got a very good voice. You ought to have it trained." That was the only comment she made.'

What no one else knew at the time was that Harry was already planning to leave. He hated the songs he was having to sing and could see that there was no scope for his plans to emulate Elvis with Dick Teague policing his movements. The only person he grumbled to though was Terry Smart who he found shared his grievances.

'We both found rock 'n' roll far more exciting than skiffle,' says Smart. 'A few times during rehearsals we had asked to try some of these new numbers but Dick didn't want to. He didn't like the sound.'

So they planned to form their own rock 'n' roll group which would rehearse on the evenings that they weren't needed to play skiffle, only breaking the news to Dick when they felt confident enough to get their own engagements. The most immediate problem though was that they were only a duo and neither of them could play guitar, even though Harry had recently bought one from a mail order firm and had been shown the rudiments by his father.

They tried to coax Brian Parker away from Dick because Parker was becoming recognized as one of the brightest guitar talents in the area. 'I can remember actually getting on a bus to go down to Hargreaves Close saying to myself, "Yeh, I'm definitely going to join this rock 'n' roll group",' Parker remembers. 'But by the time I arrived I'd changed my mind. I told him that I was going to stick with the skiffle group.'

Eventually they decided they'd pull in Norman Mitham, Harry's old friend.

'He came to me and said that if I could learn to play guitar I could be in his band,' says Mitham. 'Up until that point I'd never had a music lesson and really knew nothing about music at all.'

What he did have though was an uncle, Philip Spur, who had played professionally in dance bands and who was willing to give Norman and Harry lessons on his Gibson guitar.

'First of all uncle Philip told us what key Harry sang in and then we'd play the record we wanted to cover and he would work out the chords,' says Mitham. 'He'd teach us the chords, show us where the chord changes came and we built up a repertoire like that.

'We didn't have the musical ability to play instrumental breaks so we improvised with a sequence of chords. It was similar to what the skiffle boys did but Terry made it more rock 'n' roll by playing a definite beat. In the skiffle group he tended to play with brushes but now he was using sticks to play a more prominent beat.'

Dick Teague sensed that something was happening behind his back when Harry's legendary talent for picking songs up overnight seemed to disappear. He also noticed that Harry's friend Norman was now coming along to the group's gigs and studying his guitar chords.

Then one evening, while returning young Joan from a play session with his daughter Sheila, Walter Teague heard the sounds of a rock 'n' roll group rehearsal coming from the open windows of 12 Hargreaves Close.

'After telling Dick not to teach him how to play guitar,' says Walter, 'there he was playing as lively as you like.' A crisis meeting of the group was called for 17 January at which Harry argued that the skiffle group should include rock 'n' roll.

'The other guys said that they liked what we were playing,' remembers Dick. 'They thought that the type of material we were playing was most suited to the instruments we had. Rock 'n' roll required more competence.

'Then Terry Smart piped up that he also wanted to play rock 'n' roll. I said that there was no question about it. Either they played our sort of music or we had a split. Harry said he'd rather play rock 'n' roll but he'd prefer to do it with me because we had a good thing going. I said it wouldn't be with me.

'It wasn't unpleasant but it was a sort of agreement that the music we wanted to do was different and we just packed up that night. I just said to Terry, "Well, off you go," and I lost contact with both of them after that.'

Walter Teague solemnly recorded it in his diary: 'Harry and Terry left group after full discussion of all matters relating to future policy.' Coincidentally, the local paper ran its first feature on the group that evening beneath a photo of Harry singing at the Saints' Rhythm Club. The headline was, 'Local Skiffle Group Get BBC Audition'.

'Many people are saying that skiffle music is on the way out, but for a local group, Dick Teague and his Skiffle Group, it may well be just on its way in,' read the report.

'This local skiffle group had an audition with the BBC on Monday evening for the "Saturday Skiffle Club," which is heard every Saturday morning at l0am. The result of the audition will not be known for some time.

'Dick Teague commented afterwards: "The audition went very well, and I hope that we have passed it..."

'The group was formed just over six months ago, and its motto is "The surest way not to fail is to determine to succeed." Since its formation, the group has been rehearsing at every opportunity.

'For the first four months the group were in existence the

instrumentalists sang the songs, but in September Harry Webb joined the group as their singer.

'In its early days the group entered for many skiffle competitions but was never placed. Now they have ceased to enter for them. Dick Teague explained: "At these competitions a group is generally expected to sing Lonnie Donegan style numbers, and we don't like them. We specialise in true traditional skiffle."'

A week later Walter Teague received a letter from the BBC letting him know that the Group had not passed the audition for 'Skiffle Club'. 'Heard from BBC re. audition,' he noted in his diary. '(No go). If at first you don't succeed etc. Something attempted is something done.'

Harry's only response, when he saw the newspaper, was to think how much he looked like Elvis. His mind was already made up to leave skiffle far behind and concentrate on rock 'n' roll.

7

'Something told me he was going to be really big'

For Harry Webb, 1958 was to be the last year of normal life; the last year he could walk along a British street without being recognized, go out on a date with the assurance that he wasn't being used for his social position, or have what most people refer to as a private life. It was also the last year he would have to worry about money.

He began the year as a shy young office clerk playing skiffle in Hertfordshire village halls, and ended it under another name as a national celebrity who girls wanted to paw and their boyfriends wanted to punch.

The speed of the transition was mind-blowing. Twelve months after his first appearance with Dick Teague he was closing the show on a major tour. Elvis Presley had to wait a year and a half after cutting his first single before he was on national television, and John Lennon, who started playing skiffle in March 1958, didn't become a celebrity until 1963.

The opening months of the year were charged with excitement. Not only had his picture appeared in the paper but he was rehearsing every night at home with his own rock 'n' roll trio.

Between them Harry, Terry Smart and Norman Mitham would buy

the latest American rock 'n' roll singles on a Friday night and then Donna would painstakingly transcribe the lyrics while they worked out the chord changes. In this way they quickly learned to play 'Blue Suede Shoes', 'Heartbreak Hotel', 'Rock Around The Clock' and 'Blueberry Hill'.

Cliff's musical preferences were for the sweeter style of singers like Ricky Nelson and the Everly Brothers rather than the vaguely-threatening screams and squawks of Little Richard and Gene Vincent. He even admired Pat Boone, a white boy from Tennessee who made his name by recording cover versions of black rock 'n' roll hits in the knowledge that in a society still racially divided they would sell to the conservative white audience.

Smart suggested calling the trio the Planets. It was a topical enough name — the space race had just been inaugurated with the launch of Russia's Sputnik-1 satellite — but Harry and Norman Mitham didn't think it was quite right.

They looked up 'planet' in the dictionary and found that it came from the Greek 'planetes' meaning 'wanderer' or 'drifter'. They toyed with the idea of being the Wanderers or the Drifters and it was the Drifters that stuck. They were unaware that an American vocal group led by Clyde McPhatter had been recording under the name since 1953.

'It sounds crazy now,' says Mitham, 'but almost as soon as we started playing we decided on the cover of our first album. We hadn't recorded a single song but we said that if we ever made an LP we could have a picture of us sitting on a toboggan driving into a snow drift.'

The Drifters made their debut in March 1958 at the Forty Hill Badminton Club, between Cheshunt and Enfield, where Harry and his parents were members. It was the annual dinner and dance and they played the cabaret spot, getting the then-enormous fee of five pounds.

'I was elated that all these people were applauding me,' says Cliff, 'but it probably gave a false impression because these were people who knew me and who I played badminton with every week.'

Harry's life was incredibly full and even though he was donning a suit and tie each day to go to work, the fact that he was singing in a group reassured him that he was somehow different from all the other people there. At least he had the hope of one day breaking out. He knew that British teenagers were starved of live rock 'n' roll. There had been Tommy Steele and Terry Dene but neither of them had successfully captured the American sound.

In his already busy schedule he now found time for romance. During his last year at school he was attracted to his classmate Janice Berry who, unfortunately for him, was wrapped up in a serious relationship with Brian Cooke. A bright pupil, Janice had become head girl and passed six O levels. She was working in a two-year secretarial job with ICI in Welwyn Garden City with plans to train as a teacher when she was eighteen.

'All the time I was going out with Janice I knew that Harry wanted to go out with her,' says Cooke. 'Then one day she told me that she wasn't going out with me any more and the next thing I knew she was going out with Harry. I think she must have had him in mind when she got rid of me.'

Janice admits as much. 'It was the day I finished with Brian that he [Harry] knocked on my door and that evening we went to the cinema in Waltham Cross,' she says. 'I have to be honest and say that it wasn't entirely a coincidence. He had heard about the break-up.'

When in later years Cliff was to talk about the 'couple of times' he really believed he had fallen in love, Janice was certainly included although he has never before mentioned her by name and Janice has never told her story.

In a fan booklet published in 1959 she was referred to as 'June', a 'sixteen-year-old brunette' whom he dated for five months. 'They quietly held hands at the local cinema,' it read. 'They went to teenage parties together (spending most of the time in a corner alone), and took long country walks.'

Four years later in an interview he spoke of 'Janet', the girl he had been 'courting steadily' before he broke into show business. 'I guess she was the most serious girl I ever had,' he said.

Today he says, 'If love came into it at all, that was the first time.'

She was a dark-haired girl who lived with her mother at 242 Turner's Hill, a fifteen-minute walk from the Webbs' home. She was an only child, and her father had died suddenly while she was still at school.

She had always been part of the close-knit gang that centred on the school drama group and had often been to Hargreaves Close for tea. 'She was a lovely girl,' says Cliff's mother. 'We were very fond of Janice.'

Their brief relationship in 1958 typified the teenage innocence of the time. They would talk over coffees at the Blue Bird Café, go off on country rambles, visit the cinema or just see each other at home.

When she came along to group rehearsals she would sit in a corner quietly listening and supplying them with cups of tea. They even used her front room to practise in, setting up in the bay of the front window and leaving a threadbare patch of carpet behind as a memory.

Once, while on an evening walk, Harry surprised Janice by vaulting over the wall of a garden and picking her a flower.

'There was a beautiful magnolia bush,' she remembers. 'It was at its peak and I just happened to say something about how beautiful it looked in the evening light and he leapt over the wall, picked this flower from the tree, leapt back and gave it to me. It was a terribly romantic thing to do but it wasn't typical. That's why I remember it!

'A lot of what we did together was built around the Drifters' rehearsals. We were the same as any other boyfriend and girlfriend really. It was a loving relationship. People in those days didn't leap into bed together as they do now. Maybe some people did, but we didn't and it wasn't something that the crowd of people I was with did.

'I was certainly in love with him and, I don't know . . . I can't answer for him. Maybe it was one-sided but we both seemed to be in love.'

Dates with Janice had to be fitted in between dates with the group. They had been offered a spot at the Five Horseshoes, a pub up the road in Burford Street, Hoddesdon, where the publican was experimenting with live music during the week.

The stage was a small raised platform next to the door to the gents' toilet. There was no amplification and anyone who played had to compete with customers' chatter and the sound of darts thudding into cork boards.

When the Drifters took on the challenge one mid-week evening in March, a well-built local lad with a Tony Curtis haircut and a black leather jacket was standing at the bar. John Foster was, in his own words, a 'bit of a Ted' but he considered himself wise in the ways of rock 'n' roll because, unlike most young people in the area, he had visited the legendary 2 I's coffee bar in London's Soho. Once when he was there he found himself standing next to Terry Dene, who in 1957 had been touted as 'Britain's answer to Elvis Presley'.

What John Foster saw at the Five Horseshoes that evening impressed him deeply. It wasn't the musicianship — the group was barely mastering the most basic chords — but there was something about the singer that transcended all the failures of the act.

'I didn't look at Terry and I didn't look at Norman,' he admits. 'I looked at the singer in his white shirt and black trousers and I saw Elvis . Something told me, yes, he's going to be big. He's going to be really big. I don't know what made me do it because I was drinking with my mates at the bar, but I just walked up to the group and asked them if they wanted a manager.'

It was pure bluff. He had no experience of show business management and had never booked an act into the 2 I's. He was a driver employed on the local sewage farm. But he was on speaking terms with the manager Tom Littlewood, a former film stunt man who had the unusual business practice of paying groups to play in the cellar and then charging them a ten per cent commission for the privilege.

Being asked if you wanted to play at the 2 I's was like being asked if you would like your latest film to be shown at Cannes. For aspiring British rock 'n' rollers it was *the* place to play. It was where Tommy Steele and Terry Dene had been 'discovered' by their future managers and it had become the best-known coffee bar in Britain.

They did need a manager, especially one with such apparently good contacts. Foster even had a telephone in his home, something that neither Terry, Norman or Harry had.

'I knew I was being rather flash when I gave them my phone number,' he says. 'It was a rather impressive thing to do in those days.'

He promised them that if they met him that weekend he would arrange a spot for them at the 2 I's. No trouble.

'Foster told us to be prepared to go up to London on the 715 Green Line bus that Saturday,' remembers Mitham. 'He said it would be coming through at two o'clock and that he would be sitting on the nearside. We were to wait at the Old Pond bus stop in Cheshunt and get on when we saw him.

'We talked about it all week among ourselves. We didn't know if we were being taken for a ride. However, we turned up and waited and John was on the second bus that came, sitting up against the window. I think Harry had a lot more faith in him than I did. I didn't think he would be there.'

The 2 I's was at 59 Old Compton Street, not far from Shaftesbury Avenue. It was a small street-level coffee bar with live music in the cellar. It had been taken over in 1956 by two Australian wrestlers, Paul Lincoln and Ray Hunter, who bought it from the Irani brothers (hence the I of the 2 I's).

It was at a time when coffee bars were the latest teen sensation, providing a meeting space that was neither church youth club (where adults were concerned about your moral welfare) nor public house (which required that you be eighteen). The Gaggia machines which gushed and gurgled on the counters provided an exotic new beverage from the Continent known as 'espresso'.

At first the 2 I's had been a financial disaster. Then, on 14 July 1956, a young commercial artist called Wally Whyton dropped by and asked whether he and his skiffle group the Vipers could busk there.

'Paul Lincoln said it was OK, and within about three weeks the place was literally packed to the doors. Instead of letting us busk he charged a shilling admission and paid us two pounds a night each,' remembers Whyton. 'The basement had been a store room and when we became the resident group down there I went with Lionel Bart and a couple of others and painted designs on the walls.'

Even though they lived on the fringes of London none of the Drifters had ever ventured into Soho before. As they walked through its narrow streets they felt a frisson of excitement at the sight of the jazz clubs, foreign food stores and striptease clubs. Soho had not yet become the sleaze pit of the sixties but there was enough of an air of strangeness and naughtiness to cause a provincial lad's eyes to widen.

'I can remember someone pointing to some girls and mentioning that they were prostitutes,' remembers Mitham. 'We had never had anything to do with prostitutes and we couldn't believe that we were right in the middle of it all.'

They were met at the 2 I's by Tom Littlewood who listened to them perform two songs before telling them that they had passed the audition and could play their first show that night.

'We weren't the star attraction but at least we were on and got invited back the next day and then the day after that,' says Mitham. 'There was no screaming. The kids just listened.

'What we talked about afterwards was the fact that people had paid and they had stood there and listened. We weren't there as incidental entertainment like at the Five Horseshoes or the Badminton Club.

People had paid to watch us and they seemed to like us.

'By the time I got home that night my parents were asleep but I actually woke them up to tell them that I had played at the 2 I's.'

John Foster's bluff had paid off. The audition had led to what was in effect a two-week residency during April 1958.

'It was all very exciting for him,' says Janice, who was by this time seeing even less of her boyfriend than before. 'He obviously wanted to succeed and the fact that everybody applauded at the 2 I's reinforced the idea that he was going to.'

During the first week a sandy-haired young man on leave from the RAF, where he was just finishing his National Service, came up to them and asked if they needed a lead guitarist to boost their sound.

He was Ian Ralph 'Sammy' Samwell and like Harry had been playing in a group – the Ash Valley Skiffle Group – while really wanting to play rock 'n' roll. What the Drifters were doing summed up everything he hoped to do.

'They asked me to audition for them on the Saturday afternoon,' says Samwell. 'That became my first group rehearsal and that night I played with them and effectively joined the Drifters.'

The same night Jan Vane, a teenager from Rainham in Essex, was visiting the 2 I's as part of a treat for her sixteenth birthday from her boyfriend Eddie. The cellar was so packed that they sat on a Coca-Cola fridge and craned their necks to see.

'I can't remember what he sang that night but I just thought that he was so unusual,' she remembers. 'He was so handsome and so different.

'He was young and exciting and I had never been anywhere like that before. I was caught up in the whole atmosphere of the evening; of seeing someone live and of thinking that if he was playing at the 2 I's he must be extremely famous.'

A chatty, confident girl, she stayed behind to get Harry's autograph. After asking the usual questions about how long he had been playing and where he usually performed she asked him whether he had a fan club. Harry laughed at the question. He explained that he had only been playing rock 'n' roll for just over four weeks and apologized for having to leave so soon to get the last bus home.

'I told him not to worry because we would run him home,' says Jan. 'Eddie had a car, which was quite impressive in those days.

'So that night we all squeezed into a small green Morris Minor and drove back to Cheshunt. The group all lived in different places too so we spent half the night finding their houses.

'The main point was that we exchanged addresses. I told him I would keep in touch to see what he was doing and I started writing. Sometimes he would write back to me and sometimes his mum would write back and eventually I got invited back home.'

This was to be the beginning of the official Cliff Richard Fan Club. It started with half a dozen members who Jan would personally write to with the latest information, and rose to a 42,000-strong membership which required a full-time staff of four.

Harry Greatorex was the closest thing to an agent to spot Harry Webb at the 2 I's. He was a 35-year-old dance hall manager from Derbyshire who scoured London to find talent worth promoting in the North.

He heard the Drifters during their second week and told John Foster that he could give them work at the Regal Ballroom in Ripley. He offered a fee of five pounds with an additional ten pounds for expenses.

There was just one thing that Harry Greatorex wasn't happy with. He didn't want to bill them as a group act, but as a singer with a backing group. He didn't think Harry Webb and the Drifters sounded convincingly rock 'n' roll enough. Foster assured him that the problem could be solved within minutes and he hauled the boys to The Swiss, a pub in Old Compton Street, to dream up a new name for Harry Webb.

It wasn't unusual for English rock 'n' roll singers to ditch their given names for something more evocative. Manager Larry Parnes

◀ Cliff's maternal great-great grandparents, William and Martha Bridgwater

India, c.1924: Cliff's mother as a young girl (front, left) with her sister Olive Queenie (front, right), her uncle Vincent Bridgwater (standing, centre), her mother Dorothy Edith (standing, right), her aunt Beatrice Bridgwater (standing, left), and her grandparents, William Brock Bridgwater and Marie Beatrice Bridgwater (seated) ▼

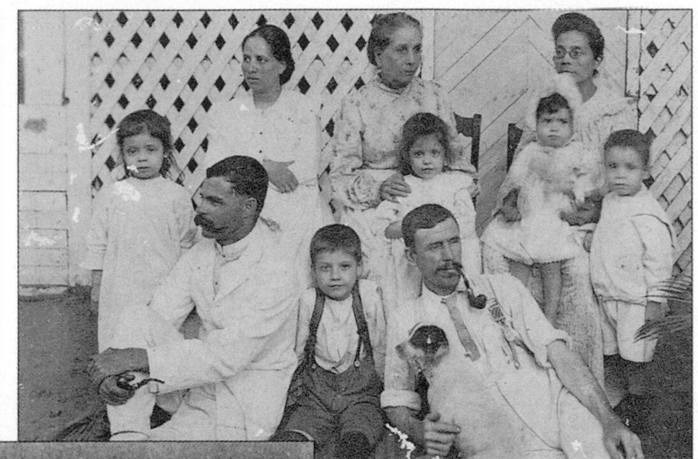

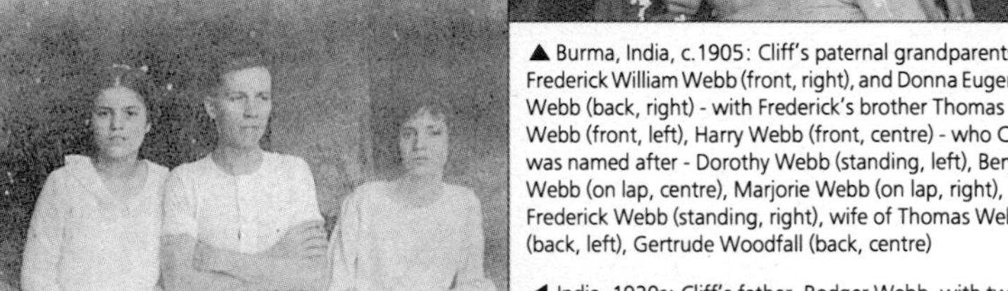

▲ Burma, India, c.1905: Cliff's paternal grandparents - Frederick William Webb (front, right), and Donna Eugenie Webb (back, right) - with Frederick's brother Thomas Webb (front, left), Harry Webb (front, centre) - who Cliff was named after - Dorothy Webb (standing, left), Beryl Webb (on lap, centre), Marjorie Webb (on lap, right), Frederick Webb (standing, right), wife of Thomas Webb (back, left), Gertrude Woodfall (back, centre)

◀ India, 1920s: Cliff's father, Rodger Webb, with two of his sisters, Joyce and Donella

▲ Anasol, India, 1935: Cliff's mother (seated, right) with Olive Queenie (seated, left) and their step brothers and sisters

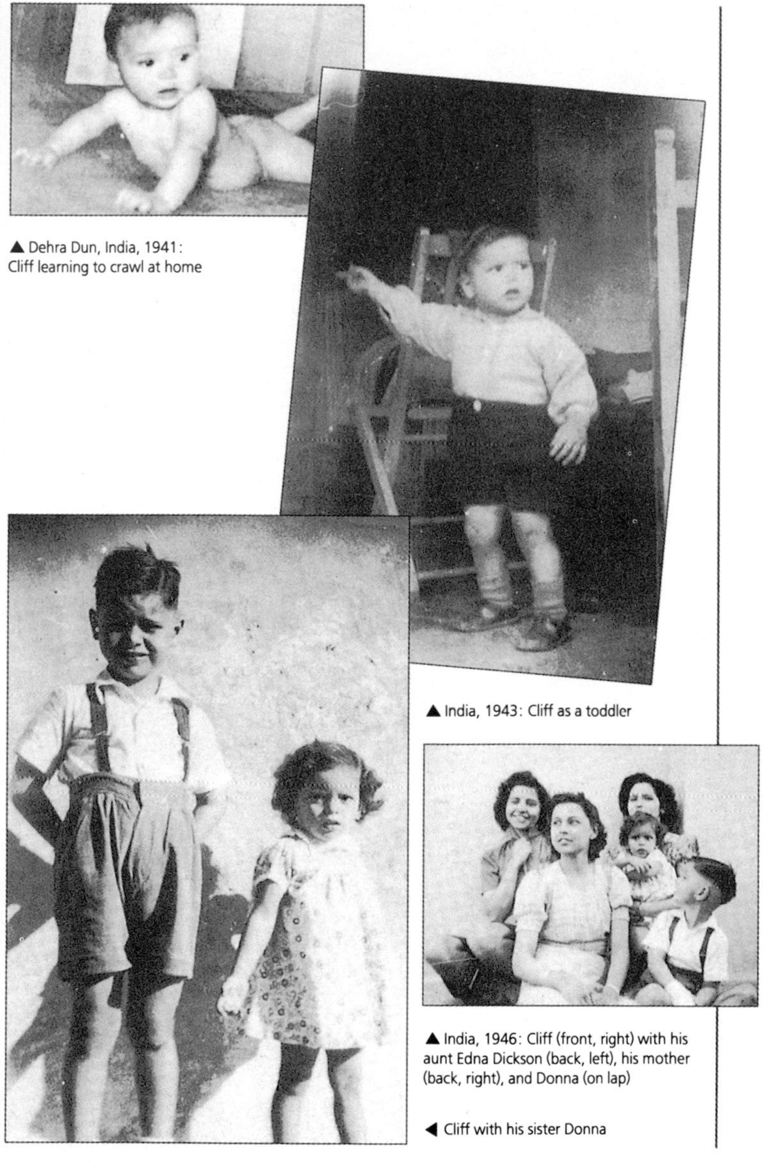

▲ Dehra Dun, India, 1941: Cliff learning to crawl at home

▲ India, 1943: Cliff as a toddler

▲ India, 1946: Cliff (front, right) with his aunt Edna Dickson (back, left), his mother (back, right), and Donna (on lap)

◀ Cliff with his sister Donna

▲ Carshalton, 1949: Cliff (right) with Sunday School friend Peter Maynard

England, 1954: Cliff's cousin Joyce Dobra (holding her son Stephen) with grandfather Frederick William Webb ▶

July 1956: The Quintones - (from left to right) Cliff, Freda Johnson, John Vince, Irene Fowler, Beryl Molineux - Cliff's first gig as featured in the Waltham and Cheshunt Weekly Telegraph ▶

◀ September 1956: Cliff and his fellow Quintones at a party at John Vince's home. Cliff can be seen third in from the left. His childhood girlfriend Betty Clarke is third from the left in the back row

1957: (clockwise from bottom) John Vince, Norman Lockwood, Doug Lee, Jay Norris, Cliff, Pete Bush, Chris Green, unidentified, at Jay Norris' home ▶

◀ The same occasion at Jay Norris' home: (left to right) Cliff, unidentified, Chris Green, John Vince, Irene Fowler

Cliff's first serious girlfriend, Janice Berry (picture taken some years after their romance) ▶

December 1957: Dick Teague's Skiffle Group - (left to right) Mick Teague, Brian Parker, Terry Smart, Cliff and Dick Teague ▼

▲ February 1958: Cliff in the kitchen of his parents' home in Cheshunt

▲ February 1958: The Drifters in its original line-up - (left to right) Cliff, Terry Smart, Norman Mitham. Taken on Bury Green Estate, Cheshunt

▲ July 1958: (left to right) Terry Smart, Cliff and Ian Samwell in the front room of 12 Hargreaves Close, Cheshunt

April 1958: The Drifters with new member Ian 'Sammy' Samwell (seated with guitar) at the 2 I's coffee bar, Soho ▶

◀ 25 May 1958: (left to right) John Foster, Cliff, Jerry Lee Lewis, Terry Smart and Ian Samwell backstage at the Kilburn State Theatre

had made an art of it – contrasting warm and friendly first names with tough and aggressive surnames: Tommy Steele for Thomas Hicks, Marty Wilde for Reginald Smith.

'All the American people had cool names anyway,' says Samwell. 'They were Chuck, Rick, Carl, Gene and things like that. None of them were called Ian or Norman.'

They started by playing on variations of Russ Hamilton, a British singer who'd had a couple of hits the year before, and came up with Russ Clifford and Cliff Russard before hitting on Cliff Richards. Samwell then suggested dropping the 's' as a tribute to Little Richard. John Foster then returned to Harry Greatorex and told him that it would be Cliff Richard and the Drifters who would be appearing in Ripley.

'I can remember him coming back home and saying that from now on he would like to be called Cliff and not Harry,' says his sister Jacqui. 'I don't think Dad ever called him Cliff but Joan, Donna and I started calling him it fairly quickly. Mum took a bit longer just because she kept slipping up. I mean, after calling your son Harry for seventeen years it is a bit difficult to call him something else overnight.'

The Ripley show, booked for Saturday 3 May, was their biggest engagement so far and their first outside London and Hertfordshire. They took a train to Derby and, on arriving, they were impressed to see posters announcing, 'Direct from the famous Soho 2 I's Coffee Bar – Cliff Richard and the Drifters'.

The Regal Ballroom was a converted snooker hall with a mock-Tudor frontage which Greatorex had taken over two years before and turned into a dance hall with events ranging from old-time dancing to skiffle. On the night Cliff and the Drifters played there was a 'top twenty record session' and support from Keith Freer and his Dixielanders .

'They had a stage with curtains which was quite something to us after the 2 I's,' says Samwell. 'The curtains parted, we were standing there and that night we really rocked. The place was absolutely jam-packed and the response was fantastic.'

After the show they had to bed down on hard benches in the venue because they were too late to get a train back home. 'It was a very exciting gig because it felt much more like the big time,' says Cliff. 'Suddenly I was fronting the band.'

Three weeks later Jerry Lee Lewis, one of the group's favourite American artists, played his first British concert. The tour was surrounded in controversy because news had leaked out that the new bride accompanying him was actually his fourteen-year-old cousin and he hadn't divorced his previous wife before the wedding.

Exposing the moral corruptness of a rock 'n' roll star was a job that the British press took to with great relish. They hounded Lewis during his stay in London and wrote editorials suggesting that the Home Secretary should deport him and teenagers should boycott his concerts.

Jerry Lee Lewis wasn't an avuncular figure like Bill Haley or a Southern gentleman like Elvis. With his narrow eyes and tight mouth he looked to be in a permanent state of mischief. His music was the look perfectly portrayed in sound – wild, sleazy, lustful, dangerous.

Cliff and the Drifters played 'Great Balls Of Fire' and 'Breathless' in their set and when they found that he was playing at the Kilburn State Theatre on Sunday 25 May they bought tickets as soon as they went on sale. The anti-Lewis publicity put out by The*People* and the *Daily Sketch* had its effect because on the night only a quarter of the seats had been sold.

'Jerry did a heck of a show that night to a poor audience,' remembers Samwell. 'There were one or two cat-calls and the people in front of us made rude noises when he stopped to comb his hair. John Foster, who was wearing his leather jacket, leant over and said, "One more peep out of you and that's your lot." They didn't make another noise.'

After the show John Foster thought of his greatest wheeze yet. He would take Terry Smart, Sammy Samwell and Cliff backstage so that he could brag about his future star. They found Lewis in his dressing room, wearing a ribbon tie and black gambler's jacket with leopardskin lapels, being photographed by a man from the *Daily Mirror*.

'I basically conned my way into the room by saying that Cliff was the latest British rock 'n' roll sensation,' says Foster. 'Of course, at that time he was nowhere near it. He'd hardly got used to the name Cliff Richard and had never been near a recording studio. Anyway, I asked if we could have our picture taken and we did, with Cliff standing right next to Jerry Lee.'

It was the closest any of them had come to a rock 'n' roll legend. Within a week Cliff was to have his own first taste of the fury and excitement that could attend rock 'n' roll.

Foster had booked the group into the Gaumont Teenage Show, a Saturday morning show at the Gaumont Theatre in Shepherd's Bush which mixed films, music, variety acts and celebrity appearances.

It was here that Cliff-mania began in a wave of frenzied screaming.

'We just weren't used to that sort of reaction from people,' says Mitham. 'It was the first reaction we had ever had to Cliff as a sex symbol. In Soho and Ripley you thought they were getting excited at the music but in Shepherd's Bush the audience was seated and they were screaming at Cliff.'

He had been playing rock 'n' roll for less than four months and had already stumbled on his natural audience. 'It didn't make sense and it felt unreal but I loved it,' he says. 'In those days the sound of girls screaming was the gauge of success.'

8

'I wanted a career so I got rid of the girlfriend'

On Saturday 14 June 1958 Cliff Richard and the Drifters returned to the Gaumont, this time as 'special guests' on a talent show.

Knowing that it was almost guaranteed to be another storming success, Sammy Samwell had been scanning entertainment newspapers to find an agent he could invite along. The names he saw meant nothing to him and so, at random, he picked on George Ganjou of George Ganjou Ltd. Entertainments, who regularly advertised on the back page of *The Stage*, and gave him a call.

What Samwell didn't know was that Ganjou was the least-likely agent to launch the career of a teenage rock 'n' roll group. Already in his late fifties, he had spent most of his life in Poland before coming to England as part of an adagio act, the Ganjou Brothers and Juanita, and when retiring as a performer he had become an agent for several variety acts. He knew nothing about rock 'n' roll beyond the fact that he didn't like it, and he proudly referred to himself as a 'square'.

Yet, to his credit, when John Foster and Sammy Samwell visited him at his Albemarle Street office on 6 June he agreed to come to the show despite the fact that it meant cancelling a weekend game of golf. He thought they were 'nice boys' and liked the looks of the singer whose photograph they showed him.

Ganjou suggested that Cliff and the Drifters should cut a demonstration record which he could play to his friends in the record industry. Early the next week they recorded two songs at a small studio above the HMV record shop in Oxford Street. They chose Elvis Presley's 'Lawdy Miss Clawdy', written by Lloyd Price, and Jerry Lee Lewis' 'Breathless', written by Otis Blackwell.

When they returned to the Gaumont that Saturday it caused an even greater storm than the debut. The audience was now primed and when Cliff hit the stage it was as if a dam had burst. His voice was barely audible above the screams and wails.

'As soon as Cliff started to sing, they all, especially the girls, went mad,' Ganjou remembered. 'They started to shout and rush towards him, and after seeing this I decided I'd better go back stage and have a talk to him.'

Ganjou's interest was aroused by show business common sense. Cliff looked good, seemed to have a pleasant personality and there was a demand for what he was doing. You didn't have to like rock 'n' roll to know you were on to a good thing here, and he had good connections with record companies through old dance band musicians who had gone on to become musical directors.

Samwell remembers being staggered when Ganjou came into the dressing room after the show and asked, 'Would you like to be on Decca or Columbia?' Samwell faked nonchalance and said his preference would be Columbia and so Ganjou said he would pass the demo disc to Norrie Paramor, a friend of his who was head of artists and repertoire for the EMI-owned Columbia label.

The scene in the dressing room that morning was a mixture of excitement and tension. There was a palpable sense that something very big was going to happen for them but also a slight fear of the teenage power that was being unleashed.

John Brunel, a reporter on the *Shepherd's Bush Gazette & Post* had been a judge on the morning's talent show (won by a local skiffle group called the Avro Boys) and described what he saw in his weekly column.

'Black-haired Cliff Richard had just been "sending" the fans and I found myself in a top floor room with the orders "Don't leave the building".

'No, I wasn't a political prisoner of the Rank Organization, but there were three hundred screaming fans down in the road below, the exit doors were being rattled and if we went out there it would have been like being thrown to the lions. So we stayed put, Cliff got out some buns (he had not had any breakfast) and we started the long wait.

'I asked a girl who introduced herself as the leader of Cliff's fan club how old he was. She did not know. Cliff ate another bun. The girls outside screamed more and we had to pretend we had left the building to kid them into leaving too.

'Who'd be a rock star? Not me.'

These experiences at the Gaumont convinced Cliff that something important was about to happen for him and he thought it was time to cool his relationship with Janice.

'I enjoyed being with her,' he says, 'but I can remember at that time feeling that I had to make a choice. I thought even then that if I was going to be a pop star my fans wouldn't want me to be married or to have a girlfriend. I could see how my sister Donna would quickly go off a pop star that she'd liked if she found out that they were engaged or married. The rock 'n' roll singer became a sex symbol and belonged to the fans.

'With Janice I had to make the decision that if I was going to go all out to be a pop star I didn't want any attachments. I didn't want anything to get in the way of me being famous and having loads and loads of girls chasing me all over the place.'

Janice had separately come to the same conclusion. She had too much self-respect to imagine herself as a bit-part player in a drama of rock 'n' roll and screaming girls.

'I can remember seeing mounted police outside the theatre and I had to stay inside while they got him out and it all worried me slightly,' she says. 'I remember thinking, "Well, this isn't me. I don't like this. I don't really like coming to these concerts."

'Cliff knew that if he was known to have a girlfriend it wouldn't be good from the point of view of his girl fans. It obviously looked better if he was a single fellow and available.

'So all these things meant that it was his and my decision that it was better if we separated.

'I remember the evening that it happened. He brought me home and we knew we were going to part anyway because we had been talking about it. We were standing in the porch of my house and he gave me the words of a song he had written for me. It said:

When teenagers love
They love for ever
When teenagers love
It's bound to be true
I'm a teenager in love
A teenager in love
I'm a teenager in love with you.

'I was literally crying on his shoulder after he handed me the piece of paper. It wasn't me saying that I'd had enough of him, it was a joint decision that this was the only thing we could do.

'I wanted Cliff to be successful. I wanted him to do well because he wanted to and I could actually see that I as in the way. I could see that he was better without a girlfriend. I don't mean without me in particular but that he was better off being single.'

It was the first of many times that Cliff would consider the options and always he has made the same choice with the same measure of apparently dispassionate calculation.

'It was far easier than it might appear looking back,' he says of the end of his romance with Janice. 'I wanted a career, I didn't want a girlfriend. So I got rid of the girlfriend. That's as brutal as I can put it. It didn't mean I liked her any less but I just made the cold-blooded choice to go for that. That's what I wanted.'

Within days of ending the relationship he was sitting in Norrie Paramor's office in Great Castle Street under consideration for the Columbia record label.

Norman William Paramor, known to everyone as 'Norrie', was forty-four years old and had been in the music business since leaving school at fifteen. He'd been a pianist, a band leader and, since 1949, a record company music director.

In common with George Ganjou he had no real experience of rock 'n' roll because he'd grown up in the big band era and, as a producer, was best known for working with old-style singers like Michael Holliday and Ruby Murray. His most recent hit was 'Lollipops' by a group called the Mudlarks.

Rock 'n' roll was still dubious music to these men who couldn't believe that the big band era was really over. They thought it was an American craze that would soon die out. Paramor had had a stab at producing the sound with Tony Crombie and his Rockets, Britain's first rock 'n' roll combo, back in 1956.

Older musicians who'd sweated through apprenticeships in dance bands and orchestras were angry at the new wave of guitar strummers and tea-chest bassists who were able to earn twice as much money with an eighth of the skill. The musical style that was liberating for a generation of teenagers was putting an older generation of professional musicians out of work.

Paramor was open-minded. He was a warm and gentle man with young daughters who were already dancing to the new music and he knew that in his position personal taste had to give way to market trends.

Although the acetate by Cliff Richard and the Drifters was crude and amateurish by professional standards, there was something about it which convinced him that they should be given an opportunity. He took it home and played it to his teenage daughter Caroline.

'She flipped when she heard it,' Paramor wrote a year later, 'and she double-flipped when I showed her Cliff's photo. This photo was not of Cliff alone but included the Drifters and American star Jerry Lee Lewis.' He arranged a meeting with Cliff. 'When he eventually turned up he brought his whole group along with him, complete with instruments. My immediate reaction was that if this youngster could go to the trouble of bringing his group along, the least I could do was to listen to what they had to offer.'

The boys plugged in their guitars and played to Paramor in his office. He later claimed that he was 'instantly filled with excitement by this thrilling sound,' but if he was, he managed to contain it for the moment and told the boys that he would make a decision over the next two weeks while he went on holiday to Tangier with his family. Cliff has since described this period as the longest fortnight of his life.

It wasn't wasted time. John Foster made up reel-to-reel tapes of a Drifters' performance and hawked them around to anyone who cared to listen. He mostly faced indifference, sometimes hostility. One record company told him that Cliff would never be a singer in a thousand years. Tommy Steele's agent told him to advise Cliff not to give up his day job.

The group carried on playing and rehearsing. On 15 June they played at the Freight Train, a coffee bar at 44 Berwick Street owned by skiffle star Chas McDevitt and named after his 1957 hit with Nancy Whiskey. Sammy Samwell wrote a letter of thanks to the coffee bar's manager who was obviously absent for the show:

'Despite the late arrival of your staff they [the Drifters] thoroughly enjoyed the evening and were pleased by the most appreciative audience. Unfortunately playing for almost three hours proved rather too strenuous, this was, however, compensated by the addition of eight new members to our "Fan" club.'

A week later they were at the Tudor Hall, Hoddesdon, supported by the Missin' Links, their main local rivals, and on 6 July they played the Astoria in Ware, sharing a double bill with a Kim Novak film. On the nights they weren't playing they would meet at Cliff's home and run through new songs.

An amusing note in the Broxbourne Borough Council files from 1958 records that on 5 July the occupant of 11 Hargreaves Close complained to them that a 'skiffle group' was playing every night at number 12 until eleven o'clock and that they should 'ask them to stop these long noisy evenings'.

The council officer obviously relayed the message to the Webb family for beneath the entry of the complaint was added the handwritten comment, 'Son not willing to co-operate'.

When Paramor returned from Tangier in mid-July, the news was good. Franklyn Boyd of the music publishers Aberbach Music had sent him a song called 'Schoolboy Crush' which had been a hit in America for Bobby Helms and Norrie thought it was a good number for Cliff to cover.

In those pre-Beatle days most artists neither wrote nor chose their own material. The power resided with the publishers and record companies. In Britain during the late fifties there was a tendency to feed out cover versions of American hits. Terry Dene had made it with Marty Robbins' 'A White Sports Coat' and Marty Wilde, Britain's latest new Elvis, had just scored with 'Endless Sleep', originally recorded by Jody Reynolds.

'Schoolboy Crush' was not a great song. It was a formula number of teenage angst in which a young student tells his 'baby doll' that even when they graduate she will be his 'steady date' because she's more than a 'schoolboy crush'.

Cliff was sent an acetate and learned the song in a day. 'Then he phoned me and told me that he'd like to come in and sing it to me,' said Paramor. 'He came up the same day with the Drifters and gave a faultless performance of the song. It impressed me enough to offer him a contract with Columbia.'

Even though it was Cliff Richard and the Drifters who had passed the audition, it was Cliff who was awarded the contract. This meant that although the group's name would appear on the record label, they would not be getting a percentage of the royalties. They would only be paid a fee for taking part in the recording session.

The most immediate problem was to find something to put on the B-side, the side of the record which wouldn't be getting radio play. The normal practice was to add a 'filler', a song with no real commercial potential. Because the 'mechanical' royalties (based on record sales rather than stage performances or radio plays) were the same as the A-side, producers often made themselves extra money by knocking up throwaway songs for flip sides and publishing them under assumed names.

Fortunately Samwell had just written his first song, called 'Move It', and they played it to Paramor. 'The arrangement was pretty rough and Cliff was not sure of the melody, but they gave such a spirited performance that I wasted no time in fixing up a session which would include Samwell's "Move It", which was to be the backing of "Schoolboy Crush".'

At the time it was virtually unheard of for a British rock 'n' roll group to record a song written by one of its members. The closest was perhaps Tony Crombie's co-writer credit on 'Rock 'n' Roller Coaster' (1957) or the writing of 'Rock With The Caveman' (1956) by Tommy Steele's friend Lionel Bart. That the song should become an A-side and then a national hit was unprecedented.

A rockabilly song with lots of American slang ('babe', 'honey', 'groove'), Samwell had written 'Move It' late in June while travelling from his mother's home in London Colney to Cliff's house in Cheshunt on a Green Line double-decker bus. He had wanted to create an authentic sounding rock 'n' roll song that would expose the pale British imitations. He sat upstairs in the back seat with his guitar on his knee and hit on the tune while deconstructing Chuck Berry licks to discover their secret.

The lyric was partly his response to a recent *Melody Maker* article by broadcaster and music writer Steve Race bemoaning the effect of rock 'n' roll on popular music. 'So rock-'n'-roll is dead, is it?' 37-year-old Race, a graduate of the Royal Academy of Music, had challenged. 'All right then. My funeral oration consists of just two words: good riddance.'

He went on to wonder whether ballads might be coming back into fashion and concluded, 'As of early June, 1958, there is no clear sign about what the next craze will be. Indeed, there may not be another craze at all. The record-buying public has not shifted its allegiance to some other kind of music: ithas merely stopped buying so many records. That, too, is all to the good. Perhaps now we shall see some sense of proportion returning to the pop music business.'

It wasn't an unusual rant for the time. There were many of his generation who were only too glad to leap in and write the obituary of rock 'n' roll. Samwell's response was:

They say, it's gonna die: Oh! Honey please, let's face it;
They just don't know what's a-goin' to replace it.
Ballads and Calypsos, have got nothing on
real Country music that just drives along.
Oh! Honey move it.

'By the time I got to Cliff's house the song was complete,' he remembers. 'I just played it to the rest of them, including my introduction. I had to rewrite the lyric out because it was full of bits and pieces and Cliff needed to be able to read it. I used to put the "ah"s and the "uh-huh"s in because you need to have every nuance there.'

Mitham became the first casualty of the new-found success. Samwell felt that his guitar added nothing to the overall sound and that it was a waste of money having three guitars when two would be adequate.

'Sammy was older than us and having served in the RAF seemed much more a man of the world, and he said that I was only duplicating

Cliff's guitar work,' says Mitham. 'What you have to remember is that Cliff and I had been friends since we were nine or ten and we had gone through a lot together. Now it had got to the stage where an outsider had turned round and said, "I think you ought to get rid of Norman." I'm sure Cliff gave it a lot of thought but he told me that was what had been suggested and I said I agreed but it's not going to stop a friendship. Then that was it. I was out of the story.'

For the recording at EMI Studios in Abbey Road on 24 July Paramor hired two seasoned session men. His original plan had been to use the Ken Jones Orchestra, whom he had used to back Michael Holliday, but Cliff was insisitent on a group sound. In 1958 there could be re-takes of a song but no overdubbing or mixing because it was all recorded onto a single-track tape, and for 'Schoolboy Crush' and 'Move It' there was only three hours of studio time booked.

Paramor brought in Frank Clarke on double bass and Ernie Shear on electric guitar. Both men were in their early thirties and had a wealth of experience playing in orchestras. To them it was just another session, Cliff was a fresh-faced young kid, and rock 'n' roll was a new musical craze they knew they'd have to get used to if they wanted to stay in business.

'Schoolboy Crush', the first track of the evening, didn't really showcase their talents. It had no fire in its belly and was covered in a souffle of background vocals from the Michael Sammes Singers . But on 'Move It' their talents combined to produce a sound that could have come straight out of Memphis, Tennessee.

The guitar introduction has become such a classic of early British rock 'n' roll that there have been arguments ever since about who invented it and how much they got paid for it. The truth is that the idea was Samwell's, and the execution was Shear's. Samwell was smart enough to know he didn't have the competence to play lead guitar on the single so he showed Shear the riff he'd come up with, and Shear then translated the sketch into a full-colour masterpiece.

Samwell, meanwhile, played rhythm guitar.

'I think we just talked about it in the studio and it developed,' says Shear. 'It was really a busking session for us even though we read music. I didn't even have a solid-body electric guitar then so I used to use a Hoffner acoustic with a D'Armond pick-up which I bought in America. To get the top sound I used to push it near the bridge. I wanted to get the toppiest sound I could get.'

When the session started, Peter Bown had been engineering but he had to leave for an appointment at the opera and so he handed over to his assistant Malcolm Addey, a junior engineer who had only been with the studio four months. There were rule books at EMI Studios in those days which even went as far as stipulating the volume at which music should be recorded. Addey allowed 'Move It' to go over the limit, and this added to its authentic sound.

It was a great performance. British rock 'n' roll records up until this date had been insipid affairs that had none of the clarity and attack of the Americans. With 'Move It' there was, at last, a single that offered a challenge to the originators.

Hearing it for the first time some twenty years later Carl Perkins, author of 'Blue Suede Shoes' and a former Sun Records artist, commented:

'That sound could have been made in Sun Studios in 1954. It's basic rockabilly music. That guitar is doing what we did. He's got some echo and he's working on more than one string. He's getting three of the bass strings and he's doubling up on the bottom. That's very good.'

Paramor quickly had test pressings made up and circulated them to his contacts, and seven days after the recording Cliff was featured in a prominent *Daily Mirror* article written by record columnist Patrick Doncaster under the headline 'New Recruit For The Disc War'.

Although he committed himself to no more than the claim that Cliff had 'a personality that shines through the grooves,' and that 'he could succeed in Discland,' it was an impressive amount of editorial space for an office lad who had yet to release his first record.

Publisher Franklyn Boyd was also doing the rounds with test pressings because of his stake in 'Schoolboy Crush' and he wanted TV and radio exposure. His first contact was Dennis Main Wilson who was producing '6.5 Special'. Wilson liked the record but couldn't use Cliff for six weeks so Boyd contacted his opposite number on independent television, Jack Good, who earlier in the year had done two pilot shows of 'Oh Boy!' and was planning an autumn series.

Good was one of the geniuses of British rock 'n' roll whose understanding of the medium was at least a decade ahead of its time. He cut an odd figure in the world of greasy-haired teenage school-leavers with tight jeans and James Dean scowls. He was a 27-year-old Oxford graduate with thick glasses and a booming voice, whose eyes would pop out with excitement when he heard something he liked. But his taste was impeccable and his faith in pure rock 'n' roll remained, and remains, unshakable.

Boyd made an appointment to see him and played a white label of 'Schoolboy Crush' on Good's office record player. Good listened politely but was non-committal. He recounted what happened next in his 'Sidetracks' column in *Disc* on 9 August, when he told the story of how he had just heard 'the most amazing first recording made by any teenage artiste in Britain'.

In a full-page article under the headline 'Just another beginner? No — this boy is really terrific!' Good wrote, 'Then he [Boyd] spins what he laughingly refers to as the "flip-side". Wham! This disc could sell 50,000 on its first eight bars alone.

'It kicks off with a forceful, dramatic guitar phrase that runs an electric shock down the spine. In comes the drum, driving a vicious beat right through the heart of the number. Then the voice rides confidently over this glorious backing — a voice with an amazingly 'non-imitative' style, considering that this kind of music ought by rights to be foreign to anyone who is not a native of the Southern States.

'The diction is clear; the phrasing authentic, professional — there is a real feeling for this country-and-western style. If this disc had been a product of Sun records of Memphis, Tennessee — the original recording company of Elvis Presley and Jerry Lee Lewis — I should not have been surprised, but would still have rated it as important and good enough to be compared, though not, of course, on equal terms, with those two giants of the beat.

'But when one considers that this is the product of a 17-year-old boy from Cheshunt, Hertfordshire, the mind just boggles.'

Good was immediately eager to see the artist in the flesh. He couldn't believe that he would look as good as he sounded. He was sure that there would be some physical drawback and that 'Move It' was just a fluke of the recording studio. An audition was arranged for the following evening at Max Rivers Rehearsal Rooms at 10–11 Great Newport Street, just around the corner from Leicester Square underground station.

In a room on the third floor Cliff and the Drifters played while agent George Ganjou lurked hopefully in the corridor outside.

'I thought it was wonderful,' says Good. 'I thought he was a good singer but there was nothing special about his physical performance. He just bounced up and down adequately and I thought he looked a bit trashy with his sideburns.'

Good's recollection is that he agreed to book him there and then and walked Cliff down to the underground while explaining to him that the guitar and the sideburns would have to go before he made an appearance on 'Oh Boy!'. Boyd doesn't think he decided that quickly.

'Jack loved him but Jack's wife, Margit, didn't like him at all. So when we came away Jack said, "Look, I like him." So I said, "Are you going to use him?" He said he didn't know and that he would try to sort it out. But his wife was quite adamant that she didn't like

Cliff. He then rang me a couple of days later and said, "OK, I'm going to use him but he's not going to be singing 'Schoolboy Crush'. He's going to be doing the B-side." '

Margit Good can't remember the audition but says that it's quite likely that she was apprehensive. 'I tended to be the more pessimistic one,' she admits. 'Jack was always totally enthusiastic about everything. I would imagine that the fact that Cliff looked like a shy little boy, definitely non-show business, would have made me wonder – what on earth are you going to do with him?'

The day that Good's article hit the news stands, and alerted the music industry to the 'exciting newcomer', was coincidentally Cliff's last day working at Atlas Lamps. Ganjou, who was the sole entertainments booker for Billy Butlin's holiday camps, had offered him a two-week contract singing at their 2,000-capacity Clacton camp and the only way to fulfil the engagement was to leave his job and turn professional.

Cliff had only ever spent one night away from his mother and father. Most young people in the fifties were naïve compared to later generations but Cliff struck those he met as having been particularly protected. Tulah Tuke was a young actress employed by Radio Butlin and recalls that her chalet mate, who was known as Randy Rene, made a play for him one night.

'He was very young and very unsophisticated and didn't know what on earth was happening. She managed to get Cliff back to the chalet but I think he brought John Foster with him as protection. I remember thinking that he was very young even for his age. He was seventeen but I thought of him as sixteen.'

Foster remembers it as a time of good clean fun. Only he and Samwell smoked (which is why they had to share a chalet), none of the boys were big drinkers and no one had time for girlfriends.

'In those days it was big news to sleep with a girl,' says Foster. 'You didn't want to set up a lasting relationship with someone who slept around. We were still all innocent boys and women were up on a pedestal somewhere.'

During the first week the camp's entertainment manager moved them around because he couldn't find the right venue for a rock 'n' roll trio. Drinkers in the camp pub, The Jolly Roger, weren't the right generation to appreciate Cliff Richard and the Drifters and they didn't contribute to the ambience of the Hawaiian style cocktail bar, so they were finally assigned to the Rock 'n' Roll Ballroom.

A poor-quality tape recording of one of their sets survives. It was made by Stan Edwards, a fellow Red-Coat entertainer, who set a reel-to-reel tape recorder on a chair in the middle of the ballroom. The guitar sound is unsurprisingly thin and limited but Cliff's vocals are already well developed although hampered by an obvious affection for Elvis. He puts a little too many 'uh-huh's into every song and doesn't yet have the confidence to match the looseness he's striving for.

The set list is dominated by songs made popular by Elvis and Jerry Lee Lewis. He starts with Eddie Cochran's 'Twenty Flight Rock', then sings 'Move It' and 'Breathless'. This is followed by five Elvis songs — 'Money Honey', 'Heartbreak Hotel', 'Hound Dog', 'I Got A Woman' and 'Milkcow Blues Boogie' — before closing with 'Move It' and 'Whole Lotta Shakin' Goin' On'.

On 'Milkcow Blues Boogie' he even follows the pattern of Elvis' Sun Records recording where the song is started as a lazy blues before Elvis stops the musicians and says, 'Hold it fellows. That don't move me. Let's get real real gone for a change' before launching into a rocked-up version. In a jive American accent Cliff can be heard saying, 'Wait a minute fellows. That don't move none. Let's get real real gone for a change, huh?'

Pre-release copies of 'Move It' had been sent by EMI to Radio Butlin which broadcast throughout the camp.

'When Cliff's acetate came in I was just grateful to have something that I could chat about,' remembers Tulah Tuke. 'I could say that he was playing on site and announce the venue. I gave the record a great plug and the next thing I knew was that Cliff and John Foster were standing at the door saying 'That's the first time we've heard it. It's great. Thanks a lot. Can we hear it again?' So they came in to my studio and I played it to them. That must make me the first person ever to play a Cliff Richard record to the public. I was certainly the first person to play a Cliff Richard record to Cliff!'

It was also while at Clacton that the group first heard the record on Radio Luxembourg. 'It was unbelievable,' says Foster. 'They may have played both sides of the single but I definitely remember "Move It" and after that they started to play it quite regularly.'

When they returned home from Butlin's there was more good news waiting for them. Mark Forster, who worked for top promoter Arthur Howes, was offering them a spot on an October tour of Britain headlined by the Kalin Twins. Their fee would be two hundred pounds a week, the most money they had ever earned.

Then there was a letter from Jack Good, who had auditioned Cliff and the Drifters for 'Oh Boy!'. They would be needed the next day, Sunday 7 September, for the first rehearsals of 'Oh Boy!'.

9

'I didn't want the real Cliff Richard. Real people on television are boring'

Jack Good invented rock 'n' roll television. He was working as an actor understudying Wilfred Lawson on a 1956 television drama when he went to see the film *Rock Around The Clock* one afternoon when he wasn't needed at the rehearsal room in Islington. The experience was to change his life.

Whereas the film *The Blackboard Jungle* had simply used Haley's song in the soundtrack, *Rock Around The Clock*, directed by Sam Katzman, was chock full of rock 'n' roll. There was not only Bill Haley but Little Richard, the Platters, and Freddie Bell and the Bellboys. For Good it was an experience of pure primitive theatrical excitement.

'I had always hated pop music,' he says, 'and therefore this rock 'n' roll appealed to me in a perverse way because I immediately realized that Frank Sinatra would hate it, and I loathed Frank Sinatra. Rock 'n' roll had a raw excitement and that was what I liked about theatre.

'To me, Laurence Olivier was an exciting actor, and Shakespeare done right was exciting. There was nothing like it. It seems ridiculous to say it, but there was something electrifying in good rock 'n' roll, and that's what I liked.'

Shortly afterwards he abandoned his short-lived career as an actor to work for the BBC where he thought there might even be opportunities to translate the excitement of rock 'n' roll into television.

His chance came when he was paired with Josephine Douglas and asked to come up with a winning formula for a teenage programme that would fit the space immediately after six o'clock in the evening. Up until then it had been left 'dark' so that parents could use the time to put children to bed. What they came up with was the '6.5 Special'.

The first show was broadcast in February 1957 but there were too many compromises for Good's liking. There was a bit of rock 'n' roll – a duo he had discovered on a United States Air Force base, called Bobby and Rudy, singing 'I'm Gonna Teach You To Rock', and a clip of Little Richard from the film *The Girl Can't Help It* – but there were a lot of features that certainly weren't rock 'n' roll: a boys' choir, a team of Hungarian acrobats, trumpeter Kenny Baker and Pouishnoff playing Mozart.

There was a conflict of ideas between Josephine Douglas, who wanted healthy Boy Scout-type features on such hobbies as stamp collecting and mountaineering, and Good who wanted to terrorize adults and excite teenagers with his vision of wild abandon.

Realizing that he was never going to have his way with the BBC, who were warning that rock 'n' roll was on its way out, Good left and joined the independent television company ABC. They allowed him to produce two trial live rock 'n' roll programmes at the Wood Green Empire in June 1958. Good called the shows 'Oh Boy!' after Buddy Holly's song.

These two half-hour shows were topped by Marty Wilde, a lanky South Londoner who had shot to prominence after an appearance on '6.5 Special', and they moved faster than anything seen before on British television.

'I wanted pace, attack and no chat,' says Good. 'I hated light entertainment. I wanted next number, next number. I'm bored with that, next number . . . so by the time you were sick of somebody they were off and the next act was on flash, flash, flash! I wanted it to jump. I wanted action. I wanted the lights to go on cue, the music to go on cue and the audience to go up in the air and everything to be like a Cadillac zooming down a freeway.

'The lighting was very important. I had seen a photo of Ricky Nelson standing in a strong spotlight which was circled on the floor, and that shot was seminal to the look I wanted. Also there was a company called Theatro Nationale Populaire who put on Shakespeare but they did it all with black and white lighting and very little in the way of sets.

'At the time I was into the psychological effect of rhythm and lights. I was into all sorts of strange books about brainwashing and the effects of voodoo. I thought I was doing the public a favour by introducing these things to television. William Sargent's book *Battle For The Mind* (subtitled 'A Physiology of Conversion and Brain Washing' and first published in 1957) was very influential.

'I wanted to create tremendous tension and excitement which I justified in my mind as being a form of catharsis as described by the Greeks. I thought that the kids would let off steam in the theatre and would then be peaceful and passive when they went back on the streets. Absolute rubbish! It worked quite the other way. I should never have been let loose.'

It was a powerful concoction and knocked spots off '6.5 Special', which was cosy and amateurish in comparison. ABC knew they were on to a winner and gave Good a spot between 6 and 6.30 each Saturday evening beginning on 13 September 1958 and lasting for as long as they could see.

Good began pulling together a show that would be transmitted live from the Empire Theatre in Hackney. He planned to keep the line-up that he'd had at Wood Green — instrumentals from the John Barry Seven, vocal harmonies from the Dallas Boys and the Vernons Girls, a Fats Domino style rhythm blast from Lord Rockingham's XI led by

Harry Robinson, Hammond organ music from South African Cherry Wainer and solo spots from Marty Wilde, Bernice Reading and Ronnie Carroll. The last-minute addition, made after hearing 'Move It', was Cliff Richard and the Drifters.

Rehearsals for 'Oh Boy!' were intensive. Cliff was needed for a full week to go through 'Move It' and 'Don't Bug Me Baby' because Good wanted to plan every move and build a persona for Cliff that would make him instantly recognizable in a crowded market-place.

His plan had swung into action the first evening they met when he told Cliff that the obvious similarities with Elvis would have to go. 'Although we were keen to have someone on "Oh Boy!" who would have the impact that Elvis did, we didn't want an Elvis impersonator. Also, Cliff clearly couldn't play the guitar very well and this would prove very limiting for the shots.'

Having eradicated the most obvious of the Elvis traits, Good set about building Cliff Richard. He was to be a young naïve teenager surging with sexual energy, but apparently unaware of it.

'He was very slim and innocent looking,' says Good. 'We presented him as if it was beyond him not to smoulder and yet he didn't mean to. That was the excitement. Elvis looked as though he'd knocked around a bit and he would bump and grind and sneer. Cliff didn't do any of that. He would be withdrawn, and the audience would come to him.'

Every day for the week before the first show Cliff would go to the 'Oh Boy!' rehearsal room at the Four Provinces of Ireland club in Canonbury Lane, Islington. Vernons Girl Maggie Streader remembers him coming in looking like a little boy lost, obviously overawed at being surrounded by hardened professionals, television executives and music business hangers-on.

'He was so sweet,' she remembers. 'He was around the same age as us but when you saw him you just wanted to look after him. There was no brashness. He wasn't "of the business" as it were. I think we girls were a bit overpowering for him.'

Good would work through the songs with Cliff line by line. Cliff was so self-conscious that he had to be tutored in a room away from the rest of the cast. Good taught him to hide the pointed tooth that still bothered him, to tilt his head at the camera and raise his eyes up and, most effectively, to suddenly grab at his arm 'as if stuck with a hypodermic syringe' at key emotional points in the songs. The word 'sex' was never mentioned.

In February 1959 Good wrote about these rehearsals in his *Disc* column.

'"Move It" was probably the most difficult number I have had to produce so far,' he said. 'Cliff and I spent some hours getting the thing absolutely right for his first TV appearance... Every blink, every change in the pose of the head, every gesture, had to be worked out and made meaningful.

'The whole song was broken down into fragments. At last, each fragment was right. Then came the very difficult job of putting all the component parts together and creating not a mass of details, but a complete and meaningful whole. Above all, the finished product must not seem to have been worked over to the nth degree. It has to seem quite fresh and unconsidered.'

For stagewear Cliff had a pink jacket and black tapered trousers (which he had made to measure by a tailor in Dean Street, Soho), pink tie, black shirt and pink socks. It was his decision to develop this image although the idea wasn't original. Elvis had been buying pink and lime-green jackets from Lanksy Brothers clothing store on Beale Street in Memphis and wearing them with black peg-legged trousers. But, in those grim post-war days when most fathers were still wearing the black or grey suits they had been issued with on leaving the armed forces, it was a fashion statement which excited the young and worried the old.

'If a woman wore shocking pink in those days it was considered quite brave,' says *Observer* journalist Janet Watts, who saw Cliff in concert in 1958 when she was a teenager. 'For a man to wear pink was alarming! For us it was liberation. It was a splash of fun and colour into what had become a very grey world.'

On the day of the broadcast there were two further rehearsals: one in the morning for vision only, one in the afternoon for sound and vision. The director was Rita Gillespie, a woman in her mid-twenties who had little experience of rock 'n' roll but saw it as an opportunity to experiment with television. It was from her carefully-prepared camera scripts, based on listening to the songs, that Good developed his stage directions.

'Cliff was very inexperienced and he wanted to be told what to do,' says Rita. 'I loved shooting him. He had the perfect face for television. I never tired of close-ups and profiles of him.

'Once, by sheer accident, I caught him singing something with a "t" or an "s" in it, and his spit was highlighted by the arc lights as a glittering tiny speck. After that I kept waiting for the same thing to happen again.'

It would complete the fairytale to say that Cliff tore the house down on his TV debut, but the response was muted. The screams were reserved for Marty Wilde, already a TV star, who was at four in the charts with 'Endless Sleep'. But the effect of the national exposure was undeniable. The following week he returned to sing 'Schoolboy Crush' and by the week ending 27 September 'Move It' had entered *Melody Maker*'s top twenty chart at number twelve.

Good's coaching had paid off. The reserved boy from Cheshunt was now regarded as both 'moody' and 'sexy'. Before the year ended he would be accused of 'crude exhibitionism' and 'short-sighted vulgarity' by *New Musical Express* (in an anonymous attack by its publisher Maurice Kinn) and the *Daily Sketch* would ask, 'Is this boy TV star too sexy?'

Good just used to laugh at these stories. Cliff took up Elvis' argument that he meant no harm — it was the beat that made him do it.

'I can't help it if people say I'm too sexy in my singing,' he said. 'I can't help it. I don't push it, believe me. I just get carried away. It's just that I do exactly what the songs tell me inside I gotta do.'

For the Kalin Twins' tour new musicians needed to be drafted in to work with Cliff. They had met a guitarist called Ken Pavey at Butlin's who had filled in for them but he'd been offered a residency in a pub in Wood Green and didn't want to pass on what looked like a secure job for the sake of a rock 'n' roll tour. This left Cliff with Samwell now playing bass, Smart playing drums and a tour due to start on 5 October. Foster went down the 2 I's to find a replacement.

'I went to meet Tony Sheridan, a very good guitarist. While waiting for him I met Hank Marvin who got his guitar out and and played a few Buddy Holly riffs and something by Ricky Nelson's guitarist James Burton. It turned out that he was already on the tour playing for the Most Brothers so I asked him to double up by playing for us as well. Hank agreed to it but he wanted to bring his mate Bruce Welch who played rhythm guitar.

'The next I heard of Tony Sheridan was when he cut his first single in Germany with the Beatles as his backing group.'

Hank Marvin and Bruce Welch were two sixteen year olds who had come to London from Newcastle to play in the finals of a talent contest with their skiffle group the Railroaders, and had never returned.

Their recent past was remarkably similar to Cliff's. They had both started playing skiffle in 1957, flunked out of school with no qualifications, changed their names to sound more American (Hank's real name was Brian Rankin, and Bruce's Bruce Cripps). Both had played rock 'n' roll and headed for the 2 I's because they had heard that this was the place where things happened.

When they arrived in London in April 1958, Cliff was already playing at the 2 I's but they didn't catch sight of him until July when Welch, who took a job in the coffee bar working the orange juice machine, went back and told Hank about the most exciting

British rock 'n' roll singer he had ever seen.

Hank was by then in the Vipers, the one-time skiffle group which Wally Whyton was updating to meet the challenge of rock 'n' roll by adding drums and electric guitars. What Whyton didn't know was that he was creating the Shadows in embryo. Besides Hank on guitar he had Tony Meehan on drums and Terence 'Jet' Harris on bass.

'We went out and had a bit of a disastrous tour,' remembers Whyton. 'We had new amplifiers which blew up and at that point I decided I didn't want to be involved with electric music. So I went off busking in the South of France and the lads asked me if it was alright if they went out with Cliff who was touring for three weeks. I said, "Do exactly as you want." '

The first rehearsal of the new Drifters was at 12 Hargreaves Close. Cliff, Hank Marvin, Bruce Welch, Terry Smart and Sammy Samwell worked through a set of 'Baby I Don't Care', 'Don't Bug Me Baby', 'Blueberry Hill', 'Move It', 'Whole Lotta Shakin' Goin' On' and 'King Creole'.

'The drumkit was set up in the living room,' remembers Hank. 'The rest of us played electric guitars through amplifiers that were the size of cornflake packets which meant that it wasn't particularly noisy. But we could see straight away that Cliff really had something going for him.'

Two days before the tour Cliff recorded another Samwell song at Abbey Road, 'High Class Baby'. Again Paramor hired Frank Clarke and Ernie Shear to beef up the sound, but this time it didn't work. It wasn't their fault. 'High Class Baby' was a colourless song.

When Cliff got home that evening he broke down and cried. He thought his career was over, that everything he had attained had been through a recording fluke. 'I thought that was it,' says Cliff 'It just didn't compare in any way to "Move It".'

The Kalin Twins' tour began on 5 October at the Victoria Hall, Hanley and Cliff Richard and the Drifters were booked to open up the second half of a show that started with sets from the Most Brothers, the Londonaires and Eddie Calvert.

Calvert was an old-time trumpeter, produced by Norrie Paramor for Columbia, who'd had several hits (including two number ones) since his chart debut in 1953 with 'Oh Mein Papa'. The Londonaires were a jazz-based trio and the Most Brothers were, according to Mickie Most, 'an Everly Brothers with bad harmonies'.

At the time the Grade Agency booked the tour, the Kalin Twins had a number one single with 'When' but it had since fallen while 'Move It' was still climbing. This put the Kalins in the unenviable position of closing the show after a set by one of the hottest acts in the country.

Hal and Herbie Kalin were not a rock 'n' roll act. They were twenty-four years old at a time when pop stars were expected to be teenagers, and had started out singing Frankie Laine and Johnnie Ray songs. What made them acceptable to a rock 'n' roll audience was the fact that they looked younger than they were, they had a hit record and they were American.

The Kalins had come to Britain expecting to discover that Cliff Richard was a nice-looking boy who couldn't sing. They had worked in America with Fabian, a handsome Italian who had trouble holding a tune in his head or keeping to the beat. But what they saw on stage in Hanley on that opening night made them realize that Cliff not only had a hit but had a voice to carry it off on stage.

'He tore the house down,' says Hal Kalin. 'Then the audience would have to go from that to, "And now ladies and gentlemen the Kalin Twins" and you'd hear a five-piece jazz band trying to outdo what the Drifters had just played. Our volume alone was half theirs! It was a constant battle.

'Then there was a shift during the last four or five dates when they arranged to put Cliff on last because it was obviously not working out with us. There was no way we could compete with an up-and-coming seventeen year old. It had become a nightmare for us.'

The second night of the tour, at the Odeon, Blackpool, was

reviewed in the *West Lancashire Evening Gazette* by someone who, in common with a lot of show business correspondents of the day, persisted in evaluating a rock 'n' roll performance as if it was a new music hall turn.

'The package, tied up by wisecracking, crewcut compère Tony Marsh, contained a collection of 'pop' musicians to the exclusion of comics, jugglers and tumblers who used to be measured amongst the choice of the music hall,' wrote the anonymous critic.

'The show pleased teenagers, but there were not enough there to fill more than a third of the house.

'The American Kalin Twins, whose disc "When" has only just slipped from the top rung of the hit parade, made the boys and girls yell for more. And Cliff Richards [sic], a new British recording star, generated almost as much excitement as he rocked and roared in a "shocking pink" jacket, surrounded by four bandsmen, dressed in sinister style in black shirts and wearing sunglasses, and the jumble of wiring and amplifiers which transmit the latest sound.'

Standing in the wings as Cliff and the Drifters played those opening nights was Jet Harris, Wally Whyton's nineteen-year-old bass guitarist who had been picked up for the tour by Mickie Most.

'I still maintain that "Move It" was the turning point for British rock and roll,' he says. 'It certainly shook me because I was a staunch jazz man. Then, partway through the tour, Cliff asked me if I'd like to beef up the sound by playing bass with the Drifters. I said "yes" straight away.'

Jet was not only older than the rest of the group but he was more worldly-wise and more experienced as a musician. Whereas Cliff and Hank looked like home-loving lads, Jet with his bleached blond hair kept in place by Vitapointe and his permanently dangling cigarette could have been the member of a street gang.

He had started playing clarinet in jazz clubs at the age of fifteen and had then switched to double bass and worked with Terry Dene, Larry Page, Tubby Hayes, Ronnie Scott, Don Lang, Wee Willie Harris and

Tony Crombie. It was the jazz drummer Crombie who suggested that he switched to a bass guitar.

'He played a Framus with a thin semi-acoustic body which sounded great at a time when everyone else was playing stand-up bass,' says Hank. 'He was also a very driving player who liked to turn up the volume and give it a lot of bottom end.

'He'd been around a lot longer than we had and had a concept of advanced chord sequences and how to play against them. To us he was like the old man of music.'

His image was that of the brooding bohemian and he added a neat rebellious hint to the Drifters. Where Cliff abstained from alcohol, Jet would drink it until he fell down. Where Cliff seemed unfazed by female attention, Jet was never without a woman. Where Cliff went home to life with mum and dad in Cheshunt, Jet returned to a basement flat in Eccleston Square, behind Victoria Station, which he shared with a collection of musicians, a fox, two monkeys, a dog, a cat and a skunk called Sam. His bedroom was carpeted with newspapers, had a broom handle fixed in the doorway as a wardrobe and was lit with a single bare light bulb.

'He looked incredible,' remembers Cliff 'He had a quiff, he was gaunt... he was everything I wasn't. Jack Good once described him as "the moody, magnificent Jet Harris" and said that only Cliff Richard could ever stand in front of him.'

Even at the age of nineteen Jet had a reputation for being edgy and unreliable. Wee Willie Harris, an eccentric piano player who was dyeing his hair pink in 1957, employed Jet and found him difficult to be around.

'He was always a bag of nerves,' he says. 'He used to drive me mental. Whenever we shared a dressing room he would be up and down like a yo-yo pacing backwards and forwards. Just watching him would get me going.'

In 1958 touring conditions were primitive. All the artists travelled in an unheated Bedford coach driven by Ron King of Timpson's

Coaches, and everyone but the headlining act had to find their own accommodation on arrival.

'They all had to pay for their own digs out of their wages,' remembers King. 'They would take the cheapest digs they could find even if it meant sleeping on the bus, which they nicknamed the "Hotel Bedford".'

The sound for performances was normally fed through two house speakers which would be positioned high up at either side of the stage. The drums wouldn't be miked and so the only sound worth checking was the sound made on the stage.

'There were no PA systems as such,' says Bruce Welch, 'and as for lights, it was just a matter of whether you wanted them on or off.'

Performances were brisk — the closing act was only on stage for eighteen minutes — and backing musicians were shared around to cut costs. Eddie Calvert 's band supported the Kalin Twins and Hank was putting in performances for all the acts except the Londonaires. Jet was now playing for the Most Brothers and Cliff.

After playing Manchester on 10 October Cliff returned to London to appear on 'Oh Boy!'. He was in Liverpool on the 12th, where in the audience was a sixteen-year-old local boy called Paul McCartney. 'My dad had a mate who used to work on the stage door,' says McCartney. 'And I can remember he got me Eddie Calvert's autograph.'

Two days later, at the De Montfort Hall in Leicester, it was Cliff's eighteenth birthday. The fans threw birthday presents on the stage and the whole audience of 2,500 sang 'Happy Birthday' to him. On 19 October, at the Colston Hall, Bristol, the tour came to an end. 'Move It' was now at number four in the charts.

10

'The kids liked him, but he didn't have an act'

George Ganjou, who had been used to booking variety acts, was already out of his depth as an agent. John Foster, not as good at business as he was at bluff, stood no chance at arm wrestling with the power brokers of British show business.

Norrie Paramor spoke to Cliff and his father about the situation and recommended Franklyn Boyd, the publisher of 'Schoolboy Crush', as a man to manage Cliff's career as he was older and well-connected in the music industry.

Franklyn Boyd had the advantage of having been a singer himself He had left the RAF in 1946 and worked with Teddy Foster's Orchestra for three years, later singing with Oscar Rabin and Eric Winstone. He agreed to handle Cliff's affairs as long as he didn't have to leave his job with Aberbach Music. John Foster was retained as road manager and put on an uncontracted salary of twelve pounds a week.

Then there was the question of the Drifters. Cliff was well satisfied with the addition of Hank Marvin and Bruce Welch but he was aware that their proficiency now exposed the weaknesses of Samwell and Smart. He knew that eventually they would have to go, and first of all he decided to get rid of Sammy.

He wasn't told right away. After the Kalin tour there were no immediate dates to play and Samwell took a break. What he didn't know was that although the Drifters weren't playing, they were hard at work practising and that his replacement on bass guitar was Jet Harris.

It was only when he turned up with a new song that he realized he had been ousted. Still he wasn't told by Cliff. 'I think it might well have been John Foster who had to break me the bad news,' he remembers.

'Even though I didn't have to do the telling, it was a hard decision because Sammy was a friend,' says Cliff. 'This sort of thing never becomes easier but I have to be single-minded when I want something new. In 1958 the decision was based on the fact that Hank was the best guitarist, Jet was the best on bass, and that meant there was no room for Sammy.'

Cliff was now becoming the star of 'Oh Boy!', much to the chagrin of Marty Wilde's manager Larry Parnes who had seen the show as the perfect showcase for his boy and others, like Vince Eager, who he was currently grooming. While Cliff and Marty remained friends, sang together on the shows and admired each other's work, Larry Parnes tussled with Jack Good over the lack of attention he felt his protégé was getting.

Parnes was the most important rock 'n' roll manager in Britain and was determined to control as much of the scene as he could. He was born in north-west London to a Jewish family in the clothing trade. After school he managed women's clothing stores before being attracted to the theatre, where he invested a small amount of money in a touring play.

His big break came in September 1956 when John Kennedy, a publicity agent, told him about rock 'n' roll and introduced him to Tommy Hicks, a merchant seaman he'd seen playing at the 2 I's. The two men took over his career, and as Tommy Steele he became Britain's first rock 'n' roll star. Marty Wilde was their second discovery.

The battle that Parnes was creating between Marty and Cliff was partly built out of resentment that Cliff didn't belong to him. A major-league rock 'n' roll star had developed in Britain and he didn't have a share of him.

On 18 October this resentment spilled over into a full-blooded row. Both Cliff and Wilde were scheduled to appear on the show and Marty turned up in a steel-grey mohair suit which Good said he couldn't wear because it wouldn't work with the lights.

'When I told him that, Parnes flew into a rage and threatened to pull him out of the show if he couldn't wear the suit,' says Good. 'In the end I had to call a security guard to usher Parnes out of the theatre.'

Wilde did the show but Parnes pulled him out of the series and didn't allow him to come back until 7 February 1959. By this time he had been eclipsed by Cliff who was now in such demand that he didn't have the time to appear regularly on 'Oh Boy!'.

Wilde then lost out on the role of Bongo Herbert in *Expresso Bongo* which Cliff was eventually offered. The reason was mainly because producer Val Guest thought that Wilde, who stood six feet three inches tall, was 'too big to feel sorry for'. Parnes put an amusing spin on the rejection when he told the press that he thought it was 'a suitable part for a smaller talent than Marty'.

The Cliff versus Marty feud made great newspaper copy and kept both their names alive.

'The "Oh Boy!" row was the best thing that ever happened to Cliff Richard and the biggest boost to his career,' says Franklyn Boyd. 'It made the front page of the *Daily Mirror*. It was unbelievable. Cliff was immediately a big star because he made the front page of a national newspaper. Having a number one record doesn't make headline news but this hullabaloo did.'

What concerned Boyd was Cliff's inexperience as a performer. Television and radio commitments were keeping him in London during the week and he was only playing out of town on Sunday nights.

'Cliff was terrible in those Sunday night concerts,' he admits. 'You had people like Rory Blackwell who had come out of the jazz clubs and they were killing him. Cliff was top of the bill but all these other stars knew what to do on stage and it killed him. I mean, the kids liked him but he didn't have an act. He didn't know how to come on and off stage. He didn't know how to take a bow.'

So Boyd booked him into three weeks of variety shows during November and December – a week at the Metropolitan, Edgware Road, a week at the Chiswick Empire and a week at the Finsbury Park Empire. Cliff was to stay with Boyd and his wife Daphne at their apartment in Barons Court. He would rehearse his 'Oh Boy!' shows during the day and then give two performances a night with the Drifters at 6.15 and 8.15, the aim being to give him an intense forty-two-show crash course in stagecraft.

The variety bills make strange reading today. At the Metropolitan, for example, Cliff shared the stage with Little Beaver and Maree, a roller-skating tap dancer called Checker Wheel, someone called Bernard Landy who mimed to records, comedian Michael Roxy, multi-instrumentalist Michael Hill, puppeteer Janet Fox and comic double act Roy Hudd and Eddy Kay.

It wasn't a happy mix. The rock 'n' roll fans weren't interested in tap-dancing roller skaters and didn't take up their seats until Cliff appeared, and the admirers of old-time variety hall acts found rock 'n' roll too loud and brash.

'If there is one thing that the appearance of Cliff Richards [sic] demonstrates at the Met this week it is the deep gulf that exists between teenage taste and the conventional variety act,' reported *The Stage*.

'It is not unbridgeable, for the youngsters often appreciate the novelty of variety, but if the bridging is to be done I do not think this bill is going to do it. It provides, in fact, a strong argument against mixing the old and the new. Young Cliff Richards is an advanced example of his kind, an acquired taste that is quite as likely to antagonize as it is to please.

'I found his almost savage approach, backed by an overloud battery of guitars and drums, most impressive and without, so far as I know, being "sent" anywhere in particular, I quite enjoyed the demonstration. But one needs to be teenage, I think, really to know what it is all about.'

Tulah Tuke, back from her stint at Butlin's, saw one of the Metropolitan shows and remembers how unpolished it seemed.

'The Drifters went on stage with their chords written out and sellotaped to their guitars. Cliff seemed very inexperienced. He was only eighteen and here he was topping the bill on a variety circuit.

'Kids weren't as streetwise as they are today anyway and Cliff's background was even more protected than most. When he became a star he hadn't had the experience of knocking around Liverpool and Hamburg that the Beatles had had by the time they started having hits.' (By the end of the Kalin Twins' tour, Cliff had been on stage fewer than a hundred times in his whole career to date. The Beatles, by contrast, played the Cavern Club alone 292 times before recording their first single.)

The reviewer who caught him at the Chiswick Empire was even more disdainful. After chiding a duo called Reggie Redcliffe and Desmond Lane, who had apparently moved around a bit too much on stage, he went on to deal with 'young Cliff Richard' who he said, disapprovingly, was 'another young artist in the long line of those who find it necessary, in order to express themselves, to jerk a leg or wave an arm as they string together a succession of extraordinary words and phrases, often repetitive, each jerk or wave producing more or less non-stop screams from youthful fans who hang on to his every word and gesture. Master Richard is backed by his Drifters — drums and electric guitars which, to the uninitiated, appear to be grossly over-amplified.

'How pleasurable, therefore, to sit back and watch someone who restricts movement to a minimum — Vendryes, who silently produces a succession of doves seemingly from thin air . . .'

Because he was so obviously popular with the girls, the boys were becoming jealous. They didn't like this pretty, smooth-skinned boy who was becoming an icon to their girlfriends. He particularly wasn't liked by Teds and Rockers who fancied themselves as hard men.

At the Finsbury Park Empire a group of Rockers turned up threatening to cause trouble.

'They were the yobs of the time,' remembers Stan Edwards, who hadn't seen Cliff since they worked together at Butlin's. 'Cliff invited them to come and meet him. We were in the dressing room and these guys arrived in heavy leather gear and they turned out to be really great blokes. So they said, "We like you and we'll make sure no one gets on stage." They had come as the aggressors and became the defenders!'

By this final week of concerts Cliff was flagging. He was now not only rehearsing 'Oh Boy!' and doing two concerts a day but was playing a small role in *Serious Charge*, a film being shot in Borehamwood. He wasn't used to working under such pressure and was clearly suffering from exhaustion.

'When it came to the last night Cliff just couldn't go on stage,' remembers John Foster. 'He came off after the first show and he just couldn't talk. So I threw everyone out of the dressing room, made him sleep and gave him honey and melted butter.

'While I was doing this Franklyn Boyd knocked on the door and when I opened it he asked, "How's my boy?" I said, "Look, get in your car, drive to Piccadilly Circus, go to the all-night chemist and get 'your boy' something for his throat because you're murdering him." I threw him out.'

He stayed in bed at home for a few days and his father began consulting Ray Mackender, at the time a fringe character in the music business, whom Cliff had met at a party thrown by Cherry Wainer, one of the cast of 'Oh Boy!'.

Mackender was a handsome 26-year-old bachelor with thick wavy hair and a public school accent. By day he worked as a non-marine broker at Lloyds of London and by night donned a pair of jeans and headed down to Battersea Town Hall where he organized a rock 'n' roll dance night. He desperately wanted to be part of the scene but hadn't yet found a role. He wrote some features for *New Musical Express*, became a disc jockey at the Poplar Theatre, and befriended many of the 'Oh Boy!' stars.

On Sunday mornings he organized coffee parties at his flat in Danvers Street, Chelsea, where the cream of Britain's young talent would gather for chat and drinks. In his visitors' book from that period are the names of Vince Eager, Jess Conrad, Sammy Samwell, Cliff Richard, Jimmy Page (later to form Led Zeppelin) and Gerry Dorsey (later to be renamed Engelbert Humperdinck).

'It was the fact of getting together in those days that was so exciting for us,' says Jess Conrad. 'We weren't drinkers. We just liked meeting and playing records and back then you really had to go somewhere else to play your records because your parents complained too much about the noise if you played them at home.'

Cliff's parents warmed to Mackender. Rodger, who was forever believing that his son was being exploited, was impressed with Mackender's position in the City and started calling him up for business advice.

'Rodger saw me as a complete Godsend at that time,' Mackender admits. 'He confided that he was thinking of getting rid of Franklyn Boyd and he thought he could become Cliff's manager if I was willing to help him out.

'Initially I thought I could but, after a few meetings with the accountants, I realized it was a much bigger job than anyone could manage part-time. I was also reluctant to give up the security of my job with Lloyds.'

Rodger Webb went ahead anyway and sent a letter of dismissal to Franklyn Boyd, who had never signed a contract. The next day the story was splashed over the newspapers: 'Cliff Richard In Rumpus. Father Gives Manager The Sack'.

'I never had any quarrel with Cliff or his mother,' says Boyd. 'It was his father who was a pain in the neck. I think Cliff should have been strong enough to say, "Look Dad, I know you're my father but this is business." But he never said it.

'I knew he was struggling a bit rehearsing and doing the variety shows but I knew he had to learn show business very quickly. If he had stuck doing Sunday concerts it would have taken him a year to get the same experience. I knew he would have a hard time but everyone goes through that.

'His father was working in a rather dull office, cycling eight miles to work each day, and now show business managers had started to wine and dine him. He was becoming quite impressed with it all. Tito Burns, Cherry Wainer's manager, had been sending limousines up to Cheshunt to bring his mother to shows. In other words, everyone was winning the parents over because they could see the pound signs in Cliff Richard.'

Boyd left at around the same time that it was decided that Terry Smart, Cliff's last link with the original Drifters, was going to have to go. It wasn't a difficult decision to make because Smart knew that he couldn't keep pace with the professionals and he was keen to join the Merchant Navy when he was eighteen anyway.

The obvious first choice as his replacement was Tony Meehan, the drummer who had worked with Hank and Jet in the Vipers.

Although only fifteen, Meehan had been drumming since he was thirteen, playing in small dance bands in the Irish belt of North London and then graduating to Soho where he played in backing groups for Adam Faith, Vince Eager and Vince Taylor.

'I went because they were complaining about how lousy their drummer was and they felt they just couldn't handle it any more,' he says. 'They were putting out feelers to see if I would be interested. So I saw him and I was impressed with what I saw. I thought he was terrific. He really was hot at that time and I was stimulated.

'Terry Smart was a real sweetheart but not a great player by any stretch of the imagination. It was a big wrench for Cliff when he left but he was quite ruthless about getting on. He was very determined. He knew that he couldn't put friendship before business.'

It was a hard time for Cliff because he was having to learn his stagecraft in the full glare of the national media and thousands of adoring fans. He was being projected as a star, yet he still found it hard to look directly at an audience. It took Cherry Wainer to coach him in the art of holding a microphone, and Franklyn Boyd to tell him how to take a bow.

By the end of 1958 he was starting to put it all together. With the addition of Tony Meehan, he had an experienced group behind him who could help paper over some of the remaining cracks.

11

'I worried for his life. I didn't want anything to happen to him'

As his life as a star expanded, so he became less and less an ordinary boy from Cheshunt. He could no longer travel on the bus or walk out alone without being surrounded by fans. Girls turned up and sat outside his home in Hargreaves Close and he often had to spend hours waiting inside the Hackney Empire until crowds dispersed. Then there was the additional threat from the Teddy boys and the slighted boyfriends.

'He didn't seem to know what had hit him,' remembers Tulah Tuke. 'When I saw him at the Metropolitan he seemed amazed and somewhat horrified that there were these little girls screaming outside. I think he was knocked back by it. He was as excited as any teenager would be but there was also that frightening dimension of not knowing exactly what might erupt.'

One night in Romford, while the girls stood outside the dressing room windows yelling for Cliff, a mob of boys started throwing bricks through the windows of the tour bus. Cliff had to be smuggled out of the building though a toilet window and driven to a rendezvous point on the road back to London.

At the Chiswick Empire some lads threw a fire hydrant from the balcony and two girls in the stalls were injured. At the Lyceum, off the

Strand, he was forced to abandon a concert after being pelted with vegetables and coins with sharpened edges.

'If one of those things hit you it would take your eye out or give you a nasty cut,' says Tony Meehan. 'We tried to play on and then one of these things came right across my cymbal and I said, "Right, that's it." So, after three numbers, we pulled the plugs. I think that was the only time we ever stopped a show. There was absolute uproar. There were hundreds of people squashed against the stage and there didn't seem to be any control. Then these people at the back started breaking up chairs and hurling them through the air. It was a horrible, horrible atmosphere.'

Events like this began to trouble Cliff's mother.

'I never worried about him being a rock 'n' roll singer but I did worry about what could happen to him. I used to try and go everywhere with him. Rodger wouldn't come. He said I was daft. But I told him that these people were doing rotten things to him and I could save him.

'There used to be rows of policemen linking arms trying to protect him from the crowds. These boys would be shouting, "Kill him! Kill him!" It was dreadful. I used to go to all these shows because I didn't want anything to happen to him and me not to be there. I used to go everywhere.'

Within months of his first hit single being released he was adapting to the abnormal lifestyle of the rich and famous. His earnings were phenomenal by the standards of his contemporaries – £15,000 for a thirty-week contract with the Grade Agency in March 1959 – but there was no time to spend it and few places to go. At the age of eighteen he was hermetically sealed into a way of life that he has never been able to escape.

His old schoolfriends gradually fell away, partly through their own inability to deal with his fame, partly through Cliff's unavailability. His new friends and acquaintances were from the world of show business: people who lived the same hours and experienced the same problems. From the cast of 'Oh Boy!' he became particularly close to Cherry Wainer, who responded to this 'little boy lost' by taking him under her wing.

Cherry was something of an oddity on 'Oh Boy!'. She was neither from the same musical background nor the same generation as the regular stars of the show. She had come to Britain from South Africa late in 1957 with her drummer Don Storer and Jack Good had spotted her playing at a US Air Force base.

'Cherry always seemed so worldly wise,' remembers Maggie Streader from the Vernons Girls. 'She was older than all of us. She was a star! She knew everybody, knew everything and called everyone "darling".'

She met Cliff at his first rehearsal and began gently to coach him and advise him on how to handle himself in the business. She saw him as vulnerable and easily exploited.

He began to share his hopes and fears with her and together with John Foster and other performers from the show he would spend evenings with her at the Lotus House, a Chinese restaurant in the Edgware Road which was a late-night hang-out for the 'Oh Boy!' crowd. Because Cliff had no means of transport and no telephone at home she also began to chauffeur him around and take messages.

Through Cherry Wainer's influence Cliff was brought together with her manager Tito Burns, who was then introduced to his parents over a meal at the Lotus House.

'His mum and dad knew nothing about show business,' says Cherry. 'Cliff became so big so fast and everywhere he went people were trying to get at him. I think he was thankful and grateful that it was happening, but it bothered him.'

Tito Burns was everything that the Webbs could have imagined a show business manager to be. He had slicked-back hair and a Groucho Marx moustache, smoked cigars and liked talking about 'wheeling and dealing'.

He was born Nathan Burns in the East End of London and had

joined a dance band on leaving school. *Melody Maker*'s annual polls voted him Britain's top accordion player, and he was also a good enough comedian to play support to Alma Cogan.

Unlike Cliff's previous managers, he already controlled several acts he could use as bargaining tools. George Ganjou had now been shunted on to the sidelines. He was still paid his ten per cent in line with the contract signed when Cliff was seventeen, but he no longer played any active part in Cliff's career.

Burns made no secret of the fact that he had no love for rock 'n' roll. He saw it as a short-term phenomenon and thought that the best insurance policy Cliff could take out would be to distance himself from the Drifters and introduce more classic cover songs into his act. Whereas Cliff had always seen himself as Elvis, Burns saw him as Frank Sinatra.

The move away from rock 'n' roll was eventually to come through Lionel Bart, Tommy Steele's songwriter. He had been approached by film producer Mickey Delamar to write songs for a film version of *Serious Charge*, a British play about a vicar who helps a juvenile delinquent who then tries to frame him on a charge of indecent assault.

At the time homosexuality was a risqué subject for cinema, and Delamar wanted a rock 'n' roll soundtrack to broaden its appeal. 'He asked me if I knew of an English kid who was an Elvis clone,' says Bart. 'I put Cliff's name forward.'

The director was 43-year-old Terence Young, later to make his name with the early James Bond films. 'I think we thought that if we put a few kids in it would draw a younger audience,' he admits. 'Otherwise it would have been strictly a television sort of audience. So the part of Curly was added for the film version.

'There were two or three singers that I went to see. I saw Cliff at the Chiswick Empire and I was sold on him right away. He seemed terribly self-assured and had a very good stage act. I thought if he could do that, then he could act.'

The film had a strong cast with former child star Andrew Ray playing the teenage delinquent, Anthony Quayle the vicar and Sarah Churchill, daughter of Sir Winston, a middle-aged parishioner with marriage on her mind. Cliff took the part of Curly, the delinquent's younger brother.

Filming took place at MGM's studios in Borehamwood and in the new town at Stevenage. Andrew Ray calls the film 'a poor man's *The Wild Ones* set in Stevenage'.

Cliff didn't have many lines and the ones he had he spat out of the corner of his mouth in a pseudo-hip accent that was far-removed from his innocent looks.

'I remember Cliff was a lovely fellow,' says Ray, 'but he was very nervous about acting. He really wanted to get on with the songs in the film.'

While filming was going on, Tommy Steele, still the reigning king of British rock 'n' roll with eleven top thirty hits, paid an unexpected visit to the set. He asked to see Cliff in his dressing room. Jess Conrad, who was playing the leader of a local gang which disrupts the vicar's youth club, remembers the tense scene as the king met the pretender to the crown.

'There wasn't friction, but Tommy was the established star and now this new boy was coming up and he asked Cliff if he had ever played "knuckles", where you had touch knuckles and if you couldn't move away fast enough you got hit.

'Tommy was very good at it and very fast. He cut Cliff's hands to ribbons. I'll never ever forget it. It was the most devious thing I had ever seen because Tommy had decided that he wanted to draw blood from the new idol. It was really awful. Cliff could never get out of the way quick enough and it went on and on. Cliff kept saying he'd play on, and yet his knuckles were red raw where Tommy had been whacking and whacking him.'

Steele had learned the game as a merchant seaman on board the liner *Mauretania*.

'To lose at "knuckles" on that ship was as bad as walking the plank,' remembers Steele. 'A young man intent on entering the arena needed to be strong, sly and very quick. Clliff was not very good at it.'

One of the songs from Lionel Bart's soundtrack was 'Living Doll'. He had written it one Sunday morning in October 1958 while reading the *Sunday Pictorial*.

'I was looking at the back pages and there was a small advert for a doll which could apparently do everything,' Bart remembers. 'I wrote the song in ten minutes.'

The advert that caught his eye was for a 99/6d 'Darling Doll' which was said to 'kneel, walk, sit and sing'. He linked this idea with the Mills Brothers' wartime hit 'Paper Doll', in which the singer asks for a cut-out paper girl because others wouldn't steal her, and she would be easier to be with than a 'fickle-minded real live girl'. Bart added his own twist to the tale.

As performed for the soundtrack, 'Living Doll' was a fast song in four-four time which Cliff hated singing. Paramor tried to thwart its release as a single by writing a song with a similar title, 'Livin' Lovin' Doll', which Cliff released in January 1959. So that no one would detect the ruse he used the pseudonym Johnny May and his friend Bunny Lewis was credited as Jim Gustard. (Paramor and Lewis went on to write Cliff's 1960 hit 'A Voice In The Wilderness', this time not hiding their identities.)

But the public was not satisfied with 'Livin' Lovin' Doll', and it only reached number twenty in the charts. There was demand for a soundtrack EP from the film and so, at the end of April 1959, Cliff re-recorded the songs.

'We told Norrie that we didn't like "Living Doll" the way it was,' says Cliff. 'We were at Sheffield City Hall doing a sound check one afternoon [14 February 1959], sitting around thinking what we could do with the song, when Bruce started strumming his guitar and he said, "What about having it as a country song?"'

Since 'Move It' had reached number two in the charts and stayed around for over four months, Cliff had been struggling to maintain momentum as a singles' artist.

He tried to achieve this initially by recording more rock 'n' roll numbers, but after 'High Class Baby' reached number seven his chart positions wavered. 'Livin' Lovin' Doll' only just made the top twenty and 'Mean Streak', because it was competing in the charts with its own flip side 'Never Mind', stalled at ten. The number of records sold had slumped to below 200,000 from a high of well over half a million.

His first LP, recorded days before the concert at Sheffield City Hall, was to be the last all-out burst of rock 'n' roll. Paramor wanted to capture the feel of those early live performances, but to do it in the controlled environment of Abbey Road's studio two. Cliff and the Drifters played to an invited audience on a make-shift stage beneath the control room.

Over two nights, Cliff belted out his favourite hits, including 'Whole Lotta Shakin' Goin' On', 'Be Bop A Lula', 'Donna' and 'That'll Be The Day'. The result was *Cliff*, which went on to reach number four in the LP charts.

The slowed-down version of 'Living Doll' became his most important recording since 'Move It'. It redefined him as a singer, was his first number one and sold almost two million copies.

'It wasn't an out-and-out rocker. But by then I was coming to see that rock wasn't a tempo but a musical culture, and that a song like "Living Doll" fitted into it,' Cliff says.

'What we were discovering was that rock 'n' roll seemed to be fairly limited as a beaty form of music because the public weren't buying it in hundreds of thousands. We were the first rock teenagers and ten year olds had no money to spend so in the end records like "Living Doll" sold because they appealed to parents who had money.

'We helped the audience to grow. By the time the Beatles came along those ten year olds were fifteen and had money. They could make a stand for rock 'n' roll. The Beatles had the benefit of all the groundwork that we had put in.'

At around the time that Cliff hooked up with Tito Burns, he moved away from home for the first time, and rented a three-bedroomed flat at 100 Marylebone High Street. At first he just shared with John Foster, but it soon became a crash pad — not only for the Drifters — but also for such singers as Billy Fury, Dickie Pride and Vince Eager. Comedian Jimmy Tarbuck often used the small spare bedroom.

'I didn't have a thing to my name back then,' says Tarbuck. 'Cliff used to let me stay at his flat when I was in London.' Cliff's mother and sister Donna would come up regularly to keep it clean and Donna would often stay for extended periods.

'We were on our own a lot of the time,' says Foster. 'We weren't really meeting new people. There weren't clubs like Tramps which you can go into today in London, and he had become so big so fast that he couldn't go anywhere. He couldn't even walk out on the street.'

The move had to be made because in 1959 Cliff started what was to become a familiar pattern of one-nighter shows which would almost always start with everyone being collected from a pick-up point in Marylebone — either Great Cumberland Place or Allsop Place — and it was too much to travel in from Cheshunt continually, especially as he didn't yet drive.

In February and March he toured the Granada circuit as part of a package which included Wee Willie Harris, Tony Crombie and Johnny Duncan with Jimmy Tarbuck as compère.

'Cliff was top of the bill,' remembers Tarbuck. 'They were fun days but the tour was so disorganized. You might be in Hull one day, Bournemouth the next and then Glasgow after that, and all of it done by coach.'

During one show, when Cliff lost his voice, Wee Willie Harris was positioned at the back of the stage to sing while Cliff mimed.

'It just shows you what it was all about in the fifties,' says Harris. 'I don't think the girls were bothered who was singing. Every time he made a sexy movement with his legs they screamed even though I was singing in full view of the audience.'

In April Cliff played for a week each at the Birmingham Hippodrome and the Chiswick Empire. It was while in Birmingham that he sent away for Hank's Fender Stratocaster, the first solid-body electric guitar to be sold to anyone in Britain.

Hank had been playing an Antoria, but the neck was bent and the tuning suspect. Like Cliff he admired the playing of James Burton, whose guitar breaks on Ricky Nelson's records epitomized American rock 'n' roll. Hank knew that Burton's instrument was made by Fender Instruments of Fullerton, California.

Hank and Cliff acquired a catalogue, pored over it and decided that Burton must have been playing a Stratocaster. The most expensive of Fender's guitars, it had revolutionized the guitar industry when it was introduced in 1954. Cliff offered to buy it for Hank (the cost was about five weeks of Hank's salary in 1959), and wrote to Dave Lilley, Ray Mackender's flatmate, to ask if he would order it:

'Dear Dave,

We've decided to have the 'Red' Fender Guitar. With A. Three pickups. B. With tremelo lever. C. Gold platted [sic] Hardware

The guitar is a 'Stratocaster'. Have marked in catalogue. When you send for it please order spare set balanced strings and also a 'Fender Case'.

Well Dave thanks a million. All the Best, Cliff.'

Hank remembers it arriving.

'A magnificent flat case with plush red lining came, and inside it was this magnificent guitar — flamingo pink with a maple fingerboard. You didn't have to play it. You just had to hang it around your neck and the audience would be totally impressed.'

The guitar, which at the time was considered to be very strange looking, changed the image and sound of the group. It was much easier to play, there was greater tonal versality and with the tremolo arm Hank was able to 'bend' notes. Within a few years solid-body guitars would be standard equipment for all rock groups.

At the Chiswick Empire, Jet met a sixteen-year-old girl in the bar. Her name was Carol Costa, and she came from Hounslow.

'She was with a chap but he wasn't her boyfriend,' remembers Jet, 'and I thought she looked terribly Brigitte Bardot-ish.' A relationship was started and the two of them moved into the spare bedroom at Cliff's flat.

Although Cliff was charming towards all the girls in his social sphere, it became obvious quite early on that he and Jet's new girl were developing a crush on each other.

They started eyeing each other at the flat. They would even hold hands discreetly at the cinema, even though Jet was sitting on Carol's other side. Then there would be parties at Carol's home in Cedar Road, Hounslow, after which everyone would crash out overnight on the floor and again there would be looks and touches between her and Cliff.

'I had always fancied Brigitte Bardot,' Cliff says. 'When I was a teenager I had a poster of her on my bedroom wall which was made up of three parts given away in *Reveille* magazine. Bardot wore eyeliner and I remember Carol being like that.

'I fell for her. It was a strange time. It was the period I refer back to when I say that all my friends got married really young. All the Drifters were going steady with girls they would marry, and there was great pressure on me to get married. That must have played a great part in our relationship, brief though it was.

'I think Jet must have been aware that she fancied me. I don't think we were as discreet as we could have been really but at that stage it was only looks and glances.'

Cliff's mother began to suspect something was going on when she visited the flat one day to clean. She discovered that Carol had slipped a letter beneath Cliff's pillow before going out. Cliff told his mother that he was frightened of her and that he didn't like what was happening, but that was only half of the truth. The other half was that he was developing feelings for her. The fear came from the fact that she was the girlfriend of one of his closest friends.

What he didn't tell his mother he poured out to Cherry Wainer in long emotional conversations. He told her that he was very fond of Carol but that he didn't want to do anything that would hurt Jet or hurt his career.

'I think Carol was prepared to break off with Jet if she knew that she could have gone with Cliff,' she says, 'but at that time Cliff's mother didn't want anything to happen to him that would affect his career. I think although he felt very deeply for her, he didn't want to argue with his parents — to say, "Yes, I'm going to do this." So that's why he stayed put.'

Matters came to a head one night at a party where Jet was sitting on a sofa with Carol perched on his knee. Without explanation, Cliff suddenly rushed out of the room and didn't return. Carol assumed he'd been taken ill.

'I asked the road manager what was wrong with him, and he said, "You know what's wrong with him,"' she says. 'I went out and found him in one of the bedrooms. He was crying. He told me that he loved me and asked me what we were going to do about it. He wanted me to tell Jet that it was over. But when I did break from Jet and move back to my parents' home he dropped me. It was just like that.

'I think someone had been talking to him. I suppose he was worried about about breaking the group up. Maybe he was worried about the effect it would have on the fans.'

At that time it was important for a young male singer to preserve his single image. His fans, who were mostly female, needed to be able to nurse the fantasy that they could be his dream girl. Terry Dene married in July 1958 and never had another hit. Marty Wilde put an end to his career as a teenage idol when he married one of the Vernons Girls in 1959.

'Without a shadow of doubt my marriage affected my record sales and my popularity,' says Wilde. 'Directly after that I really struggled. You had to change your career to survive. But we knew that would happen. I had a long meeting with my manager and he said, "I'll leave the decision to you, but you must know what you're up against." '

Cliff had thought right from the start that marriage would limit his career but an incident in 1959 confirmed it for him. He was dating a dark-haired girl called Jean who worked in a bowling alley in Wembley and had got on well enough with her to be taken back to meet her parents. Jet Harris remembers her as 'the most gorgeous girl'.

She came along to several concerts with Cliff and after one show, at the Finsbury Park Empire, she left the theatre with him and sat on his lap in the waiting car. Cliff looked out of the car window long enough to see that his fans were in tears and some of them had thrown their concert programmes into the gutter and were grinding them in with their heels.

He was shocked at the intensity of their feelings. 'When I started seeing Jean I thought, well, perhaps I could have a girlfriend but this experience underlined the fact that I couldn't,' he says. 'The fans wanted to own me, and I was happy with that.'

Franklyn Boyd reckons that early in his career Cliff's mother was also influential in keeping him single.

'She always told him not to get romantically involved with girls because it would be the end of his career.'

There can be no doubt that his image as a lonely boy just waiting for Miss Right to come along helped his career. One of the most popular magazine story ideas of the time was 'Cliff's Ideal Girl'. Cliff would always say that he liked plain-looking girls who wore no make-up and weren't too forward. In this way even the most ordinary-looking fan could think that she fitted the bill.

A typical story (featured in a romantic comic for girls) was headlined 'Cliff Richard Reveals — If Only I Could Find The Right Girl' and began, 'Although I meet pretty girls wherever I go — I haven't got a girlfriend'. What sort of girl would he like? Of course she must like rock 'n' roll, cowboy films and Chinese food but 'I like a natural looking girl . . . a girl who can let herself go without worrying if her hair is going to lose its curl in the rain, or her nose get shiny.'

Later the same year he told a fan magazine that the girl he would marry (at twenty-seven), 'needn't be too good-looking, as long as she's got a personality of her own'.

His ideal, he told *Boyfriend* in May 1959, was Hollywood actress Carol Lynley, who had been in two teen films, *Blue Jeans* and *Hound Dog Man*, because 'she seems so wholesome . . . so quiet. She's not specially good-looking. But in her very plainness there's a special kind of beauty.'

He couldn't have put it better if he'd been handed a script by a marketing executive. He was the boy with everything, surrounded by beautiful women, and yet all he wanted was a good old-fashioned plain girl who could cook him a meal and listen to records. Everyone was in with a chance. The challenge had been laid down. Even the prettiest of girls could leave off her make-up, tousle her hair up and affect just the right degree of plainness.

Jack Good was right. Cliff was too innocent to suggest the pleasures of forbidden fruit in the way that Elvis did. He was more suited to offering the promise of a romantic meal, a night at the flicks and a kiss on the doorstep that was guaranteed not to go too far. Whereas a lot of parents might have had a hard time adjusting to having Elvis around the house, Cliff was the ideal boy to invite back home: traditional but not fogeyish, proper but not prim.

Interviewed in 1964, Sammy Samwell suggested that Cliff's broad appeal was because he was a rock 'n' roll star whom parents were comfortable with and that was more important in Britain at the time than it was in America.

'In England not every home has a record player,' Samwell said. 'In many of the homes that have one, it is still something of a prized possession and if the youngsters want to play a record on it which annoys the parents, then there is trouble.

'Cliff broke this down by having the clean-cut "wouldn't mind having him for my son" type of thing. His records in this way became acceptable, so the kids were free to buy his records and play them, and still retain their own private inner image of Cliff, different from that of their parents.'

When Cliff went away in the summer of 1959 it was his first holiday since the days when he visited his grandfather in Lucknow and his first time out of England since arriving in 1948. In *It's Great To Be Young* he wrote, 'Ronnie, a chum of mine from the old days, was going out [to Italy] in his car and wondered if I'd like to join him. Would I? I jumped at it.'

'Ronnie' was Ronnie Ernstone, a 21-year-old car mechanic from Notting Hill Gate who had met Cliff at an EMI Studio party. They probably wouldn't have got so close if Ronnie hadn't had a car and promised to run him back to Cheshunt.

He was soon giving Cliff driving lessons. When, in April 1959, he wanted a Lambretta motor scooter Ernstone ordered one from friends in the motorcycle business and had it sprayed nasturtium, which was the colour of the moment. Much later, in August l9S9, he organized the purchase of Cliff's first car — a grey Sunbeam Alpine with red leather seats.

Ernstone's other useful connection was clothes. His father was a textile importer and it occurred to Ernstone that if there could be Fred Perry shirts there could also be Cliff Richard shirts.

'In those days people were wearing striped cotton shirts in bright colours,' he says. 'As it happened my father had just bought in some material like this. I showed it to Cliff and asked him what he thought about having some shirts made.'

'He thought it was a good idea so I had some samples made up. I got Cliff wearing them, had him photographed, and did a deal with Tito Burns whereby Cliff got a royalty. I interested some teenage magazines in what we called the "Cliff Richard Shirt Offer", which was a shirt in either small, medium or large, presented in a box which had a picture on the lid of Cliff wearing one of the shirts.'

The holiday in Italy came about spontaneously. Cliff had a break in his work schedule and Ernstone suggested driving on the Continent, something he had been doing with his parents since he was a child. Both Cliff and Tony Meehan agreed to go and Ernstone brought along a platonic friend called Pam who looked like Audrey Hepburn.

They drove down through Belgium, Germany and Switzerland in Ernstone's red and grey Morris Oxford Estate. Meehan sat in the front seat and navigated and Ernstone drove while Cliff sat in the back with Pam, who attempted to snuggle up to him but was apparently kept at arm's length. They made it to Viareggio on the coast of Italy in thirty-six hours.

They checked into the Hotel Regina, an old seafront hotel with creaky wooden floorboards and a grand marble staircase. After crashing out for a few hours they went out for a meal of Steak Bismarck (steak with eggs) in a local restaurant, washing it all down with a large bottle of Chianti. 'We were all eighteen then and felt we were really great,' says Ernstone (actually Meehan was still only sixteen). 'We were really putting the steak and wine away, and the truth is that we all got absolutely paralytic. We staggered back down the main street swaying all over the show and feeling as sick as dogs.'

'It was the first time for all of us,' says Meehan. 'Cliff threw up. I sat outside the hotel with my head in my hands feeling absolutely smashed. It was a beautiful evening and somehow I didn't get sick.

'But when I got back to our suite Ronnie and Cliff were just vomiting into the sink. They were very badly sick. Then they had to keep going into the shower. I cleared off out again because I couldn't stand the smell. The next day we all felt pretty fragile.'

For the next twelve days they sunbathed and swam, and listened to the music in the Italian pop charts. One night they went to a cabaret club where Cliff was pulled out of the audience and asked to sing a song. The owner, a friend of Ernstone's parents who therefore knew who Cliff was, handed him a guitar and said, 'Now, ladies and gentlemen. From London England — Richard Cliff!'

Cliff remembers it as a wonderful experience. In one way it was the last time he could be a lad among lads and spontaneously elect to drive off. In another way it was the start of his globetrotting.

'It was the beginning of it all,' he says. 'It was the first holiday I had ever afforded. I can remember we stopped to clean our teeth in a Swiss mountain stream on the way down. It was my first feeling of real freedom. I was not only able to leave my family and go off on holiday but I could afford to go to another country.'

Ever since his first press interviews Cliff had said the same thing when asked what his personal ambition was. It was 'to meet Elvis Presley', and it was on his way back from Viareggio that he made the first of several attempts.

Inducted into the US Army in December 1957, Elvis had left America in September 1958 to join the Third Armored Division in West Germany and was eventually posted to the small town of Bad Nauheim, north east of Frankfurt, where he rented a three-storey white stucco house, Goethestrasse 14.

It was well known that Elvis lived in Bad Nauheim but Cliff and his friends knew no more than that. They decided to give it a try, to drive into the town and ask around to see if they could track down the king of rock 'n' roll.

'We got to the army camp and told one of the guards that we had come to see Elvis Presley and they told us where we could find him,' says Ernstone. 'I seem to remember that his house was the third one on the left and we pulled up outside and then we just sat there in the car for about ten minutes deciding who should be the one to go and knock on the door. Tony wanted me to go and I wanted Tony to go and then I said I thought it should be Cliff who went first because he was the rock 'n' roll star.

'In the end we voted and it was decided that Cliff was going to be the one to do it. I said, "I'll tell you what. If you go and knock on the door I'll film you with my ciné camera and then when he comes out and shakes your hand, we'll have a record of it." '

The footage, exhumed after twenty-four years in Ernstone's mother's attic, shows Cliff, dressed in a striped shirt and jeans, walking slowly to the white wooden gate. He goes up a short flight of steps on the left side of the house where he drags his fingers through his hair and presses a door bell.

The door is answered by a friend of Elvis' who tells him that unfortunately Elvis is on leave in Paris but that he'll pass on Cliff's good wishes. A dejected Cliff comes back down the steps and then the camera pans along the wall in front of the house where girls have scribbled their messages of love. The picture ends up on Elvis' parked car.

'It was very disappointing for all of us,' admits Meehan. We were very keyed-up and thought it had been quite a feat for us to find his house. The guy who answered the door said that if Elvis had been around he would have loved to have met Cliff. It felt like a big let-down.'

'It would have been a great time to have met him because that's the Elvis I remember,' says Cliff. 'The second Elvis, the big fat Elvis, was not the one I wanted to meet.'

What Cliff didn't know was that Elvis was away meeting Franklyn Boyd in Paris at the time. 'I spent ten days with him there with his Memphis friends Charlie Hodge and Lamont Fike,' says Boyd. 'I'd had a call from my boss in the States, Jean Aberbach, who told me to meet Elvis at the Gare de Lyon in Paris. I talked Elvis out of coming to England. He wanted to come and I told him that he'd never get out of his hotel.'

On the same day, nineteen-year-old Terence 'Jet' Harris was marrying seventeen-year-old Carol Ann Costa at St Paul's Church, Hounslow Heath, in London. Even though Cliff must have realized that nothing permanent could have come of his flirtation with Carol, he still wasn't ready for it to end.

'I knew it was going to happen,' says Cliff. 'I must have been disappointed but I don't think I'm cut out to be married. I think I wanted the trimmings but I didn't want marriage. So, in point of fact, it was probably a good "out" for me.'

12

'America was a real eye-opener for us'

Within a day of returning from Italy, Cliff plunged into a string of concerts around Britain. Travelling on the tour was Royston Ellis, an author who had been commissioned to ghost-write a book for Jet Harris called *Driftin' With Cliff*.

Ellis was Britain's first teenage pundit. He'd started by writing poetry about coffee bars, motorcycles and rock 'n' roll and the newspapers seized on him as an erudite beatnik, an Allen Ginsberg of suburban London. The fact that he wore a beard and had worked as an office boy, duster salesman, gardener, milk-bottle washer, building labourer and farm hand by the age of eighteen helped confirm the image.

'I guess you'd call the boy in the picture a weirdie,' said the *Daily Mirror* in 1959 below a photograph of him dressed in a fur-collared jacket. 'And you'd be right. He's strictly, as they say in beatnik language, from Weirdsville.'

His first volume of poems, *Jiving To Gyp*, was dedicated to Cliff and he was soon asked by television programmmes to explain what teenagers were all about. He ended up with his own series, 'Living For Kicks', in which he explored the controversial issues of the day such as pep pills, and sex before marriage.

A cogent musical commentator – his 1961 paperback *The Big Beat Scene* still stands up as an appraisal of early British rock 'n' roll – he was soon to meet the fledgling Beatles (in May 1960) and show John Lennon and Paul McCartney how to break down a Benzedrine inhaler and sniff the strips inside to produce a mild high. This was, Lennon later recounted, their first experience with drugs.

'I wrote to Cliff saying I wanted to meet him and write about him,' says Ellis. 'I got a letter back from Ray Mackender, who was by now helping Cliff's mother deal with all the fan mail, inviting me to a broadcast that Cliff was doing with the Drifters at Radio Luxembourg.

'Cliff didn't really take me on at all because he didn't really relate to anyone in those days but Jet Harris did immediately and so my first friendship was with Jet. It was only after quite a while that Cliff decided I was harmless.'

Ellis and the Drifters worked together on some poetry and music projects, a Soho version of what America's beat poets had been doing for some years in the North Beach area of San Francisco. Ellis called it 'rocketry'.

'We did a television show and some gigs with him,' remembers Meehan. 'We didn't play our normal style of music though. It was more jazz-orientated as far as I can remember. It was different, it was interesting, and it was a bit of extra money.'

Driftin' With Cliff wasn't an in-depth account of life on the road but it did supply interesting snapshots: the communal singing of American rock 'n' roll songs on the coach, the cushion fights, the pit stops where they'd all have greasy fry-ups and Cliff would have his favourite drink of Tizer with a scoop of ice-cream.

Off stage Cliff was wearing 'a blue continental-style jacket, fawn tapered trousers and white calf-skin shoes which he had brought back from Italy'. At night he wore pink pyjamas. His favourite reading matter was science fiction and his favourite singers Connie Francis, Ricky Nelson and Elvis Presley.

Before the show the musicians would often go out to see a film.

After the show, they would play cards until the early hours of the next morning. Cliff stayed in a separate hotel to the Drifters.

'Cliff was always a mystery to me,' admits Ellis. 'He kept himself to himself. He wasn't a part of the gang. Often, when all the others were on the coach, Cliff would be in a car with his manager Tito Burns. It was very difficult to get close to him.'

One of the most noticeable differences between Cliff and the rest of the musicians was in his attitude to girls. Whereas he obviously enjoyed the mass hysteria he could provoke when on stage he never followed it through off stage. As Bruce Welch puts it, 'If there were women available we in the Drifters would be having them but Cliff wasn't interested.'

It wasn't just that he appeared to believe that sex was for marriage at that time — there were many other boys of his age who felt the same way — but that he didn't seem moved by sex at all. This was an observation made by almost all who knew him.

'From the moment I met him women were of no interest to Cliff,' says Tito Burns. 'I'm not by any means saying he's gay. Not at all. I just don't think sex meant anything to him. People find it hard to understand that there is such a thing as being completely sexless, totally unaffected by sex.'

Ronnie Ernstone thought he was 'undersexed — it just wasn't important to him,' and Maggie Streader says, 'I think there was so much going on in his life that sex played the smallest part. I think he had a very low sex drive.'

His friends didn't know what to make of this behaviour. Some thought it was naïvety. Some thought he'd grown up with an overly protective attitude to women as a result of having to look after his younger sisters. Others blamed his relationship with his mother which they felt was smothering.

When he moved back to Cheshunt from his London flat one national newspaper took the opportunity to say that Cliff was 'running back to mummy'. The accusation stung him badly and it is one of the reasons why his mother has remained wary of the press.

Alluding to this incident, Royston Ellis (writing as Jet) defended Cliff against the charge of being a 'mummy's boy' by arguing that this couldn't be so because he spent so much time away from home.

'True, he is attached to his family, but then most normal sons are,' he said. 'Then there is the question most girls are wondering — why hasn't Cliff Richard got a girlfriend? The answer is simple. Cliff hasn't found the right girl, and he has no time.'

For *Expresso Bongo*, which he started filming at Shepperton Studios almost as soon as he came off the road, his role as a virginal young pop singer discovered in a Soho jazz cellar was remarkably close to reality although it had not been written with him in mind.

Created by Wolf Mankowitz as a satire on the Tommy Steele phenomenon, it had originally been a West End play starring Paul Scofield as the manager and James Kenny as the manipulated boy star.

Bongo Herbert is supposed to be an eighteen year old so madly devoted to his music that he has no time for anything else. 'For me, it's more like a drug,' he confesses. 'Takes my mind off a few things.'

His sharp-talking manager Johnny Jackson (Laurence Harvey) introduces him to the glamorous but fading American star Dixie Collins (Yolande Donlan) who agrees to have him as a guest on her London show and she is eventually eclipsed by him.

Dixie clearly wants to seduce Bongo but he is more interested in talking to her about his love for Lambrettas. She asks him what he'd like to have behind him on the pillion seat if he was to get his motor scooter and he tells her that he was thinking of having a box fitted for his sandwiches.

In one scene, set in her luxury apartment late at night, Dixie purringly asks him whether he has a steady girlfriend.

'Why's everyone always on with this girlfriend routine?' responds a defensive Bongo. 'It's not unnatural or illegal, you know,' says Dixie.

'Girlfriends just pin you down,' says Bongo. 'They're always wanting things.' Dixie slowly sinks into a sofa and looks up at Bongo. 'Sometimes,' she says, 'the feeling is mutual, you know.'

In another prescient scene Johnny Jackson (whose character was modelled on that of Larry Parnes) tries to add a fresh dimension to Bongo's image. He suggests a song about mother love but the songwriter hired to supply the material can't come up with anything that gels.

'So far, what have we got?' asks Johnny. 'Sex. Beat. Violence... we've got it all. We've got it all except for one thing — religion! We've got to get religion!'

'I put that in because religion is always exploited in the common music hall reference out of which this type of music came,' says Mankowitz. 'Mothers and religion have always gone very well together. This suited Cliff too, I think.

'Cliff wasn't our ideal choice for the part because he didn't have the acting experience but he had the right sort of androgynous look. You could start him off quasi-innocent and have his lack of innocence as a singer come through.'

Although he had a clean-living image at the time (noted newspaper journalist Maureen Cleave had called him 'an abstemious paragon'), Cliff was not religious. He had abandoned confirmation classes because, he says, 'I couldn't understand what it was all about'. He didn't doubt the existence of a God and he would pray in times of difficulty but that was the extent of his belief. The crucifix he wore, which fans thought must have religious significance, had belonged to John Foster, who had promised to give it to him at the first sign of success.

His first public connection with a religious organization came when he opened the 59 Club in Hackney Wick and became the club President.

The 59 Club was a new kind of church youth club set up by John Oates, a 27-year-old motorcycling curate, who wanted to create a club which felt more like an espresso bar so that local teenagers could wander in and out without feeling conspicuous.

'I chose Cliff to open the club because I knew he was someone who would attract the young people,' says Oates. 'On the opening night we had 450 people turn up. The following week they all came back and brought their friends. It was chaotic!'

By the autumn of 1959 the effects of stardom were starting to tell on Cliff. The persistent clamour of fans and the lack of privacy brought him a sense of isolation.

'I honestly can't say I enjoy it much,' he grumbled when asked by *Melody Maker* to comment on his status as a 'teenage idol'. He said he worried about the 'innocent faithfulness' of the girls who screamed at him night by night and he couldn't understand why he'd lost all his friends from Cheshunt.

'When I was at school I had lots of pals. Now I've only got one real one from those days,' he said. 'Look, I'm no different. My house is still there and any of my old mates are welcome to come any time and my mother takes care of us all. But it isn't like that any more.

'Suddenly these old friends, my one-time gang, are all peculiar and stiff and strange. And they take the mickey too and try to impersonate me. Mickey-taking in any shape I can't stand – not by anybody or about anybody – but why should they? What bites them?'

The interview displayed what the fan magazines chose to ignore: his tetchiness about being criticized, his doubts about the rewards of stardom and his sense of having lost out on a normal experience of teenage life. It also revealed his competitive attitude towards the charts.

'I've just slipped from top spot in the Hit Parade,' he told the interviewer. 'Craig Douglas has taken over . . . However I think I've got something in store for Craig to worry about. It's a new song called "Travellin' Light" that I've just recorded . . . Simplicity is everything on this one and it's got a real smooth easy tempo. I think it's an even better song than "Living Doll" and I'm banking heavily on it.'

◀ July 1958: first publicity portrait taken at EMI Studios, Abbey Road

August 1958: (left to right) Terry Smart, Cliff and Ian Samwell playing Butlins as the Drifters ▼

1958: Cliff with 'Oh Boy!' producer Jack Good ▶

◀ Cliff puts Good's 'hypodermic syringe' move into action

On the road, 1959: Royston Ellis (second right) with Cliff, band members and friends ▶

February 1959:
Cliff and Donna at the first 'Oh Boy!' party at Ray Mackender's Chelsea flat ▶

February 1959: (clockwise from centre) Cliff, Donna Webb, Tito Burns, Joe Lee (chauffeur), Hank Marvin, Tony Meehan, Bruce Welch, Jet Harris, Len Saxon (road manager), George Ganjou and Dorothy Webb ▼

▲ May 1959: The 'Oh Boy!' line-up. Among the group, Cherry Wainer (front, standing), Dallas Boys (left), Billy Fury (back, third from right), Cliff (back, fifth from right)

▲ June 1959: Summer holiday in Italy - (left to right) Tony Meehan, Pam, Cliff, Ronnie Ernstone

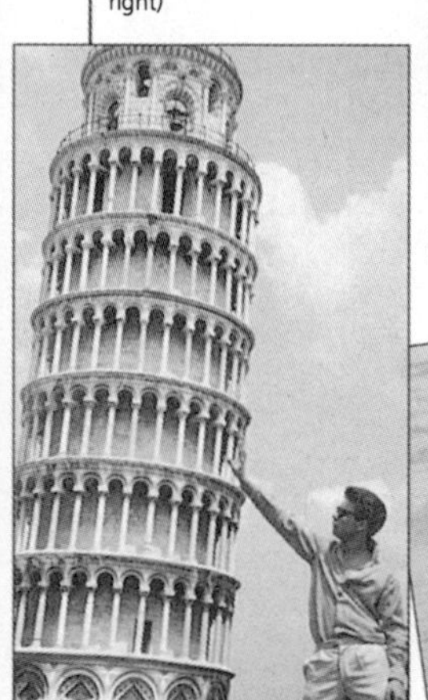

Italy: Cliff and Tony Meehan ▶

June 1959: Cliff enters the gate of Elvis Presley's home in Bad Nauheim, Germany (top left), knocks on the door (top right) and returns disappointed (bottom left)

◀ July 1959: filming Expresso Bongo

August 1959: (left to right) Rodger Webb, Dorothy Webb, Cliff and Ray Mackender ▶

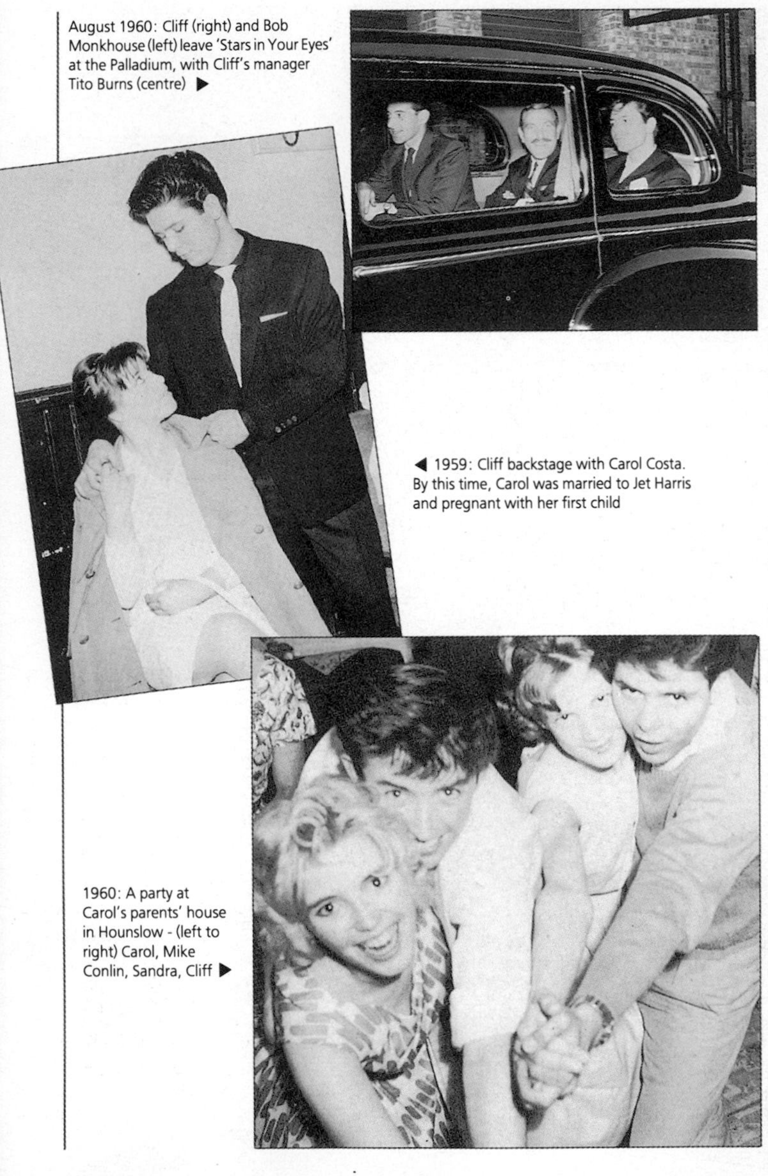

August 1960: Cliff (right) and Bob Monkhouse (left) leave 'Stars in Your Eyes' at the Palladium, with Cliff's manager Tito Burns (centre) ▶

◀ 1959: Cliff backstage with Carol Costa. By this time, Carol was married to Jet Harris and pregnant with her first child

1960: A party at Carol's parents' house in Hounslow - (left to right) Carol, Mike Conlin, Sandra, Cliff ▶

▲ February 1960: Cliff with fans in America

(above right) On tour in the US: (left to right) Freddy Cannon, Jet Harris, Hank Marvin and Johnny Paris (of Johnny and the Hurricanes)

The Shadows: Britain's first instantly recognizable rock group ▼

▲ Cliff with friend and confidante, Cherry Wainer, at the Lotus House restaurant, Edgware Road

▲ Summer 1961: Cliff with girlfriend Delia Wicks in the garden of 2 Colne Road, Winchmore Hill

▲ June 1961: Filming The Young Ones - (left to right) Cliff, Carole Gray, Melvyn Hayes, Annette Robertson, Richard O'Sullivan and Teddy Green

All Cliff's singles so far had been British-written but 'Travellin' Light', a lazy country-flavoured number, was the work of Sid Tepper and Roy Bennett, two veteran New York songwriters who had been writing together for over twenty years. By 1959 they had contributed songs to two of Elvis' films, *Loving You* and *King Creole*, writing them to order from early drafts of the scripts which would be handed out to a pool of songwriters.

'Travellin' Light' had been written in this way for a scene which was subsequently cut from *King Creole.* It was put out on the market and picked up by Cliff who, until the writing of this book, hadn't realized that it had been written for Elvis.

The sparse, almost acoustic arrangement, with Jet's stalking bass line accentuated with Meehan's tambourine and Hank's whining guitar, acknowledged the country mood of 'Living Doll'. Like 'Living Doll' it reached number one.

To rock 'n' roll die-hards, such as Jack Good, this change of pace was the beginning of the end. 'Living Doll', he claimed, was his least favourite song ever. Its lyrics were twee and its tune trite. Cliff had abandoned the true faith of rock 'n' roll.

'There was a period of cooling off between me and Cliff,' admits Good. 'I was moaning about these songs and Cliff abandoning rock 'n' roll. I think I moaned a bit in my *Disc* column. I got no direct feedback but I think he got a bit fed up with me.'

Speculation about rock 'n' roll's death had been rife since the first records were released but 1959 marked the start of a hiatus which would last until the coming of the Beatles. Elvis was in the army, Jerry Lee Lewis had been disgraced over his teenage bride, Little Richard had given up rock 'n' roll to study the Bible, Chuck Berry had been arrested on a sex charge and Buddy Holly was dead.

When Royston Ellis asked Cliff whether rock 'n' roll was dying out he had answered, 'No. It's not dying out at all. Just cleaning up.'

Asked what he thought would take its place he had said, 'I don't know, but rock is leading to a strong beat ballad style of singing,' a trailer perhaps for his second album, *Cliff Sings*, where Norrie Paramor split the repertoire between rock 'n' roll and such orchestrated standards as 'The Touch Of Your Lips' and 'As Time Goes By'. No one expected to be singing rock 'n' roll into adulthood. In *Expresso Bongo*, Bongo is asked by Dixie Collins whether his manager has made plans for his career when he's no longer a teenager. Bongo slowly shakes his head. He can't imagine what it must be like to be twenty.

Recording standard songs with an orchestra was thought to be the obvious way of extending stardom; of proving that you were a mature entertainer.

'He wants to cover everything in show business,' wrote Ellis . 'He would like to tackle every medium there is and make a success of it. This way, and this way only, will he be able to prove that he is a more talented youngster than people care to credit.'

The implication was that talent in rock 'n' roll alone was not real talent. The goal was to become an 'all-round entertainer', and Cliff was well on his way. Ballads suited his vocal style and, unlike a lot of rock 'n' roll singers, he had never abhorred the older songs.

'Although I was in at the beginning of rock 'n' roll I was also in at the end of the era that preceded it,' Cliff says. 'I knew all the songs of Bing Crosby, Frank Sinatra, Teresa Brewer and Rosemary Clooney. When Norrie suggested recording with an orchestra I thought it was a wonderful idea.'

In November he made his debut on 'Sunday Night at the London Palladium', the biggest entertainment show on British television at the time, and Sir Winston Churchill appeared at the premiere of *Expresso Bongo* (which had been rated 'X' certificate because of its stripclub scenes. Today it is rated PG).

Cliff started to dress more conservatively. In October 1959 he was wearing a black leather jacket and white buckskins but by 1960 they were hung up in favour of smart jackets, neckties and suede shoes.

'We used to talk about the teenagers and the mums and dads,' Cliff admits. 'We were very conscious that our careers depended on the mums and dads and that we needed to appeal to them to get going.'

His accent, which in *Serious Charge* sounded like a mid-Atlantic teenage drawl, was becoming more well-rounded. He was losing the Anglo-Indian lilt that he had brought to Britain and, remarkably, he hadn't inherited the North London tones of his schoolfriends.

'His most lasting influence . . . [has been] his speaking voice,' wrote rock critic Nick Cohn at the end of the sixties. 'Before him, all pop singers sounded what they were, solidly working class. Cliff introduced something new, a bland ramble, completely classless.

'It caught on. David Frost uses it. So do [disc jockey] Simon Dee, Sandie Shaw and Cathy McGowan . . . It has become the dominant success voice. I'm not suggesting anyone deliberately copied it from Cliff, but he was where it first broke through.'

That Christmas he and the group appeared in their first pantomime — *Babes in the Wood* — at the Globe in Stockton. Here Cliff made another tentative approach towards starting a relationship with a girl.

Diana Ward was a nineteen-year-old member of the chorus who came from nearby Derby. Cliff appeared to be attracted to her but was obviously too shy to do anything about it. In the meantime Hank asked her out.

'Cliff didn't pair off with anyone, and yet every single girl was out to get him,' says Diana. 'When I went to a party with Hank Cliff just followed us everywhere we went, and then the next night he asked me out.'

They saw each other throughout the season, which went on into January, but almost always with other people in tow. Their first date — a run along the beach at Redcar — included Jet and Carol and subsequent dates had Mike Conlin in position as chaperone.

It was in Stockton that Jet drove into an oncoming car while returning from a late night party with Hank, Mike Conlin and a heavily-pregnant Carol. The boys were only slightly injured but Carol, who was thrown out of the car door, suffered broken ribs and a fractured skull. She was hospitalized and it was feared that she would lose the baby.

Jet was subsequently fined for 'dangerous driving, failing to display L-plates and driving unaccompanied by a qualified driver'.

The Drifters were by now known as the Shadows. They had recorded an instrumental, 'Jet Black', and it was when they tried for a release in America that they discovered the existence of the original Drifters, who threatened them with an injunction over the name. To avoid further problems they called themselves the Four Jets for this release.

It was Jet who came up with the name the Shadows one day while they were drinking at the Six Bells in Ruislip after a ride out on their Lambrettas. He'd thought of the idea because when the spotlight shone on Cliff, as it invariably did, they were performing in the shadows. Also that year a film was released, directed by Jon Cassavettes, called *Shadows*.

On 17 January Cliff and the Shadows topped 'Sunday Night at the London Palladium' and drew a television audience of nineteen million, the most that had ever watched a light entertainment show in Britain. Eddie Cochran, on tour in England at the time, saw the broadcast and thought Cliff was 'quite a good performer but I have seen a lot better in Britain'.

'Living Doll' was Cliff's third American single and had by now become a minor hit, reaching a high point of number thirty in the *Billboard* charts. This was a considerable breakthrough at a time when British artists rarely had transatlantic success. His first two American singles, 'Move It' and 'Livin' Lovin' Doll' had flopped dismally.

Sensing an opportunity of reversing the fortunes of British pop in America, Tito Burns planned to tour Cliff and the Shadows. He eventually signed a deal with Irving Feld of the General Artists

Corporation, one of America's biggest booking agencies, who specialized in putting together top-rate rock 'n' roll package tours.

His 'Biggest Show of Stars 1957' had featured Fats Domino, Chuck Berry, Frankie Lymon and the Teenagers, the Everly Brothers, Paul Anka, Clyde McPhatter, the Drifters (the American group) and Buddy Holly. It was on his 1959 tour, 'The Winter Dance Party', that Buddy Holly had been killed.

For the 'Biggest Show of Stars 1960', Irving Feld planned to feature ten acts on thirty-three dates that would stretch from Montreal to Dallas and across to New Jersey and Philadelphia. His bill reflected the change that was happening to rock 'n' roll with good looks now taking precedence over great talent.

Before Elvis Presley, American pop had been dominated by Italian Americans — such men as Frank Sinatra, Perry Como, Tony Bennett, Al Martino and Dean Martin. Now that rock 'n' roll was apparently on the ropes it was time for the Italians to return.

Feld's billtopper was Frankie Avalon (age twenty, real name Francis Avallone), who sang anaemic high school rock and had become a star on 'Dick Clark's American Bandstand'. Symbolically, it had been Avalon who replaced Buddy Holly on tour the night after he died.

Supporting Avalon on the 1960 bill were Bobby Rydell (age seventeen, real name Robert Ridarelli) and Freddy Cannon (age nineteen, real name Frederick Picariello), both of whom sang the same bowdlerized rock 'n' roll.

Then there was Johnny and the Hurricanes who'd met at high school in Toledo, Ohio, and had had hits with instrumentals 'Reveille Rock' and 'Crossfire', Clyde McPhatter (who'd led the original Drifters), the Isley Brothers, Sammy Turner, the rhythm and blues group the Clovers, the Crests ('16 Candles') and Linda Laurie.

Cliff's name was added at the foot of the poster (mis-spelled Cliff Richards) as an 'Extra Added Attraction: England's No. 1 Singing

Sensation'. No mention was made of the Shadows. Cliff had insisted they should back him despite pressure from the promoter to use the resident tour band.

America was a thrilling place for a group of teenagers to be going to in 1960 when few of their contemporaries in Britain ever left the country. It was the land where the future had already arrived; where there were highways instead of main roads, Cadillacs instead of Morris Minors and Hollywood instead of Borehamwood.

'It was a real eye-opener for us,' says Bruce Welch. 'It seemed so far away from home at the time and it was where rock 'n' roll had come from. Just to be flying on a plane was mind-boggling enough but we were going to be meeting all these American acts and playing in front of crowds of 10,000.'

Sammy Samwell, who had become the Shadows' unofficial manager, remembers the anticipation.

'I was already steeped in American culture because I had two uncles who worked on American air bases,' he says. 'They brought back magazines which had adverts for wonderful wide cars which did about six miles to the gallon and had four happy people driving in them. I had all these wonderful images in my mind as I set off!'

The tour was booked to start in Montreal, Canada, on 22 January and so Cliff and his father, the Shadows, Samwell and Burns flew from London to New York on 18 January and were met at Idlewild Airport (later renamed JFK) by two limousines, one black and one white.

Once in New York the Shadows bought themselves trendy 'pork pie' trilby hats and checked out such legendary jazz clubs as Birdland and the Metropole. Cliff appeared on 'The Pat Boone Show', where he sang 'Living Doll' and 'Pretty Blue Eyes' and engaged in some tame scripted banter.

All the musicians on the tour met up on 21 January and left New York for Montreal on two Greyhound buses which, with their reclining seats and air conditioning, seemed like luxury to Cliff and the Shadows who'd spent the last year toiling around the B roads of

Britain on a Bedford coach.

For the first show Cliff had worked out a set of five songs: '40 Days', 'My Babe', 'A Voice In The Wilderness' (from *Expresso Bongo*), 'Living Doll' and 'Whole Lotta Shakin' Goin' On'. The only change made before the end of the tour was that 'My Babe' was replaced by 'Dynamite'.

The reaction to Cliff's set was beyond all expectations. Every night the show-stopping acts were Cliff and the Shadows, Bobby Rydell and Clyde McPhatter.

'No one could follow after we had finished,' Cliff remembers. 'The crowd were still screaming for more. It was very difficult for the next act to go on. That happened right from the first show.

'I remember there was a big black tour manager and he would get on the coach and say, "Well, I think we should all give a big hand to our friends from England," and they would all applaud us. It was fantastic and I thought we were really going to make it.

'The trouble was that I never saw anyone from my record company [ABC/Paramount] in the whole six weeks. They should have been there. My career in America is littered with lost opportunities.'

From Montreal they drove down to shows in Rochester, New York, and then to Philadelphia before returning to Toronto and Kitchener. Most of the travelling was done at night to avoid traffic and as the winter weather set in and the air conditioning failed everyone would be forced to sleep in their overcoats.

After Canada they wound down through the Midwest to Kentucky, home of the Everly Brothers, and then on to the East Coast. After five dates in North and South Carolina they flew the longest leg of the tour on to Fort Worth, Texas.

'We ran into an electrical storm and everyone was terrified,' remembers Tony Meehan. 'The plane was an old Dakota and the fact that Buddy Holly had died in an air crash on the last tour was still pretty fresh in our minds. I went to sleep though. I was that young and that optimistic.'

In Texas they played Fort Worth, Houston, San Antonio and Dallas before coming to Buddy Holly's home town of Lubbock where they played the Coliseum. Holly's family came to the show and they were moved to tears by the sight of Hank Marvin on stage with his Fender Stratocaster and horn-rimmed spectacles. From the back of the auditorium it looked like a visit from beyond the grave.

The segregation in the Southern states bemused them. They could visit clubs and see black performers such as James Brown and Bo Diddley but they couldn't eat out with black musicians Clyde McPhatter and Sammy Turner who were on the same tour. They even had to travel on separate buses for a while.

It was after the 19 February show in Wichita, Kansas, that Cliff flew back to London via New York to appear at the *NME* Poll Winners concert at Wembley Pool and then, later the same day, on 'Saturday Night at the London Palladium'.

It had been too expensive to bring the Shadows back as well so Tito Burns advised Cliff to surround himself with the best session musicians available. Cliff ignored this advice and instead hired Brian Parker's new group, the Parker Royal Five.

It was a mistake. Jet-lagged on arrival, he had to rehearse that night until half past four in the morning and didn't sleep until after the Wembley show that afternoon. When they tried to wake him in time for the Palladium he was in such a deep sleep that they had to throw cold water in his face to bring him to.

He sleepwalked his way through the performance and was roundly criticized for being lacklustre. He later apologized to his fans, admitting that 'I was just too tired to give you my best,' and then flew back to Milwaukee with his mother for the last night of the tour.

'I honestly was homesick by then,' he explained later that year, 'and I know it isn't just a place you get homesick for, it's the people. And of all the people in the world I miss most, Mum tops the list.' With the tour finally over he headed to New York with his parents for a series of press interviews to promote *Expresso Bongo*, which was opening at the Sutton Theatre in a fortnight.

They even managed a meeting with Colonel Tom Parker, Elvis' illustrious manager, at the Warwick Hotel where he was staying as he awaited Elvis' arrival from Germany. There was talk in the air of Colonel Parker being able to do something for Cliff in Hollywood.

The Colonel made an immediate impression on Cliff and his parents by asking them if they would like to join him for lunch. After they eagerly accepted the great man's offer he reached into an office drawer and pulled out three packets of sandwiches which he then handed around.

On 2 March Cliff flew back to London and was met at the airport by Ray Mackender. The next day, in Frankfurt, Elvis Presley boarded a plane for Fort Dix, New Jersey, where he was demobbed after two years as an army private.

Before he left Germany he had given an interview in which he said that he knew Cliff Richard's work and owned some of his records.

'Sure I'd love to have met him,' said Cliff later that year. 'But I wanted to get home even more. Some day we'll meet and I can think of nothing I'd like more than sharing a bill with him. That would really be something, wouldn't it?'

13

'With Carol it was the first full-blooded romance'

Despite the thousands of miles travelled and the great success of his act, Cliff hadn't made the slightest impression on the American market. You had to do much more than sound like an American to succeed there.

'I'm afraid they had about 4,000 Cliff Richards over there already,' says Tito Burns. 'They just didn't have the appetite for yet another one.'

Sammy Samwell says more or less the same thing. 'The timing was all wrong. He was a little too late and a little too generic. He was somewhere between Elvis Presley and Ricky Nelson and they already had both.'

In Britain he was rapidly becoming the country's highest-paid entertainer, commanding upwards of £1,000 a week for variety shows and £4,000 for a single television appearance. This was in addition to income from record sales, films and the granting of merchandising licenses to companies who were making everything from 2/6d photo books to 5/11d Cliff Richard pillowcases ('You can soon misplace lockets or bracelets, but you will never lose your own pillowcase. Will last for years, and will not fade in the wash').

All of this meant that at nineteen years of age Cliff Richard was rich by the standards of his contemporaries, who would have been lucky to have been going home on a Friday night with ten pounds. One newspaper calculated that he was earning more than the entire government cabinet put together. True he was paying Burns ten per cent of his income, George Ganjou a further ten per cent and had four musicians each on twenty-five pounds a week, but it still left a sizeable amount.

Yet Cliff was not a conspicuous spender. He was happy to have been able to allow both his parents to relinquish their jobs and regain their dignity after years of hardship, but he was never tempted to live particularly ostentatiously.

His pocket money was rationed to ten pounds a week until September 1960 when it was raised to fifteen pounds. His one luxury was cars. Having had the Sunbeam Alpine for almost twelve months, he traded it in at Lex Garage in Brewer Street, Soho, and bought a red American Thunderbird with a white roof for £4,000.

His parents still didn't own their own home and so in May 1960 he bought them a corner house at 2 Colne Road in Winchmore Hill, North London, for £7,000. It was unexceptional by show business standards — a neat suburban semi with a front gate and slatted garden fence — but it was equipped with what were called 'luxuries' at the time: a telephone, a stereo record player, a 21-inch television set, a radiogram, a leather-topped bar and wall-to-wall carpeting.

For a family that hadn't so long ago been sitting on chairs made out of deal packing cases and squashing four children in one bedroom it was paradise. 'This house and everything in it is all paid for,' he proudly announced to visiting members of the press. 'It will last us a lifetime.'

He tried to live as normal a life as was possible, the only difference being that 2 Colne Road was often besieged by fans and so the front gate had to be padlocked and the garden fence had to be raised two feet to prevent intruders.

Dick Teague's sister Sheila was still close to Cliff's youngest sister

Joan, and would spend weekends at Winchmore Hill. She remembers that Cliff's room was in the roof and was reached through a door on the landing which looked as if it was the airing cupboard.

'When you opened the door you went up this beautiful deep blue velvet carpet to Cliff's room,' she says. 'It was like a concealed room and I remember it being all green and yellow with sheepskin rugs.'

To a ten year old like Sheila, who was still living on a council estate in Cheshunt, the house at Winchmore Hill seemed like part of another world.

'We were all very poor and so seeing a taxi arrive for Cliff's mum to take her to the hairdresser was like watching royalty,' she says. 'Cliff wasn't big-headed though. He was very calm, very relaxed and casual.

'He showed a lot of love to his sisters and he'd often spend time in the garden with his dog getting it to bite on the end of a rag and then swinging it around. He took us all out in his car sometimes but when he tried to park he would get recognized and he found he just couldn't go shopping.'

From the outset Tito Burns' plan had been to loosen the bond between Cliff and the Shadows. He wanted to establish the idea of Cliff Richard — solo artist, so that when the beat boom was over Cliff would be able to turn his hand to almost anything.

'The way I saw his career advancing was to turn him into Cliff Richard rather than "Cliff Richard and the . . .". The "and the" was alright, providing Cliff was right up front,' says Burns.

'I wanted him to be accepted in his own right even if he didn't sing "Move It" and have three guitarists backing him. When he reached that pinnacle it wouldn't matter whether he had seventy strings or the Shadows because you'd know they had come to see him.'

Says Hank Marvin, 'Tito probably hated the music anyway and he would much rather have seen Cliff with a group of professional musicians. I don't think he understood what we did or what was happening. He gave more than an impression that he was trying to drive a wedge between Cliff and ourselves.'

Cliff was as unhappy as they were. He'd fought hard to get them on the American tour and had persuaded Norrie Paramor to give them a recording deal in their own right. As far as he was concerned, they hung together like a five-piece band for which he was the singer.

The Shadows' contract with Columbia had so far produced three singles, but none of them had made an impact. Then, after a show in Cannock in April 1960, they were played an instrumental which had been written by Jerry Lordan, who was in a band backing the other singers on the tour.

'I'd written this tune called "Apache",' says Lordan . 'It had been recorded by the guitarist Bert Weedon but I hadn't liked the result so I played it on my ukulele to the Shadows who I knew were looking for new material.'

Bruce Welch and Hank both liked it and took it to Norrie Paramor for their next single but Norrie wanted them to do a version of the traditional tune, 'Quartermasters Stores'. A compromise was reached with 'Apache' on one side and 'Quartermasters Stores' on the other.

For British teenagers the Shadows were the first home-grown group where names could be put names to faces and characters to names. The simple Gretch drum kit, the solid-body guitars and the tremolo arms completed the image of the archetypal rock 'n' roll outfit.

When the Beatles were still wearing leather jackets and jeans on stage, Brian Epstein took them to the Liverpool Empire to see a Cliff and the Shadows concert, pointing out their mohair suits, their choreographed footsteps and the way they bowed at the close of the show. Epstein told them that this was how big-time groups dressed and moved and the Beatles took his advice right down to the last bow of the head.

To maintain their separateness from Tito Burns, who never had any say in their career, the Shadows hired a young Irishman to be their tour manager. His name was Mike Conlin, and they had met him at the 2 I's. Within six months he found found himself doing the same for Cliff and moved in to 2 Colne Road so that he could be on hand twenty-four hours a day.

When on tour Cliff would be eminently sociable during the daytime, eating with the group, going to the cinema and participating in such crazes as archery, pistol shooting and home movies.

'You have to remember that he was the idol of his day,' says Conlin. 'There had never been an English pop star of this magnitude and everwhere he went he was harassed. But when he wasn't constrained by the eyes of the world being on him he was one of the lads.

'If we went to a gig I would often drive him in my car and we would sing all the way down. It wasn't until we got within ten miles of where we were going that we'd have to pull our horns in and work out how to get in the theatre.'

It was at night that they tended to live separate lives. The Shadows' idea of a fun time was to surround themselves with drink and girls and to party into the night but Cliff — who didn't smoke or drink — would only make token appearances at these affairs before disappearing back to his room.

'The Shadows thought they had the world on a string and they really did give it some,' remembers Ronnie Ernstone who would often spend his weekends on the tours. 'Cliff was a bit removed. If he came to a party he wouldn't partake.

'He had great power at the time but he chose not to use it. In fact, rather than choosing not to use it I think he just didn't want the things that he could get with it.'

Sometimes he would take long drives in the night to clear his mind. He later told Royston Ellis, 'I just drive because it's rather a strain to be with people all the time. Even my mother doesn't know this. I'll just drive around for about an hour and a half and then I'll come back and I'll feel great. I go straight to sleep and wake up feeling great in the morning.'

In May, while in Derby to play a concert, he got back in touch with Diana Ward. It was to be their last date. When she came down to London a few weeks later he arranged to pick her up from her cousin's house in Waltham's Cross, but never arrived or called to explain why.

When she wrote to him to find out the state of their relationship she received a letter:

'You ask me to be frank, so I will be. I think it would be better if you were to stop writing or contacting me. I sincerely hope that what I write doesn't upset you. Maybe we'll meet again in the near future. I hope so.'

Diana had a strong suspicion that Cliff's mother, who had only recently learned of the relationship, had stepped in. This, she feels, would explain Cliff's uncharacteristic failure to keep their date, and also the forced nature of the letter — in one breath it forbad contact, and in the next suggested that a meeting would be welcome.

'I think that he had raised his family's standard of living and they were frightened that if he became too involved with a girl and lost his popularity they would lose everything,' she says. 'He was very loving and affectionate but I think that, ultimately, fame was more important to him than anything.'

Yet it wasn't long before he found himself being drawn back into a relationship with Carol. She was now Mrs Jet Harris, and on 22 April had given birth to Ricky Brian Harris — Ricky after Ricky Nelson, and Brian after Brian Rankin (Hank Marvin).

Although they had been married for less than a year, Jet and Carol were at break-up point. The explosive arguments which had seemed engagingly bohemian when they were young lovers were now becoming bitter and increasingly violent as Jet's drinking habit got worse. He was also starting to have affairs with other women.

One night Tony Meehan saw Jet attack Carol after returning drunk from a concert. He dragged her to the floor and knelt on her arms while punching her. Meehan had to dive in and knock Jet out by smashing his head against the wall before he could pull him away.

'It was awful stuff,' Meehan remembers. 'He was out for two or three minutes, enough time to stop him doing awful damage. That's the sort of relationship they had. It wasn't a happy marriage. They weren't suited.'

The more Jet deserted and abused Carol, the more Cliff found his sympathy aroused and he began to comfort and support her. When she was pregnant he'd bought oranges for her to satisfy a craving, and when Ricky was born he was one of the first to visit Carol in hospital, bearing a giant bunch of flowers.

'I think Cliff knew more about what was going on with Jet than I did,' says Carol. It was while lying in hospital with a fractured skull after the car crash in Stockton that I discovered he was having an affair with a dancer. That was the first one I found out about.

'Cliff tried to protect me. He was more attentive and more loving than Jet ever was. When I was pregnant and had a twinge in my back, Cliff would ask if I was alright but Jet wouldn't notice. Cliff was there for me and I think a lot of it was because he knew what was going on behind my back.'

'It bothered me that Jet and Carol weren't very happy together,' says Cliff, 'and that played a part in drawing me back to her again. I never saw Jet hit her but he was obviously a bit of a rough dog. Some people can drink really well but he can't. His problems domestically and artistically were all to do with drink. His problems with Carol were due to the fact that he was drunk most of the time.'

In June Cliff began the most extended engagement of his career: a six-month stint at the London Palladium. This was Tito Burns' biggest coup so far and the show business magazines were buzzing with the story of the office clerk who was now topping the bill at the London Palladium and raking in an estimated £24,000.

Burns had managed it by striking deals with agent Leslie Grade who had exclusive booking rights for this period at the Palladium and who desperately wanted to be involved in Cliff's career.

Knowing the extent of his enthusiasm, Burns used Cliff as a bargaining tool to get other artists of his on at theatres that Grade controlled.

'I wanted to establish Cliff not just as a rock 'n' roller with a few hits but as a personality, somebody who would mean something in years to come,' says Burns.

'I left the rock 'n' roll side to Cliff while I devoted my energies to getting the right things that would further him as a stayer — like the various television shows, like the Palladium over which I battled for a month.'

Leslie Grade was one of three brothers called Winogradsky who had emigrated to London's East End from Russia. Lew and Leslie Winogradsky changed their surname to Grade, Leslie becoming a top show business agent while Lew became managing director of ATV. Linking up with the Grade agency was a significant move for Cliff, for between them the Grades had enormous power to establish an act through film, television and theatre circuits.

The third brother, Bernard, changed his surname to Delfont and became a theatre impresario. 'Stars In Your Eyes', as the Palladium show was titled, was a variety performance which attempted to feature something for everyone. There was up-and-coming comedian Des O'Connor, television actor David Kossoff, pianist Russ Conway, Canadian singer Edmund Hockridge, a team of Palladium dancers, fall-about comedian Billy Dainty, and Joan Regan, a top recording star in the early fifties.

Cliff and the Shadows closed the show with a five-song set, which was interrupted every night by David Kossoff in character as the cockney Alf Larkin from the popular television series 'The Larkins', who would scream abuse from the royal box before making his way on stage and doing a soft-shoe routine with Cliff.

'Almost nothing I said could be heard because of the screaming,' says Kossoff. 'This was to me an entirely new and frightening experience in that I was working with someone who, every time he moved his body, had the audience screaming in orgasmic delight.'

Seven weeks into the 26-week run the Shadows' 'Apache' was released and went into the top twenty. The group pushed to include it in the show but Tito Burns refused them. From his point of view it would detract from Cliff.

The Shadows were understandably resentful. It seemed to them petty to exclude one of the summer's biggest hits from a show where they were part of the headline entertainment. On 20 August 'Apache' actually knocked Cliff off the top of the hit parade when it replaced 'Please Don't Tease'.

Hank and Bruce Welch were now writing together for Cliff. The album *Me And My Shadows* was released in October, and was a prototypical beat record with over half the songs written by them or Jet, Samwell and their friend Pete Chester. It was the first time a British group had recorded so much self-written material and was an early indication of the changes that would occur in the record industry after the Beatles. Like *Cliff Sings*, it went to number two in the LP charts.

'I'm still really proud of that album,' says Cliff. 'A lot of people like Eric Clapton and the guys in Fleetwood Mac were inspired by it because of Hank's guitar work. I think we invented our own English rock 'n' roll. It wasn't American, but neither was "Rock With The Caveman".'

Committed to the Palladium for six days a week, there were still concerts out of London on Sundays. On one of these dates Jet had a brief fling with a hairdresser and word got back to Carol who threatened to leave him.

'I just went berserk that day,' remembers Carol. 'I was beside myself. I had a young child and I couldn't stand it any more. I spoke to him on the phone, told him I was leaving. Then as I was packing my car he and Cliff arrived. Jet begged me not to leave. Cliff went in the kitchen and Jet was with me in the lounge. I asked him how he could do this to me with a new baby and he just smacked me in the mouth. Cliff didn't see him do it but he saw the blood afterwards.'

Cliff drove Carol and Ricky back to her parents in Hounslow and promised to stay in touch. Within days he arrived to take her to the cinema. 'When he took me home,' says Carol, 'he kissed me goodnight and told me that he loved me. Things went on from there really.'

Over the next few weeks they met whenever they could and Cliff began to get more openly affectionate, telling her that he loved her.

The relationship had to be clandestine, not just because of Jet, but because of Cliff's career. They would meet up at the flats of trusted friends, in a central London car park close by the Palladium or they would drive out into the Essex countryside, always with Mike Conlin on hand as a lookout man.

Carol was the most sophisticated girl he had ever dated. He had previously been attracted to shy and virginal girls who were guaranteed not to put any demands on him but Carol, already a wife and mother, was recognized as being streetwise and opinionated.

'She made a beeline for him in a very subtle way which, when you're young, you sometimes mistake for mutual attraction,' says Tony Meehan. 'You don't realize you are being pursued. She had all the allure of a woman and all the forcefulness of a man and she totally dominated him.'

After a Sunday night concert in Blackpool, Carol and Cliff saw a rare opportunity to be alone. They were travelling back on an overnight train and Meehan was booked to share a sleeper with Cliff but, just after boarding, he gave up his bed to Carol. During the night things became more passionate than they had ever been before, but Cliff seemed inhibited.

'I sensed there was something not quite right, and on the Wednesday of the next week that he called me into his dressing room at the Palladium and explained to me that he was a virgin,' says Carol. 'It was then that I understood why he'd been like he had. I was quite shocked when he told me. I think I laughed — but with happiness because I was so relieved.

'I think he was frightened of going all the way because of who he was. That was the reason. He was telling me as though it was something to be ashamed of, but I told him that it was fine.'

Soon after, they did make love twice, at 52 Creighton Road, Ealing, the home of Vicky Marshall, a dancer who had appeared in *Serious Charge* and *Expresso Bongo*. Cliff told his parents that he needed to stay in London overnight for business but instead slept with Carol in an attic room.

The affair ended rather abruptly when an intimate letter sent by Carol to Cliff was opened by Cliff's mother who had assumed it was a piece of fan mail. According to Carol the letter was 'passionate' and expressed delight at the goings-on in Ealing.

'We got back from the Palladium late one night and Cliff's parents were waiting up for him,' remembers Mike Conlin. 'His mother had the letter in her hand. They asked me to go up to bed and then they talked to Cliff until the small hours.

'I never saw the letter but it more or less gave the game away. It was a hell of a lot more personal than a fan letter should have been and his mother and father talked to him all night about the evils of sin and I think that was what broke it off.'

His sister Jacqui was then only twelve but she can recall the night.

'I remember Cliff coming home and being yanked off to a room,' she says. I closed my bedroom door. I knew they were having a serious talk and I knew the subject was Carol. I don't know what was said but my dad would have been seeing it from a spiritual point of view.

'He wouldn't have been so concerned about the effect on Cliff's career or what the neighbours might think but the fact that what he'd done went against God's commandments. That's what would have been uppermost in his mind.

'I remember my mother telling me very bluntly that the Christian way was not to have sex before marriage. She said that sex was something given to married couples. That's all she said! I can remember being a bit taken aback because they didn't normally discuss things like that openly.'

Cliff couldn't bear to offend his mother and matters were made worse by the fact that his father had recently been taken ill. While playing a game of badminton at the club he had suddenly collapsed. The doctor diagnosed thrombosis. Cliff was worried that the news about Carol might kill him.

In desperation he asked Tony Meehan to make the call that would end the affair.

'He couldn't handle it so he asked me to do it and I said yes, because someone had to do it,' says Meehan. 'The relationship was destroying him and it was likely to destroy the group. It was getting too close.

'The way I looked at it was that there was no future in it because he really wasn't prepared. I asked him whether he would be willing to give up his career for this because that's what it amounted to in those days. That she was a married woman was quite a scandal in itself. I said that he would have to jack it all in for her and go away somewhere because the fans wouldn't put up with it.

'When I called up she was quite furious. Understandably so. I think he may have said a few words to her but he was definitely crying. It was a very romantic, child-like affair and it had been making a lot of demands on him.'

For Carol it was a bolt out of the blue. Only days before they had been looking through copies of *Country Life*, deciding on the home they would live in as soon as she was able to divorce Jet and marry Cliff. Now it was all over and he apparently didn't have the courage to tell her himself.

'We had been talking about getting married, we'd made love and now it was all over,' she says. 'I was devastated. I said, "What does he mean?" I insisted that I spoke to him. I wasn't going to have this from Tony Meehan.

'Cliff came on the line and told me that his mother had seen the letter and that he thought the whole thing might kill his father. They were his exact words. He said that he loved me and that he would never marry anyone else. That was it. I just had to accept it.'

The episode is surprising not because a pop star had an affair with a married woman, but because it was so out of character for Cliff, who seemed so uninterested in sex and had gone into print celebrating chaste ideals.

'I suppose in my naïvety I thought no one would either know about it or believe it,' says Cliff. 'It didn't seem to matter at the time. It went against my principles but when you are experiencing these things your principles become unimportant.

'Looking back I can see that they weren't important to me because God wasn't important in my life. He was there, but what part did he really have to play? My parents instilled values into me but possibly if I hadn't have become a Christian they wouldn't have come into play any more.

'When you live a life outside of God you think, well, even if there is a God he's there and I'm here. So what if I steal or commit adultery? I guess that was what was in my mind because I didn't really feel a great deal of guilt. I feel more guilt now over it.

'With Carol it was like the first full-blooded romance, I suppose. It was a love affair. It was one of those things people go through.'

Carol seemed an unlikely girl to have broken down his fabled resistance. She was nothing like the 'slightly shy', demure, plain-looking girl who knew 'when it was time to say goodnight' that Cliff had always claimed to be his ideal.

She harked back to the blonde bombshell fantasy of Brigitte Bardot but, more significantly, she happened to be around at a time when all the Shadows had married and he was beginning to feel lonely.

'Carol obviously got into the inner circle once she'd met Jet,' he says, 'and the next thing I realized was that she was there travelling around on tour. At the Palladium everyone would be there, Carol included, and we became a social unit. Brief encounter though it was, it was a growing-up experience for me.'

It didn't bring him the consolation he needed. Some of his friends felt that it pushed him further away from a fulfilling relationship.

'If you want to be blunt about it Carol had sex with Cliff rather than the other way round,' says Tony Meehan. 'She was tough and determined and Cliff had always been timid with women.

'I think he had a very romantic notion of romance and sex. It was like a schoolboy view. As soon as he was confronted with the reality of it, the forbidding was too strong. So, he was never able to make the jump from schoolboy to man.'

Vicky Marshall disagrees. 'I was in at the beginning, and I was there at the end when the terrible break up took place over the phone in my home,' she says. 'I was on the extension trying to calm them both down while they were crying.

'If it had happened today it would have carried on. It was a beautiful and lovely relationship. It was no quick fling. I heard him say on the phone that he would never ever fall in love again with someone else like he'd fallen in love with her.

'Carol and he were soul mates. They knew each other so well. They were right for each other. Perhaps that was his love. That was it.'

Before the Christmas of 1960 Carol discovered she was pregnant. Rather than telling Cliff, she arranged for a back street abortion.

'He didn't know about the baby,' admits Vicky. 'She made a sacrifice for him. She could have used it to pressurize him into marriage but she didn't. Somebody that can do that isn't half bad.'

Cliff says that he now looks back on the affair with a different set of values. He doesn't deny that it happened but says he is not proud of his behaviour.

He continued to like female company but he would never again have sex even though, for the next four years at least, there was no religious reason to remain celibate. 'I never got round to it,' he explains. 'There was still a fairly old-fashioned bit left in me I suppose.'

To a lot of observers in show business such a muted interest in sex was interpreted as homosexuality.

'There was much more speculation in those days because it was illegal,' says Mike Conlin. 'If someone was in the theatre and not going out with a girl it was assumed that they were gay.

'Cliff was a target for homosexuals because he was a sex symbol and he didn't have a girlfriend. The fact is that at the time Cliff was terrified of homosexuals. He never wanted to be left alone with them.'

The only time an aggressive homosexual did get close to Cliff was after a concert in Portsmouth when a man managed to get into his hotel room late at night.

'I can remember being nervous because the guy wouldn't leave,' says Cliff. 'I kept saying, "Look, this is my private time and this is my room," but he just kept advancing.

'Mike Conlin always slept in an adjoining room and I called out for him and he came and got rid of the guy.'

'Funnily enough,' says Conlin, 'at the same time that all these rumours were going around I knew that Cliff was having this affair with Carol that no one else knew about.

'Also, I spent twenty-four hours a day for months on end with him, travelling the world and sharing hotel bedrooms, and there was never a sniff of anything that you could even begin to raise an eyebrow at.

'I think that if he got burned over the affair with Carol it may have left a scar and made him loathe to go into anything else.'

In November 1960 he was interviewed by Steve Race and Royston Ellis for the BBC Radio programme 'Frankly Speaking'. He emerged as an assured, if slightly naïve, young man who was much more in control of his career than his interviewers appeared to have given him credit for.

His image was already set. He spoke of his respect for his parents, his lack of interest in party politics and his belief that he needed to be single for the sake of his career.

'Because I am a male singer,' he confessed, 'my fans like to think that perhaps they have the chance of dating me. I have to stay this way as long as I possibly can. It's not always a good thing, because people then say, "Well, he's not really relying on his singing, he's relying on the fact that girls like him." '

Royston Ellis asked whether he'd ever felt like exploiting his position to go out with as many girls as he could.

'No, I haven't,' said Cliff. 'In fact I think I've only ever dated one fan. But I found the reaction from fans wasn't too good so I just gave up on it altogether.'

Steve Race then leapt in. 'Can I speak here as the elderly parent type?' he said. 'In this teenage world you have this image that regardless of the opposition you will marry the girl you love. "They try to tell us that we're too young, but we're not" and so on. Now you're saying that "love is all, but my teenage audience want me unmarried so I won't marry". Isn't that a betrayal of your attitude?'

'Oh sure, I'll marry her eventually,' Cliff answered. 'But I shan't make it public that I'm going out with a girl. It's a sly way of doing it but I haven't met the girl I love yet anyhow. I don't think I will because at the moment I've dated perhaps four or five girls, and none of them more than two or three times each.'

It was a fair point. There was an irony in the fact that the great icon of teenage romance had to deprive himself of romance to keep his position. But that's the way things were and Cliff would admit to no regrets.

'As far as I'm concerned, it [my career] may die out next week,' he said. 'Well, I've done everything I could possibly want to do and possibly everything anybody could want to do. I've got a gold disc, I've been to America, I've filmed, I've made records. So if it all ended for me, the one thing I could say is that I've lived a fuller life than most people will ever do.'

14

'He's the person to make a film with'

Two days after Christmas 1960, Cliff's father's health took a turn for the worse and he was rushed into hospital where he stayed until 28 January. Over the autumn months he had got weaker. He was having difficulty in breathing and spent most of the days lying on a settee. During this time his relationship with Cliff slowly changed.

'Dad became helpless and I had to do everything,' says Cliff. 'I hadn't done anything before because he wouldn't let me but suddenly I had become the head of the house. Not only was I the breadwinner but I had to change the plugs.'

No one who saw Cliff and his father together ever thought there was the normal bond of familial affection. Most would say that there was no real love. Some go as far as to say that they believed Cliff resented his father. As one friend put it, 'Cliff always showed respect to his father but I don't think he ever really had respect for him.'

Cliff admits that he was always frightened of his father, but there was never any discussion of what might have gone wrong between them, even when his father was dying. 'We just didn't talk like that,' he says.

Because Cliff was still under the legal age of consent, all contracts, including those with EMI and his management, had to be approved and signed by his father, Rodger, who feared that his son could be exploited by those only interested in short-term gain. This fatherly concern naturally annoyed those who wanted a free hand in shaping Cliff's career.

Tito Burns gave him an office desk and a handsome salary of £100 a week. 'He felt that he had become beholden to his son,' says Cliff's aunt, Olive Queenie, 'and that was a terrible thing for him to feel. Instead of him supporting the family, his son was supporting the family. When Cliff gave him the job it made him feel he was doing something.'

Burns had to tolerate the arrangement because it had been he who had originally charmed Cliff's parents into giving him their boy, but privately he considered Rodger Webb the biggest drawback in Cliff's career and he resented his attempts to offer business advice.

'He was a very dogmatic man,' he says. 'He had his ideas but I thought they were all wrong. We ended up having arguments because he was quite ill and getting very edgy. He wanted my management contract with Cliff ended although he gave no specific reasons and, under the terms of the contract, there should have been.'

Burns suspected that the real reason was that agent Leslie Grade wanted more control over Cliff's career. Grade had just bought the option for his next film from Mickey Delamar for £7,500, and was courting Cliff's parents.

'I was involved in a dispute with Leslie Grade over what Cliff should be paid for the film,' says Burns, 'when in walks Cliff's father smoking a big cigar. I knew then that the only person who could have given him that was Grade.

'I think he was giving the old man money to make my severance pay. When it came within £1,000 of what I would have got if I had seen the three-year contract out, I said OK.'

When Burns' departure was announced in the press in February

1961 it was said to be 'amicable' and Rodger Webb claimed he was now 'looking after' his son. Neither of these statements was true.

Burns was furious to have been rowed out in such dubious circumstances and although Cliff's father may have momentarily held the reins that was only because he knew someone even more proficient was coming in to take over.

Peter Gormley was a 41-year-old Australian who had served in the war and then taken on various media jobs which had prepared him for his real role in life, that of being a personal manager to show business stars.

He had been a journalist, a literary agent, a film director's assistant, the manager of a circuit of cinemas and, most recently, the manager of an Australian singer called Frank Ifield. It meant he not only knew about publicity and journalism but about making and screening films. Most importantly, he knew how to get bottoms on seats.

He'd arrived in Britain in 1959 to prepare the way for Frank Ifield. Ifield was a country-style singer with a trademark yodel and Gormley had a recording contract with Columbia waiting for him in England by early 1960.

Three top fifty hits followed that year and in the summer Norrie Paramor approached Gormley to look after the Shadows now that they were a pop act in their own right. He listened to 'Apache' and saw them in 'Stars In Your Eyes' at the Palladium before he agreed to become their manager.

Peter Gormley was as unlike Tito Burns as a manager could possibly be. Where Burns oozed showbiz patter and was still appearing on television as a performer while managing Cliff, Gormley was soft spoken, modest and eager to stay out of the limelight.

The Shadows were impressed with his quiet but thorough ways and it was natural that when Burns was dismissed by Rodger, Gormley would start to manage Cliff as well.

'The request came from Rodger and Cliff's lawyer,' says Gormley.

'I was already managing the Shadows, so first of all I had to satisfy myself that it was all clean and clear between Cliff and the Shadows, and then I had to meet with Rodger to make sure there was no conflict going on, no resentments or undertones.'

Most unusually for a show business manager, Peter Gormley didn't draw up a contract, preferring to do business on trust, and refusing to take anything for the first year because it wasn't work that he had negotiated.

Two months after Gormley had taken control, Rodger had a sudden relapse and was rushed into an intensive care unit at Highlands Hospital, Enfield, where he was immediately put into an oxygen tent.

'I don't know whether he knew he was dying but he was such a stubborn man,' says Cliff. 'They actually caught him once undoing the oxygen tent from the inside so that he could have a smoke. He managed to hide a safety pin so that he could pull the zip up from the inside. He was a dominant character right to the end.'

On 15 May, at the age of fifty-six, he died. It was a shock to Cliff because he was just beginning to get close to him and felt that if he'd had the right treatment earlier he could have lived longer.

'At the funeral I can remember not being able to control my tears and it didn't bother me,' says Cliff. 'It was one of the first times I had ever cried publicly.'

By now he was in rehearsals for the first film set up by the Grade Organization's film department after the Delamar buy-out. For months rumours had been circulating. It was suggested that Cliff would star in *Hide My Eyes*, a murder thriller written by Margery Allingham. Several actresses were mentioned as being under consideration as his co-star – Carol Lynley, Heidi Bruhl, Helen Shapiro and Diana Dors among them.

Then came the announcement that Cliff's debut as a leading man was to be in an original musical produced by Kenneth Harper. None of the stars whose names had been bandied about were mentioned.

Kenneth Harper was a tall, well-spoken man in his forties who had an apartment in Mayfair and offices in a Regency terrace off St Martin's Lane.

Since coming to London after the war he had worked for a theatrical agency and, for the past six years, as an independent film producer on films such as *For Better, For Worse* with Dirk Bogarde, *Yield To The Night* with Diana Dors and Sean Connery's debut film *Action Of The Tiger*.

Now, working from within the Grade Organization, Kenneth Harper was focusing his attention on Cliff Richard.

'I found that Cliff was filling cinemas on a Sunday when films were emptying them,' says Harper. 'I went to see him and he was knocking the audience out. I thought, if he can knock an audience out on a Sunday night in a cinema that is absolutely full, then he's the person to make a film with. We hadn't made proper musicals in the UK before and no one believed we could.'

Kenneth Harper and Leslie Grade took the idea of a Cliff Richard musical to Jimmy Wallis, Head of Production at ABC (Associated British Picture Corporation), who asked them to come up with a figure. Harper asked for £110,000 and got it. When Leslie Grade later asked him how he knew it would cost £110,000 he said, 'I haven't a clue. It'll probably cost more but let's just go for a nice round figure.' It was eventually to cost half as much again.

With the money in hand Harper set about gathering a creative team. To write the screenplay and the production numbers he called on lyricist Peter Myers and composer Ron Cass who had worked together on a number of popular West End revues including *Intimacy At Eight* (1952), *For Amusement Only* (1956) and *For Adults Only* (1958).

To direct it he chose Sid Furie, a 28-year-old Canadian who had made the well-received *A Dangerous Age* when he was only twenty-four and *A Cool Sound From Hell* before coming to Britain in 1959 to make *The Snake Woman*, *Doctor Blood's Coffin* and *During One Night*.

The initial problem was finding a story to turn into a musical. The most obvious device was to do *The Cliff Richard Story* in the way that Tommy Steele had done *The Tommy Steele Story* but Harper had found Cliff's 1960 autobiography *It's Great To Be Young* so devoid of drama that he'd abandoned reading it after ten pages. He then gave to it to songwriter Herbie Kretzmer who had scolded him by saying, 'I don't know how you could conceivably make a film with any attraction at all when the only thing that has ever happened to this boy was when a microphone broke down at the Elephant and Castle when he was eighteen!'

The idea that eventually became *The Young Ones* emerged from an evening session at Kenneth Harper's flat when Sid Furie, Peter Myers and Ron Cass met together to toss ideas around. None of them wanted to make a rock 'n' roll movie but they all had affection for the old MGM musicals.

They talked about *Babes in Arms*, the Rodgers and Hart musical that starred Mickey Rooney and Judy Garland as the teenage children of retired vaudevillians who put on a show to raise money. The idea developed of a group of young people getting together to save their youth club from being torn down by a rich property developer — youth clubs and property developers were of particular interest in 1961.

'We watched every old MGM film that Mickey Rooney ever made,' says Harper. 'I didn't see anything wrong in pinching from things that have already been a huge success. Most people had forgotten them anyway. There was nothing enormously original about the plot we used but I don't believe there is anything wrong with making something which is pure entertainment. We didn't want to send a message.'

Because Cliff was such an inexperienced film actor the plan was to conceal his inadequacies by surrounding him with talented actors and dancers. The property developer, Hamilton Black, was to be played by Robert Morley; Richard O'Sullivan, Teddy Green and

Melvyn Hayes were to play the key members of the youth club gang and Cliff was to be Hamilton Black's son Nicky. The choreography would be by Herb Ross who had been working on Broadway.

Casting a female lead was difficult. If she was too beautiful the fans would resent her. If she was too ugly she would be unbelievable as Cliff's love interest. While Kenneth Harper was in New York he had been taken by Herb Ross to see a show featuring a talented Jewish girl he thought would be right for the part. Harper wasn't as convinced and didn't invite her to an audition. Her name was Barbra Streisand.

The girl who eventually got the role was Carole Gray, a young dancer from Rhodesia who had come to London and had appeared in West End stage versions of *The Boyfriend* and *West Side Story*. She had fleshy lips, a long nose and narrow eyes and was almost totally unknown. After the attention surrounding the film had subsided she would return to her anonymity. She was the perfect girl for Cliff.

Much to the annoyance of Peter Myers and Ron Cass, who were writing the soundtrack, it was decided to import half a dozen pop songs to hook the teenage audience.

'Basically we weren't given a chance to write any of the alleged pop numbers,' says Ron Cass. 'We were just the work horses who did the vital and more difficult work.'

For the songs that would hopefully be hits, Norrie Paramor, musical director for the film, turned to Sid Tepper and Roy Bennett, the writers of 'Travellin' Light'. He sent music publisher Cyril Simons to New York with a script and a commission to write three numbers.

'I arrived in New York in the morning, left the scripts with Tepper and Bennett and told them I wanted a song called "The Young Ones",' says Simons. 'I then went on to LA and when I returned forty-eight hours later they had produced three songs, one of which was "The Young Ones", one was "Outsider" and the other was "When The Girl In Your Arms Is The Girl In Your Heart", which they had already written but which no one had recorded.

'I flew back to London that day and played them to Norrie and he loved them and Cliff had two number ones from them. They recorded "Outsider" but eventually decided not to use it because nobody was one hundred per cent sold on it.' (It was used on the album *21 Today*, along with another Tepper–Bennett song, 'Catch Me'.)

Most of the filming took place at the Elstree Studios during June and July 1961 except for the vaudeville finale which took place at the Finsbury Park Empire.

Although 'Stars In Your Eyes' at the Palladium had been blighted in Cliff's memory by the clandestine affair with Carol, it had also introduced him to the next girl in his life. She was an attractive 22-year-old blonde called Delia Wicks, one of the dancers in the show, who had been selected from the line-up to play a special scene with Cliff where he sang a medley of songs about the moon and then kissed her. The girls in the audience would all shriek at this point and Delia was paid an extra four pounds a week for her hard work.

She had come to London from Leeds at the age of fifteen to learn dancing at the John Tiller School and had been a Tiller Girl for five years before joining Billy Petch's dancers at the Palladium.

They hadn't dated during the Palladium run and then, early in 1961, while making a promotional appearance at the Queen's Hotel in Leeds, he phoned her at her mother's and came to the family home in Dewsbury Road for tea. It was the start of a brief romance which no one but their families, Mike Conlin and Delia's friend Eve Sewell ever knew about.

'Our romance was very secret,' says Delia. 'He never mentioned it afterwards and so, out of respect for Cliff, I never mentioned it either. It was a wonderful time in my life because, as you can imagine, I was absolutely overwhelmed by him.'

His arrival in Leeds was a bolt out of the blue for Delia who had assumed she would never see him again after the Palladium. 'He told me that he'd missed me,' she says. 'Then he started to call me up, often very late at night, while he was touring.'

Mike Conlin's memory is that during these early months 'he pursued her like a bat out of hell', driving back to her basement flat in Stockwell after one-night stands in the north of England and grabbing every available opportunity to be at her side.

'Once he drove all the way down from Newcastle after a show to see me and I remember he hadn't shaved and he was wearing a long leather coat,' says Delia. 'He parked his car outside and felt he couldn't stay too long because everyone would see his Thunderbird.

'Another day he came running to my flat, saying "I'm so lonely, Delia. I've got to see you." He fell through the door and gave me a big kiss and I was just standing there dripping wet because I'd been washing my feet when the doorbell rang.

'We used to go out for drives in the country and I would visit him at his home. On Sundays he'd sometimes hire the whole swimming pool at Dolphin Square [London's largest complex of serviced apartments] and Mike Conlin, Cliff's mum and his sisters would come.'

It was a busy year for Cliff. A typical week would consist of several one-night stands, a couple of press interviews, a late-night recording session at Abbey Road, a promotional appearance and a radio show such as 'Saturday Club' or 'Parade Of The Pops'. Then there was the rehearsing and filming of *The Young Ones*.

In March he made his first tour of South Africa and encountered some of the most frenzied crowd scenes of his career. There were 3,000 fans at Salisbury airport when he flew in, and in Johannesburg a few days later 10,000 fans converged on the Carlton Hotel, where he was staying, bringing the city centre to a standstill. The police had to ask him to make an announcement from his balcony to pacify the crowds.

In Durban the local Indian population tried to claim him as one of their own, lining the route from the airport to the city and cheering him on. The Shadows noticed that he was disturbed by this response because it awakened the memories of the abuse he'd suffered over his racial identity when he first came to England.

Because of apartheid laws preventing mixed-race audiences Cliff agreed to do two shows — one in Harare and one in Cape Town — for a Black Africans-only audience, the profits being given to the Salisbury Society for Handicapped Africans.

Once back home his secret relationship with Delia continued. She had to promise not to mention it to anyone and when they went out they were not to be seen holding hands or kissing. At clubs and cinemas Delia had to make a separate entrance so that no one would connect them. In the street he would mask his face behind a handkerchief.

'I was prepared for the fact that these relationships would be difficult,' says Cliff. 'It was because of the kind of press I might get and what that might do. No one really knew whether it would damage your career, but I wasn't prepared to find out.

'It was hard to sustain anything that was going to have any meaning because we didn't see each other very often. I saw more of Delia during the Palladium run than I did when we later went out with each other.'

The impression Delia got was of a very harassed young man, denied a normal life, who just longed for some space in which to be himself.

'He hardly had any time to relax,' she says. 'He was always being pressured into doing things. He used to work so hard that sometimes when he came to see me he would just fall asleep in my arms.

'We were usually just so overwhelmed to see each other. You've no idea. It was such a relief for him. Everybody was always watching him and yet when he came to see me this was his big secret.'

He never mentioned his affair with Carol Costa to Delia and didn't seem about to repeat the experience. 'We kissed and cuddled but sleeping together was a bit taboo in those days,' she says. 'People didn't live together or anything like that.'

When his father died he seemed to change. Delia remembers him suddenly asking her out of the blue whether she was a Christian.

'He must have been thinking about it for a long time but it just came out like that,' she says. 'I don't think he would have carried on going out with me if I had said no.'

He also started to draw closer to his mother. Often when he came to Delia's flat he would call her to tell her where he was and he'd refuse to make decisions until she had been consulted.

'I used to ask him why he always had to ask his mother,' says Delia. 'He used to say he was very concerned about her. I suppose he felt he was looking after his family.'

One night, when Delia went to Winchmore Hill before going out with Cliff to see the American singer Peggy Lee at the Pigalle nightclub, Cliff's mother drew her aside as she was getting herself ready in one of the bedrooms.

'I can visualize it now,' says Delia. 'I was wearing a white strapless dress. She had said something before when we were downstairs but now she was saying it again. She was telling me not to get too fond of Cliff because his career was going ahead. I just shrugged it off at the time. I thought Cliff could make his own mind up.'

In August he toured Scandinavia with the Shadows and sent Delia a series of postcards which indicated that all was still well. Some were written as soon as he settled in a new hotel and all of them started 'Hi Sweetie' and were signed 'Love, Cliff'. Then, on his twenty-first birthday, he left for his first tour of Australia, playing in Singapore and Kuala Lumpur on the way. After three sell-out concerts in Sydney he travelled to Melbourne where he sat in his hotel room and wrote a letter to Delia.

'Dear Delia

'I know I haven't written for a long time, but I've been confused in my mind about you and about myself.

'I have had to make, probably, one of the biggest decisions I'm ever going to make and I'm praying that I won't hurt you too much.

'Delia, I want you to try and understand the position I'm in. Being a singer I'm going to have to give up many things in life.

'But being a pop singer I have to give up one very priceless thing – the right to have any lasting relationship with any special girl.

'Delia, you must find someone who is free to love you as you deserve to be loved, and is able to marry you.

'I couldn't give up my career. Besides the fact that my mother and sisters, since my father's death, rely on me completely, I have show biz in my blood now and I would be lost without it.

' "D" all I can say now is, goodbye and don't think too badly of me.

Love, Cliff.'

The letter arrived at the basement flat of 41 West Cromwell Road on the morning of 26 October.

'I remember that day so well,' says Delia. 'My whole world changed. I was heartbroken. I thought, "Gosh, I'll never see him again." I remember having to be at the Motor Show in Earls Court and I walked around not really seeing anything. I was absolutely dumbstruck about it because I knew he was terribly fond of me at the time.

'I never contacted him after that because I thought there was no point. I felt, "That's it". I went into mourning for about two weeks and didn't speak to anyone. I wanted to tell the whole world but I realized that I couldn't because our romance had still to be kept a secret.

'He had obviously wanted to get involved with me but then he got frightened and that was it. It was all so confusing. I've never got to the bottom of it.'

'I was a coward there,' admits Cliff. 'I didn't want to face her and tell her – and I had been away a long time anyway – and I thought that if I saw her again I could confirm it but I'd rather get it off my chest. I thought it was unfair, once I'd decided that it wasn't for me, to leave someone at home thinking that when I came back it was all going to be hunky dory.'

A brief study of postmarks and diary dates reveals that another reason for breaking off with Delia must have been the fact that he had met someone new.

At the end of August he had done his first season at Blackpool, a six-week run at the Opera House, and he had been enamoured by a nineteen-year-old dancer called Jackie Irving who appeared earlier in the show. Cliff would go out and watch her each night and remembers thinking to himself, 'Gosh. She's beautiful.'

It was an opinion shared by the rest of the Shadows. Jet Harris fancied her madly and Tony Meehan felt that she was one of the most beautiful women he had ever seen. 'After Jackie Irving was made,' he says, 'they threw away the mould.'

'Cliff was a bit timid and he asked me if I'd do him a favour,' remembers Jet. 'He asked me to introduce her to him. I thought, "Dammit! I want to introduce myself to her!" So I got hold of her, took her to his dressing room, and I said, "Cliff, this is Jackie – Jackie, this is Cliff." And then I disappeared.'

Jackie was a local Blackpool girl whose mother ran a boarding house. She had large eyes, high cheek bones, long hair and a great sense of fun.

'We started going to all the after-show parties together and I found myself more attracted to her than anyone else and so I spent more time with her,' says Cliff.

'We went out dancing, we ate out and, of course, I went back and met her mum. It doesn't take that long to realize that something like that is happening.'

She soon moved down to London, taking a flat at 102 Hatherley Court in Hatherley Grove, Queensway, and Cliff and Jackie were seen as an inseparable couple. Everyone seemed to think they were perfect together and for the first time friends and family started whispering about marriage.

15

'My career had reached a plateau'

The Shadows' line-up had remained unchanged for almost three years, during which time they had enjoyed five top ten hits and had become the best-known beat group in Britain. Hank had become a guitar hero inspiring thousands of boys to strum their cricket bats in the mirror. It was the beginning of a lineage that would produce Eric Clapton, Peter Green, Pete Townshend, Jimmy Page, Jeff Beck, Mark Knopfler and Brian May.

Yet during 1961 frictions between the four members were coming to the surface. Hank was easy-going but Welch was an often tetchy perfectionist who prided himself on speaking his mind. One of the few occasions anyone can recall Cliff becoming violent was when he and Welch squared up at 100 Marylebone High Street after Welch returned one night to discover a dog sleeping in his bed.

'We always thought of Bruce as the moody guy,' says Cliff. 'If he couldn't tune his guitar he would sling it down and drive all the way back to London. He left the Shadows a number of times.'

In *The Shadows By Themselves* ('The Kings Of Beat Music Tell Their Own Fabulous Story') each Shadow was asked to comment on his colleagues. Tony Meehan said, 'He [Welch] is a great organizer and I often feel he would make a first-rate sergeant-major in the Guards.'

It was a thinly-veiled insult which Welch was quick to recognize, mentioning in his own comment that Meehan was 'quick tempered', a 'bit of a brain' who 'knows what he wants and he'll end up getting it'.

Meehan was a precocious teenager who, despite his lack of schooling, read voraciously, was a keen student of psychology and was a great lover of jazz and blues. Whereas the rest of the Shadows confessed to liking Agatha Christie and Dennis Wheatley (if they had time to read at all), Meehan put under 'Reading Matter' in the group's biography: *Mr Jelly Roll* by Alan Lomax and *Civilisation and its Discontents* by Sigmund Freud.

Other than drumming, his interests were philosophy and psychoanalysis. Says Royston Ellis, 'Tony was the most intelligent and analytical of the Shadows.'

But after three years of hard work he was starting to slack. 'He had no respect for time,' remembers Cliff. 'The coach would be leaving, we'd be telling him that he was five minutes late, and while you were telling him he would be sitting down and ordering fried eggs and bacon. There were many times when we just had to leave him behind.'

In October, shortly before the group was due to depart for Australia, Welch and Meehan got into a flaming row which ended with Meehan walking out and suggesting they look for another drummer. Welch took him at his word and Brian Bennett, ex-Marty Wilde's Wildcats, was brought in.

'It was all getting too much for me,' says Meehan. 'We worked seven days a week, we never had any holidays and I had just started my first family. We had been worked into the ground because nobody thought it was going to last.

'When we were at the Palladium we used to work for six days a week, do three shows on a Saturday and were then put on a train to do a Sunday concert for which we would be paid five pounds extra.'

Jet was the next to go. The official leader of the Shadows, he had been causing concern for some time because of the effects of his drinking.

In *The Shadows By Themselves* he described his favourite drink as 'shandy' but the truth was that he loved whisky. 'He was a lush,' says Meehan. 'He drank himself stupid. He was a totally self-destructive creature.' None of this was known to the fans at the time who were told that Jet suffered from 'nerves' and was 'taking the plunge to go solo'.

He has since blamed his descent into alcoholism on Cliff's dalliance with Carol, but those who were around at the time say that the pattern had been established long before. 'It wasn't so much that he drank a lot,' says Cliff, 'but that he couldn't drink well.'

He would be found in theatre bars when he was due to be on stage and sometimes had to be pulled out of fights that had started when someone had suggested he must be 'queer' because he dyed his hair and wore fancy clothes. On tour in New Zealand he woke up one morning to find himself on the floor of a hut next to a Maori woman in full tribal costume. He had no idea how he came to be there.

When Bruce Welch broke the news to Jet on 15 April 1962 that he was no longer a member of the Shadows, a replacement had already been found. A month before, on 13 March, Peter Gormley had had his first meeting with Brian 'Licorice' Locking, an unassuming young bass player recommended by Brian Bennett who had played with him backing both Vince Taylor and Tony Sheridan.

What no one except Bennett knew at the time was that Locking was an ardent Jehovah's Witness who, when he was on tour, would seek out local members and carry out door-to-door evangelism. Bennett knew because he had introduced Locking to the teachings in 1958, because, although not a member himself, he had been raised as a Witness by his mother. Locking studied the teachings for two years and then became a baptized member in 1961.

'He was just a nice guy,' says Bruce Welch. 'We were twenty or twenty-one years old and you don't ask a guy his religion when he plays bass guitar. The question was whether or not he was a good musician. And we liked him.'

Although his stay with the Shadows was brief his influence was profound because it was through Locking that Cliff was led back to studying the Bible for the first time since his teens.

The biographies and autobiographies all state that Locking got into conversation with Cliff about religion while on tour in Australia, a story which can't be true because Locking never toured Australia with the Shadows. It must have taken place in England and would almost certainly have been in 1962.

'I remember the conversation,' says Locking. 'I think it was in a hotel room and it wasn't with Cliff alone. There were one or two other people from another group that was on the same tour. We were having a bit of an argument and the subject of spiritualism came up and I just brought out what I believed. But my initial conversations on the subject had been with Hank who seemed to be the most interested.'

Cliff's only comments on religion in his early autobiography make interesting reading today.

'Whatever else becomes public,' he said, 'one's own beliefs should be private. Religion is something that is in one's heart. I don't go to church a lot. Leading my hectic sort of life it's often difficult.'

His change of heart began with his father's death which pushed him into a more questioning mode. The satisfaction that he'd once received from doing a successful concert began to diminish.

'I was quite enjoying myself in showbiz... but there was this "something" missing,' he wrote in 1968. 'I'd go on stage for half an hour... and I'd be quite excited and exhilarated. Then, after the show, we'd all sit about and "wind down", talking about the show, the audience and so on. Gradually, the excitement would wear off, and I'd find myself thinking, "What a drag this all is!" This was before I began even thinking about religion.'

During the Australian tour of 1961 he idly began to contemplate the possibility of contacting his father through a medium. Some of the girls in the Blackpool show had been playing with moving glasses and he told a *Melody Maker* journalist that this had prompted him to think of 'delving into spiritualism'.

'After enjoying this new closeness with my dad just before he died I was beginning to feel dissatisfied with my career,' he says.

'I thought that if it was possible I would get in touch to find out what was happening, to find out why I was feeling this way and to see what was ahead for me. My career was going well but it had reached a plateau. I wondered where I was going.'

It was when he talked openly about contacting a medium that Locking jumped in with what the Bible said about dabbling with the spirit world.

'He jolted back and said "You shouldn't do that. It's dangerous," ' Cliff remembers. 'He said the Bible prohibited it. I told him to show me. I wasn't prepared to accept his word for it.'

Locking got his Bible and read from the Old Testament book of Deuteronomy: 'There should not be found in you anyone who makes his son or his daughter pass throught the fire, anyone who employs divination, a practitioner of magic or anyone who looks for omens or a sorcerer, or one who binds others with a spell or anyone who consults a spirit medium or a professional foreteller of events or anyone who inquires of the dead. For anybody doing these things is something detestable to Jehovah.'

Cliff was impressed with this seasoned musician who quoted the Bible with such assurance.

'I think it was a bit of a revelation to Cliff that this rocker should be involved with something so completely divorced from rock 'n' roll,' says Mike Conlin.

'I know that he used to talk to Licorice because he was trying to understand it. He was trying to put a finger on what it was that made this guy someone who one minute would be playing rock 'n' roll and the next would be putting pamphlets through people's doors.'

Although because of his background he respected the Bible, it wasn't initially what Locking said that got through to him but the zeal with which he said it. He had arrived at a point in his life when he needed more than his career to be passionate about.

The Jehovah's Witnesses had started in America during the nineteenth century and came to be characterized by their vigorous proselytizing techniques, including 'doorstep evangelism'.

They used their translation of the Bible as a source book but diverged from historical Christian teaching on key doctrines such as the trinity (Father, Son and Holy Ghost), the eternal human soul and the incarnation (Jesus as God in the flesh).

'Christianity hadn't been relevant to me before,' says Cliff. 'I didn't even know that God had a name — Jehovah. I started to read more and more. I was impressed by the prophecies they mentioned and by the fact that God could be understood rationally.'

Locking's entry into the group coincided with *Summer Holiday*, the second film put together by Leslie Grade . It was to be set in Greece because Kenneth Harper wanted to make a film which would pick up on the increased interest among young Britons in travelling abroad. He had toyed with the idea of setting a story in Spain, then untouched by mass tourism, but decided that it was too near and that Greece had more romantic connotations.

He kept the core of Cliff's gang from *The Young Ones*, Peter Myers and Ron Cass as writers and Herb Ross as choreographer. He wanted to keep Sid Furie as director but he didn't want to make another musical so Furie hired 33-year-old Peter Yates.

The problem for the writers was to get the characters from London to Athens.

'If they were basically classless, but without the money for expensive holidays, we needed a reason to get them abroad without them losing their identity as the Young Ones,' says Ron Cass.

'One day while travelling on a London bus it suddenly occurred to me that if we couldn't get them to Greece by air why not get them there on a London bus which we could convert into living quarters?'

Once the red double-decker bus had been cast in the lead role the screenplay fell into place. Cliff would be the leader of a gang of London Transport mechanics who decide to turn a bus into a hotel and drive it across Europe to Greece.

Interiors were shot at Elstree Studios but all the exteriors (except for a brief longshot in Paris) were shot on location in and around Athens starting in May 1962. Two London buses were bought for the film but the reality of getting a double-decker from London to Athens was considerably more difficult than the fiction.

Kenneth Harper remembers, 'We needed two buses because we needed one as a back-up but when they were driven overland they came across so many bridges that they wouldn't fit under. One of them actually made it eventually by road but the other one had to turn back and be sent by sea.'

There were also problems getting in the guns needed for a scene where Yugoslavian border guards challenge the bus. 'There was a most almighty fuss,' says Harper. 'My assistant producer, Andy Mitchell, was almost put in jail because they thought he was starting a revolutionary cell.'

Cliff's leading lady was nineteen-year-old Lauri Peters, a classically-trained dancer who had spent the past two years in the Broadway production of *The Sound Of Music*. She had made one previous film, *Mr Hobbs Takes A Train* with James Stewart, and was recommended by Herb Ross as someone who might appeal to potential American distributors.

As with Carole Gray in *The Young Ones* she was not the glamorous lead that might be expected, and looked unlikely as Cliff's romantic interest. Harper was furious that she had put on a lot of weight just prior to filming.

'The choice of Cliff's leading ladies was always strange,' says Tony Meehan. 'I think the notion was to pick girls who were quite plain and who wouldn't threaten the fans. I think the girls liked leading ladies who they could identify with.'

There was never any off-screen romance between the two leads.

Three days after Cliff arrived in Athens he was joined by Jackie Irving, and Lauri had just got married to a young American actor called Jon Voight, later to star in *Midnight Cowboy*.

Una Stubbs, who played one of the stranded singers, remembers, 'Like most people who have just fallen in love, Lauri was wrapped up in just one person. I think she was dreadfully homesick and pining for him. She couldn't wait for the film to finish.'

Although Jon Voight came out to Athens for one weekend he was mostly confined to New York where he was in a play. 'Lauri confided in me one day,' says Melvyn Hayes. 'She said, "Where do you think I go on a Saturday night? I must tell somebody." I told her I had no idea. She said, "I fly back to America and then come back on the Sunday night because it's costing me that much a week in phone calls home." '

She played the part of a genderless-looking stowaway who eventually melts Cliff's heart despite having been told by him, 'Girls are all very well but date them once and then run. Date them twice and they get serious ... Next thing you know, you're hooked and wondering what's hit you. No. No girl is going to own me.'

This was remarkably close to Cliff's code of caution, a code reinforced by a song which he had written with Bruce Welch which was added after the location filming had been completed. Just as Tepper and Bennett's song 'The Young Ones' forever associated Cliff with youth, so 'Bachelor Boy' connected him with a permanent state of singleness.

'We started the song just with the title,' remembers Welch. 'I wrote it with Cliff because I thought it would be a great song for him. We both wrote words and music. It was an afterthought as far as *Summer Holiday* was concerned but it became a million-seller.'

Una Stubbs was the girl in the film who many thought should have taken the lead role. She was a vivacious young dancer with a flicked-up bob haircut whose innocent freshness matched Cliff's own uncomplicated image. When Cliff saw her being auditioned he singled her out, catching the eye of the casting director and making the sign of the haircut to indicate his preference.

'I definitely think they should have cast Una in the lead role,' says Melvyn Hayes. 'They never got Cliff the right leading ladies. In *The Young Ones* he had a girl who looked as if she could have been his mother and then in *Summer Holiday* they had Lauri Peters who was great and yet wrong.'

In preparation for the filming Cliff went on a crash diet and also had his pointed tooth capped (he'd worn a temporary cap for *The Young Ones*). He'd started putting on weight during the American tour in 1960 and by the time he arrived at the Palladium run he was up to twelve stone.

Comments about his weight had been cropping up in the press since 1959 when Donald Zec, in a *Daily Mirror* interview, described him as a 'well-set, meaty youth' and Maureen Cleave had referred to 'chubby Mr Richard's tautened muscles in bathing trunks' when she reviewed *It's Great To Be Young*.

In the BBC radio programme 'Frankly Speaking', Royston Ellis had asked, 'Does your weight worry you at all? People say that you're getting too plump. Does this worry you?'

Cliff had replied that it did. 'But I don't know what to do about it. It does worry me because I should keep up my appearance. But how does one get rid of fat except by starving oneself?'

It was a comment of Minnie Caldwell, one of the original characters in 'Coronation Street', which finally prompted him to do something about it.

Transmitted in April 1962 and scripted by Tony Warren, the episode featured Minnie sitting in a park with Ena Sharples and Martha Longhurst listening to a brass band playing.

Ena Sharples: 'I'll have you know, I've got perfect pitch. To hear folks talk now you'd think everything began and ended with "Annie Get Your Gun".

Martha Longhurst: 'You can't beat the old tunes though can you?'
Ena Sharples: 'Oh I don't know. Have you ever heard *West Side Story* on Sandy McPherson?'
Martha Longhurst: 'Aye. But it doesn't seem the same thing somehow.'
Minnie Caldwell: 'Isn't Cliff Richard a lovely chubby lad?'

'He used to go to a store just off Tottenham Court Road and buy Indian sweetmeats called Jelabis,' recalls Ray Mackender.

'They had more calories in them than you can possibly imagine and the result didn't exactly enhance his photographs. The comment about him being a "chubby lad" on "Coronation Street" hurt him and from then on Jelabis were out and he became an absolute addict at keeping fit.'

By the time he started shooting *Summer Holiday* on 25 May he was down to eleven stone, the same weight that he maintains today.

Already conscious of the value of the youthfulness which he had feared was skipping away the day he left his teens, he was now, at twenty-one, becoming aware that the lean physique and the wide smile had to be worked for.

In October 1962 Cliff and the restructured Shadows toured America for the second time, this time to promote *The Young Ones* (retitled *It's Wonderful To Be Young* by Paramount and disastrously re-edited). The idea was great. The first half of the evening would be a screening of the film and the second half would be a concert.

What no one could have imagined when planning the tour was that America and Russia were to teeter on the brink of nuclear warfare that month over the issue of Soviet missiles being set up in Cuba. It wasn't until 28 October that President Kennedy called the bluff of Russian premier Khrushchev, and Khrushchev promised to remove the weapons.

The Cuban Missile Crisis was the closest that the superpowers came to conflict during the Cold War years and it meant that during Cliff's tour America was in a state of panic, with few people venturing out. As a result the concerts were poorly attended, sometimes only half full.

While in Memphis another attempt was made to meet Elvis but again it didn't work out. 'It was arranged that we should go to his home, Graceland,' remembers Locking.

'When we got there we realized he was out of town and so his father, Vernon, met us and took us on a guided tour of the mansion. He didn't say much to us and all I can remember was seeing piles of teddy bears in his bedroom upstairs.'

It may seem surprising today that Britain's biggest act was met with a lack of interest but it has to be remembered that the American fascination with British groups only built up after the Beatles. In 1962 the idea of a group of Englishmen playing rock 'n' roll appeared to have as much potential as Americans playing cricket.

The only real success to date had been Lonnie Donegan's version of 'Rock Island Line', which had reached number eight in the charts during 1956 and had been backed up with a four-month tour. Marty Wilde reached number forty-five with 'Bad Boy' in March 1960, but wasn't able to follow it up.

Although other acts, such as Billy Fury, had released singles in America, nothing had come of them. The only British acts to reach the number one slot at the time were Acker Bilk with 'Stranger On The Shore' in 1961, and Vera Lynn with 'Auf Wiedersehen' in 1952. (The Tornadoes were to have a surprise number one with their instrumental, 'Telstar', in December 1962.)

When Cliff arrived back in London on 13 November he told *Melody Maker* that despite the month-long tour and appearances on the 'Ed Sullivan Show' and 'Dick Clark's Bandstand' he was still very much an unknown in America. 'You've got to fight to make yourself known there,' he said. 'You're up against so much.'

But the tour was significant in that Cliff was able to ask more questions of Locking, and went to his first meeting of the Jehovah's Witnesses in Miami.

'We were swimming in the hotel pool one day and someone came through and asked for me,' says Locking. 'I wondered who it could be because I knew no one in Miami.

'Apparently a room maid had seen my JW Bible, which in those days had a green-coloured cover, and she'd taken a look inside to see who it belonged to because she was a Witness. She then invited me to a local meeting and Cliff and Hank joined me.'

For Cliff again it was the enthusiasm that communicated to him. 'I was just so overwhelmed,' he says. 'Everyone was just so friendly. We got big hugs and everything. It was incredible. It was the feeling of being in a charismatic [Pentecostal-style] meeting long before I knew the word charismatic. When I came back to England I introduced it to all the family.'

What Cliff didn't know was that his mother was already considering the claims of the Jehovah's Witnesses because her Uncle Vincent (Vincent Bridgwater) and his wife May, who had come to England in the early fifties, had been converted by doorstep evangelists and she had seen a lot of them after Rodger's death. One day May noticed a Bible by Dorothy Marie's bedside and talk turned to religion, beginning a conversation that went on until four o'clock the next morning.

'She then gave me a couple of magazines and asked me to read them,' says Dorothy Marie. 'She told me that she had been a very strong Roman Catholic and that nothing would move her. But she had decided that the church was doing nothing for her and she became a Witness.

'So I had the magazines, Cliff was on tour in America and when he came back he'd got copies of the same ones. He said he was interested in the Jehovah's Witnesses. So we all started studying together.'

Studying was necessarily spasmodic for Cliff, who was hardly ever in the same town two nights running. In January 1963 he returned to South Africa with Jackie Irving and Carole Gray appearing in the shows as dancers.

In Salisbury, Rhodesia, Cliff and Jackie went along with Licorice Locking to a local meeting house. That June they were back in Blackpool for a long summer season at the ABC with Dailey and Wayne and Arthur Worsley. Cliff attended JW meetings in nearby Thornton Clevelys as well as meeting twice a week with Locking and a local JW to discuss Witnesses' view of the Bible.

Locking was never sure what was motivating Cliff to study in such depth without ever committing himself, or describing himself as a Jehovah's Witness. 'I just got the impression that he was interested,' says Locking. 'He was looking for something to commit himself to.'

When *Summer Holiday* was released at the close of 1962 it broke all previous box office records for a British film. Kenneth Harper had deliberately scheduled a winter première to increase the impact of the film.

'I had told Leslie Grade to pray for snow the week that the film came out,' he says. 'We were lucky. It did snow. Everybody was frozen and they went into the cinema and it was like having a summer holiday.'

By this time Cliff had been a major star for four years in a business where runs of success were typically counted in months if not weeks.

His original opposition had by now disappeared. Tommy Steele, Marty Wilde and Terry Dene were never again to appear in the charts. Vince Eager , Duffy Power and Johnny Gentle, the great hopes of manager Larry Parnes, never had a hit single between them.

The only serious competition was from Adam Faith and Billy Fury, who had both started in the business around the same time as Cliff but whose chart careers hadn't started until 1959. By 1962 they'd both had over a dozen hits but neither of them had developed the family appeal that helped Cliff reach out beyond the original teenage audience.

Fury had a great voice — perhaps the best rock 'n' roll voice of his generation — but he was painfully shy and compensated for this by developing a writhing stage act which newspapers reported as 'suggestive'. The management of Dublin's Theatre Royal once dropped the curtain on the act because it was considered too 'offensive'.

Faith was a less threatening proposition but he also suffered from stage nerves and didn't have the voice to sustain a long career. He sang in the wavering tones of Buddy Holly, and his vocal deficiencies were expertly covered up by John Barry's string arrangements.

'I suppose I felt a certain amount of competition from Cliff,' says Faith, 'but, amazingly enough, we never got to know each other well in those days because we were both so busy. The only times we would meet would be at a transport cafe and he'd say, "I've just been to Grantham. Where are you going?" and I'd say, "Well, I'm off to Southampton." Then we'd meet at the *New Musical Express* Poll Winners concerts at Wembley Pool and we'd sit and chat. He was a nice lad, but there was a big enough audience for all of us.'

The real threat to Cliff's standing as Britain's number one pop idol was to come from the Beatles, who had their first hit single in October 1962. Appearing, with their floppy haircuts and collarless jackets, to be the challenge of the next generation, they were actually contemporaries of Cliff who had started playing skiffle at exactly the same time. John Lennon was five days older than Cliff.

The Beatles first met Cliff at a party thrown by Bruce Welch after they had played the Lewisham Odeon on 29 March 1963. Although they had never bought Cliff's records there was awe involved in meeting the man they had to topple to be Britain's best.

They gathered in Welch's kitchen and John Lennon made jokes about Cliff holding off his next release so that the Beatles could stand a chance of getting to number one with their follow-up to 'Please Please Me'.

Then they got out their guitars. Cliff and the Shadows played 'Lucky Lips' while the Beatles sang 'From Me To You', which they had recorded three weeks previously.

The one exchange of the evening that Cliff still remembers came when he expressed an interest in Ray Charles and Lennon said, 'I used to like him until everybody else started to like him.' The elitism of the comment perplexed Cliff.

'The Beatles were fairly small at the time but I remember we spent the whole night talking,' says Mike Conlin. 'They were very worried about the effect of Cliff's next release.

'We all got on very well and when we played the Blackpool season later that year I would meet up with Paul when they were doing Sunday concerts up there and he always made me feel welcome. He never made any snide remarks about Cliff.'

In April 1963, shortly after the birth of Julian Lennon, John took off to Spain for a private holiday with manager Brian Epstein. They booked into a hotel in Sitges where Cliff and the Shadows were staying while recording the album *When In Spain* in Barcelona. Mike Conlin remembers Lennon being a bit distant, as though he wanted to get into a conversation but felt it was a bit beneath him.

'It was winter time and there were no other English people around,' says Conlin. 'We used to see Brian and John every day in the street and you could see John half thinking that he'd spend some time with us but then sniffing and turning away. I never knew what effect that had but it was after that that Lennon began sounding off about Cliff.'

In a conversation which took place the following month, recorded in Michael Braun's book *Love Me Do*, Lennon said, 'We've always hated Cliff. He was everything we hated in pop. But when we met him we didn't mind him at all. He was very nice. Now when people ask us if he's a bit soft we say no. We still hate his records but he's really very nice.'

What they hated was his 'niceness' when singing rock 'n' roll. They had spent years in sweaty cellars learning how to rock audiences until they dropped from exhaustion. To the boys from Liverpool, Cliff was a British Frankie Avalon, a house-trained rock star for the family audience.

'From Me To You' went to number one, and 1963 belonged to the Beatles who had three number ones in a row. It wasn't as if Cliff had a bad year. His next three singles were all top five but it was enough to suggest that his reign as the undisputed king of British pop might be coming to an end.

It unnerved him that 'Lucky Lips' was not only beaten by 'From Me To You' but by 'Scarlett O'Hara', the second single by Jet Harris and Tony Meehan who'd teamed up after leaving the Shadows. For someone who has always been concerned with his showing in the singles charts this was a public humiliation.

He told *Melody Maker* that he became quite agitated when 'Lucky Lips' stalled at number four.

'I went home and poured my heart out to Mum and shouted, "Lucky Lips" isn't getting to the top.' You need someone to talk to. People think the showbiz life is cushy. But Jet's right in saying that you need nerves of steel. You go to bed at night wondering if things will still be the same tomorrow, if you'll still be at the top.'

In another interview he was asked whether he was buckling under the challenge of the new groups from Liverpool. 'I don't think it's that that has stopped me,' said Cliff.

'The record of mine just wasn't strong enough. Perhaps we have slipped into a rut, but it's not just a sound that sells records. They have to be good. We will just have to be more selective in choosing material. I'm certainly not going to be "Beatled" into making a disc for the sake of it.'

Getting in the lower half of the top five was hardly a disaster and the song became his best-selling single ever in Germany. But it was the start of press speculation about his future, particularly as the beat group boom was throwing up new acts every week.

After years of 'Cliff Is Tops Again' headlines, they were writing 'Is Cliff Slipping?', 'Cliff At The Crossroads' and '"We're Not Has Beens" Says Cliff'.

'These are dangerous days for Cliff Richard and he is facing them with zest, honesty and fervour,' wrote Ray Coleman in *Melody Maker*.

'After five years of glory during which he has established himself as Britain's top solo pop idol, it has been said that the route from now on can only be downhill.'

16

'I'm thinking about God'

In October 1963 Licorice Locking made the surprise announcement that he would be leaving the Shadows in order to devote more time to his religious activities.

'I love being with the group,' he told the *Daily Mail*, 'but the constant touring doesn't allow me to fulfil my promise to life. I have thought about this step for a long time. It has become a strain dividing myself into two – being loyal to the show and being loyal to my beliefs. I feel I must stay in one place and do my work there.'

Locking completed his recording commitments and was then replaced by John Rostill, a handsome young bass player the Shadows had met in Blackpool.

On 2 December, with the Beatles at the top of the hit parade with 'She Loves You', Cliff left for the Canary Islands and *Wonderful Life*, the third of his films with the Harper, Cass and Myers team and the second to be directed by Sid Furie.

Just as *Summer Holiday* had been the best received and most lucrative of Cliff's films, *Wonderful Life* was to be the worst received and least lucrative.

There were problems right from the start. To sustain the rhythm started with *The Young Ones*, filming should have been the previous summer with a release date in early 1964 but because of the

Blackpool summer season the momentum was lost.

Then there was a problem with the story that Ron Cass and Peter Myers had written. Originally Cliff was to have played the role of a dashing guardsman mysteriously called out to Mexico on the death of an uncle. While travelling through the dry Mexican countryside his train is ambushed and he is taken prisoner by a gang of bandits who blindfold him and take him to the uncle's village. When the blindfold is taken off it is revealed that the uncle was the leader of the bandits and that as his only living relative the guardsman must now adopt the mantle of The Shadow.

The rest of the film was to have shown him desperately assuming the bandit leadership while simultanously trying to ensure that those under his control committed no real crimes. 'It would have been a very different film for Cliff,' argues Ron Cass, 'and very, very funny.'

After a costing of the film based on this script Kenneth Harper broke the news that it would be impossible to do something set in Mexico.

'Andy Mitchell went out to research the possibility and found that it was absolutely out of court,' says Harper. 'So we went out looking for islands that were closer, and finally decided on the Canary Islands. That's when we realized we were going to have to change the story.'

Through changing the screenplay to fit a new location the heart was taken out of the film. Much of the final script was written on location with scenes changing day by day as weather conditions affected the shape and colour of the sand and made continuity a nightmare.

'I can't really take the same pride in the result as I did in *The Young Ones* and *Summer Holiday* because it was all over the place,' admits Ron Cass.

'I've always said that a musical should be fanciful but the idea we used of a group of young kids making a film was too fanciful. There comes a certain point where people reject "fanciful" and say "impossible". The screenplay grew rather than arrived.'

The problems didn't end when they reached the Canary Islands. The filming was held up by rainstorms, Melvyn Hayes broke his leg falling down a flight of steps and one of the leading actors, Dennis Price, had to be replaced mid-way through shooting.

'There was no excitement at all on that set,' remembers Royston Ellis, who was flown out to research a book of the film that was never written. 'There was this scandal because Dennis Price was totally drunk and incapable of filming. Cliff asked me to try and straighten him out so they could get the film done but it didn't work out. He had to be flown home and his part was taken over by Derek Bond.

'By that time Cliff was keeping very much to himself and was very into discussing religion with Una Stubbs and Hank Marvin. That was when a lot of us became aware that Cliff had got religion and word got out.'

The lack of excitement is confirmed by Melvyn Hayes, reckoned by most to be the liveliest of the cast.

He remembers a journalist from a national paper flying in to write a story along the lines of 'High Jinks On Cliff Film' and asking him what really went on. Hayes remembers, 'I turned to him conspiratorily and said, "I'll tell you what really happens. We have a wake-up call at 6.30. We do make-up. We then get into a terrible jeep which takes us forty miles to Las Palmas which is like an oven. Then we work until lunch time.

"The sun is so hot we don't enjoy our food. Then we film all afternoon until the winds start getting up at four o'clock and it starts turning cold. The sand whips into our faces and cuts us like sandpaper. But we haven't finished yet.

"We go on until the light drops and then we get back into the bus and feel sick and rough from the heat. We eventually get back to the hotel, have a bath, go to the restaurant and fall asleep."

'This wasn't good enough for the journalist so he found Richard O'Sullivan and pushed him into the swimming pool. Richard pulled the journalist in with him and when the story came out it was all about the things we all got up to at night, like throwing one another into the swimming pool.'

It was during the making of *Wonderful Life* that Cliff's relationship with Jackie Irving reached crunch point. He had now been seeing her for almost two and a half years but whereas he seemed content to have her as his high school date, Jackie wanted the relationship to mature.

'I think that for Cliff it was a very platonic relationship,' says one friend of the period. 'I don't know what Jackie would have called it. It wasn't physical. She was just the girl that he would take to things.'

His physical caution was matched with a refusal to discuss where they were headed. Newspapers had been speculating on their likely marriage since September 1963 but Cliff never mentioned the subject to Jackie.

'All this week, since these rumours that we were getting married started, people have tried to ask me about it,' Jackie told the *Daily Mirror*. 'I have just kept away from them. That kind of thing is embarrassing for both Cliff and myself.

'Obviously I like him a lot. So does my mother . . . but neither of us is planning to get married. There's nothing like that.'

Cliff's response was to say, 'Jackie is my only girlfriend.'

But although they never spoke of marriage to each other they contemplated the possibility when alone. Jackie assumed that Cliff's reluctance to put the relationship into a higher gear was because his mother was restraining him. One evening, while on tour in Birmingham, she came to Dorothy Marie's hotel room and tried to sort the matter out.

'She thought I was putting a spoke in his wheel,' says Dorothy Marie. 'I said, "My dear girl, I'm nothing to do with him. Cliff is grown up. He's a man. If he wants to get married he'll get married. If he doesn't, he won't. There's nothing that you and I can do that will change him."'

The 'forbidding' that Tony Meehan had talked about was again in evidence. He was comfortable with a schoolboyish friendship but balked at the idea of what an adult relationship might entail.

'Jackie Irving was the first girl that I thought I might marry,' Cliff says. 'I thought that if I was going to get married at all it would be to Jackie.

'I went to Peter Gormley and said, "Supposing I wanted to get married..." and Peter said, "Well, you might lose ten per cent of your fans but that doesn't mean too much." He was saying that if I got married I'd still keep ninety per cent of my fans.

'That's when I decided not to get married because as soon as the cards were dealt out and I had the OK I thought, "Ooh, I don't know if I want this anyway." '

The bottom line was that he loved being Cliff Richard so much that commitment to anyone else would be second best. There was no room in his life for a Mrs Cliff Richard. The fires of sex, which could have driven him into marriage, were never as fierce as his determination to enjoy his career.

'I don't think I'm cut out for marriage. Even though I have enjoyed the relationships I've had I have always felt fairly dispassionate afterwards and able to say I'm glad I didn't get married,' he admits. 'I obviously haven't been hit by the same bug that has hit others.'

Jackie had joined Cliff in the Canaries and it was here that he broke the news that he had decided not to see her any more.

'Obviously it takes one person to bring up the subject and I was the one to bring it up,' says Cliff. 'I said, "Look, I don't want to get married." So we called it off.

'What she felt like when I told her I don't know. I can't speak for her. I don't think she was hysterically happy but I've always felt it's best to get things said. I've never wanted to live a lie. At least I have been upfront with everybody and told them I couldn't do it.'

A brief flirtation with Una Stubbs followed but Cliff felt inhibited by the fact that although her relationship with actor Peter Gilmore was breaking up, she was still married to him.

'We had been keen on each other for quite a while,' says Una. 'Then, during *Wonderful Life*, it turned into a romance although I always kept very quiet about it. Even my closest friends didn't know.'

Cliff was still in Las Palmas when the news came that the Beatles had arrived in America to be greeted by 4,000 screaming fans in an unprecedented display of pop devotion. Like Cliff they had then appeared live on the 'Ed Sullivan Show', the difference being that they had drawn the largest audience in the history of entertainment television. To cap it all, 'I Want To Hold Your Hand' had gone to number one in the US charts.

All this must have been galling to someone who had spent five years struggling for American recognition. *It's Wonderful To Be Young* hadn't done great business, none of his ten singles since 'Living Doll' had made a mark ('Lucky Lips' had rolled around the bottom end of the top one hundred) and his new American label, Epic, was just starting to have some success with 'It's All In The Game' after having launched what it called 'one of the greatest introductory campaigns in our history'.

Now the Beatles, with a recording career of just over twelve months, were causing a sensation on their very first trip. In fact it had been the failure of Cliff's career in America that had determined the nature of the Beatles' conquest.

'Cliff went there and he died,' John Lennon told author Michael Braun on the eve of their visit. 'He was fourteenth on a bill with Frankie Avalon and George [Harrison] said that *Summer Holiday* was second feature at a drive-in in St Louis.'

To avoid such indignities the Beatles waited to take America until they could be guaranteed top billing and maximum exposure. The airport welcome was part of a well-orchestrated campaign by Capitol Records.

There were major features in the trade press, DJs were primed to announce the arrival time of the plane, Beatle souvenirs were being mass marketed and five million posters saying 'The Beatles Are

Coming' were posted all over America in December 1963.

But success on such a grand scale cannot be explained by marketing techniques alone. The Beatles captured the mood of international cultural change in a way in which Cliff never had and never would.

They were the first of a better-educated, more sophisticated generation of rock musicians who wrote their own songs and guided their own careers.

Cliff took the news philosophically. He was still Britain's most popular male singer even though, in the *New Musical Express* annual points survey, which reflected the number of weeks an act was in the charts, he was now eleventh in a list that he had topped the year before.

'We're not going to contest the beat groups,' he said. 'We won't follow trends. We will continue doing what we do until the public stops buying our records.'

There was premature talk of him retiring. At the end of 1963 he had bought Rookswood, a six-bedroom Tudor-style mansion in Upper Nazeing, Essex, where he would live with his mother and sisters. He also bought a holiday home in Portugal.

At that time the Algarve coast was completely undeveloped. There was no airport at Faro and the only way to travel there was to fly to Lisbon and drive the rest of the way. Peter Gormley heard of it through Muriel Young, then a disc jockey on Radio Luxemburg, who had built a house in Albufeira at a time when only two other British people had homes in the region.

'It was completely undiscovered,' she says. 'Peter came down initially because he was a deep-sea fisherman and he ended up buying six houses — two for Leslie Grade and one each for himself, Cliff, Frank Ifield and Bruce Welch.

'It was because these people were all so famous that the place got written about. The Algarve burst wide open six or seven years before it might have done because of the attention it got through stars such as Cliff.'

Mike Conlin remembers him being at his happiest when he was able to disappear to Portugal.

'He liked being able to get away completely from the show-business scene,' says Conlin. 'We used to go down for a month at a time. There was a fellow we knew who was at university near Lisbon and he used to take us to restaurants and introduce us to the local fishermen.

'We used to go out on the boats all night sardine fishing, things like that, and Cliff would sometimes come back and sing to the fishermen in their homes. None of them had any idea who he was and that's what he liked about it. He could go anywhere and not be recognized.'

The retirement talk had started when he had casually remarked that Portugal seemed to be the ideal place to retire. It took on added significance because Cliff was known to be deeply involved in the teaching of the Jehovah's Witnesses and some thought he might eventually follow Licorice Locking's example and quit the business.

One of those disturbed by his new obsession was Jay Norris, his old form mistress from Cheshunt, with whom he had stayed in touch over the years. Educated in a convent school, she knew enough of the Bible to know he was flirting with a quasi-Christian group, but not enough to correct him.

For help she turned to the school's religious education master, Bill Latham, a 26-year-old evangelical Christian who had an easy-going manner and an exceptional gift for communicating his beliefs. She also entertained the idea that Bill would make an ideal friend for Cliff.

'I'm a natural organizer of other people's lives and I thought they would have a lot to offer each other,' she explains.

'Cliff had no nice ordinary friends. He was stuck in the pop world where the people were often second-rate and Bill had a lot of Christian friends. Actually I thought that Bill had much more to offer Cliff than Cliff had to offer Bill. Being a pop star could be lonely and dull.'

On the surface of things Bill Latham was an unusual match for anyone to make for Cliff. The only things they appeared to have in common were a lower middle-class background (Latham was born and raised in Finchley), a father who worked in the catering business (Latham's father had worked in a Camden bakery) and an interest in religion.

Latham was not a rock 'n' roll fan and dressed comfortably rather than fashionably. He spent a lot of his evenings and weekends as a leader in an interdenominational Christian youth organization called Crusaders which arranged Bible studies and outdoor activities for teenage boys.

His own conversion, in 1952, had been through this group which happened to hold their weekend meetings in a room of the school he attended. He went with them to a summer camp in Norfolk where he understood the Christian message for the first time.

'Crusaders influenced my life very significantly, both directly and indirectly, after that,' Latham says. 'I began to be trained as a leader and that had one of the most profound shaping effects I have ever known. At the age of seventeen I was being put into positions of authority and the experience got me out of a fairly introverted life.'

Each July Jay Norris celebrated her birthday with a car rally which met at her house and then dispersed into the Hertfordshire countryside with sheets of clues imaginatively written out in rhyming couplets. In July 1964 her plan was to assign Cliff to Bill Latham's car.

'I wasn't intimidated when I met him that day at Jay's house but I was certainly curious,' remembers Latham. 'I was slightly apprehensive as to how we would get on because it was an interesting set-up. I was almost working to a brief. I was under strict instructions to get him into a spiritual discussion and this was a tall order in the context of a car rally.'

Cliff's recollection is that they 'spent the whole time arguing'. Latham thinks they didn't have the time. 'The car was full of people so there wasn't really a chance,' he says.

'I talked to him more when we got back to Jay's house but I don't think the JW thing came up. But something must have been sown because sometime later there came an invitation to go to Rookswood to talk about JWs with him and his family.'

Remembers Jay, 'I had to do it all again after the car rally because they didn't see each other. The next thing was that Cliff came to supper with me alone and talked about the JWs and I said, "I can't answer these questions but Bill can." So he asked me to bring Bill along to his home.'

After this meeting Latham felt he needed theological support as the questions were now quite specialized, focusing on differences between the teachings of Jehovah's Witnesses and those of historical Christianity. Having a fastidious mind, Cliff wanted to be absolutely sure of all the possible interpretations of the key passages in the Bible.

'None of the family were actually paid-up members at the time but they were all quite in favour and arguing from a Jehovah's Witness position,' remembers Latham.

'The discussions were very high-powered right from the word go and with my somewhat limited Crusader theology I found myself on pretty thin ice. I thought I was floundering and was aware that I needed to bring in people who had more authority than I had.'

Graham Disbrey, a friend from Finchley who was also involved with the Crusaders, was recruited for the next meeting. It took place in December 1964, while Cliff was appearing at the Palladium in the pantomime *Aladdin and His Wonderful Lamp* (for which the Shadows had written the entire score). They arrived at around eleven o'clock at night and Cliff's mother served them coffee as they waited for Cliff to return.

'It must have been after midnight when he finally got back,' says

Disbrey. 'I remember him saying, "Right, where are your Bibles? Let's get down to it!" He wanted to get on with things straight away. He went out of the room, came back armed with a Bible and we started discussing.

'I can't remember exactly what we talked about. Bill and I were very young, very naïve and terribly conservative in our views and we just fired everything we had at him and he fired everything he had at us.

'It was a heavy time and I think we were basically trying to score points off each other. The core of the discussion was about whether Jesus was alive today, whether you could enjoy a personal relationship with a loving God, and how it affected our daily lives.

'This went on for most of the night. When Bill and I got back to Finchley the dawn was breaking.'

The next person brought in to bolster the cause was David Winter, a lay-reader at Latham's local church, St Paul's in Finchley, and editor of the magazine *Crusade*. Winter had a keen intellect, a good grasp of theology and an ability to discuss it in non-specialist language.

The surprise for Winter was to find that Cliff's questions weren't those typical of an unbeliever, but of someone who respected the Bible but was unsure of the correct interpretation.

'Most people searching for Christianity have moral objections and questions,' says Winter. 'They want to know whether their lives will have to change. They don't want to be seen as nuts or religious maniacs. They can't stand church. They think Christians are weirdos. But with Cliff there was none of that.

'He would say, "I can't see how you can believe that Christ is the Son of God. The Bible doesn't teach that." What his experience with the Jehovah's Witnesses had done for him was to convince him of the authority of the Bible. He didn't want any other arguments. Arguing with him like this drove me back to the Bible and I know it drove Bill and a few others back to the same place to find the answers.'

Graham Disbrey was Latham's closest friend at the time. They had known each other since they were boys, had been Crusaders together and were now both teaching at the same school. But, following the meeting at Rookswood, Disbrey noticed that Cliff was taking his place in Latham's life.

'It was actually quite difficult for me,' he admits. 'Bill and I used to do things together and suddenly his time was taken up and he couldn't exactly say why. He was very discreet and wouldn't tell me what was happening but I would know that the big car was outside his house which meant that Cliff was there.

'I suppose I was a little envious. My nose was put out of joint. Bill used to collect me in the morning to take me to work and it was a bit difficult to know how to start a conversation at the beginning of the day. Bill wouldn't always say whether Cliff had been around the previous evening or exactly what was going on.'

Clearly Latham was becoming more than a religious adviser. Despite the gulf in their interests and in their experiences of adulthood the friendship was obviously fulfilling a deep emotional need in Cliff's life.

It wasn't as though Latham was replacing any close friends in Cliff's life. All his friends since leaving school had been business associates of one sort or another. There were no ties to cut because no ties had been made.

'I think Cliff desperately needed somebody who was wholly trustworthy and that he could look up to because everyone was looking up to him,' says Disbrey. 'He needed somebody to spend time with who was utterly reliable, absolutely confidential and I think he found that in Bill.'

It was this friendship and the wider circle of Latham's friends as much as the theological arguments that attracted Cliff to Christianity.

'I was so much into my Christian circle of church fellowship, youth fellowship and Crusader classes,' says Latham, 'that I thought the best exposure I could give Cliff was to meet Christians and introduce him to a Christian lifestyle.'

When Bill taught his Crusader class in Finchley, Cliff would sit quietly at the back listening. At first the young people were impressed to be joined by a pop singer but after a few weeks they just accepted him as one of them. He even attended church services at St Paul's, finding himself attracted to the sheer ordinariness of the people.

He was now arguing far less from the Jehovah's Witness viewpoint and was beginning to absorb the outlook of those around him. David Winter remembers that the most significant change came when he shifted to arguing from an evangelical Christian point of view.

Wonderful Life was premièred in July, the same month that the Beatles made their film debut in *A Hard Day's Night*. Whereas *Wonderful Life* had a contrived madness about it, *A Hard Day's Night* managed to communicate a refreshing irreverence, and whereas Cliff had adopted a middle-class accent and had middle-class values, the Beatles rejoiced in their working-class roots.

Cliff was beginning to look dated. Almost all the new groups had long hair brushed over their foreheads. They dressed in Cuban-heeled boots, leather waistcoats and high-collared shirts. Cliff was still neat and Brylcreemed with well-polished shoes and mohair suits.

The music too was changing. The Shadows sounded clean and clinical in contrast with the raunchy, often distorted, sounds of those who had schooled themselves in primitive rock 'n' roll and the electric blues of Chicago.

Cliff was sometimes heard commenting on the 'noise' of the Rolling Stones, or saying that the Beatles played out of tune. He failed to realize that part of the appeal of the new music was its uninhibited nature. The point wasn't to play and dress with precision, but with feeling.

The subject matter of pop was also becoming more adult. Sparkling innocence was giving way to expressions of anger, boredom and restlessness and a desire for social change. It was also no longer taken for granted that teenagers were sexually inexperienced.

A twenty-year-old 'beat fan' interviewed by *Melody Maker* in a feature which looked at shifting tastes said, 'I grew out of my Cliff Richard days a couple of years ago. When I look back I think how soppy I must have been. Groups now like the Beatles and the Stones have really got something and I can't see me getting tired of them. Not until I'm old anyway.'

It was just before Christmas 1964 that the press finally caught on to the fact that Cliff was becoming increasingly serious about religion. A *Daily Express* reporter approached him outside Rookswood and asked him about the rumours that he was a Jehovah's Witness.

'I am thinking about God,' he admitted. 'This is a very personal thing. It was Licorice Locking who set me thinking. I am not considering joining the Jehovah's Witnesses . . . I'm just thinking a lot about God. That's all. It's very important to me.'

17

'The closing of one door and the opening of another'

To his colleagues in the music business it seemed quite bizarre that Cliff's social life was now centred on a group of young North London schoolteachers. Who else, given unprecedented fame, money and female attention would eschew it all for teenage Bible classes in the leafy suburbs and the occasional drink in a Hertfordshire pub?

'What on earth do they find to talk about?' asked an incredulous Bruce Welch at the time.

Yet it was in the company of these Crusaders, none of whom knew much about pop music, that Cliff was to negotiate his re-entry into normal life.

For six years he had been living in a world where he was over-protected, over-praised and over-paid. In Finchley he could almost be Harry Webb again. No one wanted anything from him and no one appeared to be overawed by his status.

'He gave the impression of being very happy to join in my lifestyle,' says Bill Latham. 'He seemed to be glad to be doing ordinary things again. He'd had all those years of a pop star's lifestyle and now he was mixing with people who had nothing to do with show business.'

Because of the Christian ethos it was also a sexually unthreatening environment. There was no pressure to couple up because singleness didn't have the stigma it had elsewhere, and none of the group believed that masculinity was proven by sexual conquest.

Peter Graves met Cliff in September 1965 while waiting to take a diploma in education at Oxford.

'I think that one of the things that attracted him to our group was the fact that there were no girls to bother him,' says Graves. 'We were an all-male group. If girls did join us they were always on the fringe.'

During Easter of that year he joined twenty-four young Crusaders for an eight-day boat trip on the Norfolk Broads and was relieved to find himself treated as just another crew member. He played guitar for their sing-songs, cooked shepherd's pies and was subjected to pillow fights before lights-out.

The interviews he gave around this time show that these simple activities were making an impression. He wistfully envied the less-pressured lives of his new friends and could see that a great schoolteacher probably did more for the world than a celebrated pop star.

'Records don't mean all that much any more,' he told the music weekly *Disc*. 'Sometimes I'd love to have a job where I could work regular office hours and have weekends off.'

To the *Daily Express* he admitted that he was catching up with the life he had missed out on as a teenager.

'I feel I could do a lot more with my life. If this feeling continues for another year I will make a decision about my future. I could probably work in show business for the next twenty years. But if the day comes when I don't feel satisfied, I'll get out.'

For the first time in his career, Cliff was clearly out of sync with the times and apparently unconcerned. While he played cabaret at the London Palladium and put out singles like 'Wind Me Up' and 'The Time In Between', the sounds that would eventually define the decade were being produced — such songs as 'Help' by the Beatles,

'Satisfaction' by the Rolling Stones and 'My Generation' by the Who.

'Christianity had become pre-eminent in everything I did,' says Cliff. 'It changed my priorities. I had been rejuvenated and my career seemed uninteresting. At the same time the success of the Beatles and the Stones had shelved me and the Shadows. We were now the oldsters.'

He was also spending a lot less time with his mother, a situation which profoundly affected the still-young widow.

After Rodger had died in 1961 Dorothy Marie had seemed to blossom. No longer burdened with the problems of financing a home or being under the rule of a much older man she was enjoying the perks of being a pop star's mum.

'She was a totally different person after Cliff's father died,' remembers Pete Bush. 'She seemed to come out of her shell and want to be with Cliff. I don't know if it was out of wanting to be protected because of the loss of a husband but she seemed to be with him a lot more.'

Olive Queenie remembers it as a time of high excitement, 'All of these things were happening to Cliff and she was enjoying life for the first time. Instead of having to slave away to get things for people it was all coming to her easily and she was going overboard with it.

'She married her first boyfriend more or less straight from school and never knew what it was like to be adventurous and flirt and do all the things that girls do.'

She had become Cliff's constant companion as he attended film premières and ate out at fashionable restaurants. But with Cliff's involvement with the Crusaders, that began to change. Cliff no longer required her company as much as before and he was frequently absent from Rookswood for days while he stayed with Bill Latham and his mother Mamie.

'It was difficult for Cliff's mum to see him leave her and join another family,' Latham admits. 'It was compounded by the Christian dimension because she was getting more involved with the Jehovah's Witnesses. In the early days I think she thought that I had poached him and I know that she voiced this apprehension to other people.'

She began to feel lonely and it was in this state that she drew close to Derek Bodkin, a chauffeur hired for her by Cliff as she didn't drive and felt cut off living in a country house. Bodkin would take her shopping in London and to visit relatives. He would play badminton with her at a local club and later moved into a lodge at the entrance to Rookswood.

Out of this close association developed an unlikely romance between a 45-year-old mother of four children and a 23-year-old driver. At first, no one suspected anything because the two had so little in common. He wasn't a Jehovah's Witness, didn't have an interest in pop music, and admitted to being clumsy around women. Their continuing closeness was excused on the grounds that it was Bodkin's job to be at her beck and call.

'She came to see me when I was living in Manchester,' remembers Olive Queenie. 'Derek had driven her up. He was introduced to me as the chauffeur. I had never met him before. I was a little bit worried because by certain things that were said you could tell something was going on. I was thinking, "Surely not! He's younger than her son!"'

By February 1965 Cliff had become so integrated into the Crusaders set that he considered himself a Christian. When Ray Coleman of *Melody Maker* asked him what he thought of John Lennon's stinging comment that he found his singing voice 'too Christian' he responded, 'I'm glad it shows because I am a Christian and I don't want anyone to get any other idea. That's the way I am and I have no intention of covering up the fact.'

Yet his Crusader friends felt that even though he was becoming more 'Christian' by imitation he had not yet become a Christian by conviction. He appeared to regard Christianity as the highest level of decent living rather than as a change of heart.

'He was doing all the right things with all the right people in all the right places but I think that in his inner self he knew he hadn't reached the point of commitment,' says John Davey, a Crusader leader in Sussex.

'I think we all sensed that he was very close and there was a great deal of speculation between us about what would happen if he did make a public announcement.'

During a Crusader camp at Lewes, Graham Disbrey posed him the simple question: 'How can you be sure that you are a Christian?' Cliff later confessed that this was the provocation he had needed on the final stretch of his spiritual search. It bothered him that he had no answer other than to say he was British, he didn't think himself particularly evil and he believed in the existence of God.

Neither Cliff nor Bill Latham is now sure exactly when he made the decision that removed all doubt. In interviews of the period he refers back to 1965 and on 20 March 1966 he gave a talk on 'Christian Maturity' at Lewes YMCA, yet in his biography *Which One's Cliff?* he pinpoints May 1966 when he was making *Finders Keepers*, the last of his youth-orientated films.

What isn't disputed is the fact that it was in his bedroom at the Lathams' at 124 Etchingham Park Road, Finchley, that he prayed the prayer that ended the search.

A Crusader friend, Roger Stacey, had recommended that he check out verse twenty of Revelation chapter three, the last book in the New Testament. He told him that there he would find the key to his questions.

Before going to sleep that night Cliff opened his Bible and read the words of Jesus: 'Here I am! I stand at the door and knock. If anyone hears my voice and opens the door, I will go in and eat with him, and he with me.'

'I thought that this was it,' he remembers. 'I thought that if this was true I wanted to become a Christian. I didn't know how to do it though. I knew that the door was, figuratively speaking, the door of my life but I thought — how do you open it?

'I just remember saying the words, "Come on in. I want you in my life." Then I went to sleep. I didn't feel very religious the next day but, when I look back, that's when things started to change.'

June 1966 was an important month for British evangelical Christians. Billy Graham, the best-known preacher of his generation, was coming to London for a four-week crusade at Earls Court, his first in Britain since 1954.

There had been no public announcement, but word of Cliff's conversion had spread and an invitation came from the Greater London Crusade asking him to appear as a guest on the night of 16 June, a youth evening at which England cricketer Colin Cowdrey would be reading the lesson.

His career, he knew, would be on the line. If it was seen as a gimmick, it would backfire, and even if he was believed to be sincere there was no guarantee that his fans would continue to support him. In the era of drugs and mysticism Christianity was not a cool religion for a pop star to embrace.

His management were naturally concerned that Cliff could be exploited by the American evangelist, whom they knew little about, or that he could become so absorbed by religion that he would let his career slide.

'They were worried about it,' admits Mike Conlin. 'They had already had the trouble with Licorice Locking. But it was a vague worry rather than a fretful worry. They thought, "If he gets into that kind of rubbish we'll have to watch him like a hawk otherwise he'll be knocking on doors."'

The night of the appearance there were 25,000 people packed into the Earls Court arena with an additional 5,000 outside listening to the service on a sound-only relay. Cliff, who had been seated on the platform along with churchmen and dignitaries, made his way forward to the lectern, dressed in a corduroy jacket and horn-rimmed spectacles.

In a brief statement he credited his parents for rearing him on the

Bible and ended by saying, 'I can only say to people who are not Christians that until you have taken the step of asking Christ into your life, your life is not worthwhile. It works. It works for me.'

He then sang 'It Is No Secret', a gospel song which Elvis had recorded, and when he walked away from the lectern he found he was so nervous that his arms remained in their outstretched position. When the meeting ended, Cliff went outside and addressed the crowd of 5,000 who hadn't been able to get into the arena.

Two days after Earls Court his mother married Derek Bodkin at Epping Register Office. The first Cliff knew of the impending wedding was a call from someone in a public phone inviting him to the reception at Rookswood. He went and filmed the couple as they were showered with rose petals from a balcony over the front door and then they drove off for their honeymoon in an E-type Jaguar.

Confronted by the press at Pinewood Film Studios where he was shooting *Finders Keepers*, Cliff kept up his usual jaunty exterior, admitting that he hadn't known of the wedding until that morning but saying that he hoped his mother and Derek would be very happy. 'I'll be buying them a house as a wedding present and they'll be going to my place in Portugal.'

The pleasant chatter concealed his real feelings. He was disturbed by the relationship, not because he disliked Bodkin, but because he thought that the age-difference problem would be insurmountable.

Having lost Cliff to Bill Latham had she, in effect, married on the rebound? Bodkin himself may have unwittingly put his finger on the problem when he later said in an interview with the *Sunday Express*: 'I suppose I have taken over Cliff's place in Dorothy's life.'

Cliff's old way of life was fast disappearing. His mother was gone, Jackie Irving was dating his old rival Adam Faith and for the first time in six years (since 1960) he didn't appear in *NME*'s annual points list of best-selling singles.

Whatever was left standing he dismantled himself. His highly successful official fan club which Jan Vane had been running since 1958 was wound down, Rookswood was put on the market and in November 1966 he announced that he would be making no personal appearances during 1967.

'It was the closing of one door and the opening of another,' says Cliff. 'Up until that time I had felt responsible for my family. When my mother married I knew I could do what I wanted – which I did. I moved in with Bill and his mother. I wanted a different scene.'

For his fans, the most staggering news was that Cliff was considering becoming a schoolteacher. The notion had been floated a few times before, usually out of admiration for friends such as Bill Latham and Graham Disbrey, but now he appeared to be serious.

Through John Davey, a teacher at Lewes County Grammar School in Sussex, he arranged to take an O level in Religious Education and by sitting in on lessons at the school he was able to test the response of ordinary pupils to his presence in the classroom.

He also spent two months at Oak Hill, an Anglican theological college, where he studied the Bible and learned how to articulate his faith.

'I was the one who tried to get him to be a teacher,' admits Jay Norris. 'I believed that he would make a good teacher. I took him to meet the principal of Trent Park Training College in Cockfosters who said that if he got a couple of O levels they would take him.'

He was now so surrounded by schoolteachers and lecturers that it wasn't surprising that education should become his chosen alternative profession. Of his Crusader circle of friends Graham Disbrey taught art and design, Bill Latham taught religious education, John Davey taught chemistry, Peter Graves became a professor of German and John Harvey was a lecturer in aeronautics.

At the same time he was questioning whether show business was a worthy occupation for a Christian. Could he be guilty of setting himself up as a 'false idol' for teenagers? A recurring theme in interviews of the time was his desire to 'do something' with his life.

These misgivings, which had been building up long before his conversion, were confirmed by those Christians who thought that the entertainment industry was ungodly anyway. Some of them didn't own televisions on principle, never went to the cinema and maintained a Puritan attitude towards the theatre.

Coupled with a disapproval of smoking, drinking, dancing, swearing and make-up, it meant that a life on the stage was unthinkable for the thoroughly evangelical Christian because even if you weren't doing bad things you would surely be rubbing up against those who were.

The prohibition was rarely spelt out but anyone new to church circles would be quick to notice that there were no role models for committed Christians in show business. There had been actors and pop singers who had converted but the happy ending was almost always that they abandoned their worldly trappings and were now happier than they had ever been in what was known as 'full-time Christian work'. When Terry Dene had become a Christian, in September 1964, he got rid of his guitar and his records, and changed his name back to Terry Williams.

The implication was that show business, like sin itself, was something to be spurned and that anyone who secretly enjoyed the goings on at the London Palladium more than chorus singing at the church hall was spiritually suspect.

'The evangelical world had its own pressures which operated without a word ever being said,' says Cliff. 'I felt that I ought to leave show business. The majority of my friends hadn't actually said anything to that effect. They hadn't said, "Get thee out", but the pressures were vaguely there. I thought I'd move before it got any hotter and so I made my plans to leave.'

He talked it over with Peter Gormley who agreed to support him whatever decision he came to.

'I thought that was up to him,' says Gormley. 'It was his life. At one stage he asked me how much notice he would have to give to fulfil all his commitments and I can remember telling him that it would probably take twelve months.'

John Davey admits that initially his circle of friends did little to persuade him otherwise. They argued he could probably live comfortably on his earnings to date and could devote the rest of his life to worthier causes.

'He was at my parents' home in Lewes one day when the issue of him going to teacher training college came up,' Davey recalls. 'He actually rang his accountant up right there and then to find out what would happen if he didn't do any more show business work.

'He came off the phone looking quite shaken because he'd been given the news that even if he didn't do another day's work in his life he would be happily secure. He couldn't believe that he could safely sit back.'

The eventual decision to stick with pop was helped by a shift in attitude among some younger Christians who argued that evangelicals had been misguided in their rejection of the arts, media and entertainment. Even his normally conservative Crusader friends conceded that no area of culture was beyond redemption.

'I think we came to see that it would be a loss to show business if he stopped and a loss to Christianity if he didn't take advantage of the opportunities,' says John Davey. 'We realized that there was a definite job for him to do as a Christian believer within show business.'

The most encouraging discovery was a group who were meeting informally to discuss how Christians could become more actively involved in the arts. One of the group was actor Nigel Goodwin.

'We were discussing how it was possible to be a Christian and also to earn our wages as artists,' says Goodwin. 'I had this vision of a centre being created in London where Christian artists could meet and debate with their peers. Cliff started to come along to these meetings.'

David Winter was another group member, and in his role as editor of *Crusade* he chided those who withdrew from the arts and then became dismayed when other world-views came to predominate. He encouraged his readers to listen to what non-Christian artists had to say about the human condition.

Winter helped to persuade Cliff that he had two valuable assets which he shouldn't waste: his performing talent and his audience.

Independent of these discussions, Winter was involved with American film director Jim Collier in developing the story for a Billy Graham movie which would be set in contemporary London. Although Cliff wasn't under consideration at the beginning, this was to be the project which confirmed him in his growing belief that he could marry his faith to his work.

The result, *Two A Penny*, with screenplay by Stella Linden would not have merited much attention outside the Christian community had it not been for Cliff's involvement. The brief review in *Halliwell's Film Guide* called it 'Naïve religious propaganda sponsored by the Billy Graham movement and featuring the evangelist in a cameo. A curiosity.'

Yet for the Billy Graham Organization it was a departure from the conversion stories disguised as dramas which it had been making since the fifties. The main differences were that *Two A Penny* was marginally more realistic and the hero of the film, played by Cliff, didn't get 'saved' on camera. The puzzle was left with the audience rather than solved by the film maker.

Cast as a drug-dealing art student called Jamie, Cliff at least tackled the role of someone less virtuous than the squeaky-clean hero of *The Young Ones* and *Wonderful Life*. He got to fight, swear, shout and wear stubble on his chin.

'Among Cliff's Christian friends there were people who were quite pleased that he was thinking of giving it all up,' says Winter. 'But Jim Collier was the person who tipped the balance. He said, "Look what you can do! You can't throw all this away." '

Because Cliff had never been someone to whom people looked for guidance on daily living it was harder for him to find a natural way of expressing his new-found beliefs through his work. His songs didn't articulate his inner anxieties.

Show business, to be successful, had to reassure rather than disturb, to sweep people off to a fantasy world of sweetness and light rather than plunge them into debates about the security of their souls.

It was easier for novelists or those in the fine arts to incorporate spiritual discovery into their creations than it was for a man who performed other people's songs. During 1967 Cliff struggled with the issue of whether it was possible to Christianize his brand of entertainment.

His first steps towards working out an answer were necessarily faltering. There were no examples to follow. Norrie Paramor suggested that he might like to do a gospel album. After all, Elvis had recorded gospel material and it hadn't adversely affected his career.

Cliff acted on the suggestion and in February 1967 he went into Abbey Road Studios to begin recording *Good News*, a collection of spirituals, hymns and gospel songs, while the Beatles recorded their 'Magical Mystery Tour' EP in the studio next door.

Yet while the Beatles' lyrics were dissected by those keen to understand the group's shifting point of view, and only rarely were the group interviewed in depth, Cliff was increasingly being drawn into debate and argument about his faith. For producers of religious radio and television programmes he was a welcome alternative from the parade of vicars and bishops which dominated the 'God slots'. For Cliff it was an opportunity to say what he could never say in his singles.

In the 'love and peace' summer of 1967 Cliff was to be found on British television discussing his faith with Billy Graham and 'Ready Steady Go' presenter Cathy McGowan. In July he was brought into

ABC's studios to face a roasting by ex-Manfred Mann singer Paul Jones, who had just starred in *Privilege*, Peter Watkins' futuristic film of a pop singer who is tamed by the church and then used to curb teenage behaviour by making young rebels subservient to the state.

The programme, 'Looking For An Answer', began by showing a clip from the film contrasted with shots of Cliff at Earls Court with Billy Graham . Jones, then an outspoken atheist, accused Cliff of being an instrument of the established church.

Cliff denied that he was being used in this way. 'I put myself in God's hands and say, "Look, if this is the thing I ought to do I shall do it,"' he said. 'The church is just, I think, a front. You know, it's a name. We are always fooled by words and names and things.'

Jones: 'Well, one of the bishops in *Privilege* says, when he is accused of using the pop singer to further the ends of the church, "Once they used a Spanish Inquisition and this is less painful." You know, it's exactly what you have just said, really.'

Cliff: 'Before I came on the scene Graham packed out places like Earls Court. He doesn't need me.'

Jones: 'But people don't know what they're coming for. Billy Graham knows why people go to his meetings is the same reason people in American spent $125 million in one year going to fortune tellers. They are insecure; they're unsure. They don't know what they're going for. Right, so you say: "We are giving them Christ." I say you're not. You're giving them a show...'

What Cliff offered was not a dazzling display of Christian apologetics — in fact his statements were often extremely unsophisticated — but a simple admission that he had 'accepted a thing called salvation which means that if I die I can look forward to an eternal life of peace and joy and no pain'. (Interestingly, Jones went on to become a Christian himself.)

Within the next few years Cliff was to become one of the most visible defenders of the Christian faith. Just when the trend among rock musicians was to 'let the music do the talking' Cliff was pouring out the first of millions of words which would attempt to answer the public's questions on everything from Bible reading to nuclear warfare. Never before had a pop star committed so many opinions to print on behalf of something other than his own career.

With David Winter he collaborated on Christian books. The first of these was *New Singer, New Song*, a biography which had his conversion as a convenient last chapter and his confirmation by Graham Leonard (later to be Bishop of London) in December 1967 as the final page: 'It was another great turning point, in its way: like Hoddesdon, and Butlin's, and "Oh Boy!" and Earls Court; and yet so natural, so easy, that it seemed that all his life up to this moment had merely been a preparation for it. It was — and no simile could possibly please Cliff more — just like coming home.'

The next, *The Way I See It*, was a collection of answers to the sort of questions he had been bombarded with since becoming a Christian.

'We sat down with the questions and Cliff just spoke his answers into a tape recorder,' says David Winter. 'I often didn't agree with what he said but it all went in the way that he said it.'

It was a hard time to be saying the things that Cliff was saying. Although the sixties' search for alternative lifestyles was a rejection of materialistic culture, Christianity was too closely associated with the old order to merit much serious consideration.

At a time when, in the wake of the more widely available contraceptive pill for women, 'free love' was being advocated, Cliff was having to say, for instance, 'Sex outside marriage is always wrong.' At a time when recreational drugs were all the rage Cliff was saying, 'Drugs ruin your health, turn you into a sort of zombie and, in many cases, finally cause death.'

To the hippie generation, listening to Cliff was like listening to their parents who were always advising moderation or abstention and who always seemed to think that the government knew best.

One of the questions asked in *The Way I See It* was 'Do you see yourself as a conformist?'. Cliff answered that he was not a conformist because conformism is a result of peer pressure and he has never altered his views in order to gain the approval of his peers.

This is one of the paradoxes of Cliff's life, that while he always seems eager to please and his show business career is built on giving people what they want, he is determined to do things his way and never acts against his conscience.

His decision to go public as a Christian was an example of this. Faced with the option of staying quiet and continuing to fulfil audience expectations or speaking out and risking rejection he hadn't hesitated to take the more dangerous route.

'I don't think I've ever met anybody who is as sure of himself as Cliff is,' observes Tony Meehan. 'I don't think I've met anyone who was integrated in the sense that he believes he's right and that's it. He was always like that.

'The public often think of him as being soft. He's a very charming and personable man but beneath that I think it's sheer metal and that doesn't come across to the public.'

18

Dropping back into suburbia

Approaching the end of his first decade in show business, Cliff was virtually unscathed. Many of those who had shared in his success had already buckled under the pressure.

Jet Harris was an alcoholic and had suffered a nervous breakdown, Bruce Welch was on the brink of a divorce and, during a run at the Talk Of The Town in January 1968, bass player John Rostill collapsed with mental exhaustion and had to be temporarily replaced by Licorice Locking.

Yet while Cliff's level of personal contentment had risen, his creative stock had fallen. No longer 'too sexy for TV', he was beginning to dress like his schoolteacher friends, suppressing the instinct he'd once had to be beautiful and exciting.

While the younger generation indulged in a riot of kaftans and afro hairstyles Cliff was sporting a Beatles (circa 1962) fringe, tortoiseshell-framed spectacles and elephant-cord slacks. In a perverse way he seemed to be toying with the power of his fame; seeing how far from the sex idol he could move without losing the bulk of his fans.

The middle years of the sixties were a golden age for the pop single. You could take the top thirty for almost any week during 1966 and find it cluttered with songs now regarded as classics.

In June, for example, as Cliff was performing for Billy Graham, the following singles were in the top thirty: 'Strangers In The Night', 'Wild Thing', 'Sorrow', 'Monday, Monday', 'Sloop John B.', 'When A Man Loves A Woman', 'Pretty Flamingo', 'You Don't Have To Say You Love Me', 'Paperback Writer', 'River Deep, Mountain High', and 'Sunny Afternoon'.

Cliff, however, wasn't carried along on this wave of creativity. He was too busy developing his spiritual life and dropping back into suburbia.

In the years before his interest in religion he had enjoyed phenomenal chart success. Between 'Living Doll' in 1959 and 'Don't Talk To Him' at the end of 1963 he had had an unbroken run of twenty hit singles each of which sold over one million copies. Yet of the seventeen singles released between then and the end of 1967 only three had topped a million.

His domination of British pop was over. Cliff's high point had come in that dull period between Elvis' induction into the army and the Beatles' conquest of America when he pretty much had the show to himself in Britain. Now he was facing massive competition in a proliferating music market.

But the relative decline in his fortunes was also partly self-inflicted. His career had been his religion. He had worshipped it and forsaken all else for it. Now it had been toppled from this pre-eminent position in his life. 'God became more important than his career,' says Bruce Welch.

In 1966 he told journalist George Tremlett, 'I could leave show business tomorrow. It wouldn't bother me one bit. I'm sure of that. I know now that if someone was to tell me that I couldn't sing any more it wouldn't worry me at all. It's just the way I've changed. If someone had told me that four years ago I would probably have hanged myself. But I've changed a lot.'

It was a confused signal to send out to his fans. It suggested that he was half-hearted about recording and performing. Why should the public respond with passion to material that was no longer created with passion?

'That's what he wanted to do at the time and there was nothing wrong with that,' says Hank Marvin. 'The problem that resulted though was that he still wanted a career and still expected the same results while he wasn't putting the same sort of effort in. It was as though he expected things to happen by accident.'

Tony Meehan was hired to try to give him direction by introducing him to contemporary songs. Cliff had already hooked up with country producer Billy Sherrill who had taken him to Nashville and produced 'The Minute You're Gone' and 'Wind Me Up', both of which became big hits. Cliff then recorded 'Blue Turns To Grey', a song written by Mick Jagger and Keith Richards, which reached number fifteen.

'Norrie Paramor seemed to have lost direction completely at that point,' says Meehan. 'I was brought in to try and bring Cliff up to date. Norrie was very threatened by it. I was supposed to carve myself a place in the office but I didn't fit in. It was hard having been one thing in an organization and then coming back as something else.'

At the age of fifty-four Paramor, who had overseen Cliff's recording career brilliantly from teenage rock 'n' roll star to show business legend, seemed to be losing touch with a market that was being flooded with new musical influences and technology. While such bands as Cream and the Jimi Hendrix Experience spent days over one song, experimented with new instruments and stretched recording techniques as far as they would go, Cliff was still only turning up for vocal sessions and expected to get at least five numbers recorded in a session.

After the watershed year of 1966 the only million-seller Paramor was to enjoy with Cliff was 'Congratulations', written by Bill Martin and Phil Coulter. It was a massive hit, selling over two and a quarter million copies, but it nailed Cliff to a jaunty Eurovision sound at a time when rock was actually returning to its roots with the re-release of Bill Haley's 'Rock Around The Clock', 'Lady Madonna' from the Beatles and the Rolling Stones' 'Jumping Jack Flash'.

Phil Coulter had sketched out a song called 'I Think I Love You' with a lyric that went: 'I think I love you/ I think I love you/ I think the world is fine/When you say that you're mine'. He played it to his songwriting partner in their small Denmark Street office but Bill Martin found the sentiment risible.

'It was terrible,' says Martin. 'I explained to Phil, "You don't say to anyone, 'I think I love you.' You either say 'I love you' or 'I don't love you' — it's either a negative or a positive. It can't be a nebulous thing. It's got five syllables, why don't we try 'congratulations and celebrations'?" '

Martin had nursed the idea of writing a song around the word 'congratulations', thinking it might be possible to write another 'Happy Birthday' or 'White Christmas' — a jingle for any cork-popping celebration.

'Congratulations' is now one of the most recorded songs in Britain with over one thousand versions. It was played outside Buckingham Palace after the wedding of Charles and Diana, and on the dockside at Southampton when British troop ships returned from the Falklands War.

However, in 1968 when it was Britain's Eurovision entry, it lost by one vote to Spain's long-forgotten 'La La La'. It was a bemusing decision which came about in the final seconds of voting when Germany awarded Spain six points, bringing its total up to twenty-nine against Britain's twenty-eight.

'I remember that we were taken back stage to get ready to receive the award and then we were given the news that it had lost,' says Bill Martin . 'We were sure that Cliff had walked it and of course after that it became number one in all the main markets outside America.'

Under Norrie Paramor's direction Cliff had moved away from the rock 'n' roll group sound and was now almost always backed by an orchestra. By 1967, less than a fifth of all Cliff's sessions were recorded with the Shadows and in the summer of 1968 he went in the studio with the Shadows for the last time. The title of the track was 'Not The Way It Should Be'.

On 19 December 1968 Hank Marvin, Bruce Welch, John Rostill and Brian Bennett broke up and went their separate ways. The Shadows did not come into existence again until 1974 when the line-up was Hank, Bruce, Brian and John Farrar.

In ten years the Shadows had come from being Cliff's backing group to an internationally recognized group in their own right. They had had thirteen top ten hits but there had been a gap of almost three years since 'Don't Make My Baby Blue' reached number ten.

Like any band that had been together for so long and toured so hard they were beginning to irritate one another. John Rostill and Hank Marvin were constantly arguing, Bruce Welch had met Olivia Newton-John and wanted to spend more time with her and Brian Bennett had recorded a solo album titled, tellingly, *Change Of Direction*.

'We worked too hard and we saw each other too often,' says Bennett. 'If we weren't touring we were recording and if we weren't recording we were doing a film, a pantomime or television.

'In your late teens and early twenties you accept all those things as new experiences, but as you start to mature you realize that there are things that you are not going to put up with about one another.'

Cliff by now had bought a house with Bill Latham in Northcliffe Drive, Totteridge, where they lived with Mamie who looked after them as if they were both her sons.

For someone of his status, his lifestyle wasn't extravagant. His biggest luxuries were the houses, a six-berth boat on the Norfolk Broads and his two cars — an MG and an E-type Jaguar. He followed the Christian practice of tithing, which meant giving ten per cent of his income to charity, and continued to take only fifteen pounds spending money in cash each week from the office.

His holidays were now taken in August with his Crusader friends.

The group was always exclusively male and bachelor, and became known as the 'holiday gang'. If any of them married – as John Davey and Peter Graves subsequently did – they inevitably dropped out, though they remained close friends.

For the first two years they went to Portugal, driving down through France in 1966 in Cliff's E-type Jaguar and John Davey's Vauxhall Victor Estate.

'Cliff identified with the style in which we did things, which was very much on the cheap,' remembers Peter Graves.

'On the way down through France we camped and this was an entirely new experience for him. To him we were all extremely normal and he found that he wasn't put on a pedestal. There are a lot of insults flying between us, a lot of banter, and he soon got caught up in it. Once we'd all got over the initial excitement of meeting him he became an ordinary friend and that appealed to him.'

In 1968 the holiday gang – Bill, Cliff, Graham, Peter and John – met up in Los Angeles where World Wide Films had given Cliff the use of a plush apartment in Burbank and a large estate car in lieu of his fee for *Two A Penny*.

For a month they became tourists, taking VIP trips of Universal Studios and Disneyland, going to an Animals' concert at the Hollywood Bowl, seeing Tony Bennett play in San Francisco and staying at the Dunes Hotel in Las Vegas.

Neither Cliff nor Bill Latham had much time for the more traditional sightseeing. When John Davey arranged a trip to the Grand Canyon neither of them were interested in going. Similarly, a few years later, when they were all in Israel, Latham preferred to spend his time poolside at Jerusalem's Diplomat Hotel rather than visit the sites.

The Shadows couldn't wholeheartedly get behind the Christian side of Cliff's career, and he didn't expect them to feel as much a part of this work.

Bruce Welch in particular had no time for his religious beliefs and hot-footed it out of the dressing room whenever Bible studies were mentioned. This lack of empathy, plus the fact that the Shadows were suffering internal strife, gave Cliff the freedom to work with other musicians.

The first of these were the folk-rock group the Settlers. Early in 1968 he met the group's singer Cindy Kent, one of the few evangelical Christians in the business. Feeling isolated from the church after six years on the road, a friend had suggested that she turn up at one of Cliff's meetings at St Paul's church in Barnet. Afterwards, in the vestry, they were introduced.

'It was then that I mentioned to him that I was looking for a church,' remembers Cindy. 'I wanted to find somewhere where they would understand my lifestyle and the fact that I couldn't be there every week. He immediately understood my problem and suggested his church. I started going and we became good friends.'

A group from St Paul's, including Cliff and Bill Latham, later saw the Settlers at the Festival Hall. Cliff was impressed enough to ask them to be part of a special gospel tour he was planning to do on behalf of Eurovangelism, a Christian charity which sent aid to European nationals.

The international director of Eurovangelism was Dave Foster, who had met Cliff for the first time on location during the filming of *Two A Penny*. The two men had sat in the back of a van in Shepherd's Bush eating lunch and Cliff had again talked about the possibility of leaving music.

'Cliff said, "Well, what on earth can you do in the business I'm in?",' says Dave Foster. 'So off the top of my head I said, "Why not gospel concerts?" He went away and thought about it and at first he couldn't find any good Christian musicians to work with him because there was virtually no gospel scene at the time. Then one day he called and said he thought he'd found them. I hadn't heard of them but they were called the Settlers.'

Cliff hadn't done a gospel tour before but was intrigued with the possibility of creating a show that would promote his beliefs. With David Winter he discussed whether it should be a programme of hymns or whether new material should be commissioned. David suggested a concert arranged in three sections on the theme of 'Help, Hope and Hallelujah' which would involve gospel songs, spirituals and hymns alongside some thought-provoking secular material.

'The Help section consisted of songs like "Nowhere Man" which were about the longings that people have,' says Dave Foster . 'The Hope section began with "In The Bleak Mid-Winter" and concentrated on the life of Christ through to the crucifixion and resurrection. Hallelujah was a rip-roaring gospel celebration at the end.'

Peter Gormley was uncertain about this new direction and didn't want the show launched in Britain in case it failed and damaged Cliff's primary market. As a result of this Dave Foster set up the first mini-tour with dates in Stockholm, The Hague and Zagreb.

'Cliff very much became a part of us on that tour,' says Cindy Kent . 'There was no feeling of him being the star and us the humble group of backing musicians. Looking back, I can see that it was a time when he was sorting himself out, trying to discover what it was he should be doing with his music and his life.'

Even though 'Congratulations' was the biggest hit in Europe that month, Cliff had decided that this was to be his first show without hits.

'I have sung pop songs in Stockholm before,' he told the crowd of 3,000 on his opening night. 'But this evening we want to sing only gospel songs because of the special purpose of this concert.'

No one complained in Sweden but the next day in Holland they found the venue half empty despite the success of 'Congratulations' and prominent national publicity. In a confidential Eurovangelism report after the tour it was noted that this could have been because:

'Some Christians steered clear of what they expected to be an irreverent fiasco and some secular fans shunned what they thought would be a sort of staid hymn singing session.'

Says Dave Foster: 'It was an unusual experience for Cliff to see a half-empty hall. I think the analysis we came up with at the time was probably true. Something like this may have been what Peter Gormley foresaw when he was less than enthusiastic at the beginning.'

The show in Croatia, then Yugoslavia with Tito as president, was a boost for local Christians who were harassed at every turn and refused access to the media. Cliff not only used a secular venue to tell the Christian story but was also allowed to appear live on national television for three minutes before their ten o'clock news.

'We were backstage synchronizing our watches, and even changed the running order that night so that when we went live Cliff would be speaking about his faith and how he became a Christian,' remembers Dave Foster.

'At about a minute before ten he launched into "What A Friend We Have In Jesus" which then faded into the news. Yugoslav Christians, some of whom were really suffering for sharing their faith, were ecstatic that someone had got away with it on national television!'

The head of the country's Baptist Union, Dr Horak, was later called in by the head of Zagreb's secret police. Expecting a reprimand he was surprised to be offered a coffee and some mild appreciation about the concert. It turned out that the police chief's teenage daughters had been there and had loved it.

'That was really a turning point for the church in Yugoslavia,' says Dave Foster. 'The money raised was given to local Christians to help with a home for destitute children. This action helped raise their image.

'Two weeks later Dr Horak was asked to meet President Tito which was really something. Then, in 1970, Billy Graham was allowed to do his first visual relays by land line to Zagreb. I don't think any of that would have happened without Cliff.'

While his secular career entered a period of stasis, allowing challengers such as Tom Jones and Engelbert Humperdinck to snatch his crown as Britain's most popular male vocalist, Cliff was learning how to craft a show with a message, not such an easy task for someone whose success had been built on orchestrating female frenzy.

Although he had toyed with songwriting over the years, usually with Hank or Bruce Welch, it was only on becoming a Christian that he had taken it seriousiy, providing the title track of *Two A Penny* and, late in 1968, writing songs with David Winter for a Tyne Tees television series, 'Life With Johnny'.

Based on the parables of Jesus, but set in the contemporary world, the half-hour mini-musicals were the idea of religious television adviser Maxwell Dees and David Winter, and just as 'Help, Hope and Hallelujah' was an innovation for Christian music in Britain, so 'Life With Johnny' was a breakthrough for God-slot television.

Cliff was Johnny while Cindy Kent, Una Stubbs and Lynda Marchal (now known as the television writer and novelist Lynda La Plante) played his girlfriends. Twenty songs, some written by Cliff, others by David Winter and Mike Jones of the Settlers, were recorded at Abbey Road for the soundtrack.

'It was recommended at the time by the *ITV Yearbook* as one of the most imaginative bits of religious broadcasting,' says David Winter. 'There were very strong character actors in it and Tyne Tees spent a lot of money on it. Every company showed it except the four majors — Granada, Yorkshire, LWT and Anglia — who were upset that a small company had muscled in and made a programme for the main evening show.'

It was rumoured around this time that Cliff was dating Cindy Kent. After all, she did seem to fit the bill: she was wholesome, she had long hair, she liked music, she didn't wear too much make-up and she shared his Christian faith.

The *TV Times* approached her, ostensibly to write a profile, and during the interview asked what sort of man she would like to marry. She outlined her preferences and the interviewer casually suggested that it sounded as though she was describing someone like Cliff Richard. 'I suppose so,' said Cindy, and that was that.

'When the story came out it was run as part of a series titled "The Men In My Life",' says Cindy. 'They had rung Cliff's mum up to see what she thought of me.

'It was absolutely awful. Girls turned up at Cliff's house weeping, saying "It's not true, is it? He's not planning to marry Cindy, is he?" I rang him up straight away. I was so upset. He just told me not to worry.'

At the end of the sixties Cliff's secular career had settled into a dull and unadventurous rut. The only thing the singles had going for them was that they were 'catchy', in the sense that your postman could probably whistle them.

They certainly didn't have soul or musical innovation. Was it really possible to be moved by 'Good Times'? Did anyone care who played guitar on 'Big Ship' or what the lyric of 'Goodbye Sam, Hello Samantha' was attempting to describe?

A similar emptiness could be experienced by watching his television series 'It's Cliff Richard' in 1970 and 1971 where he played some of the same songs and indulged in safe humour with Una Stubbs, Olivia Newton-John and Hank Marvin (who was now one third of the group Marvin, Welch and Farrar).

Olivia seemed wonderfully suited to Cliff. With her attractive white smile and innocent beauty she looked like his female counterpart. The image of togetherness was enhanced by the duets they sang together during the series and a sketch in which they played bride and bridegroom. The public wished them on each other.

Cliff helped launch her career in Britain and Peter Gormley became her manager. After the debut on television he introduced her into his concerts and she and her friend Pat Farrar began singing backing vocals.

There was never any romance. From the time of her arrival in England in 1967 she was involved with Bruce Welch, eventually setting up home with him and getting engaged. When they split up in 1972 she had a relationship with her manager Lee Kramer before meeting dancer Matt Lattanzi on the set of Xanadu in 1980 and marrying him five years later.

But they were extremely close. Cliff kept framed photos of her at home and at the office and whenever she was in town they would end up going out together. Once they even called a radio station late at night from a hotel room and requested a song.

'I think that it was Capital Radio in London,' says Olivia. 'Cliff called up and said, "Hello, this is Cliff Richard." The DJ said, "Yes, and I'm Elvis Presley." He didn't believe Cliff! Then I called up and said, "Hello, this is Olivia Newton-John." From then on it became a running gag.

'Every DJ that took over would say, "Cliff and Olivia, are you still there? Are you having your breakfast yet?" It was all quite innocent, but that's how rumours start!'

'There was only one girl we thought had a chance with Cliff,' his mother admits. 'That was Olivia. Knowing all the girls he's been out with and knowing him I think that was his chance. If he was going to marry, she would have been the girl.'

Yet, according to Cliff, it wasn't just the fact of her boyfriends that kept them apart.

'I don't think we would have got involved anyway,' he says. 'I'm very fond of her and I guess it's because we never got involved that we can remain such good friends. I feel totally comfortable with her and would like to think she feels comfortable with me. When we see each other we hug each other to death for about ten minutes.

'We feel that close and yet I know there was no romantic thing from my point of view and I never got the romantic vibe from her. Yet, having said that, I never felt put down by it.'

In 1971 Cliff was drawn into the then-lively pornography debate which saw him on the side of Mary Whitehouse, Malcolm Muggeridge and Lord Longford against the massed ranks of the various liberation 'fronts' and Marxist–Leninist splinter groups which had emerged from Britain's alternative culture.

The Nationwide Festival of Light had been founded by Peter Hill, a young missionary who had returned home to England and been shocked by what he saw as a sharp moral decline. In a very short time he motivated thousands of Christians to register their protest in marches and rallies throughout the country. It was to be a display of solidarity and a reassertion of Christian values.

Cliff was invited to perform at the opening rally on 9 September at Westminster Central Hall in London. The Gay Liberation Front, who saw the Festival of Light as an Establishment plan to curb the freedoms they had gained in the sixties, planned to disrupt the event.

Operation Rupert Bear, as it was code-named, was organized by Dennis Lemon (later to be taken to court by Mary Whitehouse in a well-known blasphemy case when he became editor of *Gay News*) and financed by Graham Chapman of Monty Python. It involved a group of GLF members who infiltrated the crowd dressed as nuns and then, as things got going, began shouting 'Glory Hallelujah!' and 'Praise the Lord!' while releasing bagfuls of white mice.

From that point on Cliff became a particular target of left-wing groups, anarchist groups and gay liberation organizations. The homosexual activists suspected that Cliff was a repressed homosexual dealing with his repression by attacking those who had 'come out'.

When he played a thirty-minute set at the Festival of Light's final rally in Hyde Park on 25 September he was jeered and pelted with eggs.

'It was early days for Cliff as a Christian and here he was being pitched into public opposition that most of us never have to confront in a lifetime,' says Bill Latham. 'But he took it all without flinching. There was never any question of him retreating.'

19

'A time of growth'

Between 1972 and 1975 Cliff's career slumped to an all-time low. He was out of fashion, out of touch and, for long periods, out of the charts. He was a figure of ridicule to the new rock aristocracy who derided his music as too bland and innocuous.

Just as he had grown his hair, worn chunky crucifixes and started singing songs of love, peace and freedom, the rock culture he must have hoped to appear relevant to had abandoned the good vibes of the sixties for a taste of decadence.

David Bowie, who had appeared on one album cover in a full-length dress, had become the first rock singer to confess to homosexual experience. The American rock star Alice Cooper was grabbing headlines by attacking blood-filled baby dolls on stage with a sharpened axe, and Marc Bolan was draping himself with feather boas and liberally applying mascara.

With hippie culture Cliff had been able to take the buzz words of love, peace, freedom and harmony and invest them with Christian meaning. The new darker mood of hard drugs, violence and sexual perversion couldn't be given the same sort of spin. You could possibly interest a hippy in discovering 'real peace' or 'real freedom' but you couldn't honestly claim that Jesus offered the tops in decadence.

Cliff was disturbed by Bowie's use of bisexual imagery and by the mock horror of Alice Cooper. It not only offended his Christian sensitivity but it went against his natural conservativism. His acid test was always whether it would embarrass or shock his mother. If he thought it would then, in his opinion, it had gone too far. It was indecent.

He spoke out against homosexual practice and began to identify himself more with Mary Whitehouse who, as President of the Viewers and Listeners Association, had been fighting a long battle against what she saw as declining moral standards in the media. She vigilantly monitored radio and television output and encouraged her followers to complain about obscene language or scenes of violence and nudity.

'What is this Bowie man/woman image on the stage doing to young people?' Cliff asked at the time. 'He upsets me as a man. There's a great responsibility all of us singers have to the ten year olds and some of us aren't living up to it.'

New Musical Express, which in 1958 had questioned his own suitability for television, was by now on the side of those who offended respectable opinion. It gloried in tales of sleaze, debauchery and drug-taking and saw in Cliff an appropriate figure of hate.

The paper repeatedly pilloried him for his celibacy, his Christian faith and his consummate 'cleanness'. Nick Kent, whose hero of the moment was Rolling Stone Keith Richards, was sent to report on Cliff's appearance at Spre-e '73, a Christian event at Wembley Stadium at which Billy Graham was preaching.

There was no mention of the music. Cliff, he said, 'bounced around flashing his teeth' and looked as though 'he'd just come out of rigorous training for the John Denver "Wimp of the Week" sweepstakes'.

There were feeble attempts to be 'relevant' but they only served to show how out of tune he was. 'Power To All Our Friends' sounded like a belated response to 'Power To The People', but whereas John Lennon sang left-wing orthodoxy with passion and soul, Cliff sang candy-floss lyrics to a Eurovision beat.

'Take Me High' nodded in the direction of the coded drugs songs of the mid-sixties, 'Honky Tonk Angel' mined the same territory as the Rolling Stones' 1969 song 'Honky Tonk Woman' and 'Sing A Song Of Freedom' was an all-purpose anthem with no real message which drew on the popular banner-waving slogans of campus politics.

What was more worrying, for Cliff and his management, was that the fans were no longer buying the singles in such huge volumes. His entire sales between 1970 and 1975 were easily beaten by the combined sales of 'Living Doll' and 'Travellin' Light' back in the early days of his career.

His first attempt to put out a religious song as a single was a resounding flop. 'Jesus', released in 1972, was his worst-selling record to date and didn't even make the top thirty. Later the same year he lost Norrie Paramor, who retired from EMI and moved to Birmingham to conduct the Midland Light Orchestra.

Paramor might have lost his magic touch but he'd been in the studio with Cliff for almost every session since 1958, and had become an important father figure. The first single he recorded without Paramor, 'A Brand New Song', was also the first of his career not to enter the top fifty. It seemed like a bad omen.

The challenge apparently gone from his music, his desire to act was rekindled. He was approached in 1970 by the New Theatre in Bromley to take on the part of Clive Harrington in *Five Finger Exercise*, Peter Shaffer's play about the 'deep friendship' between an artistic student and a tutor.

Controversial when first produced in 1958 because of its veiled treatment of homosexual affection, it was a strange choice of subject matter for Cliff's stage debut in a dramatic role.

'It was about a young fellow discovering his sexual identity,' explains William Gaunt, who played the part of the tutor.

'We discussed the play as a cast but Cliff never related any of the emotions to himself. It was all very much, "Yes, that's interesting — let's get on with it". He didn't flinch from the subject, and he acted very capably, but at the same time I don't think he really put himself into it.

'When I visited his dressing room during the interval on the opening night I found him sitting there signing a pile of photographs. That was indicative of his attitude. It was a job he wanted to do in order to prove that he could do it.'

The local newspaper, the *Kentish Times*, felt that he couldn't ultimately master the role because of his natural niceness and his inexperience. The years hoofing it around in pantomimes and doing cute television sketches for tea-time audiences weren't an adequate training ground for serious acting.

'But within those limitations,' the theatre critic conceded, 'Cliff Richard's straight acting debut at the New Theatre Bromley was a success and a triumph for his determination to make his way in the theatre.'

Emboldened by the experience he returned a year later with his first beard to rehearse for a part in Graham Greene's 1958 play *The Potting Shed* but two days before opening night the theatre burned down and the production had to be transferred to Sadler's Wells Theatre in North London.

This time the *Kentish Times* saw an improvement: 'As the obsessed James Callifer he gives a nicely restrained performance that nevertheless has the undercurrent of poignancy and despairing drive.' Cliff has since said that this remains one of his proudest achievements.

The next year he took a part in a television drama, 'The Case', and then in 1974 he renewed his relationship with Kenneth Harper to star in *Take Me High*, with Anthony Andrews and Deborah Watling.

The story of a young merchant banker who goes to Birmingham and revives a restaurant's flagging trade by inventing the Brumburger, *Take Me High* was an artistic and commercial flop.

'We all wanted to prove that we could do a musical film without dances, and the answer is that you can't,' says Kenneth Harper.

'It was rushed into scripting and then rushed into filming. When you get to a point in the script and you think you're up a gum tree a great director can generally invent something but it just didn't happen this time. It didn't make its money back.'

Kenneth Harper and his director David Askey had made the film as if nothing had changed in the world since *Wonderful Life*. There was the same attempt at innocent joviality and coy flirtatiousness but cinema audiences no longer found the immaturity believable.

'As soon as I saw it I realized how old-fashioned it was,' says Anthony Andrews, who was then at the beginning of his film career. 'It was a hangover from a previous era. That was a slightly disappointing realization because during the making of it we'd had such fun. It was like being in *The Young Ones*.'

That year, 1974, Cliff released only one single, '(You Keep Me) Hanging On', and 1975 was his first year without a hit single. 'Honky Tonk Angel' was withdrawn after only a thousand copies had been pressed because it was brought to Cliff's attention that a honky tonk angel is not an attractive piano player but an American prostitute.

'I was at a Christian conference centre with Bill and I was taking questions from the audience when a girl asked me why my new record was about a prostitute,' says Cliff. 'It shook me rigid. I said, "You're joking, aren't you?" I promised to check it out and when I got back home I called Peter Gormley.'

Gormley wasn't sure but called some friends in Los Angeles, and confirmed that a honky tonk angel was at least a 'loose woman' who frequented honky tonk bars, if not a whore. Cliff ordered the record to be stopped, and he even went on a pre-booked 'Russell Harty Show' to explain why he wouldn't be performing his latest single.

'I had already sent copies out to the DJs on Radio 1,' says Eric Hall, then Head of Promotion for EMI. 'To make sure the record was completely withdrawn I had to go round personally and take them back because I knew that if I just told them not to play it the records would end up as collectors' items.'

Yet while the first half of the seventies was an artistic and commercial failure it was a time of great spiritual growth. The let-up of pressure gave him the time to work out how the demands of his faith should affect his work.

'It was my growth time as a Christian,' he admits. 'It wasn't planned that way but it gave me time to get my Christian life to a point where I was totally comfortable with it.'

Having moved from Totteridge into a £70,000 house in the exclusive St George's Hill estate in Weybridge, he and Bill Latham regularly began to attend Sunday evening services at Guildford Baptist Church. David Pawson, a noted Bible teacher, would preach fifty-minute sermons to a congregation that was over seven hundred strong. Often the church was so packed that the service had to be relayed to ante-rooms on closed circuit television.

Although Cliff never became a member of the church he went as often as his job would allow and a small group was organized to pray with him when he was around and for him when he wasn't.

'When Cliff came to our church I made him a twofold promise,' says David Pawson. 'One part of it was that I would never ask him to do anything unless he wanted to do it, and the other was that I would never pass on any requests I got for his services.

'I wanted him to have one place where he could come and be himself and not be bothered by anyone else. He usually came in at the last minute and because there were no seats left he would sit on the floor with most of the young people. He was accepted as one of the congregation and the lack of special attention was quite noticeable.'

The move to Weybridge in 1973 had been made possible when Bill Latham gave up his job as a teacher to work with a fledgling relief agency attached to the Evangelical Alliance, an umbrella organization which looked after the concerns of evangelical Christians in all denominations.

A dynamic young vicar in his thirties, George Hoffman, had been hired by them to organize a series of social action projects, one of which was a fund for overseas aid which had been started in 1968 from money sent in by Christians who wanted to see something done in the world's disaster areas. It became known as The Evangelical Alliance Relief Fund, Tear Fund for short.

'The work grew rapidly,' says Hoffman. 'David Winter, who was editing *Crusade* magazine in the same building, said he knew the right person to help me. That was how Bill Latham came to be my assistant. He did what I didn't do and I did what he didn't do.'

Tear Fund bought food and equipment and also sponsored workers to help on existing relief projects. Cliff had made his first donation in 1968 when the £2,000 profit from his first British gospel concert bought a Land Rover for a group in Northern Argentina.

'It was very much a venture of faith on Cliff's part,' says Hoffman, 'because there was no way that he was identifying with an established or a prestigious organization. There was only me, Bill Latham, a secretary and a lot of enthusiasm.'

In 1973, more than a decade before Bob Geldof's celebrated visit to the refugee camps of Ethiopia, Cliff became the first major British pop star to visit the sick and dying in the Third World.

He had wanted to experience Tear Fund's work first hand and in November he set off for Bangladesh, the independent republic created in the aftermath of the Indo-Pakistan War, where refugees were flooding in from North India to avoid persecution. The camps were overcrowded and filthy, the refugees sick and undernourished.

He arrived in Dacca with Bill Latham, George Hoffman and photographer Clifford Shirley and was introduced to the local team supported by Tear Fund. On the first day he was escorted by Liz Hutchison, a young nurse from Devon, who was working with children in a cluster of bombed-out buildings and makeshift shacks that was known as Mirpur Camp.

She picked him up in a Volkswagen minibus which then collected a group of severely malnourished children who needed to be bathed, fed and given medicine at a compound run by the Southern Baptist Mission.

'I don't think he'd ever seen anything like it before,' remembers Hutchison. 'It's very difficult to explain. You can see pictures but to physically touch and smell . . . it's very different.

'The children he saw were terribly underweight. Their emotional development was stunted. Some were very sick. I can remember going back with him that afternoon in the van and he couldn't say a thing. He was just staring out of the window and you knew it wasn't appropriate to talk. He was obviously trying to cope with all the impressions and emotions.'

During the rest of the stay he visited other camps dealing with similar problems. He saw adults with bullet wounds and burns and saw children dying of starvation. He began to feel a sense of shame about his own life of riches and glamour. What benefit was he to a sick and starving world? Wouldn't one month spent as a relief worker be better than all his years at the top of the charts?

At the end of each day workers and visitors met at the nurses' quarters for prayer and a Bible study led by George Hoffman. In one of the discussions that followed, Cliff expressed his longing to be of more practical use.

'He said, "You know, what I've seen today makes me feel as though I want to give it all up and come out here and work",' remembers Hoffman. 'Liz Hutchison turned to him very quietly and said, "Can you give an injection or put a person on a drip?" He said, "No, I'd be horrified." She said, "Well you go back home and raise money for us to do it. That's what you can do and this is what we do. That's what it's all about." '

This comment, made without reflection, was to mark a turning point in his life. His songs might not be the sort to change the world but the money they earned could be used to bring about change.

20

'The best thing I've done for years'

Cliff was still approaching his career with the attitudes of the fifties when singles mattered and albums didn't; when singers weren't expected to write or even choose their own material and when concerts involved singing a string of hits for twenty minutes.

He had always relied on Norrie Paramor to organize his recordings. After choosing the songs with Paramor and discussing possible musical arrangements, Cliff's only task was to drop by the studio and add his vocals — sometimes five or six in a day. Bruce Welch once said that if Cliff didn't have three hits completed by half past ten in the evening he would think it had been a bad night.

The practice harked back to the days when record companies and music publishers controlled the business and used singers to promote their product. But all this had been broken down in the era ushered in by the Beatles. Power began to return to the artists.

After Paramor's fourteen-year reign, Peter Gormley wanted to try different producers; to shift the work around much more. His first choice was Dave Mackay, a former house producer for EMI Australia, who had come to London to work with the New Seekers.

Mackay knew that Cliff's recording career needed turning round. It had lost momentum. He sat down and talked to him about contemporary music, played him tracks he liked and listened to some of the gospel material that Cliff found interesting.

One of the artists Cliff told Mackay about was Larry Norman, a Californian with shoulder-length blond hair and an acoustic guitar who was writing what the media called 'Jesus Rock'. This was a new type of Christian music that owed more to Bob Dylan and the Rolling Stones than it did to the sort of gospel music that Elvis Presley used to record.

Norman was a mesmerizing stage performer who planned every gesture for maximum effect. He often chided audiences for clapping during his concerts and developed the 'one way sign' (an index finger pointing heavenwards) to indicate where the appreciation should be directed.

Cliff went to see Larry Norman in concert at the Albert Hall and later they met up to talk.

'As soon as we met we started talking about the songs and the reasons I had for writing them,' says Norman. 'He explained the dilemma he was in having to sing music from his past, music for the future and also gospel music.

'He wasn't sure what was the most dignified or credible way to present the songs he really cared about. He seemed very wise and thoughtful about it all.'

Dave Mackay encouraged Cliff to write more of his own material and to work on his playing technique as a way of getting back in touch with the music.

'We had to break down the old routine,' says Mackay. 'I had to tell him that things had changed and that he needed to come in and work with the band. We needed to listen to songs, to work them out and to discuss the strengths and weaknesses. In the past he had only needed to decide what key to sing it in and the next time he heard the song it was already out as a record.'

Through Mackay he met a rhythm section known as Quartet, two of whose members were later to play a major part in reshaping his career.

Guitarist Terry Britten had come to England in 1969 when his band the Twilights, which had been one of Australia's top acts, broke up. Here Britten had joined up again with Alan Tarney (bass), Kevin Peek (guitar) and Trevor Spencer (drums) who had played in the James Taylor Move (nothing to do with the American singer of the same name), an Adelaide band which rivalled the Twilights.

'In those days you had to sing cover versions of pop hits in order to make a living,' says Trevor Spencer. 'But the cover bands in Australia were very good, a bit like the Irish cover bands but not as cabaret-orientated. The James Taylor Move — the singer's name was James and Kevin Peek's middle name was Taylor — played Jimi Hendrix and the Cream. The Twilights played the Hollies and the Beatles.'

Living in flats in West Kensington they had formed Quartet and signed to Decca Records. Fame though was not to come under this name but through working with Dave Mackay as session musicians and later as a working band with Cliff.

'Kevin Peek was the first to play on a Cliff session,' Trevor Spencer recalls. 'He replaced an Australian called Tweed Harris on a tour. When that tour finished they wanted Alan Tarney to join. Then Brian Bennett, who'd been playing drums, left to concentrate on the Shadows and I was brought in.'

Touring with Cliff at this point was a mixed blessing. The up-side was getting well paid for playing some of the chart hits of their youth. The down-side was the brain-deadening experience of playing songs such as 'Goodbye Sam, Hello Samantha' and 'Flying Machine' in northern night clubs where they often had to enter the stage from kitchens slippery with cooking oil.

Tales abound of musicians falling asleep on stage and losing their places in the music. There were times during runs at the Palladium when they would forget whether they were playing the matinée or the evening show. They called themselves the 'scumbags', a derogatory term for pick-up musicians, and planned to turn up wearing T-shirts reading 'Scumbag World Tour'.

'A lot of the musicians just didn't feel involved in what Cliff was doing,' says Trevor Spencer. 'They were more interested in getting drunk than playing. These were tours where we had to dress completely in black and there would be a black backdrop so that we would all merge into the background. They just about nailed the backing singers' feet to the floor so that they wouldn't distract from Cliff.'

'I found this period quite depressing,' agrees Terry Britten. 'I remember Batley Variety Club and these bleak Yorkshire days. You'd go to do the show and there'd be "Congratulations", "Living Doll" and all this stuff and you'd be sitting on a chair stuck behind a music stand, and it had the feeling of being a hired help.

'You'd do the show and there would be the clanging of knives and forks and the smell of scampi and chips everywhere. My heart wasn't in it. It was just a job. But Cliff always gave his best wherever he was.'

Some of his musicians hated the club work so much that they welcomed the annual gospel tours where, with songs like those of Larry Norman's, there would at least be a bit of speed and aggression.

Dave Mackay came into Cliff's career at its most crucial juncture. Without any more hits, Cliff was obviously destined to become a Tommy Steele or Frankie Vaughan type of entertainer who could always sell out a show but who no longer belonged on the top table.

It wasn't only Cliff who had lost his way. Rock music was suffering fatigue after the great party of the sixties. The Beatles, who had led so many of the changes, had broken up acrimoniously. Both Brian Jones of the Rolling Stones and Jim Morrison of the Doors were now dead. The British charts, which had such a short time ago been full of classics, were now laden with acts such as Chicory Tip, Donny Osmond, Lieutenant Pigeon and Terry Dactyl and the Dinosaurs.

Acts which had survived the sixties were no longer sure where they belonged. There wasn't a movement to be part of, and none of them were willing to compete with the likes of Slade, Mud and Sweet by becoming 'glam rockers' — it seemed like such a retrogressive step.

Mackay could see clearly the changes that would need to be made, but initially he wasn't in a position to make them. He had inherited the responsibility of producing a soundtrack to *Take Me High*. The songs, written by Australian Tony Cole, were vacuous and instantly forgettable. Mackay then produced the gospel album *Help It Along*.

Other than the Eurovision entry, 'Power To All Our Friends', which sold over one million worldwide, Mackay's singles were a commercial disappointment with one complete failure and three low-ranking hits.

The project which introduced the changes he had talked about was *31st of February Street*, Cliff's first proper album since 1970. Released in November 1974 it didn't get great reviews, didn't produce any singles and wasn't a best-seller but, with its softer, more introspective mood it at least helped drag Cliff into the seventies and almost half the songs were self-written.

'The recording coincided with my renewed interest in my own career,' says Cliff 'I suddenly started getting involved in the production side. I started writing.

'Dave would sit down with me and I would play him bits that I had written and he'd tell me what he thought was good and what he thought I should finish. Other than Bill and Tear Fund he was the only person ever to encourage me to write.

'That album was, to me, the turning point of my career.'

But it was Bruce Welch who was to take full advantage of Cliff's new attitude towards his music by laying the groundwork for one of the most durable comebacks in show business history. In one forty-eight-hour period in September 1975, Welch produced 'Devil

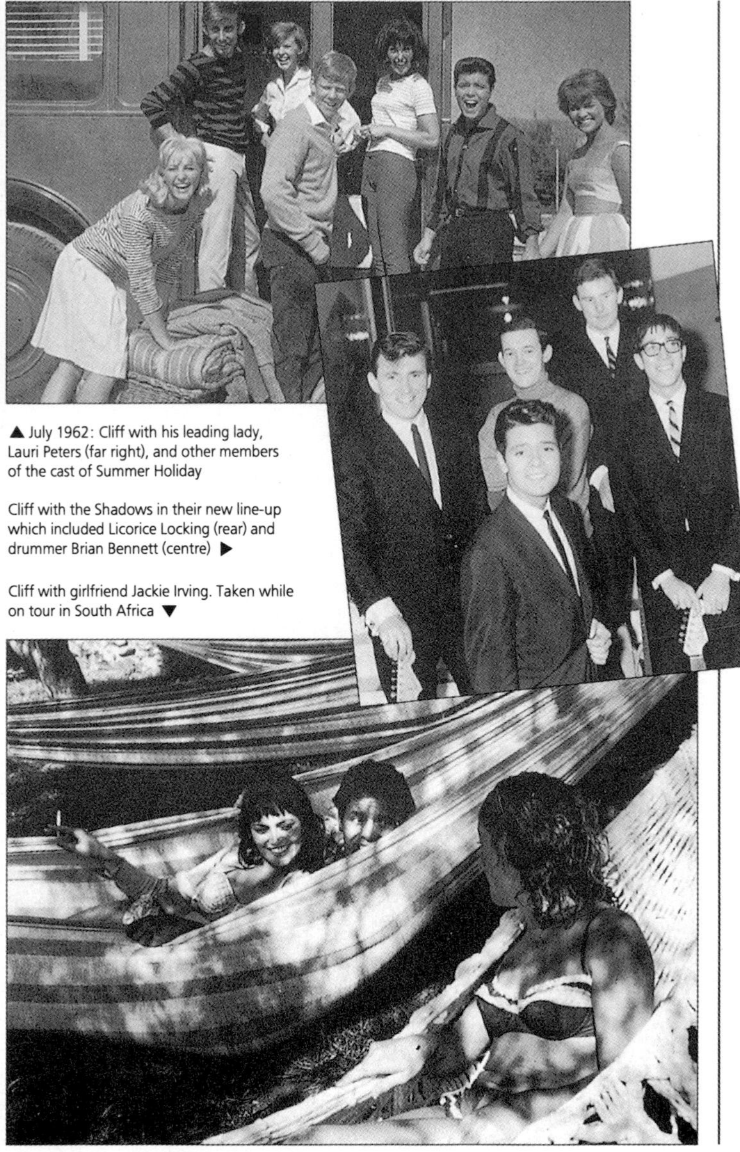

▲ July 1962: Cliff with his leading lady, Lauri Peters (far right), and other members of the cast of Summer Holiday

Cliff with the Shadows in their new line-up which included Licorice Locking (rear) and drummer Brian Bennett (centre) ▶

Cliff with girlfriend Jackie Irving. Taken while on tour in South Africa ▼

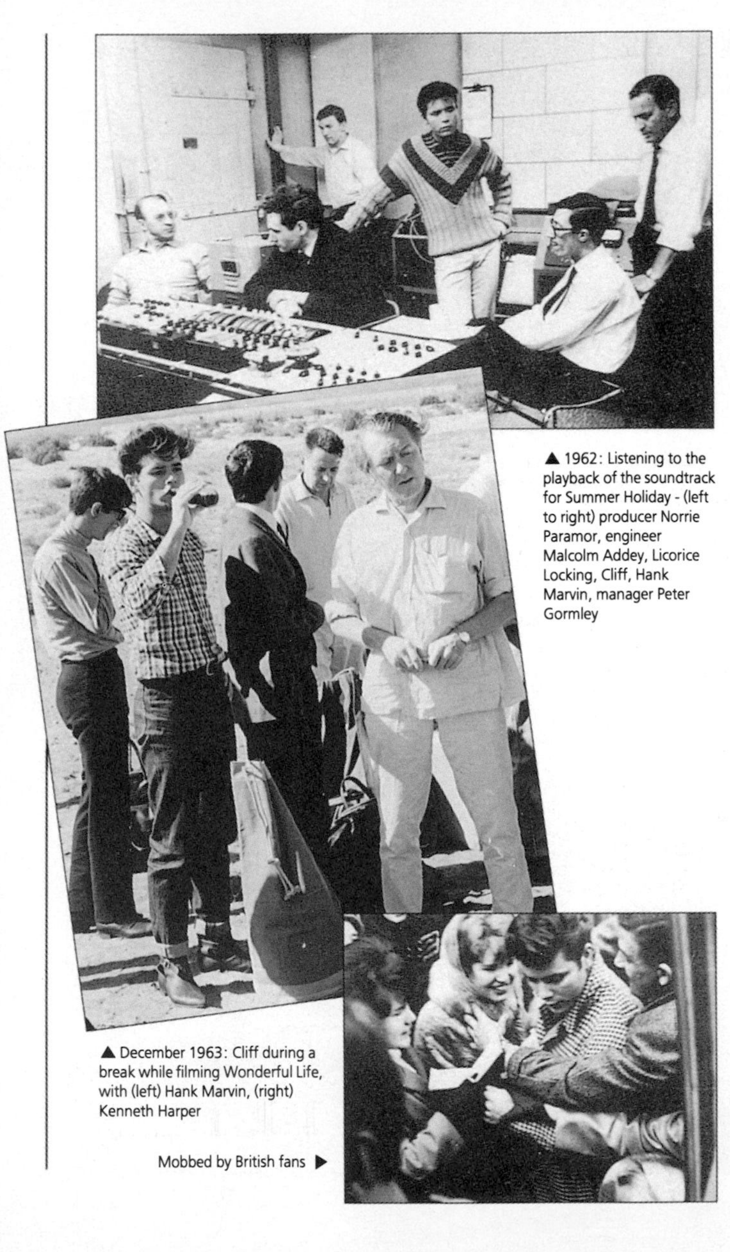

▲ 1962: Listening to the playback of the soundtrack for Summer Holiday - (left to right) producer Norrie Paramor, engineer Malcolm Addey, Licorice Locking, Cliff, Hank Marvin, manager Peter Gormley

▲ December 1963: Cliff during a break while filming Wonderful Life, with (left) Hank Marvin, (right) Kenneth Harper

Mobbed by British fans ▶

◀ July 1964: Hunting for clues during a car rally - Bill Latham and Cliff on the day of their first meeting

April 1965: Graham Disbrey (third from left) with Cliff on his first Crusader holiday on the Norfolk Broads ▶

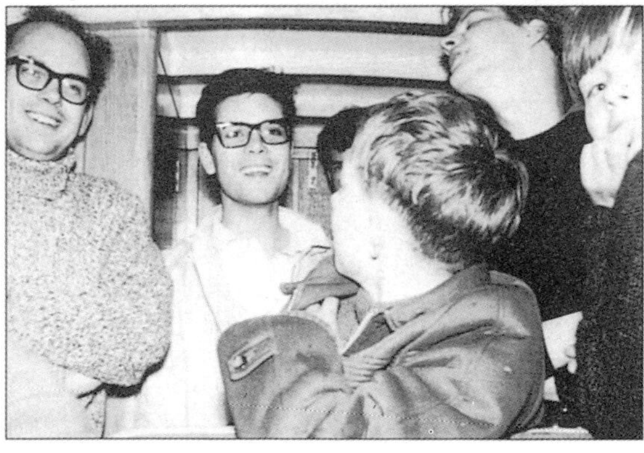

◀ Bill Latham (left) and Cliff on board one of the Crusader holiday boats

▲ 16 June 1966: Cliff addresses the crowd of 5,000 which couldn't get in to Billy Graham's Earls Court rally. This was the day Cliff's Christian faith became public

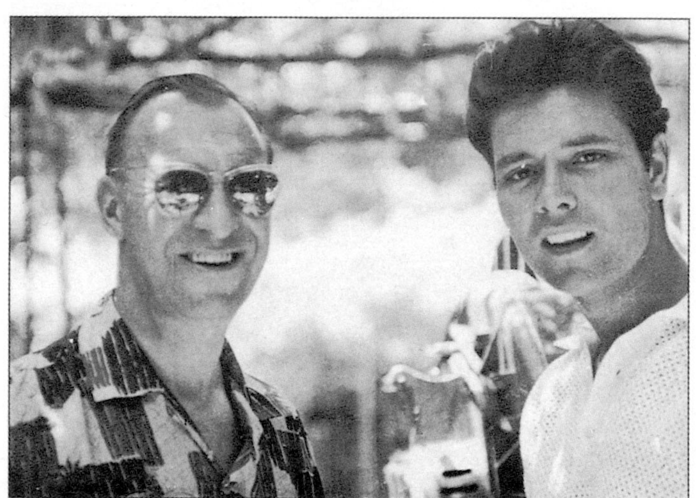

▲ Cliff with Norrie Paramor - producer, arranger and father figure

◀ July 1968, California: (left to right) John Davey, Graham Disbrey, Cliff, Bill Latham, Peter Graves, Peter Hutt

April 1968: Cliff with the Settlers - (left to right) John Fyffe, Cindy Kent, Mike Jones, Cliff and Geoff Srodzinski ▼

1968: Cliff and the Settlers returning to Britain after playing a groundbreaking gospel concert tour in Croatia (then Yugoslavia) ▶

▲ Cliff sings 'Congratulations', Britain's entry in the 1968 Eurovision song contest

▲ April 1970: Cliff speaks and sings at Kingsway Hall, London, as part of his Christian work

▲ May 1970: Cliff plays student Clive Harrington alongside actress Pamela Denton in Peter Schaffer's stage play Five Finger Exercise

◀ Cliff and Una Stubbs in his early seventies BBC TV series 'It's Cliff Richard'

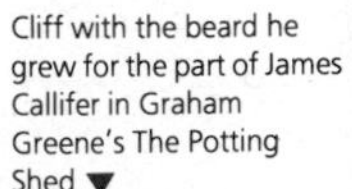

Cliff with the beard he grew for the part of James Callifer in Graham Greene's The Potting Shed ▼

October 1971: Cliff with his long-standing friend Olivia Newton-John ▶

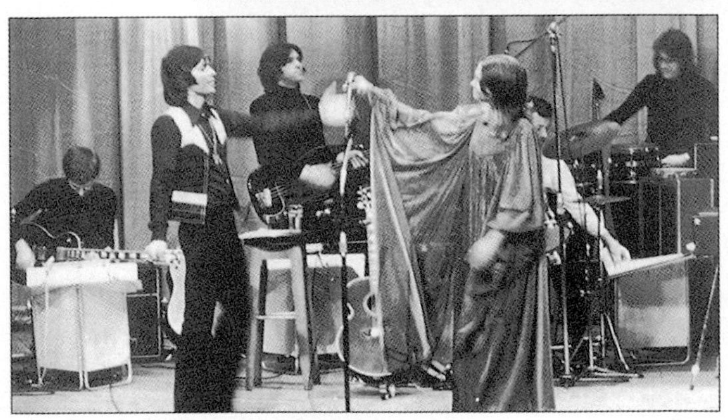

▲ On stage in the mid-seventies: (left to right) Terry Britten, Cliff, Alan Tarney, Olivia Newton-John and Trevor Spencer

Woman' and 'Miss You Nights'. These two records, more than any others, were to set the tone for the rest of his career.

There was some irony in that it was Welch who was to help relaunch Cliff's career because the two men had never been close. Privately Welch scoffed at Cliff's religious views and considered himself too down to earth and plain speaking for Cliff's liking.

'Cliff doesn't like my lifestyle and I can't believe his' was how he once put it. 'We don't have anything in common but our love of music.'

He'd come back into the picture through an off-hand remark made by Peter Gormley who was by now quite worried about the state of Cliff's record sales.

'Cliff was putting out records and they weren't becoming hits,' says Welch. 'He was making boring, bland records and he didn't seem to care. The only thing in his life was religion. Peter Gormley, who was still managing me as a member of the Shadows, happened to mention that whoever found the right songs for Cliff would have a strong chance of producing him.'

Since his successes with Olivia Newton-John (he had co-written and co-produced three of her American top ten hits) Welch was keen to do more production. He had good contacts among music publishers and songwriters and began to trawl for new songs, putting the word out that Cliff Richard was ready to shed his middle-of-the-road image. The 'Congratulations' era was over.

On a material-gathering trip to Los Angeles he met Lionel Conway, British-born head of Island Music in Los Angeles, who played him songs by his writers.

'I wasn't really struck by any of them but I said I'd take the tapes away and listen to them again,' says Welch. 'I came back to London and I was in my music room when I played them through again. I still didn't like them but I turned one of the cassettes over and there on the other side was "Miss You Nights" — a song Lionel hadn't even bothered to play me. I knew instantly that it was a smash hit.'

What he was hearing was the work of Dave Townsend, a 26-year-old writer from England, who'd recorded the song not as a publisher's demo but as a track for an Island Records album. Produced at a cost of £20,000, the album had been shelved as uncommercial. The only chance of recouping the production cost was through cover versions of the songs.

Dave Townsend had written 'Miss You Nights' while living in Somerset the year before. His girlfriend, Sally, had taken off for a solo holiday in Majorca and he had turned his feelings of longing and loneliness into a beautiful ballad with hauntingly fresh images. A swelling string arrangement by Andrew Powell on the recording had endowed it with an ethereal quality.

It was this version of the song that Welch took down to Cliff's home in Weybridge one summer evening along with 'Devil Woman' written by Terry Britten and 'I Can't Ask For Any More Than You' by Ken Gold and Michael Denne .

'Cliff put the cassette of "Miss You Nights" on in his music room and the hairs stood up on his arms,' remembers Welch. 'He'd already been given "Devil Woman" some months before but he hadn't done anything with it. I pushed him. I said, "Why on earth haven't you recorded this song?"'

'Devil Woman' had started off as a riff which Terry Britten couldn't find words for and then he linked up with Christine Holmes, a singer and children's television presenter who had been produced by Dave Mackay, and she gave it a title and wrote the story of a seductive fortune teller.

'I had my ideas about this fortune teller song in my notebook and Terry had this guitar riff and we just put them together,' says Holmes . 'We wrote it together at my flat.

'I knew it had to be a rock number. Helen Reddy had done a song called "Angie Baby" which was a really spooky song and used sounds in the mix that hadn't been used too much in pop music. In my mind that I wanted "Devil Woman" to sound similarly spooky. We both very much knew what we wanted and Cliff copied the demo exactly.'

When Cliff went into Abbey Road to record the three songs, Welch, as producer, retained Alan Tarney and Terry Britten from Dave Mackay's rhythm section but added Graham Todd on keyboards and Tony Rivers, John Perry and Ken Gold on backing vocals.

'It was a great session the day we did "Devil Woman",' remembers Terry Britten. 'The engineer Tony Clark was standing in front of the speakers as it was played back and as quick as a flash he said, "America! This is gonna be a smash in America!" '

Tony Clark remembers the emotion of the session. 'You could feel something was happening,' he says. 'The actual groove of the track was something instant. When I said it was made for America I was probably more excited than anyone else. In those days it wasn't normal to stand up in the control room and shout out loud.'

Three months later, with 'Devil Woman' and 'Miss You Nights' still unreleased as singles, the same team returned to the studio to complete an album of the songs that Welch had gathered.

'I knew what I was capable of but I'd happily got into doing family shows,' says Cliff. 'For this album I was getting songs that publishers would never normally give me because they would insist on sending me material that sounded like "Congratulations". So it was the first time in years that I'd had the chance to stretch my voice and do some rock.'

It now sounded as though Cliff was working with a band rather than dubbing his vocals over one. Although there were still ballads there was a looser, funkier feel to the tracks and a spirit of exploration that had long been missing in his music.

'I had told him that he needed to change the way he recorded,' says Welch. 'I told him I wanted rehearsals, that I wanted to make sure we got the right keys on every song. I changed the way he sang. He had never sung falsetto. He said he couldn't sing like that. I told him he could. He had just never tried it. Now he does it all the time.'

'Miss You Nights' was the first single to be released, in February 1976, because there was some concern that 'Devil Woman' might get confused with the Electric Light Orchestra's 'Evil Woman' which had entered the charts in January. It sold impressively and returned Cliff to the top twenty for the first time in two years, but it was 'Devil Woman', released two months later, which re-established him as a chart force.

'I was sitting in my kitchen in Epsom and the DJ said he was going to play a record and we should try and guess who it was,' remembers Terry Britten of the first radio play he heard. 'He played this record and my ears went up when I heard the first couple of bars.

'Then everyone started ringing in and getting it wrong and he played it again and there was this tremendous excitement that this was Cliff Richard. No one could believe that Cliff could make a record like this.'

'Devil Woman' sounded like something that the Rolling Stones or at least Elton John would record. The voice was as clean as ever but the sound of the track was dirty and swampy. Cliff had never worked around a riff like this before and the story of being seduced by a fortune teller conjured up images of dark backstreets in New Orleans; of a world a million miles away from 'Take Me High'.

The writer, Christine Holmes, says that the song is about a man who is seduced by a fortune teller.

'It's a very rude song actually,' admits Holmes. 'But I'm not sure that Cliff was aware how rude it was. My whole thing was to convey that women can be very spooky and clever when they try to snare a guy. They can force a guy into doing things he wouldn't normally do. They can be witches when they want to be.'

Cliff has indeed interpreted the lyric in a different way, believing it to be a warning against dabbling in the occult. This view was endorsed for him when a young woman from Australia wrote to him to say that the song had been instrumental in her Christian conversion. 'I heeded the warning,' she told him.

The music press was enthusiastic about the single, seeing it as a definite return to form. There was talk of the Cliff Richard Renaissance. The record climbed into the top ten, eventually becoming his biggest international seller since 'The Young Ones'.

The album, *I'm Nearly Famous*, released a month later, featured Cliff on the cover lying on a single bed with a notepad and pen transcribing the lyrics of Eddie Cochran's 'C'Mon Everybody' which is spinning on an old-fashioned monophonic turntable beside him.

On the walls are photographs of Elvis Presley, Little Richard, Chuck Berry and Ricky Nelson. Although it was hardly a return to fifties rock 'n' roll it was a return to his own roots as a working musician with band members who could write.

EMI was excited by the album and promoted it heavily, printing 'I'm Nearly Famous' T-shirts and badges which were sported by celebrities such as Elton John, Jeff Beck, Pete Townshend and Elizabeth Taylor. Although he would never be taken up by the emerging punk generation, it was suddenly OK to admit to liking Cliff.

Bruce Welch says that *I'm Nearly Famous* was the album which gave Cliff his credibility back. 'He got great reviews and he had big hits. Since that moment he's just developed and developed. His concerts have got bigger and his money has got bigger.'

Reviewing the album in *Melody Maker*, Geoff Brown wrote, 'Cliff Richard has at last made the sort of album he could, and should, have been making for years. It is with some incredulity I have to say that for the past ten days I've been playing two albums consistently. One is Marvin Gaye's *I Want You*. The other is *I'm Nearly Famous*. The renaissance of Richard, for that is what I believe this album heralds, is long overdue . . .

'I doubt whether *I'm Nearly Famous* will rid Cliff at a stroke of his straitlaced image as Mary Whitehouse's favourite son, nor, I suspect, would he want it to; for that is what he most likely is. Neither will it win him a whole new concert audience overnight.

'However, it is the best album of new songs ever and, if there are enough unprejudiced ears around, could well mark the start of a fresh Cliff Richard record-buying public. Closet Cliff Richard rock fans? Why not? *I'm Nearly Famous* is, in its way, the most surprising album for many years. Hear it.'

Brown interviewed Cliff in the next issue for a major feature which struck a similarly positive note. Cliff spoke of the forty songs that Bruce Welch had collected and how they whittled the list down to the fourteen or fifteen that were recorded.

'I think it's the best thing I've done for years,' Cliff said. 'It may be the only hit album I'll have had in years. I had more to say about how I would sing, and vocal harmonies and all that. We didn't go into the studio and say we were going to do a certain thing. What we did say was that we weren't going to record anything that sounded like "Congratulations".'

Elton John's manager, John Reid, heard 'Miss You Nights' and wanted to release it in America on his three-year-old record label, Rocket. Elton had long been a fan (he could remember seeing him in pantomime at the Palladium) and it was thought that maybe Rocket could launch Cliff in America in the way that it had recently reversed the fortunes of Neil Sedaka in his home country.

Rocket's Executive Vice President in America was Tony King, a flamboyant English bachelor who had once worked for the Beatles' Apple label, and was closely acquainted with almost everyone who mattered in the rock industry.

He listened to the album and concluded that although 'Miss You Nights' was a good song, it was 'Devil Woman' that stood the better chance of becoming a hit. He had the track remastered to match the sound quality of American radio and it was released in June.

'We cut it really hot,' says King. 'Then I brought in publicist Sharon Lawrence who said that if we really wanted to crack America, Cliff would have to be brought over for a month to do press and radio.

Peter Gormley agreed and so I went on the road with Cliff.

'Whenever I had met him before I had been in awe of him and very much on my best behaviour. The thought of spending four weeks with him made me feel a bit nervous.'

The tour party, which consisted of Tony King, Cliff, Sharon Lawrence and Peter Hebbes from Gormley Management, flew from coast to coast taking in major cities such as New York, Chicago, Boston, Memphis, Detroit, San Francisco and Los Angeles. In each city there would be a party for the media and then Cliff would spend hours being interviewed.

For Tony King it was a revelation. He had expected to wilt under withering Puritan scrutiny but instead found himself totally accepted by Cliff. The two became firm friends.

'I was pleased to find that he wasn't quite as abstemious as I had thought,' King says. 'He never got drunk but he liked a glass of wine and enjoyed getting jolly. In fact we ended up calling it the White Wine Tour of America because there would always be white wine at these receptions and by the end of the tour Cliff was getting to the wine waiter before me.

'I had always thought he might be offended if I swore and yet he just shrugged it off. I don't think he minded bad language or a clever *double-entendre*. If it was clever then he was one to laugh but what he didn't like was coarseness.

'People imagine he looks down his nose at everyone because of his Christian faith but I found him a really relaxing person to be with. He wasn't at all judgmental. We had a lot of personal talks about our lives and about religion.'

In Atlanta they caught up with Elton John and went to his show at the Omni auditorium. In Los Angeles Olivia Newton-John threw a party for them at her new home. In New York, King, who was a close friend of John Lennon and had been responsible for bringing him together with Elton John, almost managed to arrange a reunion between Cliff and the former Beatle.

'Cliff was fascinated by the fact that I was close to John,' says King. 'He would ask me lots of questions because he always wanted to know what other people were like. I think the John Lennon of that period would have got on very well with Cliff. He was a much softer character and I had told him that I thought he would find Cliff quite interesting. John was up for it.'

He was even given his third and final opportunity to fulfil his earliest rock 'n' roll ambition meeting Elvis. A magazine journalist, who said he was a personal friend, was ready to bring them together but when he then suggested bringing a photographer along Cliff changed his mind.

'The Elvis I wanted to remember was the one whose door I knocked on in 1959,' Cliff says. 'I didn't want to meet the big fat Elvis. I thought I'd wait until he got himself together.'

Cliff's career in America up to this point had been undistinguished. He'd scored a hit with 'Living Doll' and had twice been on tour but the films had flopped and Rocket was the ninth label to try to do something for him.

It was a source of frustration to him that while he'd conquered Europe, the Far East and all other English-speaking countries he had never become a household name in the country which had given rock 'n' roll to the world.

In America it was possible to have a regional hit but never to be known nationwide. The only realistic way to become a household name was to tour extensively and repeatedly and to spend at least half of each year there.

'I don't think Cliff was willing to give up his life here in England in order to make it in America,' says Peter Gormley.

'We had offers in television that would have meant staying there for up to a year compèring shows and being a part of other shows. He was offered a six-month contract with "Solid Gold" which Dionne Warwick was presenting. We toyed with the idea of flying over every week but then threw it out.'

Sharon Lawrence's game plan in 1976 was not to concentrate on Cliff's past achievements, great though they had been in Britain, nor his standing as a Christian spokesman, but to launch him as if he was a new artist. To have harped on about his string of British hits would have been to have projected him as a failure.

'We had to promote him as someone fresh,' says Tony King. '"Devil Woman"started picking up interest and getting added to secondary stations in each area but we still needed to crack a primary station. Within a month it began to edge in at the lower end of the charts and then we knew there was a chance it could make it.

'The most important radio stations to get on were those controlled by RKO. If you got on an RKO station it looked as though you were going to make it. The chain was run by a man called Paul Drew who was a friend of mine and of Elton John's and of John Lennon's but he was a tough guy and he wouldn't do anything to give me a break.

'However, because he was a friend, if he saw that I had something that looked as if it had "legs" he would maybe tip it a little in my direction. But only if the evidence was that he couldn't be accused of helping out a friend.

'When "Devil Woman" looked as though it was really happening he gave us the break that really cracked it. He gave us the number one station in Boston and that gave us a good chart position the next week. Once it performed well on that station the rest fell like dominoes.' The record entered the US charts at number eighty-eight at the end of June and slowly began to climb through July and August.

When it finally broke into the top ten Cliff was playing in Leningrad and Moscow on a ground-breaking Russian visit — the first by a Western rock artist. It was a strange experience of playing to a mixture of sober-suited party officials and excited teenagers, with security guards leaping into action every time anyone showed any visible signs of appreciation.

'We were calling back home to get the *Billboard* chart positions all the time,' remembers Terry Britten. 'The news that it was going up really kept us going out there.'

'Devil Woman' went on to reach number five in the *Billboard* charts and to become an American million-seller. *I'm Nearly Famous* became his first album to make the British charts in a decade.

21

'Age has nothing to do with it'

In September 1976 Cliff went back into the studios with Bruce Welch to record a follow-up to *I'm Nearly Famous* that would build on its success. This time there were over fifty songs to choose from because publishers no longer had him pegged as a Eurovision singer.

'I think this album is much better,' he said as he recorded what would later be called *Every Face Tells A Story*. 'I think it's more positive. With *I'm Nearly Famous* we accidentally found a new way of doing things. This one says, "Now we know what to do, let's do it!" Everything seems more confident, there's a greater sense of continuity and it's just better.'

It's part of Cliff's upbeat personality to feel that his current project is the best thing he has ever done. In the case of *Every Face* the truth was that there had been little advance. He had hits with 'My Kinda Life' and 'When Two Worlds Drift Apart' but nothing that reached the top ten. The initial American success was never built on.

'It offers no radical departure or development from *I'm Nearly Famous*,' commented *Melody Maker*. 'Bruce Welch's production is clean and powerful, the songs are, once again, attractive and the musicianship is precise if occasionally verging on the coldly clinical.'

Despite the change in the fortunes of his career, Cliff stuck resolutely to the mix of charity work and show business that had been his lifestyle since 1966 — over a decade. For his first British tour since the comeback he went out for a twenty-concert gospel tour, often staying in the homes of local Tear Fund supporters rather than hotels. He even played to an audience of 1,200 in the centre of Belfast at a time when almost no English acts would take the risk.

His Christian vision remained undimmed. He told concert audiences that his Christian faith was by far the most important factor in his life and that everything else had to take second place. Quizzed by a reporter one evening as to why he divided his career into 'pop' and 'gospel', he answered that it was out of fairness to people who didn't want to sit through an evening of gospel songs. He wanted to be fair in letting the public know what they were getting.

'I'm not misusing my platform. I still have a responsibility to those who don't want to come to a gospel concert so I do a secular tour. I still do a smattering of gospel in that, but I choose music that I think is valid musically, so nobody minds that. There's no other real reason for separating them because I think that musically all of it stands up.'

Coming off this gospel tour (which raised £37,000 for Tear Fund) he went straight into his first secular tour of Britain in two years and then in 1976 paid a return visit to Bangladesh and India.

'We thought it would be a good idea to go back and see how things had changed in three years,' Cliff said. 'And the thing was, it had changed. Things were so much better than they were. We made a film strip to encourage Christians in the West and to show them what can be done in three years.

'There weren't as many beggars in Dacca. Twenty thousand of them had been given housing in this great encampment with thatched huts and gardens. They've had a couple of good harvests as well.'

In India he performed gospel concerts in Delhi, Bombay and Calcutta, seeing the city of his childhood for the first time since his family boarded a train at Howrah station in August 1948.

It was a very different Calcutta that he returned to. He recognized the old landmarks such as Howrah Station, Chowringhee Road and the Victoria monument but was shocked at the sight of people sleeping in the street. With George Hoffman and Bill Latham he visited Mother Teresa at her hospice and spent a day watching her care for the sick and dying, later praying with her and reading from the Bible.

Because he was performing a gospel concert in Calcutta his visit was well publicized, and the Bengali community welcomed him like a local boy who'd done well in the world and was on a quick visit home. George Hoffman had notified the British Embassy in Calcutta of Cliff's visit and the party was assigned a security guard.

'He was mobbed everywhere he went,' says Hoffman. 'We could never leave the watch of the security. The crowds were just flocking around and Cliff was signing autographs all the time.'

Once back in England, he set about recording his third gospel album, *Small Corners*. It had been natural to offer the project to Bruce Welch after the success of *I'm Nearly Famous* and *Every Face Tells A Story*, but Welch wasn't interested in being involved in this side of Cliff's life.

Remembers Tony Clark: 'He was asked but said he didn't have anything to offer a spiritual album with God lyrics. Cliff was obviously determined to do it and so he chose to produce it himself using me as his engineer because by then our working relationship was very strong.'

It was harder for him to come up with good material for his gospel albums because the pool of writers available to draw on was necessarily smaller. Most of the songs on *Small Corners* were written by American writers of what was becoming known as 'contemporary Christian music', which was really Jesus Rock under a different name.

'The problem is that I don't write,' said Cliff during the recording sessions. 'If I was a writer I would probably have done more gospel albums. So I rely on the fact that I listen to a whole lot of albums and then use the best songs in my stage act. This album is full of stuff I've sung in concert for a long time but never recorded.'

While he was preparing to record *Small Corners* the Sex Pistols had become one of the better-known groups in Britain, mostly through swearing on live early evening television and getting thrown off the EMI record label for courting too much controversy. If there were two polar opposites in the music business it would have to be Cliff Richard and Johnny Rotten, who projected an arrogant petulance on stage and professed not to care about anything.

Cliff was bemused and angry about punk. It broke all the cardinal rules of show business. It was too loud, it was out of tune, it was irresponsible, it appeared to glory in images of destruction and its proponents showed neither love nor respect for their audience.

'The Sex Pistols are probably the worst band ever,' he said. 'Johnny Rotten can't sing and the band can't play. The fact that they can have any sort of a career is an indictment on the record-buying public. I know that I was criticized for being wild when I launched my career but that was by people who were relating what I did to a previous form of music. The Sex Pistols are trying to play rock 'n' roll and they're doing it badly.'

Not that the notoriety of the Sex Pistols had the remotest effect on Cliff's new rise. He was now committing himself to bigger and better tours and had left behind the club and cabaret scene.

In 1977 he went to South Africa, Australia, New Zealand and Europe. The day he returned from his summer holidays in Portugal he saw a television news flash that Elvis had been taken to hospital. He went to bed thinking it was a hoax, but at three o'clock in the morning he was woken by a call from LBC Radio asking him to comment on Elvis' death.

'I couldn't think straight,' he remembers. 'I started arguing with the guy and telling him not to be ridiculous because they had said he was alright on the television news. He then said, "I hate to tell you this but it's true." '

At the age of forty-two the one-time king of rock 'n' roll was dead from a heart attack, a bloated victim of self-indulgence. Although Cliff had never met Elvis the loss he felt was deeply personal because he knew that if it hadn't been for Elvis he would still be Harry Webb.

In January 1978 Cliff went back into the studios to record *Green Light*, his third album with Bruce Welch. By now Terry Britten was becoming Cliff's major songwriter. On *Green Light* he was involved as writer on half the album's songs.

One day during the recording, when Peter Gormley was discussing with Cliff the need to penetrate the American market, Bruce Welch suggested that the next album should have a consistent style of music.

'I had said that America was much different to Britain and Europe in that they tend to pigeon-hole you,' says Welch. 'The songs in the album have to be in a similar vein. You can't do "Miss You Nights" and then "Devil Woman", because it's wrong for America.

'I suggested that what we should do is to get the same writer, perhaps someone like Terry Britten, to write the whole album. Now this was said to my manager, Peter Gormley, and to Cliff. I didn't hear any more about it.'

Assuming that he would be producing the next album, Welch spent the following months collecting new songs. Then, in July 1978, just as he was leaving Abbey Road Studios, Welch bumped into engineer Tony Clark who supposed he would be seeing him next week in Paris. 'What do you mean, Paris?' asked Welch. 'For the new Cliff album,' said Clark.

Welch had not been told that Cliff's new album, *Rock 'n' Roll Juvenile*, was scheduled to start recording at Pathe Marconi Studios in Paris on 18 July. Not only had his advice been heeded in that Terry Britten had authored almost all the songs, but that Britten had also been made co-producer with Cliff.

Welch fumed at the news. It wasn't the fact that he'd been replaced as producer after playing a key role in the launch of Cliff's recording career but that he hadn't been told, even though Peter Gormley was his manager. It opened up a rift between Welch, Gormley and Cliff that has never healed.

'Our relationship ever since then could be described as strained,' says Welch. 'No one could call us close and I still think that someone like myself, who has been with him through thick and thin, deserves better than that.'

'I can understand him being disappointed, but not angry,' says Cliff in response. 'I'm not tied to anybody anymore. Bruce may have assumed he was doing my next album, but I didn't.'

The words to half the songs on *Rock 'n' Roll Juvenile* were written by B.A. Robertson, a tall lantern-jawed Scot who was to enjoy his own pop career the following year beginning with the hit singles 'Bang Bang' and 'Knocked It Off'.

He'd been introduced to Terry Britten by bass guitarist Herbie Flowers who had played on Robertson's debut album *Shadow Of A Thin Man* in 1976 and the two had started writing songs together.

The most successful song from the partnership was 'Carrie', which was to make number four in the charts. The riff and the title came from Terry Britten. The story was told by Robertson.

'The strength of the song comes from the fact that you're never quite sure what it's about,' says Robertson. 'You don't know whether Carrie is homeless or whether she's squatting or what.

'You don't know whether Cliff, as the narrator, is the husband, boyfriend, lover, brother or father. Nowhere does the song say what his relationship with Carrie is. It's very mysterious and musically it falls in the same groove as "I Heard It Through The Grapevine".'

Rock 'n' Roll Juvenile was an attempt to explore fresh subject matter but Terry Britten doesn't believe it worked.

'I think his fans want to hear him sing love songs,' he says. 'We did a lot of songs on that album that had very little to do with love and I honestly don't think they're liked by his fans.'

Much to Cliff and Terry Britten's chagrin the album's hit song was the one track that they hadn't produced. 'We Don't Talk Any More' was a last-minute addition, produced by Bruce Welch and surrounded in controversy.

In May 1979 Welch and Alan Tarney were producing an album for Island Records' artist Charlie Dore, and during a recording break Tarney referenced a cassette of 'We Don't Talk Any More' which he had written for his next album with Trevor Spencer. (The duo were signed to A&M as Tarney–Spencer.) When Welch heard it he immediately wanted to play it to Peter Gormley.

'I wasn't keen to lose the song but he pleaded and pleaded,' says Tarney. 'When he came in the next day he had played it to Peter and Cliff and they said they wanted to record it as soon as possible. We finished up the Charlie Dore album on the Friday and on the Saturday, which was Cup Final day, we recorded it with Cliff.'

Trevor Spencer remembers the session at R.G. Jones Studios.

'I don't think Cliff was all that keen on recording it at the time. He was so locked in to the *Rock 'n' Roll Juvenile* album. But all that was needed really was for us to remake the demo. Bruce then took the tapes to Abbey Road and popped Cliff's vocal on it.

'Alan felt sure that Cliff didn't want to do the song as he started it but then the vocal got better and better as it went on. There were only three or four takes. You can still hear him come in at the wrong point on part of the chorus. Bruce wanted to wipe that but Alan asked him not to so it remained part of the record.'

'We Don't Talk Any More' was released in July 1979 and its success meant that EMI felt it should be included on *Rock 'n' Roll Juvenile* which was scheduled to be released in September.

'Cliff and Terry didn't want it included,' says Welch. 'They said it was their album. EMI said, "But this is a monster single". I think in the end they had to half force Cliff to put it on the album.'

'We Don't Talk Any More' went to number one and sold 2,750,000 copies. It was the best-selling single of his career, and Alan Tarney was brought in to produce his next album, *I'm No Hero*, which was recorded at Riverside Studios during May and June 1980.

It was a Tarney *tour-de-force*. No longer limited to being session bass player or occasional songwriter he dominated the whole project, playing and arranging almost all the music, writing or co-writing all but two of the songs and producing everything.

From his love of the Eagles' harmonies, Todd Rundgren's synthesizer wizardry and the chord changes of Steely Dan, Tarney was creating Cliff's first identifiable 'sound' since his days with the Shadows when the twang of Hank's Stratocaster announced the arrival of a Cliff disc.

One of his great strengths was that he could produce demo tapes that were so polished that Cliff could instantly imagine the finished result. The margin for error was reduced drastically because all that was normally required was for the engineer to remove Tarney's vocals and replace them with Cliff's. The backing tracks never needed re-recording.

'He was a dream to produce,' says Tarney. 'The first thing I noticed was his voice which sounded so huge. Then I noticed that he had a good sense of the person who would be listening to the song. He doesn't need to put on a great performance, he just needs to sing the song. He'll try it out two or three times and then that's it.'

Five weeks after completing the album Cliff went to Buckingham Palace to receive an OBE, the first time a pop star had been recognized in this way since the Beatles were awarded MBEs in 1965. He arrived in his Rolls Royce, and was dressed in a black suit, red tie and red shoes.

'I've been to the palace before,' he explained. 'I know there's a lot of red about the place.'

I'm No Hero was released in September 1980 and the next month, during a five-concert run at the Apollo Theatre in London, Cliff turned forty. Just as has happened when he turned twenty and twenty-one and thirty, and when he'd been in the business for ten years and twenty years, a media hoopla ensued. How long could he go on? Did he ever think at eighteen that he would still be around at forty? Was he planning to retire?

What was extraordinary about this milestone, as he slipped into middle age, was that his career was in better shape than at any other time since the very early sixties.

Sitting in his dressing room at the Apollo the night before his birthday he said he was 'grateful and amazed' to arrive at middle age. His telephone had been ringing so much all day that he'd eventually had to take it off the hook.

'The two things that determine how well I will carry on are the quality of my voice and my own taste in music,' he said.

'If my taste in music continues to coincide with public taste then there's no reason why I shouldn't have a hit when I'm fifty. No reason at all. I've had my biggest ever single at thirty-nine!'

'I never thought I'd top "The Young Ones", "Living Doll" and "Bachelor Boy" but I have. So age has nothing to do with it. I've just got to use my integrity and hope that my voice stays intact. If it breaks down, I'll have to think of doing something else.'

The success of 'We Don't Talk Any More' around the world raised the prospect of another assault on North America and so it was that in January 1981 Cliff went on a ten-day promotional tour to Los Angeles, Toronto and New York, appearing on the Merv Griffin and Dionne Warwick shows and facing two solid days of magazine and newspaper interviews.

Interest in America was still high. 'Suddenly', his duet with Olivia Newton-John, was at number twenty in the *Billboard* charts.

Publications requesting interviews with him ranged from *People* magazine and the *New York Times* to rock magazines such as *Circus*, *Rock* and *New York Rocker*. He did a live interview on NBC's five o'clock news. He even found he was being played on some New Wave stations alongside the Police and Joe Jackson.

Cliff now had one of his most enduring bands. Backing singers Tony Rivers and John Perry had recorded with him since 'Miss You Nights' and they were joined by Stu Calver. Drummer Graham Jarvis was musical director. There were two keyboard players, Alan Park and Graham Todd, lead guitarist John Clark, bass player Mark Griffiths and rhythm guitarist Mart Jenner.

Part of the tour was filmed by a television crew putting together a four-part documentary series for the BBC. Cliff had been approached by the light entertainment department, who were keen on an eighties follow-up to 'It's Cliff Richard', but he wanted to do something other than a song-and-dance show with special guests and so suggested the documentary approach.

Nineteen years since his last American tour, Cliff flew back. It was an unambitious tour of 2,000–3,000 capacity theatres in cities where his singles had been getting heavy airplay, but the idea was to gain a foothold.

The opening night of the tour was in Seattle but that weekend before the Monday show, while the band were still in Los Angeles, the trailer containing all their equipment was stolen from outside their motel. They were left with no lighting, no sound and no instruments.

'It was horrific,' remembers David Bryce, Cliff's professional manager. 'I just had to call all the music stores around LA and ask them to stay open late for us, which they did. It was hard for the musicians because they'd lost instruments that they were familiar with and which they'd modified in little ways.'

The tour arrived in New York on 2 April to play the opening night at a new club, the Ritz, with Jack Good and Olivia Newton-John in attendance. Cliff was still expressing his disappointment at the loss of equipment.

'At the moment we're only showing half of what we can do,' he explained. 'I came here to give them our current show but we haven't been able to do it. The fact that the fans like it means that when we come back they won't know what's hit them.'

The next day there was a smaller disaster when the tour bus arrived in Baltimore, and no one knew where the venue was.

'When we got to Baltimore the tour manager realized he had left his briefcase back in the hotel in New York and that the schedule was in it,' remembers Graham Todd.

'We were driving around looking for posters to find out where we were supposed to be and when we finally got there, half an hour before show time, we discovered that the revolving stage wasn't working.'

Cliff's longest-ever American tour finished on 20 April with much the same result as the others. He had been well received but by a very small group of people and, judging by the Union Jack flags waved in some of the auditoriums, a good proportion of these may have been Brits anyway.

Once back in London he started rehearsing for a rock 'n' roll special which was to form the basis of one of the documentary programmes. The idea was to fit him up with a pink jacket, get him to sing his favourite songs from the fifties and reunite him with one of his musical heroes.

Cliff's choice of heroes for the Hammersmith Odeon concert was either Elvis' original guitarist Scotty Moore, Ricky Nelson's guitarist James Burton or Phil Everly of the Everly Brothers.

James Burton asked for too much money and Scotty Moore, who hadn't picked up a guitar since playing on Elvis' comeback TV special in 1968, couldn't be coaxed from his tape-duplicating plant in Nashville. But Phil Everly, who had become familiar with Cliff's work when touring Britain in 1959, jumped at the opportunity.

'To step on a stage and sing with Cliff reminded me so much of singing with my brother,' he said. 'It was great to be able to sing Everly Brothers songs with someone I had tremendous respect for. That was really the reason I came over.'

The concert took place on 1 May and was a precursor of the 'Oh Boy!' section of The Event in that Cliff sang rock 'n' roll songs, dressed in period costume, employed a troupe of dancers and sang duets with a star of the period. In the audience was John Foster, now a rotund man with spectacles, back home living with his mother, and the three original Drifters – Sammy Samwell, Norman Mitham and Terry Smart. They hadn't been together since Smart left to join the Navy in 1959.

At the end of the month he returned to the studios to record *Wired For Sound*, again with Alan Tarney producing and arranging. The title track was the most contemporary sounding single of his renaissance, showing that he was every bit a contender in the battle of such new techno-pop artists as Soft Cell and Human League.

The lyric, written by B.A. Robertson, was a departure from Cliff's romantic subject matter. It was a love song but this time expressing his love for the Sony Walkman and the new portable music that was revolutionizing listening habits.

'I'd never written with Alan Tarney but he called me up one night and asked me if I'd like to write a song with him,' says Robertson. 'Mickey Dolenz, who used to be in the Monkees, was coming for a meal that night so I stayed in for the starters and then drove down to Hammersmith to listen to the backing track during the main course and then arrived back home with a cassette in time for the dessert.

'I got up the next morning, put the kettle on, put the cassette in and the title came to me straight away as I listened to it. A couple of hours later, I had written the whole song and I just read the lyrics to him down the phone.'

Cliff had for some time attempted to use his position to raise the profile of various British gospel artists but although he had been able to give them exposure by producing them and inviting them on his tours, none of the acts had ever achieved general market success. The most positive outcome of his involvement was reflected in his use, for the first time, of gospel writers on a secular album.

'Better Than I Know Myself', a gospel song disguised as a love song, was written by Dave Cooke and his songwriting partner Judy McKenzie, who had been one of the pioneer Christian folk singers in the late sixties.

'Lost In A Lonely World' and 'Summer Rain' were both by Chris Eaton, a twenty-year-old writer Cliff had met at a Christian convention in 1979 when Eaton was playing in a band for Dave Pope, an evangelist and singer whose album *Sail Away* Cliff had produced.

'I'd written the title track for Dave's album and Cliff said he liked it and would like to hear more,' says Eaton. 'I sent him five songs on a tape but didn't hear anything for eighteen months. Then I got a call from Gill Snow at his office saying that Cliff wanted to do four of the songs, two of them on *Wired For Sound*.'

Wired For Sound went on to be Cliff's best-selling album since *I'm Nearly Famous*, with sales of over one million. Chris Eaton was able to give up driving taxis and beer lorries and was signed up as a songwriter to Patch Music, a music publishing company run from the Cliff Richard Organization by Stuart Ongley.

Cliff was particularly pleased with his inclusion of Christian writers in this way. In 1965, even if he had decided it was possible, there were no Christian writers of high calibre who could have contributed to his albums or singles. Now there were, and it had a lot to do with the change in attitude which Cliff and his generation had created in the church that young people were growing up considering commercial songwriting as a career possibility.

He had never felt that his faith was something stuck on to his life although, at times, his two-tier career seemed to suggest that.

'Interviewers tend to ask me certain questions and then suddenly switch to discussing Christianity,' he said. 'They don't realize that the first part of the interview was also coloured by my Christian faith. I can't separate me from me.'

22

'We're the new Charles and Di'

Since becoming a Christian in 1966 there had been no obvious romantic interest in Cliff's life. There had been girls who had adorned his arms when he arrived at film premières and charity functions but there had been no girlfriends.

The fact that this apparently abstemious period had coincided with his close relationship with Bill Latham didn't go unnoticed by the press.

Roderick Gilchrist, Entertainments Editor of the *Daily Mail*, observing that Jackie Irving had been his last serious date noted that: 'He now lives with a male friend in the show business shelter of Weybridge, with his friend's mother. Inevitably this has led to suggestions that he is "gay" — a word that had not been used in this way when he first entered show business.'

Cliff denied that he was homosexual and explained that his reasons for not bed-hopping with women were spiritual rather than psycho-sexual.

'As a Christian I don't believe in extramarital sex because God says it's wrong and I have to assume that he knows better,' he said. 'I don't sleep with women at all now. Not since my Christian conversion.'

Three years earlier he'd broken this news to pop writer John Blake, then of the *Evening News*, who commented: 'Since Cliff became an ardent Christian more than ten years ago, I am slightly stunned by this revelation.'

The story was headlined 'My Ten Years Without Sex... by Cliff Richard', as though sexual restraint because of religious conviction was a perversion in itself.

Cliff's fidelity to Christian teaching seemed beyond doubt. The deeper question was whether his celibacy was solely a matter of obedience or whether he was a celibate by nature.

If he was unmoved by sex his chastity was more an acceptance of his natural condition than a victory over seething desires. In the days before religion his lack of interest appeared eccentric but, as a Christian, there was an explanation which non-believers could understand even if they didn't approve.

'I don't particularly have any great sexual urges or needs,' he confessed to David Wigg of the *Daily Express*. 'I don't feel I have to spend my life with someone special for sexual favours. But that's my good fortune, isn't it, really?'

The implied good fortune is that he is free to devote his energies to his career. There are no distractions. There are no emotional entanglements. He is responsible to nobody but himself. His only marriage, as anyone who knows him well will say, is to his work.

This is why it was so out of character to see Cliff Richard going out with tennis star Sue Barker in the autumn of 1982. Ever since entering show business he had avoided being seen with the women he took out.

Jackie Irving, his longest-standing girlfriend, was rarely photographed with Cliff. Delia Wicks was sworn to secrecy. His romance with Una Stubbs was unknown even to his closest friends and colleagues. But on 23 March 1982 Cliff flew out to Denmark with Sue Barker to see her play an exhibition match and the next day's tabloids were full of it: 'Sue And Cliff In Love Riddle' (The *Sun*), 'Sue And Cliff Set Up A Love Riddle' (*Daily Mirror*), 'Cliff And Sue Take Off And Say There's No Love Match Blooming' (*Daily Mail*),

'Cliff, Love And Me by Sue Barker' (*Daily Star*).

The bare bones of the story were that Cliff had been spotted with Sue in a departure lounge at Heathrow Airport awaiting a flight to Copenhagen. What the press immediately wanted to know was whether this was love and whether a wedding was in the offing.

'I think he's a super person but to talk of marriage is wrong,' Sue told James Whitaker of the *Daily Star*. 'There's nothing nasty in the rumour. It just isn't accurate.'

When the couple flew back after an overnight stay Cliff was asked whether he loved her. 'I'm not going to say that,' he said. 'I don't want to embarrass her. She says she doesn't mind, but it's not fair. I've only met her four times. We'll be seeing a lot more of each other, but it's early days. Who knows what we'll feel in a year's time?'

Within three months they were a hot item. Neither of them was now pretending it was still a case of 'just good friends'. They were spotted at Wimbledon where Sue openly nibbled his ear, kissed his neck and stroked his hair while watching a game. At a pre-Wimbledon party thrown by veteran tennis designer Teddy Tinling they allowed themselves to be photographed cuddling and holding hands.

Cliff even proudly announced to reporters that he and Sue were the new Charles and Di. 'There had to be someone to take over once they got married,' he boasted. Asked if they would be following the royal example Cliff said, 'I don't know. It's early days yet. We are taking it from day to day. If we decide to get married there will be an announcement.'

Cliff and Sue's relationship had all started with Alan Godson, a Church of England vicar with a parish in Liverpool. He had helped found an organization called Christians in Sport to bring together sports people with a shared faith and to help evangelize their peers.

Godson himself was a tough-looking ex-rugby-football player renowned for his fearlessness in presenting the Christian message in dressing rooms and on playing fields. It was not unknown for him to suddenly pull up in his car and start preaching to someone in the street if he felt so called.

He had been introduced to Sue Barker by sports commentator Gerald Williams, a personal friend of his and also a supporter of Christians in Sport. At twenty-five Sue was Britain's rising female tennis star and although she had been baptized at the age of twenty-one her Christian faith had been dormant until she met Godson. For the past few years she had been involved in two intense relationships with fellow sportsmen. Now she wanted to re-dedicate her life as a Christian.

Alan Godson was aware that life as a Christian was going to be tough for her on the tennis court. Not only would she find it hard to be in regular contact with a church but there would be ridicule from fellow players and grillings from the press. The only person that he could think of who had triumphed in a similar situation was Cliff. So he called him and gave him Sue's telephone number.

'I thought that because they lived in the same area and faced similar problems he could coach her into handling the gospel publicly without getting destroyed,' says Godson. 'I thought that he was the only one with the nous to be useful as a servant to her.'

While this was happening (September 1981), Sue was playing in the Brighton Indoor tournament and coincidentally had met the Shadows who were staying at the same hotel while playing concerts on the south coast.

'Hank was the tennis nut and he came and watched me playing doubles with Virginia Wade,' says Sue. 'The next day I was due to play against Tracey Austin in the finals and Hank, Bruce and Brian came and they all got hooked. Apparently Cliff was watching the match on his television at home, and when I won I went straight over and hugged Hank. Cliff wondered what on earth was going on!

'That night, when I got home to Wimbledon, he called me. At first I thought it was a joke. I had been having this running joke with some engineers from British Telecom and I thought it was one of them playing a prank. So I just played along. I said, "Oh really!" I didn't think it was him. But then he told me that Alan had given him my number and he thought it would be good if we got together to chat.

'I was flying off to Japan at the end of that week and we had to get together on the only free night I had which was when I was actually going to see the Shadows in London.'

Sue was going to the concert at the Dominion Theatre with fellow tennis player Sue Mappin, and they were joined in their box on the night by Cliff and Bill Latham. After the show they all went out to eat together and discussion turned to the problems of British tennis. Cliff wanted to know why tennis was such a privileged sport in this country and what needed to be done to find the tennis stars of tomorrow. Out of this first meeting grew the idea of what, in ten years' time, would be the Cliff Richard Tennis Trail — a charity which helps school-age children to develop a love for the game.

At the time Cliff was not noted for his love of tennis. He was what Sue now refers to as a 'pat-a-cake' tennis player, someone who liked to knock a ball around a court but for whom 'the ball wasn't coming back very much and it wasn't much fun'.

It was Sue who stimulated his interest in playing tennis. 'He used to come and watch me train,' she says. 'I gave him a hit and he found he was getting absolutely exhausted in half an hour and he saw that if he learned to play well it would be a means of keeping fit. I think he'd played with his friends for hours but with me he was getting tired. He saw tennis as a challenge.'

From Japan Sue went down to Australia and then on to America where she lived as a tax exile. It was while she was away that the *Daily Star* broke the story that had been successfully kept a secret for over twenty-one years. Beneath the headline 'Cliff — My Secret Lover' Carol Costa told all about her brief affair in the first of a three-part series.

The tone of the story was set in the first paragraphs. 'I loved Cliff Richard, and I suppose I always will. But over the years I have come to realise that he isn't perfect.

'And that's why I have decided to tell the truth ... after keeping quiet for so long.'

On tour in the Far East at the time, Cliff had already got wind of the imminent publication because he had been called and asked for his comment on the story. He would say only that, 'Carol must have her reasons for publicizing what was very personal. She has the freedom to do that. But I also have my freedom and I don't wish to publicize anything that personal.'

He never discussed the relationship with Sue, but he did get together with Stu Calver and John Perry to pray about the situation and then he called his mother in Broxbourne and warned her what was about to happen.

'I'm sensitive about anything bad that is written in the papers,' says Cliff's mother, Dorothy Marie. 'Cliff told me not to worry. He said that if she wants to write that's entirely up to her. I was quite upset but he wasn't.'

The story had come about because Carol had been approached by Jet Harris and Tony Meehan to collaborate on a book. The three met in London with freelance book editor Carol Illingworth, journalist Sharon Ring and some media executives who promised radio and television spin-offs from the project.

Carol became uneasy with some of the angles under discussion. 'It wasn't nice at all,' she says. 'I just didn't want to know. I made my objections clear and then I was approached by people who said that if I was to tell my story it would put the record straight and squash a lot of the rumours going around about Cliff. So I pulled away from this book project and did my own thing.'

Carol was paid £12,000 for the story but insists that she did it to defend Cliff's reputation. 'If I was only interested in the money I wouldn't have sat on it for twenty years,' she argues. 'I would have got myself a fortune when I was going through really hard times with my young family.'

With Cliff still touring the Far East and Sue in America, they exchanged a couple of letters and then, in February 1982, while playing in the Dallas Tournament, Sue received a phone call from him.

'It was totally out of the blue,' she says. 'He asked me what I was doing and I told him that I was only due back in England for a long weekend and I was going to Denmark with my brother to play an exhibition match. He said, "Well, I'm not doing anything. Do you mind if I come along?" I said, "No. Of course not." We met up in London in March and flew off to Copenhagen together, and I couldn't believe what happened after that.

'It was only the second time we had met. When we got off the plane people were asking us when we were going to get married and I thought this was absolutely bizarre.

'As far as I was concerned we had been to a concert, had a dinner, written two letters . . . and I was thinking, "Blimey, I don't think we're even going out!" I didn't count it as a date. I thought, "Gosh, I'm going to put my foot in it so badly". By saying nothing you make it worse. If you say, "Of course not," you insult the other person.

'In some ways it drew us closer together. Although the press tried to make out that we were upset, we just laughed at a lot of it. We used to phone each other up and say, "Did you read that article? I didn't say any of that. I haven't spoken to them." '

Press speculation increased over the following months. Sue was playing on the European circuit and Cliff was recording his new album *Now You See Me... Now You Don't* at Strawberry South Studios in Dorking. It was during this recording that the friendship changed into something recognizably different.

'After we returned from Denmark my parents stayed with me at my flat for the few days I was in England and Cliff was doing the album and he just phoned up and said, "Look, I'd really like to see you again.

Will you come down to the studio tomorrow because I'm stuck down here."

'It was then that I sussed that something was up because we had arranged to meet in a week's time when he'd finished and my parents were gone, but he was saying "I don't want to wait a week. I want to see you tomorrow." So we did meet then. I felt the same way but I certainly wasn't going to make the phone call. I was very pleased that he had called.'

Now You See Me... Now You Don't was a further attempt to introduce the writing of his Christian friends to a wider audience, this time with an album which although regarded by EMI as a gospel project would get the same commercial push as any other release.

His choice of producer was Craig Pruess, a young American who'd been a child prodigy as a musician and had studied physics, philosophy and comparative religion at the Massachusetts Institute of Technology before arriving in England in 1973.

'He wanted this album to be more heavyweight and to break away from the pop sound,' says Pruess. 'He approached it to prove a point and he did have a point to prove. He didn't want his gospel albums to be regarded as inferior to his other albums. He felt they could be as good as anything else he did. He wanted to fuse his beliefs and his enthusiasm with his professional life.'

Pruess also noticed that Cliff was remarkably content during the period of recording. 'Of all the time I spent with Cliff I felt closest to him around that period,' he says. 'It was balanced. He could relate to couples and with my wife Jenny we went out a lot for meals as a foursome.

'I remember mixing the album at the Townhouse and Sue and Cliff were cuddling on the couch behind us. It was great. It was the happiest I had ever seen him. It helped him to loosen up. Sometimes around his band and all the people he works with he has to keep a distance for professional reasons.'

During the summer, Cliff and Sue began spending every available moment together, visiting the theatre, seeing films, playing tennis, but more often than not staying at home in Weybridge where Sue would cook a meal and they'd both watch a video. They were affectionate towards each other, they laughed a lot and there was the bonding of their Christian faith.

What was particularly refreshing about the relationship was that it took Cliff temporarily away from show business and Sue away from sport. They found they could relax and drop their guards.

'She enjoyed being with him and I think that she shook him up,' says Alan Godson. 'She brought the champagne back to his spiritual life.'

In August, Cliff and his mother left England for a three-week holiday in Bermuda. Her marriage to Derek Bodkin had recently ended in divorce after he had found another woman. Bill Latham and his mother Mamie, Graham Disbrey, Glyn MacAulay and David Rivett accompanied them on the trip. MacAulay and Rivett, both accountants with Crusader backgrounds, were the latest additions to the summer holiday gang. They stayed in a private villa in a secluded bay.

Sue went off to Marbella and when she returned on 26 August she broke down in tears at Heathrow when reporters surrounded her and surprised her by informing her that in her absence Cliff had said it was now 'Marry or break up time'. When Cliff flew back two days later Sue was not at the airport to meet him.

It was these incidents that prompted the *Daily Star* to publish its front-page headline story challenging Cliff to make his mind up.

'Cliff Richard, you are fast becoming a CAD!', wrote Sandra White on 28 August. 'You flew back from your holidays yesterday and kept quiet about your intentions. As Britain's Number One Bachelor Boy, you are too old to be coy. Do the decent thing. Make your mind up: Do you want to marry Sue Barker? Or not?'

The story went on in much the same vein and ended with a coupon 'What should Sue do?' with three boxes marked 'Marry Him Now!', 'Wait a While' and 'Give Him the Elbow'.

Cliff read the story and told Sue about it. She told him not to worry and a few days later left for the US Open and didn't return until late in September. When they linked up again Sue realized that something was different. The physical affection was now gone. Whatever romance had been there had turned into friendship.

'We were still boyfriend and girlfriend but it wasn't the same,' says Sue. 'I think during that time away we had had a lot of time to sit back and think about what we wanted to do and I think we both realized that we were spending too much time together. It certainly still felt like a strong relationship but certainly not as fast and furious as it had been.

'I think that during the summer we had probably seen too much of each other. It certainly affected my tennis in that I was so busy working out how we could see each other that I wasn't getting on with what I should be doing. I don't think it was particularly good for him either because he was dashing out to watch tournament after tournament. It was what we wanted to do though.

'It may not have been good career-wise but we were having fun. Bill must have been tearing his hair out because Cliff just wasn't around that much.'

During this time it appeared to close friends that Cliff was still mulling over his options. He spoke to married friends about the decisions he was facing and clearly saw marriage as a possibility. It had been while he holidayed in Bermuda though that he had more or less decided that he wanted to put the brakes on.

'I spoke to Sue on the phone from Bermuda because it's when you're away from people that you really start to think things through,' he says. 'I was feeling that I should curb it a bit. I don't really know why I felt that way. I still found her attractive and still enjoyed being with her.'

In 1988, he told *Woman's Own* magazine it had crossed his mind that 'marriage might be the outcome' but that one of the things that had decided him against it was an incident where Sue had become irritated when he had not told her where he was going one day.

'I suddenly realized that in the marriage relationship you no longer live for yourself,' he said. 'And, in the end, the love that I have for Sue was overshadowed by the fact that I love my lifestyle that much more.'

When Sue read this she was upset, not least because, as with Jackie Irving, during their time together he hadn't hinted that marriage was ever under consideration.

'We had a very close relationship for a few months but I needed to know someone for a couple of years before I thought of marrying them. I don't know whether he thought about marriage or whether he thought, "I've got quite close to this person — do I want it to continue? If it continues it's obviously going to involve making a decision."'

During a gospel tour of South Africa in 1981, which Cliff had played with Garth Hewitt and Nutshell (two British acts he had produced singles for), Bill Latham had struck up a relationship with an English woman who was a friend of the tour organizer. Her name was Jill Clarke, and her parents had emigrated to Johannesburg during her teens. The following year Latham was in Sun City with Cliff and Jill drove up to be with him, by which time it was obvious to friends that something serious was starting.

In the summer of 1983, with Cliff apparently contemplating the possibility of marriage to Sue, Jill flew back to England to be closer to Latham. For several months she stayed with Sue at her flat in Wimbledon and she and Latham would go out on double dates with Cliff and Sue.

Close friends of Cliff and Bill's felt that a double wedding in 1984 was definitely on the cards, during the same period if not on the same day. How things changed so drastically has never been adequately explained.

For Sue the most disappointing aspect was that it had seemed to change gear without warning. There were no explanations as to why the kissing had stopped and why the phone calls dried up.

'I had felt the need to put the brakes on but I certainly hadn't wanted it to fizzle out like this,' she says. 'I think Cliff felt it was all going too far although he wouldn't talk about it.

'It was almost as if he didn't want to front it. Without us ever having sat down and talked about it, our relationship had gone into a different stage. It slowed down to a halt where there was no romance at all.'

They kept seeing each other, mostly for meals, but Cliff no longer displayed open affection as he had done prior to Bermuda. As far as the public was concerned, Sue and Cliff were still an 'item' and as late as July 1984 Sue was speaking publicly as though it was thriving as a romance.

'I love him, he's great and I'm sure we love each other,' she told one interviewer. 'But as for being in love, I'm not so sure, it's such a funny phrase. I don't think I'm in love with him and I don't think he is with me... We're still getting to know each other. Sometimes we don't meet for weeks on end.'

The truth was that although Sue was hopeful that there might be a future she could see that Cliff was unwilling to share a lot of himself. It might have drifted on indefinitely had Sue not started dating a fellow tennis star.

'I don't remember a particular conversation with Cliff to say we've changed but we did have a conversation to say this is it,' she says. 'I remember we were in a restaurant in Sydney in October 1984. I had met someone over here who I wanted to see more of and who didn't like the attachment I had with Cliff even though by this time we were only friends.

'We went out for dinner and I told him I had met someone else. He was really pleased. He said, "I suppose that means I won't be able to see you quite so much." And that was that.'

The relationship had lasted almost two years, second only to his time with Jackie Irving, although most of it was spent apart and only a fraction of it was truly passionate. It followed the same pattern of an early intensity followed up by a sudden cooling and a reluctance to progress towards commitment.

Those who only saw the public displays of affection tend to be dismissive of the relationship. They argue that it was just a convenient time for Cliff to be seen with a girl on his arm and that it boosted his image. But among his closest friends there was a genuine belief that something could have happened.

'I don't agree that Cliff has never found the right girl,' says Peter Graves. 'Sue Barker was the right girl. She was a Christian, she understood his show business commitments, she was madly in love with him and they looked fabulous together.' But again Cliff had weighed up his options and decided to stick with the decision that he'd first made in 1968, to put the career before the girl. Says Graves, 'Now he is married to his lifestyle and that has become more important to him than any woman could ever be.'

23

'Cliff likes anything that knocks an audience sideways'

During the first half of the eighties Cliff was on the road for anything up to four months of the year in Australia, the Far East, Europe, Scandinavia, South Africa and America, as well as carrying out his annual gospel tours of Britain.

In this schedule he found time to make two further field trips on behalf of Tear Fund – the first, in 1982, a week-long stay in Kenya and the second, in 1984, a fortnight in Haiti. The purpose was to stay in touch with the charity but also to act as narrator and interviewer in two films: *Cliff In Kenya* and *It's A Small World.*

The conditions, particularly in Haiti, were far removed from the five-star luxury Cliff was used to on his tours where hotel managements fell over themselves to give him the best possible treatment and local record companies showered him with gifts.

There was starvation, poverty, disease, political violence and the menace of voodoo. In Port au Prince, the capital of Haiti, they stayed in a small hotel. On the small island of La Gonave, which could only be reached by a boat, they slept in a missionary bungalow.

'He is a tremendously adaptable person,' said George Hoffman, who had already travelled with him to Bangladesh, India, Kenya and Nepal. 'He never stands on ceremony. I've never heard him complain once, whatever the food we've been given and whatever places we've had to sleep in.'

In Kenya he reduced a group of Masai tribesmen to giggles by playing rock 'n' roll to them on his acoustic guitar.

'Their previous experience of white people was of development workers and missionaries who were all rather serious,' says documentary film director John Muggleton. 'To have this guy playing wildly on a guitar and rolling on the ground was quite amusing for them.'

Having revamped his approach to recording in the seventies, Cliff was starting in the eighties to develop his stage show. The new band were not expected to dress in black or hide behind their musical scores. He began to develop a more theatrical approach to performing: working out dance routines, acting out songs like 'Devil Woman' and incorporating ideas from science fiction films (especially *Close Encounters Of The Third Kind*) and West End musicals (especially *Starlight Express*).

Until the mid-seventies he had relied exclusively on light and sound equipment available at each venue which meant that he lagged noticeably behind the major touring acts of the day who were each trying to out-dazzle the other with the spectacular nature of their shows. Now he was investigating state-of-the-art systems: overhead trusses, motorized lights and lasers.

'Cliff liked anything that knocked the audience sideways,' says lighting engineer Bob Hellyer. 'He started to want to choreograph numbers, to have effects linked to particular lines in the songs, and so the show became part rock 'n' roll and part theatre.'

The tours abroad were almost always to countries where Cliff was established, with the exception of North America, where there were a couple of last flings, and the Far East, which was sometimes fitted in for convenience en route to Australia. Japan, once a good market, had inexplicably gone off him since his comeback with 'Devil Woman'.

In his career he had played in every significant commercial territory in the world. He'd even played in places where there was little chance of selling records, such as Jerusalem, Beirut, Bangkok, Moscow, Calcutta, New Delhi and Belgrade.

The places where he was most successful were Britain, Europe (especially France, Holland and Germany), Scandinavia (especially Denmark), South Africa, Australia and New Zealand.

'It's all down to how much attention you give each territory,' says Peter Gormley. 'In the early days he would go anywhere, he would look forward to it and he would have fun. But as you get older you lose your enthusiasm for jumping on planes and switching all over the place.'

On tour Cliff maintained a proprietorial distance from the band and road crew, appearing for after-show meals but rarely hanging out with them and always travelling first class with his tour manager David Bryce.

Bryce had become an important part of the management team. Originally he worked on the road with Cliff on behalf of agent Leslie Grade and then, in the mid-sixties, worked directly for Cliff.

He has been around show business since the end of the war when he began work as a 'call boy' in West End theatres, knocking on dressing room doors before the curtain went up.

His brother was Dickie Valentine, the most popular male vocalist in Britain before the rock 'n' roll era, who was killed in a car accident. Through him he got into the Grade agency, going out on the road with such stars as Bill Haley and Buddy Holly. Well-muscled and prematurely bald, he had the effect of intimidating people without having to resort to violence. On the road he became the liaison between Cliff and the members of the band; if there was ever any trouble it was ultimately Bryce who had to sort it out.

Although no code of conduct was imposed there was an unspoken understanding that no one would risk tainting Cliff's good name by indulging in Led Zeppelinesque on-the-road antics. If the tabloid press could get the words 'Cliff' and 'Orgy' into the same headline it wouldn't mind how tenuous the connection.

People switched on their best behaviour when they were around Cliff anyway. 'A lot of the normal banter would stop when he came in the room,' admits guitarist Mark Griffiths. 'It was just out of respect for his views. I think the sort of humour that musicians enjoy would have been a bit too strong for Cliff. You just didn't want to involve him in it.'

If anyone blasphemed by saying 'Jesus Christ' or 'God', Cliff would brush it aside by saying, 'Right name. Wrong context', but obscenities made him feel uncomfortable. During recording sessions musicians would often retire to the bathroom for a quick five-minute swear before being able to carry on.

None of this was done through fear. His naïvety, particularly over sex, made them feel protective towards him. 'To swear in front of Cliff would be like swearing in front of your mother,' as one band member put it.

On tour in Hamburg, some of the band gathered in the foyer of the hotel in preparation for a visit to the Reeperbahn, the city's notorious commercial sex district. Cliff sauntered in, saw them about to leave, and asked if he could join them.

'We were all saying, "Well Cliff, I don't think you'll want to go where we're going",' says Graham Todd. 'There was a general feeling that we had to look after him which is a bit silly when you think he's a fully-grown man. He's not at all worldly in that respect.'

In Japan in 1974 he was told by someone in the band that he would be fine to have as much *sake* as he wanted with his meal, as long as he didn't switch to another alcoholic drink. As a result he got drunk for the first time since his Italian experience in 1959.

'Naïve little me drank more than I should,' Cliff admits. 'The next day everyone said to me, "You were great! You were really one of the lads!" They were thrilled that I had got drunk. I felt dreadful. I hated it.'

Cliff was also kept in the dark about much of the practical joking that went on all around him on tour. It was assumed that he'd either disapprove or fail to see the humour.

He does have a good sense of humour — almost everyone comments on his readiness to laugh — but it was thought that some of their activities might be too much for his taste.

The bulk of the pranks centred on hotel rooms, and the priority of any touring band member was to keep his key with him at all times. Failure to do so could result either in a straightforward festooning with tea bags or the complete removal of all furniture.

Having your key didn't guarantee immunity. You could find yourself locked out by the simple trick of switching the plastic door numbers so that you tried the wrong door, or you could find yourself stuck in if a gang decided to apply adhesive 'gaffer tape' to the edges of your door.

When the management of an Edinburgh hotel released Alan Park from his gaffer-taped room it pulled away so much of the paintwork that they billed the Cliff Richard Organization for the damage and had the group banned from staying there again.

There was also no protection for those who were asleep. Dave Cooke woke one morning to find his room completely full of toilet paper and when Mart Jenner retired to his room after a heavy night of drinking the rest of the band took advantage of his comatose state to climb in through his window from a fire escape, strip him naked and cover him from the waist downwards with shaving foam.

'He didn't wake up until the middle of the night,' remembers Mark Griffiths. 'The window was open, he was frozen stiff and he had absolutely no idea what had happened to him.'

The undisputed master of the wind-up was tour manager Ron King, who'd first driven Cliff on the Kalins' tour. His practical jokes were legendary in the business because of their elaborateness. Once, while driving the coach for a British tour by American star Del Shannon, he arranged for two friends to dress up in uniforms as border guards and arrest Shannon by the roadside for attempting to enter Scotland without a visa.

His favourite joke with the Cliff band came when he discovered that Mart Jenner was involved in a dispute with his next-door neighbours and had one morning run over their son's bike with his car. Not wishing to be arrested for criminal damage, Jenner had cut the frame up and buried it in a field. His only mistake was to tell a member of the band.

While Cliff was on stage in London, King went outside the theatre and found an obliging policeman whom he brought to the side of the stage. When Jenner idly looked into the wings King pointed at him and mouthed the words 'That's him!' to the policeman who then left, his duty having been done.

At the end of the concert Jenner unplugged his guitar, leaped off the stage and ran terrified out of the theatre. He was so quick that no one could catch him. 'I couldn't get him on the phone at all,' says King, 'and then when I did get hold of him and told him what had happened he said, "Thanks a lot, Ron. You've just given me the worst weekend of my life!" '

Water bombing was the less elaborate prank the band members favoured. Plastic laundry bags were hoarded during a tour, then filled with water and released from hotel rooms. The resulting explosions were often loud enough to suggest a terrorist attack.

In fact, water bombing became something of an art form for the musicians. They started dangling a microphone from the window so that the noises could be recorded and compared. Later they compiled stereo recordings by placing another microphone at the point of impact. Cassettes of the top plops would be circulated among interested parties.

In New Zealand Dave Cooke decided that Cliff might be a repressed water bomber. 'All the others were trying to keep me quiet,' says Cooke, 'because they never wanted Cliff to know anything, but I just asked him if he fancied doing a few water bombs that night and he said he'd love to. He thought it would be great fun.

'I'd collected about sixty bags and we started throwing them out of the window and Cliff just loved it. It was all very childish, but great fun.'

Nothing more was thought about this until an incident on a gospel tour with the singer Sheila Walsh, his latest gospel protégé, when a loud explosion was heard outside the hotel one night as the band congregated in Mark Griffiths' room.

Wanting to join in whatever fun was going on they began hurling bombs from the window with Sheila Walsh rapidly filling bags from the bathroom tap. One of the bombs, however, hit the roof of a van, creating an almighty noise which alerted the hotel management. Mark Griffiths, whose window had been noted as the source of the bombardment, was later questioned by local police.

The next day, in Manchester, David Bryce gave everyone a severe dressing down, threatening Sheila with the sack. 'Cliff's career could have gone right out of the window,' he admonished them, as they tried to stifle their giggles over his inappropriate metaphor.

'Cliff was standing there being unusually quiet,' remembers Dave Cooke. 'Two or three months later we discovered why. He had been the one to throw the first bomb.'

Sheila Walsh had been brought to Bill Latham for management by her husband Norman Miller, an executive for the Christian record company Word (UK).

A television show — called *Rock Gospel* and screened by the BBC — was built around her. She became the support act on the Tear Fund tours and Cliff began to produce her with Craig Pruess. But success in the secular world proved elusive.

A hit record seemed assured in 1983 when Cliff agreed to record a duet with her for the DJM record label but the result, 'Drifting', became one of his least successful records ever, reaching a highest chart position of sixty-four.

'It was humiliating,' Sheila recalls. 'I was interviewed on Capital Radio just as the single was released and I was asked if I thought it would be a hit. I said of course it would be — Cliff could do a duet with Miss Piggy and it would be a hit. When it died a death I felt really stupid.'

Through knowing Sheila, Cliff came into closer contact with the Cobham Christian Fellowship, a non-denominational church led by Gerald Coates which practised a more informal style of worship and believed in such 'spiritual gifts' as speaking in tongues. Its meeting place was either a scout building or a school hall. The first event of theirs which Cliff attended (in 1979) was in a marquee.

The Cobham Christian Fellowship was an example of a recent phenomenon in evangelical Christianity known as the 'house church' movement. It was the fastest growing sector of the church and had started with people literally meeting in front rooms but had been forced to expand into larger premises.

One 'house church' in South London, for example, has 2,100 members. Cobham Christian Fellowship, which had started in 1971 with five people, now has a congregation of 600 locally, with a further 6,000 in associated groups.

Sheila and her husband Norman, who had sold their house for the sake of her career, had moved in with Gerald Coates and his wife Anona in their eighteenth-century home in Esher (formerly a residence of Clive of India), and it was here that Cliff developed a friendship with Gerald, whom he had first met at a social event in London.

Since leaving Guildford Baptist Church, following David Pawson's resignation in 1979, Cliff and Bill Latham had become irregular churchgoers. Initially they tried to fit in at Walton-on-Thames Baptist Church, but then tended to drift for long periods.

Cliff's attraction to the Cobham set highlighted a major difference between him and Latham. Whereas Cliff fits in naturally with uninhibited expressions of praise, believing that if it's alright to get visibly excited by rock 'n' roll then it's alright to get visibly excited by God, Latham is by nature a traditionalist who prefers the prayer-book worship of the Church of England. It was noticeable that Cliff quite often made his visits to Cobham alone.

'There was a two- or three-year period when Cliff clearly identified with us,' says Gerald Coates. 'He would come to our services, sometimes with Bill, sometimes without, and I know that he enjoyed our worship and teaching.

'Over that time Cliff and I would pray together. I think he was going through one or two things with those who were close to him and we were able to talk and I was able to advise. Bill encouraged these meetings.'

One of the hardest bits of news Cliff had to deal with during that period was the sudden death of Graham Jarvis, his drummer since 1978.

Unknown to Cliff, Jarvis had become a chronic alcoholic, sometimes polishing off a bottle of vodka before a show and another one back in his room late at night. On the last tour, which finished on 14 December 1985, the rest of the band were alarmed to notice that his skin and the whites of his eyes were turning yellow.

On 29 December he checked himself into a hospital detoxification programme in Croydon. Dave Cooke was the last group member to speak to him.

'I called him on the day before New Year's Eve and said I'd come along and play some backgammon with him,' he remembers. 'He sounded quite good. I told him I could either come that night or wait until the morning.

'I got a little Bible together for him as a present and at half past eight the next morning I called up to double check that it was OK to visit. The nurse answered and said, "Who's calling?" She then put me on to his wife Lorraine who was in tears. She said that he'd died half an hour ago.'

The shock to everyone came because they hadn't realized how seriously ill he had been. He hadn't lost his normal good humour throughout the tour and was never known to miss a beat. But, at thirty-five years of age, he was a victim of cirrhosis of the liver.

'The funeral was in North London and all the band except Mart Jenner were there,' remembers Graham Todd. 'Dave Cooke had a song cailed "Where You Are" which Graham had always liked and Cliff was going to perform it. But when it came to the time he said a few words but he was just too choked up to sing. I think he felt that if had known about it he could have done something to get Graham off the booze but I don't think anything would have done that.'

It marked the end of an era. Cliff was already planning to change the line-up. He intended to be involved in a West End musical which was planned by Dave Clark (formerly of the Dave Clark Five) and Jarvis' death provided a convenient opportunity to break the news. John Perry, Mart Jenner and Dave Cooke were phoned by David Bryce and told that they would no longer be needed.

Taking part in a West End musical had been a long-term ambition of Cliff's. Since 1980 he had been specifically talking about a production which explored the possibilities of holographic technology.

'Having had a little experience in the acting world I would like to bring that together with the kind of singing I do to create the first real pop-rock musical,' Cliff said. 'In other words, get a really great story and pepper it with songs written by people like Terry Britten, John Farrar and Alan Tarney.

'Why shouldn't something like this happen? Why shouldn't the public go to a show and hear the top twenty live on stage, performed within the framework of a play? Why not? Why do we always have to have the traditional kind of musical? I'd like to do a show where every song gave me goose pimples, songs like "Miss You Nights", "Devil Woman" and "Dreamin' ". I'd personally like to face that challenge.'

He had seen a lot of promise in a script sent to him by Chris Hutchins, a former publicist for Tom Jones and Engelbert Humperdinck, who was now a Fleet Street gossip columnist.

It was a brilliant idea of a pop star who begins to tire of his career while at his peak and who one day meets a petrol pump attendant who is his spitting image. The star realizes that he can relieve some of the pressure he's under by getting his lookalike to stand in for him by signing autographs at the stage door.

The story progresses with the lookalike taking over more and more areas of the star's life until he can perform his concerts. He then makes a move on the star's girlfriend. What excited Cliff about the idea was the possibility of having one of the characters played by himself in the form of a hologram. Unfortunately, a suitable ending was never found for the script and the project was abandoned.

The project which Dave Clark approached Cliff with in 1983 was a science fiction musical, *Time*, which Clark had not only had a hand in writing but which he was keen to produce, using his own money. He had already been recruiting stars to contribute tracks to an album which would precede the theatre opening, people such as Julian Lennon, Freddie Mercury, Dionne Warwick and Stevie Wonder. Freddie Mercury had a posthumous hit in 1992 with 'In My Defence', from the musical.

It was a simplistic moral tale of the earth's judgment by the Time Lord Melchizidek — for the usual crimes of war and pollution — the fight for a reprieve organized by earthling pop star Chris and the wise sayings of the inscrutable Akash who, although apparently not meant to represent God, looked as though he'd have a hard time bowing down to anyone.

Its origins were in a musical called *The Time Lord*, with book and lyrics by David Soames and music by Jeff Daniels, which was put on at the Overground Theatre in Kingston-upon-Thames in 1978. Dave Clark didn't see it but he read the script and heard a tape of the songs, and thought he could do something with it.

Clark met with the two writers in 1980 and they began to forge something new. The story was altered, the songs were re-written with

Clark as an additional songwriter and a collection of new songs by outside writers was added into the mix.

The gist of the musical's message was that we'd all get on a lot better if we started being kind to the earth and kind to one other. The more profound philosophical and theological issues raised by this homespun wisdom were ignored.

'It was a musical about caring,' says Dave Clark. 'Most of the bad things in life are caused through envy, bitterness and greed and unless you get yourself in order you are in no position to put the world in order.

'I believe all gods are one and that's what I tried to convey through the musical. I believe that everyone should have the right to believe in the way that they feel is right for them. As the song says, "It's in every one of us to be wise".'

In this respect Cliff's personal beliefs were at odds with the intention of the writers. But he was able to justify his role by claiming that while the musical fell short of presenting the whole truth, as he understood it, what it did say was true as far as it went.

When Akash, represented by a hologram of Sir Laurence Olivier's head, declared that love was everlasting and death was defeated Cliff felt he could add, under his breath, that this was so with Jesus. There was a sense in which it was 'in everyone of us to be wise', as the final song said, but only if we were 'born again of the Spirit'.

Some church people felt that the omissions constituted heresy rather than partial truth. The teaching that wisdom is to be found within, they pointed out, was uncomfortably close to the New Age doctrine that we need no outside saviour to reconcile us with God because God, or the energy source, is within us all.

There was a line in the original version which referred to a 'Time Lord' who went to Nazareth two thousand years ago. Cliff had this changed to 'a guiding light'.

'I respect Cliff for his religious beliefs and there was always a fine line to be walked,' admits Dave Clark. 'We had a lot of discussions about it and we ended up with no references to God at all. The challenge for Cliff was to play a part. I didn't want people to think that it was Cliff.'

Time, despite the involvement of top musical director Larry Fuller and top choreographer Arlene Philips, opened on 9 April 1986 to scathing reviews. The *Sunday Times* called it 'a spectacular load of bilge' and claimed that Cliff couldn't act his way into a deserted railway station.

Theatre critic Sheridan Morley considered it one of the century's worst musicals and Milton Shulman thought it could only really be enjoyed by children. The only aspect of the production to be universally applauded were the sets created by John Napier.

Yet no amount of condemnation heaped on the musical — for its one-dimensional characters, its lack of drama and its unmemorable score — could prevent it from being a hit. Cliff fans were faithful to the extreme, treating it as if it was a twelve-month concert run, streaming to the front of the stage during the finale and waving their Cliff scarves in the air. When Cliff's term finished there had been over 700,000 tickets sold.

Time was a big commitment for a pop star in Cliff's position to make. It not only restricted him to one city for a year and a half but it meant being tied to a daily routine. He was on stage eight times a week, a total of over a thousand hours in a twelve-month run.

He would drive up to London each day in his Volkswagen Golf and got into the habit of eating his main meal after the show, often in the company of other members of the cast. He became particularly close to Roger Bruce, the production manager, and the dancers Wayne Aspinal, Jodie Wilson and Rosemarie Ford.

'We all found it terribly difficult to wind down after a show and we liked to do something different,' says Wilson. 'Sometimes we'd even play tennis. We'd go down to the David Lloyd Tennis Centre near Heathrow and would start a game at around midnight.'

Because Sunday was his only day off, Cliff would spend the time at home rather than attend church. It marked the beginning of a withdrawal from regular church-going, a move which worried his friends who could envisage the prospect of him drifting along without the affiliations which he himself had always recommended in his books as being essential to Christian growth.

His final night in *Time* came on 11 April 1987. Cliff was congratulated on stage by Dave Clark and then said a few words himself, some of them to the critics who had panned the show. 'You should write now that this is the greatest thing that has ever hit theatre,' he said.

Without Cliff, *Time* lost the focus of its commercial appeal. He was replaced by David Cassidy but six months later the show was taken off only to return for one night in 1988 to raise money for Aids charities. It was never to open in any other country.

24

A man of today and tomorrow

Cliff had been without a smash hit album of original material since Alan Tarney worked the magic on *Wired For Sound* five years before. *Now You See Me . . . Now You Don't* (1982), a gospel album in disguise, had reached number four in the album charts but of the singles released from the album, 'The Only Way Out' just edged into the top ten and 'Where Do We Go From Here?' only reached number sixty.

Dressed For The Occasion (1983), which was recorded at the Royal Albert Hall with the London Philharmonic Orchestra, consisted mostly of back catalogue songs. *Silver* and *Rock 'n' Roll Silver* (1983), designed to mark Cliff's twenty-five years in show business, were a mixture of new material and old rock 'n' roll classics.

The Rock Connection (1984) was another of Cliff's 'co-productions', this time with his former engineer Keith Bessey. It only reached number forty-three in the charts, his worst position since the *I'm Nearly Famous* comeback. The singles picked from it did no better. 'Heart User' made number forty-six while 'Shooting From The Heart' didn't even enter the top fifty.

It was David Bryce's suggestion to bring Tarney back as producer to arrest the slide.

Ever since hearing Michael Jackson's *Thriller*, which yielded five hit singles on both sides of the Atlantic, Cliff had nursed the idea of recording an album chock-full of hits – the ultimate Cliff Richard collection.

'I had dinner with David Bryce and I said to him that I felt I had never done the definitive Cliff Richard album,' says Tarney. '"We Don't Talk Any More" should really have been on *I'm No Hero* and *Wired For Sound* was a hodge-podge of all sorts of writers. I felt I had never produced the album I could have done.'

Tarney's opportunity to do this came with *Always Guaranteed*. Recorded in September 1986 at R.G. Jones Studios while Cliff was still appearing in *Time*, it was one of his best albums ever, providing all his hit singles for the next year and the first of 1988. It was also one of his most commercial albums with sales of over 1.3 million copies.

It had been written in the studio. Tarney, who again played almost all the instruments, would arrive early in the morning to write and then Cliff would spend four hours each afternoon adding his vocals to the new backing track before disappearing to the Dominion Theatre.

'Alan liked to work on his own,' remembers engineer Gerry Kitchingham. 'He would start the day wandering around strumming the guitar and then he'd come up with a tune and he'd call me in and we'd get something on tape. That's the way he wrote "Some People". He came in with nothing and by the next day he'd got a hit song.'

Always Guaranteed illustrated Cliff's enduring ability to come back with commercial cutting-edge pop. Almost thirty years after his first hit he was still coming up with material that was effective competition for the chart acts of the day.

It has been this contemporariness that has set him apart from his peers and it's partly explained by his undiminished urge to be a chart contender. Although he's justly proud of his past achievements and will gladly recite chart positions and record sales, his main motivation is to do things of significance now.

His most animated conversation is always about the music he's currently making, not about glory days gone by. He has never basked in nostalgia, never reads books about himself and only reluctantly takes part in reunions with the Shadows.

'He doesn't keep cuttings,' says Bill Latham. 'He has no interest in old photographs. He's just not interested in talking about the past. You would expect him to have all sorts of mementoes but he only has a few things hanging up on the walls because they happened to be there. If he lost them all overnight he wouldn't care two hoots.'

It's an appropriate attitude for Britain's most consistent chart artist to have. Too much attention to his own past and he'd find himself as a golden oldie, affectionately remembered but unranked. Part of his achievement has been never to focus on a small part of his career and sell it back to the public.

There have been times when that would have been the easiest thing to do. Just as Little Richard recreates the American fifties and Gerry and the Pacemakers celebrate the Mersey boom, so Cliff could have made a handsome living out of presenting himself from the time of *The Young Ones*.

Because his commitment was to rock 'n' roll as a style of music rather than as an attitude he has never been one of those longing for a return of the excitement that surrounded the innovations of Elvis and Bill Haley. It genuinely bemuses him when old Teddy boys come up to him and wail about the death of rock 'n' roll.

'There is a new excitement today,' he says. 'If I'm asked whether I prefer singing "Move It" or my latest hit I say my latest hit because it will have a different kind of excitement. I would prefer to be excited by today's noise than yesterday's.'

He would never have been fulfilled by simply arousing memories. He needs to feel that he is a force to be reckoned with and he still regards the singles charts as a battleground where reputations are won and lost and where newcomers need to be seen off.

The stories are legion of Cliff's obsession with chart placings. When 'Devil Woman' entered the *Billboard* charts Bruce Welch walked across the stage during a concert in Hong Kong and whispered the news in his ear. In the summer of 1989, when the holiday gang were sailing off the coast of Croatia (then Yugoslavia), Cliff had his chart placings faxed to him on the boat despite the fact that all normal business was ignored during this period.

In 1990 he was delighted to have surpassed Elvis Presley's record of fifty-five British top ten hits, an achievement which meant that he was now the supreme top ten artist of all time in his own country.

The singles' market is less significant today than it was when he launched his career. Having a hit single no longer means making a fortune. Yet the top thirty remains an effective shop window for any pop artist. It ensures radio and newspaper coverage, it establishes the artist in the public consciousness and it acts as a trailer for an album.

'He really wants to remain a contemporary artist,' says Alan Tarney. 'I think he sees any newcomer as a threat to him and it's really good for him to see things in this way. He responds immediately.

'Most people stop fighting but Cliff wants to get up there and be better. If Jason Donovan is the latest heart-throb then Cliff would like nothing better than to get up there and show him how it should be done. That's what keeps him going.'

Throughout the eighties he found himself in demand by major artists wanting him to duet with them. Andrew Lloyd-Webber asked him to record a single of 'All I Ask Of You' with his then-wife Sarah Brightman, which would draw attention to his new musical, *Phantom of the Opera* .

A & M Records approached him to duet with Janet Jackson, Dave Clark had his vocals added to a track from *Time* recorded by Stevie Wonder in California and Elton John invited Cliff to join him in singing 'Slow Rivers'.

It marked the rehabilitation of an artist who, although hugely popular with the public, had never been taken to the bosom of the rock aristocracy and had received a torrent of critical abuse over the years.

His beliefs were no more popular than they had been in 1966 but he had proved that he was a man of his word, unafraid to take the 'road less travelled', and integrity has its own reward. His music hadn't become more hard-edged and rebellious but there was no shame in being an unadulterated hit maker, especially if you had never made claims to be anything else.

'I think it takes a lot of strength of character to have Cliff's choices,' says Tony King, who is able to compare Cliff with his knowledge of working closely with such stars as Elton John, Freddie Mercury, John Lennon and Mick Jagger.

'In a way his choices are more daring because they are out of step with what everyone thinks you have to be in order to be a rock 'n' roll artist. They are braver choices in that respect. Mick Jagger's choices are certainly a lot easier for young people to identify with.'

The anarchic cult comedy show of the mid-eighties, 'The Young Ones', cast one of its main characters, played by Rik Mayall, as an ardent Cliff fan (hence the tribute in the title). When the cast came to record a single for the charity Comic Relief they chose to do a send-up of 'Living Doll' and asked Cliff to join in the joke. The record sold one million copies, almost as many as the original, and reached number one.

It was a useful part of the process of keeping Cliff's name linked with contemporary pop cultural figures and also of showing him to be someone who could laugh at himself.

The only time he has been enraged by the mockery directed at him was in 1984 when the *NME* (13 October), carried a 'review' of his gospel concert at Hammersmith Odeon. It was little more than a piece of hate mail written in the style of a conversation between the reviewer and Satan.

It made no mention of the music but directed a vitriolic attack on Cliff, his fans and Christianity. It referred to Cliff as a 'Nazi', ridiculed his celibacy and described his fans as 'two-dimensional masochists'. The final paragraph was a nasty obscene insult.

Cliff responded by suing the paper for libel. He won and was awarded £5,000 damages which he immediately gave to the Arts Centre Group.

The most unlikely recording combination was that of Cliff and Van Morrison: the beaming pop star and the glowering rock idol. Where Cliff was smooth, Van was rough. Where Cliff was adored, Van was admired. Physically, temperamentally and artistically they were polar opposites, each revered for totally different reasons by totally different audiences.

Yet what they shared was stronger than these differences. They had both started out in the skiffle era, both were interested in spiritual issues and both were men who doggedly followed their chosen paths regardless of how fashionable their concerns were. It was on this level that they had first met at an Arts Centre Group supper party and a strong mutual respect built up.

When Morrison came to record his album *Avalon Sunset* he thought it would be a good experiment to contrast his tough soulful vocals against Cliff's sweet mellifluous voice. The song, 'Whenever God Shines His Light', was not one of Morrison's best, but it was one of his more clearly Christian songs in that it linked God to Christ, rather than to an anonymous natural force. It became his first top ten hit in Britain since, as a member of Them, he reached number two in 1965 with 'Here Comes The Night'.

Some purists thought that an artist of Morrison's stature should never have deigned to record with a mere show business creature such as Cliff. For them it was a like a member of the aristocracy sharing his sandwiches with a coal miner.

'Why did you choose to record a duet with Cliff Richard?' asked an incredulous *NME* reporter. 'Are you an admirer of his work?'

'Cliff Richard?' asked Morrison, making sure he'd heard the question correctly. 'You're joking, aren't you? You're kidding? I grew up with Cliff. He'd be on "Saturday Club". I was a teenager, you know...'

The same year that Cliff increased his credibility with the rock audience by helping Morrison back into the charts he had his first dance-floor hit with 'I Just Don't Have The Heart', a record produced and written by the Mike Stock, Matt Aitken and Peter Waterman team, which did wonders for Cliff-awareness among the *Smash Hits* generation.

Stock, Aitken and Waterman had been dominating the charts with danceable pop tunes with programmed drum beats and vocals by singers such as Kylie Minogue, Jason Donovan and Rick Astley. For a while they seemed invincible. The music critics hated their formula-laden music and dippy lyrics but they sold by the truck load. By 1991 they had produced or written 106 titles and seen fifty-two of them enter the top ten, making them the most successful team of producer–songwriters in British chart history.

As chart-orientated people, the SAW team and Cliff understood each other. Whereas Cliff couldn't see himself replicated in Mick Hucknall (from Simply Red) or Michael Hutchence (from INXS), he could see himself in Jason Donovan who presented a cheerful image, had an interest in musical theatre and made hit singles.

Stock, Aitken and Waterman met Cliff for the first time at the Ivor Novello Awards in April 1989 where they had won an award for writing Rick Astley's 'Never Gonna Give You Up'. Cliff was at the next table and he leaned over and said, 'If you ever come up with another song like that, give me a call.' They told him they'd love to work with him and took it from there.

'Usually we know the singers we work with very well but we didn't know Cliff and there wasn't time to find out what made him tick,' says Peter Waterman. 'We had to imagine we were Cliff and dream up an appropriate story.

'I came up with the title. I said, "Just imagine Cliff had fallen in love with this girl and then met someone else. What would he do?" We thought, he's such a spiffing chap he wouldn't have the heart to tell her, and that's where it came from. That's what the song was all about.'

'I Just Don't Have The Heart' proved, if anything, that Cliff was the consummate British pop singer, able to surf any trend. The technology had changed but pop music, at heart, remained the same: it was melodic, rhythmic music, usually about love and usually with good harmonies. One sign of the new technology was that for 'I Just Don't Have The Heart' Cliff was taped doing his warm-up vocal exercises, then a sample of it was used effectively at the beginning of the single. 'When Cliff heard it,' says Waterman, 'he had no idea whose voice it was.'

Cliff has always produced his best work when surrounded by brilliant talent brimming with new ideas. If he had been a singer–songwriter he would undoubtedly have run out of ideas by now but being an interpreter of other people's ideas means that he is constantly able to recharge his career with the fire of someone else's youth. His best songs throughout his career have been written by young men (and one woman) in their twenties or thirties.

His office is deluged by cassettes from songwriters because he is one of the few top-selling artists today who hardly ever records his own material. Stuart Ongley of Patch Music reckoned that around one thousand songs a year are sent in. These songs are now weeded out by David Bryce who then passes on what he thinks is the best to Cliff. Sometimes an outside friend, like DJ Mike Read, is called in for a second opinion.

The songwriters who've proved most successful with Cliff — such as Hank Marvin, Bruce Welch, Alan Tarney, Terry Britten and Chris Eaton — are those who've worked with him as musicians and have been able to pass songs on to him directly. They're also the first to find out what music he's currently fascinated with.

Terry Britten used to arouse Cliff's interest by playing his latest riffs through during band soundchecks. 'Cliff would then come over and say, "That's nice, Terry," and Terry would shrug and say, "Oh, it's just something I'm working on",' remembers Graham Todd. 'Then Cliff would say, "That would make a nice song." Terry was very smart in that respect.'

Cliff prides himself on being able to spot potential hits, and argues that it's this instinct, even more than his voice, which has enabled him to stay on top for so long.

Chris Eaton wrote 'Saviour's Day' in October 1989. He brought a demo of the song to the office Christmas party despite having been told by Gill Snow, Cliff's secretary, that the whole of 1990 was already mapped out, with 'From a Distance' planned as the next year's Christmas single.

'I told Cliff that I wanted him to hear this song,' says Eaton, 'so we left the party and went to sit in his Rolls where we played the tape. He loved it straight away. He said, "This is a number one song." You've got to hand it to him – he does have a feeling for what's going to make it.'

His next collaborator was Paul Moessl who was spotted playing in the house band at Blazer's club in Windsor when David Bryce went along to see Jimmy Tarbuck. He thought he sounded innovative and arranged for him to deputize during *Time*.

When Cliff formed a new band in 1987 for his 'Beyond Time' tour he retained Alan Park as his musical director, Mark Griffiths on bass and John Clark on guitar but recruited the rest of the musicians from the ranks of the *Time* musicians, including Paul Moessl on keyboards.

A year later Moessl was suddenly summoned to David Bryce's office in Esher, for a 'little talk', and assumed that he was about to be 'let go' in the time-honoured fashion. He just couldn't think what he'd done wrong.

'Then they said, "Have a listen to this song",' he remembers. 'It was "Mistletoe and Wine". I said, "Yeh, it's very Christmassy isn't it?" They said, "We want to record it and Cliff wants to give you the chance of doing it." I was completely taken aback.

'I don't know why they chose me. I put it down to youth. Cliff will always take a chance. I think he susses out young people and if he trusts that they've got an idea about what's going on he'll try and tap into that.'

'Mistletoe and Wine' went to number one and became the best-selling British single of 1988, and Paul Moessl had become the new blue-eyed boy who could carry on bringing new life to Cliff's recording career.

For *Stronger*, Cliff's follow-up to *Always Guaranteed*, Moessl was introduced as 'guest arranger' on two tracks – 'Joanna' and 'The Best of Me' – with Cliff credited as producer. 'The Best of Me', the first release from the album, went to number two and sold over 750,000 copies.

Because of the success, Moessl became arranger and co-producer for Cliff's 1991 Christmas album, *Together With Cliff Richard*, a UK-only release capitalizing on his unprecedented run of Christmas number ones, which included his part in the re-recorded 'Do They Know It's Christmas?' for Band Aid.

Instead of a great follow-up to *Always Guaranteed* and *Stronger*, his last two studio albums, he produced an uninspired collection of 'Christmas favourites' including 'Scarlet Ribbons', 'Silent Night' and 'White Christmas'. It was as if the seventies and eighties had never happened.

In 1992 Moessl was given the chance to co-produce and arrange an album of original material – *Cliff Richard: The Album*. He even wrote two of the songs with Cliff. Released in April it topped the British album charts for one week and spawned the hit single 'Peace in Our Time'.

'The original title was *Access All Areas* (taken from the badges worn backstage by those granted unlimited access to stage, arena and dressing rooms), and reflected the idea that we tried to get different song styles onto the album,' says Moessl.

'Cliff's always looking ahead. He's into fresh ideas, fresh turnover and he's always trying to do something someone else hasn't done. He had a bad throat when we were recording and he started singing in a completely different way.

'It sounded so good that we recorded the album while it was in this lapsed state. When he got better he couldn't sing in exactly the same way again. It's a bizarre way of doing things but it worked and it shows his openness towards doing things in different ways.'

At the beginning of the nineties the biggest worry among those working with Cliff was that he was only now feeling the full effect of Peter Gormley's retirement a decade earlier even though Gormley continued to offer advice. Although he was already well-established by the time Gormley took over his career, there's no doubting the effect of this quietly spoken but rock-solid Australian in guiding him steadily through the ups and downs.

Talk to Gormley about how it's done and he shrugs his shoulders. He says he never did market research ('it's all bull'), never went out to create an image for Cliff ('image creation is a term that annoys me considerably') and has no philosophy of management that he could ever pass on to anyone else.

'You did what you had to do', he says simply. 'You worked according to your own judgment. It was purely a matter of instinct and judgment. There were no methods whatsoever. We never had any arguments about it. I presume we all thought alike.'

As a manager he was more than a negotiator, promoter and protector. He was a friend and father-figure to Cliff, and his instinct for what was right extended to the choice of singles.

'He has an incredible intuition about what is right and wrong for Cliff,' says Cliff's former producer Dave Mackay.

'Sometimes you'd be slaving away over something for Cliff, trying to get exactly the right feel, and he'd just walk in and stand at the back and say, "Hate those drums, son." You'd listen to it back again and he would always be right although he's not musical. He just knows Cliff and his audience.'

With Peter Gormley gone the management was divided between David Bryce (professional), Malcolm Smith (business) and Bill Latham (charity, Christian and media). None of them had the overall control that Gormley had exercised. The fear being expressed by those within the inner circle was that Cliff would now make more unchallenged decisions, and that this wasn't always a good thing.

'Peter was the rock on which it was all built,' said one member of the inner circle who has worked with all three. 'Cliff and Peter Gormley are the greatest double act of all time. People always underestimate Peter but Cliff knows. He provided him with the ultimate platform. There is something wonderful about Cliff and Peter preserved that for thirty years. He kept it pure.

'Now he's lost that guiding figure. The next phase will be interesting to watch.'

25

Heathcliff

Typical of Cliff's desire not only to top his previous achievements but to defy his critics was his decision, made in 1992, to commission, finance and perform in a musical based on Emily Brontë's 1847 novel *Wuthering Heights*. Unlike *Time*, this musical would take to the road, playing not only in London but in Scotland, the North of England and the Midlands.

Cliff had loved *Wuthering Heights* ever since studying it under Jay Norris at Cheshunt County Secondary School in 1957. He was particularly taken with the character of Heathcliff, the foundling boy who in his pursuit of Cathy Earnshaw reveals dark and mysterious passions. It has even been suggested that it was his fascination with Heathcliff that favourably disposed him towards the name Cliff when it was suggested the following year.

Heathcliff was an unusual choice of fictional hero because he embodied many of the elements of Romanticism – a primal energy and unrestrained passion – which ran counter to Cliff's personal ideals. Heathcliff is the natural man, untamed by civilization, who strikes people as being an 'evil beast', possibly a 'devil', who has a 'half-civilized ferocity' lurking behind his brows – whereas Cliff, even prior to his Christian conversion, was never prone to wildness.

▲1973: Cliff visiting Bangladesh with the relief agency Tear Fund - (left to right) Cliff, Bill Latham, Liz Hutchison

▲1978: At home in Weybridge - (clockwise) Cliff, Cliff's mother Dorothy, Bill Latham, Bill's mother Mamie, Derek Bodkin (Dorothy's husband)

◀ 1981: Baltimore, US - Cliff at a soundcheck

May 1981, Hammersmith Odeon: Cliff with Phil Everly at the Rock 'n' Roll special which was filmed for BBC TV ▶

Same concert. The first time the Drifters had met since Terry Smart left at the end of the fifties: (left to right) Ian Samwell, Norman Mitham, Terry Smart, Cliff ▼

◀ 23 July 1980: Cliff with his mother Dorothy after receiving his OBE

Cliff with Alan Tarney, songwriter and producer of albums such as Stronger and Always Guaranteed ▼

▲ 5 July 1982: Cliff with Sue Barker at Wimbledon during the height of their romance

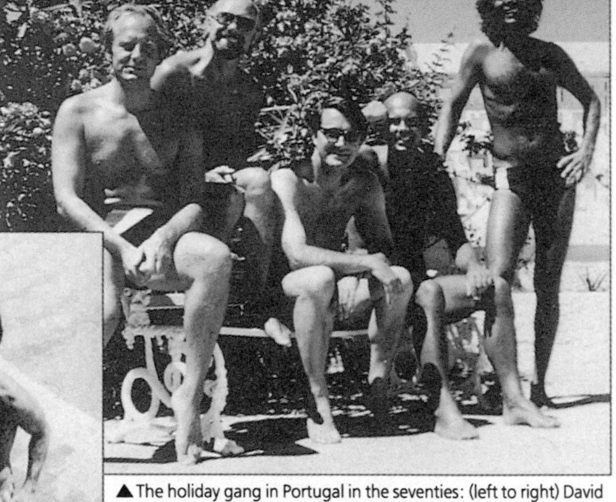

▲ The holiday gang in Portugal in the seventies: (left to right) David Rivett, Graham Disbrey, Glyn MacAulay, Bill Latham, Cliff

◀ Cliff at his villa in Portugal

◀ February 1989: Cliff and Sue Barker at a celebrity tennis match in London

August 1985: On holiday in Portugal - (left to right) Cliff, Bill Latham, Glyn MacAulay, Graham Disbrey, David Rivett ▼

▲ July 1989: Cliff's uniforms and gowns party - (left to right) Jill Clarke, Graham Disbrey, John and Carol Davey, Cliff

1986: Cliff as the rock star, Chris, in Time, with (left to right) Dawn Hope, Jodie Wilson, Maria Ventura ▶

▲Elton John's Rocket Records gave Cliff his first US top ten hit when it released 'Devil Woman' in 1976

▲The Event, June 1989: Cliff on stage with the Dallas Boys and Vernons Girls

October 1995: Cliff, after he received his knighthood at Buckingham Palace, with his three sisters: (left to right) Donna Gordon, Joan Pilgrim and Jacqui Harrison ▶

▲ July 1996: Cliff's impromptu performance at Wimbledon. Virginia Wade, former Wimbledon champion, sings along behind him

October 1996: *Heathcliff* opens, starring Cliff, and Helen Hobson ▶

Cliff was obviously not concerned with the deeper philosophical undercurrents of the book. Although he admitted that it had 'depth and complexity' he was ultimately attracted to it as 'a tragic story, a pathetic failure of manhood; the story of a man obsessed with one woman to the exclusion of all else'.

When he first announced his ambition to play Brontë's tragic hero the press were quick to point out the dissimilarities between the real-life Cliff and the fictional Heathcliff. How could this clean-living Christian whose life had been famously free of passionate entanglements play the part of the 'fierce, pitiless, wolfish man'? Surely he couldn't hope to follow in the footsteps of Laurence Olivier?

Writing in the *Independent*, columnist David Aaronovitch said, 'Cliff as Heathcliff seems as incongruous as, say, Hugh Grant playing Falstaff or Jodie Foster's Lady Bracknell... Surely the man ought to realize that you cannot be one thing for most of your life, and then expect to be allowed to become another.' Comparable miscasting suggested by other journalists included Max Bygraves as Titus Andronicus, Bonnie Langford as Medea, John Inman as Ben Hur, Michael Jackson as Othello and Perry Como as the Antichrist.

Cliff's defence was that actors didn't have to experience the lives they portrayed in order to play them convincingly. Wasn't that what *acting* meant? All they needed was insight into their own potential to behave in other ways. He asked whether it was necessary to kill someone in order to play the role of a murderer.

Yet the point being made by his critics was valid. There is such a thing as miscasting. The question was not only whether Cliff could comprehend the passion and cruelty he would have to act out, but whether his public image was so well defined that no audience would suspend its disbelief, even for an evening?

As always, the widespread conviction that he couldn't achieve something only spurred him on. He had wanted to play the part of Heathcliff for so long that no obstacle was going to stand in his way. He was even willing to sink his own money into the project so that no one but himself would lose if the venture failed.

'What goaded me on was the vehemence of the press,' Cliff admits. 'They kept saying that I couldn't possibly do this. "Mr Goody Two-Shoes? There's no way he can do it." I had thought that because we were doing something different and dangerous that they would support me. I had thought that they would at least say, "We don't think you can do it but we wish you the best of luck." But they didn't.'

He began by recruiting long-time friends as collaborators. John Farrar, who'd worked with Cliff as both musician and songwriter, was asked to do the music, and Tim Rice, who had been Norrie Paramor's assistant at EMI from 1966 until 1968, was invited to do the lyrics. Frank Dunlop, founder of the Young Vic in London and a former director of the Edinburgh International Festival, was asked to direct.

The book, which didn't aim to be a straight retelling of *Wuthering Heights*, was thrashed out in meetings between director and star. Dunlop's starting point was that he wanted the story to be told entirely in song but Cliff was adamant that he wanted dialogue. 'If I'm going to be in a show, I want to act,' he said. 'I want to speak-act, as well as sing-act.'

'Frank wrote out a basic scenario,' says Cliff. 'He's brilliant at that. Then every time I came across something in the book which I thought we had to have in I would tell him and he would slot it in. The only stuff that we had in the musical that's not actually in *Wuthering Heights* is the journey abroad which attempts to fill in the missing three years of his life.

'That idea came from both of us. We wondered where we could take him. I thought that we had to have him in Africa because I wanted to include some African rhythms. He said that he would check out that possibility and he came back and said that the period we were covering was the time of Clive of India and that the Brits at that time were going to Africa, India and China. They would pick up gold and go on to China and buy opium. So we decided to take him through that.'

As the scenario was developed, Rice would be faxed with information on the pages in the novel which needed to be translated into song. 'We would tell Tim that we needed a song here, here and there,' says Cliff. 'We would let him know the actual page numbers. He would work by taking actual words and lines from the book. For example, "Dream Tomorrow" starts with the words "I shall think it a dream tomorrow" and that is a straight lift from the text.'

Rice and Farrar (who lives in Los Angeles) met infrequently during the actual writing, both preferring to do their writing alone. Farrar was the first to get to work. He happened to have just read *Wuthering Heights* when Cliff called him and quickly wrote the music to three tracks which were then passed on to Rice.

'Whenever I've met Tim Rice over the years he has always chided me for never having recorded one of his songs,' says Cliff. 'So this time I rang him and said, "I know I've never done one of your songs – how would you like to do an album?" I told him about the project and he said that he would be delighted to be a part of it.'

It was in the spring of 1994 that the first public announcements were made. Recordings of the first songs were started in Los Angeles and at Abbey Road. Cliff was pictured visiting Brontë country in Yorkshire in the company of Jay Norris. Press launches took place in London, Birmingham, Sheffield, Aberdeen and Glasgow, the cities chosen for the musical to tour. *Heathcliff* was booked to open in November of that year and tickets went on sale.

However, three months after the press launch, it was

announced that *Heathcliff* was being postponed due to 'rehearsals being behind schedule'. In order to avoid the huge financial loss he would have made if he didn't use the pre-booked venues (a total of 27 days) Cliff swiftly arranged for a new tour to fulfil the dates and honour the tickets sold. It would be called 'Hit List' and would feature every top five single of his career.

A delay in rehearsals was the least of the problems facing *Heathcliff* at that point. The truth was that it had not yet been written and Cliff could see that there was no way that it was going to be ready by the anticipated opening night of 8 November. It was a great personal disappointment, but unavoidable in the circumstances.

'I knew that if I hadn't done something I would have been faced with a deficit of £1.5 million,' says Cliff. 'Tim and John are both people who don't take to being rushed. Quite right too. If you want quality you have to let it simmer a bit. Tim later said to me that five years is quite normal for a brand new musical.

'The interesting thing is, the bookings for *Heathcliff* had already stopped but after the 'Hit List' tour they tripled. People weren't going to come in their hordes to see the musical at that point because they hadn't yet heard anything from it. On the tour I then sang three of the songs and the bookings skyrocketed.'

The following year the singles 'Had To Be' (with Olivia Newton-John) and 'Misunderstood Man', and the album *Songs From Heathcliff* were released. The singles, which reached 22 and 19 respectively in the charts, didn't do as well as Cliff had hoped. He felt that this was in part due to a snub from BBC Radio 2, previously the natural home for Cliff's music.

Although the success of the musical wasn't dependent on BBC Radio, this action irritated him. The pop charts had been his natural home for so long and while not calling for special treatment he felt that his singles deserved to heard by the public.

'"Misunderstood Man" didn't get any airplay,' he says. '"Had

To Be" should have been number one, but it didn't get heard by anybody. Radio 2 wouldn't play it because they said it was "too dynamic". In other words, the song goes up and down. I can't understand this. I called a London radio station's phone-in programme and told them I couldn't understand this attitude. Of course, they then kept playing it and asking their listeners whether they thought it was too dynamic or whether the guitar solo was too loud.'

On 3 March 1996, at the Kensington Roof Gardens in London, Cliff finally announced the cast and the rescheduled dates. His co-star, playing Cathy, was to be Helen Hobson, and the show was to open in Birmingham on 16 October, going on to Sheffield, Manchester and Edinburgh, before coming to the Apollo in Hammersmith, London. Tickets were to go on sale the next day.

Almost immediately it was certain that *Heathcliff* was going to be a box office success. Fans were camping out overnight to make sure of getting tickets. By July, 300,000 tickets had been sold and the advance takings were estimated to be £8.5 million, a British theatre record. Cliff was invited to Tower Records in London's Piccadilly Circus to cut a celebratory cake.

When *Heathcliff* finally opened in October it received exactly the kind of critical mauling that Cliff had expected. While acknowledging that Cliff was an extremely capable singer and that the show was thoroughly enjoyed by his dedicated fans, the components of the show were mercilessly attacked. Frank Dunlop's production was 'awful', John Farrar's music was 'vapid pop pap' and Tim Rice didn't appear to have tried with his lyrics.

'I wasn't surprised by the reviews,' says Tim Rice, who himself felt the production fell between two stools in that the music was rock but the staging was traditional. 'However, I think that a lot of the critics were unnecessarily vicious. If you're a part of something which is considered to be a hit – *Beauty and the Beast*, for example – then almost everything in it gets reviewed well.

'But there were songs of mine in *Beauty and the Beast* which frankly weren't any better than the songs I did for *Heathcliff*, but because *Heathcliff* was perceived to be an artistic mess by the critics, they slagged off the songs as well.'

The main point made by critics was that Cliff was miscast; too old for the particular role, too inexperienced in musicals and plainly out of his depth. His acting was wooden, his accent, in the opinion of one reviewer, wandered 'between Weybridge, Macclesfield and New York' and it was risible to see Britain's best-behaved pop star smoking opium, acting as a passionate lover and beating a pregnant woman.

However, none of this flak affected Cliff because he deliberately didn't read a single review. He remained unshaken in his convictions. The proof, as far as he was concerned, was in the box-office pudding. He did what he thought was right, the public came in their hundreds of thousands and everyone appeared to enjoy the evening. The critics, in Cliff's opinion, didn't understand public taste, whereas his career had been built on knowing what people liked.

'The critics were wrong about *Phantom of the Opera*,' he argues. 'They were wrong about *Cats*, *Les Miserables* and *Starlight Express*. They were four of the longest-running shows in the West End. It's obvious to me that the critics have no concept of what the public actually want and because they don't know, they don't understand what people like me are trying to do.

'I'm not interested in doing something that is only liked by myself and one critic. I've never run my career like that. That's why they've written me off so often but it's also probably why I'm still here. I get written off because I don't do what people think is the thing to do. The danger with reading reviews is that you read them and you become depressed. Then you try too hard.'

Cliff's fans, as ever, were similarly not perturbed by the opinions of the experts. *The Times* interviewed one fan who had travelled from Perth, Western Australia, to see it and another who had bought tickets for 22 performances. When it closed it had been seen by almost half a million people. Additionally, the two albums *Songs From Heathcliff* and *Heathcliff Live* went on to sell 300,000 copies while the video reached the top spot in the music video charts.

By the time it was all over *Heathcliff* had taken up five years of Cliff's life – an eighth of his career so far. It was a huge investment of his time, talent and money. 'At the drop of a hat I would do it again,' he says. 'But I don't feel that now the stage run is over that I have somehow let go of it. *Heathcliff* is mine.'

The years devoted to *Heathcliff* affected his showing as a recording artist. Between 1994 and 1997 he released only five singles, one of which was a re-release ('Miss You Nights') and the rest taken from *Heathcliff*. None of them made the top ten. Likewise, the only albums released were either compilations – *The Hit List*, *Cliff at the Movies* and *The Rock 'n' Roll Years* – or *Heathcliff*-related. His projected 1998 album will be his first album of original non-*Heathcliff* material for five and a half years.

The lack of chart action didn't unsettle him. His normal pattern was to issue three singles a year to support an album. If there were no albums, it followed that there would be no singles. The compilation albums were planned by EMI. Cliff has no particular affection for compilations ('I can't understand who buys them') and didn't even listen to the entire box-set version of *The Rock 'n' Roll Years*, which consisted of four CDs and a handsome booklet.

His absence from the charts didn't mean a loss of visibility. If anything, his celebrity status rose. In 1995 he was chosen to sing for the VE celebrations in front of Buckingham Palace and to perform at the Royal Variety Performance and then, on 25 October, he became the first British pop star to be knighted by the Queen.

Even though Cliff had met the Queen many times before, he

was still overwhelmed by the award. He went to the palace with his three sisters (his mother had seen him receive his OBE) and was given a brief rehearsal before walking in and kneeling on his right knee before the Queen and being dubbed on both shoulders with the traditional sword.

'It's only after you stand up again that she puts the award around your neck and then she speaks for the first time,' says Cliff. 'I can't think what she said to me. I was so emotional I could hardly talk. I got really choked. I think she said something like "It's been a long time coming," and I just mumbled because I couldn't talk.'

The knighthood, coupled with the OBE, gave him unprecedented access. Although he had always been a reputable figure unlikely to bring disgrace on any organization which chose to associate with him, he had now been elevated to the highest echelons of British society where he could mix freely with politicians, landowners, aristocrats, captains of industry and royalty. Watching the finals at Wimbledon in July 1997 he turned to his sisters and said, 'Do you think we could ever have imagined this? Here we are sitting in the Members' Enclosure drinking tea and eating scones and you're sitting with a knight!'

His journey from among the upturned packing cases of Bury Green Estate never ceases to amaze him. He knows that few of the people he now mingles with came from such humble origins.

'When you have achieved longevity you naturally become a little bit more establishment,' he says. 'It's nowhere near as bad as people make out. I don't know why people want to knock the establishment because it's a lot better than where I was.'

He was one of only a handful of pop stars (Sting, Elton John, George Michael and Chris de Burgh were the others) to be invited to attend Princess Diana's funeral. He felt honoured to have been considered. He was in New York to watch the US Open when she died and didn't expect to be invited.

'Because it was such a terrible shock to everyone the detectives had to go through her Christmas card list to find the names of people that should be there,' he says. 'Now, I wasn't on her list but I was someone who she apparently talked about quite a lot and they knew that she had enjoyed the times we had met up and had dinner together. So they put my name down as being someone that she liked.

'I knew her quite well socially but I couldn't say that we were close. We skied from the same hotel. I sang for her boys. In fact I did my first Royal Command Performance for William out in Austria! She was a fantastic girl. She wasn't perfect because none of us are but as people go, she was really special.

'She did care about people. I've met drivers who've told me that they'd driven her just once and she'd written to thank them. She was incredible and her death is a terrible loss. Even now I find it hard to take in. To talk of Diana in the past tense seems really ridiculous. I don't think I've ever met anyone who had such a wonderful effect on people.

'We were planning to work together during the celebrations for my 40 years in show business in London during 1998. She had called me to Kensington Palace to meet some people from the Leprosy Mission and some rich Asian men. I didn't know what was expected from me. I knew I couldn't sign cheques for millions. Then one of these guys asked me if I'd be willing to do a concert and Diana immediately said, "I'd come." So they said, "Do you mean that you'd patronize the evening?" She said, "Of course I would."

It was never to happen. The next event to bring the two names together was the Diana tribute album, where Cliff's version of Paul Field's song 'All That Matters', produced by Alan Tarney, was put alongside contributions from such international megastars as Paul McCartney, Bruce Springsteen, Michael Jackson, Barbra Streisand, Celine Dion, Whitney Houston and Luciano Pavarotti.

At the start of 1998 Cliff was preparing for a year that was bound to see even more accolades rolling in, as the 40th anniversaries of almost everything that he is known for come up one after another. He'll have spent 40 years as an EMI recording artist in July 1998, as a professional musician in August, as a television performer and chart act in September, as a touring artist in October and as a film actor in December.

He was planning a tour of Australia and New Zealand followed by a tour of Britain and Europe and then the release of his 63rd album. As always he was completely buoyed up by the prospect and absolutely convinced that the record, being produced in Austria and England by American Peter Wolf, was his best ever.

'There are four fantastic singles,' he enthused. 'If I can get any airplay they are certain hits. If I don't get any airplay, I would rather do another musical. I would rather do something where you plan, spend your money, do it and have the instant gratification of a large audience. Why should I waste my time recording if no one is going to hear what I do?'

Forty years in show business plus the approaching millennium will inevitably lead to questions about how long he plans to keep performing and recording.

'I'd like to slow down a little but I don't know how I would do it,' he says. 'I'd love to wipe out the diary and just work whenever I wanted to so that if I fancied taking a whole year off I could or if I wanted to do a tour of the Far East I could do that.

'Doing something like *Heathcliff* is a career move but I would also like to do smaller things that were not career moves. I'd like to do a small part in a West End play or a short tour abroad. Things like that won't make me big money but I would enjoy doing them. I could still continue to relate to the fans and they would obviously still be able to follow me around.'

26

'My Kinda Life'

Forty years after his first (£200) tour Cliff Richard is a very wealthy man. In 1991 the *Sunday Times* valued his fortune at £50 million, ranking him at number 182 in a list of Britain's 200 richest people. In 1997 *Business Age Magazine* estimated that he was the nineteenth-richest British rock star, with £52 million. His annual earnings over the past five years were estimated at £2.5 million, despite the fact that *Heathcliff*, as a stage show, barely broke even.

To put things into proportion, Elton John's fortune was estimated by *Business Age* as being £200 million and David Bowie's as £550 million. However, everyone rated as richer than Cliff, with the exception of ex-Beatle Ringo Starr and Tom Jones, was also a songwriter.

Cliff denies that he is worth as much as that. 'When that story came out I got a note from Malcolm Smith, my business manager, which said, "Don't spend it because I haven't found it!"'

Cliff's revenue is based primarily on ticket sales, mechanical royalties on albums and singles (he has made very little from songwriting), merchandizing and videos. In the early part of his career he also made money from films and television.

His singles sales have been phenomenal. Thirty-two of them

have sold over one million copies each and his total world sales approach eighty million. His albums consistently made the top twenty from 1958 to 1966, and again from 1976 onwards. Today, a modest effort of original material can sell 500,000 and a hit album as many as 1,500,000.

But it has been his live shows which have shown the most rapid growth. Since moving out of the Empires and Odeons which characterized his touring throughout the sixties and seventies, he has been regularly filling the country's largest exhibition centres for extended runs.

Mel Bush, who has promoted several of Cliff's tours, believes that as a live entertainer Cliff could outsell any other act in the world. He is one of only seven acts that have filled Wembley Stadium for two or more nights on the strength of their name alone. (The others are Michael Jackson, Madonna, Bruce Springsteen, the Rolling Stones, Genesis and U2.)

'If Cliff had the time and wanted to do it, I think he would have absolutely no problem in playing to a million people in this country on one tour,' says Bush. 'To play to over 400,000 in 1990 we only played in four centres.'

In 1990 he played at the Wembley Arena for eighteen nights, reaching a total of 216,000 people and breaking all previous records for the Arena. His 'Access All Areas' tour in 1992 played fourteen nights at Birmingham's NEC (capacity 12,378), five nights at the Sheffield Arena (cap. 12,000), three nights at the Scottish Exhibition Centre in Glasgow (cap. 10,000), fifteen nights at Wembley Arena (cap. 12,000), four nights at King's Hall, Belfast (cap. 6,000) and three nights at the Point Depot in Dublin (cap. 4,500).

Simple calculations reveal that on that tour he played to 480,792 people and that, with seats selling for £19.50 and £17.50, this means (presuming at least a third of the audience bought the higher-priced tickets) that the gross revenue from the box office must be approaching £9 million. Production costs, which included a specially constructed stage and rehearsals at the Docklands Arena, were rumoured to be approaching £2 million, but much of that will have been covered by the smart practice of taking paid bookings almost a year in advance so that interest could accrue.

This doesn't take into account the income from merchandizing (sweatshirts, programmes, mugs, caps, badges, keyrings, torches, brooches) and the rejuvenation of his back catalogue.

All Cliff's finances are handled by Malcolm Smith, a 45-year-old chartered accountant who joined the Cliff Richard Organization as managing director in 1987 from the City firm of Touche Ross, having worked on Cliff's accounts from outside since 1985. He is a director of fifteen companies, including those which absorb the money generated by Cliff's career.

His fellow directors on these companies are the same: Cliff's mother, Michael Simkins (who has been Cliff's lawyer since 1960) and his colleague David Franks, Cliff's accountant Philip Parker and Peter Gormley. All financial decisions are made jointly.

Yet Cliff appears to be detached from his fortune. He genuinely has little idea of what he's worth, has never been a profligate spender and his pocket money is set at £40 a week, which is brought to him by Bill Latham each Thursday evening in a brown envelope made up by Gill Snow.

'That's only my spending money,' Cliff explains. 'I still have a wad of it left at the end of the week because I don't spend it. By the time six weeks have passed I'm £240 up!'

The Cliff Richard Organization, in Claygate, Surrey, has a permanent staff of eight, a bookkeeper and members of the five-strong Cliff Richard Tennis Trust. Cliff himself only employs two people: his full-time gardener Mick and his housekeeper Megan who comes in three mornings a week. He owns no valuable works of art, doesn't jet-set or gamble, and has no expensive habits other than tennis and skiing.

His main assets appear to be his home in Weybridge, bought for £1.4 million in August 1987, his Portuguese estate bought in 1992, a cottage in North Wales with 125 acres of land, the Claygate office building and his three cars – a 1990 Mercedes Benz 500 SL, a 1994 Bentley Brooklands and a 1997 Range Rover.

He has ploughed a lot of money into his holiday home, Quinto de Moinho, completely refurbishing the 19th-century Portuguese farmhouse, and planning to turn at least a third of its 35 acres into a working vineyard. He has employed David Baverstock ('the best red-wine maker in Europe' according to Cliff) to create a new wine which will blend three Portuguese grapes with a French grape. It could eventually produce up to 30,000 bottles of wine a year 'from the vineyard of Sir Cliff Richard'.

Since March 1966 he has followed the Christian practice of 'tithing', giving away at least a tenth of his income to charity. This is usually done through the Cliff Richard (Charitable Trust) Ltd which in 1991 benefited from over one million pounds and has almost no administration costs. On top of this he donates more than a tenth of his working time to charity and church events: making personal appearances, video tapes, books and Bible cassettes.

Since leaving Tear Fund in 1978, Bill Latham has managed Cliff's Christian and charity affairs, and more recently has handled the press. Together they make frequent public appearances in church situations where Cliff is interviewed about his faith and about Third World concerns.

Cliff is now so readily associated with charity work that it's easy to assume that it's second nature for him to give in this way.

Bill Latham believes that by nature he wouldn't choose to involve himself in the troubles and turmoils of the developing world and that if he hadn't been transformed by his response to the Christian gospel he would probably be an insular person.

'I think Cliff's concern for others has come about largely as a result of Christian self-discipline,' he says. 'I think the nature of the Christian faith demands that one looks outside oneself. I think he's forced himself to be aware of others. I don't think it's necessarily easy for him to do it because I think he is by nature more self-absorbed.'

The profit from all his gospel tours is automatically put into the trust, as is the income from some of his religious books. The trust then gives fifty per cent of the income to Tear Fund and the rest is spread around other charities.

He feels particularly close to the Arts Centre Group because it grew out of the group with Nigel Goodwin and David Winter that he'd been a part of starting in 1965. In 1971 he bought a mansion in Great Dunmow, Essex, which he then allowed the ACG full use of as a retreat and conference centre. It has since been sold.

'We get a lot of letters from people asking for money,' says Gill Snow. 'The answer we give is that we don't help individuals because all of Cliff's giving goes through his trust and that is authorized only to give to registered charities.

'A lot of the stories are heartbreaking but if you give to one person then you're stymied. At the moment, in the middle of a recession, ninety per cent of the requests we get are mortgage-related. People are losing their businesses or their homes. I write back to them all individually and try to be as sympathetic as possible.'

Cliff is generous to family and friends but never impulsive in the way that Elvis used to buy Cadillacs for passing strangers or Elton John has been known to hand out jewellery. He set Donna's first husband up in business and bought homes for his sisters and mother.

'It's not in Cliff's nature to throw his money around,' says Bill Latham. 'He's more cautious. He doesn't give his money away on impulse, although he has always looked after his family.'

When he does spend his money it tends to be on the house and garden. When he was living at Rookswood he discovered that

Latham and Graham Disbrey were keen tennis players, so he had a tennis court built, even though they had a chance to play on it only twice before the house was sold.

In Totteridge and at Feather Green he spent money building extensions and then promptly moved out when there seemed nowhere left to extend. At his home in Weybridge, which needs no enlarging, he has extended the garages.

He recently saw a Versace shirt he liked but when he discovered that it cost £950 – peanuts for a multi-millionaire, however small the multi might be – he threw up his hands in horror. 'I could buy a Mercedes Benz for the cost of forty-nine of those,' he said.

The amount represents a minuscule proportion of his annual income but he still thinks more in terms of the £40 in the brown envelope than of the invisible millions that are processed in Claygate.

It's often a point of annoyance to the musicians that he fails to realize the cost of living in Britain today because all his major expenses are sorted out by other people and the cash in his pocket is mainly there for tipping.

Once at a band meal he started to say that he didn't see why people had such a hard time on social security because he seemed to manage well enough on what was in his brown envelope. 'But you don't have to pay your mortgage out of that,' Tony Rivers argued. 'You don't pay your bills and buy your meals with that.'

He doesn't live a typically showbizzy life. His closest friends are not drawn from entertainment but from accountancy, teaching, sport, church and charity. He's not often spotted at openings and first nights and never goes clubbing, although he did check out a lot of plays and musicals when he was preparing *Heathcliff*.

He rarely entertains at home and if he does it will often be with a group of old and trusted friends from the Crusader days. He enjoys cooking pool-side barbecues and for bigger parties he'll hire caterers.

He loves organizing parties. For his fiftieth birthday in 1990 he had a marquee erected on the lawn and everyone had to come as they were in 1958. Recently he's held a woodland party under the trees at the bottom of his garden, an 'over the top' party where guests dressed in anything from Arab robes to space suits, and a 'ball gowns and uniforms' party.

His holidays follow the pattern that was set in 1966, which means two or three weeks in the sunshine with the 'holiday gang' where he'll swim, play tennis or sunbathe while listening to music on a personal stereo.

Most often these holidays have been in Portugal but there have been trips to California (1968), Israel (1972), Madeira (1973), South Africa, Bermuda (1983) and Florida. In 1987 and 1989 a London art dealer, David Mason, gave them the free use of his ocean-going yachts *Lindsay Jane* and *Lindsay Jane II*. On the first trip they toured the Greek islands and on the second the coast of Croatia (then Yugoslavia).

'The problem on the cruises was that Cliff had difficulty finding access to tennis courts,' says Graham Disbrey, the only person other than Bill Latham and Cliff who has been on all the 'gang' holidays. 'We managed in the end but sometimes it was half a day's venture to actually find one. In Portugal he has his own court and so after sunbathing and swimming he would be coached for one to two hours.'

Tennis has become for him little short of an obsession. Ever since playing badminton as a boy he has enjoyed racquet games but after meeting Sue Barker he changed from being a casual performer to a deadly serious contender with all the grit and determination he once displayed on the rugger field.

He started playing regularly at the David Lloyd Tennis Centre and receiving lessons. Soon he was becoming a fixture on the social circuit of the British tennis scene, turning up at

Wimbledon, organizing pro-celebrity tennis tournaments and injecting much-needed money into schemes to improve Britain's standing on the world tennis scene.

Today, he tries to ensure that he is booked into hotels that have tennis courts and on some tours he travels with a tennis pro. He plays doubles against the likes of Chris Evert Lloyd, Steffi Graf and Ilie Nastase, and friends suggest that although he professes to play only as a hobby he secretly believes that, even in his fifties, he can go on improving.

'He became infatuated with the game,' says Sue Barker. 'He can't accept not doing it well. I kept telling him that children mimic and can pick things up quite quickly but that he had no hope at his age. I think he then approached it in the spirit of trying to prove that I was wrong.

'He still doesn't look like a natural player, like someone who has been playing all his life. There is always a distinction between someone who has played as a kid and someone who has taken it up much later in life. You can see it in the flowing motion of the shots. The result is still the same, but you can feel that it's manufactured rather than natural.'

Tennis commentator Gerald Williams believes that he is better than a good club player and that he could well sneak into a minor county team.

'He's very fit and competitive and plays a good game,' he says. 'He really understands tennis. When he talks about it on radio and TV he makes more sense than a lot of people who earn a living from talking about it.'

In 1992 he and Bill Latham went on holiday to Lech in Austria with tennis partner Charles Haswell, his wife and two female friends, and here he tried skiing for the first time in twenty years. He was on the beginners' slope for just two days, graduated to the blue runs and by the end of the fortnight was confident enough to come down red runs and do parallel turns.

His involvement with skiing again shows the depth of his determination. He is never content to dabble. He has to attain complete mastery, confounding those who say it can never be done. He needs a fresh supply of challenges, however apparently insignificant they may be.

One former producer, when asked why Cliff had never married, reputedly said, 'How can someone so in love with himself ever fall in love with someone else?' The remark is quite cruel but there is a kernel of truth. How could someone so in love with their present lifestyle ever make room for the needs of another individual?

Bill Latham puts it like this: 'There is no way Cliff could have lived the life he has lived, contributed what he has contributed and achieved what he has achieved if he had been married. There is no question of that. Although he loves his home he doesn't feel tied to it and that freedom has meant that he has been able to do much, much more than if he had a family.

'It's also partly to do with the enthusiastic approach he has towards everything he touches. He always goes the extra mile. If he was to have a relationship he would give it everything. There would be no half measures.

'So because his commitments have been his career, his faith, and, more latterly, tennis, he has given himself wholeheartedly to those three activities. There hasn't been room for anything else.'

There have been no girlfriends since Sue Barker, although there has never been a shortage of women wanting to be Mrs Cliff Richard. Some of them get very close. They have been to his house and cooked him meals, accompanied him to the cinema and eaten out with him at restaurants.

Cliff will be extremely charming and pleasant to them but there is a limit to how close he'll allow them to come. As soon as he senses that they are wanting more from him than he'll ever be able to give, he cuts them off.

It's back to that scene in *Summer Holiday* where Cliff says,

'Girls are all very well, but date them once and then run. Date them twice and they get serious... Next thing you know, you're hooked and wondering what's hit you. No. No girl is ever going to own me.'

He enjoys female company, though. In the seventies he became friendly with the beautiful daughter of a wealthy landowner who, somewhat naturally, misinterpreted the signals and assumed Cliff was falling in love with her.

She went on holiday to France where she was hospitalized after a car accident. The mother, who by now assumed Cliff was her daughter's boyfriend, immediately called the office and requested that Cliff look after her and have her brought back to England. It was only then that Cliff realized the depth of the misunderstanding.

More recently he became friendly with Marietta Parfitt, the ex-wife of Status Quo guitarist Rick Parfitt. A committed Roman Catholic and a gracious hostess, she would often accompany him on double dates with Bill Latham and Jill Clarke. She was also a regular guest at Weybridge and went into print saying that Cliff had helped her through a particularly bad time in her life.

For years he has said that he's just waiting for the right girl to come along but, at fifty-eight, he has concluded that he is not the marrying sort.

'Maybe I have lived through all the things I needed to live through to find myself and what I want out of life,' he says. 'I don't think marriage is one of those things. I don't feel I'll ever get married now. I don't think I'm unique. I still have enough female company and it's fine.

'At the moment I prefer not having a romantic attachment. I find myself really free. I can do whatever I want. I don't have to look for babysitters. I shot off to Austria recently and I'd like to go again soon and I can just do things like that.

'Life for me is really quite nice and I like it the way it is. The only reason it's not selfish is because no one has to tie themselves to anyone else if they don't want to. It's a positive step in that I don't actually owe anyone anything. I don't have to be tied to anybody and I like that.'

The absence of serious romantic relationships with women and the long, close live-in relationship with Bill Latham lead many people to conclude that something homosexual is going on, despite the vigorous denials issued by both Latham and Cliff over the years.

'I have denied being gay since the idea was first mooted when I was eighteen,' says Cliff. 'I've never even contemplated the possibility that I might be gay. There's not much I can do to stop the rumours. Ultimately all that counts is what my friends and family know and they all trust and respect me.'

In 1991, while Cliff was rehearsing for a gospel tour at Bray film studios near Windsor, a group of extras working on Derek Jarman's film *Edward II* invaded the band's sound stage. They waved gay-rights placards and urged Cliff to 'come out of the closet'.

It's not an altogether outrageous assumption to make simply because it is almost impossible to name another unmarried man of Cliff's age in show business who lives with a male friend, doesn't date girls and isn't homosexual. In other words, Cliff doesn't fit any model that people know of. He doesn't appear to be the 'confirmed bachelor' of the old-fashioned type, because most of them don't dress in skin-tight cycling shorts and diamante jackets. Cliff's image is not one of fusty bachelorhood but of glamour, style and romance.

The truth seems to be that Cliff doesn't fit the clearly defined models we are used to, where if you're not Rod Stewart or Bill Wyman then you must be Liberace. It's clear that from his mid-teens until his mid-twenties he did endeavour to form relationships with women, but the desire for sexual commitment was never great enough to move beyond the stage of a fifties high-school date. Also, the more attached he became to his lifestyle, the harder it became to embark on a relationship which might threaten it.

After his relationships with Jackie Irving and Una Stubbs he seems to have become reconciled to bachelorhood, admitting (sometimes) that he wasn't bothered by strong sexual passions and was seemingly impervious to temptation.

Cliff has always had a very high view of marriage, and his conversion to Christianity can only have enhanced this. He believed he was called to live a celibate life while single and a faithful life should he marry.

This inevitably increased the significance of marriage both in his eyes and in the eyes of his fans, because there could be no euphemistic 'close friendships' or 'inseparable companions'. Serious courtship could only be conducted with marriage in mind.

At the same time, as a Christian, his single life can be looked at positively. Both Jesus and the apostle Paul said that some people are better prepared for Christian service because they are untroubled by the 'fires of passion'. It's almost certainly this that Cliff was referring to when he said that not having 'any great sexual urges' was 'my good fortune'.

When he met Bill Latham in 1964 the relationship provided him with the emotional succour that most men receive from a marriage. This 'brotherly affection', as Latham describes it, no doubt filled the emptiness that can result from living without close dependants.

But rather than being something homosexual, it confirmed his belief that he didn't need a marriage to fulfil him. His friendship with Latham, and his career, effectively replaced wife and children. There had never really been any need for sexual gratification and so that didn't constitute a lack.

If he hadn't met Latham it seems likely that Cliff would have remained single, but it's unlikely that Latham would have remained unmarried if he hadn't met Cliff. Latham had steady girlfriends in the sixties and seventies (Cindy Kent among them) and his girlfriend, Jill Clarke, shared the Weybridge house with him and Cliff for several years.

'I had never set my mind on being single,' Latham admits. 'I've had relationships in the past, am with a long-term girlfriend and am under constant pressure to marry but I don't feel that at my stage of life I would want the upheaval.

'In one sense I would have liked to have had a family but because my life has been so fulfilled in so many other ways it's not something I lose sleep over or become depressed about.'

The relationship between the two men is close but not suffocatingly so. A lot of the time they spend together is because of work, but when Cliff is recording or touring Latham carves out his own independent life.

Their interests are quite different. Latham has never been a big fan of rock 'n' roll, prefers cricket to tennis and can't stand the video games that Cliff so loves to play at home. He also has no interest in skiing. When Cliff first went to Austria, Latham sat out the skiing sessions in local coffee bars. When the next trip was set up he chose not to go.

Among close friends they often allow these tensions to come to the surface. 'I've been at meals in the last few years where there have almost been fights between him and Bill,' says one friend. 'Bill talks a lot of common sense but Cliff will come out with comments about the unemployed and homeless, and I think it drives Bill to despair. I don't think Cliff understands.'

Cliff has always appeared unashamedly right wing in his political views although he now declares that he's 'smack in the middle'. He hasn't yet met Tony Blair but thinks that 'New Labour has become like the Old Tories. There hasn't been a real change yet has there?'

In his time he has advocated birching, called for wider

censorship and suggested that the unemployed should help out in hospitals. He was a big supporter of both Margaret Thatcher and John Major. He also dismayed many of his music business colleagues by continuing to play in South Africa during the apartheid regime, a move which earned him a United Nations blacklisting and a bomb threat while touring Scandinavia.

His attitudes are a mix of those he inherited as a child of the Raj and those he has developed as a poor boy made good in England.

Thatcherism appealed to him because he had started with nothing and, through determination and talent, had become a multi-millionaire. His assumption was that anyone else with similar single-mindedness could make something of themself.

He is notably hard on people he regards as 'slackers', or who don't seem to 'pull their weight'. Seemingly oblivious to his own privileged position, he complains about those who work only to earn money.

His background in India forged a strong, almost uncritical, allegiance to those in power. Where other pop stars have questioned police behaviour, been critical of royalty, or protested against British foreign policy, Cliff has remained unstintingly loyal to the establishment.

Colleagues are often shocked by his ignorance of the harsher side of British life. Although he has witnessed the effects of Third World poverty, he knows little about the underclass of his own country.

This is not entirely his fault. Since 1958 he has lived a separate life. His encounters with the public and with officialdom are atypical because they are always in controlled situations and he is always treated with a respect not offered to the ordinary citizen. It's hard to come up with informed views about the world when the only world you experience is so protected.

'One of the causes for our disagreements is the blind spot I feel he has over the pressures in society today for people just to exist,' Bill Latham admits. 'He doesn't really understand the pressure of a mortgage, interest rates, unemployment and so on. I often feel he doesn't have enough empathy with people. I would like him actually to go to some inner-city areas in Britain to see just what the people there face.'

Yet Cliff needs Latham to shield him from the world and guard his diary. Latham plays the role of the often stern parent trying to control a naïve but talented and adventurous child who has no real perception of the adult world, no sense of time and no concept of what can and can't be done.

He admonishes him about his dress sense, reminds him of promises he has made to people, and is almost always around as the looming presence which brings conversations to an end.

'Cliff is the "Let's do everything" one and Bill is the "No, you can't do that" one,' says Gill Snow, who has worked with Cliff and Bill in different capacities for over twenty years. 'They balance each other out in that respect. Bill is very organized and Cliff, like so many artists, isn't. But, underneath it all, there's a high degree of mutual respect and they are very close friends.'

The great triumph of their relationship has been that it works. Cliff has, over a period of years, been able to integrate his professional work with his spiritual faith to the point where he has become perhaps the best-known advocate for Christianity in Britain.

'It's hard to understand Cliff without Bill,' says Graham Disbrey. 'The overriding thing is that Bill has been the most generous, kindly person and he really has made his mark on the person Cliff is today.'

Initially Cliff's proclamation of faith sat uneasily with his 'Talk of the Town' lifestyle, but it no longer seems out of place for him to speak about his love for Jesus in the middle of a show. No journalist can now write a profile of him without mentioning the fact of his Christianity because it informs everything he does.

Today, when it is quite common for rock musicians to display a passion for religion, it may not seem such an act of courage, but when Cliff did it in 1966, before the Beatles made known their allegiance to Maharishi Mahesh Yogi, it was stepping into unknown territory.

It's even more courageous for Cliff because he is essentially a people-pleaser. His musical career has been based on satisfying the public taste. Yet with the stand he has taken as a Christian he has often had to fly in the face of public opinion and this has made him the target of abuse.

'He likes to be liked professionally because if he's not liked, the career ends,' Bill Latham explains. 'He's hurt by professional criticism, but he's not really hurt or upset if he's criticized for his opinions. He may get irritated but he's not offended or hurt. Regardless of the company he's in he'll be very outspoken about the things he believes in. There will be no holds barred.'

Some of Bill and Cliff's friends feel that Latham has sacrificed his own life for the sake of Cliff, that by remaining so close he has denied himself the opportunity of pursuing a career on his own right or of marrying and raising a family. They point out that his own gifts as a communicator are no longer fully used and that he has to spend much of his time as an unacknowledged figure in the background while his famous friend grabs all the attention.

Latham denies this. 'It's not been a sacrifice at all,' he says. 'Quite the reverse. It's opened up areas of experience that have been very rewarding and fulfilling. I've seen it all as a privilege.

'Cliff and I just get on together. We work together well. Spiritually the team has been fruitful and my gut feeling is that it's right. There's a job to be done and we go out and do it.'

27

The bubble that didn't burst

If Cliff had been asked in 1958 what he would have liked to have been doing in his fifties he would probably have said 'singing'. But he could never have dreamt that his wish would come true.

That year his father was fifty-three, a gaunt, balding man with an austere Victorian demeanour. It would have been impossible to have imagined someone of his age shaking a leg and singing 'Move It'.

Realistically, Cliff thought of a career that might see him through his teens before his young audience deserted him and he was forced to get a sensible job. By the time he was twenty he openly admitted that he was saving up for that inevitable day when 'the bubble burst'.

The bubble didn't burst. He has been through trying times though. He has put out records beneath his capabilities. But never in forty years has he been less than a major star in Britain and every time he has seemed to be slipping he has come back with something bigger and better.

What makes his career doubly remarkable is that he is not simply a survivor but someone who is constantly scaling new heights.

His first decade was largely spent establishing himself as a singles artist and as a film star. During his second decade, which ended in 1978, he emerged as a star of his own television shows and, for the first time, as a serious album artist.

But even by then he hadn't done everything in his third decade, while producing his biggest-selling single ever with 'We Don't Talk Any More', he developed his stage show to new and spectacular dimensions.

By 1988 you would have thought that there was nowhere left to go. But he surprised everyone with The Event, his first stadium show, which was quickly followed by his longest run at Wembley Arena.

In his fourth decade he made the huge leap to conceive, finance and star in the multi-million pound production of *Heathcliff*, the book of which he also co-authored.

How has he survived so many changes in musical fashion? It would be easy to attribute it all to superior talent but if that were so then acts such as the Rolling Stones and Paul McCartney would have had equally consistent careers.

Part of the answer lies in the fact that most of the performers who became established in the sixties were songwriters as well as singers. Their fate has been tied up with their ability to create fresh material. Broadly speaking, they produced their best work in their twenties and early thirties. Cliff, who has always been an interpreter of other writers' songs, has not been affected in the same way.

Another part of the answer is that Cliff, because he is single, has been able to devote almost all of his energy to his work. He has been able to retain his youthful enthusiasm because he hasn't taken on the baggage of adulthood.

He is one of the most fiercely determined singers in the business, although this is often overlooked by observers because of his easygoing manner. The fighting skills he once established in the playground have been sublimated into his career.

This devotion has been supplemented by the help of good colleagues. In a business noted for sharp practice he has been extremely fortunate with those who have influenced his career. Very early on he fell in with good, honest men such as Peter Gormley and Norrie Paramor, who gave him strong fatherly direction as well as much room as possible to be himself.

Undoubtably his greatest talent has been his pure and well-rounded singing voice. It is distinctive (you can tell a Cliff record within a few notes), he has maintained it well (he took voice lessons in 1991 and now tunes up for twenty minutes before each concert) and is in perfect keeping with what the public know of his character – warm, smooth, compassionate, reassuring.

He knows what he wants. Although he has been supported by good musicians, song writers and producers, he must take credit for seeing the potential in these people. He has an eye for talent just as he has an ear for hit songs. But more than even the music itself, his continued success is due to his warm personality and to the unique relationship he has built up with his fans.

Many performers are content to churn out singles on a 'take it or leave it' basis and refuse to do anything more than the minimum of publicity. Cliff has always unashamedly given the public what it wants and has allowed himself to 'belong' to his fans.

Because he recognizes that he is an entertainer rather than an artist, he has never taken the attitude that if he likes a song it is then up to the audience to learn to like it. Entertainers are not there to confound expectations and alter perceptions. They are there to provide pleasant distractions.

Right from the early days Cliff was talking of 'doing what the fans want me to'. In 1960 he actually brought a group of fans together at Abbey Road studios to choose his next single from a collection of twenty-one recorded songs (they chose 'Please Don't Tease').

Asked in 1977 what he would do if he was faced with a choice between personal artistic satisfaction and pleasing the public, he said he would compromise. 'I would compromise with quality songs though,' he said. 'I don't want to cut the parents and grandparents out.'

Although he values his privacy he makes himself available to his fans, both in person and through chat shows and press interviews. Many performers view their dealings with the media as a chore, but Cliff approaches it all with the zest with which he records his singles.

The result has been that those who follow him hold him in great affection. This is obvious to anyone who has attended his concerts where the rapport between stage and audience is the rapport of friends rather than that of salesman and customer.

Given Cliff's huge following in the UK and many other parts of the world, his failure to crack America is surprising. His relative lack of success there must be due, in part, to the fact that the American public knows nothing of Cliff's personality in this way. He comes to them each time with no legend attached. They hear the songs in isolation and buy them when they're particularly strong and ignore them when they're mediocre. In Britain there are those who buy the singles whatever the quality because of their allegiance to Cliff.

But even if Cliff had become well known in the States, it's likely that the American public would have considered him too soft for their taste anyway. Elvis could look like a mummy's boy in his colourful jackets but he could also look like a hoodlum. Cliff never looked convincing as a hoodlum.

Softer performers have normally had to compensate by being extravagant in other ways. It was when he went to America that Elton John developed his outrageous costumes and flying leaps at the piano. You have to shout really loud in America to get noticed. It's not enough simply to make 'good' records.

Cliff's image in Britain is well defined and well known. However, interestingly enough, he has only ever employed a publicist for particular albums or film campaigns and he was not manufactured at the hands of a public relations consultant. There is no Svengali in the background.

The two strongest characteristics of this well-known image are his decency and his youthfulness. Most of that which is revered or reviled about Cliff can be filed beneath these two headings.

His decency was established right from the start. Here was someone who was kind, polite, honest and caring. He didn't swear, didn't drink, wasn't seen groping girls, dressed smartly and was frequently used as proof that not all teenagers are bad.

All this wasn't too unusual at the time because even the worst-behaved pop singers projected themselves as mother-loving milk-drinkers. It would have been folly in 1959 to brag about being drunk or to use obscenities in interviews. A hint of anti-social behaviour could end a career.

The difference with Cliff was that the image was largely true. By nature he was that dream boy who admired his mother, looked after his sisters, hated to see animals in pain, respected policemen and went to bed early.

What is amazing is that not only is the image the same forty years later, but so is the reality. All who meet him seem impressed with his genuine 'niceness'. He makes people feel comfortable in his presence, he never gossips or bitches and he always appears cheerful and optimistic. 'You feel you are a much better person after having met him,' says actor Anthony Andrews. 'His outlook on life is so positive it always has an effect on you.'

No one interviewed for this book, even those fully aware of his weaknesses, suggested that there was any sham involved in his public image. Years of scrutiny by the tabloid press have unearthed no hypocritical behaviour and he is remarkable in having created no enemies in the music business.

'He really is an ordinary guy who got caught up in extraordinary circumstances,' says Sammy Samwell. 'What you see is what you get.'

When he is criticized it is not for being phoney, but for being 'too good to be true'. His decency is sometimes perceived as a character weakness, as though it must signify a dull and unadventurous personality.

The truth is that, although he has obviously inherited an even temperament, much of what is perceived as his 'niceness' is the result of determination rather than of spinelessness. He believes it is important to love others even when you don't feel like loving. He struggles to be gracious, even when it would be more convenient to be rude.

'In the Bible, Saint Paul says that there is an "evil me" that is constantly trying to override the "good me",' Cliff explains. 'If I can let the "good me" win in front of the public as often as possible, I consider that a success rather than a fault.

'The fault is that I can't always control my thoughts, and I can't stop thinking that I'd rather be doing other things. I'd rather smash some people in the face because they really annoy me, but it's a success that I don't smash them in the face!' His Christian faith affects his thinking about everything, and there is no doubt that his greatest ambition is to express the values of Jesus in all that he does.

It's often said that the clean living that has resulted from his Christian conversion has enabled him to stay younger for longer, by protecting him from traditional show business excesses. It's also probably true to say that his face reflects his personal contentment. He doesn't appear to carry any baggage either of guilt or resentment, and the enthusiasm he exudes comes largely from a sense that he is working out God's purposes in his life.

Certainly his involvement in the Christian world has preserved his innocence by allowing him to remain unaffected by recent social upheavals. Whereas his contemporaries bear the marks of having lived through the decades of revolution in sex, drugs and politics, Cliff still appears to emerge from the Blytonesque world of the fifties, where jolly policemen push their bicycles down country lanes and people still say 'crikey' and 'gosh', while guzzling fizzy drinks.

His single status is a key element of this impression of eternal teenage. It remains important that he is available, that he can still be thought of as someone looking for the right girl.

If he had a wife, two children and a grandchild, his appeal would alter because he would no longer be seen as unshackled and able to give himself totally. In his most popular songs he allows himself to be perceived as lonely and vulnerable, a man still searching for love.

Yet the fantasy he offers remains romantic rather than sexual. He is not Tom Jones or Engelbert Humperdinck coming to offer broad shoulders and a wealth of sexual experience, but a teenager from earlier times who wants nothing more than to hold his girl tightly and tell her that he'll love her for ever. A night with Cliff, every fan knows, will end with a kiss on the doorstep.

As a consequence his followers don't respond to his overtures by throwing hotel keys and underwear on stage as they did for Elvis. The letters that come into the office show that very few of them imagine doing naughty things with him. If they fantasize at all it's about being cared for by him. They see him as someone who, unlike their present partner, would be gentle and understanding.

None of this could have been carried off convincingly if he had looked old and grizzly. The fact that he looks and acts young has become an integral part of his image. 'I wish somehow I could be Peter Pan, the boy who never grew up,' he said in 1960. 'I'm going to stay young for as long as I can.'

Yet despite all his unparalleled achievements it still irks Cliff that he hasn't had the critical accolades he feels he deserves.

That a sizeable proportion of the record-buying public likes what he does is beyond doubt, but he realizes that he has never won the respect of those who will decide his place in rock 'n' roll history and he remains surprisingly sensitive to the way in which his contribution is often dismissed.

For American rock historians he may as well never have existed. The *Rolling Stone Illustrated History of Rock 'n' Roll*, for example, gives him only three passing mentions, none of which evaluates his music.

A typical career summary from a US perspective is given by rock critic Dave Marsh in the *Rolling Stone Record Guide*.

'Before the Beatles, Cliff Richard was England's answer to American rock,' he writes. 'He began as a sort of mini-Elvis, with a back-up group called the Shadows, who included a guitarist, Hank Marvin, an important influence on many British guitarists of the Sixties. But Richard converted to England's variety of fundamentalist Christianity, and whatever spark of spunk had been in his music was snuffed, though he continued to make the British charts throughout the Sixties.'

British critics are frequently as harsh. A review of his CD back catalogue in *Q* magazine concluded, '...these are twenty-four albums of limp-wristed tosh... Maybe he should have quit after "Move it".'

Overlooked in these summaries is the importance of his role in British rock between 1958 and 1962. During this time Cliff and the Shadows were the British rock 'n' roll outfit and together helped to create the climate out of which the beat group phenomenon developed.

With their self-written songs and reliance on British craftsmanship, they sent out the message to Liverpool, London and Newcastle that a home-grown brand of rock 'n' roll was possible.

Cliff did imitate Elvis, but then so did almost everyone else at the time. For most aspiring rockers Elvis *was* rock 'n' roll and so to copy his style, intonation and movements was to follow the maker's instructions.

Cliff was also the first British singer to create scenes of mass hysteria – public expressions of teenage delight which were to climax in Beatlemania.

Also overlooked is his mastery of the pop ballad. His inclusion of slower, softer material is often dismissed as a betrayal of the promise put forward in 'Move It', whereas the Beatles' recordings of 'Yesterday' and 'Hey Jude' were greeted as being artistically adventurous departures which proved that rock 'n' roll had an expanding vocabulary.

Undoubtably the decade following Cliff's Christian conversion damaged his reputation because it seemed devoid of passion and innovation. For a while it looked as though he had settled for being an exalted end-of-the-pier entertainer providing something for everyone. That altered in 1976 when his renaissance began.

Today he is more inspirational than he is influential. There are no mini-Cliffs trailing behind him ready to take his crown, but he remains a tremendous inspiration because of his professionalism, his consistency as a hit-maker and the weight of his history.

Artists as far apart on the musical spectrum as Van Morrison and Kylie Minogue's former songwriter/producer Pete Waterman have respect for someone who has stayed on top for so long by following his tastes and his instincts.

Yet while Cliff may not be an idol for teenage musicians today, he has become a role model for many Christians. It's not that they want to emulate his lifestyle, but he has become the most visible 'layman' in the country and probably the best public example of someone struggling to integrate the traditional Christian faith with work.

His books, talks, videos and gospel albums have been

instrumental in bringing thousands of people to the Christian faith. Band members and record company executives have also been affected in the same way.

At a time when church leaders have become notably mealy mouthed when explaining the nature of the faith they are supposedly defending, Cliff has triumphed as an articulate spokesman who people respect, even when they disagree, because they know that his beliefs have been tested in the real world.

During his 'Access All Areas' tour he spoke about his first hero, Elvis Presley, and then he talked about the hero of all heroes, Jesus Christ. The tough task that Cliff has set himself has been to be a disciple of Jesus in an industry that was given its modern kick-start by Elvis.

On the wall of his poolside bar in Weybridge he has a framed stained-glass plaque. It hangs to the left of his AMI Continental juke box which is stacked with his favourite singles from the fifties. The plaque's prominent position suggests that its message has become something of a motto for him. It's easy to imagine him offering it up if ever asked what he would like his epitaph to be.

'Rock 'n' roll and God work together,' it reads, 'in the hands of someone who loves them both.'

POSTSCRIPT

Cliff read the manuscript for this book some months before it was first published in hardback. Although he had no creative control over the project, I wanted to be sure that I had the facts right.

He's not a voracious reader and not much interested in accounts of his own life, but he read a chapter of this biography each night before going to sleep. The first report I heard was that he was enjoying it. The particularly heartening news was that he considered it 'a good read'.

Biographers of living persons have ambiguous feelings about the response of their subjects to what they have written. If there is too much delight it could be because flaws have been overlooked. On the other hand, if there's too much rancour it could be because the biographer has over-emphasized weakness.

Cliff didn't disappoint me with his reactions when he finally 'phoned me up. He was enthusiastic, but had the natural reservations of a private person seeing his life unfolded before the public. He appreciated the depth of research – much of it uncovering things he either didn't know about or had long forgotten – but prickled at some comments made by former colleagues.

He felt his father had been portrayed a little too severely, that some of those who had worked with him were claiming too much glory for their roles in his success, and that he, at times, appeared weaker than he knew himself to be.

To his credit, he never even suggested that I should alter my findings to please him. I though that this in itself proved his enormous strength of character. All he suggested I might like to change were a few factual errors relating to dates, chart positions and musicians involved in sessions.

The parts I thought he might protest about – the digging up of old romances – he didn't mention, although he later told the Irish Times *that his one criticism of the book was that 'too much attention is paid to things that happened to me years ago, in one case thirty-two years ago'.*

The quote he graciously gave me for use in the book's publicity campaign was revealing in what it implied about these events. 'This book has been a learning experience!' he wrote. 'I found out more about my family tree, for instance, than ever I knew before and it revived memories I had long since buried. Even though I found it a good read, it's never easy to accept criticism about oneself or one's family. But then maybe that's what decent biographies are about.'

Six months after publication I asked him what he now thought. We both knew that he'd always resisted a detailed independent biography, and that I'd only finally succeeded in writing one because I'd made the point that if I didn't do it now then someone else would.

'Anything that deals with personal things makes me feel uncomfortable,' he admitted. 'I wouldn't like to have another book done – not immediately anyway! The most difficult thing is reading other people's opinions about you. Most people don't actually confront you with them.'

I wanted to know how he had reacted to the comments of those who had concluded that the mystery of his sexuality was explained by a low sex drive. Did it bother him to read people saying this? 'No,' he said, 'because it's all speculation.' This was a perfect Cliff answer, which displayed unflappability while neither confirming nor denying the observation.

Adding to the confusion over this issue was the fact that Carol Costa, his only sexual partner, had contacted me after publication of the book to say that Cliff had not been the poor innocent seduced by a married woman, as some had suggested. He was a more than willing partner. Was she right to claim that she hadn't been his seductress? 'I don't think she was [a seductress],' he agreed.

The most recent speculation had been over his romance with Una Stubbs. I had described it as a 'flirtation' in the book. The newspapers, almost thirty years after the event, had turned it into an 'affair', implying that 'nice boy Cliff' had been guilty of more than he's previously admitted.

'It was a flirtation,' he confirmed. 'My memory of it was that it was a sweet little time. She was having an unhappy marriage and we did a lot of holding hands. And that was it really. I did a lot of comforting. But it wasn't an "affair". We didn't go to bed together.'

Cliff is always referred to as 'born-again Christian Cliff', even when what is described happened long before his conversion.

'The thing is, I wasn't even known as a Christian in those days,' he pointed out in connection with the Una Stubbs story. 'I've been telling the press for years that I know I've changed because I know what I was like in those days.'

He finds it hard to comprehend the press's apparently insatiable appetite for personal details of this kind. I suggested it was because he remains a mystery. No one seems able to believe that what they see is what they get. People are searching for clues which they hope will resolve the mystery.

'But everyone is a mystery to everyone else,' he argued. 'I don't know anything about you, but it doesn't change anything. It's not as though I need to know. Everyone I know is a mystery to me really. You only know what they want you to know about them, and they'll never have the kind of speculation that I have as a public figure.'

Could it be that Cliff is genuinely unaware of the power of the enigmatic? This air of mystery, of which speculation is a vital component, has worked well for him. It's kept him front-page news in Britain for forty years, despite a lifestyle not given to colourful excess or nail-biting unpredictability.

'Most people don't spend their lives trying to figure me out,' he said. 'The biography brings it up or an article brings it up, but in between times nobody is bothered by me as an enigma or whether I'm a mystery or not. I either make good records and do good concerts, or I don't.'

My point is that pop stars do not live by good records alone. They need star quality. There has to be something unresolved into which the public invests its imagination.

Cliff didn't think so, and cited the example of the black American singer Morana King, whom he rated highly in the sixties, but who snubbed him when he met her in America.

'She was horrible to me. She turned her back on me and told someone else to answer my questions about her. But it didn't change my opinion.

'So I think we are what we are as people, but what we are as artists is almost something else. No one needs to know anything about me other than whether they like my music, and whether I make them feel good at a concert or whether I can act or dance or sing.'

Yet people will always want to know more. If they like what they see on stage and hear on record, they assume they will like what goes on backstage and behind the curtains at home. The performance has whetted rather than sated the appetite.

The biographer's task is to supply answers to the question, 'What's he or she really like?' The performer's task is to decide just how much of themselves they can afford to let go. If you distribute too much of yourself to too many people, you can be left with a void at the centre of your life.

'Everyone needs privacy,' Cliff said. 'If you had to live under public scrutiny the whole of the time it would be horrific. Psychologically we need things that are ours alone. We need our own space.'

Cliff has managed better than most to give to his public and also to hold back an inviolable private life. I respect him for that as I know he respects those of us who take it upon ourselves to find out where that dividing line is.

Appendix Contents

Questions about Cliff (1959)

Questions that members have asked.

Question.. "Does Cliff take sugar in his tea?"
Answer .. "Yes, and plenty of it too."
Question.. "When does 'Oh Boy' finish?"
Answer .. "On May 30th. and the show should include the one and only yes, Cliff but nothing is confirmed."
Question.. "Has Cliff got a girl-friend?"
Answer .. "No!"
Question.. "Does Cliff go out with Cherry Wainer?"
Answer .. "No, but sometimes she takes him to one of his shows in her car, or sometimes she is included in the cast that go out to dinner from 'Oh Boy'.They are just good friends."
Question.. "Can we write to Donella?"
Answer .. "Well as you know Donella is a very busy person keeping house for Cliff, Bruce and Hank (who also live at the flat) and she just doesn't get the time.
Question.. "Can we write to Cliff and will he answer?"
Answer .. "You can write to Cliff c/o this address, but please don't expect an answer. He is very busy at the moment trying to visit all your home towns that he doesn't even have time to write to his parents."
Question.. "Is Cliff a Catholic?"
Answer .. "No, but he does wear a cross and chain for luck. One that was sent to him by a fan."
Question.. "How many pairs of pink sox has Cliff got?"
Answer .. "About two dozen pairs, but new pairs are being added to the collection each day so it has probably risen to about four dozen pairs.(It was about 24 last month)"
Question.. One fan wrote this-"Does Cliff wear a vest?"
Answer .. "Don't really know, never looked!"
Question.. "If we send our photographs and autograph books in will Cliff sign them for us?"
Answer .. "Yes you can but if Cliff is away on tour it takes a good while to get them done."

JAN.

Questions to Cliff (1994)

It's difficult to ask Cliff anything he hasn't been asked before. Steve Turner fired a volley of one-liners at him in the hope of uncovering something new.

Which famous person have you been most excited at meeting?
I think it was Billy Graham. I was more nervous about meeting him than anyone else.

At what moment in your life were you most in love?
They've all felt the same to me. Each time it's happened I've thought, 'This is it'.

When were you most depressed about your career?
I've never been depressed about my career. There were times just before we kicked off again in the mid-seventies when I wondered what was happening, but I wasn't depressed. Things weren't going badly. It was just that I didn't quite know where to go. I was torn between straight acting and getting back to music. I wasn't sure if I was being any good at either of them.

What has been your most frightening moment?
I suppose it was in a plane when we flew over Nashville and the pilot circled the airport twice and we realized something was wrong. He then said that the light hadn't come on to tell him that his wheels were in position. We had to land with fire engines racing down the runway beside us. Fortunately the wheels had come down all right. It was the bulb that had broken! I prayed a lot.

What has hurt you most?
All the sexual speculation is very painful for me. It's hurtful that of all the things I do in life, so much is aimed at the sexual side of things. That area hurts a lot.

What is your favourite city?
I have a great soft spot for Lisbon in Portugal. I had a fantastic holiday there with a whole load of students one year. I enjoyed the place so much.

What do you carry in your wallet?
Some money, although not a great deal. I carry credit cards, a driver's licence and a credit card sized calculator.

What book have you enjoyed most recently?
Recently? Probably a Stephen King book.

What's the worst thing about getting older?
I suppose physically at the moment I don't notice much. I'm still fairly active. But obviously on the tennis court if I'm playing someone much younger, I'm aware that I am slower than I ever was.

What is the best thing about getting older?
Having the head you've got. I love knowing all that I know. I spoke at some churches the other day in Essex, and I was talking about age and I said that the one thing youth has is energy, but what it doesn't have, and can never have, is wisdom. You have to get older to have wisdom. I feel that as you get older you gather wisdom — so although I'm not as wise as many people I've nevertheless collected a certain amount of stuff that could be called wisdom. Certainly I'm wise enough for me and my life.

Can you remember when you first looked in the mirror and thought that you were no longer young?
That hasn't happened to me yet!

Do you have any repeated dreams?
Only one where I fly. I first remember having it as a child. There used to be a conker tree at the bottom of our close and we'd run along and jump and throw sticks into it to get conkers down. In the dream I did that and I found I flew. The more I flapped my arms the higher I flew. That has happened on and off quite a lot. I like it — it's a nice dream.

Do you ever dream of old girlfriends?
No, never.

When did you last travel on an underground train?
I think I've only ever done it once. It was in 1958 from Oxford Circus to St John's Wood.

How much is a loaf of sliced bread?
I've no idea.

A pint of milk?
Don't know.

The *Daily Mail*?
I don't know.

A first-class stamp?
Twenty-one pence?

What photos do you have in your bedroom?
I've got a photo of me holding a Bangaladeshi child whose finger Bill Latham had trodden on while we were both out there. It screamed and I picked it up. Then I've got a picture of my mum and a painting.

Are you getting better at tennis?
I am improving, but it's a slow process at my age.

When did you last check your bank account?
I don't check my bank account. My accountant tells me when I've overspent.

Who was the last pop star to shock you?
I don't think I've ever been shocked by any of them. They don't shock me at all. I find the things they call shocking are not really shocking. Is Madonna shocking? She doesn't shock me.

Which current actress is your ideal type?
Michelle Pfeiffer is pretty cool. And Kim Basinger.

Do you have one childhood memento that you cherish?
No, I don't actually.

If your house burned down while you were away on tour, which possession would you most miss?
I'd probably miss my Nintendo machine. Assuming that the dogs got out that is.

When is the last time you chatted up a girl, and what is your most successful line?
Do you know, I don't think I've ever chatted up a girl. Chatting up suggests going out of your way to pick a friendship up. It's always happened very naturally for me, so I haven't got a best line.

Where will you retire?
I don't think I'd like to retire away from Britain, but I wouldn't mind having a second home which is probably what I will have with my latest house in Portugal.

How did the rumour that you wear a colostomy bag begin?
I don't know. We think that some medical person somewhere who has had to deal with someone who was worried about having to wear one of these things has said, 'Well, famous people do have them — Cliff Richard's got one.' I suppose it's brought comfort to somebody. Funny thing is, I play tennis in all this clobber and they all see me wearing swimming trunks and it still doesn't kill the story!

Where are they now?

Malcolm Addey engineered most of Cliff's sessions until 1968 when he left EMI Abbey Road. He now lives in New York where he runs a production company and produces classical and jazz albums.

Sue Barker, 41, retired from professional tennis in 1984 and four years later she married Detective-Sergeant Lance Tankard. She lives in Walton-on-Thames, Surrey, and is a presenter for BBC TV's sports programmes.

Lionel Bart, 67, went on to write the musicals *Fings Ain't Wot They Used T'be*, *Oliver!*, *Blitz!* and *Maggie May*. *Oliver!* was recently revived in London.

Brian Bennett, 58, lives in Hertfordshire with his wife Margaret (whom he met at the 2 I's in 1957) and they have three children. When not involved in being a Shadow he concentrates on recording music for film and television. He has written theme or background music for the television series 'The Ruth Rendell Mysteries', 'Dallas' and 'Knots Landing' and the films *The American Way* and *Terminal Choice*. He has recorded several albums under his own name.

Roy Bennett, 80, with his partner Sid Tepper, wrote forty-three songs for Elvis Presley. He is now retired and lives in Flushing, New York.

Janice Berry, 57, married her husband Mike in 1962 and they have had three children – two daughters and a son. Cliff is godfather to the youngest daughter. Janice taught children with physical disabilities at a school in Stevenage until retiring last year.

Derek Bodkin, 56, remarried after divorcing Cliff's mother, and had a daughter. He has since divorced for the second time, and now works for the Post Office.

Franklyn Boyd, 70, moved to Canada with his wife Daphne. He is retired and lives outside Toronto.

Vincent Bridgwater settled in south-east London in the fifties and worked for the Post Office. He died in 1992 at the age of 79.

Terry Britten began writing for the American market and is currently teamed up with Graham Lyle, once part of the duo Gallagher & Lyle. They wrote 'What's Love Got to Do With It?', a top ten hit for Tina Turner in 1984, and 'Just Good Friends', a track on Michael Jackson's 1987 album *Bad*. He lives and works near Richmond in Surrey.

Roger Bruce, 52, was company manager for *Time* and left the theatre after working on *Journey's End* with Jason Connery. He has been Cliff's personal assistant since 1988.

David Bryce, 65, is Cliff's professional and recording manager.

Tito Burns, 75, is now almost retired after a long career in show business as performer, agent and manager. He represents French singer Sasha Distel in every territory but France and pianist Victor Borge in every territory but America and Canada. He lives in St John's Wood with his wife, Terry.

Mel Bush, 55, has been promoting concerts since 1960, working with such acts as the Eagles, Queen, The Beach Boys and Paul McCartney.

Pete Bush, 57, was a roadie for Adam Faith's group the Roulettes in the early sixties. He married in 1968 and has three children. He still lives near Cheshunt and runs his own business making window blinds.

Stu Calver, 51, suffers from cystic fibrosis and has been unable to work since 1986. He lives with his wife by the sea in Devon.

Ron Cass, 75, has composed for television, film and stage as well as writing the novels *True Blue* and *Fringe Benefits*. He was musical director for the religious TV Programme 'Highway' and lives in North London.

Tony Clark, 52, began as a tape operator at Abbey Road in 1964 and went on to engineer several of Cliff's albums as well as those of the Beatles. He left EMI in 1986 to become technical supervisor at the British Record Industry Trust Performing Arts and Technology School (better known as BRITS).

Betty Clarke, 57, married in 1961 (to a boy she met at Trinity Youth Club) and has two grown-up children. She is a typing instructor in Enfield and lives in Goff's Oak near Cheshunt.

Frank Clarke, 74, played bass on Abbey Road sessions including one for the Beatles' single 'Penny Lane', and many more for Cliff. He retired in 1989 and lives near Cambridge.

Joyce Clarkson, 83, is the last surviving member of Frederick William Webb's children. She lives in Cheshunt.

Gerald Coates, 53, is the leader of Pioneer People (the new name for Cobham Christian Fellowship) and an active Christian speaker. He is the author of many books.

Jim Collier made many more films for Worldwide including *The Hiding Place*, *Joni*, *Caught* and *The Prodigal*. He died in 1991, aged 62, after falling from a ledge beside a lake on his mountainside property outside Los Angeles. His last film was *China Cry* which he made for the Trinity Broadcasting Network.

Mike Conlin, 60, worked with Frank Ifield after leaving Cliff around 1964 and then went to Australia to manage Terry Britten's group The Twilights. He left the music business in 1970 and worked in merchant banking until the Big Bang in 1987. He married his wife Mary in 1976, and is now Senior Finance Office for a Family Housing Association in West London.

Jess Conrad, 62, made four singles as a pop singer before concentrating on acting and singing in musicals. He was the original Joseph in *Joseph and the Amazing Technicolour Dreamcoat*, a role which he toured with for ten years, played Jesus in *Godspell* and recently acted in Mike Sarne's film *The Punk*. He now takes part in rock 'n' roll revival shows, works for various charities and is proud to have made what many consider to have been the worst single of all time, 'My Pullover' (in 1961).

Russ Conway, 72, had his last top thirty hit in 1962. He continued to play but was then forced into early retirement after a nervous breakdown. In 1989 he was diagnosed as having cancer and began to perform to raise money for charities, in particular his own fund which helps cancer patients.

Brian Cooke, 57, became a trainee draughtsman on leaving school and is now managing director of his own company, C.D.K. Electronics, which specializes in refrigeration for supermarkets. He got married in 1970, lives in Cheshire and has two children.

David Cooke, 45, is married to former 'Blue Peter' presenter Tina Heath and they have two daughters. He works as a composer and arranger.

Carol Costa, 56, divorced from Jet Harris and went on to have three children with musician Rod Slade from whom she has since separated. She now has four grandchildren and lives in London where she works as a fruit buyer.

John Davey, 59, went on to become headteacher of St Brandon's School near Bristol and is now examinations officer for Trinity College of Music in London. He is married with one grown-up daughter.

Olive Dazely, married her first cousin and had two sons. She died in Felixtowe in 1996.

William Edward Dazely died in Birmingham in 1969. He had five sons, one of whom has died. He is survived by his second wife Maizie who is 86.

Dorothy Dickson, Cliff's grandmother, died in Carshalton in 1980 at the age of 77. Her husband, Richard Dickson, died in 1952.

Vincent Dickson, 69, still lives with his wife Ruth in Carshalton.

Graham Disbrey, 60, is head of Art and Design at Chauncy School in Ware, Hertfordshire.

Joyce Dobra, 72, moved to England in 1947. She married Istvan Dobra, a Hungarian refugee who died in 1975. She has two sons and four granddaughters.

Chris Eaton, 38, divides his time between Stourbridge and Nashville. He recorded his own album *The Vision* in 1986 and has since been writing for American artists such as Russ Taff, Michael W. Smith and Amy Grant.

Stan Edwards, 66, became an entertainer and then joined the Gas Board in East London before retiring in 1992.

Royston Ellis, 56, stayed on in the Canary Islands after arriving for the filming of *Wonderful Life*. He left in 1966 to live in the Caribbean where he wrote a number of best-selling plantation novels under the pen name Richard Tressilian. He now lives in Sri Lanka and works as a travel writer.

Ronnie Ernstone, 60, has worked in the car trade all his life; as a fuel injection engineer, as the owner of a tuning business and now as a prestige car dealer. He lives with his wife in West London.

Adam Faith, 57, retired as a singer in 1967 to become an actor. He worked in repertory and then, in 1971, took the title role in the TV series 'Budgie'. He later returned to the music business as manager for Leo Sayer and producer for Roger Daltry. He appeared in the films *Stardust* and *McVicar* and authors a newspaper column which offers advice on business investments. He starred with Zoë Wanamaker in the popular TV drama 'Love Hurts'. He married Jackie Irving, and has one daughter.

Paul Field, 43, works as a solo artist and has released several albums including *Restless Heart* and *Building Bridges*. He wrote 'All That Matters' for the Diana Tribute album.

Dave Foster, 64, is still international director of Eurovangelism and lives in Switzerland.

John Foster, 59, worked in public relations for Walt Disney in London for twelve years. He then became an agent and now organizes promotional and corporate entertainment from his home in North Yorkshire where he lives with his mother. He has one daughter from a marriage which ended in divorce.

Sidney J. Furie, 65, directed the films *The Ipcress File*, *Lady Sings the Blues* and *Superman 4*.

Billy Fury continued performing and recording until his death in 1983, at the age of 42, of a heart attack.

George Ganjou continued to manage variety acts until 1982. His first wife, Adela, died in 1978 and he married Georgine in 1979. He contracted Parkinson's Disease and died, aged 87, in 1988.

William Gaunt, 61, has acted and directed in most major UK repertory companies, and for two years he was artistic director at the Liverpool Playhouse. He became well known on Television as Arthur Crabtree in 'No Place Like Home' and Richard Barratt in 'The Champions'.

Rita Gillespie, 65, works for a television writer in Los Angeles.

Alan Godson, 65, is vicar of St Mary's, Edgehill, in Liverpool, and is chair of the trustees for Christians in Sport. He is married with two teenage sons.

Jack Good, 66, lives in New Mexico where he spends most of his time painting religious icons. His autobiographical musical *Good Rockin' Tonight*, which featured actors playing the roles of Cliff, Billy Fury, Tommy Steele and others, was launched in 1991. He has a daughter and is divorced from his wife Margit. He converted to Roman Catholicism in 1962.

Nigel Goodwin, 60, travels the world encouraging Christian artists and is supported by the Genesis Trust. He lives on the Isle of Wight with his wife Gillian and has three daughters.

Peter Gormley, 78, now spends his summers in Weybridge and his winters in Sydney, Australia. He is married to Audrey and has a child from a previous marriage.

Peter Graves, 55, is head of the German department at Leicester University. He is married with three young daughters.

Harry Greatorex died in 1989 at the age of 63 after a lifetime spent managing entertainment facilities in Ripley, Derbyshire, including the Rolarena, the Hippodrome Cinema and Sunset Boulevard. He was a great collector of theatrical memorabilia, owning Harry Lauder's walking stick and a pair of George Formby's shoes.

Mark Griffiths, 49, plays with the Shadows whenever they record or tour. He is a member of Plainsong, a group formed by Ian Matthews (formerly of Matthews Southern Comfort), and plays regular sessions with them. He lives in Northampton with his wife and two daughters.

Terry Harness, 59, did two years' National Service in the army before becoming a carpenter. He is now semi-retired and plays vibraphone in a modern jazz group.

Kenneth Harper, 75, married Pamela Hart, one of the dancers who acted in *Summer Holiday*. He went on to direct *The Virgin and the Gypsy* and is still involved in film production.

Jet Harris, 58, has recently married for the fourth time. His latest band is Jet and the Diamonds. His son Ricky, from his marriage to Carol Costa, lives in Weymouth and works as a tiler.

John Harvey, 62, is Professor of Aeronautics at Imperial College in London.

Melvyn Hayes, 63, became a familiar face in the situation comedy series 'It Ain't Half Hot Mum'. He continues to work in theatre and television.

Bob Henrit, 53, was drummer for the Roulettes (1963–67), Unit Four Plus Two

(1967–68) and Argent (1969–76). He currently drums for the Kinks.

George Hoffman was killed in a road accident in October 1992 at the age of 59. He had been director of Tear Fund from 1968 until 1989 and from then until his death was executive chairman of Samaritan International.

Christine Holmes, 47, was once known as Christine Sparkle and worked as a presenter on the children's TV programme 'Crackerjack', with Leslie Crowther. She has also had hit singles as a singer in Canada and Germany. She now lives in Los Angeles and has been writing jingles.

Liz Hutchison, 50, had to leave Bangladesh after falling ill with glandular fever but returned for another year before finally coming back to England and working as a health visitor. She is now married with two sons.

Jackie Irving, 55, went on to become one of Lionel Blair's Dancers before marrying Adam Faith in 1967. They have one daughter.

Paul Jones, 56, is an actor, singer and broadcaster. He plays with the Blues Band, has a blues and gospel programmes on Jazz FM and BBC Radio 2, acts in the children's television series 'Uncle Jack' and is married to actress Fiona Hendley.

Herb and Hal Kalin, 64, live near Washington DC. They both got married at the end of the sixties and went to Maryland University. Herb became a probation officer and Hal worked for the criminal justice courts. Hal retired in January and Herb in June 1992. They now plan to sing together again.

Cindy Kent, 52, became a broadcaster and consultant in media and communication skills after the break up of the Settlers in 1973. She has a son.

Ron King, 76, retired as Cliff's personal assistant in July 1988. He is now enjoying a prank-free retirement in Orpington, Kent.

Tony King, 55, left Rocket Records and went to work with Mick Jagger in New York as his personal assistant. He is now working for financier Prince Rupert Loewenstein in London.

Gerry Kitchingham, 48, is studio manager and chief recording engineer at R.G. Jones where he has worked since 1966.

Paul Lincoln, 65, went on to manage the fashionable sixties night club the Cromwellian and then in 1973 went to Australia where he dealt in the 'second-hand business'. He returned to England in 1987 and managed Charlie's nightclub in Southampton. He continued wrestling, as 'Doctor Death', until 1977. He is now retired.

Tom Littlewood ended up managing a sandwich bar in Great Windmill Street, not too far from the 2 I's. He died in 1988.

Brian 'Licorice' Locking, 59, has been an unpaid Jehovah's Witness pastor since 1963. For fourteen years he ran his own band in south-east London, playing in pubs and clubs. He now lives near Rhyl in North Wales working as a cleaner in a psychiatric hospital.

Jerry Lordan had seventeen chart entries as a songwriter, including 'A Girl Like You' for Cliff; 'A Place in the Sun', 'Atlantis' and 'Wonderful Land' for the Shadows, and 'Diamonds' and 'Scarlet O'Hara' for Jet Harris and Tony Meehan. Tax problems, a divorce and a breakdown put him out of the music business for ten years. He came back as a manager and producer but died in 1996 at the age of 61.

Glyn MacAulay, 61, was the senior partner of the accountancy firm Neville Russell & Co. He is now retired.

Chas McDevitt, 63, closed the Freight Train Club in 1968. He sang with Shirley Douglas until 1975 when he went solo. The original Chas McDevitt Skittle Group, minus the washboard player who has died, re-form around ten times a year.

Dave Mackay, 54, lives in England and writes music for television. He wrote the theme music for 'Bread' (which earned him an Ivor Novello Award), 'Making Out' and 'Auf Wiedersehen Pet'. He has also written an opera, *Pans*, which was voted Best Cast Album by a panel of critics in Australia.

Ray Mackender succcessfully managed Mark Wynter in the sixties. He moved to Canada in 1973 as a freelance tour guide, a job that entailed frequent world travel. He died in 1997 of an AIDS-related illness. He was 64.

Wolf Mankowitz, 73, has written musicals, plays, novels, screenplays, short stories, poems and histories. He was a Professor of English at the University of New Mexico 1982–86 and Professor of Theatre 1987–88. He lives in County Cork, Ireland.

Bill Martin went on to write all the Bay City Rollers' hits with Phil Coulter, 'Surround Yourself with Sorrow' for Cilla Black and 'Fancy Pants' for Kenny. The partnership ended in 1982 after sixteen years. He is now a music publisher.

Hank Marvin, 56, lives in Perth, Western Australia, with his second wife, Carol, who he met in 1968. He became a Jehovah's Witness in 1973.

Tony Meehan, 55, had several hits with Jet Harris before becoming an A & R man at Decca Records. He went on to become a prominent producer and musician, working with the likes of Eric Clapton and Paul McCartney, before becoming involved in leisure industry projects in Australia. He is married to Sue and they have two children. He also has five children from his first marriage.

Norman Miller, 55, manages gospel musicians in America. He is divorced from Sheila Walsh and has remarried.

Norman Mitham, 57, joined Mark Four on leaving the Drifters and now works as a sales rep for United Biscuits. He married in 1964 and has two children.

Mickie Most, 58, moved to South Africa in 1958 and became a big pop star by covering US rock 'n' roll hits. He moved back to England and became a producer. In 1970 he formed RAK Records. After the record company closed in 1986, Most concentrated on his recording studios and music publishing. He lives in Totteridge, London with his wife and they have three children.

Olivia Newton-John, 49, had a string of hits in America and starred in the films *Grease* and *Xanadu*. She married dancer Matt Lattanzi and they had one child.

Larry Norman, 51, has persisted as a solo artist, touring the world and now selling most of his records through mail order. His most recent album is *Stranded in Babylon*.

Jay Norris, 72, took early retirement from teaching in 1982 and now lives in York from where she still works as a drama examiner for the University of London. She is the author of *Drama Resources Cards* and co-author , with Giles Bird, of *Worlds of English and Drama*, *Dead on Time* and *In On the Act*. Her husband died in 1992 and she has two grown-up sons.

Norrie Paramor left EMI in 1968 and set up three companies of his own, although he continued to produce Cliff. In 1973 he moved to Birmingham to be principal conductor of the Midland Radio Orchestra. He died in September 1979 at the age of 65.

Brian Parker, 57, played with the Parker Royal Four and Unit Four Plus Two. He left the music business and went into computers where he stayed for twenty-six years. He's now back 'playing keyboards and guitars and absolutely loving it'.

Larry Parnes stopped managing rock 'n' roll singers in 1965 and returned to his initial interests of clothing and theatre. He died in 1989 at the age of 59.

David Pawson, 68, has been travelling the world speaking at seminars for church leaders since he left the Millmead Centre, Guildford, in 1979.

Lauri Peters, 55, left films to study classical theatre. After working as a stage actor she became a journalist, a photographer and a novelist. Then, in 1988, she took a job teaching drama in New York. She is divorced from John Voight.

Craig Pruess, 46, lives in Skelmersdale and has built his own studio where he writes music for television. He worked on *Hear My Song*, the drama about Joseph Locke, and *Assassin of the Tsar* which starred Malcolm McDowell. He has also recorded his own album, *The Eye of Jupiter*, and lectures regularly on Indian classical music. He is married with two children.

Andrew Ray, 57, continues to work in theatre, television and film. His television credits include 'Crown Matrimonial', 'Edward and Mrs Simpson', 'Tales of the Unexpected' and 'Vandervalk'.

B.A. Robertson, 47, has written lyrics for Mike and the Mechanics' songs, including the hit 'The Living Years'. He lives in Los Angeles and has been working on projects for the Disney Organization.

Herbert Ross, 71, left theatrical choreography to become a film director. Among his films are *Play It Again Sam*, *Funny Lady*, *The Sunshine Boys*, *The Turning Point*, *The Goodbye Girl*, *Pennies from Heaven*, *Flashdance* and *Footloose*.

John Rostill joined Tom Jones' band in 1969 and worked extensively in the US, where he began writing for Olivia Newton-John. He died in England in 1973 having been electrocuted in his studio. He was 31. Three months later Olivia had her first US top ten hit with his song 'Let Me Be There'.

Ian 'Sammy' Samwell, 59, wrote 'Whatcha Gonna Do About It?' for the Small Faces and later became an A & R man for WEA records in London. For the past twelve years he has lived in Sacramento, California, where he helps develop local artists. He has two sons, Ralph and Tyson. In 1991, after suffering a viral infection of the heart, he underwent a successful heart transplant operation.

Ernie Shear, 70, worked on many more sessions for Cliff and is still playing guitar. For the past thirty-four years he has been a member of the Jack Emblow Quartet which can be heard on the radio programme 'Sing Something Simple'.

Frances 'Frankie' Slade, 57, works as a painter and lives with her husband in Brighton.

Terry Smart, 56, joined the Merchant Navy in 1959 and is still serving. He lives in Harwich with his wife Cindy.

David Soames, 50, wrote the play *Teething Troubles*, the musical *Big Apple* and, with Jeff Daniels, the musical *Marriage, An Endangered Species*.

Trevor Spencer, 50, lives in Perth, Western Australia. He runs the music production company Sh-Boom! with Gary Taylor, former of the Herd.

Maggie Streader, 58, became a member of the backing vocal group the Ladybirds in

1961, and went on to work with everyone from Bing Crosby to the Beatles. She is now involved in booking singers for recording sessions and performing with a re-formed Vernon's Girls.

Una Stubbs, 61, joined the Young Vic in 1970 and has become a nationally known stage actress. On television she has been in 'Till Death Us Do Part' and 'Worzel Gummidge', as well as being a regular guest on 'Give us a Clue'. She has been married twice, first to Peter Gilmore and then to Nicky Henson.

Alan Tarney, 52, has written for Leo Sayer and Barbara Dickson and has produced Voice of the Beehive and the Moody Blues. He produced Cliff on 'All That Matters' for the Diana Tribute album.

Dick Teague, 62, is an accountant living in Lincolnshire. Mick Teague is 57. Walter Teague died in June 1993, aged 91. Mrs Teague lives near her daughter Sheila.

Sid Tepper, 80, is retired and lives in Miami Beach, Florida (see **Roy Bennett**).

Graham Todd composed eight albums of library music (one recorded by the Royal Philharmonic Orchestra) and was involved in the orchestration and production of soundtrack music for American television specials such as 'Voice of the Heart' and 'To Be The Best'. He died in 1995 at the age of 52.

Dave Townsend, 46, has his own antique furniture restoration business. He only ever had two other songs covered, 'Far Side of the Bay' by Elaine Paige, and 'That's When My Loving Begins' by Jimmy Ruffin. He has started writing again.

Tulah Tuke, 65, worked as a make-up artist for the BBC in London and Glasgow before going freelance in 1980. She is also a portrait painter.

Jan Vane, 56, married in 1961 and had her first child in 1962. She now has three children, is divorced and works for an agency which supplies temporary reps.

John Vince, 57, worked in a bank after leaving school before joining the electronics industry. In 1966 he started lecturing on computers at Enfield College of Technology and now he is a research consultant for Rediffusion. He has written books on the application of computer technology to areas of design. He is married with two teenage children and lives in Sussex.

Cherry Wainer, 66, lives in Las Vegas where she is fashion director for the Mirage and Golden Nugget hotel-casinos. On 12 June 1992 she married drummer Don Storer with whom she arrived in England in 1957.

Sheila Walsh became a popular chat show host on the CBN Network before moving to California to attend Fuller Theological Seminary. She is remarried and lives in Nashville.

Diana Ward, 57, became a dancer and contortionist. She lives in Eastbourne.

Donna Webb, 55, lives in Ware, Hertfordshire, with her husband Terry Goulden and her two adopted children Ty and Emma. She had two previous marriages – to Paul Stevens and Tim Brandon.

Dorothy Marie Webb, 77, has a 'granny house' connected to her daughter Joan's property. She is now divorced, but still goes under the name of Bodkin.

Jacqui Webb, 50, lives in Norfolk with her husband Peter Harrison. She has five children, the youngest of whom is four, and became a grandmother in 1992 with the birth of Joseph, the first child of her eldest son Rodger.

Joan Webb, 47, lives in Broxbourne, Hertfordshire, with her husband David Pilgrim. She had two previous marriages – to Colin Phipps and Peter Archer – and has three children.

Bruce Welch, 56, is involved in music publishing and production as well as being a Shadow. He has been married twice and has one son, Dwayne. He published his autobiography, *Rock 'n' Roll – I Gave You the Best Years Of My Life*, in 1989.

Wally Whyton finished with the Vipers in 1959 and became an accomplished broadcaster. He created such puppet characters as Ollie Beak and Spike McPike for television and presented country music programmes on BBC Radio and the British Forces Broadcasting Service (BFBS) for over twenty years. He also recorded a number of albums under his own name. He died of lung cancer in 1997 at the age of 67.

Delia Wicks, 59, did television advertising in the early sixties for Signal, Quality Street and Martini. She then went on to be part of the 'Black and White Minstrel Show' until she married a builder in 1970 and settled in the Midlands. She is now divorced and lives in a Cotswolds village.

Marty Wilde, 59, married Joyce Baker of the Vernons Girls in December 1959 and daughter Kim was born in 1960. He continued to perform and record but was to make more of an impact as a producer and songwriter, with his son Ricky, when Kim Wilde took up a music career in the eighties.

David Winter, 68, went on to become the BBC's head of religious broadcasting and the author of a number of books. He retired from broadcasting to become a vicar, and now lives in Berkshire.

Peter Yates, 69, went on to make the films *One Way Pendulum*, *Bullitt*, *The Deep* and *The Dresser*.

Muriel Young, 70, who was the first female announcer on commercial television in Britain (1955), now lives in County Durham and paints. Her first exhibition of paintings was in Liberty's of London.

Terence Young, 83, directed the films *Dr No*, *From Russia With Love*, *Thunderball*, *The Valachi Papers* and *Sweet Revenge*.

Memorabilia

90

20/9/57

We, the undersigned (members of Dick Teagues Skiffle group) hereby agree not to leave the group to take an individual engagement with any other musical concern without previously discussing the matter with the full group and its controlling manager.

Signed:—

Dick Teague M. Teague
T. Smart Harry Webb
[illegible] K Dunn
[illegible]

Cliff's first contract

Letter to the manager of the Freight Train coffee bar in Soho

CLIFF RICHARD AND THE DRIFTERS

Telephone: HERtford 3817

51, London Rd.,
Hertford Heath,
Hertford,
Herts.

17th June, 1958

Dear Mr. de Villiers,

Many thanks for giving CLIFF RICHARD AND THE DRIFTERS the opportunity to play at the "Freight Train" last Sunday evening.

Despite the late arrival of your staff they thoroughly enjoyed the evening and were pleased by the most appreciative audience. Unfortunately playing for almost three hours proved rather too strenuous this was, however, compensated by the addition of eight new members to our "Fan" club.

Should you require our services in the future we shall be pleased to hear from you.

Assuring you of our best intentions at all times.

Yours faithfully,

(J. FOSTER)
Manager

THE OFFICIAL CLIFF RICHARD FAN CLUB

30 Southend Road,
Rainham,
ESSEX

Dear Cliff Richard Fans,

I hope you will enjoy this, our first magazine. I have tried to make it as interesting as possible, and Stan Edwards, a personal friend of Cliff's, has contributed two fabulous articles for us.

I would like to hear whether you liked the magazine and if you have any ideas for future editions.

Your friend,

JAN

P.S. Sorry for delay but I was waiting for the theatre leaflets to come through.

May 1959: debut issue of the fan club magazine, edited by Jane Vane

The *Chestnut Weekly Telegraph* reports Cliff's first single

Cover of the sheet music of 'Move It'

Cheshunt boy makes new disc

A 17-year-old Cheshunt youth who has gained swift success since he formed his own rock 'n' roll group earlier this year is expecting one of his recordings to be on the market by the end of August.

The lad with a pleasant voice and a new beat to his guitar is Cliff Richard, otherwise known as Harry Webb, of 12, Hargreaves Close, Cheshunt, who has just been given a long-term contract by Norrie Paramor, of Columbia Records Ltd.

His new disc in the rock 'n' roll sphere is entitled "Schoolboy Crush," a ballad with a beat and a pleasant lyric. On the reverse is "Move It," a rock number that should appeal to all teenagers and jivers.

While a member of Holy Trinity Youth Fellowship, Cliff was the leading member of the club's singing group, the Chorals. Last year he joined the Dick Teague Skiffle Group as a singer, but later decided to start his rock 'n' roll group known as the Drifters.

Since then the Drifters have appeared at dances and shows, both locally and elsewhere.

Cliff was born in Lucknow, India, where his father was employed by a British wine firm. He came to live in Surrey when he was six and later moved with his family to Waltham Cross. He has lived in Cheshunt since 1950.

He was educated at King's Road County Primary School, Waltham Cross, and Cheshunt County Secondary School. For the past year he has been working at the Ferguson Radio Corporation Ltd., Enfield, as a clerk.

PAGE 10 DAILY MIRROR, Thursday July 31, 1958

ON THE RECORD . . . . . by Patrick Doncaster

Cliff Richard . . . a Presley fan.

NEW RECRUIT FOR THE DISC WAR

NEW records are few, because of the holidays. All seems quiet on the Discland front.

But it's just a front . . . Behind the scenes the battle for the autumn—when the big guns open up again—is being planned.

Making a battle-eve sortie into the Columbia camp this week, I spied a new name due to spark off on August 29. . . .

Cliff Richard, a seventeen-year-old dark-haired, dark-eyed singer and guitar twanger from Cheshunt, Herts

He is a Presley-ish type with so much promise that he has been given a big long-term contract by orchestra leader Norrie Paramor.

Norrie is Columbia's guiding light (he looks after — among others — Michael Holliday, The Mudlarks and Eddie Calvert).

"Cliff is a rock 'n' roller," said Norrie.

But isn't the rock on the rocks?

"Not quite," said Norrie, who knows what he is talking about. "I just can't see the kids giving up these personalities with a beat."

HER Verdict

Norrie has great faith in his new find. He took home a test side of the boy to let his daughter Carolyn, nearly fourteen, hear it.

A test side lasts about thirty plays. Carolyn liked it so much—that it is now worn out.

The titles: "Schoolboy Crush" and "Move It."

I think Cliff Richard, born in Lucknow, India, has a personality that shines through the grooves. He could succeed in Discland.

His favourite artist is Presley, his favourite actor is Presley. And his ambitions are (1) to win a gold disc for a million sales and (2) to meet Presley.

Daily Mirror, 31 July 1958 - Cliff's first mention in the national press

'Oh Boy!' souvenir programme

FORTHCOMING EVENTS

Regal Ballroom, Ripley

Saturday— 7.30 until 11 p.m. 4/-
BLUE JOHNS SKIFFLE GROUP
Plus Dancing to Keith Freer's Dixielanders

Sunday— (Club Members Only) 2/6
Club Four Skiffle Group and Top Records

Monday— Club Four Rock Group and Top Records 2/-

Tuesday— MODERN BALLROOM DANCING 2/6
KEITH FREER'S YOUNG MEN OF MUSIC

Wednesday— ROCK 'N' ROLL TO RECORDS 2/-

Thursday— 7.30 until 11 p.m. 3/6
OLD TIME DANCE
M.C.: E. Stanton and The Gaiety Players

Friday— ROCK 'N' ROLL TO RECORDS 2/-

Saturday, 3rd May—
Direct from the famous Soho 2 i's Coffee Bar
Cliff Richard and the DRIFTERS
Plus Keith Freer and His Dixielanders

You are invited to attend a meeting to be held (God willing) at the

CHRISTADELPHIAN HALL
HEATH ROAD
RIPLEY
at 6 p.m. on
SUNDAY, 27th APRIL
1958

When a lecture will be given on
The Return of Christ:
THE ONLY HOPE ... TROUBLED WO...

International
WRESTLIN...

1958: Cliff's first billing as Cliff Richard

... separately. Price parts list 1/9.)
MONEY BACK IF DISSATISFIED.
CONCORD ELECTRONICS
(Dept. SP.1) 69, Preston St., Brighton

Garages, Sheds, Greenhouses of equally good value and on the new attractive EASY TERMS to
SILVER MIST LTD., Dept. SS.5
Reliant Works, Brockham, Betchworth, Surrey.

SHE KNEELS, WALKS, SITS AND SINGS

In a Real Child's Voice
THE NEW IMPROVED
'DARLING' DOLL
SPEAKS LONGEST AND CLEAREST
Unique replaceable "Voice"
10/- DEPOSIT Plus P. & P. 6/6
Plus first payment of 9/6 & 14 weekly payments of 6/9.
CASH 99/6 plus P. & P. 6/6.

28" TALL

She actually says "Mary Had a Little Lamb," etc., "Twinkle, Twinkle Little Star," etc. She Sings. "London Bridge is Falling Down," etc. She Prays "Now I Lay me Down to Sleep," etc. She kneels and prays, sits in chair and pram, curtseys. Beautifully proportioned, lovely face, sleeping eyes, brushable hair. Delightful washable dress, matching panties.

Money back guarantee. Callers welcome.
PETER DARLING LTD. (Dept. S.P.1), 88, Gray's Inn Road, London, W.C.1

Knitters
The Finest Value in Wool
DOUBLE KNITTING $10\frac{1}{2}$ d. oz.
100% pure wool
THERE'S NO BETTER WOOL, CHEAPER!
Send 3d. stamp with name and address for shade cards

14 days FREE Home Trial
NEW PHILISHAVE
Sensational new shaver with luxurious case. Send 5/- deposit—refunded if not satisfied. Bal. of 15/- after trial, and 8 monthly payments 21/6. Dual volt AC/DC. Cash Price £8.15.0

GIANT PATTERN BOOK SENT POST FREE

The *Sunday Pictorial* advertisement that inspired Lionel Bart's writing of 'Living Doll'

ROUGH DRAFT.

Proposed contract between Mr.X. and

CLIFF RICHARD

Through the auspices of MR. GEORGE GANJOU

The following is a proposition to Mr. George Ganjou for CLIFF RICHARD's consideration - 1960:

(1) Period of proposed contract would be for twenty weeks during which he would work fifteen weeks as follows:-

Out of each period of four weeks, two weeks in the Theatre, and one week of six days out of seven days One-Night-Stands. Sundays by arrangement only.

(2) The type of show would be fully produced, and not just a Variety bill. The supporting bill to be approved of by Mr. George Ganjou and Cliff Richard.

(3) First Class publicity man to be provided.

(4) Chauffeur driven car to be provided, at the cost of the promoter.

(5) Accomodation to be booked, in advance, for Cliff Richard and his Party, but to be paid for by Cliff Richard.

(6) SALARY: £1,000 (One thousand pounds) weekly for Variety, and during the week of One-Night-Stands £1,200 (One thousand Two hundred pounds) which will cover any six days out of the seven.

During the week when Cliff Richard is not working he is free to accept any major T.V.show, but the Management would prefer to retain the T.V. rights at an agreed price per T.V.show.

During the week Cliff Richard is not working at all, I am prepared to pay a retaining fee for The Shadows and the Road Manager (not exceeding £150.0.0.).

Mr. .O.Webb would receive weekly the sum of £100.0.0. (One hundred pounds) cash.

(7) If Cliff Richard was to go into the London Palladium before the end of the twenty week period, the number of weeks that he would not have worked would automatically be owed for the 1961 year. This would apply equally in the case of Cliff Richard being required for any major film project in this country or America, as well as any important engagement in United States.

(8) Option for 1961 at specified and mutually agreed terms.

Draft contract for Cliff Richard drawn up by agent George Ganjou

Overseas Service
AEROGRAMME
By Air Mail · Par Avion

MELBOURNE
26 OCT
3 [illegible]
1961
VIC. AUST.

HELP
USE CH

10D
AUSTRALIA

MISS DELLIA WICKS
41, WEST CROMWELL ROAD
EARLS COURT
LONDON
ENGLAND

SECOND FOLD HERE

SENDER'S NAME AND ADDRESS.

C. RICHARD
MELBOURNE
AUSTRALIA

IF ANYTHING IS ENCLOSED OR ANY TAPE OR STICKER ATTACHED, THIS FORM MUST BEAR POSTAGE AT THE RATE FOR AIR MAIL LETTERS.

October 1961: Cliff's letter to Delia Wicks ending their relationship

MELBOURNE
AUSTRALIA.
21st OCTOBER

Dear Dellia,

I know I haven't written for a long time, but I've been so confused in my mind about you & about myself.

I've had to make, probably, one the biggest descisions, I'm ever going to make & I'm praying that I won't hurt you too much.

Dellia, I want you to try and understand the position I'm in. Being a singer I'm going to have

to give up many things in life.
But being a Pop singer I have to give up one very priceless thing — The right to have any lasting relationship with any special girl.
Delilia, you must find someone who is free to love you, as you deserve to be loved, and is able to marry you.
I couldn't give up my carreer, & besides the fact that my mother & sisters, since my fathers death, rely on me completely, I have showbiz in my blood now & I would be lost without

FOLD FLAPS BEFORE MOISTENING ADHESIVE

it.

"D" all I can say now is, goodbye & don't think too badly of me.

Love —

Cliff —

Hippodrome Birmingham

Dear Dave,
We've decided to have the "Red" Fender Guitar
With A. Three pickups.
B. With tremolo lever.
C. Gold plated hardware

The guitar is a "Stratocaster"
Have marked in catalogue.
When you send for it please order spare set balanced strings and also a "Fender Case".
Well Dave thanks a million.
All the Best
Cliff.

1959: Cliff's letter to Dave Lilley organizing the purchase of Hank Marvin's first Fender Stratocaster

1960: Cliff's billing on his first tour of America

POP STARS CLASH ON RELIGION

A CONTROVERSIAL clash between two of our leading pop stars has been recorded in a television programme which will be shown this evening.

In it Paul Jones, the 24-year-old former lead singer with the Manfred Mann group, claims that Cliff Richard is letting himself be exploited by the Church.

The programme, ABC's *Looking For An Answer*, pulls no punches from its opening shots.

It begins with a scene from the film *Privilege*, which stars Paul Jones as a pop star cynically exploited by religion and cuts to a real-life shot of Cliff Richard singing at a Billy Graham rally.

"Is the Church," asks interviewer Robert Kee, "exploiting Cliff Richard, too?"

This is the first of many hard questions for Richard in the programme.

Eight years ago he burst in on the pop scene—sideburned fat-cheeked, his thin husky voice and hip-wriggling raising hysteria among his girl fans.

His values

Two years ago, despite fame, a £30,000 country mansion and a £1,000 a week salary, he discovered a need for spiritual values. Now he appears with bishops at meetings, sings Gospel songs for Billy Graham and wants to teach divinity if he can finish his O levels.

He is single, a non-smoker and never touches spirits.

Jones went to university, and lived till recently in a converted garage in Cricklewood. He is married with two children.

Kee asks Richard if he questioned his own motives when he saw what happened to the pop star in *Privilege*?

"Did it embarrass you the slightest bit seeing that film? No one questions your sincerity as a Christian doing this. But you *are* using the mass you're able to command through your pop singing and bringing them along to a church."

RICHARD: "I put myself in God's hands and say, look, if this is the thing I ought to do I shall do it. The Church is just, I think, a front. You know, it's a name. We are always fooled by words and names and things."

JONES: "Well, one of the bishops in *Privilege* says when he is accused of using the pop singer to further the ends of the Church: 'Once they used a Spanish Inquisition and this is less painful.' You know, it's exactly what you have just said, really."

RICHARD: "Before I came on the scene, you know, Graham packed out places like Earl's Court. He doesn't need me."

JONES: "But people don't know what they're coming for. Billy Graham knows why people go to his meetings is the same reason why people in America spent 125,000,000 dollars in one year going to fortune tellers. They are insecure; they're unsure. They don't know what they're going for.

Just a show

"Right, so you say: 'We are giving them Christ.' Well, I say you're not. You're giving them a show.

"Billy Graham said in the film I've just seen of the Earl's Court thing: 'Let the bombs drop—we have joy inside.'

"You know, this is pie in the sky. This is absolutely ludicrous. If the bombs drop, you've got joy nowhere."

RICHARD: "If you become a Christian you must start immediately thinking peaceable things. Before you can ban the bomb you should know about the rest of mankind. We know that mankind, Biblically, is not going to save the world—we just know it.

"We rely on Christ's strength: so what we do first is to make the world Christian. I mean, this is what counts."

JONES: "Is this what it's all about. Until everybody's on your side. . . . ?"

RICHARD: "No, no, no—again you're using words. If I'm at all convinced, Paul, I've gotta say, 'Look, something happened to me. I've become a Christian. I've accepted a thing called salvation which means if I die I can look forward to an eternal life of peace and joy and no pain; and things like this.'

"If you ask a psychedelic what-not, or the drug-takers what they get out of it, you can treble it and multiply it by a thousand—and that's how I feel all the time."

JONES: "You know, if you ask somebody from any religion—even if his religion is acid—he'll tell you. I mean, the basic answer any religion will give you is it's the final unification of the many with the one. I mean, that's religion, that's Christian religion, and that's LSD."

KEE: "And what's your answer?"

JONES: "I say, let's get on with making the world a nicer place."

● Cliff Richard and Paul Jones argue about the Billy Graham campaign

WESTON TAYLOR'S SHOWPAGE

News World 1967: Cliff and Paul Jones debate religion

David Smith—m.—?

Vitriano Rebeiro—m.—?

George David Smith—m.—Emiline Josephine Rebeiro
(m. Calcutta 1869)

William Bridgwater—m.—Martha Walker

William Haines—m.—?

William Dazely—m.—?

Marie Beatrice Smith—m.—W.B. Bridgwater
(b. 1873/1874) (b. Hampstead 1870)

Daisy Haines—m.—Edward Dazely

Dorothy Edith Bridgwater—m.—William Edward Dazely
(b. 1902) (b. Kirkee 1896)

Dorothy Marie Dazely
(b. Lahore 1920)

Family Trees

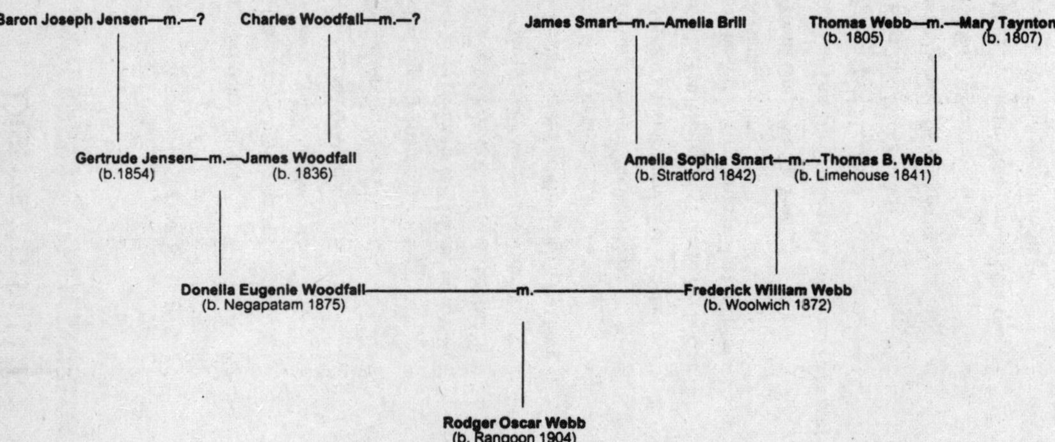

Baron Joseph Jensen—m.—?
Charles Woodfall—m.—?
James Smart—m.—Amelia Brill
Thomas Webb—m.—Mary Taynton
(b. 1805)
(b. 1807)
Gertrude Jensen—m.—James Woodfall
(b.1854)
(b. 1836)
Amelia Sophia Smart—m.—Thomas B. Webb
(b. Stratford 1842)
(b. Limehouse 1841)
Donella Eugenie Woodfall—m.—Frederick William Webb
(b. Negapatam 1875)
(b. Woolwich 1872)
Rodger Oscar Webb
(b. Rangoon 1904)

Discography (UK)

SINGLES

1	Move It/Schoolboy Crush	Aug 1958
2	High Class Baby/My Feet Hit The Ground	Nov 1958
3	Livin' Lovin' Doll/Steady With You	Jan 1959
4	Mean Streak/Never Mind	Apr 1959
5	Living Doll/Apron Strings	Jul 1959
6	Travellin' Light/Dynamite	Oct 1959
7	A Voice in the Wilderness/Don't Be Mad At Me	Jan 1960
8	Fall In Love With You/Willie And The Hand Jive	Mar 1960
9	Please Don't Tease/Where Is My Heart?	Jun 1960
10	Nine Times Out Of Ten/Thinking Of Our Love	Sep 1960
11	I Love You/'D' In Love	Nov 1960
12	Theme For A Dream/Mumblin' Mosie	Feb 1961
13	Gee Whizz It's You/I Cannot Find A True Love	Mar 1961
14	A Girl Like You/Now's The Time To Fall In Love	Jun 1961
15	When The Girl In Your Arms Is The Girl In Your Heart/ Got A Funny Feeling	Oct 1961
16	The Young Ones/We Say Yeah	Jan 1962
17	I'm Looking Out The Window/Do You Want To Dance?	May 1962
18	It'll Be Me/Since I Lost You	Aug 1962
19	The Next Time/Bachelor Boy	Nov 1962
20	Summer Holiday/Dancing Shoes	Feb 1963
21	Lucky Lips/I Wonder	May 1963
22	It's All In The Game/Your Eyes Tell On You	Aug 1963
23	Don't Talk To Him/Say You're Mine	Nov 1963
24	I'm The Lonely One/Watch What You Do With My Baby	Jan 1964

25	Constantly/True True Lovin'	Apr 1964
26	On The Beach/A Matter of Moments	Jun 1964
27	The Twelfth Of Never/I'm Afraid To Go Home	Oct 1964
28	I Could Easily Fall (In Love With You)/I'm In Love With You	Dec 1964
29	The Minute You're Gone/Just Another Guy	Mar 1965
30	Angel/Razzle Dazzle	May 1965
31	On My Word/Just A Little Bit Too Late	Jun 1965
32	The Time In Between/Look Before You Love	Aug 1965
33	Wind Me Up (Let Me Go)/The Night	Oct 1965
34	Blue Turns To Grey/Somebody Loses	Mar 1966
35	Visions/What Would I Do (For The Love Of A Girl)	Jul 1966
36	Time Drags By/The La La La Song	Oct 1966
37	In The Country/Finders Keepers	Dec 1966
38	It's All Over/Why Wasn't I Born Rich?	Mar 1967
39	I'll Come Running/I Got The Feelin'	Jun 1967
40	The Day I Met Marie/Our Story Book	Aug 1967
41	All My Love/Sweet Little Jesus Boy	Nov 1967
42	Congratulations/High 'n' Dry	Mar 1968
43	I'll Love You Forever Today/Girl, You'll Be A Woman Soon	Jun 1968
44	Marianne/Mr Nice	Sep 1968
45	Don't Forget To Catch Me/What's More (I Don't Need Her)	Nov 1968
46	Good Times (Better Times)/Occasional Rain	Feb 1969
47	Big Ship/She's Leaving You	May 1969
48	Throw Down A Line (Cliff & Hank)/Reflections	Sep 1969
49	With The Eyes Of A Child/So Long	Nov 1969
50	The Joy Of Living (Cliff & Hank)/Leave My Woman Alone/ Boogitoo (Cliff & Hank)	Feb 1970
51	Goodbye Sam, Hello Samantha/You Can Never Tell	Jun 1970
52	I Ain't Got Time Anymore/Monday Comes Too Soon	Aug 1970
53	Sunny Honey Girl/Don't Move Away (with Olivia Newton-John)/ I Was Only Fooling Myself	Jan 1971
54	Silvery Rain/Annabella Umbrella/Time Flies	Apr 1971

55	Flying Machine/Pigeon	Jul 1971
56	Sing A Song Of Freedom/A Thousand Conversations	Nov 1971
57	Jesus/Mr Cloud	Mar 1972
58	Living In Harmony/Empty Chairs	Aug 1972
59	A Brand New Song/The Old Accordian	Dec 1972
60	Power To All Our Friends/Come Back Billie Jo	Mar 1973
61	Help It Along/Tomorrow Rising/Days Of Love/Ashes To Ashes	May 1973
62	Take Me High/Celestial Houses	Nov 1973
63	(You Keep Me) Hangin' On/Love Is Here	May 1974
64	It's Only Me You've Left Behind/You're The One	Mar 1975
65	(There's A) Honky Tonk Angel (Who Will Take Me Back In)/ Wouldn't You Know It (Got Myself A Girl)	Sep 1975
66	Miss You Nights/Love Is Enough	Feb 1976
67	Devil Woman/Love On	May 1976
68	I Can't Ask For Anything More Than You, Babe/Junior Cowboy	Aug 1976
69	Hey, Mr Dream Maker/No One Waits	Nov 1976
70	My Kinda Life/Nothing Left For Me To Say	Feb 1977
71	When Two Worlds Drift Apart/That's Why I Love You	Jun 1977
72	Yes! He Lives/Good On The Sally Army	Jan 1978
73	Please Remember Me/Please Don't Tease	Jul 1978
74	Can't Take The Hurt Anymore/Needing A Friend	Nov 1978
75	Green Light/Imagine Love	Mar 1979
76	We Don't Talk Anymore/Count Me Out	Jul 1979
77	Hot Shot/Walking In The Light	Nov 1979
78	Carrie/Moving In	Feb 1980
79	Dreamin'/Dynamite	Aug 1980
80	A Little In Love/Keep On Looking	Jan 1981
81	Wired For Sound/Hold On	Aug 1981
82	Daddy's Home/Shakin' All Over	Nov 1981
83	The Only Way Out/Under The Influence	Jul 1982
84	Where Do We Go From Here?/Discovering	Sep 1982

85	Little Town/Love and a Helping Hand/You, Me and Jesus	Nov 1982
86	True Love Ways/Galadriel (both with London Symphony Orchestra)	Apr 1983
87	Never Say Die (Give a Little Bit More)/Lucille	Aug 1983
88	Please Don't Fall in Love/Too Close to Heaven	Nov 1983
89	Baby You're Dynamite/Ocean Deep	Mar 1984
90	Shooting From The Heart/Small World	Oct 1984
91	Heart User/I Will Follow You	Jan 1985
92	She's So Beautiful/She's So Beautiful (inst)	Sep 1985
93	It's In Every One of Us/Alone (inst)	Nov 1985
94	Born To Rock 'n' Roll/Law of the Universe (inst)	May 1986
95	My Pretty One/Love Ya	Jun 1987
96	Some People/One Time Lover Man	Aug 1987
97	Remember Me/Another Christmas Day	Oct 1987
98	Two Hearts/Yesterday, Today, Forever	Feb 1988
99	Mistletoe and Wine/Marmaduke	Nov 1988
100	The Best of Me/Move It	May 1989
101	I Just Don't Have the Heart/Wide Open Space	Aug 1989
102	Lean On You/Hey Mister	Oct 1989
103	Stronger Than That/Joanna	Feb 1990
104	Silhouettes/The Winner	Aug 1990
105	From a Distance/Lindsay Jane II	Oct 1990
106	Saviour's Day/Oh Boy Medley	Nov 1990
107	More To Life/Mo's Theme	Sep 1991
108	We Should Be Together/Miss You Nights (live)	Nov 1991
109	This New Year/Scarlet Ribbons	Dec 1991
110	I Still Believe in You/Bulange Downpour	Nov 1992
111	Peace In Our Time/Somebody Loves You	Mar 1993
112	Human Work of Art/Ragged	Jun 1993
113	Never Let Go/Congratulations	Sep 1993
114	Healing Love/Yesterday's Dreams/Carrie	Dec 1993

115	Miss You Nights/All I Have To Do Is Dream (with Phil Everly)	Nov 1994
116	Misunderstood Man	Oct 1995
117	Had To Be	Nov 1995
118	The Wedding	Mar 1996
119	Be With Me Always	Jan 1997

M

N

O

P

T

U

V

W

Y

Picture acknowledgments

Every effort has been made to trace the copyright holders of the photographs in this book, but one or two were unreachable. We would be grateful if the photographers concerned would contact us.

SECTION 1

page 1: Vincent Bridgwater
page 2: (top & middle) Joyce Dobra; (bottom) Vincent Bridgwater
page 3: Joyce Dobra
page 4: (top) Dorothy Willis; (middle) Joyce Dobra; (bottom) *Waltham and Cheshunt Weekly Telegraph*
page 5: (top) John Vince; (middle & bottom) Jay Norris
page 6: Jan Goring
page 7: Jan Goring
page 8: (top) Terry Smart

SECTION 2

page 9: (top) Franklyn Boyd; (bottom) Ian Samwell
page 10: (middle) Popperfoto; (bottom) Royston Ellis
page 11: (top) Ray Mackender; (bottom) Hulton Deutsch Collection
page 12: (top) Rex Features; (bottom three) Ron Ernstone
page 13: (top three) Ron Ernstone; (middle), Topham Picture Library; (bottom) Ray Mackender
page 14: David H. Hawley
page 15: (top left & right) Ian Samwell; (middle) Rex Features; (bottom) EMI Records
page 16: (top) Delia Wicks; (bottom) Topham Picture Library

SECTION 3

page 17: (top) Popperfoto; (middle) Topham Picture Library; (bottom) Rex Features
page 18: (top) Daily Express; (middle) Kenneth Harper; (bottom) Camera Press
page 19: Graham Disbrey
page 20: (top) Daily Express; (bottom) Joan Paramor
page 21: (top) Graham Disbrey; (middle) Rex Features; (bottom) Dave Foster
page 22: (top) London Features International; (bottom) Popperfoto
page 23: (top) Hulton Deutsch Collection; (bottom) Rex Features
page 24: (top left) Joan Batten; (top right) Daily Express; (bottom) Rex Features

SECTION 4

page 25: (top) Tear Fund; (middle) Ray Mackender; (bottom) Steve Turner
page 26: Steve Turner
page 27: (top) Hulton Deutsch Collection; (bottom) Retna Pictures

page 28: (top) Syndication International; (middle & bottom) Graham Disbrey
page 29: (top) Topham Picture Library; (bottom) Graham Disbrey
page 30: (top) Graham Disbrey; (bottom) Topham Picture Library
page 31: (top) Topham Picture Library; (bottom) London Features International
page 32: (top) Topham Picture Library; (middle) Rex Features, London; (bottom) Mark Bukowski

L P S

1	Cliff	Apr 1959
2	Cliff Sings	Nov 1959
3	Me And My Shadows	Oct 1960
4	Listen To Cliff	May 1961
5	21 Today	Oct 1961
6	The Young Ones	Dec 1961
7	32 Minutes And 17 Seconds With Cliff Richard	Oct 1962
8	Summer Holiday	Jan 1963
9	Cliff's Hit Album	Jul 1963
10	When In Spain	Sep 1963
11	Wonderful Life	Jul 1964
12	Aladdin And His Wonderful Lamp	Dec 1964
13	Cliff Richard	Apr 1965
14	More Hits By Cliff	Jul 1965
15	When In Rome	Aug 1965
16	Love Is Forever	Nov 1965
17	Kinda Latin	May 1966
18	Finders Keepers	Dec 1966
19	Cinderella	Jan 1967
20	Don't Stop Me Now	Apr 1967
21	Good News	Oct 1967
22	Cliff In Japan	May 1968
23	Two A Penny	Aug 1968
24	Established 1958	Sep 1968
25	The Best Of Cliff	Jun 1969
26	Sincerely	Oct 1969
27	It'll Be Me	Nov 1969
28	Cliff Live At The Talk Of The Town	Jul 1970
29	About That Man	Oct 1970

30	His Land	Nov 1970
31	Tracks 'n' Grooves	Nov 1970
32	The Best of Cliff, Volume 2	Nov 1972
33	Take Me High	Dec 1973
34	Help It Along	Jun 1974
35	The 31st of February Street	Nov 1974
36	I'm Nearly Famous	May 1976
37	Every Face Tells a Story	Mar 1977
38	40 Golden Greats	Sep 1977
39	Small Corners	Feb 1978
40	Green Light	Sep 1978
41	Thank You Very Much (Cliff and the Shadows)	Feb 1979
42	Rock 'n' Roll Juvenile	Sep 1979
43	I'm No Hero	Sept 1980
44	Love Songs	Jul 1981
45	Wired for Sound	Sep 1981
46	Now You See Me... Now You Don't	Aug 1982
47	Dressed for the Occasion (with London Philharmonic Orchestra)	May 1983
48	Silver (a second album – Rock 'n' Roll Silver – was included as part of a limited edition boxed set)	Oct 1983
49	Cliff and the Shadows	Sep 1984
50	The Rock Connection	Nov 1984
51	Always Guaranteed	Sep 1987
52	Private Collection	Nov 1988
53	Stronger	Oct 1989
54	From a Distance – The Event	Nov 1990
55	Together (with Cliff Richard)	Nov 1991
56	Cliff Richard – The Album	Mar 1993
57	The Hit List	Oct 1994
58	Songs from *Heathcliff*	Oct 1995

59	Cliff at the Movies	Aug 1996
60	*Heathcliff* Live	Dec 1996
61	The Rock 'n' Roll Years (boxed set)	Jun 1997
62	The Rock 'n' Roll Years	Jul 1997

Sources

Most of this book was researched from original sources. I conducted over 230 interviews with 199 people, the majority of whom had never been interviewed about Cliff before.

The research from interviews was supplemented by archive material from the following organizations:

BBC Written Archives, *Billboard*, British Film Institute, British Library, Broxbourne Borough Council, Butlin's Holiday Camps, Cheshunt Public Library, Chiswick Public Library, Companies House, Diocese of Calcutta, EMI Archives, Equity, Eurovangelism, Ferguson Ltd, Granada Television, Indian Tourist Board, India Office Library, Musicians Union, National Newspaper Library, National Maritime Museum, National Sound Archives, Office of Population and Censuses, Peninsular and Oriental Steam Navigation Company, Performing Rights Society, Press Association, Public Record Office Screen, Actors Guild, SOCAN, Spotlight, Sutton Public Library, Tear Fund.

There have been over thirty books written about Cliff so far although only a handful have been biographies. During research I made use of the following:

Driftin' With Cliff, Jet Harris, (Charles Buchan, 1959)

Cliff Richard (Fan Star Library, 1959)

It's Great To Be Young, Cliff Richard (Souvenir Press, 1960)

Cliff Richard: Baron Of Beat, Jack Sutter (Valex Products, 1960)

Me And My Shadows, Cliff Richard (Daily Mirror Publications, 1961)

Cliff Around The Clock, Bob Ferrier (Daily Mirror Publications, 1962)

The Wonderful World Of Cliff, Bob Ferrier (Peter Davies, 1964)

New Singer, New Song, David Winter (Hodder & Stoughton, 1966)

The Way I See It, Cliff Richard (Hodder & Stoughton, 1968)

The Cliff Richard Story, George Tremlett (Futura, 1975)

Which One's Cliff?, Cliff Richard (Hodder & Stoughton, 1977 and 1990)

Cliff, Tony Jasper and Patrick Doncaster (Sidgwick & Jackson 1981 and 1992)

Cliff Richard and the Shadows, Dezo Hoffman (Virgin, 1985)
Cliff Richard In His Own Words, Kevin St John (Omnibus Press, 1991)
You, Me and Jesus, Cliff Richard (Hodder & Stoughton, 1983)
Jesus, Me and You, Cliff Richard (Hodder & Stoughton, 1985)
The Cliff Richard File, Mike Read (Roger Houghton, 1986)
Single-Minded, Cliff Richard (Hodder & Stoughton 1988)
Cliff Richard: The Complete Recording Sessions, Peter Lewry and Nigel Goodall (Blandford, 1991).

Other books which mentioned Cliff were useful in their observations. Among these were:

Big Beat Scene, Royston Ellis (Four Square, 1961)
The Shadows By Themselves, ed. Royston Ellis (Consul, 1961)
Love Me Do: The Beatles' Progress, Michael Braun (Penguin, 1964)
Crusade '66, John Pollock (Hodder & Stoughton, 1966)
Awopbopaloobop Alopbamboom, Nik Cohn (Weidenfeld & Nicholson, 1969)
Revolt Into Style, George Melly (Allen Lane, 1970)
Land Aflame, Flo Dobbie (Hodder & Stoughton, 1972)
Spre-e'73, David Coomes (Coverdale House, 1973)
Rock 'n' Roll, Chris May (Socion, 1974)
The Guitar Greats, John Tobler and Stuart Grundy (BBC Publications, 1983)
The Story Of The Shadows, Mike Read (Elm Tree Books, 1983)
Days In The Life, Jonathan Green (Heinemann, 1988)
Rock 'n' Roll — I Gave You the Best Years of My Life, Bruce Welch (Viking, 1989)
Music Collector magazine no. 21 (January 1991)
Funny Old World: John Henry Rostill, Rob Bradford (Rob Bradford, 1992).

Articles about and interviews with Cliff are legion. Other than all the British national newspapers I consulted the following periodicals during my research:

Billboard, Boyfriend, Cheshunt Weekly Telegraph, Disc, Lucknow Pioneer, Marty, Melody Maker, New Musical Express, Newsweek, Radio Times, Record Mail, Ripley and Heanor News, Rolling Stone, Shepherd's Bush Gazette, Sutton Herald, The Stage, Tear Times, Valentine, Wallington and Carshalton Times, West Lancashire Evening Gazette.

Interviewees

Following is a list of my main interview sources for each chapter. Some sources have been left unattributed at the request of the interviewees.

CHAPTER 1

Roger Bruce, David Bryce, Mel Bush, Jimmy Henney, Sonya Jones, Hal Kalin, Linda Kay, Maggie Streader, Bruce Welch

CHAPTER 2

Vincent Bridgwater, Pete Bush, Joyce Clarkson, Rodger Cooke, Elsie Dazely, Joyce Dobra, Olive Gregory, Edna van Haeften, Gertrude Woodfall

CHAPTER 3

Dorothy Bodkin, Vincent Bridgwater, Olive Gregory

CHAPTER 4

Dorothy Bodkin, Pete Bush, Ivy Clare, Brian Cooke, Patricia Cookson, Ted Davy, Vincent Dickson, John Harris, Jacqui Harrison, Bob Henrit, Richard Holmes, Linda Lazarri, Norman Mitham, Jay Norris, Gladys Pearcy, Christine Poynter, Frances Slade, Mrs Slade, Mrs Tonks, Dorothy Willis

CHAPTER 5

Ruth Dickson, Jacqui Harrison, Betty Longhurst, Christine March, Marie Mitchell, Norman Mitham, The Rev. M.J. Bannister, Jay Norris, Terry Smart, John Vince

CHAPTER 6

Sheila Bateman, Jimmy Grant, Terry Harness, Chas McDevitt, Brian Parker, June Pearce, Frances Slade, Terry Smart, Dick Teague, Kathleen Teague, Mick Teague, Walter Teague, Wally Whyton

CHAPTER 7

Janice Berry, Dorothy Bodkin, Brian Cooke, Terry Dene, John Foster, Jacqui Harrison, Paul Lincoln, Norman Mitham, Steve Nichols, Ian Samwell, Terry Smart, Jan Vane

CHAPTER 8

Malcolm Addey, Janice Berry, Peter Bown, Franklyn Boyd, Frank Clarke, Stan Edwards, Mark Forster, John Foster, George Ganjou, Georgine Ganjou, Jack Good, Margit Good, Derek Johnson, Chas McDevitt, Norman Mitham, Caroline Paramor, Joan Paramor, Carl Perkins, Ian Samwell, Ernie Shear, Terry Smart, Tulah Tuke

CHAPTER 9

John Foster, Rita Gillespie, Jack Good, Jet Harris, Wee Willie Harris, Hal Kalin, Ron King, Hank Marvin, Paul McCartney, Mickie Most, Ian Samwell, Terry Smart, Maggie Streader, Bruce Welch, Wally Whyton, Marty Wilde

CHAPTER 10

Franklyn Boyd, Jess Conrad, Stan Edwards, John Foster, David Lilley, Ray Mackender, Tony Meehan, Sammy Samwell, Tulah Tuke, Marty Wilde

CHAPTER 11

Lionel Bart, Janice Berry, Dorothy Bodkin, Franklyn Boyd, Tito Burns, Jess Conrad, Carol Costa, Ronnie Ernstone, John Foster, Jet Harris, Wee Willie Harris, Andrew Ray, Maggie Streader, Jimmy Tarbuck, Cherry Wainer, Marty Wilde, Terence Young

CHAPTER 12

Lionel Bart, Roy Bennett, Tito Burns, Freddie Cannon, Jess Conrad, Yolande Donlan, Royston Ellis, Val Guest, Father John Oates, David Lilley, Ray Mackender, Wolf Mankowitz, Josie Pollock, Ian Samwell, Father Shergold, Maggie Streader, Sid Tepper, Diana Ward, Bruce Welch, Mark Wynter

CHAPTER 13

Sheila Bateman, Tito Burns, Mike Conlin, Carol Costa, Royston Ellis, Ronnie Ernstone, Jacqui Harrison, David Kossoff, Jerry Lordan, Vicky Marshall, Tony Meehan, Steve Race, Cherry Wainer, Diana Ward

CHAPTER 14

Roy Bennett, Stanley Black, Tito Burns, Ron Cass, Brian Crompton, Peter Gormley, Kenneth Harper, Jet Harris, Melvyn Hayes, Derek Johnson, Hank Marvin, Barry Ronger, Herb Ross, Cyril Simons, Sid Tepper, Bruce Welch, Delia Wicks

CHAPTER 15

Dorothy Bodkin, Vincent Bridgwater, Ron Cass, Mike Conlin, Royston Ellis, Adam Faith, Peter Gormley, Kenneth Harper, Jet Harris, Melvyn Hayes, Brian Locking, Ray Mackender, Hank Marvin, Tony Meehan, Lauri Peters, Victor Peterson, Una Stubbs, Bruce Welch

CHAPTER 16

Brian Bennett, Dorothy Bodkin, Ron Cass, Mike Conlin, Graham Disbrey, Royston Ellis, Kenneth Harper, Bill Latham, Hank Marvin, Jay Norris, Bruce Welch, David Winter

CHAPTER 17

Pete Bush, Mike Conlin, John Davey, Graham Disbrey, Nigel Goodwin, Peter Gormley, Peter Graves, Olive Gregory, Paul Jones, Bill Latham, Tony Meehan, Jay Norris, David Winter

CHAPTER 18

John Davey, Graham Disbrey, Dave Foster, Peter Graves, Cindy Kent, Bill Latham, Bill Martin, Tony Meehan, Olivia Newton-John, Larry Norman, Bruce Welch, David Winter

CHAPTER 19

Anthony Andrews, Terry Britten, Barrie Guard, Eric Hall, Kenneth Harper, George Hoffman, Bill Latham, Dave Mackay, Olivia Newton-John, David Pawson, Trevor Spencer, Alan Tarney, Liz Hutchison

CHAPTER 20

Terry Britten, Tony Clarke, Eric Hall, Christine Holmes, Tony King, Dave Mackay, Larry Norman, Trevor Spencer, Dave Townsend, Bruce Welch

CHAPTER 21

David Bryce, Tony Clarke, Chris Eaton, Phil Everly, George Hoffman, B.A. Robertson, Trevor Spencer, Graham Todd, Alan Tarney, Bruce Welch

CHAPTER 22

Sue Barker, Terry Britten, David Bryce, Stu Calver, Jill Clarke, Dave Cooke, Carol Costa, Chris Eaton, Paul Field, Alan Godson, Nigel Goodwin, Don Grierson, Mark Griffiths, Jet Harris, Garth Hewitt, Carol Illingworth, Bill Latham, Phil Lloyd, Hank Marvin, Norman Miller, John Perry, Craig Pruess, Mike Read, B.A. Robertson, Dan Slater, Gill Snow, Alan Tarney, Bruce Welch, Muriel Young

CHAPTER 23

Dave Clark, Gerald Coates, Dave Cooke, Mark Griffiths, Bob Hellyer, George Hoffman, Ron King, Norman Miller, John Muggleton, David Soames, Graham Todd, Sheila Walsh, Jodie Wilson

CHAPTER 24

David Bryce, Peter Gormley, Tony King, Gerry Kitchingham, Bill Latham, Paul Moessl, Alan Tarney, Graham Todd, Peter Waterman

CHAPTER 25

Tim Rice

CHAPTER 26

Sue Barker, Gerald Coates, Graham Disbrey, Charles Haswell, Bill Latham, Gill Snow, Gerald Williams

CHAPTER 27

Dorothy Bodkin, Peter Gormley, Bill Latham

Index

D

E

F

G

H

I

J

K

L